I Dread the Thought of the Place

I Dread the Thought of the Place

The Battle of Antietam and the End of the Maryland Campaign

D. Scott Hartwig

JOHNS HOPKINS UNIVERSITY PRESS | *Baltimore*

© 2023 Johns Hopkins University Press
All rights reserved. Published 2023
Printed in the United States of America on
acid-free paper
9 8 7 6 5 4 3 2 1

Johns Hopkins University Press
2715 North Charles Street
Baltimore, Maryland 21218
www.press.jhu.edu

Library of Congress Cataloging-in-Publication Data

Names: Hartwig, D. Scott, author.
Title: I dread the thought of the place : the Battle of Antietam and
    the end of the Maryland Campaign / D. Scott Hartwig.
Description: Baltimore : Johns Hopkins University Press, 2023. |
    Includes bibliographical references and index.
Identifiers: LCCN 2022033299 | ISBN 9781421446592 (hardcover) |
    ISBN 9781421446608 (ebook)
Subjects: LCSH: Antietam, Battle of, Md., 1862.
Classification: LCC E474.65 .H38 2023 | DDC 973.7/336—dc23/
    eng/20220727
LC record available at https://lccn.loc.gov/2022033299

A catalog record for this book is available from the
British Library.

Title-page illustration: The battle of Antietam—Charge of Burnside
9th Corps on the right flank of the Confederate Army. 1862. Edwin
Forbes. Library of Congress, Prints and Photographs Division.

*Special discounts are available for bulk purchases of
this book. For more information, please contact Special
Sales at specialsales@jh.edu.*

To those who died

and

their families who grieved

their loss

Never think that war, no matter how necessary nor how justified, is not a crime. Ask the infantry and ask the dead.

Ernest Hemingway, *For Whom the Bell Tolls*

CONTENTS

ILLUSTRATIONS

PREFACE

This is the story of a terrible battle and its aftermath. It is a long book, but we often rob the heart of the story lived by the participants in keeping our focus on the commanders and their decisions. Their decisions are analyzed, but the real story of a battle is uncovered when we dig into the weeds, not remain hovering above them. To understand Antietam, to sense something of what those who fought the battle—and suffered its consequences—experienced, it is necessary to venture into the woods, to walk through the corn rows, and see the battle as it was, rather than present it as some sanitized chess board.

During the writing and research for this book, I spent months reading the correspondence of Union and Confederate veterans of the battle had with John M. Gould, who was the adjutant of the 10th Maine Infantry at Antietam. Gould just wanted to know what happened, and his curiosity caused his project to grow far beyond what he initially set out accomplish, which was to determine who mortally wounded Major General Joseph K. Mansfield. The collection of letters grew to cover the whole battle that swept through the East Woods and Cornfield—and since these veterans were writing to a fellow veteran who sought the unembellished truth, that, typically, is what they gave him. I sense this was probably cathartic for many: a chance to exorcise ghosts, and to heal by committing their memories of that day to paper. Some told tall tales or had faulty recollections, but not many. Gould had a wonderful sense of humor, and the comments he wrote in the margins of letters constantly amused me. I liked Gould, and I liked nearly all the men who wrote to him. There were some blowhards, but very few. Most were straightforward and truthful. They had seen man at his worst and faced death. After what they experienced at Antietam and other battlefields, every day they lived was a gift. When I finished reading their letters, I remember coming home and telling my wife, "I am really going to miss them." I found virtually no animosity and no bitterness, in the correspondence from Confederate veterans to Gould. William Robbins, a captain in the 4th Alabama, and Gould developed a lifelong friendship through their correspondence, despite the fact that it was probably Gould's regiment that killed Robbins's brother in the East Woods. Men like Robbins did not close the book on the war and bury it. They were proud of their service and never forgot the comrades they lost. Instead, they made a conscious choice to let get go of the anger and bitterness and move on. Their choice is a lesson for the angry partisans in our country today.

Authors who have spent years digging into and writing on a subject, as I have here, often fall victim to the temptation to proclaim it is "forgotten," the "turning point," "untold," and other hyperbolic prose. Antietam is not forgotten, it was not the turning point of the Civil War, and its story, in general terms, is not untold. That it was a highly significant event in American history—*a* turning point, but not *the* turning point—cannot be denied. Antietam needs no hyperbole. It is an American tragedy and a compelling, dramatic story. I have tried my best to tell it as honestly as possible.

EDITORIAL NOTE

To avoid littering quotations with "[*sic*]," unless there might be confusion in the mind of readers with a particular word, I refrain from using it.

The Army of Northern Virginia identified its brigades and divisions by the name of the commander carried on the army's order of battle. For example, the division commanded by General Alexander Lawton at Sharpsburg was known in the army as Ewell's division, after its regular commander, General Richard Ewell, who was wounded during the Second Manassas Campaign. This can cause confusion for readers and lead to unnecessarily lengthy explanations of who the actual commander of a certain unit at Sharpsburg was. Therefore, all brigades and divisions are identified by the name of their commander *on September 17*, not the regularly assigned commander, who was not present that day.

Prologue

Weary soldiers from Wisconsin and Indiana slept soundly in a damp meadow. They had little idea of where they were—it was somewhere on a hill in a farm meadow near a village called Sharpsburg, Maryland—but few of them probably cared. Despite the discomfort of being ordered to keep their equipment on throughout the night, a drizzling rain, and the occasional outbursts of firing from in front, such was their fatigue that the men were still in a deep sleep as the fingers of dawn crept slowly across the overcast landscape. Suddenly, their division commander, Brigadier General Abner Doubleday, came galloping up the hill and commanded, "Move these troops out of here at once. You are in open range of a battery." Officers and sergeants stirred at once and began kicking, shaking, and hurrying their sleepy men into ranks. There were nearly 800 men in the brigade, and it took several minutes to get everyone up. After forming up, the brigade commander, Brigadier General John Gibbon, ordered the regiments to hurry east to get into cover on the reverse slope of the hill and behind the buildings of the nearby farm. The regiments were in a dense formation that the tactical manual called close column by division (see appendix A), so that from a distance, the 800 men looked something like a dark, moving phalanx.[1]

Major Rufus R. Dawes in the 6th Wisconsin thought too much noise had been made in awakening the brigade and forming it up, for before they had covered 60 yards, "Whiz-z-z! Bang! Burst a shell over our heads." Sergeant William Harries in the 2nd Wisconsin was so disoriented that he thought a friendly artillery battery was firing on them. A second shell followed, and it, too, burst over the column but again injured no one. The third shell was a percussion one, the type artillerymen used to find the range, since it exploded, hopefully, on contact with the ground. It fell into the midst of Company A, marching in the rear division of the 6th Wisconsin, which led the brigade. There was a flash and a deafening explosion that spewed iron fragments in all directions. When the smoke cleared, 13 men were sprawled about, mangled, torn, and bleeding. Two were dead, another man had lost both arms, and the company commander, Captain David K. Noyes, had his foot mangled so badly it would need to be amputated. A shock wave of fear rippled through the 6th, and John Gibbon was afraid it might cause the men "to scatter like a flock of frightened sheep." But the 6th's commander, Colonel Edward Bragg, a small man possessed of courage and a commanding presence, called out sharply, "Steady, Sixth. Close up!" Such was the discipline and training in the regiment that they instinctively closed ranks and swept past their stricken comrades, hurrying to gain the cover of the nearby barn and woods. "Thus opened the great battle of Antietam on the morning of the 17th," recalled Major Dawes.[2]

These 13 mangled men from Wisconsin were the first casualties in what would be an appalling day of slaughter. Antietam would be a watershed for those who experienced its fury, and a turning point for the nation. The war had unleashed forces that few had imagined, and none could predict where they would lead. Men who had hoped for a limited war, with armies deciding the conflict in the field and minimal destruction to the nation's social fabric and civilian infrastructure—either to restore the Union as it was, or to withdraw from it as an independent, enslaving republic—saw a conflict beginning to spin in directions unimagined in that bloody summer of 1862. The aspect of the war was changing, and the great bloodbath at Antietam would mark the moment when going back to the nation that existed before the war began would be both unthinkable and impossible.

THE ROAD THAT LED to the great clash at Antietam began on September 1, 1862, in the aftermath of the Confederate victory in the Battle of Second Manassas. In a remarkable campaign, stretching back to late June, Confederate General Robert E. Lee had defeated the Union Army of the Potomac under General George B. McClellan in the Seven Days Battles of June 25 to July 1 on the Virginia Peninsula. Lee then shifted his army's center of gravity to northern Virginia, to confront the newly organized Army of Virginia, under General John Pope. McClellan, who objected strenuously, was ordered to evacuate the peninsula and transfer his army to northern Virginia, to combine forces with Pope's Army of Virginia. But Lee struck before the Federals could complete their concentration of forces. From August 29 through 31, on the old First Manassas battlefield, Lee's army defeated Pope's forces and sent the Union army reeling back to Washington, DC. With northern Virginia effectively cleared of Federal troops, and despite the extremely poor logistical condition of his army, Lee seized the opportunity offered. From September 4 to 7, he and his men crossed into Maryland at the Potomac River fords near Leesburg. From what had appeared to be the brink of possible defeat, Lee and the Army of Northern Virginia now were poised to strike a crippling blow to Lincoln's administration and the Union war effort. A Confederate victory in Maryland or Pennsylvania might wipe away all the successes won by Union arms up to this point in the war.

Lee's was not the only Confederate army on the offensive that September. In Tennessee, two armies, under Generals Braxton Bragg and Kirby Smith, marched north, respectively, from Chattanooga and Knoxville and plunged into Kentucky, a vital border state Lincoln needed to keep within the Union. The war had reached a fresh crisis point. The Confederacy, apparently on the verge of collapse and defeat only 2 months earlier, now seemed on the precipice of securing its independence. Morale plummeted in the North. "The enemy have outgeneraled us," admitted Union Brigadier General John Sedgwick. "I look upon a division as certain," he continued. "The only question is where the line is to run. No one would have dared to think of this a few weeks since, but it is in the mouths of many now."[3]

"They are always going to hate us, and we them"

Confederate success on Virginia's battlefields ironically helped fuel a radical shift in Union war policy. The limited war of 1861 and early 1862, to save the Union, had largely tried to step around the thorny issue of slavery. It was well understood by all that this was *the* divisive issue that had brought on secession and war, but except for more radical Republicans, there was either hesitation in or outright opposition to attacking it. First, it was imperative to keep the border slave states of Delaware, Maryland, Kentucky, and Missouri in the Union. While Delaware had only a small enslaved population and Maryland and Missouri were relatively securely in Union hands, an open attack on slavery might push Kentucky into the Confederacy, destabilize Missouri, and fuel dissension in Maryland. To lose Kentucky alone might mean losing the war. President Lincoln needed the backing of the War Democrats, who opposed meddling with slavery, and he was rightly concerned that any radical steps toward emancipation would erode that support. There was also the fear that attacking slavery would strengthen the Confederates by confirming what the propagandists had been saying all along—that Northerners were fanatics, bent on nothing less than the complete destruction of the South's economy and society, thereby provoking Southern whites, even those who had been lukewarm toward secession, to fight all the harder.

But slavery refused to be marginalized. Everywhere that Union armies and naval forces overran parts of the Confederacy, fugitives from slavery flocked to their lines, seeking freedom. To them, soldiers in blue were seen as liberators. Yet what was to be done with these individuals who were seeking emancipation? It was well known that the Confederates were employing enslaved Blacks to labor on fortifications and for other military purposes. To return the freedom seekers to their enslavers benefited the enemy. Nonetheless, without clear direction, some military commanders felt that, legally, they had no other choice.

In May 1861, Union General Benjamin Butler, a Democrat and successful pre-war Massachusetts attorney who was commanding the Union garrison at Fortress Monroe, refused to return three fugitives from slavery who came within his lines and told him they were to be sent away to work for the Confederate army. Butler declared them to be "contrabands of war" and, therefore, could be legally seized by the government's forces. But what of the enslaved women and children and the elderly who came by the hundreds to Fortress Monroe when news spread of what Butler had done? Were they still enslaved? Were they considered contrabands of war? The answer was unclear.[4]

Lincoln approved of Butler's action, but not that of General John C. Fremont in Missouri, who, in August 1861, issued a radical proclamation that allowed, among other things, the confiscation of property and the emancipation of all enslaved people belonging to anyone serving in or supporting the Confederate cause in that state. Earlier that month, the Republicans in Congress had passed what became known as the First Confiscation Act, which authorized the appropriation of property used for the Confederate war effort, although the act did not state whether enslaved individuals seized under its authority were free or not. Lincoln signed this bill but revoked Fremont's proclamation. The general had exceeded his authority and, very likely, his declaration would have pushed Kentucky into the Confederacy, not to mention its effect on Missouri's pro-slavery Unionists. Lincoln also revoked Fremont's proclamation because he believed emancipation was a political question, and generals did not make such policy unless specifically authorized to do so.[5]

The ambiguity of the Confiscation Act caused confusion at the front, where the armies were constantly dealing with fugitives from slavery. How did one determine whether they were working for the Confederate army? Some officers felt legally bound to return those that came within their lines to their enslavers, while others refused to do so. In March 1862, Congress settled this question by passing a new article of war, forbidding army or navy officers from returning Blacks seeking emancipation, or risk facing a court-martial. At the same time, Lincoln tried to confront the slavery issue by proposing a policy of compensated emancipation to the leaders of the border states. But by then, George B. McClellan's grand campaign to capture Richmond had commenced, and hopes were high that the Confederate capital would be taken in either spring or summer and the rebellion crushed, with slavery left intact. Thus the border states' leaders rejected the president's proposal.[6]

That May, Lincoln had to deal with another general who assumed the authority to make political policy on slavery. Major General David Hunter, a crusty regular officer, commanded the Department of the South, which encompassed South Carolina, Georgia, and Florida (even though Federal armed forces only controlled the Sea Islands off South Carolina). Hunter was an oddball among Regular Army officers, in that he was an abolitionist. Before departing to take up his command, he had asked Secretary of War Edwin Stanton for permission to "have my own way on the subject of slavery."[7] Stanton provided no guidance, which Hunter assumed meant approval to proceed as he saw fit. On May 9, he issued General Orders No. 11, which declared martial law in the entire department. But the real bombshell in the orders was the final sentence: "Slavery and martial law in a free country are altogether incompatible; the persons in these three States—Georgia, Florida, and South Carolina—heretofore held as slaves, are therefore declared forever free." Lincoln learned of Hunter's emancipation proclamation in the newspapers. Since the president was still actively courting the border states to adopt a policy of gradual, compensated emancipation, he moved swiftly to revoke Hunter's order. To Secretary of the Treasury Salmon Chase, who urged the president not to retract the order, Lincoln wrote, "No commanding general shall do such a thing upon *my* responsibility without consulting me."[8]

Although Lincoln revoked Hunter's general orders, his public proclamation in retracting them contained a warning to those who continued to hope that the Union might be restored with slavery left intact. After unambiguous language voiding Hunter's orders, Lincoln stated that at any time it became a "necessity indispensable to the maintenance of the government" to declare the enslaved in any state free, this was an authority "I reserve to myself," as the commander-in-chief. Again, he appealed to the border states' leaders: "To the people of these states I now earnestly appeal. I do not argue. I beseech you to make the arguments for yourselves. You cannot, if you would, be blind to the sign of the times." The warning was clear. If the border states would not act in their own self-interest, then the unpredictable nature of war might force the president's hand on slavery.[9]

In July, Lincoln traveled to the camps of the Army of the Potomac at Harrison's Landing, Virginia, on the James River, to visit with McClellan. The general was a pre-war Whig who now aligned with the War Democrats. He had conservative views on how the war should be prosecuted. During the Peninsula Campaign, he followed a policy of carefully protecting the private property of the citizens in the path of his army. Writing on May 16, Elisha H. Rhodes in the 2nd Rhode Island Infantry observed, "Property is respected as much as it was in Washington. Even the generals sleep out of doors, and the rights of the people are respected. The men living here are surprised at this, as they were told the Yankees would destroy everything." McClellan worried about where he sensed the "fanatics" in Washington, DC, were pushing the war. In his view, radical policies toward slavery, such as those Fremont and Hunter advocated, only strengthened the rebellion. During the president's visit on July 8, McClellan handed him what has become known as the "Harrison's Bar Letter," a carefully considered document outlining the general's views on the execution of the war. Although McClellan has been criticized for overstepping his bounds in advising the president on political matters, or for acting insubordinately, his letter was entirely proper as a communication from the commander of the largest field army of the United States. Political policy directly impacted military operations.[10]

McClellan warned the president that it "should not be a War looking to the subjugation of the people of any state . . . neither confiscation of property, political execution of persons, territorial organization of states or forcible abolition of slavery should be contemplated for a minute." Although McClellan acknowledged that the rebellion "has assumed the character of a War; as such it should be regarded." While it might be necessary, as a military measure, for the government to "appropriate permanently to its own service claims to slave labor"—which was already happening—he warned against taking any extremist steps concerning this issue. "A declaration of radical views, especially upon slavery," he wrote, "will rapidly disintegrate our present armies." McClellan's expectations for the president were low. "He really seems quite incapable of rising to the merits of the question & the magnitude of the crisis," he wrote his wife Mary Ellen the day Lincoln departed. But if the president found the courage to defy the radicals and acted on his general's counsel, McClellan was confident "the country will be saved."[11]

Lincoln's biographer, David Donald, noted that the policy McClellan recommended "had been pursued for over a year and Lincoln was convinced that it had failed. He was ready to move on." So, too, were a growing number of citizens in the North, as well as soldiers in the army. "What shall be done with slavery?" Frederick Douglass asked of a Rochester, New York, audience in late March. "We have gradually drifted to this vital question. Slavery is the pivot on which turns all the machinery of this tremendous war, and upon it will depend the character of the future of our peace or want of it." Slavery was indeed the pivot and the foundation of the Confederate economy. Why should it remain untouched in a war to put down a rebellion? Was it not already clear that the Rebels were not a minority of secessionists leading a coerced majority of Southern Unionists into rebellion? Could anyone honestly consider Shiloh and the Seven Days Battles and argue that the South was not in earnest? The Confederates fought with fierce desperation. They fielded large, well-equipped armies. As Lincoln put it to August Belmont, a wealthy War Democrat from New York, "This government cannot much longer play a game in which it stakes all, and its enemies stake nothing. Those enemies must understand that they cannot experiment for ten years trying to destroy the government, and if they fail still come back into the Union unhurt." To a Southern Unionist, he wrote, "What would you do in my position? Would you drop the war where it is? Or, would you prosecute it in future with elder-stalk squirts, charged with rose water? Would you deal lighter blows rather than heavier ones? Would you give up the contest, leaving any available means unapplied[?] . . . I shall not do more than I can, and

I shall do <u>all</u> I can to save the government, which is my sworn duty as well as my personal inclination."[12]

The July 5 *New York Tribune* expressed the view of an increasing number of Northerners who were coming to understand the logic of a direct attack on slavery as a military measure: "By simply proclaiming liberty to every slave held in bondage by Rebels, and inviting all such to escape to our camps and serve the National cause to the extent of their ability, and receive a certificate of freedom and protection, we can immensely weaken the Rebels at once, paralyzing them with apprehension, and compelling them to devote a large portion of their White strength to watching and holding their negroes." Would the Union die, the *Tribune* asked, simply because it "disdainfully repelled the services of Four Millions of its children?"[13]

Within a week of his return from Harrison's Landing, Lincoln's appeal to the border states' congressional delegation to take action on his plan for compensated, gradual emancipation received a firm rejection. It was not unexpected, and Lincoln was prepared to move forward. On the same day when he received the response from the border states' delegation, he privately revealed to Secretary of State William Seward and Secretary of the Navy Gideon Welles his intent to issue an emancipation proclamation. He had been working on the document for several weeks. Four days later, on July 17, Congress passed two important pieces of legislation: the Militia Act and the Second Confiscation Act. The former included authority for the president to enroll Blacks for "any service for which they may be found competent," including in the military. The Confiscation Act authorized punishment of the rebels as traitors, ordering the seizure of their property and declaring that after a period of 60 days, Blacks held as property by rebels who did not take the Oath of Allegiance should be "forever free of their servitude, and not again held as slaves." Although Lincoln signed the act into law, he believed "Congress has no power over slavery in the states." As James McPherson points out, "The law was so confusing and poorly drawn that a good lawyer probably could have 'driven through it with a two horse team.'" Lincoln believed that whatever legal authority the federal government exerted over the practice of holding people in slavery in the states belonged to the war powers that were reserved to the president, as commander-in-chief. He intended to exercise those powers and seize the initiative from Congress.[14]

But the president needed military success to act on the topic of emancipation. Here was the rub. The tide of the war had shifted, and Secretary of State Seward argued that issuing an emancipation proclamation that summer, after McClellan's clear defeat on the Virginia Peninsula, would be viewed as a final, desperate measure by an "exhausted government." It had to be issued from a position of strength, and that meant military success. Hope for this rode on the shoulders of John Pope and his Army of Virginia.[15]

Although General-in-Chief Henry W. Halleck assured McClellan that he would have overall command when his army joined Pope's, Lincoln had no such intensions. He had lost confidence in McClellan, but because of the general's strong standing with the War Democrats, he hesitated to remove him. Lincoln circumvented this problem by detaching the army from McClellan to Pope. As the Army of the Potomac's individual corps arrived in northern Virginia, they were hurried forward to Pope, where they fell under his command. McClellan was left in a state of limbo, not relieved of his command, but without an army and with his authority dimly defined. Pope's defeat at the Battle of Second Manassas in late August brought Lincoln's maneuverings crashing down in the chaos that ensued after that defeat. The president had no choice but to select McClellan to assume command of all forces within the defenses of Washington, DC. Then, when Lee led his army into Maryland between September 4 and 7, Lincoln had no other viable options than for McClellan to command the field army. The army had to not only turn back the Confederate offensive, but the president also desperately needed it to deliver a substantial enough victory that would enable him to issue his emancipation proclamation. The great irony of the September 1862 Maryland Campaign is that the general Lincoln counted on to deliver a battlefield victory was explicitly opposed to the emancipation policy such a victory would produce.[16]

The advent of John Pope heralded a harsher attitude about the war's prosecution by the Lincoln administration, but it reflected the opinion of growing numbers of Northerners. After assuming command in July, Pope issued a series of general orders, with the president's approval, repudiating the type of war George McClellan had warned the president against pursuing in his Harrison's Bar letter earlier that month. General Orders No. 5 directed the Army of Virginia to "subsist upon the country." General Orders Nos. 7 and 11 were aimed primarily at dealing with the problem of Confederate guerrillas operating in the Union rear. Orders No. 7 authorized harsh treatment for anyone supporting or harboring guerrillas. Their houses could be burned if shots came from inside, directed at Union soldiers. When damage was inflicted on government buildings or equipment, all the civilians within 5 miles of that spot were to be turned out to repair it. Orders No. 11 instructed officers to "arrest all disloyal male citizens within their lines or within their reach." Those men willing to take the Oath of Allegiance could remain in their homes unmolested, but those who refused were to be escorted to Confederate territory. Should they return and be caught, they were to be treated as spies and dealt with through military justice.[17]

Pope's orders coincided with the Militia Act and the Second Confiscation Act. McClellan, and many other officers from the professional ranks who shared his view of a limited war, shuddered at these orders and acts. McClellan struck back with his own General Orders No. 154, issued to the Army of the Potomac on August : "The idea that personal property may be plundered with impunity is, perhaps, the very worst that can pervade an army." To his wife he fumed, "I will strike square in the teeth of all his [Pope's] infamous orders & give directly the reverse instructions to my army—forbid all pillaging & stealing & take the highest Christian ground for the conduct of the war. . . . When you contrast the policy I urge in my letter [his July 8 Harrison's Bar letter] to the Presdt with that of Congress & Mr. Pope you can readily agree with me that there can be little mutual confidence between the Govt & myself . . . we are the antipodes of each other."[18]

Many officers in both Pope's Army of Virginia and the Army of the Potomac agreed with McClellan. The idea that personal property could be "plundered with impunity" was bad for morale and discipline. The consequence of Pope's poorly worded order regarding foraging was that the enlisted ranks of the Army of Virginia, in particular, interpreted them as a license to plunder. "Most of the destruction is perfectly wanton, and not necessary, and only calculated to make the inhabitants your bitterest enemies," complained Washington Roebling, an engineer officer with the Army of Virginia. Yet, at the same time, there was grumbling in both the enlisted men's and officers' ranks with the manner in which George McClellan insisted the war be waged. Writing in mid-May, Lieutenant Charles H. Brewster in the 10th Massachusetts voiced his objections:

> All the families that remain hang out a white rag or flag of truce as it is called which ensures them protection, and we are not allowed to take anything from them even if we were to starve, and yet in nine cases out of ten, the men of the families are all in the secesh army. I think it will take ten years of Sundays to restore the Union by any such kind of war as this, the whole aim seems to be to hurt as few of our enemies and as little as possible. I go for driving every mothers son and daughter of them out of the country and settling it with Yankees. They are always going to hate us, and we them and they will take up arms again, at the first opportunity.[19]

What Brewster and many others at the front were coming to understand was that while discipline needed to be maintained in the ranks, polite respect for enemy property, particularly regarding enslaved Blacks, won them no friends among the enemy. To an increasing number of men who faced the ferocity and spirit with which Confederate troops fought at Gaines' Mill, Glendale, Cedar Mountain, Second Manassas, and elsewhere, the notion that a respectful, limited war policy would somehow win hearts and minds among the white Southern population and separate them from the secessionists seemed preposterous. They were coming to the same opinion as the president—namely, that the government could not "play a game in which it stakes all, and its enemies stake nothing." There was no consensus in the ranks about what specific policy should be pursued to achieve victory, but there was mounting agreement that dealing lighter blows rather than heavier ones would not save the Union.

"I am getting to hate the Yankees in earnest"

Pope's general orders and the unlicensed foraging they encouraged, the Militia and Second Confiscation Acts, Butler's "contrabands of war," and Fremont's and Hunter's emancipation proclamations, among other events, all served to reinforce the propaganda Confederate soldiers were regularly fed by their press and government about the fate that awaited them and their families if they were conquered by the Yankees. "Their malignity to the North will stop at nothing, however monstrous, that may be deemed effective in the prosecution of the main purpose of the complete spoliation and humiliation of the South," warned the May 22 edition of the *Richmond Daily Dispatch*. To a white Southerner in 1862, "complete spoliation and humiliation" meant the overthrow of slavery, and all that it implied. Major General James Longstreet employed this fear to inspire his soldiers before the Seven Days Battles, in a circular read to the men: "Already has the hatred of one of their great leaders [Fremont] attempted to make the negro your equal by declaring his freedom. They care not for the blood of babes nor carnage of innocent women which servile insurrection thus stirred up may bring upon their heads." Captain Harry Lewis in the 16th Mississippi, after complaining about the hardships of soldiering, wrote that he "joyfully" embraced the war "as a means of repelling a dastardly, plundering, oppressive and cowardly foe from our homes and borders," and that he was "getting to hate the Yankees in earnest." Lafayette McLaws, a former U.S. Army officer now commanding a division in Lee's army, made clear the depths of white Southerners' determination. "The enemy are only on our threshold," he wrote to his wife, "when he gets in among the people whose every man woman & child are his enemies, he can begin to realize the nature of the war." As Joseph Glatthaar has noted in *General Lee's Army*, his study of the Army of Northern Virginia, "Before the war, many had held Northerners in disdain, and some even despised them. But war enriched their venom and universalized it." As the *Richmond Daily Dispatch* advised its readers on July 25, in an editorial on John Pope, "It will not do to fight monsters with gloves on."[20]

It is a popular myth that a majority of Rebel soldiers in Lee's Army of Northern Virginia were opposed to an invasion of Maryland or Pennsylvania following their victory at Second Manassas. Believers cite, as evidence, the contention that hundreds, and perhaps thousands, of Lee's men simply refused to cross the Potomac River. There is little contemporary evidence to support this. The overwhelming majority of Confederate soldiers who left the ranks before or during the campaign did so because they were sick or exhausted, or because their logistical support had utterly broken down and they straggled behind to look for food, not because they opposed an invasion. The evidence that exists reflects strong support for an invasion of the North as a means to bring the war to a speedy end. "I do not understand the programme determined upon by Gen. Lee, but guess we will first clear Maryland of our hated tyrants, and then 'carry the war into Africa,'" wrote a Georgian. Correspondent Peter Alexander, with Ambrose R. Wright's brigade in Richard H. Anderson's division, wrote from Frederick, Maryland, on September 8: "Five days ago Maryland, chained hand and foot, writhed in the arms of the oppressor like a weeping, trembling virgin who appeals in vain to the mercy of her ravisher. To-morrow she may be free! We have come to strike the fetters from her beautiful limbs and to punish her despoiler. . . . We can never quit Maryland except as conquerors, or a broken, ruined army."[21]

With Confederate armies marching north into Maryland and Kentucky that September, the war had reached a moment of crisis and transition. The "velvet-footed" war of earlier that summer was being replaced by a war in earnest by both sides, a war in which a negotiated peace that restored the Union to its antebellum status, with slavery left intact, seemed sheer fantasy. Great things now trembled in the balance, awaiting the outcome of the Confederate offensives. On the one hand, there was the prospect of Confederate independence. On the other hand, there was the preservation of the Union, the possibility of emancipation, and the beginning of the destruction of keeping Africans in slavery in America. These momentous issues now rode on the shoulders of the soldiers in blue and gray, who would decide them amid the blood and fire of the battlefield. Crucial as Kentucky was to both the Union and Confederate war efforts, the campaign in Maryland was seen as the true crisis point by national and international communities, for Robert E. Lee and the Army of Northern Virginia appeared to be unstoppable. They had marched with impunity into Maryland and paused only 40 miles from the Federal capital.[22]

To Antietam Creek

Following a hasty reorganization around Leesburg, Virginia, from September 4 through 7, the Army of Northern Virginia crossed the Potomac River into Maryland and marched to the city of Frederick. From this central position, Lee's army posed a threat to Pennsylvania, Baltimore, and Washington, DC. His intent was to draw the Union army into the field before it had reorganized from the defeat at Second Manassas and had a chance to absorb and train the thousands of new recruits who were arriving daily in the capital in response to the government's call in July for 300,000 new volunteers. Lee let his army rest while he waited for the Federals' reaction. He was also observing the Union garrisons in the Shenandoah Valley, at Harpers Ferry and Martinsburg. These threatened his planned line of communications, but he anticipated that when his army occupied Frederick, the garrisons would be withdrawn, to avoid being cut off. The Yankees did not withdraw, however. Lee characteristically saw opportunity in this, rather than trouble. He devised a bold, complicated operation, employing three separate columns to descend on the Union garrisons. They could be destroyed in the open if they attempted to flee, or bottled up in Harpers Ferry and then surrounded and captured. When Lee conceived this plan, he learned that the Army of the Potomac had sortied forth from Washington, DC, as he had hoped. This added a potentially dangerous wrinkle that both his wing commanders, Major General Thomas J. "Stonewall" Jackson and Major General James Longstreet, thought problematic. But the Federal army was moving slowly, and Lee believed they were still badly disorganized from their recent defeats. He was confident that his army could execute the operation against the Union garrisons in the Shenandoah Valley and re-concentrate at Hagerstown, well before the Army of the Potomac came up. Thus Lee's plan prevailed.

On September 10, the Army of Northern Virginia departed from Frederick to commence the Harpers Ferry operation. In his plan, Lee divided the army into four separate columns: three columns that maneuvered against the Union garrisons, and a fourth, with Lee and Longstreet and one-third of the army, that would halt at Boonsboro, Maryland, where they could both intercept any force that escaped from Harpers Ferry and watch the mountain passes through South Mountain. But reports of the Pennsylvania Militia threatening Hagerstown, as well as information that locals were removing stores from that town, which Lee was counting on to help provision his army, caused him to modify his plan on the march. Only D. H. Hill's division was left at Boonsboro, while Lee, Longstreet, and two divisions continued on to Hagerstown, leaving the army divided into five widely scattered pieces.

The Harpers Ferry operation proceeded well, but it took longer than Lee's optimistic timetable had planned for. He expected the Union garrison at Martinsburg to be dislodged and all the Federals bottled up in Harpers Ferry by September 12, after which surrender should come quickly. The three columns moving against Harpers Ferry and Martinsburg were Jackson's three divisions; Major General Lafayette McLaws's two divisions, whose mission was to secure Maryland Heights, which commanded Harpers Ferry from the north; and Major General John Walker's single division, which was to capture Loudon Heights on the Virginia side of the Shenandoah River, commanding Harpers Ferry from the south. By the 12th, Jackson had flushed the Union garrison at Martinsburg, which withdrew to Harpers Ferry. At the same time, McLaws was fighting for possession of Maryland Heights, and Walker was a day's march from Loudon Heights.

Meanwhile, the Army of the Potomac marched methodically, but steadily, across Maryland toward Frederick. McClellan never moved rapidly, but he was hindered by the need to reorganize the army on the march; make sense of a bewildering number of often conflicting intelligence reports, many of which were also exaggerated or inaccurate; and heed General-in-Chief Henry Halleck, who feared that a large Confederate army continued to lurk in northern Virginia. On the afternoon of September 12, the advance of the army entered Frederick. The next day, September 13, as the balance of the army closed up on the city, soldiers in the 27th Indiana Infantry discovered a copy of Lee's orders for the Harpers Ferry operation—Special Orders No. 191—wrapped around three cigars and stuffed inside an envelope. The Confederate army was in a perilous situation, being widely divided, with rivers and mountains between the various forces. Mc-Clellan planned a two-pronged offensive to take advantage of his good fortune. The main force, consisting of the 1st, 2nd, 9th, and 12th Corps, as well as Sykes's 5th Corps' division of U.S. Regulars (soldiers of the United States Regular Army)—in all, over 60,000 men—would advance west from Frederick, push through Turner's Gap in South Mountain, and descend on the Confederates at Boonsboro. At the same time, the 6th Corps, reinforced by General Darius Couch's 4th Corps' division, would attack Crampton's Gap in South Mountain, which was 5 miles south of Turner's Gap, destroy McLaws's force, and relieve Harpers Ferry.

Although Lee was not aware that McClellan had a copy of Special Orders No. 191, he learned on the night of the 13th that some major Union advance was planned for the next day. He communicated with Jackson and McLaws, urging them to hasten the operations at Harpers Ferry, and, as a precaution, ordered Longstreet to march to Boonsboro on September 14 and reinforce D. H. Hill, who had been directed to march his division from Boonsboro and hold the South Mountain gaps "at all hazards."

McClellan's September 14 offensive took Lee by surprise. Although he had expected a Union advance, he had not anticipated a battle that day. Fortunately, D. H. Hill blocked the mountain passes at Fox's Gap and Turner's Gap, and the Federals were forced to fight their way through. The Battle of South Mountain was confusing and developed slowly, which enabled Longstreet's brigades to re-inforce Hill, although they lost nearly half of their men to straggling in a brutal forced march from Hagerstown. Longstreet and Hill managed to hold the mountain passes, at a cost of 2,193 men, but by nightfall the Federals, who lost 1,813 men, had seized the key terrain on the battlefield, rendering the Confederate position untenable. Unaware of McLaws's situation at Crampton's Gap or the state of the siege at Harpers Ferry, Lee nevertheless understood that McClellan's offensive had compromised his Maryland Campaign and left his widely divided army in grave danger. There was no other option than to withdraw the army to Virginia and attempt to reunite its separated parts. Longstreet and Hill were ordered to retreat to Virginia that night, via Sharpsburg and Shepherdstown. McLaws was commanded to withdraw across the Potomac River to Virginia in the best way he could, and Jackson received instructions to break off the Harpers Ferry operation and march to Shepherdstown, in order to cover the river crossing by Longstreet's and Hill's forces.

The second prong of McClellan's offensive, the 6th Corps' advance on Crampton's Gap, smashed through the thin Confederate line there and, after a fierce struggle, secured the gap. By nightfall, they were in Pleasant Valley and on McLaws's rear. Meanwhile, at Harpers Ferry, all the Confederate pieces were at last in place, and Jackson subjected the Union garrison to a heavy bombardment while he maneuvered his infantry to storm the position on September 15. When he received Lee's orders to break off the operation and march to Shepherdstown, he responded, "I will join you at Sharpsburg." Jackson knew Lee would not have him terminate the Harpers Ferry operation when they were so close to success. That evening he dispatched a more complete report to Lee, explaining that he expected Harpers Ferry to surrender on the 15th.

Longstreet and D. H. Hill's brigades began to withdraw from South Mountain late on the night of the 14th. During the movement, Lee learned of the Federal breakthrough at Crampton's Gap. It was imperative to assist McLaws by preventing McClellan from reinforcing the 6th Corps. Hoping that he would draw the Federals' main body away from McLaws, Lee changed Longstreet's and D. Hill's orders, having them halt at the village of Keedysville. He still did not intend to offer battle in Maryland. The Keedysville position was temporary and designed only to draw McClellan's main body away from McLaws's force, which was sent new orders to find a way over or around Elk Ridge to Sharpsburg, instead of retreating across the Potomac River. Before Longstreet's and Hill's men reached Keedysville, however, Lee changed his mind again. Sharpsburg appeared to be a superior point at which to establish a temporary defensive position, having Antietam Creek as an obstacle on its front and the Potomac River on the flanks. Orders were dispatched to Longstreet's and Hill's brigades, telling them to continue the march to Sharpsburg.

McClellan ordered a pursuit of Longstreet's and Hill's retreating brigades from South Mountain. All the evidence coming into his headquarters the morning of the 15th pointed to a decisive victory, with the enemy in headlong retreat for Virginia. "If I can believe one tenth of what is reported, God has seldom given an army a greater victory than this," he wrote to his wife. But as the morning progressed, the euphoria at headquarters began to dissipate. A morning message from Franklin reported that he was confronted by a strong Confederate line of battle, and that Harpers Ferry might have surrendered. Then, at 12:40 p.m., McClellan received a message from a signal station on South Mountain, reporting that "a line of battle—or an arrangement of troops which looks very much like it—is formed on the other side of Antietam Creek and this side of Sharpsburg." Lee was not running for Virginia.[23]

Yet another dramatic development altered Lee's thinking about his campaign that morning. At around 8 a.m., he received Jackson's message, written the evening before, that anticipated the enemy would surrender on September 15. This raised the possibility of salvaging the Maryland Campaign. Around noon, Lee received confirmation from Jackson of the Union surrender. Lee's next move depended on McClellan. If the Union general moved cautiously, then Jackson and the other forces in the Harpers Ferry operation could be marched to Sharpsburg and the army concentrated for battle. If McClellan acted aggressively, Lee could still withdraw Longstreet and Hill across the Potomac River to Virginia, and the Maryland Campaign would be over.

McClellan's pursuit from South Mountain was limited by a restricted road network. Only two roads were available to move some 60,000 men, artillery, and transportation, resulting in a colossal traffic jam along the Boonsboro–Sharpsburg Pike. One regiment, the 14th Connecticut, reported that it took them 11 hours to march 5 miles. McClellan had ordered that the pursuing troops be massed near wherever the enemy might make a stand, but he discovered that Major General Edwin Sumner, one of his wing commanders, and Major General Joseph Hooker, commanding the 1st Corps, had instead halted the troops along the pike, which only contributed to the traffic snarl that extended for miles to the rear. It was after 5 p.m. when McClellan reached the front and was able to personally observe the line Lee had taken up behind Antietam Creek. With sunset at 6:10 p.m., there would be no attack on September 15. The logistics of moving an army had granted Lee a day's reprieve.

That night, McClellan received confirmation of the Harpers Ferry surrender. "It releases 30,000 Rebel soldiers who will probably re-enforce the army in front of us," wrote a *New York Tribune* reporter traveling with the army. McClellan still had Franklin's 6th Corps in Pleasant Valley, with General Darius Couch's division nearby, to block a potential enemy strike into his rear by this Confederate force. But Franklin had reported that afternoon that the enemy troops in Pleasant Valley were withdrawing toward Harpers Ferry. The Confederate forces at Harpers Ferry might possibly march north along the Harpers Ferry–Sharpsburg Road to threaten McClellan's left flank. But this was a poor road for moving troops and equipment, and a more likely destination for these Confederates was to reinforce Lee at Sharpsburg. Yet a stand at Sharpsburg defied military convention about fighting with a river to your back. Lee, however, had disregarded military convention on the Virginia Peninsula, and McClellan was determined to ready his forces for either a pursuit or an attack on September 16. His inherent caution dictated his orders to Franklin. Despite the withdrawal of the enemy from Franklin's front, McClellan ordered the 6th Corps and Couch's division to remain in Pleasant Valley. The rest of the army, still massing around the village of Keedysville, were ordered to place themselves in readiness for action the next day.[24]

By nightfall, Lee had made up his mind to offer battle at Sharpsburg, despite the fact that Jackson's command and Walker's division could not arrive until midmorning on the 16th, and McLaws's and Andersons's divisions until the night of the 16th, at the earliest. It was such a daring and risky decision that historian John Ropes deemed it "so bold and hazardous that one is bewildered that he should even have thought seriously of making it." If forced to retreat across the

Potomac River, Lee's only escape route was Boteler's Ford at Shepherstown, which Lee's ordnance officer, Lieutenant Colonel Edward P. Alexander, wrote was so difficult and slow to negotiate that "this single feature of the field should have been conclusive against giving battle there." Lee was an aggressive risk taker, but he was also a carefully calculating commander. We shall never know his reasoning for offering battle at Sharpsburg, since he never provided any substantial explanation for this decision, but it is possible to deduce his logic, based on the type of general Lee was and the military/political situation he confronted.[25]

Lee undoubtedly understood the potential perils of his position at Sharpsburg. It is inconceivable that he was unaware of the condition of Boteler's Ford, as well as the hazards of offering battle with a river to his rear. But Lee did not fail to notice that the Federals had not behaved aggressively on September 15. Although they seized the Middle Bridge over Antietam Creek, they had conducted no other probes or reconnaissance of his front. Although Lee could not read McClellan's mind—he had been surprised by McClellan's offensive that resulted in the Battle of South Mountain—Lee knew him to be a deliberate commander. There would be no hasty attack on the morning of September 16. McClellan would spend the morning in reconnoitering. The earliest an attack might be delivered would be the afternoon of the 16th, but for reasons known only to him, Lee doubted that McClellan would mount a serious attack on the 16th.[26]

Why did Lee take such an immense risk? He was an opportunistic general, playing for extremely high stakes. Retreat to Virginia was the safe move, but it surrendered the initiative to McClellan and shut the door on what Lee recognized as a unique opportunity for the Confederacy to strike a damaging blow to Northern morale by achieving a battlefield victory on Union soil. Such a victory could significantly advance the cause of Confederate independence. If McClellan attacked, was repulsed, and withdrew to a defensive position, then Lee's campaign of maneuver north of the Potomac River could be renewed. The capture of Harpers Ferry secured his line of communications and enabled Lee to draw on supplies and bring up conscripts assembled at his newly established depot in Winchester, Virginia, as well as make use of convalescents who had recovered from their wounds or sickness. With a reinforced and resupplied army, Lee could march north from Sharpsburg to Hagerstown and then into Pennsylvania, via the Cumberland Valley. McClellan would be forced to pursue and, thus, be drawn far from his base of supply and the fortifications in Washington, DC, and out into the open—with South Mountain to his rear—where his army might be destroyed. Yet Lee could also overreach. He could hardly have been unaware of the dire physical condition of his army, the massive straggling that eroded its strength, and the nearly nonexistent logistical support that contributed to that straggling, but he seems to have imagined that his army could accomplish anything through sheer will.

Although McClellan understood that every passing hour raised the likelihood that Lee's forces at Sharpsburg would be reinforced by troops from the Harpers Ferry operation, he proceeded deliberately in preparing for battle. Dawn on the morning of September 16 was foggy. At 7 a.m., McClellan wrote to Henry Halleck, "This morning a heavy fog has thus far prevented us doing more than to ascertain that some of the enemy are still there. Do not know in what force. Will attack as soon as the situation of enemy is developed." Even before the fog lifted, it was evident that the Confederates remained in force behind Antietam Creek, ready to do battle. McClellan wrote later that he was "compelled to spend the morning in reconnoitering the new position taken up by the enemy, examining the ground, finding fords, clearing the approaches, and hurrying up the ammunition and supply trains, which had been delayed by the rapid march of the troops over the few practicable approaches from Frederick." This consumed the morning, and while the clock ticked, Jackson reached the field with two of his own divisions. Brigadier General John Walker's division also arrived, raising Lee's effective strength to around 24,000.[27]

There are three bridges that cross Antietam Creek, where the two armies confronted one another. McClellan's reconnaissance revealed that the Lower Bridge—also known as the Rohrback Bridge and, after the battle, as Burnside's Bridge—was closely defended by Confederate infantry. McClellan controlled the Middle Bridge, but the ground between it and Sharpsburg was swept by numerous Rebel artillery batteries. The Upper Bridge was under observation by Confederate cavalry but undefended. Besides the bridges, McClellan learned of a ford about a quarter mile below the Upper Bridge, called Pry's Ford, and his engineers believed they had located another ford below the Lower Bridge, called Snavely's Ford, which offered outflanking possibilities. McClellan concluded that his best option was to move against the Confederate left via the Upper Bridge and Pry's Ford. The stream crossing would be unopposed, and there was more room to maneuver large forces here. The general plan was to send Major General Joseph Hooker's 1st Corps across Antietam Creek that afternoon to develop the Confederate position, then to reinforce Hooker by the 12th and 2nd Corps, as circumstances dictated, so that, in theory, three Union corps would be massed against Lee's left flank. But McClellan initially kept the 12th and 2nd Corps on the east bank of Antietam Creek. The 9th Corps, under the titular command of Brigadier General Jacob Cox, but supervised by Right Wing commander Ambrose Burnside, whose wing had been broken up when Hooker's corps was detached to lead the principal attack, was to move up near the Lower Bridge during the afternoon of the 16th and, on September 17, create a diversion to prevent Lee from drawing troops from his right to reinforce his left. When the main attack and the 9th Corps' diversion were fully developed, Mc-Clellan planned to strike the Confederate center with his reserves, which then consisted of only two divisions of the 5th Corps, but, in theory, could have been reinforced by the 6th Corps.

It was a reasonable plan, but by waiting until the 17th to open the general engagement, McClellan granted Lee additional time to complete the concentration of his army. Although McClellan had discussions with both Burnside and

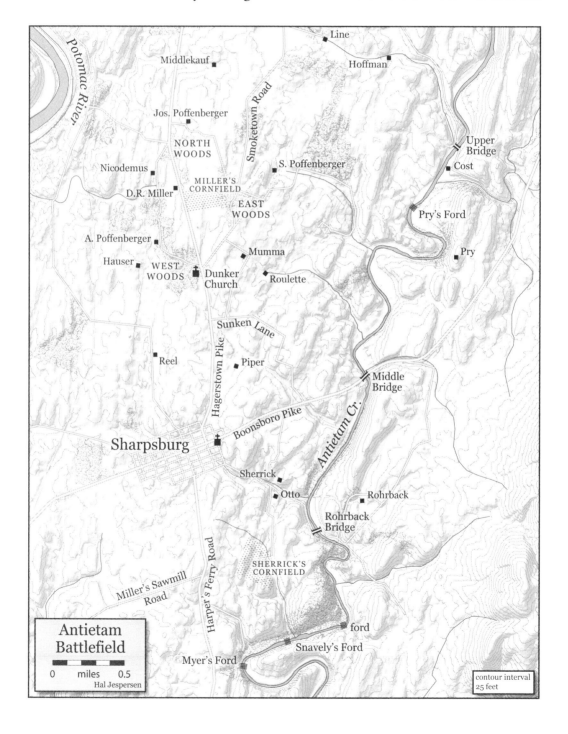

Hooker on the 16th, neither general, nor any corps commander in the army, with the possible exception of 5th Corps commander Major General Fitz John Porter, understood the general plan of attack or how their command fit into it. Of the three corps that would make the main effort against the enemy left, only the 1st Corps was to be moved across Antietam Creek on the 16th, virtually guaranteeing that each corps would enter the action successively, rather than in concert. The army's cavalry division had no role, either to screen Hooker's movement or to reconnoiter or probe Lee's position. McClellan did order Franklin's 6th Corps up from Pleasant Valley, leaving Couch's division behind, but the decision to do so was made so tardily that Franklin would not reach the field until late morning at the earliest.

Hooker commenced his movement about 2 p.m. Around dusk, his advance made contact with the Confederate infantry of Brigadier General John B. Hood's division. Sharp skirmishing ensued, lasting until nightfall ended the fighting, with the opposing sides arrayed almost within speaking distance of one another. In response to Hooker's urgent request for reinforcements, McClellan ordered Major General Joseph Mansfield's 12th Corps across Antietam Creek. Mansfield's brigades marched through a pitch-black night to a point about 1 mile north of Hooker's position, where they bivouacked and waited for morning. The 2nd Corps remained on the east bank of Antietam Creek, forbidden by McClellan to cross it until so ordered.

Lee reacted to Hooker's advance by shifting both of Jackson's divisions to his left flank. By that evening, he had three divisions confronting Hooker's three divisions. McLaws's and Richard Anderson's divisions were expected to be up by early morning of the 17th. Except for A. P. Hill's division, left at Harpers Ferry to manage the details of the surrender, Lee had completed the concentration of his army. The stage was set. At daylight on September 17, the great and terrible Battle of Antietam would begin.

1

Into the Corn

"Of all the battles that ever was fought this beats all"

Gibbon's brigade moved swiftly past the mangled bodies of the 6th Wisconsin's casualties, gaining the cover of Joseph Poffenberger's barn. They pushed on south through Poffenberger's small cornfield and walked over the soldiers of Colonel Albert L. Magilton's brigade of Pennsylvania Reserves, lying down in an open woodlot known as the North Woods. Here, Gibbon found his corps commander, Major General Joseph Hooker, mounted on his conspicuous white horse, "Colonel," in conference with Brigadier General George Meade, commander of the division of Pennsylvania Reserves. The din was deafening, as the nearby 1st Corps' artillery on Poffenberger Hill were engaging the Confederate batteries that had opened fire. Gibbon recalled that at that moment, "no enemy was in sight, but his shells were flying thick over our heads." Hooker paused in his conversation with Meade to give Gibbon his orders. He was to "advance directly to the front and attack." The balance of Doubleday's 1st Division would support him.[1]

Hooker's orders to Gibbon were characteristic of the man. He was cut from a different mold than most senior officers in the Army of the Potomac. Hooker was bold and aggressive; some believed he was positively reckless. During the advance of the army from Yorktown in May, when Hooker came up against the Confederate rear guard at Williamsburg, he knew little about the enemy's strength or position. Nevertheless, he reported that since he believed he was pursuing a retreating army, "I deemed it my duty to lose no time in making the disposition of my forces to attack, regardless of their number and position." In the ensuing action, he nearly lost his division when the Confederates proved to be both powerful and ready to fight. A month later, on the second day of the Battle of Seven Pines, when he was leading his men forward and a brigade commander from another division warned that his men could not get through a swampy area that lay ahead, Hooker roared at him, "Get out of my way. I have two regiments here that can go anywhere." His chief of artillery on the Virginia Peninsula, Colonel Charles Wainwright, who knew the general well, noted that "his bravery is unquestioned, but that he has not shown himself anything of a tactician." Philip Kearny, who rescued Hooker at the Battle of Williamsburg, and equaled him in aggressive spirit, thought Hooker was nearly overwhelmed in that battle, "because he did not know his mind" when he pitched in without a plan or any reconnaissance. Over-aggressiveness may have been a fault of Hooker's, but in an army where caution and deliberate action often characterized its senior leadership, Hooker provided a necessary jolt of combativeness. He was unafraid to pitch into the Confederates.[2]

It may have been this latter quality that caused McClellan to select the New Englander to open his attack, which only further discredits the nonsense that McClellan did not like to fight his men because he feared losing them. Privately, Hooker had little good to say about his commander. In one letter during the Peninsula Campaign, he described McClellan as an "infant among soldiers" and sharply criticized what he considered to be McClellan's excessive caution. Discretion was not a strength of Hooker's. He freely voiced his denunciations of commanders, peers, and subordinates. Charles Wainwright wrote that although Hooker was "a delightful man to serve with," Wainwright did not "like the way he has of always decrying the other generals of his own rank, whose every act he seems to find fault with." If any of Hooker's criticisms ever reached McClellan, he paid no attention to them. He had specifically selected Hooker to command the 1st Corps, because he thought the corps had poor morale and discipline and believed that the New Englander was the soldier who could "bring them out of the kinks, & make them fight if anyone can."[3]

Hooker was awake before dawn on the 17th. He spent the night in Joseph Poffenberger's barn, just in the rear of Meade's division, and listened to the outbursts of firing from the picket lines in front that flared angrily at various points throughout the night. The firing convinced him that "we might reasonably expect a violent collision at the earliest dawn," and he intended to seize the initiative and strike first. Hooker's knowledge of the ground his corps would fight on was limited. He had observed it from the high ground near Pry's farm, 1.75 miles distant, on September 15 and 16, and had a closer look during his corps' movement into position on the evening of the 16th. But it was nearly dark by the time his troops reached the area that would be the battlefield, which made it impossible to conduct any meaningful reconnaissance to understand the nuances of the terrain. He and McClellan had concluded that the key terrain to be seized was the open plateau near a large woodlot, beside what appeared to be a small white schoolhouse, but was actually the church of a small group of locals belonging to a Brethren sect known as Dunkers, because of their custom of fully immersing, or dunking, those they baptized. In studying this ground from Pry Ridge, the Dunker Church plateau appeared to command the rest of the locale that Lee had selected to defend at Sharpsburg. Capture it, and the entire Confederate position would be untenable. Directing the attack on this ground had the additional benefit of being within range of the batteries of the Artillery Reserves' powerful 20 lb. Parrott rifles, arrayed along Pry Ridge south of Pry's farm, east of Antietam Creek. Any Confederates east of the Hagerstown Pike who confronted Hooker would be enfiladed by these guns, which probably dictated the axis of Hooker's advance.[4]

Based on the resistance he had encountered the previous evening, Hooker understood it would be a hard fight to reach this objective. Two large woodlots, the East Woods and West Woods, channeled his advance into the open ground between, which Hooker estimated was between 400 to 500 yards in width. This frontage limited the size of the force he could deploy to two brigades. Since Meade's division of Pennsylvania Reserves, Hooker's most experienced unit, had borne the hardest fighting at the Battle of South Mountain and led the corps' advance on the evening of the 16th, he planned to keep them in reserve and have Doubleday's 1st Division and Brigadier General James B. Ricketts's 2nd Division lead his attack.

The 1st and 2nd Divisions of the 1st Corps were the units McClellan referred to as in the "kinks," with poor morale and discipline. There were many in these commands who would have taken umbrage at McClellan's opinion. The physical demands of the Second Manassas Campaign had created lengthy sick lists, and the two divisions had suffered 2,681 and 1,744 casualties, respectively, in the Battle of Second Manassas. Some units—such as Colonel Walter Phelps's 1st Brigade in the 1st Division, composed of five regiments—were greatly understrength. Phelps's brigade went into action at Antietam with only 425 effectives, an average of just over 80 men per regiment. The 3rd Brigade of Doubleday's division, commanded by Brigadier General Marsena Patrick, numbered only 750 officers and men in its four regiments. Holmes W. Burlingame, a private in the 104th New York of Brigadier General Abram Duryée's brigade of Ricketts's division, recalled that his entire brigade "at that time was in really bad condition, we had been without tents or blankets, with no change of clothing since we left our knapsacks in the field back near Thoroughfare Gap" in August. A shortage of officers, due to casualties, sickness, and resignations, further damaged the effectiveness of some regiments. In the 11th Pennsylvania of Brigadier General George Hartsuff's brigade, Ricketts's division, George Cramer wrote to his wife that "our company has neither captain, lieutenant, nor any sergeant, only corporals to command us. The rest is killed, wounded, or sick."[5]

Under such circumstances, discipline and combat effectiveness inevitably slipped in some units. Straggling was also a serious problem. On September 9, Hooker's headquarters notified Brigadier General John Hatch, then commanding the 1st Division, that the brigade bringing up the rear of the division's march that day moved "with great irregularity," and "the men were observed to straggle, and to quit the ranks at pleasure." Hooker sought permission to consolidate some units that were severely understrength. "For instance, it is believed that by a judicious selection of officers from the three New York regiments in the 1st brigade [Duryée's], an efficient regiment can be secured to the service in the place of demoralized fragments as they now exist," Hooker wrote to Seth Williams, the army's assistant adjutant general. Hooker also sought to remove officers he believed were inefficient or incompetent, one of whom was Brigadier General Abram Duryée. "The Brigade is in a wretched condition," complained Hooker on September 9, and "requires a commander of both intellectual and physical force, but if I cannot have a commander combining the two, I deem it indispensably necessary that he should possess at least one of these requisites." Because of the rapid pace of events in the campaign, Duryée survived Hooker's efforts to remove him and led his brigade at South Mountain and Antietam.[6]

At South Mountain, both Doubleday's 1st Division and those elements of Brigadier General James B. Ricketts's 2nd Division that were engaged were battled to a standstill by a much smaller Confederate force. It was one that fought with such tenacity that Doubleday would report he faced four times his numbers when, in fact, his three brigades outnumbered the Rebels by nearly 4 to 1. The only brigade in either division to draw attention to its performance was Gibbon's brigade, which was detached from the division and assigned to assault the formidable Confederate position in Turner's Gap.[7]

The division commanders, Doubleday and Ricketts, were experienced professional soldiers, although Doubleday had only assumed command of the 1st Division three days earlier, at South Mountain, when Brigadier General John Hatch had been wounded. Although no one questioned Ricketts's courage—he had stood with his battery at First Bull Run until he was badly wounded and the battery was overrun on Henry House Hill—the discipline and condition of his division received special attention from Hooker in his efforts to reorganize the 1st Corps. Ricketts's division had a reputation for straggling badly, and there were complaints about its performance at Second Manassas. Charles Wainwright heard after that fight that "Ricketts's division which held the extreme left on Saturday did very badly according to all accounts." Two months after Antietam, Wainwright wrote that Ricketts was "politely relieved" to administrative duties. Ricketts was ostensibly reassigned because of the severity of his wound at Antietam, but Wainwright's comment implies that there were other reasons.[8]

The ground over which Doubleday's and Ricketts's divisions would advance was a picturesque nineteenth-century pastoral landscape of meadows, cornfields, orchards, and plowed fields, separated by numerous post-and-rail, or zigzag worm, fences, and bracketed by the woodlots known after the battle as the North Woods, East Woods, and West Woods.[9] Running north–south along the axis of Doubleday's advance was the Hagerstown Pike, which provided a convenient guide for the direction of the division's advance. What Doubleday, Ricketts, and Hooker studied was not the beauty of the landscape, but the numerous obstacles the fences represented to the movements of formed troops and the abundant cover for the enemy from the woodlots, tall cornfields, and undulating terrain. Despite the known close proximity of the Confederates, none of their infantry could be seen by the 1st Corps' commanders, except those on the front of Brigadier General Truman Seymour's brigade of Pennsylvania Reserves, who were positioned at the southern edge of the East Woods.

AWAITING THE 1ST CORPS were three Confederate divisions under the operational command of Major General Thomas J. "Stonewall" Jackson, consisting of Brigadier General John R. Jones's and Brigadier General Alexander Lawton's divisions of Jackson's Wing, and Brigadier General John B. Hood's division from Longstreet's Wing. They had the additional support of four batteries with 15 guns in Colonel Stephen D. Lee's Reserve Artillery battalion from Longstreet's command, as well as Brigadier General Fitz Lee's cavalry brigade. Jackson also had the assistance of the cavalry division's commander, Major General James E. B. "Jeb" Stuart, whose contribution would be significant.

Jackson had arrived in the vicinity of the West Woods, at the head of Jones's division, around sunset on the 16th, in the midst of Hood's skirmishing with Hooker's 1st Corps. He inserted Jones's four small brigades into the undefended ground west of the Hagerstown Pike, on Hood's left. Jones's division formed into two lines immediately west of the Hagerstown Pike. Jackson tucked Colonel Andrew Jackson Grigsby's Stonewall Brigade and Captain John E. Penn's brigade into his first line, behind a ridge in a meadow about 250 yards southwest of the large cornfield of David Miller, with the northern extension of the West Woods on their immediate left. At 250 yards to their rear and just inside the West Woods, his support line consisted of Brigadier General William A. Starke's Louisiana brigade and Colonel James W. Jackson's brigade of Alabama and Virginia regiments.[10]

Jones's division was a veteran force, but the summer's campaigning had taken a severe toll from casualties and physical wear and tear. Hundreds of men in both Jones's and Lawton's divisions had straggled on the march from Harpers Ferry to Sharpsburg. Many were simply at the end of their physical and mental limits—constant hard marching, combined with uncertain and frequently inadequate rations, having worn them down. Grigsby's storied Stonewall Brigade numbered only about 300 officers and men, an average of 60 men per regiment. Penn's brigade was in a similar condition. Jackson's brigade had only about 450 effectives. Starke had the largest brigade, with about 850 from all ranks. In recalling the men of his command years later, Jones gushed with pride about how they were "ragged, tired, hungry, and barefooted—but they were <u>soldiers</u>, heroes who had marched hundreds of miles <u>during the summer of 1862</u> and fought many battles under Jackson and Lee." That they were tough is indisputable, but the staying power of these skeletal units composed of exhausted men was now in question.[11]

Jones had only commanded the division for several days. He had been wounded at Malvern Hill and then incapacitated by typhoid fever. He rejoined the army at Frederick, where he assumed command of the division through seniority.[12]

Brigadier General Alexander Lawton's division arrived in the West Woods soon after Jones had deployed. Jackson detached Brigadier General Jubal Early's brigade to cover Jones's left flank. Early formed his brigade near Alfred Poffenberger's farm, to the left of Starke's brigade, but "it was too dark to understand enough of the position to make very good dispositions" complained Early, a problem all of Lawton's brigades would share. The Louisiana brigade of Brigadier General Harry Hays massed in the West Woods to Early's right rear, as a support. Initially, the balance of Lawton's division—Colonel James A. Walker's and Colonel Marcellus Douglass's brigades—were held as a reserve in the West Woods, but during the night they were moved forward to relieve the famished soldiers of Hood's division. During the previous 3 days, Hood's men had received only a half ration of beef and some green corn. With a promise to Jackson that he "would come to support of these forces the moment I was called upon," Hood pulled his division into the shelter of the West Woods, while he rode off find provisions to feed his men.[13]

That relief took place in the pitch dark, when it was impossible for officers to understand the ground. The most Douglass and Walker could fathom was that the Yankees were to their north, in the North Woods, and to their northeast, in the East Woods. Walker deployed his brigade of 700 North Carolinians, Alabamians, and Georgians in one of farmer Samuel Mumma's plowed fields, just north of the Mumma farm lane, with Walker's left extended across Smoketown Road, facing the East Woods, which were known to be full of Federals. The men had no cover anywhere along the line, except for those near Smoketown Road's fences.[14]

The 1,150 men of Douglass's five Georgia regiments filed into a grass and clover field about 300 yards south of Miller's cornfield, on Walker's left. Two companies of the 31st Georgia, under Lieutenant William H. "Tip" Harrison, advanced as skirmishers to cover the brigade's front. Harrison pushed his line about 50 feet into Miller's cornfield, extending his left to the Hagerstown Pike and his right to near the East Woods. The remaining eight companies of Harrison's regiment formed a picket reserve about 100 yards south of the cornfield. Because the Federals might approach from both the direction of the cornfield and the East Woods, Douglass formed the main body of his brigade at a slight angle, with his three left regiments—the 26th, 38th, and 61st Georgia—facing north toward the corn, and the 13th and 60th Georgia facing northeast toward the East Woods. A rail fence, with some shrubs and small trees growing along it, which does not appear on post-battle maps but is evident in photographs taken immediately after the battle, offered some cover to Douglass's men, as did limestone outcroppings and unevenness of the ground, but much of the brigade's line lacked adequate cover. Douglass also was probably unaware that his deployment exposed his left regiments to an oblique, almost enfilading fire from the East Woods, and that his right regiments could suffer the same fate from any enemy troops that came through the cornfield. Also, neither Douglass, Walker, Hood, nor Jackson seemed to have appreciated how exposed both of these brigades were to enfilading fire from the Union batteries across Antietam Creek. They would find that out early in the fight. This may have been what prompted a member of the 13th Georgia to afterward claim that "owing to a misunderstanding of orders, we were wrongly positioned." The price of their exposed deployment would be high for both brigades.[15]

Fortunately for Jackson's thin infantry brigades, he had plenty of artillery available to strengthen the Confederate defenses. Although it is difficult to determine precisely how many batteries and guns he had, a reasonable estimate is 16 batteries with 53 guns, including 30 rifled guns. While some batteries were positioned to provide close support for the infantry, and others held in reserve, there were two important concentrations that would prove to be significant in the battle. The first consisted of the four batteries of Colonel Stephen D. Lee's Reserve Artillery battalion, with 15 guns, which were unlimbered in the early hours before daylight on the open plateau extending east from the Dunker Church to the Mumma farm lane. Jeb Stuart assembled the other concentration, which proved to be troublesome and deadly to Hooker's soldiers. Stuart had a good eye for terrain. Because he was an active soldier and had, on September 16, examined the ground that would be the battlefield on the 17th, he had identified an irregular hill that rose to a height of 500 feet, located about 200 yards northwest of the northern finger of the West Woods, as an ideal platform for artillery to deliver an enfilading fire on any Federal troops that advanced south in the direction of the Dunker Church. It had the additional benefit of being beyond the range of the 20 lb. Parrott rifles on the east bank of Antietam Creek. This irregular hill became known as Nicodemus Heights, named for the nearby Nicodemus farm. Besides the enfilading fire Stuart's guns could deliver into the open ground between the East and West Woods, any Federal troops advancing through this corridor would also be subjected to a crossfire from the guns of S. D. Lee's battalion on the Dunker Church plateau and Jackson's divisional batteries.[16]

The first battery to reach Nicodemus Heights were the four guns of Stuart's horse artillery, under the command of Major John Pelham, who parked the guns on the south slope around sunset on the 16th. When night fell, Pelham and his men went to sleep, rather than move their pieces into position under the cover of night. Robert Macknall, a member of the battery, recalled how the tramp of a horse near his head around 2 a.m. woke him from a sound sleep. Macknall demanded to know who was riding a horse through sleeping men. The rider asked where Pelham was. Macknall instantly recognized the voice of Jeb Stuart. He rose and led Stuart to Pelham, who was fast asleep beside a post-and-rail fence. Recalled Macknall, "I distinctly remember hearing him [Stuart] say to Pelham 'My dear fellow, don't you know that the corn field at the foot of the hill is full of Yankees and that you ought to have your guns in position now, for if you wait until daylight the hill will be swarming with blue coats.'" Pelham wasted no time in awakening his men, and the crews pushed the guns by hand to the crest to await morning.[17]

With Jackson's apparent blessing and complete confidence, Stuart worked through the predawn hours to mass additional firepower on the heights. He collected three batteries from Jackson's command: Captain George Washington Wooding's Danville (Virginia) battery of 4 guns, Captain Joseph Carpenter's Alleghany (Virginia) battery of 5 guns, and Lieutenant Asher W. Garber's Staunton (Virginia) battery of 2 guns. Garber's men had made camp in the West Woods after a long and tiring march from Harpers Ferry on the night of the 16th, and the men "scattered around the camp and went to sleep." Apparently Garber had allowed them to spread out for some distance, for when he was awakened with orders to report to Stuart, he was unable to locate all of his troops. One of his enlisted men recalled that "many of the men were not found and were left lying in the woods still asleep." Garber's battery was an odd choice. as the lieutenant fielded only two obsolete 6 lb. smoothbore guns, out-ranged by any guns the Yankees had. This may reflect the haste necessary in assembling batteries in the dark. Nor were the men in the Staunton battery the only ones who sought shelter in the West Woods that night. Captain Edgar D'Aquin's Louisiana Guard battery, attached to Lawton's division, also camped there. At around 1 or 2 a.m., Stonewall Jackson and his staff encountered John J. Block, a member of the battery, who was on guard where they had picketed the battery's horses. Seeing only horses, Jackson asked, "What cavalry is this?" Block replied that it was a battery. Jackson had D'Aquin roused and informed him that "this is no place for a battery, get out as quick as possible. This woods will be shelled in a short time." D'Aquin and his Louisianans cleared out in short order.[18]

On Nicodemus Heights, in the predawn darkness, Wooding's and Carpenter's gunners pushed their pieces into a small cornfield on the eastern slope and waited quietly for dawn. Lieutenant Garber brought his two guns up on the southern slope of the hill, in a meadow south of the cornfield on Wooding's right. All told, Stuart had concentrated 14 or 15 guns, including 7 rifles and 3 Napoleons, on the heights.[19]

The 27-year-old Garber had been a machinist in Staunton, Virginia, in civilian life. In the wave of fear that John Brown's raid spread through the South, Garber was elected 2nd lieutenant of a local artillery battery that formed in December 1859. They were mustered into Confederate service when the war began. Garber was wounded at First Bull Run but recovered to be elected 1st lieutenant and in command of the battery from the Seven Days Battles on. Such was Garber's focus on his getting his guns into position that, years later, he could not recollect any cornfield or any other guns nearby. "I did not see or hear them," he wrote. He did however, meet Major Pelham, who, earlier in the war, had drilled

Garber and the Staunton battery at Harpers Ferry and knew them well. Pelham no doubt advised Garber of the general direction of the Yankees and their close proximity. Because Garber had left so many of his men sleeping in the West Woods, he and his other officers were forced to help crew the guns. It was just at daybreak when they were positioned. In the early dawn light, he made out a Union battery, about 1,200 to 1,500 yards to the east, on Poffenberger Hill The former Staunton machinist ordered his guns to open fire on it. With a crack and a deafening roar, the Battle of Antietam had begun.[20]

THERE WAS AN ABUNDANCE of targets on Poffenberger Hill. Six batteries were parked in the general vicinity, which included 32 guns, 32 limbers, a minimum of 192 horses, and hundreds of sleeping artillerymen. In addition to the guns, all four brigades of Doubleday's 1st Division were bivouacked in the area, in what General John Gibbon described as "a very confused and huddled up condition," due to their arrival in the pitch-black night. Gibbon's brigade of 800 Midwestern soldiers was the most exposed, having lain down on the southwestern slope of the hill, facing Nicodemus Heights. Fortunately they had some warning before Lieutenant Garber and his artillerymen yanked the lanyards on their guns. Someone, probably a picket, saw or heard the Confederate guns going into position on the heights and alerted Doubleday, who galloped up the hill, warning Gibbon that his men "were in open range of the rebel batteries" and ordering him to move his brigade at once.[21]

William H. Humphrey, a private in Company E, 2nd U.S. Sharpshooters, could see the red in the eastern sky, although it was still "quite dark" on Poffenberger Hill when he woke that morning. He wandered across the Hagerstown Pike, beyond the main positions of Doubleday's infantry and artillery, to find a place to answer nature's call. While in this compromised position, he heard a bugle sound from beyond Union lines. Humphrey hurried back, and his path took him through the guns of Lieutenant Frederick M. Edgell's 1st Battery, New Hampshire Light Artillery. He woke Lieutenant Edwin Hobbs, one of the battery's officers, who gazed through the hazy early morning light and saw what was probably Garber's guns unlimbering on Nicodemus Heights. Hobbs shouted for the sleeping men of the battery to get up, while Humphrey ran back to his own regiment and called out, "Fall in men." Privates do not usually order regiments to fall in, and his shout produced grumbles and curses from the sharpshooters—Humphrey called the men "slow and cross"—but moments later, one of Garber's shells came hurtling into Edgell's battery nearby, cutting the throats of two battery horses, then striking the ground and bounding up and over Humphrey's regiment. "Then there was lively work falling in," he remembered.[22]

Near the summit of Poffenberger Hill, Captain J. Albert Monroe and the officers of Battery D, 1st Rhode Island Light Artillery, were gathering for breakfast.

Their cook had come up before daylight with "a pail of steaming coffee, some johnny-cakes and 'fixins,' together with cups, plates and other table ware." A blanket was spread out and the officers crouched down to enjoy their meal. Monroe recalled that it was still dark enough that they "could little more than distinguish each other." They ate undisturbed for a few minutes as dawn gradually crept around them. "We could see the first rays of the sun lighting up the distant hilltops," wrote the captain, "when there was a sudden flash, and air around us appeared to be alive with shot and shell from the enemy's artillery." To the Rhode Islanders, Nicodemus Heights, slightly more than 1,000 yards distant from Monroe's position, suddenly appeared to resemble "an active volcano, belching forth flame, smoke and scoriae." Monroe thought the first shot passed directly through the breakfast party and struck the ground only a few feet away. Everyone dropped whatever they were holding "and looked around the group to see whose head was missing." Monroe admitted that the firing commenced so suddenly, and with such rapidity, that "I felt lost for an instant." He ordered his groom to bring his horse, and by the time his mount arrived, Monroe had recovered from his momentary daze. Around him, the men of his battery and those on either side of him—Battery B, 4th U.S., and Battery L, 1st New York—had leaped to their feet and were clearing for action.[23]

The two most exposed infantry brigades, Gibbon's 4th brigade and Colonel Walter Phelps Jr.'s 1st Brigade, quickly formed up and started to move out of the line of fire. Gibbon marched his men to gain the cover of Poffenberger's barn, and Phelps, the cover of the reverse slope of Poffenberger Hill. Gibbon's brigade drew the particular attention of one of the batteries on Nicodemus Heights. It is difficult to say which one, but it was a rifled percussion shell that fell in the midst of Company A, 6th Wisconsin, and sowed bloody destruction, so it came from Wooding's, Carpenter's, or Pelham's battery.

Lieutenant Garber's and the other Confederate batteries on Nicodemus Heights had struck the first blow, but they stirred up what Captain Monroe described as a "hornet's nest." Three of the Federal batteries—Monroe's Rhode Islanders, Captain John A. Reynolds's Battery L, 1st New York, and Lieutenant Frederick M. Edgell's 1st Battery, New Hampshire Light Artillery—counting 18 guns, all Napoleons or rifles, cleared for action in "but three or four minutes" and returned fire. Poffenberger Hill became its own active volcano, belching flame and smoke as shells arced to the source of the enemy fire. During the winter of 1861, Monroe's battery and Battery L had drilled under John Gibbon, then the commander of Battery B, 4th U.S., and one of the leading experts on the technical aspects of gunnery in the pre-war Regular Army, until they achieved "great proficiency" in sighting and targeting. This training paid dividends in the artillery duel, but the miserable system of attaching batteries to divisions—and even brigades—thus rendering the chief of artillery position void of any tactical authority, meant that it was difficult for Monroe to mass firepower against specific targets. He might have used Campbell's Battery B, 4th U.S., Ransom's Battery C, 5th U.S., or Thompson's Battery C, Pennsylvania Light, all of which were close at hand, to help smash Stuart's guns, but Campbell's battery was ordered to move with Gibbon's brigade, and Ransom and Thompson took their orders from either their division commander or from Hooker, who superseded all others in the corps and acted like his own chief of artillery.[24]

One of the Federal batteries on Poffenberger Hill observed a different target than the Confederate guns on Nicodemus Heights. The night before, "through the mistake of a blundering guide," Fitz Lee's cavalry brigade had been led into a position near the heights that was under the direct observation of the Union gunners once it grew light enough to see. Before daylight, Lee realized his exposure and personally began quietly awakening his officers. The brigade mounted and, as soundlessly as a cavalry brigade can move, set out for cover. But they were spotted by one of the Federal batteries, who opened fire on them. The incoming shells drew blood before all the cavalrymen had mounted. The first shell struck alongside Lieutenant Colonel John T. Thornton, commanding the 3rd Virginia Cavalry, as he swung up into his saddle. A fragment fractured one of Thornton's arms in three places. Another piece wounded Corporal T. J. Handy, killed his horse, and threw earth over Sergeant George W. Beale in the 9th Virginia Cavalry, who was close enough to see the "shrugging of his [Thornton's] shoulders and quiver of the muscles of his face" when the fragment struck him. Thornton's wound was a frightful one, near his shoulder. The limb was amputated, but he died in the early hours of September 18.[25]

The guns on Nicodemus Heights, however, were the primary target of the 1st Corps' batteries. Once they had the range, they pummeled the graycoat gunners. Wooding's battery appears to have been the hardest hit, reporting 15 casualties from a strength of 64. Pelham ordered Lieutenant Garber, whose howitzers were out-ranged, to retire when he came under a crossfire. Despite fierce fire and casualties, the crews of the other three batteries stuck to their guns and continued to blaze away.[26]

Minutes after this gun duel erupted, S. D. Lee's batteries began shelling the North Woods and Poffenberger Hill. This drew the attention of the Union gunners manning the batteries on Pry Ridge, who now also observed Walker's and Douglass's brigades, lying in the open fields south of the East Woods, and Roswell Ripley's brigade of D. H. Hill's division, positioned in a field south of Samuel Mumma's farm. There were three batteries on the ridge, mounting eight 20 lb. Parrott rifles and four 10 lb. Parrott rifles, all with the range to strike these targets, and they opened up an enfilading fire on them. Colonel James Walker reported that his brigade "was exposed to full view of their gunners and had no shelter." Yet he found the fire mostly "annoying" and "less destructive than I at first apprehended it would be." His experience was the exception. Other Confederate brigades reported numerous casualties. A member of Douglass's brigade accurately estimated that they were under fire from three batteries, which "used shell with terrible effect" among the exposed Georgians. Captain George Ring in the 6th Louisiana of Harry Hay's brigade, which had moved from the West Woods to the open ground between Douglass's brigade and S. D. Lee's artillery battalion, wrote to his wife, "I thought, darling, that I had heard at Malvern Hill heavy cannonading, but I was mistaken. That half hour that we were lying in that field taught me to the contrary." Shells from the Federal guns killed or wounded "a good many" in Hays's regiments before they even joined the infantry action.[27]

Stonewall Jackson described the enfilading fire as "severe and damaging" and reported that his divisional batteries—those of Poague, Carpenter, Brocken-brough, Raine, Caskie, and Wooding—all responded "vigorously" to it. This sounded impressive but amounted to very little. Wooding and Carpenter were on Nicodemus Heights and were trading fire with the 1st Corps' batteries on Pof-fenberger Hill, not firing at the Union guns east of Antietam Creek, which were beyond their range anyway. Caskie had only one gun on the field, a 10 lb. Parrott, and Raine had only two 3-inch rifles. Poague and Brockenbrough counted 5 rifled guns between them. The Union 20 lb. Parrotts were at the ex-treme range of all these Confederate rifled pieces, and it is unlikely that the Fed-erals directed much, if any, fire at them when so many other targets, at closer range, presented themselves.[28]

S. D. Lee's battalion, with its concentration of guns, crews, limbers, caissons, and horses presented the largest target for Union gunners. Some months later, when Colonel Edward P. Alexander succeeded Colonel Stephen D. Lee in com-mand of his reserve battalion of artillery, Lee told him "that I might pray never to see another Sharpsburg, that 'Sharpsburg was artillery hell.'" It was necessary for Lee's battalion to face northeast, the direction in which the Union's 1st Corps was expected to advance, but this presented their flank to the Federal batteries on Pry Ridge. "I was taken in enfilade and almost in reverse by the long range guns of the enemy on the east side of Antietam Creek," Lee wrote after the war. Captain William Parker, one of Lee's battery commanders, remarked, "They got the range with the first shot, and kept it for two hours."[29]

Captain William W. Parker's battery was particularly hard hit, losing 21 men and 12 horses in 40 minutes—around a third of its manpower and horsepower—devastating losses for an artillery battery. Parker was a physician in civilian life, and he raised and organized the battery in the spring of 1862 from volunteers drawn from the Richmond, Virginia, area. It earned the nickname "The Boy Company," because it seemed to have so many young men, including some who needed the written permission of their parents to enlist, although the battery's historian noted that the average age on enlistment in the company was 25.2 years. It fell under Stephen D. Lee's command in early August, who found it poorly trained and believed it was "a very crude organization." Lee rode Parker and his men hard in the company's training. "The Captain and Company did not understand me or why I was so strict and harsh," Lee recalled, and he was deeply unpopular until the battery's first exposure to combat at Second Manassas. Then, the reason for Lee's seeming severity became evident to all.[30]

In the current battle, "men and horses fell in rapid succession," recalled Royal W. Figg, one of Parker's artillerymen. Smoke from all the firing "hung like a pall over the scene of conflict." One Union shell smashed through a caisson, and Patrick McNeil, a 35-year-old driver on the vehicle, who was miraculously unharmed, held up a set of good-luck beads given to him by some ladies in Frederick several days before, as if they were the reason his life had been spared. Joseph M. "Kenny" Richardson, age 15, was not as fortunate. His father had been attempting to get his son out of the army, but without success. Kenny was listed as a battery drummer, and when the action commenced, Parker had sent him to the battery's rear—probably with the caissons—with another 15-year-old youngster, Willie Evans. But the rapid loss of manpower forced Parker to call the lads forward to help serve the guns. Richardson had barely reached the gun line when a shell struck him, killing him instantly.[31]

THE GROWING VOLUME OF small-arms fire Colonel Walker and his infantrymen were receiving from the direction of the southern border of the East Woods was of greater concern than the enfilading artillery fire. The source of this fire was Truman Seymour's 1st Brigade of the Pennsylvania Reserves. Seymour's brigade, particularly the 13th Rifles, or Bucktails (called that because of the tail of a whitetail deer each man wore in his kepi), had borne the brunt of the fighting on the evening of the 16th. When night put an end to the combat, Seymour pulled the bulk of his brigade back to near the northern edge of the East Woods, leaving only the 13th Rifles near the wood's southern boundary. For a young man who sought danger and the opportunity to see combat, the 13th Rifles was a good choice, for few other units in the Army of the Potomac had seen as much fighting. The regiment was armed with breech-loading Sharps rifles, which consequently accorded it the bulk of the dangerous work of skirmishing and sharpshooting. They led the advance of the division at South Mountain, and again during the movement on September 16. In the action to clear the East Woods, they lost their excellent colonel, Hugh McNeil. McNeil's death left Captain Dennis McGee of Company F in command. So great was the attrition of officers in the regiment from the spring's and summer's battles that McGee was one of only two captains left with the regiment. Although he seems to have been personally courageous, McGee lacked confidence to manage the regiment in action, a view the rank and file shared, so he asked the adjutant, William R. Hartshorne, to assume tactical command.[32]

Seymour's men were worn out. They had eaten nothing since noon on the 16th, saw the heaviest combat that evening, and then lay down on their arms, with their equipment on, through the night, which was frequently punctuated by flare-ups of firing between pickets, so no one got any sleep. Angelo Crapsey, a 19-year-old private in Company I of the 13th Rifles, fired 70 rounds from his Sharps rifle in the skirmishing on the evening of the 16th and "was well satisfied to stop for the night." In the middle of that night, Seymour sent orders up to the commander of Crapsey's company, Lieutenant Frank Bell, a 25-year-old carpenter from McKean County, Pennsylvania, to take 10 men and creep up close to the Confederate pickets and wait there until morning—the equivalent of establishing a nineteenth-century listening post. Crapsey was one of the 10 soldiers Bell took with him. The group crawled up close to the southern edge of the East Woods and concealed themselves behind a log. At first light, they observed either Walker's skirmish line or the skirmishers in the 31st Georgia advancing toward the woods. "Wee let them advance & when within 12 rods [about 60 yards] wee just commenced to upset them," wrote Crapsey. "I knocked several of them & they tried to kill us but wee could hold them off as long as our ammunition held out," he continued.[33]

There had been no opportunity to resupply with ammunition during the night, and Craspey was down to only 20 rounds, which the Sharps rifles could burn through quickly. Despite their initial surprise and casualties, the Confederates fought doggedly. They managed to gain a flanking fire on the party which had wounded Bell and two others and put a ball into Crapsey's knapsack, "not more than 3 in[ches] from my back." With their position becoming untenable, Craspey and the others "just scedalted" back into the woods. But they, too, had mettle, and when they came upon dead and wounded men from their regiment— possibly from the fighting on the 16th—they gathered ammunition from them and returned to the fight.[34]

Although Crapsey may have been too busy trying to avoid being shot to notice, he and his comrades were being reinforced. Skirmishers in the 1st and 6th Pennsylvania Reserves pushed through the western side of the East Woods and the soon-to-be-infamous cornfield of farmer David Miller (referred to henceforth as "the Cornfield"), stopping at the southern border of the field and the woods. Among those scooped up in their advance was Lieutenant William H. "Tip" Harrison in the 31st Georgia, who had earlier established his brigade's skirmish line in the corn. "They told us to throw down our guns and come in, and to be quick about it," recalled a sergeant with Harrison. South of the corn, the Reserves' skirmishers opened fire on the balance of the 31st Georgia, who formed the picket reserve south of the Cornfield. The 5th Pennsylvania Reserves advanced to the left of the 13th Reserves and opened fire at Walker's regiments, who were lying down in Samuel Mumma's plowed field, about 200 yards away. Meanwhile, the 2nd Reserves moved up and relieved the 13th, whose remaining riflemen were down to their last rounds.[35]

Walker's regiments were in a difficult position. With small-arms fire in front, artillery fire in their flank, and no cover, their courage was severely tested.

"Going into battle has always been a terrible thing for me. So it is with every other man," wrote Captain Ujanirtus Allen in the 21st Georgia, shortly after Antietam. Allen carried only seven men from his company into the fight, and three of them fell out or skulked off to escape the combat. He found that anger helped him overcome his dread of battle. When his remaining four men were wounded, he carried on the fight by picking up an Enfield rifle, and "if I did not wake things up it is not because I did not try." The commander of the 12th Georgia, Captain James G. Rodgers, of whom it was said that he loved "to go about doing good," had all the fingers on his left hand shot off but refused to leave the field, continuing to pass up and down his line. Such leadership inspired Walker's men to fight with "spirit and effect" and hold Seymour's Pennsylvanians in check, despite the Confederates' exposure.[36]

Shirkers afflicted every unit when the troops came under fire. Colonel William Sinclair, commanding the 6th Pennsylvania Reserves, complained that his effective strength was greatly reduced, due to the quantity of his men who helped the wounded to the rear without orders, a problem that would diminish the numbers of many 1st Corps regiments that day. In the 5th Pennsylvania Reserves, Colonel J. W. Fisher reported that Captain Arnold D. Collins, "by some strange fatality finds his health to fail about the commencement of almost every battle," and that Lieutenant A. Percival Shaw, when their regiment was fired on in the middle of the night, "disgracefully fled . . . and gave an alarm which, had they been as cowardly as himself, might have proved disastrous." While men like Crapsey, Allen, and Rodgers inspired those around them with their courage under fire, those like Collins and Shaw could sap the courage of their men and weaken discipline.[37]

While Seymour's Pennsylvanians exchanged fire with Walker's and Douglass's regiments, the brigades of Hooker's 1st and 2nd Divisions were steadily approaching to open the attack on Jackson's line. To provide them with close support, Hooker ordered batteries from both divisions to move forward with the infantry. Hooker intended that Gibbon's and Hartsuff's brigades would lead their respective divisional assaults. The plan in Ricketts's 2nd Division was straightforward. Hartsuff's and Duryée's brigades, which had spent the night in the vicinity of Poffenberger's Woods, were to flank to the right, so both brigades would be west of Smoketown Road, and then advance to the attack, with Hartsuff leading and Duryée's men, formed in column of divisions, following to Hartsuff's right rear. Colonel William A. Christian's 2nd Brigade would advance east of Smoketown Road, on Hartsuff's left rear. The idea apparently was that Hartsuff would engage the enemy, and Duryée and Christian could either reinforce Hartsuff or maneuver. This, at least, appears to have been Ricketts's intention, but things went awry before the attack had barely begun, due to bad luck and weak leadership.[38]

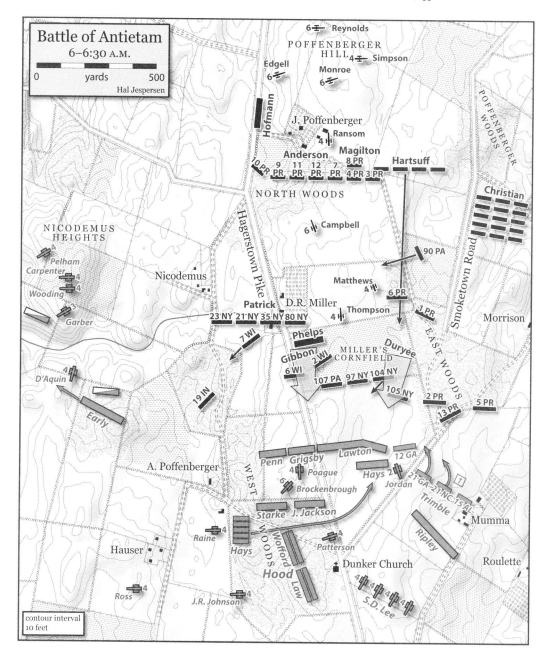

The bad luck involved Hartsuff. The general was a fine soldier, but an unlucky one. Calamity seemed to be his companion. Following his 1852 graduation from the U.S. Military Academy at West Point, he served in Texas, where he contracted yellow fever. He survived this deadly disease, but 2 years later, in 1855, his unit was ambushed during the Third Seminole War. Most of the soldiers were killed or injured, and Hartsuff, who was wounded three times, only managed to survive by hiding in a swamp. He still carried one of the bullets in his chest, which surgeons had been unable to locate. Five years later, in 1860, while crossing Lake Michigan one stormy evening on the PS *Lady Elgin*, the ship was struck amidships by a lumber schooner, and 373 passengers on the *Lady Elgin* drowned in the disaster.

Hartsuff received his orders to advance around daybreak that September 17 morning. He put his brigade in motion at once, moving through the gray, slightly foggy morning air toward the East Woods. But, after covering a short distance, he ordered his regiments to halt and lie down while he rode forward to reconnoiter, in order to gain an understanding of the situation at the front, where he could hear the firing between Seymour's, Douglass's, and Walker's men. He rode up close to the front—too close, as it turned out—and a Confederate rifleman put a bullet into his left hip. The pain was excruciating, but Hartsuff stayed in his saddle until blood loss forced him to dismount. Some of his soldiers came to his aid and attempted to help him to the rear on foot, but he collapsed and had to be carried off the field on a stretcher, out of the fight before it had barely begun.[39]

Word of Hartsuff's wounding was unusually slow in reaching Colonel Richard Coulter, commander of the 11th Pennsylvania and the senior colonel in the brigade. The result was that the brigade remained motionless near the northern edge of the East Woods for nearly 30 minutes. When Coulter finally learned that Hartsuff was wounded and he was now in command, he was unaware of Hartsuff's orders, so the brigade remained in place. Ricketts, whose job it was to manage his division's attack, had his hands full with a command failure in Christian's brigade, so he also had not noticed that Coulter was not moving.[40]

The weak reed in Ricketts's division was Colonel William Christian's 2nd Brigade—specifically, the colonel. Christian had the resumé of a soldier. He served as an enlisted man in the Mexican War—although his regiment spent the war in San Francisco—and, before the war, he had been the drillmaster for a militia unit in Utica, New York, where he was a surveyor. These credentials helped secure him a commission as colonel of the 26th New York Infantry. As long as soldiering consisted of training and drilling, Christian did well, but in the regiment's baptism by fire at Second Manassas, his courage failed him utterly. Claiming that he was debilitated by heatstroke and poison ivy, he avoided the engagement in which his regiment suffered nearly 200 casualties. He rose to brigade command by seniority when its regular commander was wounded. At South Mountain, his brigade showed poor discipline, firing off much of their ammunition after it became too dark to distinguish targets. During the march into position near Poffenberger's Woods on the evening of the 16th, some Confederate shells burst nearby but inflicted no casualties. Nevertheless, they unnerved Christian, and he was heard to remark to Colonel Peter Lyle, commanding the 90th Pennsylvania, that he had a "great horror of these shells."[41]

When Christian's brigade began to move toward the East Woods, John Vautier, in the 88th Pennsylvania, sensed something was amiss. "We done an unnecessary amount of drilling I think going into action," observed Vautier. "First it would be 'Forward guide center' then 'By the right flank' and then 'Forward guide center' again & then we would oblique to the left & so on." Vautier added that these excessive revolutions caused "no confusion, all was orderly, & every one was in his place notwithstanding the balls & shells flew thickly round us." Lieutenant Sam Moore in the 90th Pennsylvania wrote that "grape, canister and shell of every description [were] flying around like hail, cutting down trees or anything in its way." With friendly batteries nearby returning the Confederates' fire, the noise was deafening. Under such circumstances, fear was every man's companion. Christian was riding behind the 26th New York when he was seen to dismount and start leading his horse toward the rear. "He would duck and dodge his head and go crouching along," wrote Lieutenant William Halstead. Another lieutenant in the 26th, William Gifford, added years later that Christian proceeded to almost create a stampede in the rear "by shouting that our flank was turned and the lines completely broken." The disgraceful incident ended Christian's soldiering. He was allowed to quietly resign two days after Antietam. Instead of demoralizing the soldiers, Christian's behavior under fire elicited disgust from those who witnessed it, and his brigade remained steady, although it now had no leader.[42]

When it became imperative that Ricketts had to supervise the movements of all three of his brigades plus his divisional artillery, Christian's lack of morale forced Ricketts to focus his attention on the leaderless brigade. He personally ordered the regiments to deploy from column of division to line of battle, to reduce the damage the Confederates' artillery might inflict, and detailed Captain John W. Williams, his assistant adjutant general, to guide the brigade forward.[43]

These disruptions to Ricketts's advance resulted in Duryée's brigade taking the lead in the division's assault. In their initial movement from Poffenberger's Woods, Duryée's regiments flanked to the right, then moved south, part of the brigade passing over Magilton's brigade of Pennsylvania Reserves in the North Woods, before emerging into a plowed field south of the woods. The four 3-inch rifles of Captain Ezra W. Matthews's Battery F, 1st Pennsylvania, were unlimbered to the Reserve's left front, near the northwestern corner of the East Woods, and engaged in a "lively artillery duel" with S. D. Lee's battalion. Captain James Thompson led the other battery of Ricketts's division, Battery C, Pennsylvania Light Artillery, also consisting of four 3-inch rifles. Thompson followed Duryée's brigade, and before passing through the North Woods, the captain informed Duryée that he lacked sufficient manpower to crew his guns, asking whether he might be able to obtain some infantry volunteers. Although it might have struck Duryée as unusual that Thompson had waited until they were under fire to seek additional manpower, he halted his brigade and ordered Colonel Howard Carroll, commanding the 105th New York, to supply all the men

Thompson needed. Artillery service was known to generally be safer than infantry combat. Therefore, so many men in the 105th volunteered that Duryée had to personally select who would become temporary artillerymen.[44]

Detailing men to Thompson's battery only detained Duryée for a few minutes. Thompson moved his battery forward to the pasture immediately north of the Cornfield, where he unlimbered and engaged S. D. Lee's guns. Duryée had his brigade lie down approximately 100 yards to the rear of Thompson and Matthews, while these two units shelled the Confederate batteries. Thompson's and Matthews's batteries drew their share of fire from Lee's guns, a fair proportion of which passed over them and fell around Duryée's men. Duryée kept his regiments in column of divisions, which made command and control easier, but, as the experience of the 6th Wisconsin that morning illustrated, the density of the formation increased the possibility of severe casualties. John Delany, a private in the 107th Pennsylvania who would earn a Medal of Honor later in the war, recalled that "the rain of shot and shell" that reached the infantry line "was fearful." He watched as one shell exploded under the muzzle of one of Thompson's guns, knocking down three of its crew and igniting the fuse of the shell the loader, who was standing beside the muzzle, was carrying. That man was uninjured, and Delany "saw that brave fellow grab the burning fuse and extinguish it." Another round, which was a solid shot, struck directly in front of Delany's regiment and bounded over all 10 companies without injuring anyone. "I speak of these incidents because they impressed themselves on my mind most forcibly," he wrote.[45]

In his November 8 after-action report on the battle, Hooker claimed that he discovered a heavy enemy force sheltering in the Cornfield, their bayonets sticking up above the corn and glistening in the sun, and that he ordered "all of my spare batteries," of which he thought there were five or six, to open fire on the corn with canister. Hooker thrilled readers when he described the effect: "In the time I am writing every stalk of corn in the northern and greater part of the field was cut as closely as could have been done with a knife, and the slain lay in rows precisely as they stood in their ranks a few moments before." Although this passage has been quoted countless times to reflect the awfulness of Antietam, it is pure fantasy, which Hooker knew would play well in the papers. No Confederates, other than skirmishers, were in the corn, and they did not have their bayonets fixed. The corn was 7 to 8 feet tall, and there was no sun to glint off metal that gloomy early morning. Hooker had only nine batteries in the entire 1st Corps, and none of them, including Thompson's and Matthews's, which were both close to the Cornfield, were ordered to blast it with canister. They were all too busy firing at Nicodemus Heights, or S. D. Lee guns, or Jackson's batteries, to expend canister rounds on the Cornfield.[46]

After several minutes of shelling, Duryée ordered his 1,100 men forward. They passed in front of the two batteries and entered David Miller's clover field. Here,

Duryée finally deployed his regiments into line of battle and advanced into Miller's still fully intact 30-acre cornfield. Their view of what lay in front was obscured by the height of the cornstalks. The time was approximately 5:45 a.m. The enemy were very close, as was clear from the stream of shells coming from south of the Cornfield, and Duryée's men could hear small-arms fire to their left front, where Seymour's Pennsylvania Reserves were trading fire with Walker's and Douglass's brigades. Some of S. D. Lee's guns tracked the brigade's advance and, as Captain John C. Whiteside in the 105th New York wrote, "did us severe damage." Whiteside offered a graphic example of what "severe damage" meant. Rufus Barnhart, an 18-year-old private in Whiteside's company, "was struck or shot with a solid shot and his head blown from his body." Moments before his death, Barnhart—whom Whiteside described as a "noble fellow" and "brave soldier"—had been mocking the shells that passed over the regiment, calling them "little tea-pots." Despite this frightful incident, Whiteside recorded that his regiment moved on, "paying no attention to those who fell in our ranks." It seems impossible that any man could be impervious to or pay no attention to such a dreadful event, but discipline and courage held the command together, despite the casualties, and enabled it to continue its advance.[47]

SOUTH OF THE CORNFIELD, the 31st Georgia, on the right front of Douglass's brigade, had advanced to within 100 yards of the East Woods and the Cornfield to support the skirmish line, and they had been engaged with Seymour's brigade of Pennsylvanians since first light. But the rest of the 1,150 officers and men of the Confederate brigade lay behind the slight cover provided by the fence where they had formed, enduring the shelling of the Union batteries east of Antietam Creek and waiting for the enemy infantry to show themselves. "There was nothing to stop the deadly missiles but our unprotected bodies," recalled Sergeant Thomas Maddox in the 13th Georgia. Maddox's body was one that stopped some of the iron, with a fragment that struck him in the upper right breast, permanently paralyzing his right arm. His brigade commander, the 31-year-old Douglass, came from Cuthbert, Georgia, in the southeastern part of the state. As an attorney, Douglass had won a reputation "as a brilliant lawyer and an eloquent speaker." He served as a Randolph County delegate to the Georgia secession convention, where he voted to take Georgia out of the Union. Afterward, he helped recruit a company of the 13th Georgia and was commissioned as its captain. Within a month of his enlistment, Douglass was promoted to lieutenant colonel, and when the regiment's colonel died in early 1862, he was selected to command it. Brigade command fell to him by seniority when Alexander Lawton assumed leadership of the division after the wounding of Richard Ewell at the Battle of Brawner's Farm on August 28, and Douglass commanded the unit during the subsequent desperate fighting along the unfinished railroad cut during the Battle of Second Manassas.[48]

The colonel and his Georgians could not see Duryée's regiments approaching. The Cornfield and East Woods blocked their view to the north, and their position was on ground that was lower than the Cornfield. They could see some of Seymour's men at the edge of the East Woods and the southeastern edge of the corn, who were engaged with Walker's brigade and the 31st Georgia, but they were the only enemy in view. Besides the fence line the brigade had thrown down to obtain some cover, and unevenness in the ground and the rock outcroppings here and there, the men had no cover. Douglass's skirmishers probably warned him of Duryée's approach, and he gave orders for his regiments to hold their fire until the Federals were within 100 yards. Some of Douglass's regiments were armed with the .577 caliber Enfield rifle-musket, which had an effective range of up to 600 yards, although it was not accurate to that distance. The range Douglass selected for when to begin firing was favored by many infantry officers throughout the war. It was close enough for fire from a line armed with rifle-muskets to inflict considerable damage on an attacking line, yet far enough away for the men to have time to reload and fire several more times before the enemy might be upon them.[49]

Duryée's line made their way through Miller's corn. The southern edge of the Cornfield was planted in broomcorn, a variety of sorghum. As the brigade passed through this, Major Charles Northup halted the 97th New York before they reached the Cornfield's fence, probably to observe what was in front of them. A member of the regiment heard General Duryée shout, "There they are boys, give it to them!" There, slightly over 200 yards to the south, "behind a rail fence, and some bushes," were the Rebels. The New Yorkers shouldered their Enfield rifles and opened fire. Captain Henry J. Sheafer in the 107th Pennsylvania, on the far right of the brigade's battle line, recalled that the Georgians were the first to fire. "The rebels poured it into us," he remembered. Duryée's men found that the worm fence on the Cornfield's border had been dismantled, probably the night before, by Douglass's skirmishers or Hood's men, with its rails lying strewn about. The Pennsylvanians instinctively dropped down on the ground or knelt and returned the fire "for all that was in us." The 97th New York received the same reception as the 107th, but Isaac Hall, the regimental historian, recorded that the men of his unit did not lie down, but instead stood for some minutes and fired away, which may account for the fact that the 97th incurred the highest number of men in their brigade who were either killed or wounded. Despite their losses, a member of the regiment was impressed with how "steady and determined" his comrades were as they continued to load and fire. The 105th New York managed to be the first to fire when they emerged from the corn. "As soon as we came within gun shot of the rebs we gave them a volley," wrote Captain Whiteside, which the Georgians immediately returned. The 105th and 104th New York pushed past the fence line and into the meadow south of the corn, maintaining a steady fire as they did so. Their comrades in the 97th New York and the 107th Pennsylvania did not join this movement, but remained near the corn's edge, where they had some slight cover. The New Yorkers forward push exposed them to a crossfire from Walker's 12th Georgia and the regiments of Douglass's brigade on the right. They also drew special attention from S. D. Lee's artillery. Orders were shouted to lie down, but not before Colonel Howard Carroll, commanding the 105th, went down with a mortal wound, and many other casualties were inflicted. In the opinion of Captain Sheafer, everywhere across Duryée's front the Confederates "fought like devils."[50]

Douglass attempted to maneuver against Duryée by advancing the 26th Georgia, on his left flank, at a left oblique, in order to gain some higher ground nearer the Hagerstown Pike, where they might get a partial flanking fire on the 107th Pennsylvania. The 38th Georgia, to the 26th's right, moved directly on Duryée's line, attempting to gain a ledge of ground closer to the Federals, but the Pennsylvanians and New Yorkers drove them back with heavy losses. Douglass was a dynamic combat leader and exposed himself recklessly, moving up and down his line, calling to his men "to keep cool and aim well," and, at one point, exclaiming, "That's right my brave boys—pour it into them again." He paid a price for his exposure when he took a bullet "in the region of the stomach," but he refused to be evacuated and continued in command. The men in the 31st Georgia, on the far right of the brigade, thought "the fight was the hottest" where they were, but such was the intensity of fire between the opposing lines that everyone believed their part of the line sustained the worst damage. Lieutenant Colonel John T. Crowder, the 31st Georgia's commander, emulated Douglass, exposing himself and exhorting to his men, "We can't afford to give up this line!" When he moved near his regimental flag, or colors, a piece of shell struck him in the breast, and an instant later a minie ball from Duryée's line inflicted a wound in his abdomen that would leave his right leg partially paralyzed. Two of his men carried him from the field. He would survive, but his war was over.[51]

When the 104th and 105th New York advanced into the meadow south of the corn, Walker's 12th Georgia, numbering only 100 men, wheeled to their left to get cover along a ledge running parallel to Smoketown Road, from which they could bring more effective fire on the New Yorkers. They could execute this movement because Seymour's Pennsylvania Reserves regiments had fallen back from the southern edge of the East Woods. Walker aggressively followed up on Seymour's withdrawal by pushing skirmishers into the edge of the woods, where they fired on Duryée's New Yorkers, as well as the 2nd Reserves and skirmishers in the 1st and 6th Reserves, who were still within the woods. Walker noticed that the fire of his Georgians was "annoying" the 104th and 105th New York "very greatly," and with his front now relieved of fire from Seymour's brigade, he ordered the 21st Georgia and the 21st North Carolina to also wheel left, cross Smoketown Road, and get cover along the same ledge as the 12th Georgia. Walker received close artillery support when S. D. Lee ordered a section of Captain

Tyler C. Jordan's Bedford (Virginia) battery to advance close to the infantry. Jordan's men found their position to be a hot one. One of the section members, J. C. Reed, recalled later on, "As from what direction we received the most artillery & infantry fire, it seemed to me to come from <u>everywhere</u>." They managed to get off only two rounds before the storm of fire they attracted forced them to withdraw.[52]

The fusillade of bullets and shells took a steady toll on Duryée's regiments. "The battle was a terrible affair. Men [were] dropping all around—with heads and legs off. The continual roar of cannon the shot and shell flying around and the hissing of the balls all make it terrible," Charles Hayden in the 97th New York wrote to his sister afterward. Charles Barber, a private in the 104th New York, offered another picture of the carnage to his regiment in a letter home two days after the battle: "Wm Thomas got a ball through his hand Walter [Steele] got the end of his thumb shot off. . . . Capt [Henry G.] Tuthill had three fingers shot off and a ball in his leg he was carried off the field our com[pany] had two sergeants wounded two of our boys lost each a leg by a shell." The men on Barber's left and right were shot. He helped the wounded comrade on his right to the rear and then returned to the fight. This was uncommon. There were numerous volunteers eager to help the wounded off the battlefield, but few of them returned to the fighting. This was the case with most in the 104th who left the line. Francis N. Bell recalled that the regiment's line was "badly cut up" by too many leaving to assist the wounded off behind the lines. To Barber, it seemed miraculous that he was not hit. "Probably 50 bullets come in a few inches of me while my comrades fell right and left," he wrote. "I was not a bit afraid in battle but now the battle is over and I look back and see the many chances I had it makes me almost tremble now."[53]

Duryée's horse was hit early on in the fight. Some men in the 107th Pennsylvania saw the general throw himself over the back of his horse, with his head facing the horse's rump, and were under the impression that he was badly wounded, for "at every jump the wounded horse made his [Duryée's] body would sway to and fro and strike the animal's rump." Duryée departed the field in this undignified and unusual position, but he returned later, on foot. The close call evidently shook the general up, for his management of the brigade from this point on was minimal, although being dismounted did limit his mobility. His single aide-de-camp had his horse "shattered under him by a shell," which further reduced Duryée's ability to issue orders. The general's brother, the brigade's assistant adjutant general, William B. C. Duryée, exhibited great personal bravery but was of little help with command and control. Captain Sheafer thought that "I never saw a more excited man then he was in this fight, riding up & down the line like a wild man." Duryée's regiments thus fought on their own hook.[54]

As the combat raged on, a report reached Duryée that Seymour's Pennsylvania Reserves were withdrawing, and Confederates were entering the East Woods and threatening the brigade's flank and rear. This report was only partially true. Some of Walker's skirmishers had reached the southern edge of the woods, but several of Seymour's regiments remained in the woods, as they had only fallen back from the wood's edge to get better cover. With himself and his single aide-de-camp dismounted, and his brother raving like a madman, Abram Duryée had no means of investigating the report's accuracy. Instead, he somehow communicated orders for his regiments to fall back. They had been in action for nearly 30 minutes.[55]

It is relatively easy to order a retreat, but quite another thing to execute one in an orderly manner while under fire. Duryée's brigade was no exception. The chaos and confusion of battle; the cacophony of small-arms and artillery fire; the terrain, in this case the height of the corn, which blocked the view of some; the enemy, who fully occupied the attention of the fighting men; the danger, which intensified when physically carrying a message to regimental commanders and then getting the word communicated to each company—all of this made a well-ordered withdrawal exceptionally difficult. As Captain Sheafer, who commanded the four right companies of the 107th Pennsylvania recalled, "The corn was so dense that we could not see movements on our left." His regiment was in front of the corn, but apparently the boundary line of the Cornfield and the lay of the land prevented him from being able to observe the rest of his regiment and brigade. Sheafer received no orders to retreat from Captain James Mac-Thompson, his regimental commander, and was completely unaware that the rest of his brigade, as well as the left wing of his regiment, had withdrawn. He only discovered this when a man from the regiment's left wing crawled up through the corn and told him that everyone else had withdrawn, the 107th's two color bearers were dead, and the colors were lying on the ground. This meant that McThompson, who withdrew with the regiment's left wing, was either unaware that his color guard was shot down, which was possible in the confusion, or he was aware of it and simply did not attempt to retrieve the fallen colors—a grave offense in Civil War combat, where the regimental colors reflected the honor and courage of the regiment. Sheafer called for volunteers to rescue the banners, but he later stated that the enemy fire was so heavy, "I could not get a man that was with me to go down & fetch the colors." The men hugged the ground, and, admitted Sheafer, "it was really death to get up." The captain and his men fought on for several more minutes, until they had exhausted all their ammunition, as well as the ammo from the cartridge boxes of the dead and wounded. The Confederate fire had not diminished, and it actually seemed to be increasing. Sheafer knew it was time to go.[56]

The captain later claimed that he alone ran down and retrieved the flags, but John Delany, who was in one of Sheafer's four companies, remembered things differently. He saw the flags "laying under a pile of dead and wounded men," and, beyond them, observed a line of Confederates advancing toward him "on a dog trot." They may have been elements of Douglass's brigade, or Hays's Louisiana brigade, who arrived around this time to reinforce Douglass and Walker. Delany also saw Captain Sheafer and Delany's tentmate, James Kennedy. Both, he wrote, were making their way to the rear and were urging Delany to "come back." Delany claimed he yelled to them that the regiment's colors were down on the ground. "They both came bounding back," recalled Delany, "and in an instant we pulled them [the colors] out, and with our hearts in our mouths dashed away the Rebels calling out to us to drop the flags but strange to say for some reason or other, failed to fire a shot at us."[57]

Issac Hall, in the 97th New York, and his company commander, Captain Rouse S. Egleston, were so focused on the enemy that they did not realize their regiment had been ordered to fall back by Duryée's brother. It dawned on Egleston when he finally looked to his left and saw that the 104th and 105th New York were gone. He ran 30 or 40 feet to his right and found only about 20 men in the 97th who, like Hall and Egleston, had not heard the order to withdraw and were still firing. The corn probably blocked his view of Sheafer's four companies of the 107th Pennsylvania, who were farther to the right. Confederate reinforcements were seen approaching the battle zone from the direction of the Dunker Church. Egleston ordered his remnant to fall back. Lieutenant John Strang in the 104th New York, recalling the moment, wrote that "it was all confusion to us." As the 104th made their way back through the corn, Francis Bell, one of its privates, encountered a deflated General Duryée. A mounted officer, probably a staff officer from Ricketts's or Hooker's command, rode up and ordered Duryée to rally his men and "restore that broken line." Duryée replied, "I can't do it. There is all the men I have left," pointing to the remnant of the 104th. Bell described Duryée as "dismounted & demoralized." He was unaware of the condition of his brigade, and Bell thought that he did not know where the 97th New York and the 107th Pennsylvania were.[58]

As Bell and his comrades continued to wend their way through the corn, they encountered some men in the 105th New York, who were carrying the mortally wounded Colonel Carroll in a blanket. Carroll called out, "Give them another charge Boys," which was a delusional order at this point. But then Duryée's wildman brother rode up and shouted to Bell and the others, "Boys will you follow me?" There must have been something inspiring about him, for Bell and about 50 others in the 104th responded and followed the mounted officer back toward the enemy at the double-quick. They encountered riderless wounded horses running from the fight, and "shot and shell was tearing up the ground or bursting in air" around them. Emerging from the corn, they arrived at a slight elevation, probably in the northeast corner of the pasture south of the Cornfield, near the East Woods. Captain Duryée was wounded here and fell from his horse, tumbling into the arms of Major Louis C. Skinner, the 104th's commander. Sergeant John C. Cain, carrying the regiment's state colors, "defiantly" waved the flag from side to side at the approaching Confederates. "They seemed to take the challenge," noted Bell, and "poured a deadly fire into our ranks."[59]

Bell, Skinner, Cain, and the others held their ground for several more minutes. Then Hartsuff's brigade arrived to carry on Ricketts's attack, but Duryée's role in the conflict was finished. Apart from this small band from the 104th New York, by 6:30 a.m. the brigade was out of the battle. They had fought well, but the unit and its commander were used up: 59 officers and men were killed, 231 wounded, and 35 missing, totaling slightly over 30% of their strength. Captain John Whiteside remembered that his Company A of the 105th New York entered the fight with 70 men and "left it with one man & myself." Most of the missing were not casualties, but men separated from their regiments, either in the confusion of the combat and retreat, or because they assisted the wounded back to the rear. Years later, veterans would remember stories of bravery and courage. There had surely been that, but in the moment, and in the immediate aftermath of combat, more often the men simply had a dazed feeling. Some became sick, not understanding how the immense strain on their nerves could affect the body. For others, there was an absolute dread of the concept that they would have to go through the experience again. Writing just over a week after the battle, John B. Sherman in the 105th told his parents that many of the regiment's commissioned officers had resigned, and that "they are all going home if they can get away. . . . This last battle has scared them all." Then, as if fear of another Antietam was a justifiable reason to try to get out of the war if one could, he added, "I do not wonder, for of all the battles that ever was fought this beats all." In a frank admission to his mother in early October, Captain Whiteside wrote, "If we drove them [the Confederates], they in return drove us." The battle shook even the bravest. "Some of us overtaxed our physical powers," admitted Whiteside, "so that we did not get over that day's hardships yet [as of October 4, 1862], and many of us, yes very many of us will never get over it until death overtakes us."[60]

ALTHOUGH DOUGLASS'S AND WALKER'S Confederates rejoiced to see the enemy fleeing back through the corn, both brigades had been seriously hurt in the engagement with Duryée. Colonel Douglass and Lieutenant Colonel Crowder, commanding the 31st Georgia, were both badly wounded, although Douglass still remained on the field. The 13th Georgia was particularly hard hit, receiving small-arms fire from Duryée, plus a crossfire of artillery from Matthews's and Thompson's batteries to the north and the Federal guns across Antietam Creek. Their ordeal elicited little sympathy from Lieutenant Ujanirtus C. Allen, in the 21st Georgia of Walker's brigade. In a letter to a friend after the battle, he wrote how his entire regiment had a "hearty laugh" about a newspaper account that mentioned several members in the 13th who were "shocked by a shell": "Great pity that every member of these pet companies could not get a kind of honorary wound. If you could have seen the 13th Georgia Reg running

like the hounds of h——l were after it while the 21st stood like men and broke
the enemy's line you would have thought that the whole regiment was 'shocked
by a shell' and anticipated another shock." Such rivalries—and even contempt—
were not uncommon between units, but if the survivors in the 13th had run like
the hounds of hell, they had good reason to do so, for there were very few of
them left to run. Of 330 men carried into action, only 34 remained uninjured
by the end of the fight. The tally for their killed and mortally wounded alone was
44, nearly as many as for Duryée's entire brigade. Sergeant Maddox, who was
among the wounded, recorded his company's losses as 9 dead and 15 wounded,
out of 32 men. Shell fragments and minie balls cut the regimental flagstaff into
three pieces and killed or wounded three color bearers. The last of them was
lying wounded on the ground, thrusting a stump of the staff with the flag attached into the air, when a shell burst over him, shredding the banner and,
most likely, its bearer.[61]

In Walker's brigade, Captain Rodgers, commanding the 12th Georgia, who had
the fingers on his left hand shot off early in the fight, received another wound
in the thigh, but he initially still refused to leave the field. Blood loss and shock
changed his mind, but he was killed by a bullet to the head while being carried
to the rear. Nearly all of Walker's regimental leadership was down. Captain Francis P. Miller, commanding the 21st North Carolina, was killed, and Major
Thomas Glover, leading the 21st Georgia, was wounded. Captains now commanded all of Walker's regiments. Losses in the enlisted ranks were also heavy.
When Walker ordered an advance to follow up on Duryée's retreat, he saw only
about a dozen men in the 12th Georgia rise to join in the movement. The rest of
the men remained prone behind the ledge that had sheltered them. The 12th had
a reputation as a steady, tough unit, and their failure to react to his orders surprised Walker. He went over to prod forward those who had not moved, only to
discover that they were motionless because they were dead or wounded. Out of
100 effectives, 59 were casualties. The others had either helped the wounded to
the rear or slipped away in the confusion.[62]

Despite their heavy losses, the remnants of Walker's regiments trotted forward to follow up on the retreating enemy. They were joined by General Harry
Hays's Louisiana brigade, which had been dispatched by Lawton to reinforce the
boundary between Walker's and Douglass's units, as well as some elements of
Douglass's brigade who had joined in the local counterattack. But their advance
ran headlong into Union soldiers—Gibbon's brigade—who emerged from the
corn near the Hagerstown Pike, as well as Hartsuff's and Christian's brigades,
who appeared at the Cornfield's edge on the Midwesterners' left flank. The furious fighting in Miller's cornfield and pasture had only begun.

2

Men of Iron

"This dastardly work of taking the lives of human beings"

The 6th Wisconsin, leading Gibbon's brigade, deployed from column of divisions into line of battle when they reached the North Woods. Confederate shells and solid shot "whistled through the trees above us, cutting off limbs which fell about us," wrote Major Rufus Dawes. "The artillery fire had now increased to the roar of an hundred cannon," he continued, a deafening clamor that assaulted the senses. A plowed field extended south from the woods for nearly 250 yards, where it met one of farmer David R. Miller's meadows. Thompson's and Matthews's Pennsylvania batteries could be seen in this meadow to the left, firing at targets south of the Cornfield. Duryée's brigade had already advanced through the Cornfield and become engaged, although the sound of their combat may not have been audible over the roar of the artillery. David Miller's farm buildings, adjacent to the Hagerstown Turnpike, were visible about 350 yards south of the woods. The turnpike split Miller's farm. On the east side of the pike, Miller and his wife Margaret and their seven children had the family farmhouse, two tenant houses (one of which had been the original farmhouse on the site), a blacksmith shop, a summer kitchen, and several other sheds, bordered on the east side by a large peach and apple orchard and the family's garden. Miller's barn, stable, corncrib-wagon shed, and hog pens were on the west side of the road. In peacetime, Miller's farm was a charming place, but now his buildings, orchard, and fences provided cover for skirmishers from Douglass's Georgia brigade, which Duryée's advance had bypassed.[1]

John Gibbon's orders from Hooker were simple: "Advance directly to the front and attack." Gibbon's brigade was selected to lead the attack from Doubleday's division for several reasons. It was the strongest in the division, with 971 effectives; Gibbon was a talented soldier; and its performance at the Battle of South Mountain had generated attention and positive buzz about the brigadier and his men among some of the army's senior leaders. Hooker allegedly was heard referring to it as his "iron brigade." Whatever the truth was, the name would stick after Antietam. The day after South Mountain, when the brigade passed through the troops of General Edwin Sumner's 2nd Corps at Turner's Gap, the corps' adjutant general told Gibbon he was sorry his command had reached the summit so quickly, as Sumner had just sent orders to his men to cheer the Midwesterners when they passed through. Gibbon, a regular himself, was deeply moved, for "it was well known in the army that he [Sumner] was very much opposed to such demonstrations as not being proper for disciplined troops."[2]

The Civil War was a true brothers' war for Gibbon. Although born in Philadelphia, his family moved to North Carolina when he was 10, and he received his appointment to the U.S. Military Academy from that state. But, unlike most of his Southern classmates, who had resigned their commissions to serve the Confederacy, Gibbon maintained a powerful belief in the preservation of the Union, even over the emotional pull of family. Three of his brothers and two brothers-in-law took a different point of view and were now serving against him. Gibbon's professional branch of service was the artillery. He had been an assistant instructor of long arms at the Military Academy, and in 1859 he authored *The Artillerist's Manual*, which, although never officially adopted by the U.S. War Department, was the most widely read treatise on the employment of field artillery, by both Union and Confederate artillery officers, at the outbreak of the Civil War. When the war began, he commanded Battery B, 4th U.S. Artillery, but the artillery service offered little opportunity for advancement. In May 1862, he managed to secure a promotion from Regular Army captain to brigadier general of volunteers and was assigned to command an infantry brigade in Irwin McDowell's corps, consisting of three Wisconsin regiments (the 2nd, 6th, and 7th) and the 19th Indiana.[3]

Gibbon found his brigade to be an undisciplined lot. "It was not long before I discovered that reveille was a mere farce, which none of the officers attended," he wrote. He cracked down on this, but, unlike many Regular Army officers who despised volunteers and imposed draconian forms of discipline to mold their men into soldiers, Gibbon understood that harsh discipline was counterproductive. To these Midwestern volunteers, "the hope of reward was far more powerful than the fear of punishment." In one example, to improve the soldierly appearance of his men, whom he found to often be disheveled, he rewarded a well-turned-out private with a 24-hour pass and made certain the man's comrades were aware of. It was not long before the dress of the men in the brigade markedly improved. Besides these methods to foster teamwork and pride, Gibbon drilled his men relentlessly and actively worked to weed out poor officers. His regiments became so adept at drill that one veteran remembered proudly, "The brigade was not excelled in the precision and accuracy of their movements by any body of troops I have ever seen not excepting the cadets of West Point." Gibbon understood that when his men faced real bullets and shells, their proficiency at drill would instill the confidence and steadiness that would hold them together. To further build a sense of esprit in his command, Gibbon had the brigade obtain new uniforms, modeled after the uniform of the Regular Army: black Hardee hats with ostrich plumes, frock coats, and white leggings. There was considerable grumbling, since these uniforms cost more money and were harder to keep clean, particularly the leggings, but Gibbon again showed that he understood how to motivate volunteers. Before long they were being referred to as "The Black Hat Brigade," which became a source of great pride.[4]

Gibbon's efforts paid off on August 28, 1862, when his brigade was attacked by five brigades of Stonewall Jackson's command on the Warrenton Turnpike, at what became known as the Battle of Brawner's Farm. Their performance in this engagement and at Second Manassas earned high praise from Army of Virginia commander John Pope, who noted in his after-action report that Gibbon's brigade "consisted of some of the finest troops in the service." But their reputation was earned at a high price. The Battle of Brawner's Farm and the fighting that followed at Second Manassas cost the brigade 894 casualties. They added 318 more casualties just 2 weeks later, at South Mountain. These severe losses, plus the many sick men every brigade counted after the hardships of a campaign like Second Manassas, left Gibbon with only 971 effectives in his four regiments on the morning of September 17. The ostrich plumes were missing from most hats and the white leggings had worn out, but the Hardee hat remained as a mark of the brigade. The Black Hats were veterans now. "Herbert, I have seen some hard times and a good deal more than I expected to," wrote Hugh Perkins in the 7th Wisconsin to a friend. "My comrades and tentmates have fell on each side of me, and I am still alive and without a scratch . . . and I have got so that I can shoot just as cool and deliberate at them [Confederates] as I can at a prairie chicken or pidgeon."[5]

Lieutenant Colonel Edward Bragg's 6th Wisconsin led the brigade attack, which went forward in a column of regiments. Until the enemy position and dispositions were revealed, Gibbon did not want to fully deploy his brigade. He ordered Bragg to screen his movement with two companies of skirmishers, totaling about 60 men. Bragg selected Captain Alexander S. Hooe's Company C and Captain John Kellogg's Company I for this dangerous duty, and both units deployed in skirmish order at the edge of the woods. Hooe's father had been a Regular Army officer, and young Hooe excelled in the business of drilling soldiers. But he found the battlefield to be a frightening place. "He will not run but he is so terrified that he can't give a command," wrote one of his men. Skirmishing was the most dangerous assignment an officer could draw, for it required him to constantly expose himself while managing the extended front of a skirmish line. As for Kellogg, he had no military background. He had been the Juneau County, Wisconsin, prosecutor before the war, but he emerged as a natural leader, possessing great personal and moral courage.[6]

Skirmishers fought in dispersed formations, with approximately five paces between each man. Their purpose was to uncover the enemy's position and harass them, and to screen an attack or a defensive position. The drill manual afforded them considerable freedom of movement in that era of linear tactics: "They should be practiced to fire and load kneeling, lying down, and sitting, and much liberty should be allowed in these exercises, in order that they may be executed in the manner found to be most convenient." Skirmishers were directed to execute movements rapidly, in either quick or double-quick time (the latter amounting to a jog), and to seek out and use whatever cover and concealment was available. When Kellogg's and Hooe's companies, which probably averaged around 30 men each, were fully deployed, they could cover a frontage of around 250 to 300 yards, enabling their line to cover the front and flanks of the regiment. What a skirmish line lacked was firepower. A dispersed line of men with muzzle-loading rifles or muskets simply did not produce enough firepower to dislodge or stop a line of battle.[7]

When the Midwesterners emerged from the woods, the Confederate skirmishers around Miller's farm opened a "vigorous fire" on them. Kellogg, whose company deployed to the left and front of the regiment, led his men across the plowed field "at a run," and, with a "rapid flank movement handsomely executed," flushed out the Confederates and drove them back. In contrast to Kellogg's rapid movement, Hooe's company, tasked with covering the front and right, drifted leaderless. Whether it was because of the Confederates' small-arms fire, the crescendo of artillery fire, or the carnage sown earlier in the ranks of Company A by the Confederates' percussion shells, Captain Hooe became incapacitated with fear. As Lieutenant Colonel Bragg wrote years later, "He showed the white feather that morning, dodged behind a tree and grew there, letting his line go helter skelter without direction." Although Bragg commanded Hooe's Company C to "move forward that line on the right," without leadership, the men failed to respond and were left behind as the main body of the 6th Wisconsin followed Kellogg's company toward Miller's property. Hooe's collapse and the failure of his company to move forward resulted in no skirmishers covering the regiment's right flank. This would shortly lead to trouble.[8]

To facilitate command and control, Bragg divided the regiment into two wings—a fairly common tactic, and something Bragg had done at South Mountain—with Major Dawes directing the left wing and Bragg the right wing. Each wing consisted of four companies, or about 120 to 130 officers and men. When the main body of the regiment reached Miller's farmyard, Bragg's Right Wing encountered some board-paling fencing around Miller's house that was easily flattened by the onrushing line. The companies then dashed through Miller's yard and his other buildings. The men in Dawes's Left Wing were east of the buildings and encountered a stout picket fence, which enclosed Miller's large garden. Dawes "ordered the men of the left wing to take hold all together and pull the fence down." They put muscle into the effort, but Miller's fence prevailed and did not budge. Dawes could waste no more time, and he gave the order for his companies to move by the flank (in a column rather than a line) "with the utmost haste" through Miller's garden gate. He heard his "best friend in the regiment," Captain Edwin A. Brown, commander of Company E, shout "in a loud, nervous voice . . . 'Company E, on the right by file into line.'" Brown, a Fond du Lac, Wisconsin, attorney, enlisted in 1861 as a private but was almost immediately elected sergeant by his men. Promotion to lieutenant and then captain soon followed. The Second Manassas Campaign had devastated Brown's health, and one of his men wrote that the captain was "almost worn out, and so lame that he could scarcely walk." As Brown wrote to his wife at the end of that campaign, "I have seen enough of the horrors of war, imagination cannot picture it, it is too horrible to write about." He attempted to get a leave of absence, but—probably due to the emergency created by Robert E. Lee's invasion of Maryland—it was refused. Now, a moment after the exhausted captain shouted the command to move his men through the garden gate, a bullet or shell fragment struck Brown in the face, mortally wounding him. One of his privates knelt beside him, and Brown gave him some personal effects for his wife before he died. "He was [an] ever kind and noble and human man," wrote a sergeant in Brown's company, and "had not a single enemy in the whole regiment."[9]

Dawes had no time to mourn his friend's death. He led the left wing, which dashed "over briars and flower beds" through Miller's garden and into his orchard. They caught up with Bragg and the right wing by the fence at the orchard's southern boundary. There had been some Confederate skirmishers along this fence—possibly one of them had fired the fatal round at Captain Brown—and they gave Bragg's wing "a hot reception," but, wrote the lieutenant colonel, "it was unavailing to check the bullet like force of the command." The Georgians disappeared into the Cornfield. After Dawes caught up with Bragg and re-formed his companies, he studied the ground in front of him: "Before us was a strip of open field, beyond which on the left-hand [east] side of the turnpike, was rising ground, covered by a large cornfield, the stalks standing thick and high." The regiment's swift advance left them probably several hundred yards in advance of the rest of the brigade. Their movement through Miller's farmyard had also caused the three right companies of the regiment (F, G, and K) to be crowded across the turnpike around Miller's barnyard and strawstacks. The enemy skirmishers had vanished, and not another graycoat was in sight. Moreover, no friendly troops were to be seen, either in front or on the flanks. The corn and the rising ground blocked their view of Duryée's brigade to the southeast, which was still heavily engaged at this time, but no one in the 6th Wisconsin knew they were there. Remaining in the open along Miller's orchard fence and waiting for the brigade to arrive seemed like a bad option to Bragg. His orders were to attack, and he was an aggressive officer. He wasted no time once his regiment had re-formed. With what Dawes described as Bragg's "usual battle ardor," he ordered the regiment to resume its advance.[10]

The regiment moved across the strip of meadow and entered the Cornfield. This was a test of courage and discipline, for the cornstalks stood 7 to 8 feet high,

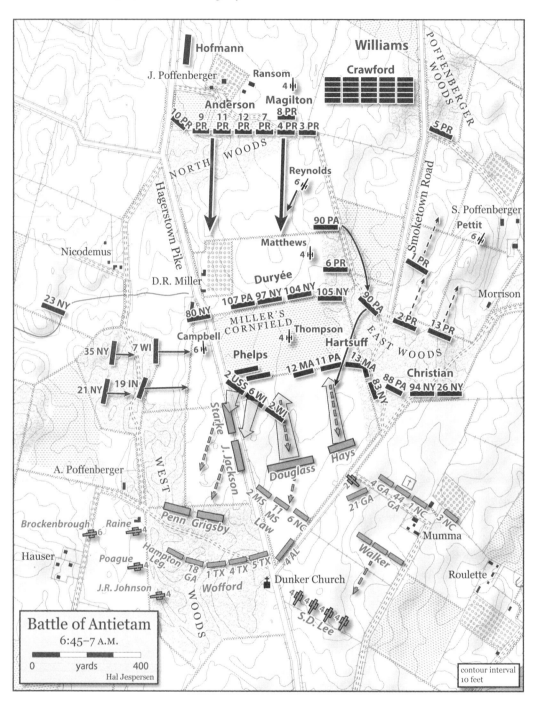

Battle of Antietam

6:45–7 A.M.

0 yards 400

Hal Jespersen

contour interval
10 feet

and although the sounds of battle were roaring around them, within the corn, Bragg's men "could neither see or be seen." The enemy skirmishers who had fired on them from Miller's farmyard indicated that the main Confederate line was close, but where?[11]

The five companies east of the pike moved through the corn cautiously, while the three companies west of the road passed by Miller's barn and nearby straw-stacks and entered a meadow. About 100 yards to their right, the northern portion of the West Woods (there were three distinct sections to it) stood on their flank. It was the duty of Captain Hooe's Company C to probe this woodlot for the enemy, but his leadership failure meant that it remained unexplored. Lying unseen among the trees were skirmishers of Captain Penn's small Virginia brigade. A considerable part of the brigade was detailed to this duty and placed under the command of an aggressive, cool-headed officer, Captain Archer C. Page in the 21st Virginia. Page concealed his men and made them wait patiently for the approaching black-hatted Federal soldiers, who were crossing the meadow in front of them, to expose their flank. The balance of Penn's brigade, along with Grigsby's Stonewall Brigade, were lying down just behind a ridge of ground that rose in front of these three rightmost companies of the 6th Wisconsin. As the Midwesterners approached this rise, a Confederate gun and limber suddenly burst into view, driving from south of the Cornfield into the turnpike. It was probably a 10 lb. Parrott rifle of Captain Hugh M. Ross's Sumter Artillery of Cutts's battalion. A section of Parrotts from Ross's battery had been deployed that morning east of the turnpike, somewhere in front of the left of Douglass's brigade. They had been ordered by Jeb Stuart to join his artillery concentration on Nicodemus Heights and may have been moving in response to these orders, or they may have been chased off by Duryée's brigade.[12]

Bragg ordered Captain Werner von Bachelle, the commander of Company F, which was advancing astride the turnpike, to push forward and shoot the horses on the limber. At the same time, he sent orders for Companies G and K, on von Bachelle's right, to keep moving forward. This was the moment Captain Page's skirmishers revealed themselves in the West Woods, firing into the flank of Companies G and K. Meanwhile, von Bachelle's company dashed to the ridge in their front for a shot at the escaping limber. Captain von Bachelle had a reputation in the regiment as something of "a character." German born, he had received a military education in Thun, Switzerland, served in the French army for a time, as well as on the staff of Garibaldi in the Italian wars, before moving to America and settling in Milwaukee in 1851, where he was active in the militia. "He was a tall and stalwart soldier," wrote Dawes, and "rigid as a disciplinarian," but he was also well respected and liked by his men. Trotting beside von Bachelle was his beloved black-and-white Newfoundland dog. The dog had wandered into the regiment's camp earlier that summer, and the men of Company F, knowing their captain's affinity for animals, gave it to him as a pet. In a short time it became von Bachelle's "most devoted friend on earth." The captain trained the dog to give military salutes and "many other remarkable things." Dog and man were inseparable—in camp, on the march, or in battle—and side by side they crested the ridge.[13]

Here they were confronted by a line of Confederates lying down on the reverse slope, southwest of the turnpike. It was Grigsby's and Penn's brigades. Combined, they mustered less than 500 men, but against a company, they possessed overwhelming firepower. They blasted von Bachelle's men. The captain was riddled with at least 12 bullets and killed instantly. For the moment, his faithful dog was spared but refused to leave the fallen captain's side. Werner von Bachelle died, wrote Lieutenant Colonel Bragg, "as he desired,—a soldier in the front line of battle."[14]

The Confederates who raked the right companies of the 6th Wisconsin were old adversaries. Some 3 weeks before, they had traded volleys at the Battle of Brawner's Farm. John R. Jones had supervised the deployment of the two brigades, although surely Jackson approved the deployment. Whoever selected the position did a poor job. It was exposed to enfilading artillery fire from the Federal guns east of Antietam Creek, and, if the enemy chased off Captain Page's skirmishers in the West Woods, the bluecoats could deliver a flanking fire from good cover. The officers and men were all physically exhausted, "in the worst possible condition for [a] fight," in the opinion of Lieutenant Thomas R. Dunn, a member of Jones's staff, "having been under arms two nights in succession, one of which, at Harper's Ferry, it rained all night, while the march from Harper's Ferry to Sharpsburg was forced." Captain Robert W. Withers in the 42nd Virginia wrote that he knew less about Sharpsburg than any battle of the war, because he was "broken down from loss of sleep and forced marching" and "therefore paid little attention to details, and cared but little whether we lived or died." During the engagement on the evening of September 16, as John Worsham in the Stonewall Brigade recalled, "we were subjected to the severest shelling experienced during the war." Exhausted, dirty, hungry, and exposed, both units were near the end of their tether before the 6th Wisconsin appeared. Division commander Jones was lost before the fight had fairly begun. When a shell burst over his head, it left him dazed and unable to command. Before he was carried off, Jones was conscious enough to have Lieutenant Dunn inform General Starke that Starke was now in command of the division.

Wounds that concussed an individual, rather than inflicting visible physical injury, were not well understood at this point, and Jones's early departure gave rise to rumors that perhaps he may have feigned injury to escape the fighting. Several months later, at Chancellorsville, he left the battle, complaining of an ulcerated leg. Lee was apparently convinced that there might be a problem with the general, and when the army reorganized for the Gettysburg Campaign, Jones was relieved of his command, and his association with the Army of Northern Virginia came to an end.[15]

The fatigue of Penn's and Grigsby's soldiers did not affect their aim. Lieutenant Colonel Bragg described their volleys, and the enfilading fire from Captain Page's skirmishers, as "murderous." Bragg acted quickly and decisively.

He ordered Company F's survivors to take cover behind the turnpike's fences and return the fire. An instant after he gave this command, a bullet struck him in the arm. "I thought my elbow fractured," he wrote to his wife afterward. Another ball went through his coat, exposing its red lining. Although his wound was painful and stunned Bragg, he remained composed enough to order Companies G and K to fall back to the turnpike, where they would have some cover and could respond to the flanking fire. This was all Bragg could manage. "There, I must confess," he wrote, "things began to look pretty dark and I felt faint." The effects of shock were becoming noticeable. Bragg then sent Sergeant Major Howard J. Huntington dashing into the corn in search of Major Dawes.[16]

Dawes had halted the left five companies of the 6th Wisconsin in the corn and the men had lain down, when the firing on the right suddenly broke out. So far as Dawes knew, he had no support on his left, and their rapid advance had left the 2nd Wisconsin, who were their support, some distance behind. Bullets, "thick, almost as hail," were clipping through the corn and spinning through the furrows in the soil. Shells were bursting all about, "tearing up the ground." They did not come from the enemy, however. It was friendly fire, possibly from Matthews's or Thompson's batteries, firing short. It proved to be deadly. One fragment killed Lieutenant William Bode of Company F, the second officer in that company to die in minutes. Possibly the same round badly wounded the last officer remaining for this company, Lieutenant John Ticknor. The Confederate artillery, Dawes noted, "shot way over our heads." Dawes observed laconically of the friendly fire, "This has happened often in the war."

Three company commanders—Noyes, Brown, and von Bachelle—were dead or wounded, another captain had suffered a physical collapse, and both lieutenants in Company F were down, yet most men in the 6th Wisconsin had not yet seen an enemy soldier. Sergeant Major Huntington suddenly came up through the corn and informed Dawes, "Major, Colonel Bragg wants to see you, quick, at the turnpike." Dawes followed Huntington back to the road and encountered a teetering Bragg, who managed to utter "Major, I am shot" before he collapsed. Dawes saw a tear in Bragg's overcoat and red showing through, which he mistook for blood. He thought the colonel had been shot through the body, so he called two men and had them place Bragg in a shelter tent and carry him to the rear. Dawes was 23 years old. "I felt a great sense of responsibility, when thrown thus suddenly in command of the regiment in the face of a terrible battle," he wrote. For a moment, he seemed uncertain about what action to take. Watching the companies along the road firing at the Rebels in the woods and on the regiment's right front, he observed a group of mounted Confederate officers some distance away and assumed it was a general and his staff. Although an officer's duty was to direct his soldiers, not fire weapons, Dawes could not resist the opportunity to personally do some damage to his enemy. He had his men hand him loaded weapons, and he fired six rounds at the group, causing it to scatter. Whether he hit anyone, Dawes never said.[17]

What steadied Dawes and helped him keep his composure and ability to command? Powerful forces worked to paralyze and demoralize him, as had already happened to numbers of other officers in both blue and gray that morning. The fighting raged about him with terrifying fury: shells burst with deafening explosions, bullets whizzed by, and dead and injured men with frightful wounds lay all about. His best friend was dead, and his commander wounded. The chaos and confusion of a battle can never be emphasized enough. Surely the training that Gibbon had put the brigade through was an important steadying factor for Dawes. Captain Hooe excelled at this business of soldiering, yet when real bullets began to fly, Hooe faltered. What was necessary in combat was the courage to control your fear and still do your duty. After the war, John Gibbon wrote about the experience of battle: "Of course it would be absurd to say we were not scared. None but fools, I think, can deny that they are afraid in battle." Soldiers like Dawes seemed to understand that only a thin line separated them from Captain Hooe, and that they might be pushed across it at some point in the future. In his reminiscences of Antietam, Dawes breathed not a word of Hooe's failure that led to the captain's resignation from the regiment after the battle. He simply noted discreetly that Hooe's company was on skirmish duty "farther to our right" and did not participate in the fight around the Cornfield.[18]

Both Gibbon and Hooker were working to reinforce the 6th Wisconsin. Lieutenant Colonel Thomas Allen's 2nd Wisconsin followed the 6th into the corn, at a distance of several hundred yards. Allen heard heavy firing from in front and, believing the 6th "had come upon the enemy in force," ordered his regiment to move at a left oblique, to bring them up on the 6th's left. To ease the pressure on Dawes's right flank, Gibbon ordered Captain Campbell, whose Battery B, 4th U.S., had unlimbered in the plowed field north of Miller's farm, to send a section under Lieutenant James Stewart forward to a position in front of Miller's barn. The 7th Wisconsin and the 19th Indiana, still in column of divisions, followed Allen's 2nd Wisconsin, but Gibbon halted them on the low ground just north of the Cornfield. When Stewart's guns came up and unlimbered, Gibbon ordered both regiments to cross the turnpike and "push forward rapidly" into the West Woods, to deal with the flanking fire from the Rebel skirmishers as well as cover Stewart's flank.[19]

WHEN GIBBON'S BRIGADE ADVANCED from the North Woods to open the attack of Doubleday's division, Doubleday ordered Colonel Walter Phelps Jr.'s small brigade to follow them, as a support. As Phelps and his men emerged from the North Woods, they encountered Hooker and his staff in the rear of Campbell's battery. Hooker told Phelps to follow Gibbon's path through Miller's farm into the Cornfield, form a line of battle, and support the Midwesterners as needed.[20]

Ironically, Phelps's 1st Brigade, which consisted of four New York regiments and the 2nd U.S. Sharpshooters, carried the nickname "The Iron Brigade." The name had been attached to the brigade back in the spring, after it completed a march of 50 miles in two days. Such a trek would not seem remarkable later on in the war—Jackson's entire command made one in the Second Manassas Campaign, and numerous Union units did so in the Gettysburg Campaign—but the war was still young then, and it was seen as an impressive accomplishment. Since that time, the brigade had shrunk away. It suffered 772 casualties at Second Manassas, and, like many other units in that campaign, experienced considerable non-battle attrition. Phelps, who missed the fight at Second Manassas, assumed command as the senior colonel. He found the brigade in a bad way, "terribly cut up," with the men bitter about how they had been handled in the recent battle. They had fought bravely, but "every officer & man in the brigade thinks it has been sacrificed," wrote Phelps. So severe was the leakage of manpower that on the morning of September 17, Phelps mustered a total of just over 400 officers and men in his five regiments.[21]

Phelps had a stain on his reputation that he had been working hard to remove. He fell ill during the Second Manassas Campaign, and on July 31 was granted 30 days sick leave to recover. Although he made every effort to get back to his regiment at the end of his leave, he could not reach them. The roads between Washington, DC, and Pope's army were thought to be infested with guerillas, and it was considered too dangerous for individuals or small groups to attempt the trip. When the army began to move into Maryland, Phelps's wife advised him of rumors circulating back home in Glens Falls, New York, that he was a coward and had deliberately avoided the battle at Manassas. A petition was said to be circulating, demanding that he be dismissed from the service. Furious, Phelps wrote home and told his wife that the petition would have to be presented to the Secretary of War and verified before any dismissal could take place. Phelps was so confident that he would be exonerated by this process that he offered to pay his enemies' expenses to Washington, DC. With their bluff called, no petition ever was ever produced, but the implication of cowardice and the blot on Phelps's personal honor could only be erased by his performance in battle.[22]

Phelps had done what he could to pull the brigade together, but there were still leadership problems. The commander of the 30th New York, Colonel William M. Searing, abandoned his regiment on September 16. An aide-de-camp Phelps sent to retrieve the absent colonel found Searing defiant. He refused to return, making the bizarre claim that "he had already lost one horse [presumably at Second Manassas] and did not want to lose another, nor risk his life to lead only fifty men to battle." Second Manassas and South Mountain may have demoralized Searing, but he left the 53 men of his regiment to fend for themselves. One of Searing's captains, John D. O'Brien, assumed command of this unhappy band.[23]

The 2nd U.S. Sharpshooters, one of the elite units in the Army of the Potomac, marched forward, deployed as line infantry with Phelps's New Yorkers. In an outstanding example of misusing special troops, someone had thought it best to employ these deadly marksmen, who wore green uniforms and carried Sharps rifles, not as skirmishers for the division, but as line soldiers. Phelps, no doubt, was happy to have them, not only for their prowess as fighting men, but also because they composed nearly 40% of his strength.

The brigade dashed across the plowed field, exposed to "a very heavy" crossfire of artillery. "The shot and shell flew around us in a way that is not very agreeable," quipped Edwin Chadwick in the 2nd U.S. Sharpshooters, but they managed to cross the open ground without loss. After clearing Miller's farm buildings, Phelps deployed into line and moved his men up to the southern edge of the corn. A worm fence still stood along the field's border—the 6th and 2nd Wisconsin had apparently climbed over it—and Phelps ordered his men tear it down. The command was misunderstood by William H. Humphrey in the 2nd U.S. Sharpshooters, who thought he heard an order to lie down, so he dropped to the ground. A shell exploded nearby and mangled the leg of one of Humphrey's comrades, and another man directly behind him was hit in the shoulder by a stray minie ball from the fighting in front. Then Humphrey heard the order again—"Down fence." This time the men understood, and "the fence rails flew like so many sticks of wood." Phelps moved his regiments over the dismantled fence to just inside the cornstalks and had them lie down. They were well to the rear of the fighting in front, but still in a danger zone. "You may try to imagine us laying there the balls going whiz, whiz, whiz within a step of us and over our heads and seeing the round shot tear up everything around us a few steps off," wrote Joseph Pettiner in the 14th Brooklyn.[24]

Brigadier General Marsena Patrick's 3rd Brigade of four New York regiments, numbering about 825 men, followed Phelps to Miller's farm and lay down a short distance to the rear of the 1st Brigade, in the narrow meadow between the Cornfield and Miller's orchard. When Doubleday came up, he ordered Patrick to drop off the 20th New York State Militia to support Campbell's battery, and then take his other three regiments and reinforce the 19th Indiana and the 7th Wisconsin in the West Woods. Doubleday had wanted his 2nd Brigade, under Lieutenant Colonel J. William Hoffman (this had been Doubleday's brigade at South Mountain) to join his attack, but Hooker detailed it to support the batteries on Poffenberger Hill. Meanwhile, in the eastern part of the cornfield and unseen by Doubleday's men, Hartsuff's brigade was moving through the corn to continue the assault by Ricketts's division. The conflict was poised to explode with even greater fury.[25]

IN THE CORNFIELD, LIEUTENANT Colonel Allen brought the 150 men in the 2nd Wisconsin up on the left of the 6th Wisconsin. Allen was the opposite of men like Colonel Searing, who sought excuses to avoid combat. Allen had been shot in the neck and wrist at the Battle of Brawner's Farm and could honorably have sought medical leave, but he refused evacuation. He led his men through the corn with one arm in a sling and the other carrying his sword. His nickname with the men was "Long Tom," and one of them wrote proudly that "he put forth every exertion in his power for the success of the regiment." When Allen came up through the corn and saw Dawes, he merely pointed his sword forward and told the major to advance. Dawes shouted to his companies, "Attention battalion, forward, guide left, march." At the same time, he sent Sergeant Major Huntington back to find Captain Philip Plummer, the Company G commander, whom Dawes believed was in charge of the three companies on the turnpike, and advise him that "if it is practicable," Plummer should move those companies forward with the rest of the regiment. When Huntington reached the pike, he found Captain Kellogg in command, which meant that his Company I had reinforced this part of the regiment's line. Kellogg sent Huntington back with the message, "Please give Major Dawes my compliments, and say that it is impracticable, the fire being murderous."[26]

Dawes's order to "guide left" meant that the companies in the corn would guide on (i.e., orient themselves on) the 2nd Wisconsin, and this would pull them away from the companies pinned down at the pike. Dawes sent Huntington back to Kellogg with the message that Kellogg's companies could find cover in the corn and that, "if it is possible," Kellogg should pull his men off the road and use the cover of the corn to rejoin the main body of the regiment. Huntington was wounded on this trip but managed to deliver the message to Kellogg, although without the crucial qualifier "if it is possible." Without this phrase, Kellogg understood the order not to be discretionary, but mandatory. The fire was so heavy that Kellogg doubted he could execute the order, but he tried. He ordered his companies up, but "so many were shot in their tracks that he immediately ordered them down again." Unless the flanking fire from Captain Page's Virginians could be checked, the companies at the pike were not going anywhere.[27]

The balance of the 6th and 2nd Wisconsin pushed on through the rows of corn. At the field's southern edge, they encountered a worm fence. As the regiments crossed it, a line of Confederates lying in the meadow to the south stood up. It was the 26th, 38th, and 61st Georgia of Douglass's brigade. Simultaneously, both lines opened fire on each other. Dawes's description of the ensuing combat is among the more memorable ones that emerged from the war: "Men, I can not say fell; they were knocked out of the ranks by dozens. But we jumped over the fence, and pushed on, loading, firing, and shouting as we advanced. There was, on the part of the men, great hysterical excitement, eagerness to go forward, and a reckless disregard of life, or every thing but victory."[28]

A member of the 2nd Wisconsin described the fire as a "shower of bullets—volley after volley was poured in by the contending parties." He then added, "In all battles I have not seen the like." The Georgians had suffered under the murderous Federal artillery all morning and fought with Duryée for nearly 30 minutes before Gibbon's assault struck them. Although they knocked over many of the attacking federals, the Midwesterners' return fire was accurate and destructive, and Douglass's regiments began to melt away. The 61st Georgia was particularly hard hit, losing its commander, Major Archibald P. MacRae, along with 15 others killed and 81 wounded, a high percentage of the regiment's strength. The 38th Georgia's commander, Captain William H. Battey, was also killed, and all but one of the remaining regimental commanders were wounded. The 13th Georgia lost its colors because, as one survivor related, "no one was left to bear it away." Of over 230 men carried into action, only around 30 remained. The death of the indomitable Douglass may also have weakened morale. It is impossible to determine when the colonel was killed, but it may have been around this time. He had continued in command despite a stomach wound received during the fight with Duryée, but now he took a bullet in the breast. When some of his men tried to gather him up to evacuate him, an artillery shell burst nearby and "mutilated one of his legs dreadfully." The wounds this time were mortal. His brigade had been mauled, with at least 565 casualties—50% of its strength—and most of its leadership killed or wounded. The half of the Georgia brigade engaged with Hartsuff's Yankees remained in the fight initially, but the regiments facing Gibbon began to retreat in confusion toward the Dunker Church, although a few hardcore members paused in their retreat to drop down behind whatever cover they could find and fire at their pursuers.[29]

The Confederate front west of the Hagerstown Turnpike crumbled at nearly the same time. Grigsby's and Penn's small brigades faced not only the small-arms volleys of the three right companies of the 6th Wisconsin, but also the fire of Lieutenant Stewart's two Napoleons, which he brought into action near Miller's barn and began lobbing shrapnel and solid shot into their ranks. This swung the fight in the Federals' favor. A soldier in the 42nd Virginia believed their position was "uncommonly exposed." James M. Day, in the same regiment, described "a terrible artillery fire at close range from the next opposite ridge, grape, canister and solid shot," that flayed their line, adding, "our loss [was] very heavy." Fleming Saunders, also in the 42nd, acknowledged the toll exacted by the Federals' small arms and artillery: "Sam Hale had his horse killed under. Sam Saunders had six men with him in the fight—two were killed dead on the field by grape shot + three wounded. . . . After removing the wounded + leaving a few men to take care of them, the 42 Reg could not collect more than 25 men. The 21st and 48th [Virginia] could not collect so many." Major Hazel J. Williams, commanding the 5th Virginia in the Stonewall Brigade, described the "fearful precision" of the Union artillery fire and both "front and enfilading fires." Grigsby sent an aide-de-camp, Lieutenant James M. Garnett, back to inform General Starke that "unless he received reinforcements he could not hold that line much longer." Garnett dashed back across the fire-swept ground to the edge of the West Woods, where he found Starke's and Jackson's brigades lying down, and delivered his message to the general. Before he could return to Grigsby, Garnett "saw the men coming back across the open field and remarked, 'There they are coming back now, General.'" Grigsby was as tough a fighter as the Army of Northern Virginia had, but he could hold his men no longer. Both brigades broke for the West Woods. The destructive fire on them had contributed to their retreat, but Grigsby had seen the 19th Indiana and the 7th Wisconsin move into the West Woods and knew they would drive off Captain Page's skirmishers and envelop his exposed left. It was up to Starke and the support line to recover the situation.[30]

William Edwin Starke was a businessman and entrepreneur, not a soldier. Born in Virginia, he moved to the Gulf Coast in his mid-20s and found success in the cotton business in Mobile, Alabama, and New Orleans. When the war came, he returned to Virginia and was commissioned lieutenant colonel of the 53rd Virginia. Despite his lack of a military background, Starke had natural leadership qualities and learned quickly. By the end of 1861, he was colonel of the 60th Virginia and distinguished himself in the Seven Days Battles, earning praise for "conspicuous gallantry" from A. P. Hill, who did not bestow such compliments lightly. He also lost his son in that campaign: Edwin B. Starke, the 7th Virginia's adjutant, who died of wounds received at the Battle of Seven Pines. Starke's reward for his own performance was promotion to brigadier general in August 1862 and command of a newly formed Louisiana Brigade. When his division commander was wounded at Second Manassas, Starke assumed temporary command and performed ably. Colonel Bradley T. Johnson wrote that what impressed him about Starke in this battle was "the force he showed in the handling of his command, the coolness and judgment which distinguished him in action, made him to me a marked man." This was a recurring assessment of Starke's performance in combat. When chaos ruled, Starke kept his composure. He also established a strong relationship with his sometimes rough and unruly Louisianans.[31]

This relationship and pride in his men brought Starke into conflict with Stonewall Jackson. When Jackson's command reached Frederick, some "brutes" in Starke's division (General John R. Jones had not yet arrived to assume command) were reported to have committed "brutal excesses" toward several young ladies in the city. The men were described as "foreigners," which to Jackson meant Starke's Louisiana brigade. The Louisianans were an oddity in the Anglo-Saxon-dominated army of the Confederacy. The 10th Louisiana, for one, had men from Greece, Ireland, England, Scotland, Germany, Mexico, France, and Italy. The 1st Louisiana Battalion (also known as Coppens's Zouaves), which was absorbed into the 1st Louisiana regiment, were just as diverse in their national origins and included a number of Swiss-born individuals. The Zouaves were a particularly hard lot, earning a reputation for insubordination and ill-discipline early on in the war. A story circulated after the Battle of Williamsburg that one of the Zouaves had smashed in the skull of a wounded Federal prisoner who had been shot in the body and was begging to be killed, which only served to enhance their reputation as dangerous hooligans. Jackson decided that Starke's Louisianans were the guilty "brutes" who had committed the alleged outrage and ordered Starke to march his brigade into the city, so the guilty might be identified. Starke refused. He appropriately demanded an investigation to determine the soldiers responsible for the offense against the ladies. Jackson countenanced no disobedience of his orders, and he placed Starke under arrest, but he did order an investigation of the incident. To his embarrassment, this determined that the "brutes" were not from Starke's brigade but from Colonel Andrew J. Grigsby's Stonewall Brigade. The investigation also concluded that the incident had been blown out of all proportion, so Grigsby's Virginians and Starke were all quietly released from arrest. The event also revealed that Starke was a man of principle and would fight for his men, even if it meant standing up to the likes of the famous Stonewall Jackson.[32]

Starke had around 1,350 officers and men in both his and Colonel Jackson's brigades. Early on in the action, Stonewall Jackson and his staff rode along their line. He paused at the 23rd Virginia and was heard to say to Lieutenant Colonel Simeon T. Walton, "Be ready, we will move up soon." An instant later, a load of what Lieutenant Richard P. Jennings thought was grapeshot, but was probably shrapnel, passed "just over our heads." It missed the men, who were lying down, but a shrapnel ball struck Jackson's horse in the leg. One of his aides-de-camp dismounted and gave the general his horse. Jackson had departed for another part of his line when Starke's forward line collapsed, so Starke ordered his reserve brigades to counterattack. His objective was the 2nd and 6th Wisconsin, probably the only Federal troops visible to him. He intended to execute a right half wheel, which would bring his brigades up to the Hagerstown Turnpike and on the flank of the Midwesterners. But when Starke made his decision, he was unaware of the 19th Indiana and the 7th Wisconsin having moved into the West Woods, as well as of the presence of Stewart's section of Napoleons, both of which would be on his flank and rear when he wheeled his line to face east. Incognizant of this set of dangers, Starke's two brigades burst from the woods and began their wheel to the road. The moment they emerged into the open, they were subjected to "a heavy shower of grape shot bombshells [shrapnel] and musket balls." Colonel James Jackson, leading the mixed Alabama and Virginia brigade alongside Starke's Louisianans, had risen to command of the 47th Alabama that summer, when the previous colonel had resigned in August. "You asked me why Col. Oliver resigned," Jackson wrote to his wife. "I don't think he was fond of the smell of burned gun powder & the rattle of shell grape & ball. Battle is a terrible thing and it takes nerves of iron to stand the battles we are having in this country." Nerves of iron would be necessary for what Jackson's and Starke's men were about to experience.[33]

LIEUTENANT COLONEL ALLEN SAW Starke's counterattack surging up toward his flank. He shouted orders to change front to meet the threat and directed his men to build a hasty barricade with nearby scattered fence rails. The 2nd and 6th Wisconsin opened "a rapid and telling fire" on the oncoming Confederates. Relieved from the flanking fire by the movement of the 19th Indiana and the 7th Wisconsin, Captain Kellogg brought his three companies up from the turnpike to join the rest of the regiment. Colonel Phelps, alertly observing that the Rebels on the left of the advancing line would partially enfilade Gibbon's men, ordered the 2nd U.S. Sharpshooters to move to their right and front and engage them. He also sent forward the 80 men in the 14th Brooklyn to reinforce the Midwesterners, while holding his remaining regiments back as a reserve. The men in the 14th wore a uniform patterned after that of the French Chasseurs, with red trousers and red kepis, which made them conspicuous. Their commander, Major William H. de Bevoise, was mounted on horseback when he went in with his men, which rendered him even more prominent. Shortly thereafter, a Confederate bullet killed his horse and sent de Bevoise tumbling. He was injured but remained with his men, who mingled with the 6th and 2nd Wisconsin. "Now is the pinch," wrote Major Dawes. "Men and officers of New York and Wisconsin are fused into a common mass, in the frantic struggle to shoot fast. Every body tears cartridges, loads, passes guns, or shoots. Men are falling in their places or running back into the corn. The soldier who is shooting is furious in his energy. The soldier who is shot looks around for help with an imploring agony of death on his face." In Company B of the 6th Wisconsin, one man was shot and cried out to his company commander, Captain Rollin P. Converse, "Captain! Captain! I am <u>killed</u>! I am <u>killed</u>!" Converse offered little sympathy—none could be allowed at that critical moment—and shouted back, "Go to <u>the rear then</u>!" Moments later, Converse was shot through both legs. He "turned very coolly," then called out to 2nd Lieutenant Charles P. Hyatt, "Damn it Hyatt I'm hit, take command," and waddled to the rear.[34]

As Starke's brigades emerged from the West Woods, Lieutenant Frank Haskell, on Gibbon's staff rode up to Lieutenant Stewart, who had his section of guns in front of Miller's barn. Haskell delivered orders from Gibbon to move the section forward about 100 yards to a slight ridge, which the general believed offered Stewart's Napoleons a better field of fire. "I could see large bodies of the enemy coming out of the woods," recalled Stewart, and he objected to the order. "I wish you would give my compliments to the general and tell him, as I have cover for my men and horses, I do not think a move of seventy-five or one hundred yards is any advantage to artillery," he told Haskell. Nevertheless, he obeyed the order and shouted the command "Action, front." His men swiftly limbered the guns and drove their teams forward. Stewart's section was distinctive, in that all the horses on the limbers and caissons were grays. As they went forward, Stewart "saw a line of battle in front of me." It may have been the 1st Louisiana, who were on the left of Starke's brigade line, who saw the Yankees approaching and changed front to meet them. Whoever they were, they greeted Stewart's section with a devastating volley that felled Stewart's horse and killed or wounded 14 of his 17 cannoneers and limber drivers—nearly the entire compliment of the section. Stewart commandeered his bugler's horse, but it, too, was quickly killed. He ordered the survivors to lie down and sprinted back to his caissons near Miller's barn. He ordered those drivers to dismount and come forward to serve the guns. "The drivers did not want to leave the horses," Stewart remembered, although they were probably less concerned about their horses than about the prospect of being shot while serving the guns. Stewart did not say what motivation or threat he employed, but the caisson drivers dismounted and followed him to the guns.[35]

Despite the fire the Federals poured into them, the two Confederate brigades pushed up to the fencing along the turnpike, which gave them limited cover. Their adversaries were between 30 to 75 yards away. When Colonel Jackson's Alabamians and Virginians reached the fence, "they all fell down & began firing." Jackson understood that a continued advance, although seemingly insane, was more likely to drive off the Federals than stopping to engage them in a firefight. He struggled desperately to get his men up and moving over the turnpike's fences, "but the fire was so destructive that they would not rise." It was a similar situation for Starke's brigade, but here many of the men apparently stood or knelt behind the fence line to get a better shot at the Federals. Starke noticed Jackson's efforts to get his men moving, and also that the left of Jackson's brigade seemed "more inclined to give way than advance." The general made his way over to assist the colonel, but this made Starke a conspicuous target, and three bullets struck him while standing by Jackson's side. He "died almost immediately," and Jackson had several men carry his body to the rear.[36]

Starke apparently had intended his counterattack to cross the Hagerstown Pike and drive off the Federals south of the Cornfield, but the movement was checked by a combination of the enemy's firepower and the turnpike's fencing. To cross these fences, reported Colonel Edmund Pendleton in the 15th Louisiana, "under the circumstances, was an impossibility."[37]

The opposing lines blazed away at one another at a range similar to the one where neighbors exchange greetings. "The fire upon the regiment was very murderous," reported Acting Adjutant James D. Wood in the 2nd Wisconsin. "All around me, men were falling," wrote Captain George H. Otis, the Company I commander, with "some begging to be carried off the field—others giving their last request to some comrade." Although part of the 2nd Wisconsin found some cover behind a hastily collected breastwork built of fence rails, most of the men in the 2nd and 6th Wisconsin and the 14th Brooklyn fought in the open. Lieutenant Colonel Allen received a bullet in his good arm and turned his command over to Captain George B. Ely. So many men in the 2nd Wisconsin were shot that Captain Otis thought only about 40 of the 150 men taken into action were still in the fight. The slaughter was so awful that Otis admitted for a moment—"with the bullets flying all around me and man after man dropping here and there"—that he thought "of the awful carnage of this dastardly work of taking the lives of human beings."[38]

The carnage in Starke's and Jackson's brigades was equally appalling. W. E. Moore was the junior captain in the 1st Louisiana, which occupied Starke's far left flank, but officer losses were so heavy that "I was in command of the regiment in less than 10 minutes after we reached our side of the lane [Hagerstown Pike]." Captain Richard Jennings, in Jackson's brigade, later recalled how "you fellows [the Federals] just mowed us down." Jennings grabbed a musket and cartridge box from one of his dead men and dashed to the turnpike's fence, where he "laid down as flat as I could to protect myself." He observed a Union soldier jump up onto the fence across the road, but when Jennings rose up to fire at him, a shell burst above him and a fragment struck his hip. Jennings rolled over behind a nearby stump, where he found Captain Thomas Michaels of his regiment, as well as a lieutenant from the 48th Virginia and a corporal who stood beside the stump, firing at the Federals. The officers tried to get the corporal to get down, but he refused and soon was killed, falling across the officers. Another bullet passed over Jennings's legs and struck the lieutenant in the knee, and then a bullet struck Michaels in the ankle. This was enough for Jennings, who, years later, admitted with refreshing honesty that he then declared, "I am going out from here." Michaels warned that he would be killed, but Jennings jumped up, his hip stiff and sore from where the fragment had struck him, and took off for the West Woods, with bullets flying about him "like a swarm of bees." Although "almost scared to death," he reached the woods safely. The Confederate line was fraying, but so, too, was that of their opponents.[39]

The casualties in this desperate firefight probably would have been higher had the black-powder weapons not produced so much smoke. As Edwin Chadwick in the 2nd U.S. Sharpshooters noted, "the smoke was so dense that we could hardly tell friend from foe." Besides obscuring targets, it also increased the chaos. Starke's advancing men were initially so indistinct through the battle fog that some men in the 14th Brooklyn and the 6th Wisconsin at first thought they might be friendly troops. Joseph Pettiner in the 14th recorded hearing a number of men saying, "Don't fire, they are friends," before the Louisianans opened fire on them.[40]

Another group of Confederates—perhaps elements of Captain Page's skirmish detachment, or parts of Grigsby's or Penn's brigades who had rallied—moved up on Starke's left rear, reaching a low stone fence midway between the northernmost finger of the West Woods and the Hagerstown Pike. Their objective appears to have been to strike either the flank of the Federals in the cornfield or Stewart's advanced section of Napoleons, or possibly both. Whatever the case, Colonel Henry A. V. Post's 2nd U.S. Sharpshooters, situated beside the turnpike, saw them coming. Initially, due to the smoke, the sharpshooters were uncertain whether the approaching force was friend or foe, but when the Confederates reached the low stone wall about 100 yards from the pike, they dropped down behind it and opened fire. "When the bullets began to whistle about our ears we were satisfied they were gray backs," wrote Edwin Chadwick, and he and his comrades opened fire on them with their Sharps rifles. Another sharpshooter, William H. Humphrey, claimed he carried 160 rounds into the action, which, if true, meant the sharpshooters could sustain a high volume of firepower with their breechloaders.[41]

While the sharpshooters engaged this threat from west of the turnpike, in the meadow south of the Cornfield the tenor of the battle swung in the Confederates' favor. The tipping point was a "heavy crossfire" on the 2nd Wisconsin, delivered by the remaining elements of Douglass's brigade, who were "concealed behind a ledge running obliquely to our front." Nonetheless, even an Iron Brigade has human limits, and though they still kept firing, "by common impulse" the line began to sag back toward the corn. A backward movement under fire was often difficult to check, but the men seemed to view this as a change of position to escape a deadly crossfire, rather than a retreat. Some moved back grudgingly. Bob Tomlinson in the 6th Wisconsin, who, early on in the war, had been marked down as a "bombastes furioso" for all his boasting about what he would do when he got into battle, "proved as good as he talked." Dawes recalled how, when the line began to fall back toward the corn, Tomlinson, "with disappointment in every feature," shouted, "God, you ain't going back are you? Not yet. I still have a few more cartridges left," and proceeded to fire them off. Besides men like Tomlinson, the 2nd and 6th Wisconsin, in particular, had excellent leadership. Dawes noted how "Captains P. W. Plummer and Rollin P. Converse, Lieutenants Charles P. Hyatt, Lyman B. Upham and Howard V. Pruyn were always in the lead. But the same is true of all of our line officers who were there." Dawes then added, in reference to everyone, both enlisted and commissioned, "Whoever stood in front of the corn field at Antietam needs no praise." Their courage was simply understood. The determination of the men and their leaders contributed to the staying power of these regiments, as well as to why, despite severe losses, they stopped when they reached the edge of the corn, dropped down behind whatever cover they could find, and resumed the fight.[42]

The balance of Phelps's small brigade played a role in steadying Gibbon's men and the 14th Brooklyn. Dawes recalled that when his men reached the corn and lay down, "another line of our men came up through the corn." This was the 22nd, 24th, and 30th New York. The three regiments combined counted only

177 officers and men, but any infusion of fresh troops boosts morale and can steady a broken line.[43]

The Confederates' jubilation at seeing the Yankees' backs was brief. Gibbon's deployment of the 19th Indiana and the 7th Wisconsin to the West Woods, and the aggressive placement of Stewart's guns, turned the tables again in this see-saw battle.

The 19th Indiana led the movement into the West Woods. The Hoosiers were commanded by 23-year-old Lieutenant Colonel Alois O. Bachman, who had assumed command after South Mountain. Their colonel, Solomon Meredith, had broken some ribs in a fall from his horse during the Battle of Brawner's Farm on August 28, and although he managed to lead the regiment through South Mountain, he was physically incapable of continuing in command after that engagement. Gibbon could not have been disappointed in the command change. He disliked Meredith and felt that the 19th lagged behind the other regiments because of the colonel's poor leadership. "The Indiana regiment had the finest material in it in the whole brigade, yet it was the worst regiment I had," wrote Gibbon. Meredith, continued Gibbon, "had not the first principle of a soldier in him," and the brigadier had sought unsuccessfully to have him removed from command. The dislike was mutual. Meredith attempted (also unsuccessfully) to pull political strings to get his regiment out from under Gibbon's command. Meredith had also hoped to rid himself of Bachman, who, as he wrote earlier in the war, was "a man of no energy and is [of] very little advantage to me." But the tall, athletically built Bachman would settle any doubts about his courage that morning.[44]

The 19th, followed by the 7th Wisconsin, crossed the Hagerstown Pike between Miller's house and barn and followed a small brook that ran perpendicular to the pike. There was a total of about 500 officers and men in the two regiments, the 19th being the larger of the two. The 7th Wisconsin was commanded by 34-year-old Captain John B. Callis, who had also led the regiment in their bloody fight at South Mountain, where they had sustained 147 casualties. A North Carolinian by birth, Callis's family had moved to Wisconsin when he was a child. He had no military background but developed into a competent soldier. As the two regiments approached the woods, Bachman detailed Company B, under 19-year-old Captain William W. Dudley, and a 7th Wisconsin company to deploy in front as skirmishers.[45]

The Yankee skirmish line quickly made contact with Page's Confederate skirmishers. In the exchange, Page was wounded and his men driven back, eliminating the flanking fire on the 6th Wisconsin. This happened at about the same time as the 6th and 2nd Wisconsin advanced out of the Cornfield and engaged Douglass's, Grigsby's and Penn's brigades. The Confederates who advanced on Starke's left (in order to hit the flank of Stewart's artillery section) and became engaged with the 2nd U.S. Sharpshooters apparently came from the central part of the woods, and they were unaware of the arrival of Bachman's and Callis's regiments on their flank and rear.[46]

The two Union regiments deployed, with the 19th Indiana on the right and the 7th Wisconsin on the left, extending to the eastern edge of the woods. Captain Callis observed the Confederate force crossing his front and saw that a change of front to the left would bring his regiment up on the enemy's left and rear. "There is no such thing in small-arms combat as a fair fight," wrote Robert H. Scales in 2015. The men in the 7th Wisconsin understood this. So did the Confederates. They presented their backs to the 7th, behind a stone wall, and believed this position gave them an advantage over Stewart's artillerymen. "It is very important for infantrymen to hate," wrote Captain Norman Allen, a Korean War veteran. This was no less true in 1862 than it was in 1951. "It's easier to meet the enemy when you do, when you're at the end of the rope—hungry, desperate, sleepless, mean, angry," continued Allen. Three days earlier, at South Mountain, Confederate soldiers had enjoyed the advantage of position and inflicted terrible damage on the 7th Wisconsin. Now the Midwesterners had the upper hand. Callis ordered his regiment to change front to the left, facing east, which brought them up to a limestone ledge at the edge of the woods—a perfect natural breastwork.[47]

The 7th Wisconsin's Sergeant George Hoyt recalled that the ledge was 2–4 feet high. Hugh Perkins of Company I, an 18-year-old private, saw that the Rebels in front "thought them verry safe as they had a stone breastwork in front of them." The 7th then opened fire. The Confederates were initially greatly confused, unable to determine where the fire striking them came from.[48] Perkins described what happened next in a letter to a friend, written days after the battle: "After they discovered our position they threw down their arms and broke for the woods (what was left of them). Then we had fun picking them off. We might have taken them all prisoner, but we wasn't in for that. We killed evry one of them; even a wounded man could not be seen creeping off without being plugged by a Minnie."[49]

This was the often cruel and pitiless war the Civil War infantryman—Union or Confederate—understood but rarely admitted to. Perkins almost certainly exaggerated when he wrote that they killed every Rebel soldier, and his statement that they shot wounded men who were creeping off is unusual but not unique. In an earlier letter, Perkins related that they were ordered to cease firing when the surviving Confederates made a break for the woods. "But it was of no use," he observed. "The boys had been fooled too much by the gray backs to let one slip," and they continued firing. Why did they shoot men who appeared to be trying to surrender? It is impossible to know with the evidence available, but it seems likely that Perkins and his comrades believed the Rebels were merely feigning surrender, in order to get the Federals to stop firing so they could escape into the cover of the woods. It would not be the last time that Union or

Confederate soldiers were shot down under such circumstances. Such instances were relatively rare, but they were more common than the "brothers' war" mythology that wrapped itself around the Civil War in the twentieth century would have us believe. Such cruelties would occur again on this terrible September day.[50]

Caught between the rapid fire of the 2nd U.S. Sharpshooters in front and that of the 7th Wisconsin from the rear, the Confederates behind the stone wall had no choice but to run or be shot down. The unraveling of the Rebel line spread to Starke's brigade, now commanded by Colonel Leroy A. Stafford. Lieutenant Stewart had his Napoleons back in action, and they were dropping shrapnel into the Louisianans. Earlier, Gibbon had observed the near disaster his orders had caused to Stewart's section, and he directed Captain Campbell to bring up the remainder of Battery B to the Scotsman's position. Campbell's guns thundered down onto the pike at about the time the Confederate line was beginning to come apart. As the guns came abreast of Stewart's section, Campbell shouted, "Action, front," and the four Napoleons unlimbered and swung into action besides their comrades.[51]

The Napoleons' fire inflicted numerous casualties. Colonel Edmund Pendleton, commanding the 15th Louisiana, reported, "We suffered greatly as well from musketry in front as from a battery on our left, which enfilated us with grape and canister [case shot/shrapnel]." Oli Claffey in the 10th Louisiana also recalled the enfilading fire from Stewart's guns. "We were in a bad spot but put up a gallant fight with only a rail fence for cover," he wrote. No more-graphic evidence of the terrible carnage in Starke's ranks is available than the series of photographs taken by Alexander Gardner on September 19. Bodies of the dead are strewn along the fence line. The fire from Campbell's guns was augmented by the rifles of either the 7th Wisconsin or 19th Indiana, the latter regiment having changed front and come up on the 7th's right flank. Captain William E. Moore, who had assumed command of the 1st Louisiana when Colonel Nolan was wounded, "discovered that we were being flanked" and ran to inform Colonel Stafford of this development. In a letter written years later, Moore acknowledged, "You can readily see, Genl., that we could not have lived long under the two fires." Oli Claffey bluntly wrote, "We were being shot to hell." Stafford ordered an immediate retreat by the right flank. In an instant, Starke's and Jackson's brigades broke "rapidly" for the West Woods. Claffey left behind a close friend, Sergeant Joe Joyce, who had been shot through the side. "I wanted to save Joe but in the smoke and slaughter . . . it was impossible to take back any of our wounded," Claffey reminisced. Joyce died at the fence and may be one of the men in Gardner's photographs.[52]

A moment before the general retreat began, a bullet struck Colonel Jackson with such force that he was temporarily knocked unconscious. When he came to his senses, he saw his and Stafford's men running for the woods. Checking his

Confederate dead, probably from Starke's Louisiana brigade. These men engaged the 2nd and 6th Wisconsin, the 14th Brooklyn, and the 2nd U.S. Sharpshooters across the Hagerstown Pike. The North Woods are in the distance. Battery B, 4th U.S., was a short way over the ridge behind the bodies. Courtesy of the Library of Congress

wound, he discovered that the bullet had penetrated to the bone, which caused the shock, but otherwise it was not a serious injury. He was able to get to his feet and hobble after his men.[53]

Around the same moment when Stafford ordered a retreat, the color bearer in the 1st Louisiana had climbed over the turnpike's fence and into the road, probably hoping to inspire an advance to follow up on the retreat of the 2nd and 6th Wisconsin and the 14th Brooklyn. He was shot and killed, and the flag fell into the road. Lewis C. Parmelee was the 20-year-old, clean-shaven adjutant in the 2nd U.S. Sharpshooters. He was popular in the regiment and entertained its members by being able to easily quote "great poets and prominent authors." He was also an aggressive soldier, and when he saw Starke's men start to fall back, he took the colors of the 2nd U.S. Sharpshooters from its badly wounded bearer and "advanced to the front cheering us on." Edwin Chadwick watched as the Confederates "began to run leaving guns, knapsacks, and everything that impeded their progress on the ground beside their dead and wounded comrades." They also left the colors of the 1st Louisiana lying in the road, in the confusion probably unaware that it had fallen. Parmelee went for the flag, along with several other men. He found that the staff had been broken off near the colors, so he jammed his sword into its broken end and raised it above his head in triumph.[54]

LYING ON THEIR FACES in the corn, Major Dawes, as well as the men of Phelps's brigade and the 2nd and 6th Wisconsin, heard a "rattling fusillade and loud cheers," which was the firing of the 7th Wisconsin and the 2nd U.S. Sharpshooters. Then the Confederates along the Hagerstown Pike suddenly began to fall back in disorder. Someone shouted, "Bully, Bully. Up and at them again. Our men are giving them hell on the flank." The Federals rose and burst out from the corn. "The whole field before us is covered with rebels fleeing for life, into the woods," recalled Dawes. The men around him were transformed into predators, bent on the destruction of a fleeing prey. "The men are loading and firing with demoniacal fury and shouting and laughing hysterically," reflected Dawes. Jackson's line had been cracked open.[55]

The survivors of the 6th and 2nd Wisconsin, Phelps's New Yorkers, and the 2nd U.S. Sharpshooters hounded the fleeing enemy toward the small white Dunker Church. Regimental integrity and alignment were gone. There were no orders to pursue; it was a collective impulse that drove them on. The 7th Wisconsin and the 19th Indiana did not join in this chase—and may not have even been able to see it from their position—so the advance lacked weight and punch. Its firepower was also diminished, not just from casualties and disorder, but also from what Dawes described as inferior powder that fouled the men's weapons. "It takes hard pounding to get the bullets down, and our firing is becoming slow," wrote the major. Looking toward the church, Dawes and the others suddenly saw "long gray lines" of men, moving steadily and purposefully, sweeping out of the West Woods and expertly deploying into line of battle, "unbroken by the fugitives who fly before us." It was John Bell Hood's division, and the tide of battle was about to turn again.[56]

3

The Pinch of the Fight

"Death seemed depicted in many countenances"

When General Hartsuff was badly wounded early in the morning of September 17, it left Colonel Richard Coulter in the 11th Pennsylvania, the brigade's senior colonel, in command. Since Coulter did not know what Hartsuff's orders were (see chapter 1), and in the absence of any instructions, he kept the brigade lying down north of the East Woods, on Samuel Poffenberger's farm. Coulter may have sent someone to find General Ricketts and get orders, but the division commander had his hands full with Christian's brigade. Whatever the situation, the brigade remained motionless for nearly 30 minutes, while the fighting raged up front.

Coulter was not one to shrink from fighting. The 34-year-old colonel was a Greensburg, Pennsylvania, businessman and attorney before the war, but he had served as an enlisted man in the Mexican War, seeing action in several battles, and remained active in the state militia between the wars. He possessed the rare combination of popularity with his men but good discipline in his command. Although he commanded respect, he had an easy familiarity with his soldiers, who referred to him in conversation as "Dick Coulter" or "Fighting Dick Coulter." At the engagement in Thoroughfare Gap, 2 days before the Battle of Second Manassas, Coulter "fought like a hero," in the opinion of Colonel Fletcher Webster in the 12th Massachusetts. George Kimball, an enlisted man in Webster's regiment, considered Coulter "one of the bravest men I ever knew." Corporal Austin Stearns in the 13th Massachusetts recalled that during the night on South Mountain, a straggler approached a group of men huddled together, trying to keep warm, and inquired, "Can you tell me where the 11th P.V.'s [Pennsylvania Volunteers] are?" The men proved to be officers, one of whom was Coulter. "Do you belong to that regiment?" Coulter asked. The soldier immediately recognized the colonel's voice and, "not daring to say anything but the truth," replied "meekly" that he did. Coulter asked the soldier if he could discern a black line some distance away, barely visible in the darkness. "Well, that is the 11th P.V.'s, and you double quick to it in no time, or I'll put you in a place where you can't straggle," he commanded. The soldier left the colonel's presence "in quick time for his regiment, well satisfied to escape so easy." This was Coulter, fair but strict.[1]

In camp, on the march, or in battle, the colonel was never without one of the more remarkable mascots in the Army of the Potomac, a Staffordshire terrier named Sallie. Sallie joined the 11th Pennsylvania as a pup when it was first organized as a regiment with a 3-month enlistment period in the spring of 1861. Soldiers and puppy established a close relationship, and before long the little dog was a celebrity to the whole brigade. George Kimball recalled how he enjoyed visiting the 11th Pennsylvania's camp when the regiment performed dress parade, just to watch Sallie. He described the "long line at 'parade rest,' the drum corps slowly marching down the front, the colonel [Coulter] with folded arms calmly looking into the faces of the men and Sallie lying at the feet of the color bearer, as if she loved to be in the shadow of the flag." Sallie also earned renown for never straggling, and after a particularly severe march, the 11th Pennsylvania could always be sure of "being represented by a colonel, a flag and a dog." She accompanied the regiment into every battle and was in her place as Hartsuff's brigade waited for orders in Sam Poffenberger's fields.[2]

Coulter had four regiments in line—from right to left, the 12th Massachusetts, 11th Pennsylvania, 13th Massachusetts, and 83rd New York (whose soldiers preferred to be called the 9th New York State Militia)—numbering about 1,100 officers and men. It was Hooker who discovered that the brigade was waiting immobile. He sent Captain William L. Candler, one of his aides-de-camp, to get it moving. Coulter obeyed immediately, ordering his regiments forward. "The men never obeyed a summons with greater alacrity," recalled George Kimball, who also remembered how the four regiments descended a knoll west of Smoketown Road, "steadily and with as good a line as we would have maintained had it been a parade." On September 19, George Smalley, a *New York Tribune* reporter who accompanied Hooker during the morning—the general understood the power of the press in creating a popular public reputation—published a major eyewitness account of the battle, scooping all the other reporters. Smalley would be what today is called an "imbedded" reporter. But Smalley sought to thrill *Tribune* readers, not write factual history. He related how Hooker's opening attack (by Duryée's brigade) had been driven out of the Cornfield, and how Rebels were "pouring out of the woods [West Woods] in endless lines" and surging toward the corn. Smalley continued with an oft-quoted passage:

> Hooker sent in his nearest brigade to meet them, but it could not do the work. He called for another. There was nothing close enough unless he took it from his right. His right might be in danger if it was weakened, but his centre was already threatened with annihilation. Not hesitating one moment, he sent to Doubleday: "Give me your best brigade instantly."

> The best brigade came down the hill to the right on the run, went through the timber in front through a storm of shot and bursting shell and crashing limbs, over the open field beyond, and straight into the corn field, passing as they went

the fragments of three brigades, shattered by the Rebel fire, and streaming to the rear. They passed by Hooker, whose eyes lighted as he saw these veteran troops led by a soldier whom he knew he could trust. "I think they will hold it," he said.

Gen. Hartsuff took his troops very steadily but now that they were under fire, not hurriedly, up the hill from which the corn field begins to descend and formed them on the crest. Not a man who was not in full view—not one, who bent before the storm.[3]

Hartsuff's men were delighted with Smalley's account, particularly his dubbing them the "best brigade," although, to a man, they were aware that his reporting was inaccurate and sometimes pure baloney. Hooker thought highly of the brigade—he had selected it to lead Ricketts's division's assault—but Hartsuff was already wounded when the brigade advanced, and it belonged to Ricketts's division, not Doubleday's. As David Chenery, a member of the 13th Massachusetts, noted, "It is not at all likely that an order came for the <u>best brigade</u>—orders did not generally come in that form & only in someone's <u>vivid imagination</u>." There was no crisis at the moment when the brigade started forward, although shortly after they began to move, Starke's counterattack struck Gibbon's and Phelps's brigades in the Cornfield, which accounts for Smalley's description of Rebels "pouring out of the woods in endless lines." That not a single soldier bent under the small-arms and artillery fire the brigade began to receive after it started forward was a fiction that would read well on the home front. The brigade's steady advance was attested to by George Kimball and others, but Kimball noted that when they first were exposed to Confederate artillery fire, "we wavered but little under this opening of the storm." There was hesitation, but it was minimal. Even the best soldiers will duck an artillery round. Considering Smalley's story years later, Sergeant Robert B. Henderson in the 13th Massachusetts hesitated to accuse the reporter "with deliberately manufacturing a lie," but added, "I have of course always known it to be not correct as to its details."[4]

As Coulter moved forward, the situation in front was fluid. Duryée's brigade was disengaging and drifting out of the fight in the direction of the North Woods, except for the handful of men in the 104th New York, who held on in the far northeastern corner of the pasture south of the Cornfield. Curiously, no one in Hartsuff's brigade remembered passing any troops other than some men of Seymour's brigade. This may be because their attention was riveted on the danger ahead, not on retreating troops, but, more likely, most of Duryée's men fell back in the direction they had advanced—toward the North Woods—and passed by the right flank of Hartsuff's line. Farther west, the 6th and 2nd Wisconsin were just emerging from the Cornfield, and the conflict on that front was exploding. Meanwhile, the Confederates on the right of Lawton's division were surging toward the East Woods and the Cornfield, following up Duryée's re-treating regiments.

WHEN THE FEDERAL ASSAULT struck Jackson's line, Lawton had the Louisiana brigade of Brigadier General Harry Hays, about 550 strong, as his reserve, tucked away in the West Woods. Lawton discovered that Jackson's deployment on the night of September 16 had left a small gap between J. R. Jones's division and his own left. When it was known that the Federals were advancing on the morning of the 17th, Lawton sent orders for Hays to "proceed to a point in our lines yet unoccupied" and fill in the gap. Hays started moving, but the orders were so vague that he had no idea what gap he was moving toward. He sent a staff officer ahead to locate Lawton and get more specific instructions. Lawton apparently realized his orders were not easily understood, for Hays's staff offi-cer met a courier en route, whom the general had sent to bring the Louisianans into position. With a guide in hand, Hays pointed his brigade in the right direc-tion, but before he had moved far, he received fresh instructions from Lawton to bring his brigade up in the rear of Douglass, where Duryée's assault had burst upon the Georgians' line.[5]

Hays led his five small regiments across the Hagerstown Pike and into the pasture south of Douglass's embattled line. This was some of the ground most exposed to the Federal artillery on the Confederates' front, and the shells "came so thick and fast" that Hays immediately ordered his men to lie down. Douglass was furiously engaged in front of them, while behind them, S. D. Lee's batteries were blazing away and also receiving their fair share of enemy artillery fire. It is hard to imagine a more terrifying position than that which Hays's men occupied. Douglass's and S. D. Lee's men could fire back at those pouring fire into their line, but Hays's men could only remain prone and take it. "We lay down under a cross fire of the artillery, the shell bursting over us and around us until the whole heavens were illuminated with flashes of light from the exploding shells," wrote Lieutenant George Lovick Pierce Wren in the 8th Louisiana.[6]

William P. Snakenberg was a private in the 14th Louisiana. The night before, knowing that combat was imminent the next day, he was overcome with a feel-ing that he would be wounded. "I never once thought that I would be killed, or fatally wounded," he reminisced, but he dreaded the idea of a surgeon cutting into his body to extract a bullet. Snakenberg wanted to say something to his commander, Lieutenant Colonel David Zable, "to look out for me and not to let me lay on the field," but he thought Zable would think he was trying to get out of the fight by being sent off on some detail, so he remained silent. He took all the letters he had received and anything else he thought unnecessary and threw them away. When Snakenberg heard the firing begin on the morning of the 17th, he rolled his blanket up, tied the ends together, and put it over his left shoulder.

"I did this to protect my left breast as best I could," he explained. We can only imagine the terror Snakenberg and his comrades felt as the Federal artillery mauled their prone line. "One shell burst and wounded three men at my side," he recalled, "and another killed and wounded thirteen on my left." Yet, despite his premonition, the private was untouched.[7]

Captain Fred Richardson's Company F, 5th Louisiana, were not as fortunate. Richardson and Lieutenant Nick Canfield were lying down in the rear of their men, with Canfield's younger brother William, a private, directly in front of them. Suddenly an enemy shell came plunging in. In an instant, four men, two of them brothers, were dead or dying in a bloody, horrific mess of mangled flesh and gore. "Oh, the anguish I felt at the sight of my poor friend," a stunned Richardson wrote afterward, "who, a moment before, was buoyant in spirits, even while the leaden messengers of death were dealing destruction around us, now in the hands of his maker, and the thought rushed fast to my mind of the feelings of his poor mother and family on hearing of the loss, the pride of her heart."[8]

Hays's Louisianans were a tough, colorful lot. Like Starke's regiments, they were a virtual foreign legion, composed of men from across Europe and North America. For example, the 8th Louisiana carried men on its muster rolls from Ireland, various states in Germany, France, England, Canada, Mexico, Belgium, Holland, Denmark, Norway, Scotland, Sweden, Brazil, Cuba, Italy, Russia, and Switzerland. They were also a rough group, particularly the 14th Louisiana, Snakenberg's regiment. During a stop in Grand Junction, Tennessee, in 1861, when the regiment was traveling by rail to Richmond, a portion of the regiment got roaring drunk and set off a rampage that left 7 dead and 19 wounded. Later, when passing through the streets of Petersburg, Virginia, the men found some whiskey, got drunk, and precipitated a drunken brawl—whether with locals or as an internal regimental clash is unclear—but the participants employed "paving stones, clubs, bowie knives, and every available weapon that was at hand." A lieutenant who bravely tried to break up the melee received three stab wounds, and when a store owner's wife complained about looters in her store, some of the men pursued her with their knives drawn. Nor was drinking confined to the enlisted men. Over a period of nine days, the brigade commander, Harry Hays, purchased five bottles of brandy, one canteen of whiskey, and one bottle of wine. Earlier that spring, the colonel of the 6th Louisiana complained about his company officers: "Some dozen or so of them are low vulgar fellows . . . [who] habituat whisky tubs."[9]

The brigade was formed in the army's reorganization after the Seven Days Battles in July. Harry T. Hays, a colonel in the 7th Louisiana, received his promotion to brigadier general during this time and was appointed as its commander. Hays was 42 years old, a Mexican War volunteer, attorney, and politician. He was hard drinking, tough, and capable of managing the unruly soldiers in his command. In the spring, General Richard Taylor praised how Hays had developed the 7th Louisiana into a crack regiment and recommended Hays's promotion to general. When this promotion was approved, Hays was still recovering from a serious wound received at the Battle of Port Republic in June. He regained enough mobility to make his way back to the army by September and joined his new command while they besieged Harpers Ferry. Sharpsburg was his first battle as a brigade commander, and it was a brutal test for Hays.[10]

Hays's regiments had a reputation as hard fighters. The 14th Louisiana suffered an appalling 51 killed and 192 wounded at Gaines' Mill. At Second Manassas, the brigade participated in some of the toughest fighting of August 29 and 30. At one point, during the Union assaults on their line on the 30th, ammunition gave out and the Louisianans resorted to throwing rocks at the Federals to help repel the attack. The carnage of these battles sobered the men. "I have got my fill of fighting, I want no more of it," wrote a 14th Louisiana lieutenant after the slaughter at Gaines' Mill. It was one thing to drink, wrestle, and brawl, but quite another to face shrapnel and canister and volleys of musketry that slaughtered men by the dozens. Besides combat, most of Hays's regiments had served under Stonewall Jackson, which meant the roughest soldiering for anyone in the Army of Northern Virginia. Despite their solid combat record, they leaked deserters and stragglers at an alarming rate. Lieutenant George Ring rejoiced when Harry Hays arrived to assume command at Harpers Ferry, for he hoped the general "will inaugurate some system to keep our men in the ranks." Ring blamed much of the dwindling numbers in the brigade on the constant fighting and marching. "Since the 1st Sept., after having fought every day for ten days, we have made a circuit through western Maryland and are now here almost where we started from," he wrote while at Harpers Ferry. "It is too much as the state of our ranks show, and if Jackson keeps on at it, there will soon be no army for him to command. I have only 11 men for duty now out of 112 four months ago, and I am most confoundedly disgusted at the idea of all the time being captain of a corporal's guard."[11]

Late in the action with Duryée's brigade, Colonel Douglass sent a request back to Hays for help. Douglass's casualties were heavy, and some men may have been running low on ammunition. But it is also possible that Douglass perceived the enemy line to be crumbling, and the moment was ripe for a counterstroke. Federal artillery had already killed or wounded "a good many" of Hays's men, but he responded immediately to Douglass's appeal. His men rose up from the ground and raised the rebel yell as they went forward, passing through battle smoke so thick that, as Lieutenant George Wren later wrote, it covered the field like a "dense fog." It proved to be a blessing, since it helped obscure the brigade from observation by Federal gunners. But, Wren noted, it was necessary to "put on a strong nerve" just to get up off the ground, for "I had never seen so many falling in as little time in any instance before." Hays's men may have been yelling, but the lieutenant observed that "death seemed depicted in many countenances" of those around him. Officers continually shouted "Forward" to urge the men on over the din of shouting, firing, and explosions. The line swept over the right of Douglass's brigade and kept on toward the Cornfield. Some of the Georgians jumped up and joined the Louisianans, and Walker's brigade added to the advance on Hays's right. Duryée's remnants disappeared into the corn. Unseen by Hays or any other Confederates in the counterattacking force, Hartsuff's brigade was moving through the corn toward them on a collision course.[12]

Hays's counterattack reflected an unwritten but understood doctrine in the Army of the Northern Virginia: to take the offensive any time an opportunity presented itself. On several occasions already that morning, although fighting a defensive action, the Confederates had mounted local counterattacks, such as Douglass's counterblow against Duryée, and Starke's against Gibbon. They had failed, but these assaults threw the Federals off balance and made the Confederates appear more numerous than they really were.

DURING THEIR APPROACH, HARTSUFF'S center and right regiments encountered Joseph Poffenberger's narrow farm lane, enclosed by post-and-rail fences, which entered the East Woods on its most northern projection and continued along its eastern edge. When the 13th Massachusetts, in the left center of the brigade, reached the lane—which one veteran described as nothing more than a cart path—the men halted, leveled the fencing, and moved on without incident. But the 12th Massachusetts, on the far right, crossed the lane north of the woods, where they were exposed to the Confederate batteries on Nicodemus Heights. Perhaps the 12th hit a newer section of fencing, for they found that "the rails ran through posts and could not be pulled down" without an unacceptable amount of exposure to the Rebel guns. Instead, the regiment scrambled over the fence and started across the plowed field west of the lane, moving toward the Cornfield, about 300 yards south of them. George Kimball thought the corn "seemed to be alive with men." The smoke obscured their identify, and Kimball did not realize they were Confederates in the 13th and 60th Georgia of Douglass's brigade, who had pursued Duryée through the corn. As these men approached, the cornstalks wavered "as if swept by the wind." Even though the range was considerable, the Rebels opened fire and hit some New Englanders as the latter climbed Poffenberger's fence and entered the plowed ground. The 12th's commander, Major Elisha Burbank, deployed Companies K and E, about 60–65 men, as skirmishers, under the command of Captain Benjamin F. Cook, in order to engage the enemy in the corn and allow Burbank to form the rest of the regiment into line.[13]

Cook was an ideal officer to command a skirmish line, being described as "brave and fearless in action, [a] strict disciplinarian; one who knows his business and does it." He cared deeply for his men and always saw to it that they were taken care of before he attended to his own needs. "He gave us to eat from the last hardtack in his lean old haversack and gave us to drink from the last drops in his battered old canteen," one of his men remembered. His unit kept up a steady fire as they advanced toward the corn. They were joined on their left by Company E of the 11th Pennsylvania, also in skirmish order. Cook decided that there were more skirmishers than necessary and ordered one of his companies to fall back to the line of battle. The two remaining companies proved to be sufficient to drive the Georgians back through the corn in a running fight. Following behind Cook in the regimental line, George Kimball noted that "bullets and shells came in pretty lively," but that most of them passed over their heads.[14]

Coulter met General Seymour as the former's brigade approached the East Woods. Seymour suggested that Coulter oblique his regiments to the right, to avoid becoming entangled with some of Seymour's men who were still in the woods. Coulter ordered the change in direction, and this brought the entire 12th Massachusetts, 11th Pennsylvania, and right wing of the 13th Massachusetts into the open, west of the woods. The left wing of the 13th, and the 83rd New York, remained in the trees and passed over Seymour's men while moving toward the woodlot's southern and southwestern boundary.[15]

Coulter's regiments on his right came into the Cornfield behind their skirmish line. Shells from both sides were continually passing over their heads, adding to the terrific din of the battle. Some Confederate shells began to find the range, one of which exploded near Corporal Austin Stearns in the 13th Massachusetts, striking him in the side with a fragment and tearing his blouse and shirt. Stearns later recounted that he "doubled up like a jack-knife and sank down on a corn-hill." Sergeant William Fay ran to him and asked "if I was hit," and a moment later Stearns's company commander, Captain Charles H. Hovey, a Boston apothecary before the war, came over and asked the same question. Stearns, when he was able to regain his breath, replied that "I was not hurt much only lost my wind." An inspection of his wound revealed that although the fragment had nicked him, the injury was superficial. Always solicitous of his men, Hovey told Stearns to "sit there till I would be able to follow on," and ran back to join his company. An instant later, another shell hurtled in, striking a limestone ledge "not a rod [5.5 yards] away" from where Stearns was recovering and "went into a thousand pieces." Miraculously, the fragments missed him, but the close call convinced Stearns "to evacuate that place rather suddenly."[16]

Covering a front of about 450 yards, extending from a short distance inside the East Woods to the center of the Cornfield, Coulter's four regiments steadily advanced. Inside the corn, nothing could be seen of the enemy, but danger lurked everywhere. Bullets whined and zipped, clipping cornstalks and occasionally striking a human target; shells burst; and the unnerving high-pitched rebel yell coming from the throats of Hays's advancing Louisianans rose above the battle roar. George Kimball admitted, "My limbs trembled at every step, for fear had taken a strong hold of me." This was typical, yet somehow most men kept their places in the ranks. In Kimball's case, he overcame his dread by focusing on "the requirements of duty and of the ridicule to which I would be subjected from my comrades should I fail." He drew courage as well from his first lieutenant, William G. White, a 22-year-old accountant from Boston. White was a bright fellow, with a deep interest in history, and was beloved by his men. During the early part of the Second Manassas Campaign, he came down with a fever that forced him to enter the brigade hospital. During the course of the campaign, he left the hospital to rejoin his regiment, but his compromised health soon landed him back in a Washington, DC, hospital. The regiment left him there when they marched into Maryland, but on the night of September 16, Kimball was awakened by a stir and bustle around him and overheard comrades saying "God bless you." He woke to discover that White had again slipped away from the hospital and returned to his company. "His face was pale, his eyes were sunken and his limbs weak, but his soul was on fire," recalled Kimball. Now, as the regiment made its way through the corn, Kimball noticed that White appeared "as cool as he would have been had he been leading his company in review." It gave the 20-year-old private confidence.[17]

At the southern edge of the corn, the 12th Massachusetts found the worm fence still standing. Orders were shouted to knock it down. A "fearful fire" greeted them when they attempted to do so, and a number of men were hit, including Lieutenant White, who lost two toes from a bullet that struck his foot. He sat down to inspect the wound, and his commander, Major Burbank, paused and advised White to go to the rear. White smiled and replied that he was "worth a dozen dead men yet." Satisfied that he still had some mobility, White rose and rejoined his company. Nearby, Kimball held a fence rail above his head to throw it behind him when it was struck by a shell fragment or solid shot that "wrenched it from my grasp with such violence that my arms were benumbed."[18]

With the fence flattened, Coulter's men entered the pasture south of the corn. The 12th Massachusetts passed over a rocky knoll (photographed by Alexander Gardner on September 19, where the 90th Pennsylvania Memorial stands today) about 50 yards south of the corn. Here, the 13th and 60th Georgia could be seen through the battle smoke, moving behind the fence line about 200 yards to the south, as well as Hays's Louisianans coming up in the gap between Douglass's and Walker's troops. Walker's regiments were farther to the left, and they engaged the 13th Massachusetts and the 83rd New York. "Never did I see more rebs to fire at than that moment presented themselves," remembered George Kimball. Abram B. Dyer, in the 12th Massachusetts's Company I, described them as "quite a nest of gray-backs." Both lines shouldered their weapons and opened fire. The storm of bullets from the Federal troops stopped Hays's counterattack in its tracks and added further damage to Douglass's already battered Georgia regiments. "We literally wiped out the rebs in our front. From a beautiful line of battle they became squads behind stumps, etc.," wrote Kimball.

But the return fire knocked Massachusetts and Pennsylvania boys over by the dozens. Jordan's or Parker's battery of S. D. Lee's battalion inflicted particular carnage in the ranks of the 12th Massachusetts. "They had one gun that fired to the right and center of our Regt. And every time they would send a shot through our ranks," wrote Sergeant Joseph E. Blake. So many men in the 12th were shot down that when Robert Shearer in the 11th Pennsylvania looked to his right, although he saw the main line of the Bay State regiment standing firm, there were so many men going to the rear that he thought, "My God, are the men running [a]way?" But then he realized that nearly all of them were wounded, limping and hobbling back or holding on to bleeding arms. To Shearer, "it seemed as if the majority of the line had been hit."[19]

Along Coulter's line, officers shouted "Give it to them, boys!" to encourage their men. The men began to shout this as well, until there was "a pandemonium of voices" mingling with the "perfect roar of musketry." Among the cacophony of sounds, George Kimball never forgot the "screams and groans" that rose from the Confederate line when his regiment's first volley struck home. In the mayhem, Kimball forgot his fear and "thought only of killing as many of the foe as I could." Sergeant Lewis Reed noted with alarm how the men in the 12th Massachusetts "were falling very fast." He watched his company commander, Captain Edward P. Reed, receive a wound in the hand. Then his friend and tentmate, Benjamin Curtis—a 21-year-old shoe cutter from Hanover, Massachusetts, who had enlisted only a month earlier—fall, "never to rise again." It was a similar story in Kimball's Company A. A "tall soldier" standing beside him, whom he did not identify for some reason, and who, the day before, had admitted to a premonition that he would be hit in the battle, lay at Kimball's feet, mortally wounded. The man's brother dragged him back behind the firing line and returned to the fight. Soon Kimball's own brother, William, was hit. George helped him behind a stump. "Go back and give it to them," William exhorted his sibling.[20]

When George W. Orne, Kimball's 2nd lieutenant, encountered Lieutenant White hobbling around along the line of their company, he told White to go to the rear. White refused. Then a shell fragment struck Orne in the right shoulder, tearing his arm from its socket and later, on October 7, costing the 38-year-old Boston carpenter his life. White, meanwhile, "seemed to be everywhere imparting courage and stimulating the efforts of his men" until another shell burst, sent a fragment into the upper part of one of his arms, and hurled him to the ground. Again, though, he managed to regain his feet, and "his voice could be heard as before above the din of battle."[21]

An oft-repeated "statistic" from the Civil War, whose origin is both murky and suspect, is that minie balls and musket balls produced roughly 90% of the deaths and wounds in combat, and artillery only accounted for nearly 10%, with bayonets, clubbed muskets, swords, and other weapons tallying some 1%. The problem is that wounds caused by shrapnel balls (which were about the same size and appearance as a musket ball) and some canister balls (which were not all the same size) could be documented by surgeons as musket ball wounds. We will never know what percentage of wounds and deaths artillery fire had inflicted at Antietam, but the circumstantial evidence is that it was considerable. Sergeant Joseph Blake wrote to his brother about the Confederate artillery fire that hit the 12th Massachusetts: "The papers say that they haven't got good gunners but they had some good ones there that day." Small-arms fire may have been the predominant killer at Antietam, but the open nature of the battlefield allowed artillery to wreak havoc on exposed infantry.[22]

In the 11th Pennsylvania, Robert Shearer faced danger from a different quarter. Shearer was in his company's front rank. The man behind him was a "very excitable" individual, and after he fired, he would step back one or two paces to reload his rifle. In his eagerness, he raised his rifle to fire from this new position, which placed those in the front rank in great danger of being shot by him. Shearer reached back and manhandled this individual into his proper position before he could discharge his weapon again. This repeated itself several times, but one time the soldier managed to load and fire before Shearer could react. The gun exploded in Shearer's ear and staggered him. When he recovered, Shearer seized the fellow and kicked him into line. This angered the man, and he threated to shoot Shearer, who replied, "Now is the time" and leveled his musket at the soldier. "That cured that notion," Shearer recalled, and they were both soon loading and firing at the Confederates.[23]

Half of the 13th Massachusetts were in the East Woods, and the others were in the Cornfield. The experience of the two halves was dramatically different. The left wing was not at the edge of the woods, but, rather, several feet back inside the woods. There was little or no underbrush, so they had good fields of fire. The woods in general and the smoke helped conceal their position, while the trees stopped many of the bullets and shell fragments. Austin Stearns, who, several paragraphs earlier, we left in the Cornfield stunned by a shell's explosion, rejoined his company in the meadow south of the corn. He recalled that the Confederates fired first, but many of the balls passed over his line. The enemy's aim quickly improved, and they began to score hits. Prince A. Dunton, a 21-year-old shoemaker who was a Company H private, had the men on either side of him shot down. "The shot and shell fell about us thick and fast, I can tell you," he wrote to a friend, adding, "I do not see how any of us got out alive." An unknown member of the regiment wrote home that the range "was short, not over two hundred yards and we can count on our man every time that distance." The Rebels got *their* man, though, for the letter writer was hit in the ankle by a musket ball in the act of firing his thirty-first round. Austin Stearns also noted how "men now commenced to drop on all sides." One of them was a close friend, whom Stearns saw throw up his hands and fall to the ground: "One little struggle more and then all was still."[24]

Stearns was so intent on loading and firing that when he heard Captain Hovey shout "Close up to the right," it was the first time he took note of his regiment's condition. "Looking to the right, and left as well, I saw that there was quite a space between me and my right hand man," he wrote. In warfare of that era, it was important to keep the ranks closed up, in order to concentrate fire and better enable officers and noncoms (non-commissioned officers) to direct their fire. A fragmented line not only lacked firepower, but also quickly lost cohesion and staying power. The closest man to Stearns's left was William Henry Gassett, a 19-year-old bootmaker, to whom Stearns repeated Hovey's order. A moment later, Gassett cried out, "Jim, I'm hit," threw down his gun, ran several feet to the rear, and fell to the ground. Stearns ran over to him and asked where he had been hit. Hovey, their compassionate captain, joined them and told Stearns to help Gassett to the rear, as he expected that the whole line was going to fall back soon. They found the private had been shot through the shoulder, but he was able to throw his good arm around Stearns's neck, and the two men started off. Another bullet struck Gassett in his left leg before they reached the woods. Stearns inspected the injury and reassured the private that it was only a flesh wound, so they pushed on until they found a massive oak in the woods they could rest behind.[25]

Hovey had only three men remaining in Company K. There were just nine left in the adjacent Company D. He ordered them to join with his men and then told everyone to keep closing up to the left, toward the regimental colors. This brought the captain within the East Woods. Delighted to "get in 'where it was safe,'" he jumped in the air and crowed like a rooster. As he did, a fragment or splinter from a spent bullet struck him in the face. Because their circumstances in combat are so extreme, soldiers are prone to rough humor, so when an inspection determined that Hovey's wound was superficial, everyone had a good laugh at the absurdity of his wounding. He took it in stride. "I got the laugh on me," he recalled.[26]

Coulter's regiments were subjected to a beating, but they took a terrible toll on their adversaries. Early on in the action, Coulter realized that he could get a crossfire on Hays's brigade by wheeling the 83rd New York and the left wing of the 13th Massachusetts through the East Woods, so they could fire across the front of the rest of the brigade. Hays's charging Louisianans, sweeping up nearly 150 yards past Douglass's line, marched directly into this kill zone. "We were in the angle the enemy had formed, they were shooting us in two directions," wrote Lieutenant Wren in the 8th Louisiana. Men fell rapidly under the crossfire. Among the casualties was William Snakenberg. During the advance, the Federal soldiers he could see in the woods appeared to be falling back, and he fired on them. As he reloaded, he felt a burning sensation in his left side, which left him stunned. For a moment he did not realize he had been wounded, then "everything seemed to turn green to me and I staggered for 20 feet and fell." He hollered to some of his comrades for help. Mike Clark helped him off the field. When they reached safety, Clark discovered that Snakenberg had been hit three times: once in his left hand, once in the left side of his body, and a third round through the blanket on his right side.[27]

Colonel Henry Strong in the 6th Louisiana was mounted on a gray horse, which made him a conspicuous target. Most field officers fighting around the Cornfield in the morning seem to have gone into action dismounted. This made command and control more difficult, but it greatly increased the odds of their survival. A dead or wounded field officer or brigade commander could seriously dent a unit's combat effectiveness. But the conflict in the mind of officers was what their men might think if they dismounted. Honor and courage have always been important to soldiers, and this strongly influenced the decision of some field and general officers about whether to assume the risk of going under fire on horseback. We cannot know what the thinking was in Hays's brigade, but in the 6th Louisiana, Strong and Henry Richardson, an enlisted man serving as his courier, were mounted, a decision that ended badly for both. Strong and his horse were both killed about 200 or 250 yards southwest of the East Woods. Two days later, Alexander Gardner photographed what was probably Strong's gray horse. It lay on its forelegs, with its head turned to the right, as if it was resting in that position. Union 12th Corps' General Alpheus Williams came across the dead animal afterward and, in a letter to his daughter, remarked that it "had died in so graceful a position that I wished for its photograph. . . . Until you got to it, it was hard to believe the horse was dead."[28]

Another Union bullet knocked Henry Richardson from the saddle. When he fell, one foot became caught in the stirrup, and his terrified horse dragged him around until another bullet killed the animal. Of the 12 officers in Strong's regiment who entered the fight, in less than 30 minutes 5 were dead and 7 wounded. One of the latter was Lieutenant George Ring, who was hit in the knee by a bullet while kneeling beside Strong's body to collect his valuables. Another ball struck Ring's arm, and two hit his sword—a testament to the volume of fire Hartsuff's men were pouring into Hays's ranks. Fortunately for Ring, none of his wounds were serious, and he limped off the field. Of the two companies he commanded in the fight, Companies K and H, which, combined, only numbered 14 men, he lost 11. "So you see I have cause to thank God that he has protected me in this great battle," Ring wrote to his wife. It was a similar story in George Wren's company of the 8th Louisiana. During the fighting, he heard General Hays shout orders to close up to the right. When Wren repeated this command, he saw that only 3 of his 18 men were still standing. Then he was hit by two bullets, one through the calf of his left leg, and another grazing the upper part of his right leg. "The balls were coming so thick at this time and [I] feared that I should never be able to get off of the field," he recorded in his diary. The Federals were indistinct forms in the murky smoke that hung over the field. Although in great pain from his calf wound, Wren struggled off, despite "a perfect storm of shot and shell" that filled the air around him. When he reached safety, he felt like a man reprieved from a death sentence. "I never felt so thankful in all my life," he confessed.[29]

Somehow, Harry Hays emerged unscathed from the maelstrom that destroyed his brigade. His staff, however, did not share his good fortune. Lieutenant Dwight Martin, his aide-de-camp, was mortally wounded before the brigade even made its charge. Captain John H. New, a Harvard Law School graduate, had his horse killed from under him during the attack and was injured in the fall. Hays presumably was mounted. If so, he was the only one to emerge unharmed. Even among the officers who were not on horseback, the carnage was shocking. The 5th Louisiana had 11 killed or wounded; the 6th Louisiana, 13; the 7th Louisiana, 11; and the 8th Louisiana, 15. These losses included every regimental commander. Considering the small size of the brigade, this made up most of the brigade's leadership. Such a large number of casualties among officers reflected either the severity of the fire they faced, or the need for them to risk increased exposure to hold their men together under the withering small-arms and artillery fire they faced.[30]

Colonel Walker, on Hays's right, had no empathy for the Louisianans. He referred to Hays's brigade as "fresh troops" who came to the support of Douglass's brigade and caused Walker to order his own brigade to advance. "But the fresh troops, which were advancing in such good order at first, gave way under the enemy's fire and ran off the field before they had been halted by their officers and almost before they had fired a gun," Walker reported. This was hogwash, and Jubal Early, who wrote the after-action report for Lawton's division, omitted the aspersions Walker cast on the Louisianans. Union reports, personal accounts, and casualty returns tell a different story than Walker's. All evidence indicates that Hays's men fought bravely, despite the Federal artillery that caused significant damage before they advanced, and then the deadly crossfire that decimated the brigade.[31]

Walker had no need to denigrate the conduct of other troops to add luster to the performance of his brigade—if that was what he sought to do. His command's performance was impressive by any calculus. They held one of the most exposed positions on Jackson's line, yet they managed to maintain their position against both Duryée's and Hartsuff's onslaughts, despite the loss of nearly all their regimental commanders. Walker's regiments were skillfully handled to take advantage of the limited cover, and this reduced their losses. Although Walker's Confederates fought for twice as long as Hays's brigade, their casualties amounted to 33%—heavy losses in normal circumstances, but significantly less when compared with Hays's 61% and Douglass's nearly 50%. Many factors influence why one unit loses more men than another, but given the exposed nature of his position, Walker did an admirable job of preserving his men's lives while inflicting significant damage on their Union adversaries and holding the enemy in check.[32]

After nearly an hour and a half of combat, from 5:30 to 7 a.m., Walker's regiments were low on ammunition, even though he had his officers and men collect all they could from the dead and wounded. They managed to hold their position, but when Hays's counterattack was repulsed, Walker had no choice but to order his men to fall back to their original line, near Mumma's farm. A fresh mass of Union soldiers advancing toward him through the East Woods also influenced Walker's decision. It was Christian's brigade in Ricketts's division.[33]

WE LEFT CHRISTIAN'S BRIGADE north of the East Woods, with their commander having suffered a breakdown and abandoned his command. Ricketts took control of the brigade, deployed the regiments into a line of battle, and appointed his assistant adjutant general, Captain John W. Williams, to lead it forward. These events caused a delay, during which Duryée advanced, fought for nearly 30 minutes, and withdrew. Hartsuff's brigade advanced in its stead and renewed the assault of Ricketts's 2nd Division. Hartsuff's regiments were hotly engaged before things were sorted out and Christian's regiments renewed their advance. There were only three regiments—from right to left, the 88th Pennsylvania, 94th New York, and 26th New York—totaling around 750 officers and men. The 90th Pennsylvania were left to support Matthews's battery, near the northwestern edge of the East Woods.

Christian's brigade entered the East Woods and halted again. Perhaps Williams was uncertain about where to go, or maybe he rode ahead to reconnoiter. Although they had concealment in the woods, it was a frightening place, as Confederate shot and shell were "tearing through the trees at a furious rate." Fortunately, most overshot the men. There were some close calls, however, such as when Charles Ackerman, a lieutenant in the 26th New York, watched a rifled shell strike a young white oak beside him and split the tree trunk up to its branches. General Seymour suddenly appeared on horseback and demanded to know why the brigade had halted. When no one could provide a satisfactory answer, Seymour ordered it forward. He wanted to relieve his own men, who were down to their last rounds of ammunition. The 94th and 26th New York kept east of Smoketown Road and advanced to a worm fence along the southeastern border of the woods, which looked out on a large plowed field that extended south to Mumma's farm, 400 yards away. The 88th Pennsylvania moved west of the road and, coming up with the 83rd New York, opened fire on Hays's men.[34]

Mumma's farm was burning furiously, set on fire by men in General Roswell Ripley's brigade of D. H. Hill's division, in order to prevent the Federals from using it as a strong point—a position of strength. Corporal Oliver P. Clarke, one of the 94th New York's color bearers, spotted a mass of Confederates moving past the farm, with the sun, which had emerged from the cloud cover, reflecting off their muskets. This was Ripley's brigade, moving up to relieve Walker's regiments, who were finally out of ammunition. Although the range was long, the 94th opened fire. Lieutenant Colonel Calvin Littlefield, the 94th's commander, could not see the Rebels from his position and thought his men were firing on friendly troops, so he shouted orders to cease firing. Corporal Clarke left his position in the center of the regiment, walked to where Littlefield was, and pointed out the enemy. The 94th resumed firing.[35]

The range was extreme for a small-arms battle. The 3rd North Carolina, and perhaps other regiments in Ripley's brigade, were armed with smoothbore muskets firing buck and ball (a round ball and three buckshot). These weapons and their ammunition were deadly at ranges of 100 yards or less, but beyond that distance, their accuracy and killing power dropped off precipitously. This may account for the comparatively light losses suffered by the 94th and 26th New York. The 94th counted only 12 wounded, while the 26th's casualties totaled 5 killed, 41 wounded, and the unusually large number of 20 missing (odd, since no prisoners were lost or taken in this action). Lieutenant Charles Ackerman in the 26th New York observed how the Confederate musket balls mostly fell short of their line, "raising the dust in front of us." Both the 26th and 94th New York were armed with Enfield rifles, which had a range to hit targets at 400 yards but required the men to understand how to adjust their sights. The New Yorkers apparently failed to make the adjustment, for Lieutenant Enoch Jones noticed how the shots from his company, in the 26th New York, were throwing up dirt in front of the Confederate line. The lieutenant ordered his men to aim higher, to account for the range. Although most of the Confederates' bullets landed harmlessly in front of the New Yorkers, some carried the distance. Ackerman was unlucky enough to be on the receiving end of a ball that struck him in the chest with enough force to knock him unconscious, even though it did not break the skin. Some of his men carried him back into the woods, where he recovered. Most of the wounds in Ackerman's regiment were slight—getting knocked out by a musket ball was considered "slight"—which William Holstead, a young lieutenant in Company C, thought was due to the range.[36]

Christian's regiments fought largely on their own hook, without any brigade leadership. Colonel Peter Lyle in the 90th Pennsylvania was the senior colonel, but since Colonel Christian was not a casualty—he had simply abandoned his brigade—Lyle received no orders to assume command. In any event, he was with his regiment, supporting Matthews's battery. Captain Williams apparently believed his job was finished once Seymour intervened and positioned the brigade. Compounding the problem, the regimental leadership in the 26th and 94th New York was mediocre. Sergeant Charles Sloat in the 94th commented that his regiment had not been resupplied with ammunition since the Battle of South Mountain, which did not reflect well on Lieutenant Colonel Littlefield. In the 26th New York, Lieutenant William Gifford, commanding Company I, wrote how he was told that Lieutenant Colonel Richard H. Richardson, the acting regimental commander, "did his duty," but Gifford, whose company was the fourth or fifth in line, never once saw his commander, who remained at the extreme right of the regiment and never ventured beyond that position. "So without field officers every captain of a company became a law unto himself," noted Gifford. Initially, Gifford had been unable to see the Confederates around Mumma's farm, but when he did make them out, he unwisely urged a charge across the plowed ground in front of it. This bad idea became irrelevant, because the virtual committee commanding the regiment could not manage such a concerted action, anyway. The men simply stood along the fence and fired off their ammunition. The line gradually began to diminish, not from casualties, but from men who decided they had done enough fighting and wandered rearward. With "no field officers in sight" and companies that were short of line officers, it became, in Gifford's words, "a sort of go as you please with the men in some companies." In such an atmosphere of slack discipline, many in these companies simply quit the battle.[37]

On Christian's right, the 88th Pennsylvania and the 83rd New York had a far deadlier engagement with elements of Hays's, Walker's, and Douglass's brigades. The Pennsylvanians and New Yorkers had cover within the woods, but the range was closer, and they were exposed to fire from S. D. Lee's battalion and other Confederate batteries. "We were drawn up as if for a dress parade," wrote Henry A. Chadeayne in the 83rd New York, to which he attributed his regiment's heavy losses. He noted that the Rebels were behind good cover, and "had we taken the same advantage as they did, we could have done as much execution and without so much loss." John Vautier, a private in the 88th, found that the enemy troops in his front were "mostly behind a fence." This was the 13th and 60th Georgia, in the shelter of the east–west fence bisecting Miller's pasture south of the Cornfield. But "heavy lines" of Confederates swept up past this fence and across the front of the two Union regiments, moving toward the corn. This was Hays's counterattack. Vautier fired "many rounds" at one of the Confederate colors and an "officer on a white horse," who very likely was the 6th Louisiana's Colonel Strong. Trees could stop a bullet or a shell fragment, but the oaks that made up the most common tree species in the East Woods were large, mature trees. If a sizeable branch was severed by a shell or cannon ball, the consequences could be lethal for those standing below. This was the fate of the 88th Pennsylvania's Jess Tyson, who was killed when a falling limb crushed him. Plenty of bullets also found human targets. The 88th lost their commander, Lieutenant Colonel George W. Gile, who received a bad leg wound. Vautier was struck three times, yet, luckily, the missiles passed through his clothing or equipment, rather than his body—an experience that would be common that day. Close calls were not a rare event. Nearly everyone in the two regiments who was not killed or wounded had bullet holes through their clothing or equipment.

Plenty of bullets, musket balls, and shell fragments hit their target, however. Losses in the 88th Pennsylvania tallied 72 killed or wounded, and the 83rd New York's were 111, almost half their effective strength.[38]

The entire color guard of the 88th numbered among the unit's casualties. This, too, would be a common occurrence throughout that awful day. Only a mounted officer occupied a position as dangerous as that of a regimental color guard. Today, with automatic weapons and camouflaged uniforms, the presence of regimental flags in combat seems a mad and unnecessary ornament, but these flags, or colors, served to bolster morale and were a means of communication in nineteenth-century warfare. A Union infantry regiment was authorized to carry two regimental colors: a national flag and a state flag. Most regiments used both flags, but some dispensed with the state colors and only carried national colors. The Army of Northern Virginia authorized their infantry commands to carry a single battle flag. The color bearers were usually sergeants, and the color guard consisted of six to nine corporals, depending on the drill manual used. Colors were placed at the center of a line of battle and were a highly visible object on which the regiment aligned itself. They also were used as a central point where a broken unit could be rallied, or where troops suffering losses under heavy fire could gather to maintain cohesion. A common command in both armies at Antietam was to "close up on the colors." Flags identified troops as being Confederate or Union, which helped reduce friendly fire. Sometimes, though, it was beneficial to conceal a unit's identity by keeping the colors furled, in order to get close to the enemy. Smoke made it difficult to discern between blue and gray uniforms at certain distances. Major Alfred J. Sellers in the 90th Pennsylvania noted that the Confederates used this tactic frequently: "The rebs had a hobby at times of concealing their colors."[39]

The true functional value of flags in combat was for communication. When noise and smoke rendered hand or voice commands unrecognizable, a commander could utilize the size and visibility of regimental standards to generate an advance or retreat. Soldiers were trained to align on the colors, so if they saw them going forward or backward, they would usually follow.

The importance of regimental flags to a unit's morale and cohesion cannot be overstated. They represented the collective body of the regiment and were inscribed with the names of the battles it had engaged in. These flags represented the honor of the regiment and the memory of those who had fallen. To lose one of the colors was a great disgrace, and capturing one was considered to be among the most dangerous and heroic acts a soldier could perform. Because of their importance to morale and communications, flags were an especial target in battle. Knock them down enough times, and this might make the enemy lose heart or cause his line to fall into disorder. Colors also attracted heavier fire, because they were conspicuous in the smoky atmosphere of Civil War battles. This was why John Vautier and others in his regiment directed their fire at the Confederate colors and at the officer mounted on a milky white horse—they stood out in the smoke and confusion. It took great personal courage to be a color bearer, and, as we shall see, Antietam repeatedly tested its limits.

The color sergeant in the 6th Louisiana was John Heil, an immigrant from the German state of Baden. He had been the color sergeant since November 1861 and carried the regimental battle flag through six engagements, including Gaines' Mill, where he was wounded. His luck ran out in the storm of bullets that targeted his regiment at Antietam, and Heil died beneath the flag.[40]

Sometimes the fire could be so deadly that keeping the colors up was deemed not worth the loss in casualties. This was the case for the 12th Massachusetts. After both color sergeants were shot, Lieutenant Arthur Dehon of Company F ordered three different men (probably corporals in the color guard) to keep the flags up. Each man was shot down in succession, and Dehon stated that he "had not the heart to order another up, so I picked them up and brought them off myself."[41]

WHEN HARTSUFF'S BRIGADE ADVANCED through the Cornfield, Captain James Thompson, in the spirit of the overall aggressive use of 1st Corps artillery that morning, ordered his battery to limber and led it about midway through the corn, to a knoll or ridge where he had a good view of the Hagerstown Pike, extending from Miller's farm to the Dunker Church. But friendly troops limited his field of fire. The 12th Massachusetts was directly south of his guns, and Gibbon's and Phelps's men obstructed the line of sight to his right front. While Thompson could see well enough, his gun crews, limbers, and horses could also be seen, and they attracted enough small-arms fire that the captain was forced to order his men to lie down after unlimbering the guns. For the moment, his guns were silenced.[42]

In front of the battery, Hartsuff's regiments, who were still in the open, were melting away under the fire being poured into them. "On the right the fire lessened every moment," reported Colonel Coulter. Unlike Duryée's men, who had mostly lain down when they came under fire, which reduced their casualties, Coulter's men generally stood and fired. Why one unit lay down and another stood is unknown. Sometimes it was a question of leaders who sought to protect their men, but other officers thought it cowardly not to stand in battle. Duryée's men hit the ground instinctively, not because they were ordered to do so. Whatever the reason, Coulter's regiments remained standing, and the exposure cost them dearly. Sergeant Lewis Reed in the 12th Massachusetts remembered that only minutes after his tentmate was killed, "I found myself on the ground with a strange feeling covering my whole body." There was no pain yet. He had been hit in the right side of his neck, just above the collarbone, and the initial sensation was numbness. Nat Phillips, a member of his company, tried to help Reed but then left for some reason. Reed's right arm was useless, so he used his left hand to search for his wound. He found his shirt and blouse filled with blood and believed he was mortally wounded. "I had the usual feelings of home and friends and thousands of thoughts ran through my mind at once," he recalled, but then, taking in the appalling carnage around him, the will to survive took hold. He discarded his equipment and struggled to get to his feet. "After many attempts I got on my knees and tried to get on my feet but not yet," he wrote. Eventually he stood up and staggered toward the rear. "How many times I fell getting there I do not know but I fainted many times" before he finally reached the East Woods, where he found help.[43]

Evacuating the wounded from the firing line proved to be problematic. In theory, there were three ambulances, with two stretchers on each one, for every Union regiment. Each ambulance had two privates assigned to it, plus a driver. This works out to a maximum of six stretchers per regiment. Each set of two ambulance privates could only manage one stretcher—barely—so a regimental commander had to detail additional men to handle the remaining three stretchers. For example, the 12th Massachusetts sustained 165 wounded in about 30 minutes. It was simply impossible for this small number of stretchers to remove, in any kind of timely fashion, the quantity of cases this many wounded produced. The system was overwhelmed. Officers had no choice but to detail able-bodied men to help carry away the seriously wounded. Although this was contrary to orders, officers often chose to ignore them, such as in the case of Sergeant Austin Stearns, related earlier in this chapter. Many men helped the wounded to the rear—without orders—as an excuse to escape the firing line. "A good many men left the ranks to help off the wounded," observed George Kimball, adding that this was against orders, and "an effort was made to prevent it," although he did not detail what that effort consisted of. The assistant surgeon in the 12th, Albert A. Kendell, made a courageous attempt to provide emergency medical attention for the wounded who were near the firing line, much as a modern-day army medic operates. But this entailed considerable risk and ended tragically when Kendell was mortally wounded.[44]

The 12th Massachusetts had difficulty in preventing the able-bodied from helping the wounded off, because the leadership of the regiment was literally slaughtered. Major Elisha Burbank, its 52-year-old commander, was mortally wounded, and his replacement, Captain David Allen Jr., "one of the most gallant officers in the brigade," was also wounded, leaving Captain Benjamin Cook in command. Of the 15 officers the regiment carried into action, 12 were killed or wounded. George Kimball recalled that he and his surviving comrades became possessed with a battle fury and paid little attention to who was leading them. "The men did not know or care who was in command," he wrote. "They continued the fight just the same and would have kept on without officers as long as a man was left." The memory of that frightful morning in David Miller's meadow remained imprinted on Kimball's mind. At one point, a bullet wrenched his ramrod from his hand as he prepared to pound home a fresh round. Another bullet struck his knapsack; a third, his haversack; and then a fourth cut both straps of his canteen, which fell to the ground. "Having lost all natural feeling, I laughed at these mishaps as though they were huge jokes," he remembered. Earlier, when his regiment was advancing through the Cornfield, Kimball had admitted to trembling with fear. That fear had now been replaced with a kind of cold detachment. A solid shot struck a man a few paces from him "squarely in the face," scattering human fragments on Kimball. "I grumbled about it as though it were something that might have been avoided," he recalled about that moment, but this reaction was almost certainly a temporary one. Such appalling, shocking events are never erased from one's memory. He also remembered how the "groans of the dying seemed louder and more dreadful every moment." At one point, he heard a shriek that pierced through the general roar of battle. It was Lieutenant White. He had received his third wound, a frightful one from a shell that shattered his hip and tore open his abdomen. Perhaps understanding that his wound was mortal, he waved off those who came to his aid.[45]

It was around 7 a.m. now. Coulter's regiments had been in action for nearly 30 minutes, and ammunition was running out. The survivors in the 12th Massachusetts searched through the cartridge boxes of the dead, but there were so few men left in the ranks that the regimental line resembled a weak skirmish line. Someone brought word that support troops were approaching. But enemy reinforcements could also be seen pouring out of the West Woods around the Dunker Church, forming up with the steadiness of crack troops and moving inexorably toward the Cornfield and the East Woods. There were only 32 officers and men left in the 12th, out of the 334 carried into action. They had sustained the highest losses of any 1st Corps regiment. The official tabulation was 49 killed, 165 wounded, and 10 missing, although Captain Cook, who later penned the regimental history, gave their actual losses as 70 killed or mortally wounded, 183 wounded, and 30 missing, for a total of 283, or 84% of the regiment's strength. The 11th Pennsylvania counted 124 casualties; the 13th Massachusetts, 136; and the 83rd New York, 114. Overall, the brigade's losses totaled 54%. One of the survivors was the 11th Pennsylvania's canine mascot, Sallie, who joined the brigade's remnants when they fell back toward the East Woods.[46]

George Kimball searched for his brother, whom he had left behind the firing line. Someone told him that his sibling had been removed to the rear. Kimball and three other comrades gathered up Lieutenant White, placed him on a blanket, and started for the woods. The air was full of "flying fragments of iron and whistling bullets." In the Cornfield, Kimball encountered greatly distressing sights. The cornstalks were trodden down, and all about were dead men and "hundreds of wounded men," crawling, creeping, dragging themselves toward the rear, or "lying down in despair to die." They carried Lieutenant White to a field hospital at Sam Poffenberger's farm. The popular lieutenant faced his inevitable death with such modest, quiet courage that Dr. J. McLean Hayward, the regiment's surgeon who examined White's wound, lost his normal equanimity "and burst into tears." White died that afternoon.[47]

BEFORE HIS LINE BEGAN to give way, Colonel Coulter went in search of help. Riding back through the East Woods, he encountered the 90th Pennsylvania, 264 strong, under Colonel Peter Lyle. They had been supporting Matthews's battery, but, minutes before, they had received orders to rejoin their brigade. The regiment was marching in column of fours and had just entered the East Woods when they met Coulter, who implored Lyle, "For God's sake come and help us out. Our ammunition is exhausted." The 40-year-old Lyle was a tobacco merchant and carriage maker in Philadelphia before the war, but he also had extensive pre-war experience in the state militia. Since 1846 he had commanded the National Guards Regiment, an elite Philadelphia militia unit. Lyle and his Guards were mustered into Federal service for 3 months, as the 19th Pennsylvania, when the war began, and after this short stint they reenlisted for 3 years as a volunteer regiment, the 90th Pennsylvania. Lyle did not hesitate at Coulter's plea for help. He ordered his men to deploy from column to line, which brought them into Miller's meadow, south of the Cornfield. They occupied approximately the same position as the right wing of the 13th Massachusetts had, about 60 yards south of the Cornfield and 160 yards west of the woods. There were plenty of targets, for Hood's men were pouring out of the West Woods, and the Pennsylvanians became engaged immediately.[48]

HOOKER'S OPENING ASSAULT HAD cracked open Jackson's line, but the Southerners had dealt out heavy punishment before their line collapsed. Ricketts's division was particularly badly mauled. Duryée's and Christian's brigades had suffered less than Hartsuff's brigades, but both of the former had been plagued by numerous stragglers, which compromised their combat effectiveness. The 26th and 94th New York remained along the south and southwestern edges of the East Woods, but their line was shaky and leaking men to the rear. The 90th Pennsylvania stood alone in the meadow west of the woods, with Thompson's battery in the Cornfield on their right rear. Both were about to receive the particular attention of Hood's advancing regiments. Farther west, Gibbon's and Phelps's men, their ranks greatly thinned and jumbled by the combat with Jones's division and Douglass's brigade, were pursuing the retreating Confederates along the axis of the Hagerstown Pike, but they lacked the cohesion and power to exploit their success. Patrick's brigade, as well as the 19th Indiana and the 7th Wisconsin, remained intact in the West Woods, and Battery B, 4th U.S., occupied its advanced position south of Miller's barn. The latter was about to experience a fight that its members would never forget.

By 7 a.m., Hooker's attack had shattered both of Jackson's divisions, except for Jubal Early's brigade. The carnage among their leadership was appalling. In Jones's division, he was stunned by a shell and incapacitated, Starke was dead, and the remnants of the division were under the command of Colonel Grigsby. Grigsby remained as combative as ever, but he was only able to rally roughly 200 to 300 men out of the entire division in the West Woods. The division had suffered about 650 casualties, which meant that 700 to 800 men, just under half its original strength, had left the fight for various reasons. Brigade commander Colonel James W. Jackson was wounded, as was his replacement, Lieutenant Colonel John F. Terry. Starke's brigade had two regimental commanders wounded, and the acting brigade commander, Colonel Leroy Stafford, suffered a severe contusion on his foot, although he remained with his men and assisted Grigsby in rallying the division's remnants. In Penn's brigade, Captain Penn and his replacement, Captain A. C. Page, were seriously wounded. In Lawton's division, Lawton was badly injured, leaving Early in command. Among the brigades in the division, Douglass's had suffered 565 casualties, approximately 50% of its strength. Douglass was dead, and four of his six regimental commanders were killed or wounded, leaving a major in command of the brigade. Colonel James Walker counted 226 casualties. Walker had his horse shot from under him and been injured by a shell fragment, but he remained in the field until his brigade was relieved by the advance of Ripley's brigade. Three of his four regimental commanders were casualties, with two of them killed. Hays's 64% loss was the highest in the division. Of his 356 casualties, only 31 were listed as missing, a testament both to the brigade's discipline and the deadly effectiveness of the enemy's fire. The devastating losses to the regimental and company leadership in this brigade have been recounted above. Stonewall Jackson would report that his men fought with "stubborn resolution," which they certainly had, but he also claimed that they faced "superior numbers," and that "fresh troops from time to time relieved the enemy's ranks." These latter two claims, however, do not square with the evidence.[49]

It may have appeared to Jackson that the Federals brought superior numbers to bear on his line, since he received successive blows on Ricketts's front, but he faced only four brigades—Duryée's, Gibbon's, Hartsuff's, and Phelps's—plus the 88th Pennsylvania of Christian's brigade. These units received crucial support from the 1st Corps' artillery and the Reserve Artillery on the east bank of Antietam Creek. In terms of numbers, Jackson had engaged seven brigades, composed of roughly 4,250 men. The Federals brought about 3,900 soldiers against them. Jackson also had the support of S. D. Lee's battalion, Stuart's guns on Nicodemus Heights, and his divisional artillery, but even though they inflicted substantial losses on Duryée's and Hartsuff's brigades, in particular, they were out-ranged and outgunned by the Federals' artillery and failed to prevent them from inflicting severe damage to Jackson's exposed infantry. We will never know how many casualties were due to the Union guns, but the anecdotal evidence is that they were numerous. Major John H. Lowe, the senior surviving officer of Douglass's brigade, reported that the enfilading fire from across Antietam Creek was the most destructive to his command, describing how it killed or wounded "many of our men." Besides the physical carnage, the shelling, and particularly the enfilading fire, were highly demoralizing. Even the toughest troops have a breaking point when subjected to a crossfire of artillery and small arms.[50]

All the assaulting Union brigades fought bravely, but Gibbon's attack, aggressively spearheaded by the 2nd and 6th Wisconsin, with crucial support from Phelps's brigade and enfilading fire from the Reserve Artillery, had been the most successful, driving back both Douglass's left and the first line of Jones's division, and forcing Starke to commit the divisional reserve. Starke's counterattack checked and drove back Gibbon's spearhead, but Phelps's support and Gibbon's decision to deploy the 19th Indiana and the 7th Wisconsin to the West Woods, and then push Stewart's section of Napoleon's far forward, proved to be decisive and repulsed the Confederate attack, with heavy Rebel losses. Jackson's line had been cracked open—not by superior numbers, but by aggressive tactics, effective maneuvers, and concentrated, well-directed artillery fire. If there were any questions about whether the 1st Corps was still in the "kinks" and would fight, their opening assault had laid these to rest.[51]

THE NIGHT BEFORE, WHEN General John B. Hood had asked Jackson to relieve his famished division, Jackson agreed, but he extracted a promise from Hood that the latter would come to the support of Jackson's men "the moment I was called upon." When Hooker's first blows struck, Hood received a message from Alexander Lawton, stating that "he would require all the assistance I could give him." Hood had anticipated a hard fight that morning. His skirmishing with the 1st Corps the night before had convinced him that the Federals had arrayed a powerful force and would strike hard at first light. At 4 a.m. he sent an aide-de-camp to D. H. Hill, inquiring whether he could spare any troops to reinforce the left. Hill said "No." Hood also queried Longstreet for help, but the Georgian, too, replied that he had no men to spare. Hood's search for reinforcements raises a question about the Confederates' command structure on their left flank. Why was Hood negotiating with D. H. Hill and sending messages to Longstreet, rather than going through Jackson, the ranking officer on the left? Why would Hood negotiate with Jackson to relieve his men, so they could get some rations and rest, but not work through him to obtain reinforcements? The official record provides no clues. Jackson is a bit of an enigma at Antietam, particularly in the early part of the engagement. While numerous officers in the 1st Corps saw Hooker frequently and received orders directly from him, Jackson's presence is scarcely noted in the existing sources, and his impact on the battle seems minimal. Jubal Early received orders from him to support Stuart's gun on Nicodemus Heights and then bring his brigade back and assume command of Lawton's division, after Lawton was wounded. Jackson was seen early on in the action along Starke's reserve line and, even earlier, in the East Woods, when he ordered D'Aquin's battery out. He may have intervened with D. H. Hill, for when the situation along Jackson's line became critical, Hill agreed to send three of his five brigades as reinforcements. But Hill did not mention receiving any orders from Jackson in his after-action report and stated that his brigades went to support Hood, not Jackson, which implies that his orders came from Lee.[52]

Ripley's brigade, in Hill's division, had already been engaged around Mumma's farm against the 26th and 94th New York. Now Hill's orders sent Colonel Alfred Colquitt's and Colonel Duncan McRae's brigades, along with Ripley's, into motion toward the embattled left flank. Early's brigade, minus the small 13th Virginia, which Early left to support Stuart's guns, was also moving to shore up the broken front of Lawton's and Jones's divisions. With Hood's division, this gave the Confederates six brigades converging to support their crumbling left flank.

For Alexander Lawton—who was seriously wounded, and with his brigades melting away under the onslaught of Hooker's brigades—the moment for Hood to come to his aid had arrived. Lawton sent a staff officer to the Kentuckian with an urgent summons: "General Lawton sends his compliments, with the request that you come at once to his support." It was approximately 7 a.m., and the morning's seesaw conflict was about to swing dramatically in favor of the Confederates.[53]

4

Hood Strikes Back

*"I have never seen a more disgusted bunch
of boys & mad as hornets"*

Peering at an early Civil War photograph of John Bell Hood,
with his thick, sandy hair, piercing blue eyes, and long beard
and face, one can almost imagine him standing at the prow of a Viking long-
ship—a fierce warrior who reveled in battle. The Viking image of Hood is further shaped by his combat record as an aggressive, fearless, and, at times, reckless, warrior. But Hood had another, sentimental side and cared deeply about the
welfare of his soldiers, at least early on in the war. People commented on his soft
voice, his kind, gentle disposition, and the smallness of his hands, all of which
were at odds with a warrior image. Although tall and powerfully built, he was
gangly, "a tall, rawboned country-looking man, with little of the soldierly appearance that West Point often gave its graduates," wrote a staff officer who
knew him, adding that Hood "looked like a raw backwoodsman, dressed up in
an ill-fitting uniform." But the Kentucky born, 31-year-old officer came, not from
the backwoods, but from a privileged childhood. His father was a physician, and
one of the wealthiest men in Montgomery County, Kentucky, with significant
holdings in land, enslaved people, and property. Hood grew up in "something
of a romantic, unrealistic world." Dr. Hood wanted his son to follow in his foot-
steps and become a physician, but it was the army that appealed to the youngster. When he came of age, a congressman uncle secured him an appointment
to West Point. He was a below-average student, 44 in a class of 52 when he graduated in 1853. During his last 2 years at the academy, he established a close relationship with Superintendent Robert E. Lee. The two men were brought together again in 1855, when Hood wrangled an assignment to the newly formed
2nd U.S. Cavalry, of which Lee was lieutenant colonel. Lee enjoyed Hood's company and saw promise in the young officer. While they were in Texas in 1857,
Lee often invited the lieutenant to join him on rides to search for a location in
which to site a permanent army post. This deepened their relationship and
strengthened Hood's admiration for Lee.[1]

Hood suffered no gut-wrenching decision when secession and war came. Although his home state did not secede from the Union, Hood did. His sympathies

were with the slaveholding South. Two days after the firing on Fort Sumter, he resigned his commission in the U.S. Army and was commissioned as a lieutenant in the Confederate States Army. Because trained officers were in demand, Hood was promoted to colonel in September and placed in command of the 4th Texas Infantry. Hood loved Texas ever since his time there with the army, and he considered it his "adopted land." He labored hard to mold the rugged, individualistic Texans into disciplined soldiers. Like John Gibbon in the Army of the Potomac, he opted to motivate his volunteers by building the unit's pride and striving to "impress upon them that no regiment in that [Confederate] Army should ever be allowed to go forth upon the battle-field and return with more trophies of war than the Fourth Texas."[2]

In the spring of 1862, Hood was promoted to brigadier general and command of the unit that became famous as the Texas Brigade, consisting of the 1st, 4th, and 5th Texas and the 18th Georgia, which was informally dubbed the "3rd Texas" by their Texan comrades. Hood's biographer, Richard McMurray, considered this promotion to be one of the mysteries of Hood's career, as he done nothing yet to distinguish himself. That soon changed.[3]

In May, during the army's withdrawal up the Virginia Peninsula from Yorktown, Hood's brigade was detailed to deal with a bridgehead that General William B. Franklin's 6th Corps had established at Eltham's Landing, on the southern bank of the Pamunkey River, to threaten the Confederates' rear. Confederate commander Joe Johnston gave orders for Hood "to feel the enemy gently and fall back," which meant to probe the enemy with skirmishers and avoid a pitched fight. Hood eschewed such tentative tactics. He believed in hitting hard and fast, and then not stopping once the enemy was on the run. He struck Franklin's Federals hard and never let them recover, driving them, in confusion, relentlessly back to the cover of their gunboats, and ending the threat the 6th Corps posed. Hood earned high praise with his division commander, who described the "conspicuous gallantry of Hood." When Joe Johnston asked Hood what his Texans would have done if he had ordered them to charge and drive the enemy back, rather than "gently feel their position," he responded, "they would have driven them into the river, and tried to swim out and capture the gunboats."[4]

Hood had a chance to test his tactical ideas again nearly 2 months later, in a far tougher situation at Gaines' Mill on June 27. The army's new commander, Hood's old friend Robert E. Lee, massed two-thirds of the army north of the Chickahominy River to crush the Union's 5th Corps and sever McClellan's supply line to the York River. The plan was sound, but its execution foundered against the powerful position the 5th Corps' commander, Fitz John Porter, had selected, as well as the failure of the Confederate units to coordinate their attacks. By the time Hood arrived on the field, late in the afternoon, the situation was critical. The Federal line had to be broken, or Lee's entire offensive might be at risk. General William H. C. Whiting's division, which included Hood's

Texas brigade, was ordered to carry the heights that were the key to the Union position. Lee personally appealed to Hood, stating how vital it was that his attack break the Union line.[5]

Hood conducted a personal reconnaissance of the approaches to the enemy position. The ground he would have to pass over was open, and thus exposed to enemy fire. Beyond it, Boatswain's Swamp ran in front of the Federal lines and would be difficult to get through quickly, or to do so in any kind of order. There were many casualties littering the ground from previous failed assaults, and Hood concluded, based on where the wounded and killed were, that the attacks failed because the men halted to return fire before crossing the swamp, thereby breaking the momentum of their attack. He returned to his command and gave strict orders that there was to be no firing until he ordered it. When the attack went forward, it tested the mettle of every man. Murderous fire struck down dozens, but Hood kept shouting "Forward!" and "Steady!" The line, accompanied by Whiting's brigade, which was commanded by Colonel Evander M. Law, kept moving forward. But with casualties mounting, when the 4th Texas neared the creek, its commander made the same error earlier attacks had and ordered his men to halt and fire. Fortunately, Hood was near his old regiment, and he immediately countermanded the order, shouting for the regiment to keep moving and "drive them out with the bayonet." This maintained the momentum of the attack, which swept across the swamp and up the slope beyond it. The Federals facing Hood had been engaged all day and were near the limit of their endurance. At the moment of Hood's attack, other Confederate units joined in at different points, and the Union line began to collapse and retreat. Lee had his victory.[6]

Much of the credit for the Confederates' success went to Hood. Stonewall Jackson, always sparing in his praise, described Hood's attack as "this rapid and almost matchless display of daring and valor." Again, Hood's tactical instincts had proven to be sound, and his leadership conspicuous. To his men, Hood appeared utterly fearless in battle, but while he understood the importance of being seen by his volunteers, he was not foolish and went into the attack on foot. Victory came at a high cost—the Texas brigade suffered 572 casualties—but they were lower than those of many other Confederate units whose attacks had failed. Along with the confidence that success gave soldiers, Hood's men also felt a sense of their superiority over the enemy.[7]

That his losses were less, compared with other units, was little solace to Hood. After spending the night seeing that his dead and wounded were removed from the field, a staff officer came upon him sitting on a cracker box, weeping. "Just look here, Major, at these dead and suffering men, and every one of them as good as I am, and yet I am untouched," Hood lamented. Yet his concern for his men did not affect his hard-hitting doctrine. Two months later, at Second Manassas, he would lead another assault that swept the enemy from his front. This time he was in charge of a division. When division commander Whiting left the army on a medical furlough, Hood assumed command as the senior officer. His tactics mirrored those he had employed at Eltham's Landing and Gaines' Mill—close quickly with the enemy and, once their line was broken, press them relentlessly. The enemy again fought stubbornly, and Hood's losses were high: 962 for the division. But Union losses were higher, and the Confederates notched another battlefield victory. The lesson Hood and his command had learned—the doctrine by which they operated—was that bold, hard-hitting attacks produced victories. Casualties were inevitable, but losses in victory were easier to accept than those suffered in defeat.[8]

A high casualty rate did not affect Hood's standing with his men. That relationship remained one of mutual admiration. Hood did not hesitate to risk their lives in battle when necessary, but he loved them. They knew it, and they revered him in return. No story better illustrates the bond he enjoyed with his men than an incident during the Battle of South Mountain. His division had just completed a brutal march from Hagerstown and was passing through Boonsboro, moving toward the fighting at Fox's and Turner's Gaps. Hood rode at the rear of his division, under arrest for a petty offense. On August 30, during the fighting at Second Manassas, Hood's division had temporarily been attached to the command of General Nathaniel "Shanks" Evans. Evans demanded that Hood turn over some ambulances his soldiers had captured, to which Hood, who seemed unaware that he had ever been subject to Evans's authority or orders, refused. Evans demanded that Hood be placed under arrest, and Longstreet directed Hood to make his way to Culpepper and wait for his case to be tried. Lee, loath to lose one of his best officers to the petty tyranny of General Evans, intervened and ordered Hood to remain with the army, although still under arrest. When Hood's division marched past Lee toward Turner's Gap, the men began to shout, "Give us Hood!" Lee summoned the Kentuckian and asked him to make some admission of regret for his refusal to obey Evans's order. Hood replied that he would not do so, for he could not "admit or see the justness" of Evans's demand. With the sound of fighting echoing down from the mountain, and Hood's men shouting for his return, Lee relented and suspended the brigadier's arrest until the battle was decided. As Hood rode to the front of his men, they raised a cheer and hollered, "Hurrah for General Lee! Hurrah for General Hood! Go to hell Evans!"[9]

In addition to tactical skill and personal courage, Hood possessed great stamina, a crucial quality in a combat leader. He needed it on the eve of Antietam. On September 14, his division completed the grueling march from Hagerstown (which was only 11 miles distant, but considerable stretches were covered at the double-quick), ascended South Mountain, skirmished at Fox's Gap, then acted as rear guard when the army retreated to Sharpsburg. It is unlikely that Hood slept at all on the night of the 14th. He did not sleep on the night of the 16th, either. That afternoon and evening, his division held the left of Lee's line, and they skirmished with Hooker's advance until late into the night. His men were famished and exhausted. When Jackson agreed to relieve Hood's division, Hood withdrew his men into the West Woods. He then rode off to hunt up his commissary wagons and get his troops some food. After finding the wagons and heading them toward the division, he spent the remaining hours of darkness communicating with D. H. Hill and Longstreet in a fruitless effort to obtain reinforcements before the anticipated Union assault struck.[10]

The summer's campaign had whittled Hood's two brigades down to around 2,000 effectives. Colonel William T. Wofford, commanding the Texas Brigade (the brigade now also included the Hampton Legion of South Carolina), counted 854 officers and men, while Colonel Evander M. Law had 1,150 in his four regiments. Although both were still colonels, Wofford and Law were among the top tier of brigade commanders in the Army of Northern Virginia. Wofford was a 38-year-old Georgian who had been a volunteer captain in the Mexican War. He was employed in work typical of a rising white Southerner of the antebellum era: planter, state legislator, newspaper editor, and attorney. He voted against secession but volunteered for service as soon as his state left the Union. Despite his limited background in the military, Wofford excelled as a soldier and jumped from being a captain in the 18th Georgia to its colonel during the army's April 1862 reorganization. He ascended to command of the Texas Brigade by seniority when Hood was promoted.[11]

Law was a 26-year-old bachelor, a graduate of the South Carolina Military Academy (now the Citadel), and came from a large family in Darlington County, South Carolina, where his father was a wealthy planter and attorney. Law taught at a military school in Yorkville after graduation, and in 1860 he moved to Tuskegee, Alabama, to teach at another military school and study law. When South Carolina seceded, he volunteered at once, recruiting young men from among his students into what would become the 4th Alabama Infantry. The volunteers elected Law as their lieutenant colonel. He performed well at First Manassas, where he was severely wounded in the left arm. By that fall he was the regiment's colonel. When General William H. C. Whiting was elevated to division command during the Peninsula Campaign, Law took command of the brigade by seniority and led it ably through all the battles that summer. During the Second Manassas Campaign, he demonstrated initiative and solid leadership when he personally discovered a route over the Bull Run Mountains that enabled the Confederates to outflank the Union defenders at Thoroughfare Gap.[12]

Hood's relationship with his brigade commanders seems to have been good, but not warm. Although Hood was gracious in praising both officers in after-action reports, he did not mention Wofford a single time in his later memoir about the war, and, while he described Law's command as a "splendid brigade," its commander only merited a boiler-plate description as "an able and efficient officer." Perhaps Hood was merely sparing with his praise, but the implication seems otherwise.[13]

Hood's soldiers were supremely confident in their superiority to the blue-coats, but they were also realistic and recognized that the Federals were hard fighters, Victories over them were neither easily nor cheaply won. "The Yankees fight well," wrote James H. Hendrick in the 1st Texas, shortly after the Seven Days Battles. "They will stand and shoot all day with us. The only way we can whip them is to charge them. They will not stand the bayonet." H. Waters Berryman, also in the 1st, echoed his comrade's sentiments after Second Manassas, writing home that "we killed thousands of the Federals but they fought very well." Hood's division was a crack outfit by any definition, yet even the best units were not immune to the stresses of war, particularly when their most efficient officers were lost. Even after all the experience he gained in the Peninsula Campaign's battles, August L. P. Varin, in the 2nd Mississippi, confided in his diary on July 20 that he had so little confidence in his regiment's other officers that, "should our colonel [John M. Stone] and lieutenant colonel [David W. Humphreys] be taken from us the 2nd Miss. would be little better than so many raw recruits." Company A, 5th Texas, lost six men who fell to the rear sick on September 14. Two were apparently legitimately ill, but the four others were all recent recruits from Texas and were subsequently deemed to be deserters. Two more men of the company fell out sick on the 16th and 17th and also deserted. For a regiment that numbered only about 176 officers and men in the ranks on September 17, the loss of six deserters from a single company was substantial. It reflects that even in the best units, there were men whose commitment to the cause and to their comrades wavered under war's harsh realities. In the 4th Alabama of Law's brigade, the adjutant, Robert T. Coles, wrote that by the time they reached Sharpsburg, there was only one man in the entire regiment "who was regarded as a downright coward." This was Joseph Frame, a farmer from Huntsville, a powerful man standing 6 feet 2 inches tall and known to be able to "whip any three of the best soldiers of the regiment when around the camp fire," but who became "perfectly demoralized at the first sound of a bullet or shell." Frame had contrived to slip away from every fight the 4th had been in. His company commander, Lieutenant James Stewart, was determined to put a stop to it and vowed that if he could not force the big private into the impending battle, "he intended to kill him."[14]

"The only way we can whip them is to charge them." No quote better reflected, in simplistic terms, the tactical doctrine Hood had instilled in his command over the summer's campaigns. One day during the Peninsula Campaign, some Texans were assigned to sharpshooting duty. They made it clear that they were not sent out "to dig trenches—that is not our style." A charge, as soldiers like James Hendrick understood, was not a headlong, reckless dash. It might be a rapid rush to a certain point without firing, such as at Gaines' Mill, or it could be a steady advance, with the men loading and firing while on the move, such as at Eltham's Landing and Second Manassas. Hood employed the tactics that best suited the situation, and thus far his judgment had never failed.[15]

If soldiers are more effective, as Korean War veteran Captain Norman Allen maintains, "when you're at the end of the rope—hungry, desperate, sleepless, mean, angry," then Hood's men were at a razor's edge. They were all of these things that morning. When the division was relieved by Jackson's men, the two brigades fell back into the West Woods, just west of the Dunker Church. When Hood rode off to track down the divisional commissary wagons, some officers decided to take matters into their own hands. Lieutenant Colonel Samuel F. Butler, commanding the 11th Mississippi, ordered details from all his companies to gather corn from Miller's field and prepare it for the regiment. David C. Love, a private in Company E, was part of one detail. He and his comrades gathered corn and some pumpkins and carried them to a point in the northern part of the West Woods. It took all night to collect the rations, carry them to the preparation point, and cook them. They finished only about an hour before daylight, and a guide directed them to the regiment, where they found everyone sound asleep. They woke the men and began distributing the rations. Wofford's commissary wagons, which Hood had ordered up, arrived around the same time, but the Texas brigade discovered, to their disgust, that their ration consisted of nothing but flour. Moreover, there were no utensils to prepare it. Dawn found the hungry men trying to "improvise some means" of turning the flour into bread. Fires were kindled and ramrods were employed as makeshift cooking implements to cook dough over the flame. Then the Federal artillery opened fire, sending some of their shells into the woods. Beyond the woods, the sounds of battle quickly ramped up to a roar that gradually moved in their direction. Orders were shouted to fall in. Rations had to be abandoned, causing the ravenous men to feel a special fury toward the foe who had upset their meal. "I have never seen a more disgusted bunch of boys & mad as hornets," recorded Lieutenant James L. Lemon in the 18th Georgia.[16]

The precise position of Hood's two brigades is unclear from the records. In his maps of the battle, Ezra Carman placed the two brigades side by side, west of the Dunker Church. After the regiments formed up, their officers ordered everyone to lie down. Lieutenant Odie Putnam in the 18th Georgia described the artillery fire as "a storm of canister shot and shell." Lawrence Daffan, with the 4th Texas, commented on how shells cut limbs from the trees and sent them crashing down among the men. Casualties were light, but those that occurred were often appalling. Captain William Robbins, acting as major of the 4th Alabama, was standing beside Lieutenant David B. King, a 20-year-old farmer from Whitesburg, Alabama, whom Robbins described as his "noble and handsome young friend," when a shell or large fragment struck King in the head, throwing a piece of his skull ten paces to the rear, into the ranks of the 11th Mississippi's

Company E. Robbins was spattered with his young friend's blood and brains. The piece of King's skull that landed among the Mississippians was hideous, but the body part came from a stranger, and they shrugged it off as one of war's horrors. It was personal for Robbins. King was his friend, and he had been killed instantly, in a most awful way, in front of Robbins's eyes, while the captain escaped unscathed. The wonder is that Robbins was able to recover from such trauma and do his duty, but he did. "The strain upon the men is terrible," noted Corporal William P. Pritchard in the 1st Texas. "It takes more than brute courage to make him stand. There must be some higher, nobler feeling to prompt him or he will run in this great moment of trial."[17]

Hood's men lay under this shelling for nearly an hour and a half, from 5:30 to 7 a.m. At 7 a.m., an aide-de-camp from General Lawton rode up to Hood to report that Lawton was wounded, sent his compliments—a seemingly obligatory phrase in that era—and requested Hood to "come at once to his support." Hood ordered "to arms" to be sounded, and both brigades rose to their feet. Marching by the right flank,[18] Law's brigade passed through the woods, emerging just north of the Dunker Church in front of S. D. Lee's battalion. They passed through gaps in the turnpike's fencing, moving into the clover field east of the pike. Wofford, also marching by the flank, followed, although his brigade may have emerged from the woods slightly farther north of Law. W. T. Hill in the 5th Texas wrote, "The Brig always moved in that order [by the flank] when moving rapidly unless under too much fire." Column was the most efficient method to move troops through an area with numerous obstacles, such as the West Woods. Nonetheless, every movement was made swiftly and efficiently, just as Hood had trained his men to fight.[19]

As the soldiers came to the lower end of the clover field, in the angle where Smoketown Road and the Hagerstown Pike meet, Law deployed his regiments into line of battle. The 4th Alabama was on the right, with (from right to left) the 6th North Carolina, 11th Mississippi, and 2nd Mississippi continuing the line. Law instructed Captain Lawrence H. Scruggs, commanding the 4th Alabama, to guide along Smoketown Road. The brigade faced northeast, toward the East Woods. All of its movements were executed "without any halt being made." Possibly because of the crowded area in which both brigades were attempting to deploy, Scruggs found his regiment astride Smoketown Road, where fences disrupted his formation, so he ordered his regiment back into column and marched it up the road, to keep up with the rest of the brigade. One of the first to fall out was Joseph Frame, the strapping young man whom battle paralyzed with fear. When Frame dropped out, Lieutenant Stewart, pistol in hand, "caught Joe by the collar" with his free hand and tried to drive him forward. But the private fell to his hands and knees and "held his position against the struggles of Lieutenant Stewart." Watching his regiment move rapidly off without him, Stewart at last gave the private "a vigorous kick," and rushed off to join his men, while Frame "made Gilpin speed back in the direction of Dunker Church."[20]

Wofford's regiments filed into the clover field close behind Law. Law reported that the Texas Brigade deployed on his left, which was only partially true. There was not enough room for the three Texas regiments, so they formed in Law's rear. This placed the Hampton Legion and the 18th Georgia on Law's left, and (from left to right) the 1st, 4th, and 5th Texas in a support line. The situation was chaotic. The crash of firing was deafening, and smoke blanketed the field, making it difficult to spot the enemy. Law could see "but few of our troops on the field, and these seemed to be in much confusion."[21]

Hood met General Lawton, who was being carried to the rear, and "about forty men" whom Harry Hays had rallied, but they were without ammunition. He suggested that Hays go to the rear, re-form his shattered brigade, and resupply them with ammunition. Although Hood reported that his division confronted "an immense force of the enemy," he actually had superiority in numbers over the Federals in his immediate front when he first deployed. The odds would change, but initially they were in Hood's favor.[22]

Confronting Hood were the remnants of Doubleday's and Ricketts's divisions. On Ricketts's line, Hartsuff's and Christian's brigades were withdrawing. The only infantry unit in the entire division that remained to oppose Hood was the 90th Pennsylvania, in the meadow south of the Cornfield near the East Woods. They were supported by Thompson's battery in the Cornfield, on their right rear, and Matthews's battery, on the ridge north of the Cornfield. On Doubleday's front, the 2nd and 6th Wisconsin and Phelps's tiny brigade, all jumbled together in confusion, were pursuing retreating elements of Douglass's brigade and J. R. Jones's division east of the Hagerstown Pike, placing them on a collision course with Hood. This was the force that immediately opposed Hood—263 men in the 90th Pennsylvania, perhaps 300 to 400 men of Gibbon's and Phelps's brigades, and two batteries containing a total of eight 3-inch rifles.

In the Cornfield, the men of Thompson's battery were lying down, but as survivors of Hartsuff's brigade began to fall back, Corporal William L. Turpin got up and stood on the trunnion of his gun "to see what was going on." He spotted "two columns of troops charging from the south of the Dunker Church obliquely toward the cornfield"—Law's and Wofford's brigades. Although the Rebels were in canister range, so many wounded Federal soldiers lay in front of the battery that Thompson feared he would hit some of them with this type of ammunition. Thus he ordered his crews to fire case shot with a 3-second fuse. Matthews also turned his guns on this new threat.[23]

Corporal John Stevens in the 5th Texas recalled that these two batteries rained "a terrible shower of shell and shrapnel on us as we advanced," causing some casualties. But the division shrugged these losses off and moved steadily

forward. Small-arms fire soon augmented that of the Union artillery. Lieutenant Colonel Martin W. Gary, commanding the Hampton Legion, a slim battalion numbering only 77 men, reported that his command came under fire from
Federal troops "near the edge of the corn-field immediately in our front" the moment they emerged from the West Woods. Lieutenant Colonel Benjamin F.
Carter, leading the 4th Texas, described the fire as "severe," but because of the
"dense smoke pervading" and Law's soldiers in front of his Texans, Carter was
unable to "see the enemy clearly."[24]

The small-arms fire came from the 2nd and 6th Wisconsin and Phelps's men,
who were about 200 to 300 yards away, on the plateau of high ground south of
the Cornfield. "Firing and yelling," the men in the mingled Wisconsin and New
York regiments had pushed south to this point in their pursuit of Douglass's
Georgians. Poor-quality powder fouling their weapons had greatly slowed their
rate of fire, and it took hard pounding to seat rounds in the rifles. Major Dawes
watched the "long gray lines of men" who had poured out of the West Woods,
crisply fronted their line toward the Federals, and then, raising the rebel yell,
begin to advance. The soldiers moving directly toward Dawes were the Hampton Legion and the 18th Georgia, only 253 men combined, but their ranks were
well formed and their weapons clean. They stopped, leveled their rifles, and fired
a well-aimed volley into the Union ranks. "It was almost like a scythe running
through the line," wrote Dawes. The effect was devastating. "Two out of every
three of the men who went to the front of the line were shot," Dawes recalled,
underlining the words to emphasize how destructive the fire was.[25]

Men near Dawes who were hit looked at him "with all the imploring earnestness of death for help." But pausing to assist the wounded was a death sentence.
All Dawes could do was shout "Get to the rear if you can," even though he knew
this was impossible for many. To Captain George H. Otis in the 2nd Wisconsin,
"it seemed as if the Secesh rose from the ground—for of a sudden a whole brigade of fresh rebels rose and poured in on our distracted men volley upon volley of Minnie balls." Someone in the 2nd U.S. Sharpshooters on the Hagerstown
Pike called out, "Look over the fence!" When W. H. Humphrey did so, he "could
see the rebs come out of the wood that surrounded the old church." He and his
comrades fired on them with their Sharps rifles. Adjutant Parmalee, who only
moments before had triumphantly hoisted the captured flag of the 1st Louisiana above his head and thus made a conspicuous target, was struck by five bullets and killed. Edwin Chadwick, another sharpshooter, saw Hood's men coming on steadily and thought, "Nothing was left for us now but to remain and be
taken prisoner or retreat." Orders were shouted to fall back, and the Federals'
massed crowd, for that was what they now were, began to withdraw, doing so
slowly at first and returning fire at the advancing Rebels. The Confederates were
not "more than a dozen rods [about 60–70 yards]" away from Chadwick when
he started to retreat. Bullets pursued him, one cutting the strap of his haversack

and striking his belt, which stopped the blow. It probably doubled him over, but he kept on moving.[26]

"The bullets of the advancing, steadily grandly advancing foe drive us in confusion back to the cornfield," wrote Dawes. What began as a stubborn withdrawal collapsed into "a race for life" as each man ran for the cover of the Cornfield, perhaps 100 yards away. Years later, Dawes admitted, with refreshing honesty, that when everyone broke for cover, he ran as "fast as I could run and I was a pretty good sprinter." In his dash to cover, he felt a sharp, cutting pain, "as of a switch," sting the calf of his leg as a bullet creased it, but he ignored his injury and kept running.[27]

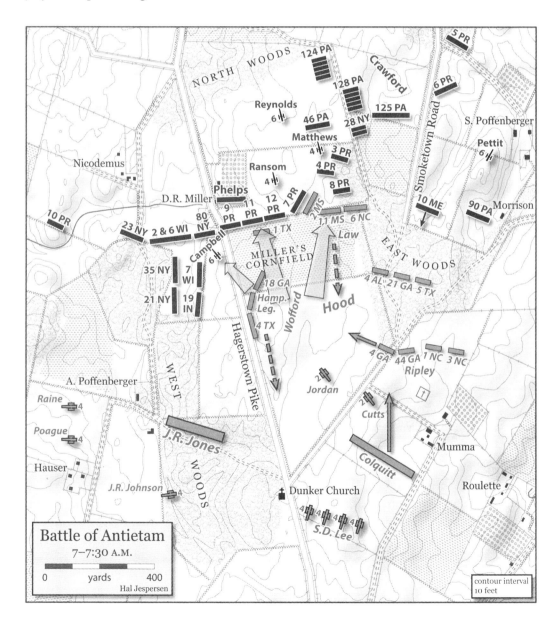

Battle of Antietam

7–7:30 A.M.

0   yards   400

Hal Jespersen

contour interval 10 feet

Colonel Wofford watched the Hampton Legion and the 18th Georgia "moving slowly forward, but rapidly firing." Riding over to them, he saw two groups of Federals through the smoke, one directly in front of the Legion and the Georgians, "and the other partly to their left." The men to the left were probably remnants of the 6th Wisconsin, the 14th Brooklyn, and the 2nd U.S. Sharpshooters. The others were the 2nd Wisconsin and the rest of Phelps's brigade. Together, the two groups were probably slightly larger than the Legion and the 18th Georgia. Hood saw them, too, and ordered Wofford to move his brigade at a left oblique, to clear away this threat. In the noise and confusion, only the Legion and the 18th Georgia received the order. The Texas regiments initially continued on in the rear of Law. Hood also told Law, whose brigade was moving in a direction that would have carried it into the East Woods, to change direction slightly to his left, to strike the 90th Pennsylvania and Thompson's battery. These orders caused the two brigades to advance in slightly diverging directions, with Wofford moving north, with his left on the Hagerstown Pike, while Law advanced in a northeasterly direction, with the Texans following.[28]

The Legion and the 18th Georgia made short work of the enemy in their front. "We charged with a yell & hit the yanks in front of the corn & they fairly flew apart & fled," recorded 1st Lieutenant James L. Lemon in the 18th Georgia. Stephen E. Welch, a private in the adjacent Hampton Legion, wrote to his parents that his battalion swept forward "like a hurricane." Welch was near his regiment's flag, carried by a 31-year-old private named Herod Wilson. A bullet struck Wilson in the arm, and he dropped the flag. "I saw it fall," wrote Welch, "but did not pick it up being hard at work loading and firing." James Estes of Company E retrieved the colors, but a bullet in his leg knocked him down after only a few steps. Corporal Christopher P. Poppenheim took the flag, but he received a serious arm wound. The Federals may have been fleeing before the Confederate onslaught, but they still had bite. Major J. Hervey Dingle Jr., a wealthy 37-year-old planter from Clarendon County, South Carolina, took the standard from Poppenheim and shouted, "Legion, follow your colors." The Legion's commander, Lieutenant Colonel Gary, reported that Dingle's words and courageous act "had an inspiring effect, and the men rallied bravely under their flag." That they "rallied" implies that seeing their regimental colors fall three times in a matter of minutes may have caused some disorder. If so, they recovered quickly and pressed ahead, "fighting desperately at every step."[29]

Stephen Welch discovered that his rifle would not fire, so he threw it down and picked up another gun lying on the ground. It, too, "wouldn't shoot," so he hunted up a third weapon. This one worked, and Welch fired five or six shots, all them directed at the Union flags, which, in the smoky haze, drew fire like a magnet. "As fast as raised they fall again," he wrote.[30]

As the Legion and the 18th Georgia drove the enemy through the Cornfield, Wofford became aware that his Texans were not following the rest of his brigade, so he ordered Lieutenant Colonel Philip A. Work, commanding the 1st Texas, to move his regiment by the left flank. Work's regiment was some 150 to 200 yards into the clover field when he received Wofford's order. When he neared the Georgians, Wofford ordered the Texans to move up on the 18th's right, to give his front more weight and firepower, as well as partially fill the gap with Law's brigade. Meanwhile, Hood halted the 4th and 5th Texas, but in the general confusion, two companies of the 4th misunderstood their orders and followed the 11th Mississippi. Lieutenant Colonel Carter had no opportunity to retrieve his errant companies, because Hood ordered him to move his regiment to the left at once, until his left flank rested on the high ground south of the Cornfield, where he would serve as a reserve.[31]

Hood also ordered the 5th Texas to the left, for Corporal John M. Smither in that regiment recalled that the 5th came up in the rear of the 1st Texas, who were exchanging fire with Union soldiers in the Cornfield at what seemed to be point-blank range. Smither had been in seven battles before Sharpsburg, and this was the first that approximated "the picture I had seen of battles in histories." The opposing lines "were enveloped in smoke; nothing to be seen above the smoke except the colors opposing, the 'stars and stripes' on one side, and on the other, the 'St. Andrews cross,' our Confederate battle flag, and in addition [illegible], the state flag of the 1st Texas, the 'Lone Star.'" It was possible to discern the legs of the men in the 1st Texas "from the knees down," but that was all. Hood, who ranged widely across his division's front, suddenly came riding out from the ranks of the 1st Texas and pulled up in front of the 5th Texas. He had seen enough to believe that the 1st could manage the enemy in front without help. Stopping in front of Captain Ike N. M. Turner, he said, "The First Texas can attend to this; oblique to the right and uncover and drive those people (pointing to a line of Federal infantry advancing out of the edge of the East Wood, to our right) out of that wood!" It was the 90th Pennsylvania. Why he did not think Law's brigade could easily overwhelm this single regiment remains a question. Perhaps Hood saw elements of Hartsuff's and Christian's brigades and, not realizing they were retreating, thought they could pose a problem for Law. Whatever the case, Turner started his regiment toward the East Woods.[32]

Law's brigade closed the distance to the 90th Pennsylvania and Thompson's battery. The slight change of direction by the 6th North Carolina and the 11th and 2nd Mississippi, in order to strike these enemy units, caused a gap to develop between them and the 4th Alabama. The 4th, which may not have received these orders, remained moving in column along Smoketown Lane. Captain Scruggs was aware of the growing gap but was confident that when his regiment arrived at the head of the lane in the East Woods, he could deploy into line and left oblique to close the gap. Long-range small-arms fire reached Law's regiments. Most of it was inaccurate, but here and there a man dropped.[33]

Until they came to the point where Smoketown Road met the Mumma farm lane, it was difficult for Union soldiers along the southern edge of the Cornfield and East Woods to see the 4th Alabama. But when the Alabamians reached this point, they immediately drew fire from the 90th Pennsylvania and the 6th Pennsylvania Reserves, who had been moved from the northwestern corner of the woods to fill the void left by the departure of Christian's regiments. "The bullets began to zip about us, very lively," recalled Captain Robbins. One of the first to be hit was Captain Scruggs, who took a bullet in the foot, which removed him from the fight. Command passed to Captain Robbins. With nearly 200 yards of open ground to cross before they reached the East Woods, Robbins thought it imperative for the regiment to get out of column and into line, and he shouted the necessary commands. "Almost without checking our forward movement," the men ripped away the fencing along the lane, formed into line, and advanced, yelling loudly and firing. As they deployed, Robbins saw a group of Confederates—he judged them to be about five small companies, who were carrying a flag—come up beside his regiment. They "called out loudly" to Robbins that they had no field officers, had been cut off from their command, and "hardly knew what to do but 'wished to go into the fight again with somebody.'" In the din, all Robbins could make out was that they were Georgians. It was many years before he learned they were part of the 21st Georgia, under Captain James C. Nisbet. There was no time for introductions and inquiries. Robbins yelled back that they should form on his right flank and go in with his regiment, which, he recalled, "they did like lightening."[34]

The 90th Pennsylvania was outnumbered nearly 4 to 1 by Law's Confederates. The 4th Alabama threatened their left flank, the 6th North Carolina bore down directly on them, and the 2nd and 11th Mississippi's line extended well beyond their right flank. Behind them, Thompson's battery was pouring case shot into the Southerners, cutting fuses first for 3 seconds, then 2 seconds, then half a second as the range narrowed. But the Rebels seemed impervious to bullets and shrapnel and responded with what 90th Pennsylvania Lieutenant Sam Moore described as a "terrific" fire. Some of S. D. Lee's guns were shooting over the heads of their infantry, and the combined artillery and infantry fire wreaked havoc, causing the Pennsylvanians "to go down very rapidly." Lee's "shot and shell" was particularly effective and "literally mowed them [Moore's comrades] down."[35]

The 90th had its origins in the Philadelphia National Guards, a militia unit dating back to 1840. The regiment's commander, Colonel Peter Lyle, had led the Guards from 1846 until the war, when he was appointed colonel of the 90-day 19th Pennsylvania, which then became the 90th and enlisted for 3 years. Despite the odds confronting him and his rising number of casualties, Lyle held his men in their position, hoping for reinforcements. He became one of the casualties when a bullet struck him in the side, but he refused to leave the field. Corporal Theodore Mason, the color bearer, was killed, and William H. Paul dashed forward to raise the fallen banner. Paul, who received a Medal of Honor in 1896 for this act, claimed that a party of Confederates attempted to capture the flag when Mason went down, and he led a group of 10 men who saved it in a deadly hand-to-hand combat. No other survivor of the 90th who reported on the battle recalled such a notable incident, and it is probably an invention of Paul's. But his courage was unquestioned. An attempt to retrieve one of the colors under the fire his regiment was receiving was a perilous act, demanding great bravery. The regiment's situation grew more untenable with each second. "We were being virtually annihilated," wrote Major Alfred Sellers. Soon, only about 100 men remained, and their ammunition was running low. They carried .69 caliber Harpers Ferry smoothbore muskets, firing buck and ball, which was deadly at 100 yards or less but was at a significant disadvantage in a firefight with any opponents armed with rifles. With no reinforcements coming, and his men being shot down rapidly, Lyle ordered a retreat. There was no stampede, as the men fell back in "comparatively good order" toward the East Woods, firing on their pursuers. Division commander Ricketts joined them as they retreated and, recalled Lieutenant George W. Watson, "encouraged us by his presence" until a bullet or shell fragment killed Ricketts's horse and sent the general sprawling. The extent of Ricketts's injuries is unclear. There were claims that he was seriously injured, but a member of his staff, writing 6 days after the battle, mentioned that the general had his horse shot out from under him but "fortunately escaped any injury." Whatever the extent, if any, of his wounds, he was able to make his way, under his own power, back to the East Woods with the 90th.[36]

Some failed to hear Lyle's retreat order over the noise of the battle. John Howell in Company B was one, and he remained shooting at the Rebels until a buckshot, fired by one of his comrades, struck him in the back of the head and knocked him unconscious.[37] Private Paul, carrying the regimental colors, refused to turn his back on the enemy, and Major Sellers recalled how he "backed in all the way to the East Woods." Paul's courage was matched by 1st Sergeant Hillary Beyer, who heard the order to retreat but remained to tend to some of the wounded, and then to carry a wounded soldier behind a boulder, before he dashed back to the woods under fire. He, too, would be awarded a Medal of Honor in 1896. The survivors in the 90th Pennsylvania made a brief stand behind a section of stone fence, which was probably along the edge of the East Woods, but they were too few to check Law's onslaught and continued their retreat.[38]

The departure of the 90th Pennsylvania left Thompson's battery with no infantry support. As Law's Mississippians and North Carolinians drew nearer, they gained defilade from Thompson's guns, due to the roll of the ground south of the Cornfield. "They suddenly dissolved, vanished," recalled William

Turpin. It was time to clear out before the battery was overrun. A mounted officer, whom Turpin thought was General Hooker, ordered them to fall back. Although Hooker ranged widely across his front that morning, Turpin's memory failed him here. The rider was Captain Thompson. The immediate danger to his battery came from the 2nd and 11th Mississippi, directly in his front. They advanced, firing at the crews as they attempted to limber the guns. Three men positioned by Thompson's right piece were shot in quick succession. The captain jumped from his horse and hooked the gun to the limber. Dismounting probably saved his life, for, an instant later, his horse was struck by three bullets. The four guns started for the rear under a hail of fire. The horses were the prime targets of the Mississippians, who sought to immobilize the battery. Thompson could see "blood spouting out of some of the horses" where bullets had struck them, but, incredibly, not a single one dropped as they heroically heaved to put space between themselves and the Confederates. Somehow, the horses hauled the guns out from the corn and past Matthews's battery, where Thompson ordered a halt. There were 24 horses pulling the four guns. When they stopped, 16 of them dropped dead or were dying in their traces, but they had saved the guns from capture. Thompson sent off details to bring up horses from the caissons and ordered everyone else to find some cover. For the moment, his battery sat abandoned.[39]

IN ONLY MINUTES, HOOD'S COUNTERATTACK had checked and then smashed Hooker's spear point on both Doubleday's and Ricketts's fronts, sending the Federals reeling back in full retreat. But in Hooker, Hood encountered a commander cut from the same cloth, one who matched Hood's aggressiveness and grasp of tactics. Hooker still had Magilton's and Robert Anderson's brigades of Meade's division in reserve in the North Woods. When Hood's men came pouring out of the West Woods, Hooker ordered Meade forward, as well as Ransom's Battery C, 5th U.S., and Captain John A. Reynolds's Battery L, 1st New York. Reynolds was already on his way to the front, in response to an order from General Marsena Patrick to provide support to his brigade, when Hooker showed up. The ruinous system of connecting batteries to brigades or divisions not only caused confusion, but also made any concentration of artillery nearly impossible. If Hooker had had a real chief of artillery, with tactical authority, he might have had guns in position that could have battered Hood's brigades. Instead, Hooker was riding around, serving as his own artillery chief. He intercepted Reynolds's guns after they had crossed the plowed field south of the North Woods and entered Miller's meadow, near his orchard. Hooker ordered Reynolds to instead move east and unlimber near the East Woods, where Ricketts's division was rapidly coming apart.[40]

Marching toward the woods, Reynolds saw Matthews's battery firing canister into the Cornfield. One of Matthews's officers rode over to warn Reynolds that it would be "folly" to unlimber where they were. There was no room to insert the battery between Matthews and the East Woods. Besides, as Lieutenant George Breck, one of Reynolds's section commanders, observed, bullets from the Confederates "were flying about us, and onward was coming the enemy." Reynolds saw Matthews's men and horses dropping rapidly, due to fire that came from barely visible Mississippians and North Carolinians in the corn. He concluded it would be "madness" to unlimber where they were, "unless we wished to lose our pieces, horses, and very probably our lives." The Union infantry of Ricketts's division, who were in sight, were retreating in disorder. "The rebels were yelling to the top of their voice, confident that the day was theirs," wrote Breck. From what he could take in, "matters looked dubious enough about now, and the tide of battle seemed to be going hotly and greatly against us." Reynolds ordered his guns to withdraw toward the North Woods.[41]

The tension was palpable among Meade's Pennsylvania Reserves, who were waiting in these woods. Although held in reserve, their position was not particularly safe. Colonel Adoniram J. Warner, commanding the 10th Reserves, recalled that the artillery fire was "one prolonged roar varied only by the change in the volume of noise. The rapid booming of guns themselves, the quick crack and thunderlike cracking of the bursting shells, the whistling, [?], shrieking of the heavy missiles laboring through the air over our heads, smashing through tree tops, was a blending of terrific sound that none but those who have heard the like can imagine and which it is impossible to describe." When the earlier infantry fighting had heated up in front, the wounded began to come back, first in a trickle, but soon in a steady stream. The firing in front was so heavy that Warner noted how "Minni bullets flew thick back even to us." Smoke rose from the fighting, "thick and heavy," and combined with the morning's thin fog, so "nothing definite could be seen where the fight was raging." A soldier from either the 2nd or 6th Wisconsin, "with his bowels all open" from a Confederate shell, was carried back and laid down near Warner's regiment. He calmly gave his name and regiment and the names of his parents, so they might be notified that "he had done his duty." Then he turned over and died. "This incident our men looked on without emotion apparently, for such is the feeling at such a time," wrote Warner. "Aye, into that cloud of battle smoke where amid the searing roar of arms thousands were going down already in dreadful struggle, we must follow! Yet but few quailed; nearly all were silent, some few winding themselves up, forced a cheerful mood and moved about as if touched with a lofty pride at being able thus to feel in that tremendous hour. . . . At such a time when nerves are stretched to their fullest tension it takes but little to lighten or darken. Hope and despair are close together then."[42]

In Frank Holsinger's company in the 8th Pennsylvania Reserves, "the shock to the nerves" from the action in front of them was "indefinable." As the men brooded about the likelihood that they were "soon to be mangled or perhaps killed," it was "a silly remark" from Joseph Mangle that lightened the somber moment. Mangle sang out loudly, "in a high nasal twang," that it was "damned sharp skirmishing in front." It was a remark so ludicrous—perhaps deliberately so, to break the tension—that, Holsinger wrote, "there is a laugh, it is infectious, and we are once more called back to life."[43]

The tension proved to be too great for at least one man in the 7th Pennsylvania Reserves, who was seen "trying to dig his way into the root of a large tree." Division commander Meade observed him and rode up "furiously" on his horse, "Old Baldy," drew his sword, "and leaning over his horse, he gave that poor fellow a stinging taste of the flat side of his old saber; and amid the hooting and jeering of his comrades the poor man rejoined his company." Frank Holsinger also witnessed the event and thought "the action was cruel and needless on the part of the general." But when he became an officer later on in the war, "I changed my mind." Sometimes, experience had taught him, such displays of humiliation and force were necessary to maintain discipline in the brutal world of combat.[44]

George Meade was known for his explosive and unpredictable temper—it had earned him the nickname "Old Snapping Turtle"—and great stress caused it to surface several times that morning. Earlier, while speaking with Hooker, one of Meade's regimental commanders, Major John Nyce, commanding the 4th Pennsylvania Reserves, rode up and interrupted their conversation. During the skirmishing the night before, Nyce had wanted to take his regiment and capture a Confederate battery, probably Poague's, but this foolish foray was fortunately nixed by his brigade commander, Colonel Magilton. Nyce declared to Meade, "General we could have taken that battery last night." Meade did not like to be interrupted. He turned on Nyce and snarled, "Well why in hell didn't you?" Nyce beat a hasty retreat. Then, minutes after whacking a terrified private with the flat of his sword, Meade spotted Colonel Magilton, allegedly "a great chum" of his, who was dismounted. Just how much of a "chum" Magilton was is questionable—the division commander referred to the colonel as a "good for nothing" in a November 16 letter after Antietam. Meade wanted his brigade commanders mounted, and he tolerated no deviation from this order. An observer watched as the general, "wild with anger," nearly "rode almost on top of our little Colonel," and "such a sulphurous bath, as he gave him I never heard equaled, unless by General Joe Hooker." People react to pressure differently. Meade's was a hair-trigger temper. Yet it did not cloud his capacity to command, which the Battle of South Mountain had shown was considerable, and the coming fight with Hood would confirm.[45]

Meade's advanced his two brigades—Anderson's 3rd Brigade on the right, and Magilton's 2nd Brigade the left—from the North Woods in column of battalions, with each regiment in column of divisions. This presented a fat target to the Confederate guns on Nicodemus Heights and S. D. Lee's battalion. Meade recognized the danger, for he had his regiments cover the open ground south of the woods at the double-quick. Both brigades were relatively small, and their combined strength was only around 1,600 or 1,700 men. Ransom's Battery C, 5th U.S. Artillery, marched beside the infantry. They were joined by Hooker, who badgered the captain with a stream of profanity and demands to hurry his guns into action. "The captain maintained his composure," wrote John Burnett in the 4th Pennsylvania Reserves, who was marching nearby, and moved his guns to a slight ridge in Miller's meadow, north of the Cornfield, about midway between the farmer's garden and Matthews's battery, where he unlimbered.[46]

The direction of their advance brought part of Anderson's brigade through Miller's farmyard. The 11th Pennsylvania Reserves confronted the farmer's garden fence, and it proved to be as impervious to the Pennsylvanians' efforts to trample or tear it down as it had to the 6th Wisconsin. The regiment had to "double-back" to get around it. Confederate shells tracked the Pennsylvanians' movements, but the speed of their advance seems to have spared them any significant damage. Colonel Warner, commanding the 10th Pennsylvania Reserves, reported that "some few were struck, but not many." When they had cleared Miller's meadow and reached the Cornfield fence, the fighting in front was "terribly raging," and Meade could see that "the enemy were driving our men from the corn-field." He ordered both brigades to deploy along the fence, covering "the withdrawal of our people and resisting the farther advance of the enemy." In the midst of this deployment, Meade received an order from Hooker to send a brigade to help Ricketts's men, whose retreat jeopardized the 1st Corps' hold on the East Woods. Meade sent Magilton, which left him with approximately 800 men of Anderson's brigade to meet the enemy, who were driving Doubleday's division pell mell, back through the corn toward him.[47]

WHEN WOFFORD'S BRIGADE REACHED the plateau south of the Cornfield, Hood attempted to halt it before the men entered the corn. Because of the cornstalks' height, he could not see what enemy forces might lie beyond it. Although he may have known that reinforcements from D. H. Hill were on their way, they were still some distance away, and pressing ahead before they arrived carried considerable risk. But it was easier to unleash the fury of his division than it was to rein it in. His men's combat experience, and his own fighting doctrine to closely pursue a fleeing enemy, proved to be stronger than orders to halt. The Hampton Legion and the 18th Georgia charged into the corn, followed by the 1st Texas on their right. Some elements of Starke's brigade, who were rallied in the West Woods by Colonels Grigsby and Stafford, emerged to join Wofford's left, who were advancing along the Hagerstown Pike, and assisted in driving back the 2nd and 6th Wisconsin and Phelps's brigade. As the Georgians, South Carolinians, and Louisianans crested the plateau and headed toward the Cornfield, they were confronted with the 6 Napoleons of Campbell's Battery B, 4th U.S. Artillery, located about 220 yards to the north, on the west side of the turnpike, along the slight ridge Lieutenant Stewart had moved his section to earlier. For the Federals, it was the rock upon which they might rally their broken line and check Hood's counterattack, while the Confederates recognized that its capture could crack open the 1st Corps' line. The fighting that ensued, even by the standards of Antietam, became one of the most desperate engagements that day.[48]

ONLY MINUTES HAD PASSED between when Captain Campbell had reinforced Lieutenant Stewart's section south of Miller's barn and Hood's attack had struck. Campbell unlimbered the four pieces he brought up on Stewart's left, with the left one setting up in the turnpike. Gibbon, Battery B's former commander, posted himself near Campbell's guns, partly because he probably could not help having an affinity for his old command, but also because he recognized that the battery was now a focal point in the action. Its location midway between the two segments of his brigade—the 6th and 2nd Wisconsin east of the turnpike, with the 19th Indiana and the 7th Wisconsin in the West Woods— also made it a crucial link that had to hold. Since he had no infantry to support the guns, Gibbon may have asked Doubleday whether a regiment from Patrick's brigade could be detached for this purpose. Doubleday communicated this order to Patrick, who selected his smallest and least favorite regiment, the 20th New York State Militia. What Patrick had against the 20th is unknown, but he had been critical of its performance at South Mountain. Officially, the 20th was the 80th New York, but the regiment preferred its pre-war militia designation. It had suffered severe battle and non-battle casualties in the Second Manassas Campaign and had been engaged at South Mountain, so it now numbered only 132 officers and men, under the command of Lieutenant Colonel Theodore B. Gates.[49]

Dividing his regiment into two equal-sized wings of approximately 65 men each, Gates deployed with his right wing in the rear of Campbell's guns and had Major Jacob B. Hardenbergh form the left wing along the fence at the southern border of the Cornfield, beside the 9th Pennsylvania Reserves. When they arrived, Gates's men could see little of the fighting to the south, because the corn blocked their view, but they heard "a terrific fire" from that direction, which moved steadily toward them. Then they caught glimpses of soldiers from the 2nd and 6th Wisconsin and Phelps's brigade, rushing back through the meadow south of the Cornfield and dashing into the corn. Close behind them came the Hampton Legion, the 18th Georgia, and elements of Starke's brigade. Enos B. Vail, one of Gates's infantrymen, noted how the approaching Confederates, in their gray uniforms, "looked like a flock of sheep." Campbell ordered his guns loaded with canister. The Rebels moved quickly, and Ira M. Slawson, a member of Battery B, watched how they used the cornstalks to conceal their approach and "were not observed until they were within almost a stone's throw of us, when they sprang to their feet, firing as they advanced," targeting the battery's horses and gun crews. The range was only 50 to 60 yards. Campbell ordered his guns to fire. Each canister round contained around 27 iron balls, an inch to an inch and a half in diameter. A single discharge by the entire battery sent over 140 of these murderous projectiles downrange. The first blast "tore great gaps" in the Rebel ranks but did not break their charge.[50]

Major Dingle, carrying the colors of the Hampton Legion, was among those killed by the storm of iron balls. It "tore immense holes through our ranks," admitted Stephen Welch, who was hit. Receiving a glancing blow to the side of his head, Welch "fell, doubled up & lay insensible awhile." When he recovered his senses, he found that his right eye was closed and his ear was filled with blood. There was a pool of blood by his side, and he saw that his rifle was thrown in one direction and his cap in another. Welch picked up his cap, which showed no damage on the outside, but the inside "was very much torn." Reflecting on his close call 5 days later, Welch marveled that he was not "torn to pieces for it appeared I never saw rain fall faster than the bullets did around us." At least one of Campbell's guns may have been firing shrapnel, rather than canister, for Lieutenant James Lemon, in the 18th Georgia, wrote that "a single shell" killed his two brothers-in-law, William and Marcus Davenport, who were privates in his company, as well as "knocked many down." Despite the carnage, the Confederates pressed the attack relentlessly, not in a reckless charge, but creeping forward along the turnpike fencing or through the corn and keeping up a continual fire on the Union battery.[51]

A full-strength gun crew consisted of nine men: five who crewed the gun; a gunner, who was a corporal; a sergeant, who was chief of the piece; and two men with the limber, who prepared the ammunition. Firing the gun required the men to work as a team. Each man had a number, which defined his duties and position at the gun. One of the men at the limber, the No. 6 or No. 7 position by the drill manual, withdrew a round from the limber chest and gave it to No. 5, who placed it in a gun pouch. He then ran forward and delivered the round to No. 2, who stood to the left of the gun's muzzle and left wheel. No. 5 might also stop to allow the gunner to examine the round, in order to ensure that its fuse was properly set if the ammunition was shrapnel or shell. Next, No. 2 inserted the round, which typically had the powder bag attached as a fixed piece of ammunition, into the gun muzzle. No. 1 rammed the round down the tube. During this process, No. 3 stood to the right rear of the gun, with his thumb, protected by a leather tool called a thumb stall, over the gun's vent, to prevent air flow and extinguish any burning embers from a previously fired round, which could cause a premature explosion when a new round was loaded. After the round was in place, the gunner sighted the piece, having No. 3 move the gun to the right or left, using a pole, called a trail spike, that was inserted into the gun trail. The gunner might also adjust the elevation screw. When he was satisfied, he stepped back, and No. 3 inserted a tool in the vent, which punctured the powder bag in-side the gun tube. No. 4 now moved up and inserted a friction primer, which was attached to a lanyard. He then stepped outside the gun wheels and pulled the lanyard taut. At the gunner's order to fire, No. 4 jerked the lanyard, which caused a spark to issue from the friction primer within the gun's bore. That set off the powder and sent the shell, ball, or canister round toward its target. What it all added up to was that loading and firing a cannon left its crew highly ex-posed to enemy fire.

Horace Ripley in the 7th Wisconsin was one of the many men from Gibbon's brigade who had volunteered for service in Campbell's battery. Ripley was a supernumerary—that is, an additional soldier who could fill in wherever needed. When the battery first went into action, he held his sergeant's horse. But early on in the fight, the sergeant was hit in the thigh, and Ripley helped him back to Miller's barn. When he returned, he was ordered to hold two horses. Shortly thereafter, one of them was hit in the side and dropped down in its death throes. The other horse took a mortal wound in the jaw, "so that a Corporal blew his brains out to put him out of his misery." Casualties among the gun crew Ripley was attached to became so numerous that he was ordered to help work the piece. Initially he carried ammunition, but soon only he and Elbridge Packard, a trans-fer from the 2nd Wisconsin, were left to serve the gun. Ripley recalled that Packard "was one of the most fearless men I have ever known." Acting as sergeant, gunner, and the No. 3 and No. 4 men on the piece, Packard, with Ripley's help, kept the gun in action. Stewart's section, on the far right of the battery, which was being crewed by the caisson drivers because of earlier casualties, was deci-mated. Henry Klinefelter, a transfer from the 7th Wisconsin, noticed so many men of the replacement crews were shot that only two men remained, and they "crawled on their hands and knees several times from the limber to the piece and loaded and fired those guns in that way until they had recoiled so far that they could not use them anymore." The toll among the battery's sergeants—the longest-serving and most experienced regular soldiers—was particularly high. The 1st sergeant, John Mitchell, was run over by a recoiling piece and severely injured, and bullets felled Sergeants William West and Joseph Herzog. Herzog was carried to Miller's barn, where, in excruciating pain from a wound in his leg, he drew his pistol and "deliberately blew his brains out."[52]

In the midst of the crisis, Captain Campbell, fearing that his left section, clos-est to the Cornfield, might be overrun, gave orders for it to limber and with-draw. Under the circumstances, it was an ill-advised command. In the deafen-ing roar, with chaos and clouds of smoke enveloping the battery, Campbell's order was misunderstood by the crews, who thought that the *entire* battery should withdraw. "Such a movement under such a fire would have been out of the question," wrote Gibbon, who instantly countermanded the order and di-rected the men to keep firing. A moment later, Campbell was hit by two bullets and his horse was killed. The bugler, 15-year-old Johnny Cook, a tough kid who was a 6th Wisconsin transfer, helped Campbell back to Miller's barn and then ran back to inform Lieutenant Stewart that he was in command of the battery. The lieutenant was well liked. He had risen from the enlisted ranks and had the "rare tact of making his enlisted men feel that he and they were comrades, without weakening his prestige as commander." Cook noticed that most of the crews were casualties. Spotting an ammunition carrier lying dead, with his full ammunition pouch on his body, Cook removed the pouch, slung it over his shoulder, and pitched in to help crew the guns.[53]

Moments after assuming command, a bullet struck Stewart's brass belt plate, knocking him over and breaking his sword belt. The injury was more serious than he thought at first—he had to use a catheter for nearly a year as a result— but he did not consider leaving to have his wound examined. Command of Battery B had been his dream, and he would allow no damage that did not utterly incapacitate him to deprive him of it. "I knew if I should allow it to be known that I was wounded," he admitted later, someone else would take his place. So he concealed the wound and remained. The situation was desperate. Rebel soldiers, who had crept through the corn, sprang up within 15 to 20 yards of the battery's left section. Joseph C. Otis, 1st sergeant in the 35th New York of Patrick's brigade, who were in the West Woods, watched some of these plucky infantrymen rest their rifles on the Hagerstown Pike's fencing to steady their aim, picking off horses and men in the battery. Stewart ordered triple canister. Double and triple canister were used in only the most extreme circumstances, because each gun only carried 16 canister rounds in its four ammunition chests, and the recoil could be dangerous, as 1st Sergeant Mitchell's injury testified to.[54]

The result was devastating. "When we fired we sent their grey rags, their haversacks, their guns and equipments a kiting, and once or twice we lifted some of the rebels clear above the corn tops," wrote Ira Slawson. The canister was augmented by "a well directed and deadly fire" from the right wing of Gates's 20th New York State Militia and elements of the 6th Wisconsin. Ira Slawson watched a member of the 6th or 2nd Wisconsin shoot down a Confederate color bearer, dash forward to seize the trophy, and return, waving the flag "exultantly and exclaiming, 'I am ready to die now—I am ready to die—I've got their flag— I've got their flag.'" Colonel Gates was awed by the Rebels' courage. They received the canister and infantry fire "without wavering" and "gave one of the finest exhibitions of manhood and pluck ever exhibited on any battle-field." By this point, Stewart's section was effectively silenced, and a third piece was down to one man: William P. Hogarty, a transfer from the 23rd New York. He single-handedly loaded the piece and fired triple charges of canister until this ammunition ran out, then fired shrapnel with the fuse cut to explode almost immediately after leaving the gun. Hogarty would be awarded a Medal of Honor 29 years later, as would bugler Johnny Cook, who received his medal in 1894. But there were so many deeds of valor in the battery that morning that it was difficult to separate out who was most deserving of special commendation.[55]

"We knew but little of what was going on beyond our immediate vicinity," recalled General Gibbon. Throughout the furious action, he remained mounted behind the battery's left piece, which was in the Hagerstown Pike, and had somehow avoided being shot. "It was the hottest of hornet's nests," he observed, and "bullets, shot and shell whistled and screamed around us, wounded men came to the rear in large numbers, and the six Napoleons of Battery 'B' hurled forth destruction in double rounds of canister." The gun near Gibbon faced the greatest threat of being overrun by men in the 18th Georgia, who had worked their way through the corn to get extremely close. Because the gun was on a slight slope, which descended north, each time it fired, the piece "recoiled a great distance down the slope." Gibbon saw that in their excitement, "the cannoneers had carelessly allowed the elevating screw to run down and every time the piece was fired its elevation was increased until now its missiles were harmlessly thrown high over the heads of the enemy in its front." He shouted for the gunner to lower the elevation but could not be heard in the din. Leaping from his horse, he ran to the gun, took the gunner's position, ran the elevating screw up until the gun tube "pointed almost into the ground in front," and then nodded to the gunner to pull the lanyard. Lieutenant John McEntee in the 20th New York State Militia—with perhaps some exaggeration—described the havoc the discharge inflicted: "The air was filled with legs, arms, heads, ears, noses, flags, blood, thunder, and smoke!" Major Rufus Dawes, who was leading the survivors of his regiment across the turnpike to support the battery, was startled by the deafening thunderclap of the gun and saw fence rails go flying high into the air downrange. This part of the battle was not over, but a turning point had been reached.[56]

WHILE BATTERY B FOUGHT for its life, the survivors of the 6th and 2nd Wisconsin and Phelps's brigade attempted to rally in the rear of Anderson's Pennsylvania Reserves. Those from the 2nd Wisconsin passed through the ranks of the 11th Pennsylvania Reserves, while men from the 6th Wisconsin and the 14th Brooklyn came through the 9th Pennsylvania Reserves. Major Hardenbergh attempted to cover the retreat of the latter two regiments by advancing his left wing of the 20th New York State Militia into the Cornfield, but they were easily driven back by Wofford's tide. Unbeknownst to Major Dawes, the national color bearer of his regiment had been shot, and the colors were left in the corn, but one of Hardenbergh's men found it and brought it back. When Gibbon saw Dawes waving his regiment's state colors to rally his men, he ran over to him. Dawes saw that the general's face was black with gunpowder. He said to Dawes, "Here, major, move your men over, we must save these guns." Dawes shouted as loud as he could, "Let every man from Wisconsin follow me," and ran across the turnpike with the blue state regimental banner. Some 60 men in his regiment and the 2nd Wisconsin followed. Major Hardenbergh also brought his wing across the road, increasing the infantry force supporting Stewart to nearly 200. But what probably saved Battery B from being overrun were the 7th Wisconsin, 19th Indiana, and Patrick's brigade, who were in the West Woods.[57]

THE 7TH WISCONSIN WAS still sheltered behind the limestone ledge parallel to the turnpike when Hood's counterattack came boiling up over the plateau south of the Cornfield. They opened a flank fire that drove the Rebels to seek cover behind the pike's fencing or in the corn. Bachman's 19th Indiana soon moved up behind the ledge, on their right, adding the firepower of some 300 more rifles. Their bullets took a toll of the South Carolinians, Georgians, and Louisianans, but it did not check them. Sergeant George Hoyt in the 7th Wisconsin watched "some of them [Rebels] going back, and others halted where protection could be found, and kept up a heavy fire, and others pressed forward and attempted to capture the guns of Battery B." In the opinion of Hugh Perkins, the Confederates fought "like mad men. . . . They will not leave the field until they are badly whipped, and sometimes they don't get a chance to leave alive."[58]

Wofford responded to this enfilading fire by facing the Hampton Legion and part of the 18th Georgia west, along the pike. Hood dispatched the 4th Texas up from its reserve position to extend Wofford's left. "Arriving on the top of the hill, at the intersection of the corn-field with the turnpike, I found the enemy not only in heavy force in the corn-field in front, but occupying a ravine in the field on the left of the turnpike, from which position they poured a destructive fire upon us," reported Lieutenant Colonel Carter, the 4th's commander. Carter pushed his Texans up to the turnpike, where they dropped down behind the pike's fencing. They found the fire from the Midwesterners behind the limestone ledge so terrific that J. M. Polk of Company I declared, "It seemed almost impossible for a rat to live in such a place."[59]

Lawrence Daffan in Company G of the 4th Texas became mingled with some of Starke's Louisianans. The courage of a man from the 7th Louisiana impressed Daffan. While everyone else along the fence was lying down to load and fire, this man was coolly and calmly standing up while loading and firing, heedless of the bullets striking nearby. Such acts of reckless courage often ended tragically, as it did in this instance, when two bullets struck the Louisianan, one in the hand and another through the heart. The dead man fell on Daffan.[60]

Casualties mounted steadily among the Texans. Company F was particularly hard hit, losing 24 of its 33 men. Some of the wounded were carried behind a limestone outcropping a short distance behind the front, but such was the volume of bullets, canister balls, and shell fragments lashing the area that several of these men were struck a second or third time. On the firing line, those who were not hit all had close calls to relate afterward. One bullet shot the top of

Charlie McAllister's hat off and it "just did miss the small of my back," wrote James Murray. He was one of the few in Company F to emerge uninjured, but the experience left him shaken. "It looks like there will not be a Texan left if this little fuss is not settled soon," he declared to his sister.[61]

The Texans noticed that the small-arms fire from the limestone ledge continued to increase until, in the opinion of Miles V. Smith, it became a "perfect rain of bullets." The upsurge in firepower marked the arrival of Patrick's brigade. After dropping off the 20th New York State Militia to support Battery B, Patrick moved his brigade into the northwestern portion of the West Woods. Here his skirmishers reported a considerable Confederate force moving through Alfred Poffenberger's cornfield, toward Nicodemus Heights. It was Early's brigade, on their way to support the batteries Stuart had placed on the heights. Patrick reported this development to Hooker, who ordered him "to watch and check the movement with one of my regiments." Patrick dropped off the 23rd New York to keep an eye on the flank, and he moved the 21st and 35th New York into the woods, behind Gibbon's men. The 21st was a solid unit, but the 35th had leadership issues. Its colonel, Newton B. Lord, was a drunkard, and at South Mountain he "manifested evident fear and trepidation," then claimed he was ill and left his regiment. Whether he was present at Antietam is unknown.[62] Leadership problems at the top often permeated a unit, and so it was with the 35th New York. Sergeant James C. Otis had nothing but contempt for his regiment's leadership: "I can't name the number of officers present, but there are many more absent than present. Battlefields do not, it would seem, possess a charm for some of the officers and men of the 35th—Never a man falls out on the retreat, but on the advance—Oh! dear, how common it is to see men taken with the gripes."[63]

When Hood's attack exploded over the plateau south of the Cornfield, Patrick had his two regiments change front to the east and move up to the ledge with the 7th Wisconsin and the 19th Indiana, effectively doubling the firepower on Wofford. They were soon joined by the 23rd New York, which came up at the double-quick after being relieved of their flank duties by the 10th Pennsylvania Reserves. The three regiments added nearly 700 men to the Federals' firing line.[64]

The alignment of the regiments along the ledge is murky. The 19th Indiana was on the far right of the line. To the 19th's left, the order appears to have been the 23rd New York, 21st New York, 7th Wisconsin, and 35th New York, with the latter two regiments partially mingled together. The 7th was nearly out of ammunition by the time the 35th and 21st New York came up, and it fell back through these regiments into the West Woods. The smoke from Battery B and heavy small-arms fire shrouded the field and helped conceal the enemy's position. This led to confusion among Patrick's men. When the 35th New York arrived at the ledge, someone shouted to them, "Stop firing! Don't you see they are our troops?" Another replied, "No, they are not; I know that flag. Don't you see the stars and bars?" The flag settled the question, and the first voice sang out, "That's so, give them Hell! They are rebels." James R. Putnam, a 20-year-old private in the 23rd New York, recalled that the smoke made the enemy so difficult to see that he and his comrades were ordered to simply fire "in the direction of the pike, and to aim low. We could see there was a fence along the pike, and we were firing into it."[65]

The "furious fire" on his front and flank had checked Wofford's charge, and he recognized that his brigade could "neither advance nor hold their position much longer without re-enforcements." He rode back to find Hood, but instead ran into Hood's assistant adjutant general, Captain William H. Sellers, to whom he reported his brigade's situation and the need for reinforcements. Hood had kept in close contact with the fighting and was aware that his attack had met fierce resistance everywhere. His gains were in jeopardy of being lost if he did not receive help. Around this time, Jackson dispatched his own assistant adjutant general, Captain "Sandie" Pendleton, into the fire-swept fields, to find Hood and "see how it goes." Pendleton's ride partly answered the question. "Such a storm of balls I never conceived it possible for men to live through. Shot and shell shrieking and crashing, canister and bullets whistling and hissing most fiend-like through the air until you can almost see them," he wrote. Pendleton never expected to survive the trip, but he was blessed with luck and reached Hood untouched. The general advised the captain to tell Jackson that "unless I get reinforcements I must be forced back, but I am going on while I can."[66]

Reinforcements from D. H. Hill's division were approaching, but they were too far off to help Wofford. His losses were catastrophic: 101 out of 176 in the 18th Georgia, 55 of 77 in the Hampton Legion, and at least 107 in the 4th Texas. The effort to take Battery B had failed, and both his dwindling numbers and the enemy's increasing strength rendered his position along the pike untenable. The survivors in his brigade had already reached this conclusion and began falling back without orders. Wofford saw no point in trying to stop them, so he gave orders to rally near their original position in the West Woods, by the Dunker Church.[67]

James Putnam thought he and his 23rd New York comrades fired between 15 to 20 rounds, which would take about 5 or 6 minutes, before the resistance along the pike began to slacken and they saw Rebels retreating. In the 19th Indiana, the men urged their young commander, Lieutenant Colonel Bachman, to seize the opportunity and charge. With more fervor than good tactical sense, Bachman agreed. Pushing his way through the ranks, he drew his sword, and "his deep bass voice rang out, 'Boys, the command is no longer forward, but now it is follow me.'" He sprinted forward, followed by his men, who charged up the open slope toward the remnants of the 4th Texas at the turnpike. In response to Bachman's assault, Patrick commanded his regiments to join the assault. The 35th New York raised a shout: "Hurrah boys! See them run! There they go! Rise up and give them a volley, and then after them!" With fixed bayonets and cheering loudly, the New Yorkers followed the Hoosiers toward the road.[68]

Many of the Texans along the pike heard no order to fall back and were still there when hundreds of Union soldiers burst out of the West Woods. One of them was William E. Barry, a private in Company G, who, with about 50 others, had scaled the pike's eastern fence and gone to the western fence, where they had a better field of fire. They blazed away at the charging Yankees, knocking some over, but the return fire killed or wounded many of those around Barry. When it became evident that the enemy would cut them off, Barry and two others attempted a dash south along the pike, toward the Dunker Church. They ran directly into what was probably the 23rd New York, who killed Barry's companions and took him prisoner.[69]

Patrick intended to employ only a limited counterattack to clear the Confederates from the turnpike and outflank any enemy remaining in the Cornfield, but the 19th Indiana and the 21st New York slipped the leash, clambered over both turnpike fences, and continued on to the plateau south of the Cornfield. One of S. D. Lee's batteries targeted the 19th Indiana and burst a shell near them when they were scaling the pike's fencing. Corporal Bob Patterson, who was one of the victims, recalled that the explosion hurled "me with a mass of broken rails high in the air." He landed unconscious, but alive, and was fortunate to be carried from the field by his comrades. His Hoosier compatriots followed the "tall athletic form" of Lieutenant Colonel Bachman to the crest of the plateau, where they came face to face with a long line of Confederates. It was the 4th and 44th Georgia of Ripley's brigade in D. H. Hill's division, moving to support Hood. The Georgians unleashed a volley that riddled Bachman and struck many others. Command fell to Captain William W. Dudley, who had just turned 20 in August but was one of those rare individuals who kept a cool head in desperate situations. Dudley considered his regiment's charge "foolhardy," and he immediately ordered a retreat to the pike, but not before he had his men gather up the bodies of Bachman and all the other casualties and carry them back. In the 50 yards or so that it took to get to the road, three of the regiment's color bearers were shot. The last time they fell, Lieutenant David S. Holloway dashed back under what one man described as "the fire of almost a whole secesh Brigade" and rescued them. His reward was promotion to captain in October.[70]

Patrick personally halted the charge of the 21st New York. They had crossed the pike on the 19th Indiana's left and rear. The general tore after the 21st, stopped them before they suffered the fate of the 19th, and led them back to the road. Nearly all of the 19th Indiana's casualties—13 killed and 59 wounded—were incurred in the brief minutes when they exposed themselves to Ripley's brigade and S. D. Lee's artillery. Patrick knew the pike was no place to remain. It was easily flanked and exposed, a point driven home when some of Starke's diehards, led by Colonel Stafford, reemerged from the West Woods, approached to within 100 yards of the 19th Indiana, and fired into their flank and rear. This convinced Captain Dudley to leave, and he withdrew his regiment back to the West Woods.

This exposed Patrick's men to the Louisianans' fire. The 21st New York took the brunt of this. Their colonel ordered his men to disperse and rally on their colors in the woods, but not before the 21st incurred nearly 71 casualties. Stafford's men then enfiladed the 23rd New York, who had 11 men in their right company killed or wounded in rapid succession. Colonel Henry Hoffman chose to fight back. He wheeled his regiment out of the road and faced it south toward the pesky Rebels, quickly driving them off. This allowed his regiment and the 35th New York to withdraw to the limestone ledge without further trouble. The counterattack to the pike could claim some success. It cleared the last vestiges of Wofford's brigade from the road and the western edge of the Cornfield, captured a guidon (one of two small flags some regiments employed to mark their right and left flanks), probably from the 4th Texas, and enfiladed the 1st Texas, who were located deeper in the Cornfield, which helped hasten their retreat. But the advance had been costly, and it underscored how quickly casualties mounted when units exposed themselves on open ground to enemy small-arms and artillery fire.[71]

WHILE THE MAIN BODY of Wofford's brigade fought and failed to capture Battery B, the 1st Texas plunged into the Cornfield in pursuit of the retreating Yankees of Gibbon's and Phelps's brigades. There they found immortality and utter calamity. The charge into the corn occurred because, in the words of the regiment's colonel, Philip Work, "it became impossible to restrain the men, and they rushed forward, pressing the enemy close." This was how they had been trained to fight, and it had never failed them: when the enemy was on the run, give them no reprieve and press them relentlessly. The 1st entered the Cornfield perhaps 200 yards east of the Hagerstown Pike and engaged in a running fight with the retreating Federals. The attempt by the 20th New York State Militia's left wing to check the Texans was easily swatted aside and driven back. But as his men moved deeper into the Cornfield, Colonel Work realized that he had no contact with Law's brigade on his right or the 18th Georgia on his left. Law's advance had diverged away from the Texans and opened a gap of over 100 yards. On the left, the Georgians were focused on capturing Battery B and had lost contact with the 1st Texas. Coordination and communication were difficult in the corn. Work could not see more than a few yards in any direction, and the dense battle smoke further limited visibility. All that Work knew was that his flanks were unprotected. He dispatched his adjutant, Lieutenant Winkfield Shropshire, followed by Private Amos G. Hanks—the fire was so heavy that Work sent two men, in case one was shot—to Wofford to report that he was driving the enemy, but his flanks were exposed. Work needed Wofford to "hurry up the regiments on my right and left to my support." Both Shropshire and Hanks were badly wounded and never reached the brigade commander. There was little he could have done anyway, for he had his hands full dealing with the threat to his left flank.[72]

The objective of Work's Texans seems to have been Ransom's battery, which they saw unlimber in Miller's meadow on the low ridge north of the Cornfield. Directly in front of them, lying down unseen, were nearly 600 men in Anderson's 3rd Brigade of Meade's Pennsylvania Reserves. After they took up their position behind the Cornfield's fence, Hooker had detached the 10th Pennsylvania Reserves and sent them west of the Hagerstown Pike, to keep an eye on the enemy force reported by the 23rd New York. Anderson placed his remaining three regiments behind the partly dismantled worm fence on the Cornfield's edge, with the 9th Pennsylvania Reserves on the right, its right flank resting on the Hagerstown Pike, and the 11th and the 12th Pennsylvania Reserves extending the line for about 250 yards east. The 9th Reserves were armed with Model 1842 .69 caliber smoothbore muskets, loaded with buck-and-ball ammunition. The 11th's and 12th's regiments carried Model 1842 rifled muskets, but they, too, were firing buck and ball rather than .69 caliber minie balls. Smoothbore ammo contained 120 grains of black powder, versus 70 grains for rifled ammunition, and it packed more punch, which most likely accounts for the choice by the 11th and 12th Reserves.[73]

Anderson's men had ample warning of the Texans' approach. First, the "deafening thunder of small arms" moved steadily toward them from the south. Then the survivors of Gibbon's and Phelps's brigades emerged in "considerable confusion" from the corn, warning that the Rebels were close behind. As these men passed through Anderson's lines, they heard Campbell's battery begin firing canister. Ransom's battery, on the ridge behind them, also opened fire, indicators that the enemy were very near. A "Dutch captain and lieutenant" in the 2nd Wisconsin—probably Captain John Stahel, the Swiss-born captain of Company K—attempted to rally his men directly in the rear of the 11th Pennsylvania Reserves, but his efforts caused so much confusion that the 11th's commander, Lieutenant Colonel Samuel M. Jackson, asked Stahel to re-form his men farther to the rear. Although it was possible to look down the corn rows, the smoke limited visibility to merely yards. "While it aided to conceal us, it also helped to fool us," wrote Lieutenant James P. George in the 11th Reserves. The first thing anyone made out was a flag sticking up above the corn and moving in the Pennsylvanians' direction. In the smoky haze, it looked to be a U.S. flag, and someone yelled not to fire, as not all the friendly troops were out of the corn. It was not a U.S. flag, however, but the state colors of the 1st Texas, the Lone Star flag. Charlotte Wigfall, the wife of the regiment's original colonel, fire-eater Louis T. Wigfall, had hand sewn it from her wedding dress. The flag had two horizontal bars, white over red, with a blue vertical bar containing a single white star. From a distance and through smoke, it could easily be mistaken for a U.S. flag. The Texans also carried a battle flag, but it was not yet seen. Due to the confusion, the Rebels closed to within 30 yards of Anderson's Pennsylvanians before their identity was revealed.[74]

The charging Texans, with their attention focused on Ransom's battery and Magilton's 2nd Brigade, which they could see moving toward the East Woods, were completely unaware of Anderson's Pennsylvania Reserves, directly in front of them. "The first notice they got of us was a volley at point-blank range which brought them to a halt," wrote Lieutenant George. The buck and ball wreaked havoc among the 1st Texas. The state flag went down and, noted Lieutenant George, "staid down." Despite the shock and carnage, the Texans doggedly pushed forward, firing as they went. Men seemed to drop at every step. "We had nothing between us [and them] only the air," noted Sergeant O. T. Hanks, and he watched men go down "almost like grain before a cradle." Observing a Pennsylvanian 30 yards away, he snapped his rifle to his shoulder to fire, but before he could squeeze the trigger, a ball struck him in the left side and came out under his shoulder blade. Hanks staggered to the rear for medical attention. Many others, however, were not as fortunate. They received disabling wounds and fell, helpless, in the corn, out of sight of their comrades. Sometimes they were hit again by the veritable gale of bullets, buckshot, and canister. Entire companies were shot down. All nine men in Company F were killed or wounded. Company E lost 18 out of 21, and Company L (the 1st had 12 companies) counted 24 out of 31 as casualties. Among the 12 company commanders, 9 were killed or wounded.[75]

H. Walters Berryman of Company I had the good fortune to miss the bloodbath in the Cornfield, being on a detached detail. But he received an itemized inventory of the wounds the men in his company received and shared this in a September 22 letter home. It cataloged the varieties of ammunition the enemy fired at his regiment, with 20 of the 24 men in his company being killed or wounded. His brother Newt was struck in the thigh "by a spent grape shot," which was probably either a canister ball or shrapnel ball, but the wound was superficial enough that Newt was not listed as wounded. Tom Boone was hit in the foot by a piece of shell. William Pritchard took a buckshot in the face and a ball in the chest, which ranged downward and "lodged in the skin of his belly," where a surgeon removed it. Lawyer Mitchell had his skull fractured by a piece of shell. Captain R. W. Cotton was shot by a ball or bullet in the head, and the effects of this wound caused his death on September 30. Ransom's battery accounted for the shell fragments, shrapnel, and canister balls, while the balls and buckshot were from Anderson's Pennsylvanians.[76]

Although his situation was growing critical, Colonel Work remained optimistic that he could hold his position if he was reinforced. Having heard nothing from his previous runners, he sent Private Charles Hicks of Company F to find Wofford and repeat his request for reinforcements. Hicks survived his journey but was unable to either find Wofford or return to Work. It was moot point, for moments after Hicks departed, Major Matt Dale, commanding the regiment's right wing, "reported that nearly every man of the right wing had been shot down, killed or wounded, and not a man would be left alive unless we withdrew at once." The noise was so deafening that Dale had to place his mouth up to Work's ear and shout, in order to be heard. As he drew back, with the two men "standing breast to breast," there was a sickening thud as a ball struck the major. Dale "straightened, stiffened and fell backwards prone upon the ground, dead." Captain Woodward then appeared from the left wing, to report that it, too, was shattered. The Confederates' situation was particularly precarious, because the advance of Patrick's regiments to the Hagerstown Pike enabled the 35th and 23rd New York to fire into the Texans' flank and rear. This fire was probably not accurate, but any enfilading fire cannot be endured for long. Work ordered Woodward to withdraw the left wing, and he would pull back the survivors of the right wing. How the two managed to communicate the retreat order to the men is unknown. Amid the limited visibility, carnage, noise, smoke, flying metal, and general mayhem, it is remarkable that they extricated anyone.[77]

Work found only a handful of men from the right wing and led them out of the Cornfield. When he emerged, he observed "a squad of perhaps thirty men" gathered around a battle flag, 30 to 40 yards away. They were probably remnants of the 18th Georgia. Work told his squad to join this group, while he remained at the edge of the corn to collect any other survivors from his regiment. One of them was Captain Woodward, who was alone. When he met Work and scanned the approximately 17 men with him, Woodward noticed that both regimental flags were missing. "The flags, the flags. Where are the flags?" he cried. Work had seen one of them—probably the battle flag—at the beginning of the retreat but lost sight of it by the time he left the Cornfield. He and Woodward "looked in every direction and they were nowhere to be seen." No one else could provide a clue as to what had happened to the flags. Woodward declared that he would find them and disappeared into the corn, but he reemerged shortly to report that the Yankees were advancing. With only a corporal's guard left in his regiment, Work had no choice but to abandon the two banners. His immediate concern was to save the few men he had left. The advance of the 19th Indiana and the 21st New York had chased off the platoon of men to whom Work had attached the survivors of the right wing and now threatened to cut off his escape. His party retreated southeast, toward Smoketown Road. Some of the Hoosiers or New Yorkers fired at them, putting a bullet through Woodward's canteen and another into Work's sword scabbard, but they were too small a party to pose a threat, and Ripley's brigade drew the Federals' attention away. It took time for Work to accurately assess the damage his regiment had sustained in the Cornfield. When he finished the final tally, of the 226 men carried into the fight, 50 were killed or mortally wounded, 132 wounded, and 4 missing, a loss of just over 82%. It would be the highest verified percentage loss of any regiment in either army that day.[78]

The story of the 1st Texas in the Cornfield has become the stuff of legend. They fought with remarkable courage and tenacity, yet had we been able to interview the survivors, they undoubtedly would have preferred to have *inflicted* an 82% loss on the enemy rather than suffering it. Although their charge generated many casualties in the 2nd and 6th Wisconsin and Phelps's brigade, and did drive them back through the Cornfield, the 1st Texas did relatively little damage to their primary adversary, Robert Anderson's brigade of Pennsylvania Reserves. Anderson's three regiments had 112 killed or wounded, but most of these casualties occurred in their engagement with Ripley's brigade, after they had repulsed the Texans. The battle was a calamity for the 1st Texas, as it was for nearly all of Hood's division. "They always take the Texians to the hottest part of the field," lamented Walters Berryman, "but her best men have fallen now and they will be more particular now, I reckon where she is carried hereafter."[79]

As Wofford's brigade receded from sight, and the 19th Indiana and Patrick's brigade advanced to and beyond the Hagerstown Pike, General Gibbon, with aggressive instincts, sensed that it was an opportune moment to land a counterblow. His own brigade was used up, so he went to Captain Samuel Dick, who was commanding the 9th Pennsylvania Reserves of Robert Anderson's brigade, and ordered him to advance. Dick obeyed and ordered his men forward. Meade was busy with Magilton's movement toward the East Woods, so Gibbon apparently appealed next to Anderson, for the rest of his brigade soon joined in the counterattack.[80]

WHEN THE 1ST TEXAS charged into the Cornfield, Evander Law's three left regiments—the 2nd Mississippi, 11th Mississippi, and 6th North Carolina—did likewise, entering about 100 yards east of where the Texans went in and extending across a front of roughly 250 yards to the East Woods. They had easily driven off the 90th Pennsylvania, Thompson's battery, and the residue of Duryée's and Hartsuff's brigades. This was the work of the 2nd and 11th Mississippi, for the 6th North Carolina did not fire their weapons until they reached the Cornfield. "We never fired at long range," wrote their major, Samuel M. Tate, and "'shoot low' was a standing order." They endured artillery fire first from Thompson, and then from Matthews. It inflicted relatively few casualties, but two of them were significant, wounding both Tate and Lieutenant Colonel Robert F. Webb, the regiment's only field officers. This left the 6th under the command of its senior captain.[81]

Matthews's battery offered the most serious resistance, firing double canister from his four 3-inch rifled guns. Canister from a rifled cannon was not as effective as that from a smoothbore cannon, due to a smaller canister charge (rifled guns had a smaller bore). In addition, the rifling caused the balls to emerge from the gun in a more random pattern, which left large gaps in the charge as it traveled downrange. But casualties among the Mississippians and North Carolinians mounted as their distance from the guns decreased. In David Love's company of the 11th Mississippi, he recalled that when they entered the Cornfield, the fire killed Sergeant Joseph C. Howarth, as well as wounded his company commander, Captain Henry P. Halbert, and a comrade, Jefferson L. Edmonds. So it went in each regiment as they moved through the corn rows, screaming the rebel yell. When they reached the north Cornfield fence, about 200 yards from the battery's position, all three regiments opened fire, driving the crews from the guns and silencing the battery. Then a new target presented itself.[82]

It was Magilton's brigade, hurrying east to reinforce Ricketts's men in the East Woods. Moving by the flank, the brigade presented a fat target for Law's men. For some reason, the 3rd and 4th Pennsylvania Reserves, in the middle of the column, took the brunt of a "withering" fire the Mississippians and Tarheels delivered. It broke both regiments, who fled to get cover behind the ridgeline. They quickly rallied, however, and were again led to the ridge, where Law's rifles and muskets drove them back once more. The 8th Pennsylvania Reserves, at the head of the column, managed to reach the northwestern corner of the East Woods intact, where they were greeted with a deadly fusillade from the 6th North Carolina. "Great God, the slaughter!" wrote Pennsylvanian Frank Holsinger. "Corporal White, my file leader, shot in the arm; Frank Dean, my rear file, wounded; my left file, James Gates, received four wounds, losing his leg and being mortally wounded." Holsinger was the only unscathed man in his section, which seemed improbable, as Gates was to his left, away from the enemy: "Just how it was possible for him [Gates] to have four bullets while I escaped, between him and the enemy, is one of the unsolved mysteries of war." The close call undid Holsinger, who admitted that while his regiment was demoralized by the volley from the North Carolinians, he was positively "stampeded." What checked his rout was a "tall thin soldier, very boyish in manner, but cool as a cucumber." Holsinger could not recall that person's name, but he never forgot how the young man stood there, swinging his cap and shouting, "Rally, boys, rally! Die like men. Don't run like dogs!" The effect was electric on Holsinger, and probably on others. "Why can I not stand and take what this boy can?" he wondered. Holsinger recovered his composure, found some cover, and began firing back at the enemy.[83]

The 8th Pennsylvania Reserves' color bearer was Corporal George Horton, whom Holsinger described as "the bravest of the brave." He had been shot through the arm at South Mountain but refused to seek medical attention. He simply tied off the wound with his pocket handkerchief. When someone asked him why he didn't go to the hospital, Horton replied, "When I go to the hospital, I will have something to take me there." He then added the fatal line of many a valiant soldier in history: "The bullet has not been moulded to kill me." When the regiment reached the edge of the East Woods, Horton planted the colors and shouted for the men to rally on them. About 50 men did, using the trees for cover. A bullet shattered Horton's ankle. He went down but determinedly kept his hold on the flag. When someone called for him to give up the colors, lest they be captured, Horton replied grimly, "Stay and defend them," and drew his pistol to do just that. A group of North Carolinians rushed him, and one of them shot

Horton through the head at a range of about 5 yards, killing him. In the close-quarters melee, Lieutenant Lewis Waltz avenged Horton's death by picking up a rifle lying on the ground and shooting the man who had killed Horton. The Confederates were driven back, and the colors saved. "The names of Horton and Waltz are unknown to history," observed Holsinger, "but their heroism is impressed on the tablets of the memories of their companions."[84]

The arrival of the 8th Pennsylvania Reserves blocked any deeper penetration into the East Woods by the 6th North Carolina. On Magilton's right, the 7th Pennsylvania Reserves performed the same function against the 2nd and 11th Mississippi. The 7th had only about 150 effectives, and they were waiting to follow the rest of the brigade in the movement to the East Woods when Law's brigade burst up through the Cornfield to its northern edge. James C. Alexander, who went by the alias "Bates," thought it a miracle that "half of the front companies were not shot down" when the 2nd Mississippi opened fire on them while they were still in column. To close the range, some of the Southerners had advanced beyond the corn into Miller's meadow. Alexander thought the Rebels got off five or six shots before he heard Major Chauncy Lyman, the 7th's commander, shout, "Deploy column on the centre, battalion by the right and left flanks, double quick march." In less than 30 seconds, the regiment formed a line almost perpendicular to the Cornfield's north fence, enabling them to fire at the Confederates by the fence and those who had crossed into the meadow. Such a deployment under fire was a test of courage and discipline. Major Lyman made sure his men did not shirk by dismounting and prowling behind his line with a drawn revolver. Griffin Baldwin decided that the Battle of South Mountain had demanded physical courage, but the fight here "required undaunted courage." He was in the front rank and knelt down to avoid the possibility of being accidentally shot from behind. It also made him a smaller target, but he nevertheless endured numerous close calls: one bullet passed through his haversack, and two more cut the straps to his knapsack, but none pierced his skin. Many of his comrades were not as fortunate. Nearly half the regiment—72 men—were killed or wounded.[85]

Ransom's battery tried their best to support Magilton, but much of their fire overshot the Mississippians. The Regulars already had their hands full with the 1st Texas, who were firing at them from inside the Cornfield. Some of the 2nd Mississippi targeted them as well. "Our horses commenced to fall, until at least twenty were killed or wounded," wrote Lieutenant Henry S. Gansevoort, one of Ransom's section commanders. "Our men fell fast—seventeen killed and wounded. My horse was shot in the flank by a Minnie ball and struck also by a piece of shell. My stirrup was broken by a ball, and I was wounded by a ball in the right cheek. It was a very narrow escape, but merely a flesh wound." The left wheel of Ransom's far left piece was hit by so many bullets that it rendered the gun useless. Lieutenant Gansevoort admitted, "We would have retired in order to save our pieces, but our horses were killed and it was impossible." Ransom had no choice but to order his crew's survivors to abandon their guns and take cover.[86]

David C. Love in the 11th Mississippi remembered how the 7th Pennsylvania Reserves were in "splendid order," but their fire "inflicted very little damage," as the 11th was on lower ground, and most of the Pennsylvanians' fire passed over their heads. An officer on a white horse appeared, riding in front of and behind the Pennsylvanians. Love presumed it was the regimental commander, but Major Lyman was on foot. It may have been Hooker, who was on this part of the field and rode a white horse, although none of the 7th Reserves' accounts mentioned seeing him. Whoever it was, the cry went up along the 11th's line to "shoot the man on the white horse." Although many tried, horse and rider escaped unscathed.[87]

"SO FAR WE HAD been entirely successful and everything promised a decisive victory," Law reported about his attack. They had done well indeed, sweeping the enemy from nearly all the East Woods; silencing Thompson's, Matthews's and Ransom's batteries; driving off the remnants of Ricketts's division; and shaking Magilton's brigade. It was nearly 7:30 a.m., his regiments had been engaged for nearly 30 minutes, and ammunition was giving out. Losses were substantial, but the brigade remained combat effective. Nonetheless, to hold on to his gains, or to proceed any farther, reinforcements were necessary. Ripley's brigade was approaching, but it was still hundreds of yards away. A report reached the brigadier from the 6th North Carolina, stating that they could see large masses of Union infantry approaching the East Woods through Sam Poffenberger's cornfield. It appeared that the enemy would win the race of who could reinforce the fight first. Law sent James Steptoe Johnston, a private from the 11th Mississippi who was serving as a courier, racing back to find Hood and ask for help. The private rode "at a furious gait" back to the clover field where the brigade had formed for the attack but "saw no troops" anywhere. He should have seen Ripley's brigade approaching from the direction of Mumma's farm, but somehow he missed them. He rode to the Hagerstown Pike and turned north, hoping to find some of Jackson's men, whom he had seen in the West Woods earlier that morning. Instead, he nearly ran into the 19th Indiana and had to ride for his life, with their bullets cutting the air around him. His horse "seemed to appreciate the exigencies of the case" and carried him to safety.[88]

By the time Johnston's life was saved by his horse, Law's situation had already resolved itself. When Johnston did not return, and nothing was heard from Hood or anyone else, Law decided that to remain any longer at his advanced position invited destruction. "No support was at hand," he complained in his October 2 report. "To remain stationary or advance without it would have caused a useless butchery," he concluded, "and I adopted the only alternative." He ordered a withdrawal. The order took David Love by surprise. In front of his regiment, most of the enemy had been driven off and their guns silenced. He heard someone shout that "our rear right was being threatened," followed by an order to retreat. Love could not see any flanking troops, but he and his comrades wasted no time in clearing out. "We retreated rapidly," he remembered. A retreat under fire is difficult to execute. There is always a level of confusion, as some men hear the orders to fall back and others do not. Moreover, since retreating soldiers are often not firing, it enables the enemy to shoot at them unhindered. This was the principal reason why units often suffered much heavier losses during a retreat than an attack. Law's men had an additional disadvantage of withdrawing up rising ground in the Cornfield, in full view of two of the batteries they had silenced. The moment they turned back, the crews of Ransom's and Matthews's batteries returned to their pieces and, along with the remaining elements of Magilton's brigade, poured fire into them.[89] The 8th Pennsylvania Reserves were inside the edge of the East Woods when Frank Holsinger felt euphoric at seeing the backs of his enemy: "The battle when it goes your way is a different proposition. . . . They [the Confederates] soon begin to retire, falling back into the cornfield. We now rush forward. We cheer; we are in ecstasies. While shells and canister are still resonant and minies sizzling spitefully, yet I think this is one of the supreme moments of my existence."[90] Like Dawes' statement, Holsinger's account was another of those relatively rare voices from the Civil War who admitted to an uncomfortable truth about combat—that one could feel absolute elation at the destruction of the enemy.

Dozens of Mississippians and North Carolinians were cut down as they attempted to escape the Cornfield. The 11th Mississippi lost its two remaining field officers—Lieutenant Colonel Samuel Butler, mortally wounded, and Major Taliaferro S. Evans, killed—both of whom had to be left behind. All but one company officer was killed or wounded. Every field officer in the 2nd Mississippi—Colonel John Stone, Lieutenant Colonel D. W. Humphreys, and Major John Blair—was wounded, and they, too, lost nearly every company commander. When the regiment reached safety, it was commanded by 2nd Lieutenant William C. Moody. David Love was among those hit, with a minie ball passing through his oilcloth and blanket, which he had rolled up and worn over his shoulder. They stopped most of the bullet's force, but the impact injured Love. With the help of some comrades, he managed to get out of the killing zone. When the 2nd emerged from the corn, "considerably disjointed," their regimental battle flag was missing. The colors had been carried into action by William Kidd, an Irish-born coachmaker, who had served as the regiment's artificer (someone who worked on the regiment's weapons) until he volunteered to carry its flag. His fate mirrored that of the 1st Texas color bearers. He had been killed in the Cornfield, and in the general mayhem, no one saw him go down or knew where the flag might be. It, too, would be lost. The percentage of casualties in the three regiments may not have been as high as Wofford's were, but all of them were wrecked, having lost every field officer, most of their company leadership, and 383 men killed or wounded out of 876, a loss of nearly 44% loss.[91]

WHEN LAW SWEPT UP through the Cornfield with the 2nd and 11th Mississippi and the 6th North Carolina, his 4th Alabama, under Captain Robbins, joined by the 5th Texas and part of the 21st Georgia, drove the remaining Federals out of the East Woods and consolidated their position. Law did not communicate the order to retreat to Robbins, so he and his Alabamians, Georgians, and Texans remained in the woods.

By 7:30 a.m., except for the outpost in the East Woods, which neither Hood nor Law apparently realized was there, all of Hood's division was in full retreat. As Hood's men disappeared into the West Woods, the Union's 12th Corps was arriving to reinforce the battered 1st Corps, while three brigades of D. H. Hill's division were approaching the Cornfield and East Woods from the south. The conflict for this contested ground was far from over.

Hood's division had lost three flags, most of their field officers, and many company officers, as well as suffering extremely heavy casualties in all other ranks. The loss of so many experienced field officers was particularly impactful, as junior officers typically did not have the leadership skills or experience to manage a regiment. As August Varin had said about his 2nd Mississippi, "Should our colonel & lieutenant colonel be taken from us the 2nd Miss. would be little better than so many raw recruits." Now, both officers were out of action. In reporting on his brigade's experience, Colonel Wofford wrote, "They fought desperately; their conduct was never surpassed." The same could be said for all of Law's regiments. The men had fought courageously and employed the hardhitting tactics that had previously always brought them victory. Why, then, had they failed? Given the level of their sacrifice, there was understandable bitterness reflected in the reports of some officers, and a casting about for who was to blame. Colonel Work in the 1st Texas angrily concluded his after-action report by stating, "If required to carry strong positions in a few more engagements, and, after carrying them, hold them unaided and alone, this regiment must soon become annihilated and extinct without having accomplished any material or permanent good." The most common and comforting explanation was the vast amount of Federal troops. This was Hood's rationalization. He reported that his small division had confronted an "immense force" of the enemy, no less than two full Union corps. Evander Law claimed his brigade faced "ten times our number" when he ordered a retreat. The theme of overwhelming enemy numbers carried over into the postwar years. Miles V. Smith in the 4th Texas reminisced about how Law's brigade of 1,000 met the Yankees, who were 10,000 strong, "in an open field," and how the two brigades were "flanked for a half mile on either side," which led to their defeat. After the war, Hood refused to acknowledge that his division had been driven back. In his 1880 memoirs, Hood claimed that after "several ineffectual efforts to procure reinforcements and our last shot had been fired, I ordered my troops back to Dunkard Church." In this telling, retreat was a choice, not a necessity.[92]

The second explanation for what happened was a lack of support. This was among the most common reasons both sides used in rationalizing defeat during the course of the war. In his report, written 10 days after the battle, Hood not so subtly implied that it was D. H. Hill and Lafayette McLaws who bore responsibility for what happened. In Hill's case, the failure of Ripley's brigade to properly support Hood's flank enabled the enemy to "pour a heavy fire upon the rear and right flank of Colonel Law's brigade." This resulted in forcing Hood, not to retreat, but "to move the division to the left and rear into the woods near the Saint Mumma church." As for McLaws, Hood was "thoroughly of the opinion had General McLaws arrived by 8:30 a.m., our victory on the left would have been as thorough, quick, and complete as upon the plains of Manassas on August 30." Never mind that Hood's division was in retreat by 7:30 a.m., or that no Union soldiers ever got around Law's right flank and rear. In a circular to his division on September 28, Hood continued this theme of overwhelming enemy numbers and lack of support, telling his men they had driven off the Yankees, who had "twenty times your number," and, "if supported, would have led on to one of the most significant victories known to the history of any people."[93]

Picking up on this theme, in early 1863 the chaplain of the 4th Texas, Nicholas A. Davis, published a small book about Hood and the Texas brigade—whether with Hood's knowledge and approval is unknown—which leveled a serious charge against McLaws. If McLaws had been up "even as late as 9 o'clock," the Confederates would have won a smashing victory, wrote Davis, echoing Hood's report but moving the time up by a half hour. Davis continued his attack on the Georgian, employing the eternal tactic of painting his target as guilty until proven innocent:

> The reasons for his tardiness, we hope, will be satisfactory, when he renders his report. But, if he moved carelessly up, stopping at the river and losing 2 hours, as we are told he did, waiting for his men to strip and roll up their clothes, to prevent them getting wet, and then halting for some time, for them to make their *toilette* on the other side, not only the loud condemnation of a country, which had, in part, entrusted him with its destiny, should fall upon him, but the strong arm of the law should take hold, and by one way or the another, remove him from a position, in which he is able to jeopardize her future weal. This is not the first time that a single man has thwarted the plans of a great army, and made its victory only half complete.[94]

McLaws was infuriated when he read Davis's book and demanded an explanation from Hood. Hood unconvincingly replied that "the book you refer to was not written under my auspices," and that he knew nothing of the inflammatory paragraph. McLaws found it hard to believe that the chaplain of Hood's original command wrote such a document without the general's knowledge. "The whole tenor of the publication is so unfounded so maliciously false that one naturally seeks for a motive which would prompt a writer to turn out of his path to utter a baseless slander," he wrote to Hood. "I am very glad that you have denied that the pamphlet of Mr. Davis was published under your auspices for I tell you frankly that it has been the opinion of many who have read it, that you must have been a party to its publication or must have known its contents before publication." Hood again responded that he had nothing to do with the book and promised to contact Davis to make a correction to the slanderous passage. McLaws dropped the matter, but not his suspicion that Hood was behind Davis's publication.[95]

Hood had received no support, but McLaws bore no responsibility for this, and D. H. Hill was only partially to blame. The real culprit was Robert E. Lee's command structure, which hindered swift communications and command decisions. It was Lee's duty to establish a command arrangement for the battle that facilitated flexibility and the ability to rapidly respond to battlefield situations. He should have placed Jackson in command of all forces on the left, including D. H. Hill. But it is clear that, apart from their arrangement that Hood should come to Jackson's support if needed, both officers understood that they belonged to separate commands and, hence, operated that way. This explains why Hood, rather than Jackson, was negotiating for reinforcements from D. H. Hill in the early morning hours, and when Hill said no, why Hood appealed to Longstreet, his direct superior, and not Jackson for more men. Hood should have been detached to Jackson, who could have communicated directly with Lee for reinforcements or ordered D. H. Hill to send them. Jackson, too, as already related, seems to have been strangely detached during the battle and exercised relatively little influence over the early morning fighting. If Hood realized the strength of the enemy in front of him on the night of September 16, why had Jackson not done so, too? Although it was commendable of Jackson to send Sandie Pendleton to Hood to inquire how Hood was getting along, Jackson certainly knew that when Hood was committed, there were no reserves left, and that his own two divisions, apart from Early's brigade, were completely used up. Was it really necessary to see if Hood needed support? Given the ferocity of the morning's fighting, this was a question whose answer seems obvious. As soon as Hood went into action, Jackson should have communicated the situation on the Confederates' left and requested reinforcements. Finally, the decision of when to move McLaws's division, and to where, lay not with McLaws, but with Lee.

Hood's claim of facing two Union corps and 20 times his division's numbers may have eased the pain and anger his men felt at their heavy losses, but it bore little resemblance to reality. He faced one Union corps, the 1st, which had already been fighting for an hour and a half. Hood's division initially encountered half of Gibbon's brigade, Phelps's very small brigade, Thompson's battery, and the 90th Pennsylvania infantry, all of which he heavily outnumbered. In Gibbon's and Phelps's cases, both units were disorganized and diminished by their earlier combat. After driving these units from the field, Hood's division engaged Anderson's and Magilton's brigades of Meade's division; Patrick's brigade; half of Gibbon's brigade; Battery B, 4th U.S.; Battery C, 5th U.S.; and Battery F, 1st Pennsylvania Light Artillery. All told, his division confronted about 3,000 Union infantry and 18 guns, hardly the overwhelming numbers Hood claimed to have faced. The guns, particularly in Battery B, which fought with extraordinary courage, took a heavy toll from Hood's ranks. Patrick's and Gibbon's men in the West Woods were perfectly positioned to take Wofford in the flank, and Meade's placement of Anderson's brigade behind the Cornfield's north fence gave his men both cover and the element of surprise. In Gibbon, Meade, and Hooker, Hood encountered tough, experienced leaders who assembled a defense in depth that drained the strength from Hood's attack and then drove him back. It is true that the 12th Corps' arrival on the field hastened the retreat of Law's brigade, but the damage to Law and Wofford was inflicted by the 1st Corps. When confronting the causes for his division's defeat, Hood might rather have echoed the words George Pickett allegedly uttered when asked why Pickett's Charge failed at Gettysburg: "I think the Yankees had something to do with it," Pickett replied.

5

The Death of a General

"It is terrible to march slowly into danger"

There was something about Brigadier General Joseph King Fenno Mansfield that made him unforgettable. The opinions were not all positive, but most were. Part of the reason was his striking appearance. He looked a bit like a Union Kris Kringle, with a massive beard and shock of hair, white as snow, even though he was only 58 years old. But, unlike the portly Kris Kringle, Mansfield was fit and trim, bubbling with energy. It was his energy that surprised those who did not know him, because he looked older than he was. Chaplain Joseph S. Evans in the 124th Pennsylvania, who encountered the general at Willard's Hotel in Washington, DC, shortly before he departed to join the army in the field, was struck by his soldierly bearing, describing Mansfield as "as fine specimen of the true soldier." He had been a soldier for 40 years when he joined the Army of the Potomac on the morning of September 15, assuming command of its 12th Corps. He had entered West Point as a 14-year-old boy and graduated 5 years later, second in his class, although still a teenager—an accomplishment that speaks to both his fortitude and intelligence. His high class ranking landed him in the prestigious Corps of Engineers. During the war with Mexico, he established a reputation as a man of action and personal courage, suffering a severe wound in the Battle of Monterrey, and earning three brevet promotions for distinguished conduct. "I never yet have seen a man so regardless of his personal safety or so eager to imperil it," wrote John Pope, who served with Mansfield in the topographical engineers in Mexico.[1]

In 1853, Mansfield was named inspector general of the army, an important and physically demanding post, since it entailed traveling great distances to visit the army's far-flung forts and outposts. He was in Texas when the secession crisis came to a head. Before South Carolina joined the Confederacy, he had seen enough in Texas to convince him that the entire South was going to secede, and war was inevitable. When it came, the government named Mansfield to the critical post of commander of the Department of Washington, which entailed the defenses of the nation's capital. Promotion to brigadier general in the Regular Army followed. Mansfield threw himself into the work of rendering the capital secure, seizing the high ground at Arlington, across the Potomac River, and commencing fortifications there, as well as tightening security in the city. The arrival of General George B. McClellan after the Battle of First Manassas did not sit well with Mansfield. The young general's new command included the Department of Washington and and Department of Northeastern Virginia, commanded by General Irwin McDowell. Neither Mansfield nor McDowell were happy with this arrangement, which placed them under McClellan's command, but it especially irked Mansfield and may have had something to do with McClellan's reorganization of the departments in August, which removed Mansfield from his post. Mansfield was first sent to the North Carolina coast and, subsequently, to a brigade command in Suffolk, Virginia. For an officer of Mansfield's rank and experience, his assignment away from the newly forming Army of the Potomac does not seem accidental. There is no evidence that McClellan harbored rancor toward Mansfield, however. In March 1862, McClellan proposed forming a new division in McDowell's 1st Corps, to be commanded by Mansfield. Nonetheless, even though Mansfield had equal or superior credentials to any corps commander with the Army of the Potomac on the Virginia Peninsula, there was no serious effort to find a position for him. For a man of action, with long service to his country, banishment to a secondary theater in the greatest crisis his country had ever faced had to be galling.[2]

A friend of Mansfield's later wrote that he was "not one of those who are constantly demanding place and reward at the hands of the government. He pleaded no political influence, and left place to follow his work, not to be sought after." This was true, yet it does not explain why someone with his distinguished service career was not actively sought after for a major field command. Alpheus Williams, who headed the 12th Corps in the Maryland Campaign until Mansfield arrived to take command, offered a possible clue when he wrote, after Antietam, that Mansfield "was an excellent gentleman, but a most fussy, obstinate officer." In another letter, Williams related that the New Englander "had a very nervous temperament and a very impatient manner." The answer may be that the War Department believed Mansfield's skills were better employed in engineering, staff work, and training troops, not in leading or directing them into battle.[3]

Following the Union disaster at Second Manassas and the army's retreat to within the fortifications of Washington, DC, Mansfield received a summons to come to the capital. If he had hoped it meant he was to receive a field command at last, those hopes were dashed when he learned he had been named to a court of inquiry investigating the charges General Pope had made against General Fitz John Porter. This time Mansfield must have made known his displeasure with his assignment, for on September 8, the army's Adjutant General's Office issued special orders, directing Mansfield to report to McClellan in the field. He would finally get his field command. Mansfield had had brushes with death before, in Mexico and, more recently, at Suffolk, when a percussion shell fired by the CSS

Virginia hit his room, knocked down his chimney, and came to rest beside him as he sat in a chair, writing. Due to a defect in the detonating device, the shell did not burst when it struck the fireplace, and Mansfield survived. But he understood the perils of service in the field, and as he made his preparations, he reflected on friends and family. On September 11, he paused to write his to early mentor, Sylvanus Thayer, a former West Point superintendent and legend at the academy: "This is only to say, if I never see you again, that I have not forgotten your inestimable favors to me." The sentence said volumes about Mansfield's character. On September 13, the day of his departure for the army, Mansfield said to a friend, "I am going into battle. If I fall have my body sent to my friends in Middletown, Ct." In a note to his wife, he reminded her of what she already knew well: "All is uncertain in the future. May Heaven's blessing rest upon you."[4]

Accompanied only by a single aide-de-camp and a Black body servant, Mansfield set out on September 13 and reached McClellan's headquarters on September 15. McClellan assigned him to command the 12th Corps, then under the temporary command of Brigadier General Alpheus Williams. It was a challenging assignment. The 12th was the weakest corps in the army, both in numbers and in leadership. The Second Manassas Campaign left it in a shambles. General Pope's poor logistical support and incessant marching put thousands on the sick rolls, and the Battle of Cedar Mountain on August 9 cost it 2,200 casualties, including one of its two division commanders and two of its five brigade commanders. By the end of that campaign, regiments were reduced to the size of companies. Brigadier General Samuel W. Crawford's brigade of four regiments mustered only 629 effectives, and these men, Crawford warned, due to exposure and lack of good food and rest, were in no condition for active field service. Granting them a period of rest and reorganization was not an option, since Lee's army was in Maryland. Instead, the 1st Division was strengthened by the assignment of five newly raised regiments—the 124th, 125th, and 128th Pennsylvania, the 13th New Jersey, and the 107th New York—which more than doubled its strength. Yet, despite the manpower increase, the 12th Corps only numbered about 9,000 effectives in its two divisions.[5]

The new regiments, which made up nearly half of its combat strength, were only slightly more than organizations of civilians in uniforms, carrying weapons. All of them had only been mustered into service in mid- to late August and had had a month or less in the service. Because so much of their time had been spent in transportation to the nation's capital and then marching across Maryland, there had been little time to teach the officers and men the rudiments of being a soldier, let alone drill them for maneuvering on a battlefield. The 124th Pennsylvania was perhaps the best of the lot in this respect, and yet it had conducted only about 10 days of regimental and company drills. There is no evidence that any of the regiments had ever fired their weapons. Colonel Ezra Carman, the commander of the 13th New Jersey and a veteran of the Peninsula

Campaign, told the colonel of the 2nd Massachusetts that before his regiment's assignment to the 12th Corps, it had done nothing but march and had never drilled in loading and firing. "I do not imagine that they will prove very valuable auxiliaries in the field," noted the 2nd's adjutant, Charlie Mills. On September 7, Colonel Carman encountered Colonel Samuel Croasdale, the 25-year-old commander of the 128th Pennsylvania, who had been a Doylestown attorney a month earlier. Croasdale asked Carman what the commands were to form a line of battle, "not knowing himself and giving as an excuse that he had no time since being commissioned to buy a copy of tactics." The same lack of experience and knowledge of army tactics was true for the other colonels, except for Carman, who had been the lieutenant colonel of the 7th New Jersey, and Colonel Jacob Higgins, commanding the 125th Pennsylvania, who had seen some service in the Mexican War and with the 1st Pennsylvania Cavalry.[6]

Proficiency in the complicated maneuvers and commands of the linear tactics employed by Civil War armies formed the difference between victory and defeat, and between excessive or acceptable number of casualties. The leaders needed to know instantly what command to issue when unexpected situations developed on the battlefield, and their men required constant drilling and training, in order to execute those commands without thinking. The tactics of the era may seem simple in comparison with what an infantry officer must know for modern warfare, but they were not. Officers and men needed to learn the proper commands and movements—for instance, to face by the rear rank; deploy into various column formations, such as column of companies or column by divisions; deploy from any column formation to line of battle, and from line of battle back to column; to change front to the rear; to change front to the right or left to meet a flank attack; to wheel left or right; to maneuver by the flank; and so on. The purpose and benefit of drilling in these maneuvers for countless hours, as Earl Hess notes in *Civil War Infantry Tactics*, was "to create an automatic response to orders from large masses of men who acted upon those orders as one." None of the new regiments in the 12th Corps were yet capable of an automatic response to orders, with most of their officers lacking the knowledge and confidence to order anything more than the most elementary maneuvers. Even forming into line of battle from column, perhaps the most important fundamental combat command, was a formidable challenge for most of them. This inexperience would significantly affect Mansfield's thinking on how he managed his troops in battle.[7]

The divisional and brigade leadership of Mansfield's new 12th Corps' command was a mixed bag. He had two solid division commanders: Brigadier General Alpheus Williams and Brigadier General George S. Greene. The 51-year-old Williams was a successful attorney and judge in Detroit before the war and had served as lieutenant colonel of the 1st Michigan in the Mexican War. He was one of the first men from Michigan to step forward and offer his services, and he rose from brigade to division command on merit. There was nothing flashy or dashing about Williams, but he was a solid tactician and remained levelheaded in times of crisis. An argument can be made that he may have been the best volunteer officer at brigade or division command in the Army of the Potomac in Maryland. Williams's counterpart, George Sears Greene, assumed command of the 12th Corps' 2nd Division when its commander was wounded at Cedar Mountain. At age 61, Greene was one of the oldest general officers in the Army of the Potomac. He was a former classmate of Mansfield's, graduating from the Military Academy in 1823, a year after Mansfield. After the tragic death of his wife and three children from disease, Greene left the army in 1836 and became a civil engineer. Like Williams, he was unpretentious, unflappable, and quietly competent, but he was generally unpopular with his men. An Ohioan in Colonel Hector Tyndale's brigade wrote that before Antietam, they would all hiss and hoot whenever Greene passed them on the road. This opinion would change for many after what they encountered at Antietam.[8]

The brigade leaders were largely mediocre or inexperienced. The Second Manassas Campaign removed all of the brigade commanders in Greene's division, either through wounds, capture, or disease, and all three brigades were commanded by their senior colonels. Of these three, only one, Colonel William Goodrich, had any pre-war military experience, having served as an adjutant to a Missouri volunteer regiment in the Mexican War. Lieutenant Colonel Hector Tyndale, commanding the 3rd Brigade, was despised by Major Ario Pardee Jr. in his own regiment, the 28th Pennsylvania, who considered him to be tyrannical and insolent. "A more disgraceful man I never met," the major wrote to his father, adding that Tyndale "has been fortunate that we were not in a regular engagement as I fear he would, if the balls of the enemy spared him, been injured by his own command." In the 1st Division, General George H. Gordon was a West Pointer, class of 1846, who had served in Mexico and resigned his commission in 1854 to practice law. "Gordon needed no watching," wrote Alpheus Williams. Williams had a lesser opinion of Brigadier General Samuel W. Crawford, his 1st Brigade commander. Crawford had initially chosen medicine as his career path. He graduated from the University of Pennsylvania's School of Medicine in 1850, and a year later he took a position as an assistant surgeon in the U.S. Army. He was at Fort Sumter in April 1861, which made him something of a celebrity. An ambitious man, Crawford sensed that there was more opportunity for notice and advancement in commanding troops, rather than in practicing medicine, and he accepted reassignment as major of the 13th U.S. Infantry. In April 1862, he won promotion to brigadier general of volunteers and was assigned to brigade command in John Pope's Army of Virginia. He did little to impress Williams. Crawford, Williams wrote to his daughter, "knows no more of military than that piebald dog I used to own." In another letter, Williams opined that

Crawford "had no more knowledge of deployment or handling troops than the green colonels of these new regiments fifteen days from home." Crawford's men loathed him, particularly the new regiments assigned to his brigade. During the march from South Mountain on September 15, the commissary wagons, issuing rations, had not caught up with the troops, and the men were hungry. When Crawford rode by the 124th Pennsylvania, the men complained that they were hungry, to which the general grumbled something about them being "Pennsylvania cattle" and rode on. This did not sit well with the new volunteers. As Sergeant William Potts recalled, "Some of the boys threatened to get square with him if opportunity offered. I told them that was very wrong, but if I was aiming at a Reb and the general got in the way, I would not stop firing on his account."[9]

Mansfield was Crawford's opposite. He paid attention to details that mattered to common soldiers. From the moment he assumed command of the 12th Corps, there was no question among the men that he personally cared about their welfare. On the same march in which Crawford dismissed his hungry new volunteers, Mansfield, who had been in command for less than 12 hours, came upon the 125th Pennsylvania, also of Crawford's brigade, who had halted and were left standing in the hot sun for some time. "Why are the men kept standing in the sun?" Mansfield demanded of the brigadier, and ordered that they be moved at once to the shade of some nearby woods. Lieutenant Thomas McCamant in the 125th wrote that he and his men did not forget "the deep interest he [Mansfield] took in us." On the night before the battle at Antietam, when some members of the 10th Maine, anxious and excited about the prospect of combat the next day, were talking too loudly, Mansfield, who had lain down nearby to snatch some sleep, understood their anxiety and ordered them not to stop talking, but to lower their voices to a whisper.[10]

While the rank and file took to their new corps commander, Alpheus Williams had some concerns. He found Mansfield to be an "excellent gentleman," but "very fussy," "very nervous," and "very impatient." It was evident that Mansfield did not have experience handling large numbers of troops in the field. John H. Keatley, an acting first sergeant in the 125th Pennsylvania, recalled how Mansfield rode up to his colonel on September 16, when they came under some artillery fire that overshot the Union batteries on the bluffs east of Antietam Creek, and ordered him to have his men load at will. Keatley had not been in the service long, but it immediately struck him as odd "that any general officer, under the circumstances, should personally communicate such an order— one usually entrusted to officers of the staff." As Williams knew, while it spoke well of Mansfield that he took a personal interest in his troops, this did not necessarily translate into the skills necessary to manage a corps in battle, where the wrong decisions and a lack of tactical experience could get men slaughtered. Mansfield understood infantry tactics, but, thus far in the war, he had never had to apply that knowledge to the unpredictable and chaotic environment of combat.[11]

SHARP FIRING FROM THE direction of Hooker's 1st Corps woke the soldiers of the 12th Corps from their sleep. It was 5:30 a.m. The firing was over a mile to the south, yet it carried clearly to their position. Within minutes, the crackle of small-arms fire was swollen by the deep bass roar of artillery. All across the farm fields of the Line and Hoffman families, the men of the 12th Corps began rising from their uncomfortable beds in fields of corn or stubble, or freshly plowed ground. How much sleep the men got depended on their experience and level of exhaustion. The veterans tended to sleep better. Adjutant John Gould in the 10th Maine slept "like a hog." A soldier in the 27th Indiana recalled that he and his comrades also slept soundly. No one slept for very long, though, since the corps had not bivouacked until nearly 2 a.m. The men of the 3rd Wisconsin had to be awakened by the "gruff voice" of their sergeant major, who walked rapidly along their line and ordered the men up for roll call. There was less sleep among those in the rookie regiments. "We slept but little that night," recalled Lieutenant Thomas McCamant in the 125th Pennsylvania. Besides nerves, part of the problem was the noise of barking dogs on Line's and Hoffman's farms, as well as the crowing of roosters disturbed by the arrival of thousands of men. Crickets joined the nighttime cacophony, as did a high-pitched chorus of katydids. Sergeant William Potts in the 124th Pennsylvania wrote that his sleep was troubled, and that he had a presentiment he would be killed or wounded that day. The men slept with their equipment on, and this added to their discomfort. William F. Goodhue in the 3rd Wisconsin woke "with a feeling of numbness in my left side," caused by his cartridge box pressing against his body.[12]

All across the 12th Corps' bivouac area, regiments were forming up. In most cases there was no need for orders. The men simply fell in and formed line of battle. As they called the roll in the 3rd Wisconsin, the firing from the south increased significantly. William F. Goodhue, in the 3rd, heard the horses and mules that would haul the ammunition wagons whinnying or braying in anticipation of their morning feed, which they would miss this day. Along the line of his regiment, Goodhue watched his comrades prepare for combat:

> Looking along the line I saw the men wiping the moisture from their muskets, for the dew had been heavy, and just now there was considerable fog. Others were changing their gun caps or adjusting a knapsack, putting canteen and haversack well behind, to give free access to the cartridge box. Others were munching hardtack, and some were smoking. Several of my comrades, with canteens, had gone for water, with the evident intention of making coffee, while others had made little fires for cooking breakfast, taking rails from an adjacent fence for the purpose; when suddenly and sternly came the order to get back into the ranks.[13]

Mansfield was up and in the saddle. He rode up to the 10th Maine, near George Line's farm buildings, and addressed the regiment. "Men," he said, "you are called upon to-day for an active duty, and I ask no more of you than to maintain the reputation you have already achieved." Lieutenant Colonel Fillebrown was struck by Mansfield's "white locks and calm expression," which "inspired confidence in all." In Gordon's brigade, General Williams rode up and quietly gave orders to Colonel Thomas Ruger, commanding the 3rd Wisconsin. Ruger turned to his regiment and shouted, "Attention, battalion! Shoulder arms! Close column by division!" This brought the regiment into a rectangular-shaped formation, with two companies deployed in a line of battle, and the other eight companies stacked directly behind them. A veteran regiment like the 10th Maine, which numbered 297 officers and men, would present a front of about 30 men—15 in each company's first rank—and a depth of 20 ranks, since each company formed in two ranks. Other regiments formed close column by companies—that is, the leading company formed a line of battle, and the other nine companies stacked up directly behind them. Close column meant that each line closed up to within 6 paces of the line in front. The formation of the 3rd Wisconsin was the same one used by Meade's two brigades of Pennsylvania Reserves when they advanced from the North Woods to the Cornfield. As Earl Hess has noted in his book, this was the most common column formation employed on battlefields throughout the Civil War. Commanders favored it because regiments and brigades were easily maneuvered, and a line of battle could be quickly formed from it. The formation's liability was the huge target it presented, particularly for enemy artillery. Because of this, infantry commanders typically only used it to move men up to the edge of the battle zone, where they then deployed into a line of battle before they came under fire.[14]

It was 6:10 a.m., according to Adjutant John Gould's watch, when the nearly 7,300 fighting men of the 12th Corps began to move. Gould's regiment, the 10th Maine, led the march, followed by the other regiments of Crawford's 1st Brigade, and then Gordon's 3rd Brigade, which was trailed by George Greene's 2nd Division. The stupendous roar of the battle ahead tested the nerve of every man. A handful came unglued under the awful strain. Sergeant William Potts's company commander in the 124th Pennsylvania, Captain Frank Crosby, was one. He announced to his men that it was "too hot for him, and if we wanted to go in we might, but he would be——if he would, and he retired to the rear." Crosby resigned his commission on September 24. Even veteran regiments were not immune. During a halt to unsling their knapsacks, William F. Goodhue in the 3rd Wisconsin observed one of his regiment's captains step from his place in the column and approach Colonel Ruger. No one could hear what was said, but the captain, "with downcast face, walked to the rear, so very far to the rear that the regiment knew him no more."[15]

The column marched west, crossing Smoketown Road, then turned south through the fields of John S. Poffenberger's and Middlekauf's farms. The head of the column tramped through a large cornfield adjacent to the road, which probably belonged to Joseph Poffenberger, and emerged into one of Poffenberger's meadows, where Mansfield called a halt and told the men to lie down. Poffenberger Hill, some 400 yards to the west, gave them cover from enemy observation and defilade (protection) from random Confederate artillery fire that overshot their 1st Corps targets. Mansfield, sitting on his horse near the 10th Maine's colonel, George L. Beal, was heard to say to Beal, "We are in reserve today, sir." Beyond the higher ground in front of them, the fighting raged on. "The roar of musketry was incessant," wrote Van R. Willard in the 3rd Wisconsin, "and the cannons boomed with the most terrific of violence, seeming almost to shake the very earth." Considerable numbers of Confederate overshots struck near enough to be uncomfortable. Adjutant John Gould in the 10th Maine observed that "the men being almost positively safe amused themselves by observing the different kinds of noises the shot made." One type of shell created "a very singular fluttering," while another "came along making a perfect whistle without the least whir or harsh sound." One solid shot drew particular notice. When it struck the ground, it plowed up "cart loads of dirt," then bounded 50 yards or more before striking the ground again, until it finally entered Poffenberger's cornfield in the rear of the 10th and came to rest. "It may look like sport now," noted Gould at the apparent indifference he and his comrades had toward the danger, but he assured postwar readers that the experience was "hard and dismal," and that the Confederate overshots were "enough to make us curse ourselves and our ill luck for ever coming to such a place."[16]

All of the shells were not so harmless. The 3rd Wisconsin halted in a piece of Sam Poffenberger's woodlot, near Smoketown Road. One shell struck a tree trunk near them, "shivering the tree into fragments," which fell down among the men. Another struck and mangled a soldier from Company D. "How pallied [*sic*] were the faces of all," recalled William G. Goodhue as he scanned the ranks. "They had grimy, sallow features and muscular bodies, lean and gaunt as hounds."[17]

A steady trickle, then a stream, of wounded men and stragglers began to appear from the direction of the fighting. The first were the slightly wounded, "hurrying out of range of the fire." They were followed by the more seriously wounded, "assisted by the stragglers." The latter, observed John R. Rankin, a 19-year-old 1st sergeant in the 27th Indiana, "have given up all hope of saving the Union, and adopt this pretext to get out of the fight, in order they may be saved whether the Union is nor not." Adjutant Gould reflected, "This day was in the grand old times for sneaks, when a gang of men could leave the battle to carry off a dead or wounded comrade." Gould had crept up to where he could observe the East Woods, out of which "there poured a current of disabled and unfaithful ones." Miles Huyette in the 125th Pennsylvania watched one young soldier who had been shot through the wrist and was writhing in pain, yet he still managed to call out as he passed by, "Go in, boys! Go in, boys! Give them Hell." The historian of the 27th Indiana recorded that most of the wounded who were passing by had something to say, of which "every word is one of encouragement and cheer." Perhaps this was so, but 1st Sergeant Rankin, who was not writing for publication, saw things differently. He noticed considerable numbers of able-bodied men leaving the fight under the pretext of helping the wounded off the battlefield. "Sometimes two or three of the stragglers were assisting one wounded man," he wrote. Observing one of these groups pass his regiment, Colonel Silas Colgrove, Rankin's regimental commander, said, so that everyone in his regiment could hear, "Boys, I don't want to see any of you at that kind of work to-day."[18]

While the 12th Corps marked time and awaited a summons to battle, Mansfield found time to speak words of encouragement to some of his regiments. Sergeant Rankin recalled that they did not know who the white-haired general was who rode up to them and asked their colonel what regiment it was. Someone passed the word that this was the new commander of the 12th Corps. Mansfield smiled at the Indianans and declared "Boys, we're going to lick em to-day," which brought cheers from the men. To Rankin and his comrades, Mansfield's manner and words "inspired confidence, and we feel that he can handle his command." Adjutant Gould wrote, "We all saw General Mansfield riding about the field in his new, untarnished uniform, with his long silvery hair flowing out from behind." The general stopped to speak with Colonel Hector Tyndale and asked if his brigade had eaten breakfast yet. When Tyndale replied "No," Mansfield ordered Tyndale to have his men kindle fires and boil water for coffee. It was such attention to the morale and well-being of his men that caused him, as Gould recalled, to find "a way to our hearts at once. . . . He made us feel that he was our father and would care for us, and you remember we needed someone high in rank to care for us then." Mansfield eventually made his way over to the far northwestern corner of the East Woods, where he could observe the fighting and determine where and when his corps would be needed.[19]

Mansfield could see little of the fighting, because of the higher ground south of his position and the smoke. He was unaware that the central section of the East Woods had been seized by the Confederates. During Hood's counterattack, the 4th Alabama, commanded by Captain William Robbins after Captain Scruggs was wounded, picked up elements of the 21st Georgia in Mumma's plowed field south of the East Woods, who formed on their right flank. The 4th numbered 270, and Robbins thought the Georgians made up half of that amount, or less. When the 90th Pennsylvania fell back into the woods before the advance of Law's brigade, Robbins led his two regiments into the woodlot in pursuit. They entered the woods "yelling fiercely" and blazing away at the retreating Pennsylvanians. They also flushed elements of the 6th Pennsylvania Reserves of Seymour's brigade, who were nearly out of ammunition. Neither regiment was

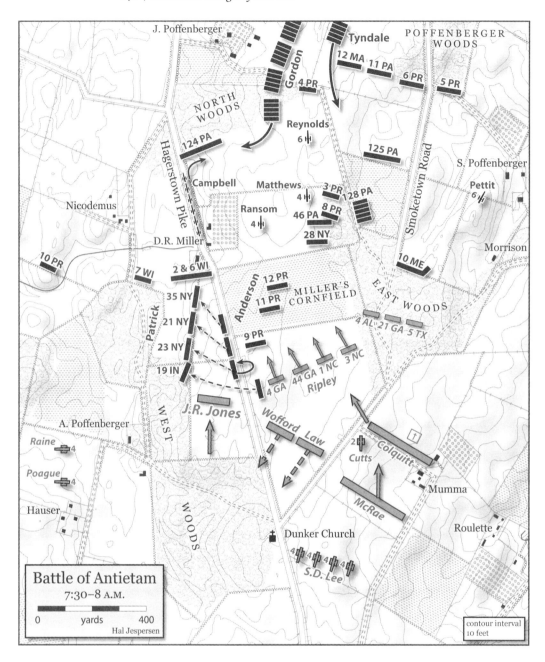

Battle of Antietam
7:30–8 A.M.

0   yards   400
Hal Jespersen

contour interval
10 feet

interested in making a stand against Robbins, and they withdrew to Poffenberger Woods. Except for parts of Magilton's brigade, who entered the far northwestern section of the East Woods, Robbins had seized control of the woodlot for the Confederates.[20]

Robbins pushed his men north to about the middle of the woods, until the left of the 4th Alabama rested along the fence on the western edge of the woodlot, about opposite to the southeastern corner of the Cornfield. Here, the

Alabamians and Georgians spread out to take any cover they could find behind live trees, logs, and limestone ledges, and they skirmished with a handful of hardcore Federals who remained in the woods or along its northern edge. Wounded Union soldiers, who had found shelter in the woods or been carried there by comrades, were liberally sprinkled about. Robbins remembered watching one Federal officer—"a fine looking man"—drag himself around behind a log on the Confederate side to get cover from the fire of friendly troops near the northern edge of the woods. Unbeknownst to Robbins, while he was supervising the advance through the woods, Captain Ike N. M. Turner's 5th Texas, sent by Hood to chase off the 90th Pennsylvania, arrived and passed in the rear of Robbins's line, and then formed on the right of the 21st Georgia. The 5th numbered only about 175 officers and men, but there were now over 500 first-rate Confederate soldiers with a firm hold on the East Woods. They lacked the strength to exploit what they had gained, but they had the numbers, morale, and cover that would make them very difficult to dislodge.[21]

Hood and Law were unaware that any of these units remained in the East Woods when the rest of the division retreated back to the Dunker Church around 7:30 a.m. Although Law's report acknowledged that the 4th Alabama and the 5th Texas "pushed into the wood" and "drove the enemy through and beyond it," he did not mention that they remained there when the rest of his brigade retreated. And neither Law nor Hood mentioned Robbins in their report, indicating that they did not understand it was the captain's initiative that secured the woods and would make that area so difficult for the Federals to regain. Robbins and the three small remaining regiments were on their own, but reinforcements that might have helped them were coming. The problem was that neither the reinforcements nor Robbins were aware of one another's presence, so there was no cooperation or coordination between them.[22]

In his report of the battle, General Daniel H. Hill stated that Hood's division was "handsomely supported by Colquitt and Ripley" in Hill's division. If Hood had read Hill's report, he would have been incredulous at this statement. In Hood's opinion, it was Hill's failure to render him any support that enabled the enemy to maul the flank of Law's brigade and force its retreat. Hood had requested support from Hill early in the morning, before the battle began, and had been told that none could be provided. Hill's problem was that his division was stretched out to cover a very broad front, extending from Mumma's farm on the left to the Boonsboro–Sharpsburg Pike on his right. Brigadier General Roswell Ripley's brigade held the division's left flank and were formed immediately south of Mumma's farm, where they could support Walker's brigade of Lawton's division. Over 500 yards to Ripley's rear, Colonel Alfred Colquitt's brigade occupied the old sunken farmland that connected the Boonsboro Pike with the Hagerstown Pike. Colonel Duncan McRae's and Brigadier General Robert Rodes's brigades extended Hill's line along the lane, to cover its northern and eastern approaches, and Brigadier General George B. Anderson's brigade covered the point where the lane joined the Boonsboro Pike. Hill had no reserve, which may explain his reluctance to send any support to Hood. Ripley was in a position to have provided help to Lawton or Hood during their respective fights, but he did not do so. What drew Hill into the Cornfield–East Woods battle is unknown—he never indicated who ordered him to forward troops into the fight—but it was probably a direct order from Robert E. Lee. It will be recalled that during Hood's counterattack (see chapter 4), Hood communicated to Jackson that unless he received reinforcements, he would be forced back. Jackson probably shared this important information with Lee, who ordered Hill to reinforce Hood.[23]

It had been an unpleasant morning for the men of Roswell Ripley's brigade, which was composed of four regiments—the 4th and 44th Georgia, and the 1st and 3rd North Carolina—numbering about 1,349 men. It had been moved up in the night to a point about 100 yards south of Samuel Mumma's farm, where they could support S. D. Lee's artillery battalion and cover the approach to Smoketown Road. Who selected the position is unknown, although it was probably D. H. Hill. Whomever it was, they chose a poor location. The men lay in one of Mumma's meadows, without a particle of cover. Mumma's farm buildings, his large orchard situated north and northeast of the barn, and the higher ground north of the farm buildings provided good defilade from any fire coming from the direction of Hooker's 1st Corps. But the position was completely exposed to the Federal batteries east of Antietam Creek, who could deliver an enfilading fire. Hill should have been aware of this, since he had observed these batteries firing throughout the day on September 16. Finally, S. D. Lee's batteries were about 300 yards in the rear. There was no question of the quality of Lee's personnel, but their Confederate ordnance prematurely burst often enough to make any deployment of infantry in front of artillery decidedly risky.[24]

Like everyone in the Army of Northern Virginia, Ripley's soldiers were ravenously hungry, having received no rations for 3 days. Somehow, the heroes of the brigade commissary scrounged some flour, with which they cooked hot biscuits on stones, one for each man, serving them warm just before daylight.[25] The farm in front of the brigade belonged to 58-year-old Samuel Mumma. He and his wife Elizabeth and their 10 children abandoned their residence on the afternoon of September 15, when a battle seemed imminent. They took some clothing and silverware, but left everything else. It was a substantial farm. Besides the two-story farmhouse, there was an 80 by 50 foot barn, a smokehouse, a springhouse, a hog pen, and other outbuildings, valued at $10,000, a considerable sum in 1862. For some reason, either Ripley or Colonel William L. DeRosset, commanding the 3rd North Carolina, decided that Mumma's residence and barn posed a problem. DeRosset claimed that he ordered its destruction. Recalling the event in 1890, he wrote, "Everything pointed to desperate work. Before the sun rose, perceiving that the Mumma house in our front, and a little to the right, was well adapted to the protection of sharpshooters, and not knowing if we were to be advanced to take in its position, I ordered its destruction and called upon volunteers from the nearest company on the right." The colonel apparently was unaware that Mumma's farm buildings were within Confederate lines, but Ripley should have known this, and one would imagine that Ripley had to approve DeRosset's destruction of civilian property. Whatever the case, DeRosset assembled five or six volunteers from Company A of his regiment, led by the regiment's 20-year-old sergeant major, James Clark. The detail set the house on fire. Whether they also torched the barn is not recorded, but this is immaterial, since the huge inferno engulfing the house also destroyed it.[26]

Besides "consuming all of the Mumma family possessions as well as all of the farmer's grain, hay and farming tools," the burning buildings attracted the attention of the Union artillery batteries on Pry Ridge, who spotted Ripley's regiments. They immediately sent what DeRosset described as a "fearful shower of shells" at the North Carolinians and Georgians. The first round to reach them was apparently a percussion shell. It struck between DeRosset's main line and a group of the regiment's officers who were lying down in front of the line. The resulting explosion wounded 16 officers and men in DeRosset's regiment. This calamity was not duplicated, but Ripley reported that for over an hour (from 5:30 to 7 a.m.), the "enemy plied his guns unceasingly" and inflicted "serious loss" on the brigade. Ripley and others noted how stoic the men remained during the shelling, but enduing a prolonged bombardment without cover is a morale-eroding experience.[27]

At some point before the brigade moved from its position, Colonel DeRosset sent an aide-de-camp of Ripley's to the general, to tell him DeRosset wanted to speak with him. There had been trouble brewing between these two officers for a considerable period, and DeRosset decided it was time this came to a head, before they went into action. Ripley rose to brigade command with solid credentials. He was a West Point graduate in the class of 1843, which included Ulysses S. Grant and William B. Franklin; served with distinction as a staff officer in the Mexican War; and also saw service in the 1849 conflict with the Seminoles. Although born in Ohio and nominated to West Point from New York State, Ripley had lived in Charleston, South Carolina, since the early 1850s, where he married and came to fully embrace the Southern lifestyle and cause. Having resigned from the U.S. Army in 1853, he joined the South Carolina militia, where he was commissioned as a major of ordnance. On November 6, 1860, only a day after Lincoln's election, Ripley wrote to offer advice to States Rights Gist, an advisor to South Carolina's governor, on where arms might be acquired and how South Carolina should proceed in leaving the Union. There was no question of Ripley's Northern birth tainting his commitment to the cause. He was a true believer.[28]

South Carolina entrusted Ripley with the defense of Charleston during the Fort Sumter crisis, which he managed competently enough, but he apparently proved to be a prickly person to get along with. In August 1861, he was promoted to brigadier general and eventually assumed command of an infantry brigade assigned to the army in front of Richmond, Virginia, arriving on the first day of the Battle of Seven Pines. In the Seven Days Battles that followed almost a month later, his performance raised questions about his courage and competency. "After the Seven days fight it was a common subject of conversation among officers & men, that Ripley was not under infantry fire during the week," wrote DeRosset. "We saw nor heard nothing of him at Mechanicsville, Cold Harbor or Malvern Hill—where we engaged infantry—after the lines started forward, nor was he known to be near his proper position at any time." The question of Ripley's personal courage prompted his entire staff—except for a single aide-de-camp, Captain Ben Reid—to leave him. For some unaccountable reason, D. H. Hill claimed to be unaware of his brigadier general's performance in the Seven Days Battles and the attitude toward Ripley in his brigade. Hill entrusted a major attack to him at South Mountain, which Ripley fumbled badly, resulting in a disjoined movement that was easily defeated by the Federals. During the retreat of the army from South Mountain, Ripley forgot about the 4th Georgia, which had been detached, an oversight that nearly resulted in its capture.[29]

Ripley did not respond to DeRosset's request to speak to him. The North Carolinian had to repeat his request three more times before the general finally rode up and asked what he wanted. As DeRosset recalled, "I spoke plainly & told him that in all the engagements I had been in I felt the need of advice from my commander and had never seen him; further that the rank & file were complaining that they had not seen their brigadier under infantry fire since he took command, & that they believed he kept to the rear to avoid the fire." Ripley "blusteringly replied that he would show them he was no coward" and vowed to go into action beside DeRosset.[30]

At 7 a.m., the same time when Hood's division began its attack, Ripley received orders to "close in to my left and advance." He reported that his men sprang to their arms "with alacrity," which is not surprising. Advancing was preferable to the terror of being used as target practice by Union artillery. Despite the orders to close to the left, for some reason the brigade first went in a slightly northeasterly direction, which may have been to keep their distance from Mumma's burning house and barn. The 3rd North Carolina had to move by the right flank to avoid them. That probably caused a rightward shift of the whole brigade, in order for the regiments to maintain contact with one another. After clearing the burning buildings, the 3rd and 1st North Carolina advanced through Mumma's orchard to the fence on its northern edge, where they halted while Ripley re-formed the whole brigade, because they came under fire from the

26th and 94th New York along the southeastern face of the East Woods. Ripley's men replied with a "rapid fire" at the Federals, who were some 300 yards away. The enemy fire inflicted a number of casualties on the 4th Georgia, who were between the barn and the Mumma family's cemetery, northwest of the house. "Our loss, while in line at this point was unusually heavy," remembered Charles T. Furlow, a Company K private serving as a courier to Colonel Doles. The rest of the brigade had better cover and suffered few casualties, but one lucky Union bullet nicked Ripley in the throat. DeRosset, who was near him, described it as a slight wound, but it stunned the general, who was carried a short distance to the rear. He recovered from the shock soon enough for DeRosset to observe him "breaking down the corn, standing in the field, going to the rear." Ripley would be back, but not during the stern test that his men soon faced.[31]

Ripley's departure left Colonel George Doles, commanding the 4th Georgia, as the acting brigade commander. Doles may have been unaware of Ripley's orders, and the brigade remained stationary around Mumma's orchard and cemetery until nearly 7:30 a.m., during which time Hood attacked and was repulsed. Given the losses his own regiment had sustained from the enemy in the East Woods, Doles may have hesitated to move his brigade across the plowed field that extended 300 yards in his front. When he saw the Federals begin to retreat "in great haste" in reaction to Hood's counterattack, Doles ordered the brigade forward. When they were about halfway across the plowed field, D. H. Hill rode up and ordered Doles to move to the left, probably to close the distance to where Hill believed Hood's right flank to be. Forming a column of fours, the brigade hurried across the field toward the meadow south of the Cornfield. Hill led them across Smoketown Road, at the southwestern tip of the East Woods, and into the meadow, where they came under scattered small-arms fire, most likely from elements of Magilton's brigade, who were pursuing Law's retreating brigade. Having started Doles in the desired direction, Hill left to get the other elements of his division moving, leaving the colonel on his own.[32]

In the meadow, Doles deployed from column to line, with the regiments aligned from left to right: the 4th Georgia, 44th Georgia, the 1st North Carolina, and 3rd North Carolina. As they formed up, a bullet found a good friend in his regiment, Major Robert S. Smith, and killed him, leaving Doles visibly distraught. Ransom's battery pelted them with canister, but it must have fired high, since it inflicted few casualties. When the 3rd North Carolina completed their formation, they opened fire on the Union Regulars. Eight of the 3rd's 10 companies were armed with smoothbore muskets firing buck and ball, and the range, which was nearly 500 yards, was 400 yards beyond what was considered to be effective. Yet their first volley silenced the guns. Then the 19th Indiana arrived, on the plateau south of the Cornfield. The Georgians and the 1st North Carolina blasted them with fire and drove them back. As they disappeared, more Yankees emerged from the southern edge of the corn. It was the 9th Pennsylvania Reserves of Robert Anderson's brigade. The 11th and 12th Reserves were also advancing, but they were farther back in the corn and not yet visible.[33]

ANDERSON'S THREE REGIMENTS ENTERED the Cornfield in staggered order, with the 9th Pennsylvania Reserves, who were closest to the Hagerstown Pike, leading, followed en echelon by the 11th and 12th Reserves. By this point the Cornfield was a horrid place, littered with hundreds of casualties. The ground where the Reserves began their counterattack was particularly thick with the dead and wounded in the 1st Texas. Though battered and knocked about in places, much of the corn was still standing, which helped to conceal Anderson's advance and limited his observation of what lay ahead. As the regiments moved through the field, Lieutenant James P. George in the 11th Pennsylvania Reserves passed over the state colors of the 1st Texas. "I then could have picked them up myself," he recalled, but he left the flag for someone else to collect. The 9th Reserves reached the corn's southern edge, peering out at the same plateau that had been fought over throughout the morning. Ripley's regiments, alert to a potential threat to their left flank by their encounter with the 19th Indiana, were wheeling in that direction when the 9th came into view. The 4th and 44th Georgia opened fire on them at once, joined by part of the 1st North Carolina. The balance of this regiment, and the 3rd North Carolina, fired at the 11th and 12th Pennsylvania Reserves.[34]

The 9th Pennsylvania Reserves had already expended a substantial portion of their ammunition in repulsing the 1st Texas. Now, as they traded fire with Ripley's brigade, their remaining supply rapidly dwindled. Captain Dick had his men scrounge ammunition from the dead and wounded. Lieutenant Colonel Robert Anderson told Dick to hold on while Anderson went to the rear to find a regiment to relieve him. Both sides suffered severe losses in the firefight. "Our boys fell as regularly and as fast as counting, one, two three," wrote J. B. R. [probably 2nd Lieutenant Joseph B. Reese] in the 44th Georgia, even though the men lay down to obtain some cover. One of the first to be hit was the letter writer's beloved company commander, Captain Charles D. Pearson, who was struck in the head and killed instantly. "The men knew nothing but to love and obey him," lamented J. B. R. But the Georgians and North Carolinians scored numerous hits on their foe, as well, and they stopped Anderson's counterattack in its tracks. The 12th Pennsylvania Reserves made it only as far as the high ground in the middle of the Cornfield, where they encountered a "terrible fire" from the 3rd North Carolina and part of the 1st North Carolina that decimated nearly half of the regiment. All the color guard of the 12th Reserves went down in this fusillade, but the colors were saved by one unnamed member who, though wounded twice, dragged the flag from the field. The 12th held its ground for several more minutes until someone, probably Meade, ordered them to fall back.[35]

The 11th Pennsylvania Reserves advanced out of the corn on the right of the 12th Reserves and met the same reception. "It was here we suffered our heaviest loss," noted Lieutenant George. Their casualties were not as heavy as those in the 9th and 12th Pennsylvania Reserves, but it was apparent that they were outgunned. We "fell back slowly bringing off our wounded," wrote Lieutenant George, as well as a number of prisoners captured from Wofford's and Law's brigades, whom the Federals had passed over in their advance and "were lying down among the corn rows."[36]

Facing the brunt of Ripley's fire, and having the greatest exposure, Captain Dick's 9th Pennsylvania Reserves sustained the worst damage in the 3rd Brigade, with 17 men killed and 66 wounded (although some of these losses occurred during the engagement with the 1st Texas), which amounted to nearly 40%. Captain Dick held his position until it was evident no reinforcements were coming, and he then ordered his men back. His regiment was damaged, but they had hurt their opponents. Lieutenant Colonel Hamilton A. Brown, whose 1st North Carolina helped send the Pennsylvanians in retreat, remembered the relatively brief combat as "furious," and "the courage exhibited by the Yankees was sublime." Doles pushed Ripley's brigade forward, advancing the 4th Georgia up to within 50 yards of the Cornfield, on the plateau the 9th Pennsylvania Reserves had just vacated. To further secure the left flank from any surprises from the direction of the West Woods, Doles shifted part of the 1st North Carolina to the left of the 4th Georgia. The balance of the brigade moved up on line with the 4th Georgia, facing the Cornfield, and sent skirmishers into the corn. It was a poor position, with fields of fire limited by the corn's height. The regiments were standing or lying exposed, without any cover, but possibly Hill had cautioned the Georgian to advance no farther than the Cornfield until he had brought up reinforcements.[37]

It was nearly 8 a.m. by this point, and the repulse of Robert Anderson's Pennsylvania Reserves precipitated a fresh crisis for the Federals. The 1st Corps was completely fought out, having sustained most of the 2,590 casualties they would suffer on September 17, which amounted to nearly 25% of its effective strength. Anderson's counterattack was its last offensive gasp. Ricketts's division was in disarray, attempting to rally its broken regiments and brigades in Poffenberger Woods. Doubleday's division still held the northern end of the West Woods and Miller's farm, but its offensive capability was spent, and the impact of Hood's and now Ripley's counterattacks left Meade's regiments scattered from Poffenberger Woods to the Hagerstown Pike. Part of Magilton's brigade still occupied the northwestern tip of the East Woods, but its grip was tenuous. If Ripley could drive them out, the Confederates would gain full control of the woodlot, providing them with an important tactical advantage. It was imperative that the East Woods be recaptured by the Federals and Ripley's advance checked, or potential disaster loomed. The moment for the 12th Corps had arrived.[38]

MANSFIELD'S CORPS WAS ALREADY in motion before Ripley arrived in front of the Cornfield. During the high point of Hood's counterattack, when the pressure on the 1st Corps' front was so great that it seemed as though it might give way, Hooker called up Mansfield to his support. It was shortly before 7:30 a.m., and minutes before Hood's attack began to recede. Mansfield's leading brigade was that of Brigadier General Samuel W. Crawford, commanding the 1st Brigade of Alpheus Williams's 1st Division. It consisted of three veteran regiments (the 10th Maine, the 28th New York, and the 46th Pennsylvania), and three newly raised regiments (the 124th, 125th, and 128th Pennsylvania) with a 9-month enlistment period. The 10th Maine, almost 300 strong, was the largest veteran unit. The 28th New York was the size of a company, with only 68 officers and men, and the 46th Pennsylvania carried 150 into action. The strength of the brigade resided in its new regiments, each numbering between 600 and 700 men.

Colonel Joseph F. Knipe in the 46th Pennsylvania understood that the general plan was for the three new regiments to lead, with the three veteran regiments following as their supports, but the urgency of events altered this. From the flow of broken units, wounded men, and stragglers coming back, Alpheus Williams realized that the 12th Corps' engagement was imminent. But the regiments of the corps were still in column of companies or double column of companies, without deployment intervals between them—that is, a regiment could not form into a line of battle without running into its neighbors. It was imperative that they deploy. Since Mansfield was absent, observing the fighting between the 1st Corps and Hood's men, Williams ordered Crawford's brigade to deploy from column to line. Before the order could be executed, Mansfield came riding back and immediately countermanded Williams's order. Although most of the Confederate shells were passing by them, Williams knew the damage a shell would do if it landed in the mass of soldiers. "Dozens of men would have been killed by a single shot," he fretted. Williams "begged him [Mansfield] to let me deploy them in line of battle, in which the men present but *two* ranks instead of *twenty*." But Mansfield refused to budge. "He was positive that all the new regiments would run away," wrote Williams. As 10th Maine adjutant John Gould pointed out, Mansfield's stubborn belief that an infantry regiment could be more easily managed in column than in line was true in the abstract or on the drill ground, but in the reality of infantry combat, it was a recipe to get men slaughtered.[39]

Whatever had originally been intended for how Crawford's brigade should go into action was now discarded. Hooker advised Mansfield to shift the three new regiments of the brigade to the right, with their right on the Hagerstown

Pike, and send the three veteran regiments to their left, toward the East Woods. This meant marching the veteran regiments across the front of the new regiments, since they were on the right of the brigade as it waited to go into action. Part of Mansfield's problem in managing his corps was that he had only two staff officers, Captain Clarence H. Dyer, who was his personal aide-de-camp, and Colonel James W. Forsyth, who would one day command the 7th Cavalry at Wounded Knee. McClellan had loaned Forsyth to Mansfield, because the latter had no staff. But Mansfield compounded his problems by personally meddling in the deployment of Crawford's brigade, rather than allowing Williams and Crawford to manage the brigade. He sent Captain Dyer off to either Williams or Crawford with orders to bring Crawford's regiment forward, but while Dyer was delivering these orders, Mansfield rode up to the 10th Maine, on the far right of Crawford's brigade, and ordered them to follow him. He may have also ordered the 46th Pennsylvania and the tiny 28th New York to move as well, for they followed the 10th. All the regiments were still in double column of companies.[40]

When Mansfield refused to allow Williams to deploy Crawford's regiments into line of battle, the division commander gathered several regimental commanders of the brigade, including Colonel Joseph F. Knipe and Captain William H. H. Mapes, commanding the 46th Pennsylvania and the 28th New York, respectively, under a large tree to discuss how they would go into action. Williams's plan was that the 46th Pennsylvania would go ahead double-quick and deploy as skirmishers, to cover the brigade's front. This would screen the new regiments when they deployed and advanced, but this plan came to nothing when Mansfield seized on the veteran regiments and led them toward the East Woods. The result was self-inflicted confusion, caused by Mansfield's haste and excitement.[41]

THE 297 OFFICERS AND men in the 10th Maine were commanded by 37-year-old Colonel George L. Beal. Beal had been an express agent in Norway, Maine, before the war, but the military was his real interest, and he was captain of the local militia company. When the war came, he was the first in his county to enlist, and when the 10th Maine was organized in the fall of 1861, Beal was named as its colonel. Although the 10th had nearly a year's service under its belt, it had participated in only one battle, Cedar Mountain. Nonetheless, that was bad enough. It suffered 173 casualties there, all but 4 of those killed or wounded. Beal and his men fought well, but the battle ended with the regiment running for their lives before a counterattack by Stonewall Jackson's men.[42]

When Mansfield beckoned the 10th forward, Colonel Beal shouted "Attention," which brought the regiment to its feet, and then "Forward." Adjutant John Gould noted that it was 7:30 a.m. by his watch. The regiment passed over the high ground in their front and moved downhill, through a plowed field and toward a 10-acre cornfield of Samuel Poffenberger, bordering the west side of Smoketown Road. As they neared Poffenberger's field, Mansfield gestured to Beal to move his regiment farther to the left. To execute the order, Beal commanded "Left oblique," which meant that each man marched at a 45-degree angle to the left. It was hard enough to maintain order on the drill field when executing this movement, but it was impossible when the regiment went "hustling and sliding" into Poffenberger's corn. The 10th "should have been badly confused" had Beal not noticed the disorder and shouted the command "Left flank!" which caused each man to face left and march east. This brought the regiment out of the corn to Smoketown Road, where scores of wounded from Ricketts's division were trying to get to the rear. The New Englanders knocked gaps in the fencing and double-quicked into a plowed field east of the road. While they were moving across the road, Hooker galloped up to them from the direction of the East Woods and asked Beal what regiment he commanded. Told it was the 10th Maine, Hooker replied, "The enemy are breaking through my lines, you must hold these woods."[43]

"A few stray bullets whizzed around us as we crossed the road," recalled Adjutant Gould. More bullets cut the air about them as the regiment hurried into the field. Once the tail of the regiment had cleared the road, Beal commanded "Right face," which had them facing to the south, toward the East Woods. Some 50 to 100 Confederates were seen, scattered along the fence on the northern border of the East Woods. "They had the immense advantage that they could rest their rifles on the fence and fire into us, massed ten ranks deep, while we could only march and 'take it,'" observed Gould. The Confederates opened fire, but most of their bullets were aimed too low or high. They scored only one hit, but it was a fatal one. John McGinty, a 30-year-old Irish-born laborer from Portland, Maine, in Company B, who had enlisted just over a month earlier, was shot in the head and had the sad distinction of being the first man in the regiment to be killed. The humming bullets and the death of McGinty underscored the fact that it was time to deploy. This maneuver meant the difference between the firepower of 60 men in double column of companies, versus that of over 270 men. Beal made this suggestion to Mansfield, who replied "No," adding that a regiment could be more easily handled in mass than in line. Mansfield rode off to bring up the rest of Crawford's brigade. Beal, who had no intention of seeing his men "uselessly butchered," due to Mansfield's outdated ideas of infantry tactics—"we were as big a target as a barn," wrote Gould—barely waited for him to get out of sight before he commanded his regiment to form line in double-quick time. "Everybody felt the need of haste," Gould noted.[44]

The 10th Maine moved from one of Sam Poffenberger's plowed fields into a meadow that gently sloped up toward the East Woods and the Confederates along the woods' edge. Moving over this open ground tested the mettle of even the best soldiers, as Gould related:

And now came the moment of battle that tried us severely, not that there was a sign of hesitancy, or show of poor behavior, but it is terrible to march slowly into danger, and see and feel that each second your chance for death is surer than it was the second before. The desire to break loose, to run, to fire, to do something, no matter what, rather than to walk, is almost irresistible. Men who pray, pray then; men who never pray nerve themselves as best they can, but it is said that those who have been praying men and are not, suffer an agony that neither of the other class can know.[45]

The Confederates behind the rail fence on the edge of the woods were from the 5th Texas, who, as Captain William T. Hill proudly recalled years later, were "as fine rifle shots as America ever produced, & I might add, as fearless." But they were also experienced enough to know that waiting to receive a volley from nearly 300 rifles was unwise, so as the 10th Maine approached, the Texans melted back into the woods, but not before they knocked over several more New Englanders. The companies of the 10th hurried to deploy into line but Smoketown Road's fencing and the bushes growing along it presented an obstacle to Companies A and H, on the right. On the left, companies F and C encountered a limestone ledge running at a northeast angle from the woods. With quick presence of mind, Captain William P. Jordan, the Company C commander who was responsible for the "division" (consisting of these two companies), directed his men to take cover behind the ledge. This placed a good portion of his men at a 45-degree angle to the rest of the regiment, but it gave them excellent cover and, as Adjutant Gould noted, "because, perceiving there was no Union force on our left, he knew it was better to have our left 'refused' [bent back] and hence not so easily 'flanked' by the enemy." Despite the obstructions from man and nature, the regiment "kept together finely," and the balance of it soon arrived at the worm fence on the East Woods' edge, where they opened fire on the Confederates, whom they could see darting about in the woods. "It made a good impression upon them," wrote Gould, but the Confederates had fine cover. The Texans, Alabamians, and Georgians in their front "were well scattered through the woods, behind numerous ledges, logs, trees and piles of cord wood, a few men only being east of the Smoketown Road," and they returned a fire that "was exceedingly well aimed." Many in the 10th, rather than standing in line behind the worm fence, which offered only a modicum of cover, leaped over or knocked through the fence and took cover inside the woods, behind trees and logs. "Not a mound or tree that gave us protection we did not improve," wrote the regiment's lieutenant colonel, James Fillebrown. "It was a squirrel hunt on a large scale as you could see our men creep along from tree to tree." This led to the regimental line more closely resembling a thick skirmish line than a line of battle, with some individuals working their way so far forward that they may have been hit "by the wild shooting of our own men in the rear."[46]

Among the first of those hit at the fence line was Colonel Beal. A sharpshooter perched in a tree toward the regiment's left flank—probably a member of the 5th Texas—targeted the colonel. His first shot missed Beal but hit his horse in the head. "The brute became unmanageable," wrote Adjutant Gould, "reeled around, tried to throw the Colonel, and at length compelled him to dismount." As Beal extricated himself from his bucking horse, the same sharpshooter put a bullet into the colonel that passed through his right thigh and lodged in his left leg. Beal's horse broke free and ran straight into Lieutenant Colonel Fillebrown's horse with such force that Fillebrown was knocked out of the saddle and fell onto the ground. Fillebrown got up and managed to catch his mount, but Beal's horse "came again with redoubled fury," separated the lieutenant colonel from his horse, and then kicked Fillebrown in the stomach with both feet, causing "the most intense pain and suffering I ever experienced." A single bullet had effectively knocked the 10th Maine's field officers out of the battle. Command fell to Major Charles Walker, who, Gould noted, "had been sick a month, but who still kept along with us, hoping, against hope and reason, that he might improve." Lieutenant Edwin W. Fowler was less tactful than Gould in his opinion of Walker's command ability. When the regiment later fell back from its position, Fowler observed Walker "and several other fireaters" lying behind a rocky knoll in the field, in the rear of the regiment's position, "making a very minute examination of the soil on rocks, glued to the earth they seemed."[47]

The riflemen in the 10th Maine got their revenge on Beal's and Fillebrown's nemesis. Several Texans were discovered concealed in the canopy of the woods off the regiment's left flank. Dennis McGoverin, a recent recruit who had joined the regiment in August, felled one, and others shot two more from their tree perches. The 10th had been supplied with an experimental cartridge, known as a "combustible envelope cartridge," which eliminated the need to tear open a cartridge, prime the rifle, and press the minie ball into the muzzle. Instead, the whole cartridge was inserted and rammed down the gun barrel. Some men discovered that it was also possible to insert the cartridge and then give the rifle a sharp rap on the ground, in order to seat the cartridge. This enabled the 10th to maintain a considerably more rapid fire than was typical for a muzzle-loading percussion rifle.[48]

While the 10th Maine traded fire with Rebels in the woods, the rest of the Crawford's 1st Brigade trickled into the fight. The 46th Pennsylvania and the 28th New York trailed the 10th Maine at enough distance that they never saw one another, and Colonel Joseph Knipe was later baffled by how the 10th managed to get from the right of the brigade to its far left without him seeing it. These two regiments—still in column of divisions, as mandated by Mansfield—marched south through the 10-acre cornfield, crossed the Poffenberger farm lane, and entered the far northwestern tip of the East Woods. They encountered men of the 3rd and 8th Pennsylvania Reserves of Magilton's brigade still fighting there. The two units were low on ammunition, and most withdrew when Knipe arrived with the 46th and the 28th, but some diehards joined the newcomers and remained in the fight. When these two regiments reached the woods, Knipe ordered them to deploy. This part of the woods was slightly elevated and gave Knipe's men a view of the 3rd North Carolina of Ripley's brigade, located in the meadow about 250 yards south of the Cornfield. The Pennsylvanians and New Yorkers immediately commenced a "lively fire" at the Tarheels.[49]

AFTER LEAVING THE 10TH Maine in the plowed field north of the East Woods, Mansfield rode back some 500 yards to the 128th Pennsylvania, standing in column of companies west of Poffenberger Woods. The rookies in the 128th were anxious and frightened. They had watched a "long line of dead and wounded" from the 1st Corps be carried past them toward the rear. "Breakfast was not to be thought of," wrote Frederick Crouse, a 27-year-old private in Company C. Crouse pulled his pocket bible out and read the 91st Psalm to comfort himself. He noticed many other comrades doing likewise. An extra 20 rounds of ammunition were issued, in addition to the 40 rounds in their cartridge boxes. The men stuffed this surplus into their pockets, haversacks, or wherever they could access it quickly. Two men from each company were detailed to act as stretcher bearers to evacuate the wounded. Officers spoke words of encouragement and, Crouse recalled, "also gave us positive orders not to fire a gun until the order to fire was given, and then to fire low." The officers put on a brave face, but they were just as anxious as their men, pondering the reality of leading everyone into the seething maelstrom before them, with the men having virtually no knowledge of even the most basic infantry tactical commands or how to execute them.[50]

The summons to join the struggle arrived when Mansfield rode up and ordered Colonel Samuel Croasdale to bring the 128th Pennsylvania forward. David Mattern, a Company B private, wrote home afterward that he could see Mansfield riding in front of the regiment "with his hat in his hand cheering us on to follow him which we did." They marched south, nearly paralleling the Poffenberger farm lane on their right; entered the 10-acre cornfield, passing through the right of the 125th Pennsylvania, which was halted there; and then went into the northern finger of the East Woods. As the regiment entered the woods, Frederick Crouse wrote that "we heared for the first time that whistle or peculiar whiz of the minnie ball." David Mattern could see the Cornfield and, beyond it, the 3rd North Carolina, who were "firing on us like two forty." Bullets struck several men. "We all began to duck our heads," Crouse observed, and, he admitted, "I felt pretty streaky and a little weak in the knees." With nearly 700 men in column of companies, the regiment made a huge target. Now that they were exposed to fire, Mansfield ordered Croasdale to deploy, an order simple to issue, but impossible for a raw regiment under fire to perform. Mansfield's apparent intent was for the 128th Pennsylvania to relieve the 28th New York and the

46th Pennsylvania, whom he probably planned to shift to fill the gap between the 128th's left and the 10th Maine's right. But from the knoll in the East Woods—soon to be known as Croasdale's Knoll—where the Pennsylvanians were attempting to deploy, Mansfield saw the 10th Maine firing rapidly into the woods. From everything he understood of the 1st Corps' position, the 10th were firing on their own men![51]

Adjutant John Gould saw Mansfield, along with General Samuel Crawford and some other mounted officers, on Croasdale's Knoll. He observed the corps' commander make motions at the 10th Maine to cease firing. "As this was the very last thing we proposed to do, the few who saw him did not understand what his motions meant, and so no attention was paid to him," Gould noted. Then Mansfield, accompanied by a single orderly, galloped down to the 10th, passing through the men of the right companies near Smoketown Road and shouting, "Cease firing, they are our own men!" Company officers at once attempted to stop their men from firing, but their instructions were attended to with "great difficulty," as the men were certain they were not mistaken about their targets. Mansfield continued along the line of the regiment, riding "rapidly and fearlessly" until he reached the point where the regiment's left flank was refused.[52] Here, Captain Jordan, commanding Company C, ran up to the fence along the edge of the East Woods and shouted that Mansfield should "look and see." Jordan and one of his sergeants, Henry A. Burnham, pointed at several men who were clearly Confederate soldiers, only around 20 yards away, and were aiming their weapons in Mansfield's direction. Mansfield pulled out his field glass to look, but his horse was shot in the right hind leg and "became unruly." Satisfied that Jordan was correct, Mansfield replied, "Yes, yes, you are right." As he said these words, a bullet punched through his right lung, but he displayed no sign of being hit to those who were watching him. He managed to turn his horse and ride back toward Smoketown Road, to a point where the rail fence along the East Woods was thrown down. His horse refused to step over a pile of rails in its way, so the general dismounted to lead the animal over the obstacle and behind the 10th's battle line. As he did, a gust of wind blew open his uniform coat, and Gould noticed that the general's whole front "was covered with blood." Gould ran over to Mansfield as the general was attempting to remount his horse and asked if he was badly hurt. "Yes," Mansfield replied, "I shall not live—shall not live," adding that "I am shot—by one of our own men," the latter statement indicating Captain Jordan had not entirely convinced Mansfield that the 10th Maine was firing on the enemy. Gould told Mansfield that his horse was also wounded and suggested he take his orderly's horse. Mansfield tried to do, so but his strength was swiftly ebbing. He asked to be helped off, repeating, "I am shot—I shall not live." Then, incredibly, he had the presence of mind to ask his orderly to look after his wounded horse.[53]

So preoccupied were the men in the 10th Maine with the enemy that, wrote Gould, "no one seemed to notice us." Several minutes passed before Gould was joined by Sergeant Joe Merrill in Company F and Private Stover Knight in Company B. The three men also "pressed into service" a young Black man—apparently a cook for a 1st Corps regiment—who claimed, incredibly, to be searching for some captain's frying pan. The four men started to carry the mortally wounded general to the rear, but, for some reason, the cook incensed Sergeant Merrill. Gould opined that it was his "sauciness, his indifference to the danger, and his slovenly way of handling the General." Race undoubtedly also played a significant role. Merrill asked the party to stop, set down the general, and then kicked and cuffed the cook "most unmercifully." By this point, other men, probably from the 125th Pennsylvania, had been attracted to the group, a blanket was acquired, and Mansfield was carried to the rear, while Gould hurried ahead to find a surgeon and an ambulance. He came upon General George H. Gordon, commanding the 3rd Brigade, 1st Division, near Poffenberger Woods and asked if he would send an orderly off for help. Gordon was busy maneuvering the raw 107th New York into position and was short of orderlies, so, Gould wrote, he "paid no attention to me." Hurrying on along Smoketown Road into the woods, Gould finally discovered an ambulance and two medical officers. They gave Mansfield some whiskey or brandy, which merely choked the general and "added greatly to his distress." Mansfield was loaded onto the ambulance and, still accompanied by Sergeant Merrill, headed back toward George Line's farm, where, only 2 hours earlier, the general had started forward toward the battle, full of energy and life.[54]

Mansfield's command of the 12th Corps was fleeting—only 2 full days and a brief part of a third. He showed inexperience in the deployment of his corps into the battle, exposing men to unnecessary losses by maintaining dense column formations until the regiments were under fire, as well as in micromanaging the deployment of Crawford's brigade, causing confusion and inefficiency in how the brigade entered the fighting. But he had also inspired his men. No one who met him ever forgot him. He displayed great personal courage and aggressiveness, signs indicating that, with experience, he might have developed into an effective corps commander. But the cruel fates of war had decided otherwise.

6

The 12th Corps Sweeps the Field

"The roar of the infantry was beyond anything
conceivable to the uninitiated"

W hen General Mansfield personally guided the 10th Maine toward the East Woods, General Alpheus Williams led Colonel Joseph Hawley's 124th Pennsylvania to the right, toward the North Woods. Williams understood that the overall strategy for Crawford's brigade was to deploy the three new regiments on the right, in the direction of the Hagerstown Pike, and the three veteran regiments on the left, toward the East Woods. He was unaware that Mansfield, by seizing the 128th Pennsylvania to reinforce the 28th New York and the 46th Pennsylvania, had again meddled in a plan on which Williams thought there was agreement. Williams guided the 124th, still in Mansfield's prescribed double column of companies, across the Poffenberger farm lane and out to the fence on the northern border of the North Woods. Williams used the fence line to deploy the regiment into battle line, ordinarily a simple process for a unit with any training, but a challenge for the 124th. "The men were of an excellent stamp," wrote Williams to his daughter, "ready and willing, but neither officers nor men knew anything, and there was an absence of the mutual confidence which drill begets." Starting one company after another moving by the flank—either right or left, depending on their position in the double column—Williams horsed the 600 to 700 rookies into a line, with the right flank resting on the Hagerstown Pike. He ordered Hawley to "go forward and open fire the moment he saw the Rebels" and then left to see to the deployment of the rest of his division. On the way, he encountered Colonel James Forsyth, from Mansfield's small staff, on his way to inform him that Mansfield was seriously wounded, and that Williams was again in command of the corps.[1]

Williams went in search of Hooker, whom he found alone in Miller's plowed field south of the North Woods. Hooker was on the higher ground at the southern end of this field and was under fire. Williams noticed that while they talked, "the dust of the ploughed ground was knocked up in little spurts all around us, marking the spot where musket balls struck." It was an uncomfortable place, yet Hooker seemed oblivious to the danger. While they discussed where Hooker wanted the 12th Corps to go, a general from the 1st Corps, whom Williams did not know, rode up and asked for "immediate assistance to protect a battery." In a letter to his daughter, Williams commented that the general "was very earnest and absorbed in the subject, as you may well suppose, and began to plead energetically, when he suddenly stopped, extended his hand, and very calmly said, 'How are you?'" The man was George Meade, and the battery he was worried about was probably Ransom's. By this point, Anderson's 3rd Brigade of Pennsylvania Reserves was retreating, and Ripley's brigade had silenced Ransom's guns. Meade feared the Rebels might capture the artillery if support was not provided quickly.[2]

While Meade pleaded for support, General John Gibbon, fresh from his epic combat with Wofford's Texas Brigade, rode up and made a similar appeal for help to protect Battery B, although he failed to mention that the crippled battery was pulling back. The situation on Gibbon's front was tenuous. Hood's attack had been repulsed, but without fresh infantry, it was unlikely that another attack could be stopped. Williams told Hooker that Gordon's brigade, from his 1st Division, was approaching, and that its line of direction would bring it up in support of Ransom's battery. Williams said he would detach the rear brigade of Greene's 2nd Division to reinforce Gibbon's position. Hooker and Williams apparently discussed the deployment of Greene's two remaining brigades, which were then marching south across Joseph Poffenberger's farm, in the direction of the East Woods. Hooker wanted Greene to move up and form with his right on the Poffenberger farm lane, and extend his left south, toward the burning Mumma buildings. In other words, Hooker desired Greene to execute a sweeping right wheel, to flank the Rebels opposing Crawford and Gordon and drive them from the field. While the generals discussed how the 12th Corps would relieve the 1st Corps, both Gordon's brigade and Greene's division came into view. Hooker pointed at them and said to Meade and Gibbon, "Gentlemen, you must hold on until Williams' men get up." With that the group broke up, with Meade and Gibbon returning to their commands and Williams riding to find Greene. Williams had no idea where Mansfield had placed the 12th Corps' artillery brigade, so, while he went to meet with Greene, Williams sent part of his small staff to find the guns and bring them forward.[3]

In the East Woods and the fields west of it, the engagement between Crawford's brigade and the Texans, Georgians, and Alabamians in the woods, as well as the 3rd North Carolina of Ripley's brigade, who were near the Cornfield, raged on. Mansfield had apparently intended to have the 128th Pennsylvania relieve the 28th New York and the 46th Pennsylvania, who would shift left to fill the space between the 10th Maine and the 128th. Mansfield's first mistake was not to deploy the 128th into line before it came under fire. His second was to imagine that this green unit could execute any of these complicated maneuvers with other units, who were already closely engaged.[4]

Young Colonel Croasdale bravely attempted to carry out Mansfield's orders, while the latter rode off and would be mortally wounded moments later. Croasdale shouted the commands to form line. He then ordered "Charge bayonet" and "Double quick march." The regiment was so large that when it deployed, most of it spilled out of the woods into Miller's meadow, north of the Cornfield. The Pennsylvanians raised an enthusiastic shout, but Major Joel B. Wanner observed "much confusion" in the regiment's effort to execute the orders. The 3rd North Carolina poured buck and ball and minie balls into the rookies, and the 4th Alabama peppered the 128th's left flank. Captain Robbins thought the Union regiment "seemed helpless, ineffective, and inclined to retire." His riflemen, some of whom climbed up into trees, did their best to sow chaos in the 128th's ranks. As the Pennsylvanians struggled to get their companies into line, a 17-year-old private, Henry A. Shenton in Company G, saw a puff of smoke from a tree along the edge of the woods, about 100 yards away. Colonel Croasdale toppled from his horse, shot through the head and killed instantly. Lieutenant Colonel William W. Hammersly, who dismounted and ran over to Croasdale, was promptly shot through the wrist and arm. This left Major Wanner, recently the mayor of Reading, in command. He dismounted, and his horse then broke free and ran off. This probably saved his life, "else the enemy's sharpshooters would have picked him off," wrote Peter Noll, a Company H private. The targeting of officers seemed so accurate to Lieutenant Michael P. Boyer that he cut off his shoulder straps and picked up a musket, so he did not stand out from the enlisted men.[5]

Major Wanner was shaken by the sudden shock and violence of his regiment's introduction to combat and was heard repeatedly exclaiming, "Too bad! Too bad!" He found it impossible to form the regiment "in the excitement and confusion." Colonel Joseph Knipe came to Wanner's rescue. With the help of Sergeant William Winthrope in the 28th New York, Knipe horsed the 128th into a semblance of a line and got the Pennsylvanians firing back at the enemy. Frederick Crouse, who was feeling "streaky" and weak kneed when he first came under fire, found that after firing two to three rounds, "that nervous feeling left me and I made up my mind that I was there to fight and I loaded and fired as fast as I could." John S. Dougherty, a private in Company C, aggressively dashed forward in advance of his company, in order to get a shot at the Rebels. "The bullets flew so fast" around the private that "I had not time to look around." He managed to fire a round or two before he took a bullet through the fleshy part of his thigh, which sent him limping to the rear through a "shower of bullets, and shell." Since standing in the open, exposed to the fire of Ripley's men and the 4th Alabama, seemed to be a bad idea for a rookie regiment, Colonel Knipe suggested to Wanner that he charge into the Cornfield and drive the Confederates out. Knipe returned to his 46th Pennsylvania and ordered it to join the 128th's advance.[6]

To Colonel William L. DeRosset, commanding the 3rd North Carolina, the 128th was so large it looked like a brigade in column of battalions, and it was moving squarely toward his exposed right flank. He went to Colonel Doles and asked for orders. According to DeRosset, Doles responded, "Colonel, I don't know what to do, have just lost my Major, and I wish you would act as you think best." As Doles later developed into a top-notch brigade commander, DeRosset's account might seem questionable, but the situation at that point was enough to test the mettle of even the most experienced officer. Doles had never commanded a brigade, so we must consider the possibility that DeRosset did not exaggerate. "Disgusted beyond measure," the colonel hurried back to his regiment and moved down his line, stopping to inform each company commander to prepare to "change front to rear on 10th company." What DeRosset wanted his regiment to do was to change from facing northwest to facing northeast, the direction from which the 128th and 46th Pennsylvania were approaching. This was an exceptionally difficult maneuver to execute under fire, as it called for each company to about face and then wheel to their left to form the new line. DeRosset's 10th was the left company in the original line of battle, but when the maneuver was complete, it would become the right company. The risk of a stampede once the men faced to the rear was considerable, and nearly 1 out of 5 in the regiment were recent conscripts, which elevated the peril. But it was the only way the 3rd North Carolina could confront the enemy's advance with the regiment's full firepower. DeRosset made it to eight of his companies, but when he reached the 2nd Company (second from the right), a bullet struck him in the thigh and traveled to his hip, inflicting a permanently disabling wound. Many others were hit at the same time. "Here the great slaughter of my officers and men took place," recalled DeRosset.[7]

Certain personal tragedies forever imprinted themselves on the memory of Major Stephen D. Thruston, who assumed command when DeRosset was wounded. He saw Lieutenant Tom Cowan in Company B supporting the head of Lieutenant Bill Quince, who had been shot in the breast and head, "in the hollow of his elbow, giving him water from his canteen," when a Federal bullet struck Cowan in the head, mortally wounding him. Captain Edward H. Rhodes, the Company G commander, a 30-year-old bachelor farmer from Onslow County, North Carolina, had "a handkerchief around his thigh vainly trying to stop life's ebbing current," before another bullet struck him in the heart and killed him. Nearby, Thruston spotted Lieutenant George W. Ward, a 29-year-old teacher from Duplin County, North Carolina, "with one arm dangling in his sleeve, and sword in his other hand waving on and encouraging 'B' Co."

Despite the murderous fire and their losses, the regiment executed the change of front, one of the most remarkable feats of battlefield discipline and maneuver under fire by troops of either army at Antietam. DeRosset, in his post-battle writing, gave the impression that the maneuver was flawlessly executed. The reality, however, was different. Smoke blanketed the field, and the noise of hundreds of muskets and rifles discharging, along with the incessant artillery fire, drowned out voice commands. During the course of the movement, every officer in companies B, C, D, E, F, G, and I were shot down, not to mention dozens of enlisted men. It is simply impossible to believe there was not some amount of confusion under these circumstances. In one postwar letter, Thruston admitted that the men "wavered" in the movement, and that he "called upon the officers to steady the men." Captain David Williams, the commander of Company K, "who knew not fear," proved to be crucial in helping to keep the men together and preventing panic. Thruston modestly downplayed his own conspicuous role in doing the same for the regiment. When he observed the corporal bearing the state colors face to the rear (the 3rd North Carolina was one of those rare Confederate regiments that carried both state colors and a battle flag), Thruston ordered him to turn around and face toward the enemy. As the corporal did so, a bullet struck and killed him instantly. Thruston caught the colors from the dying corporal and, at the same moment, saw friendly troops moving up on their right. With the flag as a rallying point, he called on the men to advance, and they responded with the rebel yell. The line then surged into the Cornfield toward the Pennsylvanians.[8]

What made Thruston's decision to charge so extraordinary was that his regiment was a wreck. Out of 547 officers and men, nearly half were casualties, including all the officers of seven companies. After such severe losses, most soldiers—with justification—would have seen the arriving reinforcements as their relief and withdrawn. But Thruston and DeRosset reflected the aggressiveness that Lee encouraged and cultivated in the Army of Northern Virginia, which made it such a dangerous opponent.[9]

Parts of the 128th Pennsylvania had advanced nearly to the southern edge of the corn when the 3rd North Carolina completed its change of front and Thruston's counterattack burst upon them. The 46th Pennsylvania had joined the 128th when it moved forward but halted at the northern Cornfield fence, from which it unleashed into the ranks of the North Carolinians "a fire so well directed that, if well supported, would have compelled the enemy to give way." The 46th probably created the bulk of the carnage in the ranks of the 3rd North Carolina, but with so many rifles, the 128th certainly scored hits as well. In their inexperience and unfamiliarity with their weapons, however, they also inflicted damage in their own ranks. "Many of our men were wounded by those behind them," complained Corporal Robert Andrews on September 21, in the sort of letter that rarely found its way into postwar regimental histories. Two of his comrades, Robert Mann and William Haldeman, were felled by fire from the rear; Mann died of his wounds, and Haldeman was killed instantly. As for Andrews, he "never expected to leave the field alive, by the way the bullets whistled by us." Frank Holsinger in the 8th Pennsylvania Reserves, who watched the 128th's charge, saw the confusion and friendly fire: "The terrible destruction that they received was due largely to their excitement—the rear division firing into the front." The 128th Pennsylvania's lack of training, their excitement, the terrain, and the enemy fire caused the line that Colonel Knipe had helped them form degenerate into more of a mob, crowding through the corn. Frederick Crouse could not see any Confederates, but their bullets, balls, and buckshot tore through cornstalks and were "doing us great damage." The fire from the 3rd North Carolina, augmented by part of the 1st North Carolina, which was on their left, checked the 128th's advance and inflicted significant damage on the big regiment, but what drove them and the 46th Pennsylvania back was a cross-fire from the 4th Alabama. Captain Robbins had alertly noticed that the enemy's flank was vulnerable and shifted part of his regiment to shoot into it. His men "poured in [fire] with all the vim from our sheltered post in the wood to their great annoyance and discomfiture."[10]

No other regiment in Ripley's brigade joined Thruston's counterattack into the Cornfield, because the brigade had minimal command and control, and they were confronted by a new threat—the arrival of General George H. Gordon's brigade on the gentle ridge about 150 yards north of the corn. Gordon's brigade had initially marked time behind Crawford, just west of the Poffenberger Woods. When Crawford's regiments began to move forward, Gordon received orders, possibly from Mansfield, to support a battery on the right. What battery this was is unknown, but also irrelevant, since before the brigade had moved any distance, Gordon received urgent orders to move with "all possible dispatch" to Hooker's support. Gordon turned his regiments at the double-quick toward where they appeared to be needed—the ridge where Ransom's and Matthews's batteries were located. Gordon, a Harvard-educated attorney and West Point graduate with a distinguished Mexican War record, was the best brigade commander in the 12th Corps. He was responsible for five regiments, totaling 2,210 men. Two were brand new—the 13th New Jersey and the 107th New York—and they constituted over half of the brigade's manpower. The other three were crack veteran units: the 2nd Massachusetts, the 3rd Wisconsin, and the 27th Indiana. Gordon dropped off his rookies before his command came under fire, sending the 13th New Jersey, commanded by future Antietam historian Colonel Ezra A. Carman, to watch the corps' right flank. He left the 107th New York as a reserve near Poffenberger Woods, advising them that the woods were to be "held at all hazards." This left Gordon with slightly over 1,000 officers and men in his three veteran regiments.[11]

The stake-and-rider fences along Joseph Poffenberger's farm lane obstructed these units' way into the North Woods. "To push these down sufficient for us to scramble over them is only the work of a moment," remembered Edmund R. Brown, a 17-year-old farm boy in the 27th Indiana. But clearing the road's fences caused enough confusion in the formation that the regiments halted in the woods to re-form and drop their knapsacks. Brown recalled that during the halt in the woods, "we can hear a peculiar singing, humming noise in the tree tops." Twigs and small branches and limbs drifted down on the men "as if an army of locusts was at work in this grove." But the workers in this instance were shrapnel, shell fragments, and bullets. As the three regiments emerged from the woods, orders were shouted: "Battalion, deploy into line of battle, double quick, march." Each regiment swiftly and efficiently moved from column into line, with the 27th Indiana on the left, the 3rd Wisconsin in the center, and the 2nd Massachusetts on the right. The movement was executed "as though we had been on a parade ground instead of a battle-field," opined Lieutenant Julian Hinkley in the 3rd Wisconsin.[12]

Beyond the woods, "a scene of horror and grandeur" unfolded before them. Battle smoke and some last vestiges of the early morning mist clung to the field, "giving a spectral appearance to objects but a short distance away." The Confederates' "shouts of exultation"—the rebel yell—was audible over the roar of the firing. John R. Rankin, a 19-year-old 1st Sergeant in the 27th Indiana, observed that "disaster and destruction were everywhere in sight. Riderless horses dashed over the field, dead and dying men covered the ground and dismounted artillery is piled up in heaps." Rankin had exaggerated somewhat. On this part of the field, there were some dead and dying, but they did not cover the ground. Nor was there any dismounted artillery—that is, gun tubes knocked from their carriages. Thompson's abandoned guns were to Rankin's left front, which is probably what he referred to.[13]

When a regiment formed a line of battle, the proper position for the colonel was in the center rear of the line, where, theoretically, he could see his entire command when mounted. But the 27th Indiana's colonel, Silas Colgrove, sensed that in this fight, his men needed more conspicuous leadership to inspire them, so he guided his horse forward, in front of the line. Colgrove was a tough disciplinarian and had been despised in the early days of the regiment, but now it was impossible not to admire his courage. Young Edmund Brown noticed how the colonel rode with a quiet ease, "setting his face straight to the front, except when it was necessary for him to turn to give commands." As the regiment moved from column into line, stray Confederate fire killed one man in the regiment and wounded several others. Yet, Brown observed, for his colonel, "there was not a twitching of a muscle, not a quaver of the voice, not a movement or condition of any kind, which indicated that he felt himself in the least personal danger, or was in any way influenced by the peculiar surroundings." Such exposure by Colgrove and others might appear to be foolish bravado, but they understood that courage—like fear—could be infectious. Rankin wrote about how each man "has to fight within his own breast" during his struggle "between conscience and cowardice." For the frightened infantryman in the ranks of the 27th Indiana, such as Sergeant Rankin and Private Brown, watching their colonel fearlessly riding in front of them gave them strength to meet the severe test ahead. The colonels of the other two regiments, Thomas Ruger in the 3rd Wisconsin and George L. Andrews in the 2nd Massachusetts, were both West Point graduates and possessed the same sturdy fiber as Colgrove. The quality of their leadership was reflected in the excellence of their regiments.[14]

Colgrove's regiment had two distinctions. The first was the two noncoms from the regiment who had discovered Lee's Special Orders No. 191 on September 13. Coincidentally, these two belonged to the company that gave the 27th Indiana its other distinction. Second, the soldiers of Company F were referred to as the "giants," with every man over 6 feet tall. The company commander, Captain Peter Kop, was just over 6 feet 4 inches, while 1st Sergeant Bloss, one of the two Federals who discovered Special Orders No. 191, stood a solid 6 feet 2 inches.[15]

In front of Gordon, a remnant of what probably was the 4th Pennsylvania Reserves of Magilton's brigade were seen clustered around their colors. To their right was a remnant of the 7th Pennsylvania Reserves. "What a reception they give us!" recalled Sergeant Rankin. These men began to yell, wave their hats, "and act as if though they want to embrace every one of us." The 4th and 7th Reserves moved out of the way to let Gordon's regiments move past them. Then, to the surprise of Gordon's men, they started to "about face, reform their ranks, and move back before us, to renew the struggle."[16]

The brigade went past Thompson's abandoned battery. As it did so, 1st Sergeant Rankin noticed a single artilleryman trying to unharness an uninjured horse from its limber. There was something odd about the man. He had his cap pulled down over his eyes, "and he moves slowly around, as though he had a whole day in which to do his work." He seemed oblivious to all going on around him, and Rankin concluded that "he is evidently in bad mental health."[17]

Gordon's infantrymen saw that the Confederate riflemen "were making serious havoc" among Ransom's battery. They had driven the crews from the guns and killed or crippled many of its horses. But Ransom's men were made of tough fiber. They waited until the infantry came up on line with their guns and then emerged from their hiding places, in order to re-crew their pieces and deal out punishment to their tormentors.[18]

The 27th Indiana and the 3rd Wisconsin arrived on the ridge first. The 2nd Massachusetts was delayed getting around Ransom's battery and arrived a few minutes later. The Midwesterners saw the 128th Pennsylvania falling back through the Cornfield toward the East Woods, with the 3rd North Carolina in pursuit. The height of the corn made it difficult to see the North Carolinians, but their regimental colors, one of them carried by Major Thruston, stuck up above the cornstalks and gave away their position. Beyond the Cornfield, Colonel Colgrove observed "three regiments in line of battle, and farther to the right, on a high ridge of ground, was still another regiment in line diagonally to our line." Colgrove accurately described the position of Ripley's regiments. The 4th Georgia was on the plateau south of the corn, deployed to meet a potential attack from beyond the Hagerstown Pike. The 44th Georgia and the 1st North Carolina were on the 4th's right, but they were facing Colgrove's line. The 1st may have been separated into battalions, which would account for why Colgrove counted three regiments south of the Cornfield.[19]

All three of these Confederate regiments immediately opened fire on the 27th Indiana and the 3rd Wisconsin when the Federals arrived on the ridge, even though the range was between 400 and 450 yards—extreme for rifled muskets, and far beyond the range for smoothbores. Only the 3rd North Carolina was close enough to inflict real damage. The Midwesterners were the Rebels' primary target, because the majority of the 2nd Massachusetts, moving through Miller's orchard and garden, were on lower ground and thus were only partially visible. Lieutenant Charlie Mills observed, "I did not see one of our men hit while we were in that orchard." The 27th and the 3rd initially had to stand and take the fire from the 3rd North Carolina, at least until the 128th Pennsylvania cleared their front. Colonel Colgrove prudently rode around in the rear of his line, where he could better direct his regiment and not present the enemy with an easy target. He permitted his men to conduct individual fire if they were certain of their target, so some shots rang out from the 27th's line, but most of the Hoosiers and everyone in the 3rd Wisconsin set their jaws and simply endured the effects from the enemy's musketry. As bullets and balls scorched through his line, 1st Sergeant Rankin admitted that "thoughts of a selfish nature begin to crowd on my mind. I begin to calculate in my chances of escape. . . . How much would I give to be away from here?" As Rankin pondered afterward, "What keeps me here in my place? Not honor, but reputation. If I could sneak away I would be willing to try to settle the matter with conscience. . . . Of course the rebels must be driven back across the Potomac, but the absence of one musket will not make any difference in the general result. I am about half Quaker, anyhow." Like thousands of others that fateful day, Rankin wrestled with his conscience—thoughts of self-preservation struggling with his duty as a soldier—but in the end he remained.[20]

General Alpheus Williams met the 128th Pennsylvania as it reemerged from the Cornfield. He directed it and the 46th Pennsylvania to withdraw to the northern finger of the East Woods and re-form. Meanwhile, on Gordon's line, some confusion existed over whether the men advancing through the corn toward them were Rebels or Yankees. Some of the rank and file in the 27th Indiana were positive they were the former, but noncoms and line officers repeated the caution of Colonel Colgrove and instructed the 27th not to fire on what they thought were their own men. Edmund Brown declared, "It was impossible, at the distance they were then away, to distinguish them from Union troops, by their appearance alone. In the haze or smoke which rested upon the field, their uniforms looked as much like blue as gray." Moreover, in the smoky atmosphere, the 3rd North Carolina's battle flag appeared to be the stars and stripes. Only 2 or 3 minutes—but which must have seemed like an eternity—ticked by while the two Federal regiments endured the enemy fire, suffered casualties, and waited for the 128th Pennsylvania to clear their front. By this point the identity of the advancing soldiers had been resolved, and Colonel Colgrove's voice "rings out like a clarion: 'Battalion, make ready!'" Rifles were shouldered and the

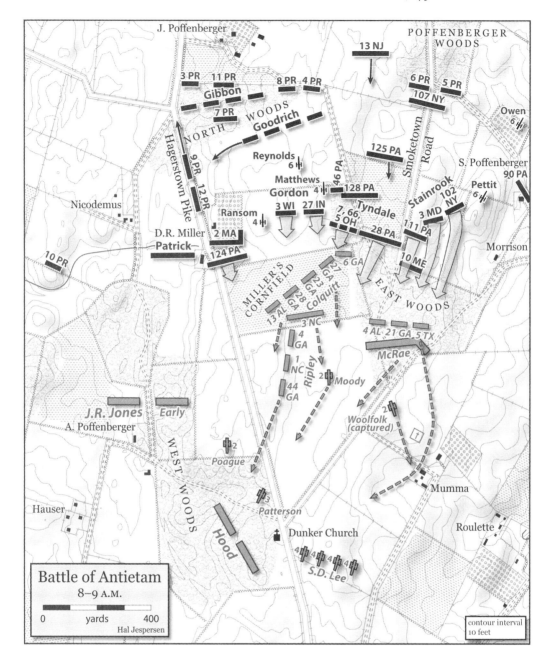

Battle of Antietam
8–9 A.M.

0   yards   400

Hal Jespersen

contour interval
10 feet

hammers pulled back into firing position. "Now, aim good and low, boys!" Colgrove instructed, which was repeated by the company officers. Then the colonel shouted, "Take aim, fire!" and a volley exploded from the 27th's line. The 3rd Wisconsin opened at the same time, with both regiments directing their volleys on the 3rd North Carolina.[21]

The shots from over 700 rifles inflicted considerable damage on the already hard-hit Tarheels. Major Thruston, carrying one of the 3rd's colors, miraculously survived the fusillade, but Edmund Brown, in the 27th Indiana, noticed that it seemed as though nearly half of the North Carolinians seemed to stumble and fall. The remainder immediately halted "and begin mixing among themselves, as if confused about something. We can see the officers exerting themselves very energetically." Both the 27th Indiana and the 3rd Wisconsin reloaded and poured steady volleys into the confused group. The Confederate survivors dropped down in the corn for some concealment and returned the fire, but heavy casualties, particularly among the regimental leadership, and a dwindling ammunition supply quickly rendered their position untenable, so they began to fall back. The North Carolinians emerged from the corn near a rock outcropping Alexander Gardner photographed on September 19, where a monument to the 90th Pennsylvania now stands. Here they were elated to be greeted by the sight of Colonel Alfred Colquitt's mixed brigade of Georgians and Alabamians hurrying up to their support. With this infusion of fresh troops, the conflict was about to begin another of its deadly surges of violence.[22]

When D. H. Hill ordered Colonel Doles to advance Ripley's brigade toward the Cornfield, he left his other four brigades in position at various points along the Sunken Lane, where they guarded the Confederate army's center. The question is why he did not send the other brigades in at the same time. Part of the answer is because there was no overall commander on this part of the field who could apprise Hill of what level of reinforcements was needed, and Hill had to balance maintaining an adequate force to defend the center with reinforcing the Confederates' left. It was not until he personally rode forward to guide Doles into position that he probably realized just how precarious the situation on the left was. Rather than moving Ripley's brigade to support Hood, which seems to have been what he understood was its mission, Hill discovered Hood's brigades in retreat. This left Ripley unsupported, except by the three regiments in the East Woods, which Hill did not know were there. It appeared to Hill that the Confederate's left was in danger of collapse, so he dispatched orders summoning three of his remaining four brigades—Colquitt's, McRae's and Rodes's—which left the center guarded by G. B. Anderson's single brigade. These brigades were not adjacent to one another, and they received their orders to move in staggered order. Because of the different distances they were from the Cornfield, they arrived in succession, although Rodes's men did not even reach it.

The first to set out was Colonel Alfred Colquitt's brigade of approximately 1,320 men, consisting of four Georgian regiments and an Alabamian one. They had spent the night of September 16 in the Sunken Lane, immediately west of its intersection with the Roulette farm lane. During the night, some men in the 27th Georgia wandered over to either Henry Piper's or William Roulette's farmhouse and discovered, to their delight, a considerable quantity of hard cider in the cellar of the house. Ben Milikin, a Company I sergeant, was part of the party, and he recounted how they knocked in the heads of the casks and started the cider flowing. The men guzzled it down on empty stomachs, until Milikin admitted that "the first thing I knew I was so drunk that I was afraid I could not get back to the regiment." For a few blissful minutes the war, with all its hardships, was forgotten, but Milikin and his inebriated comrades eventually made their way back and found their regiment. Its men were in Piper's large cornfield, south of the Sunken Lane, gathering ears of corn to roast over fires made with Piper's fence rails. Occasionally a divisional staff officer would come by and order the men to put the fires out—since it identified their position to the enemy—but after he left, Colquitt would come around and countermand the order, telling the men to start their fires again and eat their fill of roasted corn.[23]

Alfred Colquitt, a 38-year-old from Macon, Georgia, was popular in the brigade. As a young man, he had served as a major in a volunteer regiment during the Mexican War, which helped advance his career in politics and law. He married well, wedding Dollie Tarver—the daughter of a wealthy plantation owner who was a major general in the state militia—in 1848, which provided Colquitt with a plantation of his own and over 100 enslaved people. His politics largely reflected those of his father, Walter, who had served as both a U.S. congressman and a senator from Georgia. In 1850, when Congress wrestled with the question of whether holding people in slavery should extend into the territories conquered in the Mexican War, Walter advocated secession if slavery was banned. Ten years later, his son Alfred, now a state legislator, campaigned for John C. Breckinridge in the 1860 presidential election. After Lincoln won, Alfred encouraged Georgia's secession from the Union and voted for it at the state's convention on this issue. When Georgia left the Union, he immediately sought military service, securing a commission as captain in the 6th Georgia Infantry. But a man of Colquitt's intelligence, personality, and presence—he was physically powerful and had an athlete's grace—did not remain for long as a line officer. By May 1861, he was elected as his regiment's colonel. Battlefield attrition and seniority left him in command of Gabriel Rains's brigade after Rains and two other colonels were wounded at the Battle of Seven Pines. Colquitt did well in brigade command. After the Seven Days Battles, a group of officers from the brigade recommended his promotion to brigadier general. His division commander, D. H. Hill, who was notoriously spare with praise for anyone, agreed that the Georgian was deserving of a higher rank. Colquitt upheld Hill's confidence with his skillful handling of his brigade at South Mountain. The position he selected for the 23rd and 28th Georgia, part way down the mountain, defied the best efforts of Gibbon's excellent brigade to break through their line, and it enabled his men to inflict heavy casualties on the Midwesterners while suffering relatively light losses in return. Colquitt's promotion to brigadier general had been approved and would reach the army on September 17, but not until the fighting ended.[24]

It was probably around 7:30 a.m. when Hill's orders reached Colquitt. Because of their urgency, Colquitt did not wait for his skirmish battalion—one company from each regiment, who were deployed north of Roulette's farm—to be retrieved, but instead moved without them. The brigade moved at the double-quick, marching west for a short distance along the Sunken Lane. Then, leaving the lane, they skirted north along the western edge of Samuel Mumma's cornfield. Past it, they turned northwest, hurrying by Mumma's burning buildings. Here they were exposed to a "heavy artillery fire" from the Union guns east of Antietam Creek, which inflicted several casualties. Ben Witcher in the 6th Georgia, at the tail of the column, also recalled a "heavy musketry" fire, which could only have been overshots from the fighting near the Cornfield. The five regiments hurried across the plowed field north of Mumma's burning farm, toward the East Woods, out of which trickled the wounded from Ripley's brigade and Robbins's stalwart band. These injured men cheered the reinforcements, encouraging them to "give 'em hell boys." Sergeant Ben Milikin in the 27th Georgia never forgot this encouragement, for, in the coming minutes, "we went in and got hell ourselves." Colquitt and D. H. Hill met them at Smoketown Road and ordered the men to deploy. They approached the battle zone with the 13th Alabama in front, followed by the 28th, 23rd, 27th, and 6th Georgia. The first three regiments moved through the southwestern tip of the East Woods and into the meadow south of the Cornfield. It was the same moment when the 3rd North Carolina launched its counterattack into the Cornfield against the 128th Pennsylvania, and the 27th Indiana and the 3rd Wisconsin appeared on the ridge north of the Cornfield.[25]

Colonel Birkett Fry's 13th Alabama hurried west from the East Woods until they arrived near the 4th Georgia, when they then fronted north and formed into line. The 28th and 23rd Georgia came up on the 13th's right and extended the line toward the East Woods. About half the 27th Georgia was in Miller's meadow, beside the 23rd Georgia, while the other half was in the woods. The entire 6th Georgia were inside the East Woods. Since all the regiments were engaged almost immediately, there are few references to whether the regiments moved forward together or were more staggered. What evidence does exist indicates the latter. The brigade had double-quicked uphill and down, over plowed fields and meadows and across fences, for nearly a mile, so the men probably arrived winded and, possibly, were strung out. Jeremiah Stallings, a 13th Alabama private, recalled that the center of his regiment was near the large rock pile where Major Thruston and the survivors of the 3rd North Carolina had rallied. Part of the 1st North Carolina was also still in this vicinity, so there must have been some confusion in sorting out the units from one another. Colquitt asked Major Thruston if the North Carolinians would protect his left flank, which, recalled Thruston, "was done to the best of our ability"—that is, the 3rd and 1st North Carolina regiments shifted to their left to clear Colquitt's front. The major watched Colquitt's men sweep forward in "beautiful order." If there had been confusion due to fatigue or to units mingling with one another, it was quickly overcome.[26]

The 6th Georgia was the last of Colquitt's regiments to deploy. They were fired on by the 10th Maine, whom they could see on the opposite side of the woods. The regiment was already partially scattered from the nearly mile-long run they had just made, and the small-arms fire caused further disorder. Displeased with this, the 6th's commander, Lieutenant Colonel James N. Newton, ordered a halt, sent guides out to establish right and left markers for the regiment to align on, and then dressed the regiment on them until the line "was as cool as on dress parade." What worried Ben Witcher more than the bullets humming around him were some cows that had miraculously survived the fighting and were running around, terror stricken, in the woods. "I remember I was more afraid of being run over by a cow than of being hit by a bullet," wrote Witcher. Ignoring the fire from the 10th Maine, which must have been random, since they were primarily engaged with Major Robbins's mixed command, the 6th Georgia hurried forward to catch up with the rest of the brigade, which had continued on. To maintain their connection with the 27th Georgia on their left and clear Robbins's men, whom they found in front of them, the 6th moved at a left oblique, which brought the left of the regiment out of the East Woods and into the meadow south of the Cornfield.[27]

As Colquitt's regiments came within range, they opened fire on Gordon's men, who were silhouetted along the ridge north of the Cornfield. Like Ripley's regiments, they began the engagement at long range, nearly 400 yards. This probably explains why the opposing lines did not annihilate one another in minutes. It also answers why, after his men had fired only a few rounds, Colquitt concluded that trading fire at such a range was ineffective. He then ordered a charge to drive the enemy off and capture Ransom's and Matthews's batteries. Passing over windrows of casualties from the earlier fighting and raising a yell, the five regiments charged into the corn, loading and firing as they advanced. The 3rd and part of the 1st North Carolina followed them. The battle had raged like a wildfire throughout the morning, flaring up to terrible crescendos as each army fed brigades into the action, then pausing, as if to catch its breath, as the men fought themselves out and were replaced with fresh units, before roaring to life again. The arrival of Colquitt was like a bellows blowing on a fire, and the conflict surged to a new and furious level.[28]

IN THE EAST WOODS, Captain Robbins's regiments held on tenaciously, keeping the 10th Maine at bay in the front while mauling the flank of the 128th Pennsylvania when it charged into the Cornfield. The 4th Alabama and the 5th Texas had been in action since 7 a.m., for over an hour, and the 21st Georgia had been engaged off and on since first light, for over 2 hours. Because they had good cover, their losses had been moderate, although, unbeknownst to Robbins, one of his regiment's casualties was his younger brother, Madison. Madison and a comrade, Sergeant Ira Marshall, who went by his middle name Abe, were lying near the left of the regiment behind a rock outcropping about 3 feet high and wide enough to barely cover the two men. It gave them a good position to fire into the flank of the 128th during its charge. The two young men would rise up from behind the rock each time they fired. The pattern proved to be fatal, for after several rounds, when Madison rose to fire, a Union soldier in the woods, perhaps from the right of the 10th Maine or in one of the several regiments of Crawford's brigade that mingled in the northwestern part of the woods, shot him in the throat. He fell back uttering, "Abe, I'm gone," and was dead.[29]

Robbins had two problems with maintaining his hold on the East Woods: ammunition and manpower. He needed both. When he sent a runner back to General Law, asking for reinforcements, he was told, "Hold your position, Hill is moving to your support," meaning D. H. Hill. But while Hill's brigades provided some indirect support by engaging Union forces west of the East Woods and on its northwestern edge, Robbins received no reinforcements. Ammunition was critical. "I had sent two or three messengers back for more," wrote Robbins, "but somehow we in the wood were overlooked & no supply came." The riflemen raided the cartridge boxes of the dead and wounded lying nearby, and Captain Ike Turner even sent details from his 5th Texas outside the woods to search bodies for ammo. Turner also sent four different runners back to division headquarters for ammunition. None came. Yet Robbins and Turner, and their men, refused to contemplate retreat. "You will pardon me for saying that the handful that remained was pure grit," wrote Robbins. This was true, but their stubborn stand was also possible because of the excellent cover the boulder-strewn woods provided. So long as their ammunition held out, a frontal assault was unlikely to dislodge them. The difficulty of driving them out underscored why Hooker had been desperate not to lose Union control of the woods.[30]

The engagement between the 10th Maine and Robbins's command in the East Woods was utterly unlike the popular image of Civil War combat, with lines of battle standing up out in the open and blazing away at one another. It bore a resemblance to what American soldiers who fought in Afghanistan or Vietnam or World Wars I and II would have experienced. "I didn't see a single Rebel," wrote Lieutenant Edwin A. Fowler in Company A, the second company from the right in the 10th Maine. Others made the same observation. George Smith in Company E related that he and his comrades simply fired at the sound of and probably the smoke from the guns, because the Confederates were so well concealed. The men of the 10th also did their best to find cover behind trees or anything else that might stop a bullet. In Company H, Xavier Martin related that they fired at random, the Confederates in his front not revealing themselves at all. Nevertheless, noted Lieutenant Fowler, "we were under a steady fire."

Lieutenant Granville Blake thought the Confederates "were the best marksmen that we ever met." They two sides fought to a stalemate. "We did not drive the rebs, nor did they drive us," observed Lieutenant Blake.[31]

When Colonel Beal and Lieutenant Colonel Fillebrown were wounded at the opening of the action, it left Major Charles Walker in command of the 10th Maine. As related earlier (see chapter 5), Walker had been sick with diarrhea for nearly a month, a condition that could be debilitating. Whatever his difficulty, Walker gave no orders and exercised no leadership. "Each captain was his own commander," wrote Captain George Nye in Company K.[32]

The regiment's wounded caused a steady trickle of able-bodied men to leave the fighting line to assist the more seriously wounded back. One of the latter was Captain Nathan Furbish, the Company I commander, who was shot in the head when he stood up to fire his pistol. Company I was the color company, which protected the national colors, the single flag the 10th Maine carried. When Furbish fell, Lieutenant Hebron Mayhew told Color Sergeant Charles C. Graham, "we don't need them colour here just now, you and Corpl Dempsey take the captain back till you find an ambulance you can get him in to." Graham tucked the national colors under his arm, while Dempsey slung his rifle over his back, and the two men carried Furbish toward the rear to find an ambulance, despite the fact that "the brain hung out over his right eye as large as a small sized hen's egg." They found an ambulance, but the driver inspected the captain and declared him dead. Graham and Dempsey somehow convinced him to drive the mortally wounded officer to a field hospital. With their mission completed, the two men did not hurry back to their regiment. Instead, they made their way to a single tree in a field to cool off and, for Dempsey, to rest a twisted ankle. Confederate artillery rounds landing uncomfortably close flushed them from their resting place, and by the time they approached where their regiment had been, some other soldiers they met said it had been relieved.[33]

In another incident, Charles Harris of Company B was shot through the lungs, and three comrades carried him to the rear. This was how the strength of a unit in combat dissipated. Two men here, three men there, withdrawing from each company and helping wounded to the rear, steadily eroded a regiment's cohesion and firepower. Firmer leadership could diminish but not stop it. Lieutenant Edwin Fowler assessed what happened in the 10th Maine with refreshing honesty: "I don't like to say so—but it was a clear case of sneak on the part of the regt. . . . We skulked—the regiment could have stayed in the woods an hour if need be." The trouble, continued Fowler, was not the men, who were brave enough, but the officers—specifically the field officers. "If our field officers had been possessed of any courage, and had not palpably shown the white feather before the men, you would not have been obliged to search for the achievements of one man with a view to covering the deficiencies of the many." Fowler used the plural, but he most likely meant the singular. Beal and Fillebrown were wounded at the beginning of the action and out of the fight. Fowler was writing about Walker. Henry Smith in Company E encountered the major lying face down behind the line when he and another man carried a badly wounded comrade back. Smith exclaimed loudly, "For God's sake is there no one to command us today?" He was sure Walker heard him, but his exclamation brought no reaction. Lieutenant Ben Redlon, commanding Company D, was furious at the way the regiment's numbers shrank away. He spotted Walker lying behind the line and demanded, "Who commands the regiment?" Walker replied, "I don't know." Thus the 10th Maine, a good regiment, but lacking regimental leadership, gradually leaked men to the rear.[34]

Enough of the regiment kept up the fight to ensure that their position was not lost. Many of them saw the 6th Georgia and part of the 27th Georgia moving up along the western edge of the woods and fired at them. Some also saw yet another Confederate line enter the woods from the south, behind Robbins's command. It was the North Carolina brigade of Colonel Duncan McRae, the last of D. H. Hill's reinforcing brigades.[35]

MCRAE'S BRIGADE HAD BEEN battered 3 days earlier at the Battle of South Mountain, with 374 casualties, including their commander, General Samuel Garland. During the fight, four of its five regiments had been routed and forced to flee down the mountain. Internal politics and personality conflicts afflicted every volunteer command in both armies, but the problem was particularly acute in this brigade. Garland had provided firm leadership that earned his men's respect and kept the personal animosities and jealousies among the officers from affecting the brigade's battlefield performance. But with Garland dead, that restraint was removed. Duncan McRae elicited little respect throughout the brigade. The 42-year-old Fayetteville, North Carolina, attorney was intensely ambitious but dogged by controversy, most of his own making. Before the war, he was criticized for changing his party affiliation multiple times to win public office. Although a Whig, he ran as a Democrat in one election, and then as an independent against a Democrat in another. When he ran for governor in 1858, he was accused of changing his position on issues, depending on which part of the state he was campaigning in, a tactic not unfamiliar to some politicians today. He lost that election, then became a Stephen A. Douglas Democrat before he sensed this was a liability, and subsequently jettisoned his backing of Douglas to support secession. One newspaper joked, "Mr. McRae was a Democrat, then a Distributionist, then a Consul, then a Douglas Democrat and is now a disunionist, having marked all the phases through which he has passed by a candidacy for something, without a solitary election we recollect of." His morphing into a secessionist paid career dividends, however, and won McRae a commission as colonel of the 5th North Carolina Infantry. Despite lacking military experience, he managed his regiment competently and displayed courage on the battlefield. But he was widely disliked for being a strict disciplinarian, as well as having a prickly personality, being quick to pick a quarrel or take offense at the slightest provocation. One of his captains complained that the colonel was "a man whose passions and prejudices are paramount to his regard for truth or sense of justice." His first cousin, Lieutenant Colonel Thomas Ruffin Jr., who commanded the 13th North Carolina in the brigade, thought McRae a "bad, bad man" and maintained only a professional relationship with him, because Ruffin "feared [McRae] would involve me in some [of] the miserable feuds which his presence seems every where to breed."[36]

One of his quarrels had to do with Garland. When the army was reorganized on the Virginia Peninsula and Garland was assigned to command the brigade, McRae was furious. Garland was a Virginian, commanding a North Carolina brigade, and McRae believed he was the one who deserved the promotion. He complained loudly, threatening to resign, and then claimed that both Garland and D. H. Hill made "earnest solicitations" that he remain. When Garland was killed at South Mountain, McRae assumed command as the senior colonel. It was while under his command that the brigade was routed, prompting questions about his competency as a leader. But McRae made no egregious errors there. His defeat stemmed largely from poor support, which forced him to spread his brigade out over a very wide front, confronting aggressive, well-led Union troops who exploited the gaps in McRae's line. The principal problem seemed to be that Duncan McRae did not inspire confidence, either in his own regiment or in the brigade, and this led to trouble at Sharpsburg. As one Union officer observed, "Troops without confidence in their leaders are worth nothing."[37]

The losses at South Mountain reduced McRae's five regiments to only 756 officers and men. They spent the night of September 16 in the Sunken Lane, east of where the Roulette farm lane came into it. McRae estimated it was 15 minutes after Colquitt's brigade departed before he received his orders to follow the Georgian. His regiments formed up quickly and hurried west along the lane for a couple of hundred yards before turning north, skirting the hill that rises west of the Roulette farm lane and passing west of Mumma's farm. They halted near the Mumma cemetery to form a line of battle and received shelling from the Union batteries across Antietam Creek, but they inflicted few casualties and the regiments moved quickly across Mumma's plowed field toward the East Woods. Along the way, McRae received a warning from D. H. Hill that Colquitt might be in his front and not to fire on him accidentally.[38]

The brigade reached the southern boundary of the East Woods with the 20th North Carolina on the left and the 13th, 23rd, 12th and 5th North Carolina extending the line to the right. The 5th was the largest regiment in the brigade and contained a considerable number of conscripts whose exposure to combat at South Mountain had been jarring and psychologically crushing. The shelling they endured while crossing Mumma's plowed field further eroded their shaky morale. At the woods' edge, the brigade encountered a high, split-rail worm fence, which, as Adjutant Veines E. Turner of the 23rd North Carolina recorded, "disarranged our line" in crossing. They encountered some Texans emerging from the woods—possibly details Captain Turner had sent to hunt up ammunition. When they entered the woods, Captain Elijah B. Withers, commanding the 13th North Carolina, could see "an irregular line" of Confederates west of the woods, near the Cornfield, which was composed of Colquitt's and Ripley's brigades. But neither Withers nor anyone else mentioned seeing Captain Robbins's command.[39]

When the brigade entered the woods, it came under fire from what McRae described as "a slight skirmish line." This was the remnants of the 10th Maine, scattered along the woods' northern edge. With the 10th's regimental flag missing, it was difficult in the smoky atmosphere for McRae's men to determine if the line firing at them was friend or foe. Shouts rang out that it was Colquitt's brigade. McRae ordered his men not to fire until he could determine who the troops were. But the confusion continued to spread. "Here a state of confusion ensued which it is difficult to portray," reported Captain Thomas M. Garrett, commanding the 5th North Carolina. "Various conflicting orders [mere suggestions, perhaps, taking that shape] were passed down the line, the men in the ranks being allowed by the officers to join in repeating them, so that it became utterly impossible to understand what emanated from the proper authority." The brigade's movements were "vacillating and unsteady." They reached a line of boulders that extended randomly through the woods, and the men "fell down and sought shelter" behind them. For some odd reason they still did not discover Captain Robbins force, or, if they did, no one in either command mentioned it. Since the woods were largely free from underbrush, Captain Withers could look through the trees and observe U.S. flags and mounted officers moving toward them through the 10-acre cornfield north of the woods. They belonged to the 28th Pennsylvania, part of Brigadier General George S. Greene's 12th Corps division, which was about to tip the scales of the fight for the Cornfield and the East Woods.[40]

GREENE'S 2ND DIVISION FOLLOWED Gordon's brigade in the march from Line's and Hoffman's farms that morning. Like the 1st Division, the regiments marched in Mansfield's favored column of divisions. Lieutenant Colonel Hector Tyndale's 3rd Brigade led, followed by Colonel Henry Stainrook's 2nd Brigade and Colonel William B. Goodrich's 3rd Brigade. These commands were all small, having suffered heavy casualties at Cedar Mountain and even more non-battle losses during the Second Manassas Campaign, so the division numbered only 2,504 officers and men. As it marched across Joseph Poffenberger's farm, between Smoketown Road and the Poffenberger farm lane, and approached the battle area, General Williams rode up to speak with Greene. After his earlier meeting with Hooker, Williams had ridden to the northwestern corner of the East Woods, where he found the 128th Pennsylvania falling back before the 3rd North Carolina's counterattack. General confusion prevailed. He met Colonel Knipe, who was "greatly afflicted" and in tears over the death of Captain George A. Brooks, a close friend of his. Williams informed Knipe that Mansfield was mortally wounded, so Knipe was in command of the 1st Brigade. "I told him to look up the new regiments and to get the Brigade in order and do a dashing thing," recalled Williams. He also advised Knipe that Greene was approaching and would form on Knipe's left. The new responsibility inspired Knipe, "and he dashed off full of zeal."[41]

The disorder Williams saw in the corner of the East Woods convinced him not only of the urgent need to get Greene into action, but also that his deployment would need to be slightly modified to help support Knipe. Williams rode up to Greene, briefed him on Mansfield's condition, and gave him his orders. Greene was to detach Goodrich's brigade, to reinforce Doubleday's division near the Hagerstown Road. Hooker had wanted Greene to place his right on the Poffenberger farm lane and extend his left toward Mumma's farm. Williams modified these. The farm lane could still serve as a guide, but Williams wanted Greene to extend his right toward the northwestern corner of the East Woods, to give Knipe support, while still extending his left in the direction of Mumma's farm. Greene grasped the intent of his orders—to engage the enemy with his right and swing his left around and turn their right flank. The orders were Williams's, but the plan was Hooker's, who, throughout the morning, displayed a superb grasp of the tactical situation despite the smoke, mixed terrain, and confusion. The coordination he and Williams brought to the battle, and the lack of coordination on the Confederates' side, were about to prove decisive in the titanic struggle over the Cornfield and East Woods.[42]

Greene's arrival on the edge of the battle zone coincided almost exactly with the arrival of McRae's brigade in the East Woods, as well as with Colquitt's orders for his brigade to advance and drive the 3rd Wisconsin and the 27th Indiana from the ridge north of the Cornfield and capture the artillery there. That Colquitt's men responded as they did to his commands is a testament to their discipline, leadership, and morale. Ordering men who are in the open and under fire to advance is exceedingly difficult, because human nature recoils from the idea of moving farther into danger. Moreover, making orders heard and understood, and then having them executed in an environment of choking smoke, a deafening roar of weapons, and the typical confusion attendant with combat is extraordinarily challenging.

Edmund Brown, with the 27th Indiana, watched the Georgians and Alabamians approach, loading and firing as they moved, in order to keep up a constant fire on the Federal line in their front. "On and on they press," wrote Brown, "until they reach the [North Cornfield] fence, only seventy steps in front of the Twenty-Seventh. Those who observe them—how eager and persistent they are, stooping forward like a hunter stalking his prey, at last making one vigorous dash up to the fence and throwing themselves down behind it—will not soon forget the sight." "Spot! Spot! Spot! I heard their bullets striking our line," wrote 1st Sergeant Rankin. Soon thereafter came "crashing volleys simultaneously from each line." Rankin decided that "I will play the angel of mercy instead of the demon of vengeance." He would find a wounded comrade to bear back to a ravine, "a deep one, where rebel bullets can reach us not." Rankin did not have long to wait. His company commander, Captain John W. Wilcoxen, was hit. "A comrade with a heart as tender as my own takes one arm while I take the other," Rankin recorded. But Wilcoxen refused their help. "My disgust on finding the captain's hurt less severe than I had supposed is intense," fumed Rankin, who was forced to return to the dangerous firing line. Gradually, he wrote, as he loaded and fired mechanically, "I lose my desire to leave the field. . . . Thank God! My higher nature has triumphed. It has lifted me out of the mire of self and cowardice in which I floundered."[43]

Unlike the combat between the 10th Maine and Robbins's command in the East Woods, this was a stand-up fight. The Confederates had some concealment from the corn and cover from the northern Cornfield fence, but the 27th Indiana and 3rd Wisconsin were without any protection. "All stand perfectly erect," recalled Edmund Brown. "From first to last not a man lies down, kneels or stoops, unless he is hurt." While this was courageous, it led to appalling carnage. "Everyone that the eye rests upon, even for a moment, is seen to fall," observed Brown. He continued, "A soldier makes a peculiar noise in loading his gun, which attracts attention, but when we turn to look at him he falls. Another makes what he considers a good shot, and laughs over it. When others turn to inquire the cause, he falls. A third turns to tell the man in the rear rank not to fire so close to his face. Others glance in that direction, only to see both fall. All of these instances, and others, are observed by the writer at almost the same moment."[44]

A report from the 3rd Wisconsin provides detail on where the bullets made contact with human flesh—in the leg, sometimes both legs, arm, knee, foot, arm and leg, shoulder, hand, both hands, side, thigh, head, lungs, face, breast, neck, and back. Minie balls and musket balls that did not strike flesh passed through clothing and struck equipment. "Everyone standing here has bullet marks on his clothes," observed Rankin.[45]

"At times," recorded Rankin, "everything is enveloped in smoke, and we can only mark the rebel line by the red flashes from their guns." The smoke prevented the complete destruction of these two regiments, yet a breeze would occasionally push it away. During one of these times, Rankin, in the right wing of the 27th Indiana, looked to his right and saw only about 15 men standing in line to the left of the colors of the 3rd Wisconsin. In his own regiment, the right wing was also almost completely shot away. "Only twelve or fifteen remain," he observed. For some reason the Confederate fire was particularly heavy on the right wing of the 27th and the left wing of the 3rd. It also, as usual, concentrated on the colors and color guard. Sergeant Chauncy Beebe carried the national colors of the 3rd Wisconsin into the fight (the state colors were not with the regiment). He was shot in the shoulder and handed the flag to Corporal Charles Chubb, who held it for only a moment before he was hit in the hand. Chubb gave it to Corporal William Kimberly, who was also wounded in the hand. The flag then went to Henry C. Isbel, who was also wounded, although his name does not appear on the regiment's casualty report, and he gave the colors to Private John Green. Green's clothes were immediately "riddled with bullets and he received no less than seven flesh wounds," all of which he ignored until a bullet in the thigh forced him to give the flag to Corporal James G. Savage, the last member of the color guard. It was not long before Savage received a wound, which was listed as "slight." Nonetheless, he gave the flag to Lieutenant Julian Hinkley, the closest officer he could find, saying that he had to go to the hospital. Hinkley asked Private Joseph E. Collins from his company to take the colors, which he did, and Collins remained unharmed for the rest of the day. What is interesting about this succession of color bearers is that while each man was obviously brave, only Green stayed on the battlefield after being hit and thus was wounded more than once. Courage had boundaries that soldiers acknowledged and understood. It was perfectly honorable for someone like Corporal Savage to go to the rear with a slight wound, rather than remain in the fight and possibly be killed. The saga of the 3rd Wisconsin's color guard also speaks to the general inaccuracy of small-arms fire in the murky haze of Civil War combat, even at a range of under 100 yards. The colors always drew the greatest volume of fire, yet not a single member of the color guard was killed or received a mortal wound, despite standing on an open ridgeline.[46]

Although any wound gave a soldier an honorable exit from the fighting, many ignored those they considered to be inconsequential. Edmund Brown wrote that in the 27th Indiana, "there is scarcely a man on whom blood has not been drawn in some way." Sergeant John M. Bloss in Company F, one of the finders of Special Orders No. 191 four days earlier, offered some idea of what a soldier might consider an insignificant wound. In a letter home, he related that a comrade, Corporal Elijah McKnight, a 23-year-old farmer, was hit in the arm above and below the elbow, but that it was "a mere scratch and brusse, it was done in the beginning of the fight but did not disable him so he fought until it was over." In another instance, William C. Riley wrote about how he was hit in the left breast by a spent ball: "I thought it went plum thru me, it would not have hurt more if it had." He thought it strange that he did not fall down, so he felt the place where the ball had struck him, in order to find the hole where it went in. Riley discovered no discernable wound, "so I kept fighting all day." Riley's and McKnight's wounds were reported on their regimental casualty list, but there were others whose injuries were not. One such person was the 3rd Wisconsin's commander,

Colonel Ruger, who suffered a minor wound in the head and thought the injury "too slight" for his name to be added to the casualty list.[47]

In the 27th Indiana, the company of "giants" (Company F) was particularly hard hit, losing 50 men—nearly their entire strength—including everyone involved in the discovery of Special Orders No. 191. Sergeant Bloss was hit in the legs, 1st Sergeant John McKnight in the legs, Corporal Barton Mitchell in the left calf, and David Bur Vance in the hand and knee. Their company commander, Captain Peter Kop, survived the bloodbath on the ridge, only to be to hit by a stray round later in the day and mortally wounded. In his after-action report, Colonel Colgrove estimated that his regiment was engaged with Colquitt's and Ripley's brigades "for about two hours." No doubt it seemed to last that long, for it is exceptionally difficult for individuals to gauge the passage of time in combat.

Estimates of how long they were engaged vary dramatically for men involved in the same action. The 27th fired "as high as eighty, ninety, and even one hundred rounds each," which is a tremendous expenditure of ammunition. But if each soldier fired twice a minute—which is a reasonable estimate, since many would fire faster than that early in the action, and then slower later on, as their guns fouled with black powder and became more difficult to load—then the two regiments were in action for 40 to 50 minutes. For units as exposed as the 27th Indiana and the 3rd Wisconsin, this was an extraordinarily long time, even if part of that combat, against Ripley's graycoats, was at long range. Theirs was one of the most tenacious, remarkable stands by any of the regiments in the Army of the Potomac in this battle, or any battle that the army fought, yet it is little known. By standing firm against Colquitt's assault, despite appalling casualties, the 27th and 3rd served as the anvil for a Union counterattack that soon fell with devastating effect on the Georgians' and Alabamians' flank.[48]

Part of the Union hammer was the guns of Ransom's battery. When the 27th Indiana and 3rd Wisconsin took a position on the ridge to Ransom's left, they drew the bulk of the Confederates' fire, which enabled his gunners to re-crew the battery and blast Colquitt's line with canister. On Ransom's right, the 2nd Massachusetts was still in Miller's garden and orchard, where a north–south ridge to their left kept them out of view of the Confederates. The Bay Staters saw the 124th Pennsylvania lying down to their right front, in the swale north of the Cornfield and near the Hagerstown Pike, where they had halted after being sent into action earlier by General Williams. Because Colonel George Andrews's regiment was about 75 yards in advance of Ransom and the 3rd Wisconsin, he adopted an unusual formation: facing his left wing east and right wing south, so he could protect both his left flank and front, as well as fire in either direction. The right wing formed along the southern fence of Miller's orchard, and the left wing along the orchard's eastern fence. From his vantage point on higher ground, Colonel Ruger noticed that if Andrews slightly adjusted the position of his left wing, it could issue a raking, almost enfilading fire on the 13th Alabama and 28th Georgia in Ruger's front. Ruger suggested this to Andrews, who immediately made a "slight change of position" with his left wing to give it a field of fire. No one in the 2nd Massachusetts documented precisely what maneuver the left wing made. They probably crossed Miller's eastern orchard fence and moved a short distance farther east, where they had better fields of fire. Whatever it was, Lieutenant Charlie Mills described how they poured "a perfectly withering fire" into "a lot of rebels," inflicting numerous casualties.[49]

While the 2nd Massachusetts and Ransom's guns delivered fire on Colquitt's left flank, the leading elements of Hector Tyndale's 1st Brigade of Greene's division arrived opposite Colquitt's right flank. The brigade consisted of three small Ohio regiments—the 5th, 7th, and 66th—and the 28th Pennsylvania. It led Greene's column and numbered about 1,200 men. Three-quarters of them were in the 28th Pennsylvania, a huge regiment of 795 officers and men. But, unlike the other large regiments in the corps, the 28th were no rookies. They had organized in the summer and fall of 1861, and although they had participated in some skirmishes, they had not yet fought in a general engagement. They were a well-trained, disciplined, tactically proficient unit. They were also unusual, having 15 companies rather than the standard organization of 10. The Ohio regiments, in contrast, were mere skeletons. In the words of Lieutenant Colonel Eugene Powell, commanding the 66th Ohio, they had been "knocked to pieces" during the spring campaign in the Shenandoah Valley and at Cedar Mountain and never recovered. His own regiment numbered only 94 enlisted men and 4 officers. Together, the three Ohio regiments counted only 425 effectives. There had been talk that morning of combining them into a single maneuver unit, but this meant that two regiments would need to give up their colors, since there was agreement that three flags would cause confusion. No one was willing to do this, so the idea was abandoned, and the units went into action with their regimental organizations, tiny as they were, still intact.[50]

The Ohioans led the brigade. Because of their small size, they deployed rapidly, with the 7th on the right, the 66th in the center, and the 5th on the left. It took the 28th Pennsylvania's larger numbers longer to form up, so the Ohioans approached the woods ahead of them. Eugene Powell recalled that he saw some of the enemy north of the woods, who opened fire on his regiment, but his memory clearly failed him here. The 128th Pennsylvania, 46th Pennsylvania, and 28th New York were just north of the woods, where they were regrouping after Williams had pulled them back, so it was impossible that any Confederates had advanced as far as Powell claimed. What is more likely is that Powell's men came under fire from stray rounds loosed in the combat between Gordon's regiments and Colquitt's brigade. Powell rode behind his regiment, side by side with Major Orrin J. Crane, commanding the 7th Ohio. The regiments passed through the 10-acre Cornfield and over the "serious obstacle" of the Poffenberger farm lane's fences. Crane, Powell, and Major John Collins, commanding the 5th Ohio, then obliqued their commands to the right, in order to close the space between them and the 27th Indiana. Clouds of battle smoke hung like a mist and limited visibility. The smoke stayed close to the ground, rather than drifting upward. As the line advanced through the northwestern portion of the East Woods, Powell rode forward and was able to peer over the smoke from the back of his horse. He saw a line of Confederates behind a fence along the northern edge of the Cornfield. Their attention was riveted toward Gordon's men, whom they were firing at. They "did not observe or heed us," recalled Powell.[51]

It might seem puzzling that the Colquitt's men were unaware of the Ohioans' approach, but the clouds of black-powder smoke greatly limited visibility. There was also the earsplitting noise. "The roar of the infantry was beyond anything conceivable to the uninitiated," wrote General Williams to his daughter. "If all the stone and brick houses of Broadway should tumble at once the roar and rattle could hardly be greater, and amidst this, hundreds of pieces of artillery, right and left, were thundering as a sort of bass to the infernal music." Finally, it was the duty of the officers—particularly the field officers—not the enlisted men, to look for approaching threats. The enlisted men's duty was to engage the most immediate threat, which, for Colquitt, was Gordon's brigade. Officers of the 6th Georgia did observe Tyndale's approaching line, but, as we shall see, they were unable to react in time to save themselves.[52]

Powell rode back to his advancing men, pointed out where the Rebels were, and ordered them to open fire. Major Crane was certain Powell was mistaken and believed that the men in front were friendly troops. The Confederates were only 60 to 70 yards away, but even at this close range, the smoke made positive identification of friend and foe questionable. Crane attempted to stop what he was he was sure was a tragic mistake by Powell, but the colonel was equally confident it was the enemy. Getting in the first fire in such an encounter was critical. To avoid confusion, Powell ignored Crane and emphatically repeated his order to open fire. The 66th poured a volley into the 6th and 27th Georgia, immediately followed by volleys from the 7th and 5th Ohio.[53]

Ben Witcher was one of the few Georgians who may have seen Powell when he conducted his brief reconnaissance. He recalled seeing a federal officer ride forward alone and then ride back to a line of Union soldiers that suddenly appeared. Captain John G. Hanna, commanding Company B on the right flank of the 6th Georgia, also saw the Ohioans approaching and ran over to warn Lieutenant Colonel Newton that they were flanked. When he started back to his company, Hanna was killed by the initial blast of fire. This also mortally wounded Newton, who fell into the arms of Captain William H. Plane in Company H and one of Plane's men. Major Philemon Tracy, the only other field officer in the regiment, was already a casualty. He had been shot in the thigh during the attack through the corn. The bullet severed or nicked an artery, and he began to bleed out. Lieutenant Thomas Marshall in Company E paused to bandage Tracy's wound, but when he attempted to drag Tracy to a safer location, Marshall was shot in the side and had to abandon the major, who bled to death.[54]

Some of the Ohioans left the impression that the engagement between their regiments and Colquitt's was brief, and that the Georgians quickly broke, but this was not the case. Colquitt's men fought desperately to thwart the flank attack. At the other extreme, Captain Fred Seymour, of the 7th Ohio, thought the fight went on for half an hour before the Confederates broke. Seymour overestimated, but he reflected the fierce nature of Colquitt's resistance and the fact that it was not easily overcome. What destroyed the 6th Georgia and unraveled Colquitt's entire line was the 28th Pennsylvania.[55]

The 28th brought up the rear of Tyndale's brigade. As the Ohio regiments in front began to deploy, Major Ario Pardee Jr. shouted the commands, "Deploy from the right and left. First division right and left face. Double quick march." The regiment's column of divisions rapidly uncoiled into line. Sergeant William Armor in Company B was in the rear division of the regiment and could not hear Pardee's orders, which were drowned out by the roar of battle. nonetheless, Company B understood what Pardee wanted by the movements of the other companies and executed the maneuvers "as steadily as if on parade." The many months of training the regiment had gone through now paid off. Within 2 minutes, despite Confederate artillery fire and stray rounds from the fighting in front, the nearly 800 men in the 28th were deployed to bring their full firepower to bear. Pardee ordered bayonets fixed, and the enlisted men drew fearsome saber bayonets from their sheaths and attached them to their rifles. Some of Crawford's men, withdrawing from the fight and trying to get out of the way, created a certain amount of disorder, as did the stake-and-rider fences along the Poffenberger farm lane, but the well-trained soldiers quickly restored their line, which swept up toward the East Woods.[56]

Some of the 6th Georgia, and probably part of Robbins's 4th Alabamians farther south in the woods, saw the Pennsylvanians and opened what John Foering in Company D recalled was a "withering fire," wounding a number of men but failing to check the Pennsylvanians' momentum. Because of the configuration of the northern part of the East Woods, the right of the 28th entered the woods first, moving up onto what became known as Croasdale's Knoll, where Colonel Croasdale had been killed earlier. This brought the right wing of the 28th opposite the right front of the 6th Georgia, extending beyond that regiment's flank. Tyndale was riding behind the 28th, and he ordered it to open fire. No one in the 28th or the 6th Georgia ever forgot that volley. Sergeant Armor wrote that it "sounded like one gun." Joseph A. Moore, a private in Company O, described it as "one splendid burst of musketry." Joseph H. Cornet believed it was the "heaviest volley I have ever heard delivered by a single regiment—it cut down cornstalks and rebels alike." The fire was deadly accurate, and men literally went down in rows in the 6th Georgia. The right wing of the 28th raised a yell and charged forward, their saber bayonets flashing in the light.[57]

While the 28th Pennsylvania's right wing struck the exposed flank of the 6th Georgia, its left wing encountered the tough nut that was William Robbins's ad hoc command. Robbins's men, with some help from part of McRae's brigade, poured a terrific fire into the Pennsylvanians as they entered the woods. Sergeant William Armor declared it was "as hot for a little while as any battle I was in during the war." Orders to keep alignment with the colors, which advanced with the right wing, could not be obeyed, due to a "fatal flank fire." In less than 10 minutes, more than half of Armor's Company B were killed or wounded. But the Rebels soon had a new threat that relieved the pressure on the 28th. It was Colonel Henry J. Stainrook's tiny 2nd Brigade, only 587 strong. The leading regiment was Major Thomas M. Walker's 111th Pennsylvania, which, with 243 officers and men, accounted for nearly half of the brigade's strength. For some reason the 111th apparently departed from Mansfield's favored formation of double column of companies and instead were formed in column of companies. Greene directed Stainrook to establish his brigade on Tyndale's left. They crossed Smoketown Road and hurried toward the East Woods. There was no question whether the woods were occupied by the enemy. The heavy firing from the 28th Pennsylvania's left wing answered that. Major Walker instructed his companies to open fire as soon as they came on line, rather than wait for the entire regiment to form line. Some remaining elements of the 10th Maine were in Walker's front, but, seeing the 111th approaching "in fine style," they cleared out of the way.[58]

In the East Woods, Colonel Duncan McRae mounted a large boulder to get a look at the approaching troops, which some in his brigade thought were Colquitt's Georgians and Alabamians. "I saw a line of what I supposed to be about a Regmt with the flag of the U.S. flying," McRae observed. It was the 111th Pennsylvania, forming along the northern edge of the woods. McRae gave orders to fire and charge. Instead, in just moments, in what seemed a baffling calamity, his brigade utterly collapsed and stampeded from the field. The break began in the 5th North Carolina, on the right. Captain Thomas M. Garrett, its commander, saw the 111th Pennsylvania approaching. He may also have seen the 3rd Maryland and the 102nd New York, which were Stainrook's following regiments, forming on the left of the 111th. Garrett's men were lying down behind rocks and trees, but he realized that a few files (the front and rear ranks) of his men on the far right had no cover. He ordered these men to deploy as flankers and take cover behind the trees. As Garrett was directing this movement, Captain Thomas P. Thomson, the G Company commander, approached him, "and in a very excited manner and tone cried out to me, 'They are flanking us! See, yonder's a whole brigade!'" Garrett ordered Thomson to be quiet and return to his company, but the damage was done. Enough men had heard Thompson's imprudent outburst, and a sudden panic gripped the enlisted men. Despite the efforts of sergeants and officers, all except 10 men of the regiment fled from the woods toward the rear. Incredibly, one of those remaining was Captain Thomson. Despite, Captain Garrett's statement that he "manifests clearly a want of capacity to command," Thomson was not a coward. Garrett ordered this tiny band to fall back to the fence on the southern edge of the woods. The cry "They are flanking us!" swept along the brigade line, and the panic quickly spread to the other regiments. "In a moment the most unaccountable stampede occurred," wrote McRae, "and a brigade famous for previous and subsequent conduct of each of its Regts, fled in panic from the field." Field and company officers struggled to prevent the flight, to no avail. Many of them were carried along with the mob who poured out from the woods, either fleeing toward the West Woods and beyond, or back toward the Sunken Lane. McRae and a handful of officers and men were left standing bewildered at what had just occurred. They could see the 111th Pennsylvania and the right wing of the 28th Pennsylvania pushing into the woods toward them. McRae and his remnants "made haste to escape" before they were captured.[59]

McRae never mentioned seeing Robbins's line, but they saw him. John M. Smither in the 5th Texas remembered the North Carolinians coming up and taking a position to their right. Observing their age and appearance, Smither concluded that they were conscripts, which meant this was probably the 5th North Carolina. It had the largest concentration of draftees in the brigade. The rest of McRae's brigade would have formed behind the 5th Texas and Robbins's other regiments. After a single volley, Smither watched the regiment break and run: "Their officers did all they could to stop them but to no avail." Captain Ike Turner, the daredevil young commander of the 5th Texas, called for his men to fire on the fleeing Tarheels, but when his men turned their weapons to do so, he "laughingly" countermanded the order. Some officers of the brigade were still present—probably it was McRae and the handful who remained with him—and Turner went over to them. He asked what regiment it was that had just fled, apparently not aware that it had been an entire brigade. Smither recalled that the officer replied, "I'll be damned if I'll tell you! I'll resign tonight!" and departed from the woods. If this was McRae, a proud and ambitious man, now shocked and mortified, one can imagine why he would respond to Turner in such a manner.[60]

McRae always believed that his brigade's stampede was inexplicable, but the reasons seem clear enough. The men had not recovered from their experience at South Mountain; the most exposed regiment in the brigade, McRae's own 5th North Carolina, had many poorly trained conscripts; and there was a general lack of confidence in McRae's leadership. The last factor was key. In assessing the performance of units in World War II, General Matthew Ridgeway wrote, "The best of troops will fail if the strain is big enough." Ridgeway related that although he commanded some of the finest troops in the U.S. Army, the paratroopers, he still saw some units "perform miserably," and the reason was always "because of poor leadership." In McRae's brigade it only took a spark, provided by Captain Thompson's outburst that "they are flanking us," to trigger a collapse. Once the 5th North Carolina broke, the panic quickly spread to the other regiments, and no effort by the officers could check it. The adjutant of the 23rd North Carolina, Veines E. Turner, wrote that "it was impossible to maintain the broken line," and his regiment fell back to the fence on the southern border of the woods. He and the other officers attempted to rally their men here, but this proved to be undoable. They had no choice but to join the retreat, falling back to the Sunken Lane.[61]

The flight of McRae's brigade left Robbins's force alone in the East Woods. They were confronting the left wing of the 28th Pennsylvania, the 111th Pennsylvania, the 3rd Maryland, and the 102nd New York, a force that heavily outnumbered them and extended far enough east to outflank and envelop the 5th Texas. The 3rd Maryland and the 102nd New York were small regiments, with command issues. The 3rd suffered from a high desertion rate, frequently a sign of poor leadership. The regiment's major, Gilbert P. Robinson, pointed the finger at the line officers, whom he considered a "set of beats." Robinson later consolidated the regiment into a battalion to get rid of them. John M. Gould interviewed Robinson in 1891. Although Gould found him to be a perfect gentleman, the latter spent the entire hour-long interview "berating them [the regiment's line officers] individually and collectively." In the 102nd New York, the problem was its commander, Lieutenant Colonel James C. Lane. Captain Lewis R. Stegman, probably the most universally respected and loved officer in the regiment, wrote that Lane was mocked with nicknames like the "Fighting Major" or "Black Jack" and was considered an "incubus" (something that oppresses, like a nightmare). "While always on the field he never gave commands," complained Stegman, and "when his name is mentioned it is with a damn." Corporal Lyman Welton grouped Lane with "the brigade of coffee cooking, sneaking hospital bummers." Stegman proffered charges of cowardice against Lane after Antietam, but his brigade commander counseled him to withdraw them, which Stegman did. Lane remained in command until he resigned for medical reasons in July 1864, during the Atlanta Campaign.[62]

The 3rd Maryland and 102nd New York followed the 111th Pennsylvania across Smoketown Road. When they attempted to deploy from column of divisions into line, they ran into one another and mingled in confusion until officers sorted the mess out. Stray Confederate artillery rounds and small-arms fire from the Rebels inside the woods added to the general mayhem. "There seemed to be quite a force in opposition to us," recalled Milton Wing, a Company B private in the 3rd Maryland. The Marylanders and New Yorkers also found, like the 10th Maine had, that although Confederate bullets were buzzing about, the enemy were not easy to see. Under this fire, the left wing of the 3rd Maryland had difficulty re-forming. Then, when the 102nd began to form on their left, the Marylanders commenced a reckless fire, some of which had an effect on the right companies of the 102nd. Captain Walter R. Hewlett, the commander of the 102nd's Company C, recollected that the friendly fire "busted us." To escape it, the right compa-nies crowded against the left ones, bunching the men up and creating confusion. Sergeant Isaac Van Steenbergh heard Captain Mervin E. Cornell, commanding Company D, loudly complaining about other units crowding his company. But the 102nd had "a fine body of line officers and good men in the ranks," wrote Captain Stegman, and many of the officers rushed out in front of their men to urge them forward, toward the woods. A good line was formed, the regiment delivered a volley into the woods, and then it surged forward to the fence at the edge of the woods. When Captain Cornell reached the fence—a high worm fence—he began to climb it, probably to encourage his men to follow, but a Texan put a bullet through his forehead. Cornell joined Mansfield, Beal, Croas-dale, Hammersly, and other Union officers who were killed or wounded that morning by Robbins's deadly riflemen. Thirty years later, Corporal Lyman Wel-ton lamented, "How clear his [Cornell's] daring conduct comes to me now." Le-muel H. Hitchcock, a recent recruit in the 111th Pennsylvania, also gave testimony to the deadly aim of the Confederate troops opposing them. He had joined the regiment on September 1, along with 12 other recruits, and 9 of the 13 were killed or wounded. Among those who escaped uninjured, there was a close call, which Hitchcock related: "One had a ball strike his gun as he was capping it, breaking his gun, cutting the cap box from his belt, going through his canteen, haversack, coat, and shirt, and coming out without breaking the skin."[63]

Robbins's command still possessed a deadly sting, but his men had reached the end of their tether. Ammunition ran out, and there were many casualties. The stampede of McRae's brigade left them with no support. All efforts to get help or ammunition had failed. "The time arrived when our experience as sol-diers told us it was time to 'get up and git,'" wrote Robbins. Captain Ike Turner had sent 1st Sergeant J. A. Murray to find Hood and tell him that his regiment was nearly out of ammunition. The enemy were threatening to turn his left [i.e., right] flank, there were no supports on his right, and "unless reinforced he would have to fall back." Murray returned with Hood's unhelpful reply: "Go back and tell Captain Turner he *must* [emphasis in original] hold his position." Hood could offer no more than bold language, and Turner concluded that his men could not fight without bullets. Afterward, he reported succinctly, and with a touch of sar-casm, "My men were out of ammunition, the enemy not more than 100 yards in my front, no support, no ammunition; all our troops had fallen back on my left; I deemed it prudent to fall back also." All three regiments retreated at the same time, under a "withering" fire from Stainrook's regiments and the left wing of the 28th Pennsylvania. The fire was so heavy that Robbins decided he would not survive. He was determined not to die from a bullet in the back, so he exited the woods while keeping his face to the enemy, with "my comrades dropping all about me." To his surprise, he made it unscathed to the woods' edge and started a deadly dash over open ground to the West Woods. Robbins, and most of the men with him, retreated south toward Mumma's farm, where they turned southwest to enter the West Woods below the Dunker Church. He remembered that when the pursuing Federals reached the fence, at the woods' southern edge, they commenced "peppering us vigorously." When Robbins was not hit by this fusillade, "thinks I to myself I believe I shall escape after all," so he decided to make better time by turning around and running with the other survivors to the West Woods. Many did not make it. Nearly half of Robbins's regiment, perhaps 100 to 110 men, were casualties. Turner's 5th Texas counted 96 killed or wounded, over 50% of their strength. They also lost some prisoners, whom Turner did not include in his list of casualties. The losses in the part of the 21st Georgia that fought with them, are unknown, but probably they were just as heavy.[64]

EVEN BEFORE ROBBINS, TURNER, and their stalwart commands began their retreat, utter catastrophe had engulfed Colquitt's brigade. In the 6th Georgia, a comrade of Ben Witcher's warned that it was time to get out, pointing to the line of their men lying along the Cornfield fence. Witcher answered "No," stating that he thought they had numbers enough to stop the enemy, so "let them come." His comrade replied that most of the men along the fence were killed or wounded. He shook several of them, to convince Witcher, adding that "the quicker we get out of this the better." This made a believer out of Witcher, so he, his comrade (whom he never named), and two other men dashed back through the corn. Union bullets cut down every man in the party except Witcher. Out of the 33 men in Lieutenant Thomas Marshall's Company E, 13 were killed and 17 wounded. In Company K's total of 40 men, 16 were killed, 15 wounded, and 5 captured. Two companies had lost every man. All but two commissioned officers were shot, leaving the regiment in the command of a lieutenant. As Witcher recalled, 29 years later, "This battle was the most disastrous to my Regt of any in the war." Two members thought the regiment had carried about 300 men into action. "Out of this number we had 84 killed besides wounded and captured," one of them wrote. The other gave the number killed as 81. If either amount is correct, it is an astonishing figure, with the highest mortality rate of any Confederate regiment in the battle: 115 officers and men wounded, and 30 captured, for a total of around 226, a loss of 75%. Corporal Robert Johnson recalled that only 40 men could be accounted for on September 18, which meant that the 6th Georgia might have had losses as high as 87%, exceeding any other regiment in the battle.[65]

The 27th Georgia, on the 6th's left, suffered a similar fate. "Oh I tell you truly it was a perfect hail of bullets shot and shell from the time I got in until I was hit," recalled Ben Milikin. Only 4 out of 30 in Milikin's Company I emerged unscathed, and 2 of them were litter bearers. Milikin was shot during the advance through the East Woods, taking a bullet in the thigh while ramming home a cartridge. He begged a comrade to drag him behind a tree on the edge of the East Woods, since the "bullets were coming so fast." His friend did so, and probably saved Milikin's life. The carnage among the regiment's officers was dreadful. Colonel Levi B. Smith was killed; Lieutenant Colonel Charles T. Zachry fell wounded at the beginning of the brigade's charge into the Cornfield; and every other commissioned officer was killed or wounded, except for Captain William H. Rentfro, who took command of what was left of the regiment. Out of nearly 400 carried into action, only 37 men were present on the morning of September 18.[66]

Lieutenant James Hunt in the 28th Georgia later declared that he did not know what troops his regiment opposed, but "know this they knew how to handle rifles very well." Hunt's regiment lost half its men and emerged under the command of a lieutenant. The 23rd Georgia also suffered losses of 50%. Its colonel, William P. Barclay was killed, Lieutenant Colonel Emory Best wounded, and Major James H. Huggins wounded. During the retreat, the 13th Alabama lost its flag to Private John Murphy of the 5th Ohio, and Colonel Birkett D. Fry was wounded. Only Company D's losses are known. If they are representative, the regiment suffered heavily. Out of 28 men, 3 were killed, 11 wounded, and 3 captured, for a 60% loss.[67]

To escape the murderous flanking fire, Colquitt's brigade retreated southwest, toward the Dunker Church and West Woods, carrying Ripley's brigade with them. As Ben Witcher's and Captain Robbins's experiences attest, the retreat was fatal for many. Once the men left the corn or the woods, they were on open ground and came under a "withering" fire from the pursuing Federals. Lieutenant W. W. Holbert in the 4th Georgia observed, "I remember very distinctly that the fire from the Union troops swept the field in the rear of our regiment, and that the risk in getting out over that field to the rear was really greater than in line of battle." Among those cut down was Captain William H. Plane in the 6th Georgia, who, with another man, was carrying mortally wounded Lieutenant Colonel Newton. They made it to the meadow south of the Cornfield before Plane and the other man were shot. Twelve days earlier, Plane had reassured his wife that "we cannot be defeated. We may suffer much & many brave hearts may cease to beat, but the sons of the South can never be conquered by the Myrmidon hirelings of the North." Now, Plane's life ebbed away in farmer Miller's pasture.[68]

Before the infantry line collapsed, Colonel Stephen D. Lee had attempted to provide it with some close gun support. Lee's battalion had inflicted significant damage on the Federal infantry throughout the morning—far more than Stuart's artillery group on Nicodemus Heights, which was largely neutralized by the 1st Corps' batteries on Poffenberger Hill—but it had also suffered severe losses from counter-battery fire. So many horses and men had been killed or wounded in Parker's and Woolfolk's batteries that Lee pulled them off the line, to refit the units. Lieutenant William Elliot's Brooks (South Carolina) artillery exhausted its ammunition and had to be withdrawn to resupply, which left only Woolfolk's battery. During Colquitt's counterattack, Lee's battalion was joined by Captain George V. Moody's battery, armed with two 3-inch rifles and two 24 lb. howitzers. Lee inserted Moody's guns into the position Parker had occupied, near the Dunker Church. Captain James Blackshear's battery from Cutts's battalion, under the command of Lieutenant Thomas Maddox, also arrived to reinforce Lee. He inserted them into his gun line on Woolfolk's left. Once Colquitt had pushed up into the Cornfield, the infantry lines were too close together for Lee to safely keep shelling the enemy, so he ordered two guns—probably the howitzers of Moody's battery—to move up near the Cornfield. Lee also sent two guns of Woolfolk's battery, under the command of Lieutenant W. D. Terrell, into the plowed field south of the East Woods. Lee probably intended for Terrell's guns to cover McRae's right flank.[69]

Although the pursuing Federals "made slaughter" among the retreating Rebels, Sergeant William H. H. Fithian in the 28th Pennsylvania noted that the Confederates fell back fighting. They "would load, then hault, then give us a volley, then retreat." Confederate artillery also took its toll of the pursuers. Part way in the advance toward the Dunker Church, Joseph Moore, also in the 28th Pennsylvania, recalled that "a rebel shell struck our flag bearer under the arms and cut him in two. I barely escaped it, being first by his side." Another soldier picked up the flag and made it 20 steps farther before he was shot. A third man took the flag and he, too, was hit. The guns that S. D. Lee had advanced in support of D. H. Hill did their best to slow the Union pursuit, but at considerable cost to themselves. Moody's two guns were exposed "to a galling infantry fire," and Lee ordered them to the rear. Not, however, before the section's commander, Lieutenant John B. Gorey, received a bullet through the head and was killed as he sighted the one remaining gun for a final shot. Lieutenant Terrell's gun crews, in Woolfolk's battery, managed to get off only two rounds of canister before Stainrook's brigade shot all the horses on the two limbers and killed or wounded 11 of Terrell's 16 men. Terrell and his five survivors were forced to abandon the guns to the 28th Pennsylvania and flee.

Back on S. D. Lee's main line, D. H. Hill, watching his entire line collapse, ordered Lee to limber his remaining guns and withdraw to the ridge west of the Hagerstown Pike, running southeast from Reel's farm, which we shall refer to as Reel Ridge. Lee's battalion, in his own words, was in a "wrecked condition." It had lost so many horses that he was forced to abandon a caisson and limber, as well as the rear chests from a caisson in Parker's battery.[70]

When Stainrook's regiments emerged into the plowed field south of the East Woods, they came under a flanking fire from their left. It was delivered by

Colquitt's skirmish battalion, under the command of Captain William M. Arnold, which was strung out along the rail fence on the western side of a cornfield north of Roulette's farm. Some of McRae's men ran past these skirmishers when they stampeded out of the East Woods, and Arnold, an intrepid leader, "made the most earnest appeals to them to rally and stand by us." But, recalled Josiah Lewis in the 6th Georgia, "they were wild with terror & deaf as an adder." Arnold's battalion opened fire on Stainrook's men the moment they reached the edge of the woods. Josiah Lewis thought they had halted the enemy, but Major Thomas Walker, commanding the 111th Pennsylvania, remembered it only as a "scattering fire of sharpshooters." The other regiments of Stainrook's brigade reported no check to their advance. The 102nd New York returned the fire, apparently with considerable effect, for Lewis recalled the "the bullets coming like hail" at their position. His brother Sidney, who had been lying down behind the fence, decided it would be easier to load standing up. As soon as he did so, he was hit. Moments later, Captain Arnold was badly wounded in the thigh. The battalion fell back, hurried on their way not only by the fall of their inspiring leader, but also by the approach of a large Union force, advancing from their right and rear—Sedgwick's division of the 2nd Corps.[71]

On the ridge north of the Cornfield, the 27th Indiana and the 3rd Wisconsin took stock of their condition. Out of 443 men carried into action, the 27th had lost 209, with 18 killed and 191 wounded, for a loss of just over 47%. The 3rd counted 27 killed and 173 wounded out of 345 men, a nearly 58% loss. At the end of the action, the 3rd had only 43 men left. The missing were those who had left the ranks, either by helping the wounded to the rear or by simply having been jarred loose from their unit in the confusion. Word passed along the line of these two regiments to wait for an ammunition resupply, while those regiments who had suffered less damage pursued the retreating enemy. But then Hooker rode up and demanded, "What are these men doing here?" Someone replied they were waiting for ammunition. "Where-in-the-hell's-your-bayonets? Forward!" Hooker commanded. The survivors of the two shattered regiments fixed bayonets and, as Edmund Brown remembered, began "to cheer with all our might." They could see the 2nd Massachusetts advancing on their right, and Greene's division to their left front, "charging into the open ground, in splendid style." Some men in the 3rd Wisconsin noticed blood dripping from Hooker's foot. Precisely where and when the 1st Corps' commander was hit is difficult to determine. He had ordered up artillery to support the 12th Corps before riding over to Gordon's men and, by his own account, was hit while reconnoitering a position for these batteries to occupy. For the moment he ignored the wound and remained in the saddle.[72]

"The whole field before [us] was literally covered with dead and dying," wrote Captain Charles Morse in the 2nd Massachusetts, referring to the Cornfield. A sergeant found the colors of the 11th Mississippi, which he gave to Lieutenant

Colonel Wilder Dwight, who rode along the 2nd's line, waving the captured banner. "Every cap went off," recorded Morse, "and a cheer went up, you must have almost heard at Jamaica Plain [Morse's home town]."[73] When Gordon's men reached the meadow south of the corn, the number of dead and wounded Confederates seemed even greater. Robert Gould Shaw, a captain in the regiment, described the grisly scene: "Such a mass of dead and wounded men, mostly Rebels, as were lying there, I never saw before; it was a terrible sight and our men had to be very careful to avoid treading on them; many were mangled and torn to pieces by artillery, but most of them had been wounded by musketry fire. We halted right among them, and the men did everything they could for their comfort, giving them water from their canteens, and trying to place them in easy positions."[74]

Among the fallen Rebels, Colonel Andrews saw a "tall Confederate officer, whose sword had been picked up by someone connected with the 3rd Wisconsin." Andrews examined the weapon and saw that it was a presentation sword, inscribed to Lieutenant Colonel James M. Newton, 6th Georgia. Captain Plane's body would have been nearby, which helps place how far Plane and one of his men had carried Newton's body before being killed.[75]

When the Ohio regiments of Tyndale's brigade reached the Cornfield's northern fence, the number of Confederate dead and badly wounded men they found piled up along the fence line stunned them. "I was amazed, when we reached the ground where their line stood, at the terrible execution that we had done," wrote Lieutenant Colonel Powell. "The dead were piled up so thick, that we could hardly pass without stepping on them." He tried to urge his horse across the fence, but it recoiled at the number of corpses heaped against each other, and Powell had to find another way through. All around him the victorious Ohioans "were madly rushing forward." They encountered numerous dazed or wounded Southerners, but the Buckeyes did not pause, simply ordering them to the rear as prisoners.[76]

The 12th Corps swept forward from Miller's farm to the East Woods, pursuing the retreating Confederates "like a cyclone." General Greene was seen bareheaded, with his sword drawn, sitting on a trotting horse and urging his men on. Hooker and Williams pushed everything they could forward. On the right, near the Hagerstown Pike, the 124th Pennsylvania joined the advance, supported by the Purnell Legion of Goodrich's brigade. In the East Woods, the 125th and 128th Pennsylvania were ordered forward, along with the 46th Pennsylvania. Both the rookie 13th New Jersey and the 107th New York of Gordon's brigade, who had been held out of the fight, were also ordered up. From Poffenberger Hill, Hooker sent for Captain J. Albert Monroe's Battery D, 1st Rhode Island, and Lieutenant Frederick M. Edgell's New Hampshire Light from the 1st Corps' 1st Division's artillery. Williams's orders brought Captain George W. Cothran's Battery M, 1st New York, clattering up from the 12th Corps' artillery brigade. Two batteries from the 2nd Division's 2nd Corps—Captain John A. Tompkins's

Battery A, 1st Rhode Island, and Lieutenant George A. Woodruff's Battery I, 1st U.S. Artillery—also soon arrived. When all were assembled, Hooker and Williams had massed 30 guns on captured ground near the East Woods and the Cornfield. Hooker did not intend to lose this ground again.[77]

Stainrook's three regiments moved south across Mumma's plowed field to the farmer's burning buildings. The 102nd New York ended up to the left of the structures, while the 3rd Maryland and 111th Pennsylvania crossed the Mumma farm lane, which was to the right of the farm and the family's cemetery. The 102nd continued to the northern border of Mumma's cornfield, where the men began dismantling the fence along it. Some of them advanced into the corn. At this moment an officer, probably Captain J. Albert Monroe, commanding Battery D, 1st Rhode Island, rode up and asked Lieutenant Colonel Lane if his regiment would support Monroe's battery. Monroe had driven his artillery down the Poffenberger farm lane to Smoketown Road. When they emerged from the East Woods, he ordered his guns to form line abreast, in the meadow west of the woods. Sergeant Stephen W. Lockwood in Cothran's battery, which followed Monroe several minutes later, described the meadow Monroe's Rhode Islanders had entered: "The field in front of us had been fought over so many times, that the ground lay strewn with the dead and dying, dead horses, muskets and broken muskets." Monroe saw dozens of Union and Confederate casualties "indiscriminately mingled" in the path of his guns. He observed later how, unless greatly excited, horses will not tread on the bodies of men, but when harnessed and hauling a limber or caisson, "they may go so close as to cause further injury to the wounded or mutilation to the dead by passing the wheels over them." He had his teams carefully thread their way across the field, and he even stopped one limber to remove a wounded Confederate soldier in its path. Monroe's crew no doubt performed this particular merciful act, and the captain did his best to avoid crushing the dead and injured with his heavy vehicles and guns, but he softened the reality of his unit's drive across a casualty-littered field for the readers of his postwar history of the battery. In a statement to John Gould, Lieutenant Ezra K. Parker, one of the section commanders, recalled that the guns advanced at a trot, "passing over dead and wounded rebels." The question of whether Parker meant that the limbers and guns actually ran over the dead was answered by Sergeant Lockwood of Cothran's battery. In a September 30 letter, before veterans tempered the battle's realities, he wrote that "we could not get into position without running over some of the dead." When all his guns were on line, Monroe ordered them to unlimber. "We then faced directly to the plateau by the Dunkard Church," recalled Parker—that is, they faced the locale occupied only minutes before by S. D. Lee's battalion. The lieutenant thought it a poor location and suggested to Monroe that it was "no position to fire into the enemy." Just then, an aide-de-camp from Hooker rode up and ordered Monroe to move his guns forward to the plateau. Monroe limbered again, shifting his guns to the plateau and his caissons to the low ground near Mumma's farm, where they had better cover. The captain had not occupied this position earlier, because it was too far forward and exposed, but now that he had no choice, he made sure to get the support of Lieutenant Colonel Lane's 102nd New York.[78]

Monroe soon had plentiful infantry support when the other regiments of Greene's division arrived and took cover beneath the crest of the plateau. The infantry was furiously shelled by S. D. Lee's repositioned guns on Reel Ridge and by the Georgia battery of Captain George M. Patterson, located a short distance south of Mumma's cornfield. Eugene Powell described the situation as so bad, it was "about all that human nature can endure." William Fithian in the 28th Pennsylvania recorded that it created "sad havoc among our brave fellows. They fell right and left; some with heads blown off, others with legs, arms, and so on." The 102nd New York managed to bring Patterson's guns under fire and forced the Georgians to displace west of the Hagerstown Pike, but it was still too dangerous for infantry to be on the plateau. Greene's men stayed below the summit and out of sight. When Monroe neared the plateau, he encountered Greene and asked whether his infantry could support the battery, probably hoping to confirm what he had already arranged with the 102nd New York. Greene "answered in a low tone of voice that he was out of ammunition," and the captain thought "that it was a funny place for men without ammunition to be in." Nonetheless, if the infantry could hold their position with empty cartridge boxes, his six guns with full limber chests could surely hold theirs, so he ordered the guns up onto the plateau and unlimbered. Greene was only partially correct. His Ohio regiments were out of ammunition, but the rest of the division still had some remaining.[79]

As Monroe's six guns took up their position, Lieutenant Parker observed an enemy battery west of the Hagerstown Pike, which was also unlimbering and preparing to fire. It was probably one of S. D. Lee's batteries, or possibly Patterson's repositioned battery. Parker also saw Confederate infantry within rifle range. "They beat us in getting in battery in time to fire two rounds," wrote Parker, "but they fired wild—too high." The New Englanders cleared for action and, noted Parker, "fired to hit," which they immediately did. "We blew up a caisson in short order and what was left of the battery soon drew off," remarked the lieutenant. But the Confederate infantry proved to be more troublesome. They crawled up under cover near the church and "opened a deadly fire," hitting men and horses. On Private Christopher Carpenter's piece, the lead horse on the limber, and the No. 1, No. 2, and No. 4 men on the gun, were all hit. Monroe ordered a section to blast the troublesome skirmishers with canister. Although he did not think it inflicted any damage, it kept the enemy's heads down and enabled him to maintain his position for the time being.[80]

By 8:30 a.m., the entire area east of the Hagerstown Pike—encompassing the Cornfield and East Woods, and south of Smoketown Road to Mumma's

farm—had been swept clean of Confederates. In the West Woods and along the Sunken Lane, the remaining officers and noncoms attempted to rally the survivors of what had been a debacle for the Army of Northern Virginia. Every field officer in Colquitt's brigade was killed or wounded. Ezra Carman estimated Colquitt's losses at 111 killed, 444 wounded, and 167 missing—a 55% loss—but the actual losses were certainly higher. On September 18, Sergeant Silas Crosby of the 27th Georgia was ordered by Colquitt to assemble a detail and find and cook rations for the brigade's survivors. Crosby remembered precisely how many men he had issued rations to: 186. Those who had been separated from their command in the fighting rejoined the brigade later, on September 18th and 19th, and raised the number of survivors, but the actual total of men either killed or wounded may have been as high as 900. Ripley's four regiments tallied 110 killed, 506 wounded, and 124 missing, a 54% loss. The 3rd and 1st North Carolina suffered particularly heavy casualties. Among them were 24 of 27 officers in the 3rd and 330 of its 520 enlisted men, a nearly 65% loss. The the 1st counted 50 dead, 75 wounded, and 21 captured out of 315. These were appalling numbers, and although parts of both brigades would be engaged again later in the day, they were effectively destroyed as combat units. McRae's brigade suffered relatively few casualties. Nonetheless, although a small element would participate in the fighting at the Sunken Lane, the brigade ceased to exist for the rest of the battle.[81]

Knap's Battery E, Pennsylvania Light Artillery, September 19. The battery posed on the Dunker Church plateau for this image, which shows much of the terrain on the northern part of the battlefield. Smoketown Road is directly behind the battery, and beyond that can be seen the East Woods (*right distance*), the Cornfield (*center distance*), and the North Woods (*left distance*). The dead horse (*foreground*) came from Colonel S. D. Lee's battalion. Courtesy of the Library of Congress

Colquitt watched helplessly as his command was shattered. "I sent in haste to the rear for re-enforcements, and communicated to General Hill the exposed condition of my men," he reported. McRae's brigade vanished from his right flank, and Doles failed to advance his 44th and 4th Georgia to support Colquitt's left, which allowed Ransom's battery and the 2nd Massachusetts to maul his left flank. Captain Robbins's men in the East Woods provided help to Colquitt's right flank, of which he was unaware, but their numbers were not enough to prevent Tyndale's crushing flank attack.[82]

When the collapse came, Rodes's brigade were on their way to join the fight, but the distance and a delay in getting orders to him meant that just as his Alabamians left the Sunken Lane, they met elements of McRae's and Colquitt's brigades, who were retreating in confusion. As Rodes reported, "It was evident that the two latter [Colquitt and McRae] had met with a reverse, and that the best service I could render them and the field generally would be to form a line in rear of them and endeavor to rally them before attacking or being attacked." It was a prudent decision. D. H. Hill was of like mind, for just as Rodes decided that continuing to advance was a bad option, he received an order from Hill to fall back and form his brigade in the Sunken Lane.[83]

No one on the Confederate side ever seemed to understand just how conspicuous Captain Robbins's leadership was, or the importance of his stand in the East Woods. Captain Ike Turner, commanding the 5th Texas, and Captain James C. Nisbet, in charge of the 21st Georgia detachment, had also performed superbly. Turner received credit in Wofford's report on the Texas Brigade, but Nisbet and Robbins received no mention in their brigade or division commanders' reports. In Nisbet's case, his brigade commander was wounded and probably unaware of what the captain did. Robbins was ill for some time after Antietam and unable to submit a report, so it is possible that Hood and Law did not understand what he had done. This seems questionable, however, since Robbins sent requests for ammunition back to them several times, and they knew his position. The Alabamians, Georgians, and Texans who fought with Robbins demonstrated just how difficult it was to dislodge good troops from cover by a frontal attack. Had D. H. Hill understood Robbins's position and supported him better, the Confederates might not have lost the East Woods.

The outstanding performance of the 12th Corps was also not acknowledged in the initial after-action assessment by the Army of the Potomac. McClellan barely recognized their part in the battle in his first report, written in October. Alpheus Williams's important role in the fighting received no mention at all. It took a lengthy letter from Williams to McClellan in April 1863 to politely advise the then former army commander of "possible certain facts which conflict somewhat with your Preliminary Report and which are capable of proof by hundreds of witnesses." Williams proceeded to clearly lay out what the 12th Corps did that day. To his credit, McClellan gave Williams and his corps full honors for their excellent performance in his final report, published on August 4, 1863.[84]

In wording similar to what Hood employed to explain his division's defeat, D.H. Hill also implied that his brigades had been bested by overwhelming Union numbers. He reported that they confronted line after line of Federal troops, leaving the reader to imagine hordes of Yankees overwhelming his Spartan band. This was a familiar refrain Hill repeated throughout the war and afterward. Although Colquitt complained primarily about a lack of support, he also reported that the contest was "unequal," noting that if "the brigades on the right and left had advanced, we should have driven the enemy from the field." But, as in Hood's case, overwhelming enemy forces did not explain Hill's defeat. He committed three brigades to the fight, numbering 3,475 men. Added to this were the approximately 500 men of the 4th Alabama, the 21st Georgia, and the 5th Texas in the East Woods, so about 4,000 Confederate troops were engaged. The 12th Corps brought elements of four brigades into action against them, with a total of about 4,000 men, nearly 700 of whom were in the untrained 128th Pennsylvania. The odds were even, and, when we consider that some of the Union soldiers were raw recruits, were actually slightly in favor of the Confederates. Neither side had more courage than the other. Apart from McRae's brigade, whose circumstances have already been discussed, both sides fought tenaciously and with valor.

What made the difference was leadership, at both the division and corps levels. Here, the Federals shone brightly, and the Confederates did not. Hooker, Williams, and Greene, in particular, ranged close to their commands, keeping their fingers firmly on the pulse of the battle and sensing—correctly—where an infusion of troops was most needed. D. H. Hill's brigades reached the combat zone in sequence, rather than in a concentrated body. This was perhaps unavoidable, but Hill compounded the problem by exercising virtually no command coordination, leaving his brigades to fight independently, with disastrous consequences. In contrast to Hill, Hooker seemed to be everywhere along the Cornfield's and East Woods' fronts, and he accurately assessed where the 12th Corps' brigades were most needed.

This was not an easy achievement in that seething, roaring, smoke-shrouded environment. While Mansfield's initial deployment of Crawford's brigade was clumsy, and his commitment of the untrained 128th Pennsylvania into the fight was ill advised, his insistence on moving the 12th Corps up to the front in close column kept the corps well closed up, so it could be quickly committed to the fighting. Williams did an excellent job after Mansfield was mortally wounded, keeping his rookie regiments out of the way and getting his veteran regiments into action to carry out Hooker's orders. The stand of the 27th Indiana, the 3rd Wisconsin, and Ransom's battery was remarkable—one of the most distinguished actions by any of the regiments in the Army of the Potomac during the Civil War. They stopped the counterattack of the 3rd North Carolina in its tracks, and then checked Colquitt's attack. These units also joined in the subsequent counterattack, although at a terribly high price in casualties. Their ability to stand in the open and absorb the punishment that Doles's and Colquitt's infantry and S. D. Lee's guns delivered enabled Greene to bring his division into action on the Confederates' right flank. Once McRae's brigade broke, Greene's men were able to outflank Robbins and envelop Colquitt's right. Greene and most of his men performed magnificently, but it was Hooker who indicated where Greene should go in. This decision, combined with the men's stout fighting, particularly by Tyndale's brigade, led to the smashup of D. H. Hill's brigades. Had Hooker held Greene back as a reserve or sent him to the right or center—both reasonable decisions—Hill's brigades still might have been defeated, but it is just as likely that they could have held on and kept control of the East Woods, changing the course of the battle.[85]

WHILE GREENE'S DIVISION FOUND cover below the Dunker Church plateau, Gordon's three regiments, in the meadow south of the Cornfield, swung west to face the Hagerstown Pike and the West Woods. Hooker accompanied them into the meadow, his foot dripping blood, but then fell out of his saddle. A surgeon hurried forward to examine him, but Hooker was out of the fight. His loss would prove to be one of the battle's critical turning points. No one had done more to bring about the Confederates' defeat on the Union right. As a party carried the wounded general off, and the Hoosiers and Badgers moved toward the turnpike, a staff officer rode up and saucily ordered them to move out of the way, in order to allow room for General Edwin Sumner and General John Sedgwick's 2nd Division of the 2nd Corps. The time was around 9 a.m. Looking east, Gordon's men saw the big division marching in magnificent style, in a column of brigades, toward the southern end of the East Woods. The white-haired Sumner was riding proudly in front, his hat in one hand and a sword in the other. "It was a grand sight," thought Captain Robert Shaw of the 2nd Massachusetts, "and they looked as if they couldn't be repulsed." Shaw's entire regiment cheered the reinforcements. "They were in three lines, and looked splendidly," wrote Captain Morse. From a signal station established near the East Woods, General Alpheus Williams sent a situation report to McClellan, the first the army commander received from a commander at the front. "Gen. Mansfield is dangerously wounded. Gen. Hooker is wounded severely in the foot. Gen. Sumner I hear is advancing. We hold the field at present. Please give us all the aid you can. It is reported that the enemy occupy the woods in our advance in strong force. P.S. The head of Genl Sumner's column has just arrived." Another decisive moment was at hand.[86]

7

To the West Woods

"We shall not all be here tomorrow night"

There were many opinions in the army about Major General Edwin Vose Sumner, but no one questioned his discipline, punctuality, obedience to orders, and soldierly qualities. Born in Boston only 14 years after the end of the American Revolution, at age 65 he was one of the oldest active-duty general officers in the U.S. Army. Commissioned directly into the army in 1819, by the Battle of Antietam he had already served for 43 years. The army was his life, his love, and his home. Most of his service had been in the mounted arm, with the 1st and 2nd Dragoons, and then, in 1855, as colonel of the 1st U.S. Cavalry. A month before Fort Sumter he was promoted to brigadier general in the Regular Army, one of only three to hold that rank. McClellan gave him a divisional command in November 1861. In March 1862, when Lincoln ordered the creation of the army's corps, by seniority he received command of the 2nd Corps. Promotion to major general of volunteers followed. His courage was legendary. A story popular with soldiers in the 2nd Corps was that at Cerro Gordo in the Mexican War, a musket ball struck Sumner square in the forehead but fell to the ground, flattened, without breaking the skin. While the story might be apocryphal—he was wounded in the battle, but only slightly—the soldiers loved it and affectionately nicknamed him "Old Bullhead." This was shortened to "Old Bull," or just "Bull," because of his booming voice. In the battles of the Peninsula Campaign, he frequently came under fire. "He would get bullets in his hat, his coat, his boots, his saddle, his horse, sometime have his person scratched," one article said about him. During the Battle of Fair Oaks, he rode to the front of the 15th Massachusetts, heedless of the heavy fire the regiment was under. He asked who they were. When the men shouted "15th Massachusetts," Sumner thundered, "I, too, am from Massachusetts. Three cheers for the Bay State." Inspired by the general, the regiment soon drove the enemy off. The story revealed that besides an abundance of courage, Sumner understood morale and knew what motivated volunteers under fire. He built the 2nd Corps into a first-class fighting unit and established a culture of professionalism, discipline, resilience, and steadiness, which endured long after he was gone.[1]

While no one questioned his courage, Sumner has often been depicted as slow and thick headed. McClellan helped fuel this portrait with his complaint after the Battle of Williamsburg, on May 5, 1862: "Sumner has proved that he was an even greater fool than I supposed & had come within an ace of having us defeated." But Sumner was neither a fool nor a dunderhead. On more than one occasion in his career, he displayed sound diplomatic and administrative skills. In 1851–1852, he successfully diffused a conflict with the Navajo in what became New Mexico, not with a punitive expedition, but by a combination of the judicious employment of military pressure and skillful negotiations. He was sent to Kansas in 1855, where his 1st U.S. Cavalry was instrumental in helping to control the violence there. Although he personally was opposed to slavery, Sumner took no sides, and he worked to maintain law and order with impartiality.[2]

Although he commanded a division for nearly 5 months before his promotion to the leader of a corps, he never led that division in combat. Thus he essentially went from a regimental command on the frontier, with those troops scattered across a large area in company-sized garrisons and outposts, to heading a corps. At that time, there was no Command and General Staff College or War College to prepare officers for high leadership positions in the U.S. Army. Learning how to manage large formations was on-the-job training. Few men could make the mental adjustments necessary for such an enlarged responsibility. Sumner was not one of them. A good corps commander's principal responsibility was not to lead attacks, but instead to manage and coordinate assets and resources—be they his generals, his brigades and divisions, or his artillery—to work together to bring their full combat power to bear. Sumner excelled administratively. He produced good soldiers. But there was a reason General Philip Kearny wrote after the Peninsula Campaign that Sumner "has neither capacity, nor sane judgement. He is a proverbial blunderer." As a 3rd Corps artillery officer, Colonel Charles Wainwright, observed after the Battle of Williamsburg, "He [Sumner] is a great general, but I do not want to serve under him in another fight if this is a specimen." Although admirably aggressive, Sumner was unable to make the adjustment necessary to managing a corps in battle. To some degree he still thought in terms of directing smaller units, such as regiments or brigades. He could not resist the temptation to lead from the front, a fatal flaw for a corps commander who needed to take a larger view of the battle and use his staff effectively to keep him informed of circumstances beyond those which he could see. Leading from the front might make for good headlines and play well with the troops, but it did not win battles, and it often caused unnecessary casualties. Sumner's command weaknesses would reveal themselves with fatal consequences at Antietam.[3]

While McClellan never officially criticized Sumner, nor sought his removal or reassignment, the former's decisions at Antietam reflect a lack of confidence in his general's judgment. On September 15, when McClellan reached the front,

rather than consulting with Sumner, who was a wing commander and the senior officer then present, McClellan conducted his reconnaissance of the enemy
position with Fitz John Porter, a slight not lost on all those present. On the night
of September 16, he could just as easily have sent Sumner over Antietam Creek
with the 2nd Corps and ordered him to assume command of the attack in the
morning, leaving the 12th Corps in reserve on the east bank of Antietam Creek.
Instead he held Sumner and the 2nd Corps back and sent the 12th Corps across
the creek. Perhaps even more revealing, McClellan wanted Hooker, with only
2 weeks' experience as a corps commander—not Sumner, with months under
his belt—leading the attack. There is no evidence that McClellan shared any of
his plans for September 17 with Sumner, which was not particularly unusual
with regard to a corps commander, but was atypical behavior toward a wing
commander and the senior subordinate officer in the army.

Sumner's orders on the night of September 16, sent at 5:50 p.m., were to move
Mansfield's 12th Corps across Antietam Creek and "take such position as may
be designated by General Hooker." The 2nd Corps—which Sumner continued
to directly command, even though he was a wing commander—was ordered to
be ready to march 1 hour before daylight. If there was to be an attack in the morning, Sumner could see no sense in not committing his entire wing to the effort,
and he asked McClellan for permission to move the 2nd Corps across the Antietam. McClellan refused. The 2nd Corps would remain on the east bank of the
creek until ordered to move, and McClellan made it clear that those orders would
not be forthcoming until the next morning. Although Sumner is often described
as a soldier who blindly followed orders, he revealed that he could place a liberal interpretation on them when he thought the circumstances warranted. The
orders to take the 12th Corps across Antietam Creek included the sentence,
"General McClellan desires that all the artillery, ammunition, and everything
else appertaining to the corps, be gotten over without fail to-night ready for action early in the morning." The intent is clear. Sumner was to ensure that the
artillery, ammunition, and other equipment of the 12th Corps be moved over
the creek that night and be ready for action early on the 17th. But Sumner chose
to place a broad interpretation on them, to include repositioning *all of* the artillery under his command, and he quietly ordered five of the 2nd Corps' batteries
across the creek that night, too.[4]

Numerically, the 2nd Corps was the most powerful in the army, numbering
15,206 infantry present for duty in three divisions, and 859 artillerymen, who
formed seven batteries containing a total of 42 guns. The 1st and 2nd Divisions,
commanded, respectively, by Major Generals Israel B. Richardson and John
Sedgwick, were among the army's finest units. Every regiment in both divisions
had seen action during the Peninsula Campaign. The 3rd Division, under Brigadier General William H. French, was a newcomer to the corps, having completed its formation only a day earlier. It initially consisted of two brigades—a

deviation from the favored three-brigade organization—one of three veteran regiments plus a new regiment, and another of three large rookie regiments. The arrival of Brigadier General Max Weber's brigade on September 16 enabled McClellan to fill out the division, and it was assigned as the 3rd Brigade.[5]

Sedgwick's division spent the night in the fields east and northeast of McClellan's battle headquarters at Pry's farm, and within a short walking distance of it. French's brigades were massed on either side of the Boonsboro Pike, east of Sedgwick, and Richardson's three brigades were deployed to support the artillery batteries on the bluffs south of Pry's farm, overlooking Antietam Creek. The men tried their best to snatch some sleep, but it was not easy. Rain, nerves, and preparations for battle kept many awake. Lieutenant Fred Hitchcock, the adjutant in the rookie 132nd Pennsylvania of French's division, recalled that the camp around his regiment was "ominously still." The men were forbidden to sing or make any noise, and only small fires to boil coffee were allowed. There was no need to keep the men quiet. With an impending battle, all were in a contemplative mood. "Letters were written home—many of them 'last words'—and quiet talks were had, and promises made between comrades," Hitchcock noted. He never forgot how his colonel, 40-year-old Richard A. Oakford, from Scranton, gently asked him if his roster of the officers and men of the regiment was complete, "'for,' said he, with a smile, 'We shall not all be here tomorrow night.'" Interruptions were frequent. Captain Francis E. Pierce in the 108th NY wrote that his regiment was awakened at 10 p.m. to receive an additional 40 rounds of ammunition, supplied to all regiments in the corps, giving each man a total of 80 rounds. Pierce complained, "But very little sleeping was done in camp that night as we were getting rations or something all night long."[6]

Sumner had his men awakened at 2:00 a.m., almost 4 hours before sunrise. There was no reveille. Lieutenant Hitchcock observed that none was necessary. "A simple call of a sergeant or corporal and every man was instantly awake and alert," he wrote. "All realized that there was ugly business and plenty of it just ahead." In Hitchcock's regiment, facing their first test of combat, the adjutant recalled a "nervous, subdued demeanor" among the men, who were normally full of jokes and horseplay. There was none of that now. Still, nearly 14,000 men moving about produces a certain hum, consisting of low voices, the rustling of equipment, and the tramp of thousands of feet. The men stripped their equipment down to only the necessities for fighting: rifle or musket, bayonet, canteen, cartridge box, cap box, and haversack. Knapsacks were packed and then piled according to company and regiment, to be retrieved later—that is, if one survived. Daniel Bond in the 1st Minnesota was having none of this. He had lost his knapsack and personal belongings at White Oak Swamp in the Virginia Peninsula, so he opted to keep his knapsack on, which his sergeant apparently permitted, since sergeants inspected weapons and ammunition. Small fires were kindled to boil coffee and prepare a hasty breakfast. Sergeant Ben Hirst of the

14th Connecticut remembered that he ate his "as though it was going to be the last meal in this world."[7]

In the 15th Massachusetts, Archibald Hudson, a 37-year-old farmer who had joined the regiment in August, walked up to the tent of his company commander, Lieutenant Albert Prince, "and said that he did not care to go into the fight and that he believed he would go home." Prince patiently explained to Hudson that since he was now enlisted in the army, "he couldn't do as he pleased," but it took some time to convince the green, frightened soldier. The lieutenant prevailed, and Hudson went in with his company. George Fletcher, one of three brothers in Company H, had been given a *Harper's Weekly* by someone on the 16th. Not wanting to throw it away, he rolled it up and stuffed it into the pocket of his uniform blouse. In the 20th Massachusetts, Daniel McAdams was a 17-year-old who had lied about his age to enlist on August 15. He had only recently joined the regiment, along with 85 other recruits. Arms were available only to some of them, and McAdams was one of those with no weapon. Possibly because leaders had discerned his age, he was told to remain behind, but he begged his company commander, Lieutenant Leander F. Alley, a sailor from Nantucket, to be allowed to go with his comrades. Alley relented and assigned McAdams to the rear rank when the regiment formed line, advising the private and the other unarmed recruits "to pick up all the muskets we could find from all the stragglers" as they made their way forward to the battlefield.[8]

The corps was ready to march well before daylight, and they awaited orders. Hours passed. At dawn, the artillery of both armies opened up, seemingly all along the front. "Heavy firing began at 6 a.m.," noted the 20th Massachusetts's quartermaster, Lieutenant Charles Folsom, in his diary. Orders still had not arrived. Roland Bowen, a private in the 15th Massachusetts, left the ranks and strolled over to a nearby hill, where he had a view of the fighting. "Yonder Hookers men were hard at it," he wrote. "The air seemed to be alive with bursting shell and the tremendous roar of musketry showed that the Hellish work had commenced in earnest."[9]

As the morning advanced and the roar of the battle grew loader, still no orders came, and Sumner grew increasingly agitated. His son, Captain Samuel S. Sumner, serving on the corps' staff, recalled that his father was "uneasy and impatient." If the 2nd Corps was going to participate in the attack, General Sumner wanted it to get moving, so it could coordinate with the 1st and 12th Corps. Shortly after 6:00 a.m., he could stand the uncertainty no longer and rode to Pry's farmhouse with his staff, hoping, as his son wrote, "to facilitate the movement of his command." Ezra Carman, in his authoritative work, *The Maryland Campaign of 1862*, wrote that "McClellan had not yet awakened from sleep and none of his staff seemed disposed to disturb him, though the roar of the battle was sounding in their ears." Carman, a veteran of the battle and a thorough historian, had hundreds of contacts with battle veterans, but he provided no source for this damning statement. The rumor only began to circulate after the war. It may have originated unintentionally with Rufus Dawes, a major in the 6th Wisconsin at Antietam. Dawes visited the field in 1866 for the dedication of the National Cemetery and spoke with a relative of Philip Pry's, who told Dawes that Pry had shared with him the comment McClellan was in bed when the 1st Corps was engaged. But in a letter to Jacob Cox in 1887, Dawes advised that it was best not to state this, "unless other evidence confirmatory is found." No other evidence has come to light, and this story's leak may have come from Cox.[10]

We shall never know whether McClellan was asleep when Sumner rode up to his headquarters, because his staff refused to allow the wing commander access. Captain Samuel Sumner admitted that he did not know "if General McClellan was asleep or engaged inside." Evidence strongly suggests the latter. In his report of the battle, General Ambrose Burnside stated that about the time his artillery and Confederate batteries engaged in a gun duel that morning, "I received an order from the general commanding to make my dispositions to carry the stone bridge over the Antietam nearly opposite our center, but to await further orders before making the attack." Burnside did not give a specific time, but it can be easily extrapolated. Jacob Cox, the acting commander of the 9th Corps, reported that the Confederate batteries began shelling the 9th Corps "shortly after daybreak." Sunrise on September 17 was at 5:53 a.m., so these guns probably opened fire around the same time batteries on other parts of the two armies' front lines commenced firing, around 5:30 a.m. It was during the gun duel between the 9th Corps' batteries and the Confederate artillery that Burnside said he received McClellan's orders. Since this engagement lasted for some time—Captain Asa M. Cook, commanding the 8th Massachusetts battery, reported that he fired for an hour or more—there is some variance as to when the orders arrived. Cox wrote that at 7:00 a.m., he received orders from Burnside to make the necessary preparations for an attack on the bridge and the heights beyond. Therefore Burnside got them from McClellan before 7:00 a.m. It was a preparatory order, however, not a directive to attack. McClellan and some of his staff later spun a fictive tale, claiming that he sent Burnside orders to attack at 8:00 a.m.—which he did not—but the details of this will be explored more fully later (see chapter 13). A reasonable estimate would place the time they were sent at around 6:30 a.m., precisely the same time that Sumner and his staff were fidgeting anxiously on the stairs and in the yard of Pry's house, waiting for their orders.[11]

McClellan did not want to see Sumner. He had little interest in Sumner's opinion on how the 2nd Corps should be used. The "Bull" was someone to be managed, not consulted. In the implementation of his battle plan, McClellan wanted a report on how Hooker's attack was progressing before he committed the 2nd Corps. His strategy was somewhat improvisational. If it had been McClellan's intention to attack the enemy's left with the 1st and 12th Corps, supported by the 2nd Corps, as he claimed it was in his final report of the campaign, then the 2nd Corps should have been in motion for the front minutes after the guns on Hooker's front opened fire. Since McClellan offered no explanation for why he held the 2nd Corps back, we must speculate on his reasoning. What seems most likely is McClellan's belief in the enemy's superiority in numbers, which dominated his thinking. If Hooker's attack was progressing favorably, then the 2nd Corps could be committed without undue risk. But if Hooker encountered overwhelming enemy numbers or was repulsed, then the 2nd Corps, the 5th Corps, and, when it arrived, the 6th Corps would compose a formidable veteran force on the east bank of Antietam Creek, which would prevent the Confederates from following up. McClellan consistently did not think in terms of destroying his opponent, but, instead, of ensuring that his forces did not lose, and this helps us understand his management of the battle.

Sumner was left to pace on Pry's porch, feeling "uneasy and impatient," while the minutes ticked by and the sounds of a great battle rattled the farmhouse windows. While riding to rejoin his command, Captain George Noyes, a commissary officer with Doubleday's division of the 1st Corps, stopped by the house at about this time. He described an "immense cavalry escort [that] waited in the rear, staff horses picketed by the dozens around the house, while the piazza was crowded with officers seeking to read with their field glasses the history of the battle at the right." On a bluff about 100 yards west of the house, which commanded "a still better view," Noyes saw "groups of officers, newspaper correspondents, and citizens" observing the battle.[12]

Sumner's staff mingled with McClellan's headquarters staff and watched the distant battle. Someone from the headquarters staff remarked to Captain Samuel Sumner that it was only a rearguard action, and that Lee "was too much of a soldier to fight in that position with a river at his back." It did not look or sound like a rearguard action from the vantage point of the bluffs outside Pry's house, however. Besides the infantry combat on Hooker's front, artillery across the front was blazing away, causing a constant roar that continued all day. At a distance of nearly 2 miles, it was difficult to observe any details of the 1st Corps' attack. "I could not distinguish a single battery, nor discern the movement of a single brigade, nor see a single battalion of the men in gray," wrote Captain Noyes, since "smoke-clouds leaped in sudden fury from ridges crowned with cannon, or lay thick and dim upon the valleys, or rose lazily up over the trees; all else was concealed." It could not have taken long for even the most skeptical to realize that this was no rearguard action.[13]

McClellan could only follow Hooker's progress through the limited view his staff had from the porch of Pry's house and the nearby hill, or by signal message or courier. The Signal Corps had established a station on the hill clustered with staff officers, newspapermen, and civilians, which was probably another reason these people had all gathered there. This station was in communication at daylight with a station set up by Lieutenants J. B. Brooks and W. H. Hill near Joseph Poffenberger's farm, probably on Poffenberger Hill, which was the highest point on Hooker's front. There is no record that Brooks and Hill provided a situation report during the early morning fighting, but McClellan received some type of report—either via courier or a signal message—which was not entered into the record, stating that Hooker's attack was making progress. At 7:20 a.m., McClellan decided to commit Sumner, but with a hedge. Only Sedgwick's and French's divisions were released. Richardson's division would remain in support of the artillery on the bluffs of the east bank of the Antietam until they were relieved by Morell's division of the 5th Corps, which was a mile to the rear, at Keedysville.[14] Chief of Staff Marcy prepared Sumner's written orders, which read: "The Comdg. General directs that you move Sedgwick and French across the creek by the fords which Captain [George Armstrong] Custer will point out to you. You will cross in as solid a mass as possible and communicate with Genl. Hooker immediately. Genl. Richardson's Division will not cross till further orders. You will cross your artillery over the bridge and halt after you cross until you ascertain if Genl. Hooker wants assistance."[15]

These were not aggressive orders. If Hooker did not require assistance, it was implied that Sumner was not to put his troops into action until he had communicated with headquarters for further orders. No explanation was offered for why Richardson's division was being held back, or even that it would be released when Morell relieved it. Sumner did not care for McClellan's management of the battle, testifying later that he disliked sending troops into action "in driblets," but he did not question his orders. He and his staff were in their saddles immediately after receiving Marcy's communication, dispersing to get Sedgwick and French underway. Sumner obeyed McClellan, but—as he had done the night before, when he sent most of the 2nd Corps' artillery across Antietam Creek, behind the 12th Corps—he again placed his own interpretation on these latest orders. He had no intention of wasting any more time by halting after crossing the creek, in order to communicate with Hooker. Instead, he would do so while on the move. His son wrote that Sumner set out "with a definite plan to combine his two corps, and, together with General Hooker's command, make an overwhelming attack, turn the enemy's left, and force him into the angle between the Potomac and Antietam Creek, and along Burnside's front." Sumner's instincts to bring mass to bear on the enemy's lines were sound, but things would not be as he expected when he reached the front.[16]

THE SITUATION ON THE Confederates' left flank, toward which Sedgwick's powerful division was marching, was critical. The only combat-effective forces remaining from the four divisions engaged there that morning consisted of the 1,225-man infantry brigade of Brigadier General Jubal Early; a small, regimental-sized remnant of Jones's division, which was rallied by Colonels Grigsby and

Stafford; elements of S. D. Lee's battalion; and a collection of other batteries from Lawton's, Jones's, and Stuart's commands. Twelve of the 13 infantry brigades engaged in the morning's action had been mauled. Two division commanders and seven brigade commanders were dead or wounded.[17] Most of the brigades had suffered such dreadful losses that they had temporarily lost their organization. Those that still retained it, such as Hood's division, were so reduced in numbers, as well as low on ammunition, that they could not have stopped any determined attack.

There are many adjectives used to describe Jubal Early, the commander of the only intact brigade on the left flank, most of which are unflattering: sarcastic, cantankerous, eccentric, profane, abrasive. Yet he was one of the best brigade commanders in the Army of Northern Virginia. Early was a complicated man, which included his politics. In a state that was overwhelmingly filled with Democrats, he was a Whig. "I have been in a minority all my life," he quipped. When Virginia debated the question of secession, Early, a prosecuting attorney living in rugged Franklin County, vigorously opposed leaving the Union. He lamented the fall of Fort Sumter and praised Major Robert Anderson, the fort's commander, for his "gallant devotion to duty." Early was a West Pointer, class of 1837, as well as a Mexican War volunteer officer, and he viewed the enthusiasm for secession and war in the South with horror and sorrow. Nevertheless, when Virginia seceded, Early joined his state. "I offer my own head on the block as a willing victim for the good of the Commonwealth," he wrote. Despite his reluctant entry into the war, he proved to be a skillful warrior, earning praise—and promotion to brigadier general—for his performance at First Manassas. His soldiers called him "Old Jube," or "Old Jubilee." For some people, this might have been a complimentary nickname, but in Early's case, it was because rheumatism, contracted in Mexico, caused him to stoop badly and appear older than his 45 years.[18]

Although Early generated little affection from his men, he had their respect. He was fearless on the battlefield, and smart, managing his brigade with a dexterity and skill that made the task look easy, when it was not. Significantly, his successes at Cedar Mountain and Second Manassas were not accompanied by huge casualty lists, even though his brigade was in the thick of the fighting. This was a sign of tactical proficiency.

When the battle began at daylight on the 17th, Early's brigade was in a reserve position, near Alfred Poffenberger's farm, which was a short distance west of the central section of the West Woods. Soon after Hooker's attack broke on Jackson's front, Jackson, in person, ordered Early to move his brigade to support the batteries assembled on Nicodemus Heights, which were under Jeb Stuart's command. Jacob Hauser's farm was about 400 yards southwest of Poffenberger's farm. A few hundred yards west of Hauser's buildings, there were a series of irregular hills, with summits reaching 500 feet (known today as Hauser's Ridge), and a small woodlot near the northern end of this ridgeline. Early used the woods and the ridge to shield his troops from observation when they made their way to Stuart's position. En route, Early observed skirmishers of the 23rd New York, from Patrick's brigade, in the fields west of the West Woods. Patrick had detached the regiment to keep an eye on Early, because his movement had been spotted, as well as to attend to a particularly troublesome battery in Stuart's group—possibly Captain Louis E. D'Aquin's Louisiana Guard battery, which consisted of three rifled guns—located at the southern end of Stuart's artillery grouping. Early dropped off some skirmishers to entertain the New Yorkers and continued on to Stuart with his brigade. The cavalryman suggested that Early form his brigade behind the heights, where they would be sheltered from the Federals' artillery fire, then beginning to zero in on Stuart's batteries.[19]

For nearly an hour, Early's men hugged the earth, while above them, Stuart's artillery group fought courageously. Nonetheless, they took a severe beating from the Union's 1st Corps' guns on Poffenberger Hill. Although the 23rd New York caused no mischief, Stuart also observed the movement of elements of Gibbon's and Patrick's brigades into the northern end of the West Woods. Then a new threat appeared. When Meade's division advanced from the North Woods to support Doubleday's and Ricketts's attack, Hooker detached Lieutenant Colonel Adoniram Warner's 10th Reserves, from Robert Anderson's 3rd Brigade of the Pennsylvania Reserves Division, to guard the extreme right flank of his corps, west of the Hagerstown Pike. Passing just north of Miller's farm buildings, Warner found elements of the 23rd New York between Nicodemus's farm and the northern end of the West Woods. The New Yorkers were lying low, and when they learned Warner had orders to skirmish and watch the right flank, they quickly withdrew "to some stacks behind a barn [possibly Nicodemus's] and covered themselves from bullets."[20]

Warner pushed his skirmishers forward aggressively, but he kept the main body of his regiment concealed, "so that my real strength should not be seen." It was Warner's aggressive posture that convinced Jeb Stuart it was time to displace his artillery. Some of Warner's skirmishers were picking off the gunners in one of Stuart's batteries, but the more important question for Stuart was whether these enemy skirmishers might be screening a larger force that might interpose itself between Stuart and the main Confederate line. Besides, his batteries had already suffered enough. Stuart had a good eye for terrain, and he recognized Hauser's Ridge as the key to control of the West Woods and the Confederates' left flank. If the enemy gained control of the ridge and massed artillery there, it would render the Confederate position at Sharpsburg untenable. For that reason, it had to be held. Moreover, it offered excellent fields of fire for Confederate guns to sweep the western face of the West Woods, as well as fields of fire over the woods into parts of the Cornfield and East Woods area, because of its elevation. Stuart ordered his remaining batteries to move to locations along the ridge, and he directed Early to shift his brigade to the small woodlot about 400 yards west of Alfred Poffenberger's place, at the northern end of the ridge. Early would have good cover here and could prevent the enemy from penetrating to a position where they might cause real trouble.[21]

This movement to Hauser's Ridge began between 7:30 and 8 a.m., when Hood's counterattack receded and D. H. Hill's brigades arrived to renew the attack. Stuart assembled an assortment of batteries at various points along the ridge. Some had been with his group on Nicodemus Heights, and the rest came from other locales. The precise number of guns and an accounting of which batteries were present may never be accurately known. Pelham's horse battery unlimbered in Poffenberger's cornfield, on the eastern edge of the woodlot Stuart had ordered Early to occupy, where the guns had a good sweep of the approaches from the northern and central sections of the West Woods. There was also Brockenbrough's Maryland battery (three rifles, one 12 lb. howitzer); Raine's Virginia battery (two 3-inch rifles, two 12 lb. howitzers); Poague's Rockbridge Artillery (two rifles, one Napoleon); and a howitzer of D'Aquin's Louisiana Guard battery. Depending on whether the full strength of each battery was deployed (and we know Poague's Napoleon was not), between 13 and 17 guns were gathered in positions to cover the approaches from the West Woods. This was a Confederate artillery battalion's worth of firepower.[22]

Stuart managed the guns in his makeshift battalion with Pelham's capable assistance but, apparently, with no help from Jackson's divisional artillery commanders, even though most of the guns came from Jackson's two infantry divisions. Major Alfred R. Courtney, commanding Lawton's divisional artillery, shirked his duty and was not present on the field, for which he was subsequently court-martialed. John R. Jones's divisional artillery chief, Major Lindsay Mayo Shumaker, had a good reputation, but there is no evidence that he was present, either. Not that Stuart needed help. He displayed excellent tactical judgment in the placement of the guns and inspired leadership for the crews. Such leadership carried risks, however. "I was in constant anxiety for the life of my general, who was always where the carnage was greatest," recalled William W. Blackford, a member of Stuart's staff. But fortune favored the cavalier this day. Later in the morning, although his horse would be shot and a courier killed near him, he emerged unscathed from the battle.[23]

Meanwhile, Jubal Early led his brigade on a different, better-concealed route toward the small woodlot Stuart had directed him to occupy. When he reached the woods, he was met by Stuart, who informed him that Lawton was wounded and that Jackson had ordered Early to return with his brigade and take command of the division. Early left the 13th Virginia, numbering only about 100 men, to support one of Stuart's batteries (probably Pelham's) and keep back the 10th Pennsylvania Reserves, and set off with the rest of his command. He used the woodlot and Poffenberger's cornfield to screen his movement from observation. Warner's 10th Pennsylvania Reserves saw them, but Early's movements confused them. Alerted to the enemy's activity, Warner rode up a small hill near his skirmish line, where he was able to see Early's brigade. At the moment when he spotted them, the brigade was halted, and Warner thought the Confederates were "evidently puzzled to know what to do or to understand the meaning of our maneuvers. Their field officers were riding about in confusion and their ranks stood still as if awaiting some orders." Warner was not there for more than 2 or 3 minutes before Early's skirmishers fired at him. One bullet glanced off his sword, another nicked his horse, and several more hit the ground nearby. He wrongly assumed that they were stray shots. Although some of his men hollered at him to get under cover, he did not hear the warning. The next shot struck him in the hip and toppled him from his horse. Warner was a man of hard bark, though. He had some of his men remount him, and then made sure his regiment was under control and in good cover before he left to get medical attention.[24]

Plucky as Warner and his Pennsylvania Reserves were, they were no hindrance to Early's movements. The confusion Warner believed he observed was probably just a short halt, made while Early and his regimental commanders determined the best route back to the main Confederate line. Early's march along the southern border of Poffenberger's cornfield led him to the farm lane between Hauser's and Poffenberger's homesteads, which his brigade followed to the West Woods near where they had bivouacked during the night. Here he found Colonels Grigsby and Stafford, along with the 200 to 300 men they had rallied from their division. They were trading fire with some Federals in the woods. Early was unable to determine the size of the force opposing them but thought they were probably only a skirmish line. His hunch was correct. They were from Patrick's brigade and had remained in the northern section of the woods, following the counterattack against Hood's division.[25]

Despite the ad hoc nature of their command, Grigsby and Stafford had decided to advance against this enemy force and either drive them out or reveal if they screened a larger number of men. Early agreed with their plan and formed his brigade in their rear, as a support. Patrick had no interest in picking a fight. His regiments were low on ammunition, and he felt left alone after Gibbon's brigade and Battery B, 4th U.S., withdrew, following the repulse of Hood. With more caution than the situation probably warranted, when Grigsby's and Stafford's men probed his position, Patrick decided to give up the cover and defensive strength of the woods. He withdrew his brigade back to a ledge of ground a short distance north of Miller's barn, where he allowed his men to kindle fires to make coffee. While Patrick's concern for his men was admirable, his decision to abandon the woods was a poor one, and the position where he halted his brigade exposed them to fire from Pelham's battery.[26]

Aware of how weak they were, Grigsby and Early were not inclined to push their advance into the northernmost section of the woods. They halted on sloping ground about 130 yards from the northern edge of the West Woods' central section. Early thought this a good point to hold. It concealed his brigade from anyone north of his position, and the higher ground on his right, in the direction of the Hagerstown Pike, kept him hidden from Union gunners. He suggested that Grigsby and Stafford move their force to his left, in an Alfred Poffenberger meadow a short distance north of the farmer's buildings, facing the northern portion of the West Woods. Although the most direct threat at that moment appeared to be north of his position, Early took the precaution of forming the 49th Virginia to face east, at a right angle to the rest of the brigade, where it looked across open ground leading up to the Hagerstown Pike. It was a good position. Although Early had organized it principally to resist an attack from the north, if a threat emerged from the east, he could easily redeploy the entire force behind the limestone ledge that was used by Union troops earlier that morning. With nearly 1,400 men, they would not be easily dislodged.[27]

From his position, Early could see Patrick's brigade, north of Miller's barn, but could not discern that the men were making coffee, rather than preparing to attack. He believed they were "evidently endeavoring to make a movement on our flank and rear," but he had his orders to take control of the division. Leaving Colonel William Smith, commanding the 49th Virginia, in charge of the brigade, with instructions to "resist the enemy at all hazards," Early rode off to determine the location and condition of the rest of the division. We do not know precisely where his ride took him, but it was probably in the vicinity of the Dunker Church. He learned that the division had suffered heavy casualties and "fallen back some distance to the rear for the purpose of reorganizing, and that they were probably not in a condition to go into the fight again." Nevertheless, he sent Major John Parke Wilson Jr., a volunteer aide-de-camp, to hunt up the brigades and order them back. He also saw Confederate troops falling back from the direction of the Cornfield and East Woods. They were D. H. Hill's men: either McRae's brigade, or Ripley's and Colquitt's brigades. The situation looked alarming, and Early went to find Jackson. His report merely confirmed what Jackson already knew—that the left flank was collapsing and urgently needed reinforcements. Jackson had already sent his aide-de-camp, Sandie Pendleton, to Lee for help. Never one for detailed explanations, Jackson merely told Early that reinforcements had been sent for and that he must "keep the enemy in check until they arrived." Early hurried back to his brigade.[28]

WHILE JACKSON AND EARLY held their brief conversation, Sandie Pendleton raced his horse to Cemetery Hill, where Robert E. Lee had established a forward command post. He was not the only staff officer on his way to the army's commander in quest of reinforcements. D. H. Hill dispatched his assistant adjutant general, Major James W. Ratchford, at around the same time, and Hood may have also sent a staff member, via Longstreet.[29]

Lee probably slept very little on the night of September 16. His headquarters were in a woodlot just outside the western edge of Sharpsburg, at the extreme range of Union artillery rounds. He spent the night in great anxiety over whether McLaws's and R. H. Anderson's divisions would arrive before McClellan attacked. At 4:30 a.m., he took the precaution of writing to General Pendleton, asking him to "keep some artillery guarding each of the fords at Williamsport, Falling Waters, and Shepherdstown, and have some infantry with it, if possible." The Shepherdstown ford was Lee's only escape if things went awry. Williamsport and Falling Waters were critical, not only to deny them to the enemy, but also to provide access back into Maryland, should it become necessary to withdraw from Sharpsburg.[30]

AFTER AN UNCOMMONLY SEVERE march throughout the night, for which he was unfairly criticized for being slow, McLaws reached the Potomac at Shepherdstown around 2:30 a.m. and began the laborious river crossing. The head of his column arrived outside Sharpsburg between 4:30 and 5:00 a.m. On the way up from the river, McLaws received an order from Stonewall Jackson, directing his division to the army's right flank. Moving on ahead of his men in that black night, McLaws rode right by Lee's headquarters, which were never imposing to begin with, and into Sharpsburg. He remembered that the village was completely quiet, with no "indication of the close proximity of the two contending armies." Incredibly, he met no one in the village. McLaws turned around to halt his command, so he could "find someone who could tell me where to go." On the way he ran into Longstreet and his staff, heading to the front. When McLaws asked Longstreet where Lee was, the wing commander turned in his saddle and pointed to a woodlot about a quarter of a mile away, saying, "You will find him among those trees." Longstreet instructed McLaws to send R. H. Anderson's division through the town to the vicinity of Cemetery Hill and then rode on. McLaws galloped the short distance to army headquarters and found Lee "with his coat off and washing his face." Lee expressed great satisfaction for what the Georgian had accomplished but also observed, "We have I believe a hard day's work before us, and you must rest your men." He advised McLaws to halt his division about a quarter of a mile west of headquarters. "Do not let them come quite this far as the shells of the enemy fall about here," Lee warned. When McLaws mentioned that he had received an order from Jackson to go to the army's right flank, Lee replied, "Never mind that order but do as I told you and consider yourself as specially under my orders."[31]

McLaws halted his division "in plain view of General Lee's headquarters" and gave orders for the men to rest but not stray, since they were likely to be called into action soon. He continued back to R. H. Anderson and gave him the orders to march through Sharpsburg and report to Longstreet. With these details attended to, McLaws, who had not slept in nearly 72 hours and was utterly exhausted, turned his horse loose "and was asleep in the tall grass in about a minute."[32]

With McLaws's and R. H. Anderson's arrival, Lee immediately released Walker's division from reserve, ordering it to take up a position on the army's far right, guarding Snavely's Ford. Soon after issuing these orders, he and his staff mounted and rode through town to Cemetery Hill. Curiously, Lee's movements at Antietam are very poorly documented. Colonel Armistead Long, Lee's military secretary, wrote that his position during the battle "was on a hill to the east of Sharpsburg, which gave him an oversight of the whole field." This was Cemetery Hill, but as there was no one spot on this hill where Lee could view every part of his line, he probably moved about, going both north and south of the Boonsboro Pike, depending on which portion of the action he wished to see. He also left the hill several times, but when the battle opened at 5:30 a.m., Lee most likely was already on the hill. Although smoke would have obscured much of the fighting on his left flank, he could easily discern its severity by the sound of heavy firing. As the fighting continued, Lee would have seen a growing stream of stragglers and walking wounded trickling back toward Sharpsburg, and he might have spotted the battered brigades of Hays, Douglass, and Walker, in Lawton's division, falling back to a point a short distance north of the village. We do not know of any reports he received about how the action was going, but there was abundant evidence that it was not going well. Lee was experienced enough, however, to know that at the rear of a fight, things always looked bleak. He had few reserves. When and where he released them would be the most critical decisions that he made. He could not overreact and commit them until he was certain of the necessity. About 7:30 a.m., toward the end of Hood's counterattack, Lee decided on a modest reinforcement of his left. Whether it was prompted by a request for help from Jackson, Hood, or D. H. Hill is unknown.[33]

Lee tapped the Georgia brigade of Colonel George T. "Tige" Anderson, which was resting behind Cemetery Hill as a support for the batteries there. Anderson's five regiments numbered only about 590 men, but they were close by and could move out immediately. In the careless staff work typical in the Army of Northern Virginia at this point in the war, when Anderson received his orders, he was provided with no guide, nor with any directions on where he might find Hood's division. Why he was ordered to support Hood and not Jackson is another mystery, although it may be because Hood had requested the reinforcement. Anderson moved out immediately, although he did it so quickly that he left one of his regiments behind. He guided the direction of his march "by the sound of the musketry."[34]

Soon after G. T. Anderson set out, Pendleton and Ratchford arrived on Cemetery Hill in swift sequence. Who arrived first is unknown, but it was probably Sandie Pendleton. He probably left Jackson around 7:30 a.m., and, since it was just a mile's ride to Cemetery Hill, he should have reached Lee in only a few minutes.

According to Ratchford, when he relayed D. H. Hill's request for help, Lee replied that he had no troops to spare, but the major's memory failed him here. Whatever reports the two staff officers gave to Lee, they convinced him that the situation on the left was more critical than he had believed, and that it would need more than G. T. Anderson's small brigade to blunt the enemy's attack. Lee dispatched Major Walter Taylor to find McLaws and order his entire division to the left at once. Ratchford rode along with Taylor, to act as a guide for McLaws. They rode out from the western side of Sharpsburg, where they found McLaws's brigades asleep in the fields beside the road. No system existed then for marking where headquarters was. Valuable minutes were wasted searching for McLaws, who, sound asleep in the tall grass, could not be located. Taylor and Ratchford managed to find Major Thomas S. McIntosh, a young attorney from Savannah who was the division's adjutant general, and gave him the orders. McIntosh did not know where McLaws was, either, so he took on the responsibility to order the division to march. While the division assembled and started to move, Taylor and Ratchford continued their search for McLaws, whom they soon found in a grassy field beside the road. "The next thing I remember was being wakened up by an officer who was a stranger to me," recalled McLaws of the occasion when Taylor found him. The Georgian jumped to his feet and asked what Taylor wanted. "General we have been looking for you, the tall grass in which you were sleeping prevented our finding you. Your division has been called for by General Lee to move in haste, and as you could not be found it has been put in motion by your adjutant-general, we will ride together and overtake it," replied Taylor. McLaws mounted immediately, and the officers galloped off to overtake his division.[35]

Despite unjustified complaints about McLaws as a slow, plodding officer, there was no delay in the movement of his division. He overtook his brigades, and, with Ratchford indicating the direction, they marched rapidly cross-country, northwest of Sharpsburg and west of the farms of S. D. Piper and Reel, which were located just off River Landing Road from Sharpsburg to New Industry, on the Potomac River. The scenes they encountered along the way did not boost morale. Battered and broken elements of brigades and regiments were met, "with their tales of terrible fighting and great slaughter." There were scores of wounded, with some carried on stretchers and others walking under their own power or being helped by comrades. Equally distressing were the plentiful stragglers, many without armaments, putting distance between themselves and the fighting. The pressing question was whether McLaws would arrive in time to prevent disaster.[36]

BY THIS TIME, JUBAL Early had returned to his brigade and observed enemy troops in "considerable force" advancing on his position from the north and northeast. The Federals approaching from the north were Goodrich's

12th Corps brigade, supported by Patrick's brigade. To the northeast, in the direction of the Cornfield and Miller's farm, was another large formation which looked like a brigade but was, in fact, the 124th Pennsylvania. Early told his adjutant general, Major Samuel Hale Jr., to ride to Jackson and inform him that "the danger was imminent."[37]

IT WILL BE RECALLED that when Greene's division of the 12th Corps reached the field, General Williams detached its 3rd Brigade, under Colonel William B. Goodrich, with orders to report to General Gibbon near Miller's farm (see chapter 6). Goodrich's brigade was very small, with its four regiments numbering only 777 officers and men. The 40-year-old Goodrich came from the St. Lawrence River region of upstate New York. He had carved out a successful career as an attorney and newspaper editor, dabbled in the state militia, served as a volunteer in the war with Mexico, and spent a year in California during the gold rush. When the Civil War began, he promptly raised a company of the 60th New York and was commissioned as its captain. He was a pure patriot to the Union cause. "I could stay at home and enjoy the society of my family, who are dearer than life to me," he told a crowd in Canton as his company prepared to depart. "I have not taken this step rashly," he continued. "I have thoroughly considered the whole matter, and have come to the conclusion that it is a duty I owe my country, to surrender up my life if need be, in her defense." He was soon promoted to lieutenant colonel, where he learned his new trade under Colonel George Sears Greene. When Greene was promoted to general, Goodrich was elevated to colonel. At Antietam, he assumed command of the brigade by seniority. On the morning of September 16, with signs that a general engagement was imminent, Goodrich spoke with his friend, Sergeant Major Lester Willson, about the possibility of his death. He did not have a premonition but nonetheless thought it wise to make preparations. He gave Willson his wife's address and information on where to telegraph her if he were killed, so his remains could be sent home "unless they should be so badly mutilated as to not to be recognized."[38]

When Goodrich's brigade reached the vicinity of Miller's farm, around 8:30 a.m., Gibbon had already withdrawn both his brigade and Battery B, 4th U.S., back to the North Woods. Goodrich found the 124th Pennsylvania lying down in the Cornfield, and Patrick's brigade, across the turnpike near Miller's barn, making coffee. Someone (it is not clear who) ordered Goodrich to detach the Purnell Legion, place them in the rear of the 124th, "and drive them forward." The Legion's field officers thought this a strange order and instead moved their regiment up to support the greenhorns. This deduction in numbers left Goodrich with only 572 men in his remaining three regiments. Using this small force, Goodrich intended to push into the West Woods. Why he chose this aggressive action is unclear. He had no orders to do so, his force was small, and the enemy's strength was unknown. Patrick warned him about the nature of the ground in the woods and the formidableness of the Confederate position there and offered advice on how Goodrich might get an enfilading fire on the Rebels. "Knowing the ground well I directed Colonel Goodrich to advance cautiously, forming his skirmishers, until I could get reinforcements to go in on his left and front in sufficient force to drive through the corner [of the woods], where the enemy appeared to hold in masses," wrote Patrick. It was sound advice. Even though his regiments had not yet received a resupply of ammunition, by reapportioning what they had, there was enough to go around, so Patrick was willing to support Goodrich's advance.[39]

Patrick thought more troops would be helpful, and he rode to find his division commander, Abner Doubleday, to see if the general could round up additional reinforcements. Goodrich was an assertive but smart officer. He did not plunge headlong into the West Woods, but had his advance preceded by a strong skirmish line, consisting of a company from the 60th New York and, possibly, one each from the 78th New York and the 3rd Delaware. They found the woods infested with sharpshooters. "We could not get far into the woods," recalled Captain John C. O. Redington, commanding the 60th New York's skirmish company. Goodrich made the fatal mistake of visiting his skirmish line, to better assess the enemy's resistance, and one of Early's or Grigsby's men put a bullet through his right breast. It passed down behind his stomach and severed an artery near his intestines. Goodrich survived long enough to be carried back to Miller's barn, where he died.[40]

Patrick had no luck in obtaining reinforcements. When he returned, he found that Goodrich was mortally wounded and his brigade "with difficulty [was] holding its position" against Early and Grigsby. Patrick assumed command of both brigades and advanced skirmishers on the right, so that they went through the woods to the edge of Alfred Poffenberger's cornfield. But the Confederates refused to be budged, and the two Union brigades went no farther.[41]

Across the Hagerstown Pike, the 124th Pennsylvania, which had been detached from its brigade by General Williams and sent forward to Miller's farm during the 12th Corps' deployment, had taken cover in the low ground between Miller's house and the Cornfield during the furious engagement between Gordon's brigade and Colquitt's and Ripley's Confederates. When the Rebels retreated, Colonel Hawley ordered the regiment to dismantle the Cornfield's northern fence and move into the corn. They drifted slightly west in making this small advance, which pushed the right company out of the corn and into the meadow across from the pike. This exposed them to a battery beyond the West Woods, possibly Pelham's, which opened fire. Hawley ordered his men to lie down, even though they had only proceeded some 20 yards into the corn. Without any real orders, he may have been at a loss as to what to do. It seemed so to Lieutenant Joseph G. Cummins in Company G, who innocently admitted in a letter to his hometown newspaper, "We marched, not knowing really where we were going." There were some casualties from the shelling, one of them being Hawley, who, at 8:45 a.m., by his watch, received a wound in the neck. Command then went to Major Isaac L. Halderman.[42]

The shelling and Hawley's wounding shook the rookies, and they began to leak a steady stream of men to the rear. These shirkers encountered the Purnell Legion, posted to stop such cowardly business. David Herring, a sergeant in the Legion, thought the Pennsylvanians were "badly officered," which accounted for their poor discipline. The Legion's men were lying down, to avoid the same battery that was shelling the 124th Pennsylvania, but when the Keystone State men attempted to get past them, the Marylanders were ordered to stand up and "keep them from getting back." Although the 124th outnumbered the Legion by almost 4 to 1, the leveled rifles and bayonets of the veterans turned the rookies around and herded them back into the corn.[43]

Prodded and buoyed by the veterans, the 124th resumed their advance through the corn, continuing to drift in an oblique, southwesterly direction, which pushed two more companies out into the open across the turnpike. This was the same ground where, earlier in the morning, the right companies of the 6th Wisconsin had been fired on from the West Woods. Now the Pennsylvanians tasted what the Badgers had encountered earlier. Some 230 yards south of Miller's barn, these companies, numbering around 200 men, came under fire from the 49th Virginia, which was concealed in the woods. Lieutenant Joseph G. Cummins in Company D described "bullets by hundreds whizzing past our heads." Corporal David Wilkinson in Company A had his kepi removed by one bullet, another went through the right sleeve of his coat, and a third nearly took off his little finger. He and his comrades fired back, but after three rounds, another ball hit Wilkinson in the leg and removed him from the fight. The Confederates were so difficult to see that Sergeant William Potts and a comrade in Company F worked their way forward to try and fix their position. They discovered some bushes "along a ridge of rocks"—the same ledge the 7th Wisconsin and the 19th Indiana had used for cover—which were now "full of rebels," one of whom shot and wounded both of them. The right of the line, nearest the woods, pulled back, and the three companies now formed an oblique line to the pike. The men lay down to return fire, but it was a poor, exposed position. They soon fell back to better cover at the pike, and, subsequently, retreated back to Miller's barn.[44]

The balance of the 124th Pennsylvania, followed by the Purnell Legion, passed through the Cornfield and onto the plateau south of it, where they, too, felt the sting of a flanking fire from Early's men. Their officers wheeled the regiment to face west, then backed them east, to get behind the crest of the plateau for cover. The Legion also changed front to the west and formed on the 124th's right rear. Neither regiment had any encouragement or inclination to advance. Early and Grigsby had easily parried two enemy advances toward the West Woods, needing to engage no more than their skirmish line. It spoke well of the protective multiplier the woods and a limestone ledge provided for those who held them, and also of Early's astute placement of his men. But it also reflected a lack of command and control on the Federal side. Piecemeal, uncoordinated attacks would not dislodge determined defenders from such a strong position.[45]

SHORTLY BEFORE GOODRICH'S BRIGADE moved against Early, Major Hale returned to the general after Hale's talk with Jackson, bearing the message that reinforcements "should be sent immediately." This was comforting news, but just then a battery opened fire about 200 yards to Early's right and rear, almost directly opposite the Dunker Church. He presumed it was a Confederate battery, but a soldier in the 49th Virginia who was standing on the plateau that concealed the brigade from sight had a good view toward the church and called down that it was Union artillery—specifically, Monroe's battery. Major Hale, who may have seen the guns moving into position on his ride back from conferring with Jackson, also expressed the opinion that they were Yankee guns. Early had to see this for himself. He rode down to the woods' edge—he did not say to precisely which point—where he obtained a closer look. This removed all doubt. They were Federal forces, firing in the direction of Sharpsburg. Equally alarming, Early saw that the guns were supported "by a very heavy column of infantry," which was Greene's division. This was at about the same time as Goodrich began to advance into the northern section of the West Woods. "My condition," Early assessed, "was exceedingly critical." If the enemy to his right rear advanced, he could be cut off and destroyed. A less confident or audacious man might have ordered a withdrawal to Hauser's Ridge, which would have abandoned the woods to the enemy, with dire consequences for the Confederates. But Early possessed both boldness and a good eye for key terrain. "I saw the vast importance of maintaining my ground," he wrote, "for, had the enemy gotten possession of the woods, the heights immediately in rear, which commanded the rear of our whole line, would have fallen into his hands." He made the decision to hold his position, trusting that the reinforcements Jackson promised could tend to the enemy on his right rear, while he and Grigsby dealt with the threat from the north and northeast. But he kept a sharp lookout toward the Federals to his rear, to track their movements. By 9:00 a.m., the expected reinforcements were still not up, and Early watched with alarm as a large Union force crossed the Hagerstown Pike near where the battery was firing and entered the West Woods around the Dunker Church.[46]

Early again acted decisively. He would not give up the woods without a fight. He ordered Grigsby to occupy the spot where Early's brigade had just been and hold off the different Yankee forces north and northeast of their position. Early then led his brigade south, parallel to the Hagerstown Pike, toward the Federal force near the Dunker Church. The terrain worked to his advantage, for the higher ground, now on his left as he marched south, kept him concealed.[47]

THE TROOPS EARLY OBSERVED moving into the West Woods were another of the 12th Corps' rookie regiments: the 125th Pennsylvania of Crawford's brigade, around 700 strong. When the 12th Corps commenced their general advance, following the defeat of Ripley's and Colquitt's brigades, the 125th followed the path of Greene's division, moving through the East Woods and into the open ground south of the Cornfield and north of Smoketown Road. They arrived in the rear of Monroe's Battery D, 1st Rhode Island, which was firing at Confederate troops around the Dunker Church. The 125th's colonel was 36-year-old Jacob Higgins. Unlike some of the other newly raised Pennsylvania regiments' leaders, Higgins was an experienced officer. He had served as a volunteer in the Mexican War and was wounded at Chapultepec. A continuing interest in the military led him to the Pennsylvania Militia, and by 1861 he was colonel of the 1st Militia Regiment. Following First Bull Run, he raised a company of the 1st Pennsylvania Cavalry and was commissioned as a captain. Within a month, he was promoted to lieutenant colonel. He resigned from the regiment in the summer of 1862 to return home and help recruit the 125th Pennsylvania Volunteers.[48]

When Higgins's regiment came up behind Monroe's battery, the latter was just limbering up to move to the Dunker Church plateau. Higgins had some of his men clear a path for Monroe through Smoketown Road's fencing and then followed the battery, moving along the northern side of the road and passing over numerous dead and wounded, to a position on Monroe's right rear, where the colonel ordered his men to lie down. Although the serious fighting was over, an occasional bullet or artillery shell still posed a danger. The rank and file of the regiment begged Higgins and his lieutenant colonel, Jacob Szink, to dismount and avoid unnecessary exposure. They did, and a moment after Szink's feet hit the ground, a Confederate shell exploded, wounding the lieutenant colonel, tearing away the stirrup strap on his horse's saddle, and sending the animal fleeing in panic. The small-arms fire came from "men we could not see," recalled Milton Lytle, a 19-year-old Company B private who, only two months earlier, had been a law student. The Confederates were hidden "in the woods and behind the stone fences along the turnpike." While the regiment lay under this intermittent fire, Hooker rode up and asked Higgins if any troops were in the West Woods. "None but rebels," he replied. An instant later, a bullet struck Hooker's horse. The general seemed not to notice this, and when Higgins pointed it out, Hooker merely said "I see" and then rode off.[49]

In front of the regiment, Monroe's battery was having a rough go. The same Rebel skirmishers and sharpshooters firing at the 125th Pennsylvania were also picking off the battery's horses at an alarming rate. When Monroe decided the position was too exposed and ordered his artillery to withdraw, one limber had lost so many horses that it was unable to pull its gun off. Volunteers from the 125th dashed forward and muscled the piece to safety. As Monroe's guns pulled out, Lieutenant Edward L. Witman, an aide-de-camp to General Crawford, rode up to Higgins and said, "The General sends his compliments and requests you to advance with your regiment into that woods, and to hold it at all hazards." Why Crawford ordered this lone, inexperienced regiment into the woods, and then expected them to hold the position when unsupported, defies understanding. But Crawford earned no marks for his generalship at Antietam. Higgins asked no questions, but ordered Company G to deploy as skirmishers and, with the balance of the regiment following and raising a loud yell, rushed forward. It was 9:00 a.m. The Confederates along the turnpike fences and in the woods "fled precipitately" through the West Woods ahead of the mass of yelling Pennsylvanians. Higgins halted the regiment in the turnpike to correct their alignment, but Patterson's battery, or possibly one of S. D. Lee's, opened fire on them from the south, so the colonel ordered his men into the woods. During that pause in the road, Higgins came upon Lieutenant Colonel Newton Lord in the 6th Georgia. "He looked up at me and asked for some stimulant," recalled Higgins. The colonel stopped momentarily to provide aid to the dying Confederate officer, then hurried after his men.[50]

The 125th dashed about 100 yards past the Dunker Church, to the edge of the plateau of higher ground the church sits on. When they halted, their left rested within 20 yards of the church. The line faced west-southwest, with the right of the regiment just over 200 yards north of the church, across an east–west ravine that traversed the width of the woods. Higgins directed Captain John McKeage to advance his Company G through the woods toward its western edge and see what they turned up. The West Woods was a woodlot, like the East Woods and North Woods, consisting largely of mature oak trees, with very little understory or underbrush. "The forest is so open that you may drive a carriage almost in any direction," wrote a civilian who visited the site immediately after the battle.[51]

Higgins at once recognized that his position was precarious. He was well beyond any friendly troops, both his flanks were vulnerable, and he had no sense of the enemy's strength in his front. He gave his horse to his brother, Lieutenant Joseph Higgins, and sent him to Crawford to ask for reinforcements. As Joseph spurred away, Higgins detached Company B "and ordered it to watch the ravine or depression on the other side of the church, and report to me if the enemy attempted to come up to get in our rear."[52]

McKeage's skirmishers probed to about 20 yards from the woods' western edge, near Alfred Poffenberger's barn. A Confederate, probably wounded, was captured and told the Pennsylvanians that the farm was being used as a field hospital. Near the edge of the woods, McKeage's skirmishers were fired on by the

49th Virginia, who were leading the movement of Early's brigade from the north. The Federals beat a hasty retreat back toward the main line, firing at their pursuers as they went. John Keatly, a Company A private on the main regimental line, saw Early's brigade clearly. "Quite a heavy column commenced passing along from our right toward our left," he recalled. He observed another body of Confederates approaching their front from the southwest, driving in the Company G skirmishers who had advanced in that direction. This was G. T. Anderson's brigade. Higgins ordered his regiment to begin shooting at the two targets. In moments, "the firing was terrific on both sides," wrote the colonel. As the 125th Pennsylvania became seriously engaged, Brigadier General Willis A. Gorman, commanding the 1st Brigade of Sedgwick's 2nd Division, rode up to Higgins and told him that "his brigade was some distance back," coming up on the 125th's left flank, before hurrying off to meet his command. The "some distance back" was not particularly comforting to Higgins, but at least he knew that help was approaching.[53]

SEDGWICK'S DIVISION WAS IN MOTION only minutes after Sumner received his orders from McClellan. The three brigades filed downhill to Pry's Ford. Brigadier General Willis A. Gorman's 1st Brigade, 1,700 strong, led the way, followed by Brigadier General Napoleon J. T. Dana's 3rd Brigade, the largest in the division, with 1,946 officers and men. Brigadier General Oliver O. Howard's 2nd Brigade, nicknamed the "Philadelphia Brigade" for the city where its four regiments were raised, numbered 1,800 men and brought up the rear. The column stretched out for nearly a mile. There was no halt at the ford for the men to remove their shoes and socks. They plunged straight through, with the water coming up to their knees. Their army brogans slipped and slid on the creek bottom. "It was a tussle to keep on our f[ee]t going through it," noted William McLeon in the 34th New York. The soldiers in the 72nd Pennsylvania of Howard's brigade stopped long enough for the men to fill their canteens when they crossed. After clearing the creek, some regiments were given a brief pause, so they could remove their shoes and wring out their socks. Among the many miseries of an infantryman's life, wet socks and shoes ranked high, since the combination led to severe blisters and raw feet. The brigades marched north from the creek, up a gentle slope in the direction of Otho Smith's farm. This route sheltered them from observation, and the open ground south of Smith's farm was ideal terrain in which to form the brigades. After a march of about a quarter of a mile, Gorman's brigade halted and formed a line of battle, facing west. Dana's brigade deployed some 50 to 60 yards in their rear, and Howard's was the same distance in the rear of Dana. The tactical name for the formation was column of brigades, which is identical to column of regiments, except with brigades stacked one behind the other. Just as it was for Mansfield and the 12th Corps that morning, the formation was efficient for command and control, but dangerous when troops came under fire, since they presented such a large, compact target. Since the brigades were so close to one another, they could not maneuver easily against threats to their flanks, and the close intervals between brigades rendered them highly vulnerable to head-on artillery fire. A shell that overshot the front line was likely to score a hit in one of the two following brigades.[54]

While the brigades deployed, Colonel William R. Lee, a 55-year-old white-haired railroad executive from Roxbury, addressed his soldiers in the 20th Massachusetts Infantry, reminding them that were not to stop for any wounded, even for the colonel himself. The injured would be tended to by the stretcher bearers, he said. The same speech was given by the colonel of the 1st Minnesota, in Gorman's brigade, and probably in many other regiments, as well. After delivering his orders, Colonel Lee had a treat for some of his men. He had his servant, "a man named Kelly," come around with a box of cigars, which he began to distribute on the right of the regiment. Before Kelly's supply ran out, Daniel McAdams recalled that "all of the wright of the rigment was smoking a cargar."[55]

It was probably shortly after 8:30 a.m. by the time the division completed its formation. It set out at a quick step (110 steps a minute, or 2.4 mph) over undulating terrain that resembled large ocean swells. As they ascended a hill southwest of Smith's farm, they were spotted by at least one battery of the guns Stuart had assembled on Hauser's Ridge, which fired on them. Colonel Isaac Wistar, commanding the 71st Pennsylvania of Howard's 2nd Brigade, watched the first shell sail over the entire division and burst behind it. Sam Hodgman, 2nd lieutenant in the 7th Michigan, thought this same shell struck within a group of ambulances near the division, "knocking one or two of them to atoms and causing the rest to move to the rear doublequick." A second shell "exploded directly in front of the first line at not more than six or seven feet from the ground and perhaps 20 or 30 feet in front of the line," continued Hodgman, and a third "exploded directly in the second line about breast high. In both cases the lines never wavered for an instant but pressed on regardless of the storm of iron and lead which soon began to tell so fatally on their ranks." More guns joined in, until Wistar thought at least 12 were firing on them. General Gorman described the fire as "rapid and well-directed." Roland Bowen in the 15th Massachusetts wrote that the Rebels shelled "us like the Devil. . . . I tell you the shell flew some if not more. One burst in a small apple tree wich I was under, the limbs falling all around me, another burst in the ranks of Company D cleaning out 5 men." The company commander, Captain John M. Studley, stumbled and fell an instant before this shell hit, which saved his life. Such were the fates of combat. A fragment from another shell struck 1st Lieutenant John Reynolds in the 19th Massachusetts in the ankle. He hobbled away, inspected the wound, decided it was superficial, and hurried after the division to rejoin his regiment. At the other end of the spectrum of courage was Alexander Wilson, a 26-year-old deserter from the British Army who had enlisted in the 20th Massachusetts only a month earlier. Daniel McAdams remembered him as a good-looking man "but a poor soldier. . . . He got scared when they ware shelling us and commenced to shak and got terbelay confused and our Lieut his name was Ally [2nd Lieutenant Leander F. Alley] he told him whare he would go the Lieut told him to go to the infernell reagon and any whare so he left ranks."[56]

The pace then increased to a double-quick (165 steps per minute, or 4.3 mph). As the division neared the East Woods, Oliver Howard reported that "we passed through a large corn-field, skirting of woods [the southern edge of the large woodlot adjacent to Morgan Miller's farm], then a plowed field." Jogging across plowed ground is not easy, as 21-year-old Edward Chapin of the 15th Massachusetts discovered. Chapin had left Harvard in August to enlist in the regiment. He found "it was very hard travelling over ploughed ground, and that, together with the exertion of keeping in line, tired me very much." Fear helped propel the young man forward. Early on in the advance, he watched a fellow recruit, William Shoales, a Boston shoemaker, be killed instantly by a Rebel shell. "The excitement of that hour is past description," an enlisted man in the 1st Minnesota Sharpshooters, attached to the 1st Minnesota, wrote to a St. Paul newspaper two days later. Yet, even amid the excitement and danger, the soldiers of the 72nd Pennsylvania paused while dashing through an orchard to pluck apples and munched on them as they hurried forward.[57]

As the division hastened toward the East Woods, Sumner encountered Hooker, who was having his wound dressed. He learned little from the 1st Corps' commander. "I was conscious of his arrival," Hooker later testified, but admitted that he had fainted not long before Sumner reached him and "was in a state of partial consciousness at the time." Around this same time period, two dispatches from headquarters—one for Sumner, and the other for Hooker—reached the 2nd Corps' commander.[58] Sumner's orders reflected the generally positive news they had received about Hooker's attack on the Confederate left since Sedgwick's division started its march: "Gen. Hooker appears to be driving the enemy rapidly. If he does not require your assistance on his right, please push up on his left through the ravine at the head of which the house was burned this morning, getting possession of the woods to the right as soon as possible & push on towards Sharpsburg and a little [west] as rapidly as possible. Use your artillery freely." Hooker's orders merely stated, "Genl. Sumner has been directed (if you do not require him to assist you on the right) to move up on your left and push forward toward Sharpsburg. P.S. Keep the Genl. fully posted by means of his aides."[59]

The burning house was on Mumma's property. The woods to the right were the East Woods, which Sumner initially may not have realized were in Union hands. He could see nothing of Hooker's corps. He observed some troops lying down to his left, past Mumma's farm, "which I took to belong to Mansfield's command." This was Greene's division. Sumner had sent a member of his staff to discover the position of the 1st Corps. He returned, probably soon after Sumner moved on after his brief encounter with Hooker. The only 1st Corps officer of rank Sumner's staff officer was able to find was a demoralized Ricketts, who claimed "that he could not raise 300 men of the corps," and that it had been "dispersed and routed." There was not a grain of truth to the statement, but with no other evidence to contradict it, Sumner had no reason to doubt what Ricketts said. Then a staff officer from Alpheus Williams arrived and delivered a report from the 12th Corps. We do not know its contents, but it is possible to decipher them from Williams's after-action report. He explained the position of the 12th Corps' brigades (as well as they were known). He also stated that some regiments were out of ammunition, and the men were "greatly exhausted by the labors of the day and of the preceding night," adding that the woods beyond the turnpike—the West Woods—were believed to be held in strong force by the enemy. Soon after the staff officer made his report, Williams rode up. He had seen Sedgwick's division approaching the East Woods from his position near Mumma's farm and went to personally meet with Sumner. He repeated some of what Sumner had already heard about the position and condition of the 12th Corps, and then made "some precautionary suggestions as to the line of advance and care of his flanks," which the old general "did not receive well."[60]

The situation at the front was clearly not what headquarters imagined. The East Woods—the initial objective of Sumner's orders from headquarters—were firmly in Union hands, but from everything Sumner could see and every report he had heard, the 1st and 12th Corps were a spent force. Had Sumner made more of an effort to inform himself about the two corps' positions and condition, he would have found that, although damaged, both were still capable of supporting an attack. Moreover, some of the 12th Corps' brigades, once they were resupplied with ammunition, remained in condition to participate in an attack. But then there were those words in his latest orders that probably carried considerable weight with an aggressive officer like Sumner: "push on toward Sharpsburg and a little [west] as rapidly as possible." There were multiple reasons to proceed cautiously, however: the situation at the front was different than what headquarters believed it to be; there was less-than-accurate assessment of the condition of the 1st and 12th Corps; French's division would probably take half an hour to reach the front; the 2nd Corps' artillery, other than Tompkins's battery, was not up; and, finally, Sumner did not know the ground, the enemy positions, or their strength. On the other hand, it was clear that the West Woods was now the key terrain on this part of the battlefield. Waiting to consolidate strength might grant the enemy time to occupy the woods in force. If Sumner did not see the 125th Pennsylvania enter the West Woods near the Dunker Church, someone surely informed him of this, which explains why General Gorman rode forward and spoke with Colonel Higgins. Once Sumner reached the East Woods, in addition to Greene's division to the south, he would have also seen Gordon's brigade south of the Cornfield, and the left companies of the 124th Pennsylvania with the Purnell Legion to Gordon's right, beneath the plateau just south of the corn. He might have also seen the black-powder fog from the skirmishing between Grigsby and Goodrich, but there would have been plenty of other smoke from artillery fire drifting across the field, so this is uncertain. Sumner did not suffer from indecision. He dismissed the cautious course and chose to "push on as rapidly as possible." He would seize the West Woods immediately, using Sedgwick's division, without waiting for French's division to arrive. By itself, this was not a disastrous or even an incorrect decision. There simply was no clear solution to the situation Sumner confronted. But an ensuing series of tactical and operational blunders by the general would render this choice a calamitous one for the Army of the Potomac.[61]

The first of these was to abdicate his responsibility as the ranking officer on the field. It was Sumner's duty to coordinate all the combat assets of the 1st, 2nd, and 12th Corps on the Union right. The southern border of the East Woods was an ideal point in which to establish a command post to do this, because it offered a sweeping view and had contact with army headquarters, via a nearby signal station. Instead, Sumner decided to ride into the attack at the front of Sedgwick's division, like a brigade or regimental commander, sacrificing command and control over everyone except the leading brigade of the 2nd Division and leaving all other units to fend for themselves. He did not even take the fundamental step of having some staff remain in the East Woods, who could have communicated with French and Richardson when they arrived. In sending Sedgwick's division in alone to attack the West Woods, Sumner made the same mistake he later criticized McClellan for: "sending these troops into that action in driblets."[62] Moreover, despite their casualties, there was still a great deal of combat power in the 1st and 12th Corps that was available to Sumner. They simply needed leadership and someone to organize them, but he made no effort to do this, instead presuming that both of these corps were fought out. While an argument can be made for sending Sedgwick ahead to seize the West Woods and maintain the initiative, failing to coordinate support for the attack and conduct any meaningful reconnaissance to understand the terrain were inexcusable. Effecting mass—that is, a concentration of combat force—is a fundamental principle of warfare. Waiting 20 to 30 minutes for French's division and the 2nd Corps' artillery to come up, and for Greene's division to be resupplied with ammunition, would have doubled and almost tripled Sumner's striking power. Instead, Sumner attacked piecemeal. Finally, there would be Sumner's fatal intervention in the tactical formation of Sedgwick's division. The results would change the course of the battle.

AS SEDGWICK CLOSED TOWARD the East Woods, Major Herbert von Hammerstein, a headquarters aide-de-camp McClellan had attached to Hooker's headquarters at the Joseph Poffenberger farm signal station, sent a message to his commander: "General Hooker is wounded in the foot. General Sumner is moving up. The enemy is driven on our left and retiring, they open briskly on the right. General Mansfield killed."[63] Apart from the fact that von Hammerstein's statement about the Confederates being "driven on our left" and "they open briskly on the right," made little sense, it confirmed that both Hooker and Mansfield were out of the fight. Combined with Alpheus Williams's message at around the same time, sounding a cautionary note on how the battle was going, it prompted an immediate dispatch from headquarters to Sumner, timed at 9:10 a.m. It read, "General McClellan desires you to be very careful how you advance, as he fears our right is suffering," with the postscript, "General Mansfield is killed and Hooker wounded in the foot." By the time it reached Sumner, however, disaster had already struck.[64]

8

Disaster in the West Woods

"My God, we must get out of this"

Sedgwick's men passed numerous wounded individuals and stragglers on their march, but it was not until they neared the East Woods that they saw manifestations of how severe the fighting had been there. An officer unknown to the division emerged from the woods, rode up to Gorman's brigade, and, "with a countenance all triumph and enthusiasm, called to us to give a cheer, adding, 'We have them in a tight spot. Give us a cheer.'" After maintaining a double-quick for three-quarters of a mile, up and down hills and across plowed fields and numerous fences, while being shelled for much of that distance, the infantrymen were too winded to cheer, and the officer was not someone they recognized anyway. Entering the woods, Gorman's men found abundant evidence of the grim work that had preceded their arrival. "Here the broken guns, the dead and dying of our men, showed plainly that the battle had raged but a short time before," observed Edward Chapin. Gorman did not pause but had his brigade jog straight through the woods. His front extended over 560 yards. When it emerged from the woodlot, the right was in the Cornfield and the left in the meadow south of it. Here they encountered scenes that shocked hardened veterans. The 1st Minnesota, on Gorman's right flank, came upon what was probably the line occupied by the 6th Georgia, where the dead literally lay in rows. To Edward Walker, a Company D private, the sight was "startling to behold, it looked straight and regular." To a friend he wrote, "Perhaps you can't believe this but I never could have believed had I not seen it." Edward Chapin in the 15th Massachusetts found that the Confederate dead and wounded "lay thickly" in the meadow. "It seemed as though every third man must have fallen before the aim of our men," he recorded in his diary, adding, "We passed over this line, and I suppose my heart was hardened by the excitement; for I could look upon them with the utmost indifference." Roland Bowen, in Chapin's regiment, described the Cornfield and meadow as being "almost covered with dead and wounded." Fred Oesterle in the 7th Michigan of Dana's brigade found that it "was almost impossible to advance, the ground was covered so thick with dead and dying men of both sides." Bowen came upon a wounded Confederate who held up a hand and waved it, "as if to say, don't hurt me." As Bowen stepped over the man, he said, "No one will hurt you." Then he heard another wounded Confederate nearby say "I know you won't." Gorman's line hurried on, threading its way through the morning's carnage.[1]

Sumner, riding behind Gorman's brigade, accompanied Sedgwick to near the Hagerstown Turnpike. Here he noticed that Sedgwick had halted Dana's and Howard's brigades in the East Woods. "General, where are your other two lines?" he asked Sedgwick, who replied, "Just behind." Sedgwick then asked, perhaps incredulously, whether Sumner really wanted the two brigades up close to Gorman before they had made contact with the enemy. Sumner responded, "Yes, bring them up close to this line." Sedgwick had no choice, so he sent his aide-de-camp, Lieutenant Charles Whittier, galloping back to bring them forward.[2]

Sumner's micromanagement of Sedgwick's division had parallels with Mansfield's intrusion into the tactical formations his brigade and regimental commanders employed. What was odd in Sumner's case was that he had known Sedgwick for some time and considered him to be an excellent division commander. The two men had served together off and on since 1855, when Sumner was colonel of the 1st U.S. Cavalry and Sedgwick was its major. Sedgwick was held in high esteem by McClellan, who offered him command of the 12th Corps earlier in the Maryland Campaign. The Connecticut-born general turned down the promotion, declaring "he could do better service with the troops he knew, and who knew him." Such loyalty and modesty are rare commodities in any army in any time. "I do not claim he was the greatest of commanders," wrote Charles Whittier, one of Sedgwick's aides-de-camp—in other words, Sedgwick was not the best choice to command an army. But at the division and, later, the corps level, Whittier asserted, he was "most excellent." "I never knew a commander who so studied, analyzed and remembered the morning reports," wrote Whittier. "He was always out on the line of march on the hour designated for starting. He watched the march all the day and saw the regiments go into camp at night." Sedgwick's love for his men and personal interest in them was repaid in kind. They called him "Uncle John" and were utterly devoted to him.[3]

Sedgwick was a fine officer, but he embarked on the Maryland Campaign in a troubled frame of mind. The defeats on the Virginia Peninsula and at Second Manassas shook his confidence that the Union cause would prevail. "The enemy have outgeneraled us," he frankly admitted in a despondent letter home on September 4:

> Their hearts are in the cause; our men are perfectly indifferent, think of nothing but marauding and plundering, and the officers are worse than the men. . . . I am in despair of seeing a termination of the war till some great change is made. On our part it has been a war of politicians; on theirs it has been one conducted by a despot, and carried out by able Generals. I look upon a division as certain; the only question is where the line is to run. No one would

have dared to think of this a few weeks since, but it is in the mouths of many now; it is lamentable to look on but it may come to it.[4]

Sedgwick's plan appears to have been to send Gorman's brigade into the West Woods to discover the enemy's strength and position, then commit Dana's and Howard's brigades as the situation dictated. Sumner's orders upset this. Initially, when Gorman's brigade left the East Woods, they used Smoketown Road as a guide toward the West Woods. But when they crossed the Hagerstown Turnpike, they were ordered to right oblique. No report offers an explanation for this maneuver, but it is likely that Sumner instigated the command. Edward Walker in the 1st Minnesota recalled that he saw what looked like a general and his staff on the edge of the Cornfield, near the Hagerstown Pike, watching their advance: "Gen. Sumner rode up towards this group & the one who seemed to be a Gen. saluted Sumner & the salute was returned. Gen. Sumner seemed to be inquiring of that officer as to the direction of the enemy. The officer, who was also on his horse, pointed across the pike into the [West] woods and also said something to Sumner that we could not of course hear." The officer was probably General George H. Gordon, whose brigade, only minutes before, had been ordered out of the path of Sedgwick's division. After this brief meeting, Sumner rode back to the center of Gorman's brigade. Moments later, as the brigade crossed the turnpike, it was ordered to right oblique. What seems likely is that this officer pointed out the position of Goodrich and Patrick in the north end of the West Woods, and Sumner wanted to bring Gorman in on the flank of the Confederates facing these brigades. Whatever motivated Sumner's orders, they caused confusion and placed Gorman—and, ultimately, the entire division—in a vulnerable alignment.[5]

In the hurried movement across the pike, the order to right oblique failed to reach Colonel James A. Suiter, commanding the 34th New York, on Gorman's left. His regiment continued to orient itself by Smoketown Road, losing contact with the rest of the brigade and causing a gap nearly 300 yards wide between his regiment and the 15th Massachusetts. Gorman was initially unaware that Suiter had not followed the rest of the brigade, because the irregular nature of the West Woods and the lay of the ground blocked his view of Suiter's regiment. The southern section of the woods was its deepest part, extending from the Hagerstown Pike to the west for 500 yards. This piece of the woods paralleled the turnpike for about 300 yards north from the Dunker Church. Here the section turned 90 degrees west for a distance of some 200 yards, leading into the center portion. This part of the woods was only about 200 yards wide, with an open meadow between it and the turnpike. From the center section, which was about 400 yards in length from north to south, the wood line turned west again for nearly 175 yards to the northern part of the woods, which had a somewhat arched shape, being 250 yards wide and about 350 yards long. Open meadows extending for about 300 yards lay between this northern section of the woods and the pike. A northeast–southwest ravine cut through the central portion of the southern part of the woods. The limestone ledge, which had figured significantly in the early morning fighting, ran north to south from Miller's barn, extending down along the eastern edge of the woods' center section. The ground from east of this ledge to the turnpike was relatively level, but west of the ledge, the terrain dropped off sharply. Early had used this ledge to conceal his exposed flank from observation, and it would play an important part in the fighting to come.

Gorman's three right regiments—from left to right, the 15th Massachusetts, the 82nd New York, and the 1st Minnesota—crossed the pike opposite the center and northern sections of the West Woods. This brought them directly down on the exposed flank of Grigsby's command, who were skirmishing with Goodrich, Patrick, and the 124th Pennsylvania. Grigsby's men fired a handful of shots at the rapidly approaching Union line, one of which shattered the knee of Color Sergeant Sam Bloomer in the 1st Minnesota as he was crossing the western fence along the turnpike. Bloomer handed off the colors and crawled to the West Woods, where he found cover behind one of its large oaks. Only moments before this occurred, while the regiment was moving up toward the pike, Sumner had noticed that the colors were still cased. He exclaimed to Colonel Alfred Sully, "In God's name what are you men fighting for? Unfurl those colors." They did, and one of the first men to fall was the color bearer. Gorman's skirmishers, backed by nearly 1,400 men in the three regiments, easily dislodged Grigsby's Confederates, who melted away through the woods.[6]

The three regiments made no halt to dress their lines after clearing the turnpike fences, but hurried on across the intervening meadows to the limestone ledge and descended into the woods. As the 1st Minnesota made this movement, "a man came out of the brush to the right and rear," wearing an officer's hat and a rubber coat. He called out a warning that the enemy "was not far off." It was General Marsena Patrick. The turnpike fences and the speed of the advance disrupted regimental formations, and they descended into the woods "in great disorder." Roland Bowen had scarcely set foot in them when he heard firing off to his left. It was the 125th Pennsylvania, engaging Early's brigade. The Minnesotans brought their rifles to the ready position. "We knew the enemy were not far away tho we did not see them while passing thro the woods," noted the 1st Minnesota's Edward Walker. Pulses quickened and tension mounted.[7]

The 1st Minnesota entered the northern section of the woods, marching across the front of Goodrich's brigade and passing through the woods to a rail fence on the western edge. Alfred Poffenberger's cornfield lay directly in front of the regiment, partially obscuring their view. The corn was planted on a slope, however, which rose 20 to 30 feet to Hauser's Ridge, about 400 yards away, where a Confederate battery was seen. This was probably Pelham's. Edward Walker watched the battery limber a couple of pieces and move them to another hilltop

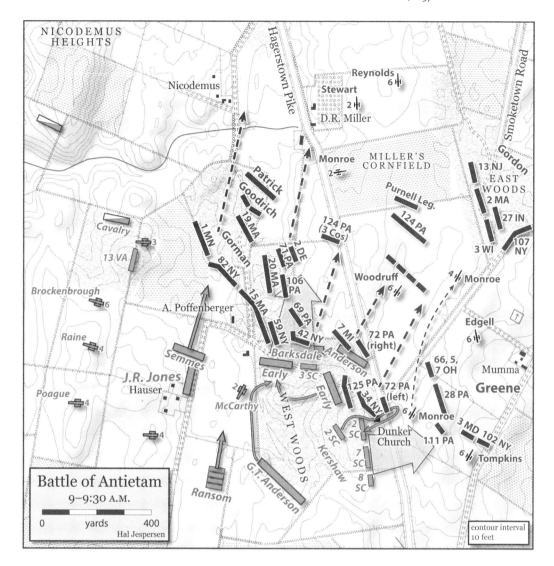

Battle of Antietam
9–9:30 A.M.

0   yards   400

Hal Jespersen

contour interval
10 feet

farther north, to get an oblique fire on the Federals. Those on the left of the regiment could see Poffenberger's farmhouse, about 250 yards to the south, and "a line of rebs" on the slope west of the house. These were some of Grigsby's men, using the farmer's fences for cover. The Minnesotans received some fire from skirmishers of the 13th Virginia, who were in the cornfield, but return volleys quickly drove the Confederates out of the corn to Poffenberger's small woodlot at the top of the hill.[8]

Colonel Henry W. Hudson's 82nd New York and Lieutenant Colonel John W. Kimball's 15th Massachusetts arrived at the western edge of the West Woods at the same time as the 1st Minnesota. The two right companies of the 82nd took cover behind the same rail fence as the 1st Minnesota, but the rest of the regiment scrambled over the fences along the Poffenberger farm lane, which ran along the western edge of the woods, and entered a meadow west of the lane. Why did they leave the cover of the woods? Hudson did not explain this, but it was probably to gain a position with a better field of fire. Then the 15th Massachusetts arrived, with its center directly in front of Alfred Poffenberger's farm buildings. The two right companies of the regiment crossed the farm lane and went into the meadow, to gain the "brow of a hill"—really more of a rocky ledge—in their front. The rest of the regiment remained behind the lane, at the edge of the woods, with the line running in the direction of the Dunker Church. This meant that the far left of the regiment was about 70 yards back from the edge of the woods. Some of Grigsby's men were seen in the direction of Hauser's farm buildings, but others, concealed in Poffenberger's barn, orchard, and grain stacks, opened fire on the Bay Staters from a range Kimball estimated as only 15 yards. There were also elements of the 13th Virginia in Poffenberger's cornfield, and they fired on the 82nd New York and the two advanced companies of the 15th Massachusetts. In addition, the Federals were shelled by a Confederate battery, possibly Raine's Virginia battery of four guns, about 500 yards away on Hauser's Ridge.[9]

The opposing lines traded fire. Edward Chapin recorded that his regiment, the 15th Massachusetts, did not even have time to re-form into a proper line of battle before the "bullets flew like hailstones." Raine's battery, wrote another man in the regiment, "was showering grape and canister upon us"—that is, shrapnel and canister. Many in the 15th Massachusetts and 82nd New York were hit. Chapin, in his first battle, watched Dennis Murphy, a 22-year-old shoemaker, be struck and killed beside him. On the other side lay 19-year-old farmer Franklin Hayden, who was mortally wounded. A third man, whom Chapin did not identify, was stretched out at his feet. Another bullet hit Chapin's gun as he was placing a cap on the piece, but it left him unwounded. Perhaps to his surprise—despite his inexperience, the nearby carnage, and his own close shave with death or wounds—he kept his composure. "I loaded and fired as fast as I could, but aimed at something every time, for I was not so excited that I knew all that was going on," he noted in his diary.[10]

Roland Bowen described the "rebs about 30 or 40 rods [150–200 yards] off in strong force" and said, "I never had a better chance in my life at them." Another soldier in the 15th wrote of how "within easy shot, were massed their [Rebel] solid columns." Through the smoke and din of firing, Gorman's men may not have realized that the Confederates in their front were being reinforced.[11]

AS MCLAWS'S DIVISION MARCHED north toward the army's embattled left flank, they met "an incessant current of wounded" flowing to the rear, as well as entire units, "apparently badly cut up," falling back in confusion. Robert Shand, a sergeant in the 2nd South Carolina of Kershaw's brigade, recalled encountering Lieutenant Colonel Martin Gary, the commander of the Hampton

Legion from Hood's division. He called out to Gary to inquire about his cousin, Henry J. Smith, a captain in the Legion. Gary, shaken by the experience his unit had passed through and its ghastly losses, replied, "Killed dead. We are all cut to pieces. Go in men and give them hell." Shand thought this was "not very encouraging, and therefore very improperly said by an officer to soldiers going into battle." The closer they came to the battle front, the faster the column was urged on. For the last half mile, they moved at a double-quick. In an army filled with fatigued, poorly fed, exhausted soldiers, McLaws's men (and R. H. Anderson's division) might have been at the top of the pyramid of misery. Except for the brief naps they were able to snatch during pauses in their various movements, the officers and men had not slept in 48 hours. The second night of their ordeal was spent making the severely taxing march to Sharpsburg, which left hundreds along the roadside, too physically spent to keep up. Most had received nothing to eat in over 36 hours, and the lucky few who had scrounged some rations had no time to cook them. "All were worn and jaded," wrote Joseph Kershaw. James Nance, the colonel in Kershaw's 3rd South Carolina, thought "our division as a whole was never in a poorer plight to go into battle."[12]

McLaws's situation bore some similarities to Sumner's. McLaws knew nothing of his own army's position or where his division was heading, and he was completely ignorant of the ground he would fight on. But McLaws would manage his approach with greater prudence and listen carefully to the advice he received from those who had been engaged on the left. While his division hustled cross-country, guided by Major Ratchford, McLaws rode on ahead of his brigades to gather what information he could. He met up with Jackson, possibly near Reel's farm, where the wing commander seems to have spent some time during mid-morning. What orders Jackson gave are unknown. McLaws never mentioned this meeting, but we know it occurred from what was written in the diary of his aide-de-camp, Captain Henry L. P. King. During McLaws's and Jackson's brief conference, a shell came hurtling in and fell at their feet. Although it wounded one of McLaws's couriers, it luckily failed to explode. Had it done so, "it would have killed both Gens," observed King. Battles are sometimes won and lost on such random events. In order to get information about the terrain, McLaws was referred to Hood, so he rode on and met the Kentuckian riding alone. Hood told McLaws that his men had been driven from the West Woods, "and the enemy were now advancing through it in large force." He gave some explanation of the ground and pointed out the direction in which he suggested McLaws advance to regain the woods.[13]

As McLaws continued forward and gained a view of the West Woods, it was evident that it was essential to get his division deployed and into action quickly. He could see groups of Confederate troops—elements of Hood's division and D. H. Hill's brigades—falling back from the woods, and Union troops "were advancing rapidly, occupying the place." The night march from Harpers Ferry had greatly depleted his division's strength, and his four brigades numbered only 2,825 officers and men. Cobb's brigade, which had been mauled at Crampton's Gap, led the column. Cobb had suffered some nervous or emotional breakdown after the traumatic experiences of that battle, and the brigade was led onto the field by its senior officer, Lieutenant Colonel Christopher Columbus Sanders in the 24th Georgia. Sanders, a graduate of the Georgia Military Institute, was only 22 years old. He was not in top form that day, being described by another officer in the brigade as feeling "very unwell." The other three brigade commanders—Paul Semmes, Joseph Kershaw, and William Barksdale—were all citizen-soldiers. The latter two were also politicians, usually considered a black mark for a Civil War general. But all three came to rank with the finest of the Army of Northern Virginia's brigade commanders. Paul J. Semmes, 47 years old, a successful Georgia planter and banker, had long experience with Georgia's militia and had authored an infantry tactical manual in 1855. William Barksdale, the most well-known of the group, was a former U.S. congressman and newspaper editor known for his aggressive pro-slavery views and his support for secession. He turned out to be utterly fearless in battle and molded his brigade into a tough, well-disciplined, hard-hitting command. South Carolinian Joseph B. Kershaw, an attorney and state senator, had also dabbled in the state militia, a not uncommon activity for aspiring politicians in both the North and the South. Early on in the war, Pierre Beauregard referred to Kershaw as a "militia idiot," but Kershaw proved that he was no fool. He mastered infantry tactics, possessed a steely determination concealed under his likeable personality, and won the devotion of his men. As a sergeant in the 2nd South Carolina wrote of him, "There was not a man in it [the regiment] who would not follow him to the death."[14]

As McLaws's brigades reached River Landing Road, where it makes a 90-degree turn to the west, just northwest of Reel's farm, McLaws directed them across the road into a plowed field, flanked on the east and west by large cornfields. Sanders's tiny brigade, which numbered only 400 effectives, was immediately ordered to file right, the intention being to move the brigade far enough to the right so the other brigades had room to deploy before they fronted and advanced toward the West Woods, generally using the Hagerstown Pike as a guide. Which brigade followed Sanders is a good question. Based on McLaws's report, it should have been Kershaw, but Kershaw stated that he formed in the rear of Barksdale and Semmes, so the South Carolinians may have brought up the rear. Whatever the case, all three brigades hurried into the plowed (some referred to it as "fallow") field in column. Barksdale's and Semmes's brigades paused briefly to shed their knapsacks, blankets, and any other equipment that might hinder rapid movement. Kershaw's regiments did not even have time to halt. The men threw their knapsacks and blankets off on the run, "so that it looked like a retreat rather than an advance," recalled Sergeant J. J. McDaniel in the 7th South Carolina.[15]

McLaws hoped to deploy all four of his brigades abreast and sweep up toward the West Woods, orienting them by the Hagerstown Pike, but several events dictated otherwise. As Barksdale's and Semmes's brigades deployed in the plowed field, Jackson rode up and ordered McLaws to send a brigade to support Stuart. Since Semmes's brigade was on the division's left and thus closest to Stuart's position, it drew this assignment. They advanced to the north, toward Jacob Hauser's farm and Hauser's Ridge, diverging away from the direction in which the rest of the division would be moving. Second, Cobb's brigade went astray. Marching through the large cornfield east of the plowed field, toward the right, Colonel Sanders failed to hear or obey McLaws's order to "march by the left flank"—that is, to front left and advance toward the woods—so they continued on until they crossed the Hagerstown Pike and encountered Rodes's brigade in the Sunken Lane. At the same time as Sanders and his brigade wandered off, McLaws observed enemy troops pouring into the woods and advancing toward its southern face—this was the 34th New York—and it was clear that he did not have time either to wait for the entire division to form or to retrieve Sanders. "As the enemy was filling the woods so rapidly, I wished my troops to cross the open space between us and the woods before they were entirely occupied," he wrote. As we have seen with Robbins's men in the East Woods, and Grigsby in the West Woods, a determined force in the cover of woods was difficult to dislodge. To buy some time, McLaws ordered Kershaw to double-quick the 2nd South Carolina forward and occupy the part of the woods projecting toward his division. The rest of the brigade could follow as it arrived.[16]

Barksdale reported that the field his brigade, Semmes's, and Kershaw's deployed in was "being raked by a terrible fire of grape and canister from the enemy's artillery," although this apparently inflicted few casualties. The source was probably Tompkins's Battery A, 1st Rhode Island, on the Dunker Church plateau, but there may have been some shells from the 20 lb. Parrott rifles across Antietam Creek, although this was at their extreme range. The 32nd Virginia, leading Semmes's column into the upper end of the field, received small-arms fire from the direction of Alfred Poffenberger's cornfield. The range was long, but the enemy fire scored some hits. Commands of "By company into line" and "Forward into line" were shouted, and Semmes's regiments hurried from column to line, their front extending west into Hauser's large cornfield. Barksdale formed on their right, while the 2nd South Carolina hurried past them toward the southwestern part of the woods. McLaws—whom, Captain King wrote, was "in every direction giving requisite orders"—did not wait for Kershaw to complete his deployment in Barksdale's rear before he waved his handkerchief, which was the signal for a general advance. This means of communication seems absurd, as well as impossible to see for those any distance away, but the division started forward, so it apparently worked. "Onward moved the line without a waver," wrote Captain King.[17]

After the war, McLaws insisted that there were no Rebel troops between his division and the enemy when he ordered his advance. He was mistaken. Besides Grigsby's diehards around Hauser's farm and Early's brigade in the West Woods, G. T. Anderson's brigade was directly in his front, lying down along the southwestern side of the West Woods. Jackson mentioned Early's brigade to McLaws, but there is no evidence that he alerted him to Anderson's brigade. Possibly Jackson was unaware of its presence, since Anderson reported to Hood. Whatever the case, both Jackson and Hood get low marks for their role in coordinating the Confederate counterattack into the West Woods. Hood helped, with an explanation of the ground and a suggested avenue of advance, but McLaws was largely left to fend for himself. The culprit was not necessarily Jackson or Hood, but the muddled Confederate command structure. That the Rebels' counterattack proved to be so successful had more to do with McLaws's superb handling of his division and the initiative and fighting spirit of brigade commanders like Early and G. T. Anderson, who coordinated with McLaws's troops without any orders from a higher authority.[18]

G. T. Anderson's Georgia brigade reached the West Woods only shortly before McLaws's division came up in his rear. His precise route from Cemetery Hill is uncertain, but the brigade apparently moved cross-country, which slowed its march, due to fences, plowed fields, and cornfields. Anderson reported to Hood, who ordered him to the southwestern part of the West Woods. The brigade marched through Reel's large cornfield, east of the plowed field where Barksdale, Semmes, and Kershaw would deploy, and emerged into the meadow that extended, for about 230 yards, to the edge of the woods. Here they came under fire from skirmishers in the 125th Pennsylvania. Anderson ordered his sharpshooters to the front. They ran forward, firing as they went, and drove the Pennsylvanians back. When the main body of the brigade reached the worm fence at the woods' southwestern edge, Anderson ordered his men to tear it down and pile up the rails, forming a breastwork. The enemy had been pushed back, but they remained an annoyance. Sergeant William H. Andrews in the 1st Georgia Regulars recalled that the Yankee bullets "were flying pretty thick." One of them struck a rail "3 inches of my head" when he peeked over the breastwork for a look. The ground in Anderson's front rose steadily, reaching the plateau where the main line of the 125th was deployed, about 400 yards away. But the Pennsylvanians were positioned back from the ridge crest and not visible to the Georgians. Anderson's brigade was a tough unit. As a member of the 8th Georgia remarked, "We had only tried and brave men here, for all those disposed to straggle or evade service were left behind." Anderson also proved to be a smart, prudent soldier. Until reinforcements arrived, he wisely held his small brigade under cover and let his sharpshooters harass the enemy.[19]

Inside the western edge of the West Woods, 400 yards north of G. T. Anderson, Jubal Early had arrived at a similar decision. His brigade had thrown back the skirmishers of the 125th Pennsylvania's Company G and prevented that regiment from any further advance into the woods. But then Early observed G. T. Anderson's brigade arriving at the woods' edge to the south, at nearly a right angle to his position. Anderson's men appeared to be preparing to advance, and Early was afraid that if he ordered his brigade forward, it would cross the Georgians' path and possibly expose his men to friendly fire. It would also "throw us into confusion, as they [Anderson] would have been at right angles." Early also had another problem. Gorman's brigade suddenly appeared and had pushed down through the woods on his left flank, and the 15th Massachusetts, which was Gorman's left regiment, halted only about 100 yards north of Early's left. Fortunately, Early heard Grigsby's and Stafford's men engage this enemy line, but he took the additional precaution of changing his front to the north, with the 31st Virginia protecting his left flank, while keeping the rest of his brigade oriented east, toward the 125th Pennsylvania.[20]

It was around 9:10 a.m. when the 253 officers and men of Colonel John D. Kennedy's 2nd South Carolina rushed forward in column, heading for the West Woods. They came up in the rear of G. T. Anderson's brigade, and Kennedy guided his regiment to Anderson's right, along the southeastern side of the woods. The edges of the woods in this area formed an angle, running northeast–southwest for approximately 280 yards, and then turning east for roughly 300 yards, toward the Hagerstown Pike. Kennedy's men approached the woods about 200 yards from the Dunker Church. They were fired on by skirmishers in Company B in 125th Pennsylvania, whom Colonel Higgins had deployed to watch his left flank. Kennedy gave orders for his regiment to deploy into line and advance. As they came into line, the two right companies found a gap in the worm fence bordering the woods and got through easily, but the fence proved to be problematic for the rest of the regiment to climb over while under fire. One of those hit here was Kennedy, who took a bullet in the foot. Command of the regiment passed to Major Franklin Gaillard. Fortunately for the South Carolinians, the Pennsylvanians were new troops, on ground about 20 feet higher, and they mostly overshot their targets. The 2nd cleared the fence and, driving the Union skirmishers before them, moved up through the woods toward the left flank of the 125th Pennsylvania. The main body of Higgins's regiment was far enough back from the crest so that Gaillard's Carolinians could not see them. Although both sides knew the enemy was close, each was uncertain about precisely where they were. The Confederates closed to within 50 yards before they and the Yankees saw one another. William H. Andrews, in the 1st Georgia of G. T. Anderson's brigade, watched the 2nd move up through the woods and recalled that "as their heads rose over the ridge the enemy opened fire on them, but not a man flinched or a gun fired until they reached the crest and then such a volley of musketry as would scare a weak kneed soldier to death."[21]

Creswell A. C. Waller, a 23-year-old student in Company F of Gaillard's regiment, thought the Federals were surprised by the 2nd South Carolina's sudden appearance on their left. They were, but their first volley nevertheless scored hits among the Carolinians. Among them was Robert Gault, an illiterate farmer who had been improperly conscripted that summer, because he was over 35 years old. Gault had successfully argued his case and was due to be discharged at the end of the campaign, but this was not to be. A Yankee bullet hit him in the heart and killed him instantly. He fell hard against Sergeant Robert Shand, a 22-year-old graduate of South Carolina College, who had been studying law in the office of Maxcy Gregg when the war started. "The battle raged horribly," wrote Shand, with "both sides firing as rapidly as they could load their muzzle-loading rifles." Creswell Waller thought the 2nd South Carolina had an advantage over the Pennsylvanians, in that the 2nd's line was looser and not so tightly bunched as the 125th's. Waller also wrote that the two companies on each flank of the regiment were crack shots. It was a lethal firefight. "Officers were yelling to men, and men shouting," recalled Shand. "Groans were heard but unheeded; some leaped forward; others drew back." Lieutenant Solomon Lorick in Company B waved his sword and called for his men to follow him forward when a Union bullet struck him the face, knocking him out of the fight. The other lieutenant in this company, Edward "Mitty" Goodwyn, received a mortal wound. Shand recalled that he resolved to "make sure that I had a killed a man, so I am aimed at the one who stood third from the color bearer in my front, and pulled trigger." He saw the soldier throw up his arms and fall to the ground.[22]

When the 2nd South Carolina started toward the West Woods, Barksdale ordered his brigade to fix bayonets, shouted some words of inspiration, and ordered them forward. As they approached the woods, he apparently maneuvered his brigade around the left flank of G. T. Anderson's brigade. This brought his regiments up to where the worm fence ran from north to south along the western face of the woods. Barksdale halted his men here, to allow Semmes to move up on his left. James Dinkens, a 17-year-old private in the 18th Mississippi (who would be discharged on December 6 for being underage), thought they paused at the fence for no longer than 5 minutes. They heard the heavy firing between the 125th Pennsylvania and 2nd South Carolina, which was taking place on the hill in their front. When Semmes's regiments fought their way up to Hauser's farm, to Barksdale's left and rear, the Mississippian ordered his regiments over the fence and into the West Woods. The brigade entered the woods at the mouth of the ravine described earlier, which led directly toward the right flank of the 125th. It was a natural avenue of approach that provided some cover, and it was undefended when Barksdale's men started up it. The Mississippians passed to Early's right, although James Dinkens, whose 18th Mississippi was on the left flank, recalled that they passed through some retiring troops, whom, he was told, were Ransom's brigade. As Ransom's brigade in Walker's division had not yet reached this part of the field, it had to have been part of Early's brigade, moving to avoid a collision with Barksdale.[23]

"We ran up the slope at the double quick," recalled C. C. Cummings in the 17th Mississippi. Like the 2nd South Carolina, Barksdale's right regiments—the 17th and 21st Mississippi—were able to approach unseen until they were less than 100 yards from the Pennsylvanians. The rookies of the 125th heard them coming, for the Mississippians charged up the ravine with "ringing shouts," which unnerved the inexperienced soldiers. Barksdale's men got in the crucial first fire: a devastating volley, followed rapidly by several more. David Peebles in the 18th Mississippi wrote that he "went to work loading and shooting faster than I ever did before." Peebles did not bother returning his ramrod to its sleeve on his rifle. Like a veteran, he held it in his fingers, to facilitate faster loading and firing. Edward Burress, a 19-year-old private from a large family of enslavers, fumed that "the cowardly dogs hardly gave us fight enough to make it interesting."[24]

As Barksdale struck the right flank of the 125th Pennsylvania, Semmes's brigade fought their way along Hauser's Ridge against fierce resistance from Gorman's brigade. Semmes's regiments deployed—from right to left, they were the 32nd Virginia, the 10th Georgia, the 15th Virginia, and the 53rd Georgia. Being on the right of the line and, therefore, the most exposed, the 32nd Virginia took the brunt of Gorman's long-range fire. Colonel Edgar B. Montague had his horse shot from beneath him. One company commander was killed, and another seriously wounded. The brigade's commissary officer, Captain Richardson L. Henley, known as "our fighting commissary," accompanied the regiment into action and was slightly injured. When Montague asked who would take command of Company C, whose badly wounded captain was the only officer with the company, Henley sang out that he would. Montague noticed that the captain was also injured and told him to go to the rear, since "he had no business to fight—it was his duty to look after the provisions for the men." But Henley would not be deterred, and the colonel let him assume command.[25]

Semmes's four regiments advanced steadily north while under fire, with the right of the brigade crossing a post-and-rail fence southeast of Hauser's farm buildings, and the left passing through Hauser's orchard and buildings. The shots from the 15th Massachusetts were particularly deadly. The Georgians and Virginians nevertheless pressed forward until the 32nd Virginia reached a rocky knoll about 130 yards from Alfred Poffenberger's barn. "When we got to the knoll the fire was so severe that we could go no further," recorded 18-year-old Corporal Jonathan T. Parham. He thought his regiment had lost half its men at this point. "Our flag was shot through seventeen times, and the staff cut in two," he recalled. The survivors took cover behind the knoll and returned fire. The rest of the brigade halted as well, taking what cover they could find and also opening fire. As severe as the losses were in the 32nd Virginia, the 10th Georgia and the 15th Virginia were hit even harder, with both losing 56% of their strengths.

But their rapid return fire began to take effect among the enemy, and the rate of casualties in the four regiments rapidly decreased. The firing from the Federals facing Semmes diminished, because they were suddenly confronted with a crisis on their left flank.[26]

WHILE SEMMES'S REGIMENTS FOUGHT their way up Hauser's Ridge and engaged the front of Gorman's brigade, more Confederates poured into the West Woods behind the 2nd South Carolina and Barksdale. Kershaw brought up his 7th and 8th South Carolina, followed by the 3rd South Carolina, in the rear of G. T. Anderson's brigade on the edge of the West Woods and asked what command they were. When told it was Anderson's Georgians, he called for three cheers, then led the 7th and 8th into the woods, with part of the two regiments passing over Anderson's line. Kershaw led them toward the right, to bring support to the right flank of the 2nd South Carolina. For some reason, Colonel James D. Nance's 3rd South Carolina did not follow the 7th and 8th, but instead adhered to Barksdale's path, entering the woods on Anderson's left. Watching the South Carolinians advance through the woods "without a bobble or a tremor in the line," caused Sergeant William H. Andrews in Anderson's 1st Georgia Regulars to contemplate the idea that horrid as war was, he could think of nothing "on this green earth half so grand as the sight of soldiers moving into action." Once the South Carolinians cleared his line, Anderson, who still had no orders, brought his men to their feet, commanded them to march double-quick by the left flank, then right face and push into the woods, slightly to the right of where Barksdale's brigade and the 3rd South Carolina had entered. There were now four Confederate brigades—Early's, Barksdale's, Kershaw's, and G. T. Anderson's, consisting of nearly 3,500 men—concentrated in the southern end of the West Woods and moving rapidly on Sedgwick's exposed flank. Bloody ruin threatened for the Federals.[27]

WHEN DANA'S 3RD BRIGADE of Sedgwick's division, followed by Howard's 2nd Brigade, emerged from the East Woods, Gorman's brigade had already crossed the Hagerstown Pike and disappeared from sight. As was mentioned earlier in this chapter, the gap had developed because Sedgwick had planned to advance Gorman's brigade and then commit Dana and Howard as circumstances and the situation dictated, but he had subsequently been ordered by Sumner to bring these brigades forward. When Dana cleared the woods and entered the meadow south of the Cornfield, he observed a line of troops lying down. It was either part of Gordon's brigade or the 124th Pennsylvania plus Purnell Legion. Dana thought it was Gorman's men, and he ordered his brigade to lie down behind them. They were scarcely prone when Lieutenant Whittier, on Sedgwick's staff, rode up and ordered Dana to advance to the West Woods at the double-quick. Dana brought his five regiments to their feet and the line hurried on, with Howard's Philadelphia Brigade following close behind. At the Hagerstown Pike, they could hear heavy firing ahead in the woods. The two brigades followed the same general route as the main body of Gorman's brigade, obliquing right and diverging away from the Dunker Church, where Barksdale's and the 2nd South Carolina's attack was just breaking on the 125th Pennsylvania and the 34th New York. Dana's left-flank regiment, Colonel Norman J. Hall's 7th Michigan, crossed the pike and reached the West Woods at the northeastern point of the southern portion of the woodlot, about 300 yards north of the Dunker Church. The other regiments marched across the meadow north of this, toward the central and northern sections of the West Woods. The five regiments numbered 1,946 officers and men and extended across a front of nearly 600 yards from north to south.[28]

Samuel Hodgman, the 2nd lieutenant in Company I of the 7th Michigan had his hands full with two of his soldiers. They had "here to fore managed to keep out of danger," and Hodgman was determined that they would do their duty this time. As the regiment approached the West Woods, one of these two men commenced vomiting. Hodgman suspected that he had deliberately swallowed his chewing tobacco, and the lieutenant evinced no sympathy. "I did not—under the circumstances feel any compunctions of conscience but placed my sword against him and pushed him along," wrote Hodgman. "By close watching & sundry threats, I got them to face the music," he continued grimly.[29]

The 402 officers and men of the 7th Michigan scaled the turnpike's fences and entered the West Woods. They faced slightly southwest as they went into the open timber, advancing for about 60 yards before halting to realign the regiment, which had become disordered when crossing the fences. The right wing of the 125th Pennsylvania could be seen through the woods, lying down about 20 to 30 yards in front of the 7th's left flank. The left of the 7th rested at the head of the ravine—the same one that Barksdale's brigade of Mississippians was currently advancing up. The center of the 7th rested on a "little rise," with the ground descending slightly to the north, where the regiment's right was located. The realignment was completed quickly, and the Michigan regiment stood in a line that, as one member recalled, was "absolutely straight." Just then some scattered firing was heard toward the left. It was the approach of the 2nd South Carolina against the left of the 125th Pennsylvania. The shooting rapidly grew heavy and spread north. Suddenly, a mass of Rebel soldiers rose up from the ravine in front of the 7th's left wing. It was Barksdale's 18th and 13th Mississippi, who had seen the 7th approaching and quickly maneuvered to engage them. The men of the 7th had been warned that Union skirmishers were in their front and to be cautious not to fire on their own men. For a fatal moment there was confusion about the identity of the approaching troops. Then the Mississippians leveled their rifles and poured in a devastating volley, followed by another before the 7th could respond. Half of the left wing went down, either killed or wounded. Oliver Chapman in Company B thought this first volley accounted for nearly all of the regiment's 39 killed in action.[30]

Nearby, the 125th Pennsylvania fought bravely for a few minutes, but the crushing fire from Barksdale's 17th and 21st Mississippi and Kershaw's 2nd South Carolina proved to be more than they could stand. Miles Huyette, a Company B private, wrote that "the crash, cheers, and cries of the wounded made a fearful din and it was impossible to hear orders." For a regiment never before under fire, the experience was terrifying in the extreme. Captain Samuel L. Huyett, commanding Company B, came up from the left and reported to Colonel Jacob Higgins that there were two regiments of Rebels approaching from behind the church. There was only one, the 2nd South Carolina, but under the circumstances, the exaggeration is not surprising. Higgins would report that on looking and "finding no support in sight," he was compelled to order a retreat. This simply was not true. The 34th New York had just arrived in the rear of his left, and the 7th Michigan was coming into position on his right. The 125th Pennsylvania managed to fire five to six rounds into their attackers—taking, say, 2 to 3 minutes—before the right wing began to disintegrate and rush to the rear. Higgins sent his adjutant, 20-year-old Lieutenant Robert M. Johnson, who was also acting as major that day, down along the left of the regiment to order a retreat, but a bullet shattered Johnson's hip on the way, mortally wounding him. The Confederates were close enough that Higgins heard them shouting for his men to surrender. He tried to order the regiment to fall back, but, in the general chaos, his voice could not be discerned over the crash of firing and yelling. The rush to the rear spread to the left of the regiment as the whole command disintegrated and began to run for their lives. "The retreat was attended with much disorder," admitted Captain William W. Wallace, commanding Company C. As the 125th collapsed, its beloved color bearer, George A. Simpson, was shot in the head and killed. Such was the confusion that, for a moment, no one realized the colors were down. Then Eugene J. Boblitz of Company H spotted the flag, with Simpson lying on top of it. Boblitz pulled it free, went several steps, was shot in the leg, and dropped the flag. It was retrieved by Sergeant Walter W. Greenland of Company C. "The rebs were not fifty yards off," Greenland noted, "but I got out safe." He was lucky, since, as he admitted, a Confederate bullet "struck my ear and stung considerably." Close calls like Greenland's were common. "Many were the hair breadth escapes and it was a common thing to see men with holes through their caps, coats, equipment, etc.," wrote Sergeant Samuel G. Baker. In the brief minutes when they were under fire, the Pennsylvanians had 28 men killed, 115 wounded, and 2 missing. Given the volume of fire poured into their ranks, they were fortunate their casualty list was not higher.[31]

The retreat of 125th Pennsylvania left nearly a 200-yard gap in the Union line between the 34th New York and the 7th Michigan, which Barksdale's brigade quickly exploited. The 34th had reached their position—about 20 yards west of the Dunker Church and to the left rear of the 125th Pennsylvania—only minutes before the 7th Michigan arrived in the woods, 300 yards to the north. The New Yorkers immediately became engaged with the 2nd South Carolina on their left. "We fire two or three tremendous volleys, which thinned their ranks; but we in turn received quite as warm a fire as we were able to give," wrote William McLeon, a Company C private. Colonel James A. Suiter recognized immediately that his left flank was in danger. When Captain Church Howe, one of Sedgwick's aides-de-camp, rode up, Suiter explained to him that "the enemy were making a move to flank me on the left." Howe, incredibly, replied "that he thought they were our friends." Lieutenant William R. Wallace, a daring soldier with Company C, volunteered to go forward to "make what discovery he could." Wallace ran ahead, survived the enemy fire, and returned to confirm Suiter's belief: "The enemy were moving upon my left flank with a strong force." The 2nd South Carolina was maneuvering to gain a position from which it could enfilade the 34th New York and the 125th Pennsylvania. At this point, which encompassed only a few brief minutes, Lieutenant Richard Gorman—Willis Gorman's son, who served as an aide-de-camp—rode up, probably sent to find the 34th. Suiter told him to go back to the general and inform him that the Confederates were flanking the 34th New York. Gorman galloped off, and moments later Sedgwick arrived. The heavy firing on his left had drawn the division commander to this spot. Riding down the line of the 34th toward its left, Sedgwick confirmed for himself that Suiter was flanked and ordered the colonel to fall back.[32]

But the situation abruptly grew worse as the 125th Pennsylvania broke and streamed to the rear, taking with it some men on the 34th's far right flank. Barksdale's 17th and 21st Mississippi took advantage of the break to push forward and engage the 72nd Pennsylvania, which arrived in the midst of the fight, and whose movements will be described shortly. G. T. Anderson's brigade was swarming up on Barksdale's right and moving directly toward the exposed right flank of the 34th New York, who were holding their own against the 2nd South Carolina. One of those Low Country soldiers noted that while the first Union line, the 125th Pennsylvania, "was very quickly driven," an oblique line, the 34th New York, "apparently older soldiers, were not so easily moved and checked us." But with the arrival of Anderson's Georgians, the advantage in numbers and position swung decisively to the Confederates. Sergeant William H. Andrews of the 1st Georgia saw "about sixty yards distant a solid line of blue, and every man working his gun for all it was worth." He spotted the national flag of the 34th New York and took aim at its color bearer, Sergeant Charles B. Barton. Fortunately for Barton, Andrews's gun misfired. But others did not. The sergeant was hit five times, although none of his wounds were mortal, and the flagstaff was cut in two. Someone who examined the colors afterward wrote that "in every part small holes appear made by balls." Sergeant Milus O. Young of the 9th Georgia thought "it seamed impossible for our Brigade to miss these chaps."[33]

The Georgians poured in a crossfire "that raked the length of our line," recorded William McLeon. He saw a Confederate standing between two trees, 40 yards away, where the 2nd South Carolina was. The Rebel raised his rifle, aiming directly at McLeon, but the private fired first and the South Carolinian disappeared. McLeon quickly loaded his rifle and saw another Confederate in the same spot, capping his rifle. McLeon fired again but did not reveal whether he hit his subsequent target. The 34th New York was heavily outgunned. Their 311 officers and men were confronted by some 850 Confederates in G. T. Anderson's brigade and the 2nd South Carolina. The New Yorkers began to fall back, "at first in good order, loading and firing as we could." Anderson sensed a wavering in the Union regiment, so he ordered his brigade to fix bayonets and charge. "There is something in a desperate charge that cannot be defined or expressed, in the onward rush to victory or defeat," noted Sergeant Andrews. The rebel yell pierced the tumult of battle. "When we were within thirty feet of the Federal line, it wavered, then broke and dashed to the rear," remembered Andrews. William McLeon concurred with Andrews's account: "The advancing of the rebels and their deadly fire was at last too much for the famed 34th" and "we broke for a time and ran about 30 rods [150 yards]," before the New Yorkers rallied.[34]

The fight had lasted "no more than 8 or ten minutes." In this brief period, the 34th suffered nearly a 50% loss: 33 killed, 111 wounded, and 10 missing. William McLeon escaped unscathed, but he had two bullets cutting so close to his right and left ears that it removed the hair on his head there. When McLeon reached safety, he, like many survivors that day, was dazed by what they had gone through. "When I sat down I felt bewildered," he wrote, "like on awakening from a dream. The experiences were incredible." And, he might have added, almost inconceivable to ever describe accurately. The losses of the 2nd South Carolina in this part of the engagement are impossible to know. They had 94 killed or wounded on September 17, but some of these losses were incurred in the fighting that followed the defeat of the 125th Pennsylvania and the 34th New York. Anderson's brigade, moving fast and pouring in a crushing flanking fire, escaped with losses of less than 90 men. The left flank of the Union line in the West Woods, however, was crushed.[35]

General Dana saw the 125th Pennsylvania burst out of the woods "in great disorder" and observed Norman Hall's 7th Michigan firing to their left oblique. The Rebel volleys were almost perpendicular to the direction in which Dana was moving the balance of his brigade, in obedience to orders. "There was no time to wait for orders," he reported—that is, in trying to find Sedgwick and request permission to realign his brigade. "The flanking force, whatever it was, was advancing its fire too rapidly on my left." Dana allowed his three right regiments—from left to right, the 59th New York, the 20th Massachusetts, and the 19th Massachusetts—to continue on and close up with Gorman, but he ordered Lieutenant Colonel George M. Bomford's 42nd New York to change front to the left and support the right of the 7th Michigan, to "meet the attack which had apparently broken through the first line on my left and front, and was now precipitated with fury on my left flank." Orders were shouted, and the 42nd began to change front to face the southern part of the West Woods. But before they even reached the woods, they took a volley from the 13th and 18th Mississippi that knocked nearly 70 men—1 in 5—down. The 42nd grimly continued to advance, but a second volley sent a shudder through their line. Bomford and his officers steadied the wavering regiment, and it pressed up to the edge of the woods, some 50 yards west of the 7th Michigan. The Mississippians, reinforced by the 3rd South Carolina of Kershaw's brigade, poured more volleys into the New Yorkers and the 7th Michigan. The enemy fire was "the most terrific I ever witnessed," reported Dana. The 42nd could stand no more. Nearly 160 men had been shot down in just minutes—almost half the regiment—with 35 being killed before the regiment had even discharged their weapons. The New Yorkers began to retreat.[36]

Dana's three right regiments continued on toward Gorman's brigade in their front, unaware of the debacle unfolding on their left. Per Sumner's orders, they closed up on the 1st Brigade until, in the words of Lieutenant Oliver Wendell Holmes of the 20th Massachusetts, "they could have touched them with a bayonet." Because of the nature of the ground, and with the 1st Brigade directly front of them, the 19th and 20th Massachusetts could do nothing except duck the small-arms and artillery fire that overshot Gorman's line. Colonel Edward W. Hinks, commanding the 19th Massachusetts, ordered his regiment to lie down. Minie balls "rained upon them, seemingly thick as hailstones, and buzz of canister shot was continual," recalled one member of the regiment. It was the same story for the 20th Massachusetts. "The enemy had cannon planted on the top and constantly swept us down with grape and shrapnel shell," wrote Lieutenant Henry Ropes. "Our line was advanced close to the first, exposing us to an equal fire, while we could not fire at all because of our first line . . . all this time we stood up and were shot down without being able to reply." Confusion reigned on the left of the line, where the 59th New York came up in the rear of the 15th Massachusetts. The 59th was on higher ground than the 15th, which exposed them to fire from Semmes's brigade and the Confederate artillery on Hauser's Ridge. "Every part of their persons were exposed to enemy fire," observed the 59th's colonel, William Tidball. Even though the 59th was in the rear of the 15th Massachusetts's left, either through poor management by Tidball and his officers or just from the general chaos and excitement of battle, the New Yorkers opened fire on their tormentors, who had closed up to Poffenberger's farm buildings. The problem was that they fired *through* the 15th Massachusetts's left wing, killing and wounding a number of men. Lieutenant Colonel Kimball made the "most strenuous exertions" to halt the shooting, but his efforts "were of no avail either in stopping this murderous fire or in causing the second line to advance to the front." The Confederates shortly resolved the friendly fire problem.[37]

Brigadier General Oliver O. Howard's Philadelphia Brigade was close behind Dana's 3rd Brigade. The 32-year-old Howard hailed from Leeds, Maine, which remains a small rural community in the southern part of the state. He attended West Point, where he did well, graduating fourth in his class in 1854. When the war began, he was appointed colonel of the 3rd Maine Infantry, which he led at First Bull Run. That September, he was promoted to brigadier general of volunteers and took command of a brigade. He had something of a knack for getting hurt. He fell on his head as a cadet at West Point; crushed his left big toe when he fell off a limber while in command of the 3rd Maine; and then, on June 1, 1862, at Fair Oaks, he took two balls in his right arm, which had to be amputated. Although outwardly mild-mannered and kind, Howard was tough and determined. By August, he taught himself to write with his left hand and returned to the army, where he was placed in command of the Philadelphia Brigade. But his toughness and determination did not translate into competence as a general officer, which he would demonstrate in the catastrophe that enveloped Sedgwick's division.[38]

Howard's four regiments numbered some 1,800 men, with the 72nd, 69th, 106th, and 71st Pennsylvania aligned from left to right. In the ground between the East and West Woods, the brigade came under severe artillery fire. Which batteries had a line of sight over the West Woods to deliver this fire are unknown, but although shells dropped "amongst us thick as need be," in the opinion of George W. Beidelman, a private in the 71st Pennsylvania, they inflicted little damage. Despite the artillery fire, Lieutenant Robert Park in Company K of the 72nd Pennsylvania remembered, "Our advance was still beautiful, the alignment perfect, but still the cautionary command of the file closers of 'steady men' [and] 'guide on the colors' was at short intervals heard." Sedgwick rode up to Howard, probably while on his way over to the 34th New York, and ordered the brigadier to "move up my entire line," which Howard interpreted as closing up on the 1st and 3rd Brigades. As the line neared the Hagerstown Pike, the men heard a rebel yell from within the West Woods piercing through the loud din of the firing. Recalled Robert Park, "We right surmised that this yell boded no good to the Union troops, for immediately from the wood in front came pouring in the utmost disorder and confusion our whole front line in wild retreat." It was the 125th Pennsylvania. Colonel Dewitt C. Baxter, the 72nd's commander, ordered the regiment to fix bayonets, to prevent their line from being broken. The effort failed, wrote Park, "for such was the rush and crush that it was beyond human power to stop the frantic retreat of the fugitives." The 72nd's splendidly formed line "was broken badly and almost rendered useless for effective work," with a portion of the regiment carried off in the rout. "But the color guard with the colors still stood firm with four or five companies intact," continued Park, and parts of the companies disordered by the 125th's retreat were quickly rallied. But the damage to unit integrity had been done and would not be repaired.[39]

Howard was riding with the 106th Pennsylvania and had crossed the Hagerstown Pike when he "noticed confusion on the left, and quite a large body of men falling back." It was the 125th Pennsylvania. Incredibly, despite the confusion he observed, and the heavy firing in the woods, Howard concluded that they were "troops that our division was relieving." Only minutes earlier, General Dana had moved two of his five regiments to meet what he believed was a strong flank attack. In contrast, Howard displayed no curiosity about what he observed and heard, but instead blindly marched on in obedience to orders. He also seems to have been unaware that the 72nd Pennsylvania had entered the woods to the left and rear of the 7th Michigan and became separated from the rest of the brigade. The 69th, 106th, and 71st Pennsylvania marched on across the open area that today is known as Philadelphia Brigade Park. When they reached the limestone ledge along the woods' edge, where the ground then descends sharply down, Colonel Joshua Owen, commanding the 69th Pennsylvania, "noticed many of the regiments to the left of Sedgwick's division falling back in great confusion." He probably saw the disorderly retreat of the 42nd New York. Owen could not have failed to hear the roar of musketry moving in his direction. There was heavy firing across Gorman's line, plus shelling from Confederate artillery, but, as Dana reported, the shooting on the division's left was particularly intense. Owen rode to Howard and "suggested the propriety of moving the brigade obliquely to the left." Howard replied that his orders were to dress to the right. He ignored the disaster unfolding on the division's left flank, which was also embracing his own 72nd Pennsylvania, and marched on with his three regiments until they entered the woods and closed up directly in the rear of Dana's 3rd Brigade.[40]

Ezra Carman, who was careful with criticism of the leaders on either side at Antietam, believed "Howard did not act as the occasion required. Had he taken the responsibility of changing front to the left with his three regiments, when he saw this attack upon his flank, either by throwing forward his right or retiring his left, or both, and forming line perpendicular to the Hagerstown road, on high and very favorable ground, he would have formed a rallying point upon which the other regiments could have formed." It is impossible to see Carman's criticism as anything but just, for what he suggested Howard should have done is precisely what Dana took the initiative to attempt with two of his regiments. Sylvester Byrne in the 72nd Pennsylvania offered a more damning indictment of Howard's leadership that day. Writing to Carman years after the battle, Byrne declared, "It has been my opinion that any non-commissioned officer of the 72nd could have handled the brigade better than it was on Sept 17 1862."[41]

Nine of the 13 regiments of Sedgwick's division—over 4,000 well-trained, veteran infantrymen, some of the army's best regiments—were now packed into the central and northern sections of the West Woods, on a front slightly over 500 yards wide and 150 yards deep. Because Sumner had insisted that the brigades close up on one another, mere yards separated them, rendering it impossible for them to change front to meet a flank attack. One of the fundamentals of Civil War infantry tactics—which Sumner violated—was to always leave enough room between brigades (or regiments) advancing in column of brigades (or regiments) for the reserve lines to change front to the right or left in the event of an unforeseen flank attack. It was essential to also leave some distance between lines, so fire directed at the front line did not strike the reserve lines. Both Dana's and Howard's regiments suffered unnecessary casualties from volleys directed at Gorman's brigade, because Sumner had insisted they close up on the front line. The consequence of Sumner's tactical blunder was a horrific slaughter.

Sedgwick first realized the scope of the Confederates' flank attack when he ordered the 34th New York to fall back. From the 34th he rode north, probably up the Hagerstown Pike, to the 7th Michigan, which he found under furious attack. He missed the 72nd Pennsylvania's arrival on the pike, to the left and rear of the 7th, by moments. Having already endured the 125th Pennsylvania crashing through their ranks, the 72nd then encountered the 34th New York rushing in disorder from the woods and passing around and through its left wing. Despite these disruptions, the bulk of the regiment reached the pike, where it quickly dressed its line to the right before advancing about 10 yards into the woods. Here, the Confederate storm broke upon them. The regiment had been under a "galling" fire as it approached the pike, but once it reached the road and entered the woods, it received a "murderous fire in front, left flank and rear, and the casualties were terrible." G. T. Anderson's regiments and Barksdale's 17th and 21st Mississippi moved swiftly to exploit the rout of the 125th Pennsylvania and 34th New York. The Rebels swarmed up through the woods, enveloping the exposed left flanks of both the 72nd Pennsylvania and 7th Michigan. Sylvester Byrne, a private in Company L (the 72nd had 15 companies at this time), thought he fired his rifle five times, which would take about 2–3 minutes, before his regiment was swept away by the Confederate attack. In these brief moments, his company had 10 killed and 25 wounded. The story was the same elsewhere along the regiment's line, particularly in the left wing, which absorbed the brunt of the Rebels' onslaught. Byrne thought no more than 5 to 10 minutes elapsed before "the enemy came round us on the left flank." It probably took less than 5 minutes. "Human flesh and blood could not stand that iron storm longer," remembered Lieutenant Robert Park in Company K, "and the command was given to 'fall back.'" The break began on the hard-hit left wing and carried the right wing with it, the regiment falling back to the northeast. "There was I am sorry to say," admitted Sylvester Byrne, "no order maintained" in the retreat. This is unsurprising. The Confederate fire mowed men down at an astonishing rate. In the 5 minutes or so when the regiment was engaged, they sustained most of their 237 casualties—the second highest loss in Sedgwick's division. There was no question of changing front or attempting a stand. That would have only increased the slaughter. The Pennsylvanians did what any veteran troops would have done under the circumstances—they ran like hell.[42]

The 7th Michigan collapsed at nearly the same time as the 72nd. Their experience mirrored that of the Pennsylvanians, with Barksdale's and G. T. Anderson's men striking their front and enveloping their left flank. "It was perfectly awful where we were," wrote Lieutenant Sam Hodgman. "Infantry in front and in flank. Artillery in flank and in front all pouring in upon us a terrible storm of iron and lead it seemed almost a miracle that any escaped." The two reluctant soldiers he had pressed into the fight at the point of his sword both went down: one killed, and the other shot through the thigh. Hodgman felt no regret. "Had it not been for me one would probably have saved his life and the other preserved his leg unhurt—however my conscience does not accuse me of murder," he wrote. The lieutenant admitted that he felt no desire to "get out of the way" until he got hit. Early on in the fight, a piece of shell struck the inside of his calf on his right leg but did not break the skin. He ignored this blow, but then a minie ball passed through his left leg, several inches above the knee. "I then had to turn my back to the enemy and was not very ambitious to see how long I could stay amongst the balls," he wrote. Bullets "were flying all around each side, over, in front, and behind me and like plums in a pudding." Besides bullets, Confederate shells were "bursting in every direction." Hodgman managed to hobble off the battlefield, where, in his opinion, "the bursting shells were the most terrible and grand part of the scene."[43]

Fred Oesterle, one of the survivors in Company E of the 7th Michigan, offered a sense of the volume of fire directed at his regiment. No bullet or shell fragment broke his skin, but "I had the button of my cap shot off, one ball went through my blouse pocket and tore my dictionary to pieces, another cut my leg just above the knee and another grazed my right arm, but not any of them severe enough to disable me." As the regimental front began to dissolve, one of its members saw Sedgwick behind him, beckoning for the men to fall back and rally on their colors, which were a short distance to the rear. It was an impossibility. The color sergeant was shot down, "then another, still another, till the fourth color bearer was down, then the Adjutant seized the colors, and was hit twice, the second time being knocked down, then a private in Company G took the flag and bore it aloft," wrote Frank Spencer. "We were nearly surrounded, each man fighting on his own orders," another recalled. Realizing the futility of attempting a stand, Sedgwick ordered the regiment to retreat. An instant later, he was hit three times: in the wrist, leg, and shoulder. He managed to stay in the saddle and rode off the field. General Dana was also badly wounded, although it is unclear whether this occurred near the 7th Michigan or 42nd New York. He, too, managed to keep in the saddle and was carried along in the retreat of these two regiments. Of the 402 officers and men with which the 7th Michigan entered the West Woods, 221 were casualties.[44]

In 10 minutes—or no more than 15—the left flank of Sedgwick's division had been destroyed. Five Union regiments, totaling around 2,500 men, had been crushed by elements of three Confederate brigades—Barksdale's, Kershaw's and G. T. Anderson's—composed of 1,741 men, or 2,007 if the 3rd South Carolina, which came up late in this part of the fight, is included. The Federals suffered 938 casualties—a 37% loss—with a staggering 173 killed. The Confederate units that were engaged reported total losses of 564, but many of these were incurred during the pursuit, when Barksdale's and Kershaw's regiments emerged into the open and came under the fire of Union artillery. A reasonable estimate would place the Rebel losses at around one-third of the Union casualties. It was a classic example of how a smaller force could smash a larger but poorly managed one. Individually, the Union regiments fought bravely, but their defense was hastily thrown together, and it lacked effective overall command and control. Dana made an effort in this area, but he was not supported. The maneuvering of the Confederates while under fire, particularly Barksdale's brigade, was remarkable. They moved hard and fast, and the Federals were unable to react quickly enough. The survivors of the 42nd New York, the 7th Michigan, and the 72nd Pennsylvania either fled north in confusion or back toward the East Woods, while the victorious Confederates came swarming out of the West Woods in pursuit or turned to fall on the open flank of the nine regiments packed into the central and northern sections of the woods. The slaughter of Sedgwick's division, however, had only just begun.[45]

BARKSDALE'S BRIGADE AND THE 3rd South Carolina surged out of the northern edge of the West Woods' southern section, into the meadow where today's Philadelphia Brigade Park is located. The 18th and 13th Mississippi moved north, driving toward the rear of Sedgwick's three brigades in the central and northern sections of the woods. The 17th and 21st Mississippi, with the 3rd South Carolina to their immediate rear and right, moved northeast, toward the Hagerstown Pike, in pursuit of the 7th Michigan, the 42nd New York, and the 72nd Pennsylvania. G. T. Anderson's brigade, however, did not join in this pursuit. After they cleared the Federals around the Dunker Church a staff officer rode up to Anderson's brigade, informed the regimental commanders that the enemy had turned the Confederates' right flank, and ordered the brigade to fall back. Anderson was temporarily away from the brigade when this took place, and when he returned, he found his command in confusion over these orders. He was unaware that part of Kershaw's brigade had just advanced beyond the Dunker Church, fighting against Greene's division on the Dunker Church plateau, and been repulsed, prompting the orders from the unknown staff officer, who may have been with Kershaw. Anderson re-formed his regiments and wisely decided that venturing beyond the West Woods, and thus exposing his brigade to Union artillery, was a bad idea. Instead, he led his men back to a spot near their original position, at the southwestern edge of the woods.[46]

On Barksdale's left, Jubal Early, who watched Dana's and Howard's brigades double-quick past his left flank, waited until the Federals around the Dunker Church and the southern part of the West Woods were cleared out. He then changed front to the north, placing his brigade on the flank of the 15th Massachusetts, the 59th New York, and the 69th Pennsylvania. Now, as Barksdale's men burst out of the woods on their right, Early's Virginians moved forward against the suddenly vulnerable enemy regiments.[47]

Sumner was with Lieutenant Colonel John W. Kimball and his 15th Massachusetts when the Confederate storm broke on Sedgwick's flank. Sumner had stopped to inquire how things were going, and Kimball gave him an earful, no doubt respectfully. He told Sumner that the 59th New York was firing through his left wing and had killed or wounded a number of his soldiers, and that he had been unable to stop the friendly fire. Sumner immediately fearlessly rode into the midst of the New Yorkers and "cussed them by the right flank," shouting and gesturing for them to cease firing and fall back. Sumner undoubtedly meant that they should fall back from the immediate rear of the 15th Massachusetts, to prevent any friendly fire, but what he did not at first comprehend was that the New Yorkers were just then beginning to receive a deadly flanking fire from Early's brigade, which was approaching their exposed left flank. The regiment began to fall back "in considerable confusion." Sumner rode back to Kimball. A moment later, Kimball's major, Chase Philbrick, pointed to the left and rear and called out in alarm, "See the rebels." It was Barksdale's men, swarming out of the woods and moving toward the division's left and rear. Sumner looked at what was happening and exclaimed, "My God, we must get out of this."[48]

He rode back to the 69th Pennsylvania, which was in the third line. Sumner then guided his horse along the front of the regiment, which was lying down, with his hat off and his white hair exposed, "in the midst of a deadly shower of shot and shell," gesturing and shouting something that could not be heard over the din. At first the Irishmen of the 69th interpreted Sumner's gestures as an order to advance, and they began to rise up and cheer. Then they, too, saw the Rebels moving toward their rear and flank and began to understand that Sumner was ordering them to fall back. Some of the men finally heard that he was shouting, "For God's sake, get out by the right flank." Under the circumstances, it was the only order Sumner could give. There was no time to change front, and Dana's men were too close to execute such a maneuver. The only hope Sumner had was to get his men out of the trap closing in around them—fast. He continued to ride down along the front of the Philadelphia brigade, waving his hat and shouting, "Back boys, for God's sake move back, you are in a bad fix." Howard, who was still with the 106th Pennsylvania, observed Sumner approaching and saw his men on the left beginning to get up and fall back in confusion. Sumner's arms were outstretched, and he was "gesturing violently, while giving some unintelligible command" that could not be heard over the din. The brigadier was later told that Sumner was shouting, "Howard, you must get out of here."[49]

Howard claimed that he interpreted Sumner's gestures to mean that the 2nd Corps' commander wanted him to change front to the left, but the existing evidence does not support this. Sumner's orders were for the 2nd Brigade to move as fast as it could to get out of the disaster about to engulf it. Writing for the public years later, Howard maintained that he "gave the necessary orders to protect my flank, by changing front to the left." Not a single officer in the Philadelphia Brigade reported receiving such an order, and Howard's claim is at odds with both his after-action report and a letter to his wife, which he wrote on September 26. In his report, Howard stated that the troops were "hastily faced about, and moved toward the rear and right in considerable confusion." To his wife, Howard admitted that "Gen. Sumner tried a movement & nobody knew in the beginning what he wanted to do—He faced [?] my troops before he let me know & they were broken or nearly so almost immediately." There were no orders to change front. The 69th and 106th Pennsylvania rapidly "faced about and took the back track in some disorder, but not at first very fast." The 69th managed to maintain some order, but veterans in the 106th admitted that their withdrawal "soon became a hasty, disorganized and disgusting retreat." The 71st Pennsylvania, on the right flank of the brigade and not directly connected to the 106th, had a different experience, which will be described shortly.[50]

When Sumner rode into the midst of the 59th New York to get them to stop firing through the left wing of the 15th Massachusetts, the regiment was already under "a terrific fire." "We were completely flanked and in two minutes more would have been prisoners," wrote Lieutenant James Peacock in Company K, had Sumner not ordered them to fall back. Caught in a crossfire from Early's brigade on their left, and Semmes's brigade and Stuart's artillery on Hauser's Ridge in front, the regiment was cut to pieces. "My men fell around me like dead flies on a frosty morning," Peacock wrote to his son. He picked up a rifle and fired at the advancing Rebels. A bullet went through his left sleeve at the elbow, another went through his right pants leg below the knee, and a third knocked his hat off. "That is all," the lieutenant noted, as if his near-death experiences were a trifle, compared with all those around him who were killed or wounded. The regiment's entire color guard was shot down. Lieutenant Colonel John L. Stetson was on the right of the regiment when it began to retreat. He desperately attempted to rally the regiment on his wing and change front to face the flank attack. Stetson was mounted, making him a prominent target. He was heard to shout, "Men, rally on your colors!" A bullet then killed him, and he toppled from his horse.

Colonel Tidball, in a letter to Stetson's father, claimed that the 59th New York were the first of Dana's brigade "to fire upon the enemy and the last to leave the field." Tidball can be excused for this exaggeration in a letter to a father who had lost his son, but neither statement was true. The 7th Michigan and the 42nd New York were both engaged before the 59th. Henry Ropes, a lieutenant in the 20th Massachusetts, on the 59th's right flank, wrote a letter three days after the battle, in which he described how the 59th "broke and gave way most disgracefully." Lieutenant Peacock made it clear that the men of the 59th had little choice. With the full weight of Early's brigade smashing into their flank, and Barksdale's regiments in their rear, it was either run for your life or be killed, wounded, or taken prisoner. Less than half of the regiment escaped. Of the 381 men taken into action, 224 were casualties, including 48 killed, for a loss of 58%.[51]

For Private Roland Bowen in the 15th Massachusetts, the first time he knew something was amiss was when a shout of "Fall back" came from behind him. Bowen and his comrades had just experienced the satisfaction of seeing the Rebels in their front—Semmes's brigade—appear to be retreating. He was confused. "Hell, ain't the rebs falling back themselves?" he thought. He continued firing at Semmes's men. Then came another shout: "Fall back, we are flanked on our left, the rebs are getting in our rear." Bowen turned and looked back. "What Great God can't be possible," he wrote. "But I saw it was no joke, the bullets actually came from the rear. My God, such confusion." George Fletcher in Company H was slightly wounded in the lip, and then a bullet struck him square in the chest. The copy of *Harper's Weekly* he had folded and stuck into his breast pocket absorbed the blow and saved his life. His brother James was not so fortunate. A bullet hit him in the head, and he fell, dead, into the arms of their third brother, Lieutenant Sam Fletcher. Lieutenant Lyman H. Ellingwood wrote of how "the men on the left fell like chaff, they were literally swept down." In his correspondence, Lieutenant Colonel John W. Kimball stated that when he witnessed Howard's brigade, and then the 59th New York, decamping to the north, he did not wait for orders but immediately ordered his men to fall back. "We retired slowly and in good order," he reported. Bowen saw it quite differently. To him, the retreat was a stampede. "In a moment all was confusion, and it was every man for himself," he wrote to a friend. To his uncle, Bowen admitted that "all hands ran for dear life." The Confederates "chased us like the devil" and poured in fire that "mowed us down." Nonetheless, Bowen escaped. "No God Damned Southerner is going to catch me unless he can run 29 miles an hour. That's my gate [*sic*]," he noted grimly. Many of his comrades, however, did not survive the gauntlet of fire. The 15th Massachusetts earned two terrible distinctions that day. Its 318 total casualties, with 98 of the men killed or mortally wounded, were the highest for either army at Antietam.[52]

In the 20th Massachusetts, on the right flank of the 59th New York, the men's attention was focused on Gorman's 15th Massachusetts and the 82nd New

York—who seemed to be gaining the upper hand in their firefight with Semmes—and on Stuart's artillery, whose shells were striking within the 20th's line. One solid shot passed between the legs of Lieutenant Henry Ropes, just grazing his knee. Lieutenant Henry L. Patten in Company E wrote home that the men in his unit were standing and watching Gorman's line—and, apparently, dodging shells and solid shot—when he heard a cry above the roar of firing: "The enemy are behind us." He turned to look, "and sure enough the rebs were not 20 rods [100 yards] from me—coming in on our left flank." The 69th and 106th Pennsylvania were bugging out, followed by the 59th New York and the 15th Massachusetts—a mass of men fleeing the danger sweeping down on them. Henry Ropes, writing to his brother just over a week after the battle, described how "the New York and Pennsylvania troops" were "rushing by us and through us like sheep." Some of the 15th Massachusetts must have been included in this bolting mass of frightened men. The left wing of the 20th about faced and opened fire on the rebels moving toward their rear. In Company G, one of Lieutenant Oliver W. Holmes's men turned around and fired to the rear. Holmes had not yet realized the unfolding disaster, and he struck the soldier with the flat of his sword, crying out, "You damn fool." Then Holmes saw the Confederates and the hundreds of fleeing men from the 2nd Division.[53]

Another of the 20th Massachusetts's lieutenants, Herbert Mason in Company H, repeated what many others in Sedgwick's division echoed about that awful day when he, in a letter to his father, related that they came under "one of the hottest fires this war has witnessed." Mason's company, like Henry Patten's, was in the left wing. Sumner rode by, shouting for the men to fall back. Patten saw him, but the firing was so loud that he could not hear what the general said. Patten saw the right wing of the 20th begin to fall back, "but I supposed they were going without orders and chose to stay a little longer." His company remained firing at the approaching enemy, perhaps purchasing some precious time for his comrades, who were trying to gain a little distance from their pursuers. But it cost Patten 17 of his 29 men.[54]

"In less time than it takes to tell it, the ground was strewn with the bodies of the dead and wounded," wrote the regiment's lieutenant colonel, Francis W. Palfrey. He was among them. A canister or shrapnel ball hit him in the shoulder and sent him sprawling. Another shell struck near Henry Ropes—his second close call with an artillery projectile—and covered him with dirt and stones. The fire on the 20th Massachusetts was so awful, Ropes related, that "the trees of the woods were crackling as if on fire." This was the sound of hundreds of minie balls striking the trunks and branches. "It was the first time I appreciated what I have often read of 'men mowed down in rows like corn' but it was so," he continued. The regiment's assistant surgeon, Dr. Edward H. R. Revere, was shot and killed while dressing a wounded man's leg. The left wing waited until nothing but Confederates were visible before they joined the retreat. Lieutenant Patten wrote that his company marched off at shoulder arms—that is, with the rifle on one's right shoulder, with the forearm parallel to the ground and a hand holding the butt—"at an ordinary pace." Henry Ropes claimed his company did likewise and "did not take one step at double quick but marched out at shoulder arms." It seems improbable that these companies could have done this, but odd things can happen in battle, some of which defy belief. Not everyone in the 20th Massachusetts marched off in order, however. Lieutenant Oliver W. Holmes admitted that he ran as fast as he could. No doubt many others did, as well. While Holmes was running, a bullet struck him in the neck and passed completely through, miraculously not hitting his spine or anything else vital. He fell to the ground unconscious. The 20th escaped with less damage than the other regiments in their brigade, but it was bad enough: 124 casualties out of 400 men.[55]

The 82nd New York, on Gorman's front line, pulled out when the 15th Massachusetts collapsed on their left. The flanking fire hit Fred Morris, a 21-year-old from New York City, passing through his bowels. Orders were being shouted above the roar. "I seemed stunned for a second as I leaned over Fred," wrote his friend, Austin Carr. "The last words I heard him say were 'give them fits boys, don't let them get me.'" Carr comprehended that the orders were to fall back, but he stood dazed beside his dying comrade. "Something within me seemed broken," he admitted, and bitter emotions overwhelmed him. "It was almost impossible to leave Fred there on the ground to the mercy of the rebels. My eyes filled with tears in spite of me." He had no choice, however, but to leave Morris behind. The regiment's color sergeant was hit six times, but fortunately none of his wounds were mortal. Part of the 82nd New York fell back in confusion, passing through the 19th Massachusetts in their rear. The rest of the regiment managed to stay together, and Colonel Hudson led them back through the northern section of the West Woods.[56]

The three far right regiments of Gorman's, Dana's and Howard's brigades—the 1st Minnesota, the 19th Massachusetts, and the 71st Pennsylvania—escaped the rout that swept up the regiments to their left by dint of position and the leadership of their units' commanders. The first inkling the men in the 1st Minnesota had that something was amiss was when bullets began hurtling in from their left. "Looking to our left we saw the line give way and the place that was occupied by our men was now full of Secesh and they pouring a fire into us lengthwise," wrote Edward Walker. An order reached Colonel Sully from General Gorman: "Move quietly and by the right flank." Gorman later explained that his intent was to "unmask the second and third lines, to enable them to direct their fire to check the rapid advance of the enemy on my rear," but the second and third lines—Dana's and Howard's brigades—were already stampeding to the rear by the time Sully received his orders. The 1st Minnesota were under a "very severe fire [by] musketry" from their front and flank, as well being shelled by a Confederate battery on Hauser's Ridge. "Such a fire as we received, I never imagined," a member of Company L declared. Thinking quickly, Sully ordered his regiment to about face and march to the rear. "We simply about faced, rear rank in front & marched straight back thro the woods, perhaps 200 yards over a stone wall & into an open field & then about faced the Regt fronting the woods and the right nearer the wall than the left was," remembered Walker. Marching either north or northeast, the regiment fell back, fighting, through the woods. "Some slinks of course run but the men generally behaved better than they did in any fight before," observed Walker. Daniel Bond was one of the few in the regiment with his knapsack on. He had refused to add it to the pile when the others removed their knapsacks before wading through Antietam Creek, for fear he would lose it. His decision nearly cost him his life. When the regiment reached the northern edge of the West Woods, they crossed a stone wall with a stake-and-rider fence over it. Confederate minie balls "were singing as cheerful as one could wish" when they reached the fence, Bond wrote. His knapsack caught on the rider as he tried to get through and required extra exertion before he could free himself. Bond made it, "but I confess the delay was more than I wished at that time."[57]

The writers of the history of the 19th Massachusetts Infantry claimed that the regiment changed front to rear on the first company, a maneuver that turned the regiment south to confront the Confederates charging toward their flank. In a letter written 5 days after the battle, however, William B. Hoitt, a 32-year-old private in Company I, stated that Colonel Edward Hinks simply ordered the regiment to march by the right flank through the woods. Hoitt is probably correct. The change from front to rear occurred when the regiment emerged from the West Woods. Hinks's quick action extricated his regiment from the closing jaws of disaster. They emerged from the West Woods immediately east of the farm lane running north from the woods to Nicodemus's farm, which was about 200 yards to the north. Here, Hinks ordered his regiment to form line, facing south. To Hinks's immense relief, he saw the 1st Minnesota emerge from the woods on the western side of the lane and begin to form a line of battle on his right. Beyond the 1st Minnesota, the elements of the 82nd New York, which Colonel Hudson had held together, were forming up on the 1st's right. There was no time to lose, for the Confederates in Semmes's, Early's, and Barksdale's brigades were pouring through the woods in vigorous pursuit.[58]

Colonel Isaac Wister and the 71st Pennsylvania were lying down in rear of the right wing of the 20th Massachusetts, in the northwest corner of the middle section of the West Woods, when the division came apart. Suddenly, an "irrestrainable rush of fugitives" came pouring through the woods at them as the regiments to their left and front collapsed under the Confederates' flank attack. Wistar, like Hinks and Sully, reacted immediately and decisively. Waving his sword, "for no word was audible" above the racket of firing and yelling, Wister brought his regiment to its feet with fixed bayonets, their rifles held "at the charge." It had the desired effect. Rather than breaking through his lines and carrying the 71st off in the rout, the mob of fleeing soldiers coming from the left flowed around the bristling bayonets of the Pennsylvanians. When all the regiments to their left and front had cleared out, the 71st began shooting at Semmes's brigade, who had resumed their advance. For a brief period the two sides exchanged "a steady and destructive fire at short distance." When the volleys on Wistar's left began to increase, he climbed up on the limestone ledge, which was only a short distance in his rear, to take a look. He was stunned at "the appalling state of facts. On our left as far away as the eye could reach all our troops had given way, and the enemy's pursuing lines were already many hundreds yards in rear of us with nothing in sight to stop them."[59]

One of Stuart's batteries, which had repositioned itself where it could partially enfilade the 71st Pennsylvania, opened with what Wistar thought was canister but may have been shrapnel. Whichever it was, George W. Beidelman, a Company C private, described the fire "pouring into us so terrifically that we could not stand it." It was time to get out. Wistar formed the regiment into column of companies and led them in a northeasterly direction. They executed the maneuver, although men "were falling at every step," either killed or wounded. Then a bullet hit Wistar in the shoulder and knocked him down. John D. Rogers, 1st sergeant in Company D, was at his side immediately. Wistar was bleeding badly, and Rogers hastily applied a tourniquet, using the colonel's pocket handkerchief and his own bayonet. Rogers offered to remain with Wistar "and was inclined to insist," but the colonel appealed to the sergeant to save Wistar's sword from capture. Rogers agreed "and was scarcely gone till the enemy's line marched over me," Wistar remembered. Lieutenant John M. Steffan in Company A recalled that the regiment made three stands as it withdrew north, in the direction of Miller's farm, "until we got to a stone wall where we made a regular halt and gave them rats." This was probably the section of stone wall along the eastern side of the Hagerstown Pike, north of David Miller's farmhouse.[60]

Unbeknownst to Wistar, his regiment may have been saved from destruction by the 106th Pennsylvania. When Sumner ordered Howard's brigade to fall back, the 106th retreated northeast, which took them out of the West Woods and into the pasture between the woods and the Hagerstown Pike. Here they came under fire from Barksdale's 18th and 13th Mississippi, which, admitted the regimental historian, Joseph R. C. Ward, a musician with the 106th, "broke our line." Colonel Turner G. Morehead, the 106th's commander, had his horse shot from beneath him. He went down hard, and his dead mount pinned him to the ground. Sergeant Joseph Taylor and Corporals William McNeal and Stephen Taylor, all in Company C, dashed back and freed the colonel. As the small squad ran toward the rest of the regiment, Morehead suddenly realized that he had lost his sword—perhaps his rescuers had unbuckled it to help free him—so he started back to retrieve it. When the noncoms warned him not to, Morehead replied, "Yes, I will, that sword was given me by my men and I told them I would protect it with my life, and never see it dishonored, and I am not going to let them damned rebels get it." Whether he found time to utter this long sentence under the circumstances is doubtful, but he did return and grab his sword. Barksdale's men were close enough to shout for his surrender, and when he turned and ran, they fired on him. Luck was with Morehead, and they missed him.[61]

While these events were occurring, the 106th Pennsylvania's color sergeant, Benjamin F. Sloanaker—along with 1st Sergeant James J. Foy and Lieutenant William B. Rose, both in Company H—set about trying to rally the part of the regiment that was still intact. It was sheltered behind the worm fence that ran east–west from the northern edge of the central section of the West Woods up to the Hagerstown Pike. Sloanaker waved the regimental colors and, like the popular song, shouted "Rally on the colors." They were joined by men from the 69th and 72nd Pennsylvania. There were enough remnants of the 69th to form an improvised company, led by some of the regiment's officers. The men of the 72nd, wrote Joseph Ward, "were halted by our men and compelled by our officers to stay." Morehead, though partially disabled when pinned to the ground by his horse, made it back to the line Sloanaker and the others had assembled. He gave the command to open fire on Barksdale's fast-approaching men. Several volleys had the effect of temporarily checking the Mississippians' advance and preventing Barksdale from cutting off the 71st Pennsylvania. But with no support, and Confederates moving on both of his flanks, Morehead's position was untenable. After a few minutes of firing, he ordered his men to retreat. As they did so, Sergeant Charles E. Hickman in Company A held his rifle across his body and marched backward, keeping his face toward the enemy and calling on his men to remain steady. Hickman's courage held the company together, which fell back, firing on their pursuers. Unfortunately, Hickman did not survive. During the retreat, a Confederate bullet killed him instantly, and Corporal McNeal, one of Morehead's rescuers, also died. When the elements of the 106th fell back across the Hagerstown Pike, the last vestige of organized Union resistance south of Miller's farm was removed. In perhaps 20 minutes of fighting, Sedgwick's splendid division had been smashed and routed from the West Woods.[62]

Barksdale's 13th and 18th Mississippi pursued the retreating Federals a short distance beyond the fence, where the elements of the 106th, 69th, and 72nd Pennsylvania had made their stand, into the pasture just west of the Cornfield. Barksdale halted here. "I did not deem it prudent, however, without more support, to advance farther, and, I therefore ordered these regiments to fall back to the woods in front of my first position," he reported. It was a wise decision. The two regiments had lost 30% and 43%, respectively, of their strength, and Barksdale had no view—or idea—of what lay behind the Cornfield or on the plateau of high ground south of the corn. He also may have seen Reynolds's Battery L, 1st New York Light, on the ridge east of Miller's farmhouse. His other two regiments, the 17th and 21st Mississippi, with the 3rd South Carolina of Kershaw's brigade on their right rear, pursued the 7th Michigan and 42nd New York across the Hagerstown Pike and onto to the plateau south of the Cornfield. Here "they perceived a very strong force moving to the right and attempting to flank them."[63]

What they saw were the 34th New York, the 124th and 125th Pennsylvania, and the Purnell Legion,—as well as elements of the 7th Michigan, the 42nd New York, and the 69th and 72nd Pennsylvania—who had rallied or were in the process of attempting to rally behind the guns of Lieutenant George A. Woodruff's Battery I, 1st U.S., and Monroe's Battery D, 1st Rhode Island. Monroe's artillery, after their ordeal near the Dunker Church, had displaced back to near the East Woods, close by Smoketown Road. Woodruff's guns had come up, following Sedgwick's advance into the West Woods, and unlimbered 150 yards east of the Hagerstown Pike and 350 yards north of the Dunker Church. Woodruff opened with canister on the Mississippians when they appeared on his right front, as well as on the 3rd South Carolina, which he spotted approaching the turnpike on Barksdale's right. Lieutenant William Cage in the 21st Mississippi wrote that they realized "we had advanced too far, (the Briggades on our right & left had not advanced), and we were in danger of being flanked both on our right and left." The Mississippians fell back across the pike, and through the West Woods, to a stone wall near where the brigade had started its advance. Woodruff's and Monroe's fire partially enfiladed Colonel James Nance's 3rd South Carolina as it approached the turnpike, moving in a northeasterly direction. Nance promptly changed front to face east and withdrew his men to a "slight hollow that afforded me protection from the artillery fire." The hollow they took cover in can be seen today, just south of the parking area for Philadelphia Brigade Park. Here, the colonel took stock of his situation. There were no troops on his right, at least that he could see. Barksdale had either pulled back or was in the process of falling back on his left. The gap on his right worried Nance the most, since he had seen considerable numbers of enemy troops in that direction. He sent off his adjutant, Lieutenant Y. J. Pope, to find Kershaw and "report the fact of no troops being on the right," requesting support there. While Nance kept his regiment out of sight, and Pope went in search of the brigade commander, Nance "kept a strict watch for any demonstrations of our forces" against the enemy in his front, waiting for an opportunity to pitch in. He would not wait long.[64]

In his history of the Antietam Campaign, Ezra Carman wrote that it "is difficult to determine the part taken by Early in the pursuit [of Sedgwick's division] through the West Woods." Early's lengthy and detailed after-action report is quite obscure regarding his brigade's role in this action. The best evidence indicates that after participating in the flank attack on the 59th New York and the 15th and 20th Massachusetts, Early's regiments advanced through the middle section of the West Woods. Semmes's brigade (whose movements will be explained shortly), in its pursuit of Sedgwick, partially moved across Early's front and absorbed the brunt of the resistance the Federals put up. Following in Semmes's path, but to that brigade's right rear, Early's brigade emerged from the northern edge of the middle portion of the woods into the pasture below and west of the limestone ledge running northeast to Miller's barn. They advanced about halfway, and possibly slightly farther, toward the strawstacks just south of Miller's barn when someone noticed that Barksdale's regiments were falling back on their right, and an enemy force was advancing in that direction. This was the 13th New Jersey and 2nd Massachusetts of Gordon's brigade, moving forward to help check the Confederates' pursuit of Sedgwick. Lieutenant Cyrus B. Coiner of the 52nd Virginia recalled hearing an "imperative order," shouted by Early, "to halt, or we would be cut off and captured." After their pursuit of the Federals through the West Woods and into the open, the brigade, in Coiner's opinion, "was not demoralized, but badly disorganized." Early managed to halt his command and pulled it back under cover in the West Woods' middle section, near where he and Grigsby had earlier confronted Goodrich's brigade.[65]

When Gorman's brigade began to waver and then fall back, Semmes gave the order for his brigade to charge, "which we did with a 'yell,'" recalled Captain William Stores in the 32nd Virginia. Corporal Jonathan Parham remembered that Corporal Bob Forrest in Company F was carrying the regimental colors. Forrest ran forward several paces in front of the regiment and stopped to wait for the line to come up to him. The fire from the 15th Massachusetts on the 32nd had been particularly deadly, and Lieutenant Henry St. Clair, from Company I, apparently thinking Forrest's nerve had suddenly failed him, went up to him and said, "Bob Forrest, why in the hell don't you go forward with the flag; if you won't go, give it to me." Parham later said the corporal was "as brave a man as ever lived." Forrest replied to the lieutenant, "You shan't have it; I will carry this flag as far as any man; bring your line up and we will all go up together." The line soon swept forward, the men yelling and firing on the fleeing Federals. The 32nd passed by Poffenberger's farm buildings and over the ground where, moments before, the right of the 15th Massachusetts, plus the 20th Massachusetts and the 71st Pennsylvania, had been. The rest of the brigade moved forward on their left. The 32nd apparently advanced through the West Woods, where the middle and northern sections met, and into the pasture west of the limestone ledge. The 10th Georgia, on the 32nd's left, and the 15th Virginia went through the eastern edge of the northern portion of the West Woods, up to the fence bordering the woods and facing Miller's barn. There the Georgians and Virginians saw a group of Union soldiers attempting to rally around the barn and Miller's strawstacks.[66]

These Federals were most of Company A, in the 106th Pennsylvania; elements of the 15th Massachusetts; and, probably, other men separated from their regiments. They fired on Semmes's men, slowing their pursuit, but then a Confederate battery that was moving north from Hauser's Ridge got their range and started dropping shells into their midst. "We were under a continual artillery fire," remembered Lieutenant Colonel John W. Kimball, commanding the 15th Massachusetts. Kimball was speaking with Captain Clark S. Simonds, a 31-year-old scythe maker from Fitchburg and commander of Company B, when a shell struck the captain square in the chest and killed him instantly. This frightful tragedy took the fight out of the Pennsylvanians and Bay Staters, and they departed toward the North Woods.[67]

Semmes's three right regiments spotted another Union force, which appeared more formidable, just north of Miller's barn. This was Patrick's brigade. When Sedgwick entered the West Woods, his men had initially formed in close support of Goodrich's 12th Corps' brigade, who were a short distance to the right rear of the 19th Massachusetts. When Sedgwick's division later collapsed and fled north, it stampeded Goodrich's regiments, carrying them along in the rout. "Everything now was in the wildest disorder," penned Patrick in his journal. He promptly ordered his three regiments (the 20th New York State Militia was still detached) to fall back to a "low spot" with some rocky knolls, a short distance north of Miller's barn, where his brigade had earlier halted to boil coffee. Patrick thought they could make a stand here and help rally some of the retreating troops. The brigade withdrew in good order, but its efforts to mobilize either Sedgwick's or Goodrich's men proved to be futile. Lewis Greenleaf in the 35th New York wrote that the fleeing men "broke through our lines in spite of all that we could do to stop them." Colonel William F. Rogers, commanding the 21st New York, and his company officers "confronted them and endeavored to check the retreat," trying to get these men to form on the 21st's right. But routed soldiers under fire are extremely difficult to rally, particularly by strangers. As Rogers recalled, "No heed was paid to our efforts, officers and men alike striving to reach the rear." Incredibly, Patrick's brigade had still not been resupplied with ammunition (one wonders what either division commander Abner Doubleday or his division ordnance officer were doing). There were only a few cartridges left per man, which meant that the brigade could offer only token resistance.[68]

With his brigade's attention fully occupied in trying to maintain their position while Sedgwick's retreating men were streaming through and around them, and hundreds of yelling Confederates were charging toward them, Patrick was unaware that the 19th Massachusetts, the 1st Minnesota, and elements of the 82nd New York had re-formed in the field just north of the northernmost section of the West Woods, and that the left of the 19th was perhaps only 75 yards to Patrick's right front. Even though the two lines were not working together, they presented a formidable front to Semmes's advance. The three 2nd Corps regiments opened fire on the 53rd Georgia as it came charging up through the

West Woods. The Georgians were checked, but not repulsed. Their men took cover in the woods and returned the fire. The historian for the 1st Minnesota thought that the manner in which the Confederates attacked gave them an advantage. Union regiments, he noted, "had been drilled and trained to present solid lines to the front in battle instead of 'taking intervals' and fighting in open order," and he believed this caused heavier casualties. The Confederates advanced "'scattered out'; a hundred of them would 'string out' for more than a quarter of a mile or cover an acre." Both armies used the same drill manual, but what the Minnesotan was describing was an adaptation the Confederates had made to the tactics. Semmes's regiments were also more dispersed, due to their rapid pursuit of the retreating enemy through the woods.[69]

The two lines exchanged fire for several minutes. The Georgians' aim proved to be deadly. They hit Colonel Hinks in the 19th Massachusetts twice. One bullet hit his right arm and fractured it. The other struck above the right hip, passed through his abdomen, nicked his colon, and exited on the left side of his spine. Edward Walker in the 1st Minnesota saw that Hinks had dismounted and was holding the bridle of his horse. He "was crouching down & hopping around." Lieutenant Colonel Arthur Devereux took command. His horse was killed, and then the former bookkeeper from Salem took a bullet in the arm, but he remained on the field. Another round severely wounded Major Edmund Rice, knocking him out of the fight. Despite their losses, the Union line outnumbered the Georgians and might have prevailed in the combat had not trouble, organized by Jeb Stuart, suddenly loomed up on their exposed right flank.[70]

When Sedgwick's division began to disintegrate and flee north, Stuart gathered up the 13th Virginia, and possibly Colonel Grigsby's and Stafford's band of hardcore remnants of Jones's division, along with parts of Poague's, Raine's, and D'Aquin's batteries, and started north, parallel to the retreating Federals. Stuart was seeking to damage the Yankees as much as possible and turn the flank of any stand they might make against McLaws's pursuing brigades. It was not a formidable number of guns. Poague had three: two 10 lb. Parrotts and a Napoleon. Raine contributed two 3-inch rifles, and D'Aquin added one or two howitzers. These guns broke up the stand of parts of the 106th Pennsylvania and the 15th Massachusetts near Miller's farm. They also scattered an attempt to rally, by some parts of the 59th New York and the 15th Massachusetts, around Nicodemus's farm. Observing the 82nd New York, the 1st Minnesota, and the 19th Massachusetts forming north of the West Woods, Stuart leapfrogged his guns forward to get an enfilading fire on the Federals, pulling his small infantry force along to help. Stuart seemed to revel in the fight. Edward A. Moore, a member of Poague's battery who served the battery's Napoleon, remembered seeing him riding "to & fro in our front" and "singing and cheering" as he led north what Moore thought was a band of stragglers whom Stuart "had transformed from a lot of shirkers to a band of heroes." The 13th Virginia and

Grigsby's men would have bristled at being called shirkers, but Moore was too busy to know who they were.[71]

Colonel Sully spied one of Stuart's batteries and Stuart's infantry force moving into position on a knoll just north of Alfred Poffenberger's cornfield and small woodlot. The Confederates were only about 260 yards away and would partially enfilade the line Sully and Hinks had formed. When Hinks was wounded, Sully had assumed command of the line, and he now ordered an immediate retreat. The 19th Massachusetts went back first, and Edward Walker, in the adjacent 1st Minnesota, noticed that they left "a blue line of men against the wall & on the ground." Preoccupied with engaging the 53rd Georgia in the woods, over whom they seemed to be gaining an advantage, many in the 1st Minnesota were surprised by the order to retreat. "There were apparently not many Rebs in our immediate front and the order to fall back was reluctantly obeyed," noted Walker. Captain Gustavus A. Holtzborn, commanding Company K, was one of the dissenters. In disobedience of Sully's orders, he ran to the stone wall in front, climbed up on it, and encouraged his men to follow him forward. A Georgian promptly shot and killed Holtzborn. Sully was heard to say, "It served him right," a seemingly harsh statement, but one that also reflected the necessity of absolute obedience to orders in combat. Sully knew that Holtzborn was a brave soldier but also recognized that his reckless action placed all of his company—and the regiment—at risk. "Experience is worth more than mere bravery," Walker observed. Sully was a case in point. His prompt response to Stuart's maneuvers prevented the regiment from being flanked and kept them from suffering even heavier casualties.[72]

Sully's line fell back at a double-quick, "accompanied with a shower of canister" from the nearby Confederate battery. The New Yorkers and Minnesotans were "almost in contact with the enemy" as they fell back. This was the 13th Virginia and possibly some of Grigsby's and Stafford's men, who followed closely. The Federals halted twice in their retreat to fire on their pursuers, who were joined by the relentless 53rd Georgia, a regiment that neither fatigue nor casualties seemed to discourage. Sully's regiments reached Nicodemus's farm, scrambling through the farmyard and orchard and into the lane on the east side of the buildings, hurried along with continual doses of canister from the Confederate guns. "In less than 20 seconds formed on our colors in the road, every man in his place," wrote Captain William Colvill Jr., commanding Company F of the 1st Minnesota, which was on the far right of the regiment. Sully ordered his regiment and the fragment of the 82nd New York, which had mirrored the 1st's movements, to right flank and double-quicked them north along the lane to the portion of the North Woods that spilled west across the Hagerstown Pike. The 19th Massachusetts joined them there, falling in on their left. Here, all turned to engage their pursuers, who had reached Nicodemus's farmyard. But their rifles were useless against the pesky Confederate artillery that continually displaced to follow their retreat. To the joy of these beleaguered Yankees, a section of Union artillery came trotting up into the stubble field west of the woods, unlimbered, and engaged the Rebel gunners.[73]

The guns were Lieutenant James S. Fullerton's section of 3-inch rifles from Captain James Cooper's Battery B, 1st Pennsylvania Light Artillery. Fullerton's section, along with the 95th New York, had been positioned west of the turnpike, several hundred yards to the north, behind a farm lane leading to Coffman's farm and the small community of New Industry, near the Potomac River, to cover the right flank of the 1st Corps. The 95th belonged to Colonel William Hoffmann's small brigade of Doubleday's division. The main body of the brigade remained near Joseph Poffenberger's farm, to support the batteries on Poffenberger Hill. Hoffman placed his command along the Hagerstown Pike, at the western base of the hill. When he saw Sedgwick's division retreating north, under orders from Doubleday, Hoffman moved his brigade across the road, changed front to the south, and followed in support of Fullerton's section when it moved forward. This infusion of fresh infantry and artillery into the fight tipped the scales against the Confederate pursuers. "The enemies battery—the same which had been following us—was quickly silenced" by Fullerton's guns, observed Captain Colvill. The infantry sparring sputtered on, but the Rebels' pursuit went no farther. When his regiment reached the Nicodemus's farm, Captain Samuel W. Marshborne, now commanding the 53rd Georgia, concluded that his men had gone far enough and done enough. Ammunition was low, and they had lost nearly 80 men out of the 276 taken into action. "It was thought prudent to fall back to the lines for a new supply," he reported.[74]

The retreat of Sully's regiments exposed the right flank of Patrick's brigade. "Battle flags of the Rebels were within a very short distance of us, both in front & rear, of our right," Patrick recorded in his journal. The flag to his right and rear was the 53rd Georgia, which sent a "brisk fire" into the flank of the New Yorkers. Those in front belonged to the 15th and 32nd Virginia and the 10th Georgia. All told, these three Confederate regiments did not muster more than 250 effectives, but Patrick, with his men down to their last cartridges and no nearby support, ordered his regiments to retire. They filed onto the Hagerstown Pike "in perfect order," Patrick wrote, which might read like a commander putting the best face on a humiliating retreat, but it was true. Colonel Henry C. Hoffmann, commanding the 23rd New York, remembered that as they marched up the pike, they caught the attention of Oliver O. Howard, struggling to rally elements of Sedgwick's division near the North Woods. Howard pointed to the New Yorkers and cried to his soldiers, "Men! That is the way to leave a field. That regiment are acting like soldiers. Do as they do, men, and we will drive them back again in ten minutes." But this was not to be the case. All the ground from Miller's farm south, which had been won with the blood of many good men that morning, was now in the hands of the Confederates. The Federals were back where they had started, around the North Woods, licking their wounds and try-ing to put their shattered units back together.[75]

ALTHOUGH REDUCED TO AROUND only 250 men, Semmes's 15th Virginia, the 10th Georgia, and the 32nd Virginia rushed forward toward Miller's barn when they saw Patrick's brigade pulling out. The 32nd, on the right, reached the straw-stacks south of the barn, where, earlier that morning, Lieutenant Stewart had parked his limbers. Calhoun Jones, in the 15th Virginia, found a "right many wounded federal soldiers, also some dead," around the stacks. The 32nd Virginia, reduced to only about 80 effectives, captured 17 able-bodied Union soldiers who had attempted to hide themselves in the stacks and sent them to the rear. A fur-ther advance from this point was discouraged by doses of canister delivered by a battery on the ridge east of Miller's farmhouse. In addition, the Confederate regiments were low on ammunition and unsupported. The 10th Georgia and the 15th Virginia passed north of Miller's barn, into the lower ground where Patrick had recently been. Here they came under fire from Union troops behind a stone wall bordering the Hagerstown Pike, north of Miller's house. It was the 71st Pennsylvania. After retreating up the pike, the regiment had taken cover behind this wall at some point between Miller's farmhouse and the North Woods. The Pennsylvanians, in Lieutenant John M. Steffan's opinion, "gave them [Semmes's men] rats, our artillery also had a chance to play on them, when they thought it best not to advance." The small-arms and artillery fire, com-bined with the limited numbers of men who were left, discouraged any further advance by the Georgians and Virginians. Their line "was very thin," remem-bered Calhoun Jones, "and scattered at that." But some bold individuals from the 10th Georgia dashed across the pike to Miller's house, where they found a number of Union wounded, as well as some uninjured men who had taken shel-ter there. The latter were rounded up and sent to the rear.[76]

The artillery that helped check Semmes's advance at Miller's farm was the very one that had fought in a desperate combat only 2 hours earlier, on the same ground these Confederates were now swarming over. It was a section of Stew-art's Battery B, 4th U.S. Artillery. Following their harrowing action against Hood's division, which cost the battery 33 horses in addition to 40 officers and men, Stewart moved his guns to the left of Ransom's battery, who, at the time, were engaging Ripley's and Colquitt's brigades. Because Gordon's brigade was in his front and blocked his field of fire, Stewart withdrew his battery to the edge of the North Woods, where he hastily "regulated the men and horses through-out the battery." Just as he completed this reorganization, he received an order from Gibbon to move his guns back to the position they had first occupied in the morning, which was east of Miller's house and garden. Because of his losses, Stewart could field only one section. He moved south with his two guns and came into position on the same ridge where Ransom's guns had been earlier, on the right of Captain John A. Reynolds's Battery L, 1st New York Light. Reynolds's guns were "under a very heavy fire from two of the enemy's batteries." Lieutenant George Breck in Battery L agreed that the Rebels were "throwing shot and shell in our midst very lively," adding that "it was a question whether we should be able to silence it." Then Sedgwick's division came rushing out of the West Woods, "very much disorganized" and "closely followd by the enemy." Stewart's gun crews came under infantry fire, but, due to the dense smoke from the musketry and Reynolds's artillery, he could not discern precisely where the enemy was. Stewart decided that he would have a better field of fire if he moved, so he ordered his guns to limber, drove them behind Reynolds, and came up onto the ridge on the New Yorkers' left. Here, Stewart noted, one of his men "reported to me that the turnpike directly in my front and about 75 yards distant was full of the enemy's infantry." The crews unlimbered and opened with canister shot, "which scattered the enemy in every direction."[77]

While Stewart's Napoleons sprayed canister at Semmes's men around Miller's farm, Reynolds's 3-inch rifles kept up their duel with the Confederate artillery, who were constantly displacing north to harass Sedgwick's retreating men and engage the New Yorkers. Reynolds's pieces made things hot for the Confederate gunners. Edward Moore, manning Poague's Napoleon, described it as "a terrific artillery fire," and John Block in D'Aquin's battery remembered their position as "a very hot place." Reynolds's shelling, combined with that of Fullerton's section of Cooper's battery, "put a stop to the firing of the hostile battery." No doubt their return fire helped silence Poague's, D'Aquin's, and Raine's guns, but so, too, did a shortage of ammunition. The Confederates had been firing for some time, and their ammunition chests were low.[78]

Semmes's men did their best to seek cover from the effects of Stewart's canister, although William Stores in the 32nd Virginia distinctly remembered that one of their men was killed after he climbed up on an old wagon frame between the barn and the strawstacks. "My brigade was thrown farther to the front than the troops on my right by about 300 yards," reported Semmes. As he took stock of his situation, Semmes concluded that he was overextended and exposed. Barksdale had withdrawn from his right, Semmes's brigade had suffered substantial casualties, and all his regiments were low on ammunition. While Semmes pondered what he should do next, the inexhaustible Jeb Stuart suddenly came galloping "at full speed" out of the West Woods and rode up to the men of the 32nd Virginia, asking what command they belonged to. When told it was Semmes's brigade, Stuart praised them: "Boys you are doing good work." He then asked, "Where is the general?" Semmes was pointed out, situated behind the ledge running southwest from the barn. Stuart rode over to him and declared, "Genl, that battery must be taken," indicating Stewart's or Reynolds's guns. Semmes had no stomach for such an adventure and replied, "Genl. my men have been engaged all the morning and are short of ammunition," adding that

"Barksdale's brigade is through the woods there," pointing in the direction where he had seen the Mississippians go. Stuart galloped off in the direction Semmes indicated. When Stuart had departed, Semmes sensibly ordered his regiments to fall back through the West Woods, where they could replenish their ammunition and reorganize. Considering their low numbers and the hardships they had endured in the march to Sharpsburg, their accomplishments were remarkable. They had paid a steep price, however. Three of the four regimental commanders were wounded, and, overall, 44% of the brigade became casualties, the highest rate of loss in McLaws's division. Semmes's withdrawal marked the end of the Confederate pursuit of Sedgwick in this sector. At the same time as Semmes pulled his brigade back to the West Woods, Kershaw's brigade met with disaster when it attempted to follow up the rout of the enemy in the southern section of the woods.[79]

9

Attack and Counterattack

"The most deadly and bloody conflict I have ever witnessed"

Afﬁter helping rout the 125th Pennsylvania, the 34th New York, and the 72nd Pennsylvania in succession, the 2nd South Carolina of Kershaw's brigade advanced to the Dunker Church. Part of the left wing passed around the north side of the building, while the balance of the regiment swung south of it. The target of their pursuit was the Union troops they had helped drive from the woods who retreated east, rather than north. The South Carolinians also saw Woodruff's battery in the meadow south of the Cornfield, about midway between the East Woods and the Hagerstown Turnpike, and probably Monroe's Rhode Island battery, which had displaced to just outside the East Woods, astride Smoketown Road. The Confederates quickly cleared the pike's fences or ran through gaps and crossed the open ground east of the church to "a prominent rock ledge, 110 yards east of the church and close to Smoketown Road." This is where the Maryland monument stands today. The 2nd South Carolina halted there, to use this ledge as a cover. They fired on Woodruff, who seemed to be getting ready "to fight or move," and at the Union infantry rallying in the rear of the battery. The regiment then faced and sent volleys toward the northeast, because, as Cresswell A. C. Waller remembered, the "enemy seemed to be bunched over there more than in my front where there were very few."[1]

Colonel James Nance, waiting for an opportunity to advance, saw the 2nd South Carolina move out "most beautifully through the woods up the open slope beyond." Although a gap of over 200 yards existed between his 3rd South Carolina and the 2nd, Nance ordered his regiment up and forward to join the attack. His men crossed the pike and entered the plowed field east of the road, advancing to the brow of the high ground there, where they faced Woodruff's Napoleons, which were only about 150 yards in their front. The Regulars greeted them with canister, and some nearby Federal infantry, possibly the Purnell Legion, added their small-arms volleys. For a moment Nance's men gamely traded fire with their adversaries, but then Nance saw the 2nd South Carolina falling back into the West Woods. He pulled his regiment back to the pike, where they were relatively safe from Woodruff's canister, and fired "for a time" at whatever targets presented themselves. They remained here only a few minutes until,

Nance reported, "a further requirement" necessitated falling back to the ravine where he had started his advance. What the "requirement" was is unknown. Most likely it was the regiment's exposure and lack of support.[2]

The retreat of the 2nd South Carolina that Nance witnessed was compelled by the sudden appearance of Hector Tyndale's 12th Corps' brigade on the Carolinians right flank. Captain George B. Cuthbert, commanding the right wing of the 2nd, attempted to advance his wing farther to the east, to gain the higher ground there. This stirred up more than Cuthbert bargained for, as Tyndale's men, fully resupplied with ammunition and lying quietly on the reverse slope of the Dunker Church plateau, suddenly rose up and fired into the startled South Carolinians. The 2nd recoiled from this threat to their flank and fell back. It was not a pell-mell retreat. Rather, the men moved "leap frog like" westward as, "one by one, men would try to get on west side of his western neighbor" to escape the fire from the right flank. Cresswell Waller, who was lying down firing at Woodruff's battery and the Union infantry in its rear, was so intent on his work that he suddenly found himself alone. He kept his position for a few moments, hoping the regiment would return, but soon gave up and made a dash for the woods. Two bullets struck the fence he climbed through, but he made it back. Woodruff was shelling the woods near the Dunker Church, so the 2nd South Carolina had fallen back nearly 150 yards west of the church, where the terrain gave them some cover and a place to rally. When they had re-collected themselves, Major Franklin Galliard moved the regiment southeast, out of the line of fire striking from near the church, to close by the southern border of the West Woods. The advance, retreat, and rally of the regiment had consumed no more than 10 minutes.[3]

It was about 9:45 a.m. when the 2nd South Carolina reached the southern edge of the West Woods. They saw the 7th and 8th South Carolina approaching to their right, marching side by side in column. Because of the smoke, the potential for accidental friendly fire was high, so Major Galliard had his color bearer mount the fence along the edge of the woods and wave the colors, to "let them know we were friends." Recognition was established, and an unfortunate incident avoided. Of the two approaching regiments, Colonel D. Wyatt Aiken's 7th South Carolina had done the hardest fighting several days earlier, on Maryland Heights, incurring 113 casualties. Nevertheless, they remained the strongest regiment in the brigade, with 268 officers and men. Lieutenant Colonel Axalla J. Hoole's 8th South Carolina fielded no more than a large company, with a lopsided ratio of 26 officers commanding a mere 45 enlisted men. After the fighting it had already engaged in, the 2nd South Carolina probably had less than 200 effectives. Combined, there were about 540 men in the three regiments. They had gun support following behind them, from Captain John P. N. Read's Pulaski (Georgia) Artillery, consisting of the typical mishmash of guns that equipped the Confederates at this point in the war: a 10 lb. Parrott, a 3-inch rifle, a 6 lb.

smoothbore, and a 12 lb. howitzer. Kershaw directed Read to move his guns to a hill about 300 yards south of the West Woods. Most of the hill was covered by farmer Reel's large cornfield, but the northeastern slope was in stubble, and the battery apparently moved to this area.[4]

As the 7th and 8th South Carolina neared the Hagerstown Turnpike, they deployed into line, with the 2nd joining on the 7th's left. "A terrible fire of shell and shrapnel" from Union artillery burst around the moving line. There were few losses, although one explosion knocked Major William C. White in the 7th down and badly bruised his face. White, a 36-year-old plantation overseer from Georgetown, South Carolina, rose, wiped the blood and dirt away, and rejoined his regiment. Under the circumstances, there was no time for Kershaw to pause and reconnoiter the situation. The enemy were on the run, and the unwritten doctrine of the Army of Northern Virginia was to pursue and hit them hard. Major Galliard might have warned Kershaw that there were a mass of Federals beyond the plateau east of the church, but it is unlikely that there was any opportunity for this. Everything happened too quickly. The three Confederate regiments went forward south of the church, cleared the pike's fences, and charged across the open plateau east of the church. Lieutenant Woodruff saw them burst from the West Woods—"a heavy mass of rebel infantry"—but the "peculiar nature" of the ground largely shielded the Carolinians from Woodruff's fire. He also had the problem of the 3rd South Carolina, which his canister had driven back from his front only minutes earlier. Changing front to better engage Kershaw's attack would present his flank to the 3rd if they came on again. Woodruff ordered his guns to limber and withdraw about 200 yards—to the position recently held by Monroe's battery, which had just withdrawn—where he hoped he might have better fields of fire and greater security.[5]

During the same time period as Sedgwick's defeat, the Federals had assembled a powerful line of batteries along the western front of the East Woods. Captain George W. Cothran's Battery M, 1st New York Light, arrived along Smoketown Road shortly after Woodruff's Battery I, passing Hooker, who was being evacuated in an ambulance along the way. The 2nd and 3rd South Carolina had advanced east of the Hagerstown Turnpike when Cothran's Federal gun teams emerged from the East Woods, "and the shot fell thick and fast in the moving battery." The captain found no one to direct him into position, so he selected his own, on Woodruff's right but somewhat closer to the East Woods, with the right gun of the battery about 70 yards from the rock pile the 3rd North Carolina had charged past earlier in the morning. As each gun unlimbered, it opened fire on the South Carolinians, helping to drive them back into the West Woods. Captain Joseph M. Knap's Battery E, Pennsylvania Light, and Captain John T. Bruen's 10th Battery, New York Light, followed Cothran at a gallop. Knap went into position in the "much trampled down" southeastern corner of the Cornfield, and Bruen unlimbered on Knap's right, in the meadow north of the corn.

Whether all these guns were in place when Kershaw's three-regiment counter-attack burst out onto the Dunker Church Plateau is not certain, but Cothran's battery was.[6]

Cothran's guns targeted Kershaw's charging Rebel regiments as they spilled onto the plateau. The moment Woodruff unlimbered after displacing to the edge of the East Woods, his Napoleons also began belching fire at the South Carolinians. Tompkins's Battery A, 1st Rhode Island, positioned to fire toward the south and southwest, was just below the crest of the plateau. This gave them defilade from enemy fire from the west, but it also meant that they initially did not see the Confederates charging toward them. "I was not aware of their approach until the head of the column gained the brow of a hill, about 60 yards from the right guns of the battery," reported Tompkins. The captain shouted orders for the guns to be faced to the right oblique and called for canister. George Greene's infantry, however, were not surprised. They saw Kershaw coming and were ready. Colonel Hector Tyndale, who, William Fithian in the 28th Pennsylvania recalled, "was ever on the watch," saw the Rebels as they poured across the Hagerstown Pike, ordering his men to lay low and stay out of sight. He intended to let them advance to point-blank range. There was risk in this, but a short-range volley could be devastating if it was accurately delivered. On Tyndale's left, Greene ordered the 111th Pennsylvania right up into the midst of Tompkins's guns to receive the attack. Part of the 102nd New York, on the 111th's left, also changed face to confront the enemy's advance.[7]

The 2nd and 7th South Carolina approached to less than 70 yards before the Union soldiers rose up from the ground. "We poured into their advancing columns volley after volley," reported Major Orrin J. Crane, commanding the 7th Ohio. Sergeant J. J. McDaniel in the 7th South Carolina remembered, "No sooner did we gain the top of the hill [Dunker Church plateau], than they opened a most murderous fire of grape and shells from batteries on our right, front and left." The storm of canister, shrapnel, shell fragments, and minie balls checked the 2nd and 8th South Carolina relatively quickly. Sergeant Robert Shand, in the 2nd, saw "the mouths of Napoleon guns pointed our way" as he came over the rise of ground. This was probably Woodruff's cannons, back near the East Woods. At this moment, Shand heard his captain calling for him to fall back. He looked around and saw "our men were falling back towards the Church." Others in the regiment kept on, however. One of them was Charles Kerrison Jr., a 23-year-old clerk from Charleston, South Carolina. He thought the fight was "the most deadly and bloody conflict I have ever witnessed." Kerrison and others made it to within 50 yards of Tyndale's infantry, whom they discovered lying down beneath the crest of the plateau. The Federals rose and poured a "destructive fire" on the 2nd, but Kerrison and his comrades took what cover they could and "opened upon them with our rifles." Kerrison believed "some misunderstanding" led to his regiment's retreat "just at the time when victory was almost in our grasp." This was an illusion. The 2nd South Carolina had taken heavy losses and lacked the strength and cohesion to make any kind of a dent in Greene's defense. In Kerrison's company, both his lieutenants were killed. Out of 13 effectives taken into action, only 5 escaped, and nearly all of these "were struck but not seriously hurt." Major Orrin Crane, whose 7th Ohio was directly in front of the 2nd South Carolina, wrote that the Confederates "fell like grass before the mower" and that the enemy retired "in great disorder." Out of 253 men carried into the fight, the 2nd had 94 killed or wounded. The survivors fell back into the West Woods.[8]

J. D. McLucas, a 2nd lieutenant in Company K, 8th South Carolina, wrote that his tiny regiment was cut up by the time it reached the Hagerstown Pike, and he did not think it advanced beyond the road. The captain of Company H, Duncan McIntyre, remembered going farther. He recalled passing an abandoned caisson, which was probably the limber that can be seen in Alexander Gardner's photograph of the Dunker Church plateau after the battle. McIntyre thought they kept on until they reached some apple trees, but there were none in the locale where his regiment advanced. In any case, however far his company-sized regiment got, McIntyre recalled that they did not stay there long before they, too, fell back, having lost a third of their strength.[9]

Of Kershaw's three attacking regiments, the 7th South Carolina managed to go the farthest and paid the steepest price. "As we reached the end of the crest, under the declivity," commented Captain Henry W. Addison, the Company H commander, "we were confronted with artillery and any numbers of lines of infantry that belched forth such destruction as I had never seen before, though no novice in the business." The guns belonged to Tompkins's battery, whose crews frantically turned them to confront the rapid approach of the South Carolinians. They opened with double canister at a range of around 40 to 50 yards. The storm of deadly iron balls and the fire of Greene's infantry pinned down the right wing of the Confederate regiment. It was possibly at this time that Colonel D. Wyatt Aiken was badly injured in the chest and knocked out of the fight. His wound was thought to be mortal, but Aiken survived, although his days as a soldier were over. The nature of the ground allowed the left wing to get closer to Tompkins's three right guns. Major White, who commanded the left wing of the 7th South Carolina, ran to the right, where he found John R. Carwile, the acting adjutant. "We can take that battery—forward," White shouted. The two officers passed through the left wing and ran ahead, side by side with the color bearer, straight for the Union cannons. Their men followed, advancing while loading and firing, and managed to drive the crews from the three guns. In the desperation of the moment, someone, perhaps Tompkins or one of his section commanders, gave the command to limber to the rear, which would have ended in disaster for the battery. Fortunately, it was not heard in the tumult, and the 111th Pennsylvania came to the aid of the beleaguered Rhode Islanders. The

South Carolinians still came on, until they were within 10 feet of the abandoned guns. "Just at this time when it seemed they would run over us a very large regiment came in from the right and helped us," observed Gideon Woodring in the 111th Pennsylvania. It was the 28th Pennsylvania, whose numbers and firepower turned the tide. Major White was hit in the cheek by a minie ball, but he grimly kept on to within 20 yards of the battery. Then a blast from one of Tompkins's guns that was still in action sent a canister ball through his ear and into his head, which killed him instantly. Every officer and man in the color company was either killed or wounded, and the 7th's battle flag—"a beautiful silk flag with blue field filled with stars, and crossed from opposite corners"—was captured by the 28th Pennsylvania. Of the 29 officers and 239 enlisted men in the 7th South Carolina, 16 officers and 124 enlisted men became casualties, totaling 52% of the regiment. With their key leaders either dead or disabled, the survivors turned "and made for the wood." Sergeant William Fithian in the 28th Pennsylvania paid tribute to the mettle of the South Carolinians in his diary. "They fought well, in fact they seemed to know no fear, brave, dareing men," he wrote, and admitted that they "did a good bit of damage to us," including shooting the horses of all the 28th's field officers. But Kershaw's attack had been repulsed.[10]

The survivors of the attack fell back across the turnpike, past the Dunker Church, and into the West Woods. They were pursued by a torrent of shell, shrapnel, and solid shot from Woodruff's, Cothran's, Knap's, and Bruen's batteries. Lieutenant Y. J. Pope, adjutant in the 3rd South Carolina, believed it was "one of the heaviest and most prolonged firing of shot and shell I can recall as coming from Field batteries. I recall seeing round cannon balls dancing over the ground." The shelling contributed to the general chaos and confusion and made it difficult to rally the broken units. Sergeant Robert Shand helped a wounded man in the 7th South Carolina to cover, but when he rejoined his regiment, he found that "so many of those ordered back had gone so far to the rear, and there had been so many casualties, that our regiment now was no larger than a company." Captain John S. Hard, who assumed command of the 7th South Carolina, admitted in a letter to his father that when he rallied "the little remnant" of his regiment, "I wept more bitterly than I have done for years." Five of his men had been shot dead alongside him, while "others paid the penalty of their bravery and can never be soldiers again."[11]

The artillery deployed to support Kershaw's advance fared little better than the infantry. Captain Read's Pulaski (Georgia) Artillery unlimbered in the stubble field northeast of Reel's barn and commenced firing, probably on the left pieces of Tompkins's battery, which were only about 500 yards away. That elicited a furious response. Sergeant Robert Shand watched the exchange and noted that "in a very short time," Read's battery "was practically wiped out." The one-sided duel lasted no more than 20 minutes. In that time, one of Read's lieutenants was killed, along with 13 other casualties; a gun was disabled; and 20 horses were put out of action, which accounted for nearly every limber horse. The Confederate battery was so badly crippled that Read was forced to abandon his damaged piece and haul the other guns off by hand.[12]

During Read's duel with Tompkins, another of McLaws's divisional batteries was brought up to the Dunker Church by Jeb Stuart. This unit was Captain Henry H. Carlton's Troup (Georgia) Artillery. Carlton had only three guns, as one had been disabled at Crampton's Gap. His battery followed the division to the vicinity of Hauser's farm, where it halted, waiting for orders. Stuart—who, it will be recalled, unsuccessfully attempted to get Semmes's brigade to charge Stewart's section of Napoleons and then possibly tried to get Barksdale's brigade to do the same thing, also without success (see chapter 8)—suddenly came tearing up to where McLaws and Jackson were observing the fighting. Stuart asked for a battery to be pushed up through the woods, perhaps thinking that if he could get artillery to engage the Federal battery he had seen, then the Confederate infantry might be able to advance against it. McLaws said "No," but Jackson, who, up to this point, had played only a minor role in the battle's tactical management, overruled the division commander, and Carlton's battery drew the assignment. It would prove to be an unfortunate decision. The cavalrymen led the three guns down past Poffenberger's farm, and then along the road that wound from Poffenberger's place up to the Dunker Church. Carlton and Stuart rode ahead of the guns to the church and paused at the edge of the West Woods to view the ground. They could see some of Greene's infantry to their right, and Carlton counted "some two or three batteries of artillery on the ridge just opposite us." These were Woodruff's, Cothran's, and Knap's guns. While Carlton and Stuart conducted their reconnaissance, riflemen from Greene's division sniped at them. Both officers' horses were shot, and a courier of Stuart's, who had accompanied them, was killed. This did not deter Stuart, however, who seemed oblivious to the hornets' nest he was placing Carlton and his men into. Stuart ordered Carlton to situate his guns at the edge of the woods "and not to let loss of men and horse cause me [Carlton] to retreat from position but to hold it" until Stuart could get infantry up. Stuart had been superb in his handling of artillery up to this point, but his placement of Carlton's battery, given what the two officers could see of what would oppose it, condemned good men and horses to destruction for no justifiable purpose.[13]

The Federal guns had the Dunker Church area zeroed in, and when Carlton's artillery arrived at the edge of the woods, they drew a storm of shells like a magnet. Captain Tompkins also turned his two right pieces on them, placing the Georgians in a deadly crossfire. Before the Confederates even unlimbered their guns, every horse pulling the limbers, plus some that were with the caissons, were killed. A total of 18 horses died. Carlton's crews struggled on heroically, hauling the three guns into position by hand and opening a rapid fire on their many adversaries. They managed to get off 109 rounds in about 10 minutes, an impressive rate of fire. But, one by one, the Union artillery knocked Carlton's pieces out of action and killed or wounded 30% of his men. When McLaws became aware of the destruction being wreaked upon the battery, he wasted no time in sending orders for the captain to abandon his guns and pull his surviving horses and men back under cover. Infantry could recover his three pieces. The battery accomplished nothing, except providing target practice for Federal artillery. Carlton had obeyed Stuart's orders, "but at the sacrifice of my entire battery," he bitterly recalled years later.[14]

The Federals made their own futile sacrifice—but with infantry, instead—at nearly the same time as Carlton's Georgians were being pounded. At some point during the rout of Sedgwick's division, Sumner sent an urgent order to Alpheus Williams "to send to the front all of my command immediately available." There does not appear to have been much more direction than this. Sumner needed every available man to help cover Sedgwick's retreat. Williams's problem was that the 12th Corps had little he could call on. Greene's division was holding a critical position at the Dunker Church plateau; Goodrich's brigade was already supporting Sedgwick (Williams may not yet have been aware that it had been routed, along with Sedgwick's men); and Crawford's regiments were scattered in different locales, so they could not be quickly concentrated. Only General George H. Gordon's brigade was available, and it was somewhat dispersed. The 107th New York were supporting Cothran's battery, while the pummeled 27th Indiana and the 3rd Wisconsin were supporting Knap's and Bruen's guns. That left the 2nd Massachusetts and the rookie 13th New Jersey, who were resting in the East Woods. With little information about where these men were needed, Williams could only offer vague instructions to Gordon. Nonetheless, the orders Gordon received were "most urgent and imperative," directing him "to move up toward the woods in front, to support the troops there." Because of the lay of the land, the retreat of the bulk of Sedgwick's division to the north was not visible to Williams. It was known that Sedgwick had met with a disaster of some proportion, but Gordon was provided with incorrect information, stating "that our forces had again entered the woods in our front." From what he could discern, his mission was to assist friendly troops who had reentered the West Woods. Since it would take too much time to assemble the entire brigade, Gordon ordered the 2nd Massachusetts and the 13th New Jersey forward, while he collected the 27th Indiana and the 3rd Wisconsin to follow these two regiments.[15]

Colonel Ezra Carman, commander of the 13th New Jersey, received his orders from an officer on Gordon's staff. They were to advance through the Cornfield, which was in Carman's front, "across the Hagerstown Pike and into the West Woods, where he was to report to the first general officer he met." Carman was cautioned that he might find elements of the 124th Pennsylvania and other units in the vicinity of Miller's farm, and he was warned twice that friendly troops would be in his front, so his men were not to fire on them. The colonel shared this information with his company commanders, who warned their troops. Although the East Woods sheltered the 13th New Jersey from enemy observation, there was much around them that the rookie soldiers found unsettling. A large number of dead and wounded from the morning's fighting were littered in front of their position. Corporal Sebastian Duncan Jr. wrote that one of them, a young soldier from the 107th New York, "lay just before us with one leg shot off; the other shattered and otherwise badly wounded; fairly shrieking with pain." E. Livingston Allen in Company K never forgot how the wounded man kept crying out, "Mother! Mother! Mother!" with increasing intensity. "Brave hearts trembled—strong men wept—indescribable emotions swept over mind and heart," he recalled. Skulkers—that is, men separated from their regiments who had no great desire to rejoin them—lurked throughout the woods. Carman managed to force several of them to carry the mangled, shrieking soldier back for medical attention. But such scenes and incidents were demoralizing to Carman's rookies.[16]

General Gordon approached on horseback as the regiment was forming up and called out to the over 600 men, whose line extended for 200 yards through the woods, asking if they would follow Colonel Carman "into those woods," indicating the West Woods. The New Jerseyites, whose nerves were taut as a bowstring, replied with "hearty cheers." Carman ordered the double-quick and the 13th New Jersey, with the 2nd Massachusetts following in their left rear, burst out of the woods. The 13th threaded their way through the Cornfield, which was strewn with the dead and wounded, as well as cast-off equipment. The 2nd stepped through the equally carnage-littered pasture south of the corn. Both regiments moved directly toward the plateau south of the corn, where so much fighting had already occurred. The cornstalks disordered the 13th, but Carman planned to reform when they reached the Hagerstown Turnpike. Due to the direction of their advance, the 13th's right reached the pike first, near the southern boundary of the Cornfield, climbed over the first fence, and entered the road. They saw a few men to the right and front but could not determine their identity. The West Woods were quiet, and no other troops were visible. The rest of the regiment began to arrive and scale the fence when "puffs of white smoke" suddenly were seen about 150 yards in front, rising from behind the limestone ledge that had sheltered troops from both sides throughout the morning. This first fire proved to be deadly, killing 5 or 6 privates and wounding 20 to 30 other men.[17]

The 2nd Massachusetts had a similar experience when they scaled the fence on the western side of the Hagerstown Turnpike. Captain Charles Morse, the commander of Company B, claimed that he saw Rebel soldiers who were so close to the road, "you could distinguish the features of the men." This caused confusion, since Colonel Andrews had been advised that friendly troops were in his front. "Instead of finding friends there, we were met by a volley of musketry," wrote Robert Gould Shaw, the future leader of the 54th Massachusetts, who was then the Company H commander. The Confederates were so well concealed behind the ledge that initially the men thought friendly troops were firing on them. The New Englanders endured the fire "for some time, thinking there was some mistake," before Andrews realized they were Rebels and ordered his men to return fire. Then, added Morse, "We gave them a volley which sent them back in quick time under cover of a natural breastwork they had there." But it was clear to the veterans that their position in the road was untenable. "We did very little execution," Shaw thought.[18]

The Confederates firing on the 2nd Massachusetts and 13th New Jersey were new troops entering the conflict over the West Woods. It was Brigadier General John G. Walker's division. Recall that Robert E. Lee had deployed this division to the army's extreme right flank (see chapter 7), where it kept an eye on Snavely's Ford, below the Rohrback Bridge. After dispatching G. T. Anderson's brigade and McLaws's division to his left, Lee concluded that from the lack of any aggressive activity by the Federals on his right flank, he could strip some of his defenses there. Lee never thought in terms of simply holding ground or checking the enemy. He consistently sought opportunities to mass his troops' strength and deal his enemy a crushing blow. At 9 a.m., Lee took an considerable risk by ordering Walker's division to leave its position guarding Snavely's Ford march to the army's left, and report to Jackson. Lee also detached Brigadier General Lewis A. Armistead's Virginia brigade of R. H. Anderson's division, which was then moving toward the Rebel army's center at the Sunken Lane. Walker's two brigades were among the army's largest, and with the two divisional batteries, they numbered nearly 4,000 effectives. Armistead's strength is unknown, but it was probably around 700. Of Lee's 34 infantry brigades on the field, he had now committed 21 to the action on the left, or almost 62% of the Confederate army's strength.[19]

Walker's precise route is somewhat vague. Carman wrote that they passed west of Sharpsburg, and this was confirmed by Lieutenant Robert T. Knox in the 30th Virginia, who remembered passing by Lee's headquarters. They probably avoided marching directly through Sharpsburg, which was the fastest route, to avoid Union artillery overshots, which were striking within its boundaries. Most likely the division followed Snavely's Lane to Harpers Ferry Road, then left the road near the village, marched around its west side, and followed the same cross-country path as McLaws. Samuel Walkup in the 48th North Carolina noted that the movement was conducted in "great haste," the whole distance of about 2 miles being covered at the double-quick. When the division reached the vicinity of Reel's farm, the brigades were halted briefly to stack up knapsacks, blankets, and anything else not needed in combat. Benjamin C. Rawlings, a young lieutenant in the 30th Virginia, decided that his new uniform coat would be too conspicuous and left it with his company's pile of equipment. Such was the excitement that Rawlings "never even thought my blood red hunting shirt was even more conspicuous."[20]

The North Carolina brigade of Brigadier General Robert Ransom Jr. led the division. The 34-year-old Ransom was an 1850 graduate of West Point, with service in the dragoons and cavalry before the Civil War. Who gave Walker the orders for his division is unknown, but most likely it was Jackson, since Walker reported to him. Ransom was sent north, perhaps because it was known that Semmes had suffered heavy losses in his fight with Gorman and could use some help. Whatever the case, Ransom led his brigade in column of regiments over the plowed field where Barksdale's, Semmes's, and Kershaw's brigades had deployed a half hour earlier. They had advanced past Hauser's Ridge and were near Poffenberger's farm when Ransom received orders from someone—he does not say whom—"to form to the right and resist the enemy, who were in possession of a piece of woods," meaning the West Woods. The nature of the orders indicates that Jackson and McLaws were unaware that Sedgwick's division had been completely cleared from the West Woods. Ransom wheeled the 49th North Carolina to the right, and it marched up to the edge of the West Woods, just south of Poffenberger's barn. The 35th North Carolina followed in the 49th's path, moving around the barn, while the 25th North Carolina passed by and around Poffenberger's house. For some reason, the 24th North Carolina, on Ransom's left, either failed to obey or did not get the orders to wheel. They continued marching north into and through the West Woods, where they ended up being commandeered by Jeb Stuart to support his guns and the army's far left flank.[21]

Ransom either did not notice the drift of the 24th North Carolina or was too busy to fetch them back. When his other three regiments completed their line along the edge of the West Woods, he ordered them forward through the woodlot. Ransom's report of this advance is a fine example of the type of sheer fantasy that sometimes made its way into these official documents. He claimed that he encountered the enemy in "strong force," and a "tremendous fire was poured into them, and, without a halt, the woods was cleared and the crest next the enemy was occupied." Division commander Walker, who also was particularly fond of exaggeration and equipped with a vivid imagination, also effused about how Ransom "advanced in splendid style, firing and cheering as they went, and in a few minutes cleared the woods, strewing it with the enemy's dead and wounded." Passages such as this played well with the newspapers but bore no connection to reality. Ezra Carman declared, "What enemy Ransom encountered and drove from the woods is a mystery to us." The truth was that there was no enemy to be driven from the woods. Semmes, Barksdale, and Early had already cleared this part of the West Woods and strewn it with "the enemy's dead and wounded," whom Walker erroneously claimed for Ransom. Ransom's advance was unopposed, except for some random artillery shells fired into the area by Knap's, Bruen's, Cothran's, or Reynolds's guns. The 25th and 35th North

Carolina moved up through the central section of the woods and halted behind the limestone ledge, while the 49th North Carolina stopped in the southern section of the woods. Ransom imprudently decided that a charge to the turnpike and beyond would be a good idea, but before he could give these orders, the 13th New Jersey and the 2nd Massachusetts appeared in front of the regiments of the 25th and 35th. The North Carolinians immediately opened what Ransom described as a "crushing fire" on the Union soldiers.[22]

The 13th New Jersey were busily firing back at men whom they were certain were the enemy when an officer dressed in blue rode out of the woods and shouted, "For Gods sake stop; you are shooting your own men!" According to Corporal Duncan, "this created considerable confusion; some ceased firing, when suddenly the Rebs poured a terrible volley into us and rushed from the woods." Although they rarely admitted to it, soldiers on both sides occasionally resorted to any number of tricks to gain an advantage. In this incident, one of Ransom's officers or men possibly donned the uniform coat of a fallen Federal officer in an attempt to confuse the Union soldiers in their front. More likely, however, in the smoky atmosphere his bluish-gray uniform looked blue to the rookies. Whatever the case, he deliberately sought to confuse these Yankees. In this moment of uncertainty, Captain Hugh C. Irish, commanding Company K, on the regiment's right, climbed over the second turnpike fence and called for his men to follow him. He was immediately shot dead, demoralizing his men. Carman ordered the regiment to fall back behind the first fence, on the eastern side of the pike. Sebastian Duncan did not hear Carman's orders, although he saw his comrades scrambling over the fence, "some of them very precipitously." Duncan lay on his stomach in the road, attempting to get his rifle loaded. He managed to get off a shot at the North Carolinians but found himself in a position where he was "liable to be shot by my comrades behind me as well as by the rebels, the balls whistled in both directions over my head." He crawled back, managed to get on the other side of the fence with the others, and sent another round "somewhere near a rebellious Southerner." But then the regiment "began to give way." Duncan thought the flight was due "to our want of discipline & our ignorance."[23]

Carman had ordered a retreat, but, amid the chaos and the noise, many of the soldiers did not hear the order. "The men were being shot by a foe they could not see, so perfectly did the ledge protect them; they scarcely knew how to load their muskets and were doing little or no execution," so Carman concluded that to "hold them longer under fire would be murder and they were ordered back to the East Woods." The 13th New Jersey's colonel claimed they fell back in good order, "under the circumstances," but Corporal Duncan's journal told a different tale. He wrote that the regiment was "thrown into disorder and finally skedaddled. Some of the officers who had driven us in now leading us out." Lieutenant John A. Fox, commanding Company I of the 2nd Massachusetts, which was on the far right of that regiment, plus his first sergeant and second lieutenant, made an effort to hold the 13th New Jersey. By "denunciations and taunts," they managed to keep part of the regiment in position on their right, "but only for a short time. They soon broke and fled in confusion, amid the jeers and hooting of the Second."[24]

The 2nd Massachusetts fought on alone for several minutes. "Our men never flinched or faltered," wrote Lieutenant Fox with pride. "They loaded and fired as coolly as ever." But Fox watched "man after man fall dead or wounded, while we inflicted but little injury upon the enemy." Although the firing "was pretty hot," Lieutenant Charley Mills could barely spot any enemy soldiers. The Rebels were in the woods, and "all I could see there, except smoke & flash, was a dim vision of two or three men in gray dodging among the trees." Captain Charles F. Morse, the Company F commander, was hit in the temple by a spent ball, "which laid me on my back for a moment, and raised a pretty black & blue spot." The captain thought he was mortally wounded, but "I soon got the better of that idea." He was able to get up and resume his duties. The regiment's beloved lieutenant colonel, Wilder Dwight, had his horse shot. Dwight dismounted and attempted to hold the frantic animal, but it struggled so violently that it broke loose and ran off. He then started moving toward Colonel Andrews. Dwight was within two feet of him and about to say something when a bullet struck the lieutenant colonel in the hip. He sunk to the ground and uttered, "That's done for me." Dwight probably intended to tell Andrews what the colonel already understood—namely, that their position was untenable. Andrews ordered the regiment to fall back. Among the wounded left in the road was Lieutenant Mills, shot through the hip and disabled. He hollered, "For God's sake help me off, some one." One of his men ran back for him and somehow managed to get Mills over the turnpike fence and back into the East Woods. The 2nd Massachusetts fell back in good order, although Morse admitted that "it was hard work getting over that high fence in our rear with much appearance of dignity." Nearly a third of the regiment had been killed or wounded, and they were forced to leave the mortally wounded Dwight behind. Twenty-nine years later, Colonel Andrews lamented the decision that sent his regiment and the 13th New Jersey up to the Hagerstown Pike: "The only effect of the order was to send the regiment into a hornet's nest to no good purpose." Captain Robert Gould Shaw viewed the sad affair philosophically. "Of course, there are mistakes made in every battle; that day we were the victims of one," he wrote to his mother.[25]

Some of Ransom's men pursued the retreating Federals up to the pike, where they were greeted with a dose of canister from Cothran's, Knap's, and Bruen's guns, which sent them back into the woods. The 2nd Massachusetts and the 13th New Jersey fell back to the East Woods, where they re-formed. Four men in the 2nd, including the regimental assistant surgeon, Lincoln R. Stone, immediately volunteered to go back and get Lieutenant Colonel Dwight. Colonel

Andrews approved, so the men made their way to the turnpike, gathered up Dwight, "all the time under a heavy fire," and brought him back. "Any of us would willingly have done anything for the brave little Colonel," wrote Captain Morse. Meanwhile, Sebastian Duncan Jr. rejoined the 13th New Jersey in the woods after helping to carry a wounded soldier to safety. The regiment had been drawn up and was "evidently dissatisfied with its conduct." General Gordon rode up and asked the members of the 13th if they would follow their colors into the West Woods again, to which the men responded with "hearty cheers." But it would not be with the same color bearer. He "gave out" and refused to carry the flag any longer. One harrowing experience under fire had been enough. Colonel Carman took the colors and called out for a volunteer. An embarrassing "moments silence" met Carman's appeal before a man, unfortunately not identified, stepped forward and said he would carry them, which he did "nobly" for the rest of the battle.[26]

Minutes after Andrews's and Carman's regiments fell back from their ill-fated advance to the Hagerstown Pike, the Confederates launched another disastrous attack from the woods around the Dunker Church. It was again directed at Greene's division. The victims this time were the men of Colonel Vannoy H.

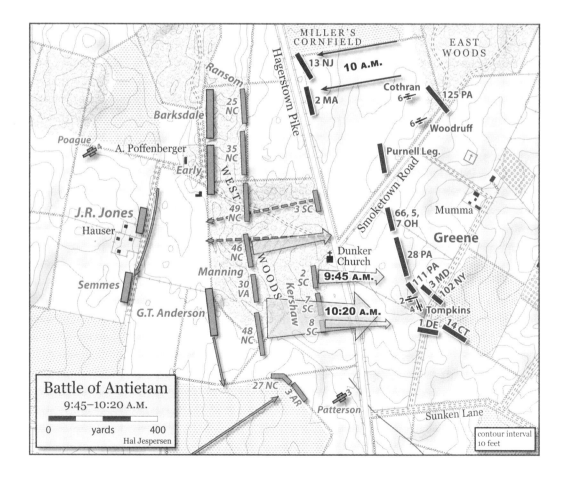

Manning's brigade. The young Manning—he was only 23—was an ambitious man who made his way from Mississippi to Tennessee and then to Arkansas in 1860, where he practiced law and dabbled in politics. When the war began, he helped organize the 3rd Arkansas Infantry, a regiment destined to win distinction as a hard-hitting combat unit. He was elected the regiment's colonel in the army's reorganization during the spring of 1862. When Walker moved up to division command, Manning assumed command of the brigade by seniority. He possessed courage in abundance, but he lacked experience as a brigade commander and made the mistake of thinking "élan," rather than reconnaissance and coordination of support, could carry any position.

Manning's brigade did not follow Ransom across the Hauser farm's plowed field. Instead, it was directed through Reel's large cornfield, toward the Dunker Church and the West Woods, probably to support Kershaw's brigade. Manning's was the largest brigade in the army, with 2,164 officers and men in three North Carolina regiments (the 27th, 46th, and 48th), plus the 3rd Arkansas and the 30th Virginia. As they passed over the high ground at the northeastern edge of the corn, Manning was ordered to drop off the 27th North Carolina and the 30th Virginia to "hold the open space between the woods and Longstreet's left"—that is, the ground between the West Woods and D. H. Hill's line in the Sunken Lane. They were also probably placed here to support the different batteries that took up position at various times on the hill that rose in the eastern part of the cornfield. The other three regiments hurried on without stopping, heading toward the West Woods under severe artillery fire. Lieutenant Robert T. Knox in the 30th Virginia remembered "the air being fairly musical with the shrieking & bursting shells." Some of Greene's men may have fired on them, as well, for Lieutenant Benjamin Rollins, also in the 30th, commented on the "terrible noise" bullets made when they struck the cornstalks. It only got worse. "A terrific fire of artillery and musketry" greeted the regiments when they reached the West Woods. At the eastern edge of the woods, just north of the Dunker Church, Colonel Edward D. Hall, commanding the 46th North Carolina on Manning's left, observed the enemy "in heavy force on an elevation distant about 200 yards, with a battery of artillery in position on the crest of the hill." This was Tyndale's brigade and the right section of Tompkins's battery. Noting how the turnpike fences between his regiment and the enemy would disorder an attack, Hall wisely deemed it "inexpedient" to attempt an assault. He placed his regiment under cover of a breastwork of rails from the turnpike's fencing that someone had assembled earlier and had his men open fire.[27]

Manning was with the 30th Virginia and the 48th North Carolina. They moved up to the Dunker Church without pause. The 48th was the largest regiment in the Army of Northern Virginia, with an estimated strength of 907. It surged up around either side of the church. Manning "came tearing up on horseback" in front of the two regiments, "& waving his sword around his head cleared the fence at a bound called to us to follow him." Lieutenant Knox wrote, "Where was the Confederate soldier then that would have held back?" But a number of them did. Lieutenant Colonel Samuel H. Walkup recorded that in the 48th, "many hesitated and took shelter behind trees & could not be forced forward." There were quite a few conscripts in the regiment. A month earlier, one of them, Constantine A. Hege, had complained, "I do not like it here, I do not like to here [sic] of going to face the cannon and the muskets," and begged his father to find him a substitute. None could be found, and Hege was among those confronted by the bullets, shells, and canister. Those in the regiment who followed Manning crossed the Hagerstown Turnpike's fences "under a most galling fire of grape & canister from the artillery & musketry." Many were killed or wounded, and the survivors began to break ranks. "I drew my pistol and threatened to shoot & scolded but with very futile effect," Walkup recorded. The terrible fire "swept everything before it" as Walkup watched his regiment disintegrate, "& the whole give way in confusion & retreat in disorder."[28]

The experience of the 30th Virginia largely mirrored that of the 48th North Carolina, although the latter managed to advance slightly farther. This regiment emerged from the West Woods in the triangle where Smoketown Road meets the Hagerstown Pike, which meant they had to clear the pike's fences, then Smoketown Road's fences, as well as the rocky ledge south of that road, where the Maryland monument stands today. A worm fence bordered the eastern side of the turnpike here, and another was on the northern side of Smoketown Road. The men fixed bayonets as they charged out of the woods "at a full run" and raised the rebel yell. The 30th "went flying over" the fences, with their color bearer in the lead. Within 60–70 yards of the plateau's crest, the Virginians saw lines of Federal infantry, who rose up from the ground "and fired point blank at us." Lieutenant Knox remembered it as "a perfect hail of bullets." Another soldier wrote how the enemy fired "Volley after Volley after us and it is a wonder to me that any of us escaped. I have often heard men talking of a Shower of Bullets, but never saw nor expierienced it untill Yesterday." In a familiar refrain for the Battle of Antietam, every member of the color guard was shot down. Lieutenant Knox picked up the flag from the last of the guard and "waved it so our boys could see we were there." A solid shot, probably fired by Woodruff's artillery, struck the flag, tearing off a corner but leaving Knox unharmed. The tempest of bullets checked the charge. The survivors took cover, either under the crest of the ridge or behind the rock ledge, and attempted to return fire. "Our men were falling every minute," wrote Knox. Besides Tompkins's guns blasting canister at them, Woodruff's or Cothran's battery "enfiladed our line with grape and canister." Lieutenant Colonel Robert S. Chew sensed the futility of their attack and ordered the regiment to retreat. Chew was hit at some point in the withdrawal. Manning was struck in the left arm and breast, yet he managed to ride over to Colonel Hall and inform Hall that he was now in command of the brigade.

The retreat began in good order, but Lieutenant Ben Rawlings noted that the "fire was so terrible that every men broke and got out as fast as possible."[29]

The Virginians streamed past the Dunker Church in disarray, heading into the West Woods. "Having no orders and no one in command [we] fell still farther back," recorded Lieutenant Knox. The 30th Virginia, as well as the huge 48th North Carolina, were both effectively destroyed in the brief assault. Of the 236 officers and men the 30th carried into the charge, 49 were killed or mortally wounded and 113 others wounded, for a loss of just over 68%. Such was the volume of fire the Virginians and North Carolinians faced that when the body of Lieutenant Benjamin L. Smith in Company C, 30th Virginia, was later recovered, they found "nineteen balls in his person." Ben Rawlings counted eight dead in his company, and double that number wounded. Knox recalled that among the regiment's survivors, "every one was helping off some wounded friend & comrade." One of the survivors in Rawlings's company was Joe Haislip. His story offers some insight into the terror the attackers experienced. Haislip's face was black and bruised, and he told Rawlings that a shell had burst in front of him, knocking him over. Rawlings sent him back to the hospital. Thirty years later, Haislip admitted to Rawlings that when the firing grew so terrible, "he decided he could not stand it any longer." He deliberately fell on his face to avoid the volleys, then took a cartridge out and rubbed the black powder on his face. This fooled the lieutenant and got Haislip out of the killing zone.[30]

Lieutenant Colonel Walkup attempted to rally the 48th North Carolina in the West Woods, where they were under the brow of the hill that extended west from the Dunker Church. His efforts were undercut by the cowardice of Colonel Robert C. Hill, who, Walkup wrote, "led the retreat." Out of 900 men in the regiment, Walkup managed to gather three officers and part of one company. The others paid no attention to Walkup's efforts to rally them and followed their colonel off the field. The conscripts, in their first action, were particularly shaken, but so, too, were veterans. The Federals shelled the woods furiously, and Walkup lost several more men. He decided to fall back beyond the range of the enemy guns. The 48th "left [although] the 2d or 22d S.C. [the 2nd South Carolina] begs us to stand by them." The South Carolinians had better cover, however, so Walkup pulled his survivors back. At a rock wall, which may have been the one at the northern end of the Reel cornfield, Walkup halted and began trying to collect what he could of his regiment. "I with difficulty retained about 100 men," mostly from three companies. Of the 907 who charged up to the Hagerstown Pike, 35 were dead, 171 wounded, and 86 missing or captured. The rest had scattered and were out of the fight for the rest of the battle. Only the 3rd North Carolina may have exceeded the 48th North Carolina's 292 casualties. In contrast to the bloody debacle Manning's aggressiveness had inflicted on the 30th and 48th North Carolina, the 46th North Carolina, whose colonel had

sensibly put his men under good cover, emerged from the fight with 5 killed and 60 wounded—serious losses, to be sure, but not devastating.[31]

Greene's division had repulsed two Confederate brigade attacks on his position, which gave the Federals some measure of revenge, but this did not erase the impact of Sedgwick's catastrophic defeat. In 30 minutes, all the advantages won by the hard fighting of the 1st and 12th Corps had been lost, and the Rebels had restored their shaken line. Given the length of the combat, the physical damage done to the Federals was shocking. Sedgwick's three brigades and two batteries suffered 2,210 casualties, most of them being killed or wounded. Francis Palfrey, the lieutenant colonel of the 20th Massachusetts and author of *The Antietam and Fredericksburg*, was badly wounded and captured in the action. He believed that "besides the immense advantages which Sumner's blunder gave the Confederates, they probably considerably outnumbered the forces they encountered." But they did not. The Confederates defeated Sedgwick with parts of five brigades, one of which was Kershaw's, and the latter committed only two of its regiments to the counterattack. The Rebels engaged 4,322 infantry against Sedgwick's 5,437.

"Where Sumner's Corps Charged." The Dunker Church plateau, looking north. The Hagerstown Pike is to the left. The abandoned limbers and dead horses came from S. D. Lee's battalion. The dead soldiers were infantrymen in Kershaw's and Manning's Confederate brigades, killed during their counterattacks against Greene's 2nd Division. Courtesy of the Library of Congress

How had they so decisively defeated a crack, veteran division that outnumbered them? Some luck was involved, as well as tactical bungling by Sumner, which prevented the full combat force of Sedgwick's division from being effectively employed. The Confederates also handled their forces more skillfully, and struck hard and fast, giving the Federals no time to rectify their faulty position. McLaws, who seems to have been criticized for everything he did during the Maryland Campaign by his superiors, peers, and historians, managed his division with consummate skill. He put his brigades into action in such a manner that they struck with power and mutually supported one another. There was no hesitation, delay, or plodding, traits that are so often attributed to McLaws. He acted decisively and quickly, and rammed the Federals with every bit of the force of Hood's counterattack earlier, except that McLaws's assault was far more successful. Had he been more tentative or defensive minded, Sumner might very well have recovered and managed to redeploy Sedgwick's brigades to better defend the West Woods. Because Jackson was present, he often gets the credit for managing the action on the Confederates' left, but other than giving McLaws some general guidance, he had a minimal impact on the tactical conduct of the fight.[32]

Jeb Stuart and the brigade commanders in the Army of Northern Virginia also deserve high praise. Stuart directed the Confederate artillery with skill and energy. His gun line on Hauser's Ridge was crucial in helping to check Sedgwick's advance beyond the West Woods. Moreover, his leap-frogging of batteries to the north after Sedgwick's defeat prevented the Federals from re-forming and checking the Rebels' pursuit. Early, Semmes, Barksdale, and G. T. Anderson all distinguished themselves in handling their brigades. Although Early attributed actions to his brigade that they did not perform, this does not detract from the ability he displayed in managing his men, before McLaws's division arrived, to prevent the enemy from seizing the West Woods. Semmes kept his small brigade in the fight despite severe losses, and then conducted a vigorous pursuit that, with Stuart's help, cleared out the Yankees nearly to the North Woods. Barksdale's ability to maneuver his brigade under fire was remarkable. Man for man, his command probably inflicted more damage on the Army of the Potomac than any other Confederate brigade at Antietam. G. T. Anderson also deserves high marks for his actions. No one gave him orders to join the assault on Sedgwick. He did so on his own initiative, and then coordinated his movements beautifully with Barksdale's and Kershaw's brigades. Finally, he wisely avoided carrying his pursuit beyond the West Woods, where the Union artillery could have mauled him. Kershaw's brigade took some very hard knocks in its charge on Greene's division, but his 2nd and 3rd South Carolina were handled deftly by their regimental commanders and did significant damage to Sedgwick. Kershaw's costly charge beyond the West Woods is perhaps explained by his belief that his brigade was pursuing a defeated enemy, rather than assaulting a well-defended position.

Sumner's tactical blunders and disastrous decision to abandon his role as a corps commander—instead essentially leading a brigade assault—have already been discussed (see chapter 8). The old warrior exhibited great courage in attempting to extricate Sedgwick's men from the position he had placed them in, as well as in helping to prevent outright panic. But the slaughter of Sedgwick's fine troops rattled him. It would be a rare man who would not be shaken by such an experience. In his history of the 2nd Corps, Francis A. Walker, who served on Sumner's staff after Antietam, wrote:

> It is not a profanation to say such a thing about Edwin V. Sumner, he had lost courage; not the courage which would have borne him up a ravine swept by canister at the head of the old First Division, but the courage, which, in the crush and clamor of action, amid disaster and repulse, enables a commander to coolly calculate the chances of success or failure. He was heartbroken at the terrible fate of the splendid division on which he had so much relied, which he had deemed invincible, and his proximity to the disaster had been so close as to convey a shock from which he had not recovered. Nor had he recovered from this shock an hour or more later when Franklin came up.

Walker's assessment remains an accurate one. It is rare that a battle as large as Antietam has a single turning point, and the defeat of Sedgwick's division was not one. The Army of the Potomac could still have won a decisive victory despite this setback. But it was *a* critical turning point in the fight, for it decisively shaped Sumner's view of the battle. As the senior officer on the army's right flank, his distorted and demoralized perception carried tremendous weight. He abandoned all thoughts of offensive action and now believed that the Union right trembled on the precipice of outright disaster. The consequences would be profound.[33]

AS THE LAST OF Manning's 30th Virginia and 48th North Carolina disappeared into the West Woods, George Greene seized the moment and ordered an advance. The accomplishments of Greene and his two small Union brigades have never truly been recognized. They smashed Colquitt's brigade; dislodged the stubborn 4th Alabama, 5th Texas, and 21st Georgia from the East Woods; routed McRae's brigade; and repulsed two assaults by Kershaw's and Manning's brigades, inflicting nearly 700 casualties. Much of their success belonged to Greene's skillful handling of his men, which enabled them to inflict maximum damage on the enemy while minimizing their own casualties. Greene now saw an opportunity to seize a lodgment in the West Woods, and he took a calculated risk to push his division forward. Greene had heard the furious fighting in the woods and would have seen the 34th New York and the 125th Pennsylvania— and others—retreating in disorder. Because most of Sedgwick's division fell back to the north and northeast, however, out of Greene's view, he was unaware of

Sedgwick's rout. He still believed Sedgwick held the main body of the West Woods. Leaving behind the 66th Ohio and the 102nd New York to support Tompkins, the rest of division raised "three rousing cheers" and went forward toward the Hagerstown Pike. Colonel Hall's 46th North Carolina delivered what he described as a "galling fire" at the approaching Federals, but as Greene's men barely mentioned any resistance, it is evident that Hall quickly recognized his single regiment had no chance of stopping the enemy. He ordered his men to fall back, which they did in good order, all the way through the woods, until he encountered Stonewall Jackson. Jackson ordered Hall to report to McLaws—a curious order, since Hall's division commander was Walker. McLaws directed Hall "to hold the woods at all hazards," so he led his regiment back to the woods' western edge, only to find it "filled with the enemy." More than his regiment would be needed to dislodge them.[34]

Colonel Nance's 3rd South Carolina withdrew around the same time as Hall's 46th North Carolina retreated. Nance also marched his regiment out of the West Woods and back near Hauser's farm, where he reported to Kershaw and McLaws. Thus the only substantial Confederate force remaining in the West Woods was Ransom's brigade, which occupied the central section behind the limestone ledge.[35] Greene's regiments scrambled over the Hagerstown Turnpike's fences and entered the West Woods, the fourth time this ground had changed hands. Major Thomas M. Walker, commanding the 111th Pennsylvania, remembered that two companies of his regiment passed north of the church, while he and the remaining eight companies went around the south side. The far right of Greene's line advanced about 200 yards west of the church, to the edge of the plateau, before halting. It was roughly the same position held earlier by the 125th Pennsylvania. Greene arranged his regiments to face west and south. The 5th and 7th Ohio held the right. To their left was the big 28th Pennsylvania, whose line extended to the fence on the southern face of the woods. The 111th Pennsylvania and the 3rd Maryland deployed along this fence, facing south at nearly a right angle to the 28th. Greene knew his right flank had no direct support, and he immediately sent for help to fill the gap between his right and where he thought Sedgwick was. It was 10:30 a.m. Although the cannons kept firing and the skirmishing continued, the conflict over the West Woods settled into a temporary lull. Both sides were exhausted and disorganized. But off to the south, in the area of the old sunken farm lane that connected the Hagerstown Pike with the Boonsboro Pike, rose the roar of a furious combat. It was here, at Lee's center, where the next crisis of the battle was unfolding.

10

General French Assaults the Sunken Lane

"May I never again see such horrors as I saw that day"

It was about 8:30 a.m. when Brigadier General Robert Rodes received orders from D. H. Hill to support the advance of Ripley's, Colquitt's, and McRae's brigades toward the East Woods and the Cornfield. Rodes's brigade contained five Alabama regiments, with a total strength of around 850. Three days earlier, at the Battle of South Mountain, they had fought valiantly but been battered, losing a third of their men. They spent the night of September 16 bivouacked not far from Newcomer's farm on the Boonsboro Pike, near the southern extension of the Sunken Lane and to the left of G. B. Anderson's brigade. Precisely how Rodes moved after receiving his orders is uncertain, but the best evidence indicates that he followed the Piper farm lane to the family's various buildings, then turned north and marched through Piper's orchard. As the brigade hurried through the fruit trees, it encountered fugitives from Colquitt's and McRae's brigades, who were retreating in confusion from the fighting to the north. It was immediately evident to Rodes that continuing on in blind obedience to orders was not a good idea. He determined that "the best service I could render them [Colquitt's and McRae's brigades] and the field generally, would be to form a line in rear of them and endeavor to rally them before attacking or being attacked." Before he could decide where to form that line, he received new orders from D. H. Hill, who had the same thought. Rodes was to halt his brigade "and form line of battle in the hollow of an old and narrow road just beyond the orchard."[1]

Rodes deployed his regiments in the Sunken Lane and went to work trying to rally Colquitt's and McRae's broken units, but most men were beyond any attempt to regroup and continued past the Alabamians toward Sharpsburg. Only a part of the 23rd North Carolina of McRae's brigade rallied, along with a handful of men from the other regiments in the two brigades. A precise number is unknown, but it was probably no more than 100 or so officers and men. Rodes placed this scratch force on his left, in the spot where the Sunken Lane met the Hagerstown Pike. The lane ran east from the pike for approximately 500 yards and then turned southeast for another 500 yards, where it then angled 90 degrees south and zigzagged for slightly over a half mile to the Boonsboro Pike.

Ezra Carman described its 1862 appearance: "By rains and usage the roadway had been much worn down to an ordinary depth of two or three feet, and in many places to a much greater depth." It was a ready-made breastwork and an ideal point in which to rally broken units, but not necessarily a desirable defensive position. Higher ground north of the lane, within close musket range, commanded much of its eastern and southeastern course. Unless the road could be occupied where it turned south, an alert attacker could outflank the position. Hill was probably aware of these vulnerabilities but chose to defend the lane for two reasons. First, it was a ready-made breastwork. Second—crucially—much of its eastward and southeastern sections could not be observed by Federal artillery, because of the intervening high terrain. This explains why Hill did not form his line on the higher ground in front of the lane, where his men would have been exposed to a crossfire from the Union batteries east of Antietam Creek and from those around the East Woods and Mumma's farm.[2]

Rodes deployed his five regiments immediately to the right of McRae's and Colquitt's rallied remnants. The Alabamian left rested about 150 yards from the Hagerstown Pike and extended to where the lane turned southeast, deploying (from left to right) the 26th, 12th, 3rd, 5th, and 6th Alabama, on a frontage of about 350 yards. There was good cover along most of the front, except for the section of the road occupied by the right wing of the 6th Alabama. This part could be enfiladed by an enemy positioned on the ridge about 250 yards to the right front.[3]

The regiments immediately went to work to build up their cover by dismantling the fencing on the sides of the road and building a crude breastwork along the northern bank of the lane. The Union batteries on the eastern bank of Antietam Creek added urgency to this construction effort by dropping some shells in the vicinity. While Rodes's Alabamians were engaged in this labor, the North Carolina brigade of Brigadier General George B. Anderson, 1,174 strong, came up on their right. Anderson had also been summoned by Hill, and he led his brigade up a ravine running northwest from the general area of Newcomer's farm. This gave the men a covered route to Piper's cornfield, which the Carolinians passed through into the Sunken Lane. Anderson placed the 2nd North Carolina on his left, connecting with the 6th Alabama, and extended his line along the southeastern extension of the lane, with (positioned from left to right) the 14th, 4th, and 30th North Carolina. Anderson's line, Carman related, which "was not a continuous one, was mostly under good cover. There were places where the road was crossed by rock ledges, and at these points there was great exposure and they were not occupied." Anderson did not have enough men to fill the lane all the way to where it turned south, so a dangerous stretch of about 150 yards was left undefended. In the military parlance of the day, Anderson's right flank was "in the air," with no natural or artificial feature to protect it.[4]

These two brigades were solid units, led by the division's two best brigadier generals. D. H. Hill described 33-year-old Robert E. Rodes of Lynchburg, Virginia, as a "capital brigadier." What rendered this praise noteworthy was that the famously sarcastic Hill was sparing with compliments, and he and Rodes were not close. Their personalities were "as diametrically opposed to each other as the opposite points of the needle." Rodes was an 1848 graduate of the Virginia Military Institute. Three years later, he took a position there as an assistant professor, teaching physical science, chemistry, and tactics, but he quit when a highly coveted full professorship was awarded to Thomas J. Jackson. Leaving academia behind, Rodes became chief engineer of the Alabama and Chattanooga Railroad in Tuscaloosa, Alabama. But the military institute sought the return of the handsome Virginian and lured him back with the offer of a full professorship, teaching applied mechanics. The Civil War intervened, however, before Rodes could accept the position. He offered Alabama his services and was commissioned colonel of the 5th Alabama. By October 1861, he was a brigadier general. Rodes trained his regiment, and then his brigade, relentlessly. No detail seemed to escape his attention. "Col Rodes inspects in person and is very particular about everything, never passes over anything and is always sure to reprimand a fellow, whenever there is anything amiss," wrote one of his men. His training regimen proved to be such a shock to his green soldiers that even "the officers now complain as much of Rodes as the privates." The regimental surgeon counseled Rodes to back off, lest he start killing men with his relentless schedule. Rodes agreed to ease up slightly, but he understood what his men were in for when the shooting started and knew that the harder he pushed his men in training, the greater the likelihood they would survive in combat. Any questions his soldiers might have had about Rodes's personal courage were settled when his brigade first went into combat at the Battle of Seven Pines. A member of his old regiment, after observing him under fire, concluded that "he has no fear."[5] Hill considered Rodes's brigade "one of the best regulated and disciplined brigades in this army," but the 12th and 26th Alabama had just lost all their field officers at South Mountain, and the brigade had not fully recovered its morale and efficiency from that battle.[6]

George B. Anderson was a 31-year-old native of Hillsboro, North Carolina. He graduated from West Point in 1852, when Robert E. Lee was serving as commandant of the academy, and was commissioned into the 2nd Dragoons. Edward P. Alexander, Lee's ordnance chief, also knew Anderson in both the old Regular Army and the Army of Northern Virginia. Alexander described him as "a six footer of fine figure with specially good legs which gave him a graceful seat on horseback, & his face was as attractive as his figure, with brown hair, blue gray eyes & general good nature in every feature." Anderson served less than 10 years in the uniform of the United States. When North Carolina seceded in

May 1861, he accepted a commission as colonel of the 4th North Carolina. Like Rodes, Anderson was exacting and demanding, but he applied his Regular Army training schedule with a lighter touch, for one of his officers described how "his men loved him from the start." He assumed temporary brigade command at Seven Pines and was in the thick of the fighting. His 4th North Carolina suffered one of the highest losses of any Confederate regiment in the Peninsula Campaign, with 462 killed or wounded out of 520, including 24 of its 27 officers. He performed so well during this campaign that D. H. Hill recommended his promotion to brigadier general, which Anderson received three days later. Although Anderson entered the Maryland Campaign with a solid record, he performed poorly at South Mountain. In the morning's action, he failed to provide adequate support to Garland's brigade, which enabled Cox's division to mass its strength and crush them. Then, during the late afternoon, Anderson ordered a reckless assault on what he may have thought was an unsupported Union battery. The battery was well defended, however, and Anderson's attack was easily repulsed, with losses to the brigade that might have been avoided by a simple pre-attack reconnaissance. Despite this blemish, Anderson was still an officer Hill could count on to get the very best from his men.[7]

A postwar writer fond of hyperbole claimed that for G. B. Anderson's Tarheels, "the crash of Napoleons, the roar of howitzers and crash of musketry always excited and exhilarated them, and as they swung into action they seemed supremely happy." If this was true, then Anderson's brigade was the most unique in any army during the Civil War. No sane soldier was exhilarated by the din of Napoleons or musketry, particularly when they were pointed at him. Even the best units faced these weapons and their missiles with dread. What set the better units, like Anderson's North Carolinians, apart was their training, discipline, leadership, and experience, which enabled the men to do their duty despite the fearful situation they faced. Anderson was also fortunate in that all four of his regiments had their colonels in command, and each of them was competent and battle tested.[8]

Colonel Risden T. Bennett, heading the 14th North Carolina, claimed long after the war that G. B. Anderson's brigade "did not occupy the road from choice but to meet the sudden and rapid deployment of the Govt forces." Bennett's memory on this point clearly failed him. D. H. Hill personally selected the position as a place to defend, a point Bennett admitted in another letter. The report of Major William W. Sillers, commanding the 30th North Carolina, made it clear that there was ample time to have selected a different locale, since the enemy would not appear in their front for another 30 to 45 minutes.[9]

As an experienced soldier, G. B. Anderson probably quickly recognized the advantages and disadvantages of his and Rodes's position. They had good cover from Union artillery, and enemy infantry approaching from the north would not see them until they were only some 50–60 yards away, which would enable the

Confederates to maul them with close-range volleys. But Anderson knew that his location could be easily outflanked on the right, and when the Federals reached the higher ground in front, they would have cover on the reverse slope to reload and reorganize. Even more dangerously, the Yankees could enfilade parts of the Sunken Lane or bring a crossfire on it. The right wing of the 6th Alabama and the left wing of the 2nd North Carolina, which met at the angle where the lane turned from east to southeast, were on terrain that sloped downhill to the east. The two wings were dreadfully exposed to a hill only 80 yards to the north, and they could be enfiladed from a hill 150 yards to the northeast of the 2nd's position. The undulating ridge north of the lane was cut by a ravine, through which the Roulette farm lane passed. The hills rising on either side of the lane dominated the position of the 14th North Carolina, who held the lowest ground in the lane, which would enable an enemy to deliver a crossfire on the regiment. Once they were under fire, the Sunken Lane would be difficult to reinforce, resupply with ammunition, or to allow evacuation of the wounded. Samuel Piper's large cornfield bordered the lane's southern edge, extending along the entire length of Anderson's line to about the center of Rodes's brigade. While this provided concealment to approaching troops who were crossing through the field, it was dominated by the ridge to the north, and anyone moving through the corn would face a gauntlet of fire before getting to the road. In short, once the enemy reached the higher ground north of the lane, the defenders would be pinned in their position, unable to maneuver and difficult to reinforce. It was not a desirable situation.

To make matters worse, Rodes's and G. B. Anderson's men would initially have to face whatever the Federals might send against them without the benefit of close artillery support. Captain Thomas Carter's King William (Virginia) battery (two 12 lb. howitzers, two 6 lb. guns, and one 10 lb. Parrott) had been in position north of the lane, beyond Rodes's left flank, in that brigade's early morning position, but when the Alabamians were ordered to the left, Carter lost his infantry support. So he limbered and withdrew, intending to relocate on Reel Ridge, the undulating ground that rose south of the West Woods and roughly paralleled the Hagerstown Pike. The captain thought his guns "could command any position taken by the division" from this ridge. Besides Carter's battery, at one point Hardaway's Alabama battery (1 Whitworth and 2 3-inch rifles), commanded by Lieutenant John W. Tullis, Captain George M. Patterson's Georgia battery (three guns), and Captain Robert Boyce's Macbeth (South Carolina) battery (6 guns of unknown type) were all deployed in front of Rodes's position in the Sunken Lane. In Tullis's case, this was not by choice. "I had rifled guns and therefore I always took position on a ridge," the lieutenant recalled, but "an infantry general," most likely D. H. Hill, forced him to bring his artillery "below the brow of the hill," to support the retreat of Colquitt's and McRae's brigades. Tullis's field of fire in front was obstructed by the hill that Tompkins's battery soon occupied, and on the right by Mumma's large cornfield. Elements in the 102nd New York of Greene's division used Mumma's corn to conceal their movements and worked their way close enough to have nearly captured Tullis's guns. The Alabamians managed to escape, as did Patterson's Georgians, who withdrew at the same time. Boyce's guns remained in place long enough to get smashed by Tompkins's battery, with four of his six pieces dismounted before Boyce beat a retreat to reach cover in Piper's cornfield.[10]

When Captain Carter and his battery reached the Hagerstown Pike, he found that the stone walls along it blocked his access to Reel Ridge, so he continued on toward Sharpsburg, looking for a gap. Nearing the village, Carter encountered his cousin, the Army of Northern Virginia's commander, Robert E. Lee, making his way north with a single orderly. Worry was etched on Lee's face. "He seemed to fear that the whole left wing, then hard pressed and losing ground, would be turned," and the Federals would gain possession of Reel Ridge, thus rendering his army's position untenable. In a letter home, Carter declared, "I never saw Genl. Lee so anxious." Lee confirmed Carter's decision to occupy Reel Ridge and ordered him to set up a position "with all the artillery that could be collected."[11]

Lee rode north from his meeting with Carter and came to the Sunken Lane soon after Rodes's arrived there. At that point, D. H. Hill was unsuccessfully trying to rally Colquitt's and McRae's brigades. Lee must have passed a considerable number of men from these two brigades, retreating in confusion along the Hagerstown Pike toward Sharpsburg. This, and the disorder he encountered at the lane, would have heightened his concern. But Lee was renowned for mastering his emotions, and he displayed a face of confidence and composure to the shaken troops. His poise, remembered a 6th Georgia soldier, steadied men who were "in a most deplorable state of affairs." Lee, accompanied by Hill, rode along Rodes's line as far as the 6th Alabama. Hill addressed the men in the regiment, telling them, "Soldiers, you fought well on Sunday, but today you must fight harder." Colonel John B. Gordon, the 6th's commander, implied that Lee encouraged them "to be prepared for a determined assault and urged to hold that centre at any sacrifice, as a break at that point would endanger his entire army." Probably it was Hill who said this, but Gordon, although an outstanding soldier, could never resist embellishing a story, and he knew it would sound better if Lee, rather than Hill, was the speaker. Whatever the case, Lieutenant John D. Perry, commanding Company G, responded to Hill's comments: "General, Company G will do their duty and I am determined to *die* with them." In the coming struggle, Perry would prove that he meant what he said, as he was killed in action at Sharpsburg. Not to be outdone in matters of oratory, Gordon called out dramatically to Hill and Lee as they rode away: "These men are going to stay here, General, till the sun goes down or victory is won."[12]

The 2nd and 14th North Carolina each deployed one company as skirmishers. The 4th and 30th North Carolina probably did likewise. A 25-year-old teacher from Warren County, North Carolina, 1st Sergeant Newsome Edward Jenkins, commanded the 14th North Carolina's skirmishers. He recalled that Colonel Bennett told him to "go out and meet the enemy," and to fall back to the main line whenever he was forced to do so. The 2nd's skirmishers only advanced to the hill 50 yards in front of their line. Sergeant Jenkins and the skirmishers from the other regiments went forward over 300 yards, to Roulette's farm buildings and orchard and Clipp's small tenant house, which sat along the Roulette farm lane about 150 yards south of Roulette's barn. The area between this cover and the Sunken Lane was open ground. The trick for survival was determining the right moment to fall back. If they waited too long, they could be cut down crossing the long, exposed expanse back to the lane.[13]

At about 9:15 a.m., some of the officers of Anderson's and Rodes's brigades walked forward to the hill in front of the 2nd North Carolina to observe any enemy activity. The group included G. B. Anderson; Colonel Charles C. Tew, the 2nd North Carolina's commander; and Captain John C. Gorman, one of Tew's company commanders. From the hill's summit they could see over 1,000 yards to the East Woods. They spotted a large Union force deploying in the woods and extending into the open ground to the east. Rodes also saw the Federals from his front and reported that they "deployed in three beautiful lines, all vastly outstretching ours, and commenced to advance steadily" south toward the Sunken Lane. Captain Gorman noted that the Yankees' oncoming lines extended "to the right and left as far as we can see, each column about 100 yards apart." He felt "my heart sunk within me, as I heard Gen. Anderson say to one of his aides-de-camp to hurry to the rear and tell Gen. Hill for God's sake to send us reinforcements, as it was hopeless to contend against the approaching columns." The soldiers in blue marching resolutely toward Anderson and Rodes belonged to Brigadier General William H. French's 3rd Division of the 2nd Corps. The Sunken Lane line was about to be tested.[14]

Behind his back, the men of Brigadier General William H. French's command called him "Old Blinkey" because of his habit of blinking constantly when excited. Observers also commented about the 47-year-old's perpetually red face. This was probably the result of a skin condition, but one staff officer thought "he looks precisely like one of those plethoric French colonels, who are so stout, and who look so red in the face, that one would suppose some one had tied a cord tightly round their necks." But this same officer also thought French looked well on horseback, and "his whole aspect was martial, not to say fierce." French graduated in 1837 in the upper half of a West Point class of 50 and was in the Regular Army's artillery branch. In the Mexican War he won brevets for battles at Cerro Gordo and Churubusco. In 1851 he feuded with none other than Thomas J. Jackson,

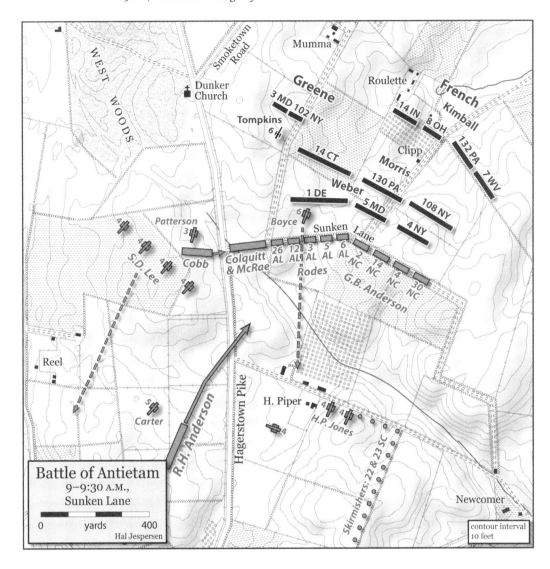

Battle of Antietam
9–9:30 A.M.,
Sunken Lane

0   yards   400

Hal Jespersen

contour interval
10 feet

who was then a lieutenant under French's command at an army post in Florida, during operations against the Seminoles. Jackson, with some reason, felt micromanaged by French, and French thought Jackson did not show him the deference due to a commanding officer. The feud escalated until French had Jackson arrested and the latter demanded a court of inquiry. Neither officer handled the dispute well—both were rigid adherents to army regulations—but French's superior came down hard on him, sending another officer to assume command and noting that French "had preferred charges successively against all the officers serving under his orders, and has shown himself incapable of conducting the service harmoniously at a detached post."[15]

Nine years later, French redeemed his tarnished reputation. He was stationed with three companies of the 1st Artillery at Fort Duncan, Texas, on the Rio

Grande. When Texas seceded in February 1861, Confederate authorities demanded that the garrison be surrendered. French ignored the ultimatum and instead slipped away with his companies, marching them down the river and picking up two more companies at another fort along the way before escaping to Key West, Florida. French might have been difficult to work for, but his escape from Texas exhibited daring, bravery, and skill. With his reputation recovered and war begun upon the land, he was promoted to brigadier general of volunteers and assigned to command a brigade in Edwin Sumner's division of the Army of the Potomac's 2nd Corps. French led his brigade through the Peninsula Campaign and performed so ably that General Israel Richardson, who became the 1st Division's commander when Sumner was promoted to head the 2nd Corps and had high standards for performance, recommended that French be promoted to command of a division.[16]

This opportunity came to pass during the Maryland Campaign, when reinforcements to the Union army enabled McClellan to form a 3rd Division in the 2nd Corps. He assigned French as its commander. This division was only 7 days old when it marched across Antietam Creek to join the current battle. Sumner assembled it from Brigadier General Nathan Kimball's independent brigade and a brigade of brand-new regiments commanded by its senior colonel, Dwight Morris, in the 14th Connecticut. A third brigade was added on September 16, when Brigadier General Max Weber's command, consisting of three regiments coming from garrison duty on the Virginia Peninsula, arrived as reinforcements.

The 3rd Division was a mixed bag, and no doubt French had concerns about how it might perform in combat. His 1st Brigade, commanded by Kimball, was in solid hands and was his best unit. The Indiana-born Kimball was 39 years old and had lived a relatively hard life. He was orphaned at age 6 and raised by his grandfather. He taught public school for a short time, farmed, studied law, and finally went into medicine. On the eve of the Civil War he was a physician, married, with four children. During the Mexican War, Kimball served as a company commander in the 2nd Indiana volunteers. He performed well, even when his regiment did not. He seemed an unlikely warrior but possessed solid leadership skills and was a staunch Republican, which could help a career in the volunteer service. Kimball served under McClellan in the western Virginia Campaign and fought ably in the victory at Cheat Mountain. When the 14th Indiana organized in the spring of 1862, Kimball was appointed its colonel. On March 22, 1862, when his division commander was wounded in the Battle of Kernstown, Kimball assumed command and proceeded to administer the only clear-cut defeat Stonewall Jackson suffered in his Shenandoah Valley Campaign. This success won Kimball promotion to brigadier general on April 16, 1862. He brought three excellent veteran regiments onto the field at Antietam—the 14th Indiana, the 8th Ohio, and the 7th [West] Virginia—and one regiment of rookies, the

132nd Pennsylvania, for a total of 1,751 officers and men. The veterans brimmed with confidence in Kimball. "We were so fortunate in the first year of our service as to [be] victorious in every encounter with the enemy," noted Thomas Loundsdale in the 14th Indiana. "We have a good opinion of Kimball as a General," wrote Charles Merrick in the 8th Ohio, for their leader asked "no one to go where he did not."[17]

Colonel Dwight Morris, the 45-year-old commander of the 2nd Brigade, had been an attorney in Bridgeport, Connecticut, 4 months earlier. Morris was well known in the state, having served in the state legislature and as judge of probate for the District of Bridgeport. Tragedy struck in 1858 when his wife of 16 years died. Her death deeply shook Morris, and he left for Europe, ultimately traveling across Asia, Russia, Turkey, Greece, and what today is Syria and Israel before returning to the United States in 1860. He lived with his father-in-law and reported the value of his personal estate as only $5,000, a modest sum for someone of Morris's profession and standing. After returning home, he left again for Africa and traveled up the Nile. Those who knew him recalled that his "personal appearance was striking, his figure erect and he carried himself with a military bearing." Morris had political connections, which helped him secure a commission as colonel in the 14th Connecticut in the spring of 1862, despite a lack of any direct military experience. But Morris applied himself. His sergeant major, Henry P. Goddard, noted in a letter home that the colonel "was never in the army, but has studied military science at home and abroad." Command of the 2nd Brigade went to Morris, due to seniority. Marion V. Armstrong, in his history of the 2nd Corps in the Antietam Campaign, suspects that Sumner permitted the inexperienced Morris to command the brigade "because he felt there was already enough turmoil within the corps command structure at the brigade level." This was true, but Sumner had several fine and experienced West Point–trained colonels who could have been assigned to the brigade, such as Colonel Norman Hall, commanding the 7th Michigan, and Alfred Sully in the 1st Minnesota.[18]

The 2nd Brigade was one of the largest in the army. Its three regiments—Morris's 14th Connecticut, the 108th New York, and the 130th Pennsylvania—totaled 2,240 officers and men, which outnumbered Rodes's and G. B. Anderson's brigades combined. The regiments were painfully green, however, having been mustered into the service only a few weeks earlier, on August 23, August 18, and August 17, 1862, respectively. There was minimal opportunity for training in the few days before the regiments were brigaded and joined the Army of the Potomac. For example, the 108th New York managed only about 3 days of drilling. For French, Morris and the 2nd Brigade were a large question mark.[19]

Brigadier General Max Weber commanded the newly arrived 3rd Brigade. He was 38 years old and had been born in the German state of Baden. He attended military school in Karlsruhe and served in the Grand Duke's army as a lieutenant.

Politically, Weber sided with those advocating liberal reforms to the repressive governments many Europeans lived under. When revolution erupted in 1848, Weber joined the ranks of the rebels, who were led by Franz Sigel. The movement ended in defeat, and Sigel, Weber, and others escaped, making their way to the United States. Weber settled in New York City and operated the Konstanz Hotel. When war came to his new homeland, Weber used his connections in the German community to raise the 20th New York Infantry, known as the "United Turner Rifles," a reference to the Turner societies, which were liberal political and athletic organizations, popular in many German communities. They traced their origin to the occupation of Germany by Napoleon in the early nineteenth century. Weber was promoted to brigadier general on April 28, 1862. After a brief command of Fortress Monroe, he led a brigade during the capture of Norfolk, Virginia, in May. From there, the brigade occupied Suffolk, Virginia, where his command remained for the rest of the summer until summoned to reinforce the Army of the Potomac in early September.[20]

Weber took two regiments from his brigade, the 1st Delaware and the 4th New York, and a third, the 5th Maryland, from a different brigade. Although they had seen no serious combat, all three regiments were well trained. William P. Seville, the 1st Delaware's adjutant, recalled that through the winter of 1861, his regiment "was able to profit by the constant exercise of every kind of field duty, guard, picket and camp, and daily drill by company, battalion, brigade and skirmishing." This period of training, along with "strict discipline, combined with judicious instruction," helped "make our regiment into one of the best volunteer organizations in the service." No doubt other regiments would quibble with that opinion, but the important point was that the 1st Delaware thought of themselves as one of the best. They and the New Yorkers and Marylanders were ready to leave Suffolk for a more active theater of operations. The weather was hot, and their monotonous duty had been almost "intolerable" to the men. They "sighed for a little excitement of some kind for a variety." The orders to join the Army of the Potomac were met with delight. "Never did soldiers pack their knapsacks for a march to meet the enemy with lighter hearts or more genuine enthusiasm," Seville remembered.

Because they were employed primarily as garrison troops, Weber's three regiments had maintained their strength and mustered a total of 1,740 officers and men. French could be confident that Weber understood his duty as a brigadier and that his regiments were proficient in tactics, but as Michael D. Doubler noted in his study of American soldiers in the European theater in World War II, "no matter how thorough or rigorous, training could not simulate battlefield conditions realistically. Soldiers under fire for the first time were stuck with the sense of fear, confusion, and helplessness that shelling and direct, heavy fire induced. Commanders and leaders had to learn how to maintain command, control, and communications, while keeping their soldiers moving despite the paralyses of fear and confusion and a hail of shot and shell." It remained to be seen how Weber and his regiments would do in their first taste of actual combat.[21]

French's division woke at 3:00 a.m. to begin its preparations for battle. Lieutenant Fred Hitchcock, the adjutant in the 132nd Pennsylvania, remembered that there was no reveille to wake the men, just "a simple call of a sergeant or corporal," and "every man was instantly awake and alert." Typically there were jokes and horseplay among the young, inexperienced soldiers, but none occurred that morning. "All realized there was ugly business ahead and plenty of it just ahead. This was plainly visible in the faces as well as in the nervous, subdued demeanor of all," observed Hitchcock. In the 130th Pennsylvania, Private Edward W. Spangler, a 16-year-old who stood all of 5 feet 2 inches tall and weighed less than 100 pounds, took out his pocket bible and read a chapter. When he finished, he handed it back to a fellow 16-year-old, Christian Good, "and suggested he read it for it might be their last chance." Spangler woke that morning in pain. He had a carbuncle on his right knee, and the joint was swollen, painful, "and stiff as a ramrod." He went to his captain, Levi Maish, a 24-year-old teacher who would eventually become colonel of the regiment, and showed him his inflamed knee. Maish advised him to stay behind, but then Spangler overheard some of his comrades muttering "invidious remarks," implying that he was showing the white feather. "This put me on my mettle" wrote the private, and he determined to go into battle, despite the pain.[22]

By about 7:40 a.m., Sedgwick had cleared the way and French's brigades started down toward Antietam Creek. The division moved in three brigade columns: Weber's 3rd Brigade on the left, Morris's 2nd Brigade in the center, and Kimball's 1st Brigade on the right. The sequence was deliberate. French's orders from Sumner, according to Ezra Carman, were to "put and keep the head of his column abreast Sedgwick's Division." This meant that when they went into action, French, who would be on Sedgwick's left, would face left and move up on line with the 2nd Division. Since both divisions would go into action in Sumner's favorite tactical formation of column of brigades, Weber's garrison troops would lead the advance. The untested group in the division, Morris's brigade, would be in support, sandwiched between more experienced soldiers, and French's best brigade—Kimball's—would bring up the rear. Azor Howitt Nickerson, a 2nd lieutenant in the 8th Ohio, heard French tell Kimball that the general placed him in the reserve position because he was "afraid that some of the new troops would not stand under the heavy fire which he knew they must encounter." Marion Armstrong points out that French's order of brigades was in keeping with the doctrine that Dennis Hart Mahan had taught at West Point, which called for the best troops to compose the reserve. "The object of the reserve is to supply the want of strength in our line of battle, and this it does by coming to the aid of the troops first brought into action, when they are weakened, exhausted, and in a partial state of disorganization from the murderous struggle," Mahan advised.[23]

The 3rd Division's crossing of Antietam Creek proceeded slowly. The banks of the creek were steep, made even more slippery by the earlier passage of Sedgwick's 2nd Division. "The fording was not an agreeable recreation," observed the 14th Connecticut's chaplain. Many of the men in this regiment, and no doubt in others, paused to fill their canteens. Some enlisted men in the new regiments stopped when they reached the creek, in order to remove their shoes and socks. In most cases they were hustled along, except those in the 108th New York. Officers hurling "red hot anathemas" at them failed to prevent a halt while the men removed their shoes and socks and rolled up their pant legs. It took time for 700 to 800 men to do this. Sergeant Ben Hirst in the 14th Connecticut noticed that during the delay at the creek, two or three men from his company "left us not to be seen again that day." Another delay occurred when an inspection of arms and ammunition—probably conducted before the division began to march—discovered that the 5th Maryland somehow had no more than 10 rounds of ammunition per man for their .54 caliber Austrian rifles. George R. Graham, then a private in the regiment, remembered that "when the shortage of ammunition of our regiment was made known, a hurried requisition was made on the corps ordnance officer, but he had none of the required size. Here was a pretty mess. General French grew impatient; Max Weber swore; Staff officers galloped about asking questions; reasons, etc., etc." None of the correct caliber ammunition could be found. Finally, in exasperation—and probably fury at the failure of Weber and Major Leopold Blumenburg, the 5th's commander, to see to such a fundamental detail before a general action—French ordered the Marylanders out of the brigade column. But just at this moment a messenger, having been sent by the 5th's adjutant to locate their ordnance wagon, rode up with thousands of cartridges strapped to his horse's backside. The cartridges were quickly distributed, 80 rounds to a man, but with over 500 riflemen in the regiment, this, too, consumed precious minutes. Because of such stops and starts, French's 3rd Division fell nearly 15 minutes behind Sedgwick, which allowed the 2nd Division to move out of sight.[24]

Once across Antietam Creek, with shoes and socks back on and ammunition sorted out, French's brigades moved along "at a rapid pace" toward the front. They encountered a discomfiting scene. "It was now quite evident that a great battle was in progress," wrote Adjutant Hitchcock in the 132nd Pennsylvania. "A deafening pandemonium of cannonading, with shrieking and bursting shells, filled the air beyond us, toward which we were marching." As they got closer to the fighting, the rookies heard the sound of musketry for the first time. "It had none of the deafening bluster of the cannonading so terrifying to new troops, but to those who had experienced its effect, it was infinitely more to be dreaded," Hitchcock noted. The volleys of small-arms fire sounded, at a distance, like "the rapid pouring of shot on a tinpan, or the tearing of heavy canvas." Hitchcock spoke for many of the men marching in the division's ranks when he admitted, "I realized the situation most keenly and felt very uncomfortable." Looking about, he saw that "the nervous strain was plainly visible upon all of us. All moved doggedly forward in obedience to orders, in absolute silence so far as talk was concerned. The compressed lip and set teeth showed that nerve and resolution had been summoned to the discharge of duty." The nervous strain, wrote the adjutant, "was simply awful."[25]

For most of the march to the front, Hitchcock rode beside his colonel, 41-year-old Richard A. Oakford, a justice of the peace from Scranton. Oakford had been colonel of the 15th Pennsylvania Infantry, with a three-month enlistment period, earlier in the war, before being offered command of the 132nd Pennsylvania. Hitchcock described him as "a thorough disciplinarian, an able tactician, and the interests and welfare of his men were constantly upon his heart." His soldiers felt their colonel's personal interest in them, and they reciprocated. He was "beloved by all his men," recalled one of his privates. In the days leading up to the battle, Oakford had taken time to reassure nervous family members that all was well. "We are all in good spirits," he wrote to his wife Frances on September 6. Six days later, he comforted another family member by writing that "you need not give yourself any uneasiness, as there is no prospect of fighting," even though Oakford knew otherwise. He reassured his 91-year-old mother the same day: "I doubt very much our finding many of the enemy as they retire before us just fast enough to get out of the way." Now, as the 132nd marched toward the terrifying din of battle, Oakford entered into a serious discussion with Hitchcock about the chances of surviving the action unscathed.[26]

Hitchcock's and Oakford's contemplative conversation was overheard by Sergeant Thomas F. (Francis) D. Galwey, an Irishman in the 8th Ohio, who was marching at the end of his regimental column and had Oakford's horse "close upon my heels." Tramping beside Galwey was Jack Shepherd, whom the sergeant described as both "a man of wild and lawless antecedents" and a "brave, generous, and conscientious fellow." Shepherd was Jewish, and his real name was Victor Aarons. He had been a sailor before the war. His disposition earned him the nickname of "Happy Jack" from his comrades, but he was a veteran and had little empathy for the fears of rookies, possibly because they stirred emotions he himself struggled to suppress. Shepherd found Hitchcock's and Oakford's discussion amusing and made fun of it to Galwey. When he heard Oakford reply piously to a comment from Hitchcock "that one must do his duty under circumstances and then leave the rest to the Providence of God, and so forth," Shepherd sneered and "ended his mockery by swearing, in the profane style that was his habit, that the bullet was not yet molded that would do him harm." He would find out soon enough whether this was true.[27]

French's 3rd Division reached the East Woods around 9:15 a.m., 15 minutes after Sedgwick's 2nd Division, and just about the same time as Colonel Tew, General G. B. Anderson, and other Confederate officers arrived on the high ground in front of their soldiers' positions in the Sunken Lane. Sergeant Galwey found the East Woods "full of stragglers," along with "some dead and many wounded" who were "passing our right towards the rear." The chaplain of the 14th Connecticut noted that there were also "huge shells crashing through the tree-tops and branches and dropping and bursting about." The frightened rookies began to waver. Sergeant Ben Hirst remembered General French riding into their midst, shouting "Forward there; forward, for Gods Sake. Forward. I'll ride over you, etc." It seemed cruel, but it steadied the men. Officers and sergeants shouted orders along the brigade columns. The men were to drop their knapsacks and "other extras," perform a final check of arms and ammunition, and fix bayonets. "We began to think something was to do," quipped Lieutenant William F. Smith in the 1st Delaware. The brigades faced left, closed up, and formed a line of battle. Just 10 minutes or so was all the time needed to complete these final preparations for combat.[28]

Other than his standing orders from Sumner to "put and keep the head of his column abreast Sedgwick's Division," French received no other instructions. Sumner was nowhere to be found, and no one from his staff had been left behind to steer the 3rd Division. Looking south in the direction his division now faced, French saw Tompkins's battery about 750 yards away, on the eastern slope of the Dunker Church plateau. Greene's division was lying down in the rear of the battery, with its left flank resting on the Mumma farm lane and its men facing both south and west. Although most of Sedgwick's 2nd Division was out of sight west of the Hagerstown Pike, French heard the the sounds of guns from their engagement in the West Woods. "The firing on our right and front was terrific," recalled Captain Daniel Woodall in the 1st Delaware. Thus French knew the direction in which Sedgwick had moved. In the area beyond Tompkins's battery and Greene's division, French observed Confederates—Rodes's brigade—in the Sunken Lane. There is no evidence that French conducted any reconnaissance to understand the terrain, nor that he attempted to communicate with Sumner or coordinate with Greene. He had his orders, and since Sumner had not modified them, they still stood. Since troops from the 12th Corps occupied the ground on Sedgwick's immediate left, French decided that for him to obey orders and keep his division "abreast Sedgwick's," he would advance on the left of Greene's division, thereby coming up to the same line he believed Sedgwick to be on, and engage the Confederates he had observed. It was not an unreasonable conclusion.[29]

French's decision to advance on Greene's left may have been sensible, but there was no tactical creativity in his plan of attack. He deployed no skirmishers, even though he did not know the terrain, the Rebels' strength, or their position with any certainty. A better tactician would have pushed a strong screen of skirmishers out in front, to get a fix on the enemy's location and enable the main force of the division to maneuver into a position from which it could inflict maximum damage. A good example of this was Cox's management of his division against Garland's brigade at Fox's Gap, three days earlier. Instead, French, like numerous Civil War commanders (and others throughout history), employed the tactics of brute force and the sheer weight of numbers to overwhelm whomever was in his path. Occasionally these tactics succeeded, but always at a high cost in men. Weber's brigade led the way, emerging from the West Woods into the plowed fields and meadow to the south. They covered a front extending for nearly 600 yards. Their direction of march was slightly southeasterly, in order to come up on Greene's left and avoid the burning Mumma farm. Weber directed the color bearer in the 5th Maryland, his center regiment, to orient on William Roulette's farm, whose buildings stood 800 yards to the south. The Mumma farm lane served as a guide for his right flank. Morris's brigade emerged 300 yards in the rear of Weber's, and Kimble's brigade was a similar distance behind Morris's. In all, 5,731 officers and men were moving directly toward the Sunken Lane, most of which remained obscured from view by the rolling terrain.[30]

Weber's brigade scaled the fences in their path and passed through both Mumma's orchard and Roulette's cornfield. Captain George Patterson's Georgia battery of Cutts's battalion, now west of the Hagerstown Pike, and another battery on the ridge south of Piper's farmhouse shelled them. The 1st Delaware took the brunt of the fire, but it did little or no damage. Most of the shells and solid shot passed over the regiment's heads. The color bearer in the 5th Maryland—the regiment apparently carried only the national flag—was a massive German, who stood over 6 feet tall and weighed nearly 300 pounds. Unfortunately, none of the existing 5th Maryland accounts identify who he was. He marched with great deliberation, while the color bearers of the 1st Delaware and the 4th New York moved at a brisker pace. Consequently, as the brigade neared Roulette's farm, the line resembled a crescent, with the wings in advance of the center.[31]

The farm buildings Weber's brigade marched toward were owned by 37-year-old William Roulette (also spelled "Rulett"). Farming was hard work, but all indications were that things were good for the Roulettes before war descended on them. When the armies arrived, William sent his family and servants off to safety, but he remained to protect his property. Now, with Rebel skirmishers in his orchard, yard, and farm buildings, and with the Yankees rapidly approaching, he retreated to the cellar of his house for shelter.[32]

Although no one mentioned it, in order for Weber's brigade to orient itself on line with Greene's division as they approached Roulette's farm buildings, they needed to execute a partial right wheel, so the brigade would face south, rather than southeast. As the 5th Maryland neared the farm, Major Leopold Blumen-berg, a former Prussian army officer who emigrated to America to escape anti-Semitism and now commanded the Marylanders, ordered his four left compa-nies to "break to the rear," a maneuver that enabled them to avoid Roulette's outbuildings by moving in the rear of the rest of the regiment. Three of the com-panies "obeyed the command as coolly as if on battalion drill," but the company on the left flank either did not hear the command or ignored it "and marched through the house yard by the flank"—that is, they made their way around the obstacles by breaking ranks. The 5th Maryland swept through Roulette's prop-erty so quickly, they marched right past a group of G. B. Anderson's skirmish-ers, who were hiding in the springhouse.[33]

As the regiment cleared the buildings and re-formed in Roulette's orchard, a half dozen or so Confederate skirmishers in the Roulette farm lane and near Clipp's tenant house fired on them, hitting two or three men in Company E. Im-mediately, parts of the 5th and 4th New York, on the Marylanders' left, returned the fire, "and they hastily fell back with a loss of several of their number." On the right, the 1st Delaware had also felt the bullets from Confederate skirmishers as it approached Mumma's cornfield.[34] 1st Sergeant Newsome Jenkins's skir-mishers from the 14th North Carolina were probably the party that fired on the 5th Maryland from near Clipp's tenant house. The return volley from the Federals killed one of the sergeant's best men and wounded several others. The survivors beat a hasty retreat along the Roulette farm lane and back to their main line.[35]

General G. B. Anderson, Colonel Tew, Colonel Gordon, and the several other officers who stood on the hill above the Sunken Lane watched French's 3rd Di-vision steadily approach. "On moved the columns, until I could distinguish the stars on their flaunting banners, see the mounted officers, and hear their words of command," wrote Captain Gorman. Tom Taylor, a lieutenant in Gordon's 6th Alabama, watched the Yankees marching "slowly but steadily on to us" and "made up my mind to give them the best that I had when they got near enough." The officers on the hill watched their skirmish line fire at the advancing host of men, then sprint back toward the main line. One of the Union officers on horseback saw the knot of Confederates atop the hill, removed his hat, and waved it at them. Tew waved his hat back, a gentlemanly gesture on both sides before the killing began. The Rebel officers then scattered back to their respective com-mands. Colonels Tew and Gordon tarried a bit longer than the others, watch-ing the enemy approach. Then Tew bounded down the hill to his regiment, shouting as he did, "Aim low, men! Aim very low!" As Gordon passed by to join his regiment, he called out, "Stick to us Tarheels! Alabama's on your left!"[36]

COLONEL JOHN B. GORDON'S oft-quoted and well-known account of the Battle of Antietam is exaggerated, self-centered, and filled with fictions—which is odd, because he was an excellent officer with no need for hyperbole—but he did accurately discern French's intentions: "Every act and movement of the Union commander in my front clearly indicated his purpose to discard bullets and depend upon bayonets. He essayed to break through Lee's centre by the crushing weight and momentum of his solid column." French did not plan to "discard bullets." The advancing Union soldiers had loaded rifles, but French had no desire to maneuver. He wanted to smash his way through. This was unimaginative, but perhaps understandable from French's perspective. The staying power of his 2nd Brigade was questionable, and his 3rd Brigade had never been in combat before. Maneuvering against a veteran enemy force with his own inexperienced troops could pay huge dividends, but it could just as likely end disastrously. It was easier to go straight at the Confederates and overwhelm them with firepower and shock.[37]

After clearing Roulette's buildings, Weber halted his brigade briefly to adjust its alignment and then sent it forward at the double-quick. On the left, the 4th New York cleared one of Roulette's fences that ran obliquely across their front and entered a pasture sloping steadily uphill toward the Sunken Lane, which was hidden on the reverse slope. The right flank of the New Yorkers guided on the Roulette farm lane. Blumenberg's Marylanders, whose left was positioned alongside the lane, encountered a plowed field as they emerged from the farmer's orchard. The right of the regiment extended into Mumma's cornfield. James K. P. Racine, a Company I private, was one of those who passed through the corn. He remembered 1st Sergeant William G. Purnell repeating the phrase "Steady, boys!" But, Racine recalled, "I would shake in spite of all his encouragements." On Purnell's right, the 1st Delaware pressed through the corn as well, trading shots with the retiring Confederate skirmishers. George Graham, a private in Company E of the 5th Maryland, glancing to his right, saw the bayonets of the 1st Delaware flashing above the cornstalks as the powerful Union line swept forward.[38]

The 1st Delaware felt the initial fire from the Confederates. The oblique line of the cornfield's southern edge—it ran northwest–southeast—meant that the right of the regiment emerged into the open ground before the left did. As the right wing came out of the corn, they began to scale the cornfield's fence, which was about 200 yards from Rodes's brigade. Rodes was ranging up and down along the Sunken Lane to steady his men and ensure they did not fire too soon. He also posted some men in Piper's cornfield, above the lane, where they could fire over the line occupying the lane. Scaling the cornfield's fence disordered the 1st Delaware's line. As the regiment attempted to re-form, Rodes ordered his brigade to open fire. McRae's and Colquitt's joint force, composed of rallied stragglers, began shooting as well. "The Balls com fust," wrote John Carey, a Delaware private on the receiving end of the volley. Captain Daniel Woodall, commanding Company F, described it as "a terribly effective and incessant fire from a double line of infantry, one of which was posted in a sunken road in front of our left and behind a stone wall in front of our right [where McRae's and Colquitt's men were], the second line was in a more exposed position on the slope of a hill in a corn field, and could fire over their front line." The volley scored many hits. Colonel John M. Andrews shouted for his regiment to lie down and return the fire. "This was our mistake," opined Woodall.[39]

On the 1st Delaware's left, the 5th Maryland charged up the hill west of the Roulette farm lane, which overlooked the Sunken Lane, yelling as they went. At the top of the hill, they were only about 50 yards from the 6th Alabama and the 2nd and 14th North Carolina. "It was an awful situation, *that waiting to fire*," remembered Captain Gorman in the 2nd North Carolina. Then, suddenly, the shouting Yankees were there in front of them. "My rifles flamed and roared in the Federals' faces like a blinding blaze of lightning accompanied by the quick and deadly thunderbolt. The effect was appalling. The entire front line, with few exceptions, went down in the consuming blast," wrote Colonel Gordon, in the adjacent 6th Alabama. One of Gordon's men thought the enemy was only 30 paces from their line when they fired. Whatever the exact range, the volley from the Alabamians and North Carolinians shot down nearly 130 men and caused the surviving Marylanders "to reel, stagger and retreat." "Oh, but the bullets did fly!" recalled a frightened James Racine, on the receiving end of this fire. "I didn't see them, but saw the effects. Men were falling all around us. Our bugler was standing near me, when a cannon-ball struck him in the head and cut it from his shoulders." George Graham remembered how the storm of bullets made even the "bravest shrink for a moment." Major Blumenberg was among the fallen, his thigh broken by a bullet.[40] It was here, at Lee's center, where the next crisis of the battle was.

The experience of Lieutenant Colonel John D. McGregor's 4th New York mirrored that of the 5th Maryland and the 1st Delaware. "We kept on till we got on the brow of a hill," wrote Albert Kennelly, a 21-year-old Company E private. Here they received a devastating volley from the 30th, 4th, and part of the 14th North Carolina. Colonel Francis M. Parker, commanding the 30th North Carolina, had given strict orders to his men "to hold their fire until I should give the command, and then to take deliberate, cool aim; that I would not give the command to fire until I could see the belt of the cartridge boxes of the enemy, and to aim at these. They obeyed my orders, gave a fine volley, which brought down the enemy as grain falls before a reaper." Nearly 150 New Yorkers went down, a quarter of the regiment's strength. Despite the shock and carnage, Private Kennelly claimed that "not a man flinched," which was surely an exaggeration. Most of the regiment flung themselves on the ground and returned the fire. Kennelly noted that the regiment's officers helped to hold the survivors together. "Our officers acted well," he wrote. "Lieut-Colonel McGregor and Major Jamison sustained their reputation for coolness." Strong leadership could avert a panic in such circumstances. The regiment also benefited from the terrain. "The brow of the hill well protected us," wrote Kennelly. The private also accurately perceived that, "on the whole, I think that we, that is, my regiment, had a better position than the enemy in front of us." The Federals were on higher ground, and the men had the shelter of the reverse slope to load their weapons. The 4th New York attempted what Kennelly described as several "mimic charges," all of which were repulsed. Their color bearer was hit in one of them. These may have been efforts to draw the Rebels' fire, or simply futile efforts by Lieutenant Colonel McGregor to break the deadlock. After their failure, the New Yorkers settled in to shoot it out with the North Carolinians.[41]

"The battle now became general all along the line," reported a member of the 4th North Carolina. "The roar of musketry was incessant and the booming of cannon almost without intermission. Occasionally the shouts of men could be heard above the awful din, indicating a charge or some advantage gained by one side or the other." Rising above this deafening racket were "the cries of wounded and dying and the shouts of brave officers, trying to hold and encourage their men." In the 5th Maryland, officers yelled for their men to crawl forward and form a line, based on where their stalwart color bearer was, since he had somehow survived to advance the colors about 30 feet farther than anyone else. The Marylanders slithered forward, all the while maintaining "a steady fire on the enemy in our front at the foot of the hill." When the bulk of the regiment reached the same spot as their color bearer, "a small body of rebels, under cover of the smoke, made a rush for our colors, but our color bearer saw them and ran back with the colors about twenty yards, while the boys in line met the venturesome rebels and sent them back quicker than they came." George Graham boasted that "there was not at any time, any confusion, nor any evidence of shrinking" in the ranks of his regiment. This was, of course, nonsense. The 5th Maryland fought bravely, but no unit could endure the fire they were under without some amount of confusion and shirking.[42]

Early on in this furious engagement, the Confederates received a small but important reinforcement. It will be recalled (see chapter 8) that Cobb's brigade of McLaws's division had wandered off from the direction of the division's advance toward the West Woods, passed over Reel Ridge, and came up to the Hagerstown Pike opposite to the place where it joins the Sunken Lane. The brigade, which numbered perhaps 400 officers and men, was commanded by Lieutenant Colonel Christopher C. Sanders in the 24th Georgia, who, despite being "very unwell," remained in command. Sanders led his small force across the pike and formed them with McRae's and Colquitt's remnants in the Sunken Lane. Rising ground in their front obstructed their field of fire, so they were unable to contribute much to the destruction of the 1st Delaware, but they added needed numbers to Rodes's left flank. Moreover, their infusion of manpower probably helped steady McRae's and Colquitt's men.[43]

The 1st Delaware exchanged fire with Rodes for several minutes, and then Colonel Andrews ordered the regiment to charge. It was a desperate, but poor, decision, reflecting his lack of combat experience. From Captain Woodall's perspective, "it was evident to the minds of all who stood in that shattered line that the time for a successful charge had passed, yet every man who was not disabled pressed forward at the word of command." The result was a slaughter. Rodes's, Colquitt's, and McRae's men spewed volleys into them. A battery, probably Patterson's, blasted them with artillery fire. The entire color guard were shot down, and the staff bearing the state flag was cut in two. Lieutenant Colonel Oliver Hopkinson advanced with the color guard and was wounded while gripping the national colors. Nearby, Color Sergeant John W. Eccles threw his body over the fallen state colors to protect them. Two captains were killed and three wounded—half of the company commanders in the regiment. Woodall was among the wounded officers. He made it to within 20 yards of the Confederate line before a ball struck him between the wrist and elbow and passed up his arm. He coolly handed his sword to his 1st lieutenant, John W. Williams, whose own sword had been shot out of his hand, and went to the rear. Colonel Andrews's horse, "Old Spot" was hit, dismounting its rider. It then wandered over to the right of the regiment and fell over dead. For a few moments the men of the 1st Delaware stood in the open and bravely but vainly attempted to respond to the "terrific" storm of bullets that flayed their line. At this critical juncture, the 14th Connecticut of Dwight Morris's brigade emerged from Mumma's cornfield in the 1st's rear; beheld a smoky, chaotic scene in front of them; and opened fire into both friend and foe.[44]

Morris's 2nd Brigade had maintained its distance of approximately 300 yards from Weber's line throughout its advance, which began in the East Woods. During the march toward Roulette's farm, a member of the 108th New York noted that "our ears were soon greeted with the whizzing of bullets and the bursting of shells." He, like hundreds of others in every regiment of the brigade, wondered, "Will the regiment stand fire—will green men who hardly know how to shoulder a musket, fight—is this the school of instruction to which we were to be sent?" Fortunately, the Confederates' artillery fire was inaccurate and did little damage. "Serious as was the occasion," the major and some of the men in the 14th Connecticut could not resist plucking apples from Mumma's orchard as they went through it. In the interval between the passing of Weber's 3rd Brigade and the approach of Morris's men, the Confederate skirmishers who were bypassed by the 5th Maryland re-emerged to fire on the 14th Connecticut and the 130th Pennsylvania as they neared Roulette's buildings. Some "belligerent" ones took cover in his springhouse. Captain Elijah W. Gibbons, commanding Company B of the 14th, which was on the left of the regiment, neatly maneuvered his men to envelop and capture the Rebels. As the Yankees collected their prisoners, Mr. Roulette emerged from his cellar and "shouted excitedly" at the Connecticut rookies: "Give it to em! Drive em!"[45]

While Roulette cheered on the Connecticut boys, the 130th Pennsylvania swept through his farm, with the 108th New York on their left flank. To negotiate Roulette's farm buildings, Companies A and F of the 130th moved by the flank between the house and the springhouse. The rest of the regiment extended down toward Roulette's barn. As Company A approached the garden, located between the house and barn and enclosed by a stone wall and white picket fence, two men were wounded by more bypassed Rebels, who had infiltrated back into Roulette's orchard. When the bulk of the 130th reached the garden fence, it was found to be too high to climb. "The boys layed hold of the fence and with a mighty pull the entire fence came down," wrote John Hemminger in Company E. Somehow the fence fell on top of 21-year-old Private Theodore Boyles in Hemminger's company. The mass of dozens of men, plus Colonel Henry Zinn and his horse, tromped over the fence, crushing several of Boyles's ribs and "otherwise seriously injuring him." The Pennsylvanians hurried through Roulette's garden and attacked its southern fence with their musket butts, smashing it to pieces. In their excitement, some of Zinn's men knocked over Roulette's beehives. "The little fellows resented the intrusion," noted Hemminger, and they launched a vigorous aerial charge on the 130th, pursuing the soldiers relentlessly through Roulette's orchard before giving up the attack. Little Edward Spangler, hobbled by his swollen knee, caught up with the regiment here and recalled how a bullet whizzed past his head, "which made me dodge" as he crossed the garden. He also watched several members of his company skulk out of the battle line to seek hiding places around Roulette's property, perhaps including some who had earlier questioned the young private's courage.[46]

The rush of the 130th Pennsylvania through Roulette's farmyard overran the handful of Tarheel skirmishers, who had no safe avenue of escape, and these Rebels chose to surrender. After clearing Roulette's buildings, Morris's three regiments followed the same route as Weber's, with the 14th Connecticut entering Mumma's cornfield; the 130th Pennsylvania positioned in Roulette's plowed field, with its left near the farm lane and its right just inside the corn; and the 108th New York located in the meadow east of the lane. The brigade quickly reformed its line and then resumed its advance, but with a quickened pace. Bullets from the fighting in front—overshots—buzzed over the men's heads or struck the ground around them with increasing frequency as the line moved forward. Morris R. Darrohn in the 108th New York remembered that when his regiment passed through Roulette's orchard, "the bullets came through the trees like hailstones." When the 14th Connecticut entered Mumma's cornfield, those who had not divested themselves of overcoats and blankets earlier now cast them aside. With their hearts thumping, the rookies pushed through the tall cornstalks, moving closer to the raging battle they heard, but which the plants concealed from their view. The tension was palpable. "Most of my men did well," wrote Captain Isaac R. Bronson, the Company I commander, "but some had to be driven forward at the point of a bayonet."[47]

As the New Englanders emerged from the corn and reached the worm fence the 1st Delaware had crossed minutes before, "a voley tore through our ranks killing and wounding quite a large number." The regimental historian described the fire that struck the regiment as "a perfect tempest of musketry." 1st Lieutenant Samuel W. Fiske thought the scene that unfolded before them was one "of indescribable confusion." Instinctively, many dropped to the ground and, observed Sergeant Ben Hirst in disgust, began "firing indiscrimately and I am sorry to think wounding some of our own men on the left of our line of battle." The 1st Delaware and part of the 5th Maryland, caught between friendly fire from the rear and hostile volleys in front, "seemed to melt away," running pell-mell through the ranks of the 14th Connecticut and into the corn. Lieutenant Fiske heard several of the fleeing men shouting "Skedaddle, skedaddle" as they ran by. "Some of our men tried to stop them," Fiske noted, "and a few of them, it must be confessed, joined in their flight." Captain Samuel H. Davis, commanding Company H, admitted that "some of my men skedaddled shamefully." Sergeant Hirst, one of those rare soldiers not rattled by the chaos of combat, "roard like a mad Bull for our men to cease firing until they could see the rebs." This was not easy. "No enemy could be seen, only a thin cloud of smoke rose from what was afterwards found to be their rifle-pits," noted the 14th's historian. Captain Davis wrote to his father that "the firing exceeded anything I ever imagined." Colonel Morris, who was present with the 14th, had, with the help of the regiment's officers, urged a charge. Part of the regiment managed to surge forward, and some elements made it for perhaps 50 yards before the hail of Confederate bullets drove the survivors back to the cornfield's fence. Other elements of the regiment joined with the 1st Delaware and loosed volleys in the direction of the Rebel position, but bedlam ruled as the firing line leaked a steady stream of men who sought an escape from danger. "I am not going to charge anyone with cowardice," complained Ben Hirst, "but there were always too many wanting to go to the hospital with any one that was wounded and they never by any means came back again until yesterday." But there were some who endured through the madness, and Hirst was one of them. He carried a badly wounded friend to safety, then ran back to the firing line—a rare act that day. Corporal Sam Watrous in Company H was another who emerged as a natural fighter. He was seen "standing up; with the bullets flying around him, and laughing and blazing away like fury."[48]

Colonel Henry Zinn's 130th Pennsylvania slogged their way through Roulette's plowed field to the rail-and-stone fence dividing it from a clover field. This was a continuation of the cornfield's fence, where elements of the 14th Connecticut and the 1st Delaware were engaged in their deadly firefight with

Rodes's brigade. Zinn halted his regiment behind the fence and ordered the men to lie down. He took the sensible precaution of dismounting and leaving his horse beneath a nearby walnut tree. "The bullets flew thicker than bees, and the shells exploded with a deafening roar," wrote a frightened Edward Spangler. The fire was directed at the 5th Maryland, whose line was only yards away, at the crest of the hill in front. As Spangler admitted, "I was seized with fear far greater than the day before. I hugged the plowed ground so closely that I might have buried my nose in it. I thought of home and friends, and felt that I surely would be killed, and how I didn't want to be!" After a pause, Zinn ordered his men to advance to the top of the hill. Here they received the same reception the Marylanders had, minutes earlier. "On the crest of the hill we had no protection from the murderous fire poured into our advancing ranks from the enemy in the old road, and from their batteries posted on the high ground beyond," reported John Hemminger. Many were hit, and the regiment dropped down in the clover. They then began to return fire "thick and fast" at the Rebels crouching in the lane below them or hiding in the corn. Edward Spangler, who had been paralyzed with fear moments before, felt a sudden surge of courage. "The moment I discharged my rifle, all my previous scare was gone," he wrote. "The excitement of the battle made me fearless and oblivious of danger; the screeching and exploding shells, whistling bullets and the awful carnage all around me were hardly noticed."[49]

On the left of the 130th Pennsylvania, 24-year-old Sergeant George S. Goff bore the national colors of the 108th New York as it marched up a long open slope, toward the ridge where the 4th New York was blazing away at the enemy on the other side. Adjacent to Goff, Sergeant Miles Casey—35 years old, "a man of noble stature," and a veteran of the British Army and the Crimean War—carried the regiment's beautiful, unstained blue state colors. Goff had been selected for this role only the day before. "It is a pretty dangerous position, but an honorable one, and I shall endeavor to do my duty," he wrote to his brother. Goff had "a noble appearance" and was popular both in the regiment and back home. He had no illusions about war. His wife had died before he enlisted, and he visited her grave with some comrades prior to the regiment's departure for the front. Standing there, Goff said sadly, "Farewell! I shall never see your grave again." His melancholy alarmed his friends, who "urged him to dispel such thoughts from his mind, but no, he was as confident of the prediction as he was that he was then alive."[50]

Like others who had never been under fire before, Captain Francis E. Pierce, the commander of the 108th's Company F, admitted that "at first I acknowledge that I felt afraid, going through the orchard and up the hill the bullets were whistling like the devil." The regiment was close enough that these overshots were not harmless, and several men were wounded by them. When they reached the post-and-rail fence below the ridge where the 4th New York was hotly engaged, the men were winded from their long, rapid advance. Colonel Oliver H. Palmer ordered them to lie down and catch their breath. Some members of the 4th New York thought the 108th New York was their relief, and they began to retreat. "We drove them back," wrote Pierce. After their brief rest, Palmer ordered his regiment forward. "The boys went in splendidly," Pierce noted. At the ridge crest, where they mingled with the 4th New York, they received a "withering fire" from the North Carolinians in the Sunken Lane and the cornfield behind it, knocking dozens from the ranks. Major George B. Force, an experienced officer who was largely responsible for the training the regiment received in the brief period between completing its organization and entering combat, was among the first ones killed. "The crest of the hill was quickly covered with our dead and wounded," observed George Washburn, an 18-year-old in Company D.[51]

Like every other regiment that encountered this murderous fire, the men of the 108th New York dropped to the ground and returned fire. Most of the color guard went down in the initial fusillade, but, miraculously, color bearers Casey and Goff were unscathed, as was Corporal James Hinds. Colonel Palmer called for Lieutenant William W. Bloss in Company A to form a detail and defend the colors. The war was quite personal for Bloss. He had been in the seed business in Lawrence, Kansas, in the mid-1850s and also edited the *Leavenworth Times*. He became caught up in the violence between the pro- and anti-slavery forces there, aligning himself with the latter side. At one point he rescued a free Black man who had been kidnapped by pro-slavery forces, for which Bloss paid a steep price. Attackers burst into his office later and shot him several times. He returned to Rochester, New York, where he endured a long, painful recovery. Now he led a squad of volunteers to protect Goff and Casey. Reaching the two sergeants, Bloss raised the national colors with Goff and shouted to his men, "Boys, come on!" The flag instantly drew the attention of the North Carolina riflemen, and to Bloss it "seemed the target of a leaden hailstorm from the rebel rifle-pits." Sergeant Casey and the state colors drew their own blizzard of bullets. Corporal Hinds would later count 48 holes in the flag from bullets and shell fragments.[52]

When Bloss turned to look back at the regiment, the view shocked him. Only minutes before, he had watched it move "into action with the steadiness of dress parade." Now it was "badly shattered. Men in portions of it were prostrate, to escape the incessant and destructive fire from the cornfield and the trenches." Sergeant Goff suddenly went down, and Bloss dropped to the ground beside him. Goff stared at the lieutenant and asked, "What did you strike me for?" Bloss saw blood on Goff's head and replied, "You were struck by a bullet, sergeant, there is a blood spot on your forehead. Are you badly hurt?" Goff answered, "o[h], yes, I can't see with my left eye." His head had been struck by a bullet or buckshot. Bloss suggested that he go to the rear. Goff crept away from the firing line and made his way back to the aid station at Roulette's farm. When one of his friends saw him there, with blood trickling down his face, Goff shook his hand and said, "I told you so. I knew it would be so." Later that day, the sergeant continued the letter he had started earlier to his brother: "I have been through one day's fight and barely escaped with my life. I was shot square in the forehead while bearing the colors toward the enemy. I think I shall get over it if inflammation does not set in." Tragically, the wound may have hemorrhaged internally, and 6 days later Goff died of his wound.[53]

Not long after Goff crawled off for medical attention, Lieutenant Bloss was struck by a ball that hit him near the bridge of the nose, passed down between his lips and teeth, came out at his chin, and traveled down to penetrate his vest and break the crystal of his watch. It also knocked him senseless. "When I came to consciousness I was lying under the shadow of a haystack in rear of our line of battle, amid a crowd of suffering comrades under surgical treatment. Captain Pierce of Company F, as I learned, had taken me from the field and members of Company A carried me to hospital quarters," he wrote. He would recover, but the lieutenant's war was over. William Woodhull, a 19-year-old private who was part of the detail Bloss had led to defend the colors, took hold of the national flag, along with another man. They were ahead of the main line, hugging the ground. To his left, Woodhull saw the colors of the 4th New York, somewhat in advance of his position. The 4th's guard was also flattened on the dirt. Woodhull and his comrade decided they were too far forward and crawled back toward the main line, "keeping as close to the ground as possible." A bullet broke the arm of the soldier with Woodhull, but the private survived unharmed and joined Color Sergeant Casey on the main firing line of the regiment. A moment later, Casey was hit in the leg, a wound that cost him his leg and, eventually, his life. Corporal Hinds took the state colors. Then Colonel Palmer, repeating the mistake of other inexperienced officers that terrible morning, ordered a charge. A hail of bullets stopped the attack in its tracks, but not before piling up more casualties. Among them was Woodhull, who was wounded in the thigh. Someone else raised the colors, while two comrades picked Woodhull up and carried him to the rear.[54]

French had hurled two brigades, consisting of almost 4,000 men, against the Confederate line in the Sunken Lane and been stopped cold. His brigades had not been defeated—elements of both remained in the fight—but their offensive capability was utterly spent and the unit's cohesion was shaken. Hundreds had left the firing line to help the wounded to the rear or to find safety from Rebel bullets and shell fragments. Those who remained continued to steadily fire on the enemy, but the slaughter in both brigades was frightful. In perhaps 20 minutes of fighting, from about 9:45 a.m. to shortly after 10 a.m., both Weber and Morris lost a quarter of their men. The 1st Delaware had 230 casualties, the highest amount in the division. In the 4th New York, 44 men were killed, a testament to the deadly fire G. B. Anderson's men laid down in front of the Sunken Lane. The system that was in place to evacuate the wounded utterly collapsed under the numbers that piled up: 138 in the 130th Pennsylvania, 182 in the 1st

Delaware, 122 in the 108th New York, and so on. In all, 795 officers and men in the two brigades were wounded, the majority in the first 20 minutes of this engagement. Many of these men were helped to the rear by comrades, and sometimes officers, who were either seeking escape from the slaughter or doing so out of genuine compassion for friends who were struck down. The consequence to unit cohesion when officers participated in these humanitarian acts is illustrated by the experience of Captain Samuel H. Davis, commanding Company H of the 14th Connecticut. He wrote how his 1st sergeant was shot right behind him. Davis helped him from the field, and when he returned, he found another sergeant, Tom Mills, who was badly wounded. Davis carried him to the rear, as well. This time, when the captain returned to his company, only 5 or 6 men out of the 70 he had carried into action remained in the fight. Without leadership, the rest had either slipped away to a place of safety or were casualties.[55]

Ambulatory wounded were directed back to Dr. Otho J. Smith's farm—a half mile northeast of Roulette's property, near where French's men had forded Antietam Creek—where the divisional hospital was established. Litter cases were taken to Roulette's barn, which had been turned into an aid station, manned by several of the division's surgeons and attendants. The available space inside the barn filled up quickly, so the medical helpers began placing the wounded elsewhere, first in the yard outside, and, when that filled up, in the house and springhouse. Ambulances brought some of the badly damaged men back to Smith's, but there were not enough vehicles to make a dent in the numbers that needed transportation. The sheer volume of injured Union soldiers who arrived at Roulette's barn in a short period of time overwhelmed the surgeons there. One of them, Arner Mast, the surgeon in the 108th New York, reported that he dressed over 100 men's wounds and performed several operations, "and this without one morsel of food from five o'clock in the morning until the day following."[56]

PRECISELY WHERE CONFEDERATE GENERAL James Longstreet observed the Sunken Lane battle is unknown, but wherever he was, he watched the repulse of Weber's and then Morris's attacks. Noting the confusion in the Yankees' ranks, he sensed an opportunity for a counterattack. Bypassing D. H. Hill, he dispatched orders directly to Robert Rodes to charge what appeared to be a shaken enemy. Rodes was not pleased. Up until this point in the action, except for the 6th Alabama, his regiments had suffered few casualties because of their excellent cover, and Longstreet's orders were more easily conceived of than executed. It was not a matter of Rodes standing up and shouting "Charge." The deafening noise of the battle made it necessary for him to communicate with each regimental commander—a dangerous task, as the length of the lane was under both infantry and artillery fire—as well as with Cobb's brigade and the fragments of McRae's and Colquitt's units. Yet somehow Rodes managed to do this. A signal was given, and the Confederates surged up and out of the

Sunken Lane. The attack foundered immediately. Colquitt's and McRae's men had little stomach for charging over open ground that was swept by bullets and shells, and they proceeded only a short distance from the lane before faltering. Cobb's brigade went on without them. The 6th Alabama, for reasons that were never explained, failed to advance at all. Perhaps Gordon never received Rodes's order, but it is also conceivable that the firing on the exposed right wing of his regiment rendered it impossible for them to move ahead. Rodes ran back to bring the 6th forward. As he did so, the rest of his brigade made their way toward the high ground to their right front. The direction of their advance exposed them to an oblique fire of shell and shrapnel from Tompkins's battery, as well as to small-arms fire in front from elements of the 1st Delaware, the 14th Connecticut, and the 5th Maryland. The Alabamians made it part way up the slope before the attack wavered under heavy fire and then collapsed into a disorderly retreat. "The men that held the center could die, but they could not fly," exulted Colonel Cullen Battle, commander of the 3rd Alabama, with a typical postwar flourish. Yet most of the brigade would have flown past the Sunken Lane, were it not for the intervention of their brigade commander. Rodes personally headed them off, "just in time to prevent the men from falling back to the rear of the road"—in other words, abandoning the Sunken Lane.[57] At the same time, Cobb's brigade reached the ridge in their front "amid a galling and destructive shower of balls" and came fully into view of Tompkins's guns. Here the brigade's colonel, Christopher Sanders, saw not only that Rodes's men were falling back, but also that Colquitt's and McRae's remnants had not kept up on their right. Since his troops were therefore exposed and unsupported, Sanders ordered his small brigade to retreat to the lane. Longstreet's counterattack had failed, costing Rodes casualties he could not afford and nearly resulting in calamity. Had Rodes not rallied his brigade, the Confederates' line in the Sunken Lane might have collapsed. The assault also settled one thing: local counterattacks were not going to budge the enemy.[58]

While Rodes's brigade charged and was repulsed, D. H. Hill was busy hunting up artillery support. He found a section of Captain William K. Bachman's German (South Carolina) Artillery, under the command of 1st Lieutenant James Simons Jr. Bachman's unit was somewhat unique in the Army of Northern Virginia, in that it was recruited from the German community in Charleston, South Carolina, and German was often spoken by its members. Simons was a 23-year-old, cultured, well-educated Charleston attorney. He had studied at the University of Leipzig and was described as "a man of much scholarship." In addition, he was a fine musician. The lieutenant had been with his battery on Cemetery Hill when his section was ordered to the left. He encountered Lee and Longstreet after passing through "a most awful fire to get there." To the young lieutenant, the two generals "appeared entirely unmoved" by the artillery fire. They ordered Simons to continue on and report to D. H. Hill. Simons found Hill near Piper's barn, and the general beckoned for the lieutenant to follow him up through that farmer's apple orchard. As the guns rumbled through the fruit trees, Simons recalled that "in spite of shells, shot and minie balls our boys could not be restrained from bagging the apples" as they passed by. No men were hit, but Simons lost a horse to a stray projectile, which prompted him to leave his guns, limbers, and caissons in the lower ground of the orchard and follow Hill by himself.[59]

Hill led Simons up to a stone wall that separated the orchard from Piper's cornfield. There was a thin line of infantry behind the wall, probably some skirmishers who had rallied in the rear of the Confederates' Sunken Lane line. The terrain here was high enough that Simons could look over the top of Piper's corn and observe the Yankee infantry only 150 to 200 yards away. "We could see them plainly," Simons remembered. "We saw just in front of us two United States flags and one blue one. So near were we, that we could almost count the stars on their flags." The colors belonged to the 108th and 4th New York. Simons noticed a small group of trees that grew on the side of the hill west of the ravine, where the Roulette farm lane ran. He told Hill, "If the enemy had any sense they would fill them with sharpshooters as soon as we came into position." Hill ignored the comment, and the lieutenant had no choice but to obey Hill's orders. He rode back, brought his guns up to the fence, and unlimbered. The crews thumped canister down the gun tubes and let fly, "ploughing up their line all around their flags." The gunners, however, stirred up a hornet's nest. "A hail storm of minie balls soon commenced to rain on us," wrote Simon, "not to speak of shell and solid shot, which tore up the very ground on which we were."[60]

The remnants of Captain Robert Boyce's Macbeth (South Carolina) Light Artillery provided some support for Rodes's brigade. Boyce began the day parked in the rear of Cemetery Hill, south of the Boonsboro Pike. As the fighting on the left intensified, Colonel Walton in the Washington (Louisiana) Artillery ordered Boyce to the left. After having been poorly placed by infantry officers in two different locations around the northern end of Cemetery Ridge, north of the Boonsboro Pike, Boyce then limbered and drove his battery through Piper's cornfield and took up a position just north of the Sunken Lane and east of the Mumma farm lane. There he engaged Greene's 12th Corps' infantry, which had advanced on him after the defeat of D. H. Hill's brigades in the Cornfield and the East Woods. As related earlier in this chapter, when Tompkins's battery arrived on the Dunker Church plateau, things deteriorated swiftly for the South Carolinians. This time the Federals' fire disabled or dismounted four of Boyce's six guns and wounded a number of crewmen, causing the captain to extricate his badly damaged battery to low ground in Piper's cornfield. Here Boyce sorted out the damage, sending his disabled pieces to the rear and moving his serviceable section through Piper's orchard into the adjacent meadow, around 170 yards south of the Sunken Lane. They arrived there about the same time as Rodes's regiments occupied the lane.[61]

Shortly after Simons's artillery were placed by D. H. Hill, a third battery arrived to buttress the Sunken Lane's defenses. This was Captain Merritt B. Miller's 3rd Company of the Washington (Louisiana) Artillery, equipped with four Napoleons. Miller's guns had been on Cemetery Hill south of the Boonsboro Pike when the fighting opened. At 9:15 a.m., Miller received orders to move his battery to the left. In what was typical staff work for the Army of Northern Virginia at Sharpsburg, Miller was not told whom to report to. It was presumed that he would find someone who needed his guns. Miller took his battery through Sharpsburg and out the Hagerstown Pike. Along the way, he "was so fortunate" as to encounter Longstreet, who told him to take his guns into Piper's orchard, where he would have some cover, and to "not to fire a gun unless the enemy was in easy range."[62]

Miller drove his guns down the Piper farm lane, passing some of those who were manning Boyce's disabled guns, which "came flying out" in the opposite direction. The Louisianans soon understood the haste with which Boyce's pieces were moving. It was a perilous journey down the lane. "A terrific fire of musketry"—overshots from French's infantry—struck all about them. Federal artillery fire was also falling into the area. One shell found its mark in one of the captain's caissons, blowing it up. Bullets and shell fragments hit so many horses and men that by the time Miller found some safety in the center of the orchard, he had only enough of both to fully crew two guns. He unlimbered these and began hurling fire at French's infantry.[63]

Courageous as the men serving these Confederate batteries were, none of them lasted long under the terrific volleys they were exposed to. Boyce probably went to the rear first, around 10 a.m., because his position was in easy range for the Federals in Weber's and Morris's brigades, which were on the ridge north of the Sunken Lane. Miller left next. Longstreet had observed the Louisianans in action and concluded that they were suffering more damage than they were inflicting, so he ordered Miller to pull his section back under cover near Piper's farm. Simons's section lasted slightly longer, but it paid a hefty price. The Federals poured "a galling fire" into the South Carolinians, killing or wounding 6 of the section's 12 horses. One of his privates had a bullet pass through the rations in his haversack, his tin plate, and both thighs. Sergeant John C. Hahn and Fritz Kassler, a cannoneer, both born in Germany, were each hit in the abdomen and died that day. Simons had his own close call. "I escaped very narrowly," he wrote later. "A piece of shell struck my sabre, and while I was pointing one of the Napoleons, a minie ball buried itself in the cheek of the gun carriage within a few inches of my head and another in the trail just barely grazing my leg." The fire emanating from the small group of trees Simon had warned Hill about was particularly troublesome. With his section rapidly being depleted of men and horses, Simon received permission from someone—possibly Hill—to withdraw back through the orchard and into cover. Guns and their crews and horses could not survive if they were within range of Union rifles.[64]

Although Rodes sustained some casualties in his counterattack, his and G. B. Anderson's overall loses were relatively light. They had the satisfaction of knowing they had either killed or wounded hundreds of Yankees, but this was tempered by the enemy's tenacity. After the repulse of the Federals' first two assaults, Captain John C. Gorman in the 2nd North Carolina noticed that "they then approach the top of the hill cautiously and lie down." Both sides poured a "continuous shower of leaden hail" into one another. "Our men are protected by about 6 or 8 inches of the wear of the road, but that is great protection," continued Gorman. "They fire cautiously, and are apparently as cool as if shooting at squirrels, taking sure aim every fire." In the 4th, Benjamin B. Ross, a 27-year-old from Beaufort County, North Carolina,, wrote that "each of us was waiting for a head on the other side to be stuck up so that we could shoot at it." But Ross also commented on the disadvantage of their position, which became apparent when the Federals occupied the high ground in their front. "It was dangerous to go down the line to carry orders—we were all 'squatting' in the road." The Sunken Lane provided adequate cover, but, as Gorman observed, its protection "is not sufficient. The air is full of lead, and many are shot as they are aiming at the enemy, and the groans of the wounded are heard amid the roar of the musketry." Gorman also noted that for those who were wounded, "it is certain death to leave the road," as "the balls fly so thick over us." Once French's infantry occupied the higher ground north of the lane, the Confederates were effectively pinned in the road. It had become impossible to resupply them with ammunition, as there was no safe way for it to reach the front. Yet help for the embattled Tarheels and Alabamians was on its way. Lee had ordered Richard H. Anderson's division to reinforce D. H. Hill's line, and Anderson's brigades were jogging across the farm fields north of Sharpsburg to join the fight. But before they could reach the front, French made a final effort to bash his way through the Confederate line with his last fresh brigade.[65]

General French observed at least part of his division's attack from the site where Tompkins's battery was located, which provided him with a panoramic view of his entire front. Around 10:00 a.m., Captain Samuel S. Sumner, General Sumner's son and an aide-de-camp on his staff, galloped up to French with orders for him to make "a vigorous attack" to support Sedgwick's division, which, by the time the command was sent, had already been smashed by McLaws's counterattack. Sumner's orders were conceived with no idea of French's situation or position. The attack order was not part of a well-defined plan or an attempt to coordinate units. It was simply an act of desperation, hurling French forward in the hope that it might relieve the pressure on Sedgwick. French had one uncommitted brigade left, his best—which was Kimball's. Its men had halted and were lying down just south of Roulette's farm, with half of the unit in Roulette's orchard and the other half in the large meadow east of the Roulette farm lane. The failure of his two leading brigades to make a dent in the Confederates' position, and the hundreds of casualties the attack incurred, did not deter French's faith in another frontal assault. He dispatched orders to Kimball to advance and carry the enemy position with bayonets.[66]

When Kimball's regiments passed through Roulette's farm, Thomas Loundsdale, a private in the 14th Indiana, on the right of the brigade, remembered how "the minie balls were by this time singing about our ears quite lively." Despite the long range, these errant rounds could still be deadly, and some men were killed or wounded. William Roulette was still standing outside his farmhouse, cheering on the Union soldiers. "Such antics as he cut I never saw before," wrote Loundsdale. "He waved his old white hat, shouted, jumped up and down [and] wanted to shake hands with all of us; we reminded him that he was in danger of being shot he replied that he had been cooped up two days and was willing to take the chances for the sake of seeing those dirty rebels drove off his farm." Thomas McEbright in the 8th Ohio also saw him and thought the farmer "did some of the tallest human hollowing and tip toe shouting I ever witnessed." The 8th Ohio and the 14th Indiana occupied Roulette's orchard, while the rookie 132nd Pennsylvania and the veteran 7th [West] Virginia extended the line into the meadow east of the farm lane. The 8th Ohio had not dropped their knapsacks in the East Woods, but they did so now in the orchard. Demoralized soldiers in Weber's and Morris's brigades were constantly coming back from the front, "singly, and in squads." The flow increased until the frightened men were retreating "at a 'Bull Run' pace, threatening to overrun everything that stood in their way." The number of stragglers threatened to disrupt Kimball's line, and he decided to put a stop to the problem. He ordered his regiments up with fixed bayonets. "By shouts of 'cowards' and threats to 'charge bayonets' on them if they did not 'halt' they were checked," wrote Lieutenant Azor H. Nickerson in the 8th Ohio. Kimball even managed to wrestle some of the frightened men into a provisional unit and placed them on his left flank.[67]

When Kimball received his attack orders from French, he trotted along the front of his brigade. There were 1,751 officers and men, more than a third of them in the 132nd Pennsylvania, and they covered an expanse of about 600 yards. He paused in his ride to address his men. Not everyone heard the brief speech, but the 8th Ohio did. Sergeant Francis Galwey remembered him shouting, "Now boys, we are going, and we'll stay with them all day if they want us to." Orders to advance rang out along the long line, and the brigade started forward. Kimball ordered the double-quick, and the men went forward with their heads bowed down, "as if under a pelting rain," wrote Galwey. To Lieutenant Nickerson, the "air seemed hissing hot with rifle balls" that passed over the Union lines in front and were striking all around Kimball's route. Some found human targets. One of them was Paul Truckey, a Vincennes, Indiana, Frenchman in Thomas Loundsdale's company of the 14th Indiana. "If ever a man really enjoyed a battle he did. I think he positively loved it," remembered Loundsdale. Early on in their movement forward, Loundsdale "heard a viscous whack and an exclamation from Truckey." The latter had been shot through the ankle and was swearing in a combination of French, English, and Choctaw. As Loundsdale recalled, "the burden of his complaint was not getting in even one shot."[68]

As Kimball's brigade advanced, he ordered a slight left wheel. The change in direction caused the left company of the 8th Ohio to cross the Roulette farm lane, going to its eastern side, which required the men to climb Roulette's "neatly painted board-rail fences," which were alongside the lane. As Francis Galwey went over the fence, a bullet clipped the strap of his haversack, the first of numerous close calls he and many other comrades would experience that morning. As Kimball's unit neared the ridge where the men in Weber's and Morris's brigades were lying down firing, Adjutant Hitchcock in the 132nd Pennsylvania noticed a sizeable group of men from the 108th and 4th New York huddled beneath a large tree a short distance below the crest. They appeared to be "doing nothing." The Pennsylvanians and [West] Virginians swept by them and over the remnants of the two New York regiments who were still fighting on the ridge. Reaching the crest, they received the same deadly reception the others had. Hitchcock described it as "a terrific fire," and Captain George W. Wilhelm, commanding Company F of the 130th Pennsylvania, called it "a perfect hailstorm of bullets." Among the casualties was Colonel Oakford, who died within minutes of receiving his wound. "He led us gallantly, and died like a brave man," lamented Wilhelm. Officers shouted for the men to lie down and return the fire, and the Pennsylvanians and [West] Virginians mirrored what the New Yorkers before them had done—that is, "lie down just under the top of the hill and crawl forward and fire over," then crawl back and repeat the process.[69]

The 8th Ohio and 14th Indiana had the same experience. Sergeant Galwey watched men drop all along the 8th's line. The 14th Indiana had the misfortune of also receiving artillery fire from Boyce's two pieces, Patterson's guns west of the Hagerstown Pike, and, possibly, Simmons's section. "Grape & canister, shot & shell screamed & whistled over us & around us till the air was dark and destruction seemed to stalk with undisputed sway," wrote Captain George Houghton. Lieutenant Nickerson in the 8th Ohio wrote of "terrible discharges of grape canister, while the bursting of heavy shells from a battery directly in our front, would create a juvenile earthquake about the head." The nine companies of the 8th that were west of the Roulette farm lane went to ground behind the hill occupied by survivors of the 5th Maryland and the 130th Pennsylvania and opened a rapid fire. Francis Galwey's company in the 8th Ohio remained east of the lane and took cover behind the same ridge as the 132nd Pennsylvania and the 7th [West] Virginia. The left of the 14th Indiana also occupied the same hill as the nine companies of the 8th Ohio, but that regiment's right companies extended into the more level ground west of the hill, where they were badly exposed. Bullets, shells, and canister inflicted frightful wounds. William Houghton, the captain of Company C, was shot through the left arm, but no bones were broken. The captain dismissed it as "only a scratch" and remained with his men.[70]

Captain Benjamin F. Ogle, commanding Company A of the 8th Ohio, documented some of the frightful carnage in his unit. His 1st lieutenant, George S. Smith, "got his left eye shot out, and his left cheekbone shot away, [but] there is some hope for his recovery." Lieutenant Creighton Thompson in Company K "had both eyes shot out, I think he will die." Others were hit in the hand, cheek, wrist, leg, head, and elbow. "The terrors of the battle were beyond the imagination," wrote Lieutenant Augustus VanDyke in the 14th Indiana to his fiancée, Angie: "Death from a bullet is ghastly, but to see a man's brains dashed out at your side by a grape shot and another's body severed by a screeching cannon ball is truly apalling. May I never again see such horrors as I saw that day."[71]

It was now around 10:15 a.m. Weber's and Morris's Federals had been in combat for nearly 30 and 20 minutes, respectively. All their regiments were in disarray, and among those who remained in the fight, ammunition was beginning to run low. When the 8th Ohio and the 14th Indiana arrived on the hill west of the Roulette farm lane, the elements of the 5th Maryland who had held this position began to pull back in small groups. The withdrawal degenerated into something of a stampede, and Weber rode into their midst in an effort to rally the men. Exposure on horseback was a magnet for bullets, and Weber received a severe wound that cost him a leg. The Marylanders fell back to the area of Clipp's tenant house and Roulette's barn, where they and elements of the 4th New York, who had also withdrawn when Kimball's men arrived, were rallied. Many in the 108th New York, the 130th Pennsylvania, the 14th Connecticut, and the 1st Delaware either remained in the fight with Kimball's regiments or fell back a short distance to a place where they had cover but could support the front line, if necessary.[72]

Adjutant Hitchcock in the 132nd Pennsylvania grew increasingly irritated with the behavior of Colonel Palmer in the 108th New York, whom Hitchcock saw lying down behind the Pennsylvanians, along with some of his men. "The horrible noise of the battle was incessant and almost deafening," recalled the adjutant, "except that my mind was so absorbed in my duties, I do not know how I could have endured the strain." It appeared to Hitchcock that Palmer was not reacting well. He was hugging the ground, and the soldiers with him, lacking leadership, were inert. Hitchcock thought this inaction was becoming "very demoralizing" for the inexperienced soldiers in the 132nd. General Kimball was sitting on his horse below the ridge the 132nd occupied and observed Palmer's behavior. He signaled for Hitchcock to come over and told the lieutenant to go to the colonel, "present his compliments," and "direct him to get his men up and at work." Hitchcock delivered the message, but Palmer, who seemed paralyzed with fear, merely turned his face up and looked at the adjutant, but made no reply. Kimball watched the exchange and called Hitchcock back, telling him this time, "with an oath," to go back and repeat the order "at the muzzle of my revolver, and shoot him if he did not immediately obey." Kimball called out to Hitchcock as he walked away, "Get those cowards out of there or shoot them." Hitchcock repeated Kimball's orders to Palmer but again received no reaction. Fortunately, he was saved from carrying out Kimball's instructions to shoot the colonel when some officers of the 108th New York rallied their men and pushed them up to the firing line.[73]

What happened to Palmer? Fear can be utterly debilitating, which may explain Palmer's behavior. It is plausible that at this particular moment, he was simply incapable of responding. We cannot know what incident may have caused his paralysis. But Palmer did not lack courage, and he eventually recovered himself. One of his captains documented that later on in the conflict, Palmer did his duty. This same captain, Francis Pierce, wrote after the battle that Palmer was popular in the regiment, adding, "He is brave but oh how he lacks in military knowledge." This offers a crucial clue to Palmer's behavior. In an action in which Hitchcock admitted he nearly could not stand the strain, Palmer—without *any* military training or preparation, with his men being wounded and killed around him, and with chaos all about—had no idea which orders to give or what to do. The result was paralysis.[74]

In contrast to Palmer, Captain Pierce found combat exhilarating. He admitted to being afraid when the regiment advanced into action and they were hearing bullets "whistling like the devil," but once he came under fire, he wrote, "I was never more cool in my life. I don't know how it was but I was perfectly indifferent, and had no more fear than I should have in your bath tub at home. In fact, I rather enjoyed it, although brave men were falling all around, dead and wounded, and being carried down to the barn which was being used as a hospital." Palmer's and Pierce's stories reflect one aspect of the reality of combat: some people can stand the awful danger and strain better than others.[75]

Another of those in their first fight who emerged as a gifted combat leader was Major Thomas A. Smyth in the 1st Delaware, an Irish-born 30-year-old carriage maker from Wilmington, Delaware. Smyth was a daring fellow—he would rise in rank to become a brigadier general and be the last general officer to die in the Civil War, as he was mortally wounded on April 9, 1865. Smyth gathered up about 150 men in his regiment and led them to the Mumma farm lane, where they gained cover from the lane's fences and nearby rock outcroppings. They were also on higher ground, which provided a better field of fire on Rodes's brigade and McRae's and Colquitt's men. Captain James L. Rickards, the Company A commander, accompanied Smyth's party and was killed here under unusual circumstances. According to the regimental historian, a limping

Confederate soldier approached their line, using his musket as a crutch. One of Rickards's sergeants raised his weapon, exclaiming, "I'll drop that fellow." The captain struck the gun down, scolding the sergeant: "You wouldn't shoot a wounded man!" The Confederate soldier suddenly raised his musket and shot Rickards dead. "The dastard rebel fell in his tracks, riddled by bullets," claimed the historian. Perhaps the incident occurred during Rodes's brief counterattack, but the idea that any Confederate soldier could have survived to hobble up to Smyth's position defies credulity, and the story of Rickards's death may well be apocryphal. Except for Rodes's brief counterattack, the Confederates in the Sunken Lane kept under cover. As the chaplain of the 14th Connecticut noted, "occasionally a rusty hat" was seen.[76]

Kimball's regiments had only been engaged for several minutes when they saw "line after line of the enemy's troops" swarming up through Piper's orchard and cornfield toward the Sunken Lane. It was R. H. Anderson's division, rushing forward to reinforce the embattled Tarheels and Alabamians in the lane. The combat suddenly swelled with renewed intensity, and the fate of the Confederates' center trembled in the balance.[77]

11

The Sunken Lane Falls

"What we see now looks to us like systematic killing"

The soldiers of Major General Richard H. Anderson's Confederate division hurried forward over a patchwork of meadows and plowed fields north of Sharpsburg toward the roar of battle in their front. All could see "smoke belching forth along the entire lines" to the east. Their march was directed towards the hottest point of this inferno.[1]

R. H. Anderson's division, it will be recalled (see chapter 7), had just completed a particularly grueling night march from Harpers Ferry that left hundreds of stragglers along the roadways. Sergeant Isaac McQuenn Auld estimated that half of the men in his 5th Florida regiment of Roger Pryor's brigade broke down, with the sergeant among this number. The 5th's experience was typical. The division, which was only 7 days old as an organization, began the campaign in poor condition and deteriorated throughout it. On paper it contained six brigades, but one of these, Parham's, had been destroyed at Crampton's Gap and carried only 84 officers and men into the field at Sharpsburg. This company-sized unit was attached to Pryor's brigade. Two other brigades, Wilcox's (Cumming's) and Featherston's (Posey's), were under senior colonels, although in the case of Featherston's command, Posey was an improvement over Featherston. Attrition from the summer's campaigns had ravaged the division's leadership. Auld's company in the 5th Florida was commanded by a corporal, and most of the other companies were led by sergeants. The 8th Florida had no field officers and no adjutant. In the 14th Alabama of Cumming's brigade, only three captains were present. Two companies were led by corporals, and two others by sergeants. The 22nd Georgia had its colonel, but he brought only about 60 officers and men into the field. The story was the same all through R. H. Anderson's division. It was a fragile, leaking ship before it entered the maelstrom of the Sunken Lane fight.[2]

While McLaws's division had a few minutes to rest after their severe march, R. H. Anderson's men had no respite. "Tired and sleepy," they marched up from their Potomac River crossing without pausing, going by "scores of wounded passing to the rear." According to Captain Charles H. Andrews, a company commander in the 3rd Georgia, "As we mounted the last hill to the village, a double quick step was taken and continued until we mounted the tableau on which the town is built." As Anderson's division hustled forward, he received orders—probably from Lee—to detach Brigadier General Lewis Armistead's brigade and send it to the left, to reinforce the sector in the West Woods. It was a significant loss, since Armistead had between 700 and 800 men, which made his one of the stronger brigades in the division. With this deduction, the strength of Anderson's remaining four brigades now totaled only about 2,600.[3]

Brigadier General Roger A. Pryor's brigade led the divisional column. The 34-year-old Petersburg, Virginia, resident had a colorful background but little military experience before the Civil War. He had been a lawyer but supposedly left his practice because of poor health. He next dabbled in journalism—although it seems unlikely that this occupation was less physically taxing than the law—and, during the 1850s, was editor of three newspapers: the *Southside* (Petersburg, VA), the *Washington Union*, and, finally, the *Richmond Enquirer*. He personally possessed no enslaved individuals, but he was a strong advocate for that practice and, when it came, for secession. Two years before the war, he was elected to the U.S. Congress. One day in 1860, during a particularly fierce argument on the floor of the House of Representatives, Pryor felt himself insulted by John F. Potter of Wisconsin and challenged the Northerner to a duel. Potter surprised Pryor by choosing Bowie knives. This cooled Pryor's enthusiasm for combat, and he backed out, claiming that Potter's choice of weapon was a "vulgar, barbarous, and inhuman mode of settling difficulties." During the siege of Fort Sumter, Pryor traveled to Charleston, South Carolina, hoping to encourage a bombardment of the fort, which he thought of as just the thing to push Virginia into seceding. There, he wrangled a position as a volunteer aide-de-camp to General P. G. T. Beauregard. When the moment Pryor sought finally arrived and he was offered the opportunity to loose the first shot on the fort, he flinched from the responsibility, claiming he could not fire the first gun of the war. He survived the bombardment but nearly died in its aftermath when, while visiting the fort with a delegation of Confederate officers, he drank a bottle of potassium iodide he found in the hospital, thinking it was medicinal whiskey. Doctors pumped his stomach and saved his life.[4]

The war opened new opportunities for Pryor. He was appointed colonel in the 3rd Virginia Infantry, but a colonel's rank did not square with his ambitions. He departed that unit in January 1862 to serve in the Provisional Confederate Congress, where, despite a lack of experience and only the most rudimentary knowledge of tactics, he was able to use his political connections and influential friends to wrangle a promotion to brigadier general. He was assigned command of a brigade on the Virginia Peninsula. He compiled an unimpressive record during the Peninsula and Second Manassas Campaigns and earned the distrust of his men. Robert E. L. Krick, one of the most astute historians of the Army of Northern Virginia's leadership, describes him as "incomparably incompetent." On July 23, 1862, a lieutenant in the 14th Louisiana wrote of Pryor, "He hoped by displaying the largest number of killed and wounded in his Brigade to obtain promotion," complaining that Pryor exposed his men unnecessarily and then mishandled his regiments in action, resulting in higher losses. Opinions of the general sank lower when, during the march to Leesburg before the army entered Maryland, Pryor ordered his brigade to open fire on stragglers. By the time R. H. Anderson's division marched toward the Sunken Lane struggle, by the fate of officer attrition, Pryor was the senior brigade commander. If Anderson went down, he would take command.[5]

The other brigade commanders were competent but not distinguished. Colonel Alfred Cumming, detached from his 10th Georgia in McLaws's division to command Wilcox's brigade, was the only professionally trained officer. He graduated from West Point in 1849 and spent 12 years in the Regular Army's infantry before he resigned to take up arms for the Confederacy. Brigadier General Ambrose Ransom Wright, a 36-year-old attorney and politician from near Augusta, Georgia, was a fearless soldier—as coming events would illustrate—and had definite leadership skills. He rose in rank from private in April 1861 to brigadier general by June 1862, but he was also impetuous and a flagrant self-promoter. Colonel Carnot Posey, a 44-year-old Mississippian who had been a U.S. district attorney and a planter before the war, had commanded Featherston's brigade as the senior colonel several times that summer during the latter's frequent illnesses, the latest having felled the brigadier general during the Harpers Ferry operation. Unlike Featherston, who was frequently absent and whose days with the army were numbered, Posey enjoyed a solid reputation. A group of officers in his 16th Mississippi affirmed this in a testimonial to Jefferson Davis, advocating the colonel's promotion: "Colonel Posey is always at his post in camp, on the march & on the field—and is ever attentive and faithful to his command."[6]

R. H. Anderson's artillery battalion of four batteries, totaling 16 guns, moved to the front separately from the infantry. When the foot soldiers left the Shepherdstown Road and started to move cross-country north of Sharpsburg, Captain Cary F. Grimes, temporarily commanding the battalion due to the illness of Major John S. Saunders, drove his guns through Sharpsburg and then turned north on the Hagerstown Turnpike. As the battalion came thundering up the pike, someone ordered the batteries to unlimber along a ridge of higher ground that rose west of Piper's orchard and extended across the pike to the hill that marked the northern end of Reel Ridge. Probably it was an individual from Longstreet's or Lee's staff who directed the deployment, as both generals were in that area. The mission of the battalion was twofold: first, to provide direct support to the infantry in the Sunken Lane; and second, to suppress enemy artillery and infantry fire long enough to permit Anderson's infantry to deploy. The assignment did not go well. Nearly half of the guns in the battalion were obsolete 6 lb. smoothbores or howitzers, good for close-range work against infantry, but pitifully outclassed against the 10 lb. Parrott rifles in Tompkins's Federal battery, which had a good bead on most of Grimes's guns. The battalion's position was also in range of the Union's 20 lb. Parrotts east of Antietam Creek, which were pouring fire into the vicinity.[7]

Which battery led the battalion is unknown, but Captain Marcellus N. Moorman's Lynchburg, Virginia, battery of three guns unlimbered about 50 yards west of Piper's barn. Grimes's Portsmouth, Virginia, battery, also with three guns, was on Moorman's left and only about 60 yards from the Hagerstown Pike. Both Captain Victor Maurin's Donaldsonville, Louisiana, battery of six guns, which included three rifles, and Captain Frank Huger's Norfolk, Virginia, battery of four guns took up positions west of the pike, on Grime's left. The artillery all arrived only minutes after Kimball's brigade had joined the Sunken Lane conflict. The 14th Indiana and part of the 8th Ohio, on the hill west of the Roulette farm lane, were the most visible to Grime's gun crews and drew most of their fire. The position of Maurin's and Huger's batteries enabled them to deliver an oblique, almost enfilading fire on the Hoosiers and Buckeyes, which was particularly destructive. "They enfilade us with their fire and it seems as though nothing could live through it," wrote Sergeant Galwey in the 8th Ohio.[8]

Only desperation could have dictated the position of Grimes's artillery. There was no cover for gun crews or limbers, and even though the batteries were between 600 and 700 yards from the Union infantry, minie balls from rifled muskets at that long range could still kill or maim. Tompkins turned four of his 10 lb. Parrott rifles on the new intruders, and the fire from the 20 lb. Parrott batteries across Antietam Creek struck the flank of Grimes's crews, although this barrage may not have been very accurate, due to smoke from the Sunken Lane fighting. Grimes's gun crews fought bravely, but their exposure to small arms and the superior firepower of the Federals' guns hammered them badly. Grimes was shot from his horse early on in the action. When several men attempted to carry him to safety, the fusillade was so severe that he was hit two more times and mortally wounded, and two of his bearers were killed. In less than 20 minutes, every rifled gun in the battalion was dismounted. The losses in personnel were not severe, but it was impossible to remain in that location without rifled guns, so the battalion was ordered to retire. Major Saunders had reached the army that morning. Learning of the position of his batteries, he joined them just as they were attempting to extricate themselves from the death trap. Saunders had the dismounted gun tubes tied to the limbers and led the battalion to safety. They had inflicted some casualties on the Federals' infantry, but the damage the Confederate units had sustained was so severe that Saunders was ordered to take his battalion across the Potomac River later that afternoon to refit. With R. H. Anderson's artillery battalion removed from the fight, the Union guns turned their firepower against his infantry brigades, with lethal consequences.[9]

It was about 10:00 a.m. when R. H. Anderson's column of infantry crested the southern end of Reel Ridge and the area of the Sunken Lane engagement came into view. A member of Wright's brigade wrote that the crash of firing became "hotter, and sometimes terrific at every step, till, finally the infantry of the enemy were plainly seen in line of battle." Captain Charles H. Andrews in the 3rd Georgia of the same brigade recalled how the Union artillery "furiously swept the fields all around us." In the 44th Alabama, Sergeant Robert Little observed that his company commander, 2nd Lieutenant Augustus Ray, was "dodging from every shell that exploded." Ray was so preoccupied by this that he failed to communicate the orders being shouted by the field officers. Finally, Ray went off at "the left oblique" and disappeared from view. Sergeant Little hollered to the company, "Boys, Lt. Ray is gone, I will have to take his place," and then told them there was no use in dodging the shells, "as you were just as apt to dodge in the way as out." In Pryor's brigade, the historian of the 14th Alabama recorded that although "the elements seemed crowded with shell," the missiles "passed harmlessly over our heads." Perhaps they did for the 14th, but the other units did not have the same experience. James J. Kirkpatrick in the 16th Mississippi of Posey's brigade recorded in his diary how "the enemy's batteries give us shot and shell in abundances, causing muscular contractions in the spinal column of our line. But all the dodging did not save us. Occasionally, a shell, better aimed than the rest would crack through our line, making corpses and mutilated trunks. A piece gave me a severe bruise in the shoulder." Alexander Chisholm, a lieutenant in the 9th Alabama of Cummings's brigade, recalled a dreadful moment when a man in his regiment named Smith was decapitated by a shell or solid shot: "His brains splattered on several of us who were close to him, I saw parts of his skull with hair attached go high into the air." Terror dogged the division's every step.[10]

At this critical moment in the division's advance, one of the many shells tracking its movement severely wounded R. H. Anderson in the thigh, removing him from the battle and placing the "incomparably incompetent" Roger Pryor in command. Since neither Anderson nor Pryor wrote a report, we have no record of what Anderson's orders were or who gave them to him. D. H. Hill claimed that R. H. Anderson reported to him, and he had directed the division commander to form his men "immediately behind my men." If this is true, it reflects how out of touch Hill was with the situation in his front. Forming immediately in the rear of Rodes's and G. B. Anderson's men was a death sentence, since the brigades would be exposed to the fire of French's infantry north of the Sunken Lane and the Federal artillery across Antietam Creek. What seems more likely is that R. H. Anderson received his initial orders from Longstreet, who directed him to Hill to find out where his brigades were needed most. Hill's headquarters were at Piper's farm, and this is probably where R. H. Anderson met the North Carolinian and where he was wounded. It took several minutes for a staff officer to find Pryor and inform him that he was now in command of the division. One of the Virginian's first acts was to send a message to Longstreet, declaring "that he [Pryor] would hold his position until the last man was taken." Longstreet was

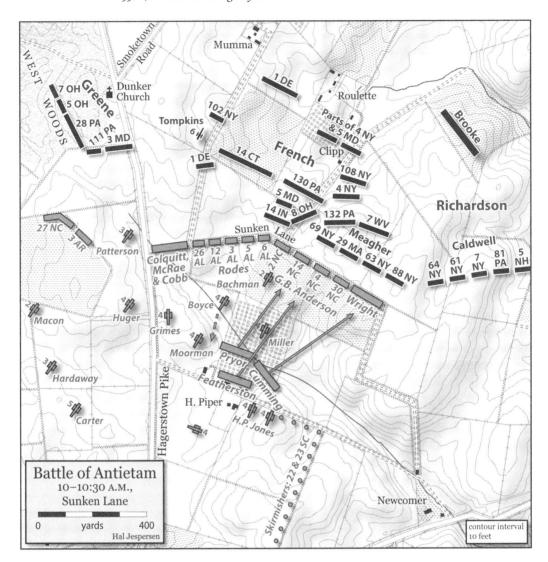

Battle of Antietam
10–10:30 A.M.,
Sunken Lane

0   yards   400
Hal Jespersen

contour interval
10 feet

not impressed by such bluster and replied, "We did not come here to be taken or surrender, we came here to fight." What knowledge Pryor had of R. H. Anderson's orders is unknown, but, based on the confusion that followed and the haphazard and piecemeal fashion in which the division was sent in, he probably knew little.[11]

Other important officer casualties swiftly followed R. H. Anderson's wounding. Under a "withering fire of artillery," Colonel Alfred Cumming was injured near Piper's farm buildings, and command of his brigade went to Major Jere Williams in the 9th Alabama. Meanwhile, around the same time when R. H. Anderson's division crossed the Hagerstown Pike, General George B. Anderson, who had been commanding his brigade from a high point in Piper's cornfield that gave him a good view of enemy movements, was informed that a new Federal force was approaching that might envelop his unprotected right flank. It was Richardson's division, advancing from beyond Roulette's farm. G. B. Anderson mounted and rode back to Piper's farm to report this news to Hill—and, no doubt, to request reinforcements. On his return, just as he reached the southern edge of the cornfield, a minie ball struck him in the foot at the ankle joint, inflicting a painful and disabling wound. G. B. Anderson sent one of his couriers, John F. Bagarly in the 4th North Carolina, to find Colonel Charles C. Tew, commanding the 2nd North Carolina, and tell him that Tew was now in command of the brigade. Bagarly had not bothered to find out how the regiments had deployed in the lane and did not know where the 2nd was on the brigade front. This became an issue, because locating Tew was a deadly task at that moment. Bagarly somehow ended up on the right of the brigade, where he found Colonel Francis Parker, who was next in seniority after Tew. Bagarly made his report, and Parker ordered his adjutant, Fred Phillips, "to proceed cautiously down the line, observe what was going on, and if possible, to find Colonel Tew." Phillips carefully made his way through the 30th, 4th, and 14th North Carolina regiments, "receiving several shots through his clothing," until he reached the 2nd and was able to ascertain that Tew was alive. Phillips risked going no farther than within "hailing" distance of Tew and shouted his message. The din of firing was so deafening that Phillips was uncertain if Tew heard what he saying, so he shouted for the colonel to make some gesture showing that he had understood. Tew rose up to indicate that he got the message and lifted his hat, making a polite bow. This movement caught the eye of a Federal rifleman, and he put a bullet through Tew's head, inflicting a mortal wound. Phillips turned back to inform Colonel Parker that he was now in command, but Phillips's luck now ran out. A bullet clipped his head, but luckily the wound was not fatal. Somehow word reached Colonel Parker that Phillips and Tew had both been hit and that he was in command. Parker started out at once to visit the left of the brigade and see how things were there, but he made it only 10 paces before he, too, was hit in the head, with a rifle ball "cutting away a narrow strip of skin and plowing a nice little furrow in the skull, leaving the membrane that covers the brain visible but uninjured." When Parker recovered enough to walk, he was helped to the rear—often a lethal journey—and command went to Colonel Risden T. Bennett in the 14th North Carolina.[12]

By the time Pryor's brigade, commanded now by Colonel John C. Hately in the 5th Florida, reached the Hagerstown Pike, they arrived around 100 yards south of the Piper farm lane. The brigade turned north up the pike until they reached the lane, which they then followed past the farmer's barn. Here the unit filed left, moving just west of Piper's orchard, in the direction of Rodes's brigade. They had not gone far when an unknown staff officer ordered them to halt. Most of the brigade was in a ravine that ran northwest from the orchard and provided cover from enemy fire, but the 2nd Florida, which led the column, was on rising ground and "very much exposed." Why Hately did not deploy is not known, but there may have been some question as to where the brigade should be sent.[13]

While Hately's regiments marked time, Wright's brigade dashed across the Hagerstown Pike north of the Piper farm lane, angled past his barn and the rear of Pryor's brigade to the lane, and followed it to nearly opposite the farmer's house. There they faced left toward the orchard and formed a line—from right to left, the 3rd and 48th Georgia, the 44th Alabama, and the 22nd Georgia. The regiments were all small, and the brigade totaled only about 400 men, covering a front of slightly over 100 yards. The orchard was enclosed by a stout oak picket fence, and Wright set his men to dismantling enough of it to permit his regiments to pass. Federal artillery was plastering this area. The right wing of the 3rd Georgia, on higher terrain just east of Piper's house, was particularly exposed, and it suffered many casualties during the effort to demolish the fence. The regiments rushed through the gaps they created and swept up across the orchard, harried as they went by the hostile artillery fire. Wright led his brigade northeast, toward the right of G. B. Anderson's line, which makes it probable that his direction of advance was ordered by D. H. Hill, in response to G. B. Anderson's warning of a threat to the Confederates' right flank.[14]

In their advance, Wright's regiments crossed another picket fence, this time on the orchard's eastern boundary, and then had to clamber over a worm fence on the edge of Piper's cornfield. Here the cornfield's terrain rose to higher ground, where today an observation tower stands. The corn provided some concealment, but Union gunners east of Antietam Creek, as well as French's infantry, saw them coming. Sergeant Robert Little in the 44th Alabama recorded that the Yankees "soon gave us a hail of lead." Another member of Wright's brigade wrote that a Union battery across the creek poured a terrible fusillade into their right flank. Lieutenant Colonel Reuben Nisbit, commanding the 3rd Georgia, remembered the artillery fire as "simply awful." The roar of the guns was so deafening, recalled Captain Andrews, "that all commands or conversation was shouted at the top of the voice to be heard at all." Wright was riding his iron-gray horse in front of the 3rd Georgia when a shell struck the poor beast's breast and exploded, "literally annihilating the animal" and hurling the general high into the air. He landed dazed but miraculously unharmed. He then continued on foot but did go far before a bullet or shell fragment went "entirely through the muscle of the leg below the knee entirely disabling him." A litter team picked up the general, but he insisted that they carry him forward to the Sunken Lane.[15]

With Wright disabled, command of the brigade went to Colonel Robert Jones in the 22nd Georgia, a pre-war Methodist minister and carriage and buggy builder in Bartow County, Georgia. Although one of Jones's men wrote that "a braver man I never seen," the colonel's harsh brand of discipline had earned "the ill will of many in the Regt." for "punishing some men unnecessarily or their punishment was too severe for the offense." One of his enemies in the 22nd apparently exacted his revenge in the excitement of the movement to the Sunken Lane. Jones was out in front of his tiny regiment when he took a bullet through his right lung. William B. Judkins, a member of the 22nd who gave out on the march up from Harpers Ferry, wrote, "It was told to me a few days after Col. Jones was wounded that he was shot by one of his own Regiment. One of Co. H I think is the one that shot him." Command went to Colonel William Gibson in the 48th Georgia, who, though amiable, was believed to be possessed of "no military genius whatsoever."[16]

The left of Wright's brigade emerged from the cornfield in the rear of the 30th North Carolina, but they were greeted by such heavy small-arms fire that they were driven back into the corn and moved toward their right. There they joined the rest of the brigade, which had occupied the Sunken Lane on the 30th's right. Only about 250 of the 400 men who started remained at this point. The Federals' 7th [West] Virginia, in Wright's left front, recoiled slightly at the appearance of this new Confederate force. This made Colonel Gibson think that the enemy were falling back. Wright, watching the battle from his litter, also thought so. He encouraged Gibson to take advantage of the situation and charge the 7th. The colonel shouted for fixed bayonets, and the brigade surged up out of the lane. One of Wright's men complained that G. B. Anderson's brigade "on our left did little to support us" when they sallied forth. Instead, the North Carolinians were astonished at what they knew was a wildly foolish assault and ignored efforts by Wright's officers to have them join the attack. Lieutenant James Shinn in the 4th North Carolina fathomed that the only explanation for the reckless charge was that "Wright was drunk."[17]

The Georgians and Alabamians spilled onto the plateau that extended for some 50 yards north from the road, where they threatened the left flank of Kimball's brigade. The Union brigadier reacted by ordering the 7th [West] Virginia and the 132nd Pennsylvania to refuse—that is, to bend their line back—and extend their line to protect the flank. "We fired such a voley into them that they soon went back and with less men," wrote Commodore P. Mears in the 132nd. But the repulse of Gibson's charge was not as easy as Mears had implied. Sergeant Robert Little and other members of the 44th Alabama remained long enough for Little to load and fire several times, as well as to count seven enemy flags in his front. Some belonged to Kimball's and Morris's brigades, but the sergeant may have also observed the Irish Brigade of Richardson's 1st Division, who were moving across Roulette's meadow to reinforce French. Some of Wright's graycoats turned their fire on Meagher's soldiers, as well as on Caldwell's 1st Brigade, which was on the Irishman's left, causing some casualties. But the firepower directed at the exposed Confederates was fearsome. "Nothing could stand such a fire," recalled Captain Andrews. In his 3rd Georgia, the "men fell on every side like leaves in Autumn." Nearly everyone around Sergeant Little was killed or wounded. "I could put my hand on 5 dead men," he later recalled. Gibson ordered a retreat, and the survivors staggered back to the road.[18]

The ill-advised charge left Wright's brigade in a shambles. Casualties totaled nearly 50%, and almost all of its senior leadership were dead or wounded. Lieutenant Colonel Charles A. Derby, commanding the 44th Alabama, was killed, and his only captain present that day was injured. Major Lawrence Lallerstedt, the only remaining field officer in the 22nd Georgia, also was hurt. Others among the wounded were the major of the 48th Georgia and its single captain. Lieutenant Colonel Reuben Nisbit, the commander of the 3rd Georgia, fell in advance of his men and was left "writhing in pain" between the lines. A bullet or shell fragment found Wright a second time, hitting him in the breast, and this time his litter bearers carried him to the rear. Gibson now was the brigade's only remaining field officer.[19]

The movement of Wright's brigade through Piper's cornfield had caught the attention of Robert Rodes and alerted him that reinforcements were at hand. When he looked to his rear, he spotted what he thought to be one regiment and part of another standing motionless, still aligned in column, beside Piper's orchard. That he could see these things tells us that Rodes's command post was on the higher ground in the rear of his brigade, where he had a better view of enemy movements than he would have in the Sunken Lane. Rodes was probably inside Piper's cornfield, on a knoll in the rear of the 6th Alabama, which gave him some concealment. The firing in his front had decreased by the time he noticed the troops near the orchard, so he went back to them and discovered that the leading unit was Captain William D. Ballentine's 2nd Florida of Pryor's brigade. Rodes asked the captain why his brigade was not moving. Ballentine and others Rodes spoke to said they had been halted "by somebody," although not General Pryor, and had received no other orders. Disgusted, Rodes told the officers that their men were needed at the front, ordered them to form into line, and directed where they should go, which apparently was toward the exposed point at the junction of his and G. B. Anderson's brigades. Rodes then came upon Pryor, who was near Piper's barn, and told him about the conduct of his brigade, adding that he had ordered them to form line and advance. According to Carman, Pryor "was unaware of the orders under which [General R. H.] Anderson was acting and did not rise to the occasion, and the consequent movements of his command were disjointed and without proper direction." This was no doubt true, but Wright's brigade definitely did have orders. Wright had told Lieutenant Colonel Nisbit in the 3rd Georgia that when Wright's brigade reached the Sunken Lane, Pryor's brigade would move up on their right, and "other troops are coming to join us." R. H. Anderson had been riding in the rear of Wright's brigade, so he may have issued these instructions before he was injured, and in the haste and confusion that followed Anderson's wounding, no one on his staff had the opportunity to impart whatever plans the division commander may have had to Pryor.[20] Whatever the case, Rodes stirred Pryor into action. The general agreed with Rodes's orders to his brigade and sent his own directives confirming them. Both Cumming's and Posey's brigades were halted near Piper's barn by this time, and Pryor ordered them to follow his own brigade through the orchard to the front.[21]

Pryor's brigade formed up quickly. Captain Ballantine's 2nd Florida deployed first, with half of the regiment in the meadow west of Piper's orchard and the other half in the orchard. The other regiments—from left to right, the 8th and 5th Florida, the 3rd and 14th Virginia, and the remnants of Parham's brigade—formed on the 2nd's right in the orchard. Colonel Hately, whose leadership was conspicuously absent up to this point, now ordered the brigade forward. The ground in the orchard sloped up to the north toward Piper's cornfield, so when Pryor's men reached the corn, they could be seen both by French's infantrymen, who were lying down along the ridge north of the Sunken Lane, and by Tompkins's battery, the nemesis of many a Confederate unit in that sector of the battlefield. In the fire that lashed the Confederate brigade's line, Lieutenant Colonel Georges A. G. Coppens—the hotheaded, brave French Louisianan who had been detached from Starke's brigade of Jackson's wing to command the 8th Florida, which had no field officers—was among the first to be killed. The senior captain, Richard A. Waller, then assumed command. He took the regimental colors and draped them over his shoulder to lead the men on, but he was killed moments later. Marshall B. Hurst, the historian of the 14th Alabama, recalled how "everything in front was obscured from view by the dense smoke; and the sound that greeted the ear can't be compared to anything but a severe hail storm, accompanied by thunder and lightning." Hurst added that "for a moment everything seemed to be in confusion." Despite heavy losses, Pryor's brigade managed to push up through the corn, arriving behind the right wing of the 14th North Carolina and the left wing of the 4th North Carolina. Colonel Hately was shot through both thighs and fell here. Colonel Joseph Mayo, commanding the tiny 3rd Virginia, was next in seniority, but he, too, was injured, so Colonel Alfred C. Wood in the 14th Alabama took command. Captain Ballantine also went down with a wound, completing the nearly total decimation of the brigade's regimental leadership. Wood did what all Confederate commanders seemed to do reflexively that day when confronted with confusion and uncertainty: he ordered a charge. Mercifully, only a part of the brigade responded to this suicide mission. "Our weary and exhausted boys rushed forward," remembered Hurst. The attack died in a hail of gunfire and melted back to the Sunken Lane. The survivors of Pryor's mangled brigade dropped down among G. B. Anderson's Tarheels in the lane and fought for their lives.[22]

Posey's brigade, trailed by Cumming's brigade, which was aligned to Posey's right rear, moved up through the orchard and arrived within minutes of Pryor's troops. Posey formed his brigade of 600 to 700 men in Piper's orchard—from left to right, the 16th, 12th, and 19th Mississippi, and the 2nd Mississippi Battalion. They covered a front of some 200 yards. Crossing nearly the same ground as Pryor's brigade, their experience was similar. The moment Posey's brigade reached the cornfield, they encountered a "sweeping fire from the Federals in their front and an enfilading fire from their batteries on the right and left." Jefferson J. Wilson, a 21-year-old private in the 16th Mississippi, called it "the hottest fires that we ever was in before." The Union infantry were difficult to see, since, besides being obscured by the smoke, only the enemy's "heads and shoulders" were visible. Posey's men also had trouble identifying their own infantry, as well, for when they came up in the rear of G. B. Anderson's North Carolinians and the survivors of Pryor's brigade, all squatting down in the lane, the Mississippians gave them a volley, inflicting several friendly fire casualties. In an act of breathtaking bravery, Lieutenant Franklin H. Weaver, a 22-year-old former student from Iredell County, stood up with the flag of the 4th North Carolina to prevent another volley. He saved his comrades from more friendly fire, but he did so at the cost of his life. He was shot dead moments after he arose.[23]

Posey's Mississippians flowed out of the cornfield into the Sunken Lane and beyond, in yet another suicidal frontal assault on French's Federals. Dozens were mowed down as the brigade encountered "a murderous fire of grape, canister, shell, and small arms." Jefferson Wilson wrote home that of the 37 men in his company, 20 were killed or wounded. The survivors recoiled and piled back into the crowded lane. One of those firing at the Mississippians was Sergeant Galwey in the 8th Ohio. He marveled at how the lines of Confederates would "come opposite us and sink out of sight in the sunken lane. It is a mystery that so many men could crowd into so small a space." Thomas Loundsdale in the 14th Indiana remembered that as R. H. Anderson's brigades came charging through Piper's corn, "How we did work then, we feared or at least I know I did, a bayonet charge and we did our best to kill them all before they could reach their ditch. It was truly pitiful to see them tumble as they came down the slope, but on they came and in splendid alignment, their colors fell as fast as they were raised, and each time they fell there was a man to seize them." But when the Rebels reached the lane, Loundsdale noted that they seemed to disappear. Within the Sunken Lane, Captain A. M. Feltus, commanding the 16th Mississippi, described how "a scene of great confusion ensued from the mingling together of different brigades." The crowding of regiments along the line originally held by the 14th, 4th, and 30th North Carolina created a dangerous disorganization that disrupted command and control and threatened to unravel the Confederates' defense of the Sunken Lane.[24]

Cumming's Alabama brigade, commanded now by Major Jeremiah Williams in the 9th Alabama, advanced through Piper's orchard in a northeasterly direction.

The four regiments had a total of about 500 men. There were only two field officers left in the entire brigade, so leadership was thin even before they came
under fire. The Alabamians entered the cornfield in the ravine through which,
hours earlier, G. B. Anderson's brigade had come up to occupy the Sunken Lane.
This spared them the lethal fire faced by Pryor's and Posey's brigades. But the
respite was temporary, for the terrain rose steadily from the ravine to a high
plateau in the northeastern portion of the cornfield. When the Alabamians
reached this high ground, Major Hilary A. Herbert, commanding the 8th Alabama, wrote that "a compact line of infantry about 120 yards in our front poured
in a well-directed fire upon us." Sergeant Zachariah Abney in the 11th Alabama
remembered it as "a perfect hail storm of bullets," noting that "it appeared to
me that every ear of corn was perforated by a bullet." In addition to the small-
arms fire, a battery at about a 45-degree angle to them across Antietam Creek,
and another at a 45-degree angle to their left—Tompkins's battery—"concentrated
shells upon us with terrible accuracy." Men fell by the score. Williams was
wounded in the head by a shell fragment, and his adjutant, James W. Wilson, died
from a shot through the head. Captain George C. Wheatley, commanding the
10th Alabama, was also killed. Bailey G. McClelen, a 10th Alabama private, was
among those who were hit, taking a bullet or shell fragment through his right
arm, which rendered it useless. He decided he should try to get to safety and
medical attention, but the odds seemed daunting. "I saw no refuge anywhere
near me," he wrote. "The bullets and shells and exploding shells, grapeshot and
canister shot came by me close, high and low." He somehow managed to reach a
limestone outcropping that offered some cover, which was already being used
by several other Confederates. His escape, McClelen believed, "seemed like a
miracle to me."[25]

Only a handful of men from Cumming's brigade reached the Sunken Lane.
The majority that were not killed or wounded dropped down in the corn and
returned the Federals' fire "rapidly and with effect." The Alabamians' experience
was a duplicate of the futile efforts of every other brigade under R. H. Anderson's command. His division's fighting strength had been sacrificed and wasted
in foolish advances into the teeth of enemy fire. Pryor deserves criticism for the
division's poor handling, but so too do Lee, Longstreet, and D. H. Hill. All three
of these officers were in the vicinity when R. H. Anderson's division reached the
field, yet no one other than Rodes provided Pryor with any meaningful guidance or help. Had Lee or Longstreet directed the division to go farther north—
where they might have advanced perpendicular to the Sunken Lane, against the
right flank of French's Federal division—they might have had a decisive impact
on the conflict there. That position also would have avoided the deadly enfilading fire from the Union batteries across Antietam Creek. But the infusion of
over 2,400 Confederate infantrymen and four Rebel artillery brigades into the

fight at the Sunken Lane was not without effect. The sheer number of additional rifles and muskets they brought into action inflicted their share of damage on the Yankees.[26]

IN RECALLING THIS CRITICAL STAGE of the engagement, when each of R. H. Anderson's brigades joined the fight, Sergeant Galwey in the 8th Ohio wrote, "The din is frightful. Alas, no words can depict the horrors of a great battle as they appear to men unaccustomed to them. We had seen a great deal of service before now; but our fighting had been mostly of the desultory, skirmishing sort. What we see now looks to us like systematic killing."[27] Lieutenant Augustus M. VanDyke in the 14th Indiana counted "eight stands of rebel colors" in front of his regiment and related how the Confederates "seemed to use every effort to break through our lines at this point." As the casualties among his regiments piled up, even tough Nathan Kimball was not immune to the effects of the slaughter. He was heard muttering "God save my poor boys!" as he rode along his line.[28]

Although it may have been imperceptible to men like VanDyke, surrounded by the carnage among those in his regiment, the Federals were slowly gaining the advantage in the lethal slugfest. The 132nd Pennsylvania, and the remnants from Weber's and Morris's brigades who remained with them, soon realized that they were perfectly positioned to deliver an enfilading fire on the right wing of the 6th Alabama and part of the 2nd North Carolina. In addition, the 8th Ohio, on the eastern slope of the hill north of the Roulette farm lane, had an oblique fire on the 14th North Carolina and those units of R. H. Anderson's division who crowded into the Sunken Lane with the Tarheels. Combined with the volleys from the front, this brought a withering crossfire against both of these exposed points on the Confederates' line.[29]

It was difficult for the Federals to tell how effective their fire was, except when R. H. Anderson's brigades made targets of themselves as they advanced through Piper's cornfield. The Confederates in the Sunken Lane kept their heads down, except to quickly rise up and fire. "It was only rarely that a head could be seen above the pile of rails," remembered Galwey. But when elements of Kimball's brigade attempted a local assault toward the lane, "the Confederates showed themselves plainly enough and met us with a murderous fire." In the 14th Indiana, Thomas Loundsdale noted that their once "splendid" line was broken up into groups and small squads of men "with blackened faces and glistening eyes. The sickening thud thud heard so constantly accounts for it numbers are to be seen lying in pools of blood while still greater numbers are writhing under the surgeon's knife." At one point in the fight, a member of Loundsdale's company, nicknamed "Old Sailor Jack," exclaimed loudly, "Faith I'm goin to have a smoke." He laid down his musket, took out his pipe and knife, carefully cleaned out the bowl, grabbed a plug of his tobacco, shredded off a bowlful, and then lit his pipe with a nearby burning cartridge paper. "All this was done as deliberately as though in a field at work," wrote Loundsdale.[30]

While most of the men on Kimball's line lay down, knelt, or sat to load and fire their weapons, Thomas Loundsdale never forgot three of his tentmates (Jim Wilson, Raleigh Kelso, and John J. Landeman) who stood up to fire at a Confederate battery—possibly one of Grimes's battalion—that was shooting at them. Wilson would shout, "Now God Damn you I'll fetch you outer thar," each time he raised his rifle to his shoulder to fire. It was Kelso's first battle, and Loundsdale described him as "wild with excitement." Loundsdale urged the young man to get down, but "No said he they can't hurt me, they have nipped me in the side a little but it don't hurt." Loundsdale went back behind the firing line for some reason, perhaps to assist a wounded comrade. When he returned, he found Kelso and Landeman stretched out on the ground, dead. Wilson remained, cursing and firing, but soon he was hit by a ball that shattered both arms. A Confederate opposite to Loundsdale mirrored the recklessness of Kelso. Loundsdale watched him stand and, with "utter contempt for our marksmanship," take careful aim "as deliberately as if he were engaged in a match." Loundsdale fired at him three or four times but missed, which offers some sense of how inaccurate much of the shooting on both sides was. While Loundsdale was loading for another shot, he saw the daring Confederate pitch forward and fall. As Loundsdale concluded, "It is bad business for a soldier to render himself unnecessarily conspicuous there was no doubt a hundred men firing at that man and there could of course be one result, death."[31]

Another bold soldier who did not survive the combat in the Sunken Lane was Jack Shepherd, Sergeant Galwey's close friend, who, hours earlier, had loudly declared "that the bullet was not yet struck that was to kill him!" Shepherd had also mocked Colonel Oakford's ruminations about his possible death. Such bravado was common with some men before a battle, and it often masked deep fears. Shepherd rendered himself conspicuous in some way and was shot a dozen times. "He never even groaned! Poor boy!" lamented Galwey. With so many dead and wounded around him and the air seemingly alive with bullets, canister, and shell fragments, the sergeant concluded "that I shall not, cannot, escape." Yet the thought did not paralyze him with fear. "I contemplate the prospect of sudden death without flinching," he recalled. "It is not heroism, but cool reason which actuates me."[32]

Terrible as the slaughter was in the ranks of Kimball's regiments, their return volleys, particularly in the places where they could bring a crossfire, began to have effects among the Confederates in the Sunken Lane. Individuals and small groups of men were seen attempting to climb out of the lane and make a break for the rear through Piper's cornfield. Loundsdale observed that "sometimes as many as twenty would spring to their feet and start to their rear then such another tumbling would take place, was pitiful to see. I am certain that not one of them ever got fifty steps away." Commodore Mears in the 132nd Pennsylvania described the same thing in his front, writing to a friend how "some of the rebs in the pit tried to make their escape through the cornfield but there was but very few that would reach the top of the hill till they would get layed [out]." One of those attempting to escape the slaughter was shot and fell over a part of Piper's cornfield fence that was still standing, his head on one side of the fence and his feet on the other. "He remained a target for the rest of the fight," wrote Loundsdale.[33]

White flags appeared at different points in the Sunken Lane that were occupied by G. B. Anderson's brigade and the reinforcing brigades of R. H. Anderson's division. Numerous soldiers from French's 3rd Division mentioned them. The 14th Indiana's Loundsdale wrote, "Soon a white flag was seen waving in the rebel line. Officers ordered the men to cease fire. The rebs called to us that they wanted to surrender." When some men in that regiment approached the Confederate line, however, they were fired on by Rebels in Piper's cornfield. The Hoosiers concluded it was a ruse, "and the fun began again fast and furious." Francis Galwey observed "white handkerchiefs at several points on Confederate line in the road." For a moment his regiment ceased firing, "but the handkerchiefs were quickly withdrawn, so we resumed our fire." In his diary. John D. Hemminger, a private in the 130th Pennsylvania, mentioned seeing small white flags or handkerchiefs at different points along the Rebel line in the Sunken Lane. "We ceased firing wondering what it meant. Suddenly they poured a deadly volley into our ranks. Many falling all about us," he recorded. The surrender signals were raised a second time, with the same result. The third time the "white rags went up our fire was withheld for a moment until every rifel could be reloaded then with deliberate aim we gave them the first volley which must have caused them greater loss than we had so far sustained." Colonel Oliver Palmer in the 108th New York saw the surrender flags as well and attempted to get his men to cease firing, but he claimed the noise was too great. A member of his regiment, writing to the *Brockport (NY) Republic* after the battle, observed the white flags and heard shouts of "Cease firing" along the line. Then a voice rang out, "No, it's a ruse," so, stated this soldier, "volley after volley kept pouring in upon the doomed foe. It was perfectly useless to attempt to stop the men."[34]

What are we to make of these incidents? They were not isolated, but instead happened to Union soldiers all along the front of French's division, although they seem to have been concentrated in the section of the Sunken Lane originally defended by G. B. Anderson's brigade. Although no Confederates mention any attempt to surrender, the evidence is overwhelming that white flags or handkerchiefs appeared at several points along their line. Was it a ruse to draw the Federals out into the open? While we like to imagine that honorable soldiers would never use such a trick, desperation can drive combatants to attempt almost anything to escape certain death. But there is some testimony that there was a sincere attempt at surrender. The officer in the 108th who corresponded with the *Brockport Republic* wrote that after the battle, he spoke to a Confederate major who had been taken prisoner and who claimed to be one of the men who had raised a white flag. "Had we [Yankees] recognized the flag he would have surrendered his whole command," the Rebel major told him, for the Sunken Lane "was a perfect slaughter pen." But when the Union soldiers kept firing, "What could I do?" asked the major. "You refused to stop firing and as a last resort, I was obliged to stay and defend myself as best I could." Colonel Palmer confirmed this story in a letter to his wife.[35]

We know from the limited number of accounts by Confederate survivors in the Sunken Lane that everywhere along G. B. Anderson's front, as well as where the 6th Alabama was positioned, was extremely dangerous, but some points were especially perilous. Newsome Jenkins, 1st sergeant in the 14th North Carolina, related that the configuration of the terrain and the lane itself gave the 4th and 30th North Carolina less protection than his regiment enjoyed. Lieutenant John Gorman in the 2nd North Carolina wrote that the cover provided by the sunken nature of the road "is not sufficient," since "many are shot as they are aiming at the enemy." He also noted, "It is certain death to leave the road, wounded, as the balls fly so thick over us." B. B. Ross, a 4th North Carolina private who served as an orderly, wrote that "it was dangerous to go down the line to carry orders—we were all 'squatting' in the road." As orders came along the regimental line, Ross "raised up every time to pass the message to Company H, and about the third time I raised up, a piece of shell struck me in the shoulder mashing me right down." At the most exposed points—the positions of the 6th Alabama and the 2nd North Carolina, and those of the 4th and 30th North Carolina—the lane was a veritable death trap, where even the wounded could not escape without being riddled. What seems probable is that at certain vulnerable portions of the line, some Confederates, believing their position to be hopeless, did attempt to surrender. There was not a consensus on this decision, however, which accounts for why Galwey noted the flags in his front were quickly withdrawn, and why others mention being fired on when they approached the tokens of surrender. This caused the Union soldiers to believe the white flags were a ruse, so they continued firing, which, in turn, prompted those Confederates who did want to surrender to have no choice but to fight on. Offering or accepting a surrender in the type of combat the two sides were engaged in at the Sunken Lane was fraught with peril. But, desperate as the situation in the lane was, the fierce resistance the Confederates continued to make indicated that the number who sought to surrender was a minority.[36]

IT WAS NOW NEARLY 10:30 a.m., and the conflict for the Sunken Lane had been raging for almost an hour. Even though French's regiments had carried 60 to

80 rounds per man into the fight, Kimball's brigade and the elements of the other regiments in the division that remained in action were running out of ammunition. "Do you remember what a dismal cry that was?" wrote Loundsdale when his comrades in the 14th Indiana reached for their last cartridges. Officers began going through the cartridge boxes of the dead and wounded, gathering up any spares, and an urgent summons to the rear brought an ammunition wagon up from Roulette's farm. "We soon had plenty," Loundsdale noted. Other regiments were not as fortunate in receiving a resupply, other than what the officers could scrounge from their fallen comrades, and their rate of fire began to diminish. It was at this crucial moment that the tide of battle swung decisively in the Federals' favor. Just then the tough veterans of General Israel Richardson's 1st Division of the 2nd Corps came sweeping up over Roulette's meadows and plowed fields.[37]

The nicknames soldiers bestowed on their commanders often reflected whether these leaders were respected or disliked—in other words, whether they were fighting officers or ones who shied from danger. By that measure, General Israel B. Richardson was exceptionally popular with his men. He had several nicknames: "Fighting Dick," "Greasy Dick," and "Old War Horse." "Greasy Dick," was a high compliment from the enlisted men, for although Richardson was an officer—and a general, at that—the rank and file considered him to be one of them. The other nicknames spoke to their respect for his courage and ability as a soldier. The men in the 1st Division believed in Richardson. The Vermont-born soldier was a West Pointer, class of 1841. His experience at the academy was difficult. He was a mediocre to poor student, particularly in mathematics, and was discharged midway through his freshman year because of his grades. Nonetheless, a small number of cadets who had displayed good conduct were permitted a second chance. Richardson made the most of this opportunity and, through hard work, managed to graduate, although it took him five and a half years to do so. Few officers survived as much combat as Richardson did in the war with Mexico, or were as distinguished in action as he was. Serving in the 3rd U.S. Infantry, he took part in nearly all the major battles of the Mexican War, serving under Zachary Taylor and Winfield Scott. Both left a deep impression on the young officer and became leadership models for him. Richardson respected officers who disdained pomp and red tape and who led by example. His standards were high, with good reason: men's lives were at stake. Richardson could never reconcile himself with tolerating incompetent, petty, or cowardly officers, which led to conflicts with some of his superiors. By 1855, his wife and child had died of disease, and the difficulties with his superiors, as well as the general harshness of frontier duty, wore Richardson down. He resigned his Regular Army commission and settled in Pontiac, Michigan, where his parents had moved to from Vermont.[38]

What followed was a difficult time for Richardson. He earned a living as a farmer, but he was unsociable and looked "queer" to the locals, who regarded him as an eccentric. When the Civil War began, he was among the first in the area to offer his services. What became the 2nd Michigan infantry was being recruited in the Pontiac region. Richardson did not seek the colonelcy of the regiment. Instead, he believed "all that I am capable of" was the rank of major. "I do not think I am fit to command a regiment of men," he added, reflecting both his modesty and a shaken confidence in his abilities. The governor and others thought differently, however, and commissioned Richardson as the regiment's colonel.[39]

Richardson's fortunes took a positive turn in the war's early days. He married Frances A. Travor, a strong-willed, attractive, younger woman, who accompanied him to the front. Then, in early July, after his regiment arrived in Washington, DC, Winfield Scott appointed him to brigade command. In the first battle of the war, at Bull Run, Richardson displayed an ability to learn from his mistakes. In a probe at Blackburn's Ford on July 18, which preceded the main fight, Richardson's over-aggressiveness nearly got his brigade into trouble. Three days later, during the general battle, his brigade again had orders to deceive the enemy but avoid a general engagement. This time, Richardson executed his mission skillfully. His brigade was detached to the division of Dixon S. Miles, who had been colonel of the 3rd U.S. infantry when Richardson had served with the regiment in New Mexico Territory. Richardson did not care for Miles, and when the division commander meddled in Richardson's defensive arrangements, the two exchanged sharp words. Richardson bluntly informed Union army commander Irvin McDowell that Miles "is drunk, and is not fit to command." The colonel's after-action report repeated his accusation that Miles was inebriated during the battle, which forced the old Regular Army commander to ask for a court of inquiry. It did not go well for Miles, as 28 out of 50 witnesses declared that the division commander was intoxicated. The court agreed, but it declined to cashier Miles. Instead, he was quietly reassigned to the then quiet posting as commander of the Railroad Brigade at Harpers Ferry.[40]

Richardson's performance at First Bull Run earned him a promotion to brigadier general on August 9, 1861, but the commission was backdated to May 17, which gave him seniority over many other newly promoted brigadier generals in the Union army. The following spring, as the Army of the Potomac prepared to embark on the Peninsula Campaign, he was elevated to division command in Edwin Sumner's 2nd Corps. Up until the start of this campaign, Richardson had maintained a good relationship with George McClellan, even though he also cultivated a close working connection with Senator Zachariah Chandler of Michigan, a Radical Republican who was one of McClellan's fiercest critics and enemies. Richardson claimed Chandler "is always ready to see me; not withstanding the number of office seekers."[41]

Richardson and his division distinguished themselves on the Virginia Peninsula as one of the best fighting units in the Army of the Potomac. On the frequent retreats during the Seven Days Battles, it was often Richardson's division that was selected to form the rear guard, a post that required considerable skill. His reward was promotion to major general on July 4, 1862. But Richardson seethed at what he considered poor generalship by McClellan. In his report on the Seven Days Battles, which was published in Michigan newspapers, he included a remarkable postscript for an official document: "If anything can try the patience and courage of troops it must be their fighting all day for five consecutive days and then falling back every night." The wording enabled Richardson to deny that he meant it as disparaging of the Union army's commander, but McClellan's critics knew what he meant.[42]

Shortly after the Seven Days Battles, Richardson took sick leave and returned to Washington, DC, where he met with Chandler and fed him damaging information about McClellan's performance on the Virginia Peninsula. Chandler used this in a verbal assault on McClellan on the U.S. Senate floor on July 16. When McClellan sought to bring his scheming division commander back into line by charging him with being absent without leave in late July and ordering him to return to his command, Richardson challenged his superior's authority by seeking protection and aid from his powerful political friends. Chandler wrote to Secretary of War Stanton that Richardson was not absent without leave, but was sick, and also that the entire Michigan delegation desired that the general be assigned to command a new division of Michigan soldiers then being raised. This was probably the real reason why Richardson was extending his sick leave. Chandler convinced Lincoln—who personally knew and liked Richardson—to intervene in army affairs on Richardson's behalf, and the president wrote to Stanton, suggesting that the Michigander be assigned to command this division. Nothing came of it, however. The Union defeat at Second Manassas threw Chandler's and Richardson's schemes askew, and any serious thoughts of reassigning the general were abandoned. Richardson rejoined the 1st Division. To McClellan's credit, despite Richardson's insubordination and political untrustworthiness, the army commander took no form of revenge that we know of. Instead, evidence indicates that he valued the return of "Fighting Dick" as an experienced combat commander, whom he needed to help defeat the Confederate invasion of Maryland.[43]

Under Richardson's leadership, the 1st Division grew into what might have been one of the two best divisions with the Army of the Potomac at Antietam, along with Sedgwick's division. It contained approximately 4,059 veteran infantrymen in three brigades. For a unit with such a fine combat record, the brigade's leadership was surprisingly average. Brigadier General John Caldwell, commanding the 1st Brigade, was an academic with no military experience before the war. He had commanded the brigade competently since the Battle of Seven Pines, when Oliver O. Howard, its original commander, was wounded. Brigadier General Thomas F. Meagher led the 2nd Brigade, famous in the army as the Irish Brigade. Meagher was an Irish revolutionary with no military training, but he possessed a charismatic personality that had rallied thousands of Irish to the Union cause and earned him a brigadier's star. The 3rd Brigade, which had originally been commanded by William French, was headed by its senior colonel, Colonel John R. Brooke in the 53rd Pennsylvania, a 24-year-old volunteer officer. He had been in charge of the brigade for only 10 days but would prove to be cool-headed and capable in the coming action.

During the time the 1st Division supported the Union batteries along Pry Ridge, a hopeful rumor began to circulate among the men "that we had been detailed as body guard to McClellan." Charlie Fuller, a 21-year-old sergeant in the 61st New York, remembered that "this comforting statement did not last long." Orders to pack up and move soon arrived, and by 9 a.m., the division was making its way down the well-trodden path to Antietam Creek. General Meagher, dressed "most gorgeously in a somewhat fancy uniform, with a gold shoulder-belt," was heard to remark that "we'd all have a brush soon." Meagher's Irish Brigade led the column, reaching the creek around 9:30 a.m. When they arrived, William H. Osborne in the 29th Massachusetts saw a flock of sheep quietly grazing on a hillside and thought they gave the place "an air of peace." For a moment, the war seemed distant and unreal—except for the sound, which assaulted the senses. "The roar of battle was awful," wrote Colonel Edward Cross, commanding the 5th New Hampshire.[44]

Richardson and his staff sat on their horses, midway in the water. As each regiment passed, the general called out to them in his "usual stern manner 'No straggling today, Colonel! Keep your men well up and in hand.'" There was no rush. The men in each regiment, when they reached the western bank of Antietam Creek, were permitted to remove their shoes, wring out their socks, and make any adjustments to equipment they thought necessary. Meagher, who was always mindful of his soldiers, ordered everyone to fill their canteens. Colonel Cross had the rolls called, to determine exactly how many officers and men he would carry into action. He then addressed his regiment: "Officers and soldiers, the enemy are in front and the Potomac river is in their rear. We must conquer this day or we are disgraced and ruined. I expect each one will do his duty like a soldier and a brave man. Let no man leave the ranks on any pretense. If I fall leave me until the battle is won. Stand firm and fire low. Shoulder arms! Forward march." And so it went until all three brigades had crossed the creek.[45]

At the moment when the 1st Division reached Antietam Creek, Sedgwick's 2nd Division was being routed from the West Woods, and French's 3rd Division was advancing from the East Woods toward the Sunken Lane. Nearly 30 minutes had been consumed by the men in each brigade removing their socks and shoes, fording the creek, putting their footgear back on, and answering roll call. Richardson's lack of haste in moving his division to the front suggests that he may have been waiting for orders from Sumner. But none arrived. This was perhaps just as well for the Union cause, since Sumner probably would have directed the 1st Division to the right, where it was not needed, rather than to the center. If Richardson sent anyone from his staff to locate Sumner and get orders, they did not find the 2nd Corps' commander, since, as of 10:15 a.m., Sumner had no idea where either Richardson or French were. What prompted Richardson to turn his division in the direction of the Sunken Lane is unknown. He was an aggressive officer and may simply have marched toward the closest sound of the guns. There is no evidence that French requested Richardson's help, or that McClellan directed where the 1st Division should go in. It is also possible that wounded Union soldiers from French's opening attacks began to come back and advised Richardson that the 3rd Division was heavily engaged to the southwest. Whatever prompted his choice, Richardson exercised his initiative and made a battlefield decision to reinforce French.[46]

Richardson marched his division southwest, parallel to Antietam Creek, with Meagher's brigade in front, followed by Brooke's and Caldwell's brigades. They passed over a high bluff overlooking the creek and descended into a ravine cut by a brook that empties into the Antietam, where Neikirk's and Kennedy's farms were located. Pushing on, they crossed another hill and went down into a second ravine, about 500 yards east of Roulette's farm. Richardson halted his brigades in this sheltered spot and ordered the men to drop all their equipment except cartridge boxes. "The sound of musketry was deafening," wrote a member of the Irish Brigade, and overshots from the fighting in their front, even at this distance, struck several men during the descent into the ravine. Using it as cover, the 1st Division deployed into line. They faced toward a large cornfield, which climbed up over a hill in its front. Meagher formed the right, with his right flank resting near the Roulette farm lane. Richardson ordered Caldwell up from the rear and directed the 1st Brigade to form on Meagher's left. Brooke was commanded to form in the rear, as a reserve. There was no artillery support, other than from the guns across Antietam Creek and from Tompkins's battery. The two batteries attached to Richardson's division had been moved across the creek during the night, and Richardson had no idea where they were. He would attack without them.[47]

There is no record of communication or coordination between Richardson and French, but evidence suggests that some transmission occurred. Wright's counterattack against Kimball's left flank took place while Richardson was deploying. It seems likely that someone from French's division asked for help to repulse this Confederate foray, since Richardson discarded his plan to attack with two brigades up front and one in reserve and instead ordered Meagher to advance before Caldwell had arrived on the Irishman's left.[48]

Meagher's brigade was one of the most famous in the army. It had fought with courage and distinction on the Virginia Peninsula and earned effusive praise in the press. A captain in the 88th New York appreciated the acclaim but thought it excessive. "Part of it is deserved and part of it is not," he wrote. "In all probability they have given the [brigade] more praise than the work we [have] done has deserved." Meagher was responsible for much of the attention. He had skill in cultivating attention from newspapers and was perhaps the most famous Irishman in America. As a young man, he had been one of the leaders of the 1848 Young Irelander Rebellion, which sought to shed British rule from Ireland. The rebellion failed, and Meagher was captured and sentenced to death, although his sentence was commuted to banishment to Tasmania. Meagher managed to escape in 1852 and made his way to New York City, where he achieved prominence as a gifted orator promoting Irish independence, and as the publisher of the weekly *Irish News*. He was a nationalist revolutionary, not a soldier, however. Initially he was ambivalent about the causes of the Civil War, but he volunteered after the attack on Fort Sumter and was commissioned a captain in the 69th New York State Militia. His performance at First Bull Run established that he possessed courage. This battle also hardened his support for the Federals' cause, and he threw himself into recruiting Irishmen for the Union army. Such was his fame in the Irish community that when he spoke at one New York City rally in August 1861, it drew an estimated audience of 60,000. His efforts produced 3,000 volunteers, who were formed into the 63rd, 69th, and 88th New York Infantry. A grateful President Lincoln rewarded Meagher with a commission as a brigadier general and command of the newly created Irish Brigade.[49]

Meagher did not get his general's star for military ability. Lincoln, a Republican, needed the support of the Irish immigrant community, which was firmly in the Democratic Party's camp, and Meagher's popularity could help with that. But bullets, shell fragments, and disease—the realities of war—eroded the initial war fervor during the summer of 1862. By the end of the Seven Days Battles, the Irish Brigade was so depleted in numbers that Meagher took leave to visit New York City, seeking new recruits. He still drew crowds. Nearly 5,000 people packed into the 7th Regiment Armory on 3rd Avenue to hear him speak on the night of July 25. But when Meagher called for 2,000 new recruits, a member of the audience shouted "Take the Black Republicans," reflecting their growing suspicion of the Union war effort and the direction Lincoln's administration appeared to be moving in regarding emancipation. Few New York City Irish were interested in risking their lives to free people who would simply become competitors for jobs. Although most attendees at the rally verbalized their support, it did not translate into enlistments. Nearly 2 months of recruiting by Meagher produced only 250 men.[50]

To reinforce Meagher's brigade, Richardson assigned the 29th Massachusetts to it on June 9. This upset its all-Irish composition. "It is doubtful if there was a regiment from Massachusetts with a larger percentage of Americans in its ranks," observed Ezra Carman. The Irish welcomed the reinforcement, however, and Yankees and Irishmen fought together effectively through the Seven Days Battles.[51]

Being spared from combat in the Second Manassas Campaign enabled the brigade to regain some of its sick and wounded members from the Peninsula Campaign, as well as to incorporate the new recruits Meagher had brought with him. Now the brigade's strength was a respectable 1,340 officers and men. The 69th New York formed on the right, closest to the Roulette farm lane. To its left were the 29th Massachusetts and the 63rd and 88th New York. Their line extended for slightly over 400 yards. When they reached one of Roulette's worm fences, located about 400 yards northeast of the Sunken Lane, they saw some of Wright's Confederates and their battle flags in the plowed field on the ridgeline in front, trading volleys with the 7th [West] Virginia and the 132nd Pennsylvania. Some of the Rebels turned their fire on the Irishmen and the New Englanders, and Meagher ordered his men to lie down while pioneers—the unit's construction engineers—cleared the fences. Nevertheless, several bullets found their target among the prone line—the 63rd New York had six men wounded here. The most accurate shooting apparently came from some of Wright's Confederates, who had found perches in a small clump of trees north of the Sunken Lane. Some of Meagher's men volunteered to trade their smoothbore muskets for rifles and were able to silence this fire. The fence was cleared in several minutes, and the brigade then arose and swept up the long slope toward the ridge where French's men were lying down, firing at the Rebels.[52]

There had been no time for reconnaissance, and French's officers offered no help regarding the enemy's position, or at least none that we know of. Even if they had, Meagher might have paid no attention to it. He was confident his Irish Brigade would sweep all before it. Yet his plan for still another frontal assault would only duplicate the failed and costly tactics of French's division. "My orders were, that, after the first and second volleys delivered in line of battle by the brigade, the brigade should charge with fixed bayonets on the enemy," reported Meagher. He counted on what he described as "the impetuosity and recklessness of Irish soldiers in a charge" and firmly believed "that before such a charge the rebel column would give way and be dispersed." The hasty retreat of Wright's men from the crest of the ridge before he began his advance might have reinforced Meagher's confidence that a pair of volleys, followed by a shock attack, would carry all before it. He would soon learn that his plan was a recipe for slaughter, no matter how brave his soldiers were.[53]

Captain Richard Stilwell, the Company K commander in the 132nd Pennsylvania, watched Meagher's forces approach. "Allow me to say that their behavior came up to my idea of the true soldier," he wrote. "They marched steadily to the brow of the hill with muskets shouldered," passing over the remnants of Morris's and Weber's brigades, who were gathered below the ridge crest, and the 132nd and 7th [West] Virginia, lying prone along the ridge. Some of these men were so inspired by the steadiness and courage of the Irish that they joined their advance. When Meagher's men came in sight of the Sunken Lane, the nature of the ground and the direction of their advance brought the left of the line closer to the enemy than the right. The 88th New York was separated from the gray-coats by only about 50 yards, while the 69th New York, on the right, was 80 yards away. Here, they "came face to face with the enemy." The Rebels were waiting, probably warned by Wright's men, who had seen the fresh Union assault approaching. An instant after Meagher's beautifully formed line appeared, the Confederate line loosed a devastating fire.[54]

The 63rd New York, on the left center, took the brunt of this initial volley. Although the brigade was on a ridge, the crest was not a straight line. Instead, it was broken by a regimental-sized depression, occupied by the 29th Massachusetts. "Our Regt has always been fortunate in Battle and owing to the ground our regt was in a little hollow under the crest of a Hill while the Regts on our Right & Left were on high ground fully exposed," wrote Major Charles Chipman in the 29th. Luck was with the Bay Staters, and not the Irish, this day. The first volley wiped out nearly the entire right wing of the 63rd New York. Major Richard Bentley called it "the most terrible volley of minie balls I could imagine." Every officer but one in these five New York companies was killed or wounded in the blast. Captain Michael O'Sullivan's Company F offered some measure of the destruction. Only 11 men were left standing in a company that probably numbered around 30 to 35 men. O'Sullivan was shot through the left thigh, the ball fortunately passing entirely through his leg without touching bone or an artery. His lieutenants did not fare as well: 1st Lieutenant Patrick W. Lyndon was shot through the heart and killed, and 2nd Lieutenant Henry McConnell received a bullet through his brain. Corporal John Dougherty was also among the dead. Two weeks earlier, he had reassured his mother that he wore some mementos she had sent—possibly rosary beads and a Celtic cross—"all the time," which "gave me a feeling of safety in the time of danger."[55]

Unsurprisingly, the color guard in the 63rd New York was hit hard. There were three sergeants and eight corporals in the guard (Dougherty may have been one of the corporals), and the 63rd was unique in that it carried three flags: national, state, and Irish. Sergeant William Daly, holding the Irish flag, was the hit in the first volley and went to the rear to have his wound dressed. These colors fell beside Corporal John Dillon in the guard, who dropped his musket and picked up the flag. Then the bearer of the national colors went down. Dillon picked it up, too, and handed the Irish flag to Martin Ratigan, a private in Dillon's Company F. Ratigan thought that flag was too heavy and asked Dillon for the national colors. Dillon replied that if he were shot, Ratigan could then have the flag. A bullet soon struck Dillon's canteen, emptying its contents. Then another bullet, or a piece of shell, hit the flagstaff and broke it. Dillon used the flag's tassel cords to splint the broken pieces together. Another round removed the eagle on the flagstaff. But Dillon's good fortune at being missed did not last. A bullet hit him in the right leg and knocked him out of the fight. Ratigan survived the slaughter, but every member of the color guard was either killed or wounded.[56]

Meagher's regiments absorbed the shock of the first volley, halted, raised their guns—the three Irish regiments were armed with Model 1842 Springfield muskets, a smoothbore firing buck-and-ball ammunition—and returned the fire. Unlike the men in French's division, who immediately dropped to the ground to get some cover, Meagher's troops stood upright, loading and firing. Because of this, they sustained frightful casualties. While most of them faced the terrifying work with remarkable courage, some did not. One of the latter was Colonel John Burke, commanding the hard-hit 63rd New York. Burke had a good record as a soldier. He had been the lieutenant colonel of the 37th New York when Meagher lured him to the 63rd as its colonel in January 1862. He was known as an excellent tactician and had been wounded in the Seven Days Battles. But at some point during the advance toward the Sunken Lane, Burke's nerve utterly failed him. He dismounted and took cover behind a hill. Major Charles Chipman in the 29th Massachusetts saw him cowering there. Chipman did not despise the colonel. Rather, he pitied him. "The best that you can make of war is it is a horrid thing however necessary it may be at times," Chipman wrote his wife. Burke would be court-martialed and dismissed from the service a month later.[57]

The murderous fire that slaughtered the right wing of the 63rd New York caused the rest of that regiment to crowd towards the right of the 88th New York, occupied by their Companies C and F. The colors of the 63rd moved with the throng and continued to draw a hail of fire. The 88th's two right companies suffered the consequences, with 16 killed and 23 wounded, 38% of the regiment's total loss and nearly half of the overall number who died. Company C was particularly hard hit, having 11 men killed, including its popular captain, James O'Connell Joyce.[58]

Meagher allowed his regiments to fire five or six volleys, hoping to beat down the opposition before ordering his charge. The 69th New York managed to struggle forward some 30 yards—coming to within 50 yards of the Sunken Lane—although losing their entire color guard in the process. Captain James E. McGee, the Company F commander, seized the fallen Irish banner and dashed in front of the regiment, in order to inspire the men. A bullet took off his hat. When he stooped down to pick it up, another bullet shattered the flagstaff and sent the captain and the colors sprawling. Somehow McGee survived, but it was evident that the assault had no hope of succeeding. The 69th was ordered to fall back to their previous position.[59]

For some reason Meagher does not appear to have ordered the 29th Massachusetts to join the charge. Located in the swale, they could neither see the Sunken Lane nor be seen by the Confederates. After shooting off several rounds, they had temporarily stopped firing. They soon resumed, however, directing it at Piper's cornfield, where it was believed Rebels might be lurking. Just how life-saving the swale was to the New Englanders is borne out by the tally of their losses and those of their neighbors. The 29th suffered 39 casualties in the battle, while the 63rd New York, on their left, lost 202 and the 69th New York, on their right, 196.[60] The 63rd New York was in no condition to charge. Men continued to fall at an alarming rate, including Lieutenant Colonel Henry Fowler and Major Richard C. Bentley, who were both wounded, leaving Joseph O'Neill as the only surviving captain. Around 50 men, out of the regiment's original strength of 341, remained in the fight.[61]

Lieutenant Colonel Patrick Kelly directed his 88th New York forward immediately after Meagher's aide-de-camp delivered the orders to charge. The regiment responded to Kelly's command by surging toward the Confederate position. Another colors-related tragedy ensued in this advance when Captain Patrick F. Clooney, commanding Company E, went down with a bullet through his knee. It was an excruciatingly painful wound, but Clooney ignored the calls of those around him to go to the rear and have his injury attended to. Instead, he seized the Irish colors—probably the bearer had been shot—and staggered forward with it. "The whirring of the bullets is music to his ears," wrote a correspondent from the brigade. Possibly it was. A handful of men find a certain strange joy in combat. But, more likely, it was pure adrenaline and fury that drove Clooney forward. He managed a few steps before one bullet entered his brain and another his heart, and the brave captain toppled over dead.[62]

The 88th New York made it some 25 or 30 yards forward when Kelly observed that the 63rd New York had not joined in the attack. He rode over and found Captain O'Neill in that regiment, who told Kelly that if there was anyone to command the 63rd, he would go forward, but since O'Neill did not know who was in command, he did not wish to give the order to advance. In the chaos, O'Neill did not yet realize that he *was* the commander. With no help forthcoming from the 63rd, Kelly was convinced that a charge had no hope, so he ordered his regiment to fall back close to their original position. Being mounted, he became a particular target and was soon hit twice: below the eye and in the jaw. These wounds may have been from buckshot, since neither injury was life threatening, and he remained in command.[63]

As the firefight continued, brigade command and control steadily deteriorated, as nearly all of Meagher's staff were wounded or injured by falls from their horses when they were shot. Meagher was conspicuous during the fight, riding along his line and encouraging his regiments. His courage under fire greatly impressed Sergeant Major William Quirk in the 63rd New York, who thought he had never seen nor read about a soldier who surpassed the general "for true heroism." Adjutant Fred Hitchcock in the 132nd Pennsylvania, who was also watching Meagher, thought differently, and concluded that Meagher "looked and acted like a drunken man." Colonel Edward Cross, commanding the 5th New Hampshire, also believed the Irishman was "drunk as usual." But there is no

reliable evidence that Meagher was intoxicated, although he did behave recklessly. Lieutenant Thomas Hamill in the 57th New York of Brooke's brigade concurred that the charges of drunkenness were not true. "I saw him several times
through that day and do believe the charges are false," he wrote, "but one thing
I must say, his brigade could have done more with less sacrifice of life, if there
was not a screw loose somewhere." The slaughter of his beloved brigade affected Meagher deeply. At one point he rode back to Caldwell's brigade, which
was halted to his left rear, and cried out to Colonel Francis Barlow, commanding the combined 61st and 64th New York, "Colonel, for God's sake, come and
help me!" Barlow replied that he was awaiting orders and would come to Meagher's aid as soon as he could. Meagher's exposure ultimately cost him. While
riding past the 63rd New York, his horse was shot, and the fall of horse and rider
knocked him nearly insensible, which explains Hitchcock's view of the general
floundering about "and swearing like a crazy man." Meagher was carried from
the field, leaving Burke, the senior colonel—who was hiding behind a hill—in
command. The brigade thus fought on without leadership.[64]

BRIGADIER GENERAL JOHN CALDWELL'S brigade consisted of approximately
1,300 men in five regiments. They had formed into line in the same ravine where
Meagher had deployed and followed some minutes behind the Irish Brigade.
When they cleared Roulette's cornfield, the brigade moved up through the
broad meadow south of the corn, toward the left and rear of Meagher. The
Confederate snipers who had fired at Meagher's brigade had been suppressed,
not run off by the Irish riflemen, and they returned to their work when
Caldwell emerged from the cornfield. Hidden in "a good sized tree heavily
leaved," they opened a deadly accurate long-range fire that sent a bullet
through the head of Captain Manton C. Angell in the 61st New York and killed
one or two more men in the same regiment before Colonel Francis C. Barlow
called for a half dozen volunteer marksman to deal with the problem. They
quickly deployed and opened fire. Soon, two Confederates dropped from the
tree, "whether dead or alive I do not know," wrote Sergeant Charlie Fuller in
the 61st. There was no more trouble from that sector.

Caldwell halted his brigade in the meadow and marked time for what Barlow thought was 15 minutes. Other than the handful of Confederate sharpshooters, no other enemy were seen, and the general contemplated advancing and
wheeling his brigade to the right to come in on the flank of the Rebel force opposing Meagher. The tactical concept was sound, but the precious time Caldwell
wasted in what even he described as "cautious" maneuvering was a problem.
While Meagher's men fought and bled on the ridgeline ahead of him, Caldwell
slowly reconnoitered to confirm that no Rebels were hidden over the crest of the
higher ground in his front. Barlow and his second in command, Lieutenant Colonel Nelson Miles, made the "air blue" with their curses over the brigade's

inaction. Meagher's plea for help only sharpened their fury. What Richardson was doing during this time, and why he allowed Caldwell's brigade to remain stationary while the Irish Brigade fought alone, is a good question. Nonetheless, the 1st Division's commander now intervened, sending a direct order to Caldwell to move at once and relieve Meagher's brigade. It was around 10:45 a.m.—at approximately the same time as the second attack at the Rohrback Bridge, a mile and a half to the south, was going forward—when Caldwell ordered his brigade to move by the right flank to bring it up in Meagher's rear.[65]

Caldwell's five regiments were formed with the Barlow's combined 61st and 64th New York on the right, with the 7th New York, the 81st Pennsylvania, and the 5th New Hampshire extending the line to the left. It was a tough, experienced unit, and it contained three fighting leaders who were as good as anyone in either army: Colonel Francis Barlow and Lieutenant Colonel Nelson Miles in the combined 61st and 64th New York, and Colonel Edward Cross, leading the 5th New Hampshire. Caldwell had commanded the brigade since June 4. He had been the principal of Washington Academy—essentially a high school—in East Machias, Maine, before the war. An Amherst College graduate, the 29-year-old Caldwell was a brilliant and likeable person. "I think I never saw a man of such remarkable memory," wrote Surgeon George Barr in the 64th New York. "He seems equally at home in the Bible Shakespeare Byron or almost any work of fiction remote or modern. As a Mathematical scholar he is said to be equaled by few in New England." Barr also added, "He is certainly the most companionable soldier I have met." Caldwell had no pre-war military experience, but his Republican Party connections helped secure him a commission as colonel of the 11th Maine Infantry. It seems likely that his intelligence and memory enabled him to learn military tactics and make the transition from educator to soldier successfully, just as they did for Joshua L. Chamberlain, another Maine preceptor turned warrior. When Oliver O. Howard was wounded at the Battle of Fair Oaks, Caldwell was tapped to replace him, a decision it is unlikely Edwin Sumner would have approved of, if he thought the New Englander was unqualified for the command. Yet Caldwell performed competently in the Seven Days Battles. If he lacked military experience, he was quick to know who his best officers were, use them effectively, and recognize their achievements.[66]

Francis Barlow moved his combined New York regiments at once after receiving his orders to relieve Meagher's brigade. He and Nelson Miles led from the front. "We followed the little Coln that wore the linen coat," wrote Ephraim Brown, an 18-year-old farm boy in the 64th New York. The 27-year-old Barlow, whose friends and family called him Frank, was small and frail looking, with a clean-shaven, boyish face. He graduated first in his class at Harvard and worked as an attorney in New York City before the war. Like Caldwell, Barlow had no previous military experience, but he was fearless. His sharp intellect and courage helped him quickly master tactics and develop into a superb soldier and leader. He was one of those rare individuals who was thrilled by the challenge and danger of combat. His wife Arabella, a remarkable woman in her own right, once declared to a friend "that he loves fighting for the sake of fighting, and is really bloodthirsty."[67]

Nelson Miles, who was only 23 years old, was cut from the same mold as his colonel. He had been a crockery store clerk at the beginning of the war. Although he did not have as much education as Barlow, he had long been fascinated with the military. Miles mastered drill and tactics rapidly and rose quickly in the ranks. The lieutenant colonel was remembered as a hard-bitten, tough, and even unlikeable soldier, all of which he was, but he did not lack a compassionate side. During the morning of September 17, while waiting for orders to join the fighting, a Confederate shell struck his favorite mount, Excelsior, sending both horse and rider down in a heap and killing the beast. Ephraim Brown witnessed the tragedy. He watched Miles jump up immediately and stand staring down at the dead animal for a few minutes, "with tears rolling off his red cheeks."[68]

Charlie Fuller, a 21-year-old sergeant in the 61st New York, remembered that they "went forward with a rush, Barlow in the lead, with his sword in the air." The speed of their movement separated them from the 7th New York, as well as from the rest of the brigade, which trailed some distance behind. The regiment came up in the rear of the 88th New York, which was still blazing away at the Confederates. With Barlow and Miles leading the men on foot, the combined regiments dashed forward through the ranks of the Irish. Rather than stop once they had cleared the 88th New York, Barlow led the men on until the two regiments were half the distance to the Sunken Lane—that is, only around 40 yards away from it. The Confederates were either pinned down from the fire of Meagher's brigade or had observed Barlow's approach and waited for them to get within point-blank range, as Ephraim Brown noted that they could not see any Rebels as they rushed forward. But about 40 yards from the lane, "up went their flags & whiz, whiz came their bulletts." Nelson Miles, writing to his brother, described how "the balls flew in storms and shells burst over my head and near enough to cover me with dust." The New Yorkers halted and poured fire back at their opponents. "We were so near to the enemy," wrote Sergeant Fuller, "that, when they showed their heads to fire, they were liable to be knocked over. It did not take them long to discover this, and for the most part, they hugged the hither bank of this sunken road." Nevertheless, the Confederates inflicted significant damage. Ephraim Brown's Company C offered an example. As they came up in front of the enemy, Ephraim Green, on Brown's right in the rear rank, tapped him on the shoulder and said, "If we die let us die at our post." The two men stepped out ahead of the front rank, and as they did so, Green called out, "Eph, See this flag to our right—lets take her down." An instant later a bullet struck Green in the heart. Brown heard an "Oh" and saw Green falling to the ground. Brown caught him and lowered him down, but the "<u>Brave Soldier</u> heard the battle no more." Then Norman Foster was shot through the head—"he never kicked"—and another bullet went through the leg of the company commander, Captain Warren Weight. One more killed William Fuller instantly. "We had a hard fight," Brown noted.[69]

Somehow neither Barlow nor Miles were shot, and, being in front of their men, they observed that the Confederate right flank was vulnerable. After giving and receiving two or three rounds, taking about 1 or 2 minutes, Barlow shouted for his regiments to about face double-quick march. Ephraim Brown thought they executed the movement in "as good order as tho on Drill." Barlow moved his men rapidly downslope and then, out of sight of the Rebels, marched them east until he believed they had cleared the enemy's flank. He now ordered "Charge Bayonets," and the combined regiments fronted and swept back into view of the Confederates. They executed a right wheel as they advanced, until they were perpendicular to the Sunken Lane and could enfilade the enemy line. By this point the other regiments of the brigade were coming up on Barlow's left and opening fire, and part of the Irish Brigade, to Barlow's right, was still loosing volleys at the Rebels. This combination of bullets and maneuvers finally unhinged the Confederate line.[70]

The remnants of Wright's brigade were the first to leave. Every field officer in the brigade, except Colonel Gibson, was either dead or wounded, and only about 200 men remained. Their ammunition was nearly out. Gibson had sent to the rear for a resupply, but none had been received—or, more probably, no one attempting to bring ammunition up had survived the journey. Barlow's rapid maneuver to gain Gibson's flank surprised the Georgians. They believed they had repulsed yet another Federal onslaught, only to have what appeared to be still one more enemy line moving toward their exposed right flank. Gibson later offered the stock excuse that the supports on his right and left both withdrew, leaving him with no option other than to retreat, but neither event was true. There were no Confederate troops on his right, and the 30th North Carolina did not go back before Gibson did. Another member of the brigade proudly claimed that it "sullenly moved off" and boasted that the 3rd Georgia, with only 40 of its 108 men remaining, gathered around their battle flag "and, coming to the about face, moved slowly off, not a man evincing any trepidation." This is unlikely. All contemporary evidence from both Union and other Confederate sources indicates the retreat was a stampede to escape the deadly crossfire that now cut through their line. In the opinion of Captain Joshua S. Pittenger, the commander of Company G, 64th New York, when his regiment gained their flank, the Rebels "ran and scattered like sheep."[71]

Gibson's retreat triggered a general and rapid exodus to the rear by the soldiers of Posey's, Pryor's, and Cumming's brigades, as well as the 30th and 4th North Carolina of G. B. Anderson's brigade. All of R. H. Anderson's brigades had suffered terrible casualties. In Cumming's unit, all the regimental commander except one, a captain, were dead or wounded. The same situation existed in Pryor's brigade, and Posey's had lost half of its regimental commanders. Survivors from the different brigades related stories of dreadful carnage in their ranks. Bailey G. McClelen in the 10th Alabama recorded that in his company, 7 were killed and 5 wounded. Since the entire regiment only carried about 100 men into action, it probably meant that McClelen's company was nearly wiped out. In Lieutenant William Fagan's Company K of the 8th Alabama, 18 out of 28 were killed or wounded. J. J. Wilson's Company C of the 16th Mississippi lost 20 of their 37 men. So it went for nearly every Confederate regiment in the Sunken Lane conflict. As Wilson wrote afterward, "I thought the battle at Richmond was a bloody battle, but that was not a circumstance compared to the battle in Maryland."[72]

When the retreat began, Posey's and Pryor's officers did not attempt to separate their men from G. B. Anderson's, because it was impossible. Benjamin B. Ross in the 4th North Carolina, lying wounded in the Sunken Lane with one of Pryor's or Posey's men stretched out, dead, across him, heard one of those brigades' officers shout, "Men, fall back," which led to a general rush out of the lane into Piper's cornfield. Colonel Risden Bennett, commanding the 14th North Carolina, described it as a "stampede," stating that the troops "broke beyond the power of rallying." Lieutenant James Shinn in the 4th North Carolina angrily blamed Wright "& some other officer," who "spoilt all, caused confusion & disorder yesterday, some by their cowardice and others by their enthusiasm." Like Gibson, Major William Sillers, commanding the 30th North Carolina, claimed that all but his regiment fell back before he ordered a retreat. This was another fantasy. The 30th was carried away with everyone else. Shinn confessed that in his regiment, even officers participated in the flight, writing how some, "I am sorry & ashamed to say left the field unhurt." The lieutenant also observed how "many men took this as a chance (from all Regt's) to leave the field entirely." It was understandable that some of the participants would single out individual officers like Wright when seeking a cause for the collapse, but the reasons for it were myriad, not the result of any one officer's decisions.[73]

Barlow's men took cruel advantage of their position on the Confederates' flank, pouring fire into the retreating men and those still trapped in the Sunken Lane. "They could do us little harm, and we were shooting them like sheep in a pen," recalled Sergeant Fuller. "If a bullet missed the mark at the first it was liable to strike the further bank, and angle back, and take them secondarily, so to speak." As the right of Barlow's line advanced, it entered the lane, which was literally carpeted with the dead and wounded. An injured Confederate color bearer, probably in Wright's brigade, sat in the lane, shot through both legs yet still firmly gripping the flag, with the staff planted between his legs. Ephraim Brown went for the colors, but "the dead & wounded [were] so thick under my f[ee]t I had a poor chance to moove my self." He seized the staff with his right hand, having shifted his rifle to his left hand. Brown told the Confederate to let go "or I'll kill you," to which the latter replied, "I'll never let go you Yankee S——n of a Bitch." By this point, Joseph Riley, a farm laborer from Big Flats, New York (near Elmira), whom Brown derided as something of a company stool pigeon, came up beside the private, switched the direction of the Austrian rifle in his hands to use it as a club, and swung it down violently, smashing the wounded man's skull. Brown then took the flag. Nearby, Lieutenant Theodore W. Greig in Company C survived a bullet wound through the neck and seized the colors of the 44th Alabama. Around Brown and Greig, the rest of the combined Union regiments were still firing at the nearly helpless Confederates. White handkerchiefs began to appear. Officers began shouting "Cease firing," but, wrote Sergeant Fuller, "the men were slow of hearing, and it was necessary for the officers to get in front of the men and throw up their guns." The cruelty of the incident with Brown, Riley, and the Confederate color bearer, as well as Fuller's testimony, does not square with a romantic view of the Civil War, with both sides behaving chivalrously toward helpless or injured foes. The savage killing frenzy that came over soldiers, whether Union or Confederate, who had gained an advantage over a foe who, moments before, had been slaughtering your comrades, could not be turned off like a light switch.[74]

At nearly the same time as the collapse of the Confederates' right flank in the Sunken Lane, the Confederates' left came apart. During the attacks of French's 3rd Division and then Meagher's brigade, the exposed right wing of the 6th Alabama was subjected to a crossfire that, according to one member of the regiment, "nothing living could stand." In the six companies on the regiment's right, only about 10 men remained unhurt. Casualties filled the road. "One could have walked the length of six companies on their bodies," wrote a survivor. Colonel John B. Gordon had been shot four times but, in a remarkable feat of courage and stamina, remained on the field. When he thought he saw wavering on his regiment's right and made his way over to steady the men, a fifth bullet struck him in the face and passed through his neck, barely missing the jugular vein. When he recovered his senses, Gordon somehow managed to crawl 100 yards to the rear, where an officer from his regiment discovered the colonel "covered with blood." With the help of others, he carried Gordon to the rear. Command then fell to Lieutenant Colonel James N. Lightfoot. Lightfoot sought out Rodes, explaining to him the critical condition of the 6th Alabama's right wing. Rodes ordered him to throw the wing back, pulling the survivors out of the lane and resetting their line to face the flanking fire. Lightfoot seemed to be clear about what was said, but amid the roar of battle and the excitement, the lieutenant colonel was rattled and either misunderstood or did not comprehend what Rodes had ordered. When Lightfoot reached his regiment, he shouted, "Sixth Alabama, about face; forward march." Major Edwin L. Hobson, commanding the 5th Alabama on Lightfoot's left, asked if the order applied to the rest of the brigade, to which Lightfoot fatally replied, "Yes." In an instant, Rodes's entire brigade, which up to this point had fought tenaciously, left the Sunken Lane and rushed toward the rear.[75]

Rodes was unable to check the flight, because shortly after he gave Lightfoot permission to pull his right wing out of the Sunken Lane, his aide-de-camp, Lieutenant John S. Birney, was hit just under the eye by a bullet or a piece of shell and fell to the ground. Rodes helped raise the young man, and when Birney determined that he could move under his own power, the general directed him toward Piper's barn to receive medical attention. Rodes followed Birney a short distance, watched him until he reached the barn and found someone who would help him, and then turned to go back to his brigade. As he did so, a piece of shell struck him hard on the thigh. Examining the wound, he found that, although painful, it was not serious. When he began walking again, to his astonishment he saw his entire command, "without visible cause to me, retreating in confusion." Rodes hurried—as fast as his injured thigh would allow—to intercept the retreating troops at the Hagerstown Pike. But it was no use. The men were beyond rallying. With the help of Major Hobson at the pike, Rodes rallied "not more than 40" men out of the entire brigade. His brigade, he wrote with unusual honesty in an after-action report, "had completely disappeared from this portion of the field."[76]

What had happened? How did a fine, well-disciplined brigade go from stubborn resistance to complete collapse in a moment? We cannot know precisely, but some evidence is available. It was not due to casualties, as it was with R. H. Anderson's brigades. The only regiment that suffered serious losses was the 6th Alabama, and they totaled 36% of its strength, which, for Antietam, was significant, but not as high as those for many other regiments in the Sunken Lane battle. The 3rd Alabama counted only 20 casualties; the 5th Alabama, 19; and the 12th Alabama, 13. The brigade's total losses were 25%. In contrast, Wright's were 62%, and Cumming's, 54%. When the Confederate regiments left the Sunken Lane, there was no cover to protect them from the fire of Tompkins's battery, the shells coming in from across Antietam Creek, or the small-arms fire from the 14th Indiana, until they reached the Hagerstown Pike. As veteran soldiers, they understood that their survival hinged on getting out of the line of fire as quickly as possible. The disintegration of the brigade may have been due to the loss of key leaders at the Battle of South Mountain, as well as to the strain of being under heavy fire for nearly 2 hours. Lieutenant Tom Taylor in the 6th Alabama wrote to his father that the retreat was so perilous, "nothing but the mercy of God saved me." Sometimes, however, panics are unexplainable. Whatever was the case, the collapse of Rodes's brigade left the 2nd and 14th North Carolina alone and exposed to destruction.[77]

Colonel Risden Bennett quickly assessed the position of these two remaining regiments and decided it was hopeless. When the right of the line disintegrated and retreated, the 29th Massachusetts of Meagher's brigade, as well as elements of the 132nd Pennsylvania, the 108th New York, the 7th [West] Virginia, and members in the New York regiments of the Irish Brigade, flowed toward the lane. Bennett spotted Barlow's 61st and 64th New York coming down on his right and rear. He gave the only command that could save the two regiments: retreat by the right oblique. In other words, the men would face to the rear and then fall back toward the Hagerstown Pike at a 45-degree angle. The retreat, reported Bennett, was attended with a "frightful loss" from the Federals' fire that raked their line. Numerous men chose to surrender rather than face what seemed like a slim chance of escape. The casualties in the two Confederate regiments bear out Bennett's testimony of frightful losses. His 14th North Carolina incurred casualties of 52%, including 52 killed, and the 2nd North Carolina lost 44%. Regimental leadership was decimated. Bennett escaped, but his lieutenant colonel, William A. Johnson, was wounded. In the 2nd, only three officers emerged unscathed.[78]

As the last two defenders of the Sunken Lane fled, Barlow's 61st and 64th New York continued their push west along the lane, scooping up nearly 300 prisoners and another flag besides the two they had already captured. The lane soon swarmed with Union soldiers. The 8th Ohio and the 14th Indiana joined in the general advance to the position that had defied all their efforts to carry it for the last hour and a half. The carnage they encountered in the lane shocked everyone. "Em if U could have seen the dead Rebels lay in the road there U would thought they wer alive because it did not seam as if we could have killed as many," wrote Ephraim Brown to his uncle. Sergeant Fuller noted, "As we found them in some cases, they were two and three deep. Perhaps a wounded man at the bottom, and a corpse or two piled over him." Several sought souvenirs. The 8th Ohio advanced to the part of the lane defended by the 2nd North Carolina, and some of their men found the mortally wounded Colonel Tew propped up against the bank of the lane, unconscious and with blood streaming down his face, but with his sword held by both hands across his knees. When one of the soldiers in the 8th attempted to take the sword, Tew drew it toward his body, then fell forward dead.[79]

The savagery that had characterized the action moments earlier now subsided, and the Federals sought to give aid to the enemy. "We at once took hold and straightened out matters the best we could," recalled Fuller, "and made our foes as comfortable as the means at hand afforded—that is, we laid them so that they were only one deep, and we gave them drink from our canteens." Corporal Charles Hale in the 5th New Hampshire found one pugnacious Confederate, probably from Wright's brigade, lying where his regiment had crossed the lane. The soldier lunged at Hale with a bayonet as the latter passed by. Hale noticed the Rebel was badly wounded and left him alone. The two men would encounter one another again soon (see chapter 12).[80]

Confederate artillery started shelling the Sunken Lane soon after it fell, particularly the eastern part, where Wright's brigade had been. By this time, Maurin's Donaldsonville (Louisiana) Battery, Carter's King William (Virginia) Battery, and Hardaway's (Alabama) Battery, which counted seven rifled pieces in total, were on Reel Ridge and had a good line of fire to the Sunken Lane. Caldwell's brigade, which was more exposed on the higher eastern end of the lane, took the brunt of the barrage. Thomas Livermore, a 19-year-old 2nd lieutenant in the 5th New Hampshire, described the bombardment as "a most terrible fire of artillery." One shell burst inside the color company, wounding eight men and tearing the state colors in two. Fragments wounded Colonel Edward Cross in several places. One struck his left cheek, another hit him over the right eye, one more knocked his hat off, and a fourth fragment impacted his right arm. None of these wounds were serious, and Cross, whose toughness was legendary, shrugged them off and kept on. His regiment, he observed with pride, endured the artillery fire "without faltering in the least" and pushed into Piper's cornfield. Others did not. Caldwell reported that the 7th New York "wavered for a few minutes" under fire.[81]

Richardson joined the advance of Caldwell's regiments as they entered the corn. He appeared on foot, with drawn sword. Lieutenant Livermore in the 5th New Hampshire heard him before he saw him. Richardson shouted, "Where's General ——?" Livermore left the identity of the general blank, but we know it was Caldwell. The lieutenant looked over his shoulder and saw Richardson, his swarthy face "black as a thunder cloud." Some of the 5th shouted back, "Behind a haystack!" to which Richardson thundered, "God damn the field officers." When Cross saw Richardson, he halted the regiment and called for three cheers for the general, which were given, along with three more for Cross. The colonel told Richardson that Caldwell was "in the rear." Richardson shouted in a loud voice, "Gen Caldwell, come up here, sir & take command of your Brigade." Whether this was because he could see Caldwell, or uttered it out of frustration, is unknown. Caldwell's behavior is a curiosity of the engagement. Less than a year later, at Gettysburg, he would lead the 1st Division with considerable skill and bravery. But there is significant evidence that he performed poorly at the Battle of Antietam. Cross was furious with Caldwell, writing that "his conduct was very singular." In another letter, Cross stated, "Gen Caldwell did not show himself either brave or skillfull; & he lost the confidence of his soldiers." Cross was a virulent Nativist and Democrat, as well as a man with an unforgiving nature, and it might be that he simply had it in for Caldwell, who was a Republican. But Surgeon George Barr in the 64th New York, who greatly liked Caldwell, had seen the general "at least 30 rods [150 yards] in rear of me sheltered from the line [?] by a ledge of rocks from that point I knew he could not observe his Brigade."[82]

The combination of Caldwell's lack of control, the Confederate artillery fire, and the height of Piper's corn caused confusion in the 1st Brigade. Barlow's after-action report on Caldwell's management was damning: "Our troops were joined together without much order—several regiments in front of others, and none in my neighborhood having very favorable opportunities to use their fire." Francis Walker, author of the *History of the Second Army Corps*, wrote that "the colonels of the regiments of Caldwell's Brigade fought the battle pretty nearly at their own discretion in the absence of direction from the brigade commander, so that the regiments were not in continuous line much of the time." This led to a disjointed troop movement that lacked the vigor the moment called for and gave the Confederates an opportunity to rally some of their men. Richardson, meanwhile, anxious to sustain the momentum of his division's attack, ordered Brooke's 3rd Brigade to reinforce Caldwell and sent aides-de-camp flying to find artillery to engage the Confederate guns that were pounding Caldwell's line. The battle for the Confederates' center was far from over.[83]

12

The Confederate Center Imperiled

"It was beautiful to see how those devils piled up"

Affairs looked very critical," admitted D. H. Hill, referring to the situation at the Confederates' center after the collapse of the Sunken Lane line. Hill's management of his division that day was conspicuous for its lack of direction: his brigades had all essentially fought on their own hook. But moments that called for great personal courage brought out the best in Hill and he rose to the crisis. Discovering the two remaining guns of Boyce's battery in their hiding place in the lower part of Piper's cornfield, he ordered them to engage Caldwell's regiments, who were advancing through the northeastern part of the corn. Boyce moved his pieces into the pasture west of Piper's orchard and blasted the Federals with canister. Nearby, in the orchard, a section of Captain Merritt B. Miller's 3rd Company of the Washington (Louisiana) Artillery, was also hurling canister at the enemy. While these guns were helping to slow down the Union advance, Hill worked energetically with surviving officers of Wright's, Cumming's, Posey's, Pryor's, and G. B. Anderson's brigades to rally their infantry. It was a formidable challenge, for all the brigades were badly dispersed and shaken. Elias Davis, carrying the colors of the 10th Alabama, wrote, "I could not see a man of our regt.," remarking that "our brigade was scattered to the four winds on that memorable day." Hill and the others paid no attention to regimental or brigade integrity. They needed bodies to stave off disaster. Hill gathered up about 200 men "who said they were willing to advance to the attack if I would lead them." Majors Hilary Herbert and Jere Williams rallied about 100 men. Believing for some peculiar reason "that the Yankees were so demoralized that a single regiment of fresh men could drive the whole of them in our front across the Antietam," Hill led his men forward in a counterattack, as did Herbert and Williams. They would discover the bluecoats were far from demoralized.[1]

While Hill, Herbert. and Williams led their bands of stragglers forward, Longstreet sought to knock the Federals off balance by hitting their flank with whatever force he could scrape together. There were few units left who retained their organization and combat effectiveness. Cobb's small brigade of 250 was one. When Rodes's brigade retreated from the Sunken Lane—which also carried

away the small element of McRae's and Colquitt's brigades on their left—
Lieutenant Colonel Sanders changed front to the rear to protect his flank. This
swung the brigade into the Hagerstown Pike, with the left of the unit resting
on the entrance to the Sunken Lane. From this position, Sanders, whether on
his own initiative or under orders, moved the brigade about 100 yards north
along the pike, so its right flank rested near the entrance to the Sunken Lane.
About 200 yards in Saunders's rear, the 3rd Arkansas and the 27th North Carolina of Manning's brigade in Walker's division were concealed in Reel's big cornfield south of the West Woods. They were skirmishing with Greene's division,
which, by this time, was in the woods around the Dunker Church. By Sharpsburg
standards for the Army of Northern Virginia, the two regiments were quite strong,
counting 675 officers and men. Longstreet sent orders to Lieutenant Colonel Sanders; to Colonel John R. Cooke, the 27th's commander, as well as acting commander of both his regiment and the 3rd Arkansas; and to General Robert Ransom, whose brigade occupied the West Woods. All of them were to attack the
right flank of the Union forces assaulting the Sunken Lane. There was no attempt to coordinate these counterattacks. It was a forlorn-hope assault, so much
so that McLaws intervened in the case of Ransom and "forbade the movement"
until he could communicate with Longstreet. On his part, the wing commander
surely knew he might be sacrificing these commands, but desperation drove the
decision. He needed to knock the enemy off balance and weaken the momentum
of Richardson's advance into the ruptured Confederate center. Longstreet also
sent for Colonel George T. Anderson's brigade, to help bolster the shaky line that
officers like Rodes were attempting to rally along the Hagerstown Pike.[2]

The war had a distinctly personal aspect for Colonel John R. Cooke. His
father was General Philip St. George Cooke, an officer of renown in the pre–
Civil War Regular Army for his service on the frontier and in Kansas. One of General Cooke's daughters married James E. B. Stuart. Another wed a man who became a Confederate surgeon. A third. however, espoused Jacob Sharpe, who
became a Union general. The war ripped the family apart. Although a Virginian
by birth, the senior Cooke remained loyal to the Union. Stuart, of course, went
on to become a renowned Confederate cavalry commander who humiliated his
father-in-law in the fighting on the Virginia Peninsula. Stuart famously declared
of Philip Cooke's decision to remain with the Union, "He will regret it only once,
and that will be continually." John Cooke had trained at Harvard as an engineer,
but in 1855 he followed his father into the Regular Army, being commissioned as a
2nd lieutenant in the 8th U.S. Infantry. In what was certainly a tumultuous and
tragic decision within the family, he resigned when the Civil War began and followed his dashing brother-in-law into the Confederate service.[3]

John Cooke—who was 27 when the war began—filled various positions in
the Rebel army until the spring of 1862, when the 27th North Carolina elected
him as their colonel. It proved to be a wise decision. Cooke was demanding but

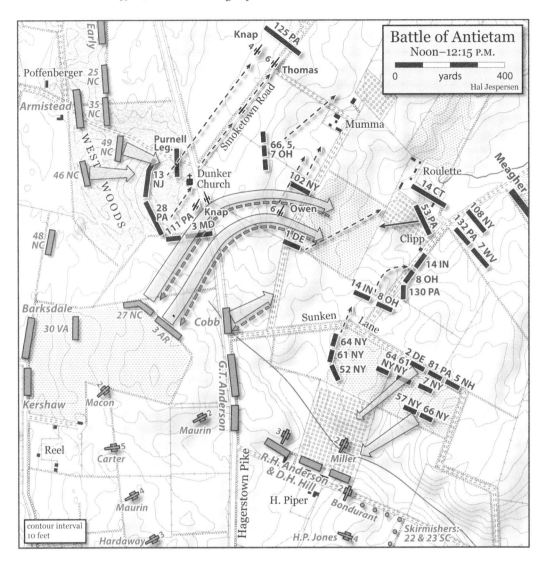

fair, which earned the respect of his men. On the battlefield, he evinced both courage and tactical skill. It will be recalled (see chapter 9) that when Vannoy Manning's brigade reached the field during the counterattack against Sedgwick, Cooke, with his 27th North Carolina plus the 3rd Arkansas, under Captain John W. Reedy, had been placed in Reel's cornfield, in order to cover the gap between the Rebel forces in the area of the West Woods and the Confederates' center. Cooke posted his men along the fence at the northern edge of the corn, with part of his regiment facing north, and the rest of the 27th and the 3rd Arkansas facing northeast, toward the West Woods. At around 10:30 a.m., when Greene's division was in the portion of the woods around the Dunker Church, Cooke's regiments had skirmished with the 3rd Maryland, the 111th Pennsylvania, and part of the 28th Pennsylvania, who occupied the southern front of the woods. The two Confederate regiments suffered some losses in the exchange, and Cooke ordered his men, except for a handful of sharpshooters, to fall back about 20 paces into the corn, both to get concealment and to hopefully lure the Federals out into the open. Cooke remained near the fence, standing behind a lone tree, where he could observe the enemy's activity. Yankee riflemen, trying to pick him off, riddled the tree with bullets but failed to hit their target.[4]

Sometime near noon, Cooke observed a Union artillery unit joining Greene. It was Lieutenant James D. McGill's section of Knap's Battery E, Pennsylvania Light Artillery, ordered—over the lieutenant's objections—by Lieutenant Colonel Hector Tyndale to move into the woods west of the Dunker Church. (McGill's story will be told in more detail in chapter 13.) Cooke watched the two guns being driven down the Hagerstown Pike for about 100 yards, going south of the church, to find a gap in the pike's fencing that would allow access for the artillery pieces. Leaving one gun in the road, the lieutenant took the other to the edge of the woods, where he waited for orders indicating what he was supposed to fire at. Watching from 200 yards away, Cooke ordered his regiment's four left companies to quietly move up to the fence. He instructed them to wait until he gave the signal and then fire at the horses that were pulling the Union guns. Just when McGill told the crew to unlimber, Cooke ordered his men to fire. At nearly the same instant, a Confederate shell cut the limb off a tree in the West Woods, sending it crashing down on the limber's horses. The volley by nearly 120 Rebel riflemen hit two horses, killed one cannoneer, and wounded another. This was not exactly devastating marksmanship, but, combined with the heavy branch falling on the limber's horses, it caused chaos. Adding to the mayhem on the Union line, at this very moment, Ransom's brigade mounted an assault on the right flank of Greene's line, causing the 2nd Division's position to rapidly unravel. By this time, Cooke had probably received his orders from Longstreet. Sensing the unsteadiness in the Union ranks, Cooke seized his opportunity and ordered both regiments to climb over the fence and charge. They raised a piercing yell—Cooke said that "such a yell he never heard before"—then scrambled over the fence and made haste toward the enemy.[5]

With over 600 screaming Confederate infantrymen bearing down on them, McGill's artillerymen abandoned the one gun in the woods and beat a hasty retreat with the other piece. Greene's infantry fled onto the Dunker Church plateau. Cooke ordered his two regiments to change direction to the right and pursue the fleeing enemy. McGill's gun was left unclaimed while Cooke and his men chased bigger game. Firing and loading as they moved, the Tarheels and Razorbacks clambered over the Hagerstown Pike's fences and charged out on the open ground east of the church, strewn with the casualties of Kershaw's and Manning's earlier failed counterattacks.[6]

Only minutes before Cooke's two regiments began their charge, Captain Tomkins's Battery A, 1st Rhode Island Artillery, was relieved by Captain

Charles D. Owen's Battery G, 1st Rhode Island Artillery. In over 2 hours of fighting, Tompkins's gunners fired 83 rounds of canister, 68 rounds of solid shot, 427 rounds of shell, and 454 rounds of case shot, an average of 172 rounds per gun. Probably no Union or Confederate battery at the Battle of Antietam inflicted as much damage as the Rhode Islanders. By 11:30 a.m. their ammunition chests were nearly empty, and Tompkins sent to Sumner for orders. Sumner, via his artillery chief, Major F. N. Clarke, ordered Owen's gunners to relieve Battery A. Owen's six 3-inch rifles were parked just north of Mumma's orchard, but it took nearly a half hour for the communications to travel between the different parties, and Battery G did not arrive to relieve Tompkins until almost noon. The moment they arrived, Owens's guns came under fire, probably from Hardaway's or Maurin's battery on Reel Ridge, about a mile away. Owen's crews swung into action quickly and replied with fused shell. After what Owen thought was nearly 20 minutes of bombardments—but probably not nearly that long—the Confederates' gunfire ceased. In the lull, Owen decided to move his artillery forward to the brow of the ridge in his front, where he would have a better field of fire at the Rebel infantry he saw milling around the Hagerstown Pike and Piper's farm. Before he could order the movement, he heard "a noise" to his right, beyond the Dunker Church plateau. Suddenly, Union infantry appeared, fleeing across the plateau from the West Woods, hotly pursued by the 27th North Carolina and the 3rd Arkansas. Turning to engage this threat was out of the question. Owen's support, the understrength 102nd New York, departed with the rest of Greene's retreating infantry. The captain ordered his guns to limber and fall back. They managed to make good their escape, but it was a close call. "When the last caisson left the ground the enemy were close upon us," Owen reported.[7]

The remnants of the 14th Connecticut who remained with its colors were in Mumma's cornfield, on Owen's left, but they withdrew back to Roulette's farmyard shortly before Owen pulled out in the face of Cooke's counterattack. No one seems to know who ordered this movement, for, as the regimental chaplain observed, "the companies seem not to have retired together." Part of the problem was that the regimental colors "had been suppressed so that they might not attract the attention of the enemy so much," which made it difficult for those separated from the regiment to find it. The farmyard was a place of confusion and carnage. Hundreds of casualties filled all Roulette's buildings and covered the ground between them. "Fragments of other regiments" from the 3rd Division were milling about, with General French and his staff struggling to reorganize them. Suddenly Cooke's yelling North Carolinians and Arkansans came trotting over the Dunker Church plateau toward Mumma's cornfield, on a straight line toward the farm. Two aggressive soldiers in the 14th, who had made their way to the Mumma farm lane to get a better shot at the Rebels around the Sunken Lane, "were so absorbed in their business" that they were not aware of Cooke's approach until the Confederates were only yards away. "Then there was a sprinting match rarely surpassed," noted the 14th's amused chaplain. Everyone could chuckle about it later, because the two lads escaped with their lives. But no one on Roulette's property was laughing as the Rebels came nearer, for it appeared as though there was nothing to stop them from reaching the farm and the rear of the Union position at the Sunken Lane.[8]

As Cooke's two regiments surged across the Dunker Church plateau, D. H. Hill personally ordered Lieutenant Colonel Sanders to join with Cobb's brigade in the assault. Although feeling "very unwell," Sanders had kept to the field until this point, but he thought this new effort was more than he was capable of, so he turned control over to Lieutenant Colonel William McRae, commanding the 15th North Carolina. Since their arrival on the field, the brigade had shed a third of its strength to enemy fire or shirkers, so McRae only had about 250 men left. Although he claimed the brigade was "eager to meet the foe" and went forward "eagerly and unfalteringly," this rings hollow. The men were exhausted and demoralized, yet they obeyed McRae's orders to attack. They sprinted over the hill in their front and ran nearly 200 yards to the fences along the Mumma farm lane, where they halted and opened fire on an accumulating number of Federals in their front. A gap of at least 200 yards separated McRae's left from the right of the 3rd Arkansas in Mumma's cornfield. Nevertheless, McRae's advance raised the number of Confederates threatening French's and Richardson's flank to nearly 1,000 men.[9]

When Cooke's regiments reached the Dunker Church plateau, the 27th North Carolina came under fire from Lieutenant Evan Thomas's Battery A, 4th U. S. Artillery, and four guns of Captain Joseph Knap's Battery E, Pennsylvania Light, which were both in position about 100 yards southwest of the southwestern corner of the East Woods. The guns were firing spherical case, and, when that failed to check the charging enemy, were switched to canister. Lieutenant James A. Graham, a bright, observant 21-year-old student commanding Company G, near the left of the Confederate regiment, wrote that the artillery fire caused "sad havoc with us," but Cooke directed the two regiments away from the guns, toward Mumma's cornfield and French's and Richardson's rear. Graham thought Cooke did this because the Union guns would be dealt with "by the troops upon our left." This was Ransom's brigade, who had driven Greene's division from the East Woods. But the guns were not Cooke's target. The rear of the enemy attacking the Sunken Lane was his goal, and he ignored the flanking fire to drive his attack home. Lieutenant Thomas breathed a sigh of relief when the Rebels swung away from his guns. "I would undoubtedly have lost my battery," he believed, had not elements of the 6th Corps arrived to support him.[10]

As the two Confederate regiments burst across the plateau, Colonel Cooke noticed his regiment's color bearer, William H. Campbell, bounding ahead of the 27th North Carolina's line. Cooke ordered him to stop two or three times, because Campbell was getting too far in front of the rest of the regiment. As

Captain Joseph C. Webb wrote, "at last Campbell told him [Cooke] he would keep stopping him till he would let that Arkansas fellow get ahead of him." Cooke left Campbell alone after that, and the private raced forward to keep abreast of the 3rd Arkansas's color bearer. The two regiments, led by their sprinting color bearers, passed over the plateau and descended toward Mumma's cornfield. Lieutenant Graham spotted what he estimated to be 200 or 300 Yankees huddled around the strawstacks at Mumma's farm. They were elements of French's or Greene's division, some of whom were out of ammunition, and they made no attempt at resistance as the Rebels came near. Some attached white rags or handkerchiefs to their ramrods or muskets and waved them at the approaching enemy. Graham's men and another company peeled off from the 27th and swept over to the group, ordering them to drop their weapons and go to the rear. In the haste of the Confederates' advance, no one remained to escort the prisoners back, so the two companies from the 27th North Carolina left the disarmed Yankees behind and hurried on to catch up with their regiment.[11]

In his account of the action for the 27th North Carolina's history, Lieutenant Graham left the impression that their charge was something of a cakewalk. "We pushed on, and soon wheeling to the right drove their line, giving them an enfilade fire, and succeeded in breaking six regiments, which fled in confusion," he wrote. Technically, there was an element of truth to this statement. Five Union regiments of Greene's 2nd Division in the East Woods—six, if we add the 102nd New York—did break and flee in confusion, but Greene's men did so because of a flank attack by Ransom's brigade. Cooke's regiments just helped hurry them on their way. In reality, however, the Union reaction to Cooke's and Cobb's counterattack was swift, decisive, and deadly.[12]

When someone alerted General Nathan Kimball of Cooke's approach, he sent orders for the 8th Ohio and the 14th Indiana to change front and contend with the attackers. Thomas Loundsdale in the 14th watched the charging Rebels "pass on the double quick their southern crosses spread to the breeze, a more hateful sight I never want to see." Sergeant Galwey estimated that the 8th Ohio had only 50 or 60 men left, and they carried only three or four cartridges apiece. The 14th Indiana was in a similar condition. Stretched out in single file, the two Yankee regiments ran down the Roulette farm lane toward the farmer's barn, in order to head off the Confederates. Cooke's men, having reached the eastern end of Mumma's cornfield, "peppered us unmercifully," wrote Galwey. Although low on ammunition and exhausted by their ordeal at the Sunken Lane, the two veteran regiments crisply formed a new line, facing west, and opened fire on the Rebels. Nevertheless, elements of the 27th North Carolina managed to reach within yards of Roulette's home. Chaplain Henry Stevens in the 14th Connecticut stood outside the basement room at the rear of the house, waiting to surrender the wounded he was tending, in order to prevent the Confederates from firing on them accidentally. But there would be no surrender, for Cooke's counterattack had reached its high-water mark.[13]

When Colonel John R. Brooke, commanding the 3rd Brigade of Richardson's 1st Division, saw Cooke's regiments coming over the Dunker Church plateau, his regiments were still north of the Sunken Lane. He immediately ordered the 52nd New York and the 2nd Delaware to change front to the right (or west) and meet the attack. Orders soon arrived from Richardson to advance and "check any attempt the enemy might make to reach our rear." Brooke called over the 53rd Pennsylvania from the left of his brigade line and gave them orders to hold Roulette's barn and orchard "at all hazards," so as to protect the hundreds of wounded collected in and around the farm buildings. Cooke's men blazed away at the 53rd as they ran to take up their position, but the volleys were inaccurate and inflicted little damage. The Pennsylvanians reached the farmyard and opened fire on the 27th North Carolina. Farther to the 53rd's right and front, Colonel William H. Irwin's newly arrived 3rd Brigade, 2nd Division, 6th Corps, was just then advancing down from the East Woods toward Cooke's left flank and rear. One of Irwin's regiments, Major Thomas Hyde's 7th Maine, charged down to the fence on the northern border of Mumma's cornfield and fired into Cooke's flank.[14]

Francis Barlow also saw Cooke's and Cobb's men. He promptly ordered a change of front to the west and hurried his regiments obliquely across the Sunken Lane, toward the hill the 8th Ohio and 14th Indiana had occupied before the lane fell. The Georgians and North Carolinians of Cobb's brigade were a little over 300 yards away, along the Mumma farm lane. The 3rd Arkansas was much closer—less than 200 yards distant—at the edge of Mumma's cornfield. These Confederates opened what Captain Pittenger in the 64th New York called a "murderous fire" on the New Yorkers, hitting several men. Barlow ordered the regiments to lie down and shoot back. A Confederate artillery unit, possibly Captain Victor Maurin's Donaldsonville (Louisiana) battery, was in position to rake Barlow's line with canister. "Charges of this deadly stuff went in front and in rear of our line," recorded Sergeant Fuller. Had the fire been more accurate, Fuller was certain it "would have destroyed our little two regiments." But, the sergeant observed, "such close calls often happen in battle."[15]

The buildup of enemy strength in his front and the advance of Irwin's brigade on his flank convinced Cooke that it was time to get out. He ordered a retreat. The 27th North Carolina and the 3rd Arkansas went back at a double-quick. "Then it was that our regiment suffered so," wrote Captain Joseph C. Webb, "for they had to retreat about four hundred yards over an open space, exposed to the fire of three regiments on their flank and three in their rear, besides a heavy shower of grape and canister." Lieutenant Graham believed the Federal infantry he saw forming on what was now their right flank were the same men his company had ordered to the rear only minutes earlier, with the Yankees seeking to take revenge on their would-be captors. Some, no doubt, were those soldiers, but the greatest damage was caused by the 7th Maine of Irwin's 6th Corps' brigade, who were joined by the 20th and 49th New York during the action. These were the three regiments, referenced by Captain Webb, who were on the 27th's flank. "Many a brave man lost his life in that retreat," wrote Graham. Sergeant Fuller in the 61st New York described the tragic demise of one of the Rebels. This individual "was considerably in rear of his comrades and he was exerting himself to get out of harms way, our men concentrated a fire on him. He was on plowed ground, and we could see the dirt fly up in front, and rear, and on each side of him as he was legging it. He was escaping wonderfully, and I felt as though he was entitled to succeed. I called out to our men and entreated them not to fire at him again, but without avail. The shooting continued, and just before he was out of range, down he went, killed perhaps, possibly wounded."[16]

Lieutenant Graham maintained afterward that "we had fairly broken the enemy's line, and had we been supported, I think, could have put them to rout." Such optimism was not uncommon among men in either army whose view of the battle was limited. The 27th North Carolina had put a scare into the Yankees, but there was no chance two Confederate regiments were going to put the forces arrayed against them to rout. Their foray into the enemy's rear cost both units dearly. The fate of the six messmates with Sergeant Major Benjamin F. J. Hyatt in the 3rd Arkansas illustrated the terrible carnage. Only Hyatt escaped unharmed from the group. All the others were wounded. In Lieutenant Graham's Company G, 3 were dead, 20 wounded, and 1 missing, which accounted for nearly three-quarters of the unit. Total losses for Cooke's 27th North Carolina were 203 casualties, or 62% of its strength, and Captain Ready's 3rd Arkansas counted 215 killed or wounded, a loss of 61%. Some of these casualties were suffered before and after the charge, but the great majority of the men were injured during the assault and retreat. The two regiments fell back across the Hagerstown Pike to the Reel cornfield, where the charge had commenced. Cooke was surprised at how quickly the survivors of both regiments rallied and reformed. While they reorganized, an aide-de-camp from Longstreet rode up and told the colonel he must hold his position at all costs. "Tell Gen. Longstreet we have no ammunition, but will hold it as long as there is a man of us alive," replied Cooke, to which the aide replied, "I know you will." This so inspired one of Cooke's soldiers that he ran out in front of the regiment and called for three cheers for the colonel, which, despite all they had just gone through, the men gave with enthusiasm. The same soldier, whose name, unfortunately, was not recorded, ran over to Cooke, patted him on the head, and announced, "Colonel, you are the man to lead North Carolina boys." Cooke could count on his men, but the fact that he was being asked to hold part of the line with no ammunition spoke to just how serious the crisis at the Confederates' center was.[17]

Cobb's small brigade, under Lieutenant Colonel McRae, retreated shortly after Cooke's regiments had cleared out. McRae tried to put the best face on his command's performance, reporting that his small force held the enemy in check "until our ammunition was expended," after which, "seeing no sign of support, I was constrained to give the command to fall back." The virtual collapse of his brigade under enemy fire probably had more to do with the order to retreat. Of the 250 men McRae had led up to the Mumma farm lane, "not more than 50" remained. Losses were not insignificant. Almost 40% of the brigade became casualties in the morning's and early afternoon's fighting, but nearly 200 able-bodied men, or half of the brigade's strength at the start of the battle, had found some pretense to leave the ranks and not return. McRae led his platoon-strength remnant of a brigade back across the Hagerstown Pike and joined Cooke's two battered regiments.[18]

Despite the extremely heavy losses incurred in these counterattacks, Longstreet's tactics succeeded in disrupting the momentum of Richardson's assault, forcing the Federals to divert a significant number of their forces to defeat the threat to their flank. It had the additional benefit, when considered with the other local counterattacks the Confederates mounted from the Piper farm area, of masking just how weakly held their center was. G. T. Anderson's small brigade was the only effective unit left in this part of the line. The rest—eight brigades— had disintegrated, and only fragments of them remained. But the aggressiveness of the Confederate counterpunches gave the Federal commanders the impression that the superior numbers of Rebels they were constantly hearing about from army headquarters might be true. The terrain and crop cover also benefited the graycoats, keeping the Yankees guessing as to what lay beyond Piper's cornfield or behind the next ridge. The Confederates' artillery played a crucial role, too. Once Owen's battery withdrew, Richardson had no direct artillery support to engage the Rebel guns on Reel Ridge or around Piper's farm, in order to draw their fire away from his infantry.

One of the counterattacks that D. H. Hill organized from the Piper farm area was directed at the 5th New Hampshire, probably around the same time as Cooke's regiments were mounting their attack on the Union right. After crossing the Sunken Lane, Colonel Cross led his regiment obliquely through Piper's cornfield, "all the time being pelted with canister from the battery in front." This was probably Miller's Washington (Louisiana) Artillery section in Piper's orchard. Sergeant Charles Hale had stopped to examine a comrade who had been shot when a blast of canister from Miller's guns passed over his head. "That was my dread," wrote Hale. "I could endure rifle bullets, but when the big iron bullets went swishing through the air with a sound as though there were bushels of them, it made me wish I was at home." Lieutenant Thomas Livermore remembered how the canister rounds "hurtled through and tore down even the slender cornstalks." But near the center of the cornfield, the regiment reached a ravine, which gave them cover from Miller's guns. They moved up near the southern edge of the corn, facing Piper's orchard and a plowed field east of it, when they spotted a line of around 100 men from Cumming's Alabama brigade who had rallied and were advancing toward them from a hill east of Piper's house.[19]

Cross ordered the regiment to halt and then summoned Sergeant Hale and another sergeant. Hale recalled that Cross shouted at him over the din of battle, "Sergeant: run and find the General [Caldwell] and tell him that the enemy is on our left flank." Hale sprinted back through the corn. He was observed by Captain Dick Cross, the colonel's brother, who knew nothing of the sergeant's mission and thought he was bugging out. The captain aimed his pistol and pulled the trigger, but, fortunately for Hale, the weapon misfired and he ran on, crossing the Sunken Lane at the same spot where, earlier, he had encountered the pugnacious Confederate who had thrust at him with a bayonet (see chapter 11). "The reb was not so pugnacious this time," Hale remembered, "though I saw him glaring at me as I picked my way over the heaps" of dead bodies. Reaching the high ground beyond the lane, Hale tried to find Caldwell but could not locate him. Looking back to the corn, he discerned "a tremendous commotion and shouting, and some sharp firing, indicating that something serious was going on." When Hale had departed, the 5th New Hampshire opened what Lieutenant Livermore described as "a withering, *literally* withering" fire on the Alabamians, who were over 300 yards away. By the time the Confederates reached the foot of the slope at the base of the hill, wrote Livermore, "there was no semblance of a line, and the individuals of what had been the line, either by reason of invincible bravery, or for the purpose of gaining shelter, ran forward scatteringly in the face of our fire, with heads down as if before a storm, to a fence which was a few yards in front of us." Cross had no support on either flank. He ordered the regiment to fall back to their right and rear, closer to the Sunken Lane, in order to close the gap between his right and the 81st Pennsylvania. Major Hilary Herbert in the 8th Alabama, one of the two leaders of the force advancing on Cross, mistook the 5th's movement for a rout and urged his men to pursue the New Englanders.[20]

Bullets began to strike in the vicinity where Sergeant Hale was looking for Caldwell. He concluded that "I was a fool standing there making a target of myself" and started back to the 5th New Hampshire on the run. His path brought him by the combative wounded Rebel in the road again, but by now the Confederate "had lost all his animosity." He called out to Hale, "Yank: For the love of God lift that dead man off'n my hurt leg." Using the butt of his rifle as a lever, Hale moved the dead body off the Southerner's wounded legs, then hurried on to join his regiment. He found the 5th nearing the northern edge of the corn, changing its front from facing southwest to south. He saw Colonel Cross with his trademark red bandana tied about his head—his hat had been knocked off earlier—"giving his whole attention to the movement." Cross's face "was streaked and smeared with powder, and with his cautionary orders he occasionally interjected an Apache war-whoop to which the men in the ranks responded." Hale reported to Cross that he could not find Caldwell. "Go to your company," the colonel yelled, since Cross already had his hands full.[21]

Moments earlier, while his regiment was still moving back toward the Sunken Lane, Cross received a warning from Lieutenant George Gay in Company D. Gay had been a lieutenant for only 4 days, but before his promotion, the 22-year-old had been the regiment's sergeant major. He was, wrote Cross, "a young gentleman of extraordinary talent, cheerful, diligent—beloved by his entire circle of acquaintance." Gay ran over to Cross and, catching him by the arm, said to him, "Col, the enemy are out flanking us." Cross thought this was impossible. "They are—come & see, quick," urged Gay. Cross and the lieutenant ran to the left of the 5th New Hampshire. The colonel, being taller than Gay, could see above some of the corn. "Sure enough the enemy were coming," Cross recalled, "a whole Brigade, I counted five battle flags & one large stand of colors." It was primarily Major Herbert, with his collection of men from Cumming's brigade, reinforced by elements of G. B. Anderson's brigade, including the 4th North Carolina. They were only 100 yards away. "In an instant the gray-backs raised their well-known battle yell and came on," wrote Cross. He shouted orders for his regiment to change front forward, a tricky movement in the middle of a cornfield that limited visibility to only a few yards. But Cross had trained his men well. General Richardson nicknamed the regiment the "Fire Proofs," because he could always count on them. The New Englanders moved at the double-quick to execute the maneuver. The Confederates were a mere 30 paces from the 5th's line before the latter completed their movement. Cross wrote with pride of how his "boys brought down their rifles as cool as on parade, & our volley tore them into fragments." Three mounted officers were seen among the advancing Confederates. All went down in the volley. Reflecting the relief and satisfaction a soldier feels at the demise of an enemy bent on his destruction, Cross added, "It was beautiful to see how those devils piled up."[22]

One volley did not stop the Alabamians and North Carolinians, however. They returned fire and kept coming. A color bearer carried his flag to within 15 yards of the New Hampshire men. Lieutenant Livermore heard one of his New England comrades shout "'Shoot the man with the flag' and he went down in a twinkling and the flag was not raised in sight again." Both sides blazed away at close range. Cross, ranging up behind his men, shouted to them to "Put on the war paint!" Livermore was on the right of the regiment. He looked to his left and saw Cross, "with a red handkerchief, a conspicuous mark, tied around his bare head and the blood from some wounds on his forehead streaming over his face, which was blackened with powder." Cross's men each opened a cartridge and streaked their faces with the black gunpowder. "Give 'em the war whoop!" shouted the colonel. The regiment then raised their best imitation of an Apache war whoop, which rang out above the roar of firing. "I have sometimes thought it helped to repel the enemy by alarming him to see this devilish-looking line of faces, and to hear the horrid whoop," thought Livermore, but even if it did not, the 5th's lieutenant believed the whooping "reanimated us and let him know we were undeterred."[23]

The Apache war whoop might have inspired the New Englanders, but it did not deter the determination of the Confederates, who continued to fight doggedly. In addition to Apache war whoops, above the tumult Livermore heard "a stream of shouts, curses, and appeals to 'Fire! Fire! Fire faster!'" from the officers and men of his regiment. The lieutenant was in the Sunken Lane—which pinpoints where the right of the 5th rested—kneeling on the body of a dead Confederate who was still clutching a Belgian rifle. Livermore noticed the weapon was capped and ready to fire. He pried it from the soldier's hands and "discharged it at his living comrades, and liking the work I looked around for another piece to discharge." Cross, who, to Livermore, seemed "omnipresent, omniscient, and omnipotent in the fight," spotted him and shouted sharply, "Mr. Livermore, tend to your company!" ending the lieutenant's fun.[24]

Major H. Boyd McKeen, commanding the 81st Pennsylvania, had seen the flags of the Rebels, who were moving to attack Cross when they passed through Piper's orchard. His regiment was in the cornfield, some distance from the 5th New Hampshire, facing north toward the threat posed by the advance of Cobb's brigade and Cooke's two regiments. McKeen perceived at once that Cross needed help, so he ordered his men to close the distance between the two regiments and form on the 5th's right. The 81st's movement apparently took them obliquely through the corn, across the Sunken Lane, and into the open ground immediately north of the lane—on the right, and slightly to the rear, of the 5th. Corporal James H. Mitchell wrote to his father that the 81st "got to close musket range," and "was in the open field and the enemy was in the edge of a corn field and behind fences." The Confederates delivered the first fusillade at the Union reinforcements, but the Pennsylvanians replied with repeated volleys that began to tip the balance of the fight.[25]

More Federals began to pour into the conflict. Colonel John R. Brooke displayed great initiative and tactical skill in his first battle as a brigade commander. Having seen Cooke's counterattack repulsed, Brooke dispatched the 57th and 66th New York and 2nd Delaware to support Caldwell. The three regiments came up on the right of the 81st Pennsylvania and advanced into Piper's cornfield. At the same time, hearing the firing from the cornfield, Francis Barlow pulled his regiment from the hill north of the Sunken Lane and, changing front, also entered the corn. The movement of Barlow's and Brooke's regiments pinched the 7th New York out of the line. The Confederates "fought with perfect desperation," in the opinion of Colonel Cross, but the buildup of five Union regiments, nearly 1,300 men, overwhelmed them. "The enemy began to waiver and break and then it was our time," wrote Corporal Mitchell. "We charged them with a shout and off they started as fast as they could travel throwing their guns away as they ran." Lieutenant Josiah Favill, the adjutant in the 57th, described the advance as "pell-mell," and added grimly that his regiment bayoneted "all who did not promptly surrender." Captain John Hughes, commanding Company G of the 11th Alabama, survived because he tripped. The Yankees were blazing away at the captain, but when he fell, they stopped shooting at him. "I have no doubt that the accidental falling saved my life," Hughes wrote, 38 years later. The number of colors that were captured provides evidence of how swift and utter the Confederates' collapse was. The 81st Pennsylvania took the colors of the 8th Alabama. Cross's 5th New Hampshire captured the state flag of the 4th North Carolina, the 57th New York seized the 11th Alabama's colors, and the 2nd Delaware collected the flag of the 16th Mississippi.[26]

Lieutenant Alexander Chisholm in the 9th Alabama described the retreat as a rout. In the 8th Alabama, their third color bearer, Sergeant James Castello, whose gallantry "had been conspicuous throughout the day," was killed. Major Hilary Herbert momentarily took the flag, but 1st Sergeant G. T. L. Robison insisted on his right to carry it. Robison went down wounded and a Company G private then took the flag. Herbert recalled how the enemy bullets played "fearful havoc in our ranks." Corporal Mitchell in the 81st Pennsylvania wrote to his father about how "we strewed the cornfield with dead and wounded rebels." One of them was the Company G private, the fifth color bearer in the 8th Alabama.[27]

What saved the Army of Northern Virginia's center from complete ruin was its artillery. Boyce's two guns apparently remained for some minutes in the meadow north of Piper's orchard and blasted Caldwell's and Brooke's regiments with canister. Captain Miller's section of the 3rd Company, Washington (Louisiana) Artillery, in the orchard, was joined by a third gun brought up by Sergeant William H. Ellis. All three were firing double charges of canister and case shot at the oncoming Union lines, the guns leaping nearly a foot into the air at each discharge. M. Napier Bartlett, a private in Miller's battery, recalled how one line of Federals, possibly the 57th or the 66th New York, "came so near us, that we could see their Colonel on horseback waving his men on, and then even the stripes on the Corporal's arms." The gunners worked "desperately, because it looked for a time as if we could not stop the blue wave from coming forward." Longstreet and his staff sat on their horses beside Miller's guns, offering some measure of how serious the situation was. The guns had become a keystone to whether the Confederates could hang on or if their center would burst open. Longstreet even put some of his staff to work crewing the pieces when their gunners were either killed or wounded, or too exhausted to work any more. Bartlett remembered how the wing commander "talked earnestly and gesticulated to encourage us." Recalling the moment years later, Longstreet wrote, "It was easy to see that if the Federals broke through our line there, the Confederate army would be cut in two and probably destroyed, for we were already badly whipped and were only holding our ground by sheer force of desperation."[28]

From across the Hagerstown Pike, along Reel Ridge, Maurin's, Carter's, and Hardaway's batteries poured fire at the Federals advancing through Piper's corn. On the Hagerstown Pike, after the initial retreat from the Sunken Lane, Lieutenant William A. Chamberlaine in the 6th Virginia discovered a 6 lb. gun near the entrance to the Piper farm lane. The gun belonged to Captain Frank Huger's Norfolk, Virginia, battery and had been abandoned when the horses on its limber were killed, possibly by fire from Tompkins's artillery. Being a soldier of considerable resourcefulness, Chamberlaine set about rallying some men to help him man the gun. He assembled an impromptu crew, and they pushed or pulled the gun nearly 100 yards north on the pike, to the top of a ridge that offered a better field of fire. They managed to get off two or three shots from this position, but the volume of small-arms fire they drew forced the lieutenant and his team to haul the gun back to near the entrance of the Piper farm lane, where they were less exposed. They were joined here by Major J. W. Fairfax, on Longstreet's staff, who helped fire the first round at the Federals. Fairfax found the experience exhilarating, clapping his hands as the murderous charges sped down range, then running to get more ammunition. Chamberlaine served as the vent man, using his coattail to cover the vent while the gun was being loaded. Colonel George T. Anderson, who helped Chamberlaine gather his volunteer gun crew, did not know the lieutenant's name but noted that he served the gun "beautifully until the ammunition was exhausted."[29]

The storm of iron projectiles and shell fragments extracted a toll from Caldwell's and Brooke's regiments. Lieutenant Colonel Philip J. Parisen, a promising officer commanding the 57th New York, was killed. A shell fragment to the head took the life of Lieutenant George Gay, who had warned Cross of the approaching Confederate flank attack, and both color bearers in the 2nd Delaware died. Captain N. Garrow Throop in Parisen's 57th received a wound in his arm that severed an artery. He was saved by General Caldwell, who happened to be standing near the captain and applied a tourniquet that Throop carried in his pocket. Confederate shelling also managed to take Francis Barlow out of the fight. While pushing his regiment forward to try to capture Miller's three guns, he was moving through the tall corn to the left of his regiment to see what was on his flank when there was an explosion, which sent a shrapnel ball into his left groin and left Nelson Miles in command.[30]

These losses, and others, began to suck the momentum from the Federals' attack. D. H. Hill, in the sort of personally courageous acts he seemed to relish, seized a musket and led a group of some 150 to 200 men through Piper's orchard to add an infantry punch to the murderous artillery fire. With typical bombast, he claimed "the Yankees were so demoralized that a single regiment of fresh men could drive the whole of them in our front across the Antietam." He and his counterattacking band had their chance to do this, but the Yankees met his assault "with a warm reception, and the little command was broken and dispersed." Most of the Union regiments remained within Piper's cornfield, which provided a certain amount of concealment from the Rebel gunners, but some elements of the 57th and 66th New York pushed on, nearly reaching Piper's house and farm lane. Walter R. Battle, a 4th North Carolina headquarters clerk who was assisting the single surgeon working in the farmhouse, which the Confederates were using as an aid station, confirmed that the Federals came to within 30 yards of them. George B. Anderson was among the injured being treated there. "General Anderson was anxious to get off before the Yankees got nearer," recorded Battle. "He did not want to be taken prisoner by them. He would prefer being shot through the head, so Capt. Gales, his A. A. General, myself, and two other men of the Ambulance Corps carried him through a field that looked like it was impossible for a man to walk ten steps without being killed, though we got out safely." Battle added that the fire on Piper's farm buildings area was terrific, writing how "the house, kitchen, trees, and everything else were torn and shot all to pieces."[31]

Their penetration to within yards of the Piper farm lane was the high-water mark of the Union's advance. Lieutenant Chamberlaine's 6 lb. gun sent two to three shots down the lane at the Yankees, and artillery on Reel Ridge no doubt targeted the exposed enemy as well, which sent them hurrying back to the cover of Piper's cornfield. Ezra Carman wrote that "there was now no body of Confederate infantry that could have resisted a serious advance of Richardson's Division, but the artillery fire rendered his position untenable." Richardson suspended the 1st Division's forward movement and called his advanced regiments back from their exposed positions in Piper's cornfield. He sent them to the reverse slope of the ridge, where French's 3rd Division and Meagher's Irish Brigade had engaged the Confederates in the Sunken Lane earlier. Although the Rebel guns continued to pour fire at them, Richardson's regiments at least had cover here, where they could take stock of their losses, reorganize, and resupply with ammunition. Richardson, meanwhile, continued his search for artillery to suppress the enemy guns and perhaps enable him to renew his advance. Unless they could drive off or silence the Confederate artillery, no attack could survive in the exposed ground beyond Piper's cornfield. Had Sumner performed his job as head of a corps and a wing commander, this was something the 2nd Corps' chief of artillery, Major Francis N. Clarke, could have attended to. But since Sumner took his staff with him, Clarke was thus swept up in the disaster befalling Sedgwick in the West Woods and was focusing his attention on Union defensive arrangements in the area of the East and North Woods. Richardson, like French, was left to fend for himself.[32]

Richardson's appeal for guns made its way to army headquarters. Orders went to Lieutenant Albert O. Vincent's section of Batteries B and L, 2nd U.S. Horse

Artillery—which had crossed over the Middle Bridge with other horse batteries and the 5th Corps' infantry—to report to Richardson. The two combined units were understrength, numbering only 4 Napoleons and around 58 of 75 authorized soldiers. Vincent's section was the stronger of the two, containing approximately 35 men, which may account for why he was sent. It was probably around 12:30 p.m., about the time Richardson's infantry was withdrawing to the reverse slope of the ridge north of the Sunken Lane, when Vincent reported to the division commander. The lieutenant probably quickly perceived that he was both out-ranged and outgunned by the Confederates' long arm. Nevertheless, he unlimbered his two guns on the high ground northeast of the point where the Sunken Lane turned south and opened fire on Miller's Confederate battery in Piper's orchard. Winfield Hancock, in his after-action report for the 1st Division, noted that Vincent's section did "excellent service," but we really know very little about what it experienced. Evidence suggests that the encounter was brief, since the battery reported no casualties.[33]

Vincent had not been firing for long before Captain William M. Graham's Battery K, 1st U.S. Artillery, from the Artillery Reserve, came trotting up. Richardson had requested rifled guns to deal with the Confederate long-range artillery on Reel Ridge, but no unemployed rifled battery was available. Therefore Graham, whose armament consisted of six Napoleons, got the assignment. Receiving his orders around noon, Graham left his bivouac near Porterstown, Maryland, crossed Antietam Creek at Pry's Ford, drove his guns down past Neikirk's farm, and, "following the ravines, under cover," made his way up to a point about 80 yards from the Sunken Lane, near where the left of Meagher's Irish Brigade had rested during its engagement. Vincent's horse artillerymen limbered up and departed. Graham's gun crews swiftly cleared for action and opened fire on a Confederate battery, located behind three haystacks in the meadow west of Piper's orchard and about 700 yards distant. This may have been Boyce's section. Whomever it was, Graham's Napoleons drove it off in about 10 minutes. The captain reported that "two heavy columns" of Confederate infantry had advanced to within "a few hundred yards" of his guns by moving through "a heavy corn-field." Whom this was is unknown, and there is a question just how "heavy" the columns could have been. Graham's guns greeted them with shrapnel and shell and quickly drove them back.[34]

These two successes were Graham's last, for things shortly turned against his battery. Miller's guns in Piper's orchard, as well as Hardaway's, Carter's, Manly's, and Macon's batteries on Reel Ridge, all directed their fire at the Union army's Regulars. The four Rebel batteries distributed along Reel Ridge mounted 7 rifled guns between them, all of which out-ranged Graham. Robert E. Lee and Longstreet observed the fire from near Hardaway's battery, which was commanded by Lieutenant John W. Tullis. Tullis recalled how the two generals "were both in 50 yards of my position," Lee off to Tullis's left, and Longstreet "always on the firing line." The Confederate batteries poured what Graham described as "a very sharp fire of shot, spherical case, and shell," at his position. One of these batteries, probably Manly's, had the additional advantage of enfilading the Union battery. Colonel David Strother, an aide-de-camp on McClellan's staff, watched the action from across Antietam Creek. He thought the Rebels concentrated the fire of "at least 40 guns" on Graham. "I saw a number of shells and overthrow[n] men and horses, and during the combat the battery sometimes appeared covered with the dust and smoke of the enemy's bursting shells," he observed. Battery K returned fire "as rapidly as possible," but Graham noticed that his solid shot, which had the greatest range for his Napoleons, were falling short of the enemy guns on Reel Ridge by several hundred yards. He reported this to Richardson, who replied that "he wished me to save the battery as much as possible," because he was expecting an order from Sumner. Richardson had apparently finally established contact with the 2nd Corps' headquarters, and whatever they had told him led him to believe that Sumner was contemplating a general advance. Sumner, as we shall see in chapter 13, was thinking strictly defensively and had no intention of ordering an advance, so either the communication was in error, or Richardson misunderstood it. While Richardson conversed with Graham, a Confederate shell suddenly burst close by, sending a shell fragment through the general's left shoulder, down through his body, and, according to his biographer, "possibly penetrating his left lung." The blow knocked him to the ground, but he somehow managed to regain his feet for several more minutes before he went down again and was carried from the field by a detail from the 14th Connecticut. Graham fired for several more minutes after Richardson was removed, but he concluded that remaining there any longer could only result in his destruction. He ordered the guns withdrawn some 200 yards to the rear. The 20 minutes under fire had cost Graham dearly: 17 horses killed and 6 severely wounded—which probably meant that every horse pulling the limbers, except one, was out of commission—as well as 4 men killed and 5 wounded.[35]

To a surgeon who examined his wound, Richardson exclaimed, "Tell General McClellan I have been doing a Colonel's work all day, and I'm now too badly hurt to do a General's." If the quote is legitimate, it does not reflect well on Richardson's opinion of his brigade commanders. Brooke had performed superbly, so the statement probably referred to Caldwell and Meagher. Richardson's wounding left the division's command in the hands of Caldwell, the senior officer. His tenure was short lived. The moment McClellan learned Richardson had been injured, he gave orders for Winfield Hancock in the 6th Corps to assume command of the 1st Division. A great deal is made of Richardson's wounding, which destroyed any prospect of a renewed assault by the 1st Division on Lee's center. To be sure, Richardson's mortal injury was a critical loss for the Army of the Potomac, because he was an excellent leader. But without substantial artillery support, there was not going to be any advance by the 1st Division, regardless of whether Richardson had remained on the field.[36]

Although the ridge north of the Sunken Lane gave most of Richardson's and French's brigades cover from enemy observation, the Confederate gunners could approximate their range and thus continued to drop shells into the vicinity. They managed to score one horrific hit on the 14th Connecticut, who were moving up from Roulette's farm to provide support to Richardson's forward line. While marching along the Roulette farm lane, out of sight of the enemy gunners, a shell suddenly dropped into the midst of Company D and exploded, with devastating consequences. Sergeant Ben Hirst had just told the company to close up "when it came to us with a whiz and the job was done," mangling seven men: three were killed and four wounded, two of whom lost an arm. Hirst spotted the body of William Ramsdell among the dead. Minutes before, he, Ramsdell, and two others had been talking about the regiment's bloody initiation to combat that morning, and Ramsdell had remarked that if he was going to be hit, he preferred to have the top of his head blown off. The shell had done precisely that to the poor man. The explosion spared Sam Burrows, August Gross, and Albert Towne, who were all nearby, from any physical damage, but they were not untouched. Hirst noted that Burrows and Gross "were covered with blood" from those who were struck. Towne had his haversack shot away but was otherwise "sound as a nut." The sergeant also remarked that "we closed up like veterans and moved on as if nothing had happened" after the casualties were tended to, but it is impossible to believe that the shell and the shocking damage it inflicted did not have a psychological effect.[37]

The 14th Connecticut's ordeal with Confederate artillery fire continued after this incident. The regiment was detailed to support Graham's battery, and it took up a position behind the limbers, about 250 yards north of the Sunken Lane. The men lay down, but shells aimed at Graham that sailed harmlessly over the battery frequently struck the area around and among the New Englanders. One passed directly beneath Hiram H. Fox, knocking the private unconscious for several hours. Another nearly cut William H. Norton in two. Two other members of the regiment died because of the inexperience and carelessness of rookie soldiers. Robert Hubbard and Thaddeus Lewis, who had survived all the ordeals of the regiment up to this point, were both accidentally shot and killed by the unsafe handling of loaded weapons by comrades.[38]

The shelling inflicted damage on other regiments, as well. The 53rd Pennsylvania, which had also moved over to support Graham, lost Lieutenant John D. Weaver, "the bravest officer in the regt," who was mortally wounded. Colonel Cross described how "shells were flying & bursting all around us—while every now & then rifle balls came whistling over our heads or striking close at hand." "About one hundred fellows" who remained in the ranks of the hard-hit 108th New York were also moved up to buttress Graham's and Richardson's position. After the "utmost exertions on the part of some of the officers," this group was formed into a line and deployed behind the post-and-rail fence about 200 yards north of the Sunken Lane, near where the regiment had been in that morning's attack. Captain Francis E. Pierce wrote, "We were in plain sight of a rebel battery and were severely shelled." The barrage, Pierce stated, "was awful" and inflicted many casualties. Although their losses were significantly fewer than when they were under small-arms fire, Pierce commented on the mental strain of the shelling: "It was a hundred times worse than when we were under a severe musketry fire."[39]

It was probably around 1:30 to 2 p.m. when Winfield Hancock received orders from McClellan to take command of the 1st Division. At that time, his 6th Corps' brigade was deployed across the western face of the East Woods. He left at once, galloping cross-country to join his new command. He found the troops there "suffering severely from the shells of the enemy" and immediately sent off requests to Chief of Artillery Henry Hunt and to the other commands located nearby for two batteries. Evidently no one on Richardson's staff was present to explain to the new division commander that Richardson had already tried this, with little luck. Hancock received the same response: no batteries could be spared. There was little more he could do than make some adjustments to the position of his brigades, in order to strengthen his hold on the ground near the Sunken Lane. A quick assessment of the situation made clear to him what had been evident to Richardson. Without substantial artillery support, no advance beyond the Sunken Lane could survive the fire the Rebel batteries could bring to bear on it. Offensive operations by the 1st Division were over.[40]

BY 1 P.M., WELL before Hancock arrived, it was clear that the over 3-hour fight for the Sunken Lane and Piper's farm had ended in a stalemate. Lee and Longstreet breathed a huge sigh of relief, for only their superiority in artillery on this part of the field had staved off disaster. French's and Richardson's blows had shattered the Confederates' center and inflicted massive losses on the infantry defenders. As mentioned earlier in this chapter, only one brigade, Colonel G. T. Anderson's small command, remained combat effective in the center. Every other Rebel brigade engaged in this phase of the conflict had been effectively destroyed. R. H. Anderson's division had virtually ceased to exist. The Confederates' losses were staggering. Wright's brigade incurred 62% casualties; Cumming's, 54%; and Pryor's, 42%. In Featherston's brigade, the 16th Mississippi lost 64% of its men. Out of 17 regiments or battalions in this division that were engaged in the fight, 13 regimental commanders were dead or wounded, and 3 of the 4 brigade commanders were wounded. A captain commanded Cumming's brigade at the end of the action, and a lieutenant led the 2nd Florida. This was a catastrophic loss of leadership.

D. H. Hill's brigades were also shattered. G. B. Anderson was wounded—mortally, it would turn out. His brigade's losses totaled at least 44%, and probably were over 50%. The brigade's leadership had been slaughtered. Every regimental commander and every field officer but one, Major William W. Sillers in the 30th North Carolina, had been killed or wounded. The 4th North Carolina had no officers left, and it was commanded by Orderly Sergeant Thomas W. Stephenson. Only three officers remained in the 2nd North Carolina. In a letter home after the battle, Sillers reflected the sorry state of what had been an excellent brigade. "I haven't the heart to speak of the condition of the brigade after the fight of the 17th ult.," he wrote. "God spare me the sight of ever again seeing it so much disorganized!"[41]

Rodes's brigade lost 25% through casualties, most of them in the 6th Alabama, but its flight from the field (see chapter 11) left "not more than 40" men remaining. Embellished accounts, like the one by Colonel Cullen Battle that depicted a heroic, unyielding defense, obscured its true condition. Writing a month after the Battle of Antietam, one of the enlisted men in the colonel's 3rd Alabama exposed the reality. His company carried only three men, including himself, into the fight. His two comrades were both wounded, and "I am shoeless and ragged," wrote the soldier, identified only as "Joe." "Nothing to supply my necesaties can be got up here. I am at a loss to know what to do. Numbers are in my fix."[42]

Confederate casualties amounted to at least 2,665 men, out of about 5,900 who were engaged, not counting G. T. Anderson's brigade. This was a 45% loss. At least six regimental colors were captured, a reflection on how badly mauled some units were. "The rebels fought with perfect desperation," wrote Colonel Edward Cross in the 5th New Hampshire, 3 days after the engagement. Their casualties confirmed Cross's statement. The Confederates fought with great courage, but their massive losses beg the question of how well their leadership—particularly at the division, wing, and army command levels—managed them. Effectively handling troops in battle does not mean fearlessly leading a group of soldiers in a counterattack with muskets in hand, as D. H. Hill did. Instead, it is maneuvering combat units so they inflict maximum damage on the enemy at minimal cost. The deployment of R. H. Anderson's division did not reflect well on anyone, except perhaps Anderson, who was wounded so early on in its movement that he had virtually no impact on it. Little thought seems to have been given to using this division to attack French's flank, following approximately the same axis that Colonel Cooke's 27th North Carolina and 3rd Arkansas used in their noon counterattack. Such a push might have relieved the pressure on D. H. Hill's brigades and pulled Richardson's arriving division away from the Sunken Lane. R. H. Anderson's wounding was also unfortunate in that it left the division in the hands of Roger Pryor, who was clearly not competent to command it. Lee and Longstreet deferred to D. H. Hill in guiding the deployment of Anderson's division, and he sent them directly into the very teeth of Union artillery and small-arms fire, which mauled every brigade before it even reached the Sunken Lane. There was no easy way to get to the lane from the south, although it was possible to follow the ravine that ran up along the east side of Piper's orchard and through his cornfield. This could have limited the troops' exposure to enemy fire until they were quite close to the Sunken Lane. Instead, Pryor's brigades were sent charging forward with little regard for whether the route left them exposed or provided some cover. Hill also displayed no concern for the vulnerable right flank of his defensive line, which is ultimately where it unraveled. Haste in pushing Pryor's brigades into action resulted in confusion within the Sunken Lane, where one brigade piled in on top of another to find cover from the murderous fire, and this helped to quicken the collapse of the line.[43]

Lee's and Longstreet's principal contribution during the main part of the struggle for the lane was to build up a powerful artillery line behind the infantry and along Reel Ridge. This saved the Confederates' center from collapse when the Sunken Lane line fell. Longstreet blundered in his decision to order Rodes's attack against French, which nearly resulted in catastrophe when Rodes's brigade, caught out in the open and exposed to the fire of Tompkins's battery, almost retreated beyond the Sunken Lane when that assault failed. Only Rodes's personal intervention prevented this. Though costly, Longstreet's subsequent decision to hurl Cobb's brigade and Cooke's two regiments against the Federals was sound. It threw the bluecoats off balance and sucked the momentum from Richardson's attack. Moreover, as D. H. Hill wrote when describing all the seemingly reckless Confederate counterattacks they mounted after the Sunken Lane line fell, "The Yankees were completely deceived by their boldness, and induced to believe that there was a large force in our center." This was partially true (although Richardson appears to have realized he was close to cracking the Confederates' center), but what really blunted the final drive of Richardson's 1st Division was the fire from the Rebel batteries. Curiously, Hill gave the artillery little credit for holding the center, opining that, overall, the Confederates' guns were badly handled in the conflict. They were generally outmatched by the superior firepower and ammunition of Union artillery at most points on the battlefield, but in the center, the Confederates did a superior job of massing their guns.[44]

The Federals paid a terrible price in breaking the Confederates' Sunken Lane line. French's division carried 5,731 men into action and suffered 1,750 casualties, or just over 30% of the division. The smallest loss for any regiment in this division, the 7th [West] Virginia, was 145, which offers some idea just how dreadful the carnage was. The casualties told only part of the story, however. Hundreds of men—particularly from the garrison regiments and new regiments-who were exposed to the shocking horrors of combat found some pretense for separating themselves from the ranks and finding safety in the rear. For example, the

108th New York took 750 officers and men into the fight. When the regiment was moved up in the vicinity of Graham's battery, only about 100 remained in the ranks, and these were only gathered up through the strenuous exertions of the regiment's officers. The 108th's reported losses were 195 killed, wounded, and missing, which means that some 450 able-bodied men—more than half the regiment—left the ranks. Private Edward Spangler in the 130th Pennsylvania noted that only 8 men in his company—out of about 70—remained when they were relieved by Richardson's division.[45]

Richardson's 1st Division had 4,059 infantry engaged in the attack and suffered 1,161 casualties, only 9 of whom were listed as missing or captured. Numerically, the Federals had greater losses than the Confederates—2,911 versus 2,665—but the percentages tell the true tale. The two 2nd Corps' divisions sustained a total loss of 29%, while the Confederates' was 45%. French won no laurels for his handling of the 3rd Division. His tactics were unimaginative and costly, but, as was discussed earlier in this chapter, he may have felt that a frontal assault was his only viable option. Yet, other than ordering his brigades into action one after the other, his impact on the fighting was almost nonexistent. Richardson performed well, although there is a question of why he allowed Caldwell's brigade to remain idle for so long, while Meagher's brigade was decimated in front of the Sunken Lane. Other than this, Richardson kept in close contact with his brigades and did all he could to obtain support for his assault. He also correctly sensed that the Rebel center was weak and aggressively pushed his troops forward after the Sunken Lane fell. They might have broken open the Confederates' line, had his troops received the artillery support Richardson sought. Of his brigadiers, Brooke performed with great skill. Caldwell and Meagher, although their brigades fought well, disappointed Richardson. Ten days after the battle, Colonel Cross wrote a letter of resignation and gave it to Caldwell, stating that he took this action "because I am unwilling to serve under Brig. Gen. Caldwell, not having any confidence in his courage or capacity." Caldwell wisely denied Cross's request to resign but requested a court of inquiry to clear his own name. Although Surgeon George Barr in the 64th New York had seen Caldwell out of position, in a place where he could not observe the maneuvers of his brigade, Barr's testimony was rejected, because he lacked military knowledge of infantry tactics. Caldwell avoided dismissal from the service and would fully redeem himself 10 months later, at Gettysburg, commanding the 1st Division.[46]

Sergeant Charlie Fuller in the 61st New York believed that the Irish Brigade fought very bravely, but "the fact remains the brigade was NOT tactically well placed. Had it advanced to where the Sixty-first and Sixty-fourth later went, it would have done much greater execution, and with smaller loss to itself." Meagher had applied the same tactics as French and had suffered the same consequences. The Irish regiments were not slaughtered due to the incompetence or callousness of some Nativist officer who despised them, but by the brave yet tactically inept Meagher.[47]

It was at the regimental level that Richardson's 1st Division shone. Francis Barlow's and Edward Cross's handling of their regiments was outstanding. Their initiative and ability to maneuver under fire reflected excellent discipline and training. These traits also reduced losses. The 61st and 64th New York suffered 91 casualties out of 442 effectives; the 5th New Hampshire, 111 out of 321. In contrast, the 63rd New York lost 202 of their 341 men; and 69th New York, 196. These first three regiments inflicted far more damage than they received. Brooke's 2nd Delaware and the 57th and 66th New York also performed with distinction, the latter two regiments nearly reaching Piper's house. Their casualties reflected the depth of their penetration and exposure. Both units lost nearly a third of their men. In French's division, Kimball's brigade fought superbly, earning the nickname bestowed by a tearful General French: "The Gibraltar Brigade."[48]

French and Richardson had inflicted terrific damage on the Confederates and carried away the Rebels' Sunken Lane line. These were notable achievements, although they were won at an appalling cost in blood. But their victory was incomplete and ended in a stalemate, with Lee's center badly damaged but holding. Apart from the fierce resistance the Confederates put up, there were three principal reasons why the attack was not more successful, and why Lee's center was not decisively broken. First, the failure of command and control was not at the division or brigade level, but at the corps level. French and Richardson fought their engagements with no direction, coordination, or support from Sumner's headquarters. As has already been related (see chapter 9), up until at least 10:15 a.m., Sumner did not even know where these two divisions were, and they were left to fight without direction or support. A crucial consequence of this command failure was the lack of artillery support. Francis N. Clarke, the 2nd Corps' chief of artillery, spent his time and focused his attention on the Federals' right, where Sumner, fearing a Confederate attack, kept him. Except for Tompkins's battery, Clarke retained every 2nd Corps' battery on the right until nearly noon, when he finally sent Owen's Battery G, 1st Rhode Island, to relieve Tompkins. At the same time as Richardson was desperately seeking rifled guns to reply to the artillery on Reel Ridge, Clark had two batteries sitting in reserve north of the East Woods, one of which was equipped with just that type of equipment. But such was the utter muddle at the 2nd Corps' headquarters that no one was aware of Richardson's need, or of the opportunity that existed at the Confederates' center. All of this resulted from Sumner's disastrous decision to ride at the head of Sedgwick's 2nd Division into the West Woods, and his subsequent loss of all perspective regarding the larger conflict that two-thirds of his corps was fighting, without his knowledge or help.[49]

McClellan bears some responsibility, as well, for the the attack on Lee's center failing to achieve greater success. Once battle is joined, the most important decision for an army commander is to determine when and where to commit his reserve. Most of the attention paid to the Battle of Antietam focuses on McClellan's management of the 5th Corps, but this was not his principal reserve, since part of it was already committed to the Federals' advance across the Middle Bridge of Antietam Creek (see chapter 14). The rest of the 5th Corps was supporting the Union batteries on the bluffs above the creek's eastern bank. McClellan's most important reserves were the two divisions of Major General William B. Franklin's 6th Corps, numbering close to 12,000 men. The operations of this corps will be covered in more detail in chapter 13, but its leading division— Major General William F. "Baldy" Smith's 2nd Division—arrived near McClellan's forward headquarters at Pry's house around 10 a.m. McClellan reported that "it was first intended to keep this corps in reserve on the east side of the Antietam, to operate on either flank or on the center, as circumstances might require." But soon after Smith arrived near Pry's farm, McClellan received a series of alarming messages from Sumner. At 10:15 a.m., Sumner signaled, "Reinforcements are badly wanted. Our troops are giving way. I am hunting for French's and Richardson's divisions. If you know where they are, send them immediately." This was followed at 10:20 a.m. by an even more urgent appeal from the wing commander: "I must have reinforcements immediately or will have to give way on the right." McClellan dispatched his assistant adjutant general, Major Nelson H. Davis, to visit Sumner and report on the situation there. Davis, who had previously served under Sumner and knew him, found the general "more affected from the state of affairs at this stage of the battle than I had ever before witnessed." Sumner related that he had been repulsed, that Hooker's 1st Corps was scattered, and that the new troops—possibly a reference to the 12th Corps— had broken. He declared, "Sir, I have rallied these troops in the woods and behind the fences and got them in line—Sir, tell the General I will *try* and hold my position—tell him, Sir, I *will* hold it, I *will* hold it, Sir!" Whether Sumner said these exact words to Davis is immaterial. They confirmed that Sumner considered the situation on the Federals' right to be perilous.[50]

Shortly after receiving Sumner's messages, McClellan decided to commit the 6th Corps as Sumner's support on the right. In his after-action report, the army commander wrote that "the strong opposition on the right, developed by the attacks of Hooker and Sumner, rendered it necessary at once to send this corps to the assistance of the right wing." On one level, McClellan's decision was understandable. Sumner was the commander on the ground and was at the front. McClellan had a low opinion of him as a general but seems to have accepted this assessment without further verifying its accuracy.[51]

The general from whom McClellan received his nickname, "the Young Napoleon"—Napoleon Bonaparte—like other great field commanders, had a talent for sensing where his enemy was vulnerable and committing his reserve toward that point. Discerning this weakness and attacking at the right moment on a seething, smoke-shrouded battlefield, with conflicting situation reports coming in that serve to obscure rather than clarify the situation, is extremely difficult. Even Bonaparte was not always successful. But French's and Richardson's assault on the Sunken Lane took place in plain view of McClellan's observation post. Few commanders in the American Civil War had as good a view of the battlefield as he had to assess the prospects for success, should he reinforce this sector. If McClellan had taken a calculated risk and ordered Sumner to hold the right with what troops he had, as well as committed the 6th Corps, with its powerful artillery support, to reinforce Richardson's attack, it is unlikely that Lee's center could have held. It would not have led to the destruction of Lee's forces—the Army of Northern Virginia was too resilient, and it had enough troops and depth of position to stave off complete disaster—but it very likely would have forced Lee to withdraw his army to positions west of Sharpsburg and retreat across the Potomac River that night, leaving many of his wounded and stragglers behind. Such an outcome would have given McClellan a clear-cut victory. Instead, McClellan made a safe decision, which preserved his right from the disaster Sumner had predicted but sacrificed the initiative and opportunity French and Richardson had won for the Army of the Potomac at such great cost. It helped ensure that Antietam would be a long, drawn-out battle.[52]

13

Stalemate in the North

"My head ached as if it would split from the constant bursting of shells"

The soldiers of General George S. Greene's 2nd Division, 12th Corps, had a newfound respect for their gray-haired commander. Before the Battle of Antietam they despised him, hissing and hooting whenever he passed by. But after they had swept the enemy from the East Woods at 10:30 a.m. and smashed two Confederate assaults against their position on the Dunker Church plateau, "we really got up three cheers for him," wrote a 7th Ohio soldier. Following the repulse of Manning's 30th Virginia and 48th North Carolina, Greene, it will be recalled (see chapter 9), aggressively pushed the bulk of his small division across the Hagerstown Pike, past the Dunker Church, and into the West Woods. Greene's right, held by the tiny 5th and 7th Ohio, stood approximately 200 yards west of the church, on the brow of a hill in the woods, looking down in the direction of Alfred Poffenberger's farm. The 28th Pennsylvania, reduced to around 300 effectives, filled the space on the Ohioans' left, extending to the worm fence bordering the southern border of the woods. The 111th Pennsylvania, the 3rd Maryland, and two companies in the 102nd New York held this fence line, which went from the 28th's left to the Hagerstown Pike (see map on page 370). Ezra Carman pinpointed the left of Greene's line as being 168 yards south of the Dunker Church.[1]

Greene's position was tenuous, but not hopeless. The troops nearest to his left flank were the small 66th Ohio and the balance of the 102nd New York, 250 yards away, whom he left to support Tompkins's battery on the Dunker Church plateau. He believed Sedgwick's 2nd Division protected his right flank, although he had no communication with that division, did not directly connect to it, and could not see it. Greene had heard the furious fighting after Sedgwick's brigades disappeared into the West Woods and could not have helped seeing some of those troops fleeing back toward the East Woods. But he was unaware that the entire division had been routed, and that the woods north of him were now full of Rebels. For those who study battles from detailed maps marking the contours of the terrain and the position of every unit, it is difficult to grasp just how bewildering a battlefield can be for those in the midst of the locale, particularly when they lack maps and any form of communication beyond the written or spoken word. While the West Woods provided Greene with cover and concealment, they also obscured what he could see. The ravine Barksdale's brigade had used in McLaws's devastating attack on Sedgwick ran along his right flank. Although the woods were free of underbrush, the nature of the terrain and foliage did not allow Greene or his men to have any sight lines beyond this ravine. His left regiments looked out over an open meadow, extending for about 250 yards to Reel's large cornfield, and traded skirmish fire with the 27th North Carolina and the 3rd Arkansas, who were largely hidden inside the corn.[2]

Initially, there was no opposition in front of the 28th Pennsylvania and the Ohioans. The 28th's Company F were deployed as skirmishers. They moved down into the hollow in front of the regiment and toward the western edge of the West Woods, about 300 yards distant. Colonel Hector Tyndale, commanding Greene's 1st Brigade, spotted what he thought was an abandoned Confederate battery. The guns were probably Read's battery of McLaws's division. Tyndale asked for volunteers from the 28th to investigate. One of them was Sergeant William Armor in Company B. Armor and the others made their way through to the southwestern edge of the woods without incident, but when they emerged into the open, "we got a shower of bullets from a line of rebs just back of the cannon, who were concealed behind a ledge of rocks," wrote Armor. The Union detail beat a hasty retreat into the woods.[3]

The Confederates, meanwhile, moved to fill the void in their line west of Greene. When Greene advanced, the 46th North Carolina under Colonel Edward D. Hall, 320 strong, withdrew from the West Woods to Hauser's Ridge. Here he encountered Stonewall Jackson, who ordered the colonel to report to McLaws. McLaws directed Hall "to endeavor to hold the woods at all hazards." As Hall prepared to return to the West Woods, he received a welcome reinforcement. Company F in the 30th Virginia, under Capt. John M. Hudgin, and 1st Lieutenant Alexander C. Jones's Company G in the 3rd Arkansas had been combined that morning into a small sharpshooter battalion under Hudgin's command. Both companies were armed with Sharps rifles, a rarity in the Army of Northern Virginia. They had been deployed along the banks of Antietam Creek above Snavely's Ford, where the creek turned sharply west. Orders to move to the left reached Hudgin well after his brigade had departed, so, despite pushing his men, sometimes at the double-quick, they did not reach the Confederates' left until Manning's brigade had attacked the Dunker Church plateau and been repulsed by Greene's division. General Walker, his division commander, initially held Hudgin's two companies back to support a battery he was positioning, but when it became apparent that the Yankees were not advancing beyond the West Woods, he ordered the captain to deploy his men as skirmishers, push into the woods, and engage them. If the Federals advanced against him with a line of battle, Walker authorized Hudgin to fall back on Hall's regiment, who were under cover alongside a rock ledge.[4]

Hudgins's two companies, reinforced by a company from the 46th North Carolina, pushed into the West Woods, reaching the hollow below the 28th Pennsylvania and the Ohioans. They immediately engaged in "sharp fighting," and several of the captain's men were killed or wounded. The skirmishing exhausted the remaining ammunition of the two small Ohio regiments, so Greene sent a request for reinforcements back to Alpheus Williams to relieve the Buckeyes and fill in the space he believed existed between his right and Sedgwick's left. Williams had limited resources with which to help Greene. Most of his regiments were either too badly damaged from earlier combats or were supporting batteries. The rookie 13th New Jersey, however, was re-forming in the East Woods and was available. Williams tapped them to reinforce Greene.[5]

It was shortly before 11 a.m. when Colonel Ezra Carman, the 13th's commander, received Williams's orders to report to Greene. He marched his regiment through the East Woods, past the batteries along the woods' edge, over the open fields south of the Cornfield, and entered the West Woods north of the Dunker Church. Greene personally placed Carman on his right, relieving the 5th and 7th Ohio, who fell back behind the Dunker Church plateau. Shortly after the 13th New Jersey took up its position, the Purnell Legion, about 200 strong, which Williams had scrounged from Goodrich's brigade, arrived as an additional reinforcement. It formed to Carman's right and rear, about 80 yards away—midway between the 13th and the Dunker Church—and faced slightly northwest. Williams reported that his "repeated efforts" to find further reinforcements for Greene were unsuccessful. These endeavors would have meant appealing to his superior, General Edwin Sumner, who believed the right flank of the Union army was on the verge of collapse. For Sumner, reinforcing Greene was out of the question. Sumner's state of mind precluded him from grasping the opportunity Greene's bold thrust provided, as well as what it said about the Confederates' strength.[6]

The addition of the 13th New Jersey and the Purnell Legion raised Greene's strength to around 1,350. When the 13th arrived, they saw some men in the 28th Pennsylvania, on their left, firing in the direction where the 27th North Carolina and the 3rd Arkansas were. Orders were shouted for the rookies not to fire until "we saw something to shoot at." They spotted Hudgin and his skirmishers darting about through the trees in the hollow, decided these Rebels were something to shoot at, and opened fire. This caused Hudgin to pull his men back to the edge of the West Woods, where they had better cover. Ezra Carman was nervous about his right flank. He knew from his regiment's recent advance toward the Hagerstown Pike that the woods north of him were full of rebels, but he could not see anything beyond the ravine on his right flank.

Lieutenant Charles A. Hopkins, the 13th's adjutant, walked up and down behind the regiment's line to keep an eye on the men. One soldier, Sergeant Edward Warren in Company B, the right company, had taken a position a little beyond the company's right front, behind a tree or rock, where he "was trying to pick off a rebel wherever he could see one." When Hopkins arrived behind Company B, Warren saw him and beckoned for the adjutant to come over to him. Warren said he had seen a glistening of rifle barrels through the woods beyond their right flank and was certain they were the enemy. Hopkins went to Carman and told him what Warren had spotted. Carman sent the adjutant to find Greene and report Warren's observations, imparting to the general "that the colonel of the regiment was thoroughly convinced, absolutely sure, that the identical position supposed to be held by Sedgwick, was, in fact, held by the enemy." Hopkins found Greene near the left of his line. The general rode over to the 13th's position immediately. When he reached the right of the regiment, he "put spurs to his horse and rode down the hill at our right," into the ravine. He may have seen the same body of troops Sergeant Warren had, but Greene concluded, without trying to make contact with them, that they were friendly. Riding back, he told Hopkins, "Adjutant, do not let your men fire to the right under any circumstances," because he believed Sedgwick's division was there, "and it is impossible to flank you." He shared the same warning with Carman and told the colonel "he was surely mistaken in the idea that the enemy were in the woods" on their right. Greene then repeated his instructions not to fire to the right under any circumstances.[7]

GREENE WAS DISASTROUSLY WRONG. Sergeant Warren had not been mistaken. The woods north of the 13th New Jersey were full of Confederates, the closest being only about 150 yards away, across the ravine. It was Brigadier General Robert Ransom Jr.'s brigade of North Carolinians. Recall that Ransom's brigade, minus the 24th North Carolina, which had drifted north and been appropriated by Jeb Stuart, had repulsed the advance of the 2nd Massachusetts and 13th New Jersey around 10 a.m. (see chapter 9). Two of his regiments, the 25th and 35th North Carolina, lay behind the limestone ledge along the eastern edge of the middle section of the West Woods. His right regiment, the 49th North Carolina, was entirely inside the southern section of the woods, with its right flank resting on the ravine. They were probably the troops seen by Warren and Greene. The three regiments contained around 1,200 men. Early's brigade was in Ransom's rear, not far from the western edge of the woods. Shortly after Greene advanced into the West Woods, Brigadier General Lewis Armistead's brigade of Richard H. Anderson's division, which Lee had detached and sent to reinforce his left, came up. They were greeted by a savage shelling that killed the commander of the 53rd Virginia and inflicted several other casualties on the unit when it passed over the high ground near Hauser's farm. Ransom had requested reinforcements and someone—probably McLaws or Jackson—ordered Armistead to support the North Carolinians.[8]

Ransom sent Lieutenant Walter McKenzie Clark, adjutant in the 35th North Carolina, to guide Armistead into position. Clark was still a boy, only 16 years old, but mature for his age, and capable. He met the Virginians near Alfred Poffenberger's barn and found Armistead in front, on foot and with sword drawn. Clark saluted him and "told him why I was there." The general replied, "gruffly I thought," recalled Clark, "& I stepped a little to his left." Armistead may have wondered how a mere boy was a lieutenant. The general had been a soldier since 1839 and lived a hard life, with service in Mexico and numerous remote posts across the American West. Tragedy dogged him throughout his life. His first wife and daughter died of disease in 1850, and in 1852, his family home in Virginia was destroyed by a fire. He married again, but their first child, a boy, died in 1854. A year later, cholera claimed his second wife. His experiences had left Armistead clad with a hard bark.[9]

The instant after Clark identified himself and Armistead made his gruff reply, "a terrific discharge burst over us" from the Union batteries arrayed across the western front of the East Woods. Clark saw a solid shot bounding down the hill through the woods, probably fired by Woodruff's battery. Armistead saw it too, and, Clark thought, "could have moved out of its course." Perhaps thinking it was a shell that was about to explode, Armistead "stood as one transfixed and did not move his foot or a muscle." Whether the ball actually struck Armistead's foot or the windage from the passing ordnance affected him is unclear, but he pitched forward on his face and went down so hard that Clark believed he was dead. Several of Armistead's men rushed to him. They discovered that his wound was not serious, but the blow left the general senseless and unable to command. His small brigade, already nervous from the shelling they had experienced while passing by Hauser's farm, came apart under this new barrage and the fall of their commander. Clark thought the entire command "instantly scattered." They may have, but Clark did not witness Colonel James G. Hodges in the 14th Virginia, who assumed command after Armistead's wounding, rallying the brigade and finding Jubal Early, who placed it in support of Ransom, while Early moved his own brigade up to the limestone ledge on Ransom's left.[10]

Because of the nature of the terrain and the woods, the Confederates north of Greene's position were as unaware of him as he was of them. They presumed that the woods south of them had been cleared of the enemy earlier, when Sedgwick was driven out. No one scouted or probed in that direction, perhaps because Early and Ransom thought someone else was attending to it. Ransom departed to hunt up his missing 24th North Carolina and left his older brother, Colonel Matt W. Ransom, commanding the 35th North Carolina, in temporary command of his brigade. The elder Ransom soon saw a section of enemy artillery drive down Smoketown Road, heading toward the Dunker Church. Believing that no Union infantry was nearby, Ransom thought he could use the cover of the West Woods to surprise and capture them. He ordered the 49th North Carolina to move into the ravine on their right, change front so the regiment faced southeast, and then charge in the direction of the church. The other two regiments of the brigade would follow in support.[11]

AFTER HIS MEETING WITH Colonel Carman, General Greene returned to his left flank, which he considered to be the most vulnerable part of his line. Soon after he arrived, a staff officer from the 12th Corps' headquarters rode up to deliver a message, the subject of which is not recorded. Greene grumbled to the officer that the rookies from New Jersey, on his right, "were laboring under the delusion that Sedgwick had been driven from the woods." The officer, surprised, replied, "Why, yes, General, didn't you know?" Greene's response to this jarring news was described as "picturesquely sulfurous." Cognizant now that his position "was very critical," Green thought not of pulling out of the West Woods, but of finding the help necessary to hold on to them. He sent a message back to Williams for more reinforcements and dispatched his son, Lieutenant C. T. Greene, to find artillery support.[12]

Williams regretfully replied that he had no other available reinforcements. Greene refused to accept this and decided to make a personal appeal. Leaving his command under Lieutenant Colonel Tyndale, he galloped to the rear. Along the way, he may have had the satisfaction of seeing artillery moving up to his aid. His son had secured an order detaching a section of Captain Joseph Knap's Battery E, Pennsylvania Light Artillery, which was positioned in the southeastern corner of the Cornfield. It was around 11:30 a.m. when Greene delivered his orders to Knap. The captain selected his first section, commanded by Lieutenant James D. McGill, located on the right of the battery. McGill limbered and drove his guns along the edge of the East Woods, across Smoketown Road, and up onto the Dunker Church plateau, where he unlimbered. It was the only viable artillery position the lieutenant saw in the area.[13]

McGill's section remained here for several minutes before Tyndale became aware of it. He rode over to McGill and ordered him to move his artillery into the woods. McGill was incredulous. Woods were no place for artillery. Besides having restrictive fields of fire, the pieces could not be easily maneuvered, and McGill could see that the enemy had good concealment in Reel's cornfield, which was within musket range of the West Woods. If the Rebels shot some of the horses and rushed toward the guns, he might lose his whole section. Tyndale was a bully. His major, Ario Pardee, declared of him, "A more disgraceful man I never met." Tyndale chose to belittle McGill and questioned his courage, saying, "If you are afraid I will get other guns." McGill answered that he was not afraid, but he "protested against a foolhardy undertaking that could lose him his two guns." Tyndale refused to compromise, and McGill felt he had no choice but to obey.

David Nichol, a sergeant in McGill's section, heard some of the conversation between the two officers and, 4 days later, in a letter home, he related, "I thought to myself it was no place for Artillery, but the Lieut. had to obey orders."[14]

McGill limbered his section and headed back to Smoketown Road. It was this movement that caught the attention of Colonel Matt Ransom. At the end of this road, McGill's crews could not drive straight ahead into the woods, because of the Hagerstown Pike's fences. Therefore the lieutenant turned his guns left at the Dunker Church and went 200 to 300 feet south on the Hagerstown Pike, near the southern edge of the West Woods, where there was a gap providing access west of the pike. McGill left Sergeant Nichols and the No. 1 gun in the road here and led the No. 2 gun, under a 17-year-old former bartender from Philadelphia, Sergeant Adam Shaw, into the woods. The infantry cheered the artillery reinforcement. Although there was some small-arms fire, Colonel Cooke kept all of his men, except a few skirmishers in his two regiments, concealed in Reel's cornfield. There was also the occasional Confederate shell that hurtled through the woods, severing limbs and branches. Before he placed his piece, McGill wanted to know what he was supposed to fire at. Tyndale pointed out some Rebels on Reel Ridge. They apparently were not easy to spot, for the colonel offered McGill his spyglass in order to see them. Sergeant Nichol presumed the enemy "must be some distance off." McGill looked through the glass for a few moments, returned it to Tyndale, rode over to Sergeant Shaw's gun, and ordered it to move to some rising ground near the edge of the woods and unlimber. This was the moment when Cooke's regiments revealed themselves and loosed a volley.[15]

The bullets decimated the crew. James Marshall was struck in the side, "uttered a piercing shriek and fell dead." Shaw was also hit in the side. Three others were wounded, one of them three times. At nearly the same instant, an enemy shell severed a large tree branch overhead. It fell on the pole team, pinning the horses to the ground. Then, simultaneously, shouting and firing sounded from the right of Greene's line, where Ransom's brigade suddenly appeared on the Federals' right flank.[16]

WHEN THE PURNELL LEGION arrived in the West Woods, its commander, Major William T. Fulton, ordered out a detachment of skirmishers to explore the woodlot north of his position. One of those in the detachment was a 19-year-old private, Pennock J. Cole. Four or five men in Cole's company went with him, and as they threaded their way through the woods, Cole was in the lead. They passed by a large pile of cordwood northwest of the Dunker Church and somehow made their way forward, coming between two lines of prone men, about 25 yards apart, who took no notice of the intruders. Cole saw that they were Confederates, almost certainly the 49th North Carolina. He signaled to his comrades to be silent and retrace their steps. When he returned to his regiment,

Cole reported what he had observed, but Major Fulton had no time to react before firing broke out in front of the 13th New Jersey, followed almost immediately by confusion.[17]

Adjutant Hopkins in the 13th New Jersey had remained on the right flank of his regiment ever since General Greene's visit, convinced that the troops he had seen earlier were the enemy. He observed the flash of rifle barrels through the trees, moving toward them, and hurried over to Colonel Carman to report this. Carman directed him to refuse (bend back) the three right companies. After giving the necessary orders, Hopkins, "on the strength of Gen. Greene's instructions, ran down the hill to make sure as to whether the force was our men or not, although I had little doubt in my own mind as to their being rebels." The foliage prevented him from making a positive identification until he reached the ravine, downslope from the regiment. Here he confirmed that they were Confederates, moving toward the 13th's right flank. Hopkins shouted back, "They are Rebs, let them have it." The regiment was already on high alert and immediately began shooting. Hopkins watched the North Carolinians swiftly deploy into line and return the fire. For a moment he was caught between the two sides and lay down to avoid being shot.[18]

The appearance of what looked like Union soldiers surprised the 49th North Carolina as it maneuvered through the West Woods to capture the section of artillery seen by Colonel Ransom. Two officers were sent forward, probably at the same time as Adjutant Hopkins was scrambling into the ravine, to determine whether the strangers were friend or foe. One was the 49th's adjutant, who identified the men as the enemy and shouted back to open fire. The other was Captain Cicero Dunham, who was mounted and rode near enough that some of the men in the 13th New Jersey hollered for him to surrender. When Dunham wheeled his horse to escape, they fired on him, but missed. The North Carolinians advanced with their weapons in the trail-arms position, which caused Samuel Toombs in Company D, as well as others in the inexperienced New Jersey regiment, to believe that the "rebs appeared as if they were going to surrender." Sebastian Duncan Jr., writing 4 days later, perceived that the "Rebs pretended to wish to lay down their arms & come in as prisoners." Orders were shouted to cease firing. The 49th had probably 400 or so effectives. They exploited the confusion in the 13th's ranks to quickly maneuver to a position where they could enfilade both the New Jerseyites and the Marylanders in the Purnell Legion. Closing to a range of 50 to 60 yards, they blasted the confused Federal soldiers.[19]

Combined, the two Union regiments outnumbered the 49th North Carolina, but the Confederates had the advantage of position. They could deliver their full fire, while only part of both Union regiments could reply. The Legion possibly loosed three volleys before Major Fulton, fearing they would be cut off, ordered a retreat. The 13th New Jersey collapsed at the same time, or only seconds afterward. Sebastian Duncan Jr. wrote, "There was nothing left but to fall back which we did in tolerably quick time. Had we stood three minutes longer the Reg would have been captured entire." Some, like Duncan, fell back fighting. "I retreated backwards from one tree to another firing as I could," he related to his mother. He even paused to pick up a "splendid sword" as a souvenir, which he subsequently had to throw away to help a wounded comrade. Private Charles Ritchie stated, with refreshing honesty, "There is no doubt if we had been disciplined enough to await orders before running we would have been all gobbled up." The 13th had 9 men killed and 60 wounded in the brief engagement. When Colonel Carman considered the volume of fire directed at his men, he was astonished that the number of casualties was not far higher.[20]

The collapse of Greene's right flank caused his entire position to swiftly unravel. Hastening the Federals' departure from the West Woods were the 3rd Arkansas and the 27th North Carolina, who emerged from the cornfield and charged toward the woods, hoping to capture McGill's two guns. By pure chance, the Rebels struck nearly simultaneously on both flanks of Greene's line. All told, there were slightly over 1,000 Confederates in the two attacking forces, so Greene had a manpower edge of over 350, but at the points of attack, the Rebels had superior numbers and the advantage of surprise. The 13th New Jersey's retreat exposed the 28th Pennsylvania's right flank. Major William Raphael, then commanding the regiment, saw Confederates to his left, front, and right and heard the rebel yell sounding toward his rear and right. He sensed annihilation if he lingered any longer, so he ordered a retreat. The rest of Greene's command immediately followed, like falling dominos. In perhaps 5 minutes, Greene's lodgment in the West Woods had been lost. His men streamed from the woodlot in confusion, flowing around the Dunker Church and across its plateau. It was now about noon. Greene had held the woods for nearly an hour and a half.[21]

On the Dunker Church plateau, Colonel Carman recalled that "officers of every grade made efforts to check the retreat," but their endeavors "availed nothing," and the men continued to pass by them, toward the East Woods. Ransom's and Cooke's Confederates aggressively pursued them, keeping up a steady fire on the retreating bluecoats. Many of Greene's soldiers recorded close calls. Corporal Ambrose H. Hayward in the 28th Pennsylvania had a ball take off his cap and nearly knock him off his feet. "I put my hand up and saw there was no blood and Smilled," he wrote. Private Joseph A. Moore, also in the 28th, turned his ankle while climbing over the breastwork of fence rails north of the Dunker Church, along the Hagerstown Pike. It had been built by some of Manning's Confederates earlier that morning. "I fell flat, as if shot," Moore stated, and he heard some of his men remark that he was killed. No one paused to check, and when Moore recovered and got to his feet, he was 100 yards behind everyone else. He sprinted after them, while "the rebel balls zipped thick and fast about me and struck the ground as rapidly as hail," he recalled. "Every step I expected to fall from the storm of bullets whistling around me," but luck was his companion that day, and he escaped. When Sebastian Duncan Jr. emerged from the West Woods, he encountered a comrade, wounded in the leg, who begged for his help. Reluctantly dropping his souvenir sword, he helped the injured man hobble along for nearly "a quarter of a mile exposed to a most terrible fire from the Rebs who were following us." The bullets gave extra energy to the injured man, and Duncan noticed that he "could hobble on a little faster & we came out safely," except for a single bullet hole through Duncan's pant leg.[22]

McGill's artillerymen were forced to abandon the No. 2 gun in the West Woods and run for their lives. Sergeant Nichol's No. 1 gun, which had remained in the Hagerstown Pike, unlimbered and fired a blast of canister at Cooke's approaching Rebels. It then limbered and drove rapidly up the pike and Smoketown Road, going toward the East Woods. McGill's men were furious. "We lost one gun, and nearly a whole gun squad, owing to a foolish order given by an officer of high rank, who I really believe did not know whether he was on his heels or his head," complained Corporal James P. Stewart. Sergeant Nichol marveled, as Colonel Carman had, that the section escaped "with such a small loss," considering the volume of fire directed at them.[23]

The target of the artillerymen's wrath did not emerge from the retreat unharmed. Tyndale had lost his mount and, on foot, fell back with his men. When he reached the haystacks near Mumma's orchard and the now nearly burnt-out barn, he paused to rally his men. Private Moore had caught up with the others by this point, and he recalled meeting Tyndale by a haystack. The lieutenant colonel went around one side, and Moore the other. During the passage around the stack, a bullet struck Tyndale in the back of the head and passed out through his cheek, beside his nose. "I fell senseless," he wrote. Despite Tyndale's unpopularity, he had behaved with great courage throughout the fighting on the plateau and in the West Woods. So 1st Lieutenant Charles Borbridge and Corporal Ambrose H. Hayward, at great peril, turned back to rescue him, even though the pursuing 27th North Carolina were within 100 yards of them. Borbridge was carrying a Confederate battle flag he had picked up after the repulse of Kershaw's or Manning's assault. He refused to relinquish it and figured out a way to keep hold of the colors while he and Hayward dragged Tyndale's limp body for nearly 50 yards to the cover of another haystack. This was possibly the same haystack where, earlier, two companies of the 27th North Carolina had peeled off to disarm the Union soldiers they found milling around it.[24]

The 49th North Carolina, with the 35th North Carolina close behind on its left, arrived at the edge of the West Woods, about 130 yards north of the Dunker Church. There they blazed away at Greene's retreating men, as well as at McGill's caissons and No. 1 gun, as they fled up Smoketown Road. In their excitement, part of the 49th dashed into the open ground to chase the Yankees. The more prudent ones took cover behind the breastwork of fence rails, thrown up earlier that morning. The Rebel pursuers attracted the attention of Cothran's, Knap's, and Lieutenant Evan Thomas's batteries, 16 guns in all. General Alpheus Williams was watching in the rear of Thomas's battery. He first saw Greene's infantry "scampering to the rear in great confusion," followed, moments later, by a line of yelling Confederates. The batteries hit the Rebels "with a tornado of canister." Williams directed two of Thomas's Napoleons to target what was probably the 27th North Carolina, who were passing over the Dunker Church plateau. Their canister appeared to strike along the very front of the Confederates' line, "stirring up a dust like a thick cloud." When the smoke from the firing cleared, the 49th North Carolina had vanished, and the 27th North Carolina had veered to the right and out of sight, heading into Mumma's cornfield. Survivors of the 49th remembered it as "the heaviest artillery fire the regiment ever experienced." No line could survive in the open ground between the West and East Woods against the firepower the Federals had arrayed across the front of the East Woods.[25] As the Confederates of Ransom's brigade disappeared into the West Woods, Williams looked back to see Major General William F. Smith, riding up at the head of a division of fresh troops. The 6th Corps had arrived.[26]

MAJOR GENERAL WILLIAM B. FRANKLIN'S 6th Corps, and Major General Darius Couch's 1st Division in the 4th Corps, both spent the night of September 16 in Pleasant Valley, Maryland. Franklin's orders from McClellan on the night of September 16 were to send Couch's division to occupy Maryland Heights, while Franklin, with the two division of the 6th Corps, was to join the main army on the 17th. There was no urgency in the orders, and no mention that a battle was imminent, but Franklin had his men up early the next morning. While they boiled their coffee and gulped down a hasty breakfast, everyone heard the heavy thump of artillery from the direction of Sharpsburg. The 6th Corps was on the road before 6 a.m., with Smith's 2nd Division in the lead. Franklin rode with Slocum and the 1st Division, an odd decision, given that the corps was now clearly marching to battle, and being near the front would have ensured that Franklin could react promptly to any developments. Franklin's choice was not a personality issue, since he had attended West Point with Smith, who was one of his closest friends and had his complete confidence.[27]

Other than Brooks's Vermont brigade, Smith's division had done no fighting at Crampton's Gap, which was why they led the march. Its three brigades numbered around 5,000 men. Division commander Smith was described as "a short, quite portly man, with a light brown imperial and shaggy moustache, a round, military head, and the look of a German officer, altogether." He was nicknamed "Baldy" early on in his military career, to set him apart from the other Smiths in the service. He had graduated from West Point in 1841 and, before the Civil War, had served with the elite topographical engineers. McClellan had a high opinion of the Vermonter, praising his "great personal courage" and "wonderfully quick eye for ground and for handling troops," but he was also clear-eyed about Smith's shortcomings. He was "too quick tempered toward those under him, very selfish, and had a most bitter tongue which often ran away with him and got him into trouble." Smith, in short, was a handful as a subordinate: openly critical of his peers, and hard on those who served under him.[28]

Despite the continual heavy firing coming from the direction in which they were marching, Smith's soldiers were in good spirits. Major Thomas W. Hyde remembered his 7th Maine as being "high spirited and happy." The 2nd Division passed through Rohrersville and continued north to Old Sharpsburg Road, which it followed to the northern tip of Elk Ridge. Here Smith was met by a member of McClellan's staff, who directed him to mass his division near McClellan's Pry farm headquarters. They then marched cross-country and reached the Sharpsburg–Boonsboro Pike at Keedysville around 10 a.m., massing on each side of the road not far from the Pry farm lane. McClellan sent for Smith, and the latter recalled that the army commander said to him, "Sumner is getting along very well on the right and I am expecting to hear Burnside's guns every minute. Keep your division where it is that I may send you where you shall be of the most service." Only minutes before, McClellan had received a signal message from his right flank, which reported that "Hooker is wounded, Sumner in command. Fighting is desperate, but we are steadily driving them." From all McClellan had personally observed, and according to the reports from the front, the assault on the Confederates' left, although meeting fierce resistance, was driving the enemy back. Orders to Burnside to open his attack on the Confederates' right had been dispatched at 9:10 a.m. Hence McClellan expected to hear an engagement open on the 9th Corps' front at any minute. The conflict appeared to be well in hand, and McClellan intended Franklin's 6th Corps to serve as his mobile reserve, "to operate on either flank or on the center, as circumstances might require."[29]

Smith did not think he was back with the 2nd Division for more than 15 minutes before he received urgent orders from McClellan to move his division across Pry's Ford and report to Sumner. There were no other details. What had prompted this sudden change in orders? Only minutes after telling Smith that Sumner was "getting along very well," McClellan received jarring news from the 2nd Corps' commander. The army headquarters' signal station received a message from Sumner, time-stamped at 10:20 a.m., that read, "I must have reinforcements immediately or will have to give way on the right." In a moment, McClellan's confidence that the battle was going well on the right had evaporated.[30]

As Smith's regiments filed down toward Antietam Creek, the men had a good opportunity to see some of the battlefield they were marching toward. Christoph Niederer in the German 20th New York noted how it "was a crackling and a screaming." Robert J. Cowden in the 49th New York believed that "never before had we heard so heavy firing of artillery and musketry." After crossing the creek, Smith's men began to encounter "hundreds of wounded" streaming back from the fighting at the Sunken Lane. While the 49th Pennsylvania re-formed after wading through the water, Winfield Hancock rode up in front of them and addressed the Pennsylvanians in his loud, commanding voice: "Men, I am about to lead you into the presence of the enemy, but stand by that old flag to-day, and it will be all right." They responded with three cheers. The small-arms and artillery fire seemed to rise to even greater heights. The fighting at the Sunken Lane was in full fury. "We all felt we had got to brace ourselves, for the trying moment must soon come," concluded Major Hyde in the 7th Maine. He and his good friend, Captain William L. Haskell, who was acting as regimental adjutant that day, shook hands with one another and "promised to die like soldiers."[31]

As Major Hyde watched his men hurrying toward the fighting, he realized how small his regiment was. There were 15 officers and about 155 enlisted men. He ordered the 8 or 10 fifers and drummers to arm themselves with any dropped weapons they could find and fall in with the rest. In the 4th Vermont, John Conline, only 16 years old, was both astonished and awed by the "deafening roar" of artillery "and the rapid fire of musketry" from fighting in the Sunken Lane. He recalled that in his youthful ardor, "from an artistic standpoint the spectacle was grand beyond description." Ben F. Clarkson in the 49th Pennsylvania noted that as they came nearer to the front, "shells were exploding in the air above us and solid shot went whizzing over our heads." A member of the 3rd Vermont thought that the scene unfolding before him "baffles description." Smith's men were veterans, but they had never seen an engagement on this scale, with such evident ferocity. As they neared the East Woods, Friedrich Meyer, a German in the 20th New York, noted that the "ground became more and more thickly littered with corpses."[32]

Smith found Sumner somewhere north of the East Woods. The 2nd Corps' commander had established his headquarters near the signal station at Joseph Poffenberger's farm, but he must have ridden from there toward the East Woods when the fighting between Greene, Ransom, and Cooke flared up in the West Woods. "On reporting to him I was told to close my division in mass facing a certain way from which point he expected an attack," Smith recalled. This position was almost certainly directed toward the northern end of the West Woods, where Sumner feared an enemy assault. While Smith waited for Hancock's 1st Brigade, which was at the head of his column, he saw an officer riding toward him at a gallop. It proved to be Lieutenant Colonel Joe H. Taylor, Sumner's adjutant general. Taylor rode straight to Smith, although Sumner was standing nearby, and pointed toward the Hagerstown Pike. The lieutenant colonel told the division commander that if "you don't get some troops out there . . . the enemy will capture all our artillery." Greene's division was in retreat, and the Confederates were emerging from the West Woods in pursuit. Smith did not consult with Sumner. During his meeting with the 2nd Corps' commander, he had detected that the general seemed "utterly demoralized."[33]

Smith rode to Hancock and ordered him to detach two regiments, stating that Taylor would show them where to go. He then rode forward to get a look at the ground Taylor was referencing. It was in the vicinity of Croasdale's Knoll, where the Cornfield abutted the East Woods. What Smith saw convinced him to order the rest of Hancock's brigade to this area, as well as to summon Captain Andrew Cowan's 1st Battery, New York Light, and Lieutenant Theodore J. Vanneman's Battery B, Maryland Light Artillery—a total of 10 3-inch rifles—to buttress the infantry line. Vanneman relieved Knap's battery in the southeastern part of the Cornfield. Hancock personally placed Cowan. The captain recalled that the general was "as usual on such occasions very excited and ordered me to get into battery on the farther side of the pasture, close up to a large cornfield, out of which infantry soldiers were running in great confusion." The position was the pasture north of the Cornfield, and the soldiers running through the corn could only have been some elements of the 13th New Jersey and the Purnell Legion. Confederates were reported to be advancing through the corn. Perhaps they were skirmishers from Early's brigade, but they could not have constituted any substantial force. Cowan gave them a dose of canister, "and they fell back promptly."[34]

Hancock's regiments passed through the East Woods and deployed in the rear of the line of batteries arrayed across the western front of the woods. Three batteries occupied the ground covered by Hancock's regiments: Cowan's 1st Battery, New York Light, in the pasture north of the corn; Captain John D. Frank's Battery G, 1st New York Light, from French's division, near the northeastern corner of the corn; and Vanneman's Battery B, Maryland Light, in the southeastern corner. The 49th Pennsylvania lay down on Cowan's right, while the 43rd New York and part of the 137th Pennsylvania filled the space between Cowan and Frank, and the 6th Maine and the 5th Wisconsin occupied the ground between Frank and Vanneman.[35]

While Hancock's infantry arrayed itself, Smith galloped to meet and place Colonel William H. Irwin's 3rd Brigade, the next of his brigades to come up. Irwin was the weak link in what was otherwise an excellent division. He was a Mifflin County, Pennsylvania, attorney who saw combat service in the Mexican War as a volunteer. His record shows that he had issues with alcohol and may have suffered from some type of mental illness. In January 1862, he had faced a court-martial on charges of neglect of duty, intoxication, and conduct prejudicial to good order and military discipline. He was found not guilty of the first two charges, although he did not deny he had been drinking, claiming it was not to excess. The court found him guilty of the third count, so he was relieved of his command for 30 days and officially reprimanded. Irwin, despite his personal problems, must have been considered competent by both Smith and Hancock, since they detached him from his regiment, the 49th Pennsylvania in Hancock's brigade, and placed him in command of the 3rd Brigade, filling a vacancy there. Smith would later claim that he was not aware of Irwin's troubles, but this seems unlikely, since Irwin was serving under Smith when he was court-martialed.[36]

Smith intended to place Irwin's 3rd Brigade on Hancock's left, but he discovered that the East Woods, to Hancock's left and rear, were full of 12th Corps' troops, so there was no need—or room—for more men in that area. The question soon became irrelevant. Irwin's regiments neared the East Woods at the same time as Greene's men were being driven from the West Woods, while Cooke's regiments and the 49th North Carolina were bursting out of those woods in hot pursuit. The Federal batteries deflected or repulsed any threat to the Union's hold on the East Woods, but Greene's defeat and the enemy's pursuit generated great excitement and consternation among some Yankee commanders, Smith being one of them. He rushed Irwin's regiments toward the threatened sector.[37]

Smith adamantly maintained that his plan was for Irwin's brigade to only advance to the Dunker Church plateau, where they could help protect and support the artillery, as well as fill the gap created by Greene's retreat. "I started out to cover the artillery exposed all the distance between Sedgwick's left, and Richardson's right, and I did it without the thought of making any assault on the confederate lines beyond the ground necessary to protect the artillery," he wrote long after the war. This might have been Smith's intention, but if he communicated this to Irwin, that officer did not understand his orders. Charles E. Stevens, a 2nd lieutenant in the 77th New York, thought his regiment's orders were "that they were to charge down on the [West] woods and drive out the enemy." He heard an anonymous officer whom they passed call out to his regiment, saying that there could not be many Rebels left in the woods, as the artillery had just shelled them furiously. One officer who did not believe this was Alpheus Williams, who was near Thomas's battery as Irwin's brigade came jogging up. Williams knew Smith from when the latter had been on duty as a Regular Army engineer in Detroit, Michigan, before the war. He watched as Irwin's regiments "fairly rushed toward the left and front." Williams "hastily called his [Smith's] attention to the woods full of Rebels on his right as he was advancing." No one seemed to listen to Williams's sound advice that day, be it Mansfield, Sumner, or Smith. Afterward, Williams complained to his daughter how "hundreds of lives were foolishly sacrificed by generals I see most praised, generals who would come up with their commands and pitch in at the first point without consultation with those who knew the ground or without reconnoitering or looking for the effective points of attacks." The criticism could have applied equally to any of those three generals.[38]

Irwin's five regiments had not completed their deployment before Smith hurled them forward. The 2nd Division's commander intended for the 33rd and

77th New York, who were bringing up the rear of the brigade, to advance as skirmishers north of Smoketown Road, toward the West Woods. Meanwhile, he directed the 20th New York, Irwin's largest regiment—with 680 officers and men—toward the Dunker Church plateau; while the 49th New York followed, echeloned to the 20th's right rear; with the 7th Maine to their left rear. The direction in which Smith guided the 20th lends strength to his assertion that he had no intention of assaulting the West Woods. The regiment marched southwest, following the axis of Smoketown Road and the Mumma farm lane, toward Mumma's farm and the ground Tompkins's battery had occupied earlier. This movement makes sense if Smith's plan was to flank Cooke's two regiments and drive them back, while the 77th and 33rd New York screened the West Woods and the right flank of the brigade.[39]

The 20th New York were known unofficially as the "United Turner Rifles." Recruited from the German community in New York City and, partially, in Newark, New Jersey, they traced their origin to the Turner societies in Germany. The Turners had developed in reaction to France's occupation of the German-speaking states during the Napoleonic Wars. They advocated physical fitness and used gymnastics to build a national, patriotic spirit, and they were active in the wars of liberation against France in 1813–1814. The societies were politically active, as well, advocating German unity. As liberals, many Turners participated in the unsuccessful revolution of 1848, which, among other things, sought a more representative government. Following their defeat, tens of thousands of German revolutionaries and their families fled from their homeland to the United States, to escape retribution. Known as the "Forty-Eighters," they settled throughout the nation, but particularly in northern cities like New York, Philadelphia, Milwaukee, and St. Louis. Politically, they aligned with the Republican Party, supporting its stand against slavery. Turner societies sprang up across the country. In New York City, young Turners performed their quasi-military gymnastics under the eye of Max Weber, who had fought with the German revolutionaries under Franz Sigel. Hundreds of these young men enlisted in 1861 to serve under Weber in what became the 20th New York Infantry. Before they left the city, speeches that marked the presentation of the regiment's colors articulated the cause these young, athletic Germans were fighting for.[40] One such peroration exhorted, "Side by side we now battle for our nation's life. For this very purpose it was that you sought this western world. You came here, that you of the present generation might enjoy that long deferred but dearly cherished object of every German heart—a comprehensive and united nationality. You left your native land, dismembered and disintegrated by long centuries of strife, that you might here breath, in freedom, the invigorating air of one great, united, indivisible republic."[41]

When the regiment left New York City, they were presented with three flags: the national standard; a crimson banner with *Bahn Frei*—meaning "clear the road"—embroidered in yellow silk; and a red, black, and gold German flag. A *New York Times* reporter, impressed by the athleticism of the young men, asserted that "they can climb like cats, bound like deer, fight like men, and run a-foot like Indians." But war was not a playing field, and the 20th New York reflected the contention that combat units were only as good as their leadership. Weber was promoted to brigadier general in the spring of 1862, and command went to Lieutenant Colonel Francis Weiss, who dismissed his soldiers as a "very overbearing, turbulent, socialistic body of men, who lacked discipline." From that unpromising start, relations between commander and commanded steadily deteriorated. Friedrich Meyer described Weiss as "miserable," and he referred to the regiment's lieutenant colonel as "that stupid bungler." Things worsened when the regiment went into combat at White Oak Swamp during the Seven Days Battles. Meyer recalled how Weiss and "most of the officers immediately fled the field" when they came under heavy artillery fire. Major Thomas W. Hyde in the 7th Maine witnessed the event and wrote how the 20th "went to pieces as the first shot struck among them as if they were made of glass." As Lieutenant Colonel William C. Alberger, commanding the 49th New York, recalled of the Germans, "The fact was we were always anxious about them. . . . While an exceedingly well drilled regiment, their original officers were of very poor material."[42]

Weiss resigned after the Seven Days Battles, and Colonel Ernst von Vegasack—a Swedish officer on furlough from his nation's army, serving on the staff of General Daniel Butterfield—was assigned to shape up the 20th New York. Vegasack spoke no German but quickly won the men over and established discipline and confidence. "He was very strict, but equally so with officers and men," wrote Friedrich Meyer. "On the march he was everywhere, now in the rear, then at the head of the column. He had a friendly or instructive word for everyone." Major Hyde believed that "of all the foreign officers I knew, and there were scores of them with us, he was the best." Now, as Vegasack's big regiment led Irwin's brigade toward the Dunker Church plateau, Hyde watched the colonel and his other field officers ride their horses close behind the regimental line, "pushing them on in a most spirited manner."[43]

Christoph Niederer noticed that the ground they advanced over was strewn with Confederate dead. One was directly in his path, and when he tried to jump over the body, he slipped and fell. He heard some of his comrades call out, "There, Christoph got his!" But Niederer leaped up and dashed forward to rejoin the others. Friedrich Meyer recalled scaling three fences before they reached the Rebels. At the second one, which may have been the post-and-rail fence that ran from Mumma's barn down to Roulette's farm, his company commander was shot and killed. When the 49th New York reached the fence at the northern edge of Mumma's cornfield, they received a volley from part of the 27th North Carolina, which luckily only managed to wound one man. The New Yorkers returned the fire, and the Rebels began to retreat from the corn, going across the Mumma farm lane and the southern face of the Dunker Church plateau. They were hurried on their way by the weight of the 20th and 49th New York and the 7th Maine converging on their exposed flank. The Confederates fell back, firing at their pursuers. Christoph Niederer noted that the 20th did not return fire, but simply continued to steadily advance against the retreating enemy. The three regiments then changed the direction of their march from south to almost due west, both to pursue the Rebels and gain the high ground of the plateau on their right. As the 20th emerged from Mumma's cornfield, Cooke's retiring men "gave them a good salvo," which knocked several from the Federals' ranks but failed to check their pursuers.[44]

The 20th and 49th New York swept up onto the plateau, with the 7th Maine running to catch up with them after veering away from the advance to engage the 27th North Carolina. As the Federals neared the summit, the soldiers of the 49th, excited to see the backs of the enemy, clamored to pursue the fleeing foe. Their commander, Lieutenant Colonel William C. Alberger, knowing that they were without support and far in advance of other friendly troops, reined his men in with considerable difficulty just before they exposed themselves on the crest. Robert Cowden thought Alberger halted them "just in time to save them from being cut down by a battery and a line of battle." Which line of battle opposed them is a mystery, although it may have been a rallied part of Cooke's two regiments. There were no other infantry in the area. The artillery probably was Captain Jefferson Peyton's Orange (Virginia) battery of five guns and two pieces in Macon's battery, positioned on the northern end of Reel Ridge, above Reel's cornfield. Alberger, who was on horseback, may have seen these guns, or he may have simply sensed that venturing onto the plateau's summit would only make his men an easy target. His quick action shielded his troops from casualties— for the moment. The 20th, on Alberger's left, made the mistake of advancing slightly farther and received a "murderous fire" from the Rebel guns. As Private Meyer recalled, they "cut a swath of death and destruction through our ranks." Vegesack allowed his men to fire a volley at Cooke's Confederates and reload. He then ordered them back a dozen paces, to get some cover beneath the crest of the plateau.[45]

The crest protected Irwin's men from Cooke's infantry fire, although Friedrich Meyer managed to get hit by a bullet that penetrated his overcoat, which he kept rolled over his shoulder. "It felt as though I had received a hefty blow from a club," he wrote. The coat absorbed the force of the bullet, saving Meyer's life. The Confederate guns were the greatest menace, hammering the area where Irwin's infantry were hugging the earth with shell, shrapnel, and canister. Union artillery added to the threat when short shells from the batteries east of Antietam Creek began detonating over their position, inflicting numerous wounds. Christoph Niederer wrote about one shell that burst near him with a deafening explosion. He felt a blow on his right shoulder and noticed that his jacket "was covered with white stuff." He checked his arm and found that it was okay, but his face was damp. When he wiped it, he saw blood on his hand. To his horror, Niederer now "first saw that the man next to me, Kessler [Philip Kessler, Company F], lacked the upper part of his head, and almost all his brains had gone into the face of the man next to him, Merkel, so that he could scarcely see." A moment later, Charles Schmidt, who was lying in front of Niederer, took a canister or shrapnel ball in the head, killing him instantly. When Niederer looked behind him, he saw "his gay and lively" tentmate, Herman Bruns, also among the dead, with a ghastly wound. Lieutenant Colonel Alberger felt some anxiety about the staying power of the 20th New York under the barrage and made his way to the top of the hill, to get a better idea of where the enemy shells were coming from. Just then, one of them burst nearby, killing two men in his right company and wounding several others, including Alberger, who was hit in the face by a fragment that broke his jaw and removed several teeth. To add to the misery, Christoph Niederer and his comrades had a badly wounded Confederate soldier lying yards away from them, at an exposed point on the plateau, who was "wailing terribly" for the Germans to pull him to safety. Niederer wanted to rescue the man, but his captain, Hermann Bennecke, refused to let the private expose himself. Then a shell exploded nearby, shattering one of the Confederate's arms. No doubt the heart-rending cries grew louder. Bennecke now relented and told Niederer and Julius Sucker to fetch the wounded Rebel. The Confederate artillery fire was still heavy, but Niederer and Sucker sprinted up to the man. "We laid him in a canvas, since we could not touch him any place without his screaming with pain," recalled Niederer, and dragged him down to the hospital at Roulette's farm. Niederer and Sucker had risked their lives to save an enemy soldier, but their heroic deed probably had less to do with compassion and more with survival. Given the carnage the Rebel artillery was inflicting, they probably concluded that it was safer to try to get to the injured Confederate soldier and escape from the front line than it was to remain and be shredded by a shell.[46]

The artillery barrage that wreaked havoc among the 20th New York barely touched the nearby 7th Maine. Only one man was wounded, even though the clamor from the nearby explosions was so frequent that Major Hyde complained, "My head ached as if it would split from the constant bursting of shells around." The difference was that Hyde kept his men under cover and concealed his regimental colors, which Confederate gunners could use as a range marker. The 20th kept their flags flying, clearly indicating their location. Hyde made his way over to Vegasack and suggested that his prominently displayed colors were drawing the enemy's accurate artillery fire, when it might be better to conceal them, like the 7th had. Vegasack, who was riding up and down behind his line with a drawn revolver to deter anyone from bugging out, replied to Hyde, "Let them wave: they are our glory." The price for glory was steep. In the 20th New York, 38 of its men were killed and 92 wounded, the highest in the 6th Corps—by a considerable margin. Perhaps Vegasack knew his men and believed that if he had lowered the colors, it might have shaken their courage. Morale can be a tenuous thing and could turn on some seemingly inconsequential matter.[47]

During the shelling, one of Hyde's men, a crack shot who carried a personal rifle that Hyde merely described as a "valuable weapon," came to the major and asked permission to crawl forward and try his hand at targeting the Confederate gunners. The soldier, whose name was Knox, crept to a rock in front of the 7th's line, which gave him cover. Every so often the men in the 7th would hear the sound of his rifle. Hyde moved to a point where he could observe the private's work. "He had driven away every one from a section of guns," wrote Hyde. "As fast as a man would come forward to fire, Knox would tumble him over." A Confederate officer and his staff rode near the guns, and Knox killed the commander's horse, sending the party hurrying back for cover. The battery that Knox targeted may have been Macon's or Peyton's. Whichever it was, the gunners, with the din of their own firing, were probably unaware of where the bullets that caused such havoc among them were coming from. The private kept up his deadly work for nearly an hour before the Rebel crews finally spotted him and turned one or more of their pieces on him. They managed to send a piece of shell into the breech of Knox's "pet rifle," destroying it. He slithered back to the main line and "disconsolately" showed Hyde his damaged gun. But he was not easily deterred from his deadly work. Gathering up three rifles left by the wounded, he went forward again and kept up his single-handed combat.[48]

Due to some confusion, the 33rd and 77th New York, who were to screen the right flank of the brigade as skirmishers, instead went forward in column, passing through Evan Thomas's battery. They went running ahead, with the 33rd north of Smoketown Road and the 77th south of it, slightly in advance of the 33rd. The only possible explanation for them proceeding in column is Smith's and Irvin's belief that the West Woods were unoccupied by the enemy. Captain Nathan S. Babcock, commanding the 77th, reported that his mission was to cut off the "flying enemy"—in other words, the 27th North Carolina and 3rd Arkansas. Moving in column was the most rapid means of covering ground. Whatever the explanation, the New Yorkers paid the price for both Smith and Irvin ignoring Alpheus Williams's warning to the contrary. The 49th and 35th North Carolina saw the Yankees coming and reoccupied the rail breastwork north of the Dunker Church, which they had fallen back from during the heavy shelling that followed Greene's retreat from the West Woods. The two regiments of New Yorkers were close to the woods "when the enemy suddenly and unexpectedly opened a heavy fire." Charles Stevens, a lieutenant in the 77th, described it as a "terrible volley." It no doubt was frightful for those on the receiving end, but in the horrific carnage of that terrible day, the New Yorkers escaped with only moderate losses: 47 for the 33rd, and 32 for the 77th. These were not insignificant, but they were considerably lower than the 145 casualties the 20th New York suffered.[49]

What probably saved these two regiments from greater damage was their discipline in reacting to the surprise volley. Even though both units were shaken by the fire, they recovered quickly. As Irvin reported, they "closed up and faced by the rear rank, and poured in a close and scorching fire" that at the least drove the North Carolinians under cover. Both Irvin and Smith saw Ransom's men appear in the West Woods and took immediate action. Irvin sent Lieutenant William H. Long, a member of his staff, galloping to the 77th with orders to withdraw immediately to the Dunker Church plateau. Smith did the same for the 33rd. Captain Babcock claimed that his regiment was so close to the enemy, "you could see the white of their eyes at the time of retiring." Smith, Irvin, and both regimental commanders maintained that after some initial unsteadiness both regiments fell back in good order to the plateau. Captain Charles Owen, who followed the advance with a section of his Battery G, 1st Rhode Island, probably intending to reoccupy his old position, saw things differently. He reported that the infantry "was quite unsteady," so he turned his guns around, fearing he might lose them. Although the North Carolinians "disappeared" back into the timber, the ordeal of the 33rd and 77th New York was not over. When these regiments reached the Dunker Church plateau, a Confederate battery, which Lieutenant Stevens believed had just gone into position, "raked the crest of the hill we had just passed" with fire that killed the 77th's color bearer. Stevens picked the flag up and joined his regiment beneath the crest, where they found some defilade. Irvin's advance had been checked, but it succeeded in reestablishing a strong Union hold on the plateau, which posed a worrisome threat to the Confederates.[50]

SMITH'S INTENTION, AFTER PLACING Irvin, was to bring Brigadier General William T. H. Brooks's Vermont brigade up on the left as a support for Irvin, as well as to build a connection between Richardson's and French's divisions and the 6th Corps. But when Smith turned to look for the Vermonters, he saw the brigade unaccountably "moving way off to the left." When Brooks reached the vicinity of the East Woods, Sumner had finally established communications with Richardson's and French's divisions, learning that French was reportedly out of ammunition and Richardson was in need of relief. Without bothering to inform Smith, Sumner gave orders for Brooks to relieve Richardson at once and impressed the urgency of their mission on the Vermonters by directing that the movement be executed at the double-quick. The soldiers immediately picked up their pace, but Brooks, who apparently did not hear Sumner's orders to double-quick—or disagreed with them—immediately countermanded them. "Not a bit of it men. Not a bit of it men," he said. "When my men go into battle I want them to go calm and cool." The 41-year-old Ohioan was as crusty and battle-tested a Regular as existed in either army. An 1841 graduate of West Point, he had served in the Second Seminole War and fought in nearly every battle of the Mexican War. His Vermonters loved him. A member of the 3rd Vermont wrote home about how, at Crampton's Gap, Brooks dismounted and went on all fours up the mountain, keeping close to the skirmish line. "With such a Gen. as this, men will go wherever ordered," he declared.[51]

When Smith caught up with Brooks, the latter explained that he had been ordered to relieve Richardson. Smith vented his fury in his after-action report: "It is not the first or second time during a battle that my command has been dispersed by orders from an officer superior in rank to the general commanding this corps, and I must assert that I have never known any good to arise from such a method of fighting a battle, and think the contrary rule should be adopted of keeping commands intact." Smith halted the Vermonters and told Brooks that Richardson's 1st Division "must take care of itself." He redirected the brigade to Mumma's cornfield, on Irvin's left. Brooks advanced his line to within a short distance from the cornfield's southern border. The Sunken Lane was only 170 yards from their front. Confederate gunners saw the Vermonters disappear into the corn but could not fix their position. "We were received by a storm of shot, shell and rifle bullets, which a kind Providence decreed should pass over us; in other words, the rebels fired too high," 16-year-old John Conline in the 4th Vermont remembered. Brooks ordered the regiments to unsling their knapsacks and had the men lie down on them in the corn. The Rebel artillery "shelled us unmercifully for perhaps twenty five minutes or more," but Brooks and his regimental commanders kept their men out of sight, and very few casualties were suffered.[52]

The Vermonters and Irvin's brigade received close artillery support when Lieutenant Leonard Martin's Battery F, 5th U.S., went into position near the Mumma family's cemetery—by Carman's precise measurement, 110 yards south of Smoketown Road—and engaged the Confederate batteries on Reel Ridge. Irvin effused enthusiastically about Martin's gunnery, writing that "the safety of my brigade may be largely imputed" to the Regulars' cannonade. "Had he not checked the heavy fire from the batteries of the enemy, they would have destroyed the greater part of my command," the colonel declared. This was not mere hyperbole. Lieutenant Robert Sawin, on the staff of Captain Romeyn B. Ayres, commanding the 2nd Division's Artillery Brigade, described the Rebel artillery barrage "as a most fearful fire of shot shell and shrapnel."[53]

BY THE TIME SMITH had his three brigades positioned, it was nearly 1 p.m., and Slocum's 1st Division, accompanied by Franklin, began to arrive near the East Woods. The division had passed through Keedysville, Maryland, where the streets were "almost blocked with ambulances waiting to unload their mangled suffering burdens." Surgeons and their assistants were seen "with coats off and sleeves rolled up—with hands and amputating instruments covered with blood." William Westervelt, in Bartlett's brigade, spoke for many when he ruminated, "It was not a pleasant sight." Although William Franklin was probably the most cautious corps commander in the Army of the Potomac, he became infused with an aggressive spirit when he reached the field. Stephen Sears has suggested that "shedding the responsibility of independent command apparently restored his confidence," which may well be true. Franklin rode to find Sumner and report his arrival. He found the senior commander "much depressed" and breathing dejection, telling the Pennsylvanian that the 2nd Corps was exhausted and not capable of further offensive action that day. But Franklin was not discouraged. After meeting with Smith and Slocum, he decided that once the 1st Division was deployed, they would assault the West Woods.[54]

Alfred T. A. Torbert's New Jersey brigade arrived first and was moved into position in the rear of Martin's battery, with its regiments straddling Smoketown Road. Newton's 3rd Brigade formed to Torbert's right, directly in front of the southwestern part of the East Woods. The batteries of Slocum's artillery brigade were distributed along the line to support the planned attack. Lieutenant Edward B. Williston's Battery D, 2nd U.S., unlimbered to Martin's right, its right gun only a dozen yards from Smoketown Road. Battery A, Massachusetts Light Artillery, commanded by Captain Josiah Porter, relieved Thomas' and Knap's batteries north of Smoketown Road, with its left gun only about 15 yards from the road. Captain John W. Wolcott's Battery A, Maryland Light Artillery, took position on the New Englanders' right, just south of the Cornfield. Although Cothran's, Knap's, and Thomas's batteries, all low on ammunition, were withdrawn, when these 6th Corps' batteries were in place, the Federals had a formidable line of 34 guns in six batteries, extending from north of the Cornfield to the Mumma cemetery.[55]

Franklin sent word to Sumner that he intended to assault the West Woods as soon as Colonel Joseph J. Bartlett's 2nd Brigade of Slocum's 1st Division arrived to support Torbert and Newton. Orders were relayed to the attacking regiments to fix bayonets. To the soldiers, it must have felt like a repeat of their experience 3 days earlier, at Crampton's Gap. Franklin then received word that Sumner had intervened, taking Bartlett to reinforce his right flank. Soon thereafter, Sumner rode up to Franklin's headquarters. As the senior officer, he ordered the 6th Corps' commander to cancel the attack, "giving as his reason for his order, that if I were defeated the right would be entirely routed, mine being the only troops left on the right that had any life in them." Sumner's decision was the correct one, but for the wrong reason. The direction of the attack Franklin planned would have sent Torbert and Newton directly into the teeth of the strongest Confederate defenses on their left. The troops would have been subjected to artillery fire over nearly the entire 500 yards of open ground they needed to cross in order to reach the West Woods. By this point the woods were occupied by Ransom's, Early's, and Armistead's brigades, as well as the remnant of Hood's division, which had been resupplied with ammunition. Across the middle and upper sections of the woods, the Confederates' infantry had excellent cover from the limestone ledge that ran north and south, where they were nearly impervious to the Federals' artillery. Any frontal attack against this position was almost certainly doomed to be a costly failure. The only possible way to attack the West Woods with any hope of success was to first seize Nicodemus Heights and then flank the woods from the north.[56]

Franklin protested Sumner's orders, telling him that "I thought it [to attack] a very necessary thing to do, and told him I would prefer to make the attack, unless he assumed the responsibility of forbidding it." Sumner took that responsibility. Major Herbert von Hammerstein, a veteran of the Austrian army and an aide-de-camp on McClellan's staff, happened to be present at the exchange between the two officers. Franklin asked him to ride back to McClellan and inform the general of Sumner's decision, as well as telling him that Franklin thought the attack should be made.[57]

AS ALREADY DISCUSSED (see chapter 8), the disaster to Sedgwick profoundly shaped and distorted Sumner's perspective, leading him to believe that things on the right were so bleak, if the 6th Corps attacked and was repulsed, the result might be an utter rout of the Union army's whole right wing. Sumner later testified to Congress's Joint Committee on the Conduct of the War that the 1st Corps was "dispersed," and that General Ricketts, of that corps, had advised him "that he could not raise 300 men of the corps." This may have been true for part of Ricketts's division, but it was not an accurate statement about the condition of the entire corps. The 1st Corps had sustained serious damage, and there had been heavy straggling, particularly in Ricketts's division. Meade, whom McClellan had placed in command of the corps after Hooker was wounded, reported that by 2 p.m., his division had reorganized in the rear of Poffenberger Hill and was prepared to either resist an enemy advance or "assist in any advance we might make." Doubleday's 1st Division had taken some hard knocks, but it, too, had reorganized near Poffenberger's farm and had one fresh brigade—Hofmann's— that had not yet been engaged. Captain John A. Kellogg in the 6th Wisconsin personally rallied several hundred soldiers—probably from both the 1st and 2nd Corps—near Poffenberger's farm and deployed them behind a stone wall on the western side of the Hagerstown Pike. The 1st Corps was not in any condition to lead an assault, but neither was it dispersed and unable to make an effective defense or support an attack. The same was true of the 12th Corps, which Sumner never mentioned. He seemed to take no notice of Sedgwick's division, which, to be sure, was in bad condition and would need more time to recover, but the overall situation was not as fragile as Sumner believed.[58]

One advantage Sumner did not refer to was the fearsome array of artillery he had assembled on the army's right. Nearly 30 guns of the 1st Corps were concentrated on Poffenberger Hill, anchoring the Union's flank. Sumner placed Abner Doubleday, an artilleryman in the Regular Army, in command of this entire group of guns, in addition to Doubleday's own 1st Division, which provided infantry support. Sumner established his headquarters at Poffenberger's farm, perhaps because of the nearby signal station, but just as likely because he believed it to be the most vulnerable point on the Federals' right. Should the Confederates suddenly come boiling out of the West Woods and manage to overrun this position, it would mean disaster. Because Sumner believed the enemy had superior numbers, he devoted nearly all of his attention to the portion of the front from the East Woods to Poffenberger Hill. Between Doubleday's massed batteries and the gun line assembled across the western face of the East Woods, Sumner's front bristled with 64 guns, and several more batteries were in reserve.[59]

As Francis Walker noted, a successful field commander must dispassionately assess a rapidly changing and chaotic situation. Hooker did this extremely well in the morning's engagement, keeping himself close to the fighting—near enough to get wounded—but never losing perspective on the larger conflict he was directing. But Sumner, with his view now shaped by Sedgwick's disaster, overestimated the enemy's capabilities and thus missed opportunities presented to him to counterpunch and regain the initiative. If the Confederates were so powerful, how had Greene's division occupied a part of the West Woods for an hour and a half? Rebel counterattacks after both Sedgwick's and Greene's defeats had been handily repulsed. A commander with his finger on the pulse of the engagement would have strained every nerve to reinforce Greene's success and concluded, from the failed Confederate counterattacks, that they lacked the strength for a major assault on the Union's right.

During this critical period, when the 6th Corps began to reach the battle front, Lieutenant James H. Wilson, an aide-de-camp on McClellan's staff, was sent to Sumner to inform him that Burnside was assaulting the Rohrback Bridge, and Sumner was to "get up his men and hold his position at all hazards." Wilson, whose account is exceptionally self-serving, recalled that he found Sumner "glum and grim," a description that others, like Franklin and Smith, confirmed. Sumner told Wilson to return to McClellan and ask if he should make a simultaneous advance with his whole line, "at the risk of not being able to rally a man this side of the creek if I am driven back." Wilson replied that McClellan's orders made no mention of an advance, but were only to "hold his position." Nonetheless, Sumner was adamant that Wilson carry his question back to headquarters, so the young lieutenant returned to Pry's farm. McClellan told Wilson to ride back and tell Sumner to "risk nothing," although the army commander did expect Sumner to hold his position. Before Wilson departed, McClellan changed his mind and told the aide-de-camp that Sumner should "crowd every man and gun into the ranks" and, if he thought it practicable, advance Franklin to carry the West Woods, supporting the attack with the 1st and 12th Corps. When Wilson returned, he found Sumner with Franklin, Smith, Howard, Newton, Gibbon, Gorman, and several other officers. This was probably sometime after 1 p.m., shortly after Sumner had cancelled Franklin's planned assault of the West Woods. Wilson remembered that he had barely delivered his message before Sumner answered, stating that he should return and tell McClellan that Sumner had no command; the 1st and 12th Corps were "all cut up and demoralized"; and Franklin had the only organized command on the field. Whether Sumner used the exact language Wilson included in his account is immaterial. The tone of what the general told the lieutenant is consistent with his earlier signal messages to headquarters.[60]

Wilson hurried back to headquarters, but, in the interim, McClellan had heard from Major Hammerstein, who carried Franklin's message questioning Sumner's decision to cancel the 6th Corps' assault on the West Woods. What Hammerstein said is unknown, but it convinced McClellan that he needed to visit his right and personally assess the situation. By this point it was probably around 2 p.m., so McClellan knew that Burnside had carried the Rohrback Bridge and was pushing the 9th Corps across Antietam Creek, and that cavalry under Pleasonton had crossed the Middle Bridge and were skirmishing with Lee's center. McClellan had updated Halleck on the battle's status at 1:25 p.m.:

> Please take military possession of the Chambersburg and Hagerstown Railroad, that our ammunition and supplies may be hurried up without delay. We are in the midst of the most terrible battle of the war—perhaps of history. Thus far it looks well, but I have great odds against me. Hurry up all the troops possible. Our loss has been terrific, but we have gained much ground. I have thrown the mass of the army on the left flank. Burnside is now attacking the right, and I hold my small reserve, consisting of Porter's (Fifth) corps, ready to attack the center as soon as the flank movements are developed. ~~It will be either a great defeat or a most glorious victory. I think & hope that God will give us a glorious victory.~~ I hope that God will give us a glorious victory.[61]

This was a familiar McClellan dispatch, replete with exaggeration, caution, fear of defeat, and hope for a "glorious victory," but containing few details—all of which drove his superiors to distraction. Possibly he thought the last two sentences too melodramatic—the difference between a "great defeat" and "glorious victory" was immense—for he crossed them out and they were not in the telegram Halleck received. The request to assert military control over the primary railroad that would forward ammunition and supplies to the Army of the Potomac made sense. This was the nearest rail communication point to the army, and McClellan wanted to ensure that no delays from civilian traffic hindered its resupply, particularly of ammunition. McClellan was a student of history, and he certainly was aware that while he was engaged in a major pitched battle, it was dwarfed by the Battles of Waterloo and Wagram, with over 200,000 troops, and the Battle of Leipzig, with upward of 600,000 men. As for his statement that "we had gained much ground," McClellan knew it was untrue. The Sunken Lane had been carried, as well as the East Woods, but no key terrain—ground that commanded or compromised the Confederates' position—had been captured. The flank movement McClellan had described against the enemy's left was over, and his senior general at that locale, fearful that the entire Federal force there might give way, clamored for reinforcements. McClellan made certain to describe his reserve as "small" and insist that he had great odds against him. If he prevailed, he had overcome superior forces; if he failed, it was because he was heavily outnumbered. Halleck may have also wondered where he should send any troops he could find. To Keedysville? To Hagerstown? To Harpers Ferry?

There were already 14,000 infantry in two divisions, subject to McClellan's orders, that he could call on as reinforcements. Darius Couch's 1st Division was at Harpers Ferry, and Brigadier General Andrew A. Humphreys's 3rd Division, 5th Corps, had been ordered from Frederick to Boonsboro. The disaster on the right had changed the army commander's mind about Humphreys, who had been ordered to continue to the front, but McClellan hesitated to remove Couch from Harpers Ferry.

Gathering up members of his staff, but leaving Fitz John Porter and Chief of Staff Marcy to monitor the conflict from the headquarters' command post, McClellan left for his right flank around 2 p.m. It was a crucial moment to depart, since Burnside's 9th Corps was pushing across Antietam Creek, and the Regulars of Sykes's division were pressing forward and skirmishing briskly with the defenders of Lee's right center on Cemetery Hill. In both of McClellan's reports on the battle, he stated how the commitment of his reserve—which, by this point, consisted of Sykes' and Morell's 5th Corps' divisions—was contingent on the success of the attacks on the Confederates' left and right. He now had strong evidence that the assault on the enemy's left had not only run out of steam, but that its senior officer feared the Union's whole right flank might give way if pressed. Burnside's attack on the Rebels' right offered the only reasonable hope left for a place where the insertion of McClellan's reserve could make a decisive difference in the battle's outcome. McClellan's decision to depart from headquarters to personally visit his right flank at this potentially critical point suggests that he feared calamity on his right more than he envisioned the prospect of success by the 9th Corps. This was consistent with his management of the overall battle. McClellan fought to win, but he consistently sought to minimize the risk that he might lose, which resulted in a piecemeal, disjointed commitment of the army's combat power and a conservative use of its reserves. Yet, in

McClellan's defense, his mission was to protect Washington, DC, and drive the rebels from Maryland. He had taken the offensive, despite his belief that he was outnumbered, so it should not be surprising that he sought to minimize the risk of another Second Manassas and thought it vital to visit his right flank and see the conditions there personally.

Where he met Sumner, Franklin, Slocum, Smith, and the others—whether at Sumner's headquarters near Joseph Poffenberger's farm, or closer to the East Woods and Franklin's front—is uncertain. At Williamsburg in May, McClellan had been contemptuous of Sumner's management of that battle. This time, curiously, for all the errors committed by Sumner, McClellan uttered not a single negative comment about the performance or judgment of the 2nd Corps' commander. Sumner spoke forcefully, expressing "the most decided opinion against another attempt during that day to assault the enemy's position in front," pointing out that many of the troops on the right "were so scattered and disorganized." Even with the 6th Corps on the field, and a powerful line of artillery stretching from Poffenberger Hill to Mumma's farm, McClellan was alarmed enough by Sumner's report that he dispatched orders for two brigades of Morell's division to reinforce the right at once. This was one-third of his reserve.[62]

Franklin disagreed with Sumner's gloomy assessment and still advocated that the 6th Corps attack. McClellan told him that "things had gone so well on all the other parts of the field that he was afraid to risk the day by an attack there on the right at that time." McClellan would prefer the certainty of a limited success over the risk of an assault that might or might not result in a decisive defeat of the Rebels. But Franklin pressed the issue. He, Smith, and probably Slocum had conducted a reconnaissance of the ground while waiting for McClellan to arrive, and it revealed to them that the key to carrying the West Woods was Nicodemus Heights. "If it could be taken we could drive the enemy from the wood by merely holding this point," Franklin testified later. He was almost certainly correct in this opinion. Possession of the heights rendered the West Woods untenable.[63]

Franklin and Smith took McClellan outside the East Woods, where the Nicodemus Heights were visible. The collection of officers and their staffs made a sizeable group—and a tempting target. When they passed by the 96th Pennsylvania of Bartlett's brigade, lying down near the Cornfield, Henry Keiser in that regiment wrote about how the Confederates opened fire with an entire battery, and their shells flew "around us thick as hail." Frank Treon in Company G lost his legs and life to a solid shot, but the generals and their staffs escaped untouched. Both Franklin and Smith pressed McClellan to allow them to attack. "I begged him to let me occupy a hill in sight [Nicodemus Heights] which I felt confident looked in behind the enemy's left," recalled Smith. Franklin noted that they had plenty of artillery focused on the heights, which could support the attack. McClellan, however, demurred. Franklin suggested that if McClellan did not wish to risk another attack that day, then the 6th Corps should attack the next morning. "I had no doubt that we could take that place the next morning, and I thought that would uncover the whole left of the enemy," he recalled. McClellan remained noncommittal, although his visit along the 6th Corps' front convinced him that reinforcement by Morell's two brigades was unnecessary, so he sent orders cancelling their movement. There was some discussion, probably initiated by Sumner, of sending Slocum's 1st Division to support Richardson at the Sunken Lane, as well as evidence that McClellan approved of it, but the movement was cancelled before it began, for unknown reasons. Offensive operations on the right were over. Leaving orders for Sumner and Franklin "to hold their positions," McClellan went back to his headquarters.[64]

While there is often value in an army commander visiting his front—such as to reanimate his men's morale, better understand a situation that may be out of his view from headquarters, or assess the state of mind of his commanders—McClellan's trip to the Federals' right seems devoid of any significant benefit. He accepted Sumner's gloomy assessment of the situation, despite the opposite opinion from Franklin, one of his most trusted corps commanders. We can only speculate why, but possibly it was because Sumner's report reinforced McClellan's belief that the enemy possessed superior numbers and was fully capable of mounting a devastating counterattack. By the logic McClellan applied to nixing an attack by the 6th Corps, he should have expected little from the 9th Corps' effort on the left. The 6th Corps had the potential support of the 1st and 12th Corps, plus Sedgwick's division—all of them battered, to be sure, but many units were still in good enough shape to assist in an attack—plus a massive amount of artillery that was well positioned to support an assault. The 9th Corps had nothing beyond its own resources. An army commander must constantly assess the odds of success and evaluate the risks in a highly charged and uncertain situation. What was happening on the right was a case in point. There was evidence available to McClellan that Franklin's instincts were sound. Yes, Sedgwick had been mauled by a powerful Confederate counterattack, but since then the enemy had not mounted anything more than local regimental- or brigade-sized counterattacks, and these had been quickly repulsed. This suggested that the Rebels lacked the strength to seriously threaten the Union army's flank, as Sumner feared, and might be vulnerable to a corps-sized attack. An assault by the 6th Corps to carry Nicodemus Heights would have required a considerable repositioning of troops, and it was not a sure thing. But then, neither was the attack by the 9th Corps on the Confederates' right. Both entailed risks. McClellan accepted one but not the other.

LEE OFFERED A SHARP contrast to McClellan in how he reacted to a far greater crisis that confronted the Army of Northern Virginia following the collapse of its center. By the time McClellan rode across Antietam Creek to visit his right flank—around 2 p.m.—Lee's situation was not yet desperate, but it was critical. His army had suffered extremely heavy losses, and thousands of stragglers were loose in the army's rear, although Lee was taking measures to collect and organize these men and prevent them from slipping down to the Potomac River and across it into Virginia. Only the artillery assembled along Reel Ridge, and the failure of the Federals to better support the 2nd Corps' assault after the Sunken Lane fell, prevented disaster. The Confederates' left was stable, but every infantry unit there, except for Armistead's and Ransom's brigades, was greatly reduced by casualties from the morning's fighting. To stabilize his left, Lee had stripped Walker's division and G. T. Anderson's brigade from the right and committed McLaws's division from his reserve. The assault on the army's center forced him to commit R. H. Anderson's division, the last of his reserves. This left him with Evans's brigade and five brigades of General D. R. Jones's division—in all, about 2,800–2,900 infantry—plus several artillery batteries, to defend the Confederates' front, which extended from Cemetery Hill to Snavely's Ford, nearly 1.75 miles. By 2 p.m., Federal cavalry and nearly 1,600 Regulars in Sykes's division, with supporting artillery, were across Antietam Creek at the Middle Bridge, skirmishing with Evans's small brigade (see chapter 14). On the right, the 9th Corps had forced its way across the Rohrback Bridge and also crossed in force at Snavely's Ford, which was below the bridge (see chapters 15 and 16).

A dispatch was sent to General William Pendleton—whose Reserve Artillery was guarding the Potomac River fords at Williamsport, Falling Waters, and Shepherdstown—to send 15–20 guns (which he could spare), along with any stragglers he could round up. He was advised to drive these laggards back to the front "at the point of the sword." The safety of the fords was not to be imperiled, and no guns essential to their protection were to be removed. If Pendleton could not send the desired number of guns, those that he could spare should be long-range ones, which were badly needed to engage the Federals' artillery. "We want ammunition, guns, and provisions," the message concluded, reflecting the urgency of the situation at the front.[65]

In every engagement, Lee always sought to seize the initiative from his enemy. What he considered now was striking a counterblow to knock McClellan off balance and play on the Federal commander's innate caution. While McClellan had surprised Lee with his aggressiveness at the Battle of South Mountain, since then he had behaved more predictably. Lee could not read McClellan's mind, but every good general takes the measure of his opponent and attempts to exploit any perceived weakness. McClellan's deliberate command style and innate caution were well established by September 1862, and Lee believed a counterblow might lead McClellan to take defensive measures and check his offensive against the Confederates' vulnerable right. There was only one point where a counterattack was possible. This was the Confederates' left, which had the greatest concentration of troops, although most were badly battered. Whether Lee rode over to meet with Jackson or simply sent him orders is unknown. What we do know is that Jackson was instructed to attempt a turning movement against the Federals' right flank. The only reinforcements Lee could offer consisted of Wade Hampton's cavalry brigade, about 1,400 strong, which had arrived from Harpers Ferry around 11:30 a.m. The rest of the flanking force would have to come from the resources Jackson had on hand.[66]

Lee was a gambler and a risk taker, but his risks were typically taken with careful calculation. This decision, however, when considered on its own, smacks of desperation, and even delusion, given the state of the Confederate army and the punishment the units on its left flank had suffered that morning. Jackson was a resourceful officer, but his available options were slim. The only fresh units were Hampton's and Fitz Lee's cavalry brigades, plus Ransom's and Armistead's infantry brigades—hardly a force to roll up the enemy's flank. Every other unit had suffered crippling losses. Jackson believed the Union troops in his front had done their worst, and the danger that his line might be pierced had passed—an assessment worthy of comparison with those of Sumner and McClellan—but powerful enemy forces remained. If Jackson weakened his front to assemble a flanking force, would the Federals detect it and renew their attacks? In any case, it would be a delicate mission to execute.[67]

Joseph Harsh, in his study of Confederate operations during the Maryland Campaign, believes that the purpose of Lee's proposed flanking attack was to open a path to Hagerstown, as a way for the army to escape yet still continue the campaign in the state. This seems unlikely. Attempting such a movement without the Army of the Potomac being driven back across Antietam Creek was so perilous that it is doubtful Lee ever contemplated it. What seems more probable is that he had heard from A. P. Hill and knew that his division would arrive from Harpers Ferry around midafternoon. Hill could reinforce the Confederate army's vulnerable right, while Jackson mounted his spoiling attack, which appears to have had no larger objective than to throw the Federals off balance and force McClellan to shift any reserves he might still have to his right. Viewed in this broader light, Lee's decision, while still highly risky, was a calculated one, with its principal intent being to relieve the pressure on his army.[68]

Jackson displayed considerable skill in executing Lee's orders. According to the often-unreliable General John G. Walker, Jackson told him that he intended "to make up, from the different commands on our left, a force of four to five thousand men, and give them to General Stuart, with orders to turn the enemy's right, and attack him in rear." Walker was to attack in his front, "as soon as I should hear Stuart's guns." Walker's memory, at least in this instance, was reasonably accurate. Jackson did entrust the turning movement to Stuart, and he had instructed Walker to attack from the West Woods when he heard Stuart's guns. Walker also recalled Jackson saying, with emphasis, "We'll drive McClellan into the Potomac," which indicates either that Jackson had no concept of the area's geography, which is unlikely, or that Walker forgot Jackson had said "the Antietam," rather than "the Potomac." Unless the two armies could somehow reverse their positions, the Confederates could never drive the Federals into the Potomac River.[69]

The forces Jackson selected to execute the turning movement indicate that, despite what he told Walker, he intended no more than a probe, not an attack. Jackson may have communicated with Lafayette McLaws, who had conducted a careful reconnaissance of the Confederate and Union positions, and concluded that "we had nothing to gain by an advance of our troops." McLaws found the enemy position to be strong, and even if the Confederates succeeded in driving the Federals back, the result would only be to "force them to concentration on their reserves, of which we had none, to weaken our lines, and scatter our troops, so that, in the event of a reverse, no rally of any considerable body could be made." Jackson pulled no troops from his front in the West Woods to reinforce Stuart. The cavalryman's flanking force consisted of elements of Fitzhugh Lee's and Wade Hampton's cavalry brigades; the 48th North Carolina, from Walker's division; and eight guns, drawn from several batteries and placed under the command of Captain John Pelham. This was not an assault force. Instead, it was a mobile reconnaissance unit to fix the whereabouts of the enemy's flank and determine its strength.[70]

Stuart assembled his force at Cox's farm on River Landing Road, about 800 yards southwest of the summit of Nicodemus Heights. It was nearly 3 p.m. before all was ready, and the column set out with the 4th Virginia cavalry in the lead. The Confederate battery commanders were unaware of their mission and suspicious that the aggressive Pelham "had gotten permission to look up a fight and were down on him for what we regarded as a most indiscreet proceeding." The column marched north, nearly to the community of New Industry, on the Potomac River, and then turned right on Mondell Road, which led to the toll gate on the Hagerstown Pike, just opposite the North Woods and Joseph Poffenberger's farm. Keeping his cavalry under cover, Stuart sent his artillery forward to some high ground north of the road, about 900 yards west of the mass of the 1st Corps' artillery on Poffenberger Hill, to test the waters. The battery leaders under Pelham's command got a good look at the number of Federal guns, which, Captain William T. Poague wrote, were in plain view, and they complained to the horse artilleryman that it was courting destruction to engage such a force with what they had. Pelham, who always seemed indifferent to danger, laughed at their concern and replied, "Oh, we must stir them up a little and then slip away."[71]

On Poffenberger Hill, the New Englanders in Battery D, 1st Rhode Island, watched a solitary horseman ride onto the high ground 900 yards west of them, followed, moments later, "by the teams of a battery," which quickly made a left about and unlimbered their guns. The Federal artillerymen on the hill quickly stirred into action. Within minutes, a deluge of shells was flying toward the Rebel guns. On the receiving end, Captain Poague described it as "a most terrific fire." A small body of trees partially obscured the Confederates, and Poague recalled that the Union gunners "could only mark our places by the smoke rising above them." Despite the great disparity in the number of guns and the weight of metal, the Confederate artillery crews fought back with great courage. Major Rufus Dawes in the 6th Wisconsin watched the duel from his position near the North Woods and described it as a "Titanic combat." Nonetheless, it was over within 15 to 20 minutes. Pelham loved a fight, but he concluded that this one was too lopsided and ordered his guns to withdraw.[72]

In a separate part of this flanking operation, French's and Branch's batteries of Walker's division drove up to Nicodemus Heights and unlimbered. They suffered the same fate. "Our fire was too frequent and well directed for anything to live upon that hill for any length of time," noted the historian of Battery D, 1st Rhode Island. By 4:30 p.m., the flanking maneuver was over. In his report, Stuart complained that he found the Federals' artillery to be so numerous and "judiciously established," with their front extending so close to the Potomac River, "as to render it inexpedient to hazard the attempt." Either Stuart, who normally read terrain quite well, was confused or, more likely, sought to exaggerate the challenge and resistance he faced, since the Union army's right rested over a mile from the Potomac. The Confederate maneuver, however, had been a success in one aspect: it determined conclusively that the Yankees' right was powerful and not vulnerable to being turned. It had also established that Franklin and Smith were correct, as the Federals' artillery on the right completely dominated Nicodemus Heights, so an assault by 6th Corps very likely would have seized this ground.[73]

Jackson apparently had already concluded that there would be no general attack by the Confederates' left, even before Stuart's guns opened fire. As mentioned earlier in this chapter, Jackson had advised General Walker that he should attack the moment he heard Stuart's guns commence firing. When Stuart's expedition was feeling out the Union right, Jackson rode over to the vicinity of Ransom's brigade. While waiting here for the sound of Stuart's guns, he had a soldier named Hood—probably Benjamin F. Hood in Company G of the 35th North Carolina—climb a particularly high tree in the West Woods and report what he could see regarding the enemy. Depending on the tree's height, Private Hood could have spotted several of the Union batteries along the front of the East Woods, and he may have been able to observe some of their supporting infantry. In an account that is probably embellished, Hood allegedly counted 39 enemy flags. He may have seen artillery guidons, which each battery carried (rather than full regimental colors, like an infantry unit), but nearly all of the Union infantry in that area were lying down, to avoid being seen, and kept their colors concealed. Whatever Private Hood saw convinced Jackson that a frontal assault from the West Woods was a bad idea, and Walker and Ransom heard no more about attacking as soon as they "should heard Stuart's guns."[74]

The muddled Confederate command structure at Sharpsburg reared its head again during Stuart's flanking movement. Around 3:30 p.m., toward the end of Pelham's one-sided artillery duel, General Walker received an order from Longstreet "to advance and attack the enemy in my front." It was the second time that afternoon that Longstreet had intervened with the units on Jackson's front. Around noon, when the Confederates' Sunken Lane line collapsed, Longstreet had sent orders for General Ransom to advance his brigade and capture the battery in his front (which battery he meant is unknown). Fortunately for Ransom's North Carolinians, McLaws caught wind of this ill-advised order and took on the responsibility to cancel it. This was command by committee, but McLaws prevented a bloody repulse, which surely would have been Ransom's fate. Longstreet was obviously seeking any means to deliver a counterpunch and prevent a catastrophic breakthrough in the Rebels' center. But unsupported, hastily organized assaults rarely accomplished more than piling up casualties. Now, as Burnside's 9th Corps began to apply serious pressure on the Confederates' right, Longstreet again sought a spoiling attack, without regard to the situation in Ransom's front. This time Walker was present with Ransom when the orders arrived, and he forbade the North Carolinian to move until Walker had personally spoken with Longstreet. Walker found the wing commander somewhere near Reel's farm and explained that Stuart was attempting a flanking movement under Jackson's orders, as well as that Jackson wanted Ransom's brigade to wait until this assault developed before the brigade advanced. To his credit, Longstreet cancelled Ransom's attack order. While the two generals were discussing the situation, Jackson rode up and reported that Stuart had been stymied in his effort, finding the Union's right to be strongly positioned. The three men reached a conclusion apparent to anyone who might ride along the Confederates' left: "The attempt to force the enemy's right with our fearfully thinned ranks and in the exhausted condition of our men was an effort above our strength."[75]

ALTHOUGH SKIRMISHING AND SHELLING would continue until dark, the battle for the West Woods, East Woods, and Miller's Cornfield was over. It had raged off and on for nearly 7 hours. During this time, the Federals' 1st Corps incurred 2,590 casualties; the 12th Corps, 1,746; Sedgwick, 2,210; and the 6th Corps, the bulk of their 439 men. This totaled 6,985 officers and men, with most of them killed or wounded. The majority of these losses occurred in the first 4 hours of combat, when units in the 1st, 12th, and 2nd Corps counted 27% of their men as casualties. The Confederate commands that were engaged— Lawton's, J. R. Jones's, Hood's, McLaws's, and Walker's divisions, and G. T. Anderson's and Armistead's brigades—lost 6,846 of their men, or 34%. No battle thus far in the war had produced such a shocking degree of carnage in a relatively small area. The result for all the bloodshed, the heroism displayed, and the great sacrifices made, was—a stalemate.

As the guns on the battlefield's northern sector faded to an angry sputter, the conflict, like a wildfire that shrinks in one sector, only to flare up suddenly in another, shifted its fearful wrath southward, to the Middle and Rohrback Bridges over Antietam Creek. Here, Lee and his Army of Northern Virginia would face a fresh crisis.

14

The Middle Bridge

"One of the coolest and bravest officers in our service"

McClellan's battle plan for September 17 did not contemplate any significant attack across the Middle Bridge. The artillery sparring on September 16 had established that Cemetery Hill, which commanded the approaches from the bridge, bristled with Confederate artillery. Apart from the ground overlooking the Rohrback Bridge, Cemetery Hill was the most formidable position on the Confederates' front. McClellan only intended to advance here once the attack on the enemy's left was well developed and Burnside had carried the Rohrback Bridge, seized the high ground south of Sharpsburg, and was rolling up the enemy's line. Only then would McClellan take the risk "to advance our center with all the forces then disposable."[1]

Around 7:30 a.m., McClellan, Porter, and parts of their staff rode to a bluff on the eastern side of the Boonsboro Pike, directly southeast of Pry's house. McClellan's aide-de-camp, David Strother, attested that the position "afforded the most comprehensive view of the field that could be had from any single point." It was also beyond the range of Confederate artillery, which Pry's house was not. A small redan of rails had been assembled, and Fitz John Porter sat behind them, "with a telescope resting on the top rail," studying the field "with unremitting attention, scarcely leaving his post during the whole day." Strother observed how Porter communicated with McClellan "by nods, signs, or in words so low-toned and brief that the nearest by-standers had but little benefit from them." When McClellan was not in conversation with Porter, Strother noted that he "stood in a soldierly attitude intently watching the battle and smoking [with] the utmost apparent calmness, conversing with surrounding officers and giving his orders in the most quiet under-tones." Chief of Staff Marcy hovered near McClellan, delivering the army commander's orders to the waiting aides-de-camp, who lingered near the periphery of the command group. It seemed odd to Strother that, with a huge battle roaring and seething before them, at the command post "everything was as quiet and punctilious as a drawing room ceremony."[2]

At 9:10 a.m., as related earlier (see chapter 13), one of the aides-de-camp galloped off with orders for Burnside to open the 9th Corps' attack on the Rohrback Bridge. Just 40 minutes later, French's first attack struck the Sunken Lane, an event under the direct observation of McClellan. With the 2nd Corps' assault hitting the Confederates' left center, and Burnside's attack on the enemy's right expected to commence momentarily, McClellan decided he would lend some assistance to both efforts by advancing artillery and other supports across the Middle Bridge and to the line of hills about 600 yards west of the bridge. Two divisions of the 5th Corps were available for this mission, but McClellan did not contemplate tapping them for it. In his second after-action report of the Maryland Campaign, published in August 1863, McClellan explained his thinking in keeping the 5th Corps east of Antietam Creek:1

> "This corps filled the interval between the right wing and General Burnside's command, and guarded the main approach from the enemy's position to our trains of supply," he wrote. "It was necessary to watch this part of our line with the utmost vigilance, lest the enemy should take advantage of the first exhibition of weakness here to push upon us a vigorous assault for the purpose of piercing our center and turning our rear, as well as to capture or destroy our supply trains. Once having penetrated this line, the enemy's passage to our rear could have met with but feeble resistance, as there were no reserves to reenforce or close up the gap."

Stephen Sears has reflected on the absurdity of this explanation: "Taken at their word, the commander of the Army of the Potomac and his principal adviser [Fitz John Porter] thus professed to believe they were at risk of an enemy attacking column that would have to cross a mile of open ground toward the narrow defile where the Middle Bridge spanned the Antietam, exposing its flank in doing so against three brigades of infantry and a division of cavalry and the concentrated fire of 80 to 100 guns positioned on commanding ground behind and on both sides of the bridge." McClellan's explanation lacked logic, as well. How could pushing a brigade or division of infantry across the Middle Bridge be construed by the enemy as an "exhibition of weakness?"3

McClellan's seemingly illogical caution becomes more understandable when given his headquarters' estimate of Confederate numbers. In a letter home immediately after the battle, the 5th Corps' chief of staff, Alexander Webb, related that "we knew they outnumbered us." They believed the Rebel army numbered between 100,000 and 130,000 men. As Stephen M. Weld, an officer in the 18th Massachusetts who also served on the 5th Corps' staff, wrote to his father on September 18, "The enemy greatly outnumber us." Neither of these officers formed their opinions of the enemy's strength randomly. Porter's headquarters did not join the Army of the Potomac until the evening of September 14. Therefore, the strength figures that Webb and Weld related were not drawn from imagination or speculation, but from what they had heard at army headquarters, where, the day before, McClellan had confidently informed Halleck that the

Confederates numbered "120,000 or more." In the minds of McClellan, Porter, Webb, Weld, and others, the Union army took a great risk in taking the offensive against such superior numbers.[4]

Great field commanders of the nineteenth century—like Napoleon and Wellington, or Lee and Grant—possessed the ability to apprise an enemy's strength relatively accurately by assessing not only the observable number of troops they displayed, but also the strength and force with which they defended and attacked. At the Battle of Antietam, McClellan had the additional advantage of a good line of observation from the signal station on Elk Ridge. Due to the undulating terrain, many parts of Lee's position were concealed from a person at this location, but enough was visible to have determined if the Confederates had 40,000–50,000 reserves behind their front lines, waiting to strike. An army of 100,000–130,000 would have required huge ordnance and commissary trains to supply it. Wagons were harder to conceal from the Union signal station than troops, and the signal officers had seen nothing in their 2 days on the hill to support the numbers McClellan claimed Lee possessed. As mentioned in the previous chapter, the evidence everywhere available to McClellan—whether from prisoners, from his observation post near Pry's farm, from the Elk Ridge signal station, or his visit to the East Woods—should have made it clear that the Rebels did not possess greater numbers or have an enormous hidden reserve waiting to launch a devastating counterattack. Despite believing that the Confederates had the larger army, McClellan still attacked, which reflected growth on his part. Nonetheless, his consistent overestimation of the enemy's strength and capabilities throughout his leadership of the Army of the Potomac was a critical failure for a field commander.

Because of his concern about a Confederate attack toward the Middle Bridge, McClellan tapped a light, mobile force—his cavalry and horse artillery—to cross the bridge and support Burnside and French. Because they could move readily, they could react quickly and disengage if a large Rebel force suddenly came boiling out from behind Cemetery Hill. It was probably only minutes after French's first attack swept up toward the Sunken Lane—shortly before 10 a.m.—when McClellan ordered Alfred Pleasonton to take his cavalry division and horse artillery across the Middle Bridge and support French's left flank.[5]

Pleasonton's cavalry and his four batteries of horse artillery were bivouacked about 600 to 700 yards east of the Pry farm lane, close to the Boonsboro Pike and just west of Keedysville. The force consisted of two cavalry brigades—the 2nd and 3rd Brigades—and the 5th U.S. Cavalry of the 1st Brigade. The four horse batteries had 22 3-inch rifles. The horse battery was a new experiment in the U.S. Army, differing from regular artillery batteries in that everyone was mounted. These guns were Pleasonton's principal firepower, since, except for the 8th Illinois, the 3rd Indiana, and part of the 4th Pennsylvania, most of his cavalry either lacked carbines, which enabled them to fight on foot, or had not had an opportunity to train in dismounted tactics. Troopers armed only with sabers and pistols were of little value in the environment to which McClellan dispatched them.

The bugler's "Boots and Saddles" sounded across the cavalry's camps, and officers and men stirred to action: checking equipment, retrieving horses, mounting, and forming up. Pleasonton wisely did not intend to send his entire force thundering across the Middle Bridge. Although skirmishers in the 12th U.S. Infantry occupied Joshua Newcomer's farm buildings immediately west of the bridge, the area around the bridge was under Confederate observation and artillery fire, and what lay beyond the ridge about 380 yards west of the farm was unknown. To probe this terrain, Pleasonton sent two squadrons of the 4th Pennsylvania Cavalry: Companies B and M, commanded by a remarkable young officer, Captain Samuel B. M. Young; and Companies A and E, led by Captain Edward Tombler. Only half of the troopers in the 4th were armed with carbines, and these four companies were almost certainly part of that half. Accompanying them was Lieutenant William N. Dennison's section of Captain John C. Tidball's Battery A, 2nd U.S. Artillery. The balance of the 4th, accompanied by Tidball's other two sections of artillery, followed in support.[6]

Sergeant Charles T. Bowen in the 12th U.S. Infantry, which was near the Middle Bridge, noted that the "rebs had planted cannon so as to completely rake it." Shells were dropping into the vicinity, probably as interdicting fire rather than ammunition aimed at a specific target, when the intrepid Captain Young and his troopers, followed by Dennison's two guns, came thundering down the Boonsboro Pike, galloped over the bridge, hastened past Newcomer's farm, and sprinted up the road toward the ridge, 600 yards away, which I shall refer to as Newcomer Ridge. At the crest, they were fired on by a 20-man detachment of Georgians, commanded by a captain with the impressive name of Hansford Dade Duncan Twiggs. Twiggs led an approximately 100-man skirmish unit from Colonel G. T. Anderson's brigade. He deployed his men that morning on a hill east of the Sherrick farm lane and about 300 yards south of the Boonsboro Pike, with advance pickets close to the pike. When an officer at a forward post notified him of the approach of Union cavalry, Twiggs sent 20 of his men on the run to a stone wall bordering the turnpike. They arrived in time to greet Captain Young and his horsemen with a blast of musketry that sent the bluecoats scampering back out of sight.[7]

Twiggs and his little band behaved as though they were backed up by powerful legions of hidden infantry. But they were more the mouse that roared, rather than the advance of a lion's pride. The Confederate defenses behind them on Cemetery Hill formed a thin, brittle crust. When the battle opened, Lee had three infantry brigades deployed at this locale, on the reverse slope of the hill. Brigadier General Richard B. Garnett's brigade of Virginians, 242 men strong, was south of the Boonsboro Pike, in the low ground southwest of Cemetery Hill. Colonel George T. Anderson's and Brigadier General Nathanial Evans's brigades were both behind the hill's northward extension, north of the pike, which I shall refer to as Cemetery Ridge. Evans had about 250 effectives. The infantry supported three batteries on Cemetery Hill—Captain William Bachman's German (South Carolina) Artillery, Captain Charles W. Squires's 1st Company, and Captain M. B. Miller's 3rd Company of the Washington (Louisiana) Artillery, with a total of 8 Napoleons and 6 rifled guns—and four batteries of Major Hilary P. Jones's battalion on Cemetery Ridge, with 16 guns of varying calibers. During the course of the morning, as pressure mounted on the Confederate army's left, and then its center, Lee began drawing off troops and guns from this locale. G. T Anderson's brigade went first, and it departed in such a hurry that Twiggs and his detachment were left behind. Twiggs admitted to sleeping late that morning, but this evidently made little difference. In the attendant haste of this movement, Anderson either had no time to call the detachment in or had orders to leave them in place. A section of Bachman's battery was plucked out to reinforce D. H. Hill. It was followed by Miller's battery, and another battery from Jones's battalion. By the time Young's squadron dashed over the Middle Bridge, the defense of Cemetery Hill consisted of two very small infantry brigades and a skirmish detail, totaling about 600 men, and four and a half batteries, with 18 guns.[8]

Both Garnett's and Evans's brigades were fragile units. They had participated in the grueling march from Hagerstown to South Mountain on September 14, fought on the mountain until nightfall, suffered substantial losses, and then marched through the night to Sharpsburg. They had been able to get some rest after reaching Sharpsburg, but the men were famished and their ranks depleted. How their morale would stand a hard fight was an open question. For example, Colonel Fitz W. McMaster, commanding the 17th South Carolina, reported that only 36 of his 141 officers and men remained after the battle at South Mountain. The regiment had 61 casualties, so 44 men—nearly a third of the regiment—were separated from the unit during that conflict. Only about half of them returned by September 17, which gave McMaster 59 effectives. Colonel Peter F. Stevens, who had tactical control of the brigade, described it as "a mere skeleton." The same was true of Garnett's brigade.[9]

Other than Twiggs's approximately 100-man detachment south of the Boonsboro Pike, the only other Confederate infantry units deployed on the forward slope of the hill that morning were two of Evans's regiments. Evans was on the field but persisted in the idea that he was a division commander, so he let Colonel Stevens in the Holcombe Legion direct the operations of the brigade. This was the same arrangement Evans had followed 3 days earlier, at the Battle of South Mountain, which had resulted in confusion and a crushing defeat for poor

Stevens and his men. The colonel sent the 22nd and 23rd South Carolina, with a total of only about 100 men, to a location midway down the eastern slope of Cemetery Ridge, where they deployed as skirmishers behind a worm fence.[10]

When Young crossed the Middle Bridge, the Federals had a fearsome array of batteries south of the Boonsboro Pike that could target Cemetery Hill and its environs. Five batteries were distributed along the ridges from near Ecker's farm to just northwest of Henry Rohrback's farm. Their 22 guns included eight 20 lb. Parrott rifles, ten 10 lb. Parrott rifles, and four 3-inch rifles. Two of the 9th Corps' batteries in this force were soon obliged to shift their fire in support of the effort to seize the Rohrback Bridge, but the remaining guns still possessed the capability for long-range fire. Six more batteries of the Artillery Reserve were positioned north of the pike, between it and Pry's farm. They fired principally at targets on the Confederates' left and center but could turn their wrath on Cemetery Hill and Cemetery Ridge, if necessary. The barrage from these various batteries drove Jones's battalion to seek shelter behind Cemetery Ridge and sent a deluge of shells sailing over the Confederate guns, to land near and among the supporting infantry. Richard Garnett remembered that morning as "an almost uninterrupted fire of solid shot, shell, and spherical case, by which a number of men were killed and wounded." Lieutenant William Wood, commanding the 19th Virginia, believed it was "the heaviest artillery fire from the enemy's guns that I had up to that time ever heard, and save one single occasion, the heaviest I ever witnessed." Behind Cemetery Ridge, Evans's South Carolinians also complained about the intense shelling. Garnett shifted his brigade around throughout the morning, trying to find a position that better protected his men from overshots. In general, all the metal the Union gunners fired at targets across the hill inflicted relatively little damage. For example, Squires's battery, which one might imagine would have been obliterated, only reported 1 killed and 12 wounded. These were not minor losses for a battery that probably numbered around 50 or 60 men, but neither were they crippling, so when the Federal horsemen attempted to bring up Lieutenant Dennison's section of artillery, this battery and Bachman's remaining sections were ready.[11]

After his repulse by Twiggs's 20 sharpshooters, Captain Young dismounted some of his men to act as skirmishers to engage the Georgians, and he detailed others to help get Dennison's guns into position. At the same time, Twiggs called up his entire force and deployed them behind the stone wall along the Boonsboro Pike. Captain Tombler supervised the troopers tasked with helping Dennison's horse artillerymen. Dennison picked a position just to the right of where the road reached the crest of the ridge. Some of the Company B troopers dismounted and tore down the fencing alongside the pike, so the guns could pass through. Hugh Crawford, one of those troopers, recalled that they had just gotten the guns up the bank beside the road, and he was lifting one of the gun's wheels to get it over some obstacle, when a Confederate battery—probably

Squires's or Bachman's—opened fire on them. The first shot struck a dead tree beside the road, just in front of the troopers and horse artillerymen. A second wounded John Irwin, one of Crawford's comrades. The third round, Crawford recalled, "got down to business." This ball, shell, or bolt (if from a rifled piece) passed under Crawford's horse, "cut both legs off my brother's [George] horse and killed the next man and horse to him. This raised a commotion among us." It also wounded John Boyce, another member of Crawford's company. Crawford hoisted the wounded man onto his back and walked to the rear find medical help.[12]

Despite the ghastly path the Confederate projectile carved through their ranks, the troopers and horse artillerymen succeeded in getting their guns into position, but this only exposed them to Twiggs's riflemen, whose bullets sent everyone diving for cover. Although Twiggs's position along the road was largely impervious to a frontal assault, its right flank was vulnerable, but the troopers of the 4th Pennsylvania did not appear to have perceived this. Perhaps Twiggs threw back some of his men to protect his flank, but Tidball, who was watching the engagement, was unimpressed with the 4th's performance, observing that "they hastily withdrew" when they came under fire.[13]

Colonel James H. Childs, the acting 3rd Brigade commander, soon arrived with the balance of the 4th Pennsylvania, which he wisely tucked behind the ridge south of the Boonsboro Pike, where they were sheltered from Twiggs's riflemen and the Confederate guns on Cemetery Hill. One of Childs's troopers recalled that it was still "a very warm place to be," for the solid shot of the enemy struck, in particular, at "a certain point upon the crest of the hill, then all at once, it seemed they began to descend, passing right over the heads of the regiment so closely that we almost unconsciously, as we did on that occasion, and often before, ducked our heads, and instantly got up again." While his men dodged solid shot, Childs rode forward to the crest of the ridge north of the pike. It was instantly apparent to him that the open, exposed ground, extending for over 1,100 yards to Cemetery Hill and Cemetery Ridge, was no place for cavalry to operate. He turned his horse and started back to the pike to report his observations to Pleasonton, as well as to also get more support up for Dennison's hard-pressed gun crews. Just below the crest of the hill, when he paused in the road to speak to members of his staff, a solid shot came over the ridge and struck him in the right hip, passing through his body, hurling him from his horse, and disemboweling him.[14]

Some of his men and staff gathered up the frightfully wounded officer and carried him to a sheltered place nearby. Despite his mortal wound, Childs, remarkably, had the presence of mind and sense of duty to send one member of his staff to report his injury to Pleasonton, and another to find Lieutenant Colonel James K. Kerr in the 4th Pennsylvania and advise him that he now commanded the brigade. Then Childs sent an orderly to find his regiment's surgeon and tell him "if he was not attending to anyone whose life could be saved, to come to him, as he was in great pain." Within an hour, the courageous colonel was dead.[15]

Tidball's other two sections had followed Childs and the 4th Pennsylvania over the Middle Bridge. While the cavalry took cover behind the ridge, Tidball led his four guns into a plowed field north of the Boonsboro Pike, where they unlimbered. The crews muscled the heavy guns up the steep slope by hand. Tidball, who was among the best battery commanders in the Army of the Potomac, had no intention of letting his battery—with its limbers, horses, guns, and men—be a target for Twiggs or the Confederate artillery. Sweat would save blood. The crews eventually reached the ridge crest at its highest point, 450 feet in elevation, which was about 160 yards north of the pike. Twiggs's men fired on them, but Tidball replied with canister, which kept the Georgians' heads down. Afterward, Tidball complained in a letter home, "For some inexplicable reason we were not supported by infantry, although there were thousands close by doing nothing." Squires and Bachman had also turned some of their guns on the Regulars, but Tidball, with a professional's detached judgment, opined that "but with some exceptions," the Confederate gunnery's "practice was bad." One of these exceptions was Lieutenant Dennison's gun team, closest to the pike, which lost every horse on its limber.[16]

The rest of the 2nd and 3rd Brigades, plus the 5th U.S. Cavalry of the 1st Brigade and the balance of the divisional horse artillery, thundered over the Middle Bridge behind Tidball and the 4th Pennsylvania. Their passage over the bridge was completed at some peril. Lieutenant Albert P. Morrow in the 6th Pennsylvania described it as "exceedingly hazardous" and noted that his regiment crossed at a full gallop. A member of the 3rd Indiana remembered how Confederate shells were "striking the road east of the bridge, the bridge itself and splashing the waters of the Antietam." The troopers thought the march down to Antietam Creek was the worst part: "The men were covered with dirt thrown up by the shells from Lee's guns which struck all about." They rode past a dead cavalryman and his horse on the bridge, and a rumor circulated that it was Childs—which it was not—but the scene still presented "a ghastly spectacle to those who were obliged to ride over his body to go into position." The danger was real, but the damage inflicted was minimal. The regiments who crossed the creek had a total of 3 killed (all in the 4th Pennsylvania Cavalry) and 17 wounded during the hours when they were under fire.[17]

Each regiment turned into Newcomer's mill and farmyard on the western bank of Antietam Creek and then sought some place in which to shelter south of the Boonsboro Pike, leaving only the 4th Pennsylvania north of the road. The men in the 1st Massachusetts moved snug up to the ridge south of the pike, formed into a column of squadrons, and dismounted. Flavius Bellamy, with the 3rd Indiana, recorded that his commander "took us behind a low hill for shelter

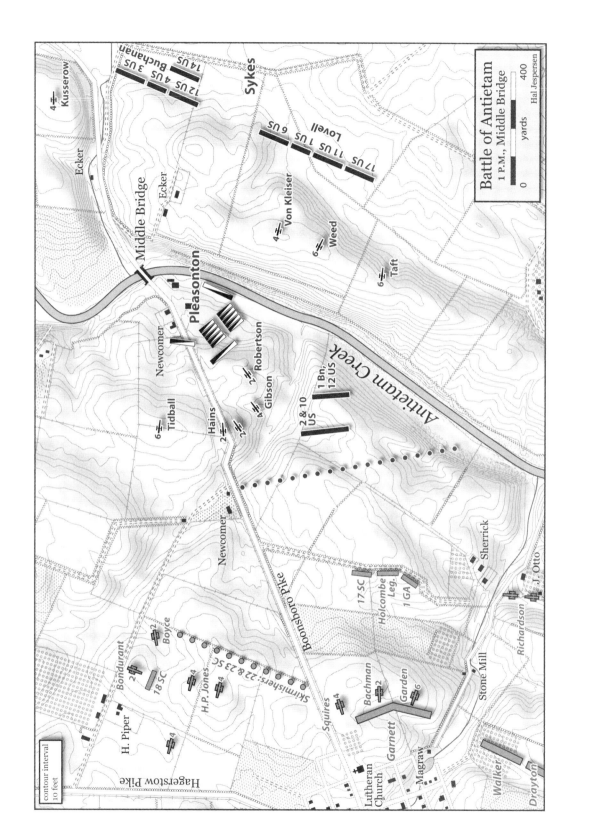

Battle of Antietam
1 P.M., Middle Bridge

Hal Jespersen

0   yards   400

contour interval
10 feet

as soon as possible but it did very little good." A shell burst close to Bellamy, and, as he watched "the curling smoke and the flying fragments a six pound shot passed over my head (grazeing [*sic*] my hat) and went into the ground." After this close brush with death, the private "made my obeisance to every one that passed very close for fear one might pass a few inches lower than that one." After several men were wounded, Major George H. Chapman moved the regiment "behind a little piece of woods and a hill that protected us." Other regiments used the big Newcomer barn or the bank of Antietam Creek for cover. Lieutenant Charles F. Adams, grandson of President John Quincy Adams and great-grandson of President John Adams, was in the 1st Massachusetts and wrote his mother afterward that it was "a terrific artillery duel which lasted where we were all day and injured almost no one." When the Federals first arrived on the western bank of the creek, "the crashing of shells and the deep reverberations from the hills were confusing and terrifying," but once the regiment got under the cover of the hill in front and dismounted, everyone gradually grew accustomed to the din. Adams admitted that he fell sound asleep on the grass, and his horse slipped away from him. Adams had company in finding the incessant racket to be a sedative. Another member of the 1st recalled that "everywhere could be seen groups of men fast asleep." In the opinion of a disgusted Major Henry Lee Higginson, speaking for the 1st Massachusetts and the rest of the cavalry in general, "We did nothing of any value during the whole day."[18]

Not everyone was sleeping or hiding from enemy shells. Elements of the 8th Illinois and the 3rd Indiana, armed with carbines, dismounted to support the arriving horse artillery south of the Boonsboro Pike. North of the pike, Twiggs's men, or parts of Evans's 22nd and 23rd South Carolina, threatened to advance on Tidball. The captain went back to the 4th Pennsylvania and asked for support. The half of the regiment armed with carbines dismounted and sprinted up the slope. Alexander C. Wikins in Company H saw a strapping man in his company drop down to the ground. When the captain stopped to check on him, the trooper claimed to be sick. As Wilkins remembered "The captain raised his sword and shouted, 'Soldiers never get sick on the battlefield,'" and told the man to get moving, which he did. At the crest, the 4th's carbines, augmented by Tidball's canister, discouraged any notion by the slim Confederate force of making a dash for the guns.[19]

Twiggs's men were dislodged around this time, when a battery across Antietam Creek—either Captain Stephen Weed's Battery I, 5th U.S., or Captain Elijah D. Taft's 5th Battery, New York Light—was alerted to the Georgians' position and opened an enfilading fire on them. Twiggs did not record whether the guns inflicted any casualties, but the shelling forced his command to "precipitately retire" in confusion. They fell back in a southwesterly direction, retreating nearly 500 yards to a stone fence running perpendicular to the Sherrick farm lane. Here Twiggs, with the help of Colonel Fitz W. McMaster in Evans's brigade, tried to rally his men. About half of them decided they had had enough and slipped by the officers, heading to the rear. Twiggs and McMaster managed to collect roughly 40–50 men, arraying them behind the wall and around some nearby haystacks. They were reinforced by skirmishers in the 17th South Carolina and the Holcombe Legion, both under McMaster's command. These two units, totaling only about 100 men, had recently been ordered forward from the reverse slope of Cemetery Ridge to support Twiggs and the skirmishers in Colonel Joseph Walker's South Carolina brigade, who were southeast of Cemetery Hill.[20]

With the menace of Twiggs's riflemen removed, the other batteries of Pleasonton's horse artillery arrived in succession and unlimbered along the ridge south of Tidball's position. The first to arrive was 22-year-old Lieutenant Peter C. Hains, a member of the June 1861 class at West Point. His Battery M, 2nd U.S., with four 3-inch rifles, relieved Dennison's section, who limbered and drove north to join the rest of Tidball's battery. Hains deployed a section of guns on each side of the Boonsboro Pike. Twiggs's and Evans's skirmishers "annoyed us some," reported Hains, but the Confederate guns on Cemetery Hill and Cemetery Ridge immediately engaged him in what he described as "hard fighting." Captain James M. Robertson's Batteries B and L, 2nd U.S., with four more 3-inch rifles, came clattering up behind Hains and unlimbered 80 yards south of the lieutenant's guns. If Hains represented the youth of the horse artillery's leadership, Robertson reflected the depth of its experience. He was 45 years old and had enlisted in the Regular Army in 1838, serving as an enlisted man until commissioned as a lieutenant 10 years later. Robertson was followed by Captain Horatio G. Gibson, a 35-year-old who had graduated from West Point in 1847, a year before Tidball. Gibson came up with Batteries C and G, 3rd U.S., armed with six 3-inch rifles. Gibson inserted his pieces into the space between Robertson and Hains. It was probably noon by the time all the guns and cavalry regiments were across Antietam Creek and in position. With these 20 pieces in action, the artillery duel began to swing in the Federals' favor. Within an hour, the Confederate gunners on Cemetery Hill and Cemetery Ridge were obliged to pull their pieces back under cover.[21]

While the artillery units battled one another, a note from McClellan, timed at 11:45 a.m., reached Pleasonton. He cautioned Pleasonton to not risk the horse artillery batteries unduly and then asked, "Can you do any good by a cavalry charge?" Even Pleasonton, who had a flair for the dramatic and for bombast, must have been incredulous. The operations of the cavalry and horse artillery were under direct observation from McClellan's command post, and the cavalry's commander might have wondered if his chief had taken leave of his senses. No mounted cavalry could survive on the forward slope of the ridge the horse artillery occupied, which was why the horsemen were hiding behind it and dodging the Confederates' shot and shell. As for the horse batteries, if there was concern for their safety, what was the point of sending them across Antietam Creek with only cavalry for support? John C. Tidball, who never shrank from expressing a thoughtful opinion, was disgusted with the management of the Middle Bridge operation and let fly in his after-action report, written 4 days after the battle: "The duties assigned to these [horse] batteries could have been performed as well by any other batteries, several of which were close by, unemployed. . . . The employment of these batteries alone with cavalry is a dangerous experiment and will most probably lead sooner or later to the loss of guns, but cavalry is not armed properly for the support of batteries, which without support are of themselves helpless." If the cavalry lacks the right type of armaments to assist the horse batteries, "as soon as the enemy opens fire the cavalry finds themselves of no service naturally and very properly retire. This, when there is no infantry at hand, leaves the batteries at the mercy of any [enterprising] party of the enemy."[22]

Around the time McClellan's message reached Pleasonton, he also received Tidball's request for infantry support to deal with Twiggs's skirmishers and the 22nd and 23rd South Carolina. The latter's long-range fire was tormenting his gun crews and could not be silenced by canister or the short-range carbines of the 4th Pennsylvania. Pleasonton rode to Captain Mathew M. Blunt, whose 1st Battalion of the 12th U.S. Infantry was stationed in the vicinity of the Middle Bridge, and asked if he would help. Blunt agreed, and he selected Company B, under 22-year-old Captain Frederick Winthrop, for the job.[23]

DURING THE CIVIL WAR, the Regulars had a reputation as being a sort of Imperial Guard—that is, an elite body of troops. Volunteer regiments swelled with pride if they learned to maneuver and behave like Regulars. Today, the Army of the Potomac's Regulars are often imagined to have been a body of hard-bitten veteran soldiers, with skin like leather from having served on the windy, sun-baked Western plains. A handful of officers fit this central casting image, such as 51-year-old Lieutenant Colonel Robert C. Buchanan, commanding the 1st Brigade of George Sykes's division. The Baltimore-born Buchanan—known by the obligatory nickname, applied to many a Buchanan, as "Buck" or "Old Buck"—was a nephew by marriage of President John Quincy Adams. The family connection helped him secure an appointment to West Point, and he graduated in 1830. Hard, dangerous service followed in various parts of the country: the Black Hawk War, the Second Seminole War, and the removal of the Cherokees to Indian Territory. In the Mexican War he participated in five major battles and distinguished himself by gallantry in action. Following that war, he served in Oregon and California. He was tough, demanding, and had something of a reputation as a martinet. But men such as Buchanan were relatively rare in the Regulars. Most officers were like Captain Winthrop, who was a 21-year-old bank clerk when the Civil War began. Coming from a well-connected New York City family, he secured a captain's commission in the 71st New York State Militia and fought credibly with it at First Bull Run. When the regiment mustered out of

Federal service, Winthrop and his family sought a commission for him in the Regular Army.[24]

At the beginning of the Civil War, the Regular Army consisted of 10 infantry regiments, 4 artillery regiments, and 5 regiments of cavalry. Numerous Southern officers in all of these regiments resigned their commissions and joined the Confederate army, leaving many vacancies to be filled. On December 31, 1860, the 10 regiments reported 8,200 men present, 1,800 soldiers short of their authorized strength. The regiments were scattered across the country, often in company-sized posts and forts. Since it would take time for the Regular regiments to be concentrated and make their way to the East, and because their numbers were so few, a decision was made early on not to break them up and use them to form a cadre for a volunteer army, but instead to retain the small number of Regular Army troops and build up the bulk of the Union army with state volunteers. This precipitated another drain on leadership in the Regulars, as many officers took volunteer commissions to secure a higher rank. Although volunteers would make up the vast majority of the Union army, a recommendation to enlarge the size of the Regular Army by adding nine regiments of infantry, and one more of artillery and cavalry, was approved. The old Regular Army regiments were organized into 10 companies, lettered A–K (there was never a Company J). The new infantry regiments, the 11th through the 19th, were recruited and organized on the French system, consisting of three battalions to a regiment, with each battalion containing eight companies, lettered A–H. Thus, at full strength, a battalion would have 800 officers and men; and a regiment, 2,400.[25]

The first order of business was to select commissioned officers. A handful came from West Point or the Regular Army. For example, the 11th U.S. had one West Pointer, who was its major, Delancey Floyd-Jones. The 12th U.S. had two West Pointers. Most of the other officers were like Frederick Winthrop, commissioned either from volunteer regiments or from civilian ranks. The newly appointed officers were then put through a brief but rigorous course in tactics and army regulations before being dispersed to recruit enlisted men. Each regiment had its own hometown recruiting depot: Fort Independence in Boston for the 11th; New York City for the 12th; Fort Trumbell in Connecticut for the 14th; and Fort Preble, a mile south of Portland, Maine, for the 17th. Recruiting officers for these regiments also traveled across the geographic regions associated with their home bases to seek recruits. This was how Charles T. Bowen, a 23-year-old farm laborer from Utica, New York, and six others from the Utica area enlisted in the 12th U.S. Infantry on August 16, 1861. Enlistees might be average U.S.-born civilians, like Bowen, but there were also many immigrants. At least nine Confederate deserters enlisted in the 12th U.S., and a number of British Regulars, who defected from their home country's regiments, which had deployed to Canada, to receive better pay and a higher rank in the 17th U.S. All enlistees ended up at the various headquarters of their regiments, where their training began. In Charles Bowen's opinion, the raw material that made up the new regiments was quite good: "We have here as fine looking body of men as could well be brought together all finely formed robust-smart looking boys, there are several here who are sons of very rich people, & quite a number have been through college."[26]

The new Regular Army regiments were initially no different from the volunteer regiments that were being raised at the same time. The Regular Army had a system of training that some volunteer regiments, particularly those led by West Pointers, followed, but these were in the minority. Regulars were held to a higher standard than the typical volunteer soldier. When the recruits in the 2nd Battalion of the 14th Infantry, known as the 2/14th, arrived at the Regulars' camp in Fairfax, Virginia, on March 4, 1862, their commander, Captain John O'Connell, reported to Lieutenant Colonel Buchanan for duty. Buchanan gazed with disapproval at O'Connell's soldiers as they marched past and snapped, "Sir, your men look like volunteers." O'Connell replied that that was exactly what they were. Buchanan then responded, "I will make them Regulars."[27]

Charles Bowen, who wrote home to his wife and family regularly and kept a detailed wartime diary, provides insight into what Buchanan meant. Each night the enlisted men were required to oil and clean their weapons "until you can see your face in the 'lock plate,' barrel, & in fact on all the iron in sight." Failure to do so landed a soldier in the guardhouse. Bayonets were "served in the same style." Clothes were kept clean and boots polished. Each morning, after wiping the oil from their guns, uniform plates and buttons were buffed to a shine, followed by dress parade. Then they had to drill, clean up, drill again, eat dinner (the midday meal), drill some more, clean up again, and drill for another hour before supper. Regular Army discipline did not equate with cruelty, as it sometimes had in the old army. Bowen's battalion commander, Major Henry B. Clitz, an 1845 West Point graduate, was revered by his men. "We all love him," wrote Bowen. "He is so kind to the soldiers, he has the privilege to ride horseback on a march & sleep in a tent at night, but he says he don't want his men to do anything more or bear any more hardships than himself." In March 1862, Bowen wrote about how his battalion went through target practice, with the targets situated 300 yards away. He placed seven rounds "in a size of a man's head with my rifle," a testament not only to Bowen's marksmanship, but also to the value the Regulars placed on training their soldiers to be proficient with their weapons. Bowen related another difference between the Regulars and volunteers when he visited the camp of the 14th New York, in Griffin's brigade of Morell's division after the Battle of Antietam: "One hour in a <u>Volunteer</u> camp is enough to sicken anyone from the life of a <u>Volunteer soldier</u>. I thought we were about as dirty & forlorn a set as could live, but our camp is a <u>parlor</u> compared to theirs & our men <u>clean</u>. I don't believe as dirty a shirt could be found in the ranks of our whole brigade, as I saw on the back of a <u>captain</u> in the 14th, & to make matters still worse, if possible, he had a beautiful (!) louse, crawling on the collar." Bowen could imagine a private having lice crawling on him, "but for a commissioned officer in camp is beyond belief."[28]

The Regulars, in short, were typically better trained, better disciplined, and better officered than the average volunteer regiment. Commanders like Buchanan held the enlisted men and officers accountable to a high standard in maintaining their equipment, being competent at drill and tactics, and ensuring the cleanliness of camp and soldier. There were volunteer regiments that vied with the quality of the Regulars, such as the 2nd and 20th Massachusetts and the 2nd and 6th Wisconsin. But in 1862, at least, the Regulars—whether one of the old regiments, like the 2nd U.S., or a newly raised one, such as the 12th U.S.—stood above the mass of volunteer regiments in quality.

BOWEN, NOW A SERGEANT, was among the two companies of skirmishers in the 1/12th (Companies B and G) who were sent forward under Captain Winthrop to assist Tidball's horse artillerymen. Numbering around 50 officers and men, they clambered over fences "where cavelry could not cross" and emerged into the open over Newcomer Ridge, south of Tidball's position and in front of Hains' and Gibson's batteries. They were to engage Twiggs's Georgian skirmishers, who had withdrawn behind a stone wall about 500 yards distant.[29]

Winthrop's advance was followed by orders from division commander George Sykes to Captain Blunt. The captain was to advance the balance of his battalion to support the skirmishers and the horse batteries. Sykes also ordered—probably after further discussion with Pleasonton—Lieutenant John S. Poland, an 1861 West Point graduate from Indiana, to take his 2nd and 10th U.S., with 402 effectives, across Antietam Creek and report to the cavalry commander. Poland led his men over the Middle Bridge and halted them near Robertson's battery, while he went to find Pleasonton. Poland was intercepted by Lieutenant Heyward Cutting on Sykes's staff, who directed the lieutenant to advance his skirmishers and drive back the Rebels harassing the Union artillerymen. Poland deployed 7 of his 12 companies as skirmishers in front of the guns south of the Boonsboro Pike and held the remaining 5 as a reserve.[30]

By the time Poland's regiment had crossed Antietam Creek, it was nearly 1 p.m., and the horse batteries were running out of ammunition. Pleasonton sent a message back across the creek, requesting relief for them. Whether the message went to McClellan or Porter is unknown, but one of them ordered Sykes to send out two of his divisional batteries. Sykes was a cautious soldier, in the mold of McClellan and Porter, and he was not feeling well on the 17th. He worried that the Confederates were concealing a large force behind Cemetery Hill and thought the order an unwise risk. Nevertheless, he obeyed and sent Lieutenant Alanson M. Randol's Batteries E and G, 1st U.S. (4 Napoleons) and Lieutenant William E. Van Reed's Battery K, 5th U.S. (4 Napoleons) to relieve the horse batteries. To provide additional security, he ordered Captain David B. McKibbin, commanding the 2/14th U.S., across the creek. An hour later, he instructed Captain Hiram Dryer, an intrepid, enterprising officer commanding the 4th U.S., to bring his regiment, along with the 1/14th U.S., over Antietam Creek and take control of all the Regular infantry there.[31]

Twenty-four-year-old Lieutenant Alanson M. Randol, ranked ninth in the West Point class of 1860, led his battery over the Middle Bridge and reported to Pleasonton, who directed him to relieve Robertson's battery on the southern end of Newcomer Ridge. The distance from this point to Cemetery Hill was slightly over 1,000 yards, in range of Randol's Napoleons, but the lieutenant was not pleased with his position, "on account of the nature of the ground and its proximity to a large corn-field and other covers, by means of which the enemy could approach to within a very short range unperceived." The only nearby cornfield was the large one that ran across the eastern slope of Cemetery Hill, which was 700–800 yards from Randol, but it did provide cover for the Rebels to infiltrate men forward to the fences on the Sherrick farm lane and into the nearby cultivated fields. The overall inequality of the terrain provided good shelter for the skirmishers, and some of them greeted Randol's gun crews with an inaccurate, but unpleasant, fire. The lieutenant turned his guns on a Confederate battery, possibly Richardson's 2nd Company of the Washington (Louisiana) Artillery, south of Sherrick's and Otto's farms. It had been engaging the 9th Corps, but Randol's gunnery forced it to displace rearward. Randol's arrival, and the subsequent gun duel, coincided with the deployment of Lieutenant Poland's seven companies of skirmishers. At Randol's request, Poland had his marksmen advance in front of the artillery and engage McMaster's and Twiggs's detachments, who had used the cover provided by walls, fences, and the uneven terrain to work their way to within long-rifle range of the guns. Poland's skirmishers pushed the Rebels back, but it did not improve Randol's opinion of his position. One wonders if Sykes had influenced his fears. Randol rode over to Pleasonton to make his case that his guns should be withdrawn. The lieutenant's battery had suffered no losses, but Pleasonton permitted him to move to the eastern bank of Antietam Creek.[32]

Randol's departure left Van Reed's Battery K, 5th U.S., as the only artillery west of Antietam Creek. Van Reed's background is curious. He was 21, and his only military service had been as a corporal in the 5th Pennsylvania Infantry, with its 3-month enlistment period. Yet in May 1861, he received a commission as a 2nd lieutenant in the 5th U.S. Artillery. He must have done well in his new occupation, for he was promoted to first lieutenant and the command of Battery K. Van Reed followed Randol and probably also inquired of Pleasonton where he should deploy his guns. He was sent to relieve Tidball's, Hains's, and Gibson's batteries, and he unlimbered between where Tidball and Hains had been. With most of the Confederate artillery cleared off of Cemetery Hill and

Cemetery Ridge, and their skirmishers pressed back, Tidball noted that "there was a lull in the battle all along the line, and what was done in relieving our batteries was done with deliberation."[33]

This lull, between around 2 to 3 p.m., was like a tempest that subsides but has not yet spent its force. Van Reed kept up his artillery fire on the Confederates, while the Union's Regular skirmishers and Twiggs and Evans's Rebels continued to spar with one another. Two things breathed new life into the combat. The first was the opening of the 9th Corps' attack on Confederate positions south of Sharpsburg, at around 3:30 p.m. The second was the arrival of Hiram Dryer, with his reinforcements. The 53-year-old Dryer was a soldier cut from a similar cloth as Lieutenant Colonel Buchanan. He enlisted in the Regular Army's Mounted Rifles as a private at the start of the Mexican War. He rose to the post of 1st sergeant, and then won a commission as a 2nd lieutenant in the 4th Infantry. He survived the transfer of the 4th Infantry to the West Coast, which cost the regiment 104 men and 1 officer, all of whom died of cholera while crossing Panama, and later volunteered to rescue a group of immigrants stranded by a severe mountain snowstorm in the Cascades. Dryer was described by a fellow officer as "one of the coolest and bravest officers in our service," but he was not a martinet. When he died of pneumonia at Fort Randall in 1876, a fellow officer remembered him as "always kind and friendly."[34]

BEFORE SYKES MADE THE decision to send Dryer and additional infantry across Antietam Creek, Pleasonton responded to McClellan's 11:45 a.m. message with a carefully worded response, timed at 2:30 p.m.: "It would be well to have some more infantry here to support my batteries. The country is broken. The indications are that the enemy are still in force in front. My cavalry is exposed." This was a diplomatic way of saying that no, a cavalry charge was not possible. The response from headquarters was not encouraging. At 3:30 p.m., Chief of Staff Marcy replied, "General McClellan directs me to say he has no infantry to spare. Confer with Major-General Porter, and if he cannot support your batteries, withdraw them." Porter and Sykes had released more infantry to reinforce Pleasonton during the period when these dispatches were traveling back and forth, but with reservations concerning the risks these two commanders had perceived.[35]

After withdrawing from Newcomer Ridge, Captain Tidball drove his battery back to a locale near Keedysville, where he found food for his men and horses and resupplied his limbers and caissons with ammunition. While his lieutenants supervised this business, Tidball rode to the top of a high hill—which was probably the hill near Ecker's farm, north of Weed's battery—where he found Porter, Griffin, and other 5th Corps officers. Tidball did not say whether Sykes was there or not. The captain recalled that he had "quite a conversation relative to matters on the other side of the Antietam" with these leaders, but unfortunately he did not share what questions Porter and Griffin had asked. Sykes, in particular, did not like the look of things across Antietam Creek and grudgingly parted with his infantry to support Pleasonton's horse artillery. He grumbled to Porter, through an aide-de-camp on Porter's staff, that he could not see "that Burnside had done a thing" on the 9th Corps' front, and that the two regiments Sykes had sent across the creek had been "driven back like sheep by the enemy's artillery." Sykes added that he believed the Confederates had a large force "under crest of [Cemetery] hill toward Sharpsburg." One wonders how Sykes came up with this report. Burnside had carried the Rohrback Bridge and was pouring troops across Antietam Creek, and, although the Regulars in the 1/12th, 2nd, and 10th U.S. were keeping under cover from the Rebel guns, no one had been "driven back like sheep." Sykes seems to have made up his mind that he did not like the situation across the creek and was looking for anything that might confirm this opinion.[36]

Tidball led his battery back across Antietam Creek shortly after 3 p.m., around the same time when Dryer, with his 4th U.S. and the 1/14th U.S., were crossing it. As his gun teams passed over the Middle Bridge to the creek's western bank, Tidball noticed Randol's guns limbering and beginning to retire. The captain led his guns back to their same position, on the right of Van Reed, returning badly needed rifled firepower to the Union position on Newcomer Ridge. Meanwhile, Captain Dryer marched his 4th U.S. and the 1/14th U.S., totaling about 640 officers and men, up to the ridge in column, then rushed them over the crest—while under fire—and down to the base of the ridge, where the Sunken Lane connected with the Boonsboro Pike. A 3-acre, triangular-shaped cornfield and a farmhouse associated with the Newcomer family stood directly in their front, which, in addition to the fencing along the lane, provided some cover. On Dryer's left, south of the Boonsboro Pike, Lieutenant Poland advanced seven of his companies over Newcomer Ridge and deployed them in an extended line, stretching from opposite to where the Sunken Lane came into the pike to the southeast, along the ravine running down in the direction of Antietam Creek. They joined Companies B and G in the 1/12th U.S., who were already established in this area, so that nine companies of Regulars, or about 300 men, now held the skirmish line south of the Boonsboro Pike, along a front of nearly 500 yards.[37]

Captain Dryer visited Poland soon after arriving at the western base of Newcomer Ridge. He told the lieutenant that he was now in command of all Regular infantry west of Antietam Creek. After evaluating the situation, the captain took immediate and aggressive action. He ordered Poland to bring up his five reserve companies to strengthen his skirmish line and then attack and seize the haystacks and stone wall serving as cover for Twiggs's and McMaster's Rebel skirmishers. Returning to his own command, Dryer ordered 26-year-old Lieutenant Caleb H. Carlton, an 1859 graduate of the Military Academy, commanding Company A in the 4th U.S., to take three companies as skirmishers and advance with them to a spot near the easternmost edge of Cemetery Ridge, north of the Boonsboro Pike. The Regulars' training in skirmish duty was about to pay dividends.[38]

THE BUILDUP OF UNION infantry and guns in front of Cemetery Hill caused a scramble in the Confederates' high command, who were trying to scrape together troops to reinforce the slim force defending the hill. No fresh infantry or artillery was to be had, so it became necessary to send ad hoc infantry commands and parts of battered artillery units. About 150 infantrymen, under the command of Captain Thomas M. Garrett in the 5th North Carolina, arrived on the hill in midafternoon. Earlier in the day, Garrett had been carried along in the rout of McRae's brigade and ended up in Sharpsburg, trying to rally stragglers. He encountered General Lee, who was riding through the village, and asked for orders. Lee advised the captain to rally all the stragglers he could lay his hands on, without regard to their command, and report to General Nathan Evans. Before the war, the 32-year-old Garrett was an attorney in Bertie County, North Carolina, and strongly opposed secession. But the events of April 1861 convinced him of the inevitability of both secession and war, and he became one of the first in his county to enlist. With the help of the assistant adjutant general in McRae's brigade, Lieutenant J. M. Taylor, and Lieutenant Isaac E. Pearce in his own regiment, Garrett gathered 50 men of the 5th North Carolina and about 100 from other commands. In the afternoon, he led his command to Cemetery Hill and reported to Evans. The brigadier general had been busy himself, rallying stragglers in the streets of Sharpsburg. With the addition of Garrett's men, he now had assembled a small ad hoc brigade of nearly 250 men. Evans divided it into two commands: one of approximately 100 men, which he assigned to Colonel Alfred Colquitt, who had somehow found his way to Cemetery Hill; and the other, which consisted of Garrett's 150 men, to Colonel Alfred Iverson in McRae's brigade. Evans then posted them in support of his own brigade and the Cemetery Hill batteries.[39]

Changes had occurred in the Confederate artillery defending the hill and the ridge. The ammunition for Bachman's guns was exhausted, and they were withdrawn from Cemetery Hill, leaving only Squires's four guns. Hilary Jones's battalion remained in the vicinity of Cemetery Ridge, along with 2 guns in Boyce's battery and 1 gun in Bondurant's. About the time that Dryer led his regiments over Newcomer Ridge, Colonel Stephen D. Lee arrived on Cemetery Hill with six guns from two batteries in his battalion. He had orders from Longstreet to relieve the Washington (Louisiana) Artillery and deploy his guns on either side of the Boonsboro Pike. Captain George V. Moody's Madison (Louisiana) Artillery, with two 3-inch rifles and two 24 lb. howitzers, took up a position on Cemetery Hill, between Squires's guns and the pike. About 150 yards north of the road, two guns of Captain Tyler C. Jordan's Bedford (Virginia) Artillery, probably the 3-inch rifle and 10 lb. Parrott, unlimbered. As they refitted, more of Colonel Lee's guns would join the fight. With the Federals' 9th Corps now pouring up from the Rohrback Bridge ravine, the Confederates also strengthened the southwestern face of Cemetery Hill, moving the four guns (two 2 lb. howitzers and two 6 lb. guns) of Captain Hugh P. Garden's Palmetto (South Carolina) Battery across Lower Bridge Road, placing them to the right of Squires and facing down the bridge road. Colonel Joseph Walker's South Carolina brigade followed Garden's battery and formed to support Squires and Moody.[40]

Moody's gun crews came under long-range fire from Poland's skirmishers as soon as they unlimbered, and S. D. Lee appealed to Garnett for infantry support. Garnett ordered Captain John B. McPhail's 56th Virginia, with only 40 effectives, to deploy as skirmishers in the cornfield on the eastern slope in front of the guns. McPhail reported that his men immediately became "hotly engaged" with the Regulars and endured "a terrific artillery fire," but their concealment in the corn and dispersal in skirmish order kept their casualty numbers low. With McPhail's 56th Virginia, there were now slightly more than 300 Confederate skirmishers on the forward slopes of Cemetery Hill and Cemetery Ridge, confronting Dryer's Regulars. The Rebel line extended from Twiggs's and McMaster's force on the right, behind the stone wall and haystacks, to Evans's 22nd and 23rd South Carolina, north of the Boonsboro Pike.[41]

It was probably around 3:30 p.m. when Poland's and Carlton's skirmishers rose up from the ground and started forward. On their left, the 9th Corps' offensive to roll up the Confederates' right flank kicked off at the same time. There were 570 Regulars in the Federals' extended skirmish line, since Poland's force included at least Company G in the 1/12th, and probably Company B in the same battalion. Managing a skirmish line was one of the most demanding and difficult duties of a Civil War infantry officer. Because it was spread out, with several feet between each man, it required a great deal of exertion and exposure to supervise its movements. It also demanded initiative from the non-commissioned officers and privates, in order to keep the line moving forward. The Regulars were well trained for this work. When Poland's skirmishers emerged from the ravine and approached the ridge east of the Sherrick farm lane, Moody's and Squires's batteries greeted them with "a heavy fire of case-shot and canister." They also received small-arms volleys from Confederate skirmishers. North of the Boonsboro Pike, Jordan's, Boyce's, and Bondurant's five guns blazed away at Carlton's companies. Sergeant Bowen, on the receiving end of Moody's and Squires' fire, wrote, "You had ought to have seen the dust fly, round shot, shell, grape, canister, & every other missel rooting up the dirt & making an unearthly noise." But for all the commotion and dust, the barrage did little damage to the dispersed Federals, and they steadily and doggedly worked their way forward.[42]

Twiggs's and McMaster's men at the stone wall and haystacks fought desperately against the approaching bluecoats. "The devils fought untill we were right up to the fence," observed Bowen. As the sergeant and his comrades rushed toward the stone wall, a Confederate "poked his musket right in my face & pulled trigger, the ball just grazed my head & the powder burnt my face he was so close." A comrade beside Bowen "put a ball through him [the Rebel] at almost the same moment." Bowen saw bayonets being crossed nearby and declared, "I tell you it was hot work." The Regulars swarmed over the wall, capturing a dozen prisoners. Years later, Twiggs wrote, "Colonel McMasters and I finding it impossible to make a stand against the large force, withdrew our commands to the apple orchard at the stone house behind the rock fence." Twiggs's account reads as if the retreat was orderly and disciplined, but McMaster offered what was probably a more truthful account. Besides the Regulars charging up in his front, Christ's brigade in the 9th Corps flanked him on the right. After firing at the Regulars for "a few moments, the Holcombe Legion and a few of the Seventeenth Regiment, in spite of my efforts, broke and ran," McMaster reported. Sensing the impossibility of holding his position, McMaster ordered Twiggs and the handful of remaining men to fall back to an apple orchard about 500 yards in their rear, located beside the stone mill on Lower Bridge Road. In Bowen's opinion, who watched the departing Confederates, it was a "skedaddle."[43]

Poland's skirmishers swept up to the Sherrick farm lane, taking cover behind its fences from the shrapnel and canister delivered by Moody's and Squires's guns. On Poland's right, some of his exuberant skirmishers, not hearing his orders to halt at the road, pushed past the farm lane. This led to unexpected results, as these men, "by a well-directed fire compelled the enemy's cannoneers to leave their guns." But just as the Confederates' defenses on Cemetery Hill began to come apart, the Union artillery accidentally came to their aid. A number of the Federals' shells, from one or more batteries across Antietam Creek, began to fall short, landing among the Regulars. "We lost a number of men by these means," observed Sergeant Bowen. Those not hit were forced to fall back to the Sherrick farm lane to get cover from the friendly fire.[44]

THE CONFEDERATES REACTED IMMEDIATELY to the threat posed by Poland's advance. Garnett ordered his entire brigade forward, heading into the cornfield on Cemetery Hill's forward slope. He sent the 28th Virginia to the left and front of the two guns in Moody's battery, which were positioned near the rail fence on the cornfield's western border. Most likely there were Moody's howitzers, which could dish out a murderous fire of canister at a range of 400 yards or less. Garnett called the 56th Virginia back from the skirmish line and ordered Captain McPhail to re-form on the left of the 28th. The 19th and 18th Virginia went into the corn on Moody's right. The men deployed in extended order, to cover more ground, with 4 or 5 feet between each man. The tiny 8th Virginia, only 22 strong, took up a position on the 18th's right and rear. All the regiments were immediately hotly engaged. "The fight was as you know terrific," wrote Major

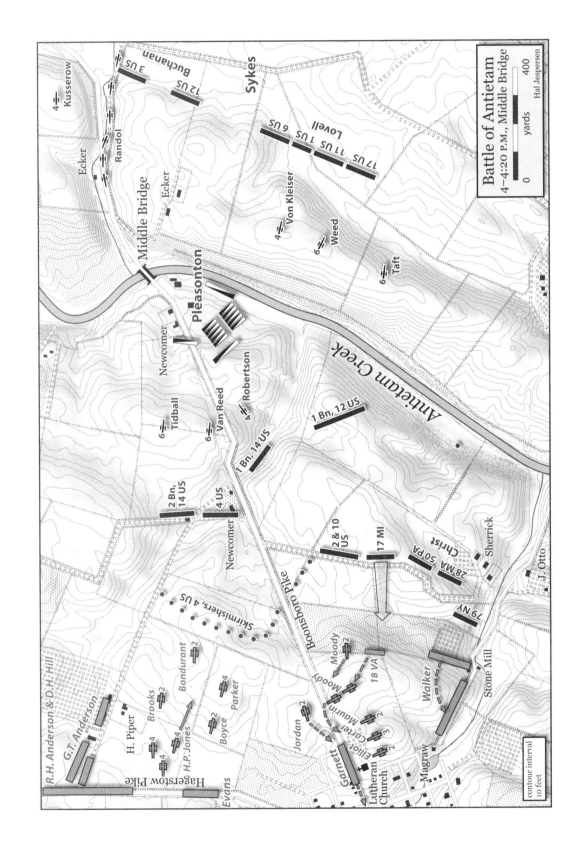

Battle of Antietam
4–4:20 P.M., Middle Bridge

Hal Jespersen

0   yards   400

contour interval
10 feet

George C. Cabell. Colonel Eppa Hunton, proudly noted that in his platoon-sized 8th Virginia, "not a man of my command faltered," unless they were wounded and went to the rear. Lieutenant William N. Wood, one of only three officers with the 19th Virginia, took courage from Moody's nearby guns, which were "worked by cool, brave men, who loaded with rapidity and sent canister thick and fast into the approaching ranks." Garnett's Virginians stabilized the situation in front of Cemetery Hill, but things were deteriorating on both of his flanks.[45]

This engagement defied the popular—but inaccurate—notion that Civil War battles were fought between two lines standing in the open, firing into one another at 100 yards or less. That type of combat occasionally happened at Antietam and elsewhere throughout the war, but it was not typical. Here, both sides fought in skirmish order, moving from one swath of cover to another, and exchanging fire at ranges of 250 to 300 yards. It was the type of combat a World War I or World War II soldier would have recognized.

North of the Boonsboro Pike, Captain Carlton's three companies of skirmishers moved forward through a small, 3-acre cornfield surrounding one of Newcomer's houses, driving back skirmishers in the 22nd and 23rd South Carolina. The Federals advanced nearly 150 yards, to the far eastern projection of Cemetery Ridge, opposite the entrance to the Sherrick farm lane. Dryer ordered his and Carlton's men to halt here, while he maneuvered his supports closer to them. The captain went back, retrieved his five reserve companies in the 4th U.S., brought them up to near the western edge of the 3-acre cornfield, and had them lie down, so the corn would conceal their position from Rebel artillerymen. On their left, Captain W. Harvey Brown led his 1/14th U.S. into the ravine south of the Boonsboro Pike, opposite to where the pike met the Sunken Lane. Captain McKibbin moved his 2/14th U.S. over Newcomer Ridge to a ravine running northwest from the Sunken Lane, on the right of the 4th U.S., and he pushed a company of skirmishers up the slope of Cemetery Ridge, which was in their front, to reinforce Carlton.[46]

The arrival of Carlton's skirmishers on the eastern edges of Cemetery Ridge triggered an aggressive response by General Nathan Evans, who sent his two straggler battalions forward, along with Colonel Stevens and the 22nd, 23rd, and 18th South Carolina—all told, about 400 officers and men—to clear the Regulars from the ridge. Carlton had only about 90 to 95 men in his three companies, and perhaps 30 to 35 more in the 2/14th U.S. company that reinforced his right flank. The Confederates had the edge in manpower, but the Regulars were backed by Tidball's and Van Reed's batteries. Moreover, they enjoyed solid unit integrity, leadership, and discipline, which most of the advancing Rebels did not. Straggler battalions with strong leadership could sometimes fight effectively for a time if they were on the defensive, but rarely did they do so on the attack. Evans's advance did not depart from this pattern. The moment his Confederate troops came under fire, the attack stalled and then came apart.[47]

Both Evans and D. H. Hill spun fictions about Evans's counterattack, which bore little resemblance to reality. Evans claimed his "little command gallantly drove the enemy from his cover in the corn-field and caused him to retreat in confusion, leaving a number of their dead and two stands of colors, the latter having been shot down by a well-directed fire of Captain Boyce's battery." Evans also maintained that a battery of the Washington (Louisiana) Artillery drove back one of the Union batteries that had crossed Antietam Creek. No colors were lost, however, by the Regulars—they were not carried on the skirmish line—and neither Tidball nor Van Reed were forced to withdraw or change position. Possibly Evans construed Randol's withdrawal as being the result of Confederate artillery fire, but it is just as likely that he invented or imagined both events. Carlton's skirmish line did give ground initially when Evans launched his counterattack, but it quickly stiffened and checked the Rebels' advance with accurate rifle fire. Never one to be outdone in exaggeration, D. H. Hill reported that Lieutenant Colonel William H. Betts in Colquitt's 13th Alabama, with only 30 men and the support of the Confederate guns on Cemetery Ridge, met Carlton's approach with "a sudden storm of grape and canister" and "drove them back in confusion." Hill imagined that he had faced Burnside's 9th Corps and cited a report in which the Federals claimed to have met "three heavy columns" who fiercely resisted their advance. "It is difficult to imagine how 30 men could so multiply themselves as to appear to the frightened Yankees to be three heavy columns," sneered Hill. One might just as well ask how Hill imagined a skirmish line to be an army corps. The Confederate soldiers who faced bullets and shrapnel on Cemetery Ridge might have found some amusement in Hill's and Evans's fabrications, but they knew their leaders' accounts bore little resemblance to the reality they had experienced.[48]

Captain Thomas M. Garrett penned a more honest statement of what happened to the Confederates' counterattack. They engaged the Regulars "with spirit, and forced them, for a moment, to give back," he wrote, which was true. But then, under the fire from Tidball's and Van Reed's guns and the Regulars' rifles, "the left of the line of which my command formed part gave way, and being left with but the men from my regiment [about 50 men], I ordered them to retire" to a large rock in a field about 50 yards to the rear. Here, Garrett kept up the fight for 25 or 30 minutes longer before being forced to retreat again. The South Carolinians—under Colonel Stevens, who was managing the tactical affairs for Evans's brigade—had been firing for some time before the counterattack started, and they quickly began to run low on ammunition. "We held against a largely superior force of the enemy for a considerable time," noted Colonel William H. Wallace, commanding the 18th South Carolina. But Stevens watched his thin line melt away under the fire directed at it, and he soon ordered Boyce's guns to withdraw. They were followed by Stevens's three regiments, who continued their retreat for nearly 800 yards, to the Hagerstown Pike. The Regulars and their supporting artillery harassed the Rebels' retreat, inflicting more casualties and scattering Stevens's command. Wallace reported that, "almost immediately," his regiment "was reduced to a handful of men." Major Miel Hilton, commanding the 22nd South Carolina, did not even pause at the Hagerstown Pike, but instead had his troops continue on to the western side of Sharpsburg, where they halted "for rest and refreshment."[49]

Although many of the Confederates fought stubbornly, the accurate fire from Carlton's skirmishers and the Federal batteries swung the engagement in the Union's favor and caused the Rebels' defense to come apart. Once the infantry had left, the remaining Confederate artillery—Jordan's battery, Bondurant's single gun, and the batteries of Hilary Jones's battalion—departed. By 4 or 4:30 p.m., Cemetery Ridge had been cleared of its Rebel defenders.[50]

Carlton's three companies and the one company of McKibbin's 2/14th U.S. worked their way up the exposed ridge. They drew fire from Lieutenant Colonel Betts and his 30 men in Colquitt's brigade, who were somewhere at the extreme northern end of the ridge. This forced the Regulars on the right of the line to halt their advance and bend back their line in order to respond to the volleys, but there was no stampede to the rear, such as the one D. H. Hill invented. Closer to the Boonsboro Pike, on the left of the Federal line, Carlton's men kept moving, climbing Cemetery Ridge until they were within 450 yards of the Lutheran Church, which was on the eastern edge of the village, and could actually see some of the buildings in Sharpsburg. It was their high-water mark.[51]

General Garnett and Colonel Stephen D. Lee were standing in the cornfield on Cemetery Hill's eastern slope, their attention fixed on Lieutenant Poland's skirmishers in the Sherrick farm lane, who were trading fire with Garnett's men and Moody's battery. Someone called their attention to Carlton's bluecoats north of the Boonsboro Pike, who were nearly even with Garnett's left flank. Lee directed Moody's two guns to turn their fire on this portion of enemy, while Garnett changed front to the north with part of the 56th Virginia, to get an enfilading fire on the Regulars. The flanking fire caught Carlton's men in the open and pinned them down. Whether Carlton might have resumed his advance became a moot point, for orders arrived from Dryer, commanding him to withdraw back on the same line with Poland, whose skirmishers had remained in the Sherrick farm lane.[52]

Dryer sent these recall orders to Carlton with the greatest reluctance. They originated from higher authority. Besides his legendary coolness and courage, Dryer was also known as "gallant and impetuous," nineteenth-century language for "aggressive." He had demonstrated superb tactical skill in his management of the fight and was sure that there were no legions of Rebels hiding behind Cemetery Hill. The Confederates' defenses were a thin shell that could be cracked open. There had been no impetuosity about his advance up to this point. It had been methodical, careful of the lives of his men, and successful. As Carlton's troops were fighting their way up Cemetery Ridge, Dryer intended to advance Poland's skirmishers on the left, supported by Blunt's 1/12th U.S., to capture Moody's battery and drive off Garnett's brigade. Captain Blunt, however, was cut from the same mold of Sykes, rather than that of Dryer. When he received Dryer's order to support Poland's assault, he sent it back to Buchanan with the comment that he thought the order inconsistent with the mission for which he believed his battalion had been sent across Antietam Creek, and thus "asked instructions." Buchanan sent Blunt's note on to Sykes, who, Ezra Carman wrote, was "very much annoyed" with Dryer. He had grudgingly sent his Regulars across Antietam Creek in the first place, and he had limited their role to supporting the artillery and dislodging the Confederates behind the haystacks and stone wall. Dryer had exceeded Sykes's orders. That Dryer was driving back the enemy was irrelevant to Sykes. It was not as if Dryer's success was unknown. Captain May H. Stacy, the adjutant in the 1/12th U.S., watched the action from his reserve position on Antietam Creek's eastern bank and jotted in his diary that "it was very handsome to see a thin line of skirmishers driving everything before them." But Sykes remained convinced of the enemy's hidden reserves in the rear of Cemetery Hill, and what he saw was a captain exceeding his orders and taking an unnecessary risk. Sykes dispatched Lieutenant William H. Powell, the adjutant general in Buchanan's brigade, to cross the creek and order Dryer to immediately cancel his orders for an attack, as well as to withdraw all his infantry back to Newcomer Ridge.[53]

When Captain Blunt sent Dryer's orders to attack back to Sykes for clarification and further instructions, his note also contained a comment that Dryer believed that only a single Confederate battery and two regiments remained in his front. Under the circumstances, it was an accurate estimate of the enemy's strength. It correctly identified the only forces remaining to be defeated: Moody's battery, plus Garnett's regiment on either side of the battery, which Dryer believed were two single regiments. Captain Thomas M. Anderson, commanding the 2/12th U.S., which remained in reserve on Antietam Creek's eastern bank, had ridden over to the high ground between Weed's and Taft's batteries south of the Boonsboro Pike, in order to observe the action with Buchanan. In an 1886 article in *Century Magazine*, Anderson noted that he had seen Sykes, Porter, and McClellan nearby, sitting on their horses and watching the action on Sykes's and Burnside's fronts. Eleven years later, in an 1897 private letter, Anderson recounted that after reading Blunt's note, Buchanan said to him, "Dryer reports center very weak and wants leave to attack," and then sent the note over to Sykes. Anderson did not admit to knowing the contents of the note until years later, but he claimed that he watched Sykes receive and read it, pass it on to Porter, who read it, and then handed it to McClellan. Buchanan was so certain they would be called to action that he told Anderson, "Fall in our men, our turn has come at last." But nothing happened. Anderson claimed that after the war, he spoke to Sykes about the incident and asked him "why our reserves did not advance upon receiving Dryer's report." Sykes replied that he remembered the moment very well and thought that McClellan was "inclined to order in the Fifth Corps," but when McClellan asked Porter's opinion, the 5th Corps' commander said, "Remember, General! I command the last reserve of the last Army of the Republic." That, in Anderson's telling, squelched any chance for Dryer's success to be reinforced and exploited. But is Thomas Anderson's account true?[54]

Porter replied to Anderson's 1886 article, stating "that no such note as 'Captain Dryer's report'" was ever seen by him, and that no discussion about using the "reserve" took place between him and McClellan. That Porter never saw "Captain Dryer's report" is probably true. But Porter's assertion that he and McClellan had no discussion about committing the 5th Corps needs an explanation. Porter was probably not present when Dryer's note arrived. He remained at the command post near the Boonsboro Pike until around 4:30 p.m., when he rode over to Sykes's position between Weed's and Taft's batteries. We know this to be true, for at 4:30 p.m., Porter sent McClellan a situation report. It is logical that he would have dispatched such a report shortly after reaching Sykes's position and being briefed on the situation. Lieutenant Powell, who carried Sykes's orders commanding Dryer to fall back, made no mention of Porter or McClellan being present when he set off, because neither one of them was there yet. This places the time of Dryer's "report" as being before 4:30 p.m. Anderson further confused the issue by implying that Dryer was the one who issued the message to Sykes. But *Dryer* did not. The note Buchanan and Sykes received came from Blunt, relating what Dryer had ordered him to do.[55]

Porter's 4:30 p.m. dispatch to McClellan lends further support to Porter's contention that he did not deliver a damning oration to McClellan about the "last reserve of the last Army of the Republic." His message is worth reading in full:

> Burnside is warmly engaged with Arty—I see no movement of anything except the gathering of infantry near Sharpsburg. Sykes skirmishers pushed up toward S and I soon saw a flank and front fire—and troops moving up. I have been looking for the advance of the infantry on my right which is still lying down. Sykes men went pretty close to ridge.
>
> 4:30 P.M. F J PORTER

> Burnside is advancing slowly. I do not think it will [do] to advance. The enemy are moving probably a brigade to our right—not much apparently. I think they are relying on their arty.
>
> F J PORTER

> The infantry on the right of Sharpburg pike I think should move up slowly and cautiously and I think they will crown the hill.
>
> F J P[56]

These are not the messages of a corps commander who dramatically warned his chief to not send in the 5th Corps. Porter was closely monitoring the Regulars' progress in front of Sharpsburg. He clearly was led to believe, most likely by McClellan, that "the infantry on my right"—that is, Richardson's (now Hancock's) 1st Division of the 2nd Corps—were going to advance to support to the 5th Corps' right flank. Because they were not moving, Burnside's advance appeared to be slow, and Sykes's skirmishers were receiving fire on their front and flank, Porter advised that he did not think it would do (although the word "do" is missing in the dispatch) to advance. But then, as events were developing before his eyes, Porter wrote in a postscript that by moving "slowly and cautiously," he thought the infantry on the right of the Boonsboro Pike—Dryer's men—could seize Cemetery Ridge.

Porter returned to the Pry house command post after visiting Sykes. *New York Tribune* correspondent George Smalley saw him there with McClellan during the height of the 9th Corps' engagement on the Confederates' right. Here Porter received a note from Pleasonton. The cavalryman sensed the same possibility Dryer had: Cemetery Hill was ripe for the taking. Pleasonton wished to move his horse batteries there, to "obtain an enfilading fire upon the enemy in front of Burnside, and enable Sumner to advance to Sharpsburg," and he requested the Porter dispatch a division for this purpose. In his after-action report, Porter wrote that the tide of battle changed between the sending and receipt of Pleasonton's note. Burnside, after reaching the heights south of Sharpsburg, was being driven back, and Sumner's troops "were held in check"—or, rather, they were not advancing. "The army was at a stand," wrote Porter, and "I had not the force asked for, and could not, under my orders, risk the safety of the artillery and center of the line, and perhaps imperil the success of the day by further diminishing my small command, not then 4,000 strong—then in the front line and unsupported and protecting all our trains."[57]

Although he refused to send the reinforcements Pleasonton had requested, Porter did advise Sykes, in a 5 p.m. note, to support the cavalryman with the forces already over Antietam Creek. "Burnside is driving the enemy," wrote Porter. "Please send word to the command you sent to Pleasonton, to support his batteries, and let him drive them." But by this point, it was too late. Sykes had already sent his orders withdrawing Dryer and his forces back to Newcomer Ridge. Nonetheless, the 4:30 and 5 p.m. messages from Porter are clear, indicating that while he was not in favor of sending more troops across the creek, he did not discourage using those already on the other side of it to support a push toward Cemetery Hill. But, because of Anderson's 1886 *Century Magazine* article, the 5th Corps' commander became a useful foil for McClellan's postwar defenders. Porter could be blamed for the failure of the Army of the Potomac to win a greater victory by smashing Lee's center.[58]

Thomas Anderson did see McClellan, Porter, and Sykes together, but not at the time when Blount's message about what Dryer planned was received. *New York Tribune* reporter George Smalley and David Strother, on McClellan's staff, both confirmed that McClellan and Porter rode over to the left—to Sykes's position—around sunset, which came at 6:07 p.m. Anderson, in a letter he wrote to the Antietam Battlefield Board in 1897, confirmed that it was at sunset—long past when Blunt's message about Dryer's orders reached Sykes—when he saw the three generals together. Smalley, who accompanied the generals and their staffs to the left, watched Sykes greet Porter and McClellan and noted that the three men "talk[ed] briefly together." While they were still in a group, a messenger galloped up and delivered a note from Burnside, urgently requesting reinforcements to hold his position west of the Rohrback Bridge. This was undoubtedly the note Anderson saw being passed between the generals. There may have been some discussion about whether any of the 5th Corps' troops could be spared, and Sykes's recollection of Porter advising against it is probably accurate, although it is unlikely that his words were in any way as dramatic as those Captain Anderson quoted in his *Century Magazine* article. The controversy surrounding the captain's account of Sykes's, McClellan's, and Porter's joint discussion is a reminder that memory, particularly under circumstances of high stress and great excitement, with numerous events crowding in on one another, can be a tricky thing to unpack accurately.[59]

Thomas Anderson and Sykes probably drew the dramatic quote attributed to Fitz John Porter from *New York Tribune* correspondent George Smalley's widely read account of the Battle of Antietam. Smalley was present at army headquarters during the 9th Corps' attack on the heights south of Sharpsburg, and he described how "McClellan's glass for the last half hour has seldom been turned away from the left." Between 4:30 and 5 p.m., A. P. Hill's counterattack struck Burnside a hammer blow. McClellan watched the 9th Corps giving ground under the assault, and Smalley observed him turn "a half questioning look on Fitz John Porter, who stands by his side, gravely scanning the field." Porter "slowly shakes his head, and one may believe that the same thought is passing through the minds of both generals. 'They are the only reserve of the army. They cannot be spared.'" The reporter did not say that any words were exchanged. Instead, he placed his own interpretation on what the look that was exchanged and Porter's head shake meant.[60]

Ezra Carman, in his history of the battle, observed that "General Porter has been severely and unjustly blamed for his inaction at Antietam." Carman is partially correct. As the army commander, McClellan bears the ultimate responsibility for not exploiting the success of the Regulars' advance, but Porter also retains some culpability. McClellan and the 5th Corps' officers went to great lengths to make the case that there were no troops available to reinforce Dryer and Pleasonton, and that to have done so was to "risk the safety of the artillery and center of the line, and perhaps imperil the success of the day." This was a weak argument. It posited that Warren's brigade had been sent to Burnside, and that Griffin and Stockton's brigades of Morell's 1st Division were ordered to reinforce the Union army's right flank, leaving Porter with a brigade of Regulars and a single brigade in Morell's division to hold the Middle Bridge and support the artillery. Warren, it is true, was unavailable. His small brigade had marched down near the Rohrback Bridge to support the 9th Corps, but Morell's two brigades—which, it will be recalled, McClellan had ordered to reinforce Sumner (see chapter 13)—had only advanced a half mile from their position near Pry's farm in the midafternoon when they were halted prior to crossing Antietam Creek. They were, at most, a 30-minute to 45-minute march from the Middle Bridge and could have been recalled to support the artillery. This would have allowed, at a minimum, the balance of Buchanan's and all of Lovell's brigades of Regulars to reinforce Dryer.[61]

Porter did not have the authority to recall these two brigades, but he could have argued for their return, in order to exploit the opportunity Dryer's advance, and the 9th Corps' assault, had opened. Considering what Dryer, with the equivalent of three regiments of Regulars, had accomplished, the addition of a single infantry brigade probably would have given the Federals possession of Cemetery Hill and Cemetery Ridge. These heights could have been occupied by Pleasonton's horse artillery, further strengthening the Union army's hold on the high ground. Burnsides's defeat by A. P. Hill, to the south, might have rendered the capture of these heights a moot point, but it is just as likely that it would have created a crisis for Lee, forcing him to commit part of Hill's division in an attempt to recapture them, with implications for Hill's counterattack against Burnside. It is unlikely that seizing Cemetery Hill and Cemetery Ridge would have led to the utter ruin and defeat of the Army of Northern Virginia, which veterans like Thomas Anderson implied in their accounts. But if these two locales could have been held by the Federals, it very likely that would have forced Lee to retreat to Virginia that night, giving McClellan a more clear-cut victory for the Union army. Porter, plus his senior officers and staff, were all victims, like McClellan, in believing that the Confederates possessed superior numbers, and that having the Army of the Potomac take the offensive against Lee on September 17 had been an act of great courage and risk. Like Sumner, they had allowed their fears to paralyze them when presented with a significant opportunity and keep them from forming a sober judgment of the Confederates' numbers and capabilities. It would stand to reason that if Lee had thousands of hidden reserves behind Cemetery Hill, he would have released them when Carlton's skirmishers were climbing the slopes of Cemetery Ridge, or when Burnside's 9th Corps' infantry was driving toward the high ground south of Cemetery Hill. If the roles were reversed, it is unlikely that Lee would have allowed the opportunity created by

Dryer to slip away. Initiative and aggressiveness were encouraged in the Army of Northern Virginia. McClellan did not necessarily discourage initiative, but he consistently sought to minimize risk, which had the same result.

WHEN LIEUTENANT POWELL FOUND Dryer and delivered Sykes's withdrawal orders, the captain, incredulous, asked if there was any discretion in the orders. Powell replied, "The order was imperative." Years later, the lieutenant wrote that had Dryer made his advance, he would have found, "instead of a single battery, some eighteen guns covering their front, and he would never have been able to reach them; and he could never have returned, after an unsuccessful charge, because he was nearly a mile away from any support whatsoever." This was nonsense. Dryer knew there were not 18 guns waiting for him. All of the Confederate artillery had been driven from the heights, except for Moody's and Garden's batteries on Cemetery Hill, and the latter was fully occupied with opposing the 9th Corps. The irony is that when Powell delivered his orders to Dryer, the Rebels were preparing to abandon Cemetery Hill. The 9th Corps was already driving the Confederates from the ridges south of the hill. When someone alerted General Garnett to this threat to his right, he looked in that direction and "could see Yankee flags appearing on the hill in rear of the town and not far from our only avenue of escape." He immediately ordered a retreat, to avoid being cut off. Walker's South Carolina brigade and Garden's battery, on the southeastern slope of the hill, had already bugged out.[62]

The Confederate retreat was precipitous. Years later, Sergeant Eugene G. Taylor in the 19th Virginia admitted, "I could hardly call it falling back in good order." Captain Benjamin Brown Jr., also in the 19th, related that the Federals were within 80 paces "when a hasty retreat down the hill with a circuitous route to the left saved us from the prisoner's cell." Garnett encountered utter confusion when entering Sharpsburg: "In this direction I found troops scattered in squads from various parts of the army, so that it was impossible to distinguish men of the different commands." By the time Captain William N. Berkeley's tiny 8th Virginia reached the village, he recalled that "there was but a remnant left" of the entire brigade. An exception to this disintegration was the 18th Virginia. Its commander, Major George C. Cabell, noticed that Moody's two guns were under a sharp fire, and their crews were having difficulty limbering them in order to escape. He ordered his regiment to halt and cover the gun crews. Moody's artillerymen had already added another feather to the laurels of S. D. Lee's battalion that day. Garnett praised the "brave and energetic manner" with which the guns were handled and credited the section with being crucial to his brigade's ability to hold Cemetery Hill as long as it did. The 18th Virginia's covering fire enabled the crews to limber their guns, and they and Cabell's infantry trotted into the cover of Sharpsburg with the 9th Corps nipping at their heels. The 18th paid a high price to save the artillerymen. Nearly half of their

75 effectives became casualties. One was Private Edward G. Sydnor, who had been studying to enter the ministry when the war began. At Second Manassas, Sydnor took the colors from a wounded color bearer and carried them throughout the battle. Apparently someone else was subsequently assigned the role of color bearer, but he fell at South Mountain, and Sydnor again rescued the flag. But his heroism ended at Sharpsburg, when a shell fragment struck him in the head and killed him. Cabell was proud of Sydnor and his whole regiment. "No man of the Eighteenth Regiment left his post until disabled," he wrote, and praised the "coolness and gallantry of my men." Cabell's words could also have applied to the rest of the brigade. Garnett, with S. D. Lee's help, mounted a skillful defense of Cemetery Hill that held Dryer's skirmishers in check. Yet, had Dryer mounted the attack he intended, which would have been in coordination with the 9th Corps' drive on the Confederates' right, there is little likelihood that Garnett could have stopped it.[63]

It is a testament to the skill and discipline of the Regulars that with approximately 600 skirmishers, supported by about 450 infantry in the 4th and 2/14th U.S., they had cleared Cemetery Ridge and nearly seized Cemetery Hill. In this instance, the Rebels could not complain that overwhelming numbers had driven them back, for in overall infantry strength, they had possessed a slight numerical advantage.

As the Confederates retreated from Cemetery Hill into Sharpsburg, an angry Hiram Dryer obeyed his orders and, gathering up his dead and wounded, pulled his men back to Newcomer Ridge. His command and Poland's had 11 killed and 75 wounded, not a small number, but at this cost in casualties, he had driven the enemy from Cemetery Ridge and nearly captured Cemetery Hill, no small feat, considering the open ground his men had to cross. In contrast, a single regiment, the 63rd New York, suffered 200 casualties, more than double Dryer's losses, in an unsuccessful attempt to storm the Sunken Lane. What Dryer and his Regulars had achieved—without orders—was remarkable, and it upheld their status as elite troops in the Union army. George Sykes lauded their performance in his report, writing that Dryer and his men "behaved in the handsomest manner, and had there been an available force for their support, there is no doubt he could have crowned the Sharpsburg crest." Dryer had exhibited great tactical skill and leadership, but the timidity of Sykes, Porter, and McClellan squandered the opportunity his enterprise had presented to them.[64]

With the sun beginning to set, and A. P. Hill's counterattack driving back the 9th Corps on the right, the Confederates quickly reoccupied Cemetery Hill. Among the first of the batteries to arrive was Captain Thomas H. Carter's King William (Virginia) Artillery, sent at the request of S. D. Lee. Carter unlimbered around 5:30 p.m. and opened fire on the 9th Corps' troops opposing A. P. Hill, but his guns drew such a savage "reverse artillery fire"—probably from the Union guns on Newcomer Ridge and those across Antietam Creek—that S. D. Lee ordered the captain to withdraw his battery. Carter drove his pieces back through the village streets, which were teeming with stragglers and the wounded, and was just about to bivouac his crews when General Lee sent for him and ordered his guns back to Cemetery Hill. He arrived there after dark.[65]

Richard Garnett, with help from the 8th Virginia's Captain William N. Berkeley and two members of his staff, managed to gather a small number of men "from among the dispersed force" that had found shelter in Sharpsburg's streets. Many shrugged off Garnett's appeal by claiming "they were hunting for proper commands," a common excuse to avoid returning to the furnace on the battlefield. Garnett led his band back to Cemetery Hill, where he found remnants of Walker's and Drayton's brigades, who had also rallied and returned.

North of the Boonsboro Pike, Major Hilary P. Jones posted a pair of howitzers from Captain Robert C. M. Page's Morris (Virginia) Artillery. They had no infantry support to speak of. General Evans claimed his brigade re-formed and "resumed its original position" on Cemetery Ridge, but if they did, it was no more than a corporal's guard. Colonel Stevens, who had the tactical management of the brigade that day, reported that the survivors were "scattering in town." He led those he was able to rally "to the rear and bivouacked for the night."[66]

It was nearly 7:30 p.m. before the Federals left Newcomer Ridge and withdrew across the Middle Bridge. Tidball's guns trotted back, having expended an astounding 1,200 rounds of ammunition in their two stretches of time there. The Regulars carried their dead back in solemn silence. They had seen enough of war to know that they had been fortunate in how they were handled by Dryer and Poland. "I hope we may go through all battles with as little loss," wrote Charles Bowman, "but men may be butchered by the ignorance of their officers."[67]

The opportunity at the Middle Bridge had been wasted. The outcome of the battle would turn now on the events on the 9th Corps' front.

15

The Bridge

"Now it was time to do our duty"

The Georgians of Brigadier General Robert Toombs's brigade reached Sharpsburg around 7 a.m. on September 15. The brigade had been left to garrison Hagerstown when Longstreet marched to the support of D. H. Hill at the Battle of South Mountain the previous day. When Lee made his decision to retreat from Turner's Gap and Fox's Gap during the night, orders were sent to Toombs to march to Sharpsburg at once and secure the village, now a vital locale in protecting the Army of Northern Virginia's access to Boteler's Ford at Shepherdstown. Toombs's orders arrived about 10 p.m. He immediately assembled his four regiments and began the 14-mile march. Arriving at Sharpsburg early the next morning, he received fresh orders from his division commander, Brigadier General David R. Jones, to send two regiments to Williamsport, Maryland, to escort Longstreet's trains across the Potomac River. Toombs detailed the 15th and 17th Georgia, leaving him with only the 2nd and 20th Georgia. These two regiments, like nearly every Confederate unit that had seen any service that summer, were small. The 2nd numbered around 130 officers and men, and the 20th, between 220 and 230. Jones's orders further instructed Toombs to "occupy the most eligible position" along Antietam Creek and Lower Bridge Road with his remaining regiments. Toombs understood his orders to mean defending the Lower Bridge—or Rohrback Bridge, as it was known locally—which was crossed by Lower Bridge Road—not the bridge 2.5 miles south that carried Harpers Ferry Road over Antietam Creek, near its mouth.[1]

Toombs's biographer describes him as "kind, pushy, funny, arrogant, charming, eloquent, sarcastic, dedicated, slovenly, candid, manipulative," and "whatever else his mood or circumstances required." He was a formidable figure and personality. Born in Georgia in 1810, Toombs was educated at Union College in Schenectady, New York, and studied law at the University of Virginia. He lost his father when he was 4 years old, but the old man left the family 2,200 acres, 35 enslaved people, and $35,000 in cash, bonds, and property, smoothing the way for Robert's life. Besides having a highly successful law practice, by 1860 Toombs owned two plantations, one in Wilkes County, North Carolina (close to the

Virginia border), and the other in Stewart, Virginia, with 48 enslaved people between them. His personal estate was valued at $250,000.[2]

Toombs's wealth opened the doors to power. He steadily climbed the political ladder, advancing from being elected to the Georgia State Assembly, to the U.S. Congress in 1844, and, in 1853, to the U.S. Senate. He was a Whig and a Unionist, helping defeat a secession movement in 1850 and embracing Henry Clay's compromise that year. When the Whig party fragmented, he became a member of the Constitutional Union Party, and when that party collapsed during the 1850s, he reluctantly became a Democrat. The rise of the Republican Party in the North coincided with a hardening of Toombs's attitude along sectional lines. Lincoln's election in 1860, with his party's platform of no extension of slavery into the territories was the final straw. Toombs resigned his U.S. Senate seat with a long, fiery, threatening speech: "We want no negro equality, no negro citizenship; we want no mongrel race to degrade our own; and as one man they would meet you upon the border with the sword in one hand and the torch in the other." To the Georgia state legislature, he thundered on about Lincoln and the Republicans: "Their main purpose, as indicated by all their acts of hostility to slavery, is its final and total abolition. His party declares it; their acts prove it. He has declared it; I accept his declaration."[3]

In contrast to his actions in 1850, when Toombs worked to preserve the Union, in 1860 he gave his full-throated support to Georgia's secession. He hoped to be named president of the Confederate States of America, but when Jefferson Davis won that post, he settled for becoming secretary of state, although he was not an admirer of Davis. He offered the Confederate president wise counsel during the Fort Sumter crisis, recommending against an attack. "You will wantonly strike a hornet's nest which extends from mountain to ocean," he warned. Toombs only lasted until July before he resigned his governmental post and was commissioned a brigadier general in the Confederate service. His worried brother Gabriel appealed to Confederate Vice President Alexander H. Stephens to use his influence to convince his brother to resign his officer's commission. "In this case my brother's zeal blinds his judgment," wrote an anxious Gabriel, "and is not according to wisdom. He has never been educated in the science of war and [has] no experience in the business, and besides is physically unfit for camp life." Gabriel's efforts failed. Robert Toombs was not accustomed to being told what he could not do. He proved to be a brave but not particularly competent soldier, who chafed under the command of professional soldiers he believed were his intellectual inferiors. During the Second Manassas campaign, he left an important ford unguarded. When this was discovered, Toombs offered a weak argument: he merely wanted his men to have an opportunity to prepare rations for their upcoming march, and he had tried to receive permission from Longstreet to remove his troops. Longstreet, unimpressed by Toombs's excuse, placed him under arrest. He was released on August 30, the second day of battle at Second Manassas, and galloped onto to the field, to wild cheers from his men. John Hennessy noted that Toombs's "skill at public display far exceeded his skill on the battlefield," yet, in this instance, he proved a boost to his soldiers' morale, even if he made little difference tactically.[4]

When the Confederate army entered Maryland, Toombs's division commander, David R. Jones, made the mistake of temporarily grouping three brigades—Toombs's, G. T. Anderson's, and Drayton's—under Toombs's command. This may have been for temporary tactical or administrative expediency, or it may also have been a way to pacify Toombs's ego by elevating his responsibility at a moment when it would cause no harm. He had done nothing to warrant promotion. In the fluid and sometimes seemingly casual command arrangements that marked the Army of Northern Virginia during this period, however, no one bothered to officially notify Toombs that his "division" had been removed from his authority when Longstreet marched to South Mountain and Jones resumed command of the brigades temporarily under Toombs's leadership. Toombs arrived at Sharpsburg still imagining himself to be a division commander, although he now headed only two regiments. Thus he delegated tactical details to his senior colonel, Henry Benning, the commander of the 17th Georgia.[5]

Politically, the 48-year-old Benning came from the same world as Toombs. But while Toombs had worked to preserve the Union through the 1840s and early 1850s, Benning had long advocated secession as a means to protect slavery. In 1849, he wrote Howell Cobb on the subject: "I think that as a remedy for the South, dissolution is not enough, and a Southern Confederacy not enough. The latter would not stop the process by which some states, Virginia, for example, are becoming free, viz., by ridding themselves of their slaves; and therefore we should in time with a Confederacy again have a North and a South. The only thing that will do when tried every way is a *consolidated* Republic formed of the Southern States. That will put slavery *under the control of those most interested* in it, and nothing else will; and until that is done nothing is done." Twelve years later, in 1861, Benning, by then a prominent justice in the Georgia Supreme Court, was dispatched by the Georgia Secession Convention to address the Virginia convention, which was then considering the question of secession. Benning's mission was to convince that convention's delegates to take Virginia out of the Union and join the Confederacy. He was not opaque in defining why he believed secession necessary: "What was the reason that induced Georgia to take the step of secession? This reason may be summed up in one single proposition. It was a conviction, a deep conviction on the part of Georgia, that a separation from the North—was the only thing that could prevent the abolition of her slavery. This conviction, sir, was the main cause."[6]

Benning had benefited handsomely from the slave society he advocated for. In 1850, his holdings included 60 enslaved people, and in 1860, his personal property was valued at $76,000. Benning stood by his convictions and, rather than take a political post in the Confederacy, raised the 17th Georgia Infantry in the Columbus area and was commissioned as their colonel. He proved to be an excellent soldier, tactically smart and respected by his men. While Toombs was under arrest during the Second Manassas Campaign, Benning assumed command of the brigade and led it ably during that battle's heaviest fighting. Toombs valued Benning's tactical skills, which was probably why he retained him at Sharpsburg, even though Benning's regiment—the 17th Georgia—was one of the two that were detached to escort Longstreet's trains across the Potomac.[7]

Toombs left the execution of Jones's orders to defend the Rohrback Bridge to Benning. With the 15th and 17th Georgia regiments having been detached, Benning had half the men he had counted on. Although Toombs described the terrain on the western bank of the bridge as "not strong," it was, in fact, a position of exceptional natural strength. "For a long distance below the bridge and for some distance above it, the ground rose very steeply from the creek for fifty or sixty yards," Benning reported. The steep and, in some places, precipitous bluffs commanded Antietam Creek and offered Benning's Georgians deadly fields of fire on all approaches to the Rohrback Bridge, while making any effort to ford the creek a sure way to be killed or wounded. George McRae in the 20th Georgia described the ground where he was posted along the creek as being "so steep it was almost a precipice." A thin scattering of trees provided some concealment along this slope, and a small quarry nearly opposite to the head of the bridge offered excellent cover for 20 or 30 men. Behind the trees, near the crest of the bluff overlooking the creek, was a rail fence with a stone wall as its base. Benning placed the 20th Georgia, under 40-year-old Colonel John B. Cumming, the former city marshal of Macon, directly opposite to the bridge. One company took up a position about 40–50 yards above the bridge, while the rest were positioned right across from it and over a short distance to the south. Nearly an entire company, or about 20 to 25 men, in Cumming's 20th Georgia filled the quarry. Lieutenant Colonel William R. Holmes, also 40 years old and a physician from Burke County, deployed the 107 officers and men in his 2nd Georgia on the 20th's right, in open order. Their line extended south along the bluffs for some 300 yards, to near where Antietam Creek curves sharply to the west. The two regiments were armed with a mixture of rifles and muskets. How these guns were apportioned in the companies is unknown, but this dictated the range in which they could effectively engage any attack on the bridge.[8]

Reconnaissance of Antietam Creek revealed that it was fordable at nearly every point above and below the Rohrback Bridge, and "in most places was not more than knee-deep." At some points this was true, but David Wilson in the 8th Connecticut, who crossed Antietam Creek at Snavely's Ford, wrote that the water was "up to the middle" of his waist, so its depth varied. The creek bottom was slippery and, in most places, its banks were steep and impassable by artillery or ammunition wagons. Antietam Creek might have been fordable nearly everywhere on Benning's front, but it was one thing to wade through it on a pleasant September day in peacetime, and quite another when Georgians with muskets and rifles waited on the opposite bank. An old, scarcely used ford existed about 1,200 yards downstream from the Rohrback Bridge, near where the creek made a bend to the west. There was also another obscure ford about 400 yards upstream from the bridge. Whether Benning was aware of either of these is unknown. Snavely's Ford, the best of the fords in Benning's defensive area, was three-quarters of a mile, as the crow flies, from his right rear and known to the Confederates. Toombs's business was to find men to defend it.[9]

When Longstreet's and D. H. Hill's men began arriving from South Mountain on the morning of September 15, a company from Wofford's Texas brigade was deployed north of the bridge, near the 20th Georgia's company. David R. Jones and his division drew responsibility for defending the ground south of the Boonsboro Pike, and after a reconnaissance of the terrain, Jones further modified Toombs's orders. The Georgian was instructed that, if his men were driven from the Rohrback Bridge, they should fall back by the right flank to a prominent hill, which reached an elevation of 500 feet, about 400 yards south of the bridge but still overlooking Antietam Creek. He was to hold this position "as long as practicable," and then fall back some 600 to 800 yards to the main line of the division, which Jones had established on the high ground east of Harpers Ferry Road and south of Cemetery Hill, which I shall refer to as the Harpers Ferry Road Ridge.[10]

Toombs's and Benning's men spent the rest of the day improving their position, becoming familiar with the terrain, and foraging for food. The defenses they constructed, which would be effective in the coming fight, were primitive compared with what these same soldiers would regularly build during the 1864 Overland Campaign. Benning reported that "the rails were taken from the fence [which ran along the crest of the bluff overlooking the creek] and built up against such trees as were in suitable situations, and where there were no such trees the rails were laid in simple piles." George McRae, a a private in the 20th Georgia, recalled that he and his comrades found positions "behind trees, some behind rocks and others in some depressions on the hillside," adding that they were scattered about "in order to find shelter" in locations away from the edge of Antietam Creek and up its steep slope.[11]

Food proved to be plentiful for some and scarce for others. Lieutenant Theodore T. Fogle in the 2nd Georgia, who attended Maryland Dental College in Baltimore before the war, wrote to his parents on September 16 that "we live pretty well here in Maryland." He sent his enslaved servant, a resourceful forager, to look for food, and, Fogle related, he "gets eggs, chickens, bread, butter & milk, but he finds great difficulty in getting the people to take 'Secesh' money." The men of the 20th Georgia found slim pickings and went without any rations on September 15 and 16. For some reason, Colonel Cummings waited until the morning of the 17th to send J. William Lokey, a Company B private, and some others on a detail to search for food. Charles F. Terrill, a well-educated and observant man who was a recent 2nd Georgia recruit, found his fellow soldiers a curious lot in their views of the world and of food. "The soldiers as a general thing literally take no note of time," he wrote. "Not one in a hundred know the day of the week or month and some not even the month itself! The present moment engages their whole attention." He also found their eating habits unhealthy, although many seemed to have adjusted to their hard life, but "it cannot be denied that imprudence in eating is the prime cause of so large a number always to be found on the sick list." His compatriots also were careless in taking care of themselves, "and unless kept within the bounds the entire army would be nothing more or less than a set of poachers and stragglers. Soldiers may be compared to children; they must be fed, washed and put to bed."[12]

It was apparent to Benning, as his men prepared their defensive positions at the Rohrback Bridge and he studied the Federals' possible avenues of approach, that he lacked the manpower to hold it. More men and artillery were needed. Thus, on September 16, D. R. Jones reinforced Toombs with the 50th Georgia from Drayton's brigade. After their mauling at South Mountain, the 50th numbered only about 100 officers and men. Toombs placed them on the right of the 2nd Georgia and strung them out in open order, extending from the 2nd's right to Snavely's Ford, to provide a means of watching over Antietam Creek. They were to pay particular attention to guard a "blind plantation road" leading down to the old ford at the bend in the creek, above Snavely's Ford.[13]

In addition to this small amount of infantry, Jones provided Toombs with considerable artillery support. The batteries of Captain Benjamin F. Eshleman's 4th Company (two 12 lb. howitzers and two 6 lb. guns), and Captain John B. Richardson's 2nd Company (two 12 lb. Napoleons and two 12 lb. howitzers), both in the Washington (Louisiana) Artillery, were placed in a stubble field on a ridge about 500 yards west of the Rohrback Bridge, where they had a field of fire on the high ground east of the bridge. Captain John L. Eubank's Virginia Battery in S. D. Lee's reserve battalion (one 3-inch rifle, one 12 lb. howitzer, one 6 lb. gun, and one gun of unknown caliber and type), was positioned about 500 yards southwest of the Rohrback Bridge, on the northern slopes of the hill that was Toombs's fallback position if driven from the bridge. This location gave Eubank a clear line of sight for approaches to the bridge from the east and southeast. Additional reinforcements arrived late on September 16, when General John Walker's division of two brigades and two batteries arrived and took up a position guarding Snavely's Ford.[14]

While Toombs, Benning, and Walker saw to the defense of Antietam Creek's crossing points, the main Confederate line took shape on high ground farther to the west. General D. R. Jones kept the bulk of his division there, close to

Sharpsburg, with Garnett's brigade in the Cemetery Hill area; and Walker's, Drayton's, and Kemper's brigades on the Harpers Ferry Road Ridge, south of the deep ravine that separated it from Cemetery Hill. Jones dared not place his infantry any farther forward, where they could be pummeled by the numerous Union batteries on Antietam Creek's eastern bank. This left Toombs's left flank exposed to an enemy force advancing south from the Middle Bridge, but Jones knew that as long as his division occupied the high ground south of Sharpsburg, such a move was unlikely.

On September 16, Benning pushed at least one company of the 20th Georgia, accompanied by part of a company of Texans from Hood's division, across the Rohrback Bridge to the eastern bank of Antietam Creek. There they skirmished with the advance troops of the 9th Corps, who pushed them back to near the bridge in the late afternoon. At this point the Texans departed to rejoin their division. Toombs appealed to D. R. Jones for a company to replace them, and early on September 17 he sent Toombs a company of South Carolinians from Colonel Walker's brigade. Companies in Walker's slender brigade averaged only about 10 men each, so, while this was probably one of Walker's stronger companies, it probably contained no more than 20 or 30 men. Toombs ordered them to relieve the company of the 20th Georgia that was posted above the Rohrback Bridge, but for some unexplained reason they failed to execute this order. Rather than making them take the position he desired, Toombs then changed his mind and ordered half of the company to occupy the space between the 2nd and 50th Georgia. He sent the other half to a position on the right of the 50th, where they could directly observe and fire on Snavely's Ford. This, then, was the sum of the Confederates' defenses when the Battle of Antietam opened on the morning of September 17. Less than 600 men defended the Rohrback Bridge and its approaches, supported by three batteries with a total of 12 guns. Farther downstream, Walker's two infantry brigades and two batteries, supported by Colonel Thomas Munford's small cavalry brigade, guarded Snavely's Ford.[15]

ON THE NIGHT OF September 16, the four divisions of the 9th Corps arrived in their pre-battle positions in pitch-black darkness. They arrived late because of McClellan's caution in moving the corps into position and then his meddling in its deployment. The only meeting between McClellan and Ambrose Burnside that day occurred in the morning, when the army commander conducted his reconnaissance of the terrain south of the Boonsboro Pike. During this meeting, Burnside learned that McClellan was detaching Hooker's 1st Corps from his wing to spearhead the attack on the Confederates' left the next morning. The 9th Corps' mission, according to McClellan's initial report on the battle, was "to create a diversion in favor of the main attack, with the hope of something more by assailing the enemy's right." Burnside learned that he would need to carry the Rohrback Bridge and should reconnoiter the approaches to it.

Burnside's reconnaissance did not include locating any fords that might enable the 9th Corps to avoid a direct assault on the bridge. Instead, this task was delegated to the theoretically "elite" topographical engineers from army headquarters. Since riding up to Antietam Creek and checking for fords was far too perilous, with alert Confederates watching every part of the creek from above the Rohrback Bridge to Snavely's Ford, how the engineers discerned the location of any fords is unknown. They managed to identify only one ford for Burnside, which, they assured him, was Snavely's Ford, but it was actually the ford 1,200 yards below the Rohrback Bridge, at the bend in the creek. This crucial error would not be discovered until the battle began.[16]

The Army of the Potomac's chief engineer, James Duane, guided the 9th Corps into position on the evening of September 16. These places were not optimal jump-off points for an assault, but rather were defensive locales, meant to guard against a potential flank attack coming up from Harpers Ferry. Brigadier General Isaac P. Rodman's 3rd Division was massed around 200 yards east of Henry Rohrback's farm, on the eastern side of Porterstown Road, where he supposedly would only be a short march from what the engineers had misidentified as Snavely's Ford. Three batteries of the 9th Corps' artillery bivouacked on a high ridge in Rodman's rear. Rodman's regiments were about 600 yards from the Rohrback Bridge. They were screened from it by high ground in their front, as well as by Rohrback's orchard and a cornfield. But they would discover the next morning that they were not hidden from the view of Confederate artillerymen on the elevated terrain west of the bridge. The division did not get settled into its position until 10:30 p.m. In the dark, it was impossible for anyone to get a sense of the terrain, their degree of exposure to the enemy, or even where the Rohrback Bridge and Antietam Creek were.[17]

Cox's Kanawha Division, commanded by Colonel Eliakim Scammon while Cox assumed temporary command of the 9th Corps, deployed its 1st Brigade, led by Colonel Hugh Ewing, in support of the artillery. This brigade was about 500 yards east of Rodman's division. The 2nd Brigade, under Colonel George Crook, was massed directly north of Rodman, just above the intersection of Porterstown Road and the lane to Henry Rohrback's farm. Cox recalled that "Crook was ordered to take the advance in crossing the [Rohrback] bridge in case we should be ordered to attack. This selection was made by Burnside himself as a compliment to the division for the vigor of its assault at South Mountain." If Cox communicated these orders to Crook, the latter, who seems to have harbored contempt for the acting 9th Corps' commander, made no effort to inform himself in any way about his surroundings, nor made any preparations for action. He worried more about the fact that his subsistence trains had not come up, so his men had to go to sleep without supper.[18]

Brigadier General Sam Sturgis's 2nd Division was placed some 500 yards northeast of Crook, with its two brigades facing south, on either side of

Porterstown Road, and just in the rear of Lovell's brigade of 5th Corps' Regulars. Brigadier General Orlando B. Willcox's 1st Division formed the corps' reserve, bivouacking nearly three-quarters of a mile east of Rodman's division. Three regiments of its 1st Brigade were detached to guard the signal station on Red Hill, located where Rohresville Road crossed Elk Ridge. In all, the four divisions and eight infantry brigades of the 9th Corps numbered approximately 11,714 officers and men, supported by seven batteries of artillery, which included a hodgepodge of pieces: 25 rifled guns, six 10 lb. James rifles, four 12 lb. James rifles, six Napoleons, five 12 lb. naval howitzers, and one 12 lb. howitzer.[19]

McClellan's dismantling of his wing command structure on September 16 rankled Burnside, and he stubbornly continued to act as if his wing were intact, but with one corps temporarily detached. Cox, the acting 9th Corps commander since Jesse L. Reno's death at Fox's Gap, urged Burnside to assume direct command. "He objected that as he had been announced as commander of the right wing of the army, composed of the two corps, he was unwilling to waive his precedence or to assume that Hooker was detached for anything more than a temporary purpose," wrote Cox. This was the spirit that comforts a bruised ego but can lose battles. Cox pressed his case. Most of Reno's staff had accompanied his body to Washington, DC, leaving Cox, with his much smaller division staff, to manage the operations of a corps. But Burnside was in no mood to be reasonable. "He met this by saying that he would use his staff for this purpose [to support Cox], and help me in every way he could till the crisis of the campaign should be over," Cox recalled.[20]

Cox managed his division well at the Battle of South Mountain, and he would go on to compile a fine record during the rest of the war, but he lacked professional training, a point he was particularly sensitive about. He spent considerable effort in his reminiscences downplaying its importance. Two of the 9th Corps' division commanders, Sturgis and Willcox, were both Regulars, although their commission date as brigadier generals made them junior to Cox. This was a point of potential friction. It made sense to Cox that, going into battle, the corps should have a leader it knew and respected. He keenly felt the "unsatisfactory position of nominal commander of the corps to which I was a comparative stranger, and which, under the circumstances, naturally looked to him [Burnside] as its accustomed and real commander." Finding that he could not overcome Burnside's obstinacy, Cox eventually accepted his position "with as good grace as I could."[21]

Cox was not the only "comparative stranger" to the 9th Corps' command team. All of the division commanders were new to their jobs. The leader of the 1st Division, 39-year-old Brigadier General Orlando B. Willcox, was a West Point graduate. He was wounded at First Bull Run, captured, and had only been exchanged in August. He was assigned to the 1st Division on September 8, replacing Isaac Stevens, who had been killed at the Battle of Chantilly. On September 3,

Brigadier General Samuel D. Sturgis, a 40-year-old West Pointer who had recently arrived from Missouri, was named commander of the 2nd Division, originally led by Jesse Reno. Cox's replacement in Ohio's Kanawha Division was Colonel Eliakim P. Scammon. Scammon had performed well in brigade command at the Battle of South Mountain, but there may have been some question by either Burnside or Cox about his capability in handling the division. They essentially removed him from exercising any real command by splitting his brigades, with Crook assisting in the operations against the Rohrback Bridge, and Colonel Hugh Ewing's brigade supporting the 3rd Division. This division was led by Brigadier General Isaac P. Rodman, a Rhode Island banker, merchant, and state legislator. The 40-year-old Rodman, like Cox, had no pre-war military experience or training. He had raised a company in what became the 4th Rhode Island Infantry and fought at First Bull Run. In October 1861, he was commissioned colonel of the regiment by Rhode Island's governor, William Sprague. Like Cox, Rodman developed into a fine soldier and impressed the major general during Burnside's 1862 North Carolina Expedition. Based on Burnside's recommendation, Rodman was promoted to brigadier general on April 28, 1862. He came down with typhoid fever, however, and was sent home to recover. After Second Manassas, Rodman heard from Burnside, who urgently needed trained officers to fill vacancies in the 9th Corps. Although not fully recovered, and against his physician's advice, Rodman answered the call and arrived to take command of his division 2 days before the Battle of South Mountain.[22]

BECAUSE IT WAS SO dark when they bivouacked for the night on September 16, some of the 9th Corps' regiments and batteries could not know if their position was exposed to enemy observation. When daylight began to creep across the landscape on September 17, the artillerymen of Captain George W. Durell's Battery D, Pennsylvania Light Artillery—which was encamped near Sturgis's 2nd Division, to which they were attached—were already busy preparing their breakfast. As the men boiled water for coffee, cooked up salt pork, or munched on hardtack, they heard heavy firing to their north, where Hooker's attack was jumping off. Without warning, Confederate artillery across Antietam Creek, unseen in the early morning light, opened fire, "filling the air with flying and bursting missiles" around the Pennsylvanians. This barrage probably came from the batteries on Cemetery Hill, and their primary target was Sturgis's nearby infantry. Although Sturgis reported that the projectiles "fell thick in our camp," they did little damage. Sturgis summoned Prussian-born Captain William C. Rawolle, an energetic aide-de-camp on his staff who also served as the division's ordnance officer, and had him position Durell's battery on the same ridge (near Antietam Creek) as Stephen H. Weed's Battery I, 5th U.S., and engage the Rebels. Durell had his battery ready when Rawolle arrived. He had shouted "Boots and Saddles" when the shelling started, without waiting for the bugler to blow the signal. Charles A. Cuffel, a private in the battery, remembered how "all was bustle and excitement in the camp; the men packing up, harnessing and hitching the horses to the gun carriages and eating breakfast, all at the same time." Within minutes, Rawolle, Durell, and his battery thundered out of camp and dashed up to the bluff overlooking Antietam Creek, arriving on Weed's left.[23]

Cox situated his headquarters "at the edge of a little grove of forest trees." This was probably the small woodlot east of Rodman's division, which ran through a depression that cut the high ridge where Benjamin's, Simmonds's, Muhlenberg's, Roemer's, and McMullin's batteries were located. The headquarters mess had just sat down to breakfast when the shelling began. The missiles in this area probably came from Richardson's, Eshleman's, and Eubank's batteries. Their targets were the Union batteries and Rodman's infantry, but some shells fell short or went astray. Cox recalled how "the rapid explosion of shrapnel about us hastened our morning meal." Breakfast was wolfed down, tents packed, and horses saddled.[24]

The shelling proved to be more lethal for the infantry. Adjutant Joseph H. Converse in the 11th Connecticut watched a collection of men from the 3rd Division gather on a nearby hill—probably the high ground in the division's rear, where the batteries were placed—to catch a glimpse of the Rebels. This caught the attention of the Confederate gunners and enabled them to accurately estimate the range. This "careless disregard of all rules of common sense" brought a deluge of shells on them. As David Wilson, a sergeant in the 8th Connecticut, declared to his mother and sister, "I want to impress upon your mind what a hideous noise a shell makes. It comes whizzing along, then presently it goes whang, and the pieces fall in all directions, whistling, snapping, cracking, squealing and yelling like so many devils going through the air." The movement of hundreds of Rodman's soldiers preparing breakfast and going about their morning chores also was noticed by the Rebel gunners, who poured shell, shrapnel, and shot at this juicy target. Lieutenant Matthew J. Graham in the 9th New York was watching Confederate soldiers on the opposite bank of Antietam Creek "shoveling and leveling the ground"—they were Benning's men, preparing their position—when the first shell arrived. Its harmless explosion sent a ripple of laughter through his regiment "at the bad shot." A second shell arrived and burst slightly closer, but again, without inflicting any damage. The New Yorkers did not understand that these were ranging shots. The third shell burst right over Graham's regiment. "When the men in gray saw the effect of this shot they opened fire in such a furious style as to give the impression that they had a dozen guns there, and every shell seemed to land in our midst," the lieutenant recalled. Charles F. Johnson, an articulate Company I private, wrote that "every one of them exploded just as nicely as they could wish, squarely over our heads, shaking its fragments among us, leaving only a harmless cloud of smoke to roll peacefully away, as if satisfied with its work and glad to return to its proper home in the atmosphere."[25]

Carnage silenced the laughter as deadly iron fragments and shrapnel found human flesh. A solid shot landed in the ranks of the 8th Connecticut, killing Sergeant George H. Marsh in Company A and three privates in Company K, as well as wounding two other men. Initially, wrote Captain Wolcott P. Marsh, "not a man in the regit. stirred excepting ambulance corps," who attended to the mangled men. But this changed as more shells followed. Another shell or round shot fell within the 4th Rhode Island, killing two men. Confusion ensued. Charles Johnson related that an order was shouted for his regiment, the 9th New York, to fall back into the small woodlot in their rear—probably the same one where Cox had his headquarters that morning—but someone blundered and ordered them up onto the open ridge in their rear, "where we would be in better range than before." Fortunately, their able commander, Lieutenant Colonel Edgar A. Kimball, roared out for the men to get into the woods via *any way,* without regard to a prescribed maneuver. "Admirable confusion" followed as the New Yorkers scattered for the woods. Shells pursued them, and Johnson watched a shell fragment knock down Corporal John McKinley, who was just 3 feet away from him. On his other side, James Shultz was felled, and Edward Dennis, a chum of Johnson's, received "a slight hurt." Dr. Nathan Mayer, the 11th Connecticut's assistant surgeon, escaped death by a hair's breadth. "Here our Lieut. Col.'s horse was wounded," he wrote, "and a solid cannon ball whizzed over my right shoulder and cut a few hairs off my horse's tail." Harrison S. Fairchild's 1st Brigade had 36 of their men killed or wounded before they got under cover. Colonel Edward Harland, commanding Rodman's 2nd Brigade, reported only that "our loss was considerable."[26]

Finding cover spared Rodman's infantry from any further casualties, and a furious response by the 9th Corps' batteries also brought them some relief. Samuel N. Benjamin's Battery E, 2nd U.S., with his 20 lb. Parrott rifles, replied first. Durell reached the ridge above Antietam Creek and opened fire at 6:20 a.m. Charles Cuffel wrote how rapidly "the air seemed to be filled with shrieking missiles, and there was ocular evidence everywhere that someone was getting hurt." While the guns blazed away, the Union army's chief of artillery, Henry Hunt, appeared behind Durell's guns. He paused to remind Durell and the other officers to fire slowly and deliberately, stating that rapid fire was a waste of ammunition that "did little execution." "He was a small grizzled man with an effeminate voice," recalled the private, but, lest anyone think Hunt's voice reflected some weakness in the man, Cuffel added that "he was an experienced and able artillerist." His advice was sound. Methodical, well-aimed fire inflicted far more damage than rapid, poorly aimed shelling. Captain Eshleman, on the receiving end of this barrage, related that his Confederate battery "was furiously shelled," and he was soon forced to displace farther south, to a position where high ground on his left gave him cover from the 9th Corps' guns. From this new position, however, he could still bring his guns to bear on Snavely's Ford. Richardson's Louisianans, posted on Eshleman's left, fared better. The captain had hidden his horses, limbers, and caissons in the low ground behind his position, leaving only his gun crews exposed to fire.[27]

John B. Richardson's crews had a lively time of it. The fire of Durell's and Benjamin's guns repeatedly drove these Rebels to cover. After his battery chased the Louisianans from their guns, Charles Cuffel watched how, after a pause and the slackening of fire from Durell, they would return in ones and twos until the guns were crewed once more and the Confederate battery reopened fire. Durell would again turn the wrath of his battery on them and send the graycoat gunners running for cover. This, Cuffel observed, was "repeated several times until finally one of Durell's shells struck one of their caissons and blew it up." The gun duel had lasted for nearly an hour before Richardson decided to keep his artillery quiet and reserve his ammunition for the Federals' infantry. Eubank's battery also fell silent during this gun duel, although who was firing at him is unknown. With the Rebel guns silenced, Durell shifted his fire to the Confederate infantry he spotted, who were 2,700 yards to the north, near Mumma's farm, while Benjamin aimed his pieces at the Rebel guns still firing on Cemetery Hill.[28]

SOMETIME BEFORE 7 A.M., Burnside received verbal orders from McClellan to "make my dispositions to carry the stone bridge over the Antietam" but to "await further orders before making my attack." Great controversy, which surprisingly continues to this day, has revolved around this directive. In his original report, dated October 15, 1862, McClellan thought the order routine enough that he did not mention it. This changed in his more elaborate report, published in August 1863. By this time, McClellan was no longer in command of any military force and his record had come under intense criticism by both the Congressional Committee on the Conduct of the War and in the press. He used his final report to rebut his critics, shape public opinion about his generalship, and burnish his reputation, sometimes at the expense of others. Burnside was an easy target to throw under the proverbial wagon. Disgraced by Burnside's subsequent bungling in the Battle of Fredericksburg in December 1862 and the subsequent "Mud March" in January 1863—an attempt, during very heavy rain, to cross the Rappahannock River and outflank Lee's army—McClellan made Burnside the scapegoat for the September 1862 failure of the Battle of Antietam to be a more decisive victory. In this second report, McClellan now claimed that "at 8 o'clock an order was sent to him [Burnside] by Lieutenant Wilson, Topographical Engineers, to carry the bridge, then to gain possession of the heights beyond, and to advance along their crest upon Sharpsburg and its rear." In 1876, McClellan solicited two letters from Delos B. Sackett, a colonel who was Inspector General of the Army of the Potomac at Antietam, to strengthen his case against Burnside. These were published in McClellan's *Own Story* and appeared to add the evidence of an eyewitness who could testify to Burnside's laziness, incompetence, and even cowardice.[29]

The "Lieutenant Wilson" was John Moulder Wilson, an 1860 graduate of West Point and a member of the elite topographical engineers. Perhaps confusingly, McClellan's headquarters staff included Lieutenant James H. Wilson, who also graduated in the class of 1860 and was in the topographical engineers. He, too, carried an order to Burnside, but did so later in the morning. In an 1894 letter, John Wilson claimed that he maintained a diary during the Civil War in which he recorded that he carried an order to Burnside at 8 a.m. "to charge and take the bridge in front of him and the heights beyond &c." There are two problems with Wilson's account, however. No one ever saw his "diary," and the order Burnside received later that morning to open his assault makes no sense if, as Wilson claimed, he was the one who had already delivered a command to attack. A careful reading of Sackett's letters to McClellan also weaken McClellan's claim of an 8 a.m. order. Sackett declared that he carried the initial directive for an attack to Burnside "around 9 a.m.," but Sackett then undermined this claim when he wrote that the wing commander greeted him testily, saying that Sackett was the third or fourth messenger sent to him that morning with similar orders. The colonel no doubt did carry a command from McClellan to Burnside, but not the initial attack orders. What seems most likely is that Lieutenant John M. Wilson carried McClellan's approximately 7 a.m. verbal orders to Burnside to make his preparations to capture the Rohrback Bridge.[30]

There is no evidence that this verbal order directed the 9th Corps to carry the bridge and "then to gain possession of the heights beyond, and to advance along their crest upon Sharpsburg and its rear." Rather, McClellan commanded the corps to *make preparations* to carry the bridge and "the heights above it by assault." Jacob Cox received these orders from Burnside at 7 a.m. He interpreted the "heights above it" to mean the bluffs commanding the Rohrback Bridge, not the Harpers Ferry Road Ridge. Cox's report, written 6 days after the battle, made it clear that his understanding of the 9th Corps' mission was to create a "powerful diversion in favor of the center and right of the army," not to roll up the Confederates' right flank in a general assault. This is consistent with the language in McClellan's October report, where he wrote that the 9th Corps was to make a diversionary attack "with the hope of something more." This is also consistent with the situation at the time these orders were sent to Burnside. Hooker's attack was meeting strong opposition but appeared to be making progress. Mansfield's 12th Corps was marching to Hooker's support from the north, and McClellan was about to give orders to Sumner—at 7:20 a.m.—to take two of his three divisions across Antietam Creek and expand the attack on the Confederates' left and center. It is inconceivable that McClellan would have ordered an all-out assault by the 9th Corps against the Confederates' right at 7 a.m., when he was so concerned about a possible Rebel counterattack that he refused to release Richardson's division of the 2nd Corps to Sumner, or before he was confident that the attack on the right was successful. Under these circumstances, a *diversionary* attack to prevent Lee from reinforcing his left made sense.[31]

After receiving his orders, Burnside immediately directed Cox to "move forward the corps to the ridge nearest the Antietam" and hold it in readiness to capture the Rohrback Bridge and the bluffs commanding it, as soon as attack orders were received. Cox wrote that in response to these orders, "Rodman was directed to acquaint himself with the situation at the ford in front of him, and Sturgis to seek the best means of approach to the stone bridge." In his after-action report, Cox stated that "the command moved forward in column as it had been formed the previous night, and took position as directed." Rodman and Sturgis may have received these orders, but there is no evidence that anyone adjusted their position at this time. Rodman's division had moved *away* from Antietam Creek to escape the shelling. Orders also went to Crook to advance skirmishers toward the creek, and he assigned the mission to Lieutenant Colonel Augustus H. Coleman's 11th Ohio. Coleman deployed three companies in the general direction of the Rohrback Bridge, with orders "to watch the enemy very closely and report any movements to him or Col. Crook." The other batteries of the 9th Corps, most of whom were on the ridge east of Rohrback's farm, cleared for action. No other movements occurred. No effort was made to determine the extent and strength of the Confederates' defenses, although the companies of the 11th Ohio did confirm that the bridge was defended. Cox may have felt that the 9th Corps' divisions were near enough to the creek, and he did not wish to expose them to more shelling by moving them closer until attack orders were received. He also may have been wary of alerting the Rebels to an impending attack and giving them time to reinforce their defenses at the bridge. This is consistent with Cox's orders to Sturgis: to reconnoiter the best approach to get his brigades near the Rohrback Bridge, but not to move until told to do so. Cox's orders to Rodman to "acquaint himself with the situation at the ford in front of him" speak to just how confused those at the 9th Corps' headquarters were to the position of their divisions in relation to Antietam Creek. The ford the topographical engineers had wrongly identified as Snavely's Ford was not in front of Rodman. Instead, it was a mile away, over very rugged, hilly terrain, with no road access leading to it. The question lingers as to why Rodman was not ordered to move his division closer to the ford, in preparation for forcing its capture. Had McClellan provided Burnside and Cox with some of his cavalry, who were then sitting around camp near Keedysville, they could have scouted for Rodman and possibly discovered that the ford everyone thought was Snavely's was not that particular one. Moreover, it was inaccessible to artillery or ammunition wagons. Overall, the 9th Corps' preparations, most notably in reconnaissance, were poorly conducted.[32]

COX JOINED BURNSIDE AT his field headquarters, located on a ridge immediately east of Antietam Creek, between Weed's and Durell's batteries and near a haystack, which Cox says "was a prominent landmark." The two generals and their staffs "anxiously watched what we could see at the right, and noted the effect of the fire of the heavy guns of Benjamin's battery."[33] As they watched and awaited orders, in the midst of the fighting unfolding before them, a curious, unsettling note, dated September 16, reached Burnside from army headquarters:

> The general commanding has learned that, although your corps was ordered to be in a designated position at 12 m. [noon] to-day [Sept. 16], at or near sunset only one division and four batteries had reached the ground intended for your corps. The general has also been advised that there was a delay of some four hours in the movement of your command yesterday [Sept. 15]. I am instructed to call upon you for explanations of these failures on your part to comply with the orders given you, and to add, in view of the important military operations now at hand, the commanding general cannot lightly regard such marked departure from the tenor of his instructions.[34]

There was no signature. The place where a signature should have been was left empty, above the title "Lieutenant Colonel, Aide-de-Camp, and Actg. Asst. Adjt. Gen." This position was occupied by Lieutenant Colonel James A. Hardie, but he did not sign the message. Cox thought Hardie "demurred to signing it" because he objected to the contents, but this appears to be speculation on his part. It is an odd document. Stephen Sears calls it "the severest rebuke McClellan ever issued." Burnside responded to Assistant Adjutant General Seth Williams, probably because he headed the Army of the Potomac's Adjutant General's Department. Cox believed the author was Chief of Staff Randolph Marcy. Whoever actually wrote it, the originator of the message and its contents was McClellan. Had McClellan held his other commanders to account for their command failures, this document would not raise an eyebrow, but he did not. Cox noted, correctly, that "the occurrence was unexampled in that campaign and stands entirely alone." As Burnside would point out in his reply, the critique of his movements on September 16 was inaccurate. *McClellan's* intervention in the movement of the 9th Corps, not Burnside's, was responsible for the late hour when the 9th Corps finally moved into position. McClellan spent time with Burnside on September 16 and could easily have asked the 9th Corps' commander about the cause of the September 15 delay. Why put it in writing? The document appears to be the sort of record a senior officer prepares against a subordinate he wishes to discredit or is building a case against for possible removal.

Whatever the intention, and why it took so long to deliver the message, is unknown. Its effect, however, was to further erode trust and a harmony of command between McClellan and one of his chief subordinates at a critical moment.[35]

Burnside's response, written by his assistant adjutant general, Lieutenant Colonel Lewis Richmond, did not address the September 15 delay but it calmly, and in detail, explained what had happened on the 16th. In an effort to perhaps diffuse a perplexingly deteriorating relationship, and politely question the harshness of the message, Burnside had Richmond add, "General Burnside directs me to say that he is sorry to have received so severe a rebuke from the general commanding, and particularly sorry that the general commanding feels that his instructions have not been obeyed; but nothing can occur to prevent the general from continuing his hearty co-operation to the best of his ability in any movement the general commanding may direct." This was the type of response a commander should wish to receive from a subordinate he had reprimanded, but McClellan made no response.[36]

AT HEADQUARTERS, MCCLELLAN AND his staff closely monitored the battle. At 7:20 a.m., Sumner had been ordered across Antietam Creek to reinforce the attack on the Confederates' left with two of his divisions. The fighting was fierce, but all indications, both in reports from the front and what the staff could observe from the headquarters' observation point, were that Hooker was driving back the enemy. Around 8:45 a.m., Lieutenant Colonel Albert V. Colburn, an assistant adjutant general on McClellan's staff, began his message to Sumner with "Gen. Hooker appears to be driving the enemy rapidly." This was tempered by General Alpheus Williams's 9 a.m. signal message, reporting that Hooker was wounded, Mansfield was dangerously wounded, and, although Union forces held the ground that had been gained, Williams implored McClellan to "please give us all the aid you can." Around this same time, word arrived that Franklin's 6th Corps was within 1.5 miles of the field, or about a 45-minute march for its leading elements. This would provide McClellan with the reserve he felt necessary to either blunt a Confederate counterattack or reinforce a success somewhere along his front. It was time to open the diversionary attack on the Confederates' right, in order to prevent them from detaching more troops to reinforce their left flank. At 9:10 a.m., Colonel George Ruggles, McClellan's assistant chief of staff, prepared Burnside's orders: "General Franklin's command is within one mile and a half of here. General McClellan desires you to open your attack. As soon as you shall have uncovered the upper Stone bridge you will be supported, and, if necessary, on your own line of attack. So far, all is going well."[37]

Burnside reported that these orders reached him around 10 a.m. Cox thought they arrived around 9 a.m., but in his *Reminiscences*, Cox said that "the judgment of the hour which I gave in my report was merely my impression from passing events, for I hastened at once to my own duties without thinking to look at my watch." Lending credence to Cox's account is the fact that Burnside received Cox's after-action report before he wrote his own and could have accepted his subordinate's timing for the order's arrival. That he did not indicates Burnside's confidence in the approximate time the orders arrived. There was no delay by Burnside or Cox in initiating the action, so there was no personal incentive for Burnside to fudge the time. When he wrote his report, there was no controversy over the timing of his orders. McClellan also accepted this as the time the directive was communicated, writing in his initial report that "the order having been communicated to him [Burnside] at 10 o'clock." The question is not *when* Burnside received his orders, but *why* it took 50 minutes for them to travel less than 2 miles.[38]

The answer may lie in the second message Colburn wrote, at the same moment when he prepared Burnside's orders. This one, also timed at 9:10 a.m., was to Sumner, and it reflected the reports from the front that were arriving at army headquarters while Ruggles was drafting Burnside's orders. The latest news was worrying. Mansfield was badly wounded, and McClellan "fears our right is suffering." The alarming reports from the Federals' right may have led to some discussion about whether to open the 9th Corps' assault, but if this occurred—and there is no evidence that it did—McClellan decided to let the attack order be delivered. Given McClellan's well-documented concern about the Confederates' superiority in numbers and the potential of a counterattack, it offers a plausible explanation for the delay. But it is just as likely that Ruggles began to write Burnside's orders at 9:10, was interrupted by the news from the right flank, and composed his message to Sumner before finishing Burnside's orders.[39]

When McClellan wrote his August 1863 report, with its claim that the attack orders to Burnside were delivered at 8 a.m., neither Burnside nor Cox could produce the 9:10 a.m. order as proof that this was a lie, because they had not saved a copy. The only copy remained in McClellan's headquarters papers, where it resided until after his death, when his son loaned the letterbooks, which contained the orders to both Burnside and Sumner, to the compilers of the *Official Records of the Union and Confederate Armies*. These were published in volume 51 in 1897. Did McClellan know this order to Burnside was in his headquarters letterbooks when he wrote his August report and prepared the text that would be published as *McClellan's Own Story*? It would be surprising if he did not.[40]

With the attack order in hand, Cox recalled that "Burnside's view of the matter was that the front attack at the bridge was so difficult that the passage by the ford below must be an important factor in the task." If Rodman could get across Snavely's Ford, he would come up in the rear of the Rohrback Bridge's Rebel defenders. The problem was that Cox and Burnside had failed to move Rodman near the ford they believed to be Snavely's. The 3rd Division had spent the morning making breakfast and keeping under cover from enemy artillery.

It would take time for this division to march to the ford, and then it was unknown whether it would encounter resistance. But orders were now dispatched to the Rhode Islander to "push rapidly for the ford." Whatever Burnside's reservations about a frontal assault on the Rohrback Bridge, the failure to move Rodman there earlier meant that it would now be necessary for Burnside to begin the attack, since his orders did not grant him time to wait for the 3rd Division to outflank the enemy's position.[41]

Anyone who had laid eyes on the terrain at the bridge, and the approaches to it, recognized that it would be a tough nut to crack. Cox provided an excellent description in his after-action report:

> The bridge itself is a stone structure of three arches, with stone parapet above, this parapet to some extent flanking the approach to the bridge at either end. The valley in which the stream runs is quite narrow, the steep slope on the right [west] bank approaching quite to the water's edge. . . . On the hillside immediately above the bridge was a strong stone fence running parallel to the stream. The turns of the roadway were covered by rifle pits and breastworks, made of rails and stone, all of which defenses, as well as the woods which covered the slope, were filled with the enemy's infantry and sharpshooters. Beside the infantry defenses, batteries were placed to enfilade the bridge and all its approaches.[42]

Burnside's and Cox's plan to capture the Rohrback Bridge by assault was a good one, but it was poorly executed. It called for the 11th Connecticut of Rodman's division to advance as skirmishers, heading directly toward the bridge and immediately south of it, to engage its defenders. While the 11th drew the fire of the Rebels, Crook's brigade would charge over Hill 415—its summit was about 200 yards east of the bridge—and storm across the bridge. Sturgis's 2nd Division, which was over 1,000 yards northeast of Rohrback's farm and astride the Rohrback farm lane, was to march down and support Crook's assault. The plan required careful timing and coordination, and this is where it failed.[43]

THE COMMANDER OF THE 11th Connecticut was 25-year-old Colonel Henry W. Kingsbury, ranked fourth in the U.S. Military Academy's May 1861 class. Two of his peers at the academy considered him "to be the best soldier, greatest gentleman, and most promising officer" they knew. He was handsome, athletic, and popular. Kingsbury's father had graduated from West Point in 1823 and made the army his career. Among the family's friends was a striking young lieutenant, Simon Bolivar Buckner, who married Kingsbury's sister in 1850. Six years later, Kingsbury received an appointment to the academy, but shortly after his arrival there, his father died. Buckner, and another of the deceased Kingsbury's old Regular Army friends, Ambrose Burnside, were named as Henry's guardians. While still at West Point, Henry met and fell in love with Eva Taylor, from Kentucky, and married her in December 1861. The Civil War thus created a division in the Taylor family. Eva's father, brother, and one of her sister's husbands sided with the Union, but another sister was married to David R. Jones, a Confederate general, whose men confronted Kingsbury's at the Battle of Antietam. Following his graduation from the academy, the high opinion of Kingsbury's talents landed him on the staff of General Irvin McDowell for the First Bull Run Campaign. Under McClellan, Kingsbury was assigned to command Battery D 5th U.S. Artillery, which he led through the early and middle stages of the Peninsula Campaign. But, like many Regular officers, he made the jump to volunteer service to gain a promotion. In June 1862, he accepted the colonelcy of the 11th Connecticut.[44]

The 11th was recruited from across the state, and when it mustered for Federal service, it lacked a commissioned colonel. Its early history was painful. The line officers "with a few brilliant exceptions, were coarse and ill-informed," and the enlisted men "were miserably disciplined." Griffin A. Stedman Jr., the regiment's major, described as "a gentleman, by birth, education, habits, conditions and opinions, a thorough bred aristocrat," replaced the original lieutenant colonel in June 1862. He began to bring some discipline to the regiment, but it was Kingsbury's arrival in July that transformed the unit from a group of poorly disciplined yet uniformed citizens into soldiers. Kingsbury "descended upon this casual band like a bolt of blue lightening." He began drilling his officers and subjected them to a short but intensive course of study in tactics. After 2 weeks, he made them take a tough examination on their abbreviated tactics course. Those who failed were pressured to resign. Kingsbury was equally hard on his slovenly enlisted men. Mary Sergent, the historian of the West Point classes of 1856–1861, wrote that "a spot of dirt or a break in step brought a reprimand. A dirty musket was a sure ticket to the guardhouse. Anyone who stepped into the company street without his coat on and every button fastened felt the wrath of the Colonel." The men and some of their officers were outraged by what they considered to be Kingsbury's tyranny, as well as furious over the relentless drilling and inspections. Kingsbury, they clamored, was a martinet, and he was the recipient of bitter, behind-his-back vitriol from the ranks. But then the men in the 11th Connecticut began to notice that soldiers from other regiments came to watch them drill. They began to take pride in the talk that they were the best-drilled, cleanest, and most orderly regiment in the division. They also became aware that while Kingsbury might be tough on them, he cared about them. He was particular about their food, even instructing the company cooks on how to prepare rice properly. When he reprimanded a soldier for a tarnished button, men noticed that he still left the individual "feeling as if the colonel were complimenting the man who wore the button." Hatred gradually gave way to respect and, eventually, genuine affection for and pride in their West Point colonel.[45]

On the morning of September 17, the 11th Connecticut numbered around 430 officers and men. Since the early morning's shelling, they had been sheltering in a ravine in the rear of Muhlenberg's, Roemer's and McMullin's batteries. Burnside personally selected the 11th for the most dangerous mission in the opening assault on the Rohrback Bridge. No one could accuse him of seeking to protect the young man who was, essentially, a stepson. Knowing the peril of the assignment, Burnside personally delivered his orders to Kingsbury. According to the survivors who overheard the exchange, or at least were told of it by those who actually did hear it, Burnside ordered the colonel to capture the bridge and hold it until Sturgis's division could cross over Antietam Creek. One officer in the regiment, writing 3 days after the engagement, thought that Burnside wanted the right wing of the 11th to arrive to the north of the bridge, and the left wing to the south, so Sturgis could pass between them when going over the structure. No mention was made of Crook, which again raises a question about the attack's coordination.[46]

Kingsbury called the regiment to arms. He knew his men and was aware that the courage of some might fail the upcoming test. Four men had already deserted. He announced to the assembled companies in the 11th Connecticut that the name of every coward and skulker would be published, so the public might know who they were. This threat of public humiliation failed to stir Sergeant David Kittler, who carried the regiment's national colors. Kittler positively refused to go forward, claiming that the 11th's understrength color guard could not properly defend the flag. It was an odd protest, and a physical confrontation ensued, during which an officer slashed Kittler across the arm with his sword. Corporal Henry A. Eastman diffused the charged and potentially demoralizing situation when he stepped forward and said he would carry the colors. The color bearer was often the most fearless man in a regiment, and the effect on morale when he refused to go forward could be serious. Fear was contagious. Kittler would be reduced to the ranks after the conflict, and Eastman promoted.[47]

To soften up the enemy's defenses, a heavy battery—probably Benjamin's 20 lb. Parrotts—shelled the suspected Confederate positions above and below the Rohrback Bridge. While the guns bombarded the opposite bank of Antietam Creek, Kingsbury readied his regiment. Companies A and B, both armed with Sharps rifles, were ordered forward as skirmishers. Kingsbury divided the remaining eight companies into two wings, giving Lieutenant Colonel Stedman the right wing, while Kingsbury led the left, which would be the most exposed. Captain John D. Griswold from Lyme, Connecticut, commanded Company A. Griswold was remembered by a Company D sergeant as an "impetuous" soldier. He had packed a great deal of living into his 25 years. An 1857 Yale graduate, he was fluent in Spanish and French and a student of chemistry and mineralogy. Griswold was a muscular intellectual, at ease discussing philosophy or classic literature and then impressing his soldiers with his sword-handling skills. Business took him to the Pacific Islands before the Civil War, but he hurried back from there when word reached him that war had begun. Griswold was the

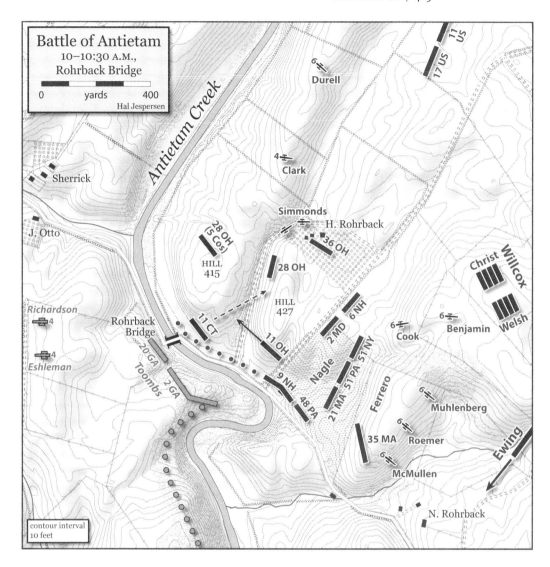

perfect soldier to command skirmishers: fearless, smart, and mentally and physically tough.[48]

When Kingsbury examined the approaches to the Rohrback Bridge, he saw that when his regiment emerged from the woods, they would cross a short meadow, leading downhill to a large cornfield, which extended for nearly 300 yards to Porterstown Road. West of this road was a plowed field, about 150 yards wide. Bordering this field's western boundary was the Rohrback farm lane, which climbed north from Lower Bridge Road. The plowed field between Porterstown Road and the Rohrback farm lane sloped steeply upward, to a hill reaching 427 feet at its crest (Hill 427 on the maps), which was nearly 100 feet higher than the ground along Antietam Creek. From this hill, the terrain descended sharply to the Rohrback farm lane and then rose rapidly to another hill, which was 415 feet high (Hill 415 on the maps), northeast of the Rohrback Bridge. Along the eastern edge of the smaller hill, a thin belt of woods paralleled the Rohrback farm lane, providing both a limited field of fire to the bridge and some cover. The most perilous part of the advance would be when the regiment emerged from the corn. From here it was about 300 long yards along the axis of Lower Bridge Road to the Rohrback Bridge. There was no cover on this route, apart from some scattered trees along the creek bank, and every step was under enemy observation.

When all was ready, Companies A and B started forward, not running, but advancing warily, scanning the opposite bank of Antietam Creek for signs of the enemy. In the cornfield they made an odd discovery: the abandoned instruments of a brass band, possibly from a 9th Corps' band that was routed by the morning's shelling. The Confederates remained invisible, but their guns continued to work, lobbing ammunition over the creek's bank. As the skirmishers neared Antietam Creek, some Rebels "were seen to emerge from the woods skirting the bank." They seemed confused at first, but then they rallied before once again appearing to disperse. Possibly the Union artillery had flushed some men from their hiding places, but it is just as likely that the Confederates were repositioning men to meet the approaching force. The New Englanders hopefully believed the shelling might have shaken the Rebels. Kingsbury maneuvered the main body of his regiment behind his skirmishers, taking advantage of the undulating terrain to shield them from enemy observation until he could get as close as possible to the bridge and the creek. As the two wings emerged from the cornfield, he ordered Stedman to take the right wing to Hill 415, west of the Rohrback farm lane, to provide overwatch (observe the terrain ahead and provide covering fire), while he and the left wing went straight toward Antietam Creek.[49]

The skirmishers crossed the plowed field and the Rohrback farm lane, then descended the southern slope of Hill 415, heading toward Lower Bridge Road. Griswold's Company A was closest to the Rohrback Bridge. As they approached the road, the men grew even more cautious and "hesitated to advance." No fire had touched them yet, but everyone sensed that danger lurked close by. Because quite a few in the 17th Georgia were armed with smoothbore muskets, Benning had probably cautioned them to hold their fire until the Federals were within good range—that is, less than 100 yards. To encourage his men, Griswold ran to the front of his line, scaled the fence bordering the road, and shouted "Come on, boys." Several others, including 18-year-old Philo S. Pearce, followed. The Georgians squeezed the triggers on their muskets and rifles, and gunfire exploded from the opposite bank of the creek. Pearce had a bullet "cut through the top of my left side but did not cut my head." He instantly dropped down into the road. Comrades around him either did the same or took cover behind Lower Bridge Road's fences. "Now it was time to do our duty," wrote Pearce. He and the others worked their Sharps rifles for all they were worth. Untouched by this opening volley, Griswold ran into Antietam Creek (a fence only bordered the eastern side of Lower Bridge Road here), urging his men to follow. Midway across, a Georgian put a bullet through Griswold. He managed to stagger to the western bank, where he lay down, his life ebbing from him. He had strength enough to call out to his men for help, but they were pinned down and unable to rescue him. Curiously, Griswold was the only man in Company A to be killed, and just two were wounded. Not a single soldier in Company B was killed in action, and only eight were wounded. Why the skirmish companies sustained such light losses is unknown, for they were engaged for quite a while. Homer B. Barnum, a 60-year-old in Griswold's company—who had told the recruiter he was 44—fired 59 of the 60 rounds he carried, and Pearce used up his entire 60 rounds, plus all the ammunition of Sergeant Irving Stevens, who was shot through the hand and gave his remaining rounds to the private. Perhaps many of the skirmishers took cover farther back from Antietam Creek and did not advance up to Lower Bridge Road. Their dispersal in skirmish order no doubt also helped to reduce casualties. But it also seems evident that they did not press their attack. Griswold's fall and subsequent death might account for this.[50]

When the two wings of the main body of the 11th Connecticut emerged from the cornfield onto the plowed ground, they broke into a double-quick. Seeing this larger, more threatening target, Benning's Georgians turned the weight of their fire on them. The 11th's more exposed left wing drew the brunt of it. "All but myself of the first eight of our company fell at their first fire, and volley after volley was poured into our flank, making fearful slaughter," wrote a member of Company K. Charles Rouse, a 45-year-old sergeant in Company F, noted that "many of our brave boys were killed" by the bullets that flayed their advance. "Language would fail me to describe the scene," recorded George Bronson, a hospital steward following in the wake of the regiment. Companies E, D, and H were particularly hard hit, with 20 men killed among the three of them. Kingsbury remained remarkably cool, despite the carnage, and could be heard calling out "not to get excited."[51]

A Confederate battery, probably John B. Richardson's, added shell and shrapnel to the hellish volleys that lashed the New Englanders. The 11th Connecticut's right wing managed to find some cover in the fringe of trees on Hill 415 and opened fire. The Confederates "were so concealed that we had very little to aim at," wrote Lieutenant Colonel Stedman, so men sighted on where smoke rose from the stream bank. The enemy's aim seemed to be unerring, and Stedman was alarmed by how many of his men were hit. Meanwhile, the companies in the left wing rushed forward to escape the line of fire from the Rebel's artillery. But this "got us into a murderous fire of sharpshooters," observed Lieutenant Francis T. Brown. Alonzo Maynard, a 19-year-old Company I private, offered an illustration of what a clichéd phrase like "murderous fire" meant. He was shot five times: one bullet pierced his right lung; another went through a shoulder, shattering his shoulder blade into four or five pieces; a third penetrated through his lungs and struck his spine, breaking a vertebra, a fourth shattered five ribs; and an unspecified body part was hit by the fifth. The private would be confined to bed for 5 years, but, miraculously, he survived his wounds.[52]

The 11th Ohio in Crook's brigade arrived at this moment. Earlier in the morning, he had detailed two companies of the 11th Ohio to skirmish with the Confederates and observe their position. These companies were firing at the Rebels when the 11th Connecticut arrived, and Stedman's left wing took up a position on the Ohioans' left.[53]

No brigade commander in the 9th Corps that day surpassed George Crook for ineptitude and bungling. On the night of September 16, even the lowliest private understood that there would be a fight in the morning. It was Crook's duty, as a brigade commander, to inform himself about the terrain on which his brigade might operate. Cox's report and reminiscences make it clear that Crook was notified early in the morning of September 17, and possibly even on the night of the 16th, that his brigade would lead the attack on the Rohrback Bridge. But he exhibited no interest in what his skirmishers learned. Instead, Crook concerned himself with having his Black body servant hunt up food for the brigade's headquarters mess. Showing resourcefulness that Crook did not, the servant found his way to what was probably Henry Rohrback's farm. Most of the family were gone, but Henry and his twin brother Jacob, and Henry's enslaved Blacks, remained at the farm, although they also may have departed before Crook's body servant arrived. Food at an abandoned farm was fair game for either army, and Crook's efficient forager discovered bread ready for baking, as well as milk and butter in the cellar. The colonel and his staff soon sat down to "a breakfast that none of us had tasted for many a day" when, instead, they should have been reconnoitering and making preparations for fighting. Shortly after 10 a.m., around the same time when Kingsbury commenced his movement to assault the Rohrback Bridge, Lieutenant Samuel L. Christie, an aide-de-camp on Cox's staff, rode to up Crook and, Crook recalled, "said the General wishes you to take the bridge." Crook replied, incredibly, "What bridge?" Christie answered that he did not know. Demonstrating his astounding ignorance, Crook then asked the staff officer where Antietam Creek was. Christie, who seems to have been singularly poorly informed, was not sure—or, at least, Crook claimed he was not. "I made some remarks, not complimentary to such way of doing business, but he went off not caring a cent," grumped Crook. Cox was generous to Crook in his after-action report, but he might have asked what, precisely, the colonel had been doing that morning. Crook also claimed in his memoirs—contrary to what was in Cox's report and reminiscences—that Lieutenant Christie said he was to cross the Rohrback Bridge *after* Sturgis's division had captured it. This is either a lie to cover for his poor performance, or evidence of a faulty memory, since Crook had maneuvered his brigade that morning like an officer ordered to attack, not *support* an assault.[54]

At least Crook put his brigade in motion after receiving his orders. He dropped off the 36th Ohio—the strongest regiment in the brigade, with nearly 800 men—in Rohrback's orchard, near the farmer's home. The 11th and 28th Ohio—with strengths, respectively, of 430 and 775 officers and men—continued down the Rohrback farm lane, going past his buildings and halting in the lane about 200 yards south of the structures. Here Crook detached four companies of the 28th, around 280 men, to advance over Hill 415 in skirmish order and join the two companies of the 11th Ohio that were already there. When these four companies emerged into the open ground north of the hill's summit, they came under fire from the 20th Georgia's company, which was north of the Rohrback Bridge, and retreated back to the farm lane. After dispatching the 28th Ohio's companies, who finally had found the bridge, Crook ordered Lieutenant Colonel Augustus H. Coleman, the popular commander of the 11th Ohio, to advance to it. As Coleman formed his regiment for the assault, Crook ordered a section in Lieutenant Seth Simmonds's battery of the Kentucky Light Artillery—probably the one with 10 lb. Parrott rifles—to move into position on Hill 415, and he sent half of the 28th Ohio to support them. Crook took the other five companies of the 28th—apparently including the skirmish companies who had retreated back to the Rohrback farm lane—around the hill to the north, hoping to find a location in which to support Coleman's attack. It did not end well.[55]

The 11th Ohio split into two wings of four companies each, for reasons neither the regiment's vague after-action report nor existing regimental accounts explain. Ezra Carman, with evidence he unfortunately did not preserve, wrote that conflicting orders—whether from Coleman or Crook is unknown—caused this partitioning into wings. The right wing crossed the Rohrback farm lane and went up Hill 415, where it joined the regiment's two skirmish companies. The left wing, accompanied by Coleman, advanced straight down the slope of the plowed field between the Rohrback farm lane and Porterstown Road, heading toward Antietam Creek, apparently to come up on the left of the 11th Connecticut. Riding his favorite horse, "Old Bull," Coleman presented a conspicuous target. One of his captains begged him to dismount. He agreed, but this did not save him. Coleman was an up-front type of officer. "He was always found, in time of danger, at the head of his regiment," noted John D. Kenney in Company A. The 2nd and 50th Georgia turned some of its fire on the approaching Ohioans, and John B. Richardson's battery shelled them. Coleman was hit twice, in his side and arm, with the fragment causing the injury to his side penetrating near his spine, inflicting a mortal wound. Assistant Surgeon Nathan Mayer in the 11th Connecticut observed some of Coleman's men take cover behind Lower

Bridge Road's fencing and return the Confederates' fire, but Coleman's debilitating injuries seem to have paralyzed and demoralized his men. Major Lyman J. Jackson replaced Coleman and promptly ordered the left wing to fall back into cover. The Ohioans' losses were light. The entire regiment only had 4 men killed and 12 wounded during the entire day, which indicates that they were not under fire for long before Major Jackson withdrew them.[56]

While Coleman's attack was quickly repulsed, Crook, with his five companies of the 28th Ohio, somehow lost the correct direction again. Rather than advance toward the Rohrback Bridge, he led them down to within 50 yards of Antietam Creek, but nearly 350 yards *above* the bridge. Here they came under fire from the company of the 20th Georgia that was situated above the bridge, which pinned the Ohioans down behind a low sandy ridge and a rail fence near the creek. Few men were hit. Although the five companies outnumbered their Confederate adversary by more than 10 to 1, no one displayed the desire or leadership to press forward across Antietam Creek. Instead, the Yankee officers and men hugged their cover, and Crook lamely reported to Cox "that he had his hands full and could not approach any closer to the bridge." Carman, who criticized sparingly, believed Crook "handled his command badly." Crook tried to transfer the blame for his brigade's poor performance on Sturgis, who, he claimed, was supposed to lead the attack. Crook would go on to compile a competent war record, but on this morning, he failed spectacularly and accepted no responsibility for the dereliction.[57]

During all this time, the 11th Connecticut struggled courageously, but futilely, to make it possible for Crook to storm the Rohrback Bridge. Assistant Surgeon Nathan Mayer heard from someone that his good friend Captain Griswold lay desperately wounded on the creek's western bank. Collecting four men and a stretcher, Mayer and his party sprinted toward the bridge, passing the regimental surgeon, who was leaning against a willow tree, banging away at the Rebels with a musket he had picked up. Mayer and his group climbed over the rail fence along Lower Bridge Road "in the face of both fires"—for here they were between the volleys of the opposing sides—waded the creek, gathered up the captain, and carried him back across the creek to a small barn or shed at the southwestern edge of Rohrback's cornfield. When Mayer told the dying captain that his wound was mortal, Griswold replied, "Then let me die quickly and without pain, if you can. I am perfectly happy, Doctor. This is the death I have always wished to die." It seems impossible that Mayer and his stretcher bearers survived this humanitarian dash unscathed. Philo Pearce, a member of Griswold's company, wrote years later that the captain was not evacuated during the fight, but that Pearce and two other men crossed the creek *after* the Rohrback Bridge was captured and carried him to a hospital. Mayer wrote his account close to the event and was consistent in his different accounts, which stated that the rescuers recovered Griswold during the fight. Lugging a dying man's body on a stretcher is hard, slow work, particularly crossing a slippery-bottomed creek, with enemy soldiers only yards away. Perhaps they were simply lucky, but this seems implausible. If Mayer was correct, and they carried Griswold away during the fight, then they could only have done so if Benning's Georgians deliberately spared them. If they did, it was an exceptionally rare act of mercy that terrible morning.[58]

Colonel Kingsbury, in particular, distinguished himself. One of his men described how he was "everywhere, inciting men to deeds of valor by his dauntless courage and the inspiration of his voice." Another member of the 11th Connecticut remembered hearing Kingsbury shouting "Forward! Come, my 11th, forward!" The man then added, "We followed him, but I doubt if we would have followed any other officer," a testament to the crucial role of leadership in getting soldiers to face mortal danger. When the 11th came near Antietam Creek, wounded Lieutenant Francis T. Brown in Company E heard Kingsbury order the left wing to find whatever cover they could and return the fire. "But there was no cover to get," wrote Brown, although a few found some behind "small trees and [others] laid behind a small pile of wood and one or two stumps." The rail fence along the eastern side of Lower Bridge Road provided the best cover, and many dropped down or knelt behind it. But the Rebels remained invisible. "We could not tell where they were," complained Brown. Kingsbury, who became a conspicuous target when dashing up and down his line, was "exposed to the most intense fire." Kingsbury was hit first in the heel, and he hobbled over to Captain James M. Pierpoint, the Company E commander, to tell him he was wounded. Then another bullet struck him in the shoulder and knocked him down. With the help of two men, Pierpoint picked up Kingsbury and started to carry him toward Hill 415. No mercy was shown to this rescue party, however. A third bullet hit Kingsbury in the right foot, and a fourth went through his right side, inflicting a fatal wound. Pierpoint and the two men helping him somehow escaped unscathed. When all of them reached the hill, they met Adjutant Joseph Converse, who called up four men. They carried the mortally wounded colonel on a blanket to Henry Rohrback's farmhouse, where he died on September 18.[59]

The survivors of the 11th Connecticut's left wing and the two 11th Ohio skirmish companies fought on, despite the latter's loss of Colonel Coleman, using up nearly all their ammunition. Major William Moegling assumed command of the left wing when Kingsbury fell, but he, too, was picked off. The wounded major was carried to the rear. With no field officers left, the remainder of the men melted away to the rear as their ammunition gave out, although some hardcore elements were still firing at the Rebels when the next effort to seize the Rohrback Bridge was made. Losses in the 11th Connecticut were frightful. Although they would see more fighting that afternoon and suffer additional casualties, the bulk of the regiment's 36 killed and 103 wounded occurred in this 30-minute engagement. The first effort to capture the Rohrback Bridge had failed.

16

The Bridge Captured

*"What the hell you doing there? Straighten
that line there, forward"*

During the time between the dispatch of Burnside's orders to open his attack on the Rohrback Bridge and the subsequent repulse of the 11th Connecticut, concern mounted at McClellan's headquarters over news arriving from the Union army's right. At 10:20 a.m., they received Sumner's troubling messages that he needed immediate reinforcements or the whole right flank might give way. The optimism prevailing when Burnside's orders were first drafted evaporated, and the operations of the 9th Corps began to assume greater importance than just a diversionary attack. McClellan considered it imperative to prevent Robert E. Lee from shifting any more troops to concentrate against his fragile right flank. Colonel David Strother detected McClellan's growing impatience with Burnside and heard him frequently exclaim, "What is Burnside about? Why do we not hear from him?" Consideration had been given to supporting the 9th Corps' attack, since McClellan had originally intended to hold the 6th Corps in reserve to reinforce a successful assault, wherever that might occur. Had he committed this corps by having it cross Antietam Creek at the Middle Bridge, or using it to reinforce the 9th Corps at the Rohrback Bridge, it might have dramatically altered the outcome of the engagement, but the decision to commit Franklin to reinforce the right eliminated this possibility. The two divisions of the 5th Corps were also available, but McClellan considered their position on the eastern bank of Antietam Creek to be indispensable to the army's safety. Instead of support that might have helped Burnside gain possession of the Rohrback Bridge by outflanking its defenders, McClellan merely sent staff officers to demand information and apply increasing pressing on the 9th Corps to capture the bridge on its own.[1]

DURING THE FIRST ATTACK on the Rohrback Bridge, Sturgis's 2nd Division moved down Porterstown Road to near Rohrback's farm. Brigadier General James Nagle's 1st Brigade also traveled on that slightly sunken road, but they went past the farm, arriving between Rohrback's cornfield east of the road and the plowed hill west of it. Nagle was a volunteer officer. He had seen service in the Mexican War, but, since then, he had earned his living as a paperhanger, painter, and sheriff of Schuylkill County, Pennsylvania, for 9 years before the war. He was tough—some in the brigade thought him a martinet—and energetic, first raising the 6th Pennsylvania, with its 3-month enlistment period, and then the 48th Pennsylvania. Jesse Reno had a high opinion of Nagle, recommending his promotion to brigadier general after Second Manassas. Two of the regiments—the 2nd Maryland and the 6th New Hampshire, which were both very small—halted in Porterstown Road east of Rohrback's farm, where the plowed hill and the slightly sunken nature of the roadbed shielded them from enemy observation. Nagle advanced the 48th Pennsylvania through the cornfield east of the road, bringing them near a shed at the southwestern edge of the field—probably the same building that Assistant Surgeon Mayer had Captain Griswold carried to (see chapter 15). Their formation faced Lower Bridge Road and Antietam Creek, but it had the men concealed in the corn. The rookie 9th New Hampshire also moved up through the cornfield to near Lower Bridge Road, where they exchanged some shots with the Georgians on the opposite bank of the creek.[2]

Colonel Edward Ferrero led Sturgis's 2nd Brigade. Ferrero was Spanish born, with Italian parents. He ran a well-respected and successful dance studio in New York City before the Civil War and authored *The Art of Dancing* and *Ethics of Politeness: Hints to Dancers*. His love of dance attracted him to military tactics and drill, and he served in the 11th New York State Militia, climbing the ranks to lieutenant colonel. Not surprisingly for a master of dance, Ferrero shaped the 11th into a unit renowned for its precision in marching and in executing drills. He was commissioned colonel of the 51st New York, which he raised at his own expense, and proved to be a competent commander. During the spring of 1862, seniority landed him in command of the 2nd Brigade, which he had led capably since that time. Ferrero followed Nagle into Rohrback's cornfield, deploying three veteran regiments—from left to right, the 21st Massachusetts, the 51st Pennsylvania, and the 51st New York. The 35th Massachusetts, a new regiment that had received its baptism of fire at the Battle of South Mountain, was placed outside the cornfield, on the western slope of the hill just below McMullin's and Roemer's batteries.[3]

It was around 11 a.m. when the first assault on the Rohrback Bridge failed. Burnside went to Sturgis and directed him to organize a new attack, impressing upon the division commander "the importance of carrying it without delay." Sturgis sought out Colonel Simon G. Griffin, a 38-year-old attorney from Keene, New Hampshire, who was commanding the 6th New Hampshire and asked him if he would like the honor of leading an assault on the bridge. Griffin may have had a look at the Rohrback Bridge by this point and seen the deadly bullet- and shell-swept approaches to it. He declined the "honor," pointing out that his regiment had only 104 officers and men and was too small to lead the attack. Sturgis made his way through the corn to the next regiment and asked some of its soldiers which unit it was. The 2nd Maryland, they replied, and Sturgis sent for their commander, Lieutenant Colonel Jacob E. Duryée.[4]

Duryée was a 23-year-old New Yorker. His father was Abram Duryée, the original commander of the 5th New York Zouaves, in which Jacob had served as a lieutenant. Father and son shared a common characteristic: a powerful ambition for rank and recognition. Abram managed to secure a coveted brigadier general's star and commanded a brigade in Ricketts's 2nd Division of the 1st Corps. His son, sporting an enormous mustache that made him look older than his 23 years, was a bright, active, strong-minded individual who thirsted for a star like the one his father wore. His connections, which reached as high as the president, secured him a promotion from lieutenant in the 5th New York to lieutenant colonel of the 2nd Maryland in September 1861. Duryée promptly set out to become the regiment's colonel. He cultivated a relationship with Burnside and Jesse Reno. The latter—possibly unwittingly—assisted him in an effort that undermined the 2nd's colonel and forced his resignation. This left Duryée the acting commander of the regiment during Burnside's 1862 North Carolina Expedition. To clear the path for gaining the colonelcy, Duryée ruthlessly purged the regiment of any company commanders that he perceived might be a threat to his promotion. "We are commanded by a northern adventurer, I mean Lieutenant Col. J. E. Duryée who will oust every one of us if possible," complained Lieutenant Charles E. Bowen.[5]

The young lieutenant colonel was an aggressive schemer when it came to his career and reputation, but he was a fine combat commander. Although he cultivated tension and resentment among his officers, Duryée displayed concern for his men, even if it brought him into conflict with his superiors, which it did on September 15. When the brigade halted for the day, after their march from South Mountain, the center of the field assigned to Nagle's brigade as its bivouac site had been plowed to the length of about a regimental front. When the brigade was ordered to camp in column of regiments, Duryée's Marylanders ended up in the plowed ground. Nagle seemed oblivious to the discomfort it would cause this unit, but Duryée would have none of it. He ignored the order and marched his men to a nearby meadow to bivouac. Nagle's wrath descended on the young officer for moving his men out of position. Duryée stood his ground and angrily responded that his men had had nothing to eat but, nonetheless, were expected to fight the next day. According to Theodore Dimon, the 2nd Maryland's surgeon, Duryée "would be damned if his men, having nothing left but sleep, should not have that tonight anyhow. He refused absolutely to obey the order and did not."[6]

More trouble followed. One of Duryée's officers, accompanied by the 6th New Hampshire's quartermaster, found two cows "that appeared to be strays," had them both slaughtered, and distributed the beef to the two regiments. This brought Nagle down upon Duryée again, this time for violating standing orders against foraging. Burnside soon arrived—it is unknown whether he was summoned by Nagle or just happened by—and he sharply questioned Duryée, asking if he had made his men sleep on the plowed ground or had taken away their beef. Duryée replied, "No, sir, and furthermore I would not have done it if I am to be cashiered for it." Theodore Dimon, an eyewitness to the scene, wrote that the wing commander replied, "You are right, and to be commended for taking care of your men, and nobody but a damned fool can think otherwise." Burnside then turned to Nagle and said, "When I ordered the Corps to bivouac in column of Brigade, I did not suppose any subordinate officer I had did not know enough to take the best advantage he could of the ground assigned to him to make his men as comfortable as possible, and I want it distinctly understood that any officer under my command who does not do this, neglects his plain and imperative duty." The rebuke pleased Duryée but probably left Nagle fuming at the upstart New Yorker.[7]

When Sturgis's summons arrived, Duryée was on the right of his regiment, along with Captain Malcom Wilson, his senior captain. They were situated in a place where they could observe the approaches to the Rohrback Bridge and watched the final stages of the 11th Connecticut's engagement. "We both saw that the road and bridge were well defended," Duryée recalled. When Duryée reached Sturgis, the general asked him, "Colonel do you want to be a general in the army?" Duryée replied, "Yes." "Then take that bridge," Sturgis said. "General Burnside says it is the key of the position and must be taken. The Sixth New Hampshire will follow you, and as you cross deploy to the right." Sturgis left the decision about the avenue of approach and the necessary attack formation up to Duryée. His focus was on arranging support for the Marylanders.[8]

From his earlier observation of the approaches, Duryée's "first thought was to avoid the road as much as possible," since he was certain the stretch of Lower Bridge Road, from where Porterstown Road and the Rohrback farm lane intersected it, was covered by Confederate small arms and artillery. Duryée did not think he could avoid Lower Bridge Road entirely, but he wanted to reduce the amount of time his regiment would be exposed on it. The plan he conceived was relatively simple. The 2nd Maryland would advance in column, marching obliquely across the plowed hill, in a southwesterly direction, to Lower Bridge Road. Then, followed by the 6th New Hampshire, they would sprint up the road and across the bridge, since speed was essential. The plan was doomed from the start, but Duryée did not have time to conduct a more extensive reconnaissance. From Sturgis down to Duryée, everyone felt the pressure of quickly taking possession of the Rohrback Bridge.[9]

To support the assault by the 2nd Maryland and the 6th New Hampshire, Sturgis ordered Lieutenant Colonel Joshua K. Siegfried's 48th Pennsylvania to move up on the southern slope of Hill 415, in order to provide covering fire for the assault. Colonel Enoch Q. Fellows's rookie 9th New Hampshire would do the same on the 48th's left, advancing into the plowed field and firing on the bank at the bend in Antietam Creek, below the Rohrback Bridge, which was a place where the Confederates could deliver a flanking fire on the attacking regiments. Sturgis also repositioned some of his artillery, ordering Captain Joseph E. Clark Jr.'s Battery E, 4th U.S., to the southern end of the ridge above Antietam Creek, where Durell was located, and summoning a section of Durell's battery into position on Hill 415. But the infantry assault went forward before these artillery redeployments could be completed.[10]

When the meeting between the lieutenant colonel and Sturgis ended, Theodore Dimon noticed that Duryée was buttoning up his uniform coat as he returned to the regiment. "This was a sign that work was at hand," noted the surgeon. Duryée ordered his men to unsling knapsacks. Dimon then asked what was up. Duryée "replied that Sturgis had asked him if he wanted to win a star and that he had said yes. 'Well,' Sturgis says, 'there is a bridge around the other side of this hill, and the Lieutenant Colonel of the 6th New York [New Hampshire] thinks his regiment too small to head the assault on it, so I offer it to you.'" It was around 11 a.m. when Duryée called his regiment to arms. With its 162 officers and men, the 2nd Maryland was not much larger than the 6th New Hampshire.[11]

Duryée led his men through Rohrback's cornfield, followed closely by the 6th New Hampshire. Colonel Simon G. Griffin, the 6th's commander, was a flinty New Englander. Both of his grandfathers had fought in the American Revolution. Griffin had been a legislator and attorney before the Civil War, but he volunteered early on as a captain in the 2nd New Hampshire. He returned to New Hampshire to accept a commission as lieutenant colonel of the 6th New Hampshire in the fall of 1861. By the following spring, he was the regiment's colonel. Griffin copied Kingsbury in his desire to make the 6th one of the best-drilled regiments in the service, starting a daily school of instruction for officers and noncoms, besides drilling the men incessantly. There were a number of former militia officers in the regiment who were offended by the notion of Griffin's school of instruction, and they refused to attend. Before long, however, the sergeants could maneuver their companies better than the officers. Soon—no doubt as Griffin had hoped and encouraged—the militia officers began to resign their commissions, enabling Griffin to promote more-worthy candidates. Their regimental dog, an ochre-colored canine that was probably a Chesapeake Bay retriever, known as the "Sixth Regiment Dog," trotted along with the Granite Staters as they marched through the corn. The men had adopted it as a puppy in Elizabeth City, North Carolina, and it was a constant companion on the march, in camp, and in battle. "Dogs generally fear firearms when discharged in volleys," wrote the regiment's historian, but "this one went fearlessly into battle."[12]

As the two regiments maneuvered toward Lower Bridge Road, the firing around the Rohrback Bridge area ceased. The silence seemed ominous to Duryée.

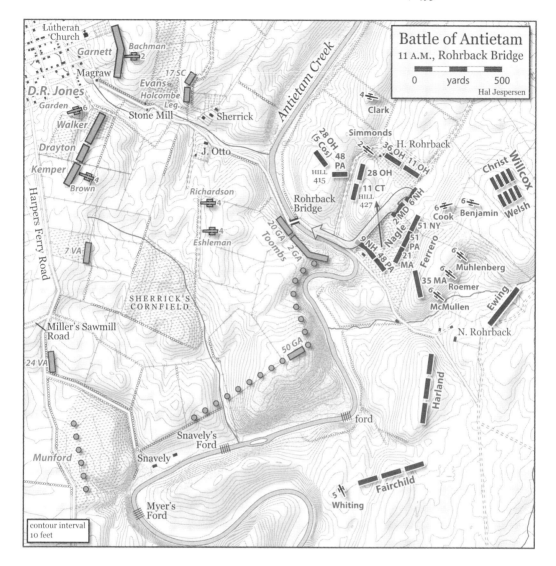

His Marylanders emerged from the corn and crossed the lower portion of the plowed field, reaching a sturdily built chestnut rail fence along the road. Neither the skirmishers of the 11th Connecticut nor the 11th Ohio had removed any of the rails during their engagement, since they had used the fence for cover. The silence continued as Duryée and several of his men struggled to dismantle a section of the fence, in order to allow the regiments to pass through into the road. It took between 5 to 7 excruciatingly long minutes to create this gap, which was accomplished with "great difficulty." Benning's Georgians let the Marylander get well into their work before they fired. The opening volleys were scattered but accurate. One of the first shots killed William Burman, and three others were wounded in rapid succession. "Instantly," wrote Duryée, "hell broke loose, the whole west bank of the Antietam was a sheet of flame." Alerted to the attack, the Louisianans in John B. Richardson's battery commenced dropping shell and shrapnel into the creek valley.[13]

Surgeon Dimon followed the 2nd Maryland and the 6th New Hampshire closely, looking for a place to establish a forward aid station. He watched men dropping onto the plowed ground as they were hit. He also saw Duryée throw down the last fence rail and then look back to see his men "shrinking and elbowing out under this tremendous fire and just ready to break." Above the din, he heard Duryée shout, "in his peculiar-keyed voice which could be, and was, heard through all that infernal noise. 'What the hell you doing there? Straighten that line there, forward.' The line straightened, like straightening your arm, and on it went for the bridge." Their objective was 260 yards away.[14]

Sprinting up the road with men falling at every step of the way, the right wing of the 2nd Maryland made it to within 50 yards of the Rohrback Bridge. By this point, a majority of men in the wing had been shot, including both color bearers. The handful of survivors dropped down along the creek bank and began to return the fire, while the left wing and the 6th New Hampshire tried to continue on toward the Rohrback Bridge. Richardson's artillery fire rained in and "inflicted the most horrible wounds," mangling and mortally wounding one of Duryée's best captains, Malcom Wilson. The Union batteries that were able bring their guns to bear added to the deafening noise, blasting the western bank of Antietam Creek with shell and shrapnel. Theodore Dimon watched "their shells bursting just at the willows and limbs of them dropping into the stream, cut off by their fragments." Since the Confederate positions could not be identified with any precision, the Federal batteries' shelling was inaccurate and failed to suppress the Rebels' fire. "We were met with a perfect hail of bullets," wrote Captain John A. Cummings in the 6th New Hampshire. The Granite Staters and the left wing of the 2nd Maryland melted away under the rain of bullets, balls, and shells. "The men sheltered themselves behind fences, logs, and whatever cover they could find as the soldiers were hit or dropped out to find cover," wrote a member of the 6th New Hampshire. Cummings dashed on until "there was only Col. Duryée of the 2d Maryland, and Capt. [Henry H.] Pearson, of our regiment, ahead. O, what a time that was." Duryée came upon 19-year-old Sergeant John A. Osborne, one of his color bearers, lying in the road, badly wounded. When Duryée offered to carry him back, the sergeant cried out, "Don't touch me! Don't touch me," I am all right here!" But Osborne was not "all right." He was dying. Duryée, Cummings, Griffin (who was also in the vanguard), Pearson, and others had shown as much courage as was humanly possible, but they now recognized that the attack had failed. Their duty now was to get their men out of the killing zone. "I had to run over dead and wounded men to get back," Cummings wrote home. Most of the men in both regiments fell back to Hill 415, but a contingent refused to retreat, stubbornly stuck to whatever cover they had, and kept up a steady fire.[15]

Because the thin strip of timber on Hill 415 only provided cover for four companies in Lieutenant Colonel Siegfried's 48th Pennsylvania, he left his other six companies in reserve, behind the hill. These four companies did their best to support the assault, blazing away at the Confederates' position. Even some of the officers joined in, "evidently enjoying the fun." One of them was Captain James Wren, commanding Company B. He was a 37-year-old machinist from Pottsville, Pennsylvania. During the engagement, a soldier in the 6th New Hampshire approached Wren and told the captain that he had a finger shot off, adding that he still had 40 rounds of ammunition left and did not want to go to the rear yet. Wren told the plucky fellow to hand him his rifle. With the New Englander biting off the ends of cartridges, the captain commenced firing until the weapon's barrel grew so hot that he had to lay it down and find another rifle. When Sturgis inspected Siegfried's position, he either did not bother to inform himself about the situation or disagreed with Siegfried's management of it. Theodore Dimon later heard the 2nd Division's commander, who was a blunt, profane individual, venting at the lieutenant colonel: "God damn you to hell, sir, don't you understand the English language? I ordered you to advance in line and support the 2nd Maryland, and what in hell are you doing flanking around in this corn, etc., etc."[16]

The 2nd Maryland was shattered, with 67 of its 162 men killed or wounded, most of the casualties being in the regiment's right-wing companies. The 6th New Hampshire miraculously escaped with a loss of just 18. Duryée estimated that only 20 minutes had elapsed between the moment when Sturgis gave him his orders and the time the attack was repulsed. He figured that the double-quick assault from the gap in the fence by the plowed field to where the attack failed had lasted only 8 minutes. Nearly all his of casualties occurred during this brief period. It was now around 11:30 a.m. Two assaults on the Rohrback Bridge had failed, with over Federals 200 killed or wounded.[17]

BENNING'S BRIGADE HAD ONLY incurred a few casualties. George McRae in the 20th Georgia noted that their excellent concealment "made it harder for the enemy to locate us" and accounted for the inaccuracy of the Yankees' small-arms and artillery fire. "The creek being immediately in front of us gave us a vast advantage over them while our ammunition held out," McRae wrote. "They would advance bravely up to the edge of the creek, some fifteen or twenty yards from us, and after standing and firing on us a while they would see the improbability of dislodging us and falling back another line would repeat the same thing over again." One man in Charles Terrill's company of the 2nd Georgia claimed he had hit 18 men. The 2nd's lieutenant colonel, William R. Holmes, relished combat. He "was insensible to fear, bombs and bullets were to him a pastime," wrote Terrill. "I verily believe that it was a matter of perfect indifference to him whether he was killed or not." Holmes had a reputation as a crack shot.

During the engagement, he took a musket and fired eight or nine times at the enemy. He then asked for a rifle and used it to drop a Union color bearer, possibly Sergeant Osborne. The Georgians also exercised superb fire discipline, not wasting ammunition until the enemy came within effective range of their muskets. With only 60 rounds per man, they had to make each shot count. After two attacks, they had burned through a substantial amount, but the ease with which they had repulsed two Union attacks filled the men with confidence. As long as their ammunition held out, no Yankee would cross the Rohrback Bridge.[18]

WHILE THE FIRST ATTACKS against the Rohrback Bridge went forward and then were repulsed, Rodman's 3rd Division was moving to flank the Confederate defenders by crossing Antietam Creek at Snavely's Ford. Everyone expected the march to the ford to be relatively short. As already related (see chapter 15), the Union army's topographical engineers had assured Burnside and Cox that Snavely's Ford was less than a half mile below the Rohrback Bridge, and the two generals' had designated a position for Rodman that should have placed him nearly opposite to the ford. There was no reason for Burnside to doubt them, since the topographical engineers were the cream of the Regular Army. Only the top graduates from the U.S. Military Academy joined their ranks. Why Burnside and Cox did not move Rodman closer to the ford after receiving McClellan's early morning preparatory order is a question already considered in the previous chapter. There is no evidence that they were aware of the presence of Walker's division near Snavely's Ford, or that his division was withdrawn around 9 a.m. to reinforce the Confederates' left. The two Union generals knew the enemy was defending all possible crossing points of Antietam Creek between the Rohrback Bridge and Snavely's Ford, but they had no idea how many Rebels were placed there. The only logical explanation is that after the Confederates' early morning shelling, Cox and Burnside thought it better to keep Rodman under cover. Since Snavely's Ford was believed to only be a short march away, they did not wish to expose the 3rd Division until final attack orders were received. Nonetheless, it would have been possible to move the division closer to the ford without exposing the brigades to enemy fire, or, at a minimum, to have a small detachment scout the approaches. The failure to do so would have serious consequences.[19]

About 10:30 a.m., Rodman's 3rd Division, followed by Colonel Hugh Ewing's 1st Brigade of the Kanawha Division—a total force of 3,734 men—moved forward from the belt of woods northeast of Rohrback's farm. They marched south in a somewhat circuitous route, in order to avoid enemy observation; crossed Lower Bridge Road, probably near Noah Rohrback's farm; and continued on to the two hills rising up steeply, opposite to the place where Antietam Creek turned from south to west. This was where Rodman had been advised that Snavely's Ford was located. Harland's 2nd Brigade occupied the hill east of the bend, which reached an elevation of about 490 feet, and Fairchild's 1st Brigade halted on a 438-foot-high hill almost directly south of the bend. The two brigades arrived there probably between 11 and 11:30 a.m. Skirmishers were dispatched to locate the ford and probe its defenses. While they descended toward Antietam Creek, the troops positioned on the hills took in the far-reaching panorama they afforded. Lieutenant Matthew J. Graham in the 9th New York described it as "an extensive view of a stretch of country toward our front and right, including much of the battlefield. . . . The air was very still, and great piles of white smoke like clouds were over and around the batteries, both the enemy's and our own." Captain Marsh in the 8th Connecticut thought the scene was "the grandest sight of my life. . . . All along the right for miles the cannon and musketry kept up a deafening roar while the air was thick with great clouds of smoke." Although the two brigades were in plain sight, they received no enemy fire. "There was no hostile demonstration made against us," wrote Graham. "Not a shot of any kind was fired at us."[20]

To support the creek crossing, Captain James R. Whiting's five 12 lb. Dahlgren boat howitzers, attached to the 9th New York in Fairchild's brigade, were placed on the hill directly south of Antietam Creek and shelled the opposite bank, including the area held by the 20th and 2nd Georgia. Unknowingly, they enfiladed the Georgians and inflicted some of the first real damage on them. Meanwhile, the skirmishers had returned from the creek to report that the ford they found seemed to be the wrong one. Its banks were steep, and the ground on the western side rose precipitously, nearly 200 feet, which even a small number of the enemy could easily defend. Valuable time had been lost. With no cavalry available for additional scouting, Rodman had to use infantry skirmishers. He ordered Colonel Harland to deploy two companies of the 8th Connecticut to search downstream and see if they could locate Snavely's Ford. He also sent someone to find a local resident familiar with the fords on Antietam Creek. Meanwhile, the division moved on, trailing behind Harland's skirmishers and feeling its way to find Snavely's Ford.[21]

AT BURNSIDE'S HEADQUARTERS, THE wing commander and Cox stayed in place, "constantly hoping to hear something from Rodman's advance by the ford." After the 2nd Maryland and 6th New Hampshire were repulsed, Cox and Burnside "would gladly have waited for some more certain knowledge of his [Rodman's] progress" before attempting another direct attack on the Rohrback Bridge. But they heard nothing, and pressure from McClellan's headquarters to capture the bridge intensified. Soon after Sturgis's failed attack, Colonel Delos B. Sackett, the Union army's inspector general, rode up with orders for Burnside "to push forward his troops without a moment's delay, and, if necessary, to carry the bridge at the point of the bayonet." McClellan, suspicious that Burnside was not exhibiting the energy necessary to get the job done, directed Sackett to remain "and see that the order was executed promptly." By this time,

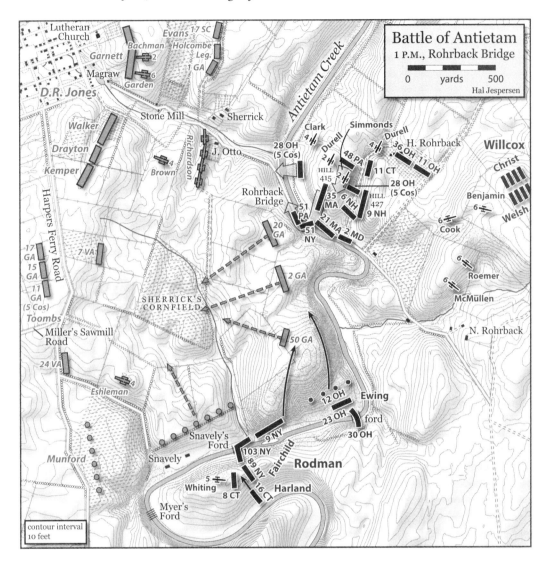

Battle of Antietam
1 P.M., Rohrback Bridge

0   yards   500

Hal Jespersen

contour interval
10 feet

Burnside would have known that Kingsbury, who was virtually his stepson, had been mortally wounded while acting under Burnside's orders, and that nearly 200 others were dead or wounded in two attacks on the Rohrback Bridge. Sackett's presence, and the insinuation that the 9th Corps was somehow not executing their orders, irritated the Rhode Islander, and he snapped at the inspector general: "McClellan appears to think I am not trying my best to carry this bridge; you are the third or fourth one who has been to me this morning with similar orders." Clearly, waiting to hear from Rodman was not an option. Another frontal assault would need to be made. Burnside gave orders that Sturgis should detail the veteran 51st Pennsylvania and the 51st New York of his 2nd Brigade to seize the bridge, and to support the attack with the balance of the 2nd Brigade and all the artillery that could be brought to bear.[22]

When Sturgis delivered his orders to Ferrero, the latter did not leap at this opportunity for glory, suggesting instead that "Nagle ought to do it," Ferrero apparently was ignorant of the fact that Nagle's 1st Brigade had tried and failed to take the Rohrback Bridge. Sturgis, never one for lengthy discussion or debate, merely replied, "Go on." Ferrero thought his men might ford Antietam Creek below the bridge, but Sturgis, who knew the steep bluffs on its western bank were well defended, "didn't see it." After Sturgis departed, Ferrero, still uncertain about how to proceed with the attack, sent one of his aides-de-camp—Lieutenant John W. Hudson in the 35th Massachusetts, an observant, intelligent, 26-year-old attorney from Lexington—to find the division commander and ask which regiments he should use in the attack. Sturgis told Hudson that the two 51sts would lead the attack, supported by the 21st Massachusetts. Hudson then anxiously inquired about the rookie 35th Massachusetts. The inclusion of his own inexperienced regiment worried the staff officer. "Nobody cared to have any part of the day *depend* upon it," he wrote. Sturgis said that the New Englanders could follow the veterans over the Rohrback Bridge once it was captured. Then, to underscore that no further delay would be tolerated, he told Hudson, "There must be no delay. General Burnside is waiting for that to be done now."[23]

Ferrero rode down into Rohrback's cornfield, arriving at the head of the 51st Pennsylvania. It was commanded by 31-year-old Colonel John Hartranft, a Norristown attorney who had dabbled in various other occupations: civil engineer, real estate developer, and deputy sheriff of Montgomery County. Hartranft had raised a company in the 4th Pennsylvania Infantry at the start of the war, but he was humiliated when the regiment, whose enlistment period expired on the eve of First Bull Run, departed for home. He, however, offered his services as a volunteer aide-de-camp to Colonel William B. Franklin. After the battle, Hartranft returned home and helped raise the 51st Pennsylvania, securing a commission as its colonel. He learned quickly and led the regiment with distinction through Burnside's North Carolina Expedition, Second Manassas, and the Battle of South Mountain. Ferrero ordered the brigade to attention and announced that it was Burnside's special request that the two 51sts seize the Rohrback Bridge. "The request was unlooked for," admitted the 51st Pennsylvania's regimental historian. "Everyone of us knew full well the meaning of that order," recorded Captain William H. Bolton in Company A. Although they had not yet seen the bridge, there was ample evidence, in the many wounded men who were limping, hobbling, and being carried to the rear, that its capture was a perilous undertaking. They had no desire for further glory when it would be purchased with their blood.[24]

After a moment's uncomfortable silence, 1st Sergeant Lewis Patterson in Company I piped up, "Will you give us our whiskey colonel, if we take it?" The regiment had lost its whiskey ration for some earlier infraction. Patterson did not imbibe, but he was happy to advocate for his men. "Yes, by God, you shall

all have as much as you want, if you take the bridge," Ferrero responded. He quickly added that the whiskey deal applied only to the 51st Pennsylvania and the 51st New York. If the commissary could not produce any whiskey, Ferrero would buy it with his own money. Then, referring to the Rohrback Bridge, he repeated, "Will you take it?" This time the two regiments replied "Yes," with genuine enthusiasm. The men had already piled their knapsacks and blankets near Rohrback's barn and filled their canteens from the farmer's spring. They were ready to move. First, though, Ferrero, Hartranft, and Lieutenant Colonel Robert Potter, commanding the 51st New York, conducted a quick reconnaissance of the approaches to the Rohrback Bridge, arranged for artillery, and organized the role the 21st and 35th Massachusetts would play in supporting the attack.[25]

A private in the 51st Pennsylvania noticed that "an air of sadness" seemed to come over Hartranft, "as if conscious of the sacrifice to be made of his fine large regiment." His unit and that of the New Yorkers each contained approximately 335 officers and men. During his reconnaissance for the assault, Hartranft encountered Duryée, who warned him, "Don't go up the road," pointing out that the Confederates' flanking fire along Lower Bridge Road was murderous. Hartranft decided that the best approach was to move the two regiments over the plowed field east of the Rohrback farm lane, to the reverse slope of Hill 415. The distance from the crest of the hill to the Rohrback Bridge was about 300 yards, over open ground. But this approach would only expose the regiments to frontal fire. Hartranft could hope that the earlier attacks had weakened the enemy's defenses and reduced the quantity of their ammunition.[26]

It was probably around 12:15 p.m. when these preparations were completed. The two regiments filed out of the cornfield and across Porterstown Road, heading toward the plowed hill. They marched by Sturgis and Ferrero, who were standing beside the road. Sturgis called out to the Pennsylvanians, "If you take that bridge, you will accomplish one of the greatest feats of the war, and your name will be recorded in History." The grim-faced men called back, "We will do it."[27] While Ferrero's infantry moved into position, two Parrott rifles in Captain Seth Simmonds's Kentucky Light Artillery, attached to Crook's brigade, were muscled into place on the northwestern slope of Hill 415. Captain Joseph C. Clark Jr.'s Battery E, 4th U.S., with four 10 lb. Parrotts, arrived on the bluff east of Antietam Creek, on Durell's left.[28]

As a prelude to the assault, Simmonds's and Clark's guns, as well as some of the artillery on the ridge east of Rohrback's farm, commenced hammering away at the hidden Rebel defenders above and below the Rohrback Bridge. "The roar of the artillery was terrific," recorded Lieutenant Albert Pope in the 35th Massachusetts. Another member of Pope's regiment, Charles Hawes, recalled how the concussion of the guns firing and shells exploding "was almost enough to take your breath away." Behind Hill 415, Hartranft's Pennsylvanians formed into close column of companies as they cleared the fence along the Rohrback farm lane; passed through the 48th Pennsylvania, who were lying down behind the hill; and started for the bridge. Potter's New Yorkers were close behind. They went forward on Hartranft's left, in column, which provided a concentrated target but facilitated command and control of the unit. The two regiments shuffled down the slope toward the Rohrback Bridge. "Tired soldiers don't go very fast," observed Ferrero's aide-de-camp, Lieutenant Hudson. Benning's Georgians opened what Major Edwin Schall in the 51st Pennsylvania described as a "murderous" fire. The hillside was strewn with dead and wounded men, but the Confederates failed to inflict enough damage to check the advance.[29]

As the 51st Pennsylvania approached the Rohrback Bridge, the firing became so severe that some of Hartranft's company commanders guided their men toward a stone wall running north of the bridge and paralleling Antietam Creek. Hartranft, who planned to storm the bridge, was helpless to prevent this rush for cover. Some of those on the left of the regiment climbed the fence along Lower Bridge Road and took cover behind the lower wing wall of the bridge. But the bulk of the regiment crowded behind the stone wall and commenced what Sergeant Thomas H. Parker described as a "terrific" fusillade at the Rebels. Potter's New Yorkers encountered the same hot reception, and their reaction checked the head of the regiment's column as it neared the bridge. "Fearing that my men being thus exposed by the flank; would be badly cut up I brought the regiment into line," wrote Potter. He obliqued his men to the rail fence along Lower Bridge Road below the Rohrback Bridge. As his men came up to the fence, they also opened fire. Hundreds of Federal rifles were now blasting the opposite bank of the creek, along with the supporting Union artillery fire, which battered the hillside with iron fragments and shrapnel balls.[30]

While the 51st Pennsylvania and the 51st New York charged down to the Rohrback Bridge, Colonel William S. Clark's 21st Massachusetts, only about 150 strong, moved into the plowed field and commenced firing volleys by rank. The Confederates were in "a mass of foliage impenetrable to the eye," so the Federals' shooting was not particularly accurate. Lieutenant Hudson, Ferrero's aide-de-camp, stood in the rear of the 21st and could see "nothing at all over the stream," but bullets from the unseen enemy struck several of Clark's men while Hudson looked on. When the two 51sts finally came near the Rohrback Bridge, Ferrero ordered Clark to move his regiment next to the 51st New York, along Lower Bridge Road, to provide closer support. As they moved forward, shells, probably from Cook's 8th Battery, Massachusetts Light, or Benjamin's Battery E, 2nd U.S., passed directly over the heads of the New Englanders and burst on the opposite bank. It kept the Rebels' heads down, but the artillery barrage was so close that at least two of Clark's men were seriously wounded by it.[31]

The fight raged on for nearly 15 minutes. It was a cacophony of sounds, accompanied by the men's sweat, fear, and determination. With about 600 rifles firing approximately every 30 seconds, Hartranft's and Potter's troops delivered roughly 1,200 bullets each minute at the Confederates. Benning's Georgians could only reply with about 400 to 500 rounds, and as their ammunition began to run low, that number diminished. Benning admitted that "the combined fire of infantry and artillery was terrific," and casualties in his brigade began to mount. "So many of the men were shot down that the officers filled their places & loaded & fired their guns," wrote Lieutenant Theodore Fogle in the 2nd Georgia. Johnnie Slade, an 18-year-old private in Fogle's company and a "splendid soldier," had stood up to watch the effect of a shot he had made "when a ball passed through the third finger of his right hand & into his stomach and liver," inflicting a mortal wound. Lieutenant Colonel Holmes fearlessly exposed himself, inspiring his men as "many bullets fell thick and fast around him." "It may be said of him that he was foolishly brave," remarked Charles Terrill. One shot finally found its mark, and Holmes went down, mortally wounded. Three men ran to him and picked him up, but this exposed the party and drew a storm of bullets. Holmes was hit three more times, and two of his rescuers were shot down. The third fled for his life.[32]

After nearly 3 hours of fighting, the tide began to turn against the Georgians. Men shouted for a resupply of ammunition. "It had now become a point of honor with them to maintain their ground," reported the *Southern Confederacy* newspaper, but a fresh supply could not reach them. There were other problems, as well. A report reached Benning that the 50th Georgia had abandoned their position, and Union troops now were approaching the old ford the Georgians had been defending, which was about 1,200 yards below the Rohrback Bridge. This was Ewing's Ohio brigade. Word also arrived that the enemy had reached Snavely's Ford in force, and that Federal troops—Crook's 28th Ohio—were wading the creek above the Rohrback Bridge. Envelopment threatened. With his fire slackening, Benning could see Union soldiers below him beginning to move toward the bridge. It was time to go. He issued orders to retreat, and gave Colonel Cummings the mission of covering the Georgians' withdrawal with two of his companies.[33]

AMONG THE FEDERALS, MARTIN G. REED, a 51st Pennsylvania private, saw Rebel soldiers emerge from their cover and disappear over the hill, although "others stuck to it with the tenacity of bulldogs." Ferrero, watching from Hill 415, could not understand why Hartranft did not rush the Rohrback Bridge, so he dispatched Lieutenant Hudson to get an answer. Hudson set off "at a good round gait." A friendly shell struck the creek in front of him just as he arrived at Hartranft's position. He found the colonel close to the bridge and asked Ferrero's question. "Does he desire it?" asked Hartranft, which, given his orders, seems an odd question, but perhaps the Pennsylvanian was incredulous at Ferrero's query. Hudson answered, "Yes." Hudson then dashed over to Lieutenant Colonel Potter, instructing him to follow the Pennsylvanians over the bridge.

Potter ran to Hartranft and asked him "what was the matter." The colonel replied that the fire was so hot, his Pennsylvanians had taken cover, and he could not budge them from it. Potter took a few cautious steps onto the bridge, survived his exposure there, and decided that an aggressive charge could carry it. Potter then asked Hartranft if he could try to lead his New Yorkers over the Rohrback Bridge. Hartranft approved, and Potter shouted at his men to follow him onto the bridge. With the din of firing, Captain Stephen B. Chase, leading the 51st New York's company that was closest to the bridge, could not hear the command and went over to Potter to ask what he wanted. "I want you to come over this bridge with me," he replied. Chase ran back and got his company moving.[34]

At the same moment when Chase's company started to move toward the Rohrback Bridge, Hartranft shouted orders for his Keystone Staters to join the advance. Company C, with the regimental colors, was nearest the bridge, and its captain, 35-year-old William Allebaugh, stirred his men from their shelter. A gate through the Lower Bridge Road's fence offered passage to the bridge, but as the Pennsylvanians crowded up to it, Benning's Georgians concentrated their fire on them, mortally wounding Davis Hunsincker, the company's first lieutenant, and hitting a number of other men. Nearly all of the casualties in the 51st Pennsylvania occurred during either the advance or this movement through the gate in the fencing. Company C counted 21 injured or mortally wounded men, including both of its lieutenants. For some reason the gate proved to be difficult to open, which accounted for the soldiers crowding up there. Corporal Levi Bolton in Company A, a Norristown, Pennsylvania, bricklayer, ran up to it. Despite receiving a severe wound in his arm, Bolton ripped the gate apart with sheer brute strength, freeing the way to the Rohrback Bridge. What was left of Allebaugh's company scrambled through this gap and onto the bridge, possibly slightly ahead of the New Yorkers. Who crossed first is irrelevant. Men of both regiments were pushing forward, eyes warily scanning the opposite bank of Antietam Creek. Some of them jumped into the creek, in order to wade across. Martin Reed watched a man in his company, who was one of the waders, pause midstream, shoot a Georgian out of a tree, and then continue on. By this point, the Confederates' fire had greatly diminished as the enemy retreated. Reed watched this same soldier climb up the creek bank, run to the body of Lieutenant Colonel Holmes, and relieve his corpse of a gold watch and two silver-mounted pistols.[35]

Two other Antietam Creek crossings by the Federals, above and below the Rohrback Bridge, sped up Benning's retreat. When the fire on them diminished, elements of the 28th Ohio discovered a useable ford 350 yards north of the bridge, at a bend in Antietam Creek, where a small feeder creek draining away from Sharpsburg joined it. Five companies, with over 350 men, splashed across here and advanced to where they could cover Lower Bridge Road. At around the same

The Rohrback Bridge. The 2nd Maryland and the 6th New Hampshire attempted to charge up the Lower Bridge Road, which is to the left of the photographer's wagon, behind the post-and-rail fence (*left*). The rail fence provided cover for the 11th Connecticut and, later, the 51st New York. The 51st Pennsylvania used the stone wall (*right*) for cover. The graves of the units' dead are in front of the stone wall (visible under magnification). Courtesy of the Library of Congress

time, two-thirds of a mile below the Rohrback Bridge, Ewing's Ohio brigade of around 900 effectives crossed the old ford there—the one the topographical engineers had thought was Snavely's Ford—shortly past noon. This movement by Ewing was presumably at the orders of Rodman, to whom Ewing was attached as support. The Ohioans met no infantry resistance from the steep western bank of Antietam Creek, because the 50th Georgia had bugged out. Friendly artillery fire was plastering the top of the hill, which partly explained the departure of the 50th, but the Ohioans noticed that some shells were coming from the opposite direction. Fortunately, these sailed harmlessly over their heads, sounding to one of Ewing's men "like a wild duck" in flight.[36]

Colonel Carr B. White's 12th Ohio led the brigade. He deployed skirmishers on the western bank of Antietam Creek, who scrambled up the steep slope and engaged the extreme right of the 2nd Georgia, driving the Confederates north, toward the Rohrback Bridge. Ewing pushed his regiments north toward the bridge, keeping them in the woods and just below the bluffs, to avoid exposing them to fire from John B. Richardson's and Brown's Rebel batteries. The Ohioans' movement steadily rolled up the 2nd Georgia's flank and threatened to envelop the regiment. In their haste to escape, the Confederates were forced to abandon some of their wounded. One of them was J. C. Spivey, a private in

Lieutenant Theodore Fogle's 2nd Georgia company. He was shot in the knee and helpless, so "we had to leave him on the field," lamented Fogle. "It was the hardest thing I ever had to do to leave him but we had to double quick to save ourselves from being taken prisoner." By the time Ewing's men had reached the 20th Georgia's front, Ferrero's troops were pushing over the bridge. Ewing's assistance in the capture of the Rohrback Bridge has long been overlooked, but Confederate sources confirm that it hastened their retreat.[37]

About the time that the two 51sts finally secured the Rohrback Bridge, the skirmishers in the 8th Connecticut reached Snavely's Ford. They were probably guided to it by the local citizen Rodman had enlisted to help find the ford. The main body of the 3rd Division halted on a bluff above Antietam Creek, overlooking this ford. The bluff provided what Lieutenant Matthew Graham in the 9th New York described as "an extensive view of a stretch of country toward our front and right, including much of the battlefield." They could see the smoke and hear the rattle of musketry from the fighting at the Rohrback Bridge, but Graham "could see no lines or masses of troops anywhere." Some Confederate batteries were visible—probably Richardson's, Eshleman's and Brown's—but otherwise the lieutenant saw only small groups of men, some mounted and others on foot, in the fields to the north. He watched a Confederate skirmish line—the South Carolinians from the small company of Walker's brigade who reinforced Toombs—move down toward Antietam Creek. Whiting's naval howitzers had been unhitched to cover the creek crossing by the Federals, and a single shot from one of these guns caused the Rebels to seemingly disappear "into the earth."[38]

Rodman detailed Fairchild's 1st Brigade to cross Antietam Creek under cover of Whiting's howitzers. Lieutenant Colonel Edgar A. Kimball's 9th New York, an excellent unit, although with a past record of being irreverent toward authority they did not respect, went first. These New Yorkers wore Zouave-like uniforms, although not the brightly colored ones of the 5th New York Zouaves. The 9th New York wore dark blue jackets, trousers with red trim, and a red fez, one of the most useless pieces of headgear in the war. Lieutenant Graham recalled that they followed an old woodlot or farm path down to the creek. Graham could not recall the ford's depth but remembered that it "was quite an effort to stem the current." To Charles Johnson, it "appeared to be rapids," rather than a ford, identifying one of the reasons why Snavely's Ford was not easy to locate. David Thompson, a Company G private, recalled that the water was waist deep, as did others, so wading Antietam Creek was not the frolic some Confederate writers claimed it to be. Midway across the creek, the Confederates, who had vanished under Whiting's shelling suddenly reappeared behind a stone wall paralleling the creek, about 150 yards away, and began shooting. "The fire was not very heavy," wrote Graham, although he overestimated the enemy's strength as consisting of two companies. The Rebels probably had no more than 20 or 25 men, which accounts for the scattered fire. The 9th New York had 373 officers and men, and the South Carolinians could do no more than harass their crossing. Still, they managed to hit two men in Graham's company, and perhaps some others. The New Yorkers did not reply, because the best tactic under such circumstances was to push quickly across the ford. Moreover, if they paused to fire, the water was deep enough that a wounded man might drown.[39]

Reaching the northern bank of Antietam Creek, the 9th New York immediately filed right, to gain the cover of the steep bluffs there. They were followed by the 89th and 103rd New York. While these units formed up, Rodman—who proved to be active, decisive, and energetic throughout—appeared on foot among the Zouaves and accompanied them up the slope, followed by the other two regiments. Starting from the creek, this bluff rose 185 feet in only about 200 yards. "The ground in front of my company was very rough and difficult and also very steep," wrote Lieutenant Graham. Fortunately, the New Yorkers met no resistance until they reached the summit, when "we came again in sight of the gentlemen who disputed our crossing the ford, but they were not having things so much their own way as they had then." These were not the same skirmishers Graham had seen earlier, as the Federals' advance had bypassed those Confederates. The ones encountered at the summit of the bluff were probably from the 50th Georgia. Whoever they were, they quickly fell back before the mass of blue uniforms.[40]

Colonel Edward Harland's 2nd Brigade dealt with the South Carolina skirmishers at the stone wall when his infantrymen followed Fairchild across Antietam Creek. Harland first dropped off the 8th Connecticut to support Whiting's battery; then sent the 4th Rhode Island, 247 strong and commanded by Colonel William H. P. Steere, forward; followed by the rookie 16th Connecticut, with over 700 men. Like many of the recently recruited regiments, the 16th had received little training, and the men acutely felt their lack of knowledge of even the most rudimentary tactical maneuvers. Jacob Bauer, a private, remembered "a kind of despondency and fear of being led into battle before we are fit which can not be overcome." During a halt on the march to Snavely's Ford, a sick call was made, which, a member of the regiment related, revealed the pre-battle jitters that gripped the greenhorns: "You would have laughed heartily had you been with us . . . of all the subjects of fits, colic, sudden faintness, taken short, heart disease, shortness of breath, diahoreah in fact all diseases known in Materia Medica had suddenly seized a hold on some." Some of the others in the 16th snuck off, slipping by their officers and noncoms. "What made it laughable," wrote William Reylea, "was that most of all these brave skulks were those same brave chaps who wanted a chance to draw a bead 'on old Jeff D.'" Reylea thought the shedding of faint hearts was a good thing. "We were now rid of the regimental rubbish," he opined.[41]

The Rhode Islanders also received a "scattering fire" from the Confederates behind the wall and around Snavely's farm buildings, west of the ford. Instead of filing right, toward the bluffs, the New Englanders headed left when they reached the northern bank of Antietam Creek, deploying Company H as skirmishers to deal with the South Carolinians and sending Company K to the left, as flankers. The balance of the regiment formed in line and followed Company H, whose men quickly dislodged the Confederate skirmishers from the wall. As the South Carolinians beat a retreat, the Rhode Islanders began to receive fire on their left, coming from the direction of a large cornfield on a hill west of Snavely's farm. This was probably some of Munford's dismounted cavalry, who were armed with rifles. They drew the wrath of Whiting's howitzers, however, and subsequently swiftly disappeared.[42]

Colonel Francis Beach's 16th Connecticut followed the Rhode Islanders and formed up in support of the 4th's left flank. Beach sent two companies to the left, past Snavely's buildings, toward the farm lane to Myer's Ford. There they took some fire from Munford's dismounted skirmishers in the large cornfield, as well as from Eshleman's battery, about 600 yards to the northwest. Beach recalled these two companies when he received orders to move his regiment toward the bluffs on the right, where he would have better cover. The 4th Rhode Island followed. Lieutenant Colonel Hiram Appelman's 8th Connecticut, 421 strong, forded Antietam Creek and joined this movement, with Harland's whole brigade advancing up a ravine running along the western base of the hill that Fairchild's brigade had climbed. This brought them to the top of the reverse slope of a ridge east of the Otto farm lane, where they joined Fairchild's brigade. Once he had located Snavely's Ford, Rodman moved rapidly and efficiently, concentrating nearly 3,700 men, including Ewing's brigade, with Sturgis's regiments on the high ground southwest of the Rohrback Bridge.[43]

"There is no doubt that an earlier appearance of Rodman on this part of the field would have rendered unnecessary much of the great loss sustained in the successive attacks on the bridge," wrote Ezra Carman in his history of the Battle of Antietam. But an earlier appearance could only have been possible if two realities were changed: first, if Burnside received his attack orders earlier than he did; and second, if the army headquarters' topographical engineers had correctly identified Snavely's Ford. In the latter instance, this presumably would have led Burnside and Cox to position Rodman farther south, but this ignores the fact that these two officers were not the ones who decided where to place their divisions on the night of September 16. Staff officers from McClellan's headquarters did that. Burnside might have moved Rodman closer to what was believed to be Snavely's Ford when he received his early morning preparatory order, but the prime responsibility for Rodman's positioning and his delayed arrival at the actual site of Snavely's Ford rests with McClellan and his headquarters staff. This is an example of the possible consequences when higher-ups sideline their commanders and meddle in the details of troop placement, thus effectively squelching initiative. Finally, if Rodman had arrived at Snavely's Ford earlier than 9 a.m., he would have found it strongly defended by John G. Walker's Confederate division. Giving the timing of his orders and the faulty information he received about the location of the ford, Rodman reached this destination and moved his division across Antietam Creek about as quickly as possible under these circumstances.[44]

MOMENTS AFTER CAPTURING THE Rohrback Bridge, Hartranft's Pennsylvanians saw a squad of Rebels rise up from behind a large log, waving a newspaper attached to a ramrod. This group consisted of 1st Sergeant Farquhard McCrimmon and several other men in the 20th Georgia who had been cut off by the advance of the 28th Ohio. Hartranft called for them to come down, but McCrimmon and the others hesitated. The moment was fraught with tension. "The ground from the entrance on the road to the end of the bridge was strewn with the heroic dead and wounded," recalled the 51st Pennsylvania's historian, and McCrimmon may have sensed that the survivors were in a savage frame of mind. Nonetheless, Hartranft coaxed them down. Major Schall observed how, "with hesitation and trembling they descend. How they plead for their lives, as if savage-like we put to the torture and death our captures!" Hartranft repeatedly reassured them that they would not be harmed, to which the Georgians replied, "We treated your wounded and prisoners well at Bull Run." The moral compass of a combat unit in moments like this can be razor thin, but Hartranft provided the leadership that protected the prisoners. They were sent to the rear unharmed, as was another Georgian that Captain George W. Bisbing found trying to escape, carrying a drum. The "tall, ungainly" fellow placed the drum at Bisbing's feet and "protested most earnestly his innocence, declaring he was a recruit, had never fired a shot, and worse of all, had been impressed into the service." The oddest capture was that of two Rebels, found under the Rohrback Bridge, who had kindled a fire and were cooking a meal. Another Confederate was discovered "hidden behind the fork of two limbs of the tree, that he could hardly be seen," even at a distance of only 25 yards.[45]

As the 51st Pennsylvania re-formed in Lower Bridge Road, the 51st New York and the 35th Massachusetts, which had advanced down to the Rohrback Bridge immediately after it was captured, moved past them to ascend the bluff overlooking Antietam Creek. In all, 21 Pennsylvanians had been killed in the action and 99 wounded, almost a third of the regiment. Potter's New Yorkers counted 19 killed and 68 wounded. While the New Yorkers and the New Englanders moved past, those in the 51st Pennsylvania stacked arms and kindled small fires to boil water for coffee. It proved to be a fatal lapse by the 51st's officers, for the smoke from their fires rose above the trees along the creek, providing Brown's battery and probably some of the guns on Cemetery Hill with a perfect target with which to calculate the range for their shells. Shrapnel and shell soon began dropping and bursting in the vicinity of the Rohrback Bridge. "The shells were well aimed," wrote one member of the 51st Pennsylvania, and they scored a painful hit. The regiment's popular lieutenant colonel, Thomas S. Bell, had just returned from meeting with Ferrero. Passing Private Hugh Brown, Bell gave him a slap on the shoulder and exclaimed, "We did it for them this time, my Boy." An instant later, a shrapnel shell burst, sending one of its balls into the side of Bell's head. Bell was knocked off his feet, and he rolled down the slope to where the regiment's rifles were stacked. The injury bled profusely, and one of those who ran to his aid cried out that the wound looked mortal. Bell retained his senses and replied, "Never say die," but the wound was as serious as they feared. Within an hour the popular lieutenant colonel was dead.[46]

The 51st Pennsylvania was still on edge, and Bell's fatal injury, from guns unseen, struck the men as somehow unfair and wicked, and it stoked a murderous anger in their ranks. As the regimental historian, Thomas Parker, frankly admitted, "Could the rebels have heard the anathemas heaped upon their heads they would have fought harder than ever to keep from falling as prisoners into the hands of the men of the 51st P. V. Had any been unfortunate enough just then to fall into their hands it would have been far more than any officer could have done to save the captives from being torn to pieces by the now infuriated regiment." Earlier, the moral authority and leadership of Hartranft had prevented any violence toward prisoners, but Parker reminds us that under certain circumstances, authority had its boundaries. Fortunately, Sergeant McCrimmon and the other Georgia prisoners were out of sight by this point, and a potentially ugly incident was avoided.[47]

The attack on the Rohrback Bridge used up much of the ammunition in Ferrero's regiments. The cartridge boxes of the 21st Massachusetts were empty, and the 51st Pennsylvania was down to about six rounds per man. The 51st New York was probably in a similar condition. But Sturgis, Cox, and Burnside wasted no time in pushing these regiments, and the rest of the 2nd Division, across the Rohrback Bridge. McClellan fabricated the myth that Burnside dawdled after the bridge had been captured, writing that "a halt was then made by Gen. Burnside's advance until three P.M." According to McClellan's account, he had to prod the plodding wing commander into action by sending his aide-de-camp, Colonel Thomas M. Key, to order Burnside forward: "That this was the time when we must not stop for loss of life, if a great object could thereby by accomplished; that if, in his judgment, his attack would fail, to inform me so at once, that his troops might be withdrawn and used elsewhere on the field." This is pure claptrap. We might ask why, if Burnside's attack was so critical, it received no support from McClellan, who had already approved the withdrawal of the 5th Corps' infantry after they had cleared the Confederates off of Cemetery Hill and Cemetery Ridge? Why would McClellan express fear that the enemy might suddenly come bursting out of Sharpsburg, in numbers so overwhelming that they would pierce his center at the Middle Bridge and capture the Union army trains, yet opine that Burnside "should not stop for loss of life?"[48]

With the Rohrback Bridge captured, Colonel Ferrero sent Lieutenant Hudson across Antietam Creek, with orders for his regiments to form in the road beyond the bridge and then advance to the crest of the bluff above the creek. Hudson's experience in trying to deliver these orders provides some insight into the friction and delay commanders often encountered when trying to get their troops moving again after an engagement. Hudson found the bridge jammed with men in the 51st New York, which tends to lend credence to the 51st Pennsylvania being the first regiment, as a body, to cross the Rohrback Bridge. The lieutenant kept shouting, "Make way for an aide," but the soldiers—who often had disdained staff officers anyway—ignored him. Hudson found "it was almost impossible to get along at all." Spotting the 51st's acting lieutenant colonel, Hudson shouted to him, asking if he would pass along an order to Lieutenant Colonel Potter. The officer replied, correctly but unhelpfully, "That is a part of your duty, sir." Hudson could do nothing but wait until the jam cleared before delivering his orders.[49]

When Hudson returned, Ferrero sent him back with orders for the 35th Massachusetts to cross the Rohrback Bridge and occupy a hill north of Lower Bridge Road. When the lieutenant came back from that errand, Ferrero sent him off again, on this occasion to determine why the 51st Pennsylvania had not left Lower Bridge Road. Hudson was on foot, and each of these deliveries of orders took time, as well as carried some risk. He had just crossed the Rohrback Bridge when the Confederates' shelling began. The first shell "burst, and whizzed along the slope just above the precipitous bank beyond the road." It was followed by a second one, which did no damage. A third burst near Hudson and sent a deadly fragment into a tree, which had an officer "coolly leaning against its opposite side." Finding the Pennsylvanians down near Antietam Creek resting and boiling water for coffee, he asked them where Hartranft was. They gestured in one direction, but Hudson saw no officer there, so he again asked where their lieutenant colonel was. "There he is sir, wounded," came the reply. One of the shells that had struck near Lieutenant Hudson had mortally wounded Bell. A party carried Bell past Hudson, and the lieutenant saw a dark blue wound above Bell's left temple, as well as the man's dimming eyes. Hartranft suddenly appeared, and when Hudson asked why he did not move his regiment up the hill, Hartranft responded, "I've no ammunition." Hudson hurried back to share this news with Ferrero.[50]

Ferrero now judged it time to stop commanding from a distance, and he ventured forward to the front. That decision nearly cost him his life. After crossing the Rohrback Bridge, Ferrero sat down on the bridge's low wall. Moments later a rifle shell hurtled in. It struck the masonry only about 15 inches below him, "tearing away nearly the whole end of the wall, without doing him a particle of harm, but a mule standing a little below the bridge received the shell just as it exploded, tearing the poor beast to atoms." A photograph by Alexander Gardner and James Gibson, taken from above the bridge only 2 or 3 days later, clearly shows the damage the shell caused.[51]

While Ferrero dodged death, the rookies in the 35th Massachusetts marched up Lower Bridge Road for several hundred yards and ascended the hill north of the road, which was situated about 300 yards east of Joseph Sherrick Jr.'s farm and reached an elevation slightly over 400 feet. The left of the big regiment extended into the deep ravine through which the road ran, but the rest of the regiment was in a plowed field near the hill's summit. They drew fire from Brown's and Garden's batteries, and possibly from some other Confederate guns on Cemetery Hill. The New Englanders described the fire as "a terrible volley." It wounded Lieutenant James H. Baldwin, a 27-year-old Boston bookkeeper; killed David W. Cushing, a 30-year-old shoemaker; and cut Luther F. Reed, a painter from Westford, in two. Lieutenant Colonel Sumner Carruth immediately ordered his regiment to fall back behind the crest of the hill and lie down. The gruesome deaths of Cushing and Reed confirmed what Ferrero might have suspected: Rebel artillery commanded the open terrain between the Rohrback Bridge and the high ground south of Sharpsburg. No assault by an infantry formation could survive in that open space without friendly artillery support to engage the Confederates' artillery.[52]

Guns were on their way. Lieutenant George W. Silvass's section of Durell's Battery D, Pennsylvania Light, had been repositioned to Hill 415 during the preparations for Ferrero's assault on the Rohrback Bridge. Because of the woods on the hill, Silvass found it impossible to see any targets clearly. Although his section received fire from a Confederate battery to their right front, the Pennsylvania crews were unable to fix its position. The Rohrback Bridge was soon captured, and Silvass ordered his section to limber and drive down to it. They crossed the bridge shortly after the 51st New York and the 51st Pennsylvania, and probably before the 35th Massachusetts. Lieutenant Gilbert H. McKibben, a staff officer with 2nd Division headquarters—an indicator that Sturgis responded promptly after the Rohrback Bridge was carried—met them on the western side of Antietam Creek and ordered Silvass to proceed toward Sharpsburg, along Lower Bridge Road. This was an unwise order, but perhaps McKibben thought Union infantrymen were in front and would support the guns. Silvass's section drove past the two 51sts, which were re-forming beside the road, and then clattered up the road to where it turned west and hugged the northern nose of the steep hill, or ridge, immediately west of the Rohrback Bridge. The lieutenant halted his section before they revealed themselves and rode forward to reconnoiter a position for his guns. He found the hill to be too steep to work his artillery. One of his sergeants, Sam Rhoads, believed the guns would have recoiled to the bottom of the hill if they were fired on its slopes. Lower Bridge Road was sharply scarped on either side of where the section had halted, which made it problematic to turn the guns, limbers, and horses around. Silvass adopted a clever solution. He ordered the guns to be unlimbered, had the limbers turned around, re-limbered the artillery, and drove back toward the bridge.[53]

Near the Rohrback Bridge, Silvass met Prussian-born Captain William C. Rawolle, the 2nd Division's ordnance officer and an aide-de-camp to Sturgis. Rawolle accompanied the section as it drove past the bridge and moved along what Silvass called a "disused road." They followed it uphill, then turned right off the road and drove through a meadow, heading toward the crest of the same hill, or ridge, they had been on the northern nose of, minutes earlier. The summit of this irregular landscape feature, between 430 to 440 feet high, was about 150 yards east of the Otto farm lane and paralleled it. This elevated terrain extended for several hundred yards from north to south, with good fields of fire. But it was commanded by the higher ground of Cemetery Hill and the Harpers Ferry Road Ridge. Silvass halted his section below the crest, while he and Rawolle dismounted and crept forward to reconnoiter. The lieutenant also detailed two of his corporals to explore a different part of the ridge and report on what they observed. Silvass's section was situated off by itself, and Sam Rhoads recalled that no friendly or enemy infantry were to be seen.[54]

The corporals returned before the officers did and declared that the guns and their crews were dangerously exposed. If Confederate infantry advanced before any friendly infantry supports arrived, they could easily be captured. Silvass and Rawolle came back soon thereafter, and the Prussian expressed an opinion markedly at odds with that of the corporals. He and Silvass had seen a Confederate battery, probably Brown's, and Rawolle thought that with some stealth, they could take the Rebels by surprise. Silvass's view of this cockeyed idea is unknown, but Rawolle outranked him, so Silvass ordered his guns unlimbered and loaded. The crews would push them by hand to the crest of the ridge and then, hopefully, blast the enemy before they were spotted. Mercifully, as the gun crews began to push their pieces forward, Rawolle suddenly changed his mind. Union infantry—Nagle's brigade—came up in their rear and began to deploy behind the guns. Therefore the Prussian decided that if Silvass started shooting, it would draw artillery fire on the infantrymen. To everyone's relief, he ordered the artillery section to stand down and remain under cover.[55]

At the Rohrback Bridge, the 21st Massachusetts, after collecting cartridges from the dead and wounded—which is yet another example of Sturgis brooking no delay in pushing troops across Antietam Creek—traversed the bridge and joined the 35th Massachusetts on the hill, or ridge, north of Lower Bridge Road. Nagle's 1st Brigade followed, except for the 2nd Maryland, which was left behind to recover after their role in the previous attempt to capture the Rohrback Bridge. The 48th Pennsylvania, followed by the 6th and 9th New Hampshire, used the same farm path Silvass's section had taken, which brought them up in the rear of his guns. The main body of the regiments lay down on the reverse slope, but they sent skirmishers forward over the crest and slightly beyond the Otto farm lane. There they were fired on by some of Benning's Georgians, who had retreated to Sherrick's 40-acre cornfield, abutting the southern end of the lane.[56]

Ewing's, Fairchild's, and Harland's brigades began to arrive soon after Nagle, and they formed in the rear of the irregular, elevated terrain. More Union guns came up as well. Captain Clark's Battery E, 4th U.S., arrived on Silvass's left, but Clark halted and began to unlimber his four Parrott rifles on the exposed forward slope. Silvass rode over to speak with Clark and his officers, perhaps to warn him about the Confederate gun positions he and Rawolle had identified. Their conversation was brief, and Silvass turned his horse to ride back to his section. At this instant a shrapnel round, probably fired by Brown's battery, burst directly over the lieutenant's head. The killing zone for shrapnel was usually the area behind where the shell burst, which was precisely what happened. Silvass was untouched, but the leadership of Clark's battery was destroyed. Lieutenant William E. Baker was killed, the other lieutenant was injured, and Clark was seriously wounded from being hit in five places. Therefore 1st Sergeant Christopher F. Merkle took command and quickly had the battery's guns put into action against their tormentors. But Brown's Virginians, who did as much damage to the Federals that day as any other battery in the Army of Northern Virginia, had calculated the range to Clark's guns perfectly. From the perspective of Lieutenant Graham in the 9th New York, lying a short distance to the rear of the Regulars' artillery, Clark's gunners "did not appear to be able do much in the way of firing, as it seemed to me that every time they would get fairly at work the rebels would concentrate such a fire on them as to silence them; and the men would be obliged to lie down in such shelter as they could get until the weight of the enemy's fire was directed to another part of the line." Graham thought the Rebel's artillery barrage "was something wonderful in its accuracy; they dropped shot and shell right into our lines repeatedly."[57]

It was now shortly after 1 p.m., and Captain Durell soon came up with the other four guns in his battery. The Southerners' artillery, Toombs's infantry in the 40-acre cornfield, and skirmishers in the 7th Virginia, located behind a stone wall about 400 yards to the west, greeted the Pennsylvanians with shells, shot, and bullets. But their fire was inaccurate, and Durell's crews quickly and efficiently unlimbered and unleashed the fury of their Parrott rifles. Brown was silenced first, and then Durell turned his artillery on the other Confederate units. Whenever he shifted his fire, Brown's dogged crews would filter back to their guns and begin shooting again. This would draw the attention of Durell's pieces back on them, and the process would repeat itself. Silvass moved his section up to join the rest of his battery, which gave the Federals 10 rifled guns in action west of the Rohrback Bridge. They were unable to completely suppress the Confederate artillery, but they ended the Rebels' unchallenged command of the terrain west of the bridge.[58]

As Sturgis, Rodman, Ewing, and Crook massed their Union forces on the western bank of Antietam Creek, Jacob Cox arrived to take a personal look at the situation. He met Sturgis, who told him that the 2nd Division was in no condition to spearhead an assault on the Harpers Ferry Road Ridge. Several regiments had sustained heavy casualties, and most of them needed a resupply of ammunition. Cox also learned that Crook's 11th and 28th Ohio required more cartridges, too. It was evident that reinforcements would be necessary to renew the 9th Corps' attack. He sent a message back to Burnside, requesting the corps' commander to send over Willcox's 1st Division, along with an ammunition train. Cox also wanted more artillery, and he summoned Lieutenant Charles P. Muhlenberg's Battery A, 5th U.S., with 6 Napoleons. Cox's decision to wait for Willcox, extra ammunition, and more artillery before renewing the 9th Corps' attack was the correct one. Critics might fantasize that he should have "hurled" Sturgis, Cox, and Scammon against the heights south of Sharpsburg, but such an attack would have been piecemeal, would have lacked adequate artillery support, and, most likely, would have failed. The Confederates on the 9th Corps' front were unshaken and undefeated, and their guns had excellent fields of fire over the undulating but largely open ground that would have to be crossed to seize the Harpers Ferry Road Ridge. The best hope to drive off the Rebel defenders and seize the ridge was for the 9th Corps to concentrate its strength, put adequate artillery support into position, and launch a coordinated assault by the entire corps. Cox's patience in doing precisely the same thing at South Mountain, with a division, paid off with a victory that swept Garland's brigade of North Carolinians from the field. He hoped to duplicate that feat with a corps this time.[59]

THE EFFORT TO CAPTURE the Rohrback Bridge had consumed over 3 hours and cost the 9th Corps approximately 101 killed, 443 wounded, and 9 missing. These losses included several key combat leaders: Colonels Kingsbury and Coleman, and Lieutenant Colonel Bell. Less than 400 Confederate soldiers had inflicted most of this damage, although they had also had effective artillery support, which rarely gets enough credit. Benning's Rebel defenders suffered about 110 casualties. Their stubborn stand was crucial in buying precious time for Lee and the Army of Northern Virginia. In subsequent memories of this part of the overall battle, their defense of the bridge has become of the stuff of absurd hyperbole, including comparisons with the Spartans at Thermopylae. Nonetheless, what Benning and his Georgians accomplished with a small force was impressive. Benning deployed his men skillfully, which reduced casualties and made it difficult for the enemy to accurately target his position. His officers and men fought courageously and tenaciously, and, crucially, exhibited superb fire discipline. This enabled them to have their 60 rounds of ammunition each—they received no resupply—last through three assaults. The cover they built, while not as formidable as it might have been had the conflict occurred in 1864, was still good enough. Lieutenant Hudson studied their position after the fight and was impressed: "The rebels were posted behind trees & natural projections of the rocky, wood covered slope, along the brow of the slope, behind little curious shelters made of rails, in the form of small lunettes & provided with loopholes (the rails couldn't be laid close you know), and in a few cases up in the trees." They had "galled the assailants of the bridge almost without being seen." Hudson thought 200 men composed the sum total of the Rebel defenders, underestimating their strength by half, but still recognizing that having additional men would only have increased the number of their casualties, without achieving anything more. The effectiveness of the Confederates' cover can be appreciated when we consider that a single small regiment, the 21st Massachusetts, fired between 5,000 and 8,000 rounds in this engagement, with little appreciable effect.[60]

The Union attackers of the Rohrback Bridge rarely receive credit, but they, too, fought with mettle and determination. Numerous leaders distinguished themselves. Kingsbury, Griswold, Duryée, Griffin, Pearson, Hartranft, Bell, Potter, and others all were conspicuous in their skill and bravery, leading their men and inspiring them to take great risks. Their management motivated the enlisted men in most regiments to fight doggedly, with many firing nearly their entire load of ammunition before they retired from the field. None of the three attacks on the Rohrback Bridge were mindless or carelessly planned frontal assaults, which is how they are typically characterized. The plan of the first attack was for the 11th Connecticut to engage the enemy as skirmishers and draw their fire, while Crook's brigade stormed the bridge. The 11th Connecticut carried out its role, but at great cost to the regiment. The attack collapsed because Crook utterly botched his mission by failing to have his brigade ready, conducting no reconnaissance, and being ignorant of the terrain and the objective of his orders. This initial repulse caused Sturgis, along with his brigade and regimental commanders, to believe that a quick dash by a couple of regiments, supported by strong covering fire, might succeed in capturing the Rohrback Bridge. In the second attack, they underestimated how long the assault troops would be exposed to the Rebels' accurate shooting, however, and they may have believed that the Federals' covering fire would be more effective in suppressing the enemy than it was. The final attack was well planned and executed, and it was better supported by artillery than the others. It also had two significant advantages: the earlier attacks had caused the Confederates to burn through most of their ammunition, and the Rebels' flanks were threatened by Ewing's and Crook's brigades.

The Rohrback Bridge would become known, derisively and mockingly, as Burnside's Bridge, with this nomenclature reflecting the alleged stupidity and futility of his effort to capture it. Henry Kyd Douglas, on Stonewall Jackson's staff, was a local resident before the war, as his home was Ferry Hill Place, on the Maryland side of the Potomac River, overlooking Boteler's Ford. He helped fuel the contempt for Burnside. Douglas wrote that with a hop, a skip, and a jump, the 9th Corps could have crossed Antietam Creek without wetting their waist belts. Douglas knew this was untrue on September 17, 1862, as there was no point on the 9th Corps' front that was not defended by Confederates, and the creek was deeper than Douglas claimed, with steep banks in the 9th Corps' sector. But after Burnside's subsequent actions at Fredericksburg in December 1862, the "Mud March" in January 1863, and the Battle of the Crater in 1864, he was an easy target to pick on as a blunderer. McClellan worked as assiduously as anyone to foster a negative view of Burnside's generalship at the Battle of Antietam, especially in his efforts to capture the Rohrback Bridge. Initially, however, McClellan breathed not a hint of censure about Burnside's management of the battle. In his October 1862 report, McClellan noted that the 9th Corps' mission was a "difficult task" and pointed out the many natural features favoring the Confederate defenders. The effort to capture the Rohrback Bridge was "obstinate and sanguinary," and it was because of the "great natural advantages of the position" that Burnside was unable to seize it until 1 p.m. on September 17. There was no criticism of the time that had elapsed between the capture of the bridge and the renewal of the 9th Corps' offensive around 3 p.m.[61]

When McClellan published his more extensive report in August 1863, covering the entire period of his control of the Army of the Potomac, circumstances had changed. McClellan had been relieved of command of the army, and his generalship at Antietam was being criticized. Fitz John Porter, McClellan's favorite subordinate, had been court-martialed and dismissed from the army. The court's finding against Porter was assisted by the Porter-to-Burnside telegrams sent during the Second Manassas Campaign, which the latter had, without malicious intent, forwarded to the U.S. War Department. Burnside, meanwhile, had failed spectacularly as commander of the Army of the Potomac and had been relieved. He was an easy scapegoat for McClellan to serve up for the army's failure to achieve a more complete victory at the Battle of Antietam. A reference to McClellan's alleged 8 a.m. attack order to Burnside first appeared in this August report. No longer was there any mention of fierce enemy resistance or the significant natural features favoring the Confederate defenders. Instead, McClellan complained that only "after these three hours delay" was the Rohrback Bridge captured, implying that Burnside had wasted time and needed continual prodding to carry out his orders. In his memoir, *Own Story*, McClellan doubled down on this theme, writing that when a second aide-de-camp returned to him with a report that the Rohrback Bridge was still in enemy hands, he sent his inspector general, Colonel Delos Sackett, with "positive orders" for Burnside to take the bridge "at the point of the bayonet," if necessary, and for Sackett to remain with Burnside, to "see that this order was executed promptly." The inference, of course, was that without this goad, Burnside would not have attacked. McClellan complained of "the very pernicious effects of Burnside's inexcusable delay in attacking the bridge," and expressed the opinion that "if Porter or Hancock had been in his place the town of Sharpsburg would have been ours, Hill would have been thrown back into the Potomac, and the battle of Antietam would have been very decisive in its results." This was pure hogwash.[62]

Burnside's subsequent record firmly established that he was no Napoleon Bonaparte, but he had performed well at South Mountain and again at Antietam. There was no delay in opening his attack on the Rohrback Bridge after receiving his orders *at 10 a.m.* When that first attack did not succeed, a second was quickly organized. When it, too, failed, a third was immediately assembled, which was successful. There were time lapses between each attack, because it was necessary for the Union officers to reconnoiter and arrange for supporting fire. Sturgis's report makes it clear that Burnside personally impressed upon him the urgency of capturing the Rohrback Bridge. Once the bridge was seized, Burnside and Cox pushed three divisions, totaling nearly 9,000 men, across Antietam Creek in less than hour, an efficient and rapid concentration of force. While it is possible to criticize the failure of these two generals to position their troops closer to the Rohrback Bridge after receiving their early morning preparatory order, the plan for each of the attacks was reasonable, given the need for haste, the enemy's concealment, and the limited number of approaches to the bridge. Burnside did not intend to simply try a frontal assault to capture the Rohrback Bridge. Based on what he had been told about the location of Snavely's Ford, he believed that Rodman could cross Antietam Creek there and outflank the bridge's defenders while they were involved in meeting the initial assault. That failure also could not be laid solely at Burnside's feet. He had no reason to suspect that the topographical engineers' reconnaissance inaccurately identified Snavely's Ford, or that they had not positioned Rodman's division close to it.

McClellan bears much of the responsibility for how events unfolded on the 9th Corps' front. His headquarters had selected the bivouac site for each of the 9th Corps' divisions on September 16, placing the corps in a defensive posture, rather than in one a corps' commander might have adopted in anticipation of being ordered to attack. Burnside and Cox were discouraged from showing any initiative. Indeed, Burnside received a blistering rebuke for the slowness of his 9th Corps in taking up their positions on September 16, when the cause for that delay had also been due to McClellan. While it is true that the Confederates guarded all the fords on Antietam Creek and made reconnaissance by the Army of the Potomac's topographical engineers difficult, there is no evidence that these elite officers collected information about the fords from residents in the area. Isaac Rodman located Snavely's Ford because he used a local guide.

The notion that Fitz John Porter might somehow have led the 9th Corps to Sharpsburg, driven A. P. Hill across the Potomac River, and secured a decisive victory for the Union army is ludicrous. Porter was a fine soldier, particularly on the defensive, but he behaved with extraordinary timidity at the Battle of

Antietam. At the Middle Bridge, Porter had his opportunity to demonstrate the aggressiveness McClellan claimed he possessed (see chapter 14). When Captain Dryer exercised initiative and, without orders, drove the Confederates from Cemetery Ridge and Cemetery Hill, real opportunity knocked for Porter, but he did not seize his chances.

It was understood at 9th Corps' headquarters that their attack was to be a diversion from the main attack on the Confederates' left and left center. McClellan's initial report sustains this. "The effect of Burnside's movement on the enemy's right was to prevent the further massing of their troops on their left," he wrote. Cox believed that McClellan's initial 10 a.m. orders to Burnside to open his attack were sent in response to the disaster caused by Sedgwick's defeat on the Union army's right. Cox was wrong in this, but correct in believing that the pressure later applied to Burnside was a result of this calamity on the right. The orders to Burnside were sent when those at army headquarters still believed that the engagement on the right was going well and knew that the 6th Corps was approaching. This was in keeping with McClellan's idea of using the 9th Corps as a diversion, to prevent Lee from stripping troops from his right to reinforce his left. It was only after Burnside's attack orders were sent that army headquarters learned of the crisis on the right. This accounts for their increasing insistence that Burnside quickly capture the Rohrback Bridge and attack the heights south of Sharpsburg. There never was any thought that the 9th Corps' attack would capture Sharpsburg and win a decisive victory in the overall conflict at Antietam, something McClellan invented in his second report and his later book, *Own Story*. It was always seen as a diversionary assault, but the attempt morphed from an attack to *assist the main effort* on the Federals' right to one that would *prevent disaster* on the right by occupying the attention of the Confederate forces south of Sharpsburg.

AS WILLCOX'S 1ST DIVISION and ammunition wagons moved to join Cox on Antietam Creek's western bank, A. P. Hill's division was on a hard march from Harpers Ferry to reach the current battlefield, and Lee was desperately collecting pieces of his other batteries to support the depleted ranks of D. R. Jones's brigades, who were defending the heights south of Sharpsburg. Would Hill arrive in time—before the 9th Corps resumed its attack? The clock was ticking, and the Battle of Antietam hung in the balance on that very question.

17

A Famous March and a Desperate Assault

"May I never be doomed to witness such a sight again"

Captain Andrew B. Wardlaw, a South Carolina planter before the war, and now commissary officer for the 14th South Carolina Infantry of Brigadier General Maxcy Gregg's brigade of A. P. Hill's Light Division, and his friend, Lieutenant Edmund Cowan, in Company G, made their way to the Shenandoah River early in the morning of September 17. It was warm and pleasant—65 degrees at 7 a.m.—and the two men enjoyed a "first rate wash" in the cool water, sluicing the grime of Maryland and Virginia from their bodies. On coming back, they found the division's camps buzzing with activity, with everything packed up, and regiments and brigades forming up to march. The previous day, the division had received orders to march to Sharpsburg at 5 a.m., and Wardlaw had been up before daylight issuing rations from the provisions they had captured from the Yankees at Harpers Ferry. They had then marched 3 miles from town before a halt was called, and the division returned to the Ferry. A. P. Hill never even mentioned this movement, but clearly either Robert E. Lee or Stonewall Jackson had summoned the division to follow the rest of Jackson's command on the 16th. Lee apparently countermanded the order, but not soon enough to save the men's legs from an unnecessary trek.[1]

This time it was not a false alarm. Hill had received orders from Lee at 6:30 a.m. to proceed immediately to Sharpsburg with his division, leaving behind whatever force was necessary to secure the remaining supplies at Harpers Ferry. The Virginian had anticipated these orders, and on the night of the 16th, he instructed his brigade commanders to have their commands ready to march early on the 17th. It took only an hour for the division to break camp and assemble its brigades. Hill selected the Georgia brigade of Colonel Edward L. Thomas to remain at Harpers Ferry and supervise the disposition of the captured supplies. The remaining five brigades of the Light Division would make the march to Sharpsburg. For the first time in quite a while, the men were not famished. They had eaten well on captured Union stores. Moreover, the Federal army had also served as quartermaster for many Confederates whose uniforms were literally in tatters. On the day of the Union garrison's surrender at Harpers Ferry on September 15, Wardlaw noted how the ground was "pretty well covered in places with old clothes which our soldiers had thrown off, substituting new ones." Their replacement apparel consisted of Union army uniforms. Sergeant Robert T. Mockbee, who was in the 14th Tennessee of Brigadier General James J. Archer's brigade, recalled that when they left Harpers Ferry, his entire brigade, "but for the tattered battle flags might have been taken for a brand new brigade from Boston so completely were they clothed in Yankee uniforms." Numerous Union soldiers who fought against A. P. Hill's men that day—far too many for it to be an error due to battlefield chaos—commented on Confederates in Union uniforms and the confusion it caused. But trickery and deception were not the reasons why many of Hill's men donned Federal trousers or jackets, and sometimes both. The division was one of the most combat-experienced units in Lee's army, and from Hill on down, every officer understood that wearing the enemy's uniform onto a battlefield entailed the great danger of being subjected to friendly fire. They probably allowed their men to don parts of Yankee uniforms because of the deplorable condition of clothing in the division after weeks of hard campaigning, which contributed to straggling and sickness, and the officers made a conscious choice to accept the risk.[2]

No unit in the Army of Northern Virginia had done more fighting than A. P. Hill's Light Division since the start of the Seven Days Battles. It incurred 4,191 casualties in the Battles of Mechanicsville, Gaines' Mill, and Glendale; 434 at Cedar Mountain; and 1,845 at Second Manassas. Straggling and sickness had further whittled the division's strength down from its original figure of 13,000 at the beginning of the Seven Days Battles to around 4,000–5,000. A popular saying was that these were the hardest, toughest men in the division, but a soldier still in the ranks probably thought of himself merely as lucky. Some of them were hard, tough men, physically able to withstand the war's adversities and mental anguish, but many were just fortunate to have been spared from bullets or disease. As we shall see, not all of the rank and file relished the idea of marching into another battle. The division's numbers may have been greatly diminished, but its officers and men knew their business as soldiers, including how to hit hard and fast on the battlefield.[3]

Everyone heard the dull thumping of artillery from the direction of Sharpsburg, which lent urgency to their preparations to march. Brigadier General Maxcy Gregg's South Carolina brigade led the division out of Harpers Ferry at 7:30 a.m. The 17-mile march to Sharpsburg would become the stuff of legends, but the participants had surprisingly little to say about it. The statement of Colonel James H. Lane, commanding the 28th North Carolina in Branch's brigade, was typical. He remembered only that "we marched very rapidly." No one mentioned singing or joking. It was a hard, relentless, grueling tramp. "The day was hot and dusty in the extreme," recalled Lieutenant James F. J. J. Caldwell, a Harvard-educated officer in the 1st South Carolina Rifles of Gregg's brigade.

Captain David B. McIntosh, one of Hill's most talented battery commanders, thought the day was "insufferably hot," adding that "the sun blazed fiercely and the dust was stifling."[4]

Hill never embraced Stonewall Jackson's system, which dictated 50 minutes of marching, followed by 10 minutes' rest. This had resulted in Hill being placed under arrest by Jackson during the march to Leesburg before the Confederate army entered Maryland. Hill could press his men on mercilessly when necessary, but he could also be careless in managing a movement. This day, his men got the hard-driving Hill. "All along the way we heard the boom of canon, almost in our front," wrote Lieutenant Caldwell. The distant rumble was a constant reminder that every minute might count. Hill had to choose between Jackson's system, which was intended to both rest the men and reduce straggling, or accept some degree of straying as the tradeoff for greater speed. His choice fell between the two options, but leaned toward the latter, allowing only a handful of very brief rest stops. Some loss from straggling was acceptable, but arriving on the battlefield with a division so fagged out that it was ineffective was not. The pace was what Caldwell described as a "rapid gait." Robert T. Mockbee called it a "quick step." The rest stops were so brief and so few that Joseph D. Joyner, a private in Brigadier General Lawrence O'Bryan Branch's North Carolina brigade, thought they made the march "without resting," but Caldwell and others noted there were two or three stops to "draw breath."[5]

At each halt, Robert Mockbee noticed that his comrades shed bits of their Union uniforms. When they departed, after having taken a brief rest, they "left the place marked by many cast off blue garments and the old faded gray coat or jacket took the place of the blue blouse or perhaps an officers fine coat." Enough men held onto to their new blue clothing, though, that from a distance—particularly in the smoky atmosphere of a battle—someone might mistake one of Hill's brigades for a Union outfit. The marching and stops left behind men, in addition to cast-off clothing. The sun, dust, and rapid pace, combined with bodies worn down by weeks of poor nutrition and exposure, caused men to give out. Ambrus R. Collins in Branch's 18th North Carolina offered an idea of what everyone had suffered in the summer's campaigning. "I hav bin on a march for 8 days and night," he wrote to his wife on September 8. "I am almost run to death and starved for water and sompin to eat and when I git water its mud and when I get my rations it is not fit to eat and when I git to lye down I have to ly on the ground." John F. Shaffner, the surgeon in the 33rd North Carolina, observed that "frequently we have subsisted on less than half rations & sometimes on none at all, but what the corn fields afforded. At other times we would have bread without meat then again beef without bread or salt. But there were occasions also on which we took more than we could consume," such as at Manassas and Harpers Ferry. The division leaked men with each mile. General Archer, who was sick and traveled for most of the march in an ambulance, reported that since so many men in his brigade had fallen out, he carried only 350 effectives onto the field at the Battle of Antietam.[6]

Not all of those who straggled were exhausted men, nor were they heroes deserving of the veneration they often receive. "Straggling is a great curse of the army, yet it seems almost impossible to prevent it," Captain Wardlaw complained to his wife. "I really believe that at least a third even of those reported present manage in some way to keep out of a fight." Dorsey Pender, commanding one of Hill's North Carolina brigades, was a strict disciplinarian. He complained that before the planned attack at Harpers Ferry, more than half of his brigade found some way to avoid combat. If Wardlaw's estimate was accurate, it meant that around 900 to 1,000 men—the equivalent of a good-sized brigade for the Confederates at Sharpsburg—left the ranks of Hill's Light Division during the march. Captain David McIntosh was disgusted to discover that not only were many of his artillerymen overcome with heat and fatigue, but the "fine looking western horses from Chicago" his men had captured from Battery M, 2nd Illinois Light Artillery, at Harpers Ferry "wilted alongside of the lead Confederate stock used to hard work and short rations."[7]

Despite all the attention A. P. Hill's march to Sharpsburg has received and the legends that surround it, in terms of distance and speed, it was not particularly notable in the Maryland Campaign. For example, Lawton's division traversed 23 miles on September 11, including climbing Turner's Gap. A. P. Hill's and J. R. Jones's divisions both tramped for 18 miles on September 10. The 15th and 17th Georgia of Toombs' brigade completed the longest march of any Confederate unit in the campaign, covering 31 miles on September 15. In the Gettysburg Campaign, General Alexander Webb's Philadelphia brigade made a trek of 35 miles in about 14 hours—a speed of 2.5 miles per hour, which is quite good—and General John Sedgwick's entire 6th Corps marched 34 miles in less than 24 hours to reach the Gettysburg battlefield. The leading elements of the Light Division reached the edge of Sharpsburg around 2:30 p.m., which meant that it took them approximately 7 hours to cover 17 miles—a speed of 2.4 miles per hour—which was a rapid pace, but not a remarkable one. Hill's march to Sharpsburg achieved prominence because Lee and his army faced defeat, and perhaps catastrophe, if the Light Division did not arrive in time.[8]

AS HILL'S REGIMENTS HURRIED on through the increasing heat and clouds of choking dust toward Boteler's Ford on the Potomac River, on the high ground south of Sharpsburg, the slender infantry brigades of Brigadier General David R. Jones's division and their supporting artillery girded themselves for the anticipated onslaught of the 9th Corps. With one of his brigades—Garnett's—busy with the advance of the 5th Corps' Regulars from the Middle Bridge, Jones was left with only four small brigades to confront the entire 9th Corps. Colonel

Joseph Walker's South Carolina brigade of 755 men lay on the reverse slope of Cemetery Hill, supporting Squires' and Moody's batteries on the forward slope. The 27-year-old Walker, colonel of the Palmetto Sharpshooters, had been a Spartanburg merchant before the war, but he had proved to be a fine military man. Later on in the war, James Kemper wrote that Walker was "a capital soldier, a good disciplinarian, and peculiarly adapted to command of our citizen soldiers." Walker had spent the morning and afternoon trying to keep his men under cover. Around 9 a.m., they had moved from their original position in Jacob Avey's orchard, south of the ravine through which Lower Bridge Road ran, to the reverse slope of Cemetery Hill, where they endured shelling that "came down upon us at a terrible rate." Dr. James R. Boulware, the surgeon in the 6th South Carolina, was in Sharpsburg, just to the rear of the brigade, and he described how the Federals' shells, intended for the Confederates' artillery and their supporting infantry, often overshot them and pierced "nearly every house in Sharpsburg—setting several on fire. We were behind one [house] when their shots came through it, one shell bursting inside and setting it on fire which some of our boys extinguished after some difficulty. Every glass window was shattered and the house (a brick building) filled with breeches in its walls, bricks were thrown over all of us, our eyes, hair and clothes filled with dust. I left that place and while passing to another place one passed (I think) in two feet of me, going through the cellar." How much damage the Union shells did to Walker's regiments is unknown, but Frank Mixson, a private in the 1st South Carolina, wrote later that "we had a good many hurt while in this position."[9]

The artillery fire buffeted the South Carolinians' morale, which was already tenuous, given the physical ordeal Walker's brigade had experienced in the last few days. They made the forced march from Hagerstown on September 14, including a punishing double-quick ascent to Turner's Gap; fought a battle there; and then retreated during the night to Sharpsburg. There were no rations for the exhausted, famished men. On September 16, Surgeon Boulware, whom we might expect fared better than the enlisted men, recorded that he had nothing but apples for breakfast and lunch, and for dinner the men were told to forage for green corn. These were their rations for at least 2 days—a recipe to play havoc with digestive systems. Adding to the general misery, the brigades were shelled throughout the day on the 16th. Nerves were taut and bellies rumbled and ached.[10]

From the ravine where Walker's right rested, the ground rose steeply to the undulating plateau of the Harpers Ferry Road Ridge. At the northern end of the ridge, which abutted the southeastern corner of Sharpsburg, where Jacob Avey's farm buildings, orchard, and small cornfield were located, the terrain reached an elevation of around 450 feet. As it continued southwest, in a rolling fashion, it climbed to just over 500 feet near where Harpers Ferry Road met Miller's

Sawmill Road. The entire length of the ridge commanded the 9th Corps' position along the bluffs west of Antietam Creek by anywhere from 20 to 70 feet—a significant advantage, particularly for artillery.

Jones placed Brigadier General Thomas F. Drayton's brigade of South Carolinians and Georgians, which had been mauled at the Battle of South Mountain, and Brigadier General James L. Kemper's Virginia brigade on the reverse slope of the northern end of this ridge, immediately south of Avey's orchard. Drayton counted just 610 men in his four units (the 50th Georgia was detached to support Toombs). Kemper's five regiments, only contained a total of 443. Both brigades were in the same state as Walker's, with the men worn out and hungry as wolves. At one point during the period between September 15 and 17, the men in the 50th Georgia complained that they went "over forty-eight hours without any thing to eat or drink." It seems impossible, with all the water near them, that they had nothing to drink, but everyone seems to have gone without rations. Instead, they were turned loose to raid orchards and cornfields for food. In Kemper's brigade, the 17th Virginia sent four men—which amounted to just over 7% of their regiment's strength of 55–2 miles to the rear at midnight on September 16 to obtain flour from their provision trains. They got the flour, but the wagons carrying the utensils to cook it had taken the wrong road and had not yet come up. The four men lugged their meager find back to Sharpsburg and began searching for someone in the village who still remained in their home. Most people had fled, and it took them some time to find a resident to talk to. Their earnest appeal obtained "one skillet and an old oven with the bottom half out." It was nearly daylight on September 17 when they finally got down to business of baking bread. By this point the Union guns across Antietam Creek began shelling Cemetery Hill, and a torrent of shells sailed over the hill and into the village, making the bakers' work perilous. The regimental historian wrote of how "two shells bursted in the yard in which they were cooking about ten yards from them; two more stuck the house behind which they were standing, and a fifth struck the adjoining house, bursted inside and set it on fire. They retreated and sought refuge in the cellar, but even that proved unsafe—a shell came down through two floors in their midst and buried itself in the ground, fortunately without bursting, else all would inevitably have been killed. From cellar to yard again they flew." Undeterred, the men carried on their work whenever they could, but it was nearly 3 p.m. before they finally had baked a batch of biscuits. Two of the cooks hurried to their regiment just as the 9th Corps began to stir from their positions near the Rohrback Bridge. The Virginians were among the most fortunate men along that slender Confederate line, for they at least had something in their bellies before they meet the advancing Yankees, due to the courage and determination of those four enlisted men.[11]

Drayton and Kemper supported Captain James S. Brown's Wise (Virginia) Battery of 4 guns (types and calibers unknown) and a section of Captain James

Reilly's Rowan (North Carolina) Artillery. These two batteries were located about 100 yards east of the Confederates' infantry, on the forward slope. Reilly's two guns sat outside the southeast corner of Avey's orchard, between it and some straw- or haystacks. Brown was situated about 150 to 200 yards south of Reilly. Both batteries had excellent fields of fire, and Reilly's guns commanded the ravine through which Lower Bridge Road ran up to Sharpsburg.[12]

Jones was forced to further deplete Kemper's small brigade in order to defend his wide front south of Sharpsburg. Sometime in the morning—probably after the departure of Brigadier General John G. Walker's division—he detached the 106 men in Colonel William Terry's 24th Virginia and posted them behind a stone wall on Harpers Ferry Road, about midway between where Miller's Sawmill Road and the Snavely farm lane join that road. They supported Captain Benjamin Eshleman's 4th Company of the Washington (Louisiana) Artillery, which was initially posted in front of the Virginians but, in the afternoon, was displaced to higher ground in the rear of the 24th, where its guns could cover the approaches from either Snavely's or Myer's Fords. Jones had also placed the Virginians here, to keep an eye on the Snavely farm lane, a likely Union avenue of approach from the ford. After the Rohrback Bridge fell, Jones raided Kemper's ranks again to detach Major Arthur Herbert's 7th Virginia—Kemper's largest regiment, with "117 muskets"—and sent them nearly 400 yards south, along the Harpers Ferry Road Ridge, into a small rectangular cornfield fronting a plowed field that extended to the soon-to-be heavily contested 40-acre cornfield of farmer Joseph Sherrick Jr. The regiment concealed itself near the eastern edge of the small cornfield and sent a strong skirmish line across the plowed ground to the stone fence separating it and Sherrick's cornfield. Sometime shortly before the 9th Corps' assault jumped off, Captain John B. Richardson's 2nd Company of the Washington (Louisiana) Artillery—which had driven through Sharpsburg, chased by a deluge of Yankee shells, when the Federals captured the Rohrback Bridge—clattered down Harpers Ferry Road and unlimbered in the 24th's rear, on a piece of high ground west of the road and opposite the southwestern corner of the rectangular cornfield.[13]

Jones's fourth brigade was that of Brigadier General Robert Toombs. The 2nd and 20th Georgia had scattered when they retreated from the Rohrback Bridge, but a portion of them, under Colonel Benning, rallied inside Sherrick's 40-acre cornfield. Here, Benning happily met the 15th and 17th Georgia of his brigade, as well as five companies of the 11th Georgia—in all, less than 300 men. They had spent the past 2 days on severe forced marches and had just arrived at the battlefield. While Benning was reorganizing the brigade, he received orders from Toombs—who continued to act like a division leader, although his only command was his own brigade—directing him to defend a "stone fence far to the right of the road from the bridge and stay there until relieved by some of A. P. Hill's troops." This fence was probably the stone fence between Sherrick's cornfield and his plowed field to the west. Since Benning's orders were to hold this position until relieved by A. P. Hill, they confirm that Hill had sent word ahead regarding where he and his men were and the approximate time of their arrival. Benning may have felt that the position Toombs wanted him to occupy was too exposed, for he let the men of the 2nd and 20th Georgia go to the rear to resupply with ammunition and moved the 15th, 17th, and 11th Georgia into a ravine in the cornfield, where they had better concealment. But someone on the 9th Corps' front detected this movement, and one or more of the corps' batteries began dropping shells into the corn. One of them had the misfortune to explode directly over Thomas Sales, the color bearer of the 15th Georgia. Ivy Duggan, a Company K private, wrote about how the explosion "tore our flag, flag bearer, and one other man all to pieces." Nat Bradford, a private in the color guard, was the second man killed by this shell, and J. Samuel Hudson, another color guard sergeant, was so terribly mangled that he died later in the day. Several others were wounded. Duggan, who witnessed the single shell's ghastly effect, declared, "A more horrid sight I have never seen."[14]

Beyond Toombs and the 24th Virginia, the only other Confederate troops on the right flank were Colonel Thomas Munford's cavalry brigade. Munford had only two regiments, the 2nd and 12th Virginia, with a combined effective strength of about 600 officers and troopers. They were spread out across a distance of nearly 2 miles, from where Harpers Ferry Road crossed Antietam Creek, near the Potomac River, to across from Snavely's and Myer's Fords. Munford deployed some dismounted skirmishers—"dangerous fellows but extremely useful to me," he wrote—near Snavely's farm. They sparred with Rodman's 3rd Division after it waded through Antietam Creek at Snavely's Ford, but they lacked the numbers and firepower to do anything more than harass a determined assault.[15]

All in all, until A. P. Hill arrived, this was everything D. R. Jones had on hand to meet a 9th Corps' assault: at most, 2,200 infantry, 600 cavalry, and 22 guns. There was no more infantry to be had, but General Lee was desperately attempting to collect every available artillery piece he could lay his hands on and send it to Jones's aid. Although Jones's force was thin, his location was probably the strongest natural-terrain position held by any of Lee's men during the conflict—except, perhaps, for the Rohrback Bridge—and was well suited for artillery. Jones also used the cornfields and undulating landscape to keep his infantry either concealed or under cover, making it difficult for the Federals to accurately gauge the strength of his infantry. The question that hung worryingly in the air for Lee, Jones, and every Confederate soldier on the Army of Northern Virginia's right flank was whether A. P. Hill would arrive before the enemy massing in front launched their attack.[16]

JACOB COX WAS WORKING hard to organize that attack. He knew time was of the essence. Every minute wasted enabled the Rebels to reinforce their position and better prepare their defense. But it was evident, from the volume of Confederate artillery fire blasting his line, that their defenses would not be breached with a hasty, uncoordinated attack. That was a recipe for a bloody repulse. He could not gauge the enemy's infantry strength, since they kept those men sufficiently concealed, but the number of guns firing at the 9th Corps indicated that the Rebels' artillery might be well supported. Cox was a volunteer officer, but he had quickly grasped the importance of concentrating strength and coordinating infantry and artillery, in order to ensure the success of his attacks. His division's late morning assault against Garland's brigade at Fox's Gap, during the Battle of South Mountain, had been a model of coordination and the application of combat power. Organizing such an attack involving thousands of troops, in an age before radio communications, was not done quickly. The men had to be moved into position under cover, objectives needed to be determined, and then they had to be communicated to the key assault formations. All of the other commands who were participating in the attack needed to know what their supporting role was. Coordination and communication consume a significant amount of time. For instance, it took Lee and Longstreet nearly 7 hours to complete the preparations for Pickett's Charge on July 3 at Gettysburg. Cox made his arrangements methodically, but there was no wasted time, despite what some of his critics might have claimed.

The rumor in Brigadier General Orlando B. Willcox's 1st Division was that they would be held in reserve on September 17. This may have been Burnside's or Cox's original intention, because Colonel Thomas Welsh, commanding the 2nd Brigade, wrote to his wife immediately after the battle, mentioning how "the general"—meaning Willcox—told him that morning "they would likely not be brought into action that day." This type of encouraging news frequently circulated among combat units before a battle. But the hope that they might get to sit this one out vanished when, sometime after 1 p.m., Willcox received orders to bring his division across Antietam Creek. Everyone understood the orders meant that they would also join the fighting. Willcox formed up his two brigades, and by 2 p.m. they were crossing the Rohrback Bridge, passing by the sobering sight of many of the Union dead who had not yet been removed and were sprawled around the approaches to the bridge.[17]

Colonel Benjamin Christ's 1st Brigade followed Lower Bridge Road to where it turned west, running up a deep ravine to Sharpsburg. The colonel had 1,395 effectives in his four regiments. They left the road here, continued north along the bank of Antietam Creek, and climbed the steep hill north of Lower Bridge Road, in order to relieve the 35th Massachusetts. The latter regiment then moved over to the hill south of the road. Christ sent the 79th New York forward, over the crest of the hill, as skirmishers and deployed the balance of his brigade on the reverse slope. Welsh's 2nd Brigade, counting 1,623 men in its four regiments, ascended the steep hill south of the Lower Bridge Road's ravine. The right of the brigade, held by the 45th Pennsylvania, rested in the ravine, with the 46th New York and the 8th Michigan extending the line up the slope toward the crest. Welsh covered his front with the 100th Pennsylvania, in skirmish order. They pushed over the crest as far as Otto's farm buildings and the farm lane that paralleled the hill's western slope.[18]

During this same period, Rodman's 3rd Division maneuvered into position behind the ridge where Clark's and Durell's batteries were located. Colonel Harrison S. Fairchild's 1st Brigade, consisting of 943 men in three regiments, deployed directly in the rear of these two batteries, with the 9th New York to the rear and right rear of Clark, the 103rd New York extending across the space between the two batteries, and the 89th New York directly in the rear of Durell. The right flank of the 9th New York rested only about 100 feet from the 8th Michigan, on Welsh's left flank. Colonel Edward Harland's 2nd Brigade, 1,848 strong, with its numbers boosted by the 750 men in the untrained 16th Connecticut, lay down in a plowed field slightly to the left and rear of Fairchild and Durell, facing Sherrick's 40-acre cornfield, which was downslope from them. Colonel Hugh Ewing's 1st Brigade of the Kanawha Division deployed about 200–300 yards in the rear of Harland, as a support. Crook's 2nd Brigade—numerically the strongest brigade in the 9th Corps, with 2,005 officers and men—massed in the rear of Welsh's brigade, along the slope of the steep bluff descending to Antietam Creek. The units in Sturgis's 2nd Division, with many of its regiments still waiting for an ammunition resupply, were concentrated in the space between Ewing and Crook.[19]

Moving sufficient artillery across Antietam Creek proved to be something of a problem, for reasons that are not well documented. Henry W. Woodbury, a 21-year-old enlisted man in the 8th Battery, Massachusetts Light, which was attached to Willcox's 1st Division, recalled that they drove down to the Rohrback Bridge sometime after it was captured but were prevented from crossing it for "several hours by reason of infantry having the 'right of way' over the bridge." A section of the battery, under Lieutenant John N. Coffin, probably equipped with 12 lb. James guns, did manage to get across and were sent forward along Lower Bridge Road to support Willcox's attack. Carman's 3 p.m. 1908 map of the engagement shows Lieutenant Charles P. Muhlenberg's Battery A, 5th U.S., positioned in a plowed field between Ewing's and Harland's brigades, but his battery suffered only 3 casualties that day, and there is no evidence that they were in this location when the attack began. Carman's early morning maps show Simmonds's, McMullin's, and Roemer's batteries placed on the ridge east of Rohrback's farm, where Benjamin's battery was located, but by the afternoon they disappear from his maps. Cox remembered Simmonds crossing Antietam Creek and being near Crook, but since Carman, who was very thorough in these matters, did not show the battery west of the creek in the afternoon, we must suppose that Cox's memory was incorrect on this point. Thus, a significant amount of firepower—four batteries, totaling 22 guns of various calibers—was not in position to directly support an infantry assault that afternoon.[20]

Was this a failure on Cox's part to assemble his available firepower to provide direct support to his infantry, which would be assaulting the formidable Confederate position? Perhaps, but we lack critical knowledge of these batteries' activities to make such a judgment. We would also need to know what Colonel George W. Getty, Burnside's chief of artillery, was doing to help Cox get guns to wherever they were needed. Perhaps Getty and Cox did not think there was space for another battery within the constricted area of the bridgehead, although Cox never mentioned this in a lengthy postwar letter about 9th Corps' artillery in the conflict. But there *was* room for one, on the hill where Christ's brigade was deployed. Such an oversight implies either that Getty and Cox failed to use all the firepower available to them, or that they did try to get guns to the front but were unable to do so before the attack jumped off. What evidence we do have indicates the latter; as both Muhlenberg's and Cook's batteries, and possibly Simmonds's, crossed Antietam Creek, but this did not happen until after the infantry assault began. Cox may have not wished to consume the time necessary to get these guns to the front and into position. Sunset came at 6:07 p.m., and he understood the need to get the 9th Corps' attack underway before he ran out of daylight.[21]

This meant that when the 9th Corps' infantry massed to make their assault, the Confederates had a significant advantage in artillery, with their 22 guns facing the 10 Parrott rifles of Durell's and Clark's batteries. Durell's battery held its own in this furious duel, but Clark's pieces, as already mentioned (see chapter 16), were repeatedly silenced. Durell's cannoneers and horses endured a "shower of bullets," both from Benning's skirmishers, who were in Sherrick's cornfield, and from the 7th Virginia's skirmishers, under cover behind the stone wall on the cornfield's western side. The Confederate volleys were long range— it was at least 500 yards to the stone wall—and more harassing than effective. For all the shells and bullets the Confederate batteries directed at Durell's Pennsylvania artillerymen, only two of the men were wounded—one of them mortally, from a shell that burst in front of their gun—and 11 horses killed or wounded. The annoying small-arms fire inflicted no casualties.[22]

The Rebels' artillery fire proved to be more unnerving to the infantry, who were lying prone in the rear of the guns, than it did to the artillerymen, who could focus on serving their guns. As Charles F. Johnson, a thoughtful 21-year-old private in the 9th New York, observed, "Soon the cannon balls mingled with the sharp play of small arms, and I noticed one of them coming like an india-rubber ball through the air. It struck the top of the hill, boring up a mass of earth, and then bounded high in the air, passing over our heads with a noise I can liken to nothing but the savage yell of some inhuman monster." Lieutenant Matthew J. Graham, positioned nearby, was equally articulate:

The practice of the rebel artillerymen was something wonderful in its accuracy; they dropped shot and shell right into our line repeatedly. They kept the air fairly filled with missiles of almost every variety, from shrapnel to railroad iron [a curious projectile, but mentioned by several other 9th Corps' soldiers]. The shrapnel or canister was very much in evidence. I saw one of our men in hospital afterward who had nine gunshot wounds in his right arm [probably shrapnel ball wounds]. I watched solid shot—round shot—strike with what sounded like an innocent thud in front of the guns, and, bounding over battery and park, fly through the tree tops, cutting some of them off so suddenly that it seemed to me they lingered for an instant undecided which was to fall. These round shot did not appear to be in a hurry. They came along slowly and deliberately, apparently, and there appeared no harm in them until they hit something.[23]

The 9th New York's commander, Lieutenant Colonel Edgar Kimball—a former Regular Army captain in the 9th U.S. Infantry who performed with distinction at Contreras and Churubusco in the Mexican War, and who seemed positively fearless to his soldiers—described the shelling as an "unmerciful fire of shot and shell" that inflicted a number of casualties in his regiment and took out his horse when a shrapnel round burst nearby. Some incident in the ranks of the nervous 16th Connecticut rookies caused "loud yelling mingled with curses," which then "gave rise to a general laugh" along the line. For some reason this outburst displeased their commander, Colonel Francis Beach, and he angrily rebuked them for their levity. This did nothing to improve the regiment's generally unfavorable opinion of Beach. Three days earlier, Jonathan Shipman, a Company C private, grumbled in a letter to a friend how, when several men in the regiment climbed a fence to raid an adjacent orchard, Beach came up, called one of the men to him, and "struck him with his sword, a favorite game with him." From what Shipman had observed, Beach and other officers "steal everything they want to eat." Opinions of the colonel were dark enough that the private declared ominously, "Many of the men swear they will shoot him if he ever goes into action with us."[24]

The deployment of Christ's brigade on the hill northeast of Sherrick's farm exposed the 28th Massachusetts to a flanking fire from either Eshleman's or Richardson's battery. The Confederates got the range and managed to "put in a few well directed shells and solid shots" before the regiment adjusted its position. But this did not happen until after a solid shot struck and killed 2nd Lieutenant Nicholas J. Barrett and Sergeant Thomas Cline in Company H, and other projectiles had caused "quite a number" of other casualties.[25]

The damage inflicted by artillery was not all one sided. The Confederates' infantry may have been concealed from view, but the Federals' gunners got their licks in on their Southern counterparts where they could. Brown's battery, which made life hell for the 9th Corps' infantry and Clark's battery, received special attention from Durell's gunners and some of the Union batteries on the eastern bank of Antietam Creek. Major William H. Palmer, commanding the 1st Virginia of Kemper's brigade, recalled that Brown's Wise (Virginia) Battery "was soon knocked to pieces by the Parrott guns across the Antietam." Only one man was killed, and Brown and three privates wounded, but Palmer's statement implies that this battery probably suffered grievous losses in horses and equipment. It was disbanded less than a month later. Garden's Palmetto (South Carolina) Artillery on Cemetery Hill—targeted principally by Taft's, Weed's, and von Kleiser's batteries on the eastern bank of Antietam Creek—had one gun dismounted by a shot striking its axle, and another put out of action when a shell struck the muzzle of the gun. Major Abner C. Beckham, a volunteer aide-de-camp in Kemper's brigade who had celebrated his nineteenth birthday just 6 days earlier, sat on his horse in front of the brigade, where he was exposed to fire. John Dooley, in Kemper's 1st Virginia, saw the young man rise up in his stirrups, cheer enthusiastically, and whirl his hat around his head when Brown's guns opened fire on the Yankees. An instant later, Dooley and others watched, horrified, as the young major "was hurled from his horse by a shot and his foot terribly mangled" by a Parrott shell. Kemper and his staff gathered around the stricken major. His foot was destroyed, but the terrible wound did not diminish his enthusiasm, and he continued cheering as Kemper and the others disappeared from view with him, heading toward the rear.[26]

To the east, and across the entire length of the 9th Corps, the crack of skirmishers' rifles added to the cacophony of noises. Willcox had two entire regiments deployed across his front: the 100th Pennsylvania, in front of Welsh's brigade, and the 79th New York, screening Christ's. As the Highlanders of the 79th cleared the summit of the hill near Sherrick's farm, "we were then in full view of the enemy's lines, on still higher ground about a thousand yards beyond," wrote their regimental historian. Rebel gunners blasted their advancing line with shell, and an order to double-quick was shouted. "It was a terrible ordeal," wrote William Todd, and men were cut down at every discharge. But their open order saved them from a heavy number of casualties. They dashed past the farm, firing at the South Carolinians under Colonel Fitz W. McMaster's command in the Sherrick farm lane, who were attempting to fend off the 2nd and 10th U.S. Infantry. With the Highlanders threatening their flank and the Regulars pressing their front, the 17th South Carolina beat a retreat southwest, heading toward the Stone Mill and house owned by Solomon Lumm.[27]

When the 100th Pennsylvania crested the hill east of Otto's farm, "we could see their riflemen firing from behind a stone wall at about 400 yards distant," wrote Corporal Fred Pettit. These were skirmishers from Drayton's brigade, who used their cover to keep themselves largely concealed. Marinus K. McDowell, a 21-year-old farmer from Lawrence County, declared, "We could not see them but fire back as best we could." McDowell did not last long in the firefight. After his first shot, he dropped to one knee to reload and was hit in the thigh. He managed to finish loading his rifle, however, and loosed a bullet at the South Carolinians around the Stone Mill or Lumm's house. His sergeant, John L. Graham, seeing that McDowell was wounded, ordered a comrade to help him to the rear, but when just one man proved to be insufficient to provide assistance, another sergeant in the company James McCreary, volunteered to help carry the private back. Thus one bullet removed three men from the conflict.[28]

The 100th Pennsylvania's greater numbers and firepower soon flushed Drayton's skirmishers from their cover. "They skedaddled to another stone fence at the further side of the field," wrote Elisha Bracken. Besides the small-arms volleys, the Pennsylvanians received the attention of "two noble batteries about 800 yards from us which piled shot, shell and grape, and railroad iron at us thick and strong." They were probably Garden's and Reilly's batteries. Fred Pettit wrote that he and his comrades concentrated first on the Confederate skirmishers, who, after a lengthy firefight, were put to flight. Then the Pennsylvanians ran forward to some strawstacks about 100 yards farther in their front and turned their rifles on the Southern artillerymen, whom Pettit now estimated were 700 yards away. The Keystone Staters soon had the satisfaction of seeing one of the batteries, probably Reilly's, limber and drive off.[29]

Charles F. Johnson in the 9th New York was on the skirmish line of Fairchild's brigade. He and the others dashed over the ridge where Durell and Clark were located and downslope to the Otto farm lane. One of Sherrick's plowed fields in front of them extended for nearly 300 yards, reaching the wall sheltering the skirmishers in the 7th Virginia. Some of Benning's Georgians were visible to their left, along the edge of Sherrick's cornfield. The 9th's rifles quickly drove both groups of Confederates under cover, and the New Yorkers then turned their attention to Brown's battery, over 700 yards away. To lessen the range, the Federals worked their way forward, going across the plowed field to a ravine that bisected their front. Soon after they reached this cover, Johnson looked back to see one of the regiments in his brigade come "thundering along at the double quick" over the ridge behind him. It was 3:15 p.m., and the 9th Corps' assault was beginning at last.[30]

The deployment of the 9th Corps was complete by 3 p.m. Cox communicated to Burnside that all was ready, and the wing commander gave his approval for them to advance, with the qualification that Sturgis's 2nd Division be held in reserve. Cox had assembled a formidable force for his assault in the 2 hours since the bridge had fallen: 8,700 men, in six brigades. Robert Toombs, no stranger to bombast, later condemned the slowness with which Cox and Burnside had built up their forces after seizing the Rohrback Bridge and the ford above it: "Though the bridge and upper ford were thus left to the enemy, he moved with such extreme caution and slowness that he lost nearly 2 hours in crossing and getting

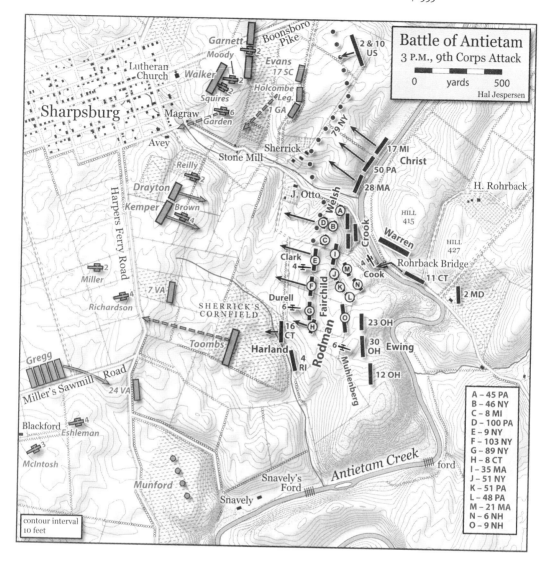

into action on our side of the river." McClellan, as has already been related in chapter 16, reinforced this uncomplimentary narrative when, in his second official report, he claimed that after capturing the Rohrback Bridge, "a halt was then made by General Burnside's advance until 3 p.m." At that point, McClellan stated, he sent his aide-de-camp, Colonel Key, "to inform General Burnside that I desired him to push forward his troops with the utmost vigor, and carry the enemy's position on the heights; that the movement was vital to our success; that this was a time when we must not stop for loss of life if a great object could thereby be accomplished." This, like Toombs's criticism, was drivel. There was no halt, no "extreme caution" or "slowness," by either Cox or Burnside. Events on a battlefield did not happen quickly, and physical communications were time consuming. Once the Rohrback Bridge was captured, Sturgis informed Cox that his division lacked the ammunition for a continued advance. Cox then requested Willcox's 1st Division to replace Sturgis, which required a staff officer to ride to Burnside's headquarters and deliver the request. Burnside immediately approved it, but then someone from his or Cox's headquarters had to ride to Willcox and deliver the orders. Then Willcox's division of 3,000 men needed to assemble, determine where they were going, march for over a mile, post skirmishers, and deploy their regiments from column to line, accomplishing all of this over difficult-to-maneuver terrain. Without *any* friction—no enemy trying to kill or maim you, no obstacles, no halts to assess the ground—it would be a 20-minute walk to cover the necessary distance. A column of 3,000 troops extends for nearly a mile, so, using this scenario, it would take 40 minutes for the tail of Willcox's division to reach its destination. But moving troops into position under enemy observation, relieving troops already in place, forming line, and deploying skirmishers is a slow process, even under the best of circumstances. That Cox managed to get all of his assault and supporting units into position and ready to advance by 3 p.m.—2 hours after the Rohrback Bridge fell—evidenced a great deal of energy and determination.[31]

As mentioned earlier (see chapter 15), Cox, in both his after-action report and postwar reminiscences, maintained that he understood the 9th Corps' attack was to be a "powerful diversion in favor of the center and right of the army." This may have been what he thought the 9th Corps' mission was, but he nonetheless prepared a sledgehammer blow, designed to sweep the heights south of Sharpsburg clean of Confederates and roll up Lee's right. Other than Hooker's morning attack, and the 12th Corps' advance that flushed D. H. Hill's division from the field to the north, no Federal assault was more carefully organized and executed that day.[32]

Cox's plan was relatively simple. Willcox, with Crook's brigade in support, would advance directly on Sharpsburg, orienting on Lower Bridge Road. Rodman, with Ewing supporting him, would first dislodge the Rebels in his front—Brown's battery and Kemper's and Drayton's brigades, located on the heights south of the village—and then change direction to the right, to bring his 3rd Division "*en echelon* on the left of General Willcox." It is clear from Cox's plan of attack that he and Burnside believed the forces in Rodman's front formed the right of the enemy's line, and when they were dislodged, the attack would roll up the Confederates' flank. The Rebel skirmishers in Sherrick's cornfield, Munford's cavalry, and the enemy artillery south of Kemper's and Drayton's brigades would be swept away by Rodman's advance, so they were not considered to pose any threat to his division's flank. The apparent flaw in the plan, however, was the exposure of his left flank as the attack progressed, when Rodman turned the axis of his attack toward Sharpsburg and the northwest. But Burnside and Cox did not see this as a problem, because their sources of intelligence informed them that no threat existed there. Before the attack went forward,

Burnside had sent a message to the signal station on Elk Ridge: "Can you see any movements of the enemy on the road or elsewhere?" The station responded, "Yes; they are moving now a strong force of infantry from Shepherdstown into the woods west of Sharpsburg and northerly to our right." This is a mystery, since no major Confederate troop movement to the north took place at this time, but, importantly, the reply reassured Burnside that the Confederates were not reinforcing their forces facing the 9th Corps. Yet the exposed flank still nagged at Burnside. Just to confirm that no enemy lurked behind the cornfields and ridges in front of his corps, he signaled back, "Can you see any movement of the enemy, particularly in rear of the corn-field in front of us?" The station responded, "I can see no movement, particularly in rear of that corn-field." The cornfield was undoubtedly Sherrick's 40-acre field, on the 9th Corps' flank. With this final reassurance that there was no danger to his flank, Burnside gave Cox approval for the assault to go forward.[33]

Unfortunately for the 9th Corps, at 3 p.m., as Cox issued attack orders to his divisions, confident that his left flank was safe from attack, a highly alarming signal message reached Burnside's headquarters. It warned, "Look out well to your left; the enemy are moving a strong force in that direction." It was A. P. Hill's division, moving precisely toward the point that had most concerned Burnside and Cox. Although signal officers claimed "this warning was in time, and it was noticed by General Burnside," it was not. By the time its contents were relayed to the wing commander, it was too late. The 9th Corps was advancing, and Hill's brigades were moving rapidly toward its vulnerable flank.[34]

CAPTAIN DAVID MCINTOSH'S PEE DEE (South Carolina) battery was the first unit of A. P. Hill's division to reach the Potomac River, arriving there between 2 and 2:30 p.m. Gregg's South Carolina infantry brigade followed. Branch's, Archer's, Pender's, and Brockenbrough's brigades, and the Light Division's other batteries, were strung out behind Gregg's men. Hill rode ahead to find Lee. Where they met is unknown. Lee greeted Hill with immense relief, exclaiming, "General Hill I was never so glad to see you, you are badly needed, put your forces in on the right as fast they come up." He directed Hill to consult with D. R. Jones for information about where, specifically, the Light Division's brigades were most needed, and to obtain details regarding the terrain. Captain Alexander C. Haskell, the acting chief of staff in Gregg's brigade, recalled that "Gen. Lee positively ordered that three brigades be held in reserve" from Hill's division. Based on how Hill committed his brigades, Haskell either misunderstood Lee's orders or his memory failed him here. It appears that Lee ordered Hill, in addition to moving at once to D. R. Jones's support, to detail part of his division to watch Snavely's Ford and Harpers Ferry Road, leading down to where it crossed Antietam Creek, near the mouth of the Potomac River. Lee could not know how many brigades Hill would need to assign, both for this mission and to blunt the 9th Corps' attack, so it unlikely that he specified a particular number to be held in reserve.[35]

While Hill met with D. R. Jones to discuss details the Light Division forded the Potomac River. John F. J. Caldwell in the 1st South Carolina wrote that "the current was quite swift, and the ledges of rock, cropping out at sharp angle, rendered the passage both difficult and painful." The men clambered up the slippery banks, but there was no halt to let them wring out their socks or dump water from their shoes. The column was urged on, the men "all wet and draggled." It appears that the division marched directly up a ravine nearly opposite the ford and then cut cross-country to Miller's Sawmill Road, accessing it where the road made a 90-degree turn east. Captain McIntosh remembered how orders to hurry "came in quick succession from the front." His teamsters urged their exhausted battery horses into a trot. The cannoneers, equally as exhausted as the horses, ran alongside. Many could not maintain the pace and fell out by the roadside.[36]

ON THE 9TH CORPS' front, Colonel Benjamin C. Christ, the 38-year-old commander of Willcox's 1st Brigade, rode up, took the colors of his old regiment, the 50th Pennsylvania, "and boldly rode forward with them" as the signal for his brigade to advance. Christ had been an educator, a coal merchant, and, immediately before the war, an innkeeper in Minersville. But he was one of those volunteer officers who excelled at soldiering. With the 79th New York deployed well to his front as skirmishers, Christ had three regiments in his brigade line—from left to right, the 28th Massachusetts, the 50th Pennsylvania, and the 17th Michigan—which had had its first baptism by fire only 3 days earlier, at the Battle of South Mountain. As the brigade crested the hill east of Sherrick's farm, Christ observed the Confederates' artillery on Cemetery Hill and Joseph Walker's South Carolina brigade advancing to their support. Looking south, he saw that Welsh's 2nd Brigade had not yet appeared. "Deeming my force alone inadequate for the attack on both artillery and infantry," Christ ordered his regiments to take cover. The only protection available was around Sherrick's farm buildings; his small orchard, which hugged the northwestern corner of his barn; and a farm lane, bordered by post-and-rail fencing, that accessed some of his fields to the north. The regiments crowded into this space while they waited for Welsh's brigade to come up. One of the Confederate batteries to Christ's left, probably Richardson's or Eshleman's, plastered Christ's men with "round shot, shell, grape, and canister [most likely shrapnel or case shot]." This bombardment, wrote Major Edward Overton in the 50th Pennsylvania, swept "the entire length of the regiment's line" and inflicted casualties in every regiment. Christ and his men were in a predicament. They could not go forward, because they lacked support on their left flank, and they would come under a crossfire from artillery in terrain that lacked any cover. To pull back now to the reverse slope of the hill near Sherrick's farm would expose the men to artillery fire for over 250 yards and, Christ concluded, "would have largely increased the list of casualties." He decided that the best of his bad options was to sit tight, trusting that his men could stand the shelling until Welsh's brigade arrived.[37]

Both Christ and Lieutenant Samuel K. Schwenk in the 50th Pennsylvania thought they had endured 30 minutes of shelling before Welsh appeared on their flank. This is probably an exaggeration, but it no doubt seemed to last this long to those experiencing the bombardment. What delayed the 2nd Brigade's advance is unknown. Colonel Thomas Welsh's orders from Willcox were simple: he was "to charge straight at the Rebels." Welsh resembled Christ in certain ways. They were self-made men who had enjoyed few advantages in life, and both were volunteer officers. But Welsh had a rougher go of it in general, and he had more military experience under his belt. He was a resident of Columbia, Pennsylvania, along the Susquehanna River. His father died when Thomas was only 2 years old. At age 8, his mother sent him to live with an uncle and work at a nail factory. He lasted only 7 months there, "not being large enough to tend the spike cutters." Over the following years he found work in odd jobs. His schooling was spotty, but he valued education and worked diligently to make up for his lack of formal training. When the war with Mexico started, Welsh was living in Cincinnati. Annoyed with how slowly Ohio was at enlisting volunteers, he crossed into Kentucky and enrolled as a sergeant in the 2nd Kentucky Volunteers. His regiment was heavily engaged at the Battle of Buena Vista. Welsh had numerous close calls in that particular conflict, writing, "I am surprised at my own good fortune in escaping death—having several bullet holes in my clothes—and my hair scorched by another." He did not escape unscathed, however. A musket ball shattered Welsh's right leg below the knee. An army surgeon managed to save his leg, but Welsh limped for the rest of his life. He returned to Columbia to recover, but before his leg had fully healed, he accepted a commission as a lieutenant in the 11th U.S. Infantry and returned to Mexico to join Winfield Scott at the siege of Vera Cruz. The wound continued to trouble him, and he was sent home as unfit for active service. Desperate to remain in the Regular Army, Welsh appealed to Secretary of State James Buchanan, a fellow Pennsylvanian, for any position that would allow him to keep his commission. Nothing came of it, however, and he was discharged. He began a business career, taking a job first as the weigh master on the Columbia–Wrightsville canal, and then as superintendent of the canal's locks. He opened a dry goods store, sold insurance, became a justice of the peace and president of the borough council in Columbia, and dabbled in politics. He was a staunch Democrat politically, but the attack on Fort Sumter stirred his martial spirit, and he raised one of the first volunteer companies in the 2nd Pennsylvania Infantry. The company elected him captain, and within days he was commissioned as the regiment's lieutenant colonel, a sign of both the respect he engendered and his ability to handle his men.[38]

When the 2nd Pennsylvania was mustered out after 90 days, Welsh was promoted to colonel and placed in command of Camp Curtin, the site where Pennsylvania volunteer units completed their organization and were processed for service at the front. Welsh exhibited a talent for administration, but he wanted active service, not a desk job. He got his wish in October 1861, when he was commissioned colonel of the newly formed 45th Pennsylvania. He molded his volunteers into one of the most well-trained regiments in the 9th Corps. One member remembered how Welsh would slowly pace up and down behind the regiment, with his hands behind him, "apparently paying no attention" to what the men were doing. But they soon learned that "nothing escaped his eagle eye." Two days before the Battle of South Mountain, when Burnside passed the 45th Pennsylvania, he paused to compliment Welsh: "Your regiment is the finest body of men that I have seen in the army during this war." At South Mountain, the men proved that they fought as well as they looked.[39]

Welsh applied these same high standards to his brigade. He thought the 100th Pennsylvania was satisfactory, but he had a low opinion of the 46th New York. That regiment "is Dutch all through and nearly worthless," he complained to his wife, reflecting his conservative Nativism, but Welsh's ire with the New Yorkers went beyond their nationality. They were poorly disciplined. In his letter, Welsh grumbled that, when he pitched into one of the 46th's captains because the regiment straggled badly and stole from civilians along the march, the captain expressed indifference toward his men's behavior, which infuriated the brigade commander. The 8th Michigan had only been transferred to his brigade from the 1st Brigade on September 16, so there had been no time for Welsh to evaluate its quality.[40]

The 2nd Brigade passed over the high bluff near Antietam Creek and moved downslope toward Otto's farm. The men advanced at a double-quick, yelling "like Indians," with their weapons at "charge bayonets." Welsh's three regiments, forming in line, were deployed with the 45th Pennsylvania on the right, close to Lower Bridge Road, and the 46th New York and the 8th Michigan extending to the left, toward Fairchild's brigade. The 45th Pennsylvania and the 46th New York descended into a depression between the ridges before climbing another ridge, which had John Otto's farm buildings and his small orchard at its northern end. These were directly in the path of the 45th Pennsylvania, who flowed around and through them, and then climbed over the farmer's fences into a plowed field that ran through another ravine. The field here was only 100 yards wide, and it was enclosed by a stone wall on its western border. Skirmishers in the 15th South Carolina had taken cover behind this, and they opened fire on Welsh's advancing Federals. After a "short, sharp encounter," the South Carolinians were forced on the run, but they retreated fighting. "The enemy retired keeping forty to sixty rods [200 to 300 yards] from us taking cover behind every hill or wall as they fell back & remaining till they were driven back," wrote

Captain Horatio Belcher, commanding the 8th Michigan's Company G. The terrain rose rapidly from the center of the plowed ground. After Welsh's men ascended the slope and scrambled over the stone wall, they entered a meadow. Reaching the crest of the next ridge beyond the wall, the Federals looked to their right front, into the ravine through which Lower Bridge Road ran, and saw the Stone Mill, as well as Lumm's house and orchard, seemingly alive with Rebels. They were Walker's South Carolinians.[41]

A SHORT TIME EARLIER, when Christ's brigade first appeared, marching over the hill near Sherrick's farm, Colonel Walker had ordered his South Carolinians forward from their position on the reverse slope of Cemetery Hill, in order to meet their advance. When the Confederate brigade emerged into the open, they were instantly exposed to the "furor of bursting shells" fired by Federal batteries across Antietam Creek. Frank M. Mixson, a private in Company E of the 1st South Carolina and orderly to Lieutenant Colonel Daniel Livingston, was jogging alongside the regimental commander under this fire when suddenly Livingston exclaimed, "Lead on, Frank, I am wounded." Whether Livingston was actually wounded or feigned injury is a question. The "Memoirs of the First South Carolina Regiment of Volunteer Infantry" relates that the lieutenant colonel fainted from the heat; a curious malady on a day when the temperature topped out at 75 degrees. Livingston's military service records do not indicate that he received any wound at Sharpsburg, but they do offer evidence that his feigning an injury to escape combat was quite possible. When he resigned his commission on March 3, 1864, his brigade commander approved it, but with a damning comment: "This officer is of advanced age [he was only 36]—limited education—lacks energy and decision of character, and, in a word, is utterly disqualified for the position that he occupies." As Livingston disappeared to the rear, Mixson shouted to the senior captain, Joseph E. Knotts, that he was now in command. It was an honor and responsibility Knotts did not desire or seek, and he would hasten to shed it.[42]

The brigade reached the edge of Lumm's small orchard, just north of his farmhouse and the Stone Mill. Here, they lay down behind a rail fence along the orchard's western border, but the Federals' artillery had tracked their movements and sent a deluge of shells at them. They struck with what one South Carolinian described as "a dreadfully fatal precision," and the fence that was their cover was shortly "shivered beyond hope of recognition and the mangled remains of unfortunate soldiers spread upon the ground in every conceivable attitude." Skirmishers in the 79th New York appeared in the brigade's front, and the South Carolinians fired on them, driving the bluecoats back. Colonel Walker spotted a stone wall along the orchard's eastern edge, which appeared to offer a superior position, and he ordered the 1st, 5th, and 6th South Carolina to advance and occupy it, in order to deal with the New Yorkers in their front. He deployed the

Palmetto Sharpshooters and the 2nd South Carolina Rifles, along with the remnants of Colonel Fitz W. McMaster's command, who were driven back by the Regulars, in and around the Stone Mill and Lumm's farmhouse, to confront the 100th Pennsylvania and Welsh's brigade, who were approaching on his right.[43]

Welsh's brigade soon came abreast of and then moved ahead of Christ's prone brigade. At that point, Christ ordered his regiments to stand up, but they advanced no farther than the Sherrick farm lane, where fire from Walker's 1st, 5th, and 6th South Carolina checked them. With Federals swarming across their front and right, Walker's men had their hands full. "We had it hot for some time but the fence was great protection to us," recalled Frank Mixson, referring to the stone wall they were crouched behind. Sometime during the fight at the wall, Captain Knotts abandoned his regiment to help his wounded brother find medical attention. This was not the behavior the Army of Northern Virginia expected of a regimental or company commander, and Knotts resigned in November. Micah Jenkins, his brigade commander, added a withering endorsement to the captain's resignation request: "Capt. Knotts, being <u>totally useless</u> as an officer it is recommended that his resignation be accepted, and he be allowed to join the ranks." Command of the 1st South Carolina fell to Captain James Stafford in Company I, but he, too, failed his test of command when he and his company found some pretense to slip away "to <u>look for rations</u>." The unfortunate regiment fought on, essentially leaderless—losing 40 men, or 40% of its strength—but many of the survivors soon found one reason or another to abandon the fight and make their way to Sharpsburg and safety. The other regiments possessed steadier leadership, and, with the excellent cover of stone buildings and stone walls, they held Welsh and Christ at bay.[44]

AT THE SAME TIME, but farther to the southeast, Lieutenant Matthew J. Graham was lying on his back the in rear of Clark's battery, along with the rest of the 9th New York, "watching the shells explode overhead, and speculating as to how long I could hold up my finger before it would be shot off, for the very air seemed full of bullets." When he heard the order to get up, "I turned over quickly to look at Colonel Kimball, who had given the order, thinking he had become suddenly insane; never dreaming that he intended to advance in that fire, and firmly believing that the regiment would not last one minute after the men had got fairly on their feet. Sure enough, there was Kimball, looking all right. He repeated the order: 'Get up the Ninth!' and I thought, looked directly at me."[45]

The rumor had already spread through the regiment that they were to charge and capture the Rebel battery—Brown's Virginians—that had been shelling them. "This narrowed the field and brought us to consider the work before us more attentively," noted David Thompson, a Company G private. The ground to be covered, by those who had managed to catch a glimpse of it, was enough to send a shudder through the bravest. "Right across our front, two hundred feet or so away, ran a country road [the Otto farm lane] bordered on each side by a snake fence. Beyond this road stretched a plowed field several hundred feet in length, sloping up to the battery." It was nearly 900 yards to Brown's battery, with all of it open terrain. Since the Confederates' infantrymen were largely hidden, no one knew what supports might be encountered as the Federals tried to reach the battery. Only the ravine below the Otto farm lane provided any defilade from the Rebels' guns. The keys to surviving an advance over such ground were unwavering discipline—and speed.[46]

The New Yorkers removed their knapsacks for greater mobility and formed up for the assault. They saw Welsh's brigade go forward on their right. Moments later, General Rodman directed Fairchild to attack. The three regiments rushed through Clark's and Durell's Union batteries and down to the Otto farm lane. Kimball's 9th New York was the battalion of direction, which meant that they selected a target or landmark to guide their movements, and the other regiments oriented on them. The objective was Brown's and Reilly's batteries and the ridge they sat on. The regiments tore at the farm lane's fencing, and by the time they had made their way through the second fence, their line was so disordered "that we hurried forward to a shallow undulation a few feet ahead, and lay down among the furrows to re-form, doing so by crawling up to the line." Their advance attracted "a perfect shower of shell and grape," but the speed of their movement preserved them from a heavy number of casualties. One among the handful who were hit haunted the memory of Charles F. Johnson, up front on the 9th New York's skirmish line. He looked back and saw a solitary soldier in Fairchild's brigade rushing over the ridge to catch up with his comrades. As Johnson recalled, "A projectile came along with its deafening death-cry, and took him right in the groin, severing his limbs completely from his body. If I could have heard his shriek, it would not have been so horrible, but to see him seize at his limbs, and fall back with a terrible look of agony, without being able to catch a sound from him—*Oh God! May I never be doomed to witness such a sight again!*"[47]

The three regiments slithered across Sherrick's plowed field and re-formed their lines while still prone. Then they lept up and rushed forward 100 feet to another undulation, where they dropped to the ground again. Brown's Wise (Virginia) Battery, noted David Thompson, "which at first had not seemed to notice us, now, apprised of its danger, opened fire upon us." Brown may have been focused on Welsh's brigade, but Fairchild posed a more imminent threat, and he redirected his guns on the New Yorkers. The first rounds went over the heads of the Empire Staters, but the Virginians adjusted their aim, and their fire began "to shave the surface of the ground." Thompson remembered looking behind him and seeing an officer "riding diagonally across the field—a most inviting target—instinctively bending his head down over his horse's neck, as though he were riding through driving rain. While my eye was on him I saw, between me and him, a rolled overcoat with its straps on bound into the air and fall among the furrows." Thompson witnessed another nearby soldier struck in the head by a shell fragment or shrapnel ball that "plowed a grove" through his skull and "and cut his overcoat from his shoulders." He heard another man swearing at a comrade for lying on him, only to discover that "he was cursing a dying man." Lieutenant Colonel Kimball was "ramping up and down the line" of the 9th New York, shouting encouragement. His men begged him to be careful, with cries of "Get down, Colonel!" or "Don't expose yourself that way!" or "Wait 'till we're ready to advance!" and other such remarks, to which he replied, "Don't mind me, boys, I'm all right" or "If you want a safe place stick close to me." Kimball would rub his palms together and then clap his hands, exclaiming "Bully Ninth! Bully Ninth! Boys, I'm proud of you! Every one of you!" Mercifully, the Rebels' iron missed him. Kimball's heroics certainly helped, but the strain of the shelling began to become intolerable. "Human nature was on the rack, and there burst forth from it the most vehement, terrible swearing I have ever heard," wrote Thompson. Moments later, Fairchild ordered them to resume their charge.[48]

The regiments rose up and "rushed forward with a wild huzzah," the shouting releasing the fear, anger, rage, and fury that had built up in each man as they lay helpless under the terrifying pounding by Brown's guns. David Thompson wrote, "In a second the air was full of the hiss of bullets and the hurtle of grapeshot. The mental strain was so great that I saw at that moment the singular effect mentioned, I think, in the life of Goethe on a similar occasion—the whole landscape for an instant turned slightly red." The brigade moved so quickly that it overran the 7th Virginia's thin skirmish line, which was behind the stone fence along the plowed field's western border, capturing it—to a man. There was no pause here, however. All three regiments continued up the long slope toward the Confederate guns.[49]

APPARENTLY BECAUSE THE NATURE of the terrain would have left them more exposed to Rebel artillery fire, General Rodman or Colonel Harland had ordered the 16th Connecticut and the 4th Rhode Island to advance into Sherrick's cornfield, where they would at least have some concealment before the general advance of the 9th Corps. Like all the ground in this part of the battlefield, the cornfield was not level. From the place where the New Englanders entered it, the land descended into a fairly deep ravine. To the west and south of the ravine, the terrain rose abruptly, anywhere from 30 to 40 feet higher than the lowest point in the ravine. Benning had hidden his main force in this ravine, but he withdrew toward Harpers Ferry Road when he received word that A. P. Hill's division was approaching. To reach the corn, the 16th and 4th crossed a plowed field, where they were exposed to the Confederates' artillery. This field, wrote Lieutenant Colonel Joseph B. Curtis in the 4th Rhode Island, "was swept by a tremendous fire of shell, grape, canister, shrapnell, and bits of railroad iron." The 16th got to the corn, but not without losses. When they were crossing the plowed field, a shell or solid shot struck Captain Newton Manross, the beloved commander of Company K, under the arm. Manross was a brilliant individual—a graduate of Yale with a degree in geology, and a doctorate in philosophy from University of Gottingen in Germany—and a world traveler. But he felt it to be his duty to serve his country, declaring to his wife, "You can better afford to have a country without a husband, than a husband without a country." A couple of Company H privates helped the grievously wounded captain to a corner of the cornfield's fence. Lester Taylor heard him say, "I am bleeding inwardly," and recalled how Manross's shoulder was so mangled "I could look down inside of him and see his heart beat."[50]

The 16th Connecticut dashed on into the corn in a state of confusion. "Our company became all mixed up and it was sometime before we found our places," wrote George Merriman, a member of Manross's Company K. The corn provided concealment but made it maddening to re-form the rookie unit. As in the Cornfield on the northern part of the battlefield, Sherrick's corn stood tall and thick. George Robbins, also in Company K, related to his wife how he "could not see anything in the corn." Commands were nearly inaudible, for, as Merriman observed in a letter home, "The cannonading at this time was most terrible. Nothing could be heard but a continual roar" of the guns. Officers managed to wrestle the unit into a line, and Colonel Beach ordered everyone to lie down. Wells A. Bigham was a Company H private, and somehow he and a few comrades were at a locale with a view outside the corn. About a half mile distant, they saw what they believed were two Union regiments approaching from the west. "They had our uniforms and flags so we thought they were all right," he related to his father 3 days later.[51]

Bigham and his comrades were not the only ones to see this force. Major Thomas W. Lion, an aide-de-camp to Harland, had returned from delivering the colonel's orders for the 4th Rhode Island and the 16th Connecticut. He reported that he and some officers in Ewing's Ohio brigade had seen what appeared to be a brigade of Confederate infantry forming on their left. This report reached Harland only moments after he had received orders from Rodman to support Fairchild's assault. He chose to obey his orders and directed his brigade to advance, but he also took the precaution to pass along Lion's report to Rodman. Harland's orders were instantly obeyed by the 8th Connecticut, who had been in the rear of the 89th New York. They jumped up and then rushed forward over the ridge and through Durell's battery. Harland's attack orders, for reasons unknown, never reached the 16th Connecticut and the 4th Rhode Island, so they remained in Sherrick's corn while the 8th Connecticut charged ahead. When Harland saw neither regiment moving, he sent an aide-de-camp to hurry them forward, then sought out Rodman and asked whether he should halt the

8th Connecticut to wait for the 16th and the 4th to come up. Rodman answered "No" and directed Harland to personally accompany the 8th and keep it moving. Rodman himself would bring up the other two regiments.[52]

AS FAIRCHILD'S AND HARLAND'S Federals burst in to view and swept forward, the 7th Virginia fell back from the small cornfield to Harpers Ferry Road, near Richardson's battery, and lay down in the roadbed. In the minutes before the 9th Corps' assault jumped off, as related earlier in this chapter, Colonel Benning received word that when Maxcy Gregg's brigade of A. P. Hill's division arrived to relieve him, he should move from Sherrick's cornfield to the right of D. R. Jones's division on the Harpers Ferry Road Ridge. But then the Union attack began, and Benning received revised orders to withdraw immediately. As he led his Georgian regiments back, Benning looked north and saw "Federals, line after line, advancing from the bridge on our lines." Captain James R. Troup, an aide-de-camp to Toombs, met Benning on the march and told him that the "General [Toombs] wished me to move faster." Benning ordered a slightly quicker step, not wishing to further fatigue his already exhausted men, but Troup soon returned with orders to proceed even faster. Benning increased the pace again, but minutes later, Troup once more came galloping up, this time with orders from Toombs to march at the double-quick. The small cornfield where the 7th Virginia had been located now blocked Benning's view to the north, and he asked Troup why such a hurry was necessary. Troup replied, "The enemy have Sharpsburg."[53]

THE REBELS WHO LOOKED like Union soldiers, whom Wells Bigham and Major Lion had observed approaching Sherrick's cornfield, were actually South Carolinians in General Maxcy Gregg's brigade, leading A.P. Hill's division onto the field. Gregg's infantry was preceded by Captain McIntosh's Pee Dee (South Carolina) Battery. The rapid pace McIntosh set from the Potomac River left most of his artillerymen behind, too physically spent to keep up with the trotting horses of the limbers and caissons. The battery's 12 lb. howitzer had been damaged at Boteler's Ford, and as they neared the front, McIntosh ordered the gun commander, Corporal W. S. Hall, to park that piece in a field to the left of Miller's Sawmill Road. He dropped off his caissons, since the horses were nearly blown, with Hall and one of his officers. Their orders were to "collect the men as fast as they came up and direct them forward." The captain pressed on with his remaining three guns: a Napoleon in the lead, followed by a 10 lb. Parrott and 3-inch rifle. About 600 yards west of Harpers Ferry Road, McIntosh turned off into the lane to Henry Blackford's farm. The guns drove to a plateau that projected southeast of the house and provided a good field of fire all the way to Sherrick's cornfield. Only two men in the detachment with the Napoleon had kept up on the jog from the river: Privates J. L. Napier, and J. J. Blake. Lieutenant William E. Zimmerman, a section commander, dismounted and assisted

Blake with unlimbering and positioning the gun. They saw a column of Union soldiers—either Fairchild's brigade or the 8th Connecticut—that Napier later recalled were only about 300–400 yards away, moving across their front. More likely, however, it was three times that distance. Blake selected a round and cut the fuse, while Napier carried it to the gun, and Zimmerman rammed it home. The resulting discharge signaled that A. P. Hill's division had arrived.[54]

The Napoleon got off two rounds, and the other guns one each, before Captain Richard H. T. Adams, A. P. Hill's signal officer, galloped up to McIntosh and ordered him to limber and report at once to General Kemper, who was "on the left of the cornfield." Adams meant the small rectangular field the 7th Virginia had just withdrawn from, adjacent to Harpers Ferry Road. Looking in that direction, McIntosh recalled that "I could then see no troops of ours to the front or to the flanks." It looked like a dangerous place for his artillery. As the battery limbered up, about 20 of their stragglers arrived. McIntosh mounted them on the limber chests, and his drivers lashed the horses to a gallop. The cannoneers held on for dear life as the guns raced around the western side of Blackford's farm buildings, traversed Miller's Sawmill Road, and then headed cross-country, bearing directly on Harpers Ferry Road, where it and the rectangular cornfield met. Although no one in the battery mentioned it, there had to have been several halts to clear the fencing along both Miller's Sawmill Road and the fields the guns went through north of it, which were crisscrossed with rail fences.[55]

They arrived at Harpers Ferry Road and either found or made an opening in the post-and-rail fence to enter the roadway. There was a plank fence and a drainage ditch on the road's eastern side, so McIntosh's South Carolinians had to drive nearly 100 yards north and past the corn before they found a gate and a bridge over the ditch that gave them access to the field. As they reached this point, Brown's battery came thundering back toward them. The Virginians had exhausted their remaining ammunition, failed to stop Fairchild's advance, and narrowly escaped being overrun. While the South Carolinians waited for the Virginians to pass, a nervous artilleryman piped up to McIntosh, "Captain, see those men are leaving there, we had better not go in." The captain grimly replied, "I was ordered to go in there and go to fighting." With Brown's guns having gone past them, McIntosh led his battery into the meadow north of the rectangular cornfield and unlimbered just below the crest of the ridge. J. L. Napier recalled that there were only 21 officers and men to drive the vehicles and crew the guns. Napier's Napoleon, on the right of the battery, unlimbered about 50 yards north of the corn, with the two rifled pieces on its left. Looking north, the private observed "a few men, not more than 100, to the left and in our front, huddled together behind a rail fence firing for all they were worth." It was Kemper's brigade, in a death struggle with Fairchild's New Yorkers. Napier then saw Union soldiers, 200 or 300 yards directly in front of him, "swarming up the hill like Pharaoh's Locusts." They were the 8th Connecticut.[56]

From his position on horseback, McIntosh saw the approaching Federals before Napier did. Because of the way the terrain fell away in his front, McIntosh "could see little or nothing to the front except the banks or ridges on the far side of the stream." Moments after his guns unlimbered, he saw one of the enemy's colors appear just above the ridge crest in his front. He watched the flag bobbing along but could not see its bearer. Then the heads of Union soldiers came into view. Initially, they seemed to be moving by the left flank, toward his right, but then they suddenly changed direction and began moving obliquely, to his left. As they did so, it brought them fully into McIntosh's view. It was the 8th Connecticut. McIntosh ordered double canister. The first discharge blew terrible gaps in the blue line and knocked their colors down, but it failed to break their advance. The ordeal of the Pee Dee battery had barely begun.[57]

IT IS NOT CLEAR which infantry brigade from A. P. Hill's division followed McIntosh onto the field, but evidence indicates that it was Maxcy Gregg's South Carolinians. The march from Harpers Ferry had trimmed the brigade down to only about 800 effectives. "All wet and draggled" from crossing the Potomac River, the brigade jogged up Miller's Sawmill Road toward Blackford's farm, near where A. P. Hill had established his command post. Past the farm, the ground crossed by Sawmill Road rose toward Harpers Ferry Road. When Gregg's men reached this point, they came under fire of the 9th Corps' batteries positioned east and west of Antietam Creek. Colonel Thomas Munford, commanding the small cavalry brigade watching Myer's Ford and the bridge over the mouth of Antietam Creek, had his headquarters at Blackford's farmhouse. He noticed that there "was great commotion of flags and couriers" at the Federals' signal station on Elk Ridge—a locale he had kept under observation all day—when Hill's infantry came into view.[58]

The 48-year-old Maxcy Gregg had limited military experience before the Civil War, serving as major of a regiment of South Carolina volunteers who were recruited for the Mexican War but did not reach the front in time to participate in any combat. Gregg, an attorney by profession, was one of South Carolina's ultra-radicals. He actively supported the 1851–1852 movement that sought to take South Carolina out of the Union, with or without the support of any other slave state. Its failure did not deter Gregg's advocacy for secession and protection for the practice of enslavement. He was one of the leading voices for reopening the African slave trade, which he and his fellow secessionists knew would not be possible if they remained in the Union. When the second opportunity to withdraw from the Union presented itself in 1860, Gregg and his ilk were better organized and prepared, and this time they succeeded. Intending to fight for his newly created slave republic, he secured a colonel's commission. By December 1861, Gregg was promoted to brigadier general. He proved to be a good soldier, and it was said that "he had an extraordinary reputation for self-possession and *sang froid* in battle." By the time his brigade arrived in Sharpsburg, the men were tough, battle-experienced, and as good as any in the Army of Northern Virginia.[59]

As Gregg and his regiments hurried up from the Potomac River, his chief of staff, Alexander C. Haskell, recalled that "a peremptory order came from Gen'l Lee that officers must dismount." Although this dramatically reduced their mobility, as well as their ability to command and control their troops, Gregg and his field officers obeyed. To avoid the Federals' artillery, Gregg led his regiments off Sawmill Road and marched them in a southeasterly direction, where the ground gave them defilade. They crossed Harpers Ferry Road north of the Snavely farm lane and deployed from column to line. Hill may have warned Gregg about the threat of an enemy advance from Snavely's Ford, for he sent his leading regiment—Lieutenant Colonel William D. Simpson's 14th South Carolina—to take up a position behind a stone wall north of the Snavely farm lane where it commanded the approaches from the ford. Gregg then formed a line with the next three regiments that came up: from right to left, the 1st, 12th, and 13th South Carolina. Their line faced northeast, toward Sherrick's cornfield. Lieutenant Colonel James M. Perrin's 1st South Carolina Rifles formed in the rear of these units, as a reserve. Skirmishers were deployed, and the line began to advance toward the cornfield. This was all done with the speed and efficiency of veteran troops.[60]

Brigadier General Lawrence O'Bryan Branch's North Carolina brigade, with about 900 men, followed Gregg. Branch came from a wealthy family in Enfield. His uncle, John Branch, had been governor of North Carolina and secretary of the navy under Andrew Jackson. Like many young Southern men from elite families, he received an excellent education, graduating from Princeton in 1838. From there he followed a now-familiar path: newspaper editor, attorney, president of the Raleigh and Gaston Railroad Company, and, in 1854, election to the U.S. House of Representatives. As a passionate Democrat and defender of slavery, he supported secession in 1860. When North Carolina left the Union on May 20, 1861, Branch, caught up in the excitement of the moment, enlisted as a private in an infantry company. It was an emotional, symbolic gesture, but powerful and prominent young men like Branch did not remain as privates in the Confederate army. Before the day was out, he was named quartermaster and paymaster of North Carolina's troops, with the rank of colonel. By September he was colonel of the 33rd North Carolina, and in January 1862 he was promoted to brigadier general. His first command, at New Bern, North Carolina, was a responsible post for someone with no military experience, and things ended disastrously when he was soundly beaten by many of the same 9th Corps' regiments he would face at Sharpsburg. He emerged from this debacle with his reputation ruffled but largely unscathed. His brigade was transferred to Virginia, where, on May 27, 1862, at the Battle of Hanover Court House, he suffered a second defeat as an independent commander at the hands of the Union's 5th Corps. This time there was carping within the brigade about "General Branches bad management." Transfer to A. P. Hill's Light Division relieved Branch of independent command, where he had done poorly, and placed him under the leadership of a professional and aggressive officer. Branch and his brigade thrived under Hill, and the North Carolinian even earned the praise of Stonewall Jackson for how he handled his command at the Battle of Cedar Mountain.[61]

Branch's regiments trotted up Miller's Sawmill Road, shedding both water and exhausted soldiers. "Our clothing was saturated with water from the hips down," wrote a member of the 18th North Carolina. The 7th North Carolina, at the front of the column, reached the high ground on Miller's Sawmill Road, northeast of Blackford's farm, where "a cannon shot or two, sped across the brow of the hill." Branch, probably guided by someone on Hill's staff, led his troops along the same route Gregg's brigade had followed, to avoid the artillery fire. They went through a large pasture, where "there were hogs and sheep, and also a considerable orchard." The movements of the brigade at this point are somewhat obscure, but it appears that the 7th crossed Harpers Ferry Road, deployed into line, faced left, and advanced up slope to a farm lane, bordered by split-rail fencing, that bisected Harpers Ferry Road. This led to a "not so well gotten up" solitary barn or storage shed, the owner of which is unidentified. At the fence on the northern side of this lane, they observed what Lieutenant James S. Harris in Company B thought was a Union regiment "in the open field on the slope of a ridge" west of Sherrick's cornfield. This was probably Company H of the 16th Connecticut, which had advanced as skirmishers to the southwestern part of the cornfield and, apparently, moved beyond the corn. Colonel Edward S. Haywood ordered the 7th North Carolina to open fire. After two or three rounds, Haywood ordered his regiment forward, and the Federals vanished back into the corn. Since his regiment had moved well in front of the brigade, Haywood ordered it back toward the farm lane and re-formed its ranks. By this point the Tarheels could see the 8th Connecticut crossing their front, at a distance of several hundred yards, and moving away from them to the northeast. Branch brought Captain William G. Morris's 37th North Carolina, which was trimmed down to only about 50 men by the forced march, up on the 7th's left flank. Both regiments sent out skirmishers and advanced to the north, the direction in which the New Englanders had disappeared. Such was their focus on the Yankees' movements that no one in Branch's brigade recalled seeing Gregg's South Carolinians, but they may have disappeared into a ravine south of the cornfield and not been visible.[62]

When the 18th and 33rd North Carolina arrived, Branch formed them as a support for his first line. His fifth regiment, Colonel James H. Lane's 28th North Carolina, was intercepted by A. P. Hill, who galloped down Harpers Ferry Road, pulled up in front of the regiment, and called out, "Who commands this regiment?" Lane stepped forward and replied that he did. "Take your regiment up

this road at a double quick, defend that unsupported battery near the stack &
drive back the enemy's sharpshooters advancing through the corn," replied Hill.
The battery he referred to was John B. Richardson's, which was west of the rectangular cornfield. The enemy were elements of the 8th Connecticut. Lane's men
double-quicked north for some 350 yards, passing the tiny 7th Virginia. Halting
in front of Richardson's guns, and with the rectangular cornfield immediately
on their left front, they found good cover in the road's drainage ditch. Lane sent
his skirmishers into the cornfield to make contact with the Federals. As the Tarheels established their position along the road, another body of troops ran past
them, heading toward Sharpsburg. This was Brigadier General James J. Archer's
brigade.[63]

The 45-year-old Archer made the journey from Harpers Ferry in an ambulance. Nicknamed "Sallie" at Princeton, because of his slight build, Archer struggled with poor health throughout the Civil War. A Maryland native from Harf-
ord County, northeast of Baltimore, Archer was a practicing attorney when the
Mexican War began. He managed to secure a commission as a captain in the
newly raised Regiment of Voltigeurs and Foot Riflemen, an experimental unit
that paired each mounted trooper with a rifleman who was on foot. The regiment was never issued any horses, but instead was organized as a rifle regiment,
armed with Model 1841 rifles. Archer performed ably in the Mexican War, particularly at Chapultepec, where he was cited for bravery. His regiment was mustered out in 1848, and Archer returned to his law practice. But he missed the
army, and in 1855 he was recommissioned as a captain in the 9th U.S. Infantry,
with which he served in the Pacific Northwest. When the winds of war began
to blow, Archer's sympathies lay with the states that had seceded. On May 14,
1861, he resigned his commission in the Regular Army and made his way to Texas,
where he had been stationed for some months during the Mexican War. There
he landed a commission as colonel of the 5th Texas Infantry. The Texans, however, did not care for him. "They all say he is not the man to lead them into battle,
that he is from a state too far North and too near Yankeedom for Texas to trust
as their commanding officer," wrote one lieutenant. Another Texan described
him as a "little fellow" who possibly was efficient if commanding Regulars, but
he was not the man to "control or *give satisfaction* to Texas volunteers." Archer
gradually won grudging respect from his Texans, and he even was senior colonel of what became the famous Texas Brigade for a short time, before the
command was transferred to John Bell Hood. On June 3, 1862, Archer received
promotion to brigadier general, assigned to the brigade he would lead at
Sharpsburg.[64]

Archer's Tennesseans, Georgians, and Alabamians found their commander to
be strict, but he was a soldier who knew his business. They nicknamed him "Little
Game Cock," suggesting respect, rather than contempt. He revealed something
of his grit and character when, although sick with fever, he accompanied his

brigade on the march from Harpers Ferry. When it reached the battlefield at Sharpsburg, he left his ambulance to personally assume command.[65]

Before Archer was able to take over, Colonel William McComb, commanding the 14th Tennessee and the senior colonel in the brigade, supervised its initial deployment. As had happened with every other brigade in A. P. Hill's Light Division, dozens of men had fallen out during the rapid march, and only about 350 men remained in the four regiments when they reached Sharpsburg. They were greeted by the same blast of Union artillery fire that had welcomed Gregg and Branch when they reached the high ground on Miller's Sawmill Road, northeast of Blackford's farm. Captain Tilghman Flynt in the 19th Georgia remembered it as "a well aimed destructive volley," fired by guns on the eastern bank of Antietam Creek. The first shell landed in the middle of the brigade, killing or wounding several men. When the brigade reached Harpers Ferry Road, Hill directed them north, along the same path where, moments before, he had sent Lane's 28th North Carolina. The little regiments hurried past the 7th Virginia and the 28th North Carolina. McComb halted his 14th Tennessee, the leading regiment, on the North Carolinians' left, directly opposite the rectangular cornfield and only about 30 yards from Toombs's brigade, whom he saw lying down in the road to his left. On his left front, in the meadow north of the cornfield, he saw three abandoned guns from some unknown battery. McComb rode over and talked with an officer from Toombs brigade, possibly Benning, and inquired what troops were in their front. Benning's men had just been in a firefight with a company of the 8th Connecticut and driven the New Englanders below the crest of the ridge, but these were the only troops they had seen. McComb asked if they had sharpshooters out front, but the Georgian replied that there had been no time to do so. McComb immediately ordered skirmishers to deploy and directed them to scour the cornfield. The balance of the 14th Tennessee took cover against the road's bank and and its plank fencing. Such was their haste in these movements that the regiment formed a line by the rear rank, to save time. They received some small-arms fire that seemed to originate from the cornfield, but they could not locate the source. As the other regiments hurried into position beside the Tennesseans, Archer arrived, mounted, and assumed command of the brigade. It was apparent to Archer, as it was to every officer in A. P. Hill's Light Division as they came onto the battlefield, that the situation in their front was critical. The three guns McComb had seen abandoned were McIntosh's battery, which had been overrun. The Federals were also driving back D. R. Jones's units.[66]

AS A. P. HILL'S INFANTRY and artillery began to arrive on the field, the Federals in Willcox's 1st Division and Rodman's 3rd Division struck D. R. Jones's Confederate division a hammer blow along the Harpers Ferry Road Ridge and in front of Cemetery Hill. Walker's South Carolinians stubbornly clung to their position in Lumm's orchard and the fortresslike stone buildings of his home and mill. On Cemetery Hill, in their rear, Garden's Palmetto (South Carolina) Artillery, badly outgunned with a pair of 12 lb. howitzers and two 6 lb. smoothbores, courageously ignored the Union artillery fire directed at them and focused their shelling on the infantry in Willcox's division. Lieutenant Samuel M. Pringle, one of Garden's section leaders, seemed to thrive on the danger. When one of his guns landed an effective shot among the Yankees, "he would wave his hat and shout out his joy." Close calls with enemy projectiles were also commonplace within the South Carolinians' battery. Corporal James H. Rice had a solid shot pass beneath his upraised arm. He was untouched, but the missile's force hurled him to the ground and left him senseless. Captain Garden raised up Rice's body, which was limp, as though he had been killed, and ordered two men to carry him to the rear. Moments later, another solid shot struck Pringle, amputating his left leg above the ankle, a frightful wound that claimed his life a week later. Other Union projectiles killed 9 horses and disabled another 5, accounting for nearly all the steeds who pulled the four limbers. One gun took a direct hit that dismounted the tube from the carriage, and another was struck near its muzzle, rendering it useless.[67]

Below Garden's battery, in the area around Lumm's mill and orchard, the firefight between Joseph Walker and Willcox reached its climax. Recognizing that he needed some extra firepower to help dislodge the Rebels from their stone redoubts, Willcox brought Lieutenant Coffin's section of Asa M. Cook's 8th Battery, Massachusetts Light, into action. Coffin had exchanged fire with Garden for a short time early on in the 1st Division's advance, but when the infantry butted up against the Confederates' strongpoint, Willcox found a superior position in the orchard just above Otto's farm buildings, where missiles from the New Englanders' artillery would have a plunging effect when fired on Lumm's solid buildings. The pair of guns manned by the Bay Staters dealt canister at the Rebels, which Lieutenant Coffin believed had a "terrible effect." It no doubt had an impact, but two other factors dislodged the stubborn South Carolinians from their stronghold. The 45th Pennsylvania—with support from Coffin's guns, as well as from the rest of their brigade and Christ's brigade—fought their way forward, crossed Lower Bridge Road west of Lumm's buildings, and outflanked the Rebels there. This was possible because Fairchild's brigade, as we shall see a little later in this chapter, drove Kemper's and Drayton's brigades from the Harpers Ferry Road Ridge and exposed Walker's right flank. Walker ordered the Palmetto Sharpshooters and the 2nd South Carolina Rifles to change front to the south, to protect his flank. At the same time, he withdrew his men closer to Sharpsburg, behind a bluff that took his regiments out of the line of Federal fire from Coffin's guns and Willcox's infantry.[68]

Company K of the 45th Pennsylvania mopped up the Confederates' defenses at the Stone Mill and Lumm's house. The center of resistance here was not

Joseph Walker's South Carolinians, but Colonel F. W. McMaster's small band, along with the redoubtable Captain Hansford Twiggs, who had been driven here by Dryer's Regulars during the Middle Bridge fight. Knowing the strength of his position, McMaster, Twiggs, and their men fought on, even after Walker's regiments pulled out. When it became evident that they would be surrounded and captured, however, McMaster ordered a retreat. Captain Twiggs and the 10 men who remained behind, either to cover the retreat or because they had not heard McMaster's order, became prisoners of Company K. Some Union accounts of the action gave the impression the Confederates' resistance was easily and quickly overwhelmed, but it seems clear that Walker's and McMaster's men fought stubbornly from their stronghold and forced the Federals to expend prodigious quantities of ammunition to drive them out. Welsh handled his men skillfully and patiently throughout the fight, however, and kept his losses low. Writing to his wife several days later, he stated that they "were exposed to a terrible storm of bullets, shell grape & canister yet strange to say the 45th had but one man killed & 38 wounded." Walker's brigade, conversely, sustained substantial losses, counting 26 dead and 195 wounded, a third of his men.[69]

Seeing Walker's South Carolinian brigade retreating, Colonel Christ unleashed the 17th Michigan in a charge to capture Garden's Palmetto (South Carolina) Artillery and a section of guns from Moody's battery on Cemetery Hill. John F. Holahan, a 45th Pennsylvania private, watched them go: "They are charging again, the brave idiots! No line what ever! They go in one great crowd around their flag!" Garden did not wait to receive their attack. Instead, he had his men haul their functioning guns into a ravine near Sharpsburg's southeastern corner, where he used his caisson horses to haul them off. He tied the two damaged guns, one of which had lost both wheels, to the surviving horses and made good his escape, dragging the wheel-less gun through the streets of Sharpsburg. The Michigan rookies came to within 100 yards of Moody's guns before their Rebel crews, along with the 18th Virginia, who were in support, retreated into the village.[70]

Although the Confederates were on the run, Christ grew cautious. This happened at about the same time when the Regulars were falling back on his right. As Christ reported, "I did not deem it prudent to advance after his artillery had retired, for the reason that the woods [on Cemetery Hill] were lined with his sharpshooters, and I would only have exposed my command to their fire without gaining anything." This was not entirely true. It was clear, even to a private, that Cemetery Hill was key terrain for the Federals to possess. Twice within a period of 3 days, the exuberant Wolverines had successfully charged and driven off the enemy. Nonetheless, Christ now ordered them to halt and fall back to the Sherrick farm lane. The men of the 17th could see that the Rebels were abandoning Cemetery Hill. Although they obeyed orders, they sensed that an opportunity had been lost. But what they did not know, and Christ may have, was that things on the 9th Corps' left flank were coming apart rapidly, and a deep thrust to Cemetery Hill might have ended in catastrophe.[71]

Welsh's 2nd Brigade, led by the 45th Pennsylvania, pursued the retiring Confederates up the slopes of the Harpers Ferry Road Ridge to Avey's orchard, where they made contact with Fairchild's brigade, who had just driven Drayton and Kemper off the ridge. They came under fire here from Walker's South Carolinians, who were positioned on the lower part of the southeastern slopes of Cemetery Hill. The men in the 45th sensed that the enemy was reeling and the way into Sharpsburg was open. Some began to move toward the village. "There is no telling where we would have halted," opined one member. He also complained bitterly that reports about the Battle of Antietam in the "New York papers," which soldiers often turned to for news, did not give his regiment the credit he felt it deserved. Welsh was aggressive, but he was also prudent. Christ was pulling back on his right, and some type of Rebel counterattack appeared to be developing on the left, beyond Fairchild's men. Welsh halted the forward movement of the 45th Pennsylvania and consolidated his brigade in Avey's orchard. His men would go no farther to the front that day.[72]

WHILE WILLCOX'S 1ST DIVISION dueled with Walker's South Carolina brigade and the Confederate guns on Cemetery Hill, Fairchild's New Yorkers stormed up the slopes of the Harpers Ferry Road Ridge, heading straight for Brown's battery. Unseen behind it, however, were Kemper's and Drayton's brigades. For sheer raw courage, this assault by Fairchild's brigade was not surpassed by any unit that day. Reilly's Rowan (North Carolina) Artillery pulled out early during the Federals' attack, probably due to Willcox's approach. Then Brown's Virginians, their captain badly wounded and their battery badly used up, recognized that they were not going to stop Fairchild's assault, so they "hastily limbered and drove off." But this did not relieve the New Yorkers from the terror of artillery fire. John B. Richardson's Louisiana battery, located on the rise just west of Harpers Ferry Road and the rectangular cornfield, had a line of sight over the corn, and they delivered an oblique, almost enfilading fire into the New Yorkers that exacted a dreadful toll. George Eaglesfield, the 40-year-old color sergeant of the 89th New York, was cut down by a shell fragment that struck his head, killing him and bathing the regiment's banner with his blood. "He never knew what hurt him," wrote Barton P. Harper. In the 9th New York, a bursting shell killed eight men in one company, and a solid shot decapitated 19-year-old James Conway, a Company G private. "The loss was frightful," recalled Lieutenant Matthew Graham. "I could see the regiment—the line—shortening perceptively as we advanced. We could hear the crash of the missiles through the ranks, and strange as it may seem, that sound brought forth like a flash to my mind a saying of [Marshal Jean] Lannes when describing the Battle of Austerlitz: 'I could hear the bones crash in my division like glass in a hailstorm.'"

During a brief halt in the advance, Graham "glanced back at the field we had just crossed and saw it sprinkled all over with our dead and wounded, all lying with their heads toward the enemy, presenting the appearance of a thin field of cornstalks I had seen some place, all rolled down to lie in the same direction for convenience in plowing them under."[73]

Many others were wounded by the iron fragments, canister balls, and solid shot. David Thompson remembered passing a hollow in the field, "about 15 f[ee]t across & with such steep sides that the farmer who owns the field had not ploughed it." A dozen wounded men had taken shelter there. The regiment's sergeant major was assisting them, and, seeing a blanket on Thompson's back, called out to him to help carry a critically wounded Lieutenant Edward C. Cooper to the rear. Thompson also recalled seeing a recent recruit among the wounded: John Devlin, whose arm "had been cut short off." All of the injured soldiers begged for water, but Thompson had none to offer them. Despite the frightening casualties, the survivors in Fairchild's regiments closed ranks and grimly pushed on up the ridge.[74]

In their position behind the crest of the Harpers Ferry Road Ridge, Kemper's and Drayton's small brigades had cover from observation by Union artillerymen, but there was a limited field of fire in their front. The crest of the ridge was about 60 yards east of their position, which meant that the enemy's approaching infantry would be "invisible until they arrived on the top of the crest opposite and in pistol shot distance, or point blank range." Alexander Hunter in the 17th Virginia claimed that they could hear Fairchild's Federals approaching, remembering "the stern commands of their officers, the muffled sound of marching feet." If they could indeed hear the enemy, it was the rustling sound of many men running, not that of a measured, methodical march. The 17th's colonel, Montgomery Corse, cautioned his troops: "Don't fire, men, until I give the word." Hunter and his comrades hunkered down behind the stone fence that sheltered them and fingered the triggers of their muskets, waiting for the Yankees to appear. Shortly thereafter, "we saw the gilt eagles of the flagpoles emerge from the top of the hill, followed by the flags drooping on the staffs, then the tops of the blue caps appeared." "Blue caps" meant that Hunter was looking at the 89th New York. Some of the New Yorkers pulled up and fired at the graycoats behind the fence, but Kemper's and Drayton's regiments got in the first devastating volley.[75]

Lieutenant Matthew Graham in the 9th New York vividly remembered "a crashing volley of musketry." Everyone around him hit the ground. Some were struck by the Confederates' missiles, but others avoided them. Graham was one of those who were hit, although it was by a canister ball from a round fired by McIntosh's or John B. Richardson's battery. The blow shattered his foot and stunned him for a moment. When he regained his senses, he saw "everybody was down on the ground." All of the color guard lay prone nearby, and the flags were on the ground, their bearers having been hit. One by one members of the color guard attempted to raise the colors, but they were shot down "like ten pins." "Then there was what seemed a spontaneous rush for them by a dozen or more men from several companies, who were shot down in succession as each one raised his flag," recalled Graham. French-born Adolphe Lebaire, the 22-year-old captain in Company E, known as a "quiet" and "modest" individual who never swore, finally ran to one of the flags. He raised it up and, swinging it around his head, shouted at his men, 'Up, damn you, and forward!' Shocked—not only because he was not immediately hit, but also by his forceful language—the survivors of the 9th were inspired by Lebaire's heroics. Captain Lawrence Leahy picked up the unit's other colors, and Lieutenant Robert McKechnie in Company H sprinted forward toward the Rebels with his cap perched on his sword. The impasse was broken, and the 9th and 89th surged forward, firing as they moved.[76]

John Dooley in the 1st Virginia estimated the Federals "to be at least two thousand in number." They may have appeared to be that many for those on the receiving end, but the two charging regiments, after all the casualties suffered during their advance, barely outnumbered Kemper's and Drayton's Confederates. Nonetheless, the Yankees had momentum, as well as a savage fury, that propelled them forward. The 89th New York, wrote Alexander Hunter, "poured a deadly volley into us that settled the matter. It killed or wounded every officer and man in the regiment except five, of whom I was fortunate enough to be one." The Confederates' defense collapsed. James Napier in McIntosh's battery watched the charge overrun and scatter the Rebels' line, and he judged that it was all over "in less than a minute after we took position." Hunter was among the prisoners Napier saw gathered up. "Just as the bluecoats were climbing the fence I threw down my musket and raised my hand in token of surrender," Hunter wrote. Given the rage some of the men in the Union ranks felt after the slaughter of their comrades, Hunter was fortunate. His surrender was accepted without incident or violence. John Dooley and his comrades in the 1st Virginia fled back through Avey's cornfield, in their rear, heading toward Harpers Ferry Road:

> "Oh, how I ran! Or tried to run through the high corn, for my heavy belt and cartridge box and musket kept me back to *half* speed. I was afraid of being struck in the *back* and I frequently turned half around in running, so as to avoid if possible so disgraceful a wound. It never entered my head to thrown away gun or cartridge box; but, encumbered as I was, I endeavored to keep pace with my captain, who with his long legs and unencumbered would in a little while have far outstripped me but that he frequently turned towards the enemy, and, running backwards, managed not to come out ahead in this our anything but credible race."

The charge routed Kemper's and Drayton's brigades, and the survivors streamed back into Sharpsburg or to Harpers Ferry Road, where only a handful from both commands were rallied.[77]

In the general melee at the stone wall, Private Thomas Hare, a 19-year-old in the 89th New York, captured one of the colors from a South Carolina regiment, either the 15th South Carolina or the 3rd South Carolina Battalion of Drayton's brigade. How Hare captured it is unknown. His Medal of Honor citation stated only it was taken "in a most gallant manner." That Hare took a flag from a regiment in Drayton's brigade, which was in front of the 9th New York, reflects the general confusion and mixing of commands that occurred during their retreat. Hare did not survive the day, and he may not have lasted long after capturing the flag. Major Edward Jardine, detached from the 9th New York to command the 89th, was seen shortly thereafter with the colors in his hand. Jardine seemed impervious to the danger that swirled about him. His "face was as calm and his manner as cool as though he was going through the ceremony on Parade," remembered Charles Johnson. Sergeant Asa L. Howard in the 89th also found Jardin's performance impressive and declared him "one of the *bravest, coolest, most energetic* men that I ever saw."[78]

Kemper and Drayton were routed but some of their men fell back fighting. Sergeant Howard accorded a grudging respect to them when he admitted that "every inch of ground was hotly contested by the half naked, half starved, dirty, sneaking Grey Backs." One of Charles Johnson's memories was seeing the Rebels "quite plainly through the smoke and dust of the [Avey's] cornfield, going through the motions of firing and loading." But organized resistance by these brigades had dissolved. The 9th and 89th New York had suffered grievous losses in their assault and were greatly disorganized. Jardine and Kimball attempted to halt and re-form the regiments at the wall they had just captured. But restraining furious men who had watched their comrades be slaughtered by the dozens proved to be difficult. Charles Johnson admitted that when he reached the wall, "I was in a delirium; I was mad." Lieutenant Matthew Graham remembered how "many of the men flushed with enthusiasm and the intense, almost savage desire for vengeance on those who had slain so many of their comrades, continued in pursuit of the fleeing enemy down the hill toward the village." A considerable number of the 9th and 89th New York pursued the Confederates to "not much over 300 yards from the town square." One member of the 9th New York was later found shot dead on a street in Sharpsburg. Lieutenant James Horner, the acting adjutant of the 9th, had to run down Sergeant Peter J. L. Searing, who had been wounded in the assault and was literally berserk with rage, and threaten him with his revolver. "He was not inclined to submit, even when so threatened by the officer," recalled Graham. "All the latent tiger in his nature had been awakened and aroused by the sights and sounds of the last quarter of an hour, and it required decidedly pointed demonstrations on the part of the acting adjutant to recall him to the condition of the obedient and well-disciplined non-com of ordinary times."[79]

While the New Yorkers attempted to re-form their shattered ranks, their officers noticed that some of the Rebels they had driven from the stone wall were rallying in Harpers Ferry Road. Colonel William DeSaussure, an excellent soldier and the commander of Drayton's 15th South Carolina, had gathered a group of men together in the road, and this may have been the force Fairchild's officers saw. Whomever it was, Major Jardine led part of the 89th New York in a bayonet charge that drove them back. But the menace to Fairchild's exposed left flank continued to build. Benning brought Toombs's regiments up, and although the 8th Connecticut was their primary target, part of the brigade fired at the New Yorkers. Charles Johnson was one of their targets. Two bullets hissed by him "in rather too close proximity to my head." A third round, "as if to convince me, that it was an earnest game," struck the ground nearby and ricocheted into his hip. The 103rd New York, and then the 89th New York, were realigned to face this threat. But it would be the 8th Connecticut who bore the brunt of the enemy's counterattack.[80]

WHEN THE 8TH CONNECTICUT saw Fairchild's regiments leap up and dash over the ridge in front, everyone knew their orders to advance were imminent. "This was the movement that showed who were men. Our white-feathered ones began to tremble and drop out of the ranks," observed Sergeant David Wilson, a noncom with no tolerance for the faint of heart. Lieutenant Colonel Hiram Appelman, a pre-war merchant, farmer, and attorney from Mystic, shouted to his soldiers "to fight like men and obey orders." He then gave the command "Forward." The regiment jumped to its feet, crossed the ridge at the double-quick, and passed over the Otto farm lane and the farmer's plowed field west of it. The moment they crossed the first ridge, "a terrible fire was concentrated upon our little band but on we pushed." Traversing the plowed ground was particularly terrifying, and Sergeant Wilson noted how "all the white-livered devils" who had not already dropped out of the ranks found some pretense to abandon the attack here. He dismissed their falling out as no great loss, as now "there was no one in the ranks then but men—those who came to fight for the good old flag."[81] The 8th Connecticut emerged from the plowed field into the meadow or pasture west of it and began the ascent toward the Harpers Ferry Road Ridge. There they came under scattering fire from skirmishers in Branch's brigade, several hundred yards away on their left flank. Some New Englanders paused to fire back, but Harland, knowing that Rodman was bringing up the 16th Connecticut and the 4th Rhode Island, expected that these troops would attend to the Rebels, so he led the 8th on up the slope.[82]

At almost the same instant when McIntosh's Pee Dee (South Carolina) Battery unlimbered north of the rectangular cornfield, Fairchild's New Yorkers overran Kemper's and Drayton's brigades. The fire from these guns may have deterred the 89th and 103rd New York from advancing in their direction, but the pursuit of Kemper and Drayton was mainly what took the New Yorkers away from the South Carolinians. It was the 8th Connecticut who posed a more direct threat to the artillerymen. When McIntosh first saw them, the New Englanders were "moving by their left flank in my front, but so far under the hill that only the colors could be seen in motion, and the heads of some of the men." Then the Federals began to move obliquely across his front, on a north-westerly bent, following the direction Fairchild's brigade had taken in their assault. McIntosh ordered his guns to be loaded with double canister and aimed at the 8th's flags, which were visible just above the ridgeline. When the main body of the Federals came into view, they were only about 250 to 300 yards away. The guns bucked and roared, spewing the contents of the deadly canister rounds downrange. "At each discharge great gaps were torn in the enemy's lines and the colors went down more than once," recalled McIntosh. Lieutenant Henry C. Hall, the acting adjutant of the 8th Connecticut, reported that "as we rose the hill to the fence [the same one, slightly farther north, defended earlier by Kemper and Drayton] a terrible burst of every description of missile from the battery was showered upon us." Elements of Fairchild's brigade, probably part of the 103rd New York, absorbed some of this fire as well, and Hall watched them break and run back down the hill.[83]

McIntosh's canister pinned down the 8th Connecticut, but the New Englanders fought back, shooting at the exposed gun crews and detaching Company K, under Captain Charles L. Upham, to flank the Rebel battery. Durell's guns also poured fire into the nettlesome South Carolinians. Both sides inflicted their share of damage. At the beginning of the fight, 19-year-old Baxter Rollins was the Confederate battery's guidon bearer. Seeing how thin the artillery crews were, he stuck his flag in the ground and joined the men working the Napoleon. As he prepared to pull the lanyard on the gun, a shell burst sent a large fragment into his side. In falling, his weight jerked the lanyard, the gun went off, and, in the recoil, a wheel ran over Rollins's foot, mangling it. Friends evacuated him, but his wounds were mortal. So many horses were hit in rapid succession by bullets and shell fragments that not enough remained to move the guns. McIntosh spotted Benning's Georgians, who ran up Harpers Ferry Road behind him and took cover in the road's drainage ditch. Seeing these infantrymen now in place, McIntosh shouted for his crews to disperse and save themselves. Bill Gilchrist, one of the limber drivers, managed to move his limber off the field, using its two surviving horses, one of which had its right forefoot shot away. The guns and the other two limbers, their dead horses still in the traces, were abandoned. Napier estimated that the Yankees in Upham's Company F were only 50 to 75 yards away when he and his comrades made a run for Harpers Ferry Road.[84]

McIntosh's battery was silenced, but Upham and his company never reached their prize. Benning's Georgians fired on them, and members of Company F thought they heard the rebel yell to the south. Upham sent some men to investigate, and they returned to warn him that Confederates were approaching through the rectangular cornfield toward the company's left flank. It was the 7th and 37th North Carolina of Branch's brigade. Then Archer's brigade arrived on their front, along Harpers Ferry Road. Enemy soldiers seemed to be materializing everywhere across the front and flank of the Federals. Upham ordered his men to fall back to the regiment.[85]

While Company K moved against McIntosh, the main body of the 8th Connecticut advanced over the crest of the Harpers Ferry Road Ridge, coming to within about 120 yards of the road. Here they exchanged volleys with a handful of Kemper's and Drayton's men, who had taken cover behind the road's fencing and in its drainage ditch, and with Toombs's Georgians. The "bullets came in terrible showers and from all sides of us," wrote Captain Wolcott P. Marsh, commanding Company F. A Confederate battery on Cemetery Hill—probably Captain Thomas H. Carter's three rifled guns, and two of Lieutenant William Elliot's rifled pieces from his Brooks's (South Carolina) Battery in S. D. Lee's battalion—poured what Charles S. Buell, a Company E private, described as "grape and canister" into their exposed right flank. "It shows poor generalship, that our generals did not discover the trap," lamented Buell. But Buell's commander, Colonel Edward Harland, indeed had spotted it. So had General Rodman. Both saw the advance of Branch's North Carolinians toward the 8th Connecticut's exposed left flank. Harland recognized immediately that if the 16th Connecticut and the 4th Rhode Island did not check this threat, "it would be impossible to hold this part of the field." For some reason, neither regiment had emerged from Sherrick's cornfield. Harland spurred his horse, seeking to find out what had happened and see if he could get these units up. Rodman, meanwhile, was riding to find Harland and tell him about the orders he had just given to the two regiments. Neither man would reach their destination. The 9th Corps' attack had arrived at its high-water mark.[86]

18

The Counterattack

"Now was a scene of terror every man for himself the bullets flying thick and fast men falling all around"

The 16th Connecticut lay on their faces in the ravine running through Sherrick's cornfield. Around them the fighting roared furiously, but the corn limited their view to only a few yards. The green soldiers could not have been in a worse position. They had never held "a battalion drill, but one dress parade, and scarcely knew how to form in line of battle." In an open field, the officers might have been able to manhandle the men into a semblance of a formation and exert some command and control, but inside the cornfield, this was impossible. The nature of the terrain where Sherrick had planted his corn added to the challenge confronting Colonel Francis Beach. Ezra Carman described it: "From its northeast corner the ground descends directly to the ravine [where the 16th was located], but in the southwest part of it there is a plateau, from which the ground descends quite abruptly 30 to 40 feet." Carman also noted that within the corn and 130 yards east of the stone fence that was along the field's western border, there was a stone ledge running north–south "upon which was an old board fence, partially thrown down and neglected, and its line was marked by trees." A spur of the plateau Carman described extended to a hill in the extreme southern part of the cornfield. This hill, and the plateau, dominated the ravine where the 16th lay and were the key to the conflict in Sherrick's cornfield.[1]

Beach had advanced Company H, under Captain Frederick M. Barber, through the corn as skirmishers. Since Barber's company had no training in tactics, we can imagine they had little idea of how to perform that service, other than to advance cautiously through the corn and see what was on the other side. Barber's men were noticed by skirmishers in Gregg's Confederate brigade, who reported that the enemy were advancing. Minutes later, those members of Company H who appeared at the western or southwestern edge of the cornfield were driven back into it by fire from Branch's 7th North Carolina. General Gregg was an aggressive, decisive officer, and he reacted immediately to this report from his skirmishers. He ordered his three leading regiments, the 12th and 13th South Carolina and the 1st South Carolina Provisional Army, to advance into

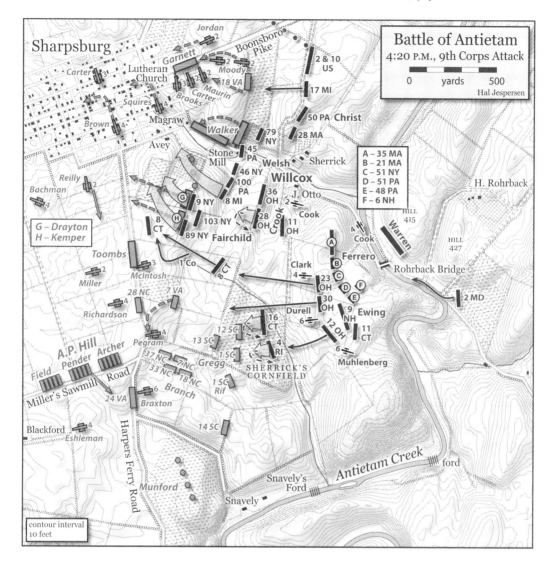

Battle of Antietam
4:20 P.M., 9th Corps Attack

0   yards   500

Hal Jespersen

A – 35 MA
B – 21 MA
C – 51 NY
D – 51 PA
E – 48 PA
F – 6 NH

G – Drayton
H – Kemper

contour interval
10 feet

the corn and repel the Yankees. Gregg's orders, almost certainly delivered verbally by a staff officer, were not interpreted in the same way by his commanders, who were all civilian volunteer soldiers from the political world of South Carolina. Colonel Oliver E. Edwards, a state legislator before the Civil War, was the 42-year-old commander of the 13th South Carolina. He understood them as defensive orders, so he halted his regiment when it reached the stone wall at the edge of the corn. Colonel Dixon Barnes, the 12th South Carolina's commander, 45 years old and a pre-war state senator, was an aggressive individual. He led his regiment into the corn, looking for someone to fight. The brigade historian wrote of Barnes's pugnacity, "Indeed, so fierce and impetuous were his charges, that it was sometimes necessary to recall him." Colonel Daniel H. Hamilton's 1st South Carolina Provisional Army, on Barnes's right, also entered the cornfield at its southwestern corner. Hamilton was 46, an attorney and the former U.S. marshal for the District of South Carolina. He came from solid secessionist stock. His father was James Hamilton Jr., who was a congressman and governor of South Carolina; a powerful advocate for slavery's expansion; and one of the leaders in the Nullification Crisis of 1832–33, when his state declared federal tariffs to be null and void within its borders. His son was not a gifted soldier. Gregg's chief of staff, Alexander Haskell, wrote of Hamilton, "The brigade had no confidence in him for he had never shown any capacity."[2]

General Rodman had received warning of Gregg's approach. When Rodman reached Colonel Beach, he ordered him to change front to the southwest, to meet the South Carolinians. He also sent orders to Colonel William H. P. Steere to move the 4th Rhode Island up to support the 16th Connecticut. Rodman then galloped off to find Harland and advise him of the revised orders for the 16th and 4th, as well as, perhaps, to redeploy his 3rd Division to meet the Confederates' attack on his flank. Because Rodman had probably sent the members of his small staff off on various mission, he rode alone. We shall never know what he intended to do, for, on the way, he was mortally wounded when shot from his horse, most likely by soldiers in the 7th or 37th North Carolina, who were near the fence running north from the eastern edge of the rectangular cornfield.[3]

The men in the 16th Connecticut could hear but not see the approach of the 12th South Carolina and the 1st South Carolina Provisional Army. Colonel Beach shouted out orders, calling the regiment to its feet and telling it to change front. It was an order that was easily uttered but impossible for these greenhorns to execute. Adjutant John H. Burnham "was tearing about in that corn from one end of the line to the other" to deliver Beach's directives to each company. In the excitement, and due to their inexperience, many company commanders either did not understand the orders or found they were unable to reorient their line in the corn. The result was sheer confusion. One officer exasperatedly cried out to Beach, "Tell us what you want us to do and we'll try to obey you." Beach shouted back in frustration, "I want my men to face the enemy." Some of Gregg's Confederates wore parts of, or complete, Union uniforms, which heightened the bewilderment in the New England regiments' ranks. Many later maintained that the line approaching them carried the national flag. Writing to his sister 6 days later, George Robbins in Company K declared that the "Rebs came on them with Ohio state flag and national colors." Adjutant Burnham wrote, "I did not see their flag to notice particularly myself but I can find fifty men and some officers in our regt and in the 8th Conn and the 4th Rhode Island who would willingly take their oath that they carried our flag." So many men in these regiments and the 16th Connecticut were positive that the Rebels carried the U.S. flag that it cannot be discounted as a mistake made by rookie soldiers in the excitement of combat. Robbins did not state where his information came from regarding which flags the Confederates carried, but the colors of three Ohio regiments—the

32nd, 60th, and 87th—were captured at Harpers Ferry, and Gregg's men were among the first into the Union camps after they were surrendered. We shall probably never know with certainty whether some of Gregg's regiments carried captured Union flags onto the field and used them to deceive the Federals, but it was not unknown for soldiers in combat to employ tricks to gain an edge in a what was a murderous business.[4]

Some members of the 16th Connecticut began to shoot at the advancing force, but then a cry of "Don't fire on your own men" was heard from the soldiers who were approaching the 16th. Adjutant Burnham wrote to his family that he heard this "distinctly in front of us myself and supposing it to be from some regiment of ours who were in advance of us I ordered the men near me to cease firing and they did so." As Jacob Bauer in Company G related to his wife, "This put us in utter confusion and the devils advanced until our very noses touched theirs." After arriving at point-blank range, Barnes's 12th South Carolina pulled up and fired a crushing volley into the milling New Englanders. "You can have no idea of it; it was like a hail storm—our men fell on every side," Robert Kellogg, an 18-year-old private, wrote to his father. In his diary, Kellogg tallied the comrades who fell all around him: Robert Speirs, William Maxwell, Newton Willey, and Arthur DeN. Talcott, all wounded, and Charles W. Pease, killed. Some of the men in the 16th now began to fire back, even though officers were still shouting for them to cease fire. Someone else, probably Beach, ordered the regiment to fix bayonets. A few heard the command, but most did not, and it only added to the bedlam. "The most helpless confusion ensued," recalled Bernard F. Blakeslee, a corporal in Company A. Captain Barber in Company H was one of the first in his company to be hit. As he fell, one of his soldiers, Wells Bingham, heard him cry out, "Oh My God . . . I'm killed . . . goodbye boys . . . you have lost your Captain. Farewell . . . Farewell." Company D's captain, Samuel Brown, a graduate of Bowdoin College and a schoolteacher in Ellington, Connecticut, "got a little excited and roundly swore at his men" when they were unable to execute his orders. Brown turned to his 1st sergeant, German-born Peter Grohman, and remarked wryly, "I believe I swear too much for a man in battle." A moment later, Brown was killed.[5]

The 247 officers and men in the veteran 4th Rhode Island heard heavy firing in their front as they moved into Sherrick's corn to support the 16th Connecticut. Suddenly, groups of frightened men from the 16th collided with the right of the 4th, throwing that part of the latter regiment into confusion. Colonel Steere ordered a movement by his left flank to avoid the fugitives, which the Rhode Islanders managed to execute. The Yankees were receiving fire from their front, but Lieutenant Colonel Joseph B. Curtis and others clearly observed a U.S. flag above the corn, in the direction the volleys were coming from. "We thought our own men were firing upon us," wrote Curtis. The 4th was situated in a gully, so Curtis and Steere ordered the regiment to squat down while they discovered who was loosing volleys at them. They called for a volunteer lieutenant—the most expendable officer in the army—to go forward and find out who the shooters were. Two brave souls, Lieutenants George E. Curtis and George H. Watts, agreed to perform the hazardous duty. They were joined by the regiment's equally courageous national color bearer, Corporal Thomas B. Tanner, a steamboat hand before the war. With Curtis and Watts—both carrying a pistol in one hand and a sword in the other—flanking Tanner on either side, the little party started uphill through the corn, toward where Curtis had seen the U.S. flag. They halted near the summit, and Tanner waved his flag back and forth, unaware that Hamilton's South Carolinians were within 20 feet of him. A blast of gunfire instantly killed the color sergeant. Miraculously, Curtis and Watts were unscathed. The former pulled the colors from Tanner's grasp and dashed back downhill, followed by Watts. Steere and Lieutenant Colonel Curtis then shouted for their men to rise up and open fire. Curtis was an aggressive officer, and he sensed that, under the circumstances, the best tactic was to charge the enemy. He suggested this to Steere, who agreed, as long as the 16th Connecticut also joined in the attack. Curtis ran through the corn to the 16th but could find no one in authority. The lieutenant colonel appealed to the officers and men he encountered, but he was unknown to them, and fear was palpable among the greenhorn soldiers. "At the very idea [to advance] they crowded back," Curtis wrote, "and some almost ran over me. I struck at them with my sabre, cursed them, and called them cowards." Fear and panic are powerful human emotions, and the efforts of a single officer swinging his sword, cursing, and calling the men cowards had no effect. Curtis ran back to Steere to report that they could expect no support from the 16th. On the 4th's firing line, the enlisted men sensed the same thing Curtis had. They were yelling that they should charge. Steere still hesitated to advance without help. Instead, he ordered Curtis to go to the rear and see if he could find any support.[6]

The New Englanders and South Carolinians blazed away at one another. The engagement's confusion was not one sided. The movement of the 4th Rhode Island, up on the left of the 16th Connecticut, threatened the right flank of Hamilton's 1st South Carolina Provisional Army. Hamilton had only 140 effectives and was considerably outnumbered, but the corn concealed his lack of men and, like nearly every regimental commander in Gregg's brigade, his first instinct was to hit back. Hamilton ordered his three right companies to draw back at an angle, to protect the flank, and kept up the fight. Then an officer warned the colonel that an enemy regiment had "gained the hill in my rear." Whether it was the mixture of Federal uniform parts or a flag that caused the muddle is unknown, but instead of Yankees, Hamilton looked back and happily saw "our own bonny blue flag" of South Carolina. The "enemy" were the 1st South Carolina Rifles, moving up in support. Hamilton's men fired so rapidly that ammunition began to run short, weapons fouled, and "in some instances the men were obliged to use stones to hammer the charges down." Berry Benson, a 19-year-old private in Hamilton's regiment, recalled how the Federals were grouped in a disorderly line "in a little hollow in the corn at the foot of the hill." He and his comrades "poured volley after volley" into them. It was the only time in the war that Benson recalled firing on order, rather than at will, noting how Captain T. Pickney Alston, acting as major, repeatedly shouted, "Right wing—ready—aim—fire—Load! Left wing—ready—aim—fire—Load!"[7]

Hamilton probably reported the threat to his flank to Gregg. The brigadier's response was characteristically hard-hitting. He ordered the 1st South Carolina Rifles, with 194 officers and men, to advance from their reserve position into the corn, on the right of Hamilton, and attend to it. Lieutenant Colonel James M. Perrin, a 40-year-old Abbeville attorney and Mexican War volunteer, brought his men, who were unseen, up through the corn, arriving directly on the left flank of the 4th Rhode Island. "We delivered a destructive volley into it before our presence seemed to be realized," reported Perrin.[8]

The volleys from Perrin's regiment were so accurate that Lieutenant Colonel Curtis thought they had been flanked by an entire brigade. Henry Spooner, a lieutenant in the 4th Rhode Island, described the fire as "the hottest I ever encountered, the bullets whistling around us like hives of loosened bees." The lethal enfilading fire tipped the scales. The Federals had superiority in numbers, but experience, discipline, and training counted for more in this fight, and the Confederates had a clear advantage there. All was confusion with the hapless 16th Connecticut. The natural tendency of untrained soldiers who come under fire is to bunch up, which only increased the number of casualties. Then, because the bonds of discipline had not been fully developed, unit cohesion disintegrated, and it became every man for himself. "Some of our boys went one way, and some another," admitted Wells Bingham to his father. William H. Reylea, a Company D private, related how "I had loaded and was going to fire the third time when happening to look around I saw only dead men laying where they fell. I very quickly decided it was no place for me." Elizor D. Belden, another private in Company C, came to the same conclusion, writing in his diary, "Now was a scene of terror every man for himself the bullets flying thick and fast men falling all around." Belden ran with the others, but as he climbed the fence on the cornfield's edge, he was hit in the thigh. He then crawled to a depression where other wounded men had gathered. The 16th's regimental leadership was decimated, with both Lieutenant Colonel Frank W. Cheney and Major George A. Washburn being injured. In addition to the three company commanders who had already been killed or mortally wounded, four more were felled with injuries. Among the field officers, only Beach survived unscathed, but he had two horses killed beneath him. Jacob Bauer, an enlisted man with no love for his colonel, declared unsympathetically, "He is too ugly a man for even a bullet to touch him."[9]

Colonel Harland arrived in the midst of this mayhem. En route from the 8th Connecticut, the brigade commander had his horse shot out from under him—probably by the same skirmishers in Branch's brigade who shot Rodman—so he made the rest of his journey on foot. Somehow Harland discerned that the Confederates' right flank was vulnerable, and he ordered Beach to change front, in order to strike the enemy's flank. Whether this change of front was the same thing Rodman had ordered earlier, or if it was a modification of that order, is unknown. Harland reported that the 16th Connecticut executed this maneuver, "though with some difficulty," but there is no evidence from anyone in the 16th that this ever took place. It all became moot when the 1st South Carolina Rifles arrived and opened their enfilading fire. At this point, sensing the hopelessness of further resistance in a cornfield where his men could see only a few yards in any direction, Beach ordered a retreat. This, Jacob Bauer confessed, "was accomplished in a Bull Run fashion." At nearly the same time, Colonel Steere attempted to extricate the 4th Rhode Island in some semblance of order by giving instructions for the regiment to withdraw by the right flank. The retreat started in an organized fashion, but, under the "tremendous fire of the enemy," fear overwhelmed discipline and the Rhode Islanders joined in the general stampede.[10]

Everyone who survived the flight from the cornfield had a distressing tale to tell or described a brush with death or injury. In a story that was a familiar one at several locales during the hard fighting on Antietam's battlefields, Lieutenant Henry Spooner in the 4th Rhode Island noted that he "had two shots through his clothing and a slight contusion on his hip from a bullet striking the swivel of my saber." Moreover, he believed, scarcely "one of our officers or men did not bear the mark of at least one bullet upon some part of their clothing or equipments." When Robert Kellogg in the 16th Connecticut burst out of the corn, "a soldier near me fell with an awful shriek but I kept on until I gained the shelter of a fence at the top of the hill." William H. Reylea encountered a desperately wounded man in the 8th Connecticut, propped up against a fence, who was "crazed by his wounds and cursing horribly in his raving saying repeatedly 'Don't run boys. Give the S—— B—— hell. See 'em over there.'" Reylea was so exhausted that, as he later admitted, "it was a useless exhortation to me I could not run if I tried," so he stopped to attend to the man, who was bleeding profusely from a nasty wound in his thigh. Cutting off a piece of the soldier's coat "and the splinter of a rail," Reylea improvised a tourniquet. He gave the man a drink of water, and then, as he turned to leave, Reylea nearly stumbled over the body of Captain Samuel Brown in Company D. He found it hard to move quickly across the plowed field east of the corn, and the bullets striking the ground knocked dirt up into his mouth and eyes. It seemed impossible to survive the gauntlet of fire, and Reylea found himself repeating over and over, "You'll never get out alive. Your wife's a widow. I'll never get out alive." Fear of dying then gave way to fury, and at one point he paused, turned, and shook his fist at the Rebels before moving on. Three days later, he returned and found the man he had helped still lying against the rail fence, dead.[11]

"In our retreat we were forced to pass over a space where nothing shielded us from the showers of shot and shell hurled upon us with such deadly effect," wrote the 4th Rhode Island's Colonel Steele. It was a shooting gallery, with human targets, for Gregg's South Carolinians. "The enemy suffered greatly while attempting to fall back as there was no obstructions to hinder shooting them & that was the only time I drew my pistol and shot at any person," Major William H. McCorkle in the 12th South Carolina recalled. Knapsacks, weapons, and the dead and injured were abandoned by by those who were still on their feet, in a desperate effort to escape the killing zone. Among those who fell during the retreat was Colonel Steere, with a serious wound in his thigh. As the Federals fled the corn, Berry Benson watched "an officer, mounted upon a black horse, waving his sword," who galloped into the midst of the retreating men and attempted "to rally the scattered line." His identity is unknown. The officers in the 4th Rhode Island were dismounted. It could have been the lieutenant colonel or the major of the 16th Connecticut, but existing evidence indicates that they were wounded in the corn. Instead, it may have been one of Harland's or Rodman's staff officers.[12]

Lieutenant Colonel Curtis greatly exposed himself to enemy fire trying to check the rout. He wrote that "I begged them to keep in the ranks. I tried to keep them back with my sword. It was no use. I waited till the last company passed me, trying to rally them; then I walked back after them up toward the lines, amid such a storm of bullets, shell and grape, as I never conceived of." Death lurked at every step. Men fell on all sides of Curtis, and at times he had to step over their bodies. Emerging from the corn into the plowed field, he saw Ewing's Ohioans advancing to cover their retreat. He also observed Lieutenant Charles P. Muhlenberg's Battery A, 5th U.S. Artillery, which had arrived during the cornfield fight and unlimbered a couple of hundred yards to the left and rear of where Durell's battery had been. This looked like a good place for Curtis to rally his broken regiment. He faced about and shouted, "I go back no further! Whatever is left of the fourth Rhode Island forms here!" It was a brave but useless gesture. Watching the collapse of the infantry, Muhlenberg's battery pulled out. Without the moral support of the big guns, the infantry had no strong point to rally on. Only Captain Martin P. Buffum and three or four men joined Curtis. He picked up a dropped musket and attached his little squad to the 51st Pennsylvania, which had come up to defend the ridge east of the Otto farm lane.[13]

Gregg's men extracted a terrible toll from the New Englanders. The 4th Rhode Island counted 21 killed, 77 wounded, and 5 captured, a 41% loss. The 16th Connecticut had 42 killed, 143 wounded, and 20 captured, a 27% loss. But the casualties only told part of the story. The 16th was so badly scattered that even on the morning of September 18, less than a third were present at roll call. Survivors trickled in over the course of the following days, but a handful had deserted and never returned. Lieutenant Colonel Curtis was unable to re-form the 4th Rhode Island's survivors until they had crossed to the safety of Antietam Creek's eastern bank. The Confederates had crushed Harland's left flank with just three small regiments, numbering no more than 500 officers and men. The odds were 2 to 1 in the Federals' favor, but Gregg and his regiments demonstrated the shock power of veteran soldiers who were deployed decisively, swiftly, and aggressively. Nonetheless, the casualties were not one sided. Barnes's 12th South Carolina was hard hit, with 102 out of 162 killed or wounded, a 63% loss. Among the wounded was Barnes, who took a bullet in the thigh, a frightfully painful wound that would kill him within 3 days. Gregg's other two regiments in the engagement suffered relatively light losses: 34 in the 1st South Carolina Provisional Army, and only 12 in the 1st South Carolina Rifles.[14]

JACOB COX HAD RECEIVED warning of the Confederates' advance toward the 9th Corps' left flank before they struck Harland's regiments in Sherrick's cornfield. He responded by ordering Colonel Ewing to shift his brigade south, but after they had moved nearly a quarter of a mile, Cox recalled them. Cox undoubtedly did so to fill the 600-yard gap in his front that had developed between the 16th and the 8th Connecticut, toward which Branch's brigade was advancing. When Cox made his decision, he may have believed—because Sherrick's cornfield obstructed his view to the southwest—that the 4th Rhode Island and the 16th Connecticut could contain the attack on his flank, but if he did not fill the gap in his front, the Rebels' counterattack would envelop the 8th Connecticut, Fairchild, and Willcox. Ewing, after returning to his starting point in the rear of Durell's and Clark's batteries, received orders to advance to the stone wall on the western border of Sherrick's cornfield and plowed field. The 23rd and 30th Ohio sprinted over the ridge crest, through the two batteries, and down the slope to the Otto farm lane. The 30th, on the left, crossed the southeastern part of the plowed field and entered the cornfield, passing over the dead and wounded of the 16th Connecticut, as well as going by some survivors. Most of the 16th, along with the 4th Rhode Island, had fled out of the eastern side of the corn at around the same time as Ewing's regiments began their advance, which accounts for why the two groups did not collide. Despite some small-arms and artillery fire, the 30th Ohio successfully reached the wall, but the 700-yard run, nearly half of it across soft plowed ground or through corn, left everyone exhausted. Carman described their position in precise detail: "It was on a hillside sloping to the north, its left on the highest part of the hill and 240 yards from the southwest corner of the corn; its right at the base of the hill, close to the ravine, beyond which was the 23rd Ohio."[15]

The 23rd Ohio were equally spent when they got to the stone wall on the 30th's right, but both regiments immediately opened fire on the 37th and 7th North Carolina, who were moving across their front to envelop the 8th Connecticut. The Buckeyes were so fatigued, though, that Major George H. Hildt in the 30th Ohio reported that their fire "was necessarily, slow and desultory." Ewing became aware of the collapsing situation in Sherrick's cornfield just as his brigade stepped off. In response, he ordered Colonel Carr B. White, commanding the 200-man 12th Ohio, which was on the left of the brigade, to change front slightly to the southwest and attend to Gregg's flank attack in the corn. When the 12th reached the northeastern corner of Sherrick's field, they came under severe shelling from the batteries A. P. Hill had assembled on the Harpers Ferry Road Ridge, north of the Snavely farm lane. Gregg's men, who remained on the higher ground of the cornfield, also directed small-arms volleys toward the Ohioans. This fire checked any further advance by the 12th. For the moment, Ewing's regiments held their own, but there was a large gap between the 12th and 30th Ohio. The Confederates were rapidly concentrating forces that would make trouble for the Buckeyes.[16]

While Ewing's brigade attempted to shore up the 9th Corps' buckling left flank, on the Harpers Ferry Road Ridge, the 8th Connecticut engaged in a desperate death grapple with growing numbers of Confederates who seemed to materialize on nearly all sides of the New Englanders. In their charge up the ridge, the regiment passed over the fence where the 89th and 9th New York incurred such heavy losses in their fight with Kemper and Drayton. To Sergeant David Wilson, it looked like at least 500 of the New Yorkers were strewn about, either dead or wounded. Fairchild's regiments were not to be seen, having advanced over the ridge in a northeasterly direction, toward Jacob Avey's farm. Wilson wrote that Harland, thinking Fairchild must be in front of the 8th, "ordered us to keep on, and we advanced full 500 yards farther." This movement diverged to the left of the direction Fairchild's regiments moved in, and this brought the 8th to within 120 yards of Harpers Ferry Road. There they came under fire from some rallied elements of Drayton's and Kemper's men, who taken cover behind the road's fencing and its drainage ditch. Minutes later, more Confederates were seen, running north along the road. The moment they cleared the rectangular cornfield, they began firing at the New Englanders. It was Toombs's brigade.[17]

When Colonel Benning reached Harpers Ferry Road, after pulling out of Sherrick's cornfield, he was joined by the 20th Georgia, who had resupplied with ammunition. They did not pause by the road, since Benning's orders were to double-quick to where McIntosh's battery had just been abandoned and Drayton's and Kemper's brigades were routed by Fairchild's New Yorkers. Captain John A. Coffee in the 20th remembered seeing A. P. Hill at this point, either on or near the road, and recalled how Hill "was in his shirt sleeves his coat was strapped to the horn of his saddle and he seemed to be on his mettle and eager for the fray." The five companies of the 11th Georgia led off, followed by the 17th and 15th Georgia, then about 50 officers and men of the 50th Georgia, and, finally, the 20th Georgia. All told, Benning had about 500 men. Lieutenant Peter A. McGlashan, a member of the 50th Georgia, wrote that "I shall never forget the scene that met my gaze as we reached the top of the hill." As the Confederates cleared the rectangular cornfield, they could see McIntosh's abandoned guns in the field to the east, "no living soul about them, no caissons or gunners; the ground lay strewed with dead horses and men." Some of the South Carolina artillerymen who had taken cover by the road cried out to the passing infantrymen to retake their battery. As Benning cleared the cornfield, he saw what he took to be an enemy brigade, "standing composedly" in line of battle "not 200 yards from the road," apparently waiting for their supports to come up. It was the 8th Connecticut.[18]

There was no time to form, and the Georgians simply piled into the drainage ditch along Harpers Ferry Road or behind the road's fences and blazed away at the enemy. The 8th immediately replied. Although the firing by both sides was "very spirited," Benning thought it was inaccurate, with the Yankees "shooting over us, we under them." In the Union regiment, Captain Wolcott P. Marsh recorded how the "bullets came in terrible showers and from all sides of us." Those all around him "now returned their fire and the men went to their work as cooly as if on drill." Lieutenant Colonel Appelman's voice could be heard over the noise, calling to his men: "Remember what State you are from, and preserve the honor of her flag and your regiment." Benning testified to the stubborn resistance of the Nutmegs, reporting that the enemy "showed a determination to hold their position stubbornly" and fought "with a vigor."[19]

A new threat assailed the 8th Connecticut's left flank when skirmishers of the 37th and 7th North Carolina, followed by the main body of their regiments, came up through the rectangular cornfield and the plowed field east of it. Their fire drove Company K, which had been sent to secure McIntosh's abandoned battery, back to the main body of the regiment. Lieutenant Colonel Appelman adjusted the position of his regiment to meet this attack. The shooting between these foes was more accurate. As Joseph D. Joyner, a 7th North Carolina private, wrote, "About half the men in my company were killed and wounded—both men on my right hand were shot down." Sergeant Wilson thought the Tarheels' fire on his regiment was "awful." Appelman ordered his men to lie down to reduce their target profile, but casualties still mounted rapidly. "The whistle of the iron hail was terrible and it did not seem possible that anyone could escape unhurt," wrote 1st Lieutenant and Acting Adjutant Henry C. Hall to his sister. A bullet shattered the right arm of 19-year-old Lieutenant Marvin Wait in Company D, and he was told to go to the rear. Wait refused to do so. His steadfastness cost him his life when he was hit three more times: in the left arm, leg, and, mortally, in the abdomen. When Peter Mann, a Scottish-born private in Company B, took a bullet through the body, he was heard to utter, "I have done all I can to save my country." He died of his wound 10 days later. Charles Buell thought he and his comrades "fought with undaunted bravery." When his friend John E. Tuttle was shot through his heart, Buell carried his dead body the long distance back when the 8th Connecticut retreated.[20]

Archer's brigade soon arrived on Harpers Ferry Road, in the rear of the rectangular cornfield, bringing more Confederates into the engagement, but what swung the fierce firefight decisively in the Rebels' favor was artillery. John B. Richardson's battery was able to bring some guns to bear on the 8th Connecticut, as, probably, was Carter's battery, newly arrived on the western side of Cemetery Hill. Both sets of guns, noted Sergeant Wilson, enfiladed his regiment's line from different directions. Sergeant Frank Spaulding in Company F related how "the men fell on every side" and "grape and canister, with thousands of bullets, mowed down our noble fellows." Lieutenant Colonel Appelman received a leg wound, and command fell to Major J. Edward Ward. It is possible that Rodman reached the regiment before he was mortally wounded, since Ward reported that the general ordered a retreat. Whomever it was that gave Ward the command, he had to repeat it three times before it was heard and acknowledged by the survivors. "The red flag of the rebs was now coming steadily upon us from three sides," wrote Acting Adjutant Hall, "and in a few moments the open space between us and our friends would have been filled with foes." The 8th's entire color guard had been slaughtered. A private, Charles Walker, picked up the national colors, a seemingly suicidal action, but, in that era of warfare, a crucially important act of courage. Some of the men were ignoring Ward's order to retreat, but when Walker raised the flag, the major shouted to his men, "in a pleading tone, 'Boys will you follow your colors rally around them and follow me.'" The word "colors" observed Captain Marsh, "brought the men to their senses and the devoted little band rallied around them." These flags were vital for preserving unit cohesion in perilous moments, when chaos and heavy numbers of casualties threatened to tear it apart. The Nutmegs fell back fighting. Lieutenant Roger Ford noted how his men gave their pursuers "lead & we sent some of them to their homes." But the Rebels also dispatched plenty of Connecticut men to their graves or caused them to suffer from wounds. The 8th lost most of their 34 dead, 139 wounded, and 21 missing—almost 50% of the regiment—on the Harpers Ferry Road Ridge in probably no more than 15–20 minutes of fighting.[21]

Ivy Duggan in the 15th Georgia thought the Yankees maintained "an admirable line," considering the fire they were under. Another Georgian noted that when the New Englanders began to retreat, they initially retired "in good order," but as it became apparent that speed was essential to escape, the Federals began to run. By this point, Toombs had joined his brigade in Harpers Ferry

Road. This was the sort of moment the Georgia politician delighted in. He ordered his mixed command to charge. "We leaped the fence, raised the yell, and pushed the scattered fugitives over ground strewn with their own fallen," wrote Duggan. Someone else in the brigade commented, "I must remark the perfect indifference of every man to danger." He then described how, even while the fighting raged, their men stopped to pick up canteens, blankets, swords, pistols, and, particularly, boots and shoes from the dead. The performance of Toombs's brigade at Sharpsburg clearly established them as a crack unit, but even the best had numbers of men who were *not* indifferent to danger. Captain Jonathan A. McGregor, commanding the 17th Georgia, went to considerable effort in his after-action report to name every soldier in his regiment who failed to do his duty that day. Bryan Beeman, Richard Jackson, and Pinkney Head all "failed to stand to the colors." Thomas McDonald and Josiah C. Cohen "fell out while going to the field and did not report until next day." E. McCleod and W. J. Wimberly, who were detailed to bring water, "did not return until after the fight." All told, 19 soldiers found some pretense with which to absent themselves from the ranks. McGregor did not give the strength of his regiment in the action, but it probably was similar to that of the 15th Georgia: 115 officers and men. This represented slightly over 16% of the 17th's strength.[22]

Seeing the backs of running Yankees fired Toombs's ardor. With more enthusiasm than tactical sense, he urged his men to pursue them beyond the crest of the Harpers Ferry Road Ridge. This was really a plateau of higher ground, and it was not clear what Union forces might be beyond it, because they could not be seen. Benning thought charging into such uncertainty was ill advised, and he discreetly suggested this to the brigadier: "We could not see what was below the crest of the hill, but I knew a very large force of the enemy must be somewhere below it, for I had from our late position seen three or four successive long lines of them march out from the bridge." Benning recommended that they halt the brigade and only send those men armed with rifles to the crest of the ridge. Toombs was bombastic and saw glory being added to his resume if they charged over the hill. But, to his credit, he paid heed to Benning, whom he realized was his superior in tactical matters. Toombs ordered only his riflemen to the crest to harass the enemy.[23]

THE DEFEAT OF THE 8th Connecticut, in turn, exposed Fairchild's brigade to envelopment. The New Yorkers, it will be recalled (see chapter 17), had pursued Kemper's and Drayton's men in a northeasterly direction, down the northern slope of the Harpers Ferry Road Ridge to the vicinity of Avey's orchard and cornfield. Since he could not see the 8th Connecticut from there, Colonel Fairchild was unaware of their retreat. He noticed that things were amiss when Rebels appeared, moving toward his left flank and rear. Fairchild gave orders for all of his regiments to withdraw, going about 300 yards to the stone wall on the western edge of Sherrick's plowed field. According to Robert Bowne, a 19-year-old private in the 89th New York, it was Rodman who warned Fairchild of the threat to his flank and gave orders to extricate the brigade from potential disaster. If this is true, Rodman performed heroic work before a Confederate bullet felled him. The 89th and 103rd New York fell back under a terrific fire from the guns of Carter's, Maurin's, and Brooks's batteries, who had returned to Cemetery Hill as the threat from the 5th Corps receded. Browne wrote of how the men in his regiment fell "thick and fast around us" as they crossed the exposed ground to reach the wall.[24]

Fairchild reported that the 89th and 103rd New York retired "in good order and without confusion." This is doubtful. Private Browne described his regiment, which lost half of its men, as being "terribly cut to pieces." Lieutenant William W. Athey in the 17th Virginia captured one of the colors of the 103rd New York. Since Kemper's brigade had been routed earlier, Athey had probably fallen in with one of the groups of men who had been rallied and joined one of the local counterattacks. That he captured one of the Union brigade's flags is powerful evidence of the confusion in Fairchild's retreat. The two regiments did not stop when they reached the stone wall, but continued on to the ridge near the Rohrback Bridge. The 9th New York, under fiery Lieutenant Colonel Kimball, either failed to receive Fairchild's order to retreat, or Kimball ignored it. It had cost the colonel a large percentage of his regiment to seize the position he held, and he had no intention of relinquishing it. Kimball had rallied about 100 of his men, and they were trading fire with "scattered groups of the enemy" while he waited "anxiously for the reinforcements which were momentarily expected to appear." How Kimball failed to see the rest of his brigade depart is unknown, but the inequalities of the terrain and the crop cover made this possible. General Willcox noticed that the colonel did not follow the other regiments of the brigade, and he sent an aide-de-camp, Lieutenant Levi C. Brackett, to advise Kimball that he was in danger of being cut off and should retreat at once. Kimball refused. He still imagined a large number of reserves were coming to his support, who would deal with any Confederate threat to his flank. Kimball also pointed out the obvious demoralization of the Rebels, whom the 9th's assault had driven off the ridge. "The order should be to advance instead of retreat," he argued. Being only a lieutenant, and from a different division, Brackett "hesitated to give an absolute order to fall back," and he left to discuss the situation with Willcox.[25]

A debate broke out among the 9th's surviving officers as Brackett departed. Several were of the opinion that they should heed the lieutenant's orders. The regiment's position seemed to be greatly exposed, the men were running short of ammunition, and Kimball's fellow officers may have pointed out the obvious—the other regiments of the brigade had vanished. Kimball refused to submit to reality. He replied, "We have the bayonets. What are they given to us for?" This was the fighting spirit armies need to win battles, but, when taken to an extreme, it can also lead to disaster. Fortunately for the 9th's survivors, Willcox settled the dispute when he came up and gave the pugnacious Kimball definitive orders to retreat. This time the lieutenant colonel obeyed, but as his men fell back, he was heard saying to Willcox, "Look at my regiment! They go off this field under orders. They are not driven off. Do they look like a beaten regiment?" Kimball insisted Willcox acknowledge that his regiment retreated under orders, not because they were defeated. Kimball had ample reason to be angry about giving up the ground his men had captured. His regiment had lost 63% of its strength—235 officers and men, which was the largest number in any 9th Corps regiment.[26]

JACOB COX WATCHED HIS 9th Corps' attack from near Clark's Battery E, 4th U.S., on the ridge east of the Otto farm lane. As A. P. Hill's counterattack developed, driving back the Federals' left flank, the Confederate general brought several of his Light Division batteries into position along the southern end of the Harpers Ferry Road Ridge, where they could enfilade the 9th Corps' advanced forces, Cox recognized "that it would be impossible to continue the movement to the right"—that is, toward Sharpsburg. Therefore he sent orders for Willcox and Crook to pull the left of their lines back and for Sturgis to bring his 2nd Division forward. The order was timely, since many of Willcox's regiments were out of ammunition, or their supply was low enough that they would have had difficulty resisting a determined attack. Referring to his troops, Willcox reported that "every regiment marched back in perfect order." The 1st Division's withdrawal was orderly, but it was not carried out in "perfect order." For example, Horatio Belcher, a 43-year-old captain commanding Company G in the 8th Michigan related that his regiment did not receive any orders at all. When the other regiments in his brigade began to fall back, Belcher's commander and many other officers in the 8th followed them, leaving the captain and about 70 other Wolverines behind. This might have been pure dereliction of duty, but it might also merely reflect the confusion inherent with any retreat in the face of the enemy. A Rebel regiment—possibly the 37th North Carolina or an element of Toombs's brigade—was spotted about 100 yards away, approaching Belcher's left flank. He coolly ordered his men to change front to the south and position themselves behind a board fence, where he spread them out in a skirmish line. Belcher cautioned them to rest their rifles on the bottom rail, stay calm, and aim well. They opened an accurate fire that drove the Confederates to cover and enabled Belcher to safely extricate his men. But for Belcher's levelheadedness and his men's steadiness, the Rebels "would have taken us prisoners in ten minutes."[27]

Ewing's 23rd and 30th Ohio provided crucial help to cover the retreat of the 8th Connecticut and Fairchild's 1st Brigade by temporarily driving back Branch's 7th and 37th North Carolina with a flanking fire. From this initial success, things rapidly went downhill for the Ohioans. Immediately after this volley, the

30th Ohio began to receive "a withering fire" from an unseen force in Sherrick's cornfield, on their left flank. Major James M. Comly, commanding the 23rd Ohio, was on the right of his regiment, where the terrain rose to give him a good view of the ground around their position. He detected movement in the corn on the 30th's left and watched what he took "to be a heavy body of our troops advancing toward our left through the corn." Then, to Comly's surprise, some men in the 30th Ohio began to fire at these soldiers. The major was confused, because the force the 30th was shooting at "used the national colors." Instead of Federals, however, it was Maxcy Gregg's brigade. Comly's hesitation gave the South Carolinians a crucial advantage, since the major ordered his regiment not to fire. This enabled Gregg's men to close to within "feeling distance" of the 30th Ohio and open a "furious attack" on the two Buckeye regiments' left flank.[28]

At nearly the same time, Archer's brigade assailed Ewing's front. After assuming command of his brigade and observing the retreat of the enemy from the Harpers Ferry Road Ridge, Archer ordered his troops to join the counterattack. The small brigade, preceded by their skirmishers, pushed through the rectangular cornfield. George Gleaton, a private in the 19th Georgia, was one of the skirmishers, and he remembered tramping across the length of the field without encountering any other troops. At a rail fence on the eastern side of the corn, he "saw a Union force behind a rock fence at the foot of a hill across a plowed field." It was the 23rd and 30th Ohio. The 14th and 7th Tennessee, on the left of the brigade, passed through the corn without incident and joined the skirmishers at the field's eastern edge. The right of the brigade, however, bumped into the 37th North Carolina, which was withdrawing from the enfilading fire from Ewing's regiments, resulting in confusion. Shouts by the 37th's officers for their men to retreat were heard by the officers of the 19th Georgia and the 1st Tennessee. In the disarray inherent with command and control in a dense cornfield, they thought the order came from Archer and promptly ordered their regiments to fall back.[29]

George Gleaton followed his comrades, and when he reached the plank fence at Harpers Ferry Road, the Southerners encountered Archer, angrily demanding to know who had ordered a retreat. Colonel Turney, commanding the 1st Tennessee, answered that he thought Archer had given the order. The general replied that "he never done any such thing" and directed the 19th Georgia and the 1st Tennessee to turn around, fix bayonets, trail arms, and attack.[30]

Archer's advance encouraged Toombs to order the 15th and 20th Georgia to join the attack. He also ordered John B. Richardson's battery to displace to the Harpers Ferry Road Ridge, in order to provide artillery firepower. The combined assault of Archer and Toombs, with a force of around 600 and 700 men, on the front of the 23rd and 30th Ohio coordinated perfectly, although entirely accidentally, with Gregg's attack on the Ohioans' left flank.[31]

In the minutes before Archer's brigade burst out of the rectangular cornfield and confronted the Buckeyes' line, Colonel Ewing, in response to Gregg's flank attack, ordered Major Comly to have the 23rd Ohio, who were in the plowed field, change front to the south and meet the Rebels' assault. At the same time, he sent orders to Lieutenant Colonel Jones in the 30th Ohio to withdraw from the stone wall and form on the 23rd's left flank. If both regiments could execute these movements, they would shift from facing west to pointing south. Jones ordered his regiment to move by the right flank—that is, he intended to have them exit the corn by turning to the right and marching forward—but in the din and confusion, only the four right companies heard the order. They moved off in the direction Jones wanted, but the other six companies, amounting to about 200 men, remained at the stone wall. By this time, A. P. Hill had brought up three more of his divisional batteries—Crenshaw's, Pegram's, and

Braxton's—unlimbering them at various points on the southern end of the Harpers Ferry Road Ridge. They sent a deluge of shells at the 30th and other targets nearby. Wayne Jacobs in the 30th Ohio wrote about how these batteries plastered their line with "grape, shell, shrapnel, canister, railroad iron, spike nails, glass bottles, and every other conceivable missile of destruction." Then Archer's brigade burst out of the rectangular cornfield and hurled themselves across the plowed field, directly at Theodore Jones's companies at the stone wall. The Buckeyes blazed away, and among those hit was George Gleaton, who was wounded "50 or 60 steps from rock fence." But the combined onslaught by Archer, Gregg, and A. P. Hill's artillery was more than the six companies could handle, and the Federals "broke ranks and ran even faster than they had advanced back toward the Antietam." Ewing attempted to extricate them before the break occurred, sending orders via his aide-de-camp, Lieutenant Reese R. Furbay, but Furbay was riddled with bullets and killed before he could reach them.[32]

Confederate minie and musket balls, canister, shell, and solid shot chased the fleeing Buckeyes. "The balls flew like hail through the corn," recalled Wayne Jacobs. The 30th's adjutant, Lieutenant Charles Duffield, was hit in the leg and disabled, and then was mortally wounded while being carried to the rear. The courage of Sergeant Nathan J. White, carrying the regiment's national flag, was conspicuous. He stood in the corn "amidst the rain of bullets and defiantly waved the color toward the advancing enemy." But courageous color bearers rarely escaped unscathed at the Battle of Antietam, and White was no exception. A Confederate drilled White through the breast, and one more life was lost in Sherrick's cornfield. White's counterpart, Sergeant William Carter, who was bearing the state flag, managed to reach the edge of the corn before he was shot through the head and killed. Corporals in the color guard picked up both fallen banners and saved them from capture. The regimental commander, Lieutenant Colonel Jones, however, did not escape. Archer's rapid advance swept up Jones and 17 others in the regiment as prisoners.[33]

The 30th Ohio was hurt, but they were not whipped yet. Elements of the six companies fell back into the ravine in Sherrick's cornfield, where they found a handful of men from the 16th Connecticut. They had remained hidden there, rather than risk flight to the rear. Meanwhile, Archer, thinking he had the enemy on the run, followed the unwritten doctrine of the Army of Northern Virginia and pursued them into the maze of the corn. Tilghman W. Flynt, a 19th Georgia captain, recalled how he made it about 100 yards into the cornfield before they stumbled into a knot of resistance by the Ohioans and New Englanders. The Federals inflicted enough casualties on the Tennesseans and Georgians—including Flynt, who was badly wounded in the leg—that Archer ordered his brigade to fall back to the stone wall. Ezra Carman believed that friendly fire from the 12th South Carolina might have accounted for some of Archer's losses. Deep inside the cornfield, the Carolinians were unaware that friendly troops were crossing their front and continued shooting toward the north, through the corn. The 23rd Ohio might have also helped turn back Archer, as their change of front placed them on his flank. But they, in turn, were outflanked on their right by Toombs's 15th and 20th Georgia. Eliakim P. Scammon, the Kanawha Division's commander, had seen Toombs's men coming down the slope of the Harpers Ferry Road Ridge and managed to withdraw the 23rd Ohio, along with the four companies of the 30th, before the Georgians could do any real damage.[34]

While these events were unfolding, the 12th Ohio had advanced for about 50 yards, into Sherrick's cornfield near its northeastern corner, but they came under a terrific fire from A. P. Hill's batteries on the southern end of the Harpers Ferry Road Ridge. Their colonel, Carr B. White, reported that it "threatened the destruction of the regiment." He pulled his command back to the eastern edge of the corn, but friendly artillery in their rear—probably Muhlenberg's Battery A, 5th U.S.—was trading cannonades with A. P. Hill's guns, and some of its shells were bursting prematurely, placing the Buckeyes under both hostile and friendly artillery fire. Then the 9th New Hampshire came up in White's rear and, in the day's fading light, mistook the 12th for the enemy and opened fire. Fortunately, the rookies fired high and inflicted no damage. White sent Sergeant John M. Snook running back to stop their volleys. While Snook carried out his mission, White led his regiment back to its original position—a short distance inside the corn, where it had concealment—and remained there a short time before Scammon sent orders for it to withdraw to the bluff above Antietam Creek.[35]

Through no fault of their own, Ewing's brigade had done little more than serve as a momentary check on the Confederates' counterattack. Compared with other 9th Corps' brigades, their losses were not high: 28 killed, 134 wounded, and 20 missing or captured, but this was still a 20% loss. Ewing was bitter about what he believed had been the incompetent handling of his brigade, directing his wrath at Cox. On the night of the 18th, George Crook encountered the colonel and several other officers full of "jig water." Ewing, Crook recalled, "ventilated himself on Gen. Cox, abusing him for being a coward and imbecile, and declaring that he would never obey an order of his again, etc." Ewing may have had a personal grudge with Cox, but he was also known to be closely attached to his men. Thus he might have been bitter over his losses, incurred with so little damage done to the Rebels. Whatever the reason for Ewing's outburst, the decision to use his brigade to fill the gap in Harland's line made sense when the orders were given. Had Cox or Scammon known that Harland's left was going to collapse, or if they had been aware of how strong the Confederates' counterattack was, they almost certainly would have deployed Ewing differently.[36]

FOR ALL ITS SIZE, Crook's brigade of 2,005 officers and men accomplished the least of any in the 9th Corps. When Willcox attacked and drove the Confederates from Lumm's house and the Stone Mill, Crook moved the 28th and

36th Ohio across the plowed field west of Otto's farm buildings and up to the stone wall on the western edge of the field. This wall was the northern extension of the same wall the 23rd and 30th Ohio formed behind, farther south. Crook halted the 11th Ohio, as a reserve, in the Otto farm lane, near the farmer's home and barn. These maneuvers cost the brigade a few losses, but one of the casualties hit the 36th Ohio hard. While crossing the plowed field, the regiment came under artillery fire, and its commander, Lieutenant Colonel Melvin Clarke, ordered the regiment to hit the dirt inside a shallow depression. "Lie down. Men, lie down, every one of you," he was heard to yell, while gesturing with his sword. He preserved his men's lives, but at the expense of his own. A Rebel shell struck Clarke in the right thigh, near where it met his hip, hurling him from his horse and killing him. Clarke was "deeply respected, honored and loved by his men," and the gruesome spectacle of his death shook them. Once the 28th and 36th reached the stone wall, they remained there until darkness ended the fighting. The brigade suffered only 68 casualties on September 17, a loss of 3%, which was a remarkably small figure, considering the heavy fighting nearby. A major reason for this small number was Crook's leadership. He would eventually compile a good record in the Civil War, but at the Battle of Antietam, he was extraordinarily cautious and exhibited no initiative.[37]

When Cox commanded Willcox to withdraw and Crook to refuse the left of his line, he also ordered Sturgis's 2nd Division up from its reserve position on the bluffs near Antietam Creek. Ferrero's 2nd Brigade filled the void in the lines left by the defeat of Rodman's 3rd Division, with Nagle's 1st Brigade in support. Because harassing Confederate artillery fire continued to drop in the vicinity of the Rohrback Bridge, ammunition wagons had been unable to safely cross the creek and resupply Ferrero's regiments with ammunition. At this critical moment, the ammunition for Durell's and Clark's Union batteries gave out, so they were forced to withdraw to replenish. Moreover, Lieutenant Coffin's section of Cook's 8th Battery, Massachusetts Light, which had been firing from near Otto's farm, was also forced to displace to cover by shelling from John B. Richardson's battery. The only artillery Cox had left to help his infantry hold the bluffs above Antietam Creek were the six Napoleons of Lieutenant Charles P. Muhlenberg's Battery A, 5th U.S. Artillery, which had crossed the Rohrback Bridge and unlimbered on a knoll about 450 yards directly east of the eastern edge of Sherrick's cornfield.[38]

In contrast to the diminishing artillery firepower on the 9th Corps' front lines, the Confederates, aided by energetic actions by Robert E. Lee and his staff to round up every available gun they could find, built up a formidable force of artillery units on the army's right. A. P. Hill's Light Division brought up Pegram's, Braxton's and Crenshaw's batteries, totaling 4 rifled pieces, six 6 lb. guns, three Napoleons, and a 12 lb. howitzer, placing the guns at various advantageous points, ranging from just south of the rectangular cornfield to around to a hill

300 yards north of Snavely's Ford. The two 12 lb. howitzers of John B. Richardson's 2nd Company, Washington (Louisiana) Artillery, mentioned earlier in this chapter, had moved up and unlimbered near McIntosh's abandoned battery. More full and partial batteries rolled up throughout the fight. A section of Napoleons from Miller's 3rd Company, Washington (Louisiana) Artillery, which had been engaged in the Sunken Lane conflict, resupplied with ammunition and came into position on the ridge west of Harpers Ferry Road, southwest of the rectangular cornfield. Joining them there were Richardson's two Napoleons, a 10 lb. Parrott rifle from Squires's 1st Company, and two rifled guns of Reilly's Rowan (North Carolina) Artillery. The five guns in Captain Thomas H. Carter's King William (Virginia) Artillery of D. H. Hill's division arrived on Cemetery Hill, and, as already mentioned, played a significant role in driving the 8th Connecticut from the Harpers Ferry Road Ridge. Carter was joined by the two remaining guns in Captain Robert Boyce's Macbeth (South Carolina) Artillery. The rest of the battery had been wrecked in the Sunken Lane fight. But Boyce, with the spirit that wins battles and prevents calamitous defeat, reorganized his survivors, resupplied his remaining section with ammunition, drove it up to Cemetery Hill, and joined the battle. The Confederates assembled so much artillery that they were able to position some in secondary defensive positions. Bachman's German (South Carolina) Artillery put four pieces on a hill 450 yards west of Harpers Ferry Road, just south of Sharpsburg. Two rifled guns of Captain John P. W. Read's Pulaski (Georgia) Battery in McLaws's division, by order of General Lee, unlimbered on a hill 600 yards west of Bachman. South of Miller's Sawmill Road, four pieces from the 4th Company in Eshleman's Washington (Louisiana) Artillery were deployed at the eastern end of a lane leading to Blackford's farm. Around sunset, with the fighting subsiding, a section of Captain Roger P. Chew's Ashby (Virginia) Battery of horse artillery, and four guns in Captain William Brown's Chesapeake (Maryland) Battery of Ewell's division, which had been left at Harpers Ferry, apparently made the march to Sharpsburg with A. P. Hill, arrived on Miller's Sawmill Road. All told, the Confederates massed 30 guns along their front, with 16 more in reserve, thus gaining thorough artillery superiority over the Union's 9th Corps.[39]

Major Edwin Schall, with the 51st Pennsylvania, wrote to his hometown newspaper that when his regiment reached the ridge east of the Otto farm lane, "everything looked dark and gloomy." Harland's 2nd Brigade and Ewing's 1st Brigade were falling back in confusion, friendly artillery was departing, hostile artillery rounds were shrieking and exploding or thudding all along the ridge, and yelling Rebel infantry seemed to be appearing all across the 9th Corps' front. "We were saluted with a tempest of bullets," continued Schall, and "the artillery of the enemy at the same time plowed our ranks with fearful effect." Brigade commander Edward Ferrero had left Lieutenant Colonel Sumner Carruth and the 35th Massachusetts near the Rohrback Bridge, with orders to turn back all stragglers attempting to cross Antietam Creek. Cox called them up from this duty, ordering Carruth to advance over the ridge east of the Otto farm lane, both to help cover Ewing's retreat and protect Crook's left flank. Ferrero's aide-de-camp, Lieutenant John W. Hudson, was unaware of Cox's orders to the 35th Massachusetts, and when he saw the regiment forming to advance over the ridge, he ran to Carruth and said he was forming in the opposite direction from what Ferrero had ordered. "Yes, sir, but you see I've got another order from that Brigadier General, and I suppose I must execute it," responded Carruth, nodding or pointing at Cox. Cox was not well known in the 9th Corps and Hudson had to look carefully at the officer to be certain who he was. Convinced that it was Cox, he agreed that Carruth must carry out his order. But believing that Cox may not have understood what Ferrero had intended the 35th to do, Hudson made his way to the acting 9th Corps' commander to explain. Hudson was dismounted, and when he reached Cox, he became immediately aware that the Confederates behind the stone wall on the western side of Sherrick's plowed field "were shooting minies our way very uncomfortably." Cox seemed utterly oblivious to the danger and calmly replied to Hudson's explanation: "Yes, I know that; but the regiment must move at once—you see the need for haste." Hudson *did* see, and he happily left the ridge for somewhere that was less exposed.[40]

The 35th Massachusetts lacked training and experience, but with over 700 effectives, they had the numbers that Cox needed to plug a gap. Carruth had just started his regiment forward when Lieutenant Coffin's section, withdrawing from its position near Otto's farm, came thundering "full speed into us," scattering soldiers in all directions to avoid being run over. Fortunately, no one was injured, and the rookies re-formed, rushing over the ridge at the double-quick. They were greeted with a "shower of shot and shell" but, as Lieutenant Clipton A. Blanchard wrote home proudly, the regiment maintained a "steady and bold line." They halted at the worm fence on the eastern side of the Otto farm lane. Some men climbed through or over the fence, into the lane, while others dropped down behind the fence. All opened fire on the closest target, which was Toombs's 15th and 20th Georgia, 250 yards across the plowed field, ensconced behind the stone wall on the edge of the field. They attracted a deluge of return fire from the Georgians, the Confederate artillery nearby, and Archer's and Gregg's men, who were in Sherrick's cornfield. The barrage was so terrific that Lieutenant Albert Pope thought his regiment was outnumbered by 4 to 1. Looking about for support from the rest of their brigade, they noticed that the other regiments had not crossed over the ridge. Instead, they were lying down just below the crest.[41]

The men in the 51st Pennsylvania, on the left of Ferrero's line, found the Confederates in Sherrick's cornfield "as thick as bees in a hive." Everyone in the 51st Pennsylvania, the 51st New York, and the 21st Massachusetts was prone, "for no man could stand up and live one minute." The shelling was terrific. "Shells, balls, grape and canister was flying around us in every direction," wrote Henry W.

Brown, a 20-year-old farmer from Thompson, Connecticut, who had enlisted in the 21st Massachusetts. Some men were hit, the shells "tearing them all to pieces." One shell or solid shot passed directly through the 51st's state colors. Although the Pennsylvanians considered it to be "one of the most violent discharges of case-shot and shells" they had ever experienced, they gratefully noticed that most shells burst directly over the regiment, which sent the bulk of the projectiles' deadly contents 15 to 20 yards to the rear. This was why it was necessary to have these shells burst in front of an enemy line, rather than over it. As it was, men were still killed or wounded, but losses were low, considering the volume of fire directed at them.[42]

The 35th Massachusetts suffered dreadfully in their more exposed position on the forward slope of the ridge. The regiment carried Enfield rifles, and they discovered that the paper on their factory-fresh ammunition was "of the toughest description." This made it difficult for fingers to tear open a cartridge to reach the minie ball and powder, and it reduced their rate of fire to about one round a minute. Officers and file closers—the latter deterred shirkers and closed up any gaps that might occur—ranged along the line, directing the fire of their men or shouting encouragement. Captain Tracy P. Cheever, who had been a Chelsea attorney only a few weeks earlier, could be heard calling to his men, shouting "Pop away, boys! Pop away!" "Our wounded accumulated rapidly," reported the regimental historian. To be struck by a minie ball, musket ball, or piece of shell or shrapnel, one of the New Englanders recorded, "is astonishing; it comes like a blow from a sledgehammer, and the recipient finds himself sprawling on the ground before he is conscious of being hit; then he feels about for the wound, the benumbing blow deadening sensation for a few minutes." Unless a man was struck in the head or heart, the mortally wounded continued to live for some time after being hit, "often in great pain, and toss about upon the ground." Lieutenant Clipton A. Blanchard reported home with pride that "not a man left his post," in his Company C. This was probably true, but it was also evident to the men that running from the fight by going up the exposed slope in their rear was more dangerous than staying and fighting behind a rail fence.[43]

Several officers in the 35th Massachusetts proved this point, although they were not running from the fight, but going for help. The first of these was its commander, Lieutenant Colonel Carruth. He was hit in the neck, close to his jugular vein, a near-fatal injury from which he luckily recovered. Captain William S. King, the acting major, tried a similar dash late in the engagement and was also wounded. King was followed by Captain John Lathrop, who survived the journey over the ridge and back to the regiment with the heartening word that relief was coming. But it never did. The regiment still fought on. About a half hour into the engagement, Gregg's and Archer's Confederates in Sherrick's cornfield adjusted their position, so they could get a crossfire on the New Englanders. This partially enfilading fire, observed Lieutenant Albert Pope, "mowed our men down at a fearful rate." With so much shooting, the barrels of some Enfields grew extremely hot, and the men could not hold the rifles in their hands. Others found their weapons so clogged with powder residue that it was nearly impossible to ram a bullet home. But there were so many wounded and dead that plentiful weapons lay about to replace disabled guns or those too hot to handle. Some Federals went through two or three rifles in the course of the fight.[44]

Cartridges began to run out in Ferrero's veteran regiments. The 51st Pennsylvania's ammunition was used up first. Lieutenant Colonel Joshua Sigfried's 48th Pennsylvania of Nagle's brigade was ordered to relieve their fellows from the Keystone State. Noted Captain Oliver C. Bosbyshell, the 23-year-old commander of Company G, "It wasn't healthy to exhibit much of one's person in that locality, and care was exercised in this respect." The 48th crawled up the ridge to reach the 51st's position, while the men in the latter regiment slithered and slid down. "My! that was a hot place!" exclaimed Bosbyshell. "Thermometer way up above the nineties [metaphorical rather than actual temperature]. Whiz! whip! chung! the bullets came pelting into the ranks." An enemy shell, "with a bang and a splutter," struck in the midst of the 48th's ranks. It filled Lieutenant Jacob Douty's eyes with dirt and bruised his shoulder, tore off one of Sergeant John Seward's legs, mangled Sergeant William Trainer's right arm, and drove the ramrod he was holding into the chest of his 1st lieutenant, William Cullen. The lieutenant, Bosbyshell remembered, "jumped to his feet, tore open his shirt to show his captain the wound, and then dropped dead at [Captain William] Winlack's feet."[45]

Shortly before the 48th Pennsylvania relieved the 51st, Nagle advanced the 9th New Hampshire, which had been supporting Muhlenberg's Battery A, 5th U.S. Artillery, to a position on the left of the 51st Pennsylvania. They were exposed to what Charles H. Little in Company K described as a "murderous firing" of artillery, which killed or wounded a number of men, including Little, who was hit by a shell fragment in his left leg, above the ankle. The artillery fire rattled the inexperienced soldiers, which may account for why the 9th fired into the 12th Ohio. Lieutenant Curtis C. Pollock, in the 48th Pennsylvania, had little good to say about the Granite Staters. He complained about how they had "gone ahead of us," although he could not know the reason for that, and then "broke and ran to the bottom of the hill"—meaning backward, toward Antietam Creek. But only some in the 9th decamped, for when the 48th moved up to replace the 51st Pennsylvania, the rookies cheered them. Pollock would have none of it and complained to his mother that he considered the greenhorns to be "miserable cowards." They were not. Rather, they were untested soldiers sent into combat without training, and many in their ranks stood the severe shelling that afternoon like veterans.[46]

Gregg's, Archer's, and Toombs's men were reinforced during this long and fierce firefight by Branch's North Carolinians. After falling back to escape the enfilading fire of Ewing's 23rd and 30th Ohio, the 7th and 37th North Carolina advanced across the trail of Archer's brigade. The 7th swung right, across the plowed field that stretched between Sherrick's cornfield and the rectangular cornfield, and arrived at the stone wall between Archer's left and Toombs's right. Captain William G. Morris's 37th North Carolina, changing front to the east, came up on the 7th's right flank and advanced a short distance into Sherrick's cornfield, where they fired at the retreating Ohioans. The 18th and 33rd North Carolina, which Branch had held in reserve, followed the 7th and 37th, although they had no orders to do so. When they passed across the rear of the 7th and 37th, Captain Morris pulled his regiment out of the corn and followed the 33rd. That unit, and the 18th, marched past Toombs's two small regiments and wheeled, taking a position on their left. Branch, who, for unknown reasons, seemed to have lost control of his brigade for a brief period, now intervened before they completed their movement and halted the 18th behind Archer. He allowed the 33rd to move up to the stone wall, where they were soon joined by the 37th North Carolina, who squeezed themselves in between Toombs's Georgians and the 33rd's right.[47]

The stone wall provided reasonable cover, but there were still losses. Colonel William McComb, commanding the 14th Tennessee in Archer's brigade, was wounded, and popular Colonel William T. Millican, the commander of Toombs's 15th Georgia, was killed. The men in the 15th felt Millican's loss deeply. "He had the entire confidence and respect of every man in his regiment," lamented Ivy Duggan. The most significant loss however, was Lawrence Branch. At this point it was probably near 6 p.m., and the sun was dropping behind the Harpers Ferry Road Ridge. Firing along the front still flared in certain places, but it was diminishing as both sides ran low on ammunition. Branch rode up and joined Major William McCorkle, now commanding the 12th South Carolina in place of the mortally wounded Colonel Dixon Barnes, as well as Colonel Oliver E. Edwards, the commander of the 13th South Carolina, at the stone wall, along the western edge of Sherrick's corn. These two regiments were to the right of Archer's brigade, on a knoll that provided a view over the corn to the Federals' position, which also meant that it was under enemy observation. The three officers struck up a conversation about the action. Branch raised his field glasses for a better view, and a minie ball pierced the general's right cheek, killing him instantly. Major Joseph A. Engelhard, the brigade's acting adjutant general, told James Lane, who had assumed command of the brigade, that Branch was the victim of a stray bullet. This seems unlikely, given the location of the wound and the fact that Branch, being mounted and using field glasses, was obviously an officer. These devices were typically only possessed by those of higher rank, and thus were a sure way of attracting the attention of a sharpshooter.[48]

AS THE SUN DISAPPEARED below the horizon, the situation along much of the 9th Corps' front was critical. Rodman's 3rd Division and most of Ewing's 1st Brigade had been defeated and scattered, and several units had sustained devastating casualties. Willcox's 1st Division was intact, but most of its regiments were either low on or out of ammunition. Sturgis's 2nd Division was fighting stoutly, but it, too, was critically short of cartridges. Only Crook's 2nd Brigade in the Kanawha Division remained truly combat effective. Ammunition could not be brought forward in any meaningful amount because of the Confederates' continual shelling of the Rohrback Bridge area, which made it too dangerous for the ammo wagons to cross Antietam Creek. Ferrero's aide-de-camp, Lieutenant Hudson, remarked how "the rebels gained a point by making the bridge impassable to teams." To underscore the seriousness of the munitions crisis and the lack of any reserve troops, when the adjutant of the 21st Massachusetts found Hudson and Lieutenant Alfred F. Walcott, who was detached from the 21st to serve as an aide-de-camp to Ferrero, and told them that the regiment had no more cartridges and needed relief, Walcott left the security of the stone wall he and Hudson were sharing and went down near the bridge to find Sturgis. Neither staff officer knew where Ferrero was, and neither wished to get shot trying to find him. Walcott was gone so long that Hudson went in search of him, finally locating the lieutenant near the Rohrback Bridge. Sturgis had just arrived, and when Walcott told him about the situation with the 21st Massachusetts, the general replied, "By G——d they *must* hold it. We've nothing else to hold with." If the Rebels kept attacking, the 9th Corps possibly might be driven into Antietam Creek. Cox communicated the depth of the emergency to Burnside, who sent to McClellan for reinforcements.[49]

McClellan, after returning from his visit to the army's right flank, was riveted by the operations on the 9th Corps' front. From headquarters, it was possible to follow the action with the naked eye. "The advance was distinctly visible from our position," wrote aide-de-camp Colonel Strother, and it "was one of the most brilliant and exciting exhibitions of the day." They watched as Burnside's infantry carried the heights south of Sharpsburg, and then saw the furious Rebel counterattack that sent the Union infantry streaming to the rear in retreat, observing how "the last rays of the setting sun shone upon the bayonets of the enemy crowning the hill from which ours had just been driven." George Smalley, the *New York Tribune* reporter, was present at headquarters then and noted that "McClellan's glass, for the last half hour, has seldom been turned away from the left."[50]

Shortly before 6 p.m., McClellan decided that he needed a closer look at the situation on the 9th Corps' front. The army commander, "followed by his whole retinue," rode down to the vicinity of Weed's and von Kleiser's batteries, which were on the bluffs south of the Boonsboro Pike. This is where Burnside's request for reinforcements reached him (see chapter 14). According to Smalley, who tagged along with the gaggle of horsemen, Burnside's message was sharp but brief: "I want troops and guns. If you do not send them I cannot hold my position for half an hour." This is probably nonsense. If Smalley, as a newspaper correspondent, knew anything about the contents of Burnside's message, it was at second or third hand, not by direct knowledge. As bad as things were on the 9th Corps' front, there is not a shred of evidence anyone thought the situation was so bad that they could not hold their position for half an hour unless they were reinforced. Sturgis's comment to Ferrero's aide-de-camp offers one piece of evidence to refute Smalley. According to the reporter, McClellan gazed at the western sky, toward the setting sun, then answered the aide-de-camp slowly and deliberately: "Tell General Burnside that this is the battle of the war. He must hold his ground till dark at any cost. I will send him Miller's battery. I can do nothing more. I have no infantry." Smalley's article stated that as the aide-de-camp began to ride off with this message, McClellan called to him: "Tell him if he cannot hold his ground, the bridge, to the last! always the bridge! If the bridge is lost, all is lost." Smalley may have actually heard McClellan's reply, for the words he attributes to the army commander were consistent with McClellan's initial report of the battle, Colonel Strother's journal, and Burnside's testimony to the Committee on the Conduct of the War, where he said that McClellan ordered him to hold the Rohrback Bridge at all costs. McClellan did have a flair for dramatic statements and very likely stressed the importance of Burnside maintaining possession of the bridge, but whether he actually uttered these exact words, or they were an invention by Smalley, is unknown. Nonetheless, they have the ring of the latter.[51]

In his journal, Strother expressed an opinion that might have reflected McClellan's thinking about reinforcements: "It was too late to repair errors or initiate any new movement, and they were not sent." But McClellan included an interesting statement in his first after-action report when he wrote that "Burnside had sent to me for reinforcement late in the afternoon, but the condition of things on the right was not such as to enable me to afford them." This provides insight into McClellan's thinking at this critical moment. His belief in the fragile condition of the right, despite its reinforcement by the entire 6th Corps, combined with his certainty regarding Lee's overwhelming numbers, paralyzed him, keeping the Union army's commander from taking any action to help the 9th Corps. The contrast with Robert E. Lee cannot be starker. Although Lee had no infantry to send to his embattled and collapsing right flank, he rounded up every battery or gun that was not essential to holding the front and sent them to bolster his defensive force. The arrival of A. P. Hill's infantry was key in repulsing the 9th Corps' attack, but the concentration of big guns assembled by Lee proved to be equally vital, providing Hill's infantry with artillery superiority.[52]

Although Jacob Cox maintained that he understood the 9th Corps' attack to be a "strong diversion" rather than a main effort, reporter Smalley's widely read account of the engagement gave the assault a far more prominent role when he wrote that at army headquarters, "it is understood that from the outset

Burnside's attack was expected to be decisive." Smalley may have misunderstood the difference between officers hoping an attack might be successful and pinning all hope for a battle's overall outcome on a particular assault. McClellan's orders and decisions support Cox's interpretation of the 9th Corps' mission. If this was a main effort, as Smalley claimed, why were there no reinforcements? Why, as discussed in chapter 14, did McClellan not insist on supporting the right flank of the 9th Corps' offensive strike with the 5th Corps and horse artillery, instead of passively allowing Sykes to withdraw his infantry? In a sentence often overlooked in McClellan's first after-action report, he explained exactly how he viewed the 9th Corps' role: "The effect of Burnside's movement on the enemy's right was to prevent the further massing of their troops on their left, and we held what we had gained." This is entirely consistent with Cox's interpretation of his orders. McClellan considered the 9th Corps' effort on his left to be a diversion, because, by the time the afternoon assault was ordered, he no longer sought to crush Lee's Army of Northern Virginia. Instead, it was an attempt to prevent the Confederates from massing their forces for a counterattack against the Union right that might recover all the ground gained at great cost by the Federals that morning.[53]

There was no criticism of Burnside's generalship or the 9th Corps' repulse in this first report by McClellan. He explained mildly, "It became evident that our force was not sufficient to enable the advance to reach the town, and the order was given to retire to the cover of the hill which was taken from the enemy earlier in the afternoon." It was not until McClellan's second report, published in August 1863, that he began to exaggerate Burnside's failures. Now, McClellan claimed that if the 9th Corps' forward assault "had been consummated two hours earlier, a position would have been secured upon the heights from which our batteries might have enfiladed the greater part of the enemy's line, and turned their right and rear. Our victory might have thus have been much more decisive." After the Army of the Potomac's debacle at the Battle of Fredericksburg, when it was led by Burnside, McClellan knew that the public would more readily believe command failures by Burnside at the Battle of Antietam were the principal reason the Union victory there was not decisive, rather than because of errors McClellan might have made. In his memoir, *Own Story*, McClellan leveled an even more damning indictment at Burnside's generalship when he stated that the ground the 9th Corps held on the western bank of Antietam Creek "was so strong that he [Burnside] should have repulsed the attack and held his own. He never crossed the bridge in person!" The implication was that Burnside had been an absent commander and botched the Federals' defense. Yet McClellan was fully aware that Cox was responsible for the tactical direction of the 9th Corps, not Burnside. There was no reason for Burnside to cross the creek. What difference would it have made had he done so? Most likely it would simply have confused things. The best help Burnside could have given Cox was to send reinforcements and ammunition across Antietam Creek, which was precisely what Burnside did. Among the list of Civil War generals, Burnside will never rank high. But, in his Civil War actions through 1862, he always demonstrated good sense by surrounding himself with competent tactical officers—such as Jesse Reno, Isaac Stevens, and Jacob Cox—letting them do their job with minimal interference and providing military support for them.[54]

In his history of the Battle of Antietam, Ezra Carman gave Jacob Cox high marks for his handling of the 9th Corps: "No corps commander on the field displayed more tactical ability than Cox, both in the attack and the dispositions quickly made when reverse, for which he was not responsible, came to his left." Cox had done extremely well, but did he display more tactical ability than Hooker? Cox's performance was not error free. He seemed slow to appreciate the strength of the Confederates' defenses at the Rohrback Bridge, and his afternoon assault, while well organized, did not provide enough protection for the Federals' vulnerable left flank. Then again, before Burnside approved Cox's assault, he had assurances from the Union army's Signal Corps that no Confederate force of any significance existed south of those that were already known to be on the Harpers Ferry Road Ridge (see chapter 17). In that light, Cox's formation for the attack makes sense. Cox got little credit for his performance, particularly within the 9th Corps, where he was a newcomer and largely unknown. The Regular Army's division commanders, particularly Willcox, seem to have been somewhat jealous of Cox or had contempt for his volunteer-officer background. Reading Willcox's September 25 letter to his wife, as well as his memoirs, gives the sense that without the 1st Division commander's presence, the 9th Corps' entire position would have collapsed, and they would have been routed from the field. In his memoirs, Willcox wrote, "On the falling of Rodman and the consequent confusion and partial disintegration of his command, I rode over to his division, and, with the aid of Scammon, rallied the broken ranks, and pointing to what appeared to be a clear road from my front to Sharpsburg, I succeeded in restoring confidence among the officers sufficiently for another joint movement forward." In this telling, Cox, Sturgis, and other officers disappeared from the battle, and it was Willcox and Scammon who rallied the broken units and restored order. If Willcox actually believed the 9th Corps could renew its attack in the less than 30 minutes of daylight that remained, then he most likely was the only one in the entire corps who thought such a reckless idea was feasible. When he mentioned Cox or Burnside, it was to denigrate them: "I do not remember seeing General Cox during the day, but I suppose he was fully occupied on the left. But this was the time when we felt the loss of Reno. As for my friend Burnside, I do not know how he was handicapped, but I did not see him among us after our crossing the Antietam." Willcox received his orders from Cox, and he obeyed them. There is little doubt that he saw Cox if, as Willcox claimed, he and Scammon were helping to rally broken troops on the 9th Corps' left.

Lieutenant Hudson's testimony tells us precisely where Cox was. As for Burnside, Willcox was well aware that with Cox directing the tactical movements of the corps, the wing commander could be more effective by pushing up logistical support and trying to get reinforcements than he could by riding over the Rohrback Bridge to be seen by others.[55]

Willcox's idea of a counterattack, if he ever actually entertained such a thought, was, at best, delusional. It would have sounded like a cruel jest to the 9th Corps' fighting men, who were holding the front in the waning hours of daylight. Those in the 48th and 51st Pennsylvania, the 51st New York, and the 21st Massachusetts had no ammunition, so they kept the enemy at bay with fixed bayonets. Other units, like the 8th and 16th Connecticut, the 4th Rhode Island, and all of Fairchild's New York regiments, were cut to pieces. They were so disorganized and scattered as to be completely combat ineffective and needed to be withdrawn across Antietam Creek to be reorganized. Only Crook's brigade had the ammunition and organization for offensive action. Robert Kellogg in the 16th Connecticut wrote to his father that when the fighting ceased, his captain was the only one of the unit's 10 company commanders who remained with the regiment, and his company mustered only 6 men out of the roughly 75 they began the day with. "We were <u>murdered</u>," he vented angrily. "A green regt placed unsupported in a cornfield." Some of the rookie soldiers were badly shaken. Lieutenant Richard Green, also in the 16th Connecticut, "was terribly excited and rather lost his bearings at the terrible disaster that had befallen the regiment and he came out of the trouble with his ideas somewhat mixed. He sat down on the road side wringing his hands in anguish, as his body swayed to and fro, he kept muttering 'Big 4th of July' 'Darn big 4th' 'Biggest 4th of July I ever saw' 'Biggest darn 4th.'" When the 8th Connecticut re-formed on the eastern bank of Antietam Creek, they counted only 130 present from the 421 men carried into action. Captain Wolcott Marsh, in the same regiment, described the men who gathered as "a sad exhausted little company." Although Colonel Harland appeared and ordered up rations for them, the "men were so completely exhausted that they did not wait for them to come up and so ate nothing till morning."[56]

Hundreds of stragglers wandered about in the 9th Corps' rear, either skulking or jarred loose from their unit in the confusion. A guard was placed at the Rohrback Bridge to prevent anyone except the wounded crossing over it from west to east, but this was easily circumvented by simply wading the creek. Yet for all the confusion and the severity of their defeat, the 9th Corps lost very few of their men as prisoners—reporting only 115—which reflects positively on how the retreat was managed. Nevertheless, as daylight faded, the situation across the corps' front, particularly on its left, was shaky. "Had the enemy known how few there were to resist their onward march, they would have never halted on yon height and corn field to our left," wrote Major Edwin Schall in the 51st Pennsylvania, "but fortunately for us, and for our country, they knew it not."[57]

In the last light of day, the greenhorns of the 35th Massachusetts grimly fought on, despite heavy casualties. Men writhed or slumped with a myriad of wounds: broken arms and legs, as well as injuries to the head, arms, legs, fingers, side, foot, hip, wrist, and breast. Some had more than one wound. Captain William S. King, the Company K commander, was reportedly struck seven times. Ammunition began to run short for those still fighting, and several of the regiment's captains made their way along the line, removing the cartridge boxes of the dead and disabled and distributing the rounds to the able-bodied. To one of the Bay Staters, the "disabled seemed as numerous as the fighting men." Those in the 35th cast anxious looks to the rear for relief. Rumors spread along the line that help was on its way, "but none came." Why Cox left this regiment on the forward slope of the ridge is a question. The most likely explanation is that its position there protected the exposed left flank of Crook's brigade, which was near Otto's farm, from possible envelopment.[58]

It grew dark enough that gunfire from the Confederate line "twinkled like a display of fireworks." As the men loosed their last cartridges, the surviving senior officers decided that they had done enough, and word was spread along the line to fall back over the ridge to their rear. The Rebels sent a "perfect storm of bullets" at them, but darkness helped the Bay Staters, who were burdened with their many wounded, escape with few additional losses. The bullets and darkness caused confusion, however. As had happened with other regiments, both veteran and rookie, many men became separated from their unit, either deliberately or by accident. One of those in the 35th Massachusetts was Lieutenant Albert Pope, who lost contact with his regiment and ended up down near Antietam Creek. He eluded the guard at the Rohrback Bridge by fording the creek, and he later mingled with men in the 9th New York. In what was unbelievable behavior for an officer, Pope failed to rejoin his regiment for 2 days, spending September 18 wandering around to field hospitals to see if anyone from the 35th was there. He then claimed that he was so weak, he could not make the hike to find his comrades. Pope did not say whether his feebleness was from nerves or physical hunger. Probably it was a combination of both. Combat places enormous stresses on the body, and soldiers react differently to the harrowing experience. In the new regiments, such as the 35th Massachusetts, there were dozens like Pope, who emerged from the fighting dazed, confused, exhausted, shaken, and ravenously hungry. They wandered around in the rear, unable to return immediately to their regiments and face a possible renewal of what they had just survived. The 35th had 48 men killed, 160 wounded, and 6 missing or captured—the second highest regimental loss in the 9th Corps. When this regiment reassembled near Antietam Creek after their withdrawal, only about 200 of the 780 men they carried into action remained. Over 40% of the survivors—men like Lieutenant Pope—were scattered in the rear and did not rejoin the regiment until the next day or on September 19. But it should not be interpreted that these men, after their first true exposure to combat, had abandoned their cause and comrades and now sought to escape the army life they had volunteered for. Of the over 350 men in the 35th Massachusetts who were separated from their unit after their retreat from the Otto farm lane, a scan of the regiment's muster roll reveals that only 3 deserted on September 17. What these soldiers needed most was time to recover, both physically and emotionally. The idea that some general, like Willcox, could have rallied such discombobulated men and hurled them at the enemy was preposterous.[59]

Had the Federals been aware of the situation with their foes, there would have been little concern that the Rebels might drive the 9th Corps into Antietam Creek. On the plus side, A. P. Hill's brigades all remained combat effective. He had only engaged three of the five he brought onto the battlefield. The two others, Pender's and Brockenbrough's brigades, were deployed along the Snavely farm lane. From this location, they could support the divisional batteries on the high ground north of them and, to the south, watch the approaches from Antietam Creek along Harpers Ferry Road and Snavely's Ford. Captain Haskell, Gregg's chief of staff, related that Robert E. Lee had personally directed Hill hold these brigades in reserve (see chapter 17). We do not know who was responsible for where they were positioned, but their location reflects Lee's concern that the Federals might still have the manpower to threaten the Confederates' extreme right flank. These two brigades represented the only unengaged infantry in the entire Army of Northern Virginia. Although A. P. Hill's brigades were intact, his men were utterly exhausted from their 17-mile forced march, followed by over an hour of fierce fighting. Numerically, their losses were light, compared with the damage they had inflicted on the Federals, but their casualties were still significant for the number of men engaged: Gregg lost around 20%, and Archer, 30%. Through the night, however, these losses were probably made good as stragglers from the march caught up with their regiments.[60]

But if Hill's division remained an effective fighting force, D. R. Jones's division was a wreck. Only Toombs's brigade, part of Walker's, and the 7th and 24th Virginia in Kemper's brigade remained intact, but, in terms of numbers, they represented less men than the makeup of a strong regiment. Hardcore elements of Drayton's and Garnett's brigades, and the main body of Kemper's, had rallied, but they amounted to a corporal's guard. Hundreds of stragglers milled about in Sharpsburg, dodging both enemy shells and officers who sought to rally them and return them to the front. General Garnett reported that when he retreated into the village, he found "troops scattered in squads from various parts of the army, so that it was impossible to distinguish men of the different commands." When Garnett encountered stragglers and called on them to join the small group he had gathered, they would inevitably respond that they were "looking for their proper commands" and move on. Captain Peter McGlashan, a company commander in the 50th Georgia of Drayton's brigade, related that there were only 55 soldiers in his regiment by the day's end. They had endured "over forty-eight hours without anything to eat, and the men were utterly exhausted." Surgeon James R. Boulware in the 6th South Carolina of Walker's brigade was in Sharpsburg when the 9th Corps' assault swept up the Harpers Ferry Road Ridge and came perilously close to the village. He observed that "our forces did not stand up to their duty as formerly and we came very near having a panic." No other unit seems to have fallen apart as completely as the 1st South Carolina in Walker's brigade. Walker declared that the regiment's officers were "a disgrace to the service and unworthy to wear a sword." Frank Mixson, a private in the regiment, gave an example to illustrate what Walker meant. When the fighting had subsided, Mixson went in search of an officer to command the 10 men who were still with the colors. He found Lieutenant Lawrence J. Sweat, the only commissioned officer left, and informed him that the lieutenant was now in command. Sweat positively refused to do so and told Mixson that Sergeant Major Jim Hagood should take command, which he did. (Hagood would soon become the regiment's colonel.) The historian of the regiment summarized the effect of its inept leadership: "When two commanding officers leave the field without permission and only because <u>they</u> deem their presence no longer necessary, how is it possible for one to expect the private soldiers to continue at their posts?"[61]

A. P. Hill justly earned great credit for his march to the battlefield and his counterattack, which averted a disaster for the Army of Northern Virginia. There is little to criticize in how the slender and fiery general managed his division's arduous trek from Harpers Ferry to Sharpsburg, and, when it arrived, orchestrated its deployment and engagement. Hill was a visible and inspiring presence. Numerous officers and men recalled seeing him or directly receiving orders from him. He commanded his troops closely enough to the front that Captain Henry E. Young, an aide-de-camp to General David R. Jones, was hit by three spent balls carrying a message to Hill. With a force of less than 2,000 effectives, plus the help of Toombs's small brigade, he defeated an enemy two to three times his size. Hill achieved this by acting decisively and aggressively—hitting hard and fast. He did not divine the enemy's vulnerability by himself, however. Hill gave credit for that to the quietly competent David R. Jones. Jones, Hill reported, "gave me such information as my ignorance of the ground made necessary." Having been in the vicinity since late morning on September 15, Jones was well acquainted with the terrain his division occupied and was able to suggest the best approaches for Hill's brigades to follow, in order to avoid the Federals' artillery and close with their infantry.[62]

Moreover, Hill's counterattack never would have happened had Benning and his Georgians not defended the Rohrback Bridge for nearly 3 precious hours. Toombs's name is often associated with the stand at the bridge, because the soldiers doing so were from his brigade. But Benning, not Toombs, made the dispositions, managed the battle, and deserves the credit—along with his soldiers, who fought with tenacious courage against great odds. Had the 9th Corps carried the Rohrback Bridge sooner on the morning of September 17, given the success their afternoon attack had in rolling up the Confederates' flank, an earlier assault very likely would have forced a general retreat by Lee, in order to prevent his army from being cut off from Boteler's Ford. Hill's Light Division would only have arrived in time to cover that withdrawal and prevent disaster. Viewed in this context, the Union command failures already discussed—by army headquarters, Burnside, and Cox—that led to the poorly coordinated effort to capture the bridge loom large in the failure of the Army of the Potomac to win a more decisive victory in the Battle of Antietam.

Ezra Carman estimated the Confederates' losses, both in the 9th Corps' assault and the Rebels' defeat of that attack, at around 1,000, with A. P. Hill's division incurring 404 casualties; D. R. Jones's division, 565; and the artillery, around 40. These figures may be at the lower end, since casualty records for many of the units that were engaged there are incomplete or unreliable. The Rebels inflicted 2,349 casualties on the 9th Corps, an impressive victory for the Confederates. With approximately one-third the strength of the Federals, they had delivered losses of 2 to 1 on them.

As darkness fell across the blood-soaked, desolate battlefield, the guns gradually sputtered to silence. There were the wounded to be evacuated, ammunition to be brought up and distributed, and regiments to be re-formed and reorganized. But many of that day's survivors simply collapsed into the sleep of those who are completely spent, both in body and mind. The scene in the hard-hit 35th Massachusetts that evening was repeated by many units on both sides as the battle subsided. The men stacked their firearms and dropped to the ground. For those in the 35th, "inquiries for friends passed around; hands were shaken when chums met, as if after a long absence; and low talk was busy about the events of the day. It had been an afternoon in the valley of death." Except for one final, tragic flare-up near Piper's farm at the close of the day, the Battle of Antietam was over.[63]

19

Return to Virginia

"Another such march I do not care to make"

Major Thomas W. Hyde's head was still throbbing from the shelling his regiment had endured earlier in the afternoon. But he took satisfaction from knowing that he had tucked his 7th Maine into such good cover that they only had one man wounded, while the nearby 20th New York had sustained severe losses. It was nearing 5 p.m., and the principal sounds of battle Hyde and his men heard came from south of Sharpsburg, where the 9th Corps was grappling with A. P. Hill. The 7th was lying down with their brigade on the reverse slope of the Dunker Church plateau, nearly in the same location Tompkins's battery had occupied throughout the Union attacks on the Sunken Lane. The Rebels in front of the 7th, around the Piper farm and along the Hagerstown Pike, had been quiet and kept their infantry under cover. But then Captain John B. Cook, commanding Company K, reported movement on the enemy's front. It was probably Colonel G. T. Anderson's brigade, which moved from the Confederates' left to their center and was deployed on the northern end of Cemetery Ridge, southeast of the Piper house, to support their artillery there. Anderson's line was perpendicular to the 7th's position, and Cook thought some well-placed artillery could enfilade the Rebels. He went to Hyde to make that suggestion.[1]

Unbeknownst to Cook, Captain Emory Upton, the bright, ambitious commander of the artillery brigade in the 1st Division, 6th Corps, was conducting a reconnaissance along the front of that division's 3rd Brigade (which the 7th Maine belonged to) at the same time, "and there saw a rebel regiment drawn up in line of battle that could be enfiladed from that position." Upton showed brigade commander Colonel William H. Irwin the target and "earnestly advised" him to request a battery to engage it. In attempting to justify the tragedy that ensued, Irwin exaggerated Upton's report into a dire threat to the security of his brigade's position. "Not a minute could be lost," Irwin reported dramatically. "The enemy were massing in front with the evident design of throwing a powerful column against my left, and they could not be seen, except from that part of the line." Upton said nothing like that, and Irwin omitted the fact that to reach him, the Confederates had to cross a half mile of open ground, rendering the likelihood of an attack extremely remote. Brigadier General William T. H. Brooks, who commanded the Vermont brigade on Irwin's left, mentioned no threat in his front, other than a "galling fire of both artillery and sharpshooters" that tormented his men and inflicted some casualties. Hyde's report of Captain Cook's observation only strengthened Irwin's conviction that the enemy intended mischief for his brigade, and that he urgently needed artillery in his front. His request for a battery to General William Smith, his division commander, was approved, and Irwin sent Upton to fetch one.[2]

Irwin also failed to mention that the Confederates he believed posed a threat to his unit were shelled by six 10 lb. Parrott rifles in Captain William Hexamer's Battery A, New Jersey Light, which was in front of Richardson's division. Hexamer targeted G. T. Anderson's brigade. Although he inflicted no damage on them, it caused the Georgian to shift his brigade behind a ridge just west of Piper's barn, which paralleled the farm lane to the Hagerstown Pike, where his men disappeared from sight. It was most likely this movement that Irwin interpreted as the enemy massing in his front. There were some other Confederates— remnants of D. H. Hill's and Richard H. Anderson's divisions—who could be seen along the Piper farm lane and the Hagerstown Pike, but their numbers were small and they showed no inclination to attack. Nonetheless, Irwin was not shaken from his opinion that his brigade's position was in danger. Soon a three-gun section of 3-inch ordnance rifles from Captain John W. Wolcott's Battery A, Maryland Light, rumbled up and unlimbered in front of the 7th Maine and the 16th New York. According to Irwin, this artillery played "on the masses of the enemy with great effect for half an hour." There is no evidence that the shelling caused any casualties, but it provoked an immediate reaction by the Rebels. They infiltrated skirmishers into Piper's orchard, and they began firing on Wolcott's section from a range of nearly 600 yards. Other sharpshooters and skirmishers around Piper's barn and nearby haystacks joined in. Irwin had stirred up a hornet's nest.[3]

If Irwin's after-action report serves as a guide, he was excitable and prone to exaggeration. He had a reputation for drinking heavily, and in January 1862 he had been court-martialed for neglect of duty, intoxication, and conduct prejudicial to good order and military discipline. The court did not find him guilty of intoxication—even though Irwin did not deny he had been drinking—but it upheld the third charge. The colonel received a 30-day suspension and an official reprimand. This was not Irwin's first court-martial, however. In November 1861, Brigadier General Winfield Hancock court-martialed him for impeding a grand review of the Union army by McClellan and President Lincoln when Irwin stopped his regiment and started drilling it in front of the reviewing stand. In this instance, Irwin lost his rank and pay for 60 days. The history of Irwin's regiment, the 49th Pennsylvania, documents other examples of the colonel's blunders that also drew Hancock's wrath. Thomas Hyde believed Irwin's judgment was impaired by alcohol on September 17, but the major's claim has never been corroborated. Irwin's principal problem was that, while he may have been "a gallant man"—Hyde's description of him—he possessed poor judgment and exceeded his capabilities by commanding a brigade.[4]

Wolcott's battery reported 1 man killed and 12 wounded at Antietam. Whether these losses occurred in the section that was in front of the 7th Maine is unknown, but the Confederates' long-range sharpshooting was destructive enough that Wolcott "complained bitterly" to Irwin about it, pointing out that the most accurate fire was coming from near some haystacks west of Piper's barn. Irwin's initial reaction made use of textbook tactics. He ordered Major Hyde to deploy one company as skirmishers and drive the Rebel riflemen back. But Irwin may not have realized how small the 7th Maine was. They numbered only 181 officers and men, and the company Hyde selected, Lieutenant Joseph G. Butler's Company D, only had 15 men in it. When Irwin saw this tiny band start forward, he rode up to Hyde and said, "That is not enough, sir; go yourself; take your regiment and drive them from those trees and buildings." Irwin's standing orders from the 2nd Division "were positive not to advance my line," but he thought that advancing a small regiment to clear his front of sharpshooters did not violate them. Hyde attempted to reason with Irwin, telling the colonel that he had observed what he thought were two Rebel brigades moving into the area he was being asked to attack. Irwin was unmoved and, like a classic bully, questioned Hyde's personal courage. "Are you afraid to go sir?" he blustered. Incredulous, Hyde asked him to repeat the order and point out the ground again. "He did so, quite emphatically, in near the same words, and added with an oath, 'those are your orders, sir,'" the major reported. Then Irwin proceeded to repeat this command several more times. Years later, Hyde reminisced, "I wish I had been old enough, or distinguished enough, to disobey orders." But he was neither at this moment, and the tragedy was set in motion. Hyde had no illusions about what awaited him and his men. "When we moved down into the fatal valley no man of us expected to return," he wrote to his mother a week later.[5]

Hyde shouted "Attention," and the regiment came to its feet. There were two teenagers—Johnny Begg and George Williams, 19 and 18 years old, respectively—who carried the regiment's guidons. Hyde ordered them to the rear, considering them unnecessary for the perilous movement the regiment was about to make, as well as wishing to protect the young men. Instead, they waited until the major's attention was diverted and snuck back into the ranks, with tragic consequences for them both. For reasons he did not explain, Hyde also decided to take the regiment's colors—they carried only a national flag—from Corporal Harry Campbell and to give it to Sergeant Perry Greenleaf. The motive appears to have been the same as the one that caused Hyde to order Begg and Williams to the rear—Hyde's compassion for his soldiers. Campbell was a corporal, and Greenleaf was a sergeant. It was a sergeant's duty to be a color bearer, and

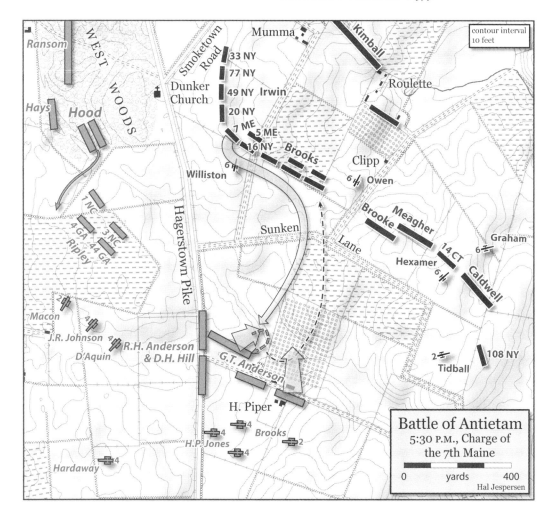

Battle of Antietam
5:30 P.M., Charge of
the 7th Maine

0   yards   400
Hal Jespersen

Hyde apparently felt it was more justifiable to ask a sergeant to assume the risk of carrying the colors in an attack. But Campbell was so disappointed at what he felt was a demotion that Hyde changed his mind and let him keep the flag.[6]

Irwin's objective for Hyde was to clear the Rebels from around Piper's barn and the haystacks west of the barn. To accomplish this, the major planned an indirect approach. If his regiment advanced straight south, it would take them over open ground, where they could be enfiladed by the Confederates' artillery along Reel Ridge. It also would not take into account the enemy skirmishers on the 7th's left, who were in Piper's cornfield and orchard. Hyde sent Butler's Company D toward the southwest, to drive these Rebels off. The rest of the regiment advanced to the post-and-rail fence in front of the brigade and formed into line. Hyde led them by the left flank (east), across the Mumma farm lane. That brought the 7th Maine in front of the 16th New York in Bartlett's brigade and Brooks's Vermont brigade, whose men were lying down in Mumma's cornfield.

As the 7th passed by, the colonel in the 4th Vermont asked Brooks if his regiment could support the attack. Brooks, who knew better, responded, "Too dangerous, sir. You will never see that Regiment again."[7]

When the 7th Maine reached a point about parallel with Piper's cornfield, Hyde ordered the men to face front and advance. This took them over the Sunken Lane, in the area that had been defended by the 6th Alabama's right wing. Hyde found it "so filled with the dead and wounded of the enemy that my horse had to step on them to get over." He directed the regiment into Piper's battered cornfield. He halted it there, in order to quickly re-form ranks and fix bayonets. He set their objective "on a point to the right of Piper's barns" and ordered a charge. The 7th burst out of the corn and sprinted across the meadow west of the orchard. Fearing that they would be outflanked, the Confederate skirmishers in the orchard "broke and ran," temporarily eliminating the threat to Hyde's left flank. The major experienced a feeling of "great exhilaration" as he watched the Rebels run. He glanced along his advancing solid line and saw his close friend, Captain William L. Haskell, the acting adjutant, on the left. Haskell—who was riding "Whitey," the magnificent white horse of the regiment's absent colonel— was urging the men on. Hyde's moment of euphoria vanished when one of Wolcott's guns fired what was probably a canister round at the Rebels, which instead took out four men in the 7th's right company. Then, in the first burst of fire from the enemy, "Whitey" and Haskell went down. The Confederates around Piper's farm buildings, however, began to flee. The 7th surged on toward the barn. Hyde rode out in front of them, just in time to see a line of Rebels suddenly rise up from behind a stone wall along the eastern side of the Hagerstown Pike. These were elements from R. H. Anderson's and D. H. Hill's divisions. They fired a volley that did little or no damage, which Hyde thought was because his regiment was moving so quickly. He shouted "Left oblique," which moved his men behind a rise of ground that gave them cover from this fire.[8]

This movement took the 7th Maine toward the ridge west of Piper's barn, which paralleled his farm lane. Hyde continued riding some 20 feet in front of the regiment. When he crested the ridge, he saw a line of men lying down behind it, weapons at the ready, poised and waiting. It was G. T. Anderson's brigade.[9] Anderson had his 500 or so effectives well in hand, but the other Confederates on Hyde's front and flanks were "all in more or less disorder." Before the 7th's attack, D. H. Hill had been walking up and down the Piper farm lane, encouraging the disorganized remnants gathered there. When Hill heard his skirmishers in the orchard and cornfield start firing, he went up to the ridge near Piper's barn and saw the 7th Maine approaching. He warned Anderson, who readied his men to meet the attack. General Hill then directed some of his own men to hurry toward Piper's house, to position themselves on the Yankees' left flank. It was this movement that Hyde probably misinterpreted as the enemy fleeing from his assault.[10]

The instant Hyde saw G. T. Anderson's brigade, he shouted "Left flank," which his veterans executed immediately. This caused the regiment to march parallel to the Piper farm lane, heading toward a "clump of trees where there was a fence and cow yard," and, just beyond that, Piper's orchard. Hyde now saw another Confederate force running toward the orchard, in order to head him off. These men were remnants of Cumming's Alabama brigade in R. H. Anderson's division, which was now under the command of Major Hilary A. Herbert. The brigade was very small—for example, the 8th Alabama had rallied only 8 survivors from the Sunken Lane disaster—and mustered, at most, about 100 men. Some stout souls in Ripley's and Ambrose Wright's brigades joined them, adding an extra dollop of muskets and rifles. The total force was tiny, but it moved aggressively to cut off the Federals.[11]

The 7th Maine now reached the fence enclosing Piper's orchard. Although the men were able to get through it easily, Sergeant Andrew M. Benson had to dismantle it further to provide passage for Hyde and his horse. As he did so, a bullet or shell fragment struck his haversack and sent his rations flying through the air. Despite the close call and the danger rapidly approaching them, Hyde, Benson, and the others nearby "had to laugh at the flying hardtack." The laughter ceased moments later, when the regiment—still advancing at the double-quick—reached a rise of ground running through the orchard and was confronted by Major Herbert's force. The Confederates fired several volleys at the New Englanders and then charged. At the same moment, G. T. Anderson's brigade, along with a gaggle of stragglers whom a musket-wielding D. H. Hill had rallied around Piper's house, advanced on Hyde's men from the west.[12]

Earlier in the morning, when Cumming's brigade had advanced to the Sunken Lane, they followed approximately the same route the 7th Maine was using to escape the forces closing in on them. Lieutenant Alexander Chisholm in the 9th Alabama, who was with Major Herbert's group, heard some of his men saying "Ground them to the fence," or "We will get them at the fence." They were referring to the picket fence around the orchard that had been an obstacle to their escape earlier, during the retreat from the Sunken Lane. Chisholm's soldiers sensed an opportunity to turn the tables on these Yankees and trap them against the fence.[13]

Hyde called a halt on a ridge of higher ground about midway through the orchard and had his men fire on Herbert's force, to prevent it from cutting them off. But driving back Herbert's men meant not resisting the other Confederates who were closing in. The 7th was fired on from three directions: front, right, and left. To add to the mayhem, a Confederate battery started lobbing shells at them. One passed so close to Hyde's leg that he lost any feeling in it. Then his horse was shot in the mouth and hip by buck and ball. It reared and went down, taking Hyde with it. His soldiers were falling rapidly, but the survivors poured a "terrible fire" into the converging group of Rebels. This gave Hyde a moment to examine his horse and discover that although it had lost some teeth, its hip injury was superficial. He managed to get the animal up, then remounted and ordered a retreat. He heard his color corporal, Harry Campbell, crying out "Major, Major, help." Earlier in the attack, Campbell had been hit and showed his bloody arm to Hyde. There was no time to stop, and Hyde could only say, "Take the other hand, Harry." Campbell did, carrying the flag with his good arm before he was wounded again, this time mortally. Hyde turned back to help the corporal and save the regimental colors. The fruit trees, although relatively short, limited Hyde's view, but as he hurried along, he caught a glimpse of Confederate soldiers running through the orchard between him and his regiment. One of them carried a battle flag and was close enough for Hyde to be able to read "Manassas" as one of its battle honors. He was forced to make the agonizing decision to abandon Campbell, in order to save himself and the others. "I shall never forget that agonizing cry," he wrote to his mother about that moment.[14]

Urging his mount on, Hyde reached the high picket fence along the orchard's northern edge. He found "no means of exit" through the fence, which was too tall for his horse to jump over. A group of Confederates were closing in on him when he heard Sergeant Henry F. Hill shout, "Back boys and save the Major." Hill and his squad ran back to the fence and fired a volley into the Rebels, at a range of 10 yards. Hyde thought he saw six men fall. This check bought precious moments for the sergeant to dismantle a section of the fence with his saber bayonet, enabling the major and his horse to get through.[15]

Colonel Irwin, watching the debacle his orders had created unfold before him, searched frantically for support to cover the 7th Maine's escape. Knowing he had no authority to order any other regiment from his brigade forward, he went to the regiment of Brooks's brigade that was on his left and asked its commander if he would advance. The reply was no, not without the approval of Brooks, and there was no chance of obtaining it. Captain Upton provided some help when he relieved Wolcott's rifled section of artillery, which had exhausted its ammunition, with the six Napoleons of Lieutenant Edward B. Williston's Battery D, 2nd U.S. Artillery. Williston blasted the forces converging on the 7th with shrapnel. Hyde wrote that this "aided us much," although the rounds burst so close, "we were more afraid of the grape [shrapnel balls] than of the enemy." Confederate accounts confirmed the effectiveness of Williston's fire. "We could not pursue them as far as I wished, because of the severe fire of artillery directed against us from long range guns that we could not reach," reported G. T. Anderson.[16]

When Hyde emerged from the orchard, he encountered the sole survivor of the color guard, who was carrying the national flag he had rescued from Campbell when the corporal was hit. Hyde gathered the 68 survivors of his regiment around their colors, and they marched back to friendly lines. As they approached

Brooks's brigade, the Vermonters rose up, waving their hats "and made the wel-kin ring" with cheers. Nearly every man in the 7th Maine bore the marks of bullets through their clothing or equipment. Hyde was "splashed from head to foot with blood" and thought he had been injured, but further examination showed that the blood was from his wounded horse. Everyone was emotionally and physically shaken and angry. The regiment returned to its position minus 51% of its strength, with 12 dead, 62 wounded, and 20 missing. The men threw themselves down on the ground and, as Hyde wrote to his mother, "*all* were cry-ing like children and execrating the man who had made us lose so many of our comrades by his foolish order." Irwin lavished praise on the unit he had sent to its destruction. "No words of mine can do justice to the firmness, intelligence, and heroic courage with which this regiment performed its dangerous task," he wrote. Of Hyde, Irwin declared that "conduct like this requires soldierly quali-ties of the highest order." His commendation of Hyde and the 7th was deserved, but it could not mask the criminal incompetency that delivered the regiment up for slaughter. All Irwin would have needed to do to protect Wolcott's guns was to deploy the regiment as skirmishers, engaging the Confederates in the or-chard and around Piper's house, which would have drawn the Rebels' fire away from the artillery and kept casualties low.[17]

The reputation of Hyde and his regiment were burnished by this tragic epi-sode. The major was called to the headquarters of 2nd Division's commander, William F. Smith, the following morning, where General Smith met Hyde with "tears in his eyes." Smith was joined by two of the 6th Corps' other major gener-als, William B. Franklin and Henry W. Slocum, in heaping praise on the young man. The 7th Maine was pulled from line duty and reassigned as guard for the 2nd Division's headquarters. Irwin was temporarily relieved of command and, Hyde heard, "severely censured." Nonetheless, Irwin kept his commission, which Hyde thought he might lose. Instead, Smith and Franklin transferred the 49th Pennsylvania and Irwin to the 1st Brigade, which removed him from bri-gade command. But his flagrant blunder received barely a mention in Smith's after-action report, in which he praised Irwin as "particularly gallant" and only stated that the colonel's orders to the 7th "were not made known to me till after the regiment moved forward." The only consequences from the sad affair were for those who became casualties and their families, as well as the bitter memo-ries the survivors carried with them.[18]

Night

Mercifully, the sun set at 6:07 p.m., and the day of frightful violence sputtered to silence. Two armies totaling nearly 120,000 men had mauled one another for nearly 13 hours. The carnage stunned veterans of the Peninsula and Second

Manassas Campaigns. Later battles in the Civil War, such as the Crater, Fort Pillow, and the Mule Shoe at Spotsylvania, would exceed Antietam for viciousness, but not for the scale of slaughter in such a relatively short time. Ezra Carman estimated that the Army of the Potomac engaged approximately 56,000 men, with 2,108 killed, 9,549 wounded, and 753 missing or captured, for a total of 12,410, or 22%. For comparison, the U.S. Army landed 55,000 men on the Normandy beaches on D-Day and incurred 4,649 casualties, or 8%.[19]

Carman estimated the engaged strength of the Army of Northern Virginia at 37,351. There will be endless haggling about the Confederates' strength, but we will never know with any precision how many men they had. Stragglers were being driven forward to join their commands throughout the battle, and officer losses were so heavy that some units simply never knew beyond a rough estimate how many men they took into action. Carman's numbers are as good as any we are likely to discover. Incomplete and inaccurate Confederate casualty returns for the *entire Maryland Campaign* (cavalry skirmishes and the Battles of South Mountain, Crampton's Gap, Harpers Ferry, and Sharpsburg) gave their losses as 1,567 killed and 8,724 wounded, with none reported as missing or captured. These figures are so inaccurate that they are of relatively little value. Nonetheless, some examples can provide a sense of the actual damage the Confederate army sustained. The 5th Florida officially reported no losses, but the regiment was decimated, with 30 killed, 93 wounded, and 36 missing or captured out of 240 men who were engaged, for a total of 66%. The 6th Georgia's casualties are listed as 10 killed and 13 wounded in the returns, but the actual figures were a staggering 81 killed, 115 wounded, and 30 missing or captured. Carman's careful study of Confederate losses at Sharpsburg concluded that there were 1,546 killed, 7,752 wounded and 1,018 missing or captured, for a total of 10,316, or just over 27%. But there is evidence that even Carman's numbers are slightly low, and casualties do not fully reflect the effect a battle has on unit organization. The Army of Northern Virginia would not experience another day in which so many brigades were rendered combat ineffective until the end of the Civil War. "Many gallant commands were torn as a forest in a cyclone," wrote Longstreet. The list included all of R. H. Anderson's brigades: Cumming's, Posey's, Parham's (which only brought 75 men onto the battlefield), Pryor's, and Wright's. In David R. Jones's division, Drayton's, Garnett's, Kemper's, and Walker's brigades; Evans's independent brigade; Douglass's and Hays's brigades in Lawton's division; Grigsby's, Jackson's, Warren's, and Starke's brigades in John R. Jones's division; and Ripley's, Rodes's, McRae's, Anderson's, and Colquitt's brigades in D. H. Hill's division. This was 21 of the army's 39 infantry brigades. Although all of these tattered units managed to rally small groups of survivors, they were company sized (or perhaps had enough for a couple of companies), such as those Major Herbert collected from Cumming's brigade. Some even occupied positions along the front line, like the remnants of Colquitt's and McRae's brigades at the Sunken

Lane. But all were exhausted and famished, and key leaders were missing, due to casualties. "We were so badly crushed that at the close of the day ten thousand fresh troops could have come in and taken Lee's army and everything he had," opined Longstreet. We shall return to the damage the army sustained and how it recovered in chapter 21, but its condition on the evening of September 17 was critical.[20]

As night crept across a field of slaughter, senior officers reported in at Lee's headquarters, on the western edge of Sharpsburg, to make their reports. Colonel Stephen D. Lee, in an 1896 article which appeared in the *Richmond Dispatch*, claimed that Robert E. Lee "had summoned his corps and division commanders to meet him," a meeting the colonel described as a council of war. This gathering of officers, which also included some artillery battalion commanders, was described by Lieutenant William M. Owen, adjutant of the Washington (Louisiana) Artillery, who attended it with Colonel John B. Walton. Owen saw Stonewall Jackson, D. H. Hill, A. P. Hill, Jubal Early, John B. Hood, and David R. Jones there. Lafayette McLaws and John G. Walker apparently were not present, but we may presume that both made a report of their respective divisions' conditions. James Longstreet and Charles Marshall were emphatic in stating to Ezra Carman that S. D. Lee was wrong. They claimed that it was not a council of war, but a typical post-battle reporting session that allowed Lee to take the pulse of his army and assess the damage it had sustained. The intent was *not* to poll his commanders for their opinions on what he should do.[21]

S. D. Lee's account of the meeting is the most detailed, but he was either mistaken in important particulars, or simply invented them. He claimed that Lee asked each of his officers as they arrived, "General, how is it on your part of the line?" Lee may have done so, but S. D. Lee claimed that the first officer to speak was Longstreet and even asserted that he remembered exactly what the wing commander said. The problem was that Longstreet had not yet arrived to utter anything. When the fighting had subsided, and Longstreet was certain that the enemy's attacks were finished for the day, he rode along his front and gave general instructions to his commanders for that night and the next morning. Since his front stretched from near the West Woods to D. R. Jones's division in front of Sharpsburg, this took time. He was further delayed from reporting to Lee by coming across wounded soldiers "hidden away under stone walls and in fence corners, not yet looked after." Then he met a family whose home had been set on fire by a shell and helped to get assistance for them. By the time he reached headquarters, all the other officers had made their reports, and Lee was concerned that Longstreet may have been wounded. Lieutenant Owen recalled him anxiously asking, "But where is Longstreet?" A staff officer replied, "I saw him at sundown, all right." Minutes later the wing commander rode up, "smoking the cigar which he had held all day, unlighted, between his clenched teeth." When he dismounted, Lee approached him "very hurriedly for one of his dignified manner," threw his arms on Longstreet's shoulders, and said, with evident relief, "Here is my old war-horse at last."[22]

In S. D. Lee's telling, Longstreet, Jackson, and D. H. Hill all were of the opinion that the Army of Northern Virginia should retreat across the Potomac River that night. Perhaps Jackson and Hill did make such a recommendation—although there is no other confirmatory evidence—but Longstreet definitely did not. His memory of what he told Lee was clear. He pointed out that Lee had seen with his own eyes the damage the Confederate army had sustained. He spoke to Lee alone, not in front of a group. There was "little said," and "not one word was noted or referred to the withdrawal from our position." It was after Longstreet's report that Lee told his officers "he would not be prepared the next day for offensive battle, and would prepare only for defense," to which Longstreet added, "as we had been doing." While there are probably elements of truth in S. D. Lee's account, it reads like an attempt to burnish Robert E. Lee's reputation by highlighting his audacity and prescience in reading his opponent's mind. Longstreet's advice to Carman regarding S. D. Lee was that "all accounts of post bellum make should be taken with a grain of salt, and unless supported by other and reliable persons, or by circumstances that justify faith, should be salted away."[23]

Practical considerations, not reckless boldness, guided Robert E. Lee's decision to remain at Sharpsburg on September 18. He had nearly 8,000 injured men, and, as Longstreet had found, many still needed to be collected and transported to field hospitals. The walking wounded and those who could safely be moved by wagon or ambulance were to be evacuated to Virginia—a slow, complicated, delicate process, given the sorry state of the Confederate army's transportation. The troops holding the front lines were worn out and famished. Demanding that they make yet another night march and a river crossing might have posed more of a risk than letting them remain in position for another day. This way Lee and his officers could rest and feed the men, push up stragglers, and make the necessary preparations for an orderly withdrawal. In his official report of the Maryland Campaign, Lee wrote that on September 18, "though still too weak to assume the offensive, we waited without apprehension the renewal of the attack." There are two possible interpretations for what he meant. One, Lee believed that his army, in its more compact position, could hold its own if McClellan attacked again. Two, Lee did not expect McClellan to attack once more on the 18th. Longstreet offers a possible clue to Lee's thinking. Lee, in an opinion expressed later, thought that McClellan "could be relied upon to conform to the strictest rules of science in the conduct of war." All good commanders take the measure of their opponents, and McClellan was a highly predictable general. He had behaved uncharacteristically only once—on September 14, at the Battle of South Mountain. Lee had correctly believed McClellan would not attack on September 16, and he seems to have applied the same logic to September 18, thinking that

McClellan would use the day to reorganize and bring up reinforcements before renewing the battle. Lee's decision to remain at Sharpsburg for another day was not without peril, for he could not be certain that McClellan would not attack, but it was not a decision made with reckless audacity, as Lee's admirers are fond of claiming. It was, instead, a coolly calculated risk. The Confederates would hold their positions and remain quiet.[24]

"BY EIGHT O'CLOCK THE wailing cries of the wounded and the glare of the burning buildings alone interrupted the silence and darkness which reigned over the field of the great battle," wrote McClellan's aide-de-camp, Colonel David Strother. McClellan led his headquarters party from where they had observed the final stages of the 9th Corps' attack and repulse toward the Army of the Potomac's administrative headquarters in Keedysville. He did not return to the Pry farm, because it had been transformed into a field hospital, with General Israel Richardson and General Joe Hooker among its patients. Before departing for Keedysville, McClellan received a signal message from the Elk Mountain station reporting an "immense train of enemy's wagons" on the road to Shepherdstown, which appeared to be halting a mile south of that village. Was the enemy retreating? McClellan forwarded the message to Burnside at 6:15 p.m., with directions "that if there is any truth in it, he desires you to push the enemy vigorously. Let the general know if the enemy is retreating, and he will push forward with the center." It was an odd communication, given the circumstances at that hour, but the signal station's warning may have arrived before McClellan received Burnside's message about the present situation the 9th Corps was facing. Clearly, based on Burnside's report, the enemy were not retreating, and McClellan arrived at his Keedysville headquarters pondering whether "to renew the attack again on the 18th or to defer it, with the chance of the enemy's retirement after a day of suspense."[25]

Burnside arrived at army headquarters around 8:30 p.m. to report on the situation on his front. In his testimony to the Joint Congressional Committee on the Conduct of the War in March 1863, Burnside related that he met with Chief of Staff Marcy and "some other staff officers," who may have been shielding an emotionally drained McClellan, and expressed the opinion "that the attack ought to be renewed the next morning at 5 o'clock." The staff informed Burnside that "our right had been so badly broken that they could not be got together for an attack," that "very little of Hooker's corps was left," and that Sumner "advised General McClellan not to renew the attack," but to wait for reinforcements before recommencing the fighting. Nevertheless, Marcy thought McClellan should hear Burnside's report and admitted him to the general's tent. Burnside testified that he "expressed the same opinion" to his chief about an early morning attack, stating that if he could be reinforced with 5,000 fresh troops, "I would be willing to commence the attack on the next morning." McClellan replied he was thinking the matter over "and would make up his mind during the night." He then asked Burnside to leave a staff officer at headquarters, adding that "if he [McClellan] concluded to renew the attack, he would send me the necessary men."[26]

In his initial report on the Battle of Antietam, McClellan made no mention of this meeting with Burnside, merely stating that the wing commander had sent for reinforcements late in the day. At that point, McClellan felt he could not spare any, because "the condition of things on the right was not such as to enable me to afford them." Ten months later, however, in his final report—with Burnside's testimony on record, and criticism of McClellan's management of the battle mounting—the army commander was silent about Burnside's request for reinforcements on the night of September 17. Instead, McClellan claimed that on the morning of the 18th, Burnside asked for an entire division as reinforcements, "to assist in holding his position on the other side of the Antietam," and that "he gave me the impression that if he were attacked again that morning, he would not be able to make a very vigorous resistance." In his book, *Own Story*, McClellan went further, alleging that besides begging for reinforcements on the morning of the 18th, Burnside "told me that his men were so demoralized and so badly beaten the day before that were they attacked they would give way." He also added the damning indictment that "Burnside was in no condition to know the real state of his command, as he had not been with it."[27]

To lend credibility to these accusations, McClellan solicited the reminiscences of Colonel Delos B. Sackett, the inspector general of the Army of the Potomac. Sackett claimed he was in McClellan's headquarters tent when Burnside arrived. Sackett recalled that the Rhode Islander requested permission to withdraw his troops across Antietam Creek, "giving as a reason the dispirited condition of his men; stating further that if he remained in his present position and an attack was made by the enemy, he very much feared the result." According to Sackett, McClellan replied that the 9th Corps must hold its position, to which Burnside responded that he would need a reinforcement of 5,000 men to do so. At this point in the conversation, according to Sackett, other general officers arrived and he left the tent. But, as has already been discussed (see chapter 15), Sackett was not a neutral observer.[28]

Under close scrutiny, McClellan's and Sackett's allegations of a *demoralized* Burnside crumble, while the latter's testimony to the joint congressional committee is strengthened. Burnside was careful to mention that he expressed his opinion that the Union army should renew its attack on the Confederates in the 9th Corps' front on the 18th not only to McClellan, but also to Marcy and other staff officers. Had Burnside lied about this, any one of them could have provided McClellan with testimony to the contrary, but none did—until Sackett spoke up 13 years later, and then only at McClellan's prompting. As for Burnside's claim in his congressional testimony that Marcy and other staff officers told him the army's right had been "badly broken," Hooker's corps was decimated, and Sumner thought the attack should not be renewed, those opinions were all consistent with the impression McClellan had formed from his visit to the right flank in the afternoon of September 17 and his meeting and correspondence with Sumner. The staff were merely repeating what was believed at headquarters. While it is well documented that there was considerable confusion on the 9th Corps' front at the close of the engagement, there is no evidence that the corps was demoralized or that Burnside advocated withdrawing it across Antietam Creek. Cox angrily denied that any part of the 9th Corps, "except part of Rodman's division was not in good condition & heart on the evening of the 17th." Orlando Willcox, who never failed to take advantage of blowing his own horn or knocking down his "friend" Burnside, did not breathe a word about demoralization or withdrawal in his immediate post-battle letters.[29]

Burnside was not alone in advocating that the fight be renewed the next day. When McClellan met with Franklin during his visit to the army's right on September 17, the 6th Corps' commander outlined a plan to seize Nicodemus Heights the next morning. McClellan "assented to this, and it was understood that the attack was to be made," Franklin recalled, years later. But Franklin and Burnside held a minority opinion within the Army of the Potomac's high command. Testifying before the joint congressional committee in February 1863, Sumner rejected the idea that the army could have successfully attacked again on the 18th. He maintained his opinion that Hooker's 1st Corps "had been dispersed and routed," and "troops are not exactly prepared to make a rapid pursuit the next day after such a battle as that." George Meade wrote to his wife that the Union army "was a good deal broken & demoralized," and it was "deemed hazardous to risk an offensive movement on our part until the reinforcements arrived here." Even Franklin, in private, harbored doubts. "Between ourselves I was not sorry that it was so, for our Army is too tired & too diminished in numbers to be able to do a great deal of work," he confided in a letter to his wife. Colonel Alexander Webb, the 5th Corps' chief of staff, expressed the point of view prevailing at his corps' headquarters when writing to his father on September 24: "Now that all is over you will hear that we ought to have advanced the next day. Well I say that myself but no one thought so at the time. . . . I know of no advocates for a continuance of the battle on the 18th." The Confederates in the Army of Northern Virginia had fought desperately at every point, and there was a widespread belief that their strength was greater than that of the Army of the Potomac. General Marsena Patrick, in the 1st Corps, was thankful his men were not attacked by the Rebels on the night of the 17th. "We had all that we could do to hold our ground yesterday, and, if we had attempted to push the enemy today, with the same troops, I think we should have been whipped," he wrote in his diary. Webb believed the enemy had 100,000–130,000 men, while a fellow staff officer in the 5th Corps, Stephen M. Weld, firmly believed that "the enemy greatly outnumber us."[30]

Besides Burnside, the only other corps commander McClellan apparently consulted that night was Fitz John Porter. McClellan offered an idea of their discussion in his first report: "To renew the attack again on the 18th or defer it, with the chance of the enemy's retirement after a day of suspense, were the questions before me." We do not know what advice Porter offered, but given his concern for "the safety of the artillery and center of the line," it is unlikely that he encouraged a renewed offensive before reinforcements arrived. As Sumner testified several months later, September 17 "had been a very severe action—uncommonly severe." McClellan accepted Sumner's opinion that Hooker's 1st Corps was wrecked and the 12th Corps was only in marginally better shape. Losses in Sumner's 2nd Corps were heavy, and the 9th Corps had been driven back on the left, losing nearly 20% of its strength in casualties. Only the four divisions in Porter's 5th Corps and Franklin's 6th Corps were in any condition to lead an assault. There were two possible points at which to strike: a renewed assault toward the Rebels on Burnside's front, or an attack with Franklin's corps against Nicodemus Heights. Burnside's front was the least promising. The Confederates controlled the high ground dominating all avenues of approach here; the beachhead across Antietam Creek was shallow; and, if Porter reinforced the 9th Corps to lead an attack, who would guard the Union army's center? Franklin's plan was the most promising, and it had the advantage of powerful artillery support from all the guns that were already assembled there, extending from Poffenberger Hill to across the front of the East Woods. But, other than the 6th Corps, McClellan considered all the other troops on this part of his front to be unreliable in an attack.[31]

There was also the question of ammunition. The 20 lb. Parrott rifles in Hays's Artillery Reserve had nearly exhausted their supply in their daylong bombardment of the enemy's lines. McClellan requested that the army's chief of ordnance, General James W. Ripley, "force some 20-pounder Parrott ammunition through to-night, via Hagerstown and Chambersburg, to us, near Sharpsburg, Md." Ripley responded immediately that a special train would depart the next morning for Hagerstown with munitions for the 20-pounders, and that additional supply for artillery and small arms would follow, arriving in Frederick and Hagerstown as quickly as the rolling stock and ammunition could be collected. This was all good news, but it confirmed for McClellan that his heavy batteries on the east bank of Antietam Creek would be unable to provide the same support they had on September 17 for an attack on the 18th.[32]

"A careful and anxious survey of the condition of my command, and my knowledge of the enemy's force and position, failed to impress me with any reasonable certainty of success if I renewed the attack without reinforcing columns," wrote McClellan in his initial after-action report. But he actually had three sources of reinforcements, two of which he controlled. The first was Brigadier General Andrew A. Humphreys's newly formed division, consisting of eight regiments of Pennsylvania infantry—seven of which were untrained, consisting of recently raised troops—with a strength of slightly over 7,000 men. This unit, which was assembled in Washington, DC, and designated as the 3rd Division of the 5th Corps, experienced a rocky start. Humphreys had no assigned staff to attend to the myriad details necessary to ready his division to take the field. His orders were to march promptly, but also to "keep my troops fresh on the march." He found the former a difficult challenge to meet. His brigades arrived later than expected at their assembly points in the capital on September 12. Then he learned that his 1st Brigade had insufficient rations, and the 2nd Brigade "had no rations whatever." Moreover, 900 rifles in this latter brigade were defective and had to be replaced. Humphreys also discovered that Porter, the 5th Corps' commander, had made no transportation arrangements for this new division. The 2nd Brigade had no wagons for ammunition or supplies, and the 1st Brigade had only eight wagons to haul supplies for 3,500 men. Some regiments had no ambulances. By a herculean effort, Humphreys addressed his most serious problems and marched at daylight on September 14, 2 days later than planned. Arriving in Frederick on September 16, he received orders from Porter to defend the approaches to the city from Harpers Ferry. He was completing his arrangements to do this on the 17th when, at 3:30 p.m., he received orders to march to Boonsboro. These had been sent at 7:15 a.m. that morning. Humphreys assembled his division and set off for his new destination. During the march, he received a series of increasingly urgent communications. The first was to continue to Keedysville. The next was to "come on as soon as possible, and hurry up with all haste. Do not render the command unfit for service, but force your march." At 5 p.m., he received a curt message from Porter: "Get here before daybreak." Humphreys ordered a forced march through the night. His 3rd Division leaked at least 1,000 stragglers in the grueling trek, but it reached the battlefield on the morning of September 18.[33]

McClellan's second source of reinforcements was the 4th Corps' 1st Division, commanded by General Darius Couch. McClellan had dispatched it to occupy Sandy Hook and Maryland Heights when he summoned the 6th Corps to Sharpsburg on September 16. Sometime during the late morning of the 17th, McClellan tapped Couch to send one of his three brigades to the battlefield. Couch picked his 1st Brigade, under Brigadier General Charles Devens Jr., which had advanced its regiments toward Sandy Hook and up to Elk Ridge, by way of Solomon's Gap. On Elk Ridge, the men in the 2nd Rhode Island "obtained a most sublime view" of the fighting at Sharpsburg and were watching in fascination when their orders to march arrived. A forced march, some of it at the double-quick, brought the brigade to within 2 miles of the Federals' left by nightfall, when they were allowed to bivouac. McClellan hesitated to pull Couch's other two brigades from Pleasant Valley, believing they were necessary to guard against an enemy advance from Harpers Ferry. By midnight he changed his mind, probably due to intelligence that the Confederates only had a small force in that vicinity. McClellan ordered Couch to bring the rest of his division to the field "as soon after daylight as you can possibly do so." This was another example of an order easily made but nearly impossible to execute. The distance to Keedysville was slightly over 12 miles, a 6-hour march in daylight. Orders to Couch sent at midnight would not reach him until 2 a.m. at the earliest. Then it would take time to call in the pickets and detachments. A late morning arrival was the *best* McClellan could hope for.[34]

The third potential source of reinforcements was the Pennsylvania Militia, who were reported to be assembling around Chambersburg, Pennsylvania. Governor Andrew Curtin had wired McClellan on September 15, claiming that the state would have 10,000 militiamen reach him by that night, under the command of General John Reynolds. It proved to be a chimera. The next night, a deflated governor wired President Lincoln that "we have no infantry or artillery sufficiently well organized to march into Maryland." Support from the Pennsylvania Militia amounted to nothing, and Reynolds returned to the Union army on September 28, grumbling to George Meade how he was "very much disgusted with his Pennsylvania campaign and militia, who he [Reynolds] says behaved very badly, and would not have stood five minutes if attacked by one-tenth their numbers."[35]

The reinforcements McClellan believed were necessary to give a September 18 attack a "reasonable certainty of success" were late in arriving—not because of external factors, but due to his caution in calling them up. Because his intelligence gathering about the Confederate army was so poor, he imagined that they possessed the force to fight a major action at Sharpsburg *and* mount a significant incursion into his rear from Harpers Ferry. There is no other explanation for why McClellan left Couch in Pleasant Valley and Maryland Heights all day on September 17 and ordered Humphreys to defend the approaches to Frederick from Harpers Ferry, rather than continue his march to Keedysville. Yet he gave the time of their arrival as one of the reasons he did not renew the offensive on September 18, even though his own decisions were what dictated their arrival time.

McClellan probably made his choice to not attack on September 18 before he ordered Couch's division up from Pleasant Valley. In his initial after-action report, he briefly explained that "I felt the duty to the army and the country forbade the risks involved in a hasty movement, which might result in the loss of what had been gained the previous day." In his final report, written 11 months later, he advanced a more detailed defense of his decision:

> I am aware of the fact that under ordinary circumstances a general is expected to risk a battle if he has a reasonable prospect of success; but at this critical juncture I should have had a narrow view of the condition of the country had I been willing to hazard another battle with less than an absolute assurance of

success. At that moment—Virginia lost, Washington menaced, Maryland invaded—the national cause could afford no risks of defeat. One battle lost and almost all would have been lost. Lee's army might then have marched, as it pleased, on Washington, Baltimore, or New York.

While it was true the national cause could not afford another defeat, it was an exaggeration to claim that "all would have been lost." Any successful general in history might have pointed out that no battle has an "absolute assurance of success." All involve risk. McClellan then piled on additional reasons for not attacking: the troops were too fatigued and exhausted by the battle and the "night marches to which they had been subjected during the previous three days"; the men suffered from hunger because their supply trains were in the rear; and Hooker's 1st Corps and Sedgwick's 2nd Division in the 2nd Corps were too scattered and demoralized to brought into action again. It was a laundry list for inaction that any student of the Peninsula Campaign would recognize.[36]

Colonel Strother recalled that sometime after midnight, he was awakened by couriers coming and going at headquarters. He heard McClellan say to one staff officer, "They are to hold the ground they occupy, but are not to attack without further orders." The officer could have been from any one of the army's corps, for these were McClellan's standing orders for September 18. Franklin's planned morning attack was cancelled, and Burnside received no reinforcements. While some officers in the Union army expressed surprise that the battle was not renewed, others, like General Marsena Patrick, were overwhelmed with relief to learn "that McClellan's orders were 'not to attack' & if possible have re-inforcements come up." In Patrick's opinion—and there were many who shared it—"only Madcaps, of the Hooker stripe, would have pushed our troops into action again without very strong reinforcements."[37]

McClellan had studied what was done by Napoleon Bonaparte, the Duke of Wellington, and George Washington, and he had served under Winfield Scott in Mexico. He learned much about army organization and administration, the technical aspects of army command, and the growing role of technology in warfare. But he failed to learn the most fundamental lesson these generals' campaigns and battles provided, whether it involved Napoleon in Italy, Wagram, or Austerlitz; Wellington in Spain; Washington in New Jersey in 1777; or Winfield Scott's campaign in capturing Mexico City. All of these commanders were able to sense their enemy's vulnerabilities and know when to demand more from their troops. They never permitted a battered opponent to have a chance to recover. Although the Confederates had fought desperately and skillfully on September 17, there was considerable evidence available to McClellan that the Army of Northern Virginia was exhausted and not as strong as he believed. The Rebels had struck two major blows during the day: at the West Woods against Sedgwick, and A. P. Hill's counterattack. No one would question the ferocity of these attacks, but both were eventually contained. At all other points, McClellan's soldiers had gained ground and held it, results defying all the characteristics of Robert E. Lee that McClellan had learned on the Virginia Peninsula. Lee would seize the initiative and strike hard, *if he had the numbers to do so*. On September 17, hundreds of Confederate prisoners were taken during the day on all fronts. George Meade described those captured by his 1st Corps as "ragged, shoeless, and half starved, and certainly in a most pitiable condition," a description consistent with those from other sections of the Union army. They reflected an enemy army at the end of its logistical rope. Soldiers will make great sacrifices, within reason, when a leader asks it of them. Lee understood this well, as did Grant. If either of them had used the same logic McClellan applied in not attacking on September 18, Grant would not have counterattacked on the second day at the Battle of Shiloh, because his men were too fatigued, hungry, and demoralized, and he could not guarantee an absolute assurance of success; and Lee would have abandoned his Seven Days Battles' offensive after his repulse at Beaver Dam Creek. McClellan's choice granted Lee a day to rest his troops, fortify his position, bring up his stragglers and any reinforcements he could muster, and resupply his men with ammunition—a consequential error. In McClellan's view, his army had done enough, and the battle would only be renewed if Lee refused to withdraw to Virginia.[38]

THAT NIGHT, WHILE LEE and McClellan contemplated the weighty decision of what their respective armies would do on September 18, the officers and men on the front lines dealt with more immediate concerns. Officers detailed men to bring up water, food, and ammunition—which often was not a simple matter. For example, the soldiers in McLaws's division had nothing to eat for 36 hours, and some had tasted no rations for 3 days. The division's commissary wagons were south of the Potomac, and since it was not considered prudent to bring them across the river, rations had to be cooked near Shepherdstown and hauled nearly 5 miles to the front, resulting in the uneven arrival of food for the men. Robert Shand's 2nd South Carolina got their meal soon after dark, but the 7th South Carolina, in the same brigade, did not receive theirs until the next morning. Everyone who had been under fire during the day was physically and emotionally spent. What is sometimes referred to as "combat stress reaction" causes fatigue, an inability to focus, indecision, and confusion. How debilitating it might be depends on the individual. This is not post-traumatic stress disorder (PTSD), which is a longer-term condition. Instead, it is an immediate reaction after exposure to violence, extreme danger, and intense stress. Yet pickets still needed to be posted, and a schedule of reliefs for them had to be organized throughout the night. Casualties on the battlefield who could be reached by rescuers had to be collected and carried to field hospitals. This was normally the duty of the ambulance corps, but the day's fighting produced so many wounded men that they eclipsed the capacity of this organization, and line troops had to assist. Surviving officers and sergeants attempted to take stock of which men were present, or were known to be casualties, or were missing. They also tried to reorganize the survivors. Some units had no officers left. The 4th North Carolina in G. B. Anderson's brigade was one example. Not only had the regiment lost all its officers, but just one noncom—an orderly sergeant—remained, and the rest of the brigade was in a similarly depleted condition. The list of correspondingly affected units in the Army of Northern Virginia was long. Fleming Sanders wrote that his 42nd Virginia went in with 120 effectives, yet mustered only 25 men that evening. A mere 50 soldiers constituted Paul Semmes's brigade by nightfall. The 1st North Carolina in Ripley's brigade only had 66 enlisted men remaining from about 300 who were taken into action. And so it went. In Semmes's case, it would be determined there were 310 casualties out of an initial strength of 709. The 1st North Carolina formally tallied 50 dead, 75 wounded, and 21 missing or captured. In these two units, this meant that 349 men in Semmes's brigade, and about 90 in the 1st North Carolina, were separated from their units and somewhere in the Confederate army's rear. Determining who was dead, injured, or missing could be difficult. As Major Rufus Dawes in the 6th Wisconsin pointed out, "the wounded man, when shot, went to the rear and availed himself of the first assistance found." This meant that the injured did not always end up at the hospital for their division or corps. Sometimes it would take days or weeks for units to determine these men's whereabouts and condition.[39]

Thousands of stragglers roamed the rear of both armies. Some were malingerers, and others were severely traumatized or sick, but many had simply helped the wounded to the rear and found one pretense or another to delay returning to their units. The rest were simply jarred loose from their comrades in the chaos of combat and found their way back during the night or the next day. The Army of Northern Virginia also had thousands of stragglers who fell out along the route to Harpers Ferry, as well as those who had recovered from being sick or wounded in the Virginia Peninsula and Manassas Campaigns and were being rushed up from the depot at Winchester, Virginia. Lieutenant Melvin Dwinell in the 8th Georgia was in this town on September 16, and he watched as large numbers of the men who had recently arrived from hospitals in Richmond were organized into companies according to what brigade or division they belonged to, and sent out on the nearly 35-mile trek to Maryland. Many of those who broke down on the march from Harpers Ferry but had recovered enough to resume their journey made their way to Sharpsburg. Thus a stream of men was constantly arriving through the night of September 17 and during the next day to rejoin their units. On the other hand, there were thousands who were too physically run down to continue, or who had their fill of marching and fighting for the time being, and they sought refuge in private residences scattered across the lower end of the Shenandoah Valley.[40]

THE NIGHT OF SEPTEMBER 17 was pitch black. Felix Viskniskki was a 20-year-old private in the 49th New York, selected as part of a detachment to establish a picket line about 200 feet in front of that regiment, along the eastern slope of the Dunker Church plateau. The shooting had ceased, but Confederates were close by, and the danger was palpable. Any noise could draw enemy fire. "Every move had to be made with great caution," Viskniskki recalled, and orders to the picket detail "were given in very low tones or whispers." He and his comrades went forward "on their hands and knees or pulling themselves along on their bellies" until they reached the desired position. They remained there, lying flat on the ground and staying silent until they were relieved several hours later. Captain Edwin Drake's company in the 43rd New York of Hancock's brigade was detailed to help picket its front, which extended from the Miller farm south through the Cornfield. Drake led his company through the corn to take up their post. "Oh, such piles of dead bodies!" wrote the captain. "I could hardly take a step without stumbling over them, and in some places they lay three and four across each other." He posted part of his company as pickets and held the rest in reserve, to provide a rotating relief. Despite the macabre scenes all around them, the men in the reserve immediately fell asleep. When it came time to relieve the forward line, Drake stumbled through the corn to find his dozing men and shake them awake. With so many dead bodies, and the night so dark, Drake found it impossible to distinguish slumbering men from the dead, and he frequently ended up shaking corpses, to his distress. "The sight was truly frightful," he wrote to his father. But the dead at least were silent. What the captain and his men found most heartrending and frightening were the cries of the wounded and the dying. There seemed to be hundreds of them. Drake had to endure their constant, desperate pleas for water, "and others begging me to end their existence." His job was to manage the picket line, not evacuate injured men, and he had no escape through the long night from the torment of the sufferers' shrieks, moans, sobs, groans, and dying gasps. Contemplating this experience 11 days later, Drake exclaimed, "Oh, may I never be permitted to pass another such night."[41]

Drake's experience was not unique. It was typical of everywhere across the front lines. "We slept last night amid the dead and wounded, mutilated in every shape and form," wrote Captain Henry Royer in the 96th Pennsylvania to his father. "One rebel General, two Colonels, and a Major, lie dead about fifty yards from me. Right in front of us lies a Company, I judge, of dead Georgians, some still hanging on the worm fence where they were killed." When Felix Viskniskki was relieved from the picket line and returned to his regiment, he found it impossible to discern the difference between his sleeping comrades and the many dead who were sprinkled throughout the area. He dropped down beside what he thought was a comrade but woke to find he was staring into "the glassy eyes and frothy mouth" of a dead Confederate lieutenant, an experience he found more unnerving than his regiment's advance into battle the day before. Roger B. Yard, the 1st New Jersey's chaplain, reached his unit, where the men were lying down in Mumma's plowed field south of the East Woods, shortly before dark and found the scene there to be shocking. "Around, among them, and beyond, the field was literally covered with dead and wounded rebels," Yard related to the editor of the *Monmouth Democrat*. "A few feet in front of them was a line of dead bodies, lying just as they had fallen in their ranks, numbering hundreds, and extending over the field, the most horrifying spectacle I ever witnessed." The pleas of wounded Rebels in front of him moved Yard to risk a sharpshooter's bullet to see what help he could provide. A young Alabamian, wounded in five places, including through the bowels, attracted Yard's attention "by his pleading look and evident distress." Yard took the man's name and address and told him what the soldier already understood—that his wounds were mortal. "Tell my friends after the war, that I am going to Heaven and hope to meet them there," said the Confederate. "After offering him some Christian consolation," Yard made his way to other injured men nearby before a sharpshooter's bullets warned him to return to his lines. Those he passed on his way back thought he was a surgeon, and Yard was followed by their piteous pleading: "O, doctor! can't you help me?" or "Will you not give me a drop of water?" or "Just turn me over a little, won't you, doctor?" or "Water! Water! etc., etc." Bullets hurried Yard along, and all he could do was encourage the suffering men to be patient. In Richard H. Anderson's division, a member of the 44th Alabama found night to be a relief, for "it removed from view the sufferings of the wounded, and the mangled bodies of the dead." But it did not stifle the voices. The sounds made by hundreds of tormented and dying men, Chaplain Yard recorded, "filled the air, and were borne to our ears from distant fields, and even from the enemy's lines." Of that terrible night, Sergeant Ephraim Brown in the 64th New York could only scribble "The Lord have Mercy" in his journal.[42]

Day

Captain Henry L. P. King, on McLaws's staff, was up before daylight on September 18 in anticipation of renewed fighting, but he found all was quiet. Sunrise was at 5:54 a.m., and the light that broke over the horizon cast "a hot sunshine on the faces of the Porr Dying Boys" who lay in front of Ephraim Brown's position near the Sunken Lane. "We were all surprised at the quiet with which the morning came," wrote Chaplain Yard. The cannons were silent and no masses of troops were moving, but sharpshooters went to work as soon as it was light enough to see. Then the chaplain watched as a "white flag was seen moving over the field" from the Union lines. Captain King met the flag bearer, stopped him, and then rode back to consult with McLaws about how they should handle this Yankee messenger. McLaws sent him to Jackson, who was meeting with Jeb Stuart. They sent the captain back to find out what, specifically, the Federals were requesting. King discovered that it was only the device a surgeon was using as cover to retrieve wounded men, not a truce flag. The latter, however, soon made it appearance, carried by Major Hiram C. Rogers, the assistant adjutant general of Slocum's 1st Division, who was accompanied by two other staff officers. The major explained to King that they proposed to "exchange the wounded at any intermediate point agreed upon." King galloped back to Jackson, and this time found General Lee with him. The latter said "that no partial or informal proposition could be entertained," but if the Union army commander proposed a formal truce, "it would be referred to Gen. Lee for consideration." The Confederate army's commander had a record in the war of sticking to strict formality regarding truces, but in this instance, he probably was also wary of a temporary cease-fire, which might enable the enemy to discover just how vulnerable his army was. The popular memory of Lee is that of a kind, compassionate soldier, but he was also capable of cold, pitiless decisions that left the helpless wounded to die when he felt the situation warranted it.[43]

When Major Rogers received Lee's response from King, he said he would attempt to find McClellan and return as soon as possible. In the discussion, the major mentioned that Franklin commanded the force opposite to the Confederates. When King replied that Jackson was in charge of the Confederates' left, he noticed that "there was a very significant look exchanged between the three Yankee officers." Rogers would not be back, for McClellan refused to propose a general truce. Nonetheless, he, like Lee, allowed informal local truces to be negotiated by subordinate officers at various points along the two armies' fronts.[44]

One of these was the space between the West Woods and the Dunker Church plateau, extending to the East Woods. Although Jackson, McLaws, and other senior commanders issued orders for skirmishers to fire on any Union soldiers who exposed themselves, a member of Kershaw's brigade of South Carolinians noted that "there existed on the left a tacit understanding between the antagonists, that burial parties would not be interfered with." Along the front of Slocum's 6th Corps' division, there was agreement between Union and Confederate officers that the wounded could be retrieved and the dead buried, so long as no one attempted to cross opposing picket lines. This proved to be difficult when details might see injured men or dead bodies from their side just inside the enemy's picket line, and local officers sometimes bent the rules for humanitarian reasons. In one example, a group of Rebels under a flag of truce edged too close to the picket line of Torbert's brigade, and Lieutenant Smith G. Blythe, the acting adjutant in the 1st New Jersey, was sent to warn them off. To Blythe's astonishment, the Confederate officer with the group, a quartermaster in

Kershaw's brigade, was a college roommate and pre-war friend. He was searching for the body of Major William C. White in the 7th South Carolina. Blythe apparently resolved the problem by having a detail of men from his brigade carry White's body to the Confederate lines.[45]

Local truces were not without danger, for not all combatants in the area might be aware of them. This was the experience of Lieutenant Robert H. Brett in the 33rd New York, who allowed Confederate parties that were collecting some of their wounded to get quite close to his picket line in the Dunker Church plateau area. While Brett observed the litter teams at work, Rebel sharpshooters in the West Woods fired at him three times. They "were just going to make fresh meat of me" when he heard the colonel of a North Carolina regiment, who was with the rescuers, shout, "God dam you stop that shooting don't you see he lets our men come get the wounded."[46]

Another local truce was negotiated in the space encompassed by the Cornfield and the meadow south of it, which were littered with hundreds of casualties. James S. Johnston in the 11th Mississippi, serving as a courier for Colonel Evander Law, noted that "many from either side met in the space between the lines." While the wounded were gathered up and some of the dead buried, the soldiers "chatted as though they had never done each other harm." This truce, however, appears to have been somewhat uneven, for Sergeant Major Howard Huntington in the 6th Wisconsin reported that throughout it, "the pickets keep firing." The shooting however, was not to kill, but to deter burial details, souvenir seekers, looters, or any others from venturing too close to one side's picket line. Samuel H. Walkup, the 48th North Carolina's lieutenant colonel, was lenient with Union stretcher parties, allowing them to gather some of their wounded inside his picket line, which went through the West Woods. Some of the Federal officers tried to engage him in a discussion about the war, but Walkup cut them off, saying, "That is not a subject we could hold discussion, however glad we would be for the war to end." The colonel took note that the injured Confederates who were brought in had been well cared for, and he mused that the Yankees had treated them "better than we do of theirs I fear." Lieutenant James L. Lemon in the 18th Georgia used the truce to locate the bodies of two brothers in his company who were killed near the Hagerstown Pike by a shell from Battery B, 4th U.S. Lemon took only a young sergeant, J. J. O'Neill, to help. The two men carried the bodies to a point 20 paces from the northeastern corner of Dunker Church and buried them. "I read a passage of scripture over them," wrote Lemon, "& if I am able I will try to return & bring them home."[47]

Colonel David Strother, on McClellan's staff, rode through the Cornfield and East Woods area during the morning and found dreadful scenes in every direction. A profusion of dead littered the ground: "Many were so covered with dust, torn, crushed, and trampled that they resembled clods of earth, and you were obliged to look twice before recognizing them as human remains." He came upon a stretcher party with a Confederate soldier sitting upright on their stretcher, with his two carriers "laughing and swearing in great astonishment." One said to Strother, "Colonel, look at this Reb; he has got up himself and asked for a drink of water!" On closer examination, Strother saw that a musket ball had hit the unfortunate man in the head where the eyebrows meet and exited from the back of his head, where his brains were protruding. The wound was clearly fatal, yet the colonel watched in gruesome fascination as the poor man "sat up and without support and drank heartily of the water offered by the soldier." Near the Hagerstown Pike, he encountered a burial party who had laid some 20 or 30 bodies "in a rain-washed gully, and were covering them carelessly by shoveling down the loose dirt from the sides." In the East Woods he passed some 6th Corps' troops, who were "strangely hilarious and recklessly at their ease," despite the awful odors and carnage all about them: "Some were cooking, and apparently enjoying their bit of breakfast although the mephitic atmosphere would have tried the stomach of a horse. Others laughed, talked, smoked, and sung snatches of droll songs." Various men were sleeping so soundly that Strother "was frequently unable to distinguish the living from the dead," except by the color of their hands or the heaving of a chest. This was one of the hardest things to fathom for those unused to a battle's aftermath—soldiers going about their daily business seemingly oblivious to the horrid scenes around them.[48]

The West Woods fell inside the Confederate picket lines, and soldiers in Walker's and McLaws's divisions used the truce to bury their dead, collect equipment, and hunt for clothing or souvenirs without fear of Union shelling or sharpshooters. Many of these men had been in the Seven Days Battles, but the carnage they encountered here left them stunned. Edward Burruss, a private in the 21st Mississippi and son of a wealthy planter, wrote home that "it is no figure of speech, metaphor or anything but a simple fact to say that there were frequently places where for 50 to 60 yards you could step from one dead Yank to another & walk all over the ground without once touching it with your foot. On one little knoll about 25 or 35 yards square I myself counted 189 dead Yankees & they were no thicker there than in many other places." Robert Shand in the 2nd South Carolina, who was a former law student in the office of Maxcy Gregg, ventured out early among the Union dead in search of a pair of shoes. He found one body wearing some that looked to be his size and began to remove them when the supposed corpse opened its eyes and exclaimed, "Can't you wait until I am dead?" A stunned Shand replied "that I really thought he was dead and that even then I would not have disturbed him but for the fact that I was barefoot." He gave the wounded man water and let him keep his footwear. "I got my shoes from another," recounted Shand, "first making sure he was dead."[49]

The local, informal truces between the lines were not observed in the area from the Sunken Lane to the Piper farm. The Federals sent a flag of truce requesting permission to retrieve their wounded, which made its way to General Roger

Pryor. Pryor probably referred this to Longstreet, who refused to agree to it. He could not allow the Federals to get a close look at just how weakly held the Confederates' center was. The pickets and sharpshooters on both sides here remained vigilant—and deadly. Thomas Hamill in the 57th New York wrote that in this area, "neither friend nor foe could walk over [it] next day and live," adding that "four of our men in attempting to bring in one of the wounded next day, had one killed and the others wounded." Charlie Fuller in the 61st New York lost a man in his company, killed by a sharpshooter, and remarked that anyone who showed himself was fired on. In the 64th New York, Sergeant Ephraim Brown's close friend, Johnny Orr, was killed on picket duty while cutting a piece of meat for a comrade. The 5th New Hampshire's picket line ran through the center of Piper's cornfield, which provided some concealment from sharpshooters. During the morning, a wounded Confederate just outside the New Englanders' line called a picket over to him and handed him a slip of paper, requesting that he give it to a Freemason. The paper contained "some mystic signs in a circle," made "with a bit of stick wet in blood." It was carried back to Colonel Edward Cross, a Master Mason. Cross could not make out the symbol, so he sent for a member of higher rank, who told him it was from a brother Freemason who was in great peril and must be rescued. Cross rounded up four other Masons in his regiment who agreed to undertake the dangerous mission. "At great risk," the rescuers crawled through the corn and found the officer, who proved to be Lieutenant John Oden in the 10th Alabama, and removed him. Oden told the party about another wounded Mason in the corn, and Cross and his fellows located the lieutenant colonel of a Georgia regiment, possibly Lieutenant Colonel Reuben B. Nisbet in the 3rd Georgia, and rescued him, as well.[50]

Risks were also taken to remove the non-Masonic dead and wounded. Sergeant Ephraim Brown and a comrade were detailed to collect the corpses of men from their company, who lay on the ridge north of the Sunken Lane. They carried a flag of truce, hoping to deter sharpshooters, but when they picked up the body of Ephraim Green, a Confederate marksmen sent five balls at them. "This was a close call but we would not drop him if we fell by his side," wrote Brown. Despite the danger, the two Yankees returned thrice more to collect the bodies of three others, all of whom were carried nearly 500 yards to near Roulette's orchard, where they buried them. Brown even ventured into the Sunken Lane, where he located the Confederate color bearer a comrade had killed with a clubbed musket (see chapter 11). Searching through the Rebel's knapsack, he found a razor, which he "took as a keep sake & will keep it the remainder of my days." This was more than just a souvenir for the sergeant. It was a tangible reminder of the horrific combat he had survived, the friends he had buried, and the brave color bearer whose life Brown's comrade had taken.[51]

The southern end of the battlefield was equally as lethal as the center. Sharpshooters and pickets shot to kill when anyone exposed himself. Lieutenant

Colonel James M. Perrin, commanding the 1st South Carolina Rifles, discovered that the Federals had deployed skirmishers who were under the cover of a fence to his right and front—probably the one on the eastern side of Sherrick's cornfield—and kept up a harassing but dangerous fire, lasting all day. His orders were "to do nothing to bring on a general engagement," so Perrin simply keep his men under the best cover he could find. His 1st Rifles and the other Confederate regiments also deployed their own sharpshooters and pickets, who traded fire with the Federals. The sharpshooters spared no one. Even those prodded to action by the piteous pleas for help from the many wounded who lay between the lines were offered no mercy. When a soldier in the 7th Virginia was killed trying to aid some wounded Federals, "this puts a stop to any humanity or charitable movements towards the enemy's wounded" by the other men in Kemper's brigade. But William Powers in the 89th New York found that "men in the agonies of death, pleading for water and for assistance, is enough to melt the stoutest heart." Some soldiers risked a sharpshooter's bullet to render aid. One of them was David Johnston in the 7th Virginia, who had watched a man from his regiment be shot and killed—at a range of 800 yards—while trying to help the Union wounded. Nevertheless, Johnston could not resist the cry of an injured Federal soldier nearby, who begged him "Friend, will you give me a drink of water? If you will and I ever get well I will do anything on earth for you." Johnston slithered forward to the man and "not only gave him a drink and bathed his wound, but filled his canteen and cup and sat them by him." Sometimes the injured crawled to find help. Henry E. Bugbee in the 16th Connecticut was wounded in his right side, right wrist, and the fingers of his right hand. He had lain all night in Sherrick's cornfield. In the morning he dragged himself to the Confederate lines, which were closer to him than his own. The Rebels showed compassion, giving him a freshly roasted ear of corn and piloting him to a hospital for medical attention.[52]

Sharpshooters made even routine duties dangerous. William B. Nixon, a hospital steward in the 89th New York, received a thigh wound when he attempted to haul hot coffee up to his regiment. The North Carolinians in Branch's brigade lay along the stone wall on the western boundary of Sherrick's cornfield. A spring, which was to their rear, was the water source for Branch's men, as well as Archer's and probably Gregg's. The trick was to get to it and back safely. In the gallows humor soldiers adopt to endure the rigors of war, those who were not part of the water details found the gyrations of their comrades, who were trying to avoid being shot as they worked their way to the spring, highly amusing to watch. "I several times joined in the laugh at some of my men dodging the Federal picket bullets when they went for water," recalled Colonel James Lane, years later. Such was one of the oddities of war. Men could laugh at comrades darting and diving to escape bullets, as long as they survived their journey. But if a bullet found its target, a grim silence would replace the laughter.[53]

The firing continued all day. Lieutenant Samuel K. Schwenk, whose company in the 50th Pennsylvania occupied the skirmish line from 7 a.m. to 6 p.m., wrote that each man in the company fired an average of 200 rounds. Schwenk's account offers evidence that most of the bullets did not hit anything. While seemingly pointless and heartless, it had its purposes: to deter looters, harass the enemy, and, in the case of the Confederates, prevent the Federals from forming any estimate of their strength.[54]

AT 6 A.M., MCCLELLAN had Marcy send orders to Pleasonton to push out cavalry for a reconnaissance across the Union army's right, left, and center to ascertain the "strength, position, and movements of the enemy." This seemed to offer a promise of offensive action as soon as the reinforcements and artillery ammunition arrived. But it soon became evident that this was nothing more than routine probing—of the sort the cavalry should have conducted on September 16 but did not. McClellan continued to fret about Harpers Ferry and the possibility that the Confederates had forces there who could threaten his flank or rear, or who could be marching to reinforce Lee. Orders were delivered to Burnside to send a scouting party "toward, and as far down as, Harper's Ferry," to investigate the situation. Burnside was also told to post some of his limited cavalry force to keep the portion of Harpers Ferry Road near the mouth of Antietam Creek under observation.[55]

Brigadier General Andrew Humphreys reported to army headquarters around 7 a.m. He had halted his 3rd Division, 5th Corps, along the turnpike nearby to rest, eat breakfast, and allow stragglers to catch up. For a division composed almost entirely of untrained new recruits, it had performed extraordinarily well. After an all-night forced march, which included climbing two mountain ranges, Humphreys arrived with 6,000 effectives out of his original 7,000 men. He learned from Seth Williams, the army's assistant adjutant general, "that the question of attack that day was not yet decided upon." McClellan ordered Humphreys to mass his men in the rear of Morell's 1st Division, which was supporting the Reserve Artillery along the Antietam Creek bluffs south of the Pry farm. By 9:30 or 10 a.m., Humphreys's division was "refreshed by their rest and coffee" and in position behind Morell, ready for action. Later, with no small degree of annoyance and incredulity, Humphreys read McClellan's first report of the campaign. The army commander gave as one of the reasons the battle was not renewed on September 18 was because Humphreys's 3rd Division, "fatigued with forced marches, were arriving throughout the day, but were not available until near its close." This read as if the brigadier general had managed the march poorly and allowed his soldiers to string out along the road. Humphreys demanded a court of inquiry to clear the record and establish the facts. The rumpus caused McClellan to slightly amend his language regarding Humphreys' division in his final report, giving them credit for the speed of their march, but he could not resist adding that "they were, of course, greatly exhausted, and needed rest and refreshment." Humphreys' reaction to this is unknown, but—given his nature—it was most likely colorful and profane.[56]

At 8 a.m., after his meeting with Humphreys, McClellan paused to write two letters: one to his wife Mary Ellen, and the other to General-in-Chief Henry W. Halleck. The note to Halleck was sparse on details, other than to say that the Army of the Potomac had been engaged for 14 hours on September 17: "we held all we gained except a portion of the extreme left that was obliged to abandon a part of what it had gained"; losses were very heavy, "especially in General officers"; and "the battle will probably be renewed today." He also asked Halleck to "send all the troops you can by the most expeditious route." Information was power, and McClellan did not share anything more with his chief than what he deemed necessary. Reading this, we can imagine Halleck's questions. What was gained? Was the battle undecided or a victory? How heavy were the losses? Which general officers were lost? Such opaqueness seems to have been the point of McClellan's message. Vague generalities about heavy losses and ground gained, as well as a suggestion that the battle would probably be renewed, gave McClellan leverage to pry additional reinforcements away from Washington, DC.[57]

His letter to Mary Ellen contained details he withheld from Halleck. McClellan told her the names of several generals who were either killed or wounded, and, oddly, that the fighting on both sides "was superb." He then continued, "The general result was in our favor, that is to say we gained a great deal of ground & held it. It was a success, but whether a decided victory depends upon what occurs today." This was an interesting analysis. The Army of the Potomac had actually gained relatively little ground and virtually no commanding terrain, other than to control Poffenberger Hill and the East Woods. They had been driven out of the West Woods; failed to seize Nicodemus Heights, Cemetery Hill, and Cemetery Ridge; and lost the Harpers Ferry Road Ridge to the enemy's counterattack. Yet he was not wrong to gauge the day's fighting as a success. Even though the Federals had not seized most of the key landscape features, the army had fought extremely well and had broken the Confederates' positions at numerous points. They had gained an advantage that, if followed up, might deliver a more decisive result. But McClellan equated a "decided victory" with Lee's retreat, rather than anything else the Army of Potomac might do. This was in keeping with McClellan's interpretation of his orders, which were to drive the enemy from Maryland and protect Pennsylvania from invasion. He found the battle at Antietam to be "sublime," and the grandest spectacle "I could conceive of." McClellan also stated that "those in whose judgment I rely tell me that I fought the battle splendidly & that it was a masterpiece of art." We do not know what sycophant shared this opinion with the general, but it did not come from Colonel Strother, his aide-de-camp, who was furious with how the advantages gained on September 17 were being squandered. "The enemy undoubtedly will escape, and we have spent the day gathering up a few thousand worthless muskets and a few hundred lousy prisoners," he vented in his journal.[58]

After breakfast, although "well nigh tired out by anxiety & want of sleep," McClellan collected his staff and set out for the front, riding by Humphreys's division on their way. McClellan claimed to have visited Burnside and made the decision to reinforce the 9th Corps with Morell's division. Strother, however, who accompanied the general, made no mention of a visit to Burnside that morning, nor did Burnside or Cox. What is more likely is that McClellan rode no farther than Morell's headquarters, notifying Burnside—via a staff officer—that he was sending the 5th Corps' 1st Division as a support for the 9th Corps, but it was not to be used in offensive operations. From here the party rode north, crossing Antietam Creek at Pry's Ford, and coming to Sumner's headquarters at the Poffenberger farm. The two generals "remained for some time in consultation," although neither left a record of what they discussed. Nonetheless, it is possible to piece it together from Sumner's subsequent testimony to the Joint Congressional Committee on the Conduct of the War. He maintained that the 1st, 2nd, and 12th Corps were in no condition for offensive operations, and that it would be prudent "to halt a little after that severe action until his re-enforcements [Humphreys and Couch] came up."[59]

From Sumner's headquarters, McClellan rode over to the East Woods and met with Major Generals Franklin, Smith, and Slocum. At 10 a.m., Franklin had written to McClellan that the Confederates were moving a battery to Nicodemus Heights and asked, "Cannot that hill be occupied?" He also mentioned that the enemy held the West Woods with infantry and artillery, and Rebel prisoners said that 10,000 men, plus extra ammunition, came up during the night as reinforcements for Lee. Whether McClellan received this message before or after his visit to Franklin is irrelevant, as the two generals no doubt discussed its contents during their meeting. Whatever argument the 6th Corps' leader made failed to change his commander's mind. The report of 10,000 fresh Confederate troops only strengthened McClellan's conviction not to renew the battle. His consultation with Sumner and Franklin "failed to impress me with any reasonable certainty of success if I renewed the attack without re-enforcing columns." What he had seen in the 1st, 2nd, and 12th Corps, and what officers like Sumner and Meade had reported about them, convinced McClellan that their "shattered" condition "sufficed to deter me from pressing them into immediate action, and I felt that my duty [to] the army and the country forbade the risks involved in a hasty movement, which might result in the loss of what had been gained the previous day." His meeting with Franklin concluded like the one with Sumner, with the plan being to hold their position and observe the enemy.[60]

McClellan and his staff rode back to Keedysville, passing several field hospitals along the way. The number of wounded men "seemed immense" to Strother. They may also have gone by Couch's 1st Division in the 4th Corps, for it reached the front around 11 a.m., sending its 3rd Brigade forward to relieve Irwin's brigade in Smith's 2nd Division, and massing its other two brigades in the rear of Brooks's brigade. McClellan's reinforcements were in place by noon, but if the battle was renewed that day, it would not be started by the Army of the Potomac.[61]

THE PRISONER OR PRISONERS who had told Franklin that the Confederates had received 10,000 reinforcements during the night were not far off. But these "reinforcements" were stragglers, some of whom came up of their own accord, while others were driven up by the cavalry. Divisions such as McLaws's, Anderson's, and A. P. Hill's, whose marches were the most severe, accounted for the largest numbers. Captain King, on McLaws's staff, noted that so many of their stragglers rejoined the division that "we had a larger force than when we went into action." McLaws thought the number who rejoined his division was equal to his losses on September 17, which was about 1,200 men. William Fagan, a lieutenant in the 8th Alabama, was near Boteler's Ford. He watched the stragglers reach the Maryland shore, where they were formed into ad hoc companies and regiments, marched to the front, and then dispersed to their home units. For those who were reluctant to do so, Colonel Chilton advised General Pendleton, whose Reserve Artillery was defending the ford, to "take any cavalry about there and send [the laggards] up at the point of the sword." Colonel James D. Nance, commanding McLaws's 3rd South Carolina, judged that "at least 10,000 stragglers" arrived through the night, making the army on September 18 "better prepared for fighting than the first day." Nance's estimate concurred with that of the prisoners interrogated by Franklin's 6th Corps, which suggests that this was a figure circulating among the troops. Ezra Carman, who had many contacts among former Confederate officers and men, thought Nance's figure was too high, believing instead that the amount was closer to 6,000. Whatever the quantity, it was not enough to cause Lee to consider offensive action.[62]

Lee joined Longstreet for some time that morning and personally observed the arrival of Couch's division on the Federals' front. They also took note of the mass of artillery still deployed on the eastern bank of Antietam Creek, "apparently to meet an attack from us." Longstreet's assessment of the Confederates' options was that "it was impossible to make any move except a direct assault upon some portion of the enemy line," which had no hope of success. He certainly shared this opinion with Lee, but the Rebel army's commander departed without revealing his thoughts and seemed to Longstreet to be "in perplexity" over what course of action to adopt. Longstreet misread Lee. He was not perplexed, but, rather, wanted to be certain that no offensive opportunities existed. Although Robert E. Lee's movements on September 18 are impossible to accurately reconstruct, it appears that he visited Jackson after leaving Longstreet, asking Stonewall to have another look at the Union's right flank and ascertain if there was any vulnerable point. Jackson apparently took Colonel Stephen D. Lee along with him, probably to have the opinion of an artilleryman. The colonel provided the only existing account of this reconnaissance, which must be used with caution. He claimed that he and Jackson rode to Nicodemus Heights, where they observed the Federals' flank to be solidly placed and bristling with artillery. Jackson's report confirmed for General Lee that he had no good offensive options. Around 2 p.m., Longstreet penciled a note to Lee, "suggesting preparations to withdraw during the night." With Jackson's report in hand, Lee had already arrived at the same conclusion. He rode over to Longstreet's command post before the wing commander's note even reached him and said that the Confederate army would retire to Virginia that night.[63]

Lee had anticipated that his army would have to fall back to Virginia, so he had ordered his trains and any wounded who were capable of being transported to start crossing the Potomac River that morning. William W. Sherwood in the 17th Virginia was detailed to cook rations for his regiment and reported that he and his helpers had hardly begun their work when orders came to pack up and drive across the Potomac, which they did around 10 a.m. This early start was crucial, for passage through Boteler's Ford by the supply trains and ambulances was painfully slow. It was essential to get them across before the main body of the Army of Northern Virginia, who would withdraw during the night. There were multitudes of details to be attended to. Surgeons had to decide who among the wounded were capable of travel, organize transportation for them and then have them driven to the field hospitals, which were scattered across the army's rear. A certain number of surgeons and attendants were detailed to remain with the seriously wounded, who would, by necessity, be left behind. A timetable and order of march needed to be determined, in order to establish the process of evacuating the line without alerting the Federals, as well as to minimize confusion and crowding at the single ford the army would use to cross the river.[64]

During the late afternoon, a heavy rain came down, which diminished to an uncomfortable, foggy drizzle by nightfall. The rain brought relief to the wounded who were still lying between the lines, but it turned the roads into muddy pathways. The Confederates built numerous campfires along their front, in order to produce smoke that concealed the preparations for retreat from Union eyes— particularly the signal station on Elk Ridge. On the Confederates' right, sharpshooters and skirmishers increased their fire, driving their Federal counterparts to cover and creating the impression that an attack was imminent. The ruse worked well. The 1st Brigade in Morell's division had relieved part of the 9th Corps in the afternoon, and Captain Francis A. Donaldson in the 118th Pennsylvania, one of that brigade's regiments, described the small-arms fire as "incessant," and those "to the right of us amounted almost to a battle." The brigade's regimental commanders were ordered "to be extremely watchful, as it was feared the enemy would attempt to retake our position."[65]

Night

Sunset arrived at 6:06 p.m. It was still warm and humid when darkness enveloped the battlefield. The weather station in Frederick recorded a temperature of 72.5 degrees at 9 p.m. The fog, mingling with the smoke of the fires built by the Confederates, lent a surreal and disorienting effect that night. When Walton's Washington (Louisiana) Artillery received their orders to pull out, they assembled their entire battalion—except for one battery, which was detached to support Stuart's cavalry, who were screening the retreat—on Shepherdstown Road. The gun crews were ordered to walk, and the instructions to their colonel were to have his staff "occupied getting everything along" and to "please exert yourself and staff to the utmost to prevent delay." Similar orders went to every unit in the army. Lieutenant William M. Owen, the artillery battalion's adjutant, was sent to deliver orders to the battery Walton had selected to support Stuart. "The fog was dense," wrote the lieutenant, "and the camp-fires burning alongside the road were blinding." Riding toward Sharpsburg, he encountered a constant stream of infantrymen filling the road—probably D. R. Jones's division. Owen, trying to get by them to deliver his orders, "was saluted by curses loud and strong" from the foot soldiers, furious because his horse was pressing against them. One man sang out angrily that Owen was a "cavalryman going after buttermilk." Extricating himself from the crush of the infantry, the lieutenant found a spot that he knew his battalion would pass in order to enter Sharpsburg, where he could pluck out the battery he needed. He soon heard the jingling and clatter of a battery approaching through the fog. It was Captain James Reilly's Rowan (North Carolina) Artillery in Hood's division. This battery had rifled guns, which is what Stuart needed for rearguard work. Owen decided that Reilly's pieces would do quite nicely, saving him from having to wait for his own battalion to come by, so he notified the captain that he was being detached to serve with the cavalrymen. Reilly did not receive the orders well, grumbling, "Devil take it now, can't somebody else do this? My men are tired out,—let me go beyond the river." Owen stood his ground, pointing out that service with the rear guard was a post of honor. He then made good his escape, leaving the irate captain damning "all posts of honor."[66]

General David R. Jones received his orders at 8:30 p.m. As the division quietly assembled, General Toombs and two aides-de-camp, one of whom was Lieutenant James R. Troup, were overseeing the withdrawal of their pickets when a group of five or six cavalrymen appeared out of the gloom. It was impossible to make out the color of their uniforms, and Troup called out, "Who comes?" The riders answered, "Friends—don't shoot." They drew very close to the others before Troup and Toombs identified them as Federals. At this point the Union horsemen produced revolvers and opened fire, hitting Toombs in the arm and possibly wounding Troup. They then wheeled their mounts and galloped off.

"Great excitement prevailed but no other guns were fired to increase the alarm in the Confederate lines," recalled 1st Sergeant Herman H. Perry in the 2nd Georgia. The riders were part of a reconnaissance detail by a squadron of the 1st Massachusetts Cavalry, probing to ascertain what the Confederates were up to.[67]

There were no other interruptions by the enemy, but the Confederates' movement nevertheless proceeded slowly. D. R. Jones's brigades did not begin to march until midnight, 3.5 hours after the division had assembled. Jubal Early reported that Lawton's division, along with Armistead's brigade in Richard H. Anderson's division, were the last to depart on Stonewall Jackson's front, and they were not relieved by Fitz Lee's cavalry brigade until sometime between 10 and 11 p.m. Walker's division set out around then, too. Whatever timetable Lee, Longstreet, and Jackson might have worked out to regulate the Confederate army's movement to the Potomac River broke down in the confusion inherent in a night march. This resulted in most of the army streaming down toward Boteler's Ford at the same time. "No one can imagine the crowd and pressure on such occasions unless he has been present in such a time," noted Surgeon James Boulware, with Jones's division, but he noticed "no confusion" around him. This accorded with the opinion of Captain Osmun Latrobe, D. R. Jones's inspector general, who felt that the march was made in "good order." Good order, however, did not equate with comfort. Night marches are always difficult, and this one was particularly unpleasant. E. B. Tate, 1st Sergeant in the 15th Georgia, remembered it as "one of the most disagreeable nights I ever experienced on the march." Colonel Walkup, in Walker's division, described an all-night march "through mud & by very difficult road, crowded by 2 or more brigades abreast." A member of Drayton's brigade declared, "Another such march I do not care to make."[68]

About a mile west of Sharpsburg, as the brigades and batteries came up near the Stephen Grove house, they were directed down a farm lane running south to Miller's Sawmill Road, which they followed to where the road turned sharply south. Here they took the same route as A. P. Hill's division, which was along a farm lane that descended through a ravine to Boteler's Ford. Lee's chief of artillery, General William N. Pendleton, had command at the ford. He had established one of his battalions of Reserve Artillery to cover this ford on September 16. On the 18th, he was ordered to ensure that the road leading to the ford and the banks on either side of it were in sufficient condition to handle the approaching traffic. He put every available man he had to work—"and such others as could be gathered," principally the small 4th South Carolina battalion—"removing obstructions, preventing collisions, having lights at hand as needed, and promoting the orderly movement of vehicles on the several routes." Despite Pendleton's best efforts, crowding and confusion ensued as units that were arriving at the same time began to pile up on the Maryland shore. When Lieutenant Owen reached Boteler's Ford with the Washington (Louisiana) Artillery, he found "artillery, infantry, ambulances, wagons, all mixed up in what appeared to be inextricable confusion in the water; and the ford, too, was full of large bowlders. Immense fires were blazing on the banks, which had the effect of blinding both men and animals. Staff-officers stood on either bank, shouting to the drivers of vehicles and artillery where they should land. Drivers were whipping their animals, and loudly urging them on. Altogether there was a terrible racket." The ford was deep and rocky, and negotiating it with wagons was tricky and slow. When these vehicles reached the Virginia shore, they had to drive up a narrow road, which climbed a steep bluff and had a sharp precipice on the river side of the road. Captain Andrew B. Wardlaw, the commissary officer in Gregg's brigade of A. P. Hill's division, found it to be so crowded with vehicles, men, and horses that "I did not attempt to pass on horseback for fear of being crushed or thrown off." It took him 3 hours to cover the 2 miles to Shepherdstown, Virginia. Jedediah Hotchkiss, Stonewall Jackson's cartographer, reported encountering the same traffic jam, and he even saw some wagons pushed into the C&O canal by the crush.[69]

The experience of Lieutenant Colonel Sam Walkup and his 48th North Carolina provides a sense of how slowly the Potomac River crossing progressed. His brigade left its position in the West Woods around 11 p.m. The distance to Boteler's Ford was about 4.5 miles, yet they did not cross the river until daybreak. D. R. Jones's brigades did not pass through the ford until 7 a.m., almost 12 hours after forming up to march. By this time the riverbanks were slippery with mud. In the 48th North Carolina, "almost every man fell down" when they both entered and exited the ford. Clothing was wet from the rain and the river, and everyone was hungry and sleep deprived. John Dooley in Kemper's 1st Virginia was startled when he took a long pull on his canteen and discovered that it contained whisky, not water. A company wag had filled about a dozen of the regiment's canteens, including Dooley's, from a whisky barrel he found in Sharpsburg during a halt the brigade made there. There were many in the army who would have delighted in a mouthful of spirits that damp night, but Dooley, a dutiful, religious young man, traded his canteen for one without alcohol. Walkup's men staggered from the Potomac River to the top of the bluffs on the Virginia shore. Then everyone collapsed and instantly fell asleep beside fires that were started along the road, so the soldiers could dry their clothing and warm themselves. Things might have been worse had Jackson's quartermaster, Major John A. Harman, not taken control. Harman was described as "big-bodied, big-voiced, untiring [and] fearless of man or devil, who would have ordered Jackson himself out of his way if necessary." Henry Kyd Douglas considered him to be the "genius of this retreat." Jed Hotchkiss related how Harman "cussed" the Confederate army over the river and believed the way the major sorted out the confusion at Boteler's ford was so vital that "but for his dogged persistence we would have lost our military trains as well as our artillery."[70]

While the bulk of the Army of Northern Virginia made its way across the Potomac River at Boteler's Ford, Lee dispatched Stuart, with Hampton's brigade, to cross the river above Shepherdstown and march to Williamsport, "so as to create a diversion in favor of the movement of the army." They crossed "at an old unused ford," where only one man at a time could wade it, and then marched through the night and all the following day to reach the river town, where they crossed back into Maryland at Dam No. 5.[71]

An anxious Lee sat his horse at Boteler's Ford, "close by the river bank, mounted and motionless as the night itself." He was accompanied by General James Kemper, who was acting as the Army of Northern Virginia's provost marshal, and watched his troops lumber over the Potomac River. Shortly after 7 a.m., A. P. Hill's division, which was the army's rear guard, arrived and began to cross. Gregg's brigade covered the division's crossing, and he deployed it in a line of battle to screen the ford. It took nearly 2 hours for Hill's first four brigades to get across. Around 9 a.m., Gregg called his regiments in, and they formed up to wade through the water. Then a report arrived that Federal cavalry were approaching. Gregg dispatched Captain Joseph N. Brown, with two companies of the 14th South Carolina, to drive them off. Brown advanced nearly a quarter of a mile from the ford and easily forced the Union horseman back. When the rest of his brigade was safely over the Potomac, Brown called his men in and they marched across, unmolested. The captain found Lee still sitting on his horse by the Maryland side of the river, along with A. P. Hill and Gregg. They complimented him on his management of the rearguard action. By 10 a.m. the ford was traversed by Fitz Lee's cavalry brigade, the final soldiers in the army to cross. Robert E. Lee joined the last of them. His relief was palpable. He had safely extricated his army to Virginia. The mood of the troops, as they dragged themselves up the river bluffs and dropped down to rest, was somber. It contrasted sharply with their feelings 2 weeks earlier, when they had splashed across the Potomac River into Maryland, filled with hope and confidence. Now they were sneaking off in the night, leaving behind their unburied dead and their seriously wounded men. For someone like Major William Robbins in the 4th Alabama, who left his brother's body in the East Woods, the foray into Maryland tasted of defeat. But Lee, who seemed possessed of inexhaustible energy and irrepressible optimism, did not think first of food, rest, and recuperation when he reached Virginia. Instead, his active mind contemplated how he might still revive his Maryland Campaign. Seemingly oblivious to the condition of his army, he mulled over marching it to Williamsport, which Stuart had secured, and then returning to Maryland. But Lee commanded men, not automatons, and reality would assert itself against his plans.[72]

20

Shepherdstown

"Help me, Captain, for God's sake don't leave me here"

In both of his reports on the battle, George McClellan maintained that he issued orders on September 18 for "a renewal of the attack at daylight." He did not mean a general attack, however, such as occurred on the 17th. His orders were for a probe—that is, a reconnaissance in force. There was no realignment of troops during the night, no massing of units for a decisive attack, and no orders to corps commanders, except one, to renew the offensive at dawn. The army's posture was defensive, not offensive. His sole attack order had been to Franklin at 5:45 p.m.—to advance a single brigade the next morning to seize Nicodemus Heights, while holding his entire corps in readiness to support them, if necessary. But even this modest movement was tempered by a timid postscript: "push your pickets forward at an early hour in the morning to ascertain whether the enemy is in force in your front." Franklin's interpretation of this sentence is unknown, but it breathed caution. He was also advised that Sumner 2nd Corps would replace Franklin's troops in the line, but there was not a word about coordination or support from any of the other corps in the area.[1]

It all became moot when, at 11:30 p.m., Sumner sent word that his pickets reported the Confederates were withdrawing and felling trees on their retreat route. For some reason it took nearly 4 hours for this message to reach headquarters. It could not have surprised McClellan. The many campfires along the enemy's front that evening seemed designed to blind his signal stations, in order to cover some movement by the Rebels, most likely a retreat. Colonel Strother recorded in his diary that reports were continually being received throughout the night, and he "heard enough to confirm my surmises that the enemy would retreat during the night." Chief of Staff Marcy responded to Sumner at 4 a.m., directing him to "mass your troops in readiness to move in any direction." This was an odd order, since there was only one direction the Confederates could have disappeared in, which was west. Orders went to Franklin and Meade 30 minutes later, as well as to the other corps commanders, to send their pickets ahead. If the enemy had retreated, they were to mass their commands. Pleasonton was ordered to advance "small parties of cavalry on the various roads leading from our position in the direction of the enemy's retreat to ascertain the nature and degree of the obstructions therein." But there were no orders to pursue the enemy.[2]

At dawn, pickets confirmed that the Army of Northern Virginia was gone, apparently in the direction of the Potomac River. Pleasonton assembled elements of Farnsworth's and McReynolds' cavalry brigades, his horse artillery brigade, and several signal officers, and they all set out on the Boonsboro–Sharpsburg Pike around 8 a.m. The command, wrote a *New York Timers* reporter who accompanied them, "dashed on at a hurried trot" through Sharpsburg. As the cavalry swept through the village, an elated McClellan sent a wire to his wife: "Our victory complete. Enemy has left his dead & wounded on the field. Our people are now in pursuit. Your father and I are well." Chief of Staff Halleck, however, had to wait another half hour for news. McClellan's report to him stated that the Confederates had abandoned their position, leaving their dead and wounded, and that the Union army was in pursuit. "I do not know whether he is falling back to an interior position or crossing the river," McClellan continued. Nevertheless, "We may safely claim a complete victory."[3]

To describe the movement of the Army of the Potomac that morning as a "pursuit" is generous. It was more like the movements of a broom, seeking to sweep any residue of the Confederate army across the Potomac River, rather than an action to bring a supposedly defeated enemy to battle. As they passed through Sharpsburg, Pleasonton's troopers and horse artillerymen took in the numerous hospital flags flying from the buildings and the crowds of Confederate wounded gathered around them; the many dead horses dotting the fields on either side of the turnpike; and the still-smoldering campfires from recently evacuated sites. But, observed the *Times* reporter, "there was no particular evidence of haste in their mode of departure." After leaving Sharpsburg, the cavalry split up, with part of the force following Shepherdstown Road, and the rest turning off into the farm lane near Stephen Grove's house and marching down to Miller's Sawmill Road. It was this force that Captain Brown's two 14th South Carolina companies had engaged and driven back (see chapter 19).[4]

The 8th Illinois Cavalry in Farnsworth's brigade came to a high, open hill, off the Shepherdstown Road, known locally as Douglas, or Ferry, Hill, over a mile north of Boteler's Ford. It overlooked the Potomac River and Shepherdstown and included the large home owned by the family of Stonewall Jackson's staff officer, Henry Kyd Douglas (see chapter 16). There the Federals were greeted by "very rapid and accurate" artillery fire from the Virginia side. Fortunately, it was not all that accurate, since the projectiles sailed over the horsemen's heads and burst behind them. The troopers did not linger to allow the Southern gunners to adjust their aim, but instead hurried to find cover. Pleasonton then summoned his horse batteries. All four of them came thundering up the hill, unlimbered on either side of Shepherdstown Road, and returned the fire. The *New York*

Times reporter, who was a spectator to this exchange, thought that the Confederate battery may have been short of ammunition, as it "was very economical in its expenditure." Pleasonton penciled a note to McClellan, stating that the Rebels had withdrawn to Virginia. He added he had captured 167 prisoners, probably stragglers or wounded; one gun, which had been abandoned; and one flag, which was probably not the regimental colors, but a guidon. It was a very small haul from the enemy's allegedly beaten army.[5]

Pleasonton followed this dispatch with several more, reporting on the situation at the front. "The enemy have a circle of batteries bearing upon the ford and have a crossfire upon each position I can take," he wrote in a message with no time signature. The brigadier general recommended that Burnside move up on his left, where the latter's artillery might be able to enfilade the Confederates' guns, and that Sumner cross the Potomac River above Shepherdstown and turn the enemy's other flank. At 10:20 a.m. Pleasonton wrote that the Rebels had at least eight batteries in position across the river, and he would need to be reinforced by additional Union artillery and infantry. Then, 25 minutes later, at 10:45 a.m., Major Albert Myer, who had accompanied Pleasonton with the signal party, reported that he could see a large wagon train parked north of Shepherdstown but could not be certain whether it was moving toward Harpers Ferry or Winchester. Lieutenant Louis Fortescue, a member of Myer's party, wrote that when he peered into the streets of Shepherdstown through his powerful glass, he saw "confusion," with "wagons, ambulances, women and children moving out household goods." Fortescue thought it "had the appearance of a stampede." But his personal opinion did not find its way into Myer's report, which said nothing about disorder in Shepherdstown.[6]

PLEASONTON'S ESTIMATE OF THE Confederates' artillery strength was remarkably accurate for an officer who delighted in exaggeration. There were actually parts of 12 batteries arrayed to defend Boteler's Ford, with 33 guns deployed in positions to fire directly on the ford and 11 in reserve. Lee had entrusted the defense of this vital crossing to one of the least capable officers in the Army of Northern Virginia: Brigadier General William N. Pendleton, the Reserve Artillery commander. Pendleton's shortcomings during the retreat across the ford have already been outlined (see chapter 19). Overall, he was a weak leader, held in contempt by his subordinates. Earlier in the Maryland Campaign, many held Pendleton accountable for spreading panic in the Confederates' reserve battalions over a reported Federal cavalry attack. Afterward, Colonel Allen S. Cutts, the commander of one of those battalions, confronted the general and declared in his blunt, profane manner that he "would leave the corps either by death resignation desertion or some other way that the corps never had fought any [enemy] and never would fight any, that it was an absolute disgrace to the army and that through all future time it would be a reproach to any man that had ever belonged to it." Rather than disciplining Cutts for insubordination, Pendleton meekly attached his battalion to D. H. Hill's division. One of Pendleton's fiercest critics—Lieutenant John "Ham" Chamberlayne, an assistant adjutant general to Lieutenant Colonel Reuben L. Walker, commanding A. P. Hill's artillery battalion—held the opinion that "Brig. Gen. Pendleton is an absurd humbug; a fool and a coward. Well known to be so among those who see and know, & do not hear." Lee could not have been oblivious to these feelings about Pendleton, and his decision to leave an important rear-guard position to him is unusual. Two factors probably influenced the choice: Lee's personal fatigue, and the fact that Pendleton had been commanding troops at Boteler's Ford since September 16 and knew the ground.[7]

On the night of September 15, Lee ordered his artillery chief to use his two reserve battalions to defend the fords at Shepherdstown, Williamsport, and Falling Waters. Pendleton sent Colonel John T. Brown's battalion to defend the latter two fords, and moved Major William Nelson's entire battalion to Shepherdstown. The general found that there was a great deal of work to be done: placing Nelson's batteries; repairing the roads to Boteler's Ford, in order to handle the heavy army traffic; and constructing a bridge over the C&O Canal. Lee added to Pendleton's responsibilities by assigning him the task of rounding up and driving stragglers forward during the fighting on September 17. On the 18th, when a report was received of an enemy movement toward Shepherd's Ford—which was 4 miles to the north, upriver from Shepherdstown—Pendleton detached one of Nelson's batteries, along with a scratch force of infantry stragglers, to its defense. Two weeks earlier, Pendleton had experienced what he called a "crisis of a diarrhoea" and was still not fully recovered. The army's retreat on the night of September 18 forced him to "work like a beaver," supervising the various duties of those under his command: "removing obstructions, preventing collisions, having lights at hand as needed, and promoting the orderly movement of vehicles on the several routes." This meant that Pendleton had to stay in his saddle throughout and got no sleep for a second night. The army's safe passage to Virginia brought him no respite from the demands of command, however, since he and Nelson were kept busy selecting and placing guns from the Confederate army's divisions to add more firepower to the defense of Boteler's Ford.[8]

In addition to the five batteries in Nelson's battalion, Pendleton secured the whole or parts of five other batteries from different divisions. Nelson only had five rifled pieces, so priority was given to obtaining more. The extra batteries contributed 11 rifled guns and 1 Napoleon. There was also one more battery, with 6 lb. guns, which was personally placed with the others by Lee's military secretary, Colonel Armistead Long. In total, Pendleton had 44 guns at his disposal. He, Nelson, and Long were able to find positions for 33 of them. The remaining 11 pieces were short-range guns and howitzers, which were placed in reserve. Two infantry brigades were added to the artillery reinforcement: Douglass's Georgia brigade in Early's division and Armistead's brigade in R. H. Anderson's division, both apparently detailed for this mission by Longstreet. Whoever was responsible for their selection was either sleep deprived, incompetent, or ignorant of the condition of these units. Together, they only numbered about 600 effectives, and both had lost their brigade commanders at Sharpsburg. Douglass's brigade had emerged from the hell of Sharpsburg with only 95 men—for example, the 13th Georgia went into action with 230 and came out with 15—so the additions to bring its strength up to around 300 were stragglers or lightly wounded soldiers pressed back into the ranks. The morale of Armistead's brigade was shaky. When Walter Clark in the 35th North Carolina of Ransom's brigade was guiding Armistead's brigade into position in the West Woods on September 17, he wrote how it had "instantly scattered" when the general was wounded by a shell. The physical state of the men also influenced their morale, with one member of Armistead's brigade reflecting that he had not eaten in 48 hours: "You may not possibly know how it feels to go that long, and to be marching night and day; I assure you that a man is not in the best of spirits." In place of Douglass and Armistead, the two brigades were commanded by their respective senior colonels: Colonel John H. Lamar in the 61st Georgia, and Colonel James G. Hodges in the 14th Virginia. They were capable officers but could only accomplish so much, given the condition of their commands.[9]

Pendleton benefited from being on strong defensive terrain. A line of steep bluffs, rising to 150 feet above the Potomac River, completely commanded the Virginia side. There was scarcely any vegetation on them, which gave Pendleton's artillery excellent fields of fire. He and Nelson arrayed 15 guns, 10 of which were rifled, south of Boteler's Ford, and 18 guns, including 7 rifled ones, north of it. The rifles were deployed 200 to 300 yards from the river, where they could cover the approaches to the ford and engage in counter-battery fire, if necessary. The short-range guns, consisting of 6-pounders and 12 lb. howitzers, were placed close to the edge of the bluffs, to either strike the ford with crossfire or sweep the River Road on the Maryland side with fire. Pendleton met with the two infantry brigade commanders, although, astonishingly, he failed to inquire about the strength or condition of their commands. Pendleton ordered them to "keep their force at the ford strong, vigilant, and as well sheltered as occasion allowed, and to have the residue well in hand, back of adjacent hills, for protection till needed." He also directed them "not to fire merely in reply to shots from the other side, but only to repel any attempt at crossing, and to guard the ford," presumably to ensure that the men did not waste ammunition or draw fire upon themselves. Pendleton was pitifully short on staff to manage his rear guard. Besides battalion commander Nelson—a 53-year-old pre-war farmer who had developed into a fine artillery officer—he only had a single aide-de camp, Lieutenant Charles Hatcher, and Sergeant Major Robert Jones to assist him.[10]

Pendleton's orders from Robert E. Lee, written by Chilton, reached him by midmorning: "The commanding general says that if the enemy is in force in your front you must retire to-night. If not in force, being merely an artillery force, withdraw the infantry forces, directing them to join their respective divisions on the march to-morrow, a few guns and a small cavalry force being sufficient to guard the fords."[11]

Pendleton may have pondered how he would determine whether the Federals were merely demonstrating or present in force, since much of the ground on the Maryland side was screened by trees and bluffs. Neither Lee nor Pendleton anticipated aggressive action by the Yankees, however. Lee wrote in 1866 that he "believed Gen. McClellan had been so crippled at Sharpsburg, that he could not follow the Confederate Army into Virginia immediately." Pendleton expressed the opinion to his wife that the reason the Federals had not renewed the battle on September 18 was because "they were too much shattered to renew the attack." Lee judged McClellan correctly, but for the wrong reasons. McClellan's caution, and his belief that shooing the enemy across the Potomac River achieved his campaign goals, was what dictated the movements of the Federals, not the damage his army had sustained on September 17. But Lee and Pendleton both failed to anticipate that subordinate Union commanders might seize the initiative and make trouble.[12]

WHEN MCCLELLAN HAD CONFIRMATION that the Rebels had retreated from Sharpsburg, he ordered Burnside to advance the 9th Corps to the mouth of Antietam Creek, where there was also a ford over the Potomac River. The rest of the Union army was directed to move forward west of Sharpsburg and establish a defensive line. Pleasonton's subsequent report that the enemy had withdrawn to Virginia made this precaution unnecessary. McClellan wired Halleck at 10:30 a.m.: "Pleasonton is driving the enemy across the river. Our victory is complete. The enemy is driven back into Virginia. Maryland and Pennsylvania are now safe." There had been no driving, however. The enemy had *withdrawn*—unmolested. McClellan had no plans to pursue the Army of Northern Virginia across the Potomac River. Maryland was "entirely freed from the presence of the enemy" and "no fears need now be entertained for the safety of Pennsylvania." To McClellan, the objective of the Maryland Campaign had been fulfilled. In response to Pleasonton's description of the Confederates' defense at Boteler's Ford, however, McClellan did decide to reinforce the cavalry with infantry and artillery. He sent Porter, with the 1st and 2nd divisions of his 5th Corps, as well as batteries of the Artillery Reserve. Porter's orders have not survived, or they may have been verbal, but there is evidence that what he was ordered to do was limited. Franklin was directed to advance the 6th Corps, so its batteries could gain an enfilading fire on Rebel columns in the Shepherdstown area, but he was cautioned to "not attempt to cross the river without further orders." Pleasonton received orders at 1:15 p.m. from Chief of Staff Marcy: "General McClellan directs me to say that he does not propose to cross the river, and he does not desire you to do so, unless you see a splendid opportunity to inflict great damage upon the enemy without loss to yourself." Porter certainly received identical instructions.[13]

Porter's 1st Division led the way. It was commanded by Major General George W. Morell and consisted of three infantry brigades, the attached 1st U.S. Sharpshooters (also known as Berdan's U.S. Sharpshooters), and a three-battery artillery brigade—totaling about 5,400 men. The division had assembled in the vicinity of the Rohrback farm and the Rohrback Bridge on September 18, and Porter sent its 1st Brigade across to the west bank of Antietam Creek to relieve part of the 9th Corps late in the afternoon. McClellan later claimed that Burnside sent Morell's entire division across the creek and withdrew all of the 9th Corps' troops to its eastern bank, but this simply was not true. When Morell received his marching orders on September 19, he crossed the Rohrback Bridge with his 2nd and 3rd Brigades, collected the 1st Brigade, and marched into Sharpsburg along Lower Bridge Road. Morell was 47 years old and a West Point graduate, but he had only served in the Regular Army for 2 years before resigning to work as a civil engineer for two different railroads. He ran a genial headquarters and was well liked by his men, but he lacked energy and initiative. Porter's opinion was that Morell "was of bright, clear mind, familiar with his duties and always true to them, though not initiatively very active or pressing" A staff officer in the 5th Corps recalled that Morell "was not a dashing officer and he had so little idea of making an effect, that he missed favorable opportunities."[14]

Morell's men noticed how "nearly every house" in Sharpsburg had been struck by solid shot or shell. "Things look rough," noted Lieutenant John Bancroft in the 4th Michigan. Lieutenant Samuel S. Partridge in the 13th New York found the village "literally riddled with balls—one church [probably the Lutheran Church on the west side of Cemetery Hill] alone had thirty-two cannon ball holes in it to say nothing of innumerable little bullet marks." Many residents had emerged from their homes or were returning from where they had taken shelter. They greeted the 5th Corps' soldiers with unrestrained elation. "We were received by the inhabitants with every demonstration of joy, men, women and children vying with each other in their desire to make us welcome," observed Captain Francis Donaldson in the 118th Pennsylvania. Lieutenant Bancroft remarked on how women "point out the houses of those who have given the rebels shelter and where rebel flags are concealed," and on how even "children swear vengeance." The soldiers in the 9th Massachusetts encountered an enraged man standing in the doorway of his home, cursing the Confederates for stealing his carpeting, quilts, and blankets and encouraging the Yankees to overtake the scoundrels and "blow them to h——." Donaldson was amused when thinking about Lee's proclamation to the people of Maryland, explaining why his army had entered their state. "How ridiculous seemed the bombastic order of General Lee," wrote the captain. "He had come to stay, he had come to give them <u>freedom</u>, and right here, in this town, close to the border of Virginia, were the people he had come to <u>liberate</u>, hailing with joy the expulsion of these 'liberators'—very curious and funny to us <u>narrow minded</u> Yanks."[15]

The Federal troops found the village filled with injured Confederates. Donaldson noted how "every available place [was] turned into a hospital." In many locations, the wounded, lying on litters of straw, overflowed onto the yards of the private homes and public buildings. Lieutenant Colonel William S. Tilton, commanding the 22nd Massachusetts, paused to give one Rebel soldier who caught his eye an apple, and the appreciative man asked God to bless him. On the west side of the village, Morell turned left at the Grove farm, onto the same farm lane part of Lee's army and some of Pleasonton's cavalry had followed. A collection of Confederate prisoners, who were perched on a fence beside the road, perked up when they saw Tilton pass by. He had been wounded and captured at the Battle of Gaines' Mill but then was exchanged, and these Confederates had encountered him at some point in this process. "Isn't that the old cock we had in Libby?" Tilton heard one Rebel ask another, who replied that it was. Tilton, mimicking the drawl of the prisoners, replied, "Ya-a-ss, tha-a-at's him, but you will never get him again."[16]

The 1st Division arrived near the Potomac River around 1:30 p.m. and turned into the fields north of Boteler's Ford, where they massed under cover of a line of bluffs. They were followed by Sykes's 2nd Division, with about 3,000 infantry in three small brigades. This division had a powerful collection of guns from the 5th Corps and the Artillery Reserve: Captain Stephen H. Weed's Battery I, 5th U.S; a single Napoleon from Lieutenant Alanson M. Randol's Batteries E and G, 1st U.S.; Lieutenant William E. Van Reed's Battery K, 5th U.S.; and Captain Charles Kusserow's Battery D and Captain Robert Langner's Battery C, both in the 1st Battalion, New York Light. These 19 guns were in addition to the 18 guns with Morell's division, as well as the horse artillery already in place and trading fire with the Confederates.[17]

The 5th Corps was a bastion of support for McClellan. "I do actually believe there never was a General loved, or rather worshipped by rank & file as McClellan is by the 'Grand Army of the Potomac,'" wrote Sergeant Charles Bowen, in the 12th U.S. Infantry, to his mother on September 26. But when Bowen and his comrades reached the Potomac River, they were loud in their condemnation of the "mismanagement in allowing them [the Rebels] to cross the river. All appear to think that there should have been a force to cut them off, & thus kill or capture the entire crowd." J. Smith Brown, the adjutant in the 1st U.S. Sharpshooters, believed Jackson had commanded the Confederate army. In a post-battle letter to his hometown newspaper, Brown pondered angrily, "All I have to say is that I do not understand why Jackson was allowed to take his army safely away."

Yet so great—and unquestioning—was their confidence in McClellan that it did not register with them that managing a pursuit to cut the Rebels off was the responsibility of their beloved commander.[18]

Arriving in the vicinity of Douglas Hill, Fitz John Porter assessed the situation and concluded that he would "clear the fords, and, if possible, secure some of the enemy's artillery." By this time, Pleasonton's Horse Artillery had been trading fire with General Pendleton's Reserve Artillery guns for over an hour. Porter ordered the 1st U.S. Sharpshooters and the sharpshooters in the 2nd Independent Company, attached to the 22nd Massachusetts, to "get as near as possible to their batteries, but not to show a man nor fire a gun" until he could get his Artillery Reserve and the 5th Corps' batteries into position. When the Federals' big guns began firing, the sharpshooters were encouraged "to pick off artillerymen and horses," as well as, more generally, to "fire at every one they saw moving." The dozen sharpshooters in the 2nd Company worked their way to the bank of the Potomac River, unseen by the Confederates. Concealing themselves in brush and behind trees, they observed what were probably Johnson's and Kirkpatrick's batteries, which were closest to Boteler's Ford, and their infantry supports. The adjutant in the 1st U.S. Sharpshooters, J. Smith Brown, wrote that the more numerous green-uniformed riflemen in his regiment "rushed up to the brow of the hill, and lay down a moment before charging down the bare bank, where there was no cover. At the word, we rose and ran down to the river, receiving a heavy fire from the enemy in so doing." They leaped into the empty C&O canal, which served as a ready-made trench, and dispersed along it.[19]

When all was ready, Porter's guns opened fire. They were immediately joined by the sharpshooters, armed with their Sharps rifles. Under ideal conditions, a Sharps was capable of hitting targets at 1,000 yards, and the range here was only between 340 and 400 yards. "Of all the unearthly din I ever heard that was the worst," wrote the lieutenant colonel in the 20th Maine, Joshua L. Chamberlain, when all the guns began firing. Pendleton described the Yankees' artillery fire as "furious," and the volleys by the sharpshooters were "an evil not slightly trying, since it exposed our cannoneers to be picked off, when serving their guns, by the enemy's effective infantry rifles." He confided to his wife that the Federals had planted a number of powerful batteries, "compared with which ours were mere pop-guns." Merit Seay, serving one of the 6 lb. guns in Huckstep's 1st Fluvanna (Virginia) Artillery, wrote that Porter's long-range guns "very near cut us to pieces while we couldn't hurt them with our little six pounders." Despite the superior position, ordnance, and ammunition of the Federals, the Confederate artillerymen stubbornly and bravely continued to serve their guns. Their losses were light, but this was because the Union's artillery and sharpshooter fire gradually drove the Rebels from several of their batteries and forced the crews to seek cover.[20]

As the afternoon wore on, Pendleton's situation steadily deteriorated. Colonel Hodges reported that "we have not a piece of artillery in position, firing, and the enemy have, as far as he [Colonel Edward C. Edmonds, 38th Virginia] could ascertain, twenty-odd. There is nothing to prevent the enemy from crossing except the line of sharpshooters." Another message arrived from Colonel Thomas Munford, whose small cavalry brigade was watching the ford near the mouth of Antietam Creek, 2 miles away. It stated that the enemy—it was the 9th Corps— had arrived across the Potomac River in force "and could not be prevented crossing unless I [Pendleton] sent him some infantry." In response to Hodges' message, the brigadier general ordered 200 of his infantrymen held in reserve—30% of his overall numbers—to reinforce the skirmishers defending the guns. To support Munford, Pendleton sent what he believed was between 100 and 200 soldiers in his remaining infantry, but apparently this help only consisted of the 9th Virginia in Armistead's brigade, which only contained 50 or 60 men. At this critical point, Pendleton become aware for the first time of just how weak his infantry force was. "In providing, therefore, for protecting right and left, as described, I was not aware of [the] infantry weakness for the ford itself," he admitted in his after-action report. Yet he made no request for reinforcements from Lee. Perhaps he believed that he could hold on until nightfall permitted him to withdraw. He shared no assessment of the Federals' strength with Lee. They kept their infantry under cover, but the number of batteries in action against him indicated that he probably faced—at a minimum—a division.[21]

A "continuous roll of musketry" and shells from Union artillery raked the Confederate position. As sunset neared, both Lamar and Hodges reported to Pendleton that the pressure on their slender force "was becoming too great to be borne." He asked them to hold on for an hour longer, as "sunset was at hand, and I had communicated with Colonel Munford, who promised at dark to be with us." He planned to have Munford screen the withdrawal of his batteries. But if a plan is to have any hope of success, all of those involved in implementing it must know what it is. This was the rub, for no one else was aware of what Pendleton intended. Pendleton had to rely on Nelson, plus their tiny staffs, to coordinate a retreat in the dark, under enemy fire. It was a recipe for disaster. The first evidence of real trouble was a string of reports from several battery commanders, who reported that they had exhausted their ammunition and asked permission to pull out. Pendleton had never been fully in control of the engagement, but it now began to slip completely from his grasp. He replied that a battery could withdraw, using routes "where they could get back unseen," but it was "not deemed wise" for the others to attempt it. Thus the decision about whether to withdraw was left to each individual battery leader's discretion, depending on whether he believed he and his gun crews could return to the main body of the army unobserved. Pendleton further confused the situation by following up this communication with another, directing the batteries to retire "in specified order, as dusk deepened to conceal them in so doing." This implies that there was some prearranged plan to withdraw the guns, but with no radios to issue the command simultaneously to all the batteries, the staff officers were only able to deliver it in a staggered sequence. There was also the possibility that they might miss a battery or gun section in the dark, and the order was almost certainly verbal, which increased the chances of it being misunderstood or misinterpreted. The result was confusion. Then the Federals struck.[22]

With the Confederate guns largely silenced and the sun setting, Fitz John Porter, with commendable initiative, decided to mount a limited, yet risky, assault to try and capture some of the Confederates' artillery. Around 5:30 p.m., he assembled a force consisting of the 1st U.S. Sharpshooters; the 4th Michigan, whose colonel volunteered his regiment; and 50 volunteers each from the 18th and 22nd Massachusetts and the rookie 118th Pennsylvania. Orders were issued to ford the Potomac River and pitch into the Rebels. Porter also sent a directive for Sykes's 2nd Division to send a storming party over to the Virginia side, but due to some blunder, the order never reached him. It would not be the last staff snafu for the 5th Corps at Shepherdstown.[23]

Captain John B. Isler, in charge of the 1st U.S. Sharpshooters, shouted orders to cease fire and advance across the river. His line was so extended, however, that only about 60 of his men heard and responded to his command. The rest, presumably, continued shooting. As Isler's men scrambled up out of their cover in the dry C&O Canal, the 300 or so men of the 4th Michigan poured down the bank behind them to lay down a covering fire. Adjutant J. Smith Brown was part of the small contingent of sharpshooters who ran down to the river. "Well, now to tell the truth, I hated to go," he wrote. "I thought of Ball's Bluff"—an earlier battle where many Federals were driven down the site's steep slope and drowned or shot in their attempts to cross back over the Potomac River. The 60 soldiers who went forward seemed a pitifully small number to Brown. But the volleys from the 4th Michigan—as well as those from Colonel Gouverneur K. Warren's small New York brigade in Sykes's division, which had moved up to the bluffs—and the artillery, gave heart to the sharpshooters. Carrying their rifles and ammunition above their heads, they entered the river. No one was sure where Boteler's Ford was, and some men found the water where they crossed to be waist deep or higher. Hodges's and Lamar's Confederate infantry fired what Brown described as "tremendous volleys," but the shooting was either not as intense as the adjutant claimed or inaccurate, for only four Yankees were hit while traversing the river. The sharpshooters were immediately followed by the 4th Michigan and the volunteers from the other regiments.[24]

Lieutenant George M. Barnard was one of the volunteers with the 18th Massachusetts, and he wrote to his mother about how soldiers from the division crowded around them as they made their way to join the assault force. "For the time being we were all made heroes," he observed. He thought the Confederates fired on them "in a pretty lively manner" when they reached the Potomac River, but they dashed over a bridge that spanned the C&O Canal—probably the one built by Pendleton for the Confederates' retreat on September 18—and paused behind trees along the riverbank. The officer assigned to guide Barnard's party led them into water that came up to their necks. Barnard thought the scene must have seemed ludicrous to anyone who was watching. "Fancy us all in full dress with nothing to be seen but twenty heads above the water, all sputtering and shivering, ammunition wet, guns full of water," he wrote. Three of his men floated away. Barnard thought they had drowned, but they somehow survived their dunking. His part in the Federals' Potomac River assault ended ingloriously when the 18th's major shouted from the Maryland bank that their target—the Rebel battery—had departed and they should all come back. The dispirited men returned to Maryland cold, soaked, and "in a pretty exhausted condition."[25]

The sharpshooters, the 4th Michigan, and the other volunteers had greater success than Barnard, managing to actually get across the Potomac River. Lieutenant William H. Nash was at the forefront of the sharpshooters and would have been the first in his regiment to set foot on the opposite shore, but the river's slippery bottom sent him tumbling into the water. Nash's spill put Lieutenant William W. Winthrop in the lead, and he was the first to reach Virginia. Lamar's and Hodges's infantry delivered a "very sharp" fire at these Yankees, but it was dark, with the enemy targets difficult to make out, and the Rebels' shooting was ineffective.[26]

By this point, the Confederate infantry had been under small-arms and artillery fire for hours. Many of their men must have been low on or out of ammunition, for it is unlikely that those nearest the Potomac River could have been resupplied under the fire directed at them. Two years later, D. H. Hill, who could always be counted on to offer a caustic opinion, even when he was not an eyewitness to events, wrote, "Our men were so much demoralized that a whole Brigade [Lawton's] had thrown down its arms the night before & fled without firing a shot at the Yankees as they crossed the river." Lamar's and Hodges's men had not acted as Hill claimed they did, but they became demoralized and eventually fled their positions, actions that were generally acknowledged by other officers in the Army of Northern Virginia. Henry Kyd Douglas wrote that the "affair disgusted General Jackson beyond words." During a flag of truce on September 22, Colonel William H. F. "Rooney" Lee, commanding the 9th Virginia Cavalry, told Captain Stephen M. Weld, a former Harvard classmate and staff officer in the 5th Corps, that when the 1st U.S. Sharpshooters and the 4th Michigan crossed the Potomac River, "they drove a whole brigade of rebels, who ran shamefully." Hill, Lee, and others implied that Lamar's and Hodges's men bugged out, rather than being commanded to retreat, but those two officers had received orders from Pendleton that the guns should withdraw first, and then be followed by the infantry, who would be screened by Munford's cavalry. If Lamar and Hodges had communicated these orders to their men, it is entirely possible that when the foot soldiers saw the Confederate batteries limbering up, they considered it to be the signal for their own retreat. Whatever the cause, all cohesion and discipline quickly evaporated when the men began to fall back, and their movement degenerated into "a state of disorder akin to panic."[27]

Pendleton was south of Boteler's Ford, along the bluffs near Charles Town Road, which bisected his position. His staff had departed to deliver orders for the withdrawal, and he was alone. In ignorance of the actual situation on his front, he believed "everything appeared likely, under favoring Providence, to result in effecting the withdrawal planned." But the Almighty abandoned the general that evening. While calmly waiting for his staff to return, he saw groups of infantrymen suddenly appear out of the darkness, rushing past him in a state of disorder, bordering on panic. He managed to stop some of them and learned that the Federals had crossed the Potomac River. He probably had listened to the small-arms fire at the river, and he may have heard the exultant shouts of the 4th Michigan when they reached the Virginia side of the riverbank.[28]

Pendleton encouraged the Rebel infantrymen he had stopped to "be steady and useful in checking disorder," offering enough resistance "to make the enemy cautious." Possibly a handful heeded his appeal, but the majority hurried on, in order to get beyond the range of the Yankees' artillery. Pendleton stood alone, confused and uncertain about what he should do. He had no idea what the situation at the Potomac River was. He had seen some of his batteries withdrawing, but he heard others still firing. He considered his position to be personally perilous, as he was exposed to "easy capture" by the enemy. With no sign of Munford's cavalry to cover a retreat, Pendleton hastily weighed his options. He believed the Federals would either halt 100 or 200 yards from the river and not advance any farther in the darkness, or would press forward and try to capture as many of the Confederates' guns as possible. He claimed to believe that the Yankees would do the former, but insisted that he had to provide for the possibility of the latter. His ensuing decisions and actions reflected a commander who, no longer having control of the conflict, did not necessarily panic, but definitely lose his composure. Peter Carmichael writes that "after the battle he [Pendleton] created a smoke screen of half-truths and falsehoods to obscure his actions and appalling lack of firsthand knowledge." Having seen some of his artillery driving out Charles Town Road, the brigadier general made his way along a path exposed to heavy enemy shelling until he eventually reached this road. On the way, he was joined by his two staff members. At Charles Town Road, they came up to what Pendleton believed was the rear of his withdrawing artillery column. What batteries these were is unknown, but his description of a "column" implies a sense of order, when the reality along the length of the Confederates' line was chaos, with the Rebel batteries taking any route possible to escape. Most avoided

Charles Town Road, because it was under Union artillery fire. Captain Victor Maurin, commanding the Donaldsonville (Louisiana) Artillery, reported that when he withdrew his two Parrott guns he could not use this road, because of "it being commanded by the enemy's artillery," so he was obliged "to cut across fields and fences and a country entirely unknown to me, without a guide." It was every man for himself.[29]

Rather than ride to the front to personally view the situation, Pendleton left the field with the battery he encountered on Charles Town Road. In a September 22 letter to his wife, he admitted that he left his artillery "to the result of my orders,—should the enemy not press on,—but rather anticipating its capture, with William Nelson and the other officers." Pendleton had decided that the situation was hopeless, abandoned his command, and fled. Fortunately, Nelson and the remaining battery commanders were made of sterner stuff and worked furiously to extricate their guns before the yelling Yankees swarming up from the Potomac River overran them. The darkness aided their escape, but they still did extraordinarily well. Nonetheless, Maurin's battery lost 20 horses in the engagement, over 50% of the horsepower in his artillery unit. The animals that pulled one of his two escaping Parrott rifles were so exhausted that they fell behind, so that gun had to be spiked and abandoned. Milledge's (Georgia) Battery lost their 12 lb. howitzer and caisson; Johnson's (Virginia) Battery, another 12 lb. howitzer; and Huckstep's 1st Fluvanna (Virginia) Battery, a 6 lb. gun and a limber. The latter two were nearest the Potomac River and thus had the most difficult time getting away. That only four guns were captured was something of a miracle. Moreover, by the standards of 1862, three of those four pieces were obsolete. Where Pendleton failed, Nelson and his battery commanders succeeded, but it was a hairbreadth escape.[30]

The 1st U.S. Sharpshooters and the 4th Michigan scrambled up to the top of the steep Potomac River bluffs. "No rebels could be seen, save a few wounded and sick ones," wrote Sergeant James W. Vesey in the 4th Michigan. Corporal Cassius Peck, an intrepid soldier, led a small party of sharpshooters and drove off the artillerymen from two guns in different Confederate batteries. To ensure that a Rebel counterattack did not recapture them, Peck and his squad pushed the guns over the riverbank. Enemy fire was mostly negligible, but some of the sharpshooters came upon a knot of resistance, where some Confederates fought to cover the withdrawal of Pendleton's hospital camp. But the fighting soon subsided. The Federals established a picket line and scoured their position for prisoners and equipment. A staff officer from Hood's division, with orders for Douglass's brigade, rode straight into the Union sharpshooters' lines, as did several Southern correspondents, who blundered into the 4th Michigan's lines. Porter, considering his foray to be a success, ordered a recall of the his expeditionary force. Around 10 p.m., the men descended from the bluffs and forded the Potomac River back into Maryland. At a cost of 3 killed and 11 wounded (some of whom were hit before the assault), the audacious attack netted four enemy guns, two limbers, two caissons, two forges, and a handful of prisoners. It had been a textbook river assault. Porter allowed his artillery and small-arms fire to gain superiority and wear down the enemy throughout the afternoon, before sending his infantry across. By waiting until late enough in the day, dusk helped provide some concealment for his infantry and greatly reduced their losses. With no means to remove the captured guns and equipment, however, they were left on the Virginia shore. Porter intended to retrieve them in the morning.[31]

AFTER RETREATING 2 MILES from the Potomac River, Pendleton came upon General Roger Pryor, commanding R. H. Anderson's division. Pryor, a soldier whose "military ineptitude exceeded even Pendleton's," was resting with his division beside Charles Town Road. Explaining the crisis at the river and the possibility that much of the artillery there had been captured, Pendleton asked if Pryor would send a force to recover it. Pryor chewed on this and concluded that it was a "responsibility too serious for him to assume," so he referred Pendleton to Hood, whose division was nearby. Pendleton pressed on and found Hood's staff in the road. They told him the general was unwell and thus unavailable. Pendleton was referred to "another and another" unit, with no success. When he asked where Longstreet was, no one knew. The Army of Northern Virginia was in an exhausted, muddled state, stumbling through the pitch-black darkness like a wounded animal. In the end, Pendleton set out to find Robert E. Lee. This, he reported, "in the extreme darkness and intricacies of unknown routes, proved a task of no little difficulty and delay." It was nearly 1 a.m. when Pendleton found the Confederate army commander and his staff, asleep under an apple tree. Lee was awakened, and a nearby staff officer overheard Pendleton explain that the Federals had crossed the Potomac River and seized the bluffs, capturing the Confederate guns there. "All?" Lee allegedly asked. "Yes, General, I fear all," Pendleton was heard to answer. The unidentified staff officer claimed this announcement "lifted me right off my blanket," and he had to walk away, lest he betray his outrage at Pendleton's report. The gist of the conversation may be true, but Pendleton knew that *all* the artillery at the river had *not* been captured, since he had escaped with some of it. What certainly alarmed Lee was that his artillery chief had no idea how many guns were captured, or even what the situation at the Potomac River was.[32]

According to Pendleton, Lee told him they would do nothing until the next morning, and the Reserve Artillery commander, ill and completely spent, went to sleep besides Lee's staff. Lee probably detected that Pendleton was badly rattled and might handicap any recovery effort. It was better to let him rest. While he slept, Lee sought answers to what the situation at the river was like, and what could be done about it. The general confusion then gripping the Confederate army, and the pitch darkness, rendered the precise whereabouts of Jackson and

Longstreet uncertain. Lee found D. H. Hill and, according to Hill, asked where Jackson's command was camped. Hill was unaware of their location—no one in the Army of Northern Virginia that night seemed to know where anyone else was—but he offered an alternative: his division was "ready to move and awaits your orders." Lee allegedly responded, "I do not know what to tell you to do. I hear from one messenger that the enemy have crossed the river and captured a few pieces of artillery, by another that they have crossed in force and have possession of all the reserve artillery. I can hear nothing reliable." Hill mentioned that he had received orders to follow Early's division to Boteler's Ford, to which Lee seemed "much perplexed" and expressed the opinion that the order might be in error. Lee himself then left to find Longstreet.[33]

It is doubtful that Lee was as befuddled and indecisive as D. H. Hill claimed. Hill sought to buttress his account of that night with an 1869 recollection by James W. Ratchford, who had served on Hill's staff. Ratchford claimed that he never saw Lee so excited over the condition of his army. Perhaps, but Ratchford was intensely loyal to Hill and may have had his reasons to sustain his former commander's account. Moreover, Hill had no love for Lee and was not adverse to portraying him poorly. Hill's statement that he had received orders to follow Early's division to Boteler's Ford in the morning raises suspicion. The only person who could have sent those orders to Hill was Jackson, yet, when Lee asked him, Hill had claimed not to know where Jackson was. A second strike against Hill's account is that Jackson never mentioned ordering D. H. Hill's division to the ford—just Early's and A. P. Hill's divisions.[34]

By the night of September 19, Lee was seriously sleep deprived, and his legendary endurance might have slipped, rendering him indecisive about how to respond to the Union incursion across the Potomac River. The available evidence, however, disputes D. H. Hill's and Ratchford's depiction of him. Sometime early on September 20—possibly after his meeting with Pendleton—Lee wrote an update on the Army of Northern Virginia's situation to Confederate President Jefferson Davis, in which Lee stated that he feared much of the Reserve Artillery might have been captured. This letter was written by a man clearly in full control of his faculties: "I am now obliged to return to Shepherdstown, with the intention of driving the enemy back if not in position with his whole army, but, if in full force, I think an attack would be inadvisable, and I shall make other dispositions." This is the first definite acknowledgement that Lee had finally comprehended the fragile condition of his army and now intended to avoid a general engagement. It also implies that he had delivered orders for the movement back to the Potomac River. This brings into question the account of another eyewitness with no more credibility than D. H. Hill: Jackson's staff officer, Henry Kyd Douglas. Douglas claimed that when Jackson learned of the debacle at the Potomac River, he did not wait for orders, but instead "took matters in his own hands," ordering A. P. Hill's and Early's divisions to return to the river in the morning and drive the Federals back. Jackson was a decisive soldier, but stating that he ordered two of the Confederate army's nine divisions to initiate an engagement against an enemy force of unknown strength—*without* communicating with Lee—defies credulity. What seems most plausible is that Lee, after learning of the disaster at the river from Pendleton, sought clarification about its extent. Even before Lee received this intelligence, however, he probably ordered Jackson to attack if the enemy were not present in full force, but to avoid a battle if their whole army were crossing. A. P. Hill, whose division led this advance, did not receive his orders until 6:30 a.m. on September 20, which indicates that the Confederates did not react impulsively or instantaneously, as some of their postwar accounts imply, but instead spent the hours after Pendleton appeared at Lee's headquarters gathering information about the situation at Boteler's Ford before acting.[35]

PORTER SPENT PART OF the night of September 19 interrogating the Confederate prisoners his men had captured in their river assault. These Rebels were cavalrymen, probably from Munford's brigade, and they informed the 5th Corps' commander that no Confederate troops were near the Potomac River, except some cavalry pickets. This confirmed all the other evidence Porter had assembled—namely, that the enemy was retreating toward either Charles Town or Martinsburg in [West] Virginia. On the basis of this information, Porter notified army headquarters at 9 p.m. that he intended to cross the river at daybreak the next morning, in order to determine the direction in which the Army of Northern Virginia had retired. He also requested the support of cavalry and horse artillery for this operation. It was to be a reconnaissance in force, for Porter planned to push the entire 5th Corps across the Potomac River, including Humphreys's division, which he had called up from Keedysville. Curiously, since Porter counted on the support of cavalry, sometime that afternoon or evening he sent Pleasonton's two brigades back to their camps near Keedysville, in order to refit the men and reshoe their horses. Even more curiously, he issued this order, supposedly on the authority of McClellan, through the Union army's chief of cavalry, General John Buford, even though McClellan and Chief of Staff Marcy were unaware of it. Pleasonton was not with his brigades when they received this order. Their return to Keedysville caught him by surprise and left him fuming at Porter's interference in his cavalry division's operations. Thinking his men would spend the night near Boteler's Ford, he had ordered his supply trains to drive forward, so his men and their horses could be fed. Porter's order meant that the troopers and their mounts missed the wagons and thus went hungry. It was the first of a series of communication snafus that would lead to tragedy on September 20.[36]

Besides the operations at Shepherdstown, McClellan was paying careful attention to reports of Confederate activity at Williamsport and remained concerned about the possibility that Lee might punch into his rear from Harpers Ferry. To secure the latter point, at 12:15 p.m. on September 19, he ordered Sumner to send Alpheus Williams' 12th Corps to occupy Maryland Heights. As for Williamsport, sometime that evening a report was received from Colonel Arno Voss, whose 12th Illinois Cavalry—part of the contingent that had escaped from Harpers Ferry several days earlier—was posted at Jones's Crossroads, south of Hagerstown, and was picketing the Williamsport area and the Potomac River crossing below that town. Voss reported the presence of 1,000 Confederate infantrymen and one artillery piece at Williamsport. In response to this, at 8:15 p.m. McClellan issued orders to General Darius Couch to detach a brigade plus a battery to surround and capture this force. But soon after these commands went out, a more worrying report from Voss arrived. The colonel passed along a note received from "a Captain Smith"—probably Captain Norman M. Smith with the Anderson Cavalry, an independent cavalry company raised in Pennsylvania, which was a detachment of the 15th Pennsylvania Cavalry. It was picketing the Potomac River at Dam No. 4, located about midway between Shepherdstown and Williamsport. Smith wrote that he had "positive information" that Jeb Stuart, with 4,000 cavalry and 6 guns, was marching to Williamsport, and 10,000 infantrymen "came down from Winchester." "This news is reliable," Smith added, and Voss vouched for the trustworthiness of the intelligence. It was not clear that Smith meant that the 10,000 foot soldiers were marching to Williamsport, but it was easy to draw this conclusion from the construction of his message, which is what McClellan and Marcy did. Fresh orders were sent to Couch to take his entire division and arrive at Williamsport by daylight.[37]

McClellan also altered Pleasonton's mission for September 20, and revised orders went out at 11 p.m. Pleasonton was notified that a report had Jeb Stuart, with 4,000 cavalry and 10,000 infantry, marching to Williamsport, so he should split his force, sending half of his division, with two horse batteries, to report to Porter at daybreak, and the second half, with his two other batteries, to Jones's Crossroads, in order to link up with Couch and Voss for the attack on Williamsport. Pleasonton was already displeased over Porter's meddling with his division, and he found little to like with these instructions. He replied at 12:15 a.m., questioning Captain Smith's report and pointing out that "the rebels would hardly present the anomaly of having an army running away to Winchester & another advancing from the same place." Pleasonton also complained that the business of dividing his cavalry "will impair its efficiency and break up my system of obtaining information." But the orders stood. Pleasonton's cavalry division would have a dual mission for September 20.[38]

SUNRISE WAS AT 5:57 A.M. on September 20. Even before the sun had cracked the horizon—"as soon as it was light enough to see"—Brigadier General Charles

Griffin, commanding the 2nd Brigade of Morell's 1st Division, sent the 4th Michigan and the 62nd Pennsylvania, with men and horses from Lieutenant Charles Hazlett's Battery D, 5th U.S., across Boteler's Ford to retrieve the enemy guns and equipment left on the Virginia side of its bank. The detachment crossed without incident, and the infantrymen even found time to forage for flour, geese, and turkeys. They also discovered the abandoned colors of the 38th Georgia in Douglass's brigade. Hazlett's artillerymen brought back three guns and several caissons. One of the guns was the 10 lb. Parrott rifle from Maurin's battery. Inspecting the piece, General Griffin discovered, to his delight, that it was one of the pieces from Battery D, which was captured at First Bull Run when Griffin had commanded that battery. By 8 a.m., the expeditionary force was back in Maryland with their captured guns, equipment, geese, flour, turkeys, and Rebel battle flag.[39]

Porter had issued orders to Sykes and Morell to begin having their divisions ford the Potomac River at 7 a.m., as well as to have them send out advance guards to probe the roads to Charles Town and Shepherdstown. Porter expected that Pleasonton would be at the river by daybreak, so he had informed his division commanders that the cavalry would precede the infantry across the river. George Sykes had his 2nd Division under arms and ready to march at the appointed time, intending to send the 1,060 Regulars of his 2nd Brigade, under Major Charles Lovell, to reconnoiter down Charles Town Road before moving his other brigades over the Potomac River. But Morell was behind schedule, and the brigade he had detailed to lead his 1st Division—Colonel James Barnes's 1st Brigade, with 1,711 men—did not reach Boteler's Ford until around 9 a.m., 2 hours after Sykes. With commendable energy and curiosity, Sykes accompanied Lovell to the river and found no cavalry there.[40]

The troopers were running late but were on their way, accompanied by a still-irate Pleasonton, who wrote to Marcy at 6:30 a.m., reporting that his command was just getting underway, as well as complaining about Porter. "I trust, after the past experience of yesterday, the general commanding will not permit corps commanders to interfere with the cavalry under my command, for it breaks up all my systems and plans," he huffed, and then added hopefully, "I shall do everything in my power to make up for the time we have lost." This included everything *except* communicating with Porter. There seems to have been a mutual dislike between the two men, so rather than conveying information to each other directly, they used army headquarters as their proxy.[41]

Porter was at his headquarters at the Stephen Grove farm, west of Sharpsburg on Shepherdstown Road, when Sykes sent word that the cavalry had not shown up at the intended hour. Porter wrote to McClellan that "our trophies increase"—a reference to the guns captured by General Charles Griffin's early morning expedition—and that he had "not seen Pleasonton." Porter stated that he planned to take his men through Boteler's Ford anyway, and he asked if there were any new orders. At 8 a.m., Porter complained to Marcy that the cavalry had still not reported, "nor can I learn that any have been in the vicinity." At this point, Porter was annoyed but not concerned. He had not pushed a large force across the Potomac River, and, in any event, according to Confederate prisoners who were captured the night before, there were no enemy forces on the opposite side, except for cavalry pickets. By the time Marcy replied at 9 a.m., stating that no cavalry was present because Porter had ordered them back to Keedysville the previous evening, the question about new orders was a moot point, since Sykes had taken Lovell's brigade through Boteler's Ford shortly after 7 a.m.[42]

When Major Lovell's brigade completed its river crossing, he received orders from an aide-de-camp of Sykes, directing him to continue along Charles Town Road and march as far as a belt of woods about a mile and a half from the Potomac River, a landmark clearly visible from the bluffs on the Maryland side. Charles Town Road wound its way up the steep river bluffs for nearly half a mile before it reached the level summit. Beyond the bluffs, the ground was mostly under cultivation. There were two woodlots that broke up the pastoral landscape: a smaller one about a mile to Lovell's right front, and a larger one beyond that, which was his objective. A brick farmhouse, barn, and outbuildings belonging to the Osbourn family stood east of the smaller woodlot. The Osbourns also had a large cornfield on both sides of Charles Town Road.[43]

When Lovell's column came abreast of the corn, the major thought he saw a horseman dart across the road in front of him and disappear. Since there were no friendly troops beyond his, this instantly put Lovell on the alert. He already had Company E in 11th U.S., under Lieutenant George E. Head, screening his march as skirmishers, but he now halted the column and ordered the 11th's entire battalion, under Major DeLancey Floyd-Jones, to reinforce the skirmish line. The column pressed on, with everyone now carefully scanning their front for trouble. Jones's skirmishers had reached the large woodlot and advanced to within 30 or 40 paces of its southern edge when they saw a large enemy force approaching in the distance. It was A. P. Hill's division. Lovell immediately deployed his brigade on either side of the Charles Town Road, with the 1st, 6th, 2nd, and 10th U.S. on the south side, in the woods, and the 17th U.S. in the corn, north of the road. While his brigade formed into line, Lovell sent word back to Sykes that a substantial force of Rebels was advancing toward him.[44]

While Lovell deployed his men, Pleasonton arrived at the Potomac River with two of his cavalry brigades and two horse batteries. Even though he passed Porter's headquarters, he ignored the 5th Corps' commander, not even bothering to send a staff officer to report his arrival or coordinate operations. He sent part of Farnsworth's brigade across Boteler's Ford with a horse battery, instructing him to follow Charles Town Road. Meanwhile, George Sykes had received Lovell's report. In Civil War communications, officers frequently failed to note the time of their report or provide estimates of the enemy's strength, other than in general terms. Lovell's report, however, was a model of precision. He judged the Confederates' strength—remarkably accurately—to be 3,000 men and said they were "rapidly approaching," with artillery support. Sykes was a cautious soldier, but decisive. He wasted no time in sending a message speeding back to Lovell, telling him to "fall back slowly to the crest of the river bank and hold it."[45]

The back-and-forth of these messages consumed a half hour, so it was approaching 9 a.m. before Lovell received his orders to retreat. Withdrawing in the face of an assertive, stronger enemy force is difficult, so the major chose to maintain his battalions in line, to present a solid front, and have them simply turn around and fall back slowly, screened by their skirmishers. Pleasonton's cavalry came up as the Regulars were starting to change their position, and the troopers learned that Lovell's men were being followed by a superior force. When word of this reached Pleasonton, he ordered Farnsworth's detachment back across the Potomac River, while he began placing his horse batteries to cover Boteler's Ford—again doing all of this without any communication to or coordination with Porter.[46]

While these events were transpiring, Morell finally got his 1st Division moving. His orders to Colonel Barnes, whose 1st Brigade would lead the movement, were brief: "In pursuance of orders from headquarters of the corps, the commanding general directs that you push your brigade across the river to Shepherdstown and vicinity, and report what is to be found there." There was no mention of Lovell's brigade, of coordinating with Sykes, of what Barnes should do if he found the Confederates to be present in strength, or of any support he could call on. Barnes reached the Potomac River around 9 a.m., where he met Pleasonton's cavalry and Gibson's Batteries C & G, 3rd U.S., returning to Maryland. The infantrymen and troopers exchanged their typical good-natured insults with one another, but the foot soldiers learned from Gibson's horse artillerymen that "there were no enemy anywhere around." Armies are notorious rumor mills, and gossip can race through them with astonishing speed, but in this instance, the artillerymen remained blissfully unaware that the reason they were returning to Maryland was because of the approach of a large Rebel force.[47]

When the rookie soldiers in the 118th Pennsylvania reached the Potomac River, the men began removing their shoes and socks for the crossing. No fight was expected, and the mood was light. Yet the acting 1st sergeant in Captain Francis Donaldson's company, Thomas M. Coane, a young man the captain knew well and thought highly of, suddenly "became perfectly demoralized, and in the face of the company, was taken suddenly sick and went to the rear." Donaldson was stunned. Coane's moral collapse left him with only one lieutenant, Purnell Smith, to manage the company—the other lieutenant was sick in Washington, DC—and Smith, "although a good, willing little fellow, is of no earthly good to me, and requires as much attention and looking after as the whole company." His original 1st sergeant, John H. Kenner, whom Donaldson referred to as "the fraud," had disappeared earlier in the Maryland Campaign and was still missing. It was a situation that was fairly typical in a new infantry regiment, which had not had enough time to winnow out misfits and poor leaders. The Pennsylvanians followed several other regiments in Barnes's brigade over Boteler's Ford. There was "much merriment, laughter and fun among the men" as they waded across, "especially when some more unfortunate one, losing balance, would fall in the water."[48]

Donaldson was a veteran of the 71st Pennsylvania and had left that regiment for a captain's commission in the 118th. He had been at the disaster at Ball's Bluff with the 71st and felt uneasy as his regiment scrambled up from the ford. He detected an "apparent want of caution" in Colonel Barnes's management. Looking up at the steep bluffs, only accessible by Shepherdstown Road, Charles Town Road and a couple of deep ravines, it "called vividly to mind Ball's Bluff." About 400 yards above Boteler's Ford, Donaldson observed a dam, built decades earlier, to provide water for a brick cement mill, which was constructed by Henry Boteler and George Reynolds in 1829. Not much water was flowing over it, and this only in places where the wood had rotted away from neglect. There was a 20-foot fishway in the dam, near the bank on the Virginia side of the river, and here "the water rushed rapidly through." The Cement Mill stood 350 yards above Boteler's Ford and close to the bluffs. It had been burned by Federal troops in 1861 and stood abandoned. Above the mill and on the right side of Shepherdstown Road were three limekilns, where workers had hauled the claylike soil from the nearby bluffs and fired it to extract limestone, from which a high-quality cement was produced. Shepherdstown Road paralleled the Potomac River for some distance above the mill and kilns before it wound its way up a steep ravine to the top of the bluffs.[49]

After a halt to allow the men to put their shoes and socks back on, Barnes's regiments re-formed and started up Shepherdstown Road. When those in the 22nd Massachusetts, at the rear of the brigade, were going through this process, they were startled by a loud crack and bang, followed by others in quick succession. It was friendly artillery positioned on the heights in Maryland, firing over their heads at some targets beyond the bluffs on the Virginia side of the Potomac River. While Barnes's men were crossing, Sykes rode up and told the colonel that a strong force of Confederates had been reported, 2 miles down Charles Town Road. He had sent an aide-de-camp to verify this information, but, as a precaution, he asked Barnes to keep his brigade by the river until the aide returned. Barnes agreed, and Sykes directed him to place his leading regiment, Lieutenant Colonel Joseph Hayes's 18th Massachusetts, just below the crest of the bluffs, north of Charles Town Road. Walter Carter, one of the 18th's enlisted men, watched Hayes and the other field officers dismount before they moved up the slope. He suspected that serious business might be at hand.[50]

While Sykes waited for his aide-de-camp's return, he wrote a message to Porter, timed at 9:15 a.m., relating that Lovell was three-fourths of a mile from the Potomac River, while at least a brigade of the Confederates were advancing, with artillery support. Sykes also reported that he had ordered Barnes up to the bluffs as a precautionary support for the Regulars. The 2nd Division's commander planned to bring General Gouverneur Warren's small brigade through Boteler's Ford "as soon as I can," but he recommended that "more troops ought to be here, and some one in authority." The last point was key. Porter had appointed no one to supervise operations on the Virginia side of the river. The cavalry had come and gone, and the two brigades already there were from different divisions. Barnes had agreed to obey Sykes's orders, but the situation was ripe for confusion.[51]

While Sykes briefed Porter, Barnes brought the rest of his brigade up to the bluffs. The approximately 260 soldiers in the 18th Massachusetts scrambled up a ravine near the Cement Mill to reach the summit. When the 13th and 25th New York arrived, Barnes sent them to the 18th's right, which required the Empire Staters to march to another ravine, north of the one the New Englander's had used. Both regiments were small, with only about 150 officers and men each. The rookie 118th Pennsylvania, 737 men strong, followed the New Yorkers. The 118th was under Colonel Charles M. Prevost. He had been an insurance agent in Philadelphia before the war, but Captain Donaldson considered him to be "a polished gentleman." Barnes joined Prevost at the head of the regiment. As they made their way up Shepherdstown Road, an aide-de-camp galloped up and informed Barnes that a heavy Confederate force was advancing beyond the bluffs. Barnes asked Prevost, "Can you get your regiment on top of the bluff?" The colonel replied, "I will try sir." Prevost dismounted and led his regiment into the same ravine the 25th had used, following a "narrow, unfrequented path that led through the glen." Barnes galloped back to the river, where the tail end of the 118th still had men putting on their shoes and socks. He urged, "Men, hurry up—you are wanted on top of the hill." This silenced the merriment and sobered the green soldiers, who hurried after those of their comrades beginning to ascend the ravine.[52]

As the 118th Pennsylvania slowly climbed up the glen to form on the left of the New Yorkers and help fill the gap between them and the 18th Massachusetts, Barnes rushed his last three regiments—the 1st Michigan, the 2nd Maine, and the 22nd Massachusetts—across the Potomac River. These were all under-strength units, with only about 150 men each. Barnes ordered them up the same ravine the 18th Massachusetts had used and told them to deploy on either side of that regiment.[53]

Of the nine divisions in the Army of Northern Virginia, A. P. Hill's was possibly the only one left with the combat power capable of smashing Porter's reconnaissance. Hill's brigades were worn out from lack of sleep and the hard marching and fighting they had experienced in the past week, but they had not suffered the crippling casualties and serious loss of leadership the other divisions had. The Georgia brigade of Colonel Edward L. Thomas, which had been left at

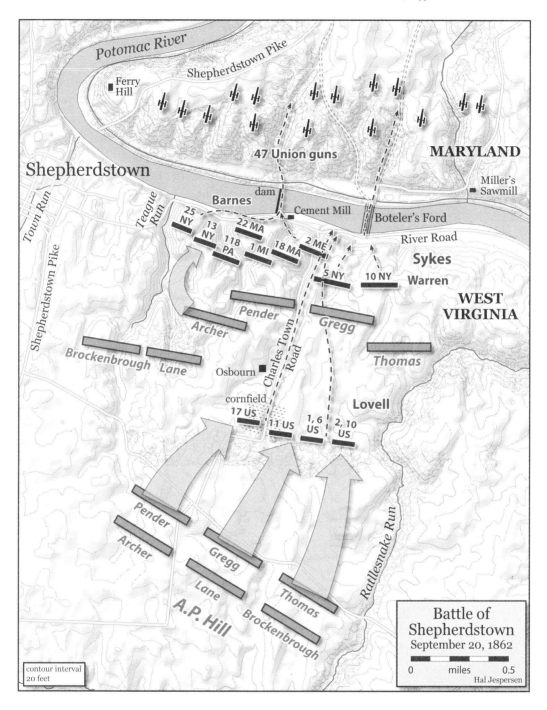

Potomac River

Shepherdstown Pike

Ferry
Hill

47 Union guns

MARYLAND

Shepherdstown

Miller's
Sawmill

Town Run

Teague Run

dam

Barnes

Cement Mill

Boteler's Ford

25
NY

13
NY

22 MA

118
PA

1 MI

18 MA

2 ME

River Road

Sykes

Shepherdstown Pike

5 NY

10 NY

Warren

WEST
VIRGINIA

Pender

Gregg

Archer

Thomas

Brockenbrough   Lane

Osbourn

Charles Town Road

cornfield

Lovell

17 US

11 US

1, 6
US

2, 10
US

Pender

Archer

Gregg

Rattlesnake Run

Lane

Thomas

A.P. Hill

Brockenbrough

Battle of
Shepherdstown
September 20, 1862

0   miles   0.5

Hal Jespersen

contour interval
20 feet

Harpers Ferry on September 17 to secure the equipment captured from the
Union garrison, rejoined the division on the 19th. Thus Hill had all six brigades
of the Light Division on hand when, at 6:30 a.m., he received orders from Jackson "to take my division and drive across the river some brigades of the enemy
who had crossed during the night." Hill had perhaps 3,000–4,000 effectives, and

he promptly put his brigades on the road. Jackson ordered Jubal Early's division to follow, as a support. At this point, Early only had three brigades, as Douglass's had not reconstituted itself since the previous night's disaster. Two of these three brigades—Hays's and Walker's—had been mauled at Sharpsburg, leaving Early's own brigade as the only truly combat-effective one.[54]

A. P. Hill moved rapidly, and the troops arrived within a mile of Lovell's brigade by 8:30 a.m. Sighting the Federals, Hill deployed skirmishers. They traded fire with a similar line of Union Regulars, who did not seem disposed to fight and fell back steadily. Reaching the woods south of Osbourn's farm, Hill deployed his division into two lines, with (from left to right) Pender's, Gregg's, and Thomas's brigades in the first line, and Archer's, Lane's, and Brockenbrough's forming the second. Early deployed his three brigades in Hill's rear. Marion Hill Fitzpatrick in the 45th Georgia was serving on the skirmish line and wrote that "we sallied forth and gone but little ways before we routed the Yankee skirmishers," who "trotted handsomely, while our boys poured it into them thick." Fitzpatrick could not know that the ease with which they drove away the Federals was because the latter were ordered to fall back.[55]

A. P. Hill's main body swept through the woods and into Osbourne's cornfield, which extended north for nearly 200 yards. When they emerged from the corn, they came into open country that extended for over half a mile to the river bluffs. Now the numerous Union batteries on the Maryland bluffs and hills opened fire on them with a fury. Hill, who had probably faced more heavy bombardments by Federal batteries in the war than any other Confederate, described it as "the most tremendous fire of artillery I ever saw." Andrew B. Wardlaw, the commissary officer in Gregg's Brigade, who watched the assault from a safe vantage point—"commissaries in this army do not go upon the field of battle," he wrote—and described it as a "perfect torrent of shot & shell." Gregg's men, who were on the eastern side of Charles Town Road, seemed to have drawn the greatest attention. Lieutenant Colonel James M. Perrin, commanding the 1st South Carolina Rifles, was forced to deploy his regiment at short intervals—almost in skirmish order—on either side of the road, in order to spread his men out. The 14th South Carolina were hit so hard that Captain Joseph N. Brown thought "it appeared our regiment would be destroyed." Barry Benson in the 1st South Carolina Provisional Army thought it "the best artillery shooting I ever saw. Every shell seemed to burst immediately in front of our line, the colors being the target. I saw one shell burst in front of a Ga. Regt. bringing down the colors and four men." Gregg quickly found terrain that gave his regiments some defilade, but not before the 14th South Carolina had nearly 55 men killed or wounded. Despite heavy losses, Hill's infantry pressed steadily forward. The historian in Gregg's command thought the three brigades in the front line "moved as one man, as steadily, coolly, deliberately, as if on the drill ground." The advance was superbly disciplined—Union accounts confirm this—but it was not a drill-field movement. The Confederate brigades paused to take cover, dispersed their formations, and maneuvered to gain protection from undulations in the ground. It was not one long, unchecked, precise movement, but it was a fearsome advance.[56]

A. P. Hill noted that the Union infantry's opposition to Gregg's and Thomas's brigades, along Charles Town Road and east of it, "was but trifling." Nonetheless, the Federals appeared to be massing in Pender's front, seemingly with the intent of turning his left flank. This was Barnes's brigade. The sudden appearance of the 13th and 25th New York on the bluffs, and then the big 118th Pennsylvania, worried Pender. He placed two of his regiments fronting the 18th Massachusetts, but under cover from the Union artillery's fire, and put his other two in position to protect his left from the New Yorkers and Pennsylvanians. Pender then sent back to Archer for help in dealing with the flank attack. Hill had placed his second line under Archer's tactical control, and the Marylander responded immediately to Pender's call for help, ordering his three brigades to move by the left flank, extending the Confederates' front farther west, in order to confront the enemy flankers.[57]

This perceived threat to Pender's flank was purely accidental, for the Federals had no aggressive intentions. Lovell's 2nd Brigade executed a disciplined, skillful, 1-mile withdrawal, heading back to the river bluffs with only a handful of casualties. Meanwhile, Sykes brought Warren's small brigade across Boteler's Ford around 10 a.m. and moved it into position on Lovell's left. This was only to purchase time by slowing the Confederates' advance. Sykes conveyed to Porter that a large force of Rebels were moving toward him, and the "Virginia side of the river was no place for troops until a proper reconnaissance was made." Porter agreed and sent back orders for Sykes and Barnes to withdraw to Maryland. By around 10:30 a.m., Warren's and Lovell's brigades, covered by their artillery and skirmishers, executed an orderly retreat over the Potomac River. Although some of Thomas's and Gregg's skirmishers worked their way forward to bring long-range, small-arms fire on the ford, it was inaccurate, and neither Union brigade suffered any losses there. In their entire operation south of the river, Warren only had one man wounded, while Lovell had one killed and eight wounded. Had Barnes's 1st Brigade escaped in a similar condition, the fighting at Shepherdstown would be forgotten as merely a trivial skirmish. But Barnes's withdrawal encountered a glitch, which resulted in a tragic ending.[58]

When his regiments began to deploy along the bluffs, Barnes believed that the main strength of the Confederates was to his left, on Lovell's and Warren's front. But as each of these regiments reached the top of the bluffs, their skirmishers immediately became engaged, and Barnes was advised that not only were the Rebels approaching in heavy numbers on the left, "but that they were also in equal numbers advancing on our front and on our right." They seemed to suddenly spring "from the bushes and corn-fields which had concealed them," appearing at close range, and opened "a rapid and vigorous fire." Adding to the bedlam, one or more of the friendly batteries in the rear began shelling Barnes's line, either because of defective ammunition or confusion over where the enemy was. Two shells burst in Walter Carter's company in the 22nd Massachusetts and mortally wounded two men. Captain Frederick K. Field, a carpenter in civilian life, was commanding Company B, which was the recipient of one of the two shells. The captain, "without an instant's hesitation," stepped out to where he was clearly visible to the Federal artillery crews across the river—but also to Rebel skirmishers—and waved his hands, indicating that the guns needed to fire higher. "How he escaped I cannot explain," recalled Edwin C. Bennett, a Company G lieutenant. Whether Field's heroics were responsible for the change is unknown, but the Union guns shifted their aim.[59]

Barnes's orders to retire did not reach him until he saw Lovell and Warren falling back toward Boteler's Ford. This was a consequence of having brigades from two divisions being on the Virginia side of the Potomac River. Sykes had accompanied Lovell across the ford, so he was in a position to immediately communicate Porter's orders to withdraw. Morell, however, had remained on the Maryland side, which meant that Barnes's orders to withdraw went to the division commander first, and then to Barnes. This added to the delay and explains why Barnes did not receive his orders until Sykes's brigades were already withdrawing. By this point, extricating his brigade was going to be tricky. The support that Lovell and Warren had provided on his left flank was gone, and the Confederates were aggressively moving toward him. Brigade commanders typically had very small staffs, and Barnes's regiments were separated by two deep ravines, which did not allow good lateral communications. Therefore, transmitting commands and having them obeyed in a coordinated fashion was difficult. Barnes personally ordered the 2nd Maine, the 1st Michigan, and the 18th and 22nd Massachusetts to fall back. He sent his aide-de-camp, Lieutenant W. S. Davis, to withdraw the 13th and 25th New York, and dispatched an orderly to deliver the same orders to the 118th Pennsylvania.[60]

By the time Barnes's regiments began to reach Boteler's Ford, more of Thomas's and Gregg's skirmishers had reached the bluffs south of Charles Town Road and could deliver more effective fire onto it. "Our crossing the river was no joke," Walter Carter wrote home. The water was up to his armpits, and the river bottom was full of slippery rock ledges. Carter struggled to both keep his ammunition dry and hold up a comrade who had fallen three times and was in danger of drowning. Behind him, "the rebs appeared on the banks, and the bullets whistled into us good." Carter and his comrade made it across, but he was "so exhausted that I could hardly stand" by the time he reached the opposite bank. Lieutenant Edwin Bennett, with Carter in the 22nd Massachusetts, thought they were saved from significant losses by the artillery fire that pounded the bluffs on the Virginia side of the Potomac River and kept most of the Rebels under cover.

Carter thought the 1st U.S. Sharpshooters were just as important. They lined the C&O Canal and targeted any Rebels that showed themselves on the bluffs. Carter maintained that without them, "we would none of us reached the shore alive."[61]

This covering fire enabled Barnes's regiments to successfully disengage and start filing down to the river, with one exception—the 118th Pennsylvania. During their climb up a rough trail to the top of the bluffs, Captain Donaldson noticed a battery wagon, with four horses still alive and attached in their harness, that had fallen off the path during the Confederates' retreat the night before. The horses "appeared to be suffering intensely," and Donaldson watched as Captain Joseph W. Ricketts, a "noble, generous soul," climbed down to them and cut them free. Near the crest of the bluff, Donaldson encountered his friend, Lieutenant Lemuel Crocker, and repeated the concern he had expressed earlier—the terrain bore an uncanny resemblance to Ball's Bluff. Reaching the top, Donaldson noted that "the enemy were in plain view, large bodies of them, seemingly a division being massed in front of a range of woods at least a mile away." He saw the Osbourn farm about a half mile away and observed that "the ground was well cleared of timber, and we had a good commanding view of the country." To the right, the roofs and church spires of Shepherdstown were visible. As the companies got to the crest of the bluff, Colonel Prevost gave the command "Right by file into line," uttered in a voice "indicative of an urgency that demanded speedy execution." The morning before, on the 9th Corps' battlefield at Antietam, Prevost had drilled his rookies for several hours, focusing particularly on the movement "right by file into line," a standard maneuver for shifting an infantry unit from column into line. Now, 24 hours later, the companies were executing this in combat. Significantly, unlike the veteran regiments in the brigade, who made sure to take advantage of any available cover, Prevost deployed his regiment over open ground, which gave them good lines of sight but left them exposed.[62]

As the big Pennsylvania regiment slowly completed its maneuver, Prevost ordered Company E, under Captain Levis Passmore, to deploy as skirmishers. Passmore was a condescending fellow and treated Captain Donaldson, who was younger, "patronizingly," earning the latter's intense dislike, even though Donaldson admitted that Passmore was a fine tactician. But proficiency in garrison duty was often not a predictor of how an individual would behave when bullets began to fly. Passmore utterly failed this stern test. Donaldson wrote that Passmore "not only did not obey the order, but actually turned [his] back upon the enemy, abandoned his company and regiment," and fled to the other side of the Potomac River, where "he awaited in safety the issue of the battle." Passmore's two lieutenants, however, rose to the occasion and established a line that immediately became engaged in a "savage skirmish" with the Rebels.[63]

As each company in the 118th Pennsylvania climbed out of the ravine and formed into a line, they immediately opened fire by file—that is, a way of shooting that delivered constant but independent fire along the regiment's front, and thus lacked the shock effect that simultaneous volley firing delivered. Captain Donaldson did not like the exposure of the position Prevost had selected. Donaldson had learned a hard lesson about the value of taking cover earlier in 1862, at the Battle of Seven Pines during the Peninsula Campaign, when he was with the 71st Pennsylvania. When that regiment was ordered to lie down, thus creating smaller targets, Donaldson thought that an officer should show himself. He recklessly remained standing and took a bullet in his shoulder, which fortunately passed clean through it without doing serious damage. Now, at Shepherdstown, as his company came up and he formed it into line, Donaldson saw that other companies, whose men were standing up, incurred numerous casualties. He wisely ordered his men to kneel. "From the beginning the fire of the enemy was tremendous, reported the regimental historian. Donaldson thought the Confederates' fire "was appalling," for "they seemed to fire by Companies as the rush of bullets sounded like a hurricane." Casualties quickly mounted in the companies on either side of Donaldson, but thus far his company had suffered none. Then Lieutenant Colonel James Gwyn, a brave but inexperienced and impulsive officer, came walking along behind the line, "shouting and yelling" encouragement. When he reached Donaldson's company, Gwyn said, "Make your men stand up Captain, make them stand up like men." Before Donaldson could explain, Gwyn waded into the company, brandishing his sword and shouting "Damn you, stand up and act like men." An agonized Donaldson ran to him and yelled, "Let my company alone Colonel, I know how to fight them, don't you see I am doing more execution than anyone else and haven't lost a man?" But Gwyn was beyond hearing what was said, and the damage was done. Donaldson's men, confused by the lieutenant colonel's orders, started to stand up. Immediately, numbers of them began to be hit.[64]

Colonel Barnes's aide-de-camp, Lieutenant Davis, was returning from delivering orders for the 13th and 25th New York to withdraw when he saw the 118th still heavily engaged on the bluffs. What had happened to the orderly tasked with delivering Barnes's retreat orders to Prevost is unknown. Perhaps he had been shot or had abandoned his mission as being too dangerous. Davis shouted up to Lieutenant Henry K. Kelly in Company F, the only officer he could see from his position, and told him to tell Colonel Prevost that Colonel Barnes ordered him to withdraw at once. Kelly relayed this message to his captain, who sent him on to communicate it to Prevost. He found the colonel in front of the regiment's center, observing his left companies, who were still struggling up the bluff from the ravine and then forming into line. Prevost asked Kelly who had given him this order. Kelly replied that it was Lieutenant Davis, on Barnes's staff. "I do not receive orders in that way," thundered Prevost. "If Colonel Barnes has any orders to give me, let his aid[e] come to me." With that, the fate of the 118th was sealed. Had Prevost been more experienced, he might have recognized

that this was not a moment to stand on ceremony, insisting that proper proto-
col be observed.[65]

Moments after Lieutenant Colonel Gwyn had forced Captain Donaldson's
company to stand up—with fatal consequences—the captain was surrounded
by frantic men, who said something was terribly wrong with their Enfield 1853
pattern rifles. Inspecting one of them, Donaldson found that the soldier had put
the minie ball in before the powder. Another gun was filled with unfired bullets. But it was not soldiers' errors causing problems with most of the weapons
the captain examined. Instead, it was defective manufacture. In some rifles, the
hammer spring was not strong enough to cause the fall of the hammer to explode
the percussion cap. In other cases, the nipple—where the percussion cap was
placed—broke off when the hammer struck it. Andrew Humphreys had discovered a similar problem with the firearms in five of his regiments when his division first mobilized on September 12 (see chapter 19). In the noise of the current
conflict on the Potomac River bluffs near Shepherdstown, many of the 118th's
inexperienced soldiers also were unaware that their Enfield rifles had malfunc-
tioned, so they continued to load the guns until the weapons were nearly filled
with unfired cartridges. At that point, they finally recognized the problem and
brought the Enfields to their officers. Prevost estimated that fully one-quarter
of the regiment's rifle-muskets were defective, while Gwyn thought it was closer
to 50%. When Donaldson looked about, he saw men in every company of the
118th Pennsylvania "running hither and thither without pieces and loudly calling for them." He was appalled and vented angrily to a friend afterward, "God!
Just think of it!—sending such troops to fight the veterans of A. P. Hill and
Stonewall Jackson."[66]

Pender's North Carolinians, reinforced by Archer's brigade, pushed hard
against the Pennsylvanians, using bits of cover to work their way to within 50
yards, all the while delivering a steady fire that inflicted "casualties with frightful fatality." With the 13th and 25th New York gone, the 118th had no protection
on their right flank, which the Confederates quickly exploited. They infiltrated
into the ravine in the regiment's right rear to deliver a flanking fire. Someone
called Prevost's attention to this, pointing out Rebels on the trail the 118th had
used to ascend out of the ravine. Colonel Prevost now exhibited remarkable coolness and presence of mind, considering that he had never commanded a unit in
combat and was leading a green regiment whose firearms were failing at an
alarming rate. He somehow managed to bend back his two right-flank companies. Their volleys quickly swept the ravine trail clear of Rebels.[67]

The men in the 118th Pennsylvania's center, not understanding the movement
of the regiment's two right companies, thought it was a retreat and began to fall
back. Prevost "had the overwhelming mortification of seeing the colors coming
at the 'double-quick' to the rear." He took the flag from the color sergeant,
walked to the front of his line, and shouted at his men to halt and re-form. They

did, and Prevost restored his line. But he made the mistake of continuing to hold and wave the colors to inspire his men. This drew the attention of Pender's North Carolinians, one of whom put a bullet through the colonel's shoulder and knocked him out of the fight. Corporal Francis Daley ran to Prevost's side and assisted him to the rear. They passed Lieutenant Colonel Gwyn, and Prevost told him to take command. Daley and Prevost then made their way down the ravine. Near the Potomac River, they ran into Colonel Barnes, who claimed to be riding toward his right to make sure his orders to withdraw were being carried out. His assertion is somewhat suspicious, for he knew the 13th and 25th New York had already withdrawn, and everyone could hear the heavy firing on the bluffs where the 118th Pennsylvania was located. Barnes asked Prevost where his regiment was and received an unsettling response: "Fighting desperately on top of the hill, Sir, where you placed it." Barnes immediately spurred his horse up the ravine and "on to the ground occupied by his [Prevost's] regiment," where he gave the order to retreat. That Barnes actually rode up to the regiment itself is disputed in the 118th's regimental history. It maintained that Barnes rode only as far as a wounded private, John Sider, whom he encountered on the ravine trail, and told the private to communicate the order to his regiment. Whatever actually happened, the orders reached James Perot, the 118th's adjutant, and he personally communicated them to Gwyn.[68]

By this point, the 118th's situation was growing desperate. "Shouts, cheers and orders were drowned in the roar of musketry and the defiant yells of the foe," wrote the regimental historian. Captain Donaldson, looking about for functioning rifles that had been dropped by casualties, encountered Lieutenant Crocker, who was doing the same thing. Crocker exclaimed, "God! Captain, was Ball's Bluff like this?" Donaldson replied, "Crocker, we are beaten and you had better look to the rear for a safe retreat for the men." As Crocker left him, Donaldson heard the rebel yell "rend the air" and saw the enemy coming on "in perfect line, with their Red Cross battle flags waving." Lieutenant Colonel Gwyn, uncertain what command he should issue with a potential stampede pending, shouted for fixed bayonets. Those who heard his order seemed to be steadied by it, but, in the racket, most did not. Company officers like Donaldson and Crocker were doing their best to prevent a panic and hold their men together, but at this crucial moment, the Confederates picked off several other key leaders. Captain Joseph Ricketts was wounded while firing at Rebels who had closed to within pistol range and then was killed by another shot. Captain Courtland Saunders, commanding Company G, was slain instantly by a bullet through the head, and Lieutenant J. Mora Moss in Company K died from a ball piercing his heart.[69]

It could only have been moments after Gwyn ordered fixed bayonets when Adjutant Perot delivered Barnes's orders to retreat. The lieutenant colonel had a loud voice, and he made his way along the regiment from right to left, shouting an order to retreat, starting with companies on the right. When Captain

Donaldson received the command, he called out to his men "to be steady and follow me." Because of his experience at Ball's Bluff, Donaldson had studied the ground when they ascended the ravine and had already picked out a line of retreat for his company, should it become necessary. He passed by Company C, on his right, "who seemed to be undecided what to do or which way to go." The captain led his men through a belt of woods, where they came upon a path that led them to the ravine trail. Donaldson plunged down this so rapidly that he nearly killed himself when he suddenly encountered a huge tree, knocked down by artillery fire, that was lying across the trail. He saved himself by quickly dropping to the ground and sliding beneath it, closely followed by his company.[70]

In the words of the regimental historian, the scene that followed the order for the 118th Pennsylvania to retreat "almost beggars description," and the men who "had contended so manfully against these frightful odds broke in wild confusion for the river." At the same time, General James Archer brought all three of his brigades up on the left of Pender's North Carolinians, and as each Rebel unit came on line, they charged at the double-quick. Looking back, Captain Donaldson saw the Confederates crowding up to the edge of the bluffs and firing down on the fleeing Pennsylvanians. Andrew J. Proffit was one of them. Less than one month earlier, he and his brother Alfred had enlisted (or been conscripted) in the 18th North Carolina of Lawrence O. Branch's brigade. "We give them fits," Andrew wrote his mother and father. "A N [Alfred] & I shot as long as we could see a blue coat exposed to the fire of 3 batteries the bombs burst round our heads with terrific fury and showers of grape and canister fell mingled with limbs of trees thick around us." Donaldson attested to the toll Proffit and his comrades took within the 118th. "The slaughter became dreadful," the captain wrote, with "men being shot as they ran, and their bodies left supported by the trees were afterwards seen by us from across the river when the fight was over." Lieutenant Crocker, in a letter to his parents, declared that they were exposed to "such a shower of lead I never want to take the risk again of coming out of." Some men, in their panic to escape, plunged down over the sheer cliffs of the bluffs, falling to their deaths or being severely hurt. Adjutant Perot, due to an injury sustained in civilian life, could not run, so he was left alone on the bluff with the dead and the wounded. He rested his pistol on his left arm and emptied it at the approaching Confederates before one of them wounded him and he became a prisoner. Numbers of Confederates slid down the bluffs and entered the abandoned Cement Mill, taking up positions on its roof or inside its windows and doors, from which they began to pick off the Federals running along the riverbank or trying to ford the Potomac. A large group of Pennsylvanians, terrified at the prospect of crossing the river under fire, sought cover behind the limekilns. Others jumped into the river at a spot where they knew it was deeper, so only their heads were exposed. Donaldson stood in the water near the fishway, encouraging "such of my company willing to venture across." He watched, "with aching heart," the "utter demoralization and rout of this fine body of men, who, beaten, dismayed, wild with fright, all order and discipline gone, were rushing headlong towards the dam, across which alone lay safety and escape."[71]

The 118th Pennsylvania's regimental history related a story of how its color bearer hesitated to ford the Potomac River when he saw the number of men being shot there. Major Charles B. Herring caught up to him, grabbed the flag, and thrust it into the hands of Private William Hummel, ordering him forward. Herring shielded the private with his body, and they miraculously survived the perilous crossing. But Donaldson's contemporary account casts doubt on this tale. The regiment carried both the national and state colors. Donaldson saw the two flags floating in the water above the dam and ordered a nearby soldier to retrieve them. The man did so and managed to carry the colors safely to the Maryland side. Possibly this was Hummel, and perhaps Herring helped him over—although Donaldson saw Herring following the wounded Colonel Prevost across the river—but this is a reminder that regimental histories, while valuable, are often selective in the details they include and omit.[72]

Captain Donaldson, who was still standing in the water near the dam, noticed his lieutenant and some men in his company paralyzed with indecision about whether they should chance fording the river. He caught their attention, pointed out that they were a target for the Confederate riflemen in the Cement Mill, and said they should immediately cross the river at the dam. Then a 20 lb. Parrott battery, probably Captain Robert Langner's Battery C, 1st Battalion, New York Light, commenced pounding the Virginia shoreline. The barrage was intended to drive off the 118th Pennsylvania's Confederate pursuers, but either through an elevation error or confusion over who was whom, Union shells began bursting around the limekilns. "A cry of horror went up from our men," wrote Donaldson. He saw several soldiers attaching white handkerchiefs to their ramrods as a token of surrender. He was about to shout to them to come to the river when a shell struck one of the kilns, "tearing to pieces 12 or 15 of the poor devils crowded therein." A group of the panic-stricken survivors ran uphill toward the Rebels, waving their white handkerchiefs. "By heavens! Think of it! These poor fellows had to run for safety to the enemy, lest their own people would kill them," raged Donaldson. The Pennsylvanians were saved from further destruction by the quick action of two signal officers—Captain Benjamin F. Fisher and Lieutenant Louis R. Fortescue—who were standing with the battery, watching the firing through their field glasses, and "could see these shells dropping among our men." They immediately called Langner's attention to it, and he ordered the elevation on the gun tubes to be adjusted, but not before the Union battery had inflicted numerous friendly-fire casualties.[73]

Lieutenant Crocker wrote that when he arrived at the dam, "I think my cheek blanched, for it seemed to me certain death to cross it." The Confederates in the Cement Mill and along the bluffs were calmly "picking off our poor fellows." To remain there was to court death or imprisonment, so he accepted the risk, jumped in, and made it safely to the Maryland side. Donaldson was still trying to coax his frightened lieutenant, Purnell Smith, to wade in, but the young man thought his uniform and sword would make him a preferred target. "I told him I would be obliged to leave him," wrote Donaldson. Smith then tossed his sword away, seized an enlisted man's overcoat to cover his officer's clothing, and made it over without injury. Meanwhile, John Fisher, one of Donaldson's privates who had been by the captain's side throughout the retreat, decided that Smith's decision to conceal his rank, while not courageous, was prudent. Fisher ran to a dead soldier on the riverbank, pulled his coat off, and put it on Donaldson. The captain did not stop this act of kindness or comment on it, but merely started for the dam, with Fisher following. Donaldson ran "as fast as the slippery and broken boards would admit." Bullets struck all around him, and he saw men "shot in various places of the body, some falling, others again staggering and struggling to make the other side, and all hurrying wildly on with the consciousness of the desperate chances they were taking." Halfway across, the soldier in front of Donaldson was shot and rolled over several times. He ended up against the captain and seized his overcoat, pleading, "Help me, Captain, for God's sake don't leave me here." Pausing was a death sentence, and Donaldson, in an act that probably replayed itself repeatedly in his memory, unfastened his overcoat and left it in the man's hands, telling him he couldn't stop but "would send after him as soon as I got across." The man, whom Donaldson did not identify, died there on the dam.[74]

What saved Donaldson, Crocker, and the others was the covering fire from the 1st U.S. Sharpshooters and Warren's 3rd Brigade, who lined the empty C&O Canal and kept up a constant fire on the Confederate pursuers. The Federals' artillery, except for poorly aimed shells from Langner's battery, was also crucial. "This is all that saved our regiment," wrote Lieutenant Crocker, since the combined small-arms and artillery fire for "a short time prevented a rebel in taking a risk of showing himself." But just how perilous getting over the mill dam could be was illustrated by William Madison, a 46-year-old private in Donaldson's Company H. "He seemed to be chosen as a special mark for the enemy's resentment" and was shot five times, with the last bullet, which passed through his cheek, tongue, and jaw, striking him just as he reached the Maryland shore. Miraculously, Madison survived his wounds. Lieutenant J. Rudhall "Ruddy" White in Company G was not as fortunate. When he stepped up onto the Maryland riverbank, he exclaimed, "Thank God! I am over at last." Then a Confederate bullet struck him in the groin, and he bled to death while being carried off in a blanket.[75]

In Lemuel Crocker's opinion, whoever had ordered and managed the reconnaissance across the Potomac River "ought to be court-martialed." Many in the 118th Pennsylvania shared his anger. The regiment ended the day with 63 killed, 101 wounded, and 105 missing or captured. Only the 15th Massachusetts in

Sedgwick's 2nd Division had suffered a greater loss in the Maryland Campaign. The rest of Barnes's brigade incurred only 52 casualties. The responsibility for the debacle lay mainly with war itself, and the chaos and confusion that are synonymous with combat. General Sykes and Colonel Barnes both conducted themselves appropriately in attempting to extricate their men from a dangerous situation, and they would have succeeded, with only small losses, had Colonel Prevost obeyed the initial orders he received to withdraw. But Prevost was inexperienced in how things were done in battle. His decision to keep fighting was the wrong one, given the circumstances, but it was understandable. Prevost was a personally brave man experiencing his first taste of combat, who expected orders to always come through official channels. Moreover, had he followed the actions of Donaldson and ordered his entire regiment to either kneel or lie down when they became engaged, or had he not deployed them in such an exposed position, Prevost might have dramatically reduced his losses.[76]

If Porter's operations on September 19 had a been model for how to conduct a river assault, his September 20 expedition was a case study in how not to carry out a reconnaissance over a river. The original decision to push the entire 5th Corps into Virginia on the morning of September 20 and reconnoiter toward Charleston and Shepherdstown was sound, given the intelligence Porter had gleaned from Rebel prisoners and the chaos his assault troops encountered when they crossed the Potomac River on September 19. Everything indicated that the Confederates were retreating in disorder and had no forces, other than some pickets, near the river. The blunders began with Pleasonton, whose cavalry was to precede the infantry and scout out the area. He arrived late, and when he did reach the river, despite orders to coordinate with Porter, Pleasonton ignored that officer and operated independently of the 5th Corps. He then withdrew when he learned the Confederates were advancing, again without communicating with Porter. The 5th Corps' leader should not have allowed his infantry to cross the river until Pleasonton arrived, but once he learned that his infantry had encountered superior enemy numbers, he acted promptly to withdraw his bridgehead—that is, his advance into hostile territory. Had all the troops across the river been under a single commander, such as Sykes, the tragedy that befell the 118th Pennsylvania might have been avoided. The delay in Barnes's orders, which probably passed through Morell on the Maryland side of the river, consumed valuable time and created the circumstances that exposed the 1st Brigade to a critical situation.

The performance of A. P. Hill and his division was, once again, superb and upheld its reputation as one of the best divisions in the Army of Northern Virginia. From the moment Hill received his orders from Jackson to drive the Federals back across the Potomac River, he moved quickly, decisively, and aggressively, just as he had done at Sharpsburg. Although his division incurred substantial losses from the Federals' artillery, the speed of his advance kept those losses lower than they might otherwise have been. It also enabled his brigades to envelop the 118th Pennsylvania and inflict devastating losses on that regiment. Hill's imagination got the better of him, however, when he reported on his division's victory. When the Federals were driven to the river, "then commenced the most terrible slaughter that this war has yet witnessed," and the "broad surface of the Potomac was blue with the floating bodies of our foe." He claimed that the Yankees themselves reported "3,000 men, killed and drowned, from one brigade alone." This played well in the Southern press, but the reality was that Hill had 291 men killed or wounded, and the Federals had a total of 348 casualties, of which the 118th Pennsylvania accounted for nearly 80%. Hill's most important accomplishment was to emphatically slam the door shut on any pursuit by the Army of the Potomac, and to strengthen McClellan's belief that the Rebel army remained strong and dangerous. Robert E. Lee desperately needed breathing space from the enemy, so his army could recover, and Hill gave it to him.[77]

The need to drive back Porter's bridgehead temporarily disrupted Lee's idea of maneuvering the Army of Northern Virginia to Williamsport and then returning to Maryland. A report from Stuart that afternoon or evening shut the door on this plan. On September 20, Stuart had probed east of Williamsport with Hampton's brigade and bumped up against elements of Couch's 1st Division and Pleasonton's cavalry. Despite the Federals' considerable superiority in numbers, Stuart boldly skirmished with them all day and then withdrew to Virginia when it became dark. Lee's scouts may have also advised him of the arrival of the Union's 12th Corps at Brownsville, in Pleasant Valley, on the night of September 19 and their occupation of Maryland Heights early on the 20th. What Lee did not know was that on the evening of September 20, McClellan had ordered Franklin's 6th Corps to reinforce Couch's division at Williamsport. With one corps there, one at Maryland Heights, and four in the Sharpsburg–Boteler's Ford area, McClellan had effectually sealed off any avenue Lee might have contemplated for a return to Maryland.[78]

But the crisis generated by Pendleton's rout at Boteler's Ford seems to have opened Lee's eyes to the dire condition of the Army of Northern Virginia. He had seemed oddly oblivious to this before. His position at the ford during the retreat on the night of September 18 gave him an opportunity to assess his army's condition, and it could not have been encouraging: brigades reduced to the size of small regiments, or even companies; men exhausted, with their uniforms literally in tatters; and crowds of stragglers everywhere. In a September 21 letter to President Jefferson Davis, Lee acknowledged that the massive number of stragglers "greatly paralyzed" the army's efficiency. The disaster at Boteler's Ford on September 19, particularly the flight of the Rebels' infantry brigades, was worrying, as was the lethargy that seemed to grip the Confederates in organizing a counterattack to recover Pendleton's reportedly captured Reserve Artillery. All of these factors pointed to an army pushed to the limit of its endurance, and whose offensive punch was spent. Risking another active operation involving rapid maneuvers and more hard fighting, without having even modest logistical support, courted potential catastrophe. Following the defeat of the 5th Corps' reconnaissance over the Potomac River, Lee slowly withdrew his army toward Martinsburg, camping beside Opequon Creek, where he could provide cover for his depot at Winchester, resupply, and "restore the efficiency of the army for the work before it." Lee reluctantly surrendered the initiative and assumed a defensive posture. The Maryland Campaign for the Army of Northern Virginia's Maryland Campaign was over.[79]

It was finished for the Army of the Potomac, as well. Although McClellan issued orders late in the afternoon of September 21 for Porter to occupy Shepherdstown "as soon as it can be done with safety to your command," all his dispositions were defensive. While Porter reestablished a bridgehead across the Potomac, Sumner and Meade were ordered to march their 2nd and 1st Corps to "a point opposite Harpers Ferry," joining the 12th Corps there. Sumner was to supervise the reconstruction of a pontoon bridge, then occupy Loudoun and Bolivar Heights, which would protect Harpers Ferry. McClellan's dispositions on September 20 through 22 were prudent defensive measures, blocking the only places in the region where Lee could return to Maryland. They also provided McClellan with secure locales from which to move against the Confederates, should he choose to do so. But he had no plans for offensive operations. Although he boasted to his wife that "I feel some little pride in having with a beaten and demoralized army defeated Lee so utterly, & saved the North so completely," his actions were not those of a commander who believed his enemy was vanquished.[80]

McClellan found time on September 20 to nurse grudges against his enemies and trade written blows with Halleck. McClellan's irritation had some justification. He had done an acceptable job of communicating developments to Halleck on September 18 and 19, and the general-in-chief had not uttered a word of thanks for Lee having been driven back across the Potomac River. Privately, though, McClellan seethed with contempt for Halleck and Secretary of War Stanton. He imagined that his victory at Antietam had accrued him enough political leverage "to enable me to take my stand" and demand both the removal of Stanton and the replacement of Halleck as general-in-chief with himself. "I will *not* serve under him [Halleck]—for he is an incompetent fool—in no way fit for the important place he holds," McClellan wrote.[81]

At Boteler's Ford on September 21, Lieutenant Lemuel Crocker and the survivors of the 118th Pennsylvania gazed across the Potomac River at the distressing sight of their dead, strewn along the line of their retreat, and some of their wounded—unattended—in agony. Crocker was deeply disturbed and went to Colonel Barnes to ask if Porter would propose a flag of truce to enable a detail to cross the river and "bring off our wounded, and to bury the dead." Barnes took Crocker's appeal to Porter, who met it with "a flat, emphatic refusal." This was war, and Crocker would have to accept its cruelty. But Crocker would have none of it. "In positive disregard of instructions," the lieutenant—wearing the full uniform of an officer, with sword and pistol—boldly started across the river. Probably surprised, or curious, at a single soldier doing this, no Confederate fired at him. Crocker made his way up the ravine to the bluff where his regiment had stood. He located the bodies of Captains Saunders and Ricketts, as well as that of Lieutenant Moss, and carried them, one by one, to the river—an incredibly physically challenging feat. He also found Edward Mishaw, a private in Crocker's company, who was still alive with a bad leg wound, and carried him down, as well. News of Crocker's act of mercy made its way to Porter. He dispatched an aide-de-camp to advise the lieutenant that if he did not return at once, they would shell him out with a battery. Crocker, by now "absolutely covered with blood and dirt," answered, "Shell and be damned."[82]

This exchange took place before Crocker had retrieved Mishaw. As he made his way back up to the bluff to collect the private, he encountered a Confederate general and his staff. It was probably General Fitz Lee, whose cavalry brigade was in the area that day. Whoever it was, one of the general's aides-de-camp rode up to Crocker and demanded to know on whose authority he had entered Confederate lines. Crocker explained how he came to be there and voiced his opinion that "humanity and decency demanded that they [the dead and wounded] be properly cared for." Since no one else was attempting to do this, "he had determined to risk the consequences and discharge the duty himself." The Confederate leader asked Crocker how long he had been in the service. "Twenty days," answered the lieutenant. "I thought so," the general replied. He told Crocker to continue his work until he was done, pointed out a boat near the Virginia shore that he could use to transport the bodies across the Potomac River, and deployed a cordon of cavalry pickets to protect the lieutenant from disturbance by other Confederate troops who might not know about his mission. Humanity and compassion were sometimes shared by both sides in this war.[83]

After finishing his self-appointed task, Crocker was arrested and hauled before Porter, who harangued the courageous young man about the laws and army regulations that determined how flags of truce worked and described how Crocker had violated them. But a scolding was all that he received. Porter wisely believed a reprimand was sufficient and ordered the lieutenant back to his regiment. Perhaps Porter felt like Crocker's friend, Captain Donaldson, who wrote, "The daring of this man Crocker is beyond all precedent," and his courage "is beyond my comprehension."[84]

Crocker's bravery and sense of humanity were extraordinary, but his mission of mercy also reflected the fact that although the military operations of the Maryland Campaign were over, the struggle to cope with its aftermath and understand its meaning were only beginning.

21

Aftermath

"The bitter wound in my heart to last forever"

Wounds

Brigadier General George B. Anderson had just returned from visiting division headquarters at the Piper farm when he received a disabling wound in one of his ankles. He was hit at the southern edge of Piper's cornfield and near the northeastern corner of the farmer's orchard. The Federals' fire was severe, and there was no time to examine his wound. "With difficulty and danger," his staff carried him back to Piper's farmhouse, where Dr. L. A. "Gus" Stith, the 2nd North Carolina's surgeon, had established an aid station with two assistants. Stith was no doubt swamped with casualties, and his hasty examination of Anderson's wound determined that a shell fragment had struck the ankle and bounced off. While the injury would hobble the general for some time, it was not serious.[1]

When the Sunken Lane line collapsed around noon and Union soldiers were approaching to within 30 yards of Piper's farmhouse, Anderson declared that he would prefer to be shot through the head than captured by the Yankees. Walter R. Battle, a 4th North Carolina headquarters clerk; Captain Seaton Gales, the brigade's assistant adjutant general; and two ambulance corps men carried him "through a field that looked like it was impossible for a man to walk ten steps without being killed." Battle did not say whether they conveyed Anderson in a blanket or on a stretcher, but it was probably the latter. After reaching safety, he was transported, probably by horse-drawn ambulance, to the home of Mrs. Boteler in Shepherdstown, where he remained until Friday, September 19. The retreat of the Confederate army to Virginia again raised the prospect that Anderson would fall into enemy hands. Desperate to see his wife and infant son, and despite the counsel of friends that he not travel, he arranged for a wagon to take him and his brother—Lieutenant Robert W. Anderson, who had been wounded in the shoulder—to Staunton, Virginia, the nearest point of rail service. This was a 125-mile journey that took several days to complete and, as Robert K. Krick observes, it was probably an "exhausting ordeal." From Staunton, Anderson and his brother traveled by train to Raleigh, North Carolina, arriving there on September 26. For the first time, Anderson's wound was carefully examined by his personal physician, Dr. Charles E. Johnson, who discovered and removed a minie ball that was embedded in the ankle joint. The damage had been done, however. Infection had already set in, accompanied by "intense suffering." On October 8, surgeons amputated Anderson's foot. The fatality rate for ankle-joint amputations, as compiled by the U.S. Army in the Civil War, was 25%, but this percentage jumped significantly when the operation was performed more than 48 hours after a wound was inflicted. In such cases, infection typically set in, as it had with Anderson. The amputation failed to prevent its spread, and the general died on October 16, almost 1 month after he had been wounded.[2]

MARINUS K. MCDOWELL, A 6-FOOT, 21-year-old farmer in the 100th Pennsylvania, was on the skirmish line near the Otto farm when he was shot in the thigh by a minie ball. His sergeant ordered one of McDowell's comrades, John Graham, to help him to the rear. Graham was unable to handle the big farm boy alone, so the sergeant allowed James McCreary to help. With one helper on each side of McDowell—who could hop on his good leg—they slowly made their way to the Rohrback Bridge. They found the bridge area to be under such heavy shelling that the three climbed down into Antietam Creek and took cover underneath the bridge. When the shelling subsided, McDowell dropped his rifle, which he had carried up to this point, and the party made their way down Lower Bridge Road to an "old log barn," which was probably a grain storage shed, in the southwestern corner of Henry Rohrback's cornfield. They found several other wounded men there. Graham and McCreary collected some hay and laid McDowell on it. Within 10 minutes, a Rebel shell passed directly through the barn, "knocking out logs at both ends." The three agreed that it was not safe to remain there any longer, so they moved along, hunting for a safer location in which to deposit McDowell. They ended up in Henry Rohrback's orchard, where they found hundreds of injured men. McDowell's comrades laid him beneath an apple tree and departed to rejoin their regiment. By this point, the private and his comrades had traveled nearly a mile.[3]

The field hospital at the Rohrback farm was either overwhelmed or disorganized, since McDowell lay all night beneath the apple tree without receiving any attention. He awoke the next morning, "stiff as a poker." A stretcher party tasked with moving all of the wounded who could not walk found McDowell and carried him to Rohrback's farm buildings. The house, barn, and outbuildings were all full of injured men, but the stretcher-bearers found room beneath the barn shed and placed McDowell there. As he gazed about at the "suffering, groaning, dying" men all around him McDowell considered himself to be lucky, since "I had escaped so well." He remained at this hospital for 2 weeks and, according to his account, received "absolutely no attention from the doctors." An ambulatory wounded comrade and some other strangers fetched water and hardtack for him, and he poured water on his injury to keep it wet, believing that this would reduce any inflammation. At the end of 2 weeks, McDowell was among those selected for transferal to a hospital in Frederick, Maryland. He made the trip in a two-wheeled ambulance with no springs and stated that the 25-mile ride over bumpy roads was excruciating. "Torture was no name for it," he wrote. On arrival, he was deposited at Camp A Hospital, one of two tent hospitals established in the city to handle the overflow of wounded from the battlefield. McDowell's tent contained 18 patients, attended by one nurse, who was a soldier detailed from a combat unit for this duty, and a hospital steward, who was essentially the pharmacist for McDowell's ward.[4]

The hospital staff promptly cut away McDowell's dirty and vermin-infested uniform and dressed him in clean clothing. Doctors visited him daily, occasionally using metal probes with porcelain tips to search for the bullet in his thigh. These attempts were unsuccessful, and the ball remained in the wound until Christmas Day, when McDowell located it and called the surgeon's attention to it. The bullet apparently had worked its way to near the surface of his skin, for the surgery was done without any anesthetic. Infection set in, discharging "pus and matter by the cupful for a week," and McDowell's condition worsened. Surgeons concluded that they needed to amputate the private's leg. McDowell's regular ward surgeon happened to be absent the day this decision was reached. Fortunately, he returned shortly before the operation began and convinced the head surgeon not to proceed with the amputation, but instead allowing him to treat the wound. McDowell's ward surgeon was well up on the latest medical knowledge, and he treated the gangrenous wound with what probably was nitric or carbolic acid. The private wrote that the liquid "burned, fried smoke and sizzled." The ward surgeon applied this treatment three times a day until the wound started to appear free of infection. McDowell immediately began to improve. He received emotional support from the Catholic Sisters of Charity, who visited frequently to bring food and religious tracts. McDowell recalled that the nuns "were so good and kind to us all I shall never forget their merciful ministrations." In March 1863, after 6 months in the Frederick facility, McDowell was deemed to have recovered enough to be transferred to a Baltimore hospital, where he remained for a month before being medically discharged from the Union army on April 7, 1863. McDowell improved enough that he reenlisted in an independent infantry company in August 1863 and served until July 21, 1864. He lived a long life and died in 1926, at age 85.[5]

DURING THE COUNTERATTACK OF his brigade toward David Miller's cornfield (i.e., the Cornfield), Lieutenant George L. P. Wren, commanding Company G, 8th Louisiana, in General Harry Hays's brigade, was shot through the calf of his left leg. At the same instant, another bullet creased the top of his right leg, just barely breaking the skin. The fire directed at his position was terrific. When Wren was hit, only 3 of the 18 men in his company had not been killed or wounded. "I started and amid a perfect storm of shot and shell and succeeded in getting off," he wrote in his diary. "When I was out of danger I never felt so thankful in all my life." No one helped Wren, and he limped for 4 miles to the Potomac River under his own power. There he found a field hospital treating a number of men from his company who were injured before he was. He did not record what medical attention he received, but he probably had his wound examined, cleaned, and dressed. On the evening of September 18, Wren, accompanied by William C. Morrow, a private in his company who was detached to attend to him, set out in an ambulance for Winchester. They were delayed in crossing the Potomac River because the Confederate army was retreating, and its trains clogged the approaches to Boteler's Ford. Wren spent the night in the ambulance and did not reach the opposite shore until the morning of September 19. The subsequent 31-mile journey to Winchester lasted until noon on September 20. Wren found the hospitals in the town "very full and very disagreeable to stay in," so he arranged for accommodations in a private home. His wounds were painful from "the long and tiresome ride in the ambulance," but with one of his men to attend to him and a "comfortable house with a pleasant family," he began to improve.[6]

His injuries kept him bedridden, but the tedium was relieved by pretty local women who stopped by to visit. "Oh! What a consolation to have the sympathy of strange lady friends, towards a wounded soldier," he wrote. A surgeon visited him on September 25 and was pleased with how well he was healing. By September 30, he was able to leave his bed and move about the house on crutches. On October 2, having grown restless with how slowly he seemed to be recovering, he ventured forth on his crutches to seek a medical transfer to Staunton, where he could obtain a furlough and catch a train home to recuperate. His move to Staunton was approved, but he was unable to find transportation. Wandering about on his crutches led to a fall when he was trying to enter his room, which landed him back in bed for an entire day. His luck improved on October 5 when he arranged for a seat on the stagecoach to Staunton. It departed at 4 p.m. on October 6 and reached Staunton at dawn on the 7th. Wren went directly to the local headquarters and obtained a 40-day medical furlough. He then booked passage on the next train to Lynchburg, Virginia, where he had family. He arrived there on October 8 and remained with his relatives for a day, resting, before beginning the long train trip home to Louisiana. He departed with conflicting emotions, thinking about the men in his company who had been wounded and left in the enemy's hands, as well as his own lucky escape from the clutches of death. "The only desire I have in going home is that I fear it may be the last opportunity I will have as I feel confident I shall never go through the same danger again without facing a worse fate," he wrote in his diary. Wren remained at home for 3 months and did not rejoin his regiment until March 9, 1863. His injury had removed him from the Confederate army for nearly 6 months.[7]

WHEN THE 125TH PENNSYLVANIA was driven out of the West Woods by McLaws's division, James Randolph Simpson, a sergeant in Company C, crossed the Hagerstown Pike and spotted a comrade who had paused behind a lone tree in the field east of the road, preparing to shoot at the enemy. Simpson ran beside him and began loading his rifle. By the time he was placing the percussion cap on his weapon, the Rebels—"hundreds of them"—were within 50 feet, pouring into the pike and firing at his retreating regiment. Simpson had just finished that preparatory step when his rifle dropped from his left hand. Looking down, he saw blood "spurting out of my breast at a great rate." He had been shot through the right side of his chest but did not know exactly where he had been hit or the severity of his wound. He whirled about and walked rapidly after his retreating comrades. After what he estimated to be 300 feet, he caught up with Robert C. Morrow in his company. Morrow called to another soldier for help in assisting Simpson. They only made it about 50 feet before Simpson collapsed. His comrades laid him on a blanket and carried him toward the rear until they found a stretcher detail, who transported the sergeant to an ambulance, probably on the northern or eastern side of the East Woods. The ambulance took Simpson, who was drifting in and out of consciousness, to the Sarah Hoffman farm, about a mile northeast of the East Woods, where part of the 12th Corps had bivouacked the night of September 16, before the battle. Simpson's ambulance probably followed Smoketown Road, which brought it by the George Line farm. A field hospital had been established there, but it probably already contained so many wounded that Simpson's ambulance driver was waved on.[8]

By the end of September 17, the field hospital at Hoffman's farm had received nearly 1,200 casualties. Journalist Charles Carleton Coffin, who passed by the farm before Simpson arrived, found the site to be appalling, with wounded men lying in rows, awaiting treatment, and groups of medical personnel busy spreading straw over the farm fields to create more space in which to lay the newly arriving wounded. Simpson was placed on straw in Hoffman's barn. He remained unconscious until after midnight, when his company commander and a surgeon managed to wake him enough for Simpson to hear that the surgeon would draw up instructions for the sergeant to be sent home as soon as he could be safely moved. Simpson was unable to speak, but he could hear the groans "and distressing cries of comrades in all parts of the barn." Having lost a considerable amount of blood, he remained very weak and unconscious throughout Thursday, September 18. The next day, two men assisted Simpson to an ambulance and drove him "some distance" to what was probably a transfer point for casualties being moved to hospitals in other towns and cities with better facilities. He was laid on the ground alongside a fence line and remained there, unattended, during Friday afternoon and night. The next morning, September 20, he discovered the wounded man lying beside him was also from the 125th Pennsylvania and had worked for Simpson's brother-in-law before enlisting. He told Simpson that he had made arrangements with a local farmer who was hauling some of the wounded to Hagerstown Maryland, and expected him to return around midnight.[9]

During the afternoon, a Christian Commission wagon came by and distributed biscuits to Simpson and the other injured men. It was the first food Simpson had eaten since Tuesday, September 16—over 72 hours earlier. The farmer arrived, as promised, around midnight. He had cushioned his wagon with new-mown hay or clover and loaded Simpson, his comrade, and as many of the other casualties as would fit. They arrived in Hagerstown around 8 a.m. on Sunday morning, September 21. Simpson was taken to a school that had been turned into a hospital, filled with wounded, where he received the first treatment he was conscious of. A surgeon found that the bullet had struck the sergeant in the right nipple and exited his body under his right shoulder blade. He dressed the wound and helped make his patient comfortable. Simpson received some food, but the crowding in the hospital cut his stay short. Around 4 p.m., he was placed in an ambulance, driven to the Hagerstown train station, and deposited on the floor of a freight car, along with other casualties being transferred to Harrisburg, Pennsylvania. Simpson recalled that the train journey "was frightful," because "freight cars do not have any springs," and the moans and groans from the wounded who were jolted about "was fearful." Simpson's sister Anna and a friend of his from Huntingdon, Pennsylvania, met him at the Harrisburg station when his train arrived at 3 a.m. on Monday, September 22. They had booked passage for themselves and Simpson on a sleeper train to Huntington and arrived there at 6 a.m. that same day. Neighbors carried him to his father's house. We can only imagine the emotions of John Simpson, the sergeant's father, when his son arrived. Two days before, he had received a telegram from a friend informing him that another son, George, the 125th's color bearer, had been killed, and that James was wounded. There was rejoicing that James was alive, mingled with grief for George. Simpson was confined to bed for several months. His sisters, Anna and Lydia, certainly played a crucial role in his recovery, both in the physical work of attending to a badly injured individual and in keeping their brother's spirits up. He received a medical discharge on April 3, 1863, but it was years before the muscles on his right side, which were cut by the bullet, had healed enough so that Simpson no longer needed to keep his arm in a sling.[10]

G. MERRILL DWELLE WAS a corporal in Company L, 1st Minnesota. The company had originally organized as the 2nd Minnesota Sharpshooters and been assigned to the 1st U.S. Sharpshooters before being reassigned to the 1st Minnesota. Dwelle and his comrades in Company L carried .52 caliber breech-loading

Sharps Rifles and were, in all respects, an elite unit. When the order to retreat reached the 1st Minnesota during the catastrophe that befell Sedgwick's 2nd Division in the West Woods, Dwelle cautioned his men to make it a steady withdrawal. As he gave this command, a bullet struck him in the thigh and exited his leg. He fell down, then managed to get back up and hobble after his regiment, but he did not go much farther before he collapsed, exhausted. He rolled to a fence corner, where there was some cover, and disabled his rifle before Confederate soldiers—probably in Semmes's brigade—swarmed around him "thick as bees." Dwelle struck up a conversation with them and soon found the Rebels "as social as any of our own people." These officers and men treated him "very kindly," as if they were friends, not enemies who moments before had been trying to kill one another. Although no artery was cut, Dwelle's wound bled freely. He took a handkerchief from his pocket and tied two knots in it, one to fit in the entry point, and the other in the exit hole. This stopped the bleeding, but then Union artillery began blasting the area and drove the Confederates off. The concussion from nearby explosions started Dwelle's leg bleeding again. He was so weak that he was not sure he could stand, but he decided there was more danger in remaining where he was. Using his disabled rifle as a crutch, he made his way toward the Union lines. Shrapnel and shell burst around him, shattering fence rails and sending slivers flying through the air, but Dwelle escaped unharmed. He continued north until he encountered a Union cavalry captain, who helped him "to a house," which was probably either the Nicodemus or Miller farmhouse. Here he was placed in a two-wheeled ambulance, which drove him to Smoketown Hospital, located on the south side of Keedysville Road, directly north of the George Line and Sarah Hoffman farms. This hospital would later become known as Antietam General Hospital. According to Jonathan Letterman, the Army of the Potomac's medical director, its purpose was to treat casualties from the right-hand sector of the army whose "lives would be endangered by their removal." It eventually consisted of 80 tents and two buildings at the Catherine Showman farm, on the north side of Keedysville Road, but the hospital was just being set up and there were no tents when Dwelle arrived.[11]

Conditions at Smoketown were rough. The rapid influx of patients overwhelmed the staff. Dwelle was set down under an oak tree, where he lay for 5 days, enduring "two severe rains storm" without so much as a blanket for shelter and only "three miserable hard crackers a day" for food. A North Carolinian prisoner, with whom Dwelle struck up a friendship, helped him survive by slipping out to farmhouses and foraging or purchasing—Dwelle did not say which—food for the two of them. "He was a good fellow and I should not fear to fall into his hands if I should ever be taken prisoner," Dwelle recalled. The general neglect and abysmal conditions, however, finally caused the corporal to vent his fury about his poor treatment on "the Dr in charge," probably Dr. B. A. Vanderkeift in the 102nd New York, who was the head of the hospital. "After talking as mean as I could to him I got better treatment," Dwelle wrote to his sister Carrie. After 5 days at Smoketown, Dwelle was moved to the hospital at the Hoffman farm, "where the fare was better" but the stench from men's wounds "was unbearable." He remained there for 3 or 4 days and then was transferred by ambulance to one of the Frederick field hospitals, probably arriving around September 29 or 30. That hospital had 850 patients, including some Confederates. The food was only marginally better than what he had encountered at Smoketown. He complained to his sister that "I have been nearly starved" on rations consisting of a slice of bread and a piece of meat, which he considered "unpalatable food for a sick man." Any hope that he might get a medical furlough to recover at home was dashed by an order from McClellan, which stated that furloughs would only be issued in cases where it was considered necessary to save the patient's life. Since Dwelle's injury was not deemed life threatening, he was out of luck. Dwelle railed about this injustice to his sister, but the Union army had no intention of having to track down thousands of wounded men, scattered across the country, to determine whether they were medically fit to return to duty. It was more efficient to keep them in its medical system, where their recovery could be more easily tracked.[12]

Although Dwelle considered his wound to be of a "slight character" he was uncertain "whether it will permanently disable me or not." With no chance of a furlough to go home, Dwelle became depressed. He had trouble sleeping, and he wrote about how dismal it was to hear the groans of his wounded tentmates at night. By October 18 he still could not walk, although he could "get around a little" with the help of crutches. What helped lift Dwelle out of his despondency were the women of Frederick, who visited the wounded every day and brought along "goodies" of various foods. There was never enough to share with all the injured soldiers, but just making conversation and seeing a friendly female face did wonders for the suffering men. "All thanks to them for the effort they make," exclaimed Dwelle. The women ignored the Confederate wounded, but Dwelle felt empathy toward these Rebels. "There has been no ladies to see them but once," he wrote. His injury healed slowly, and by February, 5 months after being hit, he still remained at the hospital. On February 17, he wrote to his sister that everyone in his camp had received a new shirt, which, for some, was the first change of clothing they had in 4 weeks. The garments were probably rejects from a manufacturer, since they came in a hodgepodge of sizes and patterns, with some shirts being so long they reached the floor, while others were absurdly short. "If Barnum had a number of the most curious ones on exhibition for a few days his museum would be crowded until the novelty wore off," joked Dwelle. Things began to look up for the corporal when he received a commission as a 2nd lieutenant in the 3rd Minnesota Light Artillery. He was discharged sometime in early March and returned to Minnesota to begin duty as an officer, 6 months after being wounded.[13]

THESE FIVE CASE STUDIES are not "typical," since every injured soldier had his own unique experience, but they include some themes regarding what individuals faced in their path from being wounded to either their recovery or death. They also help us understand the depths of pain and struggle a person experienced to achieve partial or full recovery. There were at least 17,301 men injured in the Battle of Antietam on September 17. When this figure is combined with those from the other battles and skirmishes, the Maryland Campaign produced 21,389 wounded, with nearly all of these occurring between September 14 and 17. The system developed by both armies after the Peninsula Campaign was that stretcher parties, positioned in the rear of the firing line, would carry casualties to aid stations, located at some sheltered position in the rear, where the wounded would receive emergency first-aid treatment, such as the application of tourniquets to control bleeding. Ambulances would then transport non-ambulatory patients in need of more complex medical care to field hospitals, hopefully located beyond the range of artillery. This was the theory, but none of the men in our case studies were evacuated from the front lines by stretcher-bearers, and instances of this are rare in the existing accounts we have from the wounded. They were either helped to the rear by comrades or made their way back under their own power, sometimes having to travel considerable distances. Lieutenant Sam Hodgeman in the 7th Michigan had to walk nearly 2 miles to receive medical attention, and Sergeant Edwin Coghill in the 30th Virginia walked 4 miles to Shepherdstown.[14]

The sheer number of casualties arriving in such a short time period overwhelmed this system for evacuating and treating the wounded. After reading through personal accounts of injured men who endured poor treatment and great suffering, it is easy to imagine that no such system existed. But it did, and it saved many lives. Walter Battle's account of Surgeon Gus Stith at the Piper farm illustrates how closely the Confederates attempted to locate medical services to their front lines. Dr. James Boulware in the 6th South Carolina had his aid station so near to the front that the house he was in had every window shattered and "bricks were thrown over all of us, our eyes, hair and clothes filled with dust." When he left that location for another, he had an enemy shell pass within 2 feet of him (see chapter 17 for additional details). The Federals also positioned their aid stations very close to the fighting. Edward H. R. Revere, assistant surgeon in the 20th Massachusetts, followed his regiment into the West Woods with Sedgwick's 2nd Division and was killed while tending to a wounded man. Surgeon George Barr in the 64th New York wrote about how he located his aid station "in an advanced position in the rear of my regt," and worked there until nightfall. Surgeon Isaac Scott in the 7th [West] Virginia, along with Dr. Thomas McEbright, the 8th Ohio's surgeon, set up an aid station directly in the rear of French's division. On September 17, Scott estimated that they dressed the wounds of some 1,500 men while bullets, shells, and cannonballs were "whistling around our heads like hail all day." During the opening assault on the Rohrback Bridge, Dr. Nathan Mayer, assistant surgeon in the 11th Connecticut, established his aid post "between the hills of corn" in Henry Rohrback's cornfield, only a few hundred yards from the bridge. George Bronson, a hospital steward who was with Mayer, remarked that "the way the bullets whistled around us is better imagined than described." Mayer, in a letter to his brother, declared that he had enough close calls that "I thank God that no bullet had hit me." J. Franklin Dyer was an assistant surgeon in the 19th Massachusetts. He and Josiah N. Willard, the regiment's surgeon, along with their medical attendants, marched with their regiment to the front during the fighting, and "most of the surgeons of our corps" did likewise. Dyer and Willard established a dressing station on the eastern edge of the East Woods. While Sedgwick's division marched on into the West Woods, they began treating the wounded from the earlier fighting, who lay about in considerable numbers. The gunfire on their position became so severe—Dr. Willard's horse was wounded by it—that when Sedgwick was driven from the West Woods, they were forced to abandon their aid station and displace to the rear. Here Dyer met the 2nd Corps' medical director, who ordered him to take charge of the field hospital at the Hoffman farm. Here he was inundated by nearly 500 wounded who arrived within an hour. There simply were not enough stretchers and ambulances to manage numbers like this, and they piled up extremely quickly.[15]

Ambulances did transport some seriously wounded men, like Simpson, directly to field hospitals during the battle, but they were more commonly used to move patients, such as Dwelle, from aid stations to hospitals. In the days after the conflict, ambulances took casualties from field hospitals to Maryland hospitals in Frederick and Hagerstown. The latter town was served by the Cumberland Valley Railroad and offered transportation to hospitals in other Northern cities. The problem was not enough medical transportation in either army—particularly not in the Army of Northern Virginia—to accommodate the numbers who needed it. Simpson's story illustrates this. It was through a comrade's arrangement with a kind-hearted farmer that Simpson was able to reach Hagerstown. Such improvisational measures were common. Ludolph Logenhery, a musician in the 7th Wisconsin who was detailed to assist the wounded, recorded that on September 18, between 7 a.m. and 8 a.m., citizens from Hagerstown began to arrive in buggies, carrying food and helping to transport injured men back to the city. Captain William Bolton in the 51st Pennsylvania traveled to Hagerstown in a private wagon, thanks to negotiations by his brother. G. B. Anderson and George Wren were able to reach Staunton, Virginia, because they made their own arrangements to get there. When this is the experience of officers, the situation for enlisted men can scarcely be imagined. The Confederates had serious transportation shortages, which, as Medical Director Lafayette Guild lamented, "compelled us to leave many wounded in exposed positions, and they have fallen into the hands of the enemy." There is also a question of how efficiently the transportation they did have was managed. Moving Lieutenant Wren and the unwounded enlisted man who accompanied him from the southern bank of the Potomac River to Winchester, Virginia, by ambulance may have been justified, but it points to inefficiency and a failure to prioritize medical transportation. It seems extravagant to take an ambulance out of service for more than 2 days to evacuate a single wounded officer, when it might have made multiple trips moving other injured men to closer medical facilities.[16]

Ambulances were efficient for transporting casualties, but the two-wheeled models lacked springs. As Marinus McDowell attested, the wounded suffered agonizingly when these were driven on rutted, uneven country roads and lanes. Late on September 17, Captain Andrew Wardlaw, the 14th South Carolina's quartermaster, had a disquieting moment when he met an ambulance carrying Colonel Dixon Barnes, the badly injured commander of the 12th South Carolina. "It was very distressing & a sad commentary on the horrors of war to hear such a man shrieking out with pain as the vehicle passed over rough places in the road," he wrote. Despite the discomfort they caused, and the fact that there were not enough of them for the vast numbers of casualties, the ambulance system actually worked relatively efficiently and moved thousands of injured to medical assistance. This was particularly true in the Army of the Potomac, which had its first opportunity to implement the sweeping changes to the Ambulance Corps instituted on August 2, 1862, with General Orders No. 47. William Clark, a commissary sergeant in the 28th Pennsylvania, described seeing upward of 1,000 ambulances on September 18 (although this number most likely was an exaggeration) continually hauling wounded men from the field. A member of the Vermont brigade in General William Smith's 2nd Division of the 6th Corps related how the ambulances in that division worked all night on September 17, carrying off the Union and Confederate wounded. The challenge the Ambulance Corps confronted at the Battle of Antietam is illustrated by the situation at the William Roulette farm, where an aid station was established when French's 3rd Division in the 2nd Corps assaulted the Sunken Lane. Ambulances positioned here transported casualties from the aid station to field hospitals established at the farms of Dr. Otho J. Smith, Henry Neikirk, R. F. Kennedy, and Sarah Hoffman. By the regulations in General Orders No. 47, French's and Richardson's division should have had a total of 46 two-wheeled and 23 four-wheeled ambulances, as well as 23 transport carts available. Each ambulance was equipped with two stretchers, for a total 138 litters. Transport carts were of little value, being described as "useless in the ambulance department of an army." Two men and a driver were assigned to each ambulance, while one driver handled a transport cart. How many men an ambulance carried depended on the nature of the injuries to the men it was transporting. In an emergency, a four-wheeled ambulance could hold three litter cases, but it might also convey one litter case and 12 wounded who could sit upright, or other combinations. In 3 hours, French's and Richardson's divisions sustained 2,254 wounded. This explains why Chaplain H. S. Stevens in the 14th Connecticut, who was at the Roulette farm, wrote, "All day men who could not be carried further to the rear for want of ambulances were brought there and laid upon the grass, or within the house, spring-house or barn." The numbers of injured men utterly swamped the system.[17]

Such numbers help us understand why soldiers like McDowell could be at a field hospital for 2 weeks and claim to have received no medical attention, or Merrill Dwelle could lie beneath an oak tree for 5 days with no shelter and no examination of his wounds. Conditions at Union field hospitals were considerably better than those at Confederate ones, since the former had more personnel and superior medical supplies. Lieutenant Wren offers some sense of just how awful conditions at Confederate hospitals could be when he declared that a hospital at Winchester, which was located far from the front, was too full, and had such disagreeable conditions, for him to even contemplate staying there. Many Confederates mention finding lodging at private homes. James Kent Lewis in the 16th North Carolina, who was admitted to a Winchester hospital, penned a description of it to his mother on September 18: "I have left the hospital now. It was so filthy and the food they gave us so utterly unfit for sick men I had to leave and now I am lying out in the woods." The superb Georgia newspaper correspondent Peter Wellington Alexander was blunt in his criticism of the Confederate army's medical services. He wrote that few men knew the location of their respective brigade or division hospital, and Alexander personally witnessed many wounded soldiers, unable to find a hospital, "faint and even lay down to die by the wayside." Of this army's surgeons, he noted that some "perform their work skillfully and conscientiously," but others "do it hurriedly or ignorantly; whilst a few do it in a manner that can only be properly characterized as brutal." Moreover, the object of many Rebel doctors "seems to be to get through with their work, in some sort of fashion, as soon as possible." There were also those who felt it "to be their solemn duty, every time they administer brandy to their patient, to take a drink themselves." But Alexander leveled his harshest criticism at the surgeons serving Virginia hospitals in Winchester and Warrenton. He considered these doctors to be the worst of the lot. They were of "little value" to the major hospitals in Richmond and were unwilling to serve at the front with the army. Instead, they staffed interim hospitals, such as the one at Winchester. Alexander also considered the management of the Winchester hospitals to border on the criminal. He reached a sad conclusion: "One thing has impressed me more painfully than all others connected with the army. It is the little concern which the government, its officers and surgeons show for the preservation of the lives of their troops."[18]

No doubt elements of Alexander's criticisms of the Confederate medical system were valid, but from the surgeons' point of view, they were treating huge numbers of casualties where minutes and seconds might mean the difference between life and death. The dreadfulness of the work was overwhelming, and it took its toll. If doctors appeared callous to their patients, this often was a defense mechanism that allowed them to maintain their sanity. Writing to a Northern friend 4 days after the Battle of Antietam, Surgeon J. M. Greene in the 17th Mississippi of Barksdale's brigade wrote, "'I have supped' so 'full of horrors'—have seen death, crime, shame and despair so busy at their work that my head has whitened and my very soul turned into stone. A long vista of human blood shuts out the dear past and a boundless expanse of the same crimson fluid stretches before us in the future. I see no end to it."[19]

The quality of medical personnel was an issue in both armies, although the majority of surgeons were more competent than is commonly supposed. The problems that bedeviled the Confederate medical services were the quantity and quality of supplies, as well as transportation. Robert E. Lee had left it to his medical director, Lafayette Guild, with "all the means of transportation at our command," to deal with the injured from Second Manassas when he invaded Maryland. Then came the Battles of South Mountain, Harpers Ferry, and Sharpsburg, with thousands more wounded men who had to be transported to Shepherdstown, Winchester, or other points in Virginia. The means to handle such numbers simply did not exist, and approximately 2,500 Confederate casualties were left in Union hands. Many of these were seriously wounded and could not be moved safely, but there were plenty of others who could not be evacuated for lack of horse-drawn vehicles. Each of these battles also consumed quantities of the Army of Northern Virginia's limited medical supplies and equipment. Other than the capture of some stocks from Union hospitals in Frederick, there was no resupply during the Maryland Campaign. The result was suffering for a vast number of men, but it is difficult to see how Lee could have alleviated this situation.[20]

Although the Army of the Potomac was considerably better supplied and staffed than the Army of Northern Virginia, the Federals' medical services at Antietam also experienced serious shortages of all types of supplies, for many of the same reasons as the Confederates. In addition, some of the medical resources, transferred from the Virginia Peninsula in August, still had not caught up with the army. The Confederates' destruction of the railroad bridge over the Monocacy River in Maryland also disrupted the flow of supplies, since everything had to be unloaded from the railroad cars, reloaded onto wagons, and then hauled over Catoctin and South Mountains to Keedysville. This, complained Medical Director Jonathan Letterman, led to "a great deal of confusion and delay," which "seriously embarrassed the medical department." Compounding this problem, the Union army's Medical Department had no dedicated transportation, other than ambulances, and it was reliant on the Quartermaster's Department, which controlled the army's wagon trains. Dr. C. R. Agnew, a member of the U.S. Sanitary Commission, was upset about this situation and angrily declared, "I solemnly affirm that great loss of life has occurred and will occur, among the wounded, as the direct result of an inability on the part of the medical authorities to furnish, by rapid and independent means of transportation, the surgical and medical appliances needed within the two days immediately subsequent to the battles." This explains some of the neglect that McDowell, Dwelle, and Simpson all experienced at battlefield field hospitals. Assistant Surgeon Benjamin Howard, a remarkable individual who worked directly under Letterman, served as his "eyes and ears" during the Battle of Antietam by riding to different points and "keeping me informed of medical affairs." Howard reported that "hospital tents were entirely wanting," and there were "no reserve supplies of medicine and hospital stores." Some of the surgeons in newly raised regiments departed from Washington, DC, before they could draw anything more than emergency supplies. Writing 2 days after the Battle of Crampton's Gap, Assistant Surgeon Daniel Holt in the 121st New York, one of the new regiments, complained that "our medical supplies are all gone and we feel the need of it terribly. We have not a *pound of all*—not enough to hold one surgeon's call with, and so we have been for several days."[21]

Dr. Theodore Dimon, the surgeon in the 2nd Maryland, left perhaps the most detailed account of any doctor in either army about the challenges he faced in organizing, staffing, and administering the field hospital he was in charge of. If one word could describe his experience, it would be "improvisation." The organization of medical services in the field had not yet progressed to where specialty officers would relieve doctors of their many administrative and logistical duties, so they could focus on treating the wounded. A surgeon had to be a jack-of-all-trades—and be proficient at all of them. Lives hung in the balance, depending on how well they juggled their many tasks. On September 17, Dimon worked from an aid station in a storage barn that may have been part of the Noah Rohrback farm. That evening he went to the rear, a short distance from Keedysville, stopping at what became known as Locust Spring Hospital, the largest hospital established on the southern end of the battlefield. Here he learned "that some distance further on there was a party of wounded with no surgeon and no supplies." Dimon went on to this locale, which he stated was the Millard farm, located immediately east of Keedysville.[22]

Dimon found the farmhouse filled with wounded men, as was the barn attached to the house. There was also separate log house, which was either another farm building or possibly a structure that housed enslaved individuals. "There was nothing detailed for me to begin with and I had to form everything from the foundation," he wrote. The medical director of his division "had deposited 140 wounded on the bare floors. They had not even straw under them. There was not a cook, nurses or anything for them, and no provisions, dressings or anything else." In the barn he found "some stragglers, calling themselves sick, with an ambulance," who were "making themselves comfortable." Dimon recognized at once that "I must have power to control all acting under my orders." He routed the stragglers out of the barn and promptly set about organizing them. He picked 6 to form a guard, then detailed 5 as cooks, 12 as nurses, and 1 as his steward. The "broken ambulance" was dispatched to acquire "dressings, medicines, food and candles." His hospital staff were some of the army's riff-raff, and he could permit no breach of discipline or deviation from his orders. When he discovered some of the cooks and nurses and one of the military guards "making themselves very comfortable out of the stimulants provided for the wounded," he had them taken to a nearby apple orchard and tied up by their thumbs, "so that their toes would just touch the ground." It was cruel, but effective. "For a day or two, I had some apple tree suspensions and after that everything went smoothly," he noted.[23]

Dimon wrote to his wife about what consumed his days: "Surgery, surgery, surgery. Food, food, food. Nurses, nurses, nurses. Cooks that get drunk. Everybody employed looking out for No. 1; nobody caring for anybody else. Surgeons come here to get me to take care of their sick, not knowing or caring to do anything but shirk them off on to me, in addition to my other cases." Despite these challenges, he gradually established order and an efficient routine at his hospital. Nurses (all male) were organized into reliefs, "assigning each one a given number of the wounded to take care of and fixed the relief roll for each." His nurses were stragglers who were "picked up on the road, my guard halting and taking possession of all passers till I filled my quota." The daily routine required each wounded man to be examined, with clean and fresh dressings applied, if needed. He had "all the premises carefully policed," to keep the hospital as clean as possible on a farm. Given the shirking nature of his nurses, Dimon came down hard on them if they were derelict in their duties. "The nurses think I am a savage I suppose, for if they neglect anything I arrest the one at fault and send him off to the Provost Marshal," he noted. "You have no idea of the labor and bother of organizing out of nothing all the mere necessities for the care of wounded at a moment's notice, with nothing at hand and not knowing where to get it," he continued. "I rode 14 miles to find where I could get food." Incredibly, his medical director abandoned him on September 18 to escort a wounded brother-in-law back to New York. On top of Dimon's myriad headaches in running his hospital, he suffered from "an exhausting diarrhea." By September 25, however, he could tell his wife, with satisfaction, "Now things go smoothly and well."[24]

Dimon's hospital was a small affair, compared with some others. The one at the Roulette farm was an example of a far larger hospital/aid station, and conditions there were dreadful. Visiting that facility on the evening of September 17, Adjutant Fred Hitchcock in the 132nd Pennsylvania found the wounded lying "so thickly that there was scarce room for the surgeons and their attendants to move about among them." Hitchcock observed "piles of amputated arms, legs, and feet, thrown out with as little care as so many pieces of wood" near the operating tables. Edward Spangler, a young private in the 130th Pennsylvania, also visited the hospital. Everywhere the private went, he encountered distressing sights. Some of the injured "screamed with excruciating pains," while others "ripped out a succession of oaths that must have required years of sedulous preparation" or shrieked in the "agony and throes of death." He left the hospital badly shaken and concluded that "no one can adequately depict this horrible spectacle and pandemonium of distressing and heart-rending sounds."[25]

As Merrill Dwelle's story illustrates, both Union and Confederate surgeons attended to wounded men from the opposing army. The existing evidence indicates that although doctors were obliged to minister to their wounded first, and then the enemy, most were color blind when it came to casualties. Sergeant Ben Milikin in the 27th Georgia of Colquitt's brigade was shot through the thigh near the East Woods, and he had a comrade drag him behind a tree there for some cover. Yankees soon swarmed over his position. Milikin noticed they were careful to avoid stepping on him, and several times soldiers stood over him with crossed rifles to prevent their comrades from treading on the sergeant. Other Federals filled his canteen with water and collected nearby haversacks, so he would have food available. He was carried from the field around 10 a.m. and taken to a nearby farmyard that was filled with injured men. A surgeon cut open his pants and underdrawers and located the wound in his thigh. The bullet had passed clean through his leg, but, to make sure, the surgeon—in a practice that was common but often infected an injury—put a finger in each side of the wound and probed until they met in the middle. As Milikin recalled, "This hurt a good deal worse than the wound and when I first got [it] and then I felt like my foot and leg would burst all to pieces." The medical attention he received was no different than that for the Union soldiers around him. Although Milikin would be on crutches for more than a year, he recovered from his injury. Captain Tilghman W. Flynt in the 19th Georgia, who was seriously wounded and could not be evacuated when the Confederate army retreated, praised the kindness of the Federals he came in contact with. He recalled how General Morell and Colonel T. B. W. Stockton, one of Morell's brigade commanders, "looked especially after my eating and <u>drinking</u>, as well as other kindnesses." In addition, a New Jersey officer he shared a room with gave Flynt half of everything he received in care packages from home.[26]

JOHN H. NELSON, IN his exhaustive study of Union hospitals at Antietam, identified over 120 of them. In addition to farms, various churches, courthouses, schools, a female seminary in Hagerstown, hotels, private homes, the Keedys-ville town hall, and public buildings all became temporary hospitals. Their size varied widely, ranging from a handful of soldiers at the Sarah Snyder farm to 850 and 1,400, respectively, at the George Line and Sarah Hoffman farm hospitals. Thousands of wounded men were transported by rail from Hagerstown or Frederick to more well-equipped hospitals in Chambersburg, Harrisburg, York, and Philadelphia in Pennsylvania; Baltimore; New York City; Washington, DC; and Alexandria, Virginia. The long journey through the army hospital system—and the uneven quality of treatment—that many experienced is illustrated by Nathan B. Jordan, a private in the 19th Massachusetts, who was shot in the upper chest, near his collarbone, in the West Woods. His initial care was at an aid station in a schoolhouse. A civilian drove him to the Washington County Courthouse in Hagerstown, where he remained for a week. "Nothing was done to my wound, only washed off," Jordan wrote of his minimal treatment there. He and other injured men were then placed in boxcars, like John Simpson was, and carried to Chambersburg, Pennsylvania, where he was admitted to a hospital in a schoolhouse on King Street. He found the medical care there to be abysmal. Jordan grumbled that "the doctors here were men who drank," and the night nurse was so neglectful of his charges that one evening a patient threw an old shoe at him. In December he was moved to a Philadelphia hospital and, not many days later, relocated to a facility in Germantown, a few miles away, where the conditions met with Jordan's approval. In April 1863, his medical odyssey continued when he was transferred again, this time to a General Hospital in Fort Schuyler, New York. "On the whole," he found it to be "a miserable hospital." Jordan never recovered sufficiently to return to his regiment, and in September 1863, a year after receiving his wound, he entered the Veteran Reserve Corps.[27]

Jonathan Letterman understood that it was imperative to consolidate the numerous field hospitals as quickly as possible and transfer the wounded to hospitals in Frederick and other Northern cities, as soon as they could safely travel. Since there was no rail service to Sharpsburg, procuring and hauling the necessary supplies to treat and feed the Union and Confederate wounded was a huge and complicated undertaking, made more difficult with injured men scattered in over 100 field hospitals throughout the Sharpsburg–Keedysville area. Consolidating smaller hospitals into fewer, larger hospitals—such as Smoketown and Locust Spring—helped ease the quartermasters' burden in supplying rations, and the transfer of casualties to Frederick and other points began to reduce crowding at the battlefield hospitals. Letterman's staff established a regular ambulance train from the battlefield to Frederick, a trip of 18 to 19 miles. A halt was made at Middletown, both to feed the patients and rest the men after the jolting ride over South Mountain. The complexities of managing this operation were immense. A mundane detail—like making sure the food prepared in Middletown was adequate and would "always be provided at this place at the proper time and for the proper number"—was crucial. The arrival of the wounded in Frederick had to be carefully regulated, so "that the hospitals at Frederick should not be overcrowded; that the ambulances should not arrive too soon for the trains of cars at the depot at Frederick, and that the ambulance horses should not be broken down by the constant labor required of them."[28]

A great deal of manpower was necessary for the system to function efficiently. Letterman reported that the Frederick hospitals employed 62 surgeons, 15 medical cadets, 22 stewards, 539 nurses, and 127 cooks to manage 5,353 patients. This worked out to approximately to 1 surgeon for 86 men, and 1 to 19 for nurses, if the nurses worked 12-hour shifts. The neglect soldiers like Simpson, McDowell, Dwelle, Jordan, and others experienced at field hospitals where they were treated was partly a consequence of the sheer numbers of injured, but it was also because there were not enough surgeons and nurses to attend to so many casualties. This was a known problem, whose solution had been stymied by bureaucrats who were unable to fathom the dire conditions medical personnel confronted. A proposal to increase the number of people in the medical department and create a dedicated Hospital Corps met with firm opposition from General-in-Chief Halleck, who complained that "our armies are already much too large and [it would] very seriously impede the movements of our troops in the field," as well as that "the presence of noncombatants on or near the field or battle is always detrimental." Secretary of War Stanton agreed with Halleck. When Surgeon General William A. Hammond proposed a plan to create an Ambulance Corps for all the Union forces, Stanton rejected it. McClellan's General Orders No. 47, which were Letterman's medical reforms for the Army of the Potomac, were an effort to circumvent Stanton by applying the reforms only to that army. Stanton nevertheless still intervened and nixed the plan, using the same twisted logic Halleck employed to kill the creation of a Hospital Corps. Theodore Dimon's experiences in establishing his field hospital reflect the consequences of such short-sighted, ignorant thinking. Instead of a dedicated staff of trained nurses, stewards, and cooks, Dimon was reduced to employing shirkers, whom he forced into duty at gunpoint. Even when the field hospital's staff members were augmented by bandsman or other individuals detailed from infantry regiments, there simply were not enough to provide necessary attention to the numbers of injured a battle like Antietam produced. Moreover, very few had any training in caring for the wounded.[29]

The human cost of medical staff shortages could be heart rendering. Sergeant Jonathan Stowe in the 15th Massachusetts, who was gravely wounded in the West Woods and taken to the Hoffman farm hospital, offers an example. In his diary, he detailed the wretched conditions he endured. On September 21, he complained about the difficulty in getting nurses to attend to his needs and the wounded men around him. A day later, he wrote that no one provided chamber pots for those who were unable to move. "How ludicrous for 2 score men to help themselves with diarrhea," he wrote. On September 23, he complained of a "long fearful night," since "what difficulties we have to contend . . . relief can hardly be found." Conditions slowly improved during his time there, but the early neglect may have had an effect on Stowe's eventual outcome. He died on October 1.[30]

Letterman worked tirelessly to prevent tragedies like Stowe's by combing the North for additional medical personnel. On the night of September 17, he ordered up 60 to 70 surgeons from army hospitals in Washington, DC. A special train took them to Monocacy Junction, where they arrived on the morning of September 18. Some were assigned to work in the Frederick hospitals, while the rest were sent to the front. Civilian volunteer surgeons from across the Northeast also answered the call. In one example, the city of Lancaster, Pennsylvania, dispatched five surgeons and three assistants late on September 17. These additions helped, but the most important succor Letterman received came from two civilian agencies formed in 1861: the U.S. Sanitary Commission and the U.S. Christian Commission. The Sanitary Commission's mission was to improve the life of the soldiers, with particular attention on their health and hygiene. It was the larger of the two organizations, with nearly 7,000 aid societies in communities across the North during the Civil War. The Christian Commission had a similar aim, but it also sought to address the spiritual needs of the combatants. The partial overlap in their missions fostered some jealousy and competition between the two organizations, but in a huge humanitarian crisis, such as the aftermath of the Battle of Antietam, there was more than enough need to occupy the full attention of both. Despite their crucial role in aiding the sick and wounded, Secretary of War Stanton considered them a nuisance. Letterman and his staff did not share this view, and they counted on the two organizations to compensate for what the government failed to provide. The generally positive view Letterman and his surgeons had towards the commissions and their work was not always reciprocated. George Templeton Strong, the Sanitary Commission's treasurer and one of its founders, visited Antietam soon after the battle. He produced a scathing report on the ineptitude of the Army of the Potomac's medical services and their reliance on the commission's generosity. "The Medical Department is utterly destitute and shiftless as usual," he vented in his diary on September 24, "and confessedly is leaning on the Commission for supplies and looking to it for help to get forward its own stores, waiving all its official dignity under the pressure of work for which it made no adequate provision and in an attitude of general supplication and imbecile self-abasement." But Dr. Cornelius R. Agnew, a distinguished physician and also a Sanitary Commission founder, used a completely different tone on in a September 22 report. He acknowledged that there were shortages and problems in getting medical supplies to the front, but he asserted, "I hope I never shall forget the evidences everywhere manifested of the unselfish and devoted heroism of our surgeons, regular and volunteer, in the care of both Federal and rebel wounded. Wherever I went I encountered surgeons and chaplains who had given themselves no rest in view of the overwhelming claims of suffering humanity." Of Letterman and the doctors he encountered, Agnew affirmed that "the country should be proud of those faithful men, who labor day and night to alleviate the sufferings of the battle, without hope of 'honorable mention' or a 'brevet' in this world."[31]

Both commissions were already at work in Maryland when the Battle of Antietam was fought, helping with the casualties from the combat at South Mountain and Crampton's Gap, and they responded promptly and efficiently to this new challenge. Some sense of the scale of the Sanitary Commission's aid is evident in a letter Frederick Law Olmstead, the commission's general secretary, wrote to its president, Reverend Henry Bellows. In it, Olmstead itemized supplies that were delivered to the army. By September 24 they had shipped "28,763 pieces of dry goods, shirts, towels, bed-ticks, pillows, &c., 30 barrels old linen bandages and lint; 3,188 pounds farina [milled wheat]; 2,620 pounds condensed milk, 5,000 pounds beef stock and canned meats; 3,000 bottles of wine and cordials, and several tons of lemons and other fruit, crackers, tea, sugar, rubber cloth, tin cups and hospital conveniences." In addition to these supplies, Olmstead reported that 4,000 sets of hospital clothing were on their way to the front by special train and would reach Frederick by September 24, "if money and energy can break through the obstructions of this embarrassed transportation."[32]

Besides supplies and surgical help, the Sanitary and Christian Commissions dispatched numerous women from their organizations to help at the field hospitals and the general hospitals in Frederick. The importance of their contributions in saving lives and alleviating suffering is incalculable. One of the themes running through all the case studies examined at the beginning of this chapter is the centrality of women in the recovery, or hope of recovery, for each patient. Brigadier General George B. Anderson may have taken unnecessary risks in his desperation to reach his wife and young son in North Carolina. Lieutenant George Wren wrote of the importance visits from the ladies of Winchester, Virginia, had in maintaining his spirits. Marinus K. McDowell never forgot the "merciful ministrations" of the Catholic Sisters of Charity in Frederick who made his difficult experience at the hospital there bearable. The women of Frederick, who may have been associated with the Sanitary Commission, were vital in Merrill Dwelle's recovery. John Simpson's sister Anna made the journey to the front to find her brother and bring him home, and she then helped in his recovery. Clara Barton, a volunteer nurse who probably worked in the field hospital at the John C. Middlekauf farm, is the most famous woman who arrived to help after the battle, but there were many others from local communities and across the North who selflessly pitched in. The Ladies' Union Relief Association of Hagerstown went to work transforming tablecloths into bandages and collecting other supplies before dispatching some of their numbers to the battlefield as nurses. The women in the Hoffman family, whose farm was decimated by its use as a hospital, brought "fruit, cakes, pies, etc.," to the wounded there for weeks. George

Allen, a hospital steward at Mt. Vernon German Reformed Church Hospital in Keedysville, wrote of how he would never forget a woman from Philadelphia who worked there: "Night or day, rain or shine, Mrs. Husbands was omnipresent." Maria Hall, age 26, was legendary among the patients at Smoketown General Hospital. A fearless, determined, and attractive woman, Hall was an experienced nurse by the time the fighting at Antietam occurred, having served as a volunteer during the Peninsula Campaign and at the Patent Office Hospital in Washington, DC.[33]

On September 21, a friend alerted Hall to the desperate need for supplies and help on the battlefield. Friends from New Jersey provided her with a "large trunk of hospital stores," and she left for the front on September 22 without any idea of where she was needed. In Frederick she met a party of men and women on their way to provide relief to the wounded in the 35th Massachusetts. She accompanied them to Keedysville where she encountered Colonel Francis Barlow being tended by his wife, Arabella, a woman whose determination equaled Hall's own. Mrs. Barlow told her of some individuals that the latter knew who were serving at the Hoffman farm hospital, and Hall worked there for a time. Next, she went to the Stephen D. Grove farm, west of Sharpsburg, which was primarily a Confederate field hospital; then moved to the Dr. Otho J. Smith farm hospital, which treated the wounded from French's division in the 2nd Corps; before finally ending up at Smoketown General Hospital, where she remained until it closed in May 1863. Her work principally consisted of preparing food and serving it to the patients, but she also wrote letters home for those unable to do so. In addition, she sat by the men's beds and talked with or read to them. Depression stalked injured soldiers who were confined for weeks and months to a hospital bed or had experienced an amputated limb. The role of women like Hall, in helping to give hope and keep spirits up, was inestimable. Yet, daily, Hall also encountered tragic outcomes among her patients who succumbed to their wounds. She recalled how "many last messages were taken and many precious treasures were committed to our charge to be sent home with a lock of hair and the last words to the sorrowing ones at home." Her story is a reminder that courage not only consists of facing bullets and shells. It can also encompass taking countless last messages from dying men but still carrying on. Her patients never forgot her. A sergeant in the 78th New York wrote, "Her self-sacrifice is worthy of something more than newspaper notice." Another patient observed of Hall, and others like her, "No, words or gold could not repay you for your sufferings, privations, the painful hard sights which the angels of the battlefield are willing to face—no, God alone can reward you."[34]

LIKE GENERAL G. B. ANDERSON, hundreds of wounded men in both armies died of their wounds within days or months. An analysis of 29 Union regiments from every corps except the 6th gives a total of 2,837 injured, of whom 378 did not survive, for a death rate of 13%. Within this sample, there was considerable variance among individual regiments. For example, the 28th Massachusetts had a death rate of 38%, while that for the 5th New Hampshire was only 4%. On the Confederate side, Greg Mast, who has carefully studied North Carolina casualties, found that in the 14th North Carolina, 15 of their wounded died—a rate of 31%. Numerous variables explain why these percentages were higher in some units. Closer range engagements produced more dangerous wounds than those where the shooting was at long range. Artillery fire, particularly with its shell fragments and solid shot, produced frightful wounds. Where a soldier was hit was crucial in determining his chances of survival. Of injuries that penetrated the chest cavity, the death rate was just over 65%. Spinal wounds were fatal roughly 55% of the time, and abdominal ones, nearly 49%. This number fell precipitously—to 6.5%—when an injury was in the outer extremities. The speed with which a wounded soldier received medical attention was also critical, as was the quality of that care. G. B. Anderson received timely medical aid, but it was hasty and missed discovering the bullet in his ankle, which proved to be fatal. Jonathan Stowe in the 15th Massachusetts described his painful experience at the Hoffman farm hospital, where he was treated for a severe wound in the right knee. He lay in the West Woods for 2 days before receiving aid and did not have his leg amputated until September 20. The later an amputation was performed, the less the chances of survival, which was the case with G. B. Anderson. Stowe also bore this out, as he died on October 1, due to infection. Surgeons understood the need for performing amputations soon after a wound was inflicted, but they did not yet understand how infections worked. The likelihood of survival was also significantly increased by moving injured men to better equipped, cleaner, and more fully staffed general hospitals in cities like Frederick. Jonathan Letterman reported that in the two large camp hospitals established there, a total of 5,353 patients were received during the month of October, of whom only 253 died, or slightly less than 5%. But, if the 13% death rate in our sample of 29 Union regiments is applied to both armies, it meant that nearly 1,500 Federal and a minimum of 1,000 Confederate soldiers died from their wounds as a result of the battles in the Maryland Campaign.[35]

For those who survived their wounds, the road to recovery was long. Both Merrill Dwelle and George Wren, who received disabling but not life-threatening wounds, returned to active service, but each of them spent 6 months rehabilitating. There were thousands, like Marinus McDowell and John Simpson, who never rejoined their units. Simpson was medically discharged, and he was still suffering from the effects of his wound when the war ended in 1865. McDowell was able to enlist in an independent infantry company that performed light guard duty. Of the 14 men who were listed as dangerously or seriously injured on the original casualty return for the 8th Connecticut, all of them survived— which is a testament to their medical treatment—but each of them received a medical discharge and never returned to the army. The grievously wounded did occasionally recover and rejoin their units, but they were few in number. The majority were discharged from the service or reassigned to non-combat duties.[36]

Despite the vast, almost unimaginable suffering endured by those who were injured at Antietam, Jonathan Letterman's system for evacuation and treatment worked well, considering the enormity of the challenges and the conditions it operated under. The Confederates had more problems and experienced greater suffering, due to several factors. Their medical director was still dealing with the aftermath of Second Manassas, supplies were limited, transportation was insufficient, and their army was far from any rail communications to summon additional medical help or supplies. No battle during the Civil War produced as many wounded in a single day as that at Antietam. The pressure on the medical systems of both armies was unprecedented. While it is possible to find stories of incompetent or uncaring surgeons or medical staff, the majority were capable, dedicated, and struggled heroically to save lives. The U.S. Sanitary Commission did not fail to hold the Union army's medical services to account for its shortcomings and failures, yet one of the commission's founders, after an inspection of field hospitals, lauded what he described as the "heroic" work of regular and volunteer surgeons in their care for the wounded men from both armies. There was no glamour in the job of repairing the damage inflicted on the human body by weapons of war, and it produced much to test the emotional and mental stability of those who performed the work. Routine often helped them get by. Eight days after Antietam, Dr. Theodore Dimon, shared a description of this with his wife.

> During the day I dress wounds, draw rations, look after cleaning up everything, see to serving out food, etc., etc., and make records of everything done. During the evening and night I make out some of the thousand reports necessary to be made to various quarters of the army. Last night at eleven o'clock after three hours of writing the names, regiment, company, rank, wounds, when received, how treated, etc., etc., I went to bed and for the first time in a month I dreamed of home and you. I hope the dreams will come true.[37]

As the days and weeks passed, the field hospitals gradually were shut down as the wounded were transferred to Frederick or other points, until only Smoketown and Locust Spring (or Big Spring) hospitals remained. Locust Spring closed in April 1863, and Smoketown folded its tents and shut down on May 11, almost 8 months after the great battle.[38]

Carnage

Many soldiers commented on how troubling they found the sights and sounds of a field hospital, but a landscape littered with dead bodies stirred different emotions. There were a handful who claimed they could look on the dead with no feelings at all, but it was a rare individual who could stand at the southern end of the Cornfield, or on the edge of the Sunken Lane, and not be profoundly disturbed by what they saw. At the end of the day's fighting, 2,108 Union and at least 1,546 Confederate soldiers were killed or died of their wounds. Five days after the battle, H. Waters Berryman in the 1st Texas could not shake images of the slaughter from his mind. "Oh! Ma, you never saw such destruction of human life," he wrote. "Some lying with their arms and legs off, some shot in two. Some with their brains out and still living." A member of the 13th Pennsylvania Militia, out of curiosity, visited the field on September 20. "The spectacle was revolting and horrible in the extreme," he shuddered, referring to his drive down the Hagerstown Pike.[39] Lieutenant Henry Ropes in the 20th Massachusetts walked over the field on September 19 and recounted his observations to his brother John:

> It was really a most awful sight. The dead were really piled up and lay in rows. The slaughter was more awful than anything I ever read[?] of, for it is not a small field on which the dead lay thickly scattered as if there were a desperate fight at that one place, but a vast extent of country several times as large as the common, where there is no place which you can stand and not see the field black with dead bodies as far as the eye can reach.[40]

Soldiers in the Army of the Potomac or the former Army of Virginia had few combat successes thus far, as well as little exposure to a battlefield after the fighting. They found it sobering, and numerous men remarked that this single experience cured them from ever wishing to view another. A soldier in Brooks's Vermont brigade wrote a vivid description in a letter to his hometown paper on September 20:

> I never realized what a battle was before, and God knows I am sick, sick of these scenes of blood. . . . I saw men compelled to lay within four feet of dead bodies that were so mangled that they were almost alive with maggots. And in the night the boys would break off ears of corn to throw at the hogs who would have eaten of the bodies. I tell you, sir, we could not have stood it much longer. We were literally dying by inches—suffering from head-ache and sick to vomiting, lying in one position so long.

Lieutenant Colonel Nelson Miles in the 61st New York was as tough and brave a soldier as existed in the Army of the Potomac, yet the scenes at the Sunken Lane and the Piper cornfield shocked him. "The ground over which we had fought was fearful to behold," he wrote to his brother. "It surpassed anything I have seen before. It seemed as I rode along, that it was the Valley of Death. I think that in the space of less than ten acres, lay the bodies of a thousand dead men and as many more wounded. I hope you will never witness such a sight." A 2nd Massachusetts soldier who wandered over part of the Cornfield area on September 19 confessed in his diary that the sights were so appalling, it was "too much for me to describe," adding that he hoped "it will never fall to my lot to witness such an awful scene again." When Major Rufus Dawes and his 6th Wisconsin survivors marched down the Hagerstown Turnpike the same day, he found it "indescribably horrible," with "great numbers of dead, swollen and black under the hot sun," lying beside the road and in the fields beyond. "My horse, as I rode through the narrow lane made by piling the bodies beside the turnpike fences, trembled in every limb with fright and was wet with perspiration." After the war, he considered the horrors he had seen at various battles—the Bloody Angle at Spotsylvania, Cold Harbor, and Fredericksburg—and compared them with what he observed at Antietam. He believed "that the Antietam Turnpike surpassed all in manifest evidence of slaughter." This, as the soldiers in the Army of the Potomac learned, was what victory looked like.[41]

In October, citizens of New York City had a rare opportunity to witness what soldiers on the battlefield had seen. Photographers Alexander Gardner and James F. Gibson, employed at Matthew Brady's studio in Washington, DC, followed the Army of the Potomac across Maryland and probably arrived at Keedysville on September 18. When it was established that the Confederates had retreated on the 19th, the two photographers went to work. Over the next 3 days, they captured a series of remarkable images: Confederate dead in Starke's Louisiana brigade littering the fencing along the Hagerstown Pike (see chapter 2); a burial detail at work on the Miller farm; bodies of Rebels in Kershaw's and Manning's brigades on the Dunker Church plateau, strewn beside the dead horses and damaged limbers of S. D. Lee's artillery battalion (see chapter 9); the dead horse of Colonel Henry B. Strong in the 6th Louisiana, whose rider was also killed in the counterattack of Hays's brigade in the Cornfield; a long line of Confederate dead gathered for burial near Smoketown Road; and piles of dead in the Sunken Lane (see below). They also took a series of images of the Rohrback Bridge (see chapter 16) and some of the 9th Corps' battlefield beyond, and several detailed views of the field hospital at the Dr. Otho Smith farm. But documenting the conflict's carnage was Gardner's and Gibson's primary purpose. In a most careful study of these two cameramen's work, William Frassanito has identified 70 images that were taken within 5 days of the Battle of Antietam. Brady took a select group of these to his New York City studio on Broadway and Tenth Street in October and put them on display.[42]

An October 6 announcement about this exhibit in the *New York Times* emphasized its macabre content. Viewers would see "blackened faces, distorted features," and "expressions most agonizing." The public thronged to the display. It was a *Times* reporter, whose review of the exhibition was published on October 20, who captured the crux of what Brady, through Gardner's and Gibson's work, had accomplished: "If he has not brought bodies and laid them in our dooryards and along the streets, he has done something very like it." Among the multitudes crowding into the studio, he found "a terrible fascination" with the horrifying images "that draws one near these pictures, and makes him loth to leave them." Everyone, he continued, understood in an abstract way the reality of battles like Antietam, but they were distant events, unless one was personally impacted. What Brady had done was "to bring home to us the terrible reality and earnestness of war," with images so clear it was possible to distinguish individual features of the dead, and "we would scarce choose to be in the gallery" should a relative of one of the dead recognize "a husband, a son, a brother, in the still, lifeless lines of bodies."[43]

CIVILIANS WHO LIVED WITHIN a carriage ride or walking distance of the battlefield could see its carnage for themselves, if they chose. Hundreds—perhaps thousands—of them did so following the Confederates' retreat. Joseph C. Otis, a 1st sergeant in the 35th New York, described citizens "flocking in by hundreds," some of whom had traveled 35 or 40 miles on foot. Many were from Pennsylvania. Some came to see what help they could offer, while others were frantic family members, desperate for information about a son, husband, or father. But the largest number were curiosity seekers, for whom a "broken gun, piece of shell or battered bullet seem to reward their curiosity." Ten days after the battle, James M. Smith, a musician in the 5th Pennsylvania Reserves, reported to his friends that "citizens from all parts of the North are buisy carrying away relics from the field daily." Josiah M. Favill, the adjutant in the 57th New York, was supervising a burial detail on Friday afternoon, September 19, in the Sunken Lane/Piper cornfield area. He was disgusted with the spectators "who flocked to the battlefield like vultures, their curiosity and inquisitiveness most astonishing." Favill and his men watched with a mixture of amusement and anger as they observed hundreds of these people "eagerly searching for souvenirs in the shape of cannon balls, guns, bayonets, swords, canteens, etc." They seemed uniformly "jubilant over the Rebel defeat," and the adjutant was amused by the way "they stared at me. Had I been the veritable Hector of Troy, I could have scarcely excited more curiosity than while in command of this burial party."[44]

Among these civilians on the battlefield was Oliver Wendell Holmes Sr., who had traveled there in search of his wounded son. He took time one day to visit the site, walking over the area of the East Woods and the Cornfield. The dead were mostly buried by the time he arrived, but he nevertheless found the ground "strewed with fragments of clothing, haversacks, canteens, cap-boxes, bullets, cartridge-boxes, cartridges, scraps of paper, portions of bread and meat. I saw two soldiers' caps that looked as though their owners had been shot through the head." He stopped by the dead gray horse of Colonel Strong in the 6th Louisiana, which was photographed by Alexander Gardner. At a position that had been occupied by the Confederates, he found bits of uniforms from both sides, stained dark with blood. He picked up a Confederate and then a Union canteen and contemplated taking them as souvenirs, but he found that "there was something repulsive about the trodden and stained relics of the stale battle-field. It was like the table of some hideous orgy left uncleared, and one turned away disgusted from its broken fragments and muddy heel-taps." He only removed a couple of bullets, a belt plate, and a letter from a wife to her husband, who served in a North Carolina regiment. Holmes kept the missive in the hope, "if it comes in my time," that he could find a way to get it to the woman.[45]

Although both armies buried some of the dead during the local truces of September 18, the bulk of the battlefield burials began the following day. Usually, units that had been engaged—and even some that had not—sent out burial details of varying sizes, commanded by an officer, to do this work, but sometimes entire regiments were assigned to it. This was the case with the 130th Pennsylvania in Morris's brigade of French's 3rd Division in the 2nd Corps, who were convinced they received the unpleasant task of interring the Confederate dead in the Sunken Lane and the Piper cornfield area as a punishment, because Morris disliked them. Lieutenant Favill's burial party was more typical. He was assigned to this duty by his brigade commander, Colonel John R. Brooke. Selection for a burial detail was often voluntary. Edwin Chadwick, a sergeant in the 2nd U.S. Sharpshooters, chose to do so because he wanted to find the bodies of their adjutant and a friend from his company. Griffin L. Baldwin in the 7th Pennsylvania Reserves declined to participate, noting that "I have no great desire to visit a battlefield." Ghastly as the work was, many saw it as a sacred duty to inter their comrades. It was often deeply personal and emotional. Sergeant Ephraim Brown in the 64th New York carried his dead comrades over 500 yards before burying them. Chadwick found the sights on the field "awful," with the bodies of the dead "swollen and disfigured so that we could hardly recognize them except by their clothes." Lieutenant Sam Fletcher commanded the burial party from the 15th Massachusetts regiment, which had 57 officers and men killed. His orders were to be "as quick as I could." They found the ground in the West Woods difficult to dig in.[46] Roland Bowman, who was not a member of Fletcher's group, but came upon them while searching for a dead friend, described how they buried the regiment's dead:

> The trench was 25 feet long, 6 feet wide and about 3 feet deep. The corpes [*sic*] were buried by Co., that is the members of each Co. are put together. Co. H was buried first in the upper end of the trench next the woods. They are laid in two tiers, one [on] top of the other. The bottom tier was laid in, then straw laid over the head and feet, then the top tier laid on them and covered with dirt about 18 inches deep. Henry [Ainsworth, Bowen's family friend] is the 3rd corpes from the upper end of the top tier next to the woods. Mr. Ainsworth, this is not the way

we bury folks at home. I am sorry, but it is too late to have it different. Then there is a board put up at each end of the trench with the simple inscription, '15th Mass. buried here.' There is 39 men in the trench with Henry.[47]

The weather was warm on September 19—75 degrees by 2 p.m.—and Fletcher recorded how the bodies were getting soft, making them more difficult to handle and move. "It was very unpleasant," he admitted, and "I tasted the odor for several days." The 130th Pennsylvania buried nearly 100 Union dead. Their system was to bury each body individually. The body was wrapped in a blanket and interred with a headboard that included the soldier's name and unit. Since there was not yet any governmental cemetery system, the grave identification was to help family members locate a body and facilitate its removal to a home cemetery. Adjutant John Burnham in the 16th Connecticut, who supervised the burials in the spot where his regiment fought in Sherrick's cornfield, sent information on where the regiment's dead were interred to the *Hartford Courant*, so it might be seen by family members. A headboard with the man's name and company marked each grave, but Burnham included a very specific description of where these graves were located, "so that in event of the signs being displaced by the elements or otherwise, they may be found."[48]

During the day, Lieutenant Favill and his men, working at the eastern end of the Sunken Lane, buried 53 Union soldiers on one side, 173 others in two graves on the opposite side, and 82 Confederates. "We dug ditches wide enough to hold two bodies, feet together, heads out, and long enough to hold all those the men had collected. When they were all carefully laid away, we threw over them some army blankets gathered on the field, and then replaced the earth. How many shattered hopes we buried there none of us may ever guess." Favill did not record how many soldiers he had in his detail—except to note that it was "a strong fatigue party"—or how long it took them to bury 308 bodies. Adjutant Burnham's 16th Connecticut group worked from noon until 11 p.m. For one of its members, "the day [the 19th] is a never to be forgotten one to me." They found their dead officers stripped of every bit of "outward clothing." All the bodies—both enlisted men and officers—had their shoes and any valuables removed. When the group finished their work late that night, this man "was glad to rest from the horror of it all." But the gruesome experience lingered, and he remembered how, for the next 6 months, everything he ate or drank "had an odor of dead men in it."[49]

The smell of death—of decomposing bodies—was awful. David Frantz in the 130th Pennsylvania found it "so great it was all most impossible to endure." The 13th Pennsylvania Militia member who visited the field on September 20, detected "an intolerable stench" well before they reached the battlefield. Leander Davis in Battery M, 1st New York Light Artillery, 12th Corps, wrote to his wife that "the stench was so bad that I did nothing but puke for two days." Gardner and Gibson photographed what may have been members of a burial detail

A Union burial detail, possibly the 130th Pennsylvania. The men were standing by the section of the Sunken Lane (*right*) defended by the 6th Alabama. Notice the breastworks, now largely dismantled, that the Alabamians had built from the lane's fencing (*center* and *bottom*), with the rocks (*center left*) probably coming from a nearby stone wall. Also note the large amount of discarded equipment (e.g., *bottom right*). The rise of ground behind the officer on horseback (*top center*) is where the 5th Maryland, the 130th Pennsylvania, and the 14th Indiana engaged the Alabamians. Courtesy of the Library of Congress

sitting on the rock outcropping south of the Cornfield, seemingly calmly gazing on the bodies of seven dead Confederates. The smell of the corpses must have been terribly offensive, yet none of the men in the photographs appear to be wearing bandanas or handkerchiefs over their mouths and noses to ward off some of the odor. Perhaps they found this made no difference, as the fetidness could penetrate anything.[50]

Among the dead interred by Lieutenant Sam Fletcher's 15th Massachusetts burial party was his younger brother James, whom, 2 days earlier, Sam had caught in his arms when James was shot in the head (see chapter 8). James was described by his sergeant as a "brave soldier" and "a sample for a young man to follow, faithful and true." Now Sam buried James with his own hands in Alfred Poffenberger's garden. Sam left no record of his feelings, possibly because remembering the moment was too painful. Wells Bingham, a private in the 16th Connecticut whose brother was killed on September 17, could not bring himself to look at the body when the burial detail found it, because Bingham was afraid he would resemble the other dead he had seen. Private Austin Carr in the 82nd New York was one of the few who recorded his feelings after interring his best friend. His diary entry offers a sense of the emotions men like Sam Fletcher experienced. Carr had volunteered for his regiment's burial detail, hoping he could find his best friend, Fred Morris, who had been cut down during the rout in the West Woods. Morris's last words to Carr were to "give them fits boys, don't let them get me." Carr admitted that "something within me seemed broken" when he had to abandon Morris in order to reach safety. They found Morris's body and Carr helped bury him. "Somehow I felt bitter in my heart against this thing called war," he wrote. "The shoes had been stripped from his feet, a gold ring had been torn from his finger, he had been robbed of the little things that were so very dear to him. . . . We buried him away from the others, on the side of the hill. I could scarcely bring myself to look upon his crude grave, tears gushed down my face in spite of all my efforts to stop them, & so I bid him good-bye & left him there to sleep. The bitter wound in my heart to last forever." Seth Plumb in the 8th Connecticut, who also lost a close friend, was more resigned to the fates of war and its cruelty. "Such are the fortunes of war and we are obliged to accept them," he remarked.[51]

As emotionally anguishing as these experiences were for men like Carr, Fletcher, or Bingham, they provided some measure of closure, as the living knew that their brother, husband, son, or friend, received as decent a burial as circumstances permitted. Confederate soldiers had no such comfort. Except for the relatively small number interred on September 18, the majority of their dead were abandoned, with the Union army having to bury them. Leaving them behind when the Army of Northern Virginia retreated was anguishing. Post-battle letters of survivors are generally silent on this subject, probably because it was too painful to write about. It may also have been to spare those at home further distress by reminding them that their loved ones were left unburied, at the mercy of the enemy. Waters Berryman in the 1st Texas was one the few who did comment on this. He watched his friend Tom Cook fall but was uncertain whether he was killed or wounded. Berryman lamented to his mother, "You have no account of how much I suffer on account of Tom, poor fellow, left in the hands of the Yankees and probably dead."[52]

It was customary for the army that controlled the field after a battle to bury its dead first, then attend to those belonging to the enemy. So it was at Antietam, where the Army of the Potomac assumed this dreadful task. On September 20, a Pennsylvania militiaman watched a burial party at work near the Dunker Church. The Confederate bodies had been on the field for 3 days and "were enormously swollen in limb and features, and their faces blackened." He watched as "men with rails approached a dead rebel, a rail was placed under his knees and another under his shoulders, when the men at each end of the rails carried him to a convenient spot, where they were placed side by side, to the number of from twenty to fifty. A file of men dug a trench at their heads, the dead were placed therein carefully, and then covered. We saw several trenches which had been filled and a shingle placed at the head." The inscription on one of these markers read, "Here Lies 39 DEAD REBS. Killed in Battle, Sept. 17, 1862." Lieutenant Fred Hitchcock, the adjutant in the 132nd Pennsylvania, watched the 130th Pennsylvania and other details bury the Confederate dead at the Sunken Lane and Piper's cornfield. "The work was rough and heartless, but only comporting with the character of war," he wrote. "The natural reverence for the dead was wholly absent," and the corpses were handled as "though they had been so many logs." No blankets covered their bodies, and the graves were sometimes so shallow that body parts were exposed after a rain. David Frantz in the 130th Pennsylvania was one of those whom Hitchcock watched work. Frantz related how they buried 140 corpses in one trench, but "the stench was so great that we could hardly handle" the bodies. They interred the dead until 3 p.m. on September 20, then returned the next morning and worked until noon to get all of the bodies in the area into the ground. By the 21st, the condition of the still-unburied bodies was so offensive that Oliver H. Roe in the 1st Minnesota wrote, "Today the soldiers commenced burning the rest of the dead Rebels, they have decayed so that we have to burn them."[53]

As news of the crudeness of battlefield burials made its way to the home front, it drew criticism, to which a Huntington, Pennsylvania, soldier responded on October 9:

> A report reaches us to-day from "ye ancient borough" which does injustice to many men. It is a complaint by persons in regard to the manner of interring the men who were killed at the battle of Antietam. As you are aware, for 2 days after the battle was fought, the army was in line of battle, expecting a renewal of the engagement. During that time, details from every brigade, were busy collecting the dead and bringing in all the wounded. Now, that you may know how impossible it was to give any better judgment, imagine yourself surrounded by hundreds of dead, not as much as a dozen of picks and shovels among the whole party to work with, and you may judge the disadvantages labored under. Our men secured 2 picks, and took a couple of boards and sharpened them at the end to use as shovels, and with those kind of tools buried 42 men. No one who has any knowledge of the scenes on a battle-field would, for a moment, suppose it possible to get a coffin for any one. . . . No one regrets more than us, that no better burial could be given, but, after doing all that could be done, is it justice to those who did their best, to be talked about for doing it? Not a man who helped lay their companions in their graves, expect any better fate, if it should be their lot to fall on the battle-field. . . . Yet I hear we are greatly blamed. I hope those who blame us may come, and if another battle should take place, they may see for themselves the facilities we possess, in cases of that kind. I assure those same persons, that I very much doubt if they would run the same risk to secure any of us as good an internment.[54]

Trauma

David Hackworth, a highly decorated veteran of the Korean and Vietnam Wars, writes how one of the best noncoms in his company—"a fearless leader"—fell apart in a particularly brutal action in Korea. "He was not a coward—nor, I discovered, were most men who lost their nerve on the battlefield." Hackworth uses the metaphor of a bottle to explain how combat effected people. Each exposure to it filled the container a little. How much an individual could stand varied considerably. "Some bottles are smaller than others," he notes. When a soldier broke down during a firefight, Hackworth describes it as "his bottle has filled up and overflowed," and "no amount of gunpowder will ever make him a real fighter again."[55] In their psychological reaction to combat, the soldiers who fought at the Battle of Antietam 89 years earlier were no different from those who fought with Hackworth in Korea in 1951.

Since the conflicts in Afghanistan and Iraq in the 2000s, a great deal of attention has been paid to post-traumatic stress disorder, as well as to combat stress, or combat trauma. Through the years, the latter has also been called battle fatigue and shellshock, among other names. The two conditions are related, but different. PTSD is long lasting. Emotional trauma from exposure to horrific events in combat may result in PTSD, but it also may gradually subside, allowing the soldier to resume normal activities. Although evidence of the psychological consequences of combat was regularly encountered in the Civil War, they were not understood. Physicians referred to what today we would recognize as combat stress or PTSD as "nostalgia." This term had a broad meaning, and it included soldiers who suffered from depression that may not have been related to their military service.[56]

Post-battle accounts from Antietam survivors include numerous references to the conflict's impact on their physical health. On September 23, Colonel Thomas Welsh, a brigade commander in the 9th Corps, wrote about this to his wife: "I was quite unwell yesterday but this morning I feel alright and in good trim. I had been under such tremendous excitement for several days, that when it passed off the reaction made me quite feverish." Lieutenant Fred Hitchcock, the 132nd Pennsylvania's adjutant, admitted that on September 21, he felt so miserable "as to be scarcely able to crawl about." He also related that the 132nd's lieutenant colonel and major were displaying the same symptoms. "This was due to the nervous strain we had passed through," Hitchcock believed, as well as to the bad food he was consuming. Captain William H. S. Burgwyn on the 35th North Carolina recorded in his diary that he was quite unwell for a number of days following the battle. Writing 29 years after the Battle of Antietam, Captain William M. Robbins in the 4th Alabama related that he was sick for a month afterward and, because of this, never filed an after-action report. Yet his military service records do not indicate that he was ever admitted to a hospital, due to illness. During the fighting, a friend of his had been beheaded by a shell while the two were talking in the West Woods. A short time later, Robbins's brother was killed in the East Woods, and his body had to be left behind when his regiment retreated. We cannot know what accounted for Robbins's absence in the month after Sharpsburg, but stress and emotional trauma seem to be likely reasons. Six days after the conflict, Major Rufus Dawes in the 6th Wisconsin disclosed in a letter that "I have for a day or two been suffering from a severe attack of bilious sick-headache, a result of the late terrible excitement and trying times." This same day, Nelson Dodge in the 2nd Vermont wrote a friend that he could not bear to think of the scenes he had observed on the battlefield. "I feel perfectly lost since the fight for my mess was all killed or wounded that was along with me," lamented the 16th Georgia's Eli P. Landers, after Crampton's Gap. Later on in this letter, he confessed, "My mind is so confused I can't write as I would wish to." Writing a month after the battle, Captain Edwin Drake in the 43rd New York still had not recovered from the harrowing night he spent on September 17 in the terrain immediately south of the Cornfield, among hundreds of the dead and wounded, with many of the latter begging for water or for Drake to kill them (see chapter 19). He told his father that he was utterly worn out and did not know how much longer he could remain in the field. On October 27, 32-year-old Lieutenant James Peacock in the 59th New York, whose men "fell around me like dead flies on a frosty morning," admitted to still being so fatigued that he felt like he was 60 years old. As Sidney Spaulding, an 18-year-old private in the 9th New Hampshire, wrote to his father on September 20, "I hope I shant be in nothr fit I have seen all the fiting I wanted to see." James P. Stewart in Knap's Battery E, Pennsylvania Light, declared to his mother 9 days after the battle, "I will never forget Sharpsburg and vicinity. It is indelibly engraved on my mind."[57]

The slaughter in the West Woods caused Colonel William R. Lee, commanding the 20th Massachusetts—who was an officer of acknowledged courage—to completely come undone. "It seems the horrors of Antietam, his previous fatigues & his drinking, completely upset him," Captain Henry Abbott divulged to his father. Lee was visibly distraught after the battle and refused to give orders or literally do anything. In a September 27 letter, Lieutenant Henry Ropes told his brother John, in confidence, that the colonel "ought to resign immediately," as "he is completely broken down and is not fit for duty." On the morning of September 18 Colonel Lee mounted his horse and disappeared. George N. Macy, another captain in the regiment, discovered him the next day in a Keedysville stable, drunk, with no money, his uniform soiled by diarrhea. Horrified, Macy found a house whose occupants were willing to take the colonel in. Macy undressed him, cleaned him up, and put him to bed. Colonel Lee was able to rejoin his regiment 3 days later, when they had moved to Bolivar Heights, outside Harpers Ferry, but Abbott found him "livid & shaky" and Macy described him as "just like a little child wandering away from home." Lee's wife was summoned, and her presence seemed to help stabilize him, but his soldiering was finished. He resigned on December 17, with a discharge for disability.[58]

Combat was only one of the stresses soldiers in both armies experienced. The Confederates were exhausted from lack of sleep, extremely poor nutrition, and severe marches, which impacted their ability to endure the strain combat placed on the mind and body. Many in both armies were weakened by illness, typically diarrhea from poorly cooked food or bad water. They were not so sick as to be unable to perform their duty—that is, go into battle—but it could affect how they were able to handle severe stress.

Survivors of the Battle of Antietam understood that combat was not a test of manhood. It was draining, debilitating, and traumatizing, producing its own category of casualties, from which some recovered and others did not. David Thompson in the 9th New York wrote that he and his comrades regularly read about how eager the Union army was to be led against the enemy: "But when you came to hunt for this particular itch, it was always the next regiment that had it. The truth is, when bullets are whacking against tree-trunks and solid shot are cracking skulls like egg-shells, the consuming passion in the breast of the average man is to get out of the way. Between the physical fear of going forward and the moral fear of turning back, there is a predicament of exceptional awkwardness from which a hidden hole in the ground would be a wonderfully welcome outlet." Abner Small, a lieutenant in the 16th Maine, observed how "the bravest front, bolstered by pride and heroic resolution, will crumble in the presence of the agony of wounds. Wading through bloody fields and among distorted dead bodies of comrades, dodging shells, and posing as a target to hissing bullets that whisper of eternity, is not conducive to a continuity of action, much less of thought."[59]

Unlike the campaigns and battles of 1864 and 1865; or the experiences of a soldier in Iraq or Afghanistan at the peak of those conflicts; or the fighting in the Hurtgen Forest in 1944, Okinawa in 1945, or the Argonne in 1918, where soldiers were exposed to death or wounds and shocking scenes for days or weeks without respite, Antietam's combatants had nearly 3 months before they engaged in combat again. This period was crucial in helping the survivors process their experiences with comrades who had shared the same ordeal. This allowed them to heal together from the trauma they had experienced. Writing also seems to have aided their recovery. While some men sought to shield their friends and family from war's realities, many used their post-battle letters to document the horrors they had witnessed. "Twas an awful fight mother! And death reigned like an avenging angel over us," penned Captain William Houghton in the 14th Indiana. In his lengthy letter, he described how "I saw my brave boys fall like sheep led to the slaughter. Bryant was shot through the brain. McCord was shot near the heart and while the life blood was gushing from the wound he sat up and with an almost heavenly smile playing in his features, he told us 'he was dying but to mind him not—he was happy and we must go on and avenge his death.'" Captain David Beem, another 14th Indiana officer, expressed his thankfulness to his wife that he had been spared when "at least a half dozen men were killed within six yards of me, and some of them fell at my feet." The *Memphis Daily Appeal* published an extract from a letter from Captain Fred Richardson in the 5th Louisiana, "particularly for the benefit of the numerous friends" of Lieutenant Nick Canfield and his brother William, who were both killed by the same shell that landed in Richardson's company. The shell "plunged through my poor camp, passing first through the body of William, then cut off the leg of John Fitzsimmons, then both feet of D. Jenkins, and passed through my poor friend Nick, entering at the small of the back, coming out of his breast, tearing out and exposing his heart of our lamented friend." Why did Houghton, Richardson, and others feel it necessary to include such gruesome, disturbing details in their letters? Perhaps it was partly to make their recipients understand the cruel realities of the war. Yet such missives were also therapy and release for the writers documenting these frightful things and unburdening their minds to someone they loved and trusted at home.[60]

No one who entered the vortex of combat at Antietam was spared. Men like Fred Hitchcock, Thomas Welsh, William Robbins, and Rufus Dawes recovered and resumed their duties. Others, like Edwin Drake, accepted a discharge in February 1863. Colonel William Lee's war ended soon after the battle. "His bottle has filled up and overflowed," as Hackworth would say. But although Dawes, Robbins, and the others recovered, they were not unscathed. In Hackworth's metaphor, the Battle of Antietam added to what their bottles could hold. How long each could stand the shocks, trauma, and tragedy that lay ahead was unknown, for no one truly got over what they had seen and done. They simply learned to live with it and go on.[61]

22

Civilians

*"When we came back, all I could do was jist
to set right down and cry"*

When the Civil War arrived on his doorstep on September 17, 37-year-old William Roulette had farmed his 198 acres for 9 years. His family included his 27-year-old wife, Margaret; six children, ranging in age from 20 months to 13 years old; and two African American employees. The latter were a young man named Robert Simon, who helped William with the farm work, and 40-year-old Nancy Campbell, who had been enslaved by Margaret's uncle until he freed her in 1859. Nancy assisted Margaret with domestic chores and childcare. Margaret had lived on the farm her entire life. Her brother, John Miller IV, was part of a long line of Millers who had farmed this land for decades. In 1853, John sold the property to Roulette, who grew up on an adjoining farm. It prospered under Roulette. He grew rye, corn, oats, hay, and Irish potatoes; raised sheep for wool; and produced butter and honey. The honey came from beehives Roulette maintained on the west side of his house. South of the farmhouse, he had a 4-acre orchard that provided the family with a plentiful supply of fruit and, possibly, a surplus that Roulette could market. A large vegetable garden was located between the house and the barn. As of the 1860 farm census, he had 8 horses, 14 cows/cattle, 11 sheep, and 20 hogs. There were chickens and turkeys, as well. In addition to the farmhouse, there was a large bank barn east of the house, an icehouse, smokehouse, springhouse and summer kitchen, corncrib, storage building, servants' quarters, and a tenant farm building south of the barn, where a man named A. Clipp lived.[1]

Roulette's neighbor to the south was Henry Piper, who owned a 231-acre farm, bordered on its southern edge by the Boonsboro Pike and, to the west, by the Hagerstown Pike. Piper reflected the difficult political middle ground that Maryland occupied. He was a Unionist, like Roulette, but he had six enslaved people, five of them children. He also employed John Jumper, a free 16-year-old African American man. The racial composition of Piper's and Roulette's households was not unusual in the Sharpsburg area. Nearly 10% of Washington County's population in 1860 were African Americans, of whom 1,677 were free and 1,435 were enslaved. Piper's household, with its mixture of five enslaved and one free African American reflected the county's hybrid economy of slave and free labor by Blacks.[2]

Whether Piper was a true Unionist or adopted that stance to protect his enslaved laborers is unknown, but he reflected the dilemma of those who held people in slavery in this part of the state. As Barbara Jean Fields writes in *Slavery and Freedom on the Middle Ground*, for individuals like Piper, "the middle ground on which unionism and slavery fought as allies had begun to heave and shift." These Marylanders had remained aloof from the Confederates when they occupied the state, because "to join the rebellion would be to sacrifice their remaining leverage with the federal government; and their property, which would become subject to confiscation, lay within easy reach of federal authority." Their enslaved people, particularly after the announcement of the Preliminary Emancipation Proclamation, recognized that the Union army in their midst was now an army of liberation. Farmers like Piper had to walk a tightrope with the Union authorities, to convince them of their loyalty, and those they had enslaved, lest they escape to find employment and freedom within the Federal army.[3]

Roulette's northwestern neighbor was 58-year-old Samuel Mumma, who managed 182.5 acres with his wife Elizabeth and a large household of 10 children, whose ages ranged from 1 to 24. Mumma prospered, like his neighbors Roulette and Piper, which was reflected in his spacious, well-built farm buildings. He was a devout member of the German Baptist Brethren, or Dunkers, and had the financial security in 1851 to donate 4.5 acres for the construction of a permanent church, which became known as the Dunker Church.[4]

When the Confederate army began to arrive in the Sharpsburg area on September 15–16, all of these landowners were advised to evacuate their farms and move their families to safety. The Mummas departed in haste on the afternoon of September 15, with the parents and young children in a two-horse carriage, and the other children on foot. They traveled 6 miles north, to the meetinghouse of the Manor congregation of the Brethren. One of the older sons took their other horses to a safe location, but the family left in such a hurry they brought along no possessions, other than Samuel's gold watch, which he grabbed on his way out of their house. The Pipers fed dinner to Generals Longstreet and D. H. Hill on September 15 and then left immediately afterward, at Longstreet's suggestion. They, too, departed in haste. One of their daughters recalled that they took "only the horses and one carriage." The family drove north to Henry's brother's farm and mill, located along the Potomac River. Roulette remained until September 16, but the growing likelihood of a battle caused him to take his family and employees to the Manor church, where they joined the Pipers and others. Roulette decided not to leave his farm unattended, however. He returned the same day to see to his animals and protect them and his family's personal property from hungry Confederate soldiers. Mumma sent two of his sons on a similar mission to their farm, but the Confederates had already been there. For soldiers in both armies, a vacant home was fair game for foraging or looting, and Mumma's sons found their home in a mess. One of them returned to the Manor church, but Daniel chose to remain, perhaps hoping he could protect their property from further depredations. By the morning of September 17, when the battle began, he reconsidered and left for safety.[5]

Roulette stubbornly refused to leave, and he took shelter in his house's cellar. When Morris's brigade passed through his farmyard, Roulette emerged from his cellar and "shouted excitedly" at the soldiers of the 14th Connecticut: "Give it to em! Drive em!—Take anything on my place, only drive em! Drive em!"[6] But Roulette could not have fathomed the havoc that day would bring to his life. He probably saw the flames and smoke rising from Sam Mumma's farm. One shell went through Roulette's house. Soldiers in the 130th Pennsylvania destroyed his garden fencing, trampled the garden, and knocked over his beehives, for which the bees exacted some revenge. Nonetheless, these were inconveniences, compared with what followed when the army appropriated Roulette's home and farm buildings as an aid station. Throughout the morning, hundreds of wounded men poured in, filling his house, barn, farmyard, and every other building. For men engaged in the work of saving the lives of those torn by bullets and shell, the Roulette family's personal possessions meant nothing. Anything that helped in treating the wounded was appropriated for use: curtains, linens, tables, chairs, blankets, and sheets. Chaplain H. S. Stevens in the 14th Connecticut remembered how "the rooms were stripped of their furnishings and the floors were covered with the blood and dirt of a field hospital."[7]

Several weeks later, Roulette documented his losses. They included all his destroyed beds, comforters, pillows, and quilts. More consequential were the 110 bushels of old corn, 337 bushels of corn, 65 bushels of oats, 10 bushels of rye chop, 6 bushels of seed rye, 60 bushels of wheat, 155 bushels of potatoes, 220 bushels of apples, 350 pounds of bacon, 300 pounds of lard, 200 pounds of sugar, and 11 barrels of vinegar, as well as his hogs, sheep, turkeys, 3 calves, and 12 young pigs. He also noted that 700 soldiers were buried on his property, removing this land from what he could cultivate. He claimed $2,779.99 in household damages and $720.15 for grain and forage, which were sizeable sums in 1862. But the federal government's reimbursement was only $377.37 for those damages directly related to his farm's use as a hospital. While this paltry figure seems heartless, it was better than what many received. Sorting out which damages were incurred by the U.S. Army in appropriating food or personal belongings for the use of the government, as opposed to what was destroyed by an act of war, was often unclear and difficult to accurately document.[8]

The Pipers returned on September 19 and found either 2nd or 6th Corps' troops camped on their farm. One daughter, 22-year-old Elizabeth, described the scene:

When I reached home, I could scarcely recognize the place. I entered the yard, which was covered with bloody clothing, straw, feathers, and everything that was disgusting. I went up the steps and opened the dining room door and was thunderstruck. Great Heaven! What a sight met my gaze. The room was full of dead men! Pools of blood were standing on the floor. I only looked one glance and passed on. I next went into the parlor. The dead had been removed from here, but the carpets were full of stains, the furniture broken up, and everything destroyed. The house had been pillaged from garret to cellar.[9]

The Pipers discovered the bodies of two Confederate soldiers under the family's piano. Astonishingly, most of their livestock had survived the battle and the Confederates' occupation of the farm, but these animals were soon appropriated and consumed by the Union army. Piper's buildings were intact, with minimal damage, for which Piper only requested $25 in compensation. His principal losses were in livestock, grain, household goods and similar items, stored food, and destroyed fencing. A Board of Survey, organized by General John F. Reynolds, who returned from his detachment to Pennsylvania to assume command of the 1st Corps after the battle, assessed these depredations at $2,488.55. In their report, however, the survey members noted that Piper had not produced "any certificate of loyalty." Despite the board's calculations, Piper never received any reimbursement for damages, and this question of loyalty may explain why.[10]

The experience of Maryland landowners after the Battle of Antietam bore many similarities to that of Pennsylvanians after the Battle of Gettysburg. The federal government did not cover damages that resulted from combat, and it only reimbursed farmers when they were lucky enough to get a receipt from the commanders of troops who occupied their property. Philip Pry, whose home was used for a time as McClellan's battle headquarters and as a hospital for 2 months after the fighting had ended, and whose property was occupied by large numbers of troops in the 2nd and 5th Corps, is an example of the frustrations some landowners experienced in working with governmental bureaucracy to recover the cost of damages caused by the U.S. Army. The cavalry escort at McClellan's army headquarters consumed 800 bushels of Pry's wheat. He also lost 20 acres of corn, 150 bushels of apples, 10 sheep, 22 hogs, and nearly all his fencing, which was used as firewood by the troops and the hospital's staff. It took 3 years—until November 1865—before Pry received $2,662.50 in compensation. Compared with Piper, Pry's recompense was quite reasonable, even if it was late. Seven years later, in 1872, he received an additional $1,581.83 for two other outstanding claims. But then someone in the federal government's accounting department determined that Pry had been overpaid, and he was billed $1,209.38. Once one of the most prosperous farmers in the area, the battle had reduced Pry to financially treading water, and this blow was the last straw. Confronted with mounting legal fees and a large repayment owed to the government, Pry was forced to sell his farm in 1874 to pay these bills. He moved to Tennessee.[11]

Roulette's and Piper's losses were serious, but their homes and farm buildings survived the battle intact. Samuel Mumma was not as fortunate. His farm was the only one on the battlefield that was deliberately destroyed. Mumma's springhouse and smokehouse were all that survived the conflagration set by Roswell Ripley's orders (see chapter 5). All of the family's personal possessions and farm equipment were consumed in the blaze. Remarkably, considerable quantities of his corn, wheat, hay, and firewood survived. This was promptly requisitioned by a Union army quartermaster after the battle. When Mumma apparently asked about a receipt for the 592 bushels of corn, 75 bushels of wheat, 16 tons of hay, and firewood that the army had hauled away, he was told that none was necessary, because a government commission was going to settle such accounts. The quartermaster was probably referring to the Board of Survey, which assessed damages to the Piper, Roulette, and Mumma farms. They calculated Mumma's losses at nearly $10,000, but when he filed a repayment request for the supplies taken by the Union army, it was denied, with the declaration that these depredations "were a direct result of the battle and therefore ineligible for reimbursement." His son wrote that his father was greatly discouraged by his devastating losses, but he apparently rebounded and went to work rebuilding his farm and his life. A member of the Army of the Potomac who visited the battlefield in mid-July of 1863 spoke with Mumma: "He has not set down and pined and moaned at his loss. A new house is up, fences are rebuilt. The place has been busy, and now the reaper is in his fields, cutting the grain, ranker, richer, fertilized with human blood."[12]

WARFARE IN THE MID-NINETEENTH century did not cause the type of devastation it would 50 years later with the introduction of high explosive artillery, which leveled entire towns and villages. The buildings on farms like David Miller's and Henry Piper's, which were in the vortex of some of the fiercest fighting, sustained damages but survived intact. The most badly damaged structures typically were in the line of fire from artillery. Even though the guns at Antietam did not wreak the havoc created by those in World War I, a 20 lb. or 10 lb. shell could still cause significant destruction. David Reel's barn, located on Reel Ridge, west of the Hagerstown Pike, was set on fire by Federal guns. The blaze spread so quickly that it killed some of the Confederates' wounded, who were inside the barn and could not be removed in time. The village of Sharpsburg received a deluge of Union shells that overshot Cemetery Hill. A delegation from Lancaster, Pennsylvania, who accompanied a group of volunteer surgeons to the battlefield immediately after the fighting found the buildings in the village "much injured" by artillery. A correspondent with the *Columbus Daily Ohio State Journal* reported that "many houses are pierced with shot and shell, and some burned to the ground; one church was nearly destroyed, and others injured. The largest brick house in the place, owned by a secesh, was pierced five times by shot and shell—one going through the roof, and exploding in the parlor." Lieutenant

Samuel S. Partridge in the 13th New York, who passed through the village on September 19, noted that its buildings were "literally riddled with balls—one church [probably the Lutheran Church on the west side of Cemetery Hill] alone had thirty-two cannon ball holes in it to say nothing of innumerable little bullet marks." Accounts like Partridge's, and the one written by Lieutenant John Bancroft in the 4th Michigan, who noted that "things looked rough" in the village, might suggest a scene of utter desolation, but it cannot be compared with the devastation a French village suffered in 1915. Nevertheless, several structures caught fire, and nearly every residence and public building in Sharpsburg was struck by artillery projectiles.[13]

Reactions by the residents to this damage to their homes and property varied. Elisha Bracken, who came through the village on September 19 with the 100th Pennsylvania, encountered "a buxom lass" who emerged from her home "and hurrahed for the Union, saying that she had been robbed by the dirty, lousy, ragged, half-starved, ornery wretches of rebels." She pointed to "a hole through the house made by a cannon ball, [that] had been made by the Union men and she gloried in it." Bracken then met another woman whose home had been looted by the Confederates and riddled by artillery fire, and she "appeared to be crazy and tore around in a frantic manner."[14]

Except in the handful of cases like Mumma's and Reel's, foraging and looting by the two armies and the use of farms as field hospitals inflicted far greater damage than shells and bullets. The novelist John T. Trowbridge visited Sharpsburg in 1865 as part of his tour of the South and the Civil War's battlefields. A woman who lived on the edge of the village told him that, like most of the other residents, she had left her home before the conflict began. It was a decision she regretted: "When we came back, all I could do was jist to set right down and cry." Her house had been plundered, denuded of food and personal belongings. "Them that stayed at home did not lose anything," she lamented, but vacated homes were fair game. Trowbridge asked who had plundered the most, the Confederates or the Federals? "That I can't say, stranger," she replied. "The Rebels took; but the Yankees took right smart." They consumed all of her food, and her house had been used as an aid station. This latter operation destroyed the family's clothing and bedding, which was used for bandages or as a place to lay the wounded on. Tears welled up in the woman's eyes when she solemnly said to Trowbridge, "It was a right hard time, stranger. I haven't got well over it yet." Moreover, she had lost her father in 1863, after he exhausted himself working to repair and replace their fencing, which had been destroyed in the battle. Of the war's impact on her village, she concluded, "The place a'n't what it was, and never will be again, in my day."[15]

The Hagerstown *Herald and Torchlight* wrote on September 24 that "the amount of personal property—horses, cattle, hogs, sheep, corn, hay, and other provender—which was taken from the farmers was enormous, the whole lower portion of our county has been stripped of every description of subsistence." Much of this was the work of the Confederates. Robert E. Lee's army behaved with good discipline and restraint in Maryland, paying for the supplies it requisitioned with Confederate currency or receipts. Both were worthless to a Maryland farmer, but at least there was a system to the Confederates' procurement methods. There is anecdotal evidence, however, that not everyone obeyed Lee's strict instructions for requisitioning supplies and horses. Aaron Cost, a Keedysville resident, was forced to part with his animals at gunpoint. When Confederate soldiers showed up at Henry Neikirk's farm, looking for the 11 horses he was reputed to own, his stable was empty. First they tried to burn it down. When that failed, they hung Neikirk up by a leather halter, to force him to reveal where he had hidden the animals. Neikirk survived the encounter, however, and the Rebels never did locate his horses. How prevalent such incidents were is unknown, but the evidence we have suggests that they were rare. Stragglers were the ones most likely to commit such acts, and Lee's army left a trail of thousands of them in its maneuvers across Maryland and Virginia. These men were often sick and desperate for food. Others, however, were the the riff-raff of the Army of Northern Virginia and were not bound by the discipline the army exerted within its lines. Lee acknowledged this as a serious problem. On September 22, he wrote to Longstreet and Jackson about "the depredations committed by this army" and the "disgrace and injury to our cause arising from such outrages committed upon our citizens." Lee demanded that these generals work to ensure "greater efforts be made by our officers to correct this growing evil."[16]

It was clear to many Marylanders that Lee's decision to invade the state and offer battle at Sharpsburg had brought calamity to their door. The emptiness of his September 8 proclamation was evident to anyone who took notice. "No constraint upon your free will is intended; no intimidation will be allowed within the limits of this army, at least. . . . It is for you to decide your destiny freely and without constraint. This army will respect your choice, whatever it may be; and while the Southern people will rejoice to welcome you to your natural position among them, they will only welcome you when you come of your own free will," Lee reassured Marylanders. Yet their choice and free will, as was commented on by many in Lee's army, was that they did not view the Confederates as liberators from oppression. Instead, the citizens wished for them to leave their state. Union artillery shells may have inflicted damage on the villagers' homes and caused the fire at David Reel's barn, but it was Lee's decision to make Sharpsburg a battlefield that created the circumstances leading to it. When the Marylanders' free will met the Army of Northern Virginia's strategic considerations, the needs of the Confederacy prevailed, with dire consequences for the civilian population. Captain Francis Donaldson in the 118th Pennsylvania saw this clearly when passing through Sharpsburg on September 19. He remarked on the delight of its inhabitants at the departure of the Confederates and observed that here "were the people he [Lee] had come to liberate, hailing with joy the expulsion of these 'liberators.'"[17]

While Marylanders suffered as a result of the Confederates' invasion and the fighting that resulted from it, they did not lose their freedom. There is no evidence that the Rebels seized any free African American people in Maryland, as they would do 9 months later in Pennsylvania during the Gettysburg Campaign, on the pretext that they were fugitives from slavery. But this restraint in Maryland did not apply to the nearly 1,200 African Americans, including both free and self-liberated enslaved people, who had taken refuge with the Union garrison at Harpers Ferry and were captured when that post surrendered on September 15. A. P. Hill, as the officer charged with handling the administrative details of the garrison's surrender and parole—that is, their pledge of honor as prisoners of war to fulfill the stated conditions of their release—was responsible for how these people were processed. There does not appear to have been any effort to separate free individuals from those who had been enslaved. All were branded as "contrabands of war." Some may have been returned to enslavers who came to repossess their property, but at least two train-car loads of this group of unfortunate people—including men, women, and children—were deemed undesirable as "servants after having associated with the Yankees" and were shipped to Richmond to be sold. First they were marched 125 miles to Staunton, Virginia, and then were transported by rail to Richmond. They arrived there on September 23 and vanished into the enslavement system of the Confederacy. Who provided the escort—whether it was Hill, detaching troops from his division, or the landowners who had held them in slavery—is unknown. What is telling is that the Confederacy allocated at least two train cars from their precious rolling stock to move these people to Richmond, while their army went hungry for lack of supplies.[18]

WHEN UNITS OF THE Army of the Potomac entered Sharpsburg on September 19, the residents greeted them "with every demonstration of joy, men, women and children vying with each other in their desire to make us welcome." But in the days and weeks that passed, the novelty of having a huge army camped in the neighborhood wore off. The field hospitals, which included nearly every farm in the rear of the front lines, proved to be a particular burden. The Federal government was remarkably stingy in compensating these families for the damages incurred. This was partly because the system of compensation was ripe for abuse, which made the governmental agents tasked with investigating such damage claims hypervigilant for potential dishonesty in itemized damages. Yet—even considering the possibility of padding or cheating, which certainly happened—the length of time over which many such requests dragged on, and the number of them that were denied, seems high. For example, Catherine Showman, whose farm was appropriated for Smoketown General Hospital, filed for damages amounting to $1,103.75. An investigating agent awarded Showman $605.50 but was overruled by an appraiser, who reduced the amount to $275.50. Her case was not concluded until 1878. Showman's son Hiram submitted a claim for $6,559 in 1874, but this was rejected, because he could not provide evidence proving he had been loyal to the Union. George Line, whose farm became a large field hospital, asked for reparations amounting to $608.25, but he did not do so until 1873. Why he waited this long to file is unknown, but an investigating agent noted that "short of blood stains," no damage was done to the house and recommended the claim be denied. Joseph Nicodemus, whose farm gave Nicodemus Heights its name, had a number of wounded men on his property for several days. He submitted a claim for $420.37 and received $38.80. But there were also examples of individuals who received relatively fair compensation, such as John C. Middlekauf, whose farm sat in the rear of the 1st Corps' lines and was used as a hospital. He asked for $1,066.87 and received $708.95. Whether evidence of loyalty to the Union influenced who was recompensed and who was not would be a subject worthy of further study.[19]

As Trowbridge's encounter with the woman in Sharpsburg showed, the Army of the Potomac was responsible for its own share of depredations to and burdens on the local community. Major elements of the army remained in the Sharpsburg-Shepherdstown-Williamsport area for weeks after the battle. By September 30, returns gave the army a strength of nearly 100,000 men. This number was half the population of Baltimore, and more than ten times that in Frederick. A visitor from Altoona, Pennsylvania, marveled at the amount of ground the army covered. "The country in this section appears to be naught but a vast military camp," he wrote. "Every field and wood contains a regiment or brigade, and all the roads leading to the camps are filled with baggage wagons. No one can form an idea of the scope of country which it requires to accommodate an army of the size of that now under Gen. McClellan, or the number of baggage, provision, and ammunition wagons necessary to keep it supplied, unless they go and see as we did."[20]

In addition to the large number of soldiers, over 30,000 horses and mules drew the army's artillery and wagon trains and served as mounts for its cavalry and officers. They required immense quantities of grain and hay for feed. Supply depots were established at Hagerstown and Harpers Ferry, as well as in Frederick after the railroad bridge over the Monocacy River was repaired. A system was established where quartermasters could purchase supplies from the local community to make up for shortages from the depots. There were serious kinks in the system, however, that needed to be worked out, and shortages existed. Lieutenant Abner Small in the 16th Maine noted that the issuance of "full rations of good quality" was a rare occurrence, which encouraged the enlisted men to steal food from the locals. He stated that "good food was a luxury. Officers might pay for it, but privates could not afford it unless they foraged and got it for nothing." Army rations that reached the troops were "scanty and bad," and although such raids were forbidden, "it was generally practiced" by hungry soldiers. On

October 1, McClellan issued General Orders No. 159, which reminded officers that "we are now occupying a country inhabited by a loyal population, who look to us for the preservation of order and discipline, instead of suffering our men to go about in small parties, lawlessly depredating upon their property." He required armed patrols to be sent out daily, "to arrest all officers and soldiers who are absent from the limits of their camps" without written permission. To ensure compliance, corps commanders were required to furnish evidence, within 24 hours of receipt of the General Orders, that they had been published in every company in their corps. "The commanding general is resolved to put a stop to the pernicious and criminal practice of straggling and marauding, and he will hold corps commanders responsible for the faithful execution of this order."[21]

While McClellan had issued strict orders against foraging, their effectiveness was only as good as the officers implementing them, and they often looked the other way. Moreover, underfed soldiers were good at eluding the provost guard—and their more diligent officers—in forays to supplement their rations. General George Meade was one of those who firmly enforced McClellan's orders, but he once strayed from a strict application of the regulations. One day in October, Charles S. Wainwright, the 1st Corps' chief of artillery, watched Meade berate and then knock down a soldier in his division who had stolen "a great bundle of corn leaves" and was passing by Meade's tent. The soldier picked himself up, faced Meade, and said, "If it warn't for them shoulder straps of your'n, I'd give you darn'dst thrashing you ever had in your life." Meade, "very much ashamed of himself, cleared out."[22] Many officers were not as vigilant as Meade, however. As a 9th Corps' artilleryman wrote home on September 21, "We are faring well—have plenty of fresh beef every day, coffee, sugar, crackers, as also the corn and apples needed, from the orchards, which are thoroughly cleared. This is a nice country, but the soldiers destroy all the farms they encamp on." The same party of visitors from Altoona were stunned when residents of Hagerstown told them that the Confederates "behaved themselves very well, with the exception of eating them out of everything in the eatable line," but the Pennsylvania Militia "did more damage than the rebels." Henry Brown, in the 21st Massachusetts of the 9th Corps, wrote to his parents on October 2, grousing that because guards were placed by the orchards near their camps "we have to go off 3 to 7 miles to get anything. We go out foraging pretty often but we are in a loyal state and it won't do to steal to much." McClellan's orders did not eliminate the problem, but, as Henry Brown related to his parents, they did make such practices more difficult.[23]

Problematic as the foraging and thievery were, the presence of tens of thousands of soldiers also proved to be a boon to the local economy. Austin Stearns, a corporal in the 13th Massachusetts, related, "If we were willing to travel far enough to some of the farm houses, and had any money, we could get milk and other luxuries." Kathleen Ernst, in her study of Maryland civilians and the Maryland Campaign, describes how "civilian entrepreneurs quickly tried to fill the gap between soldiers' appetites and army food." Local women charged the men for plates of stew or loaves of bread. Others, like John Koogle, hauled apples, potatoes, and cider from some distance away to Sharpsburg, for sale to those in the Union army. But the sheer number of soldiers and the limited amount of food civilians and sutlers could sell them drove prices up, which had the effect of pushing the enlisted men to forage, because they could not afford the prices.[24]

Bullets, shells, foraging, and pilfering all paled in the damage they inflicted on the local population, however, in the face of one other cause. Disease was the most lethal consequence the armies brought to Sharpsburg. Soldiers carried typhoid, dysentery, and smallpox, among other contagions, all of which which caused outbreaks of illness among the locals. Some effects, while noxious, were not deadly. Alexander Root, an enslaved man on the Joseph Nicodemus farm, related how he buried nearly 20 soldiers who were killed or died of their wounds on the farm, "but the smell hung on for a month, there were so many dead men and horses that was only half covered. The stench was sickening. We couldn't eat a good meal and we had to shut the house up as tight as we could of at night to keep out that odor. We couldn't stand it, and the first thing in the morning when I rolled out of bed I'd have to take a drink of whiskey. If I didn't I'd throw up before I got my clothes on." Surgeon Daniel M. Holt in 121st New York wrote of how a great many men in his regiment "are on the sick list with diarrhoeas and dysanteries, and so reduced that we have to get rid of them as soon as possible by sending them to hospitals." On October 8, General Lee informed Confederate Secretary of War George W. Randolph that nearly 4,500 sick soldiers, the size of a large division in the Army of Northern Virginia, "are now accumulated in Winchester, and they are principally, if not altogether, the conscripts and recruits that have joined since we have been stationary. They are afflicted with measles, camp fever, &c." Locals had significant contact with the carriers of these diseases, particularly at the hospitals around Sharpsburg.[25]

Adam Michael's family was particularly hard hit. The 65-year-old Michael was a successful farmer and wagonmaker, with a wife and five grown children who lived at home. He had a farm on Mondell Road, north of Sharpsburg (the road McLaws's division followed to reach the West Woods area), as well as a house in the village. Michael was a Confederate sympathizer, and he and his wife and daughters resisted the efforts of Union surgeons to use their farmhouse as a hospital. Nevertheless, they could not avoid contact with soldiers. Michael's 41-year-old daughter Elizabeth sickened with what was probably typhus and died on October 24. His wife Nancy died a month later. Caleb, their youngest son, who was 27 years old, and another daughter, Catherine, also became ill. They survived, but Caleb "never fully recovered." Typhoid also claimed the life of William and Margaret Roulette's 19-month-old daughter, Carrie May, on October 21. Jacob Miller—who lived in Sharpsburg, across from Adam Michael's home in the village—lost his brother Daniel to dysentery. He noted that "many other citizens and hundreds of soldiers have been taken with the same [typhoid fever and dysentery], and many died." Smallpox arrived in Sharpsburg and Hagerstown in November. How many lives smallpox, typhoid, dysentery, and other diseases took from the civilian population remains unknown, but anecdotal evidence, such as these examples, implies that the numbers were not insignificant.[26]

THE SHARPSBURG AREA SLOWLY recovered in the weeks and months after the Battle of Antietam. Chaplain Henry S. Stevens in the 14th Connecticut visited the Roulette farm at the end of September and was astounded at how the family had transformed their home from the shambles Stevens remembered on September 17. He found their house "cleansed, repainted and refurnished." Roulette's wife Margaret was "presiding at a beautifully and bountifully spread table," with William and their children "safely and cozily about her." Stevens would have had a hard time imagining that disease would penetrate the walls of this happy household and take the life of Margaret's youngest daughter within 3 weeks. When Colonel Ezra Carman visited the battlefield on October 31, although evidence of the fighting remained in the "completely riddled" Dunker Church and trees in the West Woods that were "skinned and seamed" by musket and rifle balls, the ground looked "very differently from what it did two days after the battle," with the dead all buried "and many of the fields ploughed under." A veteran who had viewed the ruins of Samuel Mumma's farm on September 17 would not have recognized it by the summer of 1863, with its fields replanted, fences repaired, and buildings replaced. Yet, on closer inspection, plentiful evidence of the conflict remained for a curiosity seeker or relic hunter. In May 1863, a visitor from Maine found multiple items on the 9th Corps' battlefield: "The ground is about strewn with knapsacks, haversacks, cartridge boxes, cap pouches, boots, shoes, socks, shirts, hats, caps, all tattered and torn—and many other things. Graves and long trenches filled with decaying bodies, are in nearly every field." An Ohio veteran of Antietam who went to the battlefield in mid-July 1863 found a similar situation at the Roulette farm. He wrote that "the ground here is strewn with knapsacks, clothing, hats, caps, cartridge boxes—knapsacks mildewed, mouldy—the names of the owners all obliterated, those who wore them gone, the most of them to long and silent homes." Yet this survivor nevertheless sensed that the land and its people were healing. Standing in Roulette's fields, he took in how "the gentle breeze of the morning rustles the bearded grain—sweet music! It is peaceful here to-day. A stranger would hardly discover that so terrible a conflict had been waged within a year. Time, although a waster, is also a repairer; if he wounds he also heals."[27]

WHILE THE RESIDENTS OF Maryland who were in the path of the two armies felt the most immediate effects of the battles on their soil, the shock waves of Antietam rippled across the nation—from Minnesota to Maine, and from Texas to Florida. Few parts of the North and the South were spared the pain of what had occurred there. The earliest news arrived by reports from correspondents. Much of it was pure rubbish. The September 30 edition of Charlotte, North Carolina's *Western Democrat* shared a story published in the *Richmond Enquirer*, which declared, "We have the gratification of being able to announce that the battle resulted in one of the most complete victories that has yet immortalized Confederate arms." The *Memphis Daily Appeal* reassured its readers on October 1 that although the newspaper did not yet have satisfactory accounts of the great battle, "we know enough to be assured that McClellan has not forgotten how to lie," adding that the Yankees "gained no great victory," and "the advantage of the day was clearly ours." Northern papers had more correspondents traveling with the army, so they had better opportunities to get their stories into print faster than Southern reporters could. The *New York Herald*, in its headlines on September 18, proclaimed, "The Great Rebel Invading Army Annihilated," reporting that it had been surrounded and was out of ammunition. In Evansville, Indiana, the September 19 edition of the *Daily Journal* reported "terrible slaughter of the rebels." It stated that Longstreet and his whole division were captured, the Rebels were in retreat, and "The Lord is on our side." Sensationalism, exaggeration, and pure bunkum were to be expected in the days immediately following a great battle. Major Rufus Dawes related how, later in the day on September 17, two reporters—one from the *New York Times*, and the other from the *New York Herald*—were near his regiment, collecting the names of casualties, when they came under Confederate artillery fire. The *Herald* reporter "got down and hugged the ground like an old soldier," but the *Times* reporter, L. L. Crounse, fled the field on his horse, "a spectacle amusing to the soldiers." The soldiers laughed at Crounse and cheered as he galloped off. The *Herald* reporter's story may have been more accurate, but Dawes noted that Crounse "doubtless got his report in first."[28]

There was shoddy reporting, to be sure, but there was also accurate and honest work from correspondents on both sides. George Smalley, with the *New York Tribune*, left the battlefield at 9 p.m. on September 17 and managed to find transportation to New York City, writing his column on the train from Baltimore. He reached his paper at 5 a.m. on September 19, and his story was published in that day's edition. Smalley described a hard-fought, bloody conflict. He judged the battle's outcome to be "partly a success," but "not a victory," which stood in stark contrast to the outlandish claims of the *New York Herald*, declaring that the Rebel army was annihilated. The *Boston Journal*'s Charles Coffin had a similar experience. He rode to Hagerstown, where he managed to work out rail transportation to Boston. The tone of his column was similar to Smalley's: "Present evidence is not sufficient to warrant any definite conclusion whether the battle was to us a victory or a defeat." For the Confederates, the reporting of Georgia's Peter W. Alexander and Felix G. DeFontaine—who wrote for South Carolina's *Charleston Mercury* and *Charleston Daily Courier* under the pseudonym

"Personne"—stood out for its honesty. In describing a makeshift hospital on the battlefield, DeFontaine did not spare readers from its terrible scenes: "Some were in the last throes of death, and some so mangled and disguised in the clotted blood upon their persons, that their nearest friends would fail to recognize them." Although DeFontaine believed Confederate arms had secured a victory, he admitted that the Union army "fought well and were handled in a masterly manner." Alexander also comforted readers with information that McClellan had been repulsed "with very heavy slaughter," but he concluded that the battle was a draw. He reminded readers of what their sons, husbands, and fathers were experiencing by noting that he was writing his story from a field hospital "in the midst of wounded and dying, amputated arms and legs, feet, fingers, and hands cut off, puddles of human gore, and ghastly, gaping wounds. There is a smell of death in the air, and the laboring surgeons are literally covered from head to foot with the blood of the sufferers."[29]

NEITHER GOVERNMENT HAD ANY system in place to notify the families of those who were killed or wounded. They relied on reporters, state agents, and soldiers to communicate this heartbreaking news to the home front. Casualty lists began to appear in newspapers within days of the battle, sometimes submitted by reporters—such as the ones Dawes encountered on September 17— but often sent directly, by telegram, from army officers. The October 9 edition of the Selma, Alabama, *Daily Reporter* contained a detailed list of every casualty, by regiment, in Rodes's brigade, covering the battles at South Mountain and Sharpsburg. It was provided by Captain Moses Green Peyton, the acting adjutant general of the brigade. If anyone in Selma still imagined that the Battle of Antietam had been a Confederate victory, Peyton's casualty report made it clear that it had been dearly bought. Peter Alexander compiled one of the first casualty lists, which was published in the *Savannah Republican* on September 26. "Col. Newton of the 6th Georgia, Capt. Nisbet commanding 3d Georgia, and Lieut. Colonel Barclay of the 22d Georgia, reported killed," wrote Alexander. The list continued on, filling nearly an entire column of the newspaper and striking grief into the hearts of readers who found the names of family members in it. The *Globe* published Captain George McCabe's September 18 casualty list for Company O, 28th Pennsylvania, on both October 1 and 8. Most compilations simply recorded the men as killed, wounded, or missing. McCabe, however, gave details that helped family members better gauge the severity of wounds: James O'Neal had his leg taken off; Calvin Tobias was wounded in the arm; and John Morningstar in the breast, but only slightly. The captain also appended a sad note: "You will see every third man was either killed, wounded or missing. My Company is about the same as the rest of our regiment. Ed. McCabe was hit three times, but he is not much the worse. Not a man of my company but what has a mark of balls some place on his clothing or arms. My men fired 204 rounds, and were under fire 7 hours. The battle was desperate." Newspapers in the major metropolitan areas had rosters that filled multiple columns, enumerating, by regiment, those killed, wounded, or missing. For example, the September 24 edition of the *Philadelphia Public Ledger* contained a list that filled nearly two entire columns of the front page—in small type—for several Philadelphia-based regiments.[30]

These post-battle catalogs were impersonal. Their purpose was to get information about which men were casualties to the public as efficiently and quickly as possible. But they generated frantic questions. Was a family member really killed? Could it be a mistake? If they were wounded, how seriously? Where were they located? What did "missing" mean? Were they captured, or killed? Thousands of Northerners left their homes to travel to Sharpsburg and find answers. In "My Hunt After the Captain," which appeared in the December 1862 edition of the *Atlantic*, Oliver Wendell Holmes Sr. provided a marvelously detailed account of his odyssey in traveling from Boston to the battlefield to find his son, Oliver Wendell Holmes Jr., who had been wounded in the West Woods with the 20th Massachusetts. Most were unable to afford such a journey, so for them, details about the fate of their loved ones most often came from comrades, officers, or chaplains. Holmes received news of his son's injury by telegram, which arrived late at night on September 17, illustrating how quickly news could travel. In a more typical example, Chaplain William Earnshaw in the 7th Pennsylvania Reserves wrote a letter to Annie Colwell on the night of the 17th: "My Dear Madam, It becomes my painful duty to inform you of the death of your brave husband Capt Colwell who fell while gallantly leading his company on the field of battle." Earnshaw assured Annie that Colwell had been "carefully buried," with the chaplain personally conducting the burial service "while our Regt standing mournfully around gazed upon the scene." The grave had been carefully marked, should she wish to recover his remains, and his lieutenant had possession of his personal effects. Earnshaw offered his deepest sympathy and reminded her that "you have much to be proud of—in such a husband and father. He was heroic, generous & brave—and so he fell—while defending his flag." Annie, as yet unaware of her husband's fate, wrote to him on September 18, expressing her great anxiety "in not having heard from you for so long a time." She mentioned the glowing accounts they were receiving of McClellan's victories, "but the sad after part, the list of killed & wounded, is very much of a mystery." With the Union army being in Maryland, perhaps she could find a home to stay at nearby, "so that I could see you sometimes. Then my mind would be at rest." She next added, like wives and mothers across the North and the South: "My husband may heaven spare your life through all these struggles. Oh! How fervently I pray for your return." The next day Annie received Chaplain Earnshaw's missive, along with two letters, dated September 13 and 14, that her husband had written to her, although they had not entered the postal system until the 18th. Annie may never have learned that her husband had survived the early morning's heavy fighting, only to be felled by a shell, which also killed or mortally wounded four privates in his company, when Sumner ordered the regiment into what one of its members called an "unnecessary position" to cover the retreat of Sedgwick's division. "Poor dear Annie is perfectly overwhelmed with grief," wrote a cousin that same day. She had four young children to raise, and this may have been what enabled her to continue on from the blow that had devastated her life. But her world, like that of thousands of others, was permanently upended.[31]

On September 20, Captain David E. Beem in the 14th Indiana sat down to write to Emaline Lundy, the wife of Porter B. Lundy, Beem's 2nd lieutenant, who had been killed. "I have now to perform the most painful duty of my life," he began, "and one which fills me with grief and sadness. No doubt the intelligence of your husband's death has already reached you, but I would not feel I had done my duty were I not to write you the circumstances of his death." Beem related how Lundy "was cheerful and ever himself," and that "he was near me when the ball struck in the back of the head by what I supposed to have been the fragment of a shell." In these letters, it was important to provide some comfort and meaning for the sacrifice a family had offered the nation. Therefore, Beem added, "Although nothing can repair the terrible loss which you sustain in the death of your affectionate companion, yet it may to some extent soften your sorrow to know that your husband died the death of a brave soldier in defense of his country's right, and in the full performance of his duty. Tell his children that their father died a glorious death; when they arrive at maturer years, they will know they lost an affectionate parent in the great struggle for a priceless government." Beem had tried, with the help of his colonel and brigade commander, to have Lundy's corpse embalmed and sent to her, but it was simply impossible. "It may be a satisfaction to you, however, to know that we buried him decently in a country cemetery [possibly the Mumma cemetery] under a beautiful tree, and have a suitable head board at his grave, so that his resting place can be identified in after years."[32]

Susan Eaglesfield, whose husband George, from Binghamton, New York, was the color bearer in the 89th New York, received a letter from Eli Crocker, a 32-year-old private in George's company. He began, "Dear Friend: My duty is a painful one, and how I wish I was more able to accomplish it. Friend Eaglesfield is gone! Oh! that I could say soothing words. He fell at the battle of Sharpsburgh, on the 17th inst. He was shot through the head while his Regiment was making a most desperate charge against superior numbers of the Rebels." Crocker wrote that he and a comrade had personally buried George. "The Rebels stripped everything from his person, even the likeness [photograph] of his family," but Crocker had cut off a lock of George's hair, which he enclosed, along with the regimental numerals from his cap. A tangible item from the deceased, such as some hair, or a sword, or a pistol and belt—which David Beem sent to Porter Lundy's widow—were crucial in helping families accept the reality of death. In the absence of a body, they would still have a physical reminder of their loved one to comfort them. Drew Gilpin Faust, in her landmark study, *This Republic of Suffering*, has noted how such tokens often helped family members find some resolution when dealing with "the unfathomable and intolerable news that confronted them."[33]

An enduring myth of the Civil War is that because fatalities from disease were more prevalent then than they are today, people were more inured to death and not as devastated as might be the case now. Faust's book and the evidence from Antietam—as well as every battle of the Civil War—demolish this myth. The sudden, violent demise of a loved one is always calamitous. Faust relates the story of Elizabeth Stuart Phelps. The man she loved was killed at the Battle of Antietam. Phelps subsequently wrote a novel, *The Gates Ajar*, published in 1868, about a woman named Mary Cabot, whose brother was killed in the war. Phelps stated that she wrote the book to "say something that would comfort some few . . . of the women whose misery crowded the land." Females were Phelps's primary audience for her novel: "The helpless, outnumbering, unconsulted women; they whom war trampled down, without a choice, or protest." In other words, the Susan Eaglesfields, Emaline Lundys, and Annie Colwells of the nation. Thousands of these indirect victims of war embraced Phelps's work, and she related how, for many years after the novel's publication, "I was snowed under by those mourners' letters . . . signs of human misery and hope."[34]

With the sheer number of casualties from the Battle of Antietam, mistaken identities were inevitable, and the consequences were always tragic. On September 19, a sergeant in the 6th Wisconsin had been sent to Hagerstown to telegraph the news to Fond de Lac that Captain Edwin A. Brown had been killed, and his body was being shipped home. But the noncom blundered, wiring instead that Lieutenant Colonel Edward Bragg had been killed, and it was his body that was being sent. How the sergeant made this mistake is unknown, but the information plunged Bragg's family into grief. "The news was considered reliable almost beyond a doubt," reported the local newspaper. The city council made preparations for a proper funeral for Bragg and sent a delegation to meet the body when it reached Chicago. On September 21, the contingent, to their horror, discovered that the corpse was not Bragg, but Brown. A member of the group then sent a telegraph to Fond du Luc: "The body is Capt E A Brown instead of Bragg. Will be home tomorrow. *Chicago Times* report Bragg wounded in arm." This news brought joy to Bragg's family, and "a dark cloud threw its shadow across another threshold"—that of Brown. "What was gained in one direction, was lost in another." "The results were sensational and very sad," recalled Rufus Dawes, who had been Brown's close friend. On October 1, Bragg's brigade commander, Brigadier General John Gibbon, wrote to Bragg's wife: "I sympathize with you in the distress you have suffered, and as these mistakes are a frequent occurrence the best advice I can give you is that given my own wife. Never to believe your husband is dead until he himself writes you it is so, for ninety nine chances out of a hundred newspaper and telegraph reports are false." Gibbon exaggerated, since most reports from the field were reasonably accurate, considering the conditions under which casualty lists were compiled. But errors did occur, and the results were often heartbreaking.[35]

Soldiers sometimes sought to buoy the morale of those at home by bringing up the cause for which so many had died. "Here let me say to the friends of those who fell on the field, that they died with their guns in their hands, and their face to their foes. But they need no eulogy from my weak pen. Who sacrifice his life in this great struggle will live forever in the memory of his countrymen," wrote a member of the 23rd Ohio in the *Elyria Independent Democrat*. But others offered a more nuanced, less uplifting view. For example, on September 22, James Carr Murray in the 4th Texas wrote to his sister that "both sides stood their ground. Both sides were badly whipped." After listing the many casualties in his company, he concluded his letter by postulating, "It looks like there will not be a Texan left if this little fuss is not settled soon." Thomas Hamill, a private in the 57th New York whose September 30 letter to his brother-in-law was published in the *Brooklyn Daily Times*, was highly critical of the handling of Meagher's Irish Brigade:

> I again assert, that had the officers done their duty promptly, and mistaken no orders, there would not have been such slaughter to record in the Irish Brigade. It may appear very well to see the names of all the noble heroes who fell on that memorable day, heralded in print in the various journals to a gaping multitude; but if through incompetency, cowardice, or other causes, these noble fellows were sacrificed through blundering officers, 'tis but a poor consolation to their friends to see the name of the loved one arranged alphabetically in the newspaper column as an item of news. Give me the commander who will cause the greatest loss to the enemy, with the least possible loss to his own command; such a one was poor Colonel Parisen."[36]

Even before the Battle of Antietam, support for the war in the Irish community in New York City was declining. On July 25, Thomas Meagher's appeal for recruits, delivered to a crowd of 5,000 in the city's National Guard Armory, managed to attract only a paltry 120 volunteers. Antietam's carnage in the brigade's ranks only strengthened the growing opinion among New York City's Irish population that their sons, husbands, and fathers were being sacrificed in a war that offered their people nothing but more suffering. Lincoln's Emancipation Proclamation, followed by the bloodbath of the Battle of Fredericksburg in December 1862, added more fuel to their opposition to the Civil War, which continued to build until it exploded into the violence of the New York City draft riots in July 1863.[37]

LEMUEL STETSON, FROM PLATTSBURGH, New York, was among the thousands who traveled to Sharpsburg to find answers about the fate of a family member. Stetson had a distinguished career as an attorney, a politician—including serving in the U.S. Congress from 1843 to 1845—and a judge. His son John was a lieutenant colonel in the 59th New York of Sedgwick's division. He had seen his son's name on the list of casualties published in the September 19 edition of the *Albany Journal.* Stetson started for the battlefield that night and reached Baltimore the next afternoon, where he went to Jarvis U.S. General Hospital in that city, hoping he might learn something about John. Here he met two wounded privates from the 59th who had just been brought in. They gave Stetson little hope. As far as they knew, his son had been killed. Joined by "many others," Stetson boarded a special train that carried him to Frederick where his group found transportation to the battlefield via wagon and ambulance. Reaching Keedysville, he found the hospital for Sedgwick's division. The many wounded men within it from the 59th confirmed what the privates had already told him—that his son John had been killed. The regimental commander, Colonel William Linn Tidball, had written this news to Stetson on September 20, but Stetson did not receive the letter, because he was traveling. When he visited the regiment in the field, he learned that his son's body had been rifled by Confederates, who stole his hat and boots. They also took John's wallet, but a Confederate officer returned it to a wounded lieutenant in the 59th New York, "saying it contained nothing of value which they wished to keep." Stetson drove to the West Woods, where he easily found his son's grave, which was "rude and imperfect, like all soldiers' graves upon the field." The trees near it were scarred by bullets, and 8 feet east of it, the top of an oak tree, felled by an artillery round, lay on the ground. "The marks upon the trees are so thick that it is wonderful that any one could have stood there in that conflict unharmed," Stetson observed. He was able to assemble a detail of men from the 59th, and on the morning of September 23, he had them dig a more substantial grave. Later, he had the body removed for reburial in Plattsburgh. Stetson never shared his emotions on finding where his son was initially interred, but he did record how visiting some of the field hospitals in the area, terrible as they were, lifted his spirits. Within them, he found "men with bodies otherwise disfigured, and yet men who talked and cheered, smiled and thanked God that it was no worse with them," even though they were missing an arm or a leg. Stetson, a lifelong Democrat who had campaigned for Stephen Douglas in 1860, left Sharpsburg strengthened in his belief in the justness of the cause for which his son had fallen. "The curse of mankind, war, is upon us," he wrote in a letter published in the *Albany Atlas and Argus* on October 2, "and yet it is only by war—vigorous, earnest, resolute war to the knife—war in the minds and hearts of our people at home, as we see and feel the horrors of the front, and in the track of the battle, that we can save our nationality and preserve to us, or recover for us, the respect of mankind."[38]

Many who came to the battlefield searching for the graves of family members never found the closure Stetson did. A local woman recalled a young wife "whose frantic grief I can never forget." By the time she reached the battlefield, her husband had been dead for two days and was buried. She refused to believe he was killed and insisted on seeing his body. When they brought her to the grave and began to open it, the woman threw herself on top of it and, "in her agonizing grief, clutched the earth by handfuls where it lay upon the quiet sleeper's form." The men uncovered enough of the corpse to reveal her husband's face, which drove home the reality of her loss. "Passive and quiet beneath the stern reality of this crushing sorrow," she departed. Another woman, whose brother in the 12th New York died from his wounds on October 16, wrote to those who had interred him, thanking them for their care and for seeing to the burial. But a month or so later, she wrote again, asking them to reopen her brother's grave, to make certain "that it was *indeed* her brother." Such tragedies were common in the weeks following the battle. Medical Director Jonathan Letterman complained of the "great many citizens" who arrived at hospitals to remove their injured family members, in the belief that if they could only get them home, they might save their lives. "It was impossible to make them understand that they were better where they were, and that removal would probably be done with the sacrifice of life," he wrote. "Their minds seemed bent on having them in a house. If that could be accomplished, all would, in their opinion, be well." Letterman did not yet understand why good air circulation was important to healing, but he knew from experience that the wounded did badly in spaces without it. Letterman was rightly proud of the work of the medical services, but, as we have seen, the conditions at some field hospitals, particularly in the period immediately after the fighting, were so awful that families probably increased the prospect of recovery for their wounded loved ones by removing them.[39]

WIVES AND MOTHERS OF Union soldiers who were killed or who died from their wounds in the Maryland Campaign could at least seek some financial compensation for their loss by applying for a pension. An Act to Grant Pensions, which Congress passed on July 14, 1862, made it possible for wives, children under 16, and mothers who were widows and could prove that a son was providing financial support to apply for a pension if their husbands, fathers, and sons had been in the service and lost their lives or were disabled in combat. This system, like the one for damage claims, was ripe for abuse, which made the approval process tedious and lengthy. A wife was required to submit proof of the marriage. Then the Pension Bureau had to verify the deceased or incapacitated soldier's service, his death or disability, whether there were children under age 16 (with proof of their birth dates), and the loyalty of the individual applying for the funds, among other things. All of this took considerable time and a lengthy correspondence. If granted, the benefit was meager—$8 a month for a private, $16 a month for a first lieutenant, and so forth—but for some families, it could mean the difference between utter destitution and the ability to avoid eviction and keep food on the table. After the death of her husband George, Susan Eaglesfield began the process of securing a pension on November 18, 1862, when she entered the office of Charles O. Root, the clerk for Broome County, New York. Susan brought two witnesses with her who could attest that she was who she claimed to be, as well as Jesse Richards, the justice of the peace who had married Susan and George on January 21, 1846. She also documented the ages and birth dates of her five children, all of whom were still living at home with her. On January 14, 1863, the Adjutant General's Office acknowledged receipt of the application and confirmed both George's service in the 89th New York and his death at Antietam. It took until October 19, 1863, however, before Susan was approved for an $8 per month benefit, plus an additional $2 per month for each child until they reached their sixteenth birthday. The pension was backdated to September 17, 1862, and included the provision that if Susan remarried, she would forfeit further payments.[40]

Susan Eaglesfield's was a typical, straightforward case. Some were more complicated. One such involved Catherine Brown of Brookfield, Massachusetts, the widow of Shepherd Brown in Company F of the 15th Massachusetts, who was killed in the West Woods. They were married in 1860 and had no children. She did not file for a pension until February 11, 1863, and was eventually approved to receive $8 a month. In 1870 she took a position as a housekeeper for Henry M. Spencer. Soon afterward, she stopped collecting her benefit monies, admitting 7 years later she had done so because "scandalous reports were circulated in regards to my relations with him [Spencer] to the effect that I was living in adultery with him and that on that account my pension would be stopped and fearing that assaults would be made upon my character I forbore the attempt of its collection." Spencer was married, but he had been separated from his wife "for a long time." Unbeknownst to Spencer and Catherine, his wife had passed away. After they learned this, they were married on August 29, 1877. After the marriage, Catherine wanted the missed pension payments she believed were due to her, but which she had not collected for the last 7 years. Remarkably, the Pension Bureau—known for being tight-fisted and ever suspicious of corruption—investigated, agreed with her request, and approved the payment.[41]

The Confederacy had no pension system for wives, widows, children, and parents. But the family could seek to recover whatever back pay was owed to the deceased. The restitution procedure was no more efficient or faster than the U.S. government's pension system. Sergeant Joseph R. Herring, a farmer from Wayne

County, North Carolina, was among those killed in the Sunken Lane with the 2nd North Carolina. On November 25, 1862, Alvia Herring, Joseph's father, entered the office of John Coley, the justice of the peace for Wayne County, to make a claim for his son's unpaid wages up to the time of his death. He brought George C. Moses with him to verify that Alvia was Joseph's father, and that Joseph had neither a widow nor a child who could request this money. The claim slowly wound its way through the Confederate bureaucracy, which needed to verify Herring's service, his pay records, and any bounties owed to him—as well as his death. On July 10, 1863, a clerk at the Comptroller's Office of the Treasury Department confirmed that Alvia Herring was due $77.63 in back pay and a $50 Confederate States bounty from his son's account. In another instance, it took Victoria A. Vickers, the widow of Benjamin Frank Vickers in the 6th Alabama, until September 10, 1863, to receive $85.63 from her deceased husband's back pay and clothing allowance. Colonel John B. Gordon had written that "there was no better soldier in either army than Vickers." During the fighting, Gordon asked for a volunteer to carry a message to G. B. Anderson's brigade. Vickers immediately offered to do so, "with some characteristic remark which indicated his conviction that he was not born to be killed in battle." He made it a few steps before a bullet through his head ended his life and left Victoria a widow, with meager compensation for his courage.[42]

FAMILIES ACROSS THE NORTH and South who had lost fathers, sons, brothers, sweethearts, and relatives at Antietam grappled with finding meaning in their deaths. In the North, some families, like that of Captain Edwin Brown, were able to have the corpse shipped home for burial. Embalming facilities in the Sharpsburg area after the battle were limited, which made it difficult to transport bodies over a sizeable distance. The graveside services for those whose remains made it home gave communities an opportunity to grieve for the loss of a son or sons, provided closure for the family, and both extolled the character of the deceased and articulated what he or they had died for. The body of Captain Albert Bartlett in the 35th Massachusetts was sent to Boston, arriving there on September 23. It was transported from there to Newburyport, Bartlett's home town, by a group of town councilmen and alderman. When the group arrived, "all the bells in the city were tolled, flags were displayed at half-mast, and the citizens generally closed their stores and suspended business for several hours." The coffin was carried into Pleasant Street Church, "which was literally jammed with soldiers and citizens." A dirge was played, scripture was read, and there were remarks by two men who had known him. Then the funeral proceeded through town to the cemetery. Boston's *Saturday Evening Express* reported that "the collection of people was immense, the streets through which the procession passed being one mass of humanity." That same day, in Kittaning, Pennsylvania, funeral services were held for Captain Wilson Colwell in the 2nd Wisconsin, who had been mortally wounded at the Battle of South Mountain. "His remains were brought to this, the home of his childhood, to be deposited in the cold, narrow grave," wrote Frank Hatch, Colwell's original first lieutenant, who had been wounded and discharged after First Bull Run and was in attendance. At his grave, "the heart bleeding widow," plus Colwell's mother, his sisters, and friends and relatives, said their final goodbyes. Hatch employed a realistic but determined tone in assessing the meaning of Colwell's death: "Farewell, fond loving husband and father; faithful son and loving brother, kind, genial and noble friend; brave soldier and patriot—farewell!—buried, but not forgotten; dead, but still living— living in the hearts and memories of a grateful people, as one who died in de- fense of his country and the glorious cause and sacred rights of humanity." The "unnatural and wicked rebellion" cried out for "more blood—more sacrifice— more weeping, more treasure," yet, Hatch counseled, "the reward will be equal to the sacrifice, and by the graves of our brave dead, will we trace the history of our government; and learn the value of our country."[43]

When it was not possible for a physical body to be present, a memorial arti- cle in a local newspaper might take the place of a funeral service. On December 3, the *Charleston Mercury* published a laudatory piece about Major William Capers White in the 7th South Carolina, killed during his regiment's assault across the Dunker Church plateau. It was written by a member of the regiment and ex- pressed themes similar to those in countless other funerals or memorials across the North and South. "When example was necessary to stimulate his men to great exertion," White "was foremost in deeds of heroic sacrifice and daring." As the regiment charged across the plateau, his last words were, "We can take that battery—forward!" The Federals sent his body on through the Confederates' lines on September 18, and his comrades buried him near Cemetery Hill. "Thus ended the career of a truly brave and noble man, whose life had been usefully and honorably spent, and whose death illustrated the heroism of his nature." Drew Gilpin Faust has remarked that these sermons and memorials about the dead serve to "ensure that dying was not an end, not an isolated act, itself un- dertaken in isolation, but a foundation for both spiritual and social immortality— for eternal life and lasting memory." They also gave meaning to a person's death and strengthened the public's commitment to what that individual had died for. In the case of Colwell, he was killed "in defense of his country and the glorious cause and sacred rights of humanity." White's "noble sacrifice" was done for "his country's good," and this made his example and memory "precious in the esteem of his fellow citizens, while his country records his name among those of her cherished sons who have nobly perished in her defense." White's memorial dif- fered from Colwell's in one significant element. The major had been an overseer before the war and had brought an enslaved "old negro" with him when he joined the Confederate army. The major and his Black body servant clearly had a per- sonal bond. When the latter learned of White's death, the old man "sat down and wept like a child." He asked permission to pass through the lines to recover the major's body, and when this was refused, "his grief seemed to increase tenfold." All day on September 18, he sought an opportunity to reach White's corpse, and when he was ordered to the rear, he begged the memorial's author "to use every means to recover his master's remains." On the morning of the 19th, as the army began its retreat to Virginia, apparently aware that White had been buried, the Black man packed up the major's personal belongings and left for South Carolina. "An instance of greater devotion I never saw." In this encomium, composed after Lincoln's Preliminary Emancipation Proclamation, the writer used White's life and death, and his body servant's grief, for the additional purpose of affirming and reassuring worried readers about the loyalty of their enslaved people.[44]

Not everyone could find meaning in the death of their family members, or comfort in sermons or memorials that spoke of the glorious cause for which they had given their lives. The father of the 11th Connecticut's Alvin Flint Jr. was one who found no solace in his son's demise beside the Rohrback Bridge on September 17. Alvin Sr. had followed his oldest son into the army in the summer of 1862, at age 53, along with his youngest son, George, who was only 13. The two enlisted in the 21st Connecticut. In the previous 13 months, Alvin had lost his wife and daughter to consumption, and he may have been driven to join the army by the painful memories surrounding him at home. He was sent to Sharpsburg in October and detailed to the Ambulance Corps. During his time there, he attempted, unsuccessfully, to locate his son's grave. In a letter he wrote to the *Hartford Courant*, he referred to Antietam as "'Antie-dam,' where my boy was brutally murdered." Attending a church service provided him with no comfort. "Oh that I could have viewed the text as Jacob did, but to me the place was dreadful in the extreme, where my dear boy had been cut down in a moment with no one to say a word to him about the future. Oh how dreadful was that place to me, where my dear boy had been buried like a beast of the field!"[45]

THE CARNAGE, HORROR, AND tragedy of Antietam shocked both the North and the South, but it did not weaken the resolve of either side or inspire a spirit of reconciliation or compromise. Bloody battles rarely do. Typically, they accomplish the opposite. Many prayed for an end to the wicked rebellion and for peace—but on terms that brought victory for their side. If anything, the scale of the sacrifices and the vast quantity of spilled blood served to strengthen their determination to avenge their losses by doubling down on the righteousness and justice of their cause, thereby steeling themselves for a long, brutal conflict. Even in his grief, Alvin Flint Sr. did not think of abandoning the war that had taken his son's life. He declared, "If my life is spared, I shall knock out some of the props that hold up this uncalled for, and worse than hellish, wicked rebellion!"[46]

23

Emancipation

"We like the Proclamation because it lets the world know what the real issue is"

Despite McClellan's claim that he had "defeated Lee so utterly," in purely military terms, the Battle of Antietam was a tactical draw. Lee's subsequent retreat to Virginia gave McClellan a crucial *operational* victory in the campaign, but it was President Lincoln who seized the moment and turned Antietam into a *strategic* victory. At a special meeting on September 22, only a day after confirmation that the Confederates had evacuated Maryland, the president presented his Preliminary Emancipation Proclamation to his cabinet. He invited their critique of the document, but not their opinion on whether it was the proper moment to publish it. "He was satisfied he was right," recorded Secretary of the Navy Gideon Welles. "His mind was fixed, his decision made, but he wished his paper announcing his course as correct in terms as it could be made without any change in his determination." A "long, earnest," and, Welles thought, "harmonious" discussion ensued. Postmaster General Montgomery Blair expressed the opinion that while he approved of the proclamation's principle, he objected to it on the grounds that he believed the Border States would secede from the Union the moment it was read, and that it would give Democrats a club "of which they would avail themselves to beat the administration." Lincoln had long considered these risks and was willing to accept them. He replied to Blair's objections by noting that he had made every effort to find a compromise acceptable to the Border States, without success. It was time to move forward without them. As for the Democrats, "their clubs would be used against us take what course we might." Welles reflected the other cabinet members' general opinion of the proclamation when he recorded in his diary, "It is momentous both in its immediate and remote results, and an exercise of extraordinary power which cannot be justified on mere humanitarian principles, and would never have been attempted but to preserve the national existence. The slaves must be with us or against us in the War. Let us have them."[1]

Although Lincoln made the proclamation public that same day, its provisions would not take effect until January 1, 1863, giving the Confederates time to reconsider their rebellion and return to the Union. No one except dreamers imagined this would happen, but Lincoln could at least say he had offered fair warning of what was coming. Others have discussed the politics of the Emancipation Proclamation more thoroughly than is appropriate here, but in a strategic sense, it struck two vital blows for the Union. On its surface, which was as far as many people went in considering it, the proclamation was ludicrous. Enslaved people in the Border Sates were not freed, nor were those in areas under Federal control, such as Tennessee, western Virginia, and other points in the South. The overwhelming majority of of them remained behind Confederate lines. Thus the proclamation appeared to free those individuals over whom the Union had no control. Lincoln understood that the U.S. Constitution did not give him the right to move against slavery in areas loyal to the Union. Only a constitutional amendment could do that. But by exercising his war powers as president, he had seized the moral high ground in the conflict. Union armies would now be armies of liberation. Federal forces would now fight not only to preserve the Union, but also to destroy slavery. Coming on the heels of McClellan's military success in Maryland, the proclamation sucked much of the wind out of the sails of those in Europe lobbying for recognition of the Confederacy. Before the Battle of Antietam, momentum had been building in Britain to offer mediation to end the conflict in America. In France, Louis Napoleon, a Confederate sympathizer, supported such an idea, but he did so for his own imperial and colonial reasons. In Britain, News of Lee's retreat to Virginia cooled the enthusiasm of Prime Minister Viscount Palmerston, who wrote in October that the battles in Maryland appeared to have "set the North up again," and "the whole matter is full of difficulty, and can only be cleaned up by some more decided events between the contending armies." As James McPherson has observed in his Pulitzer Prize–winning history of the Civil War, *Battle Cry of Freedom*, "to accept the notion that the South fought for independence rather than slavery required considerable mental legerdemain." As long as emancipation was not a Union war objective, Britons could exercise such mental dexterity, but Lincoln removed this with the Emancipation Proclamation. Frederick Douglass was someone in the United States who saw this clearly. He wrote that the proclamation

> places the North on the side of justice and civilization, and the rebels on the side of robbery and barbarism. It will disarm all purpose on the part of European Government to intervene in favor of the rebels and thus cast off at a blow one source of rebel power. All through the war thus far, the rebel ambassadors in foreign countries have been able to silence all expression of sympathy with the North as to slavery. With much more than a show of truth, they said that the Federal Government, no more than the Confederate Government, contemplated the abolition of slavery.[2]

Foreign Secretary Lord John Russell and Chancellor of the Exchequer William Gladstone nevertheless attempted to push forward with a plan for mediation, but it died in cabinet. A second effort by Louis Napoleon's France to push for a 6-month armistice likewise failed when Russia, followed by Britain, rejected it. Military victory in Maryland and the Emancipation Proclamation had helped Lincoln secure his international flank. It was not an impregnable line, as emancipation would only be achieved by an overall Union victory on the battlefield, but it was a crucial strategic and political success.[3]

The proclamation also struck a powerful blow at the foundation of the Confederacy's economy and its ability to make war. Enslaved people provided the Confederacy with an immense labor force in agriculture and industry, which allowed it to mobilize large numbers of able-bodied white men into the army, while still producing the matériel of war and food to sustain their armies. When the U.S. Sanitary Commission's inspector, Lewis H. Steiner, observed what he estimated were 5,000 enslaved African American accompanying the Army of Northern Virginia when it passed through Frederick on September 10, he noted how the Confederacy employed its enslaved people to its advantage. In the Union army, white soldiers had to be detailed from the line regiments to perform some of the same tasks done by enslaved individuals in the Confederate army. Although the Confiscation Acts encouraged those held as slaves to escape to Union lines, the Emancipation Proclamation provided the legal justification to declare them free when they arrived there. This meant that the Confederacy would need to maintain a certain percentage of its manpower on the home front, to prevent leaking its captive labor force to freedom. The proclamation also fueled the long-standing Southern fear of a slave insurrection. Lincoln understood that such a rebellion was extremely unlikely. First, because organizing one required a level of coordination that was almost impossible among the enslaved population. Second, many of the white male Southerners were mobilized into armies, which could easily crush any insurrection. Third, most of those who were enslaved had no wish to kill anyone. They simply wanted their freedom. What held more significance for Lincoln was that as his armies pushed into the South and Blacks who were not free fled to Union lines, not only did the Confederacy lose the labor represented by these individuals, but the males often found work with the Union army as teamsters and laborers, which meant that their enforced labor was now turned against their enslavers. When the final proclamation was issued on January 1, 1863, Lincoln included a provision that enabled the Union army to enlist African Americans, including those who were fugitives from slavery, into the Union army, turning the Rebels' enslaved labor force into a weapon that could be used against the Confederacy. Ultimately, nearly 200,000 African Americans—nearly 10% of the Union's total armed forces—would serve in uniform by the war's end.[4]

REACTIONS TO THE EMANCIPATION Proclamation in the Army of Northern Virginia were unsurprising. Robert E. Lee, who had his hands full with rebuilding and reorganizing his army and getting control of his problem with stragglers, made no known reference to it until a letter on October 2 to President Jefferson Davis, where he referenced both the Emancipation Proclamation and Lincoln's suspension of the writ of habeas corpus on September 24. Referring to Maryland and the prospect that it might be drawn into the Confederacy, Lee wrote, "The military government of the United States has been so perfected by the recent proclamations of President Lincoln, which you have no doubt seen, and civil liberty so completely trodden under foot, that I have strong hopes that the conservative portion of that people, unless dead to the feelings of liberty, will rise and depose the party now in power." It was not until January 10, 1863, in reaction to an order from Union General Robert H. Milroy to the citizens of Winchester and those in other parts of Frederick County, Virginia, regarding enforcement of the Emancipation Proclamation, that Lee offered his opinion about Lincoln's policy in a letter to Confederate Secretary of War James Seddon. Milroy had pronounced that anyone who resisted the peaceful implementation of the proclamation would "be regarded as rebels in arms against the lawful authority" of the Federal government. This meant that any civilian who was perceived to be resisting the terms of the proclamation could be considered an enemy combatant. Enraged, Lee denounced this "savage and brutal policy he has proclaimed, which leaves us no alternative but degradation worse than death, if we can save the honor of our families from pollution, our social system from destruction, let every effort be made, every means employed, to fill and maintain the ranks of our armies, until God, in his mercy, shall bless us with the establishment of our independence."[5]

Many of Lee's soldiers, their days consumed with practical matters—such as finding enough to eat, or obtaining shelter and adequate clothing—never bothered to comment on the Emancipation Proclamation at all. To most, it was merely a confirmation of what they had believed from the beginning of the war—the Yankees were bent on destroying slavery and smashing the entire fabric of Southern society. Before the Seven Days Battles, Longstreet invoked former Republican presidential candidate and Union general John C. Fremont, whose own emancipation proclamation (which Lincoln rescinded) in Missouri in August 1861, in order to remind his men what they were fighting for: "Already has the hatred of one of their great leaders attempted to make the negro your equal by declaring his freedom. They care not for the blood of babes nor carnage of innocent women which servile insurrection thus stirred up may bring upon their heads." As John F. Shaffner, the 33rd North Carolina's surgeon, wrote in early October, "The recent proclamation of Lincoln have infused new determination among our soldiers, and therefore cannot possible do us additional harm. . . . To declare our slave free & to free them are quite different things. There is danger now that we may drift into a wholesale war of extermination."

Samuel A. Burney, an enlisted man in Cobb's (Georgia) Legion, seethed to his wife, "What a spectacle will that be when Abraham Lincoln stands before his God with the blood of hundreds of thousands of his countrymen's flesh on his hands." In his classic study of the Army of Northern Virginia, Joseph Glatthaar has observed that "Southerners perceived Yankees as a distinct set of beings, wholly different in behavior and motivations from themselves." Some even referred to Yankees as a distinct race of people. Aaron Sheehan-Dean points out that both Northerners and Southerners "believed that each had an exclusive claim to a just cause," and that these avowals "revolved around competing visions of the meaning of freedom." For the Confederates, theirs "was a vision of freedom that required slavery." To Lee's soldiers, the Emancipation Proclamation was merely a reminder of the "degradation worse than death" that defeat in the war would mean for them and their families.[6]

REACTIONS IN THE ARMY of the Potomac were mixed. The narrative that existed for many years was that the soldiers broadly rejected the tenets of Emancipation Proclamation, but the reality is that opinions in the Union army were divided along political lines. In September 1862, there was a considerable body of men whose views were still being formed and, thus, adopted a wait-and-see stance. Democrats generally opposed the proclamation, and Republicans mainly supported it, although there were exceptions in both camps. McClellan's reaction was predictable. Lincoln had done precisely what McClellan had explicitly warned him not to do in his Harrison's Bar letter in July (see the prologue). Two days after learning about the proclamation, he wrote his wife that it was doubtful he would remain in the service much longer. "The Presdt's late Proclamation, the continuation of Stanton & Halleck in office render it almost impossible for me to retain my commission & self respect at the same time. I cannot make up my mind to fight for such an accursed doctrine as that of a servile insurrection—it is too infamous." A day later he wrote to New York businessman William H. Aspinwall, a longtime supporter who, before the Civil War, set McClellan up as superintendent of the Ohio and Mississippi Railroad. The general respected his political counsel, even if he did not always act on it: "I am very anxious to know how you and men like you regard the recent Proclamation of the Presdt inaugurating servile war, emancipating the slaves, & at one stroke of the pen changing our free institutions into a despotism—for such I regard as the natural effect of the last Proclamation suspending the Habeas Corpus throughout the land." If McClellan's name was removed from this correspondence, one might imagined these could be the letters of a Confederate officer. As McClellan's biographer, Ethan Rafuse, has pointed out, the army commander believed slavery was already being gradually destroyed, and the Emancipation Proclamation was an unnecessarily inflammatory document that would not hasten its end, but only prolong Southern resistance. On that point, Lincoln would have vigorously disagreed. America's experience with slavery had established its resiliency.[7]

Fitz John Porter, McClellan's most loyal subordinate and fellow conservative, used his back channel with the sympathetic press to serve as a proxy for his chief in condemning the Emancipation Proclamation. In an extraordinary 14-page letter to Manton Marble, editor of the *New York World*—which Zachery Fry, in his *A Republic in the Ranks*, notes was considered "the gold standard of antiradical journalism"—Porter shared his opinion on Lincoln's emancipation policy. Whether McClellan encouraged Porter to write the letter or not, Ethan Rafuse states that it "so well articulated McClellan's own views that there can be little doubt that Porter received considerable input from his commanding general as he wrote it." Porter offered a vigorous defense of McClellan's decision not to renew the fighting at Antietam on September 18 and cast blame on his chief's enemies in Washington, DC, whom he believed were undermining McClellan's ability to renew operations against the Confederates. But it was toward the proclamation that Porter directed his most incendiary language. He claimed it "was ridiculed in the army—causing disgust, discontent, and expressions of disloyalty to the views of the administration, amounting I have heard to insubordination." He argued that soldiers like himself and McClellan sought to bring about an honorable end to the conflict, but their efforts were being "upset by the absurd proclamations of a political coward." Porter believed "all such bulletins tend only to prolong the war by rousing the bitter feelings of the South—and causing unity of action among them—while the reverse with us. Those who fight the battles of the country are tired of the war and wish to see it ended soon and honorably—by a restoration of the union—not mere suppression of the rebellion." The way to accomplish this was "a conservative political policy," and the "exclusion of politics from the military sphere"—an amusing statement, considering the inherently political nature of his letter. This, Porter believed—in his magical way of thinking—would soften the opinion of Southerners who would understand that the North did not wish to oppress them, but only desired to reestablish the government all had enjoyed before the war. Porter thought such a policy would enable the Union armies to penetrate deeper into the Southern interior, which would lead to slavery's demise, "for where the army goes slavery disappears." But such a policy "must be done under McClellan's mind—not the present chief." Porter was entitled to his personal opinion of Lincoln and the government's policies, but attacking them through a back channel with the press crossed the line of military-political ethics. This was not opinion, but borderline sedition. A high-ranking army officer, obliged to carry out the policy of the elected civilian government, instead was actively working to undermine that policy and negatively shape the public's opinion toward its chief executive.[8]

The timing of Porter's subversive missive was particularly curious, since the case of Major John Key, the brother of Colonel Thomas Key, a member of McClellan's staff, was known within the army. John Key served on the staff of General-in-Chief Henry Halleck. A week after Antietam, Key engaged in a discussion about the battle with Major Levi C. Turner in the Judge Advocate's office. When Turner questioned why the Army of the Potomac had not pursued the retreating Confederates more vigorously, Key replied that the destruction of the Rebel army was not the game plan: "The object is that neither army shall get much advantage of the other; that both shall be kept in the field till they are exhausted, when we will make a compromise and save slavery." Key's statement stunned Turner, who reported it to his superior, and it traveled up the chain of command until it reached Lincoln's desk. On September 26, Lincoln wrote to Key and related the substance of the latter's conversation with Turner. The president requested the major to "prove to me by Major Turner, that you did not, either literally, or in substance, make the answer stated." Key responded that yes, that was essentially the language he had used, but then added, "I have often remarked, that the Rebels would never let this contest be decided, if they could help it—by a decided battle between us, but would protract this war—as they hoped to make a compromise in the end & that they were fighting with that end in view." Lincoln summoned both Key and Turner to the White House. Key did not deny he had used the language reported by Turner, but also avowed "that he was true to the Union." Lincoln responded that if "there was a 'game' ever among Union men, to have our army not take an advantage of the enemy when it could, it was his object to break up that game." He ordered Key to be dismissed from the service at once. Key petitioned Lincoln for reinstatement 2 months later, arguing for and documenting his loyalty. The president crafted a measured but firm reply:

> In regard to my dismissal of yourself from the military service, it seems to me you misunderstand me. I did not charge, or intended to charge you with disloyalty. I had been brought to fear that there was a class of officers in the army, not very inconsiderable in numbers, who were playing a game to not beat the enemy when they could, on some peculiar notion as to the proper way of saving the Union; and when you were proved to me, in your own presence, to have avowed yourself in favor of that 'game,' and did not attempt to controvert that proof, I dismissed you as an example and a warning to that supposed class. I bear you no ill will; and I regret that I could not have the example without wounding you personally.

Although Porter did not advocate the same "game" that Key suggested, Lincoln's actions were a warning shot to officers who held similarly strong conservative views and disapproved of government policy, affirming that there were limits to what would be tolerated.[9]

The other corps commanders did not reflect Porter's claim of universal disgust and discontent over the Emancipation Proclamation. Sumner, who never ventured into politics, and Burnside, who typically supported the administration's policies, offered no public or private views that survive. Neither did Franklin, although he agreed with Porter that Lincoln should leave military operations to the professionals. George Meade, who had reverted back to division command when John Reynolds returned, expressed no outright opinion. He did, however, observe on October 1, after hearing that the Confederates had sent peace commissioners to Washington, DC, "that the day has gone by for any terms to be granted them except complete submission! Either one extreme or the other will have to come to pass—the day for compromise, for a brotherly reconciliation, for the old Union, in reality as well as name, has passed away, and the struggle must be continued till one side or the other is exhausted and willing to give up." Alpheus Williams, still in temporary command of the 12th Corps, also kept his opinion to himself, although, as he admitted to his daughter on October 28, "I have repeatedly said that I was prepared to sustain any measure I thought would help put an end to this cursed rebellion." He did not, however, see how "slaves will be freed any faster than our troops get possession of Rebel territory." The intensely ambitious Hooker embraced any policy that might elevate him to McClellan's position. "Hooker is a Democrat and anti-Abolitionist—that is to say, he was," wrote George Meade. "What he will be, when the command of the army is held out to him, is more than any one can tell, because I fear he is open to temptation and liable to be seduced by flattery."[10]

Opinions varied widely among the Union army's field and line officers and its enlisted men, often depending on their political beliefs, education, intellectual curiosity, and home state. It was possible to find some who were so furious with the government's emancipation policy they left the army and went over to the enemy. Captain William T. Magruder, an 1850 West Point graduate and a company commander in the 1st U.S. Cavalry, was already turning against the war by the summer of 1862, but the proclamation was the final straw. He resigned his commission on October 1 and offered his services to the Confederacy, which commissioned him a captain and placed him on the staff of Brigadier General Joseph Davis. Magruder was killed near the Brian farm at the height of Pickett's Charge at the Battle of Gettysburg, less than a year later. But Magruder was an extreme and rare example. A visitor to the 107th Pennsylvania's camp related in a September 24 letter that newspapers containing the president's Emancipation Proclamation had just been received and widely read throughout the regiment, but that "no opinions have been advanced *pro* or *con*. One officer remarked that soldiers must fight and would fight for the Union, but he could not see why the Negro was brought into the contest at all." Colonel Charles Wainwright, who assumed command of the 1st Corps' artillery immediately after the Battle of Antietam, was a staunch Democrat. He also claimed that he did not hear much talk of the proclamation in the army, but those that did speak of it "all think it unadvised at this time; even those most anti-slavery." Zachery Fry believes Republican officers "would have laughed at Wainwright's evaluations." Numerous officers in Wainwright's own corps expressed positive opinions about the proclamation. Gibbon's brigade, now nicknamed the "Iron Brigade" for the fighting prowess it displayed at the Battles of Brawner's Farm, South Mountain, and Antietam, was a particular bastion of support. A member of Company I in the 2nd Wisconsin believed "the President's late Proclamation receives the favor of the greater part of the army." He found that many officers considered it to be "untimely, yet believed it proper to acquiesce and a policy if pursued by the government, which would cripple the foe." That writer placed little confidence in proclamations, however, expressing the opinion that only by the bayonet would "peace be insured to this distracted nation." When Major Rufus Dawes in the 6th Wisconsin returned home to Marietta, Ohio, on furlough in March 1863, he was asked to give a public address about the Union army. One of the subjects he discussed was the Emancipation Proclamation: "If there remains any one in the army, who does not like this Proclamation, he is careful to keep quiet about it. We are hailed everywhere by the negroes as their deliverers." He added that the practicality of the policy was obvious to the men: "Slavery is the chief source of wealth in the South, and the basis of their aristocracy, and my observation is that a blow at slavery hurts more than battalion volleys. It strikes at the vitals. . . . We like the Proclamation because it hurts the rebels. We like the Proclamation because it lets the world know what the real issue is." While Dawes and the 2nd Wisconsin correspondent might have represented the prevalent view in the Wisconsin regiments of the brigade, the soldiers in the 19th Indiana, with many transplanted New Englanders and Germans in their ranks, did not share them. As one member of that regiment declared, "I came to fight for the old flag instead [of] fighting for the negroes."[11]

Even for the corps that had been on the Peninsula Campaign and were bastions of support for McClellan, many in the rank and file did not reflect Porter's claim of opposition to the Emancipation Proclamation—a view that amounted to insubordination. Roland Bowen, in the 15th Massachusetts of the 2nd Corps, writing a friend about the proclamation, reflected a relatively common sentiment both inside and outside the army: "I fear it won't do any good because we can't enforce it, time will tell." Sergeant Charles T. Bowen (no relation to Roland) in the 12th U.S. of the 5th Corps, in a September 28 letter to his mother, related his thoughts about the proclamation: "My opinion, of course, is in favor of it, & as a matter of course the opinion of most Democrats is against it, they being the ones who have upheld slavery for the last thirty years, of course do not like it, but if that same thing had been done a year ago I do believe it would have done more to weaken the rebels arms than the capture of Richmond itself." Lieutenant Colonel Charles Albright in the 2nd Corps' 132nd Pennsylvania felt so strongly about the proclamation and the army's inactivity after Antietam that he wrote directly to President Lincoln on October 20. He stated, "I have not yielded my right as a citizen to think and to look at things through the eyes of common sense" and explained that the proclamation "was and is hailed with intense satisfaction by the army except perhaps a few pro-slavery political officers." But, like Roland Bowen and others, Albright expressed the opinion that "it will be without virtue and effect if the Union army does not march through the seceded states victoriously and bearing down all opposition." Albright, however, may have misjudged the opinion of Democrats. Although many opposed the proclamation, substantial numbers tolerated it. One of them was the 118th Pennsylvania's Captain Francis Donaldson, who railed about the fall elections in an October 20 letter to his brother: "I presume all the 'nigger' worshippers have all been elected," adding, "I am a Democrat, first, last and all the time, but as long as the rebels are in arms I will sustain the government's efforts to put down [the] rebellion—with my life if necessary. I think there should be but one party, one issue in the North as long as the war lasts."[12]

Nonetheless, opinions about the Emancipation Proclamation were neither immovable nor unchanging. Although McClellan privately opposed the proclamation, he sounded the political waters on the issue before issuing any public statement. On September 27, he heard from Postmaster General Montgomery Blair, who shared details about the Major Key incident. Blair warned that it would probably plant suspicion "in the minds of large numbers of honest people of the country" that McClellan shared Key's opinion about the war. For this reason, Blair believed it would "have a salutary effect" if the general publicly clarified his views on slavery. The government official's father, Francis P. Blair, a powerful former newspaper editor and advisor to President Andrew Jackson, followed up his son's letter with one of his own on September 30, encouraging McClellan to "manifest in every way, a fixed purpose to give full effect to the proclamation." "Slaves," the senior Blair counseled, "supply the enemy with everything. They are literally the sinews of war." Both Blairs believed that McClellan could help silence his enemies by publicly throwing his support behind the Emancipation Proclamation. By remaining silent, he only fueled their accusations that his sympathies lay with the views expressed by Major Key.[13]

Several days after the proclamation's publication, McClellan invited Major General Burnside, Brigadier General Jacob Cox, and Brigadier General John Cochrane, a brigade commander in Couch's division, to a dinner at his headquarters. On the surface, it seemed like an odd assembly. Cox and Cochrane made some sense. The former had powerful connections in the Republican Party in Ohio and, as Cox related, "McClellan perfectly knew my position as an outspoken Republican" who "looked forward to Mr. Lincoln's proclamation with some impatience at the delay." Cochrane was a prominent Democrat from New York City who nonetheless had strong connections within the Lincoln administration, and he had advocated giving arms to the slaves in November 1861. The inclusion of Burnside makes less sense, given the recent friction in his relationship with the army's commander, but McClellan believed Burnside had the president's confidence and insight into the administration's thinking. According to Cox, McClellan told them "frankly that he had brought us there for the purpose of asking our opinions and advice with regard to the course he should pursue respecting the Proclamation." McClellan related that he had been encouraged by both politicians and army officers "who were near to him" to put himself "in open opposition" to it. What he desired was their opinion on "whether we thought he should say anything or should maintain silence on the subject." The three officers questioned McClellan about his attitude on the slavery question. He replied with the same reasoning Porter had expressed to the *New York World*'s editor, stating that he believed the war would "would work out the manumission of the slaves gradually and ultimately," but that the proclamation was premature. McClellan believed the president had been pushed to issue it by radical influences within his administration. Even though Cox had never met Cochrane before, and although he and Burnside rarely discussed politics, he found that all three were of the same opinion in their advice to McClellan: "Any declaration on his part against the Proclamation would be a fatal error," and "any public utterance in his official character criticizing the civil policy of the Administration would be properly regarded as a usurpation." McClellan agreed, but pointed out that he had been assured that his support in the army was so overwhelming that they would enforce any decision he made regarding war policy. This was extremely dangerous talk, and Cox offered the rejoinder that "those who made such assurances were his [McClellan's] worst enemies" and "knew much less of the army than they pretended." Cox believed that not even "a corporal's guard" would stand by McClellan if he departed from the principle of subordinating the military to civil authority. Cox was on solid ground here, and he had a better sense of the army's pulse than officers like Porter did.[14]

McClellan took no action following this meeting, but he continued to seek more opinions. Lincoln visited the army from October 2 to 4 (see chapter 25), but there is no evidence that the two men discussed the emancipation policy. When Lincoln departed on October 4, William Aspinwall arrived to meet with McClellan and urged "that it is my [McClellan's] duty to submit to the Presdt's proclamation & quietly continue doing my duty as a soldier." McClellan may have received similar counsel from a seemingly unlikely source—Colonel Thomas M. Key, the brother of recently dismissed Major John Key. The colonel served as McClellan's confidential aide-de-camp and political advisor. On September 15, Thomas Key had expressed the opinion to Jacob Cox that he "had greatly modified his views on the subject of slavery, and he was now satisfied that the war must end in its abolition." On October 7, 3 days after the president departed and 2 days after Aspinwall's visit, McClellan at last issued a general order to the army regarding the Emancipation Proclamation. Cox considered the order to be one of McClellan's "most laudable actions," but also one of his most "misrepresented and misunderstood" ones.[15]

Colonel Key, who typically drafted communications of a political nature, probably was the order's author. It stated that the army had been raised and was being supported "simply to sustain the Civil authorities and [its members] are to be held in strict subordination thereto in all respects." Debating policy "beyond temperate and respectful expressions of opinion tend greatly to impair & destroy efficiency of troops by substituting the spirit of political faction for that firm steady & earnest support of the Authority of the Government which is the highest duty of the American soldier." The order was firm and clear—the soldiers in the army were obliged to follow the policies of the elected government. While some press outlets praised the order, it generated no enthusiasm in Lincoln's administration. There were several reasons for this. It had taken McClellan 2 weeks to produce the order, and it was known that Aspinwall claimed credit for its publication, which gave it a political aroma. Then there was the sentence stating that "the remedy for political error if any are committed is to be found only in the action of the people at the polls." Colonel Key may have meant this in an honest, neutral way, but it could easily have been interpreted as encouraging soldiers to try and influence the votes of their friends and family at home in the upcoming congressional elections. Finally, McClellan's inaction since Antietam (see chapter 25) had expended the political capital he had accrued with his victories at the Battles of South Mountain and Antietam. Although McClellan had rejected the advice of those who had encouraged him to openly oppose Lincoln's policy, the October 7 orders were a clear statement that even though he personally disagreed with that policy, he would uphold it.[16]

Within the army, opinions on emancipation would continue to take shape in the weeks and months ahead. There was no moment in time when one could poll its members and produce an unwavering opinion. External factors, such as the Federals' defeat at the Battle of Fredericksburg in December 1862, had and would influence morale and shape political opinions, causing them to fluctuate. Some would turn against the government, and others would embrace a harder stance toward winning the war against the Rebels. But McClellan's prediction in his Harrison's Bar Letter on July 7—that a radical policy on emancipation would disintegrate the army—and Porter's claim of widespread "expressions of disloyalty . . . amounting I have heard to insubordination," proved to be highly exaggerated. As Zachary Fry persuasively argues in *A Republic in the Ranks*, after a demoralizing, depressing winter of 1862–1863, the Army of the Potomac, through the active encouragement of line and field officers, steadily grew to overwhelmingly support Republican policies, largely because they saw them as the best path to winning the war.

24

Recovery

"We have experienced terrible times since my last and are now sleeping without blankets—living on poor and insufficient food and one fourth of us shoeless"

While the country reacted to the Emancipation Proclamation, Robert E. Lee and the Army of Northern Virginia recovered along Opequon Creek, north of Winchester, Virginia. With people's opinions shaped by newspapers, the Southern public may have imagined the army's Maryland Campaign had been a resounding success with the capture of Harpers Ferry and A. P. Hill smashing of the Union army's incursion across the Potomac River at Shepherdstown. But Lee probably evaluated the campaign's strategic results with a more sober, realistic judgment and found them to be disappointing. On the plus side, his expedition into Maryland had generated considerable fear in parts of the North, and any exaggeration of his army's ability to threaten their cities and other strategic points aided his objective of undermining Northern morale. The capture of Harpers Ferry stunned the North, inspired the South, and provided the Confederates with needed equipment and small arms. The Army of the Potomac had been kept on the frontier of the Confederacy for all of late summer. As days and weeks passed after the Battle of Antietam, with no sign of action by the Federal army, it stirred hope that the Yankee forces had been badly damaged in the fighting.

The strategic negatives on the Maryland Campaign's ledger more than offset its gains. Politically, it appeared to be a failure, particularly since Lee had been forced to withdraw from Maryland after only 2 weeks in the state. Hope that Marylanders might welcome a Confederate army was conclusively dashed, and the slim prospects for European recognition—which Lee had little faith in—were dealt two heavy blows: the Army of Northern Virginia's retreat, followed by the Emancipation Proclamation. There was still some glimmer of hope that the victories in the Seven Days Battles and Manassas, and the fear generated by the invasion of Maryland, would damage the Republicans in the upcoming congressional and gubernatorial elections, but the perception of a Union victory at Sharpsburg would surely help Republican Party candidates. Lee had greatly overestimated the Federals' demoralization after their defeats on the Virginia

Peninsula and at Second Manassas. Instead, they had recovered quickly and struck hard blows at the Battles of South Mountain and Sharpsburg. The capture of Harpers Ferry in no way compensated for the terrible damage the Confederate army had sustained in Maryland. Casualties were frightful. At Sharpsburg, over 10,316 men were killed, wounded, or captured, with an additional 2,193 at South Mountain, and 896 at Crampton's Gap. Three of their nine division commanders were wounded, and 16 out of 40 brigade commanders—40%—were killed or wounded. The latter figure did not include the replacements for these brigade commanders, who also became casualties. For example, Starke's brigade in J. R. Jones's division lost Starke, who was killed, and two of the colonels who took his place wounded. The depredations among the Rebels' regimental and company leadership were also severe. Joseph Glatthaar has estimated that a total of 140 officers were killed, 649 wounded, and 48 missing or captured at Sharpsburg. This was nearly 30% of the army's leadership. Alexander Lawton's division, which kept careful statistics, offers an example of just how extensive this was. It reported 24 officers killed, 110 wounded, and 2 missing or captured on September 17. On August 22, immediately before Second Manassas, it had 550 officers present. One month later, after Sharpsburg, they had 288 officers, a 52% decrease. In G. B. Anderson's brigade, the general and every field officer were casualties, except for Major William W. Sillers in the 30th North Carolina, who temporarily headed the brigade. Every field officer in Colquitt's brigade was killed or wounded. At the end of the battle, a lieutenant commanded the 6th Georgia, and captains led the other four regiments. Nearly every brigade in R. H. Anderson's division was in similar condition. This was a catastrophic loss of leadership, and it came on top of a summer campaign that had already decimated regimental command.[1]

Also worrying was the number of brigades that had come apart during the fighting at Antietam and had effectively ceased to exist by its close, which amounted to more than half of the army's order of battle—that is, its hierarchical organization, command structure, and strength. Many had fought superbly, however, before their internal organization collapsed. One example was Rodes's brigade. It had ably defended the Sunken Lane until a mistaken order caused it to fall back, after which Rodes managed to rally only about 40 men out of the 800 taken into action. Jackson's old division, commanded by General John R. Jones, shared a similar experience. It fought well against the onslaught of Hooker's 1st Corps, but after this engagement, only about 200 to 300 men, commanded by two colonels, remained combat effective from four brigades. In nearly all of these brigades, some soldiers who had melted away were later rallied and remained in the fight, but they typically numbered less than 100, the size of a strong infantry company. Colonel R. F. Floyd in the 8th Florida, who had been sick and only joined his regiment after the fighting ended, wrote that when he encountered some of the wounded from his regiment and asked them where the unit was located, they replied, "They are all killed, wounded or dispersed." This proved to be true. Floyd reported that on September 18, "it was difficult to find any men at all of these [Florida] Regts [in Pryor's brigade], except the wounded who were brought off." A private in the 3rd Alabama of Rodes's brigade related that there were three men in his company, including himself, who went into action on September 17. Two were wounded, leaving the surviving soldier distraught: "I am shoeless and ragged. Nothing to supply my necesaties can be got up here. I am at a loss to know what to do. Numbers are in my fix." Corporal Robert G. Johnson Jr. in the 6th Georgia of Colquitt's brigade stated that only 40 of the 300 men his regiment took into action remained on September 18. Two companies did not have a single man left, and only two officers remained in the entire regiment. The 4th North Carolina of G. B. Anderson's brigade was commanded by an orderly sergeant. Anderson's entire brigade had suffered such catastrophic losses of leadership that its sole remaining field officer lamented, "God spare me the sight of ever again seeing it so much disorganized!"[2]

Casualties explain the collapse in some brigades—such as Douglass's, Colquitt's, Hays's and G. B. Anderson's. In others, such as Garland's, the cause more likely was a lack of enough respected and competent leaders. But in some instances, the demoralized 3rd Alabama's private provided an important clue. Many were at the end of their tether, both physically and psychologically. They were poorly fed and clothed, which increased their problems from both exposure to the elements and the likelihood of sickness; worn down by brutally hard marching; and subjected to enormous stress on their nervous systems in combat. A sizeable part of the Confederate army had been campaigning and fighting since April. In a fairly typical letter, written on September 21, Captain Charles C. Kibbee in the 10th Georgia described how "we have experienced terrible times since my last and are now sleeping without blankets—living on poor and insufficient food and one fourth of us shoeless." In a letter to the *Western Sentinel* in Charlotte, a member of the 48th North Carolina wrote that there was "not a blanket for every half dozen men, and many of them barefooted. They are half starved, half clothed, hard marched, hard fought, and make but little complaint. Something must be done for them, in the way of bed clothing in particular, and that quickly." Sergeant John F. White in the 32nd Virginia, writing to a friend on October 12, referred to the suffering he had witnessed as "indescribable." On October 1, Lieutenant James L. Lemon in the 18th Georgia observed that almost every man in his company was barefoot, and he nearly was. Few highlighted the plight of Lee's soldiers to the public more vigorously, however, than newspaper correspondent Peter Wellington Alexander. On October 18, he wrote about a Richmond paper that described the excellent condition of the troops and how all they needed were additional blankets. "Such statements as this may be gratifying to the public, but they are *a cruelty to the army*," he complained, noting that the majority of troops were in deplorable condition, lacking clothing and shelter for the approaching colder weather.[3]

In his September 22 letter, Henry E. Young, a volunteer aide-de-camp to General David R. Jones, expressed his opinion that "Lee has made some patent errors—viz. he has marched the army to death. 2/ He has half starved it—one day's rations has often supplied three days and this has forced the men to live on green apples and green corn which together with this miserable limestone water has resulted in diarrhea among the men. All the causes have reduced our army to at least 1/3 or 1/2 its original strength. To give an instance, Drayton's brigade numbered, when at the Rapidan [River], effective strength 2600. Now it numbers 700." Lee may not have disagreed with Young's assessment. During the Maryland Campaign, he had seemed oblivious to both the condition of his army and the extent of his straggling problem, driving his men hard in order to achieve his objectives. But in Sharpsburg's aftermath and the retreat to Virginia, he became fully aware of its deplorable state. Straggling, in particular, exploded into a full-blown crisis, threatening the very existence of his army. This issue dominated his correspondence with President Jefferson Davis. The bulk of Lee's September 21 letter to Davis, his first full dispatch since the army had returned to Virginia and repulsed the Federals' probe at Shepherdstown, was devoted to the straggler problem. Lee admitted that the Army of Northern Virginia's "present efficiency is greatly paralyzed by the loss to its ranks of the numerous stragglers. I have taken every means in my power from the beginning to correct this evil, which has increased instead of diminished. A great many men belonging to the army never entered Maryland at all; many returned after getting there, while others who crossed the river kept aloof. The stream has not lessened since crossing the Potomac, though the cavalry has been constantly employed in endeavoring to arrest it." He provided Davis with specific examples. Evans's brigade had only 120 effectives on September 18, and Garnett's, only 100. Armistead's and Douglass's brigades, left to defend Boteler's Ford, merely numbered about 300 men each. "This is a woeful condition of affairs, and I am pained to state it," Lee continued, but he needed Davis to understand how widespread this difficulty was, so the government might take some action that would help him gain control of the problem.[4]

Lee returned to the straggler crisis the next day, in a September 22 letter to Davis, remarking on how the damage to private property by such laggards "occupied much of my attention." These soldiers consumed all they received "from the charitable and all they can take from the defenseless, in many cases wantonly destroying stock and other property." Lee acknowledged that any large army has a negative impact on the area it camped in or passed through, but what he saw now was "much unnecessary damage." He argued that it was impossible, given the Confederate army's current state of organization, to remedy the situation by issuing orders. "When such orders are published they are either imperfectly executed or wholly disregarded." Lee wanted an inspector general who could see to the execution of these orders. No law currently existed to establish such a position, but Lee, always careful to show deference and to appeal to Davis's vanity, hoped, if the creation of such a position did not meet with the president's approval, "that, in your better judgment, you will devise some other" means for addressing the straggling problem. In any event, Lee requested that Lieutenant Colonel Edwin J. Harvie, who had been an acting inspector general with the Army of Northern Virginia when it was near Richmond, along with Captain G. W. Latham, Harvie's assistant, be sent to him. With officers of such lower rank, however, Lee did not anticipate that he could accomplish much. What was needed was "an officer of rank, standing, and reputation to act as inspector-general, with sufficient assistants, and some tribunal to accompany the army, with power to inflict prompt and adequate punishment."[5]

An inspector general of rank, armed with the authority to enforce orders, was only one piece in a solution. Part of the problem, as Joseph Glatthaar, in *General Lee's Army*, has observed, was that army culture in the Civil War was not always a top to bottom flow. This was particularly true for the Army of Northern Virginia. In the absence of the Confederate army's high command developing "an effective military culture, a vacuum formed, and the troops themselves forged one that drew heavily from the civilian world. Military regulations circumscribed their day-to-day existence more rigidly than in civil life, but they could not snuff out vestiges of Southern society," which emphasized the rights of the individual. Particularly at the regimental and company levels, discipline was poorly enforced by officers and noncoms, many of whom were elected. Glatthaar points out that before Lee's arrival, Generals P. G. T. Beauregard and Joseph E. Johnston "had set the example by their lack of uniform discipline. Soldiers escaped punishment for the destruction of property and equipment." Brigadier General Cadmus Wilcox, a West Pointer with long experience in the Regular Army before the Civil War who returned to command his brigade after Sharpsburg, found that "we have no discipline in our army, it is but little better than an armed mob," since "where our army marches & camps desolation follows." On September 25, Lee admitted to Davis that it had been his intention, after the retreat from Sharpsburg, to reenter Maryland at Williamsport and advance on Hagerstown, forcing McClellan to react to the threat to his rear, "but the condition of the army prevented it." Lee still believed a turning movement toward Hagerstown was his best move, and he would not hesitate to attempt it "did the army exhibit its former temper and condition; but, as far as I am able to judge, the hazard would be great and a reverse disastrous. I am, therefore, led to pause."[6]

Morale was also an issue, but not to the extent it would be after the Confederates' defeat at the Battle of Gettysburg. Many soldiers were demoralized, not because they doubted or abandoned their cause, but because of poor health, inadequate clothing and food, and grueling marches that wore them out. They straggled because they were too broken down to keep up, and because loose discipline made it easy to do so. "The talk therefore of our defeat demoralization &c, is ill founded," wrote Surgeon John F. Shaffner in the 33rd North Carolina. "Our men are nearly exhausted and greatly need the rest they are now enjoying." An enlisted man in the 5th Alabama wrote to his parents the day before Sharpsburg, declaring that he had always been opposed to the war and had many opportunities to defect since the army entered Maryland, "yet I cannot bear the disgrace of being called a deserter." Their adversaries in the Army of the Potomac concurred that there was no flagging of resolve among the Rebels they faced at Antietam. As a sergeant in Battery M, 1st New York Light Artillery, wrote to his hometown paper in Lockport, New York, "The rebels are no cowards. They fought desperately that day, and were it not for the unequalled bravery of the Union troops, I fear the Union would have been sunk that day to rise no more." While recovering from his wound, Colonel Francis Barlow told Maria Daly, a friend of his wife Arabella, "how much he admired the rebels, what constancy, endurance, and discipline they showed, and with what bravery they fought. . . . They were terrible and fearful from their fierce hate." Captain Francis Donaldson in the 118th Pennsylvania explained to his brother that "I am not one of those who disparage the fighting qualities of the Confederates. They are a brave people, a very brave people, and splendid soldiers"[7]

While some in the Army of Northern Virginia claimed Sharpsburg as a victory, most who commented on the Maryland Campaign took a more pragmatic view. Rufus Felder in the 5th Texas wrote to his sister on October 1, noting that "the slaughter on both sides was terrible; there was very little ground gained on either side. Both sides were too exhausted to renew the fight the next day." Of the famous Texas brigade that he was a part of, Felder opined, "They have been in so many fights, and have suffered so much they would be willing never to go into another fight." James Steptoe Johnston, a courier who served Colonel Evander Law, believed that "the battle was as near a drawn fight as we have had since the war, and if there was any advantage the Yankees had it." Although both Felder and Johnston expressed hope for a peaceful settlement that would grant independence to the South, neither voiced any doubt about their cause or their ability to win that independence. As Lee's ordnance officer, Lieutenant Colonel E. P. Alexander, recalled, "Our successful defense at Sharpsburg & our last day's defiance of the enemy had given us renewed confidence that we could not be whipped." But after a summer and fall of bitter fighting, it was clear to veteran soldiers on both sides that "many a bloody battle will have to be fought and many a life sacrificed" to achieve victory.[8]

Lee recognized that while the Confederate army "had had hard work to perform," with long marches and poor rations, he believed that the root of his straggler problem was "great dereliction of duty among the regimental and company officers, particularly the latter." Unless something was done about it, "the army will melt away." Repairing this, however, was only one of the crises he faced in the aftermath of the Maryland Campaign. What helped fuel straggling and sickness was an utterly broken supply system. This also crippled Lee's ability to reorganize and rebuild his army. Although he had established a depot at Winchester for supplies and ammunition, it was too small to meet the army's daily needs. Conventional military wisdom, given the dire condition of the army, would be for Lee to withdraw up the Shenandoah Valley to Staunton, Virginia. This would shorten his supply lines and place him in direct rail communications with Richmond. Remaining near Winchester meant that the army's limited number of already overburdened wagon trains and teams had to haul supplies 95 miles from Staunton. Conscripts and formerly ill and injured soldiers who had recovered would need to travel the same distance to rejoin the army. Yet Lee, with sound reasoning, rejected any thought of withdrawing to Staunton. His absent men—stragglers, plus the sick and wounded—were "scattered broadcast over the land" at the lower end of the valley. Winchester alone had thousands of casualties in its hospitals and private residences. A movement to Staunton would have meant closing these hospitals and transporting the patients over long distances by wagon—a huge and time-consuming operation—and would have meant abandoning thousands of men who were not readily accessible and could therefore be captured and paroled by the Federals. Lee knew that the lower end of the Shenandoah Valley could supply his army's food needs, and he was loath to leave this rich agricultural region to the enemy. Therefore, he accepted the inconvenience of a long supply line in order to recover his numerous stragglers and recuperated sick and wounded men and avoid the logistical nightmare of evacuating thousands of casualties.[9]

This strategy was not without risk. For it to succeed, Lee needed the Federal army to leave him alone, so his commissary officers could gather supplies without the risk of being intercepted or attacked by Union cavalry. Lee understood that McClellan was a highly conventional field commander. If the Rebels remained in the lower end of the valley, rather than falling back on their rail communications—as strategic prudence would dictate—then it could only be because they remained powerful and well supplied enough to pose a continued threat to Maryland and Pennsylvania. A. P. Hill's victory at Shepherdstown played a crucial role in strengthening the belief by McClellan, and key subordinates like Fitz John Porter, that the Confederates had superior numbers. Lee reasoned that as long as his army remained in the vicinity of Winchester and Martinsburg, this would keep the Union army in the Sharpsburg-Williamsport-Harpers Ferry area, guarding the line along the Potomac River and thinking defensively. Lee's scouts and spies provided him with accurate information about the Federals' dispositions. When the 2nd and 12th Corps occupied Harpers Ferry on September 22 and returned to Bolivar Heights and Maryland Heights, Lee immediately learned about this. He correctly judged that McClellan would not attempt a general advance south of the Potomac until the railroad bridge over the river at Harpers Ferry was repaired. "When the railroad is open to Harper's Ferry he may possibly advance up the valley, where I shall endeavor to occupy and detain him," Lee wrote to Davis on September 25. A week later, Lee surmised—correctly—that McClellan "for the present seems disposed to be inactive." That same day, he wrote to Secretary of War George Randolph: "I think it is probable that as yet General McClellan is only able to procure supplies for his army from day to day, and that he is employing the time in recuperating his army from the effects of the recent battles." If McClellan did advance, Lee believed it would be from Harpers Ferry, which was the approach the latter most desired. So long as Lee could keep the Federals in western Maryland and Harpers Ferry, McClellan "will have less time this year for field operations." This meant more time for Lee to rest and rebuild his army.[10]

To reinforce McClellan's idea that the Confederate army was powerful and keen to reenter Maryland, Lee had Stuart adopt an aggressive posture by pushing his cavalry pickets up close to the Potomac River and Harpers Ferry. On October 9, he ordered Stuart and a carefully selected force of 1,800 troopers, accompanied by four pieces of horse artillery, to mount an expedition into Pennsylvania. The raid had multiple objectives: to keep the enemy off balance; seize supplies; and, most significantly, "gain all the information of the position, force and probable intention of the enemy which you can." Stuart proved to be resourceful, daring, decisive, and smart in his management of the raid, and he achieved an impressive success. Crossing the Potomac River above Williamsport early on October 10, the Rebel force made its way to Mercersburg, Pennsylvania, and then traveled 17 miles northeast to Chambersburg, where they seized or destroyed quantities of supplies destined for the Army of the Potomac. They continued east, toward Gettysburg, before turning south to Emmitsburg, and proceeding through Liberty, New Market, and Hyattstown, cleverly eluding all enemy detachments sent to find them. They then avoided a strong Union force assembled at Poolesville, dispersed the pickets defending White's Ford on the Potomac River, and returned to Virginia on the October 12, without a single man being killed in the entire operation. Stuart confirmed that the Federals had detached no troops to the east. The Army of the Potomac had been substantially reinforced but displayed no evidence of preparations for a forward movement. The raid had the added benefit of greatly embarrassing McClellan, whose forces looked hapless and foolish in their efforts to trap Stuart. Most importantly, it reinforced the thinking in the Union high command that the Rebels had sufficient numbers and resources to threaten Maryland and Pennsylvania.[11]

WITH THE ENEMY LEAVING him alone, Lee went to work tackling the problems afflicting his army. On September 21, he wrote to the quartermaster general in Richmond, Colonel A. C. Myers, about the "great deficiency of clothing in this army (particularly under-clothing and shoes), and for the want of which there is much suffering." Lee had learned of a recent purchase of 4,000 to 5,000 pairs of shoes by the Quartermaster's Department and wished them to be sent to his army, although this amount would not come close to meeting the army's needs. McClellan's defensive posture enabled Lee to disperse his army slightly, which made supplying the men easier, and gave his quartermasters the freedom to move throughout the region to seize food and forage for the men and the horses. His quartermasters and commissary officers were instructed to purchase what was needed, whether the citizens "are willing to sell or not," since some people in this borderland region were reluctant to accept Confederate currency. If the locals refused to sell at prices established by the Confederate government, Lee authorized his supply officers to seize what they needed, while leaving the family or establishment with enough for personal needs. In so doing, they were to provide a certificate documenting what was seized and indicating that the offer to purchase the items at market value had been refused. Such a system did not win friends, but Lee could not afford to allow reluctant or unsympathetic citizens—or "capitalists," as he referred to some—to deny his troops the provisions they required. The army's supply forays produced "plenty of beef and flour for our troops, hay for our horses and some grain." Obtaining *sufficient* forage for the horses and mules proved to be less successful, but with no pressure from the enemy, quartermasters and commissary officers could range widely in search of supplies. Detachments traveled as far west as Hardy and Hampshire Counties—20 to 30 miles west of Winchester, in the foothills of the Appalachians—where they procured a good number of cattle and, Lee hoped, would also be able to gather more horses and recruits for the army. Appropriating these supplies was not only beneficial to his army but, as Lee observed to Secretary of War George Randolph, "we are consuming provisions that would otherwise fall into the hands of the enemy." In addition to food and forage, Lee sent his chief quartermaster out "to purchase all the cloth, leather, shoes, &c., that can be found in this country." In November, he identified 271 shoemakers in the ranks and detailed them to produce greater numbers of desperately needed shoes. The supply situation gradually improved, but the shortage of clothing, shoes, and shelter were never fully resolved. Even as late as November 15, Major Sillers in 30th North Carolina confided to his sister, "It is not one or two who are without shoes and half-clad; but it is the greater part of every company in our regiment who are in this condition." Nevertheless, Lee's vigorous efforts in September and October succeeded in collecting sufficient food and forage for the Army of Northern Virginia, which was a critical achievement— and also directly addressed one of the core causes of straggling.[12]

While Lee worked to improve his logistics, he also took forceful action to address the prevailing culture that permitted straggling. Cavalry detachments were dispatched to begin rounding up the thousands of laggards scattered throughout the Shenandoah Valley. On September 22, he had his assistant adjutant general, Richard H. Chilton, draw up orders for Longstreet and Jackson—which were to be immediately implemented—to begin repairing the lax discipline prevalent in many regiments. Because roll calls were being neglected, and company officers were often "ignorant of the true condition of their commands" and thus unable to account for absentees, each day at reveille, soldiers were to appear under arms, and roll call would be taken. This would force officers to confirm which men were present or absent, and, therefore, easily determine who might have "thrown aside" his arms or equipment. A weekly inspection would be mandatory. Each brigade would form a guard, who would be charged with driving stragglers back to their commands. After establishing camp, these brigade guards would supply protection for private residences, to prevent depredations. Officers designated as inspectors by their division commanders would regularly review company and regimental records, to see that accountability for equipment and personnel was being maintained. Regimental commanders were expected to arrest company officers who failed to maintain good order on the march. To provide some additional teeth for this directive, each wing of the army would form a provost guard, which, "in addition to their duties as guard, will perform provost duty in correcting and punishing violations of orders coming under their observation." Chilton decreed that it was necessary for Longstreet, Jackson, and their subordinates "to infuse a different spirit among our officers, and to inspire them in making every necessary effort to bring about a better state of discipline." It was through "better discipline, greater mobility, and higher inspirations" that the Confederate army might overcome the matériel and numerical advantages the enemy possessed.[13]

Longstreet responded to these directives by appointing an assistant inspector general and issuing a general order that held company commanders to "strict accountability for all arms, equipments and ammunition that may be issued to them." It included a curious sentence: "Soldiers must understand that their ammunition must only be used against the enemy." Perhaps this was a reference to cartridges being used to kindle fires or dispatch livestock. To crack down on officers and men being absent in search of food, leisure, or mischief, no one was permitted to leave camp without written permission from brigade headquarters. Jackson apparently issued similar orders, which included, in Jacksonian fashion, a significant uptick in court-martials.[14]

These changes soon began to have an effect. When General Robert Rodes returned to his brigade after recovering from his Sharpsburg wound, he assembled his officers and noncoms and announced that the brigade would become "a model of military discipline with a view to the redemption of the Confederate army from the lethargy and inactivity and carelessness of duty into which it had fallen." Some of his officers knew no more of their duties than "would a 'Miss in her teens.'" Rodes believed company commanders were responsible for "murdering one-third of the men lost in this campaign, by not properly providing them with comfortable clothing, and other necessities to a vigorous campaign." He ordered each company to be divided into six squads, with a noncom responsible for each one. It would be their duty to make sure the men washed their hands, face, and feet each morning. No further officer resignations would be accepted. Those who had already given up their commissions would be handed a musket and placed in the ranks. No doubt many thought Rodes a madman and martinet, but he recognized and tackled a core problem common throughout the Confederate army—namely, officers who might be brave in combat but neglected the health of their men, and who were casual about discipline off the battlefield. Dirty, poorly clad soldiers got sick, and lax discipline gave them license to straggle and plunder.[15]

Alfred Iverson, promoted to brigadier general and command of Garland's North Carolina brigade on November 1, ordered that anyone absent without written permission at a daily roll call would be "bucked." This was an uncomfortable and embarrassing punishment, where the offending soldier was seated, with his knees drawn up between his arms. A rod was then inserted under his knees and over his arms, which were bound together by rope. Iverson also took on the issue of "familiarity and companionship of officers with Soldiers." It did not matter what station someone had occupied in civilian life. The army, Iverson reminded his command, must adhere to a strict hierarchy, which was a foundation of discipline.[16]

The great straggler roundup produced startling results. Brigadier General J. R. Jones, one of Jackson's division commanders, was detailed to conduct it. On September 27, he reported that he had already collected between 5,000 and 6,000 loiterers and sent them on to join the main body of the army. "The country is full of stragglers," he noted, and the number of officers among their numbers "was most astonishing." When he gave his attached cavalry orders to arrest all officers and men found in the rear without proper leave, "it created quite a stampede in the direction of the army." Jones's straggler hunters ranged widely, going south to Front Royal, nearly 20 miles from Winchester; east to Clarke County, 15 miles away at its eastern boundary; and out to the western reaches of Virginia's Frederick County, 14 miles distant. On the day of J. R. Jones's report, a patrol to Pughtown, in Frederick County, netted 150 dawdlers "found loafing at the various farm houses." He also reported a camp of some 1,200 barefoot men in the Winchester area. He believed a large number of them had thrown away their shoes to remain in camp and avoid duty.[17]

Charles F. Terrill, a well-educated enlisted man in Toombs's brigade, wrote his brother on September 25 that "no less than eight thousand stragglers" were driven up to the army on September 18. Although Terrill may have overestimated their numbers, between September 18 and 27, when J. R. Jones wrote his report,

Lee recovered the equivalent of an army corps in laggards. Thousands more remained at large, but the free ride they had enjoyed was over as the roundup details combed the farmhouses, towns, and villages in the Shenandoah Valley.[18]

In addition to stragglers, many men who had recovered from illnesses or from wounds received in earlier battles, those previously assigned to various details, and conscripts returned in a steady stream through September and October. On October 5, Captain Peter McGlashan in the 50th Georgia charted the recovery of his regiment. It had numbered 55 officers and men by the end of the day at Sharpsburg. But now, "stragglers and conscripts are coming in very fast," and the regiment's strength reached 350, a nearly seven-fold increase. James L. Coker in the 6th South Carolina of D. R. Jones's division related how only a handful of his company remained after Sharpsburg, but by the time they reached Winchester, several days later, it had grown to 38. Most of the returnees had been wounded in battles on the Virginia Peninsula and had recovered. On October 18, William L. Cage in Barksdale's 21st Mississippi wrote to his wife that the Confederate army was now "one fourth stronger than it ever was." In the 4th North Carolina, Lieutenant James Shinn reported the arrival of 70 conscripts on September 28. The Army of Northern Virginia steadily grew, and its returns chart that recovery. On September 22, there were 2,732 officers and 33,686 enlisted men present for duty. The efforts to round up stragglers, and the arrival of those who had been sick or wounded, began to show up on the September 30 return, which counted 3,857 officers and 48,933 enlisted men present for duty, a 29% and 31% increase, respectively. By October 20, the numbers rose to 4,933 officers and 63,100 enlisted men. Three weeks later, on November 10, the amounts reached a plateau at 5,229 officers and 65,680 enlisted men, nearly double the force present on September 22. Morale rose with the increasing numbers. Moreover, so long as a core cadre of experienced officers and noncoms remained, units recovered their fighting edge quickly. Captain Peter McGlashan's October 5 letter reflected the confidence many now felt as the Confederates' strength grew: "The army is now in splendid condition and woe betide 'Little Mac' if he ever crosses the Potomac."[19]

The fluidity of the army's organization had long bothered Lee. Initially, he did not have the legal authorization to form army corps, so he had grouped his divisions into two wings—under Jackson and Longstreet—but this was provisional, and the confusion attendant with units coming and going—either directly reporting to Lee or being attached to one of the wings—had been partly responsible for the disastrous loss of Special Orders No. 191 (see the prologue). It had also led to confusion, such as Robert Toombs and Nathanial Evans imagining they were still division commanders at the Battles of South Mountain and Sharpsburg. On September 18, the Confederacy's congress approved the creation of army corps, commanded by a lieutenant general. Without question, command went to Longstreet and Jackson. Longstreet's First Corps consisted of five divisions: Lafayette McLaws's; Richard H. Anderson's; David R. Jones's, now under

George Pickett, after Jones became ill from heart disease; John B. Hood's; and John G. Walker's. Jackson received four divisions: A. P. Hill's; D. H. Hill's; Lawton's, temporarily under Jubal Early; and J. R. Jones's, reassigned to Brigadier General William Taliaferro. The creation of these corps relieved Lee's headquarters of a huge administrative burden, which could now be attended to by the corps' staff. It firmed up the army's organization and built esprit among the troops, who identified with the defined organization they now belonged to.[20]

The reorganization included numerous promotions and—importantly— some transfers of misfits, poor performers, and troublemakers. Howell Cobb departed, as did Thomas Drayton and Roger Pryor. Robert Toombs, who left to recover from his wound, would not return and was replaced with Henry Benning. Toombs was brave, but also a troublesome subordinate. John G. Walker was promoted to major general and transferred to the Trans-Mississippi Department. Walker was a mediocre performer, and his reassignment opened a vacancy for General Robert Ransom Jr. to fill. Some of these departures enabled Lee to rearrange more brigades along state lines, as President Davis wished, even though Lee was personally averse to this policy. The reorganization also included a major overhaul of the Confederate army's artillery. It had fought with great courage at Sharpsburg, but at nearly every point on that battlefield, it had been dominated by the Federal guns. A large part of the problem came from poorly officered or badly depleted units, which lacked the firepower or leadership to hold their own against the superior range and ammunition of Union artillery. Now, understrength batteries were consolidated, and inefficient ones were broken up, with their officers reassigned and enlisted men and horses detailed to other units. Some batteries with good records, but so badly reduced that they could not be rebuilt without extraordinary effort, were lost, but most of those that were eliminated were poorly run affairs, and their purging benefited the army. An additional advantage to these changes was the creation of a more standardized size for divisional artillery groupings, compared with the wide disparity that existed at Sharpsburg. Continued improvements to the overall organization of the army were possible and would continue to occur, but this major restructuring resulted in a stronger, more efficient fighting force, with better soldiers and administrators in brigade and division posts.[21]

There was a period of about 3 weeks where the Army of Northern Virginia, crippled from Sharpsburg and the leakage of thousands of stragglers, was extremely vulnerable. But Lee masked this weakness with an aggressive posture, and McClellan failed to pay heed to the abundant intelligence reports available to him about the Rebel army's condition, or to probe it to test its strength and response. He made a disastrous error, leaving the Confederates free to gather supplies and carry out their recovery and reorganization unhindered. In the months ahead, the soldiers in the Army of the Potomac would reap the consequences of that failure at the Battles of Fredericksburg and Chancellorsville.

25

End of an Epoch

"Such a sight I shall never see again"

When it became clear that the Confederate army had re-treated to Virginia, at 1:30 p.m. on September 19, McClellan reported to Halleck "that Maryland is entirely freed from the presence of the enemy" and that "no fears need now be entertained for the safety of Pennsylvania. I shall at once reoccupy Harper's Ferry." There was no hint that he intended to pursue a beaten enemy and follow up his victory. The implication was clear—the Army of the Potomac had achieved a great success in thwarting the Rebel invasion of the North, and the nation should be satisfied and gratified by that result. His report received a characteristically curt message from Halleck the next day, complaining that "we are still left entirely in the dark in regard to your own movements and those of the enemy. You should keep me advised of both, so far as you know them." McClellan had been doing so, but, unbeknownst to both generals, his reports for some reason were slow to reach Washington, DC. Later that day, McClellan fired off a testy reply, providing information on the Union army's position and the enemy's whereabouts. He then admonished the general-in-chief: "I regret that you find it necessary to couch every dispatch I have the honor to receive from you, in a spirit of fault finding, and that you have not yet found the leisure to say one word in commendation of the recent achieve-ments of this army, or even to allude to them." Two days later, on September 22, McClellan prepared the groundwork for the argument that his army had accom-plished enough, and that it needed rest and reorganization before beginning a new campaign. Its efficiency was "much impaired," he believed. The Battles of South Mountain and Antietam had removed 10 general officers "and many reg-imental and company officers, besides a large number of enlisted men." All of the infantry corps were "badly cut up and scattered by the overwhelming num-bers brought against them in the battle of the 17th instant, and the entire army has been greatly exhausted by unavoidable overwork, hunger, and want of sleep and rest." McClellan also claimed there was a lack of transportation "to furnish a single day's supply of subsistence in advance"—a curious statement, since the existing modes had kept the Union army provisioned since it left Washington, DC. For these reasons, and McClellan's persistent belief in the enemy's clear superiority in numbers, he did not feel it prudent to cross the Potomac River, which might rise to flood stage with heavy rains at any time and leave him stranded and vulnerable on the Virginia side of the river. He recommended that the sensible course was to rest and reorganize the army before resuming active operations.[1]

McClellan had a right to be sensitive and proud of the Federal army's achievements, as well as of his own accomplishments. He had taken a defeated, demoralized, and dispirited force; restored their confidence; reorganized it on the march; defeated Lee at the Battle of South Mountain; and battered him so badly at Antietam that the Confederates retreated to Virginia. All this was against an enemy he believed outnumbered him. Nor were they minor achievements. His soldiers had fought superbly. So much attention is paid to the resistance that Lee's smaller numbers put up at the Battle of Antietam that the performance of the Army of the Potomac is often given short shrift. In both conflicts, they had carried the fight to the enemy with aggressiveness and courage. The 1st and 12th Corps, the two McClellan considered to be his biggest question marks, hammered the Rebels harder than any other units in the Federal army. But it came at a high cost. The 1st Corps suffered from such heavy straggling during the fighting that George Meade described it as "startling." Of its three divisions, the worst numbers were in Ricketts's, which contained only 74 officers and 890 enlisted men on September 18, but rose to 266 officers and 5,748 enlisted men 4 days later, after the absentees returned to their commands. The 9th Corps, another newcomer to the army, also fought well, but its performance was clouded by the length of time it had taken to seize the Rohrback Bridge, as well as by the defeat administered by A. P. Hill's counterattack. The storming of the Sunken Lane by the 2nd Corps was another example of the Union army's fighting spirit. Despite appalling casualties, they had pressed home their attack and overran the enemy position. Yet, in his September 22 report to Halleck, McClellan focused on negative aspects of its condition, not on these achievements and the potential his troops had shown. At various times in the Civil War, of which the Maryland Campaign was a prime example, Lee could be guilty of demanding more from his men than they were capable of giving. McClellan suffered from the opposite condition. He regularly expected and demanded less of his men than they were able to deliver. He fostered a culture that lingered with the Union army throughout the war: being satisfied with limited gains, and focusing on what the *enemy* might do next, rather than what the *Federal forces* planned to do.[2]

In Antietam's aftermath, McClellan had access to an abundance of intelligence sources that, if tapped, could have provided him with an accurate picture of the Confederates' strength, condition, and organization. His army had taken hundreds of Confederate soldiers as prisoners in the Battles of South Mountain and Antietam, along with many stragglers. Thousands of wounded and sick Confederates also fell into Union hands. Altogether, they represented every division in the Army of Northern Virginia. A systematic interrogation of them would have produced an accurate order of battle of the Rebel army, a good sense of its size, and confirmation of how poorly supplied it was. Yet nothing of the sort was done. McClellan's staff seemed more interested in affirming the narrative emanating from headquarters—that the army had been outnumbered by the Rebels in Maryland—than in seeking reliable data that was readily available to them. When General Joseph Hooker assumed command of the Army of the Potomac in early 1863, he would complain that "there was no means, no organization, and no apparent effort to obtain" information about the Confederates' strength and organization, and that "we were almost as ignorant of the enemy in our immediate front as if they had been in China." Yet evidence that the Rebels were poorly supplied was abundant—if one bothered to look. Fitz John Porter admitted that "starvation [in the Confederate army] had accomplished half the victory" for Union arms at Antietam. Henry Royer in the 96th Pennsylvania wrote home on September 18, mentioning how the Rebels he encountered "are naked and discouraged with their losses and cool reception in Maryland, besides, in a starving condition." In a letter written 2 days later, a soldier in the 89th New York described the Confederates as "ragged, poor fed, disheartened creatures." After encountering a group of Rebel prisoners, Adjutant John Burnham in the 16th Connecticut made a similar assessment: "Their hair was long and uncombed and their faces were thin & cadaverous as though they had been starved to death. It is of course possible that it is the natural look of the race but it appeared mightily to me like the result of short fare, and they were the dirtiest set I ever beheld. A regiment of New England paupers could not equal them for filth, lice, and rags." These were casual observations by individuals, but they offer a sense of what a methodical questioning of Confederates prisoners might have revealed, had McClellan been interested in hearing it. He would have learned that the enemy's forces were not as strong as he believed; their logistics were largely nonexistent; and, as long as Lee remained near Winchester and Martinsburg in Virginia—far from rail communications—he would be forced to subsist off the lower Shenandoah Valley communities, which rendered him vulnerable. Yet no effort to made to tap this rich source of information that lay at McClellan's fingertips.[3]

Instead, McClellan pushed his narrative of the Confederates' superior strength. In his September 22 letter to Halleck, he referred to "the overwhelming number" of the enemy at Antietam. Then, 5 days later, he assured the general-in-chief that "in the last battles the enemy were undoubtedly greatly superior to us in number, and it was only by very hard fighting that we gained the advantage we did." McClellan warned that if the Army of Northern Virginia obtained reinforcements and he received none, "it is possible that I may have too much on my hands in the next battle." On October 7, General Darius Couch passed along an information report to Chief of Staff Marcy. It was received from "an intelligent lad of eighteen," who had passed through the Confederate lines when coming from Martinsburg. He reported that Stuart's cavalry, located 2 miles from that town, numbered 9,000, and the main Rebel army in the Shenandoah Valley was 150,000 strong. That Couch would even deign to forward such an absurd report reflects just how deeply the Union army headquarters' prevailing view of enemy numbers had percolated down the command chain. Couch sent on the report because such numbers were believed to be credible.[4]

McClellan's intelligence gathering failed to produce realistic estimates of the Confederate army's strength, organization, and capabilities. This had a paralyzing effect on his operations and encouraged a defensive posture and mindset, which, in turn, provided fodder for McClellan's political enemies, who sought justifications for his removal. The army commander's belief in the enemy's superior numbers profoundly influenced how he managed the fighting at Antietam, ranging from his hesitation to reinforce Hooker's 1st Corps with Mansfield's 12th Corps on the night of September 16; to keeping Richardson's division in the 2nd Corps in support of the artillery until it could be relieved by Morell's division in the 5th Corps; to sending off the 6th Corps to reinforce the right flank, rather than committing them to the center or the left, where their presence might have proved to be decisive; and, finally, to holding back the bulk of the 5th Corps when Dryer's Regulars revealed that the Confederates' center was a hollow shell. In each instance, the specter of a massive Confederate counterattack by troops Lee kept hidden from view caused McClellan to choose the most conservative course. The ferocity of A. P. Hill's assault at Shepherdstown only confirmed McClellan's certainty in his estimate of the enemy's strength and his decision that the Federals' most prudent strategy was to guard the line along the the Potomac River while resting, rebuilding, and reinforcing his army. The reoccupation of Harpers Ferry, including Bolivar Heights and Maryland Heights, by the 2nd and 12th Corps on September 22; Porter's and Burnside's presence in the Sharpsburg-Shepherdstown area; and Franklin's deployment to a position near Williamsport and Hagerstown—a front of over 20 miles—were defensive in nature. It was designed to block the fords on the Potomac River that were most likely to be used in a renewed Confederate offensive into Maryland. Although McClellan thought the occupation of Harpers Ferry "gives us a great advantage of a secure debouche," he had no plans to use it as such. In any case, until the railroad bridge there was repaired, he believed that "we cannot otherwise supply a greater number of troops than we now have on the Virginia side at that point."[5]

Once the fall rains would cause the Potomac to rise enough to prevent Lee from crossing into Maryland, McClellan told Halleck he contemplated concentrating the full strength of the Union army at Harpers Ferry and then "acting according to circumstances," either by moving on Winchester "if from the position and attitude of the enemy we are likely to gain a great advantage by doing do," or else devoting time to organizing the Army of the Potomac and instructing the new troops joining it. He had no fear of a Rebel attack on Washington, DC, from the direction of Manassas, which was a concern of Halleck's. Instead, "I rather apprehend a renewal of the attempt in Maryland should the river remain low for a great length of time and should they receive considerable addition to their force." What became clear to Halleck and Lincoln was that the Federal army's commander had no intention of taking advantage of the victory at Antietam. McClellan's principal worry was that the Confederates would renew their offensive. His preference, which he expressed repeatedly, was to remain quiet, refit the army, and keep an eye on the enemy—but from a respectful distance.[6]

Halleck might have asked McClellan if, until the railroad bridge at Harpers Ferry was repaired, only a single corps of the Union army on the south bank of the Potomac River could be supplied, how, then, was it possible for the Confederates to maintain a force larger than the Army of the Potomac in the Shenandoah Valley, 95 miles from their nearest rail communications? Moreover, how could Lee accomplish this on the Confederate rail system, which—as both Halleck and McClellan should have known—had nowhere near the capability of carrying the tonnage of goods needed to supply a large army as the Northern rail lines did? Halleck also might have asked how was it possible for the Confederate army—which, only 10 days earlier, McClellan had claimed was soundly defeated, and "no fears now [need] be entertained for the safety of Pennsylvania"—to currently present a threat to Maryland? But Halleck did not ask such probing questions, because he was equally guilty of imagining the Army of Northern Virginia to be stronger and more capable than it was. In addition, Halleck was served by even worse intelligence information than McClellan. Despite the overwhelming evidence that the main strength of the Rebel army in Virginia had engaged McClellan at Antietam, and it continued to confront him from the lower end of the Shenandoah Valley, Halleck still harbored an irrational fear for the safety of the nation's capital. He wrote to McClellan on September 26, stating that he hoped the Federal forces would cross the Potomac River at a point below Harpers Ferry, "so as to cover Washington by your line of operations." Halleck imagined that, with McClellan remaining in his present position, the enemy somehow threatened both the Union army and the nation's capital at the same time. As for reinforcing McClellan, "the number of troops to be left here will depend upon the amount of protection to be afforded by your army in the field." In other words, if McClellan wanted any more men, he must restrict his line of operations to one that covered Washington, DC. On September 30, Halleck told McClellan he had received information indicating "that the enemy is massing a strong force at Culpeper," and, 4 days later, on October 4, that "Longstreet is moving to Leesburg, with intention to cross the river, while Jackson holds you in check at Harper's Ferry." Ten days later, in the aftermath of Stuart's cavalry raid, Halleck sounded a fresh alarm—the Rebels were massing 7,000 to 10,000 cavalry near Leesburg, for another raid "into Maryland or on Washington." All of these warnings proved to be false, but they wasted the energy of McClellan's cavalry and infantry, which had to investigate and guard against these phantom forces.[7]

The result of Halleck's and McClellan's mistaken exaggeration of the Confederates' strength and capabilities was to create an overall inertia in the Federals' war effort in the Maryland-Virginia theater and engender a defensive mindset. Besides supervising the actions of the Union army and advising the president, Halleck's role as general-in-chief was to develop grand strategy, at which—despite his deep thinking on the subject—he was a failure. McClellan's job was to construct plans for how to use the Army of the Potomac to suppress the rebellion. This required offensive strategies. But no such activity by the army's commander existed in Antietam's aftermath. It was to his wife, Mary Ellen, that McClellan revealed his true intentions. "I look upon the campaign as substantially ended & my present intention is to seize Harper's Ferry & hold it with a strong force. Then go to work to reorganize the army ready for another campaign," he informed her on September 22. In a letter 3 days later, he stated, "My own judgement is to watch the line of the Potomac until the water rises, then to concentrate everything near Harpers Ferry—reorganize the army as promptly as possible & then if secesh remains near Winchester to attack him." But this was little more than idle talk. On September 29, he wrote that he believed the Rebels had withdrawn from the Martinsburg area to Winchester: "If he had gone there I will be able to arrange my troops more with a view to comfort & if it will only rain a little so as to raise the river will feel quite justified in asking for a short leave." A general contemplating taking leave from his army had no intention of resuming active operations.[8]

Instead of developing operational plans, McClellan spent considerable time working his political connections to arrange for the downfall of his enemies—Halleck and Staunton—or probing the political waters for how best to respond to Lincoln's Emancipation Proclamation. He imagined that he had acquired political capital with his success in Maryland, and he intended to spend it. He revealed to Mary Ellen that "an opportunity has presented itself" through a conference of Northern governors, scheduled to meet in Altoona, Pennsylvania, on September 24, to orchestrate his plan "that Stanton shall be removed & that Halleck shall give way to me as Comdr in Chief." In another letter to his wife later that evening, he announced, "Unless these two conditions are met I will leave the service," believing that "I have at least the right to demand a guarantee that I shall not be interfered with—I know I cannot have that assurance so long as Stanton continues in the position of Secy of War & Halleck as Genl in Chief." Who agreed to present McClellan's demands is unknown, although Stephen Sears has speculated that it was Ohio's Governor David Tod, whom the general knew during his days with the Ohio and Mississippi Railroad. The maneuver backfired spectacularly. Tod and other governors who were friendly to McClellan not only failed to introduce McClellan's conditions, but they also ended up having to fend off a proposal by Republican governors for his removal.[9]

McClellan also dispatched his intelligence agent, Allan Pinkerton, to do some sleuthing for him with the president. From the moment he had been placed in command of the field army after Second Manassas, McClellan had, with good reason, never felt that he had the full confidence of Lincoln or his administration. Now, with his successes at the Battles of South Mountain and Antietam, McClellan was curious to sound out where the president stood vis-à-vis his army commander. Pinkerton met with Lincoln on September 22, the same day as the Preliminary Emancipation Proclamation was issued. The interview resulted in Lincoln doing some detective work of his own by asking Pinkerton several leading questions. Why had the Union army failed to relieve its garrison at Harpers Ferry? What was the strength of the opposing armies at Antietam? Why was the fighting not renewed on September 18? How was the Rebel army able to escape back into Virginia without further damage? Lincoln so disarmed Pinkerton with his folksy charm that the detective left the interview convinced of Lincoln' sincerity and friendship toward McClellan, being "highly pleased and gratified with all you had done." But as Lincoln's biographer, David Donald has observed, it was the president who drew the information he wanted from the spy and concluded "that Antietam had not been a great victory but a lost opportunity squandered by the high command of the Army of the Potomac."[10]

On October 1, McClellan wrote to Halleck that since it was probable Harpers Ferry would be permanently garrisoned, no matter what line of operations the Army of the Potomac ultimately adopted, a permanent bridge should be constructed across the Shenandoah River there, as well as a permanent wagon bridge built across the Potomac River. This was in addition to his earlier request to repair the damaged railroad bridge over the Potomac. These were reasonable recommendations, but Halleck sniffed out that McClellan's ulterior motive was to use the bridge building as a reason for further delay in resuming active operations. He replied that if McClellan planned to adhere to Harpers Ferry as his base, "why not cross at once and give battle to the enemy? Unless I am greatly deceived in regard to the enemy's numbers, this can be done now while the river is low. If you wait till the river rises, the roads will be such as to greatly impede your operations." Halleck's suggestion made sense, even though it came from one who careened from fearing a phantom Rebel army was going to attack Washington, DC, to questioning why McClellan was not undertaking a new campaign into Virginia. Knowing his man, Halleck added that whether building the recommended bridges was approved or not, the government would not contemplate any delay in the Federal army resuming its operations. The bridges were a question for the War Department (meaning Stanton) and the president, who, Halleck added almost as an aside, "will be with you today, and you can consult him there."[11]

This was the first McClellan knew that Lincoln was coming to visit, learning that the president would arrive in Harpers Ferry that very day. Gathering his staff, McClellan rode out to meet him there. When they were together, Lincoln told the general he had come to see the troops and the battlefields, but McClellan suspected "that the real purpose of his visit is to push me into a premature advance into Virginia. I may be mistaken, but think not." He was right to be suspicious, for the president had not ventured from the capital merely to sightsee. He came to visit his army commander, observe the troops, and look at the scenes of the fighting. Most crucially, he came to gauge the army's loyalty. Were the sentiments Major Key had expressed regarding a compromise attitude toward the Confederates (see chapter 23) and the army's continued inaction in any way connected? Did the senior officers give their allegiance to the elected government and the nation, or to the man who led the army?[12]

Reactions within the Army of the Potomac to the president's visit depended on the individual and, often, their party affiliation. Colonel Charles Wainwright, commanding the 1st Corps' artillery and a stalwart Democrat, was disgusted. On October 2, he encountered Lincoln, who was riding in an ambulance with "some half-dozen western looking politicians." During the president's arrival to review the corps, which had been patiently waiting in formation for nearly 2 hours. "I should have preferred to see the President of the United States travelling with a little more regard to appearances than can be afforded by a common ambulance, with his long legs doubled up so that his knees almost struck his chin, and grinning out of the windows like a baboon," the colonel snarled. Lincoln, he declared, was not only "the ugliest man I ever saw, but the most uncouth and gawky in his manners and appearance." A member in the 9th Corps' 51st Pennsylvania had an entirely different experience. He observed that when Lincoln, McClellan, Burnside, Cox, and other officers conducted their review of that corps, "perfect order and silence prevailed," and everyone was "anxious to get a close view" of their president. Their reaction may not have been enthusiastic, but "it was of that calm and dignified kind of respect, suited to his position under present circumstances." In this soldier's opinion, Lincoln's visit "had a good effect upon the soldiers." Even though the 6th Corps' commander, William B. Franklin, acknowledged that Lincoln was very kind to him and complimented him for his victory at Crampton's Gap, privately Franklin was contemptuous of the president, confiding to his wife that Lincoln looked "like a miserable old man as he rode around hat in hand." Franklin took pride in the fact that his corps did not cheer. "They were entirely silent to my pleasure," he gloated. When Lincoln, McClellan, and a large entourage of officers toured the Antietam battlefield on October 2, Charles Wainwright was "astonished to notice how little interest Mr. Lincoln took in the recital." But George Meade, who was also with the party, thought the president seemed "very interested in all the movements of Hooker's corps," and Jacob Cox noticed that Lincoln was "observant and keenly interested in the field of battle, but made no display of sentiment." The latter, depending on the observer, might have been interpreted as disinterest.[13]

In the days he was with the Army of the Potomac, Lincoln made it a point to meet with McClellan and all of his senior officers. Those who left a record of their encounter with the president found him genial and complimentary of the work and sacrifices the army had made. General Alpheus Williams, still in temporary command of the 12th Corps, "had quite a long talk with him, sitting on a pile of logs." Williams thought him "the most unaffected, simple-minded, honest and frank man I have ever met." He liked Lincoln but wished "he had a little more firmness" in managing the country. Jacob Cox, with more experience in politics, recognized the astute, incisive brain that lay behind the "unaffected, simple-minded" front Lincoln often presented to disarm people. "His unpretending cordiality was what first impressed one," Cox wrote, "but you soon saw with what sharp intelligence and keen humor he dealt with every subject which came up." He noticed that Lincoln made no criticisms of the Maryland Campaign. "There was enough to praise, and he praised it heartily," observed Cox. Lincoln gave thanks that the Confederates' invasion into the North had been thwarted. He was probably being disingenuous, however, when he told Fitz John Porter that the latter's dispatches to Burnside, which were so critical of General John Pope, had been helpful and that he was "satisfied" with them—which he was not. But, in general, Lincoln employed his talent for humor and modesty to put those he spoke with at ease, as well as rendering them prone to underestimate the president and judge him to be little more than "a political coward" or "simple-minded." This helped loosen tongues and draw out a less guarded, more honest opinion than would have been possible had the officers sensed that Lincoln was making any judgments or might use what they told him to punish them.[14]

Lincoln spent his time with McClellan discussing the military situation. Earlier, McClellan had voiced complaints about the president and his civilian advisors: "These people don't know what an army requires & therefore act stupidly." But the president apparently employed the same tactics with McClellan that he had with the other generals, disarming him with praise. "The President was very kind to me personally," McClellan wrote to Mary Ellen on the day of Lincoln's departure, and "told me he was convinced I was the best general in the country, etc., etc." Yet we know Lincoln also spoke to McClellan about his excess caution and the urgent need to take advantage of the Union army's victory at Antietam. He may have done so in such an oblique fashion, however, that the McClellan missed the advice. For his part, McClellan believed he made Lincoln aware "of the great difficulty" the Army of the Potomac had faced at the Battles of South Mountain and Antietam, as well as its need to reorganize and refit before beginning a new campaign. The army's commander was not alone in believing this had been impressed upon the chief executive. George Meade opined, "I think, however, he was informed of certain facts in connection with this army that have opened his eyes a little, and which may induce him to pause and reflect before in interferes with McClellan by giving positive orders."[15]

Lincoln departed on October 5. The atmosphere of distrust between McClellan and the administration had not been cleared away, but the president had resolved a crucial question in his own mind. On his first morning at the battlefield, while looking over the army's extensive camps, he famously remarked to O. M. Hatch, a neighbor from Springfield, Illinois, who accompanied him on the trip, that they were gazing not on the Army of the Potomac, but on McClellan's bodyguard. This probably reflected Lincoln's uncertainty over whether the army's loyalty was with McClellan, or the nation. His experience with Major Key posed the worry that it might be the former. But, during his discussions with the army's leadership, he found that although they thought highly of McClellan, their first loyalty was to the country. Empathy with Major Key's point of view existed, but it was a minority opinion. This knowledge strengthened Lincoln's hand and opened the path to removing McClellan, but the president intended to give the general one more chance to preserve his position. Lincoln probably also learned that Burnside remained extremely popular with the 9th Corps and was generally well regarded in the others. This would have confirmed his conviction that if it became necessary to relieve McClellan, Burnside remained the best choice as his replacement.[16]

The belief by McClellan and his generals that they had educated the president on the need for the army to resupply and refit was exploded the day after Lincoln left. On October 6, Halleck telegraphed that, by order of the president, McClellan was to "cross the Potomac and give battle to the enemy or drive him south. You army must move now while the roads are good." He was promised 30,000 reinforcements if his line of operations covered Washington, DC. If he chose to operate in the Shenandoah Valley, he would only receive 12,000–15,000 men. Lincoln favored the former, but he did not dictate which line McClellan should choose. What he demanded was a plan—and action.[17]

McClellan had given little thought to a fall campaign. Now, confronted with the need to produce a plan, he found little to like about either of the options Halleck offered. After consulting with his corps commanders, he responded to Halleck on October 7. McClellan had little enthusiasm for any overland advance into Virginia, but he chose the Shenandoah Valley line, because he believed it was only one that provided Maryland and Pennsylvania with cover from a Confederate offensive, and because he considered any advance between the Shenandoah Valley and Washington, DC, to be of little strategic value. An advance up the valley only had merit if the enemy remained near Winchester. "I do not regard the line of the Shenandoah valley as important for ulterior objects," he added, noting that if the Confederates withdrew up the valley, he could not follow them. "The country is destitute of supplies," he believed—even though Lee had been sustaining his army there for weeks—"and we have not sufficient means of transportation to enable us to advance more than 20 or 25 miles beyond a railway or canal terminus." What McClellan proposed was to fight the Rebels near Winchester, if they would offer battle, or force them to abandon the Shenandoah Valley, "then to adopt a new & decisive line of operations which shall strike at the heart of the rebellion." This meant a return to the Virginia Peninsula and the James River, which he considered the true line of operations. This reflected McClellan's strategic thinking that Richmond was the heart of the rebellion, when it actually was their armies that sustained the Confederacy, not a geographic location. Nonetheless, it was a moot point, because it was highly unlikely that Lincoln would have approved a plan to return the Union army to the peninsula.[18]

In whatever direction the Army of the Potomac moved, it could not do so until it received "shoes & other indispensable articles of clothing, as well as shelter tents &c." McClellan assured Halleck that the moment these needs were met, "not an hour shall be lost in carrying your instructions into effect." Within the Lincoln administration, the general was famous for producing reasons not to move, so there was immediate suspicion this was merely another smokescreen to delay an advance. The president knew otherwise. He had seen the army up close and could not help but notice the ragged condition of many units. The Union army's supply problems were real, and they were abundantly evident to anyone who bothered to look. Holmes W. Burlingame, a teenage private in the 1st Corps' 104th New York, related how, in the weeks after the Battle of Antietam, his brigade was "in really bad condition, we had been without tents or blankets, with no change of clothing since we left our knapsacks in the field back near Thoroughfare Gap." With no tents or rubber blankets, the men slept right against the damp ground. "Our clothes were ragged our shoes no better." For those with shoes, socks were in short supply, so the shoes rubbed against their ankles, causing raw sores. A member of the same brigade, John B. Sherman in the 105th New York, grumbled in a September 28 letter that "we are a pitiful set of beings now. We have no blankets no tents no cloths [*sic*] half of us not even a shirt and not half enough to eat and these cold nights it seems as if we should freeze." In early October, a visitor to the 2nd Delaware in the 2nd Corps learned that the men had not been paid in 5 months, nor had a change of clothing since they left the Virginia Peninsula in August. The men were "without shirts, and are dirty, ragged, and very much discouraged." As late as October 20, George Meade complained, "I have hundreds of men in my command without shoes, going barefoot, and I can't get a shoe for man or beast." Horseshoes were virtually nonexistent. Colonel Charles Wainwright, the 1st Corps' artillery chief, noted on October 10 that although standing requisitions had been placed at the supply depots in Hagerstown and Harpers Ferry, "we have not got a single shoe." His artillery batteries had not had their ordnance requisitions filled or been provided with any horses to replace those lost in the Maryland Campaign. It was a deplorable situation, although the truth was that some corps were worse off than others.[19]

A great deal of time was wasted by Halleck, McClellan, and others as to deciding whether a supply problem even existed, as well as determining who was at fault and why such items were not reaching the troops. The situation was serious enough that some officers suspected it might be deliberate withholding. "It seems almost as if they purposely kept them [supplies] back at Washington, or else they have not got them," fumed Colonel Wainwright in his journal on October 19. The truth was more complex than an evil conspiracy to bring down McClellan, although it was true that Stanton took little interest in helping to sort things out. Part of the problem was that the supply system established to support the Union army either on the Virginia Peninsula or northern Virginia could not could quickly reorient itself to western Maryland. With a massive scale of operations, it took time to redirect and then start supplies flowing to where they were needed. Army bureaucracy also contributed to the problem. This was particularly true for horses. Thousands of animals that McClellan wanted for his cavalry and artillery were issued to units concerned with the defenses of Washington, DC. Administratively, they fell under McClellan's command. Thus the Army of the Potomac technically was receiving the number of horses requested. "If General McClellan will instruct the officers authorized to approve requisitions in his name to confine this approval to issues to be made on the Upper Potomac, all the horses will be sent there till his wants are fully supplied," wrote the army's quartermaster general, Montgomery C. Meigs, "but if by his authority or in his name they approve requisitions for the troops in front of Washington, the horses will be issued to these troops under his direction."[20]

The Army of the Potomac was like a vast city—it was half the size of Baltimore—and meeting its daily needs was an immense logistical and administrative challenge. But apart from the bureaucratic issues and difficulties in establishing new lines of supply, McClellan bore some blame for his situation. Had he moved aggressively after the Battle of Antietam, or even produced a clear campaign plan to carry the war back into Virginia, this would have applied pressure on the government to solve the logistical problems sooner. So long as no operations were planned, or if the organizers were uncertain about what line the Union army would operate on, there was no urgency to reorient resources to smooth out supply systems to reach western Maryland.

Inevitably, various corners of the press began to question the Federal army's inactivity. The *Chicago Tribune*'s editor thundered, "What devil is it that prevents the Potomac army from advancing?" Many in the army, however, took a dim view of this latest version of the "On to Richmond" hue and cry. "I see by the newspapers that an uneasy and impatient public are demanding an immediate advance," General Alpheus William observed on October 17, "yet these anxious souls know nothing of our preparations, nothing of the force or resources of the enemy."

When Colonel Wainwright reached the army right after the fighting at Antietam, he was surprised that they had not immediately pursued the enemy, "but the more I know of the condition of the army, and other matters, the less certain does it appear that we could have done so to advantage." At the end of September, Halleck released 20 newly raised regiments to McClellan, amounting to a reinforcement of 18,667 men, the equivalent of an entire army corps. McClellan welcomed their numbers, but it burdened him with the responsibility of training them. It would have made more sense to have sent the 3rd or the 11th Corps to McClellan and established camps of instruction for the new regiments within the capital's defenses, rather than saddle a field army commander with the burden of raw recruits. As Alpheus Williams, whose corps received 13 new regiments during and after the Maryland Campaign, explained, "You can well fancy that these green regiments give an infinite increase of work to get them into shape." Williams was impressed with McClellan's energy and care in bringing these new units up to standard. "Nothing seems to escape his attention or his anticipation. Every endeavor is made, and constantly kept up to enforce drill and discipline and to create an *esprit de corps* and confidence. I have met no officer at all his equal in this respect."[21]

Yet, as the fine fall weather passed by with no activity, some in the Army of the Potomac began to question their idleness. Even George Meade, who had sympathized with the need for pausing to resupply and refit after Antietam, began to lose patience. On October 13 he grumbled, "I am getting very tired of inactivity, and although I am not fond of fighting, yet if we have to do it, the sooner we get at it and have it over the better." Colonel Thomas Welsh, commanding a brigade in Willcox's 1st Division of the 9th Corps, reached this point much earlier, seething to his wife on September 23, "I am thoroughly disgusted with the management of this army that it really makes me sick to contemplate the result." He believed the whole Rebel army could have been destroyed or captured before they escaped across the Potomac River and wondered if McClellan had purposely let them escape. In his October 20, 1862, letter to the president, Lieutenant Colonel Charles Albright in the 132nd Pennsylvania expressed his opinion that "soldiers would rather fight than be idle in camp." He believed that if the current mode of operations continued, they would not "end this war in six years." Welsh's opinion was a minority one, as most soldiers had implicit faith in McClellan, but even some of the general's supporters were beginning to question the army's inactivity. There had been good reason for the long period of preparation in the fall and winter of 1861. But with a core of seasoned, veteran troops, that argument was no longer valid.[22]

Despite McClellan's promise to Halleck that not an hour would be lost in moving the Army of the Potomac the moment it was fully supplied, he found time on October 10 to sneak off to New Jersey to retrieve Mary Ellen and bring her back with him. It was not unusual for generals to have their wives visit when troops were in winter quarters, but it was highly irregular when the general in question had just received orders from the president to move. If McClellan had hoped to conceal his trip, his attempt failed. This escapade made its way into the newspapers the next day, and Secretary of the Navy Gideon Welles noted in his diary that the general had been seen at the Continental Hotel in Philadelphia. McClellan permitted other senior officer, such as Franklin and Porter, to also bring their wives to the army's encampment. The optics of this decision were awful. It did not foster good morale when soldiers went without shoes, blankets, or tents, but generals could provide the means to have their wives and children in camp. To compound matters, Jeb Stuart mounted his Pennsylvania raid at the very moment McClellan brought his wife to Maryland.[23]

Stuart's and his men's escape to Virginia after the raid without any damage, and the apparent utter ineptness of an army of nearly 100,000 to catch him, struck another hammer blow to McClellan's insecure relationship with the Lincoln administration. Even among his supporters in the army, there was a feeling of humiliation and anger. "This is the third time the rascal has successfully accomplished this feat [riding completely around the army], and I think it is almost time we learned how to meet and defeat him," wrote General George Meade. Colonel Charles Wainwright described the raid and the Federals' failure to catch the Rebels as "a burning disgrace" and opined that "our cavalry is an awful botch." It was true that the Army of the Potomac was short on cavalry. The troopers it did have were dispersed along the Potomac River, in order to watch its fords and provide warning of Confederate raids. On October 4, a raid toward Cumberland, Maryland, by the enemy's cavalry, under Colonel John D. Imboden, caused McClellan to send an entire brigade of his cavalry under General William W. Averell to catch and thrash the Rebels. Averell failed to do so, and his departure made it easier for Stuart to slip through the Union picket screen along the Potomac. McClellan blamed the raid on the Federals' "deficiency in the cavalry arm," which was partly true. But Stephen Z. Starr, in *The Union Cavalry in the Civil War*, notes that "McClellan failed to take one step that might have enhanced the effectiveness of the cavalry he did have." His mounted troops were widely dispersed, with brigades existing "mainly for administrative purposes," and his excellent chief of cavalry, General John Buford, who might have instituted substantive changes to improve the service, was relegated to the duties of a staff officer, having no real authority. Lincoln, who was furious at the impunity with which Stuart carried out his raid, put his finger on another reason such forays were possible. He commented, through Halleck, that "if the enemy had more occupation south of the river, his cavalry would not be so likely to make raids north of it."[24]

Lincoln might have been furious, but his patience with McClellan remained remarkable. On October 13, a day after Stuart's escape, the president wrote the general an extraordinary letter, principally about military strategy in the

Virginia-Maryland theater. But it was also a final attempt to nudge the army commander into action. When governors and cabinet members had demanded McClellan's removal, Lincoln let him remain, but there were limits to how much the political climate and the president's patience could stand. Lincoln started his letter by reminding McClellan of having spoken to him about "what I called your overcautiousness." "Are you not overcautious when you assume that you cannot do what the enemy is constantly doing?" he asked. Lincoln referenced a recent message the general had sent to Halleck—stating that he could not provision the Union army at Winchester unless the railroad from Harpers Ferry was repaired—and pointed to an obvious contradiction. How was it possible that the Confederates, "at a distance nearly twice as great from railroad transportation as you would have to do," were able to supply their army there? He then continued, "I certainly should be pleased for you to have the advantage of the railroad from Harper's Ferry to Winchester, but it wastes all the remainder of autumn to give it to you, and in fact ignores the question of time, which cannot and must not be ignored." Lincoln pointed out that one of the standard maxims of war was to operate against the enemy's communications without exposing your own, yet "you seem to act as if this applies against you, but cannot apply in your favor."[25]

Further, if the Rebels advanced into Pennsylvania—something McClellan fretted over—they would expose their communications, "and you have nothing to do but to follow and ruin him." Lincoln pointed out that the Army of the Potomac's position was nearer to Richmond than Lee's army. "Why can you not reach there before him, unless you admit that he is more than your equal on a march? His route is the arc of a circle, while yours is the chord." If Lee prevented McClellan from threatening his communications, "I would press closely to him; fight him, if a favorable opportunity should present, and at least try to beat him to Richmond on the inside track. I say 'try'; if we never try we shall never succeed." If Lee made a stand at Winchester, then fight him there, "on the idea that if we cannot beat him when he bears the wastage of coming to us, we never can when we bear the wastage of going to him." Lincoln saw Lee's position in the lower end of the Shenandoah Valley as an *opportunity*, rather than a threat, while the latter was how McClellan perceived it. "In coming to us he tenders an advantage which we should not waive," the president went on. "We should not operate as to merely drive him away. As we must beat him somewhere or fail finally, we can do it, if at all, easier near to us than far away." He also offered his views on why he favored the Union army advancing into Virginia on what he called the "inside track," east of the Blue Ridge Mountains. In addition to being the most likely approach that could bring Lee to battle under circumstances favorable to McClellan, in a movement across Virginia, the army would have access to good, secure lines of supply the entire time. Lincoln was sometimes guilty of armchair generalship during the Civil War, as well as of not comprehending the reality of circumstances on the ground. But this was as good and as sound an example of strategic advice as any general received during the Civil War, and it reflected far deeper thinking on the subject than McClellan's headquarters—or Halleck—had produced in nearly a month since the Battle of Antietam. The president saw clearly what McClellan did not. Lincoln complained that "General McClellan thinks he is going to whip the rebels by strategy; and the army has got the same notion. They have no idea that the war is to be carried on and put through by hard, tough fighting . . . and no headway is going to be made while this delusion lasts." The Confederates would only be trounced by defeating their armies, and any strategic plans should focus on how to draw them into battle on terms favorable to the Union forces. The Rebels were well led and active, so plodding, chess-like advances—such as the Peninsula Campaign—were a recipe for failure against such a foe. "It is all easy if our troops march as well as the enemy," Lincoln concluded in his letter to McClellan, "and it is unmanly to say they cannot do it.[26]

For some reason, it took 3 days for Lincoln's letter to reach McClellan. He acknowledged its receipt at once and noted that even though he had told Halleck he planned to move against the enemy in the Shenandoah Valley, McClellan now claimed he was "not wedded to any particular plan of operations." After reflecting on the matter for 5 more days, on October 22, McClellan informed Halleck that "I have decided to move upon the line indicated by the Presdt in his letter of the 13th inst." Several more days of correspondence followed this declaration. These letters focused on the sorry condition of the army's cavalry and the attempts to determine where all the horses supposedly sent to the Army of the Potomac were actually going, as well as on the need to get the cavalry properly mounted before the army could move. On October 25, McClellan forwarded a report from Colonel Robert Williams, commanding the 1st Massachusetts Cavalry, underlining the deplorable state of the cavalry's horses. It reached Lincoln's desk, and the president lost patience. He wrote directly to McClellan: "I have just read your dispatches about sore-tongued and fatigued horses. Will you pardon me for asking what the horses of your army have done since the battle of Antietam that fatigues anything?" It was the sort of message that does not help resolve a difficult situation, but the president was at his wits' end over what it took to get the army moving.[27]

Lincoln's missive drew an immediate response from McClellan, outlining all the work his cavalry had performed since Antietam. To his wife, he seethed about the president's message as one of "those dirty little flings that I can't get used to when they are not merited." The disconnect between the two men had now reached the point where they were talking past one another. McClellan believed he was doing everything possible to get his army in shape to advance, while Halleck and the War Department—"blind & foolish they will continue to the end"—failed to forward the needed supplies. Lincoln was not unsympathetic to the supply shortages of the Army of the Potomac, but the nation was at war. As long as the weather was good, armies could not constantly wait to move until all its needs were met. Relations were frayed to near breaking point. On October 24, Lincoln relieved General Don Carlos Buell of command of the Army of the Ohio. Buell was cut from the same mold as McClellan. He had refused to move his army into Tennessee after his victory in Perryville, Kentucky, on October 8, despite the need to secure eastern Tennessee and protect the largely Unionist population there, and Lincoln could no longer shield Buell from the calls for his removal. It was also a clear warning shot to McClellan.[28]

The Army of the Potomac stirred at last on October 26. McClellan remained unsatisfied with the condition of his cavalry, and numerous units were still awaiting resupplies of clothing, shoes, and tents, but he recognized that he could delay no longer. His plan was to advance into Virginia in two columns. The 2nd and 5th Corps would cross the Potomac River at Harpers Ferry, and the 1st, 6th, and 9th Corps would use a pontoon bridge thrown across the river at Berlin, about 6 miles downriver. The 12th Corps was left in the vicinity of Harpers Ferry, to guard the army's rear. One of the advantages of this line of advance— which greatly influenced McClellan's decision to adopt it—was that when the army reached the Manassas Gap Railroad, about 30 miles south of the Potomac River, it would be reinforced by the 3rd and 11th Corps, as well as a cavalry brigade, drawn from the defenses of Washington, DC. This would add roughly 20,000 troops to the 116,000 already with the main army. McClellan welcomed the prospect of additional support but had little enthusiasm for an overland movement. As his biographer, Ethan Rafuse, has observed, "McClellan clearly would have preferred not to undertake a major campaign before winter and instead wait until 1863 to return the army to its proper line of operations on the Peninsula." Others shared McClellan's skepticism about the overland advance. One was the 12th Corps' general, Alpheus Williams, whose experience in Virginia during the Second Manassas Campaign convinced him "that we cannot successfully invade Virginia from this point [Berlin-Harpers Ferry]. We must have water transportation or large railroad carriage to subsist our troops the moment we leave our depots." The roads in Virginia were awful, and soldiers could not survive on green corn alone. Later in the war, Hooker, Meade, and Grant managed overland campaigns without major supply issues, but the logistical infrastructure that supported those campaigns was far better developed and robust than what McClellan had available.[29]

The only possibility for the overland campaign to have any hope of success was if the army moved rapidly and seized the passes through the Blue Ridge Mountains before Lee got there, forcing the Confederate general to either fight to protect his communications up the Shenandoah Valley, or retreat and surrender northern Virginia to the enemy. This was what Lincoln had emphasized— speed was essential to bring the elusive and canny Lee to battle. But, with the Union army's shortage of cavalry and McClellan's belief in the enemy's superior numbers, he had no intention of risking a rapid advance. Herein lay the seeds of his demise, for the president had privately decided that if McClellan allowed Lee to get across his path to Richmond, Lincoln intended to relieve McClellan of his command. McClellan planned an advance similar to his movement across Maryland, with cavalry screening the infantry and his corps proceeding by measured marches, always being in mutual support of one another. It was a reasonable strategy if he expected to be attacked, but if the hope was to force Lee to fight at a disadvantage, it had no chance of success. Only rapid movements, entailing risk for those units that might be pushed forward, had any prospect of seizing a positional advantage over Lee. Although McClellan, as Rafuse has noted, hoped "for an opportunity to strike a decisive blow," he had no intentions of taking "any unnecessary risks in a campaign that he considered merely a temporary expedient to placate Washington and put himself in position to return the Army of the Potomac to its true line of operations on the Peninsula."[30]

It took 8 days for the army to cross the Potomac River. The movement was a huge and complex operation, yet the length of time it took for the army to get past the river, and its subsequent chess-like advance down the Loudoun Valley, did not bode well for the prospect of bringing Lee to battle on McClellan's terms. His mood during this period waffled between anger—fuming to his wife about having to submit to the "mean and dirty dispatches" he received from Halleck and Lincoln, and grumbling that "there never was a truer epithet applied to a certain individual than that of the 'Gorilla,'"—and jubilation that success in this campaign might enable him to quash not only Lee, but also his greatest enemy, Secretary of War Stanton. "If I am successful in this campaign I think it will end in driving Stanton out—as he was good enough to say that he held office only for the purpose of crushing me, it will afford me great pleasure if I can in any honorable & open way be instrumental in consigning the rascal to the infamous fate he deserves. If I can crush him I will—relentlessly and without remorse," he wrote to Mary Ellen.[31]

Lee reacted immediately and decisively to McClellan's advance. Uncertain whether the Union army commander intended to move against his communications in the Shenandoah Valley or strike toward Richmond, Lee divided his forces, ordering Longstreet's former right wing—now the 1st Corps—to Culpepper on October 28, while keeping Jackson's corps in the Shenandoah Valley to threaten the Federals' flank and their communications. McClellan reacted as Lee had hoped: moving carefully and making sure Jackson would not suddenly come pouring through one of the gaps in the Blue Ridge Mountains and smash into the Union army's flank. George Meade, who well understood how vital it was to get ahead of the enemy, was also clear eyed about how unlikely it was that the Federals would succeed in doing so. In a remarkably candid admission about the Confederates' greater mobility, he wrote that the Union army's advance in Virginia was "an operation I never had the remotest idea we would or could succeed in, as they are much less encumbered by trains than we are, and are much better marchers." By November 3, Longstreet had arrived in the Culpepper area and established good defensive positions that were squarely across McClellan's path to Richmond. The Union general's fate was sealed, but Lincoln waited to act until after the results of the New York State congressional and gubernatorial elections. On November 5, when it was certain that Horatio Seymour—the antiwar, anti-Lincoln Democrat—would win the governor's race, Lincoln made his move, drawing up orders for Halleck to relieve McClellan; assign Burnside to command of the Army of the Potomac and General David Hunter to command of the 9th Corps (an appointment that mercifully did not come to pass); and remove Fitz John Porter, designating General Joseph Hooker as his replacement.[32]

Halleck had his assistant adjutant general, E. D. Townsend, draw up General Orders No. 182, supplanting McClellan with Burnside, at the president's orders. Fearing possible defiance by McClellan, Secretary of War Stanton assigned Brigadier General Catharinus P. Buckingham, a War Department staff officer, to carry these orders. He was handed two sets, in separate envelopes: one with orders for McClellan, and the other with those for Burnside. He was to deliver the orders to Burnside first, and, if the latter positively refused to take command—since he had already turned down the offer to head the Army of the Potomac twice—Buckingham was to return to Washington, DC. Stanton also gave his emissary an additional card to play. If Burnside balked, Buckingham was to tell him that command of the army would then go to Joseph Hooker, one of the few men Stanton knew Burnside detested.[33]

As Buckingham journeyed forth on his delicate mission, McClellan, ironically, had just completed a relatively rapid movement that brought the army's advance to Warrenton, Virginia. He was deeply satisfied with this progress but admitted to Mary Ellen that the Federal army was a machine that "is so huge & complicated it is slow in its motions." A nor'easter swept through on November 6, dumping freezing rain that then changed to snow on November 7, which made marching difficult and created miserable conditions for the troops. Burnside's 9th Corps was strung out over 5 miles between Waterloo and Orleans in Virginia, after completing a tortuous march over slick, muddy roads during the day. Burnside retired early to his quarters, which were somewhere in this general region, and was asleep when Buckingham arrived. Burnside reacted as expected to the bombshell the staff officer delivered, offering several excuses: he was incapable of managing so large an army; he was under great personal obligations to McClellan; and it was a bad idea to change commanders in the midst of a campaign. Buckingham then laid down his royal flush, explaining that McClellan was going to be relieved, regardless of Burnside's decision, and if his replacement was not Burnside, then it most likely would be Hooker. This instantly changed the dynamics. After conferring with members of his staff, Burnside agreed to accept the command. Buckingham recommended that they ride and meet with McClellan at once, even though the snowstorm was still howling, and it was getting late.[34]

The two generals reached McClellan's headquarters in the small village of Rectortown, on the Manassas Gap Railroad, around 11 p.m. They found him alone in his tent, finishing a letter to Mary Ellen. A half hour later, McClellan related to his wife that when he read the order Buckingham handed him, he was sure that, although the staff officer was watching closely, "not a muscle quivered nor was the slightest expression of feeling visible on my face." Burnside, he noted, "feels dreadfully, almost crazy—I am sorry for him, & he never showed himself a better man or truer friend than now." This was an ironic statement from a man who would go to great lengths to destroy his friend's reputation in the months and years ahead, and who, just over a month before, complained that he "ought to rap Burnside very severely & probably will" in his campaign report, as Burnside "is very slow & is not fit to command more than a regiment." McClellan believed "they"—Lincoln, as well as his enemies Halleck, Stanton, and all the Radical Republicans who had sought his downfall—"have made a great mistake—alas for my poor country—I know in my innermost heart she never had a truer servant." McClellan mastered his emotions and revealed none of his feelings to Buckingham or Burnside. He read the orders, looked at Burnside, and said, "Well, Burnside, I turn the command over to you."[35]

Because Burnside would fail so spectacularly as commander of the Army of the Potomac, and had twice expressed the opinion that leadership of the army was beyond his abilities, it is easy to condemn Lincoln's selection. But, at the time, Burnside was the obvious choice. He was extremely popular with his own corps, and he was known throughout the army. He was the only senior commander with a successful independent operation on his résumé, and he was politically neutral. What Lincoln misjudged was the Union army's senior leadership's opinion of Burnside, and this general's ability to deal with subordinates who did not give him their full support. General Alpheus Williams, who knew Burnside's strengths and weaknesses well, wrote that he "is a most agreeable, companiable gentleman and a good officer," but—critically—"he is not regarded by officers who know him best as equal to McClellan in any respect."[36]

McClellan agreed to stay on for a couple days to go over his plans and the army's dispositions with Burnside. He drew up a circular announcing the change of command and, expressing his love for the officers and men, mentioned their shared "perils & fatigues" and how "the strongest associations which can exist among men, unite us still by an indissoluble tie."[37]

Although rumors had been swirling for weeks that McClellan might be relieved, the news that it had actually occurred sent shock waves through the ranks. Except for the unhappy interlude with John Pope, McClellan was the only commander the Army of the Potomac had ever known. He had organized them and made them soldiers. George Meade, in an opinion that was widely shared, expressed surprise at the ouster of McClellan, "as I thought the storm had blown over. If he had been relieved immediately after the battle of Antietam, or at any period before he moved, I could have seen some show of reason on *military* grounds." Meade suspected that the timing of the change was entirely political. This, of course, was partly true. The congressional and gubernatorial elections had influenced the choice of when Lincoln's decision was made. He had respect for McClellan's popularity with the army and recognized that the general had performed well in reorganizing a dispirited army and driving the Confederates from Maryland. Lincoln initially had stood by McClellan, despite enormous pressure to remove him, because the president saw that despite the general's shortcomings, no one inspired the army like he did, or seemed to possess his administrative abilities. He gave McClellan every opportunity to save his position after the Battle of Antietam. To have removed him *before* a new campaign began made sense from a purely military perspective. But, in Lincoln's mind, allowing McClellan to start such a campaign was logical, for the same reasons why Lincoln had stood by him up to this point. It also afforded the general a final chance to preserve his position. Had McClellan brought Lee to battle, or reached Culpepper ahead of the Confederates, he might not have been removed. When he failed to accomplish either possibility, Lincoln felt compelled to remove him from command of the Army of the Potomac. The *timing* may be questioned, but the president had an ample past history with McClellan, as well as sufficient cause to act.[38]

The troops were not privy to the private communications of their commander or his interactions with the Lincoln administration. They knew what they saw, or heard in camp gossip, and their opinions were often poorly informed. Sergeant George Bowen in the 12th U.S. spoke for many when he penciled his opinion in his diary on November 9: "There is not a mouth in the army of the Union but what cusses the act which removes him." The more some of the men contemplated McClellan's removal, the angrier they became. After a night spent commiserating with others on the issue, Bowen wrote that "the boys are mad as mad can be, & some even swear they will not fire another shot. I confess I feel about the same. . . . If I was a prisoner Id take the oath not to serve against the rebs again in the war." Captain Francis Donaldson in the 118th Pennsylvania, a stalwart McClellan supporter, stated that when he first heard the news about McClellan being supplanted, he refused to believe it, but when he saw the order, and word of a final review on November 10 reached him, "I entirely lost my self control, lost my grip, so to speak, and gave way to tears of indignation and words of bitter reproach." His despair was so deep that, "could I have gotten home, I would have done so, as I no longer had the heart to fight for such an ingrateful country." He had no enmity for Burnside, but "we do not think he can command this army." Donaldson believed the reputation Burnside had gained in the North Carolina Expedition "was not through any merit of his own."

Others, although lamenting the loss of McClellan, were less emotional. Alonzo Quint, the chaplain in the 2nd Massachusetts, expressed the opinion that the "intimations that the army would not fight under anybody else, are perfectly foolish. Our men fight for their *country*, not for a *man*." In the 6th Wisconsin, Major Rufus Dawes wrote that there "was considerable expression of feeling," but no acts of insubordination occurred. Some officers in the 6th talked of resigning, but their colonel, Lysander Cutler, ended this when he informed the regiment's officers that any man who tendered his resignation in the face of the enemy would be recommended for dismissal from the service. No one dared call his bluff. Dawes, like many others, took a wait-and-see attitude. "I did not make a fool of myself at the time of McClellan's removal as some officers did," he wrote to a friend who exulted over the general's downfall. Rather, he would "wait and see how much better Burnside does, before 'rejoicing' over the removal of McClellan." There were also those—particularly in the 9th Corps—who greeted the news with a shrug. Captain James Wren, in the 9th Corps' 48th Pennsylvania, mentioned in his diary that Burnside had been named as army commander but breathed not a word about McClellan.[39]

In an act of generosity and respect for McClellan, Burnside arranged for the general to conduct a final review of the 1st, 2nd, 5th, and 6th Corps, who were all near Warrenton, on November 10. As McClellan prepared to make his final ride through the army, an onlooker heard him remark, "I can hardly bear to see my soldiers again." When he made his appearance in front of the troops, Colonel Charles Wainwright in the 1st Corps declared, "Such a sight I shall never see again." Some men "wept like children," while others gazed "after him in mute grief, one may almost say despair." In the 5th Corps, "whole regiments broke and flocked around him, and with tears and entreaties besought him not to leave them, but to say the word and they would soon settle matters in Washington." The Irish Brigade in the 2nd Corps crowded so closely to the general "that further progress was impossible." The brigade's regiments threw their colors down on the ground for him to ride over—apparently in their grief and anger at a government that would take such a general away—but McClellan made them pick up the flags. Captain Francis Donaldson heard General Andrew A. Humphreys, another fervent McClellan supporter, say to another officer that "he wished to God Genl. McClellan would put himself at the head of the army and throw the infernal scoundrels at Washington into the Potomac." It was, documented Donaldson, "a tumultuous scene beyond description." Humphreys was not alone in openly talking of mutiny to keep McClellan in command. After the review, McClellan met with officers from the different corps. Wainwright noted that among the 1st Corps' officers, some used expressions "with regard to his removal which they had no right to use, and a few even going so far as to beg him to resist the order, and saying that the army would support him." Although McClellan may have fantasized about using the army's loyalty to dictate terms to the administration, it was not something he seriously considered when the moment arrived. He "gently but strongly" reproved those advocating sedition. He urged the 5th Corps' officers, who were among his most loyal cohorts, to do their duty "to our new commander as loyally and as faithfully as we had served him. By doing so we would pay him the greatest honor, and as he had only the welfare of his country at heart he would follow with his prayers and good wishes the future of the grandest army the continent ever saw." Wainwright heard the same thing when McClellan met with 1st Corps' officers. In the end, the review and McClellan's encounters with officers afterward was cathartic for the army. It helped those most affected by the command change to accept its reality and go on. It also was a remarkable moment in American history—one never to be repeated. Other generals would be popular with their troops, but none ever evoked the emotions and loyalty McClellan did. Whatever his shortcomings as a general, he had charisma and an ability to inspire people that few possessed.[40]

For McClellan, the day produced a gut-wrenching roller coaster of emotions: the tear-streaked faces of his beloved veterans; the flags; the cheers bursting from thousands of throats; the surge of men crowding around him, begging him to stay; faces burning with emotion. It was impossible not to be overwhelmed by it all. "I never before had to exercise so much self control," he wrote to his wife that afternoon. "The scenes of today repay me for all that I have endured." The experience was so overwhelming, so extraordinary, that he seemed to be at a loss, or perhaps emotionally unable to elaborate further. On November 11, a special train carried the general and accompanying staff members from Warrenton Junction to Washington, DC. An epoch in the history of the Army of the Potomac had ended.[41]

Many in the Union army, and in the nation's newspapers that had supported the general, suspected the work of Republican Radicals in his downfall. Even though Edwin Stanton was not a Republican, he was a favorite target. Captain Donaldson railed against the secretary of war in a November 10 letter: "Stanton the unblushing humbug, [the] low minded, unscrupulous fellow who thinks he knows more than anyone else in the whole country. Oh! How I hate and despise him! I care not whether you make public these sentiments. They are flagrant violations of the Articles of War, but they are held by the whole army, and the truth should be told." An editorial in the pro-Democratic *New York Herald* likened the general to Cincinnatus and George Washington and asserted that relieving him "was a political, not a military necessity." The writer believed McClellan "will either again lead our armies or be at the head of the nation. Such a man as he cannot be crushed by slanders any more than the sun can be extinguished by a breath."[42]

It was true that Stanton and others in Lincoln's administration, as well as Radical Republicans in the U.S. Congress and Republican governors, all actively sought and worked for McClellan's removal, but the general had as much to do with his own demise as any of his enemies did. Although he performed well in the Maryland Campaign, he evinced little growth as a general. Nonetheless, his organizational skills were unquestioned, and he was generally a good judge of personnel. His selection of staff officers, such as Seth Williams and Rufus Ingalls, served the Union army well for its entire existence. He promoted aggressive officers like Hooker, despite their criticism of his generalship. Yet he also had significant administrative failures. His intelligence service was extremely poor and consistently failed to produce even a reasonably accurate picture of the Confederate army's organization or its strength. And, despite his background in the cavalry, his use of that branch was unimaginative, and he never developed its potential as an offensive force, as Hooker would do in the spring of 1863. Both of these deficiencies had serious consequences. A competent, systematic system for intelligence gathering would have revealed to McClellan just how badly off the Army of Northern Virginia was after the Battle of Antietam. There is no question that the Army of the Potomac was in need of rest, reorganization, and refitting from the wear and tear the withdrawal from the Virginia Peninsula and the subsequent Second Manassas and Maryland Campaigns subjected it to, but the Confederates were in far worse shape. Such opportunities as existed after Antietam were rare in the Civil War. The risks run by George Washington at Trenton and Princeton, or Winfield Scott in the campaign to Mexico City—or even Robert E. Lee in Maryland—are relevant examples that could apply to McClellan's situation. All of these military leaders faced either critical supply shortages or hazards to their communication systems, yet they accepted the perils, because the potential reward was so great. Lee's army was badly hurt, and it was vulnerable for a short period of time after Antietam. The dangers McClellan would have faced by taking his army into Virginia were more than offset by the potential to inflict a decisive blow to the Confederate war effort in the East. At a minimum, had McClellan wished to avoid a pitched battle, he could have crowded Lee—thus reducing the Confederate general's ability to forage for supplies and gather up his stragglers, plus the sick and wounded, who were scattered all over the lower end of the Shenandoah Valley—and used his cavalry to harass Lee's communications and supply operations. This would have hurt Lee almost as much as another battle, and it might have forced him to retreat up the Shenandoah Valley or toward rail communications at Culpepper. In a remarkable statement in Lincoln's October 13 letter to McClellan, which is sometimes overlooked, he pointed out that if the roles were reversed—if Lee were in McClellan's position, and vice versa—"think you not he would break your communications with Richmond within the next twenty-four hours?" If McClellan was surprised by this analogy, with the president clearly stating that he believed the enemy commander to be bolder, more active, and daring than his own army's leader, he gave no indication of it.[43]

Two weeks later, on October 26, the president expressed another fundamental military truth: by moving the Union army into Virginia, it would force "the enemy to concentrate, instead of foraying in squads everywhere." Yet Mc-Clellan behaved as if this applied to the enemy, but not to him. If Stuart had been employed protecting the Confederates' communications and foraging parties, he could not have mounted his raid into Pennsylvania. McClellan's choice to surrender the initiative and leave the Rebels alone, allowing them to lick their wounds and repair the damages to their army, forced him to adopt a defensive posture, which meant spreading his insufficient cavalry out for miles, in order to guard his line along the Potomac River against Confederate raids, which wore down the men and the horses.[44]

On October 18, Secretary of the Navy Gideon Welles noted in his diary that McClellan was not accused of corruption, "but of criminal inaction. His inertness makes the assertions of his opponents prophetic." McClellan regularly supplied ammunition for his enemies to use against him. His lack of any scheme for aggressive action following the Battle of Antietam fueled conspiracy theories that he did not want to hurt the Rebels and eroded confidence in him by those with less radical views. Even after McClellan failed to pursue Lee's army into the Shenandoah Valley, Lincoln might have allowed 2 to 3 weeks of rest so the Union army could refit, had the general produced a concrete strategy. A plan for action might also have facilitated the faster movement of supplies to the army. In another blunder, after receiving a direct order from the President to cross the Potomac and bring the Confederates to battle, McClellan instead snuck off to Philadelphia to retrieve his wife and allowed his senior commanders to summon their spouses, rather than finding the time to visit Washington, DC, and brief Lincoln and Halleck on his plans. It is no wonder Lincoln lost confidence in him. Stuart and his cavalry's untouched ride around the Union army—at the same time when the generals' wives were visiting—was yet another blow to McClellan's sinking reputation. Gideon Welles observed how the general's "opponents will triumph in this additional evidence of alleged inertness and military imbecility." During this time, McClellan did nothing to strengthen his relationship with Lincoln, who was the one individual who could protect—and had protected—him from enemies seeking his removal. Instead, he snapped in anger about the "gorilla" when the president pressed him to act.[45]

Those who claimed McClellan's replacement as commander of the Army of the Potomac was a political act ignored the general's own participation in Machiavellian politics. Stephen Sears, one of McClellan's biographers, makes the point that "the general had become the most prominent opponent of the administration and its policies," adding that this "was not a role forced on him by unscrupulous supporters (as some would believe) but one he had chosen deliberately and pursued for a year and more." McClellan corresponded regularly with power brokers in the Democratic Party, such as William Aspinwall and Samuel Barlow, about the Lincoln administration's policies and personalities. He also had proxies, like Fitz John Porter, who fed opinions from inside the army to the certain members of the press, which they could use to undermine and attack the administration. Nothing changed after McClellan's brush with removal during the Second Manassas Campaign. To the detriment of his Army of the Potomac, he persistently schemed to bring about the removal of Stanton and Halleck. He also tested the political waters for nearly 3 weeks before issuing a circular to the army about the Emancipation Proclamation. As commander of one of the most important field armies in the Union, he had every right to express his opinion on policy to the president, since his troops had to carry out that program. But McClellan behaved more like a politician than an army commander in his efforts to shape those decisions, manipulating the levers of power behind the president's back. Unquestionably, mutual suspicion existed between McClellan and Lincoln, but the former's covert maneuverings and lack of openness with the administration had much to do with creating it. The wonder is not that politics played a role in McClellan's loss of command, but that the president stood by a general who clearly opposed most of his policies for as long as Lincoln did.[46]

McClellan's influence on the Army of the Potomac cannot be overstated. In certain respects, the army struggled with the culture he developed for the rest of its existence. Many of his effects were positive, such as building the army's professionalism and organization, including significant advances in medical arrangements, logistics, and administration. He recognized and developed numerous good leaders, such as Reynolds, Meade, Slocum, Hooker, Hancock, and Sedgwick. But he also imbued the army with an inherent caution, a general lack of initiative, and a belief that the enemy was always capable of more remarkable feats than it was. One of the most well-known examples of the latter was an incident on the night of May 6, 1864, in the Battle of the Wilderness. One of the generals exclaimed to General-in-Chief Ulysses Grant that Lee was going to cut the Union army off from the Rapidan River. Grant replied that he was heartily sick of hearing such talk about Lee. The commander of the Federal forces demanded that *this* army "think what we are going to do ourselves, instead of what Lee is going to do."[47]

While the Union army fought well under Grant, he never fully succeeded in eliminating McClellan's influence on how it functioned. Many of its senior leaders—such as Sedgwick, Humphreys, Hancock, and Gibbon—who privately agreed with McClellan's conservative views on the war continually cultivated them. The debacle by McClellan's replacement—Burnside—at the Battle of Fredericksburg and his subsequent, disastrous leadership with the "Mud March" in January 1863, confirmed, in many soldiers' minds, that only McClellan possessed the competence to lead them. Around this time a songwriter published a piece that became popular in the army, titled "Give Us Back Our Old Commander." Lieutenant Henry Ropes in the 20th Massachusetts, who initially had been willing to accept McClellan's removal, changed his tune after Fredericksburg and pronounced that the only thing that could save the Union army from utter demoralization "is the restoration of McClellan with full, unrestrained powers, and the utter overthrow of Halleck and Stanton." Hooker restored the army's morale when he assumed command from Burnside, but his defeat at the Battle of Chancellorsville in May 1863 reignited the cry for McClellan's return. So powerful did the former commander's name remain within much of the army that, during the 5th Corps' grueling night march to reach Gettysburg, Pennsylvania, on the early morning of July 2, 1863, some officers spread a rumor that McClellan was back in command, in order to inspire their men. This caused the troops to become "perfectly wild with joy." After Gettysburg, Sedgwick—one of McClellan's strongest loyalists who still remained with the army—proposed raising funds for a testimonial to the general, ostensibly as an opportunity for the troops to express their gratitude to their former commander. George Meade, the head of the Union army at this time, went along with the proposal. Zachery Fry has called this "the loyal gesture of a politically tone-deaf professional." By this point, however, some cracks were forming in the army's devotion to McClellan, and the proposed testimonial generated some controversy. "No longer was McClellan the undisputed leader or the sacrificial lamb to harmful political interests in Washington," notes Fry. Stanton ultimately killed the project.[48]

The testimonial's defeat marked the beginning of the decline in the Army of the Potomac's worship of McClellan's name. Many factors brought this about: an increase in political activity by Republican officers within the army; Hooker's furtherance of the easier distribution of pro-administration newspapers, while creating obstructions for Democratic, anti-administration papers; and, in April 1863, the publication of the Joint Committee on the Conduct of the War's report on the campaigns in 1862, which included the Peninsula, Second Manassas, and Maryland Campaigns. The report, which deliberately reflected badly on McClellan, was eagerly devoured within the Union army. It surprised some, who had believed the general's complaints that the Lincoln administration had caused the army's failures in the Seven Days Battles and Second Manassas. But the most influential event in turning troops against their former commander was when McClellan aligned himself with the Democratic Party and was selected as its presidential candidate in 1864. He was unable to shed the pro-peace platform advocated by the party's leaders, and this produced a strong reaction within the Army of the Potomac. As one soldier declared, "For my part, I am done with McClellan now and forever." In the 1864 election, voters in the army overwhelmingly rejected McClellan in favor of Lincoln. Politics had at last undone the general's relations with his soldiers. As one of his admirers in the 12th Illinois Cavalry noted, "My belief is as strong as ever in *the* McClellan of the old Army of the Potomac, but he can never have our support with the backers he surrounds himself with; or upon the platform on which he stands."[49]

ANTIETAM WAS NOT THE turning point of the war. No single event or battle determined its outcome. Yet this conflict, and the Maryland Campaign in general, surely rank as *one* of its turning points, particularly when considered alongside the failure of the Confederates' offensive into Kentucky. The defeat of Lee's invasion of the North was crucial in stabilizing Northern morale, even if it only temporarily did so. The Preliminary Emancipation Proclamation was a vital step forward on the road to destroying the principle of slavery, but that practice had proven to be remarkably resilient over the decades, and the proclamation did not guarantee its end. That would demand the Union army's advance into Confederate territory, and battles—with rivers of blood—at Fredericksburg, Stones River, Chancellorsville, Gettysburg, Vicksburg, and countless other places. It would need enslaved people risking everything to flee to safety behind the lines of the Union army. It would require a hard-fought victory to pass the 13th Amendment. When McClellan left the army in November 1862, the war's outcome, the restoration of the Union, and enslavement's future all remained very much in doubt. Despite the North's advantages in manpower and industry, it still could have lost the Civil War. Some of its darkest days lay ahead, with lopsided Confederate victories at Fredericksburg in December 1862 and Chancellorsville in May 1863. Only a month after the latter battle, on June 6, Robert E. Lee's confident and powerful Army of Northern Virginia marched north again, destined for Pennsylvania, with hope for a victory over the Army of the Potomac that would undermine the Lincoln administration and fuel a growing Northern peace movement. The hard-luck Army of the Potomac made forced marches across Virginia to catch up with the Confederates and bring them to battle. In the midst of this new campaign, on June 18, after a particularly severe march to Leesburg, Virginia, Rufus Dawes, now the 6th Wisconsin's lieutenant colonel, relaxed with a recently purchased newspaper. The headline immediately caught his attention: "Rebels in Pennsylvania— Another Battle at Antietam on the tapis." It stirred powerful, troubling memories. "I hope not," he wrote. "I never want to fight there again. The flower of our regiment were slaughtered in that terrible corn-field. I dread the thought of the place."[50]

ACKNOWLEDGMENTS

Bringing forth this story of the 1862 Maryland Campaign has been a long, fascinating and rewarding journey. There was rarely a day when I worked on the project that I did not learn something or be surprised by some new piece of information. No one completes an undertaking of this size and scope alone, however.

Numerous people and research facilities have greatly helped me along the path and made both this book and *To Antietam Creek* possible. Again, I am deeply indebted to Tom Clemens of Keedysville, Maryland, one of the top authorities in the country on the Maryland Campaign and president of the Save Historic Antietam Foundation, where he has done so much to preserve and protect the Antietam battlefield. He shared sources with me, offered constructive criticism, and answered dozens of questions on any number of subjects. John Hoptak and Mike Snyder read every chapter of the manuscript, and their reviews made this a far better book. John, a fine historian, is an authority on Antietam, where he worked at the national battlefield before moving on to Gettysburg National Military Park. He seems possessed of an encyclopedic mind on all things Civil War–related, as well as on the band Queen! Mike is also a fine historian and is sharp eyed on grammar and sentence structure.

My wife, Barb Sanders, her sister Joanie, and friends Eric and Lori Fischer helped index this volume, for which they deserve a special medal. Jeff Stocker shared dozens of period newspaper accounts with me—typically letters home from soldiers, most of which have not been seen since the war—that dramatically enriched the narrative and told an often different story from what appeared in nostalgic postwar accounts. Marc and Beth Storch photocopied the entire Antietam Studies collection at the National Archives for me, for which I am eternally grateful. Marc also shared items from his superb collection on the 2nd Wisconsin and pointed me to other Maryland Campaign sources he and Beth discovered in their research. David Ward provided me with copies not only of his prodigious research into primary sources relating to the campaign, particularly on Connecticut forces at Antietam, but he also included numerous Union and Confederate collections from many other states.

Zack Waters happily hunted down sources from Georgia and Florida and uncovered ones I probably never would have found. Clarence Hollowell combed the Southern Historical Collection at the University of North Carolina at Chapel Hill and the State Archives of North Carolina. David Guest provided me with a stack of information from wartime Alabama newspapers, which were particularly helpful for Rodes's Alabama brigade. Daryl Smoker, an excellent researcher, shared numerous primary source accounts with me that he had uncovered on his research trips. My friend Pete Carmichael, a Gettysburg College professor, guided me to several excellent sources, including some outstanding 14th Indiana collections. I am indebted to my friend Greg Coco, who passed away from cancer in 2009. He always encouraged me and steered me to many sources I might have missed. Brad Graham, who makes historical documentary films—with whom I worked on an Antietam documentary—has long been a friend and supporter of this project and has always been able to view the Maryland Campaign from different perspectives, which I found helpful.

There are many others to thank: John Banks (who maintains a superb blog, *John Banks' Civil War Blog*), Gregory Acken, Steve Stottlemeyer, Jim Rosebrock, Dr. Keith Bohannon, Ed Root, Richard Jacoby, Dr. Gary Gallagher, Dr. Carol Reardon, John Fuller, Jim McClean, Gerry Gaumer, John Stoudt, Mike Phipps, Tim Smith, Scott Hahn, the late Brian Pohanka, Russell Beattie, Terry Johnston, Nicholas Picerno, Bob Gale, John Hough, and Scott Sherlock. Dr. Ben Dixon, at the State University of New York at Oneonta, has always been a friend and advocate for this project. There are others I may have forgotten, for which I apologize.

Many of my colleagues in the National Park Service were always helpful and encouraging, and they shared or guided me to source material. At Antietam National Battlefield, the late Ted Alexander made their excellent library available to me, and Stephanie Gray, who manages the library now, could not have been more helpful. At Fredericksburg-Spotsylvania National Military Park, I thank Bob K. Krick, John Hennessy, Frank O'Reilly, Mac Wyckoff, Greg Mertz, and Don Pfanz—all now retired, except for Frank. From Gettysburg National Military Park, I count my good friend John Heiser and Eric Campbell, and at Richmond National Battlefield Park, Bobby E. L. Krick. Todd Bolton, retired from Harpers Ferry National Historical Park, was my earliest supporter for tackling a narrative history of the Maryland Campaign.

I also am grateful for the work of the National Park Service, the Save Historic Antietam Foundation, and the American Battlefield Trust for their outstanding efforts in preserving, protecting, and interpreting the Antietam battlefield.

The U.S. Army Heritage and Education Center (formerly the U.S. Army Military History Institute), holds the finest collection of manuscripts about the Union army in the country, as well a good body of material on the Confederate army. The staff were always consistently knowledgeable, professional, and helpful. My especial thanks go to Dave Keough and Louise Arnold-Friend, and the late Dr. Richard Sommers, for their generous help and assistance over the years.

I consistently received outstanding service from the manuscript division of the Library of Congress and, at the National Archives, from archivists Mike Musick and Trevor Plante. Gettysburg College allowed me to use their microfilm reader so I could look through the entire voluminous correspondence in the Gould Papers. Numerous other institutions assisted me along the way. They include the Connecticut Historical Society, Duke University, the Huntington Library, the Massachusetts State Historical Society, the New Jersey Historical Society, the Rutherford B. Hayes Library, the State Historical Society of Wisconsin, the Southern Historical Collection at the University of North Carolina at Chapel Hill, and the Virginia Historical Society. Robert J. Brugger, the now retired senior acquisitions editor at Johns Hopkins University Press, believed in this project. He provided wise guidance and support that made it better. Kathleen Capels, my copyeditor, was brilliant as always and made this a far better book, and Terence Yorks used his eagle eye to make sure the tables and orders of battle and myriad other details were correct.

I am everlastingly grateful to my parents, who always encouraged and nurtured my love of history. It was my father who took me on my first visit to Antietam, sparking a lifelong interest in the campaign and battle. Thanks also to Jason, Lindsay, and Matt, my three grown children, for their love and encouragement. I experienced some of the anxiety the families of those who served in the Maryland Campaign felt when my son Jason deployed as a combat platoon leader with the 4th Infantry Division in Iraq and Afghanistan. Lastly, I give thanks for the love and constant support of my wife, Barb.

A Tactics Primer

American Civil War infantry tactics can be confusing, even for those with knowledge of the war's battles. What are *skirmishers*, or *column of companies*, or *column*, or *marching by the flank*? Eyes may glaze over as we read these terms, but to a Civil War infantry unit, their ability to execute tactics proficiently was often the difference between life and death—and victory or defeat. What follows are some of the principal tactical terms readers may encounter in this book.

Skirmishers

Skirmishers were soldiers who fought in a dispersed formation—the tactical manual called for 5 yards between each man—and were encouraged to use terrain and cover to their advantage. Depending on the situation, an infantry regiment might deploy one or two of its 10 companies as skirmishers. These soldiers would fan out across the front, and possibly the flanks, of the regiment or brigade, usually about 100 to 200 yards in advance of the main line. Their role in an attack was to discover where the enemy was, both to prevent surprises and harass the enemy's defenses. On the defensive side, they served as an early warning system and also could slow the attackers. Skirmishers lacked the firepower to stop an infantry line of battle, and only in the most desperate circumstances would they be expected to assault or defend against one. Skirmish duty also required greater initiative and leadership from officers and noncoms, because of the extended or dispersed nature of the formation.

Line of Battle

A *line of battle* was the standard infantry fighting formation, consisting of a two-rank line, with the soldiers almost shoulder to shoulder and only a pace or two separating the two lines. Noncoms and lieutenants would deploy across the rear of the line, to serve as file closers. Each front and rear rank of soldiers were known as a *file*, so a *file closer's* job was to ensure that no one shirked their duty and ran, as well as to close up gaps that might occur, due to casualties or confusion caused by terrain or man-made features. Soldiers had a tendency to clump together during an engagement, which reduced firepower and created larger targets. So it was also the file closer's job to prevent this. The purpose of a line of battle was to concentrate firepower and enable the field officers, who were mounted, to more easily direct the movements of the regiment or brigade. This was an era where communications still consisted of hand signals, voice commands, or the movement of regimental colors. The latter served a critical purpose—maintaining a unit's alignment by giving it an easily identified target to rally around, if the unit was broken up; or as an object to follow, in an advance, if hand signals and voice commands did not work. Since these flags were large and easily seen, in the murky atmosphere of black-powder warfare, they became prime targets for the enemy to aim at, and losses among color bearers were appalling.

Column

A *column* consisted of a unit marching with four soldiers abreast. It was an efficient way to move men and was easily directed by commanders. A column, however, was highly vulnerable to small-arms and artillery fire, and leaders always tried to deploy their men from column to line *before* they came under fire.

COLUMN OF COMPANIES

In this formation, a regiment or brigade would deploy, with each regiment presenting the front of an entire infantry company in a line of battle. Thus, if a regiment had 400 men, with about 40 men per company, each company would have a front of 20 men, because a line of battle was two ranks deep. Therefore, the company in our imaginary regiment would have 20 soldiers in the front rank and 20 in the rear rank. The 10 companies of a regiment would stack up one behind the other. They might form in *close column of companies*, which meant that each company was within yards of the one in front. This made communication easier and shortened the amount of ground a regiment would take up. But they also might form in *column of companies at half distance* or *column of companies at full distance*. These confusing terms meant that the companies would be spaced either at half the distance required for the following company to move and deploy to the right or left of the company in front, or at the full deployment distance required for the company to do so. Why choose one over the other? *Close column* could be used if it was known that the flanks of the advancing unit were secure and the enemy would only be encountered at its front. *Half distance* might be used if a commander wanted some space between units, in the event that they came under artillery fire, but they would still be close enough to allow the formation to be easily moved. *Full distance* would be used if the flanks might be threatened, or if it was likely that the men might encounter artillery fire. At full distance, it was relatively easy for a unit to quickly deploy into line to its right or left.

DOUBLE COLUMN OF COMPANIES

In this formation, the commander would deploy two companies in front, which broadened the alignment of a unit. Our imaginary infantry regiment, in *double column of companies*, would thus present a front of 40 men, rather than 20. Instead of 10 companies stacking up one behind the other, two companies would form the frontage, and the remaining eight would be lined up behind them at close, half, or full distance. From a distance, a unit in double column of companies would look very much like a Greek phalanx. The advantage of this double-column formation is that it made the unit even more compact and easy to maneuver, as well as adding a bit more firepower to the front of the column. This was the formation in which most 12th Corps' regiments approached the battlefield on September 17. General Alpheus Williams, however, fearing that they would be mauled by artillery fire, begged corps commander Joseph Mansfield to allow him to deploy the regiments into line.

COLUMN OF REGIMENTS
OR BRIGADES

This concept was the same as a column of companies, except on a larger scale. If a brigade adopted a *column of regiments*, such as Gibbon's brigade did in the opening Union attack, then the leading regiment deployed in a line of battle, and every other regiment was positioned in their rear, at whatever distance from the regiment in front of them the brigade or division commander desired. *Column of brigades* was a favored formation of General Edwin Sumner and the 2nd Corps, and all three of his divisions employed it at Antietam. It proved to be disastrous for Sedgwick's division, however, since Sumner insisted on the brigades deploying at close distances to one another, which rendered them unable to change their front to meet the flank attack of the Confederates.

Marching by the Flank

Marching by the flank is a term encountered frequently in the after-action reports of officers throughout the Civil War. It could mean that a unit formed in column of fours marched to its right or left. An officer would describe this as marching by "the left flank" or "the right flank," depending on the direction of the movement. But soldiers in a line of battle might also receive an order to march by the right or left flank. In this instance, if the situation was urgent, the soldiers might not form a column of fours, but simply face left or right and go in that direction. This was a simple, efficient method to get a regiment or brigade out of a difficult situation, move it to a threatened point, or maneuver it to gain the enemy's flank. The danger was that if the regiment or brigade came under accurate fire while moving by the flank, it was easier for the unit to become disorganized and break up, since the line was both thin—only two ranks—and extended.

APPENDIX B

Opposing Forces at Antietam

Union Army of the Potomac
Maj. Gen. George B. McClellan, commanding

GENERAL HEADQUARTERS

Escort
Independent Company, Oneida (NY) Cavalry—Capt. Daniel P. Mann
Company A, 4th U.S. Cavalry—Lt. Thomas H. McCormick
Company E, 4th U.S. Cavalry—Capt. James B. McIntyre

Volunteer Engineer Brigade—Brig. Gen. Daniel P. Woodbury
15th NY—Col. John McL. Murphy
50th NY—Lt. Col. William H. Pettes

Regular Engineer Battalion—Capt. James C. Duane

Provost Guard—Maj. William H. Wood
Companies E, F, H, & K, 2nd U.S. Cavalry—Capt. George A. Gordon
Companies A, D, F, & G, 8th U.S. Infantry—Capt. Royal T. Frank
Company G, 19th U.S. Infantry—Capt. Edmund L. Smith
Company H, 19th U.S. Infantry—Capt. Henry S. Welton

Headquarters Guard—Maj. Granville O. Haller
93rd NY—Lt. Col. Benjamin C. Butler

Quartermaster's Guard
Companies B, C, H, & I, 1st U.S. Cavalry—Capt. Marcus A. Reno

1ST ARMY CORPS
MAJ. GEN. JOSEPH HOOKER (W)
BRIG. GEN. GEORGE G. MEADE

Companies B, C, H, & I, 2nd NY Cavalry—John E. Naylor
3rd PA Cavalry—Col. Samuel W. Owens

1st Division—Brig. Gen. Abner Doubleday

1st Brigade—Col. Walter Phelps Jr.	2nd Brigade—Lt. Col. J. William Hofmann
22nd NY—Lt. Col. John McKie Jr.	7th IN—Maj. Ira Grover
24th NY—Capt. John D. O'Brian (w)	76th NY—Capt. John W. Young
30th NY—Col. William M. Searing	95th NY—Maj. Edward Pye
Capt. John H. Campbell	56th PA—Capt. Frederick Williams
84th NY (14th Brooklyn)—	
Maj. William H. de Bevoise	
2nd U.S. Sharpshooters—	
Col. Henry A. V. Post (w)	

3rd Brigade—Brig. Gen. Marsena R. Patrick	4th Brigade—Brig. Gen. John Gibbon
21st NY—Col. William F. Rogers	19th IN—Lt. Col. Alois O. Bachman (k)
23rd NY—Col. Henry C. Hoffman	Capt. William W. Dudley
35th NY—Col. Newton B. Lord	2nd WI—Lt. Col. Thomas S. Allen (w)
20th NY State Militia (80th NY)—	Capt. George B. Ely
Lt. Theodore B. Gates	6th WI—Lt. Col. Edward S. Bragg (w)
	Maj. Rufus Dawes
	7th WI—Capt. John B. Callis

Artillery—Capt. J. Albert Monroe
1st Battery, NH Light—Lt. Frederick M. Edgell (6 Napoleons)
Battery D, 1st RI Light—Capt. J. Albert Monroe (6 Napoleons)
Battery L, 1st NY Light—Capt. John A. Reynolds (6 3-inch rifles)
Battery B, 4th U.S.—Capt. Joseph B. Campbell (w)
        Lt. James Stewart
        (6 Napoleons)

2nd Division—Brig. Gen. James B. Ricketts

1st Brigade—Brig. Gen. Abram Duryée	2nd Brigade—Col. William A. Christian
97th NY—Maj. Charles Northrup	Col. Peter Lyle
104th NY—Maj. Lewis C. Skinner	26th NY—Lt. Col. Richard H. Richardson
105th NY—Col. Howard Carroll (mw)	94th NY—Lt. Col. Calvin Littlefield
107th PA—Capt. James MacThompson	88th PA—Lt. Col. George W. Gile (w)
	Capt. Henry R. Myers
	90th PA—Col. Peter Lyle
	Lt. Col. W. A. Leech

3rd Brigade—Brig. Gen. George L. Hartsuff (w)	Artillery
Col. Richard Coulter	Battery F, 1st PA Light—
16th ME[1]—Col. Asa W. Wildes	Capt. Ezra W. Matthews
	(4 3-inch rifles)

---

1. Detached from the brigade on Sept. 13 to serve as a railroad guard.

12th MA—Maj. Elisha Burbank (mw)
   Capt. Benjamin F. Cook
13th MA—Maj. J. Parker Gould
83rd NY (9th Militia)—Lt. Col. William Atterbury
11th PA—Col. Richard Coulter
   Capt. David M. Cook

Battery C, PA Light—Capt. James Thompson
   (4 3-inch rifles)

3rd Division—Brig. Gen. George G. Meade
   Brig. Gen. Truman Seymour

1st Brigade—Brig. Gen. Truman Seymour
   Col. R. Biddle Roberts
1st PA Reserves—Col. R. Biddle Roberts
   Capt. William C. Talley
2nd PA Reserves—Capt. James N. Byrnes
5th PA Reserves—Col. Joseph W. Fisher
6th PA Reserves—Col. William Sinclair
13th PA Reserves (Bucktails)—
   Capt. Dennis McKee

2nd Brigade—Col. Albert L. Magilton
3rd PA Reserves—Lt. Col. John Clark
4th PA Reserves—Maj. John Nyce
7th PA Reserves—Maj. Chauncey A. Lyman
8th PA Reserves—Maj. Silas M. Baily

3rd Brigade—Lt. Col. Robert Anderson
9th PA Reserves—Capt. Samuel B. Dick
10th PA Reserves—Col. Adoniram J. Warner (w)
   Capt. Jonathan P. Smith
11th PA Reserves—Lt. Col. Samuel M. Jackson
12th PA Reserves—Capt. Richard Gustin

Artillery
Battery A, 1st PA Light—Lt. John G. Simpson
   (4 Napoleons)
Battery B, 1st PA Light—
   Capt. James H. Cooper
   (4 3-inch rifles)
Battery C, 5th U.S.—Capt. Dunbar R. Ransom
   (4 Napoleons)

2ND ARMY CORPS
MAJ. GEN. EDWIN V. SUMNER

Company D, 6th NY Cavalry—Capt. Henry W. Lyon
Company K, 6th NY Cavalry—Capt. Riley Johnson

1st Division—Maj. Gen. Israel B. Richardson (mw)
   Brig. Gen. Winfield S. Hancock

1st Brigade—Brig. Gen. John C. Caldwell
5th NH—Col. Edward Cross (w)
7th NY—Capt. Charles Brestel
61st & 64th NY—Col. Francis C. Barlow (w)
   Lt. Col. Nelson A. Miles
81st PA—Maj. Boyd McKeen

2nd Brigade—Brig. Gen. Thomas F. Meagher (w)
   Col. John Burke
29th MA—Lt. Col. Joseph H. Barnes
63rd NY—Col. John Burke
   Lt. Col. Henry Fowler (w)
   Maj. Richard Bentley (w)
   Capt. Joseph O'Neill

69th NY—Lt. Col. James Kelly (w)

Maj. James Cavanaugh

88th NY—Lt. Col. Patrick Kelly

3rd Brigade—Col. John R. Brooke

2nd DE—Capt. David L. Stricker

52nd NY—Col. Paul Frank

57th NY—Lt. Col. Philip J. Parisen (k)

Maj. Alford B. Chapman

66th NY—Capt. Julius Wehle

53rd PA—Lt. Col. Richards McMichael

Artillery

Battery B, 1st NY Light—Capt. Rufus D. Pettit

(6 10 lb. Parrotts)

Batteries A & C, 4th U.S.—Lt. Evan Thomas

(6 Napoleons)

2nd Division—Brig. Gen. John Sedgwick (w)

Brig. Gen. Oliver O. Howard

1st Brigade—Brig. Gen. Willis A. Gorman

15th MA—Lt. Col. John W. Kimball

1st MN—Col. Alfred Sully

34th NY—Col. James A. Suiter

82nd NY—Col. Henry W. Hudson

MA Sharpshooters—Capt. John Saunders

MN Sharpshooters—Capt. William F. Russell

2nd Brigade—Brig. Gen. Oliver O. Howard

Col. Joshua T. Owen

Col. Dewitt C. Baxter

69th PA—Col. Joshua T. Owen

71st PA—Col. Isaac J. Wistar (w)

Adjut. Richard P. Smith (w)

Capt. Enoch E. Lewis

72nd PA—Col. DeWitt C. Baxter

106th PA—Col. Turner G. Morehead

3rd Brigade—Brig. Gen. Napoleon J. T. Dana (w)

Col. Norman J. Hall

19th MA—Col. Edward W. Hinks (w)

Lt. Col. Arthur F. Devereux

20th MA—Col. William R. Lee (w)

7th MI—Col. Norman J. Hall

Capt. Charles J. Hunt

42nd NY—Lt. Col. George N. Bomford (w)

Maj. James E. Mallon

59th NY—Col. William Tidball

Artillery

Battery A, 1st RI Light—Capt. John A. Tompkins

(6 10 lb. Parrotts)

Battery I, 1st U.S.—Lt. George A. Woodruff

(6 Napoleons)

3rd Division—Brig. Gen. William H. French

1st Brigade—Brig. Gen. Nathan Kimball

14th IN—Col. William Harrow

8th OH—Lt. Col. Franklin Sawyer

132nd PA—Col. Richard A. Oakford (k)

Lt. Col. Vincent M. Wilcox

7th [W]V—Col. Joseph Snider

2nd Brigade—Col. Dwight Morris

14th CT—Lt. Col. Sanford H. Perkins

108th NY—Col. Oliver H. Palmer

130th PA—Col. Henry I. Zinn

3rd Brigade—Brig. Gen. Max Weber (w)
   Col. John M. Andrews
1st DE—Col. John W. Andrews
   Lt. Col. Oliver Hopkinson (w)
5th MD—Maj. Leopold Blumenberg (w)
   Capt. E. F. M. Faehtz
4th NY—Lt. Col. John D. McGregor

Artillery
Battery G, 1st NY Light—Capt. John D. Frank
   (6 Napoleons)
Battery B, 1st RI Light—Capt. John G. Hazard
   (6 Napoleons)
Battery G, 1st RI Light—Capt. Charles D. Owen
   (6 3-inch rifles)

4TH ARMY CORPS

1st Division—Maj. Gen. Darius N. Couch[2]

1st Brigade—Brig. Gen. Charles Devens Jr.
7th MA—Col. David A. Russell
10th MA—Col. Henry L. Eustis
36th NY—Col. William H. Brown
2nd RI—Col. Frank Wheaton

2nd Brigade—Brig. Gen. Albion P. Howe
62nd NY—Col. David J. Nevin
93rd PA—Col. James M. McCarter
98th PA—Col. John F. Ballier
102nd PA—Col. Thomas A. Rowley
139th PA—Col. Frank H. Collier

3rd Brigade—Brig. Gen. John Cochrane
65th NY—Col. Alexander Shaler
67th NY—Col. Julius W. Adams
122nd NY—Col. Silus Titus
23rd PA—Col. Thomas H. Neill
61st PA—Col. George C. Spear
82nd PA—Col. David H. Williams

Artillery
3rd Battery, NY Light—Capt. William Stuart
   (2 Napoleons, 2
   10 lb. Parrotts)
Battery C, 1st PA Light—Capt. Jeremiah
   McCarthy
   (4 10 lb. Parrotts)
Battery D, 1st PA Light.—Capt. Michael Hall
   (4 10 lb. Parrotts)
Battery G, 2nd U.S.—Lt. John H. Butler
   (4 Napoleons)

5TH ARMY CORPS
MAJ. GEN. FITZ JOHN PORTER

1st Division—Maj. Gen. George W. Morell

Escort
1st ME Cavalry (detachment)—Capt. George J. Summat

1st Brigade—Col. James Barnes
2nd ME—Col. Charles W. Roberts
18th MA—Lt. Col. Joseph Hayes
22nd MA—Lt. Col. William S. Tilton
1st MI—Capt. Emory W. Belton
13th NY—Col. Elisha G. Marshall

2nd Brigade—Brig. Gen. Charles Griffin
2nd DC—Col. Charles M. Alexander
9th MA—Col. Patrick R. Guiney
32nd MA—Col. Francis J. Parker
4th MI—Col. Jonathan W. Childs
14th NY—Col. James McQuade

2. Arrived Sept. 18. Attached to the 6th Corps.

25th NY—Col. Charles A. Johnson
118th PA—Col. Charles M. Prevost
2nd Co., MA Sharpshooters—
    Capt. Lewis Wentworth

3rd Brigade—Col. Thomas B. W. Stockton
20th ME—Col. Adelbert Ames
16th MI—Col. Norval E. Welch
12th NY—Capt. William Huson
17th NY—Lt. Col. Nelson B. Bartram
44th NY—Maj. Freeman Conner
83rd PA—Capt. Orpheus S. Woodward
Brady's Co., MI Sharpshooters—
    Lt. Jonas H. Titus Jr.

62nd PA—Col. Jacob B. Sweitzer

Artillery
Battery C, MA Light—
    Capt. Augustus P.Martin
    (6 Napoleons)
Battery C, 1st RI Light—
    Capt. Richard Waterman
    (6 Napoleons)
Battery D, 5th U.S.—Lt. Charles E. Hazlett
    (4 10 lb. Parrotts, 2
    Napoleons)

2nd Division—Brig. Gen. George Sykes

1st Brigade—Lt. Col. Robert C. Buchanan
3rd U.S.—Capt. John D. Wilkins
4th U.S.—Capt. Hiram Dryer
1st Battalion, 12th U.S.—
    Capt. Matthew M. Blunt
2nd Battalion, 12th U.S.—
    Capt. Thomas M Anderson
1st Battalion, 14th U.S.—
    Capt. W. Harvey Brown
2nd Battalion, 14th U.S.—
    Capt. David B. McKibbin

2nd Brigade—Maj. Charles S. Lovell
1st & 6th U.S.—Capt. Levi C. Bootes
2nd & 10th U.S.—Capt. John S. Poland
11th U.S.—Maj. DeLancey Floyd-Jones
17th U.S.—Maj. George L. Andrews

3rd Brigade—Col. Gouverneur K. Warren
5th NY—Capt. Cleveland Winslow
10th NY—Lt. Col. John W. Marshall

Artillery
Batteries E & G, 1st U.S.—
    Lt. Alanson M. Randol
    (4 Napoleons)
Battery I, 5th U.S.—Capt. Stephen H. Weed
    (4 3-inch rifles)
Battery K, 5th U.S.—Lt. William E. Van Reed
    (4 Napoleons)

3rd Division—Brig. Gen. Andrew A. Humphreys[3]

1st Brigade—Erastus B. Tyler
91st PA—Col. Edgar M. Gregory

2nd Brigade—Col. Peter H. Allabach
123rd PA—Col. John B. Clark

3. Arrived Sept. 18.

126th PA—Col. James G. Elder
129th PA—Col. Jacob G. Frick
134th PA—Col. Matthew S. Quay

131st PA—Lt. Col. William B. Shaut
133rd PA—Col. Franklin B. Speakman
155th PA—Col. Edward J. Allen

Artillery
Battery C, 1st NY Light—Capt. Almont Barnes
                    (2 3-inch rifles)
Battery L, 1st OH Light—
        Capt. Lucius N. Robinson
        (6 Napoleons)

Artillery Reserve—Lt. Col. William Hays
Battery A, 1st Battalion, NY Light—Lt. Bernhard Wever (4 20 lb. Parrotts)
Battery B. 1st Battalion, NY Light—Lt. Alfred von Kleiser (4 20 lb. Parrotts)
Battery C, 1st Battalion, NY Light—Capt. Robert Langner (4 20 lb. Parrotts)
Battery D, 1st Battalion, NY Light—Capt. Charles Kusserow (6 32 lb. howitzers)
5th Battery, NY Light—Capt. Elijah D. Taft (4 20 lb. Parrotts)
Battery K, 1st U.S.—Capt. William M. Graham (6 Napoleons)
Battery G, 4th U.S.—Lt. Marcus P. Miller (6 Napoleons)

6TH ARMY CORPS
MAJ. GEN. WILLIAM B. FRANKLIN

Escort
Companies B & G, 6th PA Cavalry—Capt. Henry P. Muirheid

1st Division—Maj. Gen. Henry W. Slocum

1st Brigade—Col. Alfred T. A. Torbert
1st NJ—Lt. Col. Mark W. Collet
2nd NJ—Col. Samuel L. Buck
3rd NJ—Col. Henry W. Brown
4th NJ—Col. William B. Hatch

2nd Brigade—Col. Joseph J. Bartlett
5th ME—Col. Nathaniel J. Jackson
16th NY—Lt. Col. Joel J. Seaver
27th NY—Lt. Col. Alexander D. Adams
96th PA—Col. Henry L. Cake
121st NY—Col. Richard Franchot

3rd Brigade—Brig. Gen. John Newton
18th NY—Lt. Col. George R. Myers
31st NY—Col. Calvin E. Pratt[4]
32nd NY—Lt. Col. Francis E. Pinto
95th PA—Col. Gustavus W. Town

Artillery—Capt. Emory Upton
Battery A, MD Light—Capt. John W. Wolcott
                    (8 3-inch rifles)
Battery A, MA Light—Capt. Josiah Porter
                    (6 Napoleons)

4. According to a newspaper clipping, Pratt commanded the regiment at Antietam. See "From Washington—Wednesday, May 21," 31st New York Infantry Regiment's Civil War Newspaper Clippings, New York State Military Museum and Veterans Research Center, https://museum.dmna.ny.gov/index.php/?cID=2113/ [accessed May 2021]. Francis E. Pinto returned to command the 32nd NY. See "City Intelligence—Our Returning Volunteers," 32nd New York Infantry Regiment's Civil War Newspaper Clippings, New York State Military Museum and Veterans Research Center, https://museum.dmna.ny.gov/index.php/?cID=2116/ [accessed May 2021].

Battery A, NJ Light—Capt. William Hexamer
(6 10 lb. Parrotts)

Battery D, 2nd U.S.—Lt. Edward B. Williston
(6 Napoleons)

2nd Division—Maj. Gen. William F. Smith

1st Brigade—Brig. Gen. Winfield S. Hancock

6th ME—Col. Hiram Burnham

43rd NY—Maj. John Wilson

49th PA—Lt. Col. William Brisbane

137th PA—Col. Henry M. Bessert

5th WI—Col. Amasa Cobb

2nd Brigade—Brig. Gen. W. T. H. Brooks

2nd VT—Maj. James H. Walbridge

3rd VT—Col. Breed N. Hyde

4th VT—Lt. Col. Charles B. Stoughton

5th VT—Col. Lewis A. Grant

6th VT—Maj. Oscar L. Tuttle

3rd Brigade—Col. William H. Irwin

7th ME—Maj. Thomas W. Hyde

20th NY—Col. Ernest von Vegesack

33rd NY—Lt. Col. Joseph W. Corning

49th NY—Lt. Col. William C. Alberger (w)
           Maj. George W. Johnson

77th NY—Capt. Nathan S. Babcock

Artillery—Capt. Romeyn B. Ayres

Battery B, MD Light—
           Lt. Theodore J. Vanneman
           (6 3-inch rifles)

1st Battery, NY Light—Capt. Andrew Cowan
           (4 3-inch rifles)

Battery F, 5th U.S.—Lt. Leonard Martin
           (4 10 lb. Parrotts)

9TH ARMY CORPS
MAJ. GEN. AMBROSE E. BURNSIDE[5]
BRIG. GEN. JACOB D. COX

Escort

Company G, 1st ME Cavalry—Capt. Zebulon B. Blethen

Unattached

6th NY Cavalry (8 companies)—Col. Thomas C. Devin

3rd Independent Company, OH Cavalry—Lt. Jonas Seamen

Batteries L & M,[6] 3rd U.S. Artillery—Capt. John Edwards Jr. (4 10 lb. Parrotts)

Battery L, 2nd NY Artillery—Capt. Jacob Roemer (6 3-inch rifles)

1st Division—Brig. Gen. Orlando B. Willcox

1st Brigade—Col. Benjamin C. Christ

28th MA—Capt. Andrew P. Caraher

17th MI—Col. William H. Withington

2nd Brigade—Col. Thomas Welsh

46th NY—Lt. Col. Joseph Gerhardt

45th PA—Lt. Col. John L. Curtis

---

5. Exercised command of the Right Wing (1st and 9th Corps) until Sept. 16, when GBM suspended the wing command structure.

6. Detached to guard the army's left flank and not engaged at Antietam.

79th NY—Lt. Col. David Morrison
50th PA—Maj. Edward Overton (w)
        Capt. William H. Diehl

100th PA—Lt. Col. David A. Leckey
8th MI—Lt. Col. Frank Graves[7]

Artillery
8th Battery, MA Light—Capt. Asa M. Cook
               (4 12 lb. James rifles,
               2 12 lb. howitzers)
Battery E, 2nd U.S.—Lt. Samuel N. Benjamin
               (4 20 lb. Parrotts)

2nd Division—Brig. Gen. Samuel D. Sturgis

1st Brigade—Brig. Gen. James Nagle
2nd MD—Lt. Col. J. Eugene Duryée
6th NH—Col. Simon G. Griffin
9th NH—Col. Enoch Q. Fellows
48th PA—Lt. Col. Joshua K. Sigfried

2nd Brigade—Brig. Gen. Edward Ferrero
21st MA—Col. William S. Clark
35th MA—Maj. Sumner Carruth
51st NY—Col. Robert B. Potter
51st PA—Col. John F. Hartranft

Artillery
Battery D, PA Light—Capt. George W. Durell
               (6 10 lb. Parrotts)
Battery E, 4th U.S.—Capt. Joseph C. Clark (w)
               Lt. George Dickenson[8]
               (4 10 lb. Parrotts)

3rd Division—Brig. Gen. Isaac P. Rodman (mw)
           Col. Edward Harland

1st Brigade—Col. Harrison S. Fairchild
9th NY—Lt. Col. Edgar A. Kimball
89th NY—Maj. Edward Jardine[9]
103rd NY—Maj. Benjamin Ringold

2nd Brigade—Col. Edward Harland
8th CT—Lt. Col. Hiram Appelman (w)
          Maj. John E. Ward
11th CT—Col. Henry W. Kingsbury (mw)
          Lt. Col. Griffin A. Stedman
16th CT—Col. Francis Beach[10]
4th RI—Col. William H. P. Steere (w)
          Lt. Col. Joseph B. Curtis

Artillery
Battery A, 5th U.S.—Lt. Charles P. Muhlenberg
               (6 Napoleons)

7. Transferred to the 2nd Brigade on Sept. 16.
8. 1st Sgt. Christopher F. Merkle is credited with commanding the battery in the fighting after Clark was wounded.
9. Jardine was detached from the 9th NY.
10. Assigned to the brigade on Sept. 16.

Battery, Co. K, 9th NY—Capt. James R. Whiting
(5 12 lb. naval howitzers)

Kanawha Division—Brig. Gen. Eliakim P. Scammon

1st Brigade—Col. Hugh Ewing	2nd Brigade—Col. George Crook
12th OH—Col. Carr B. White	11th OH—Lt. Col. Augustus H. Coleman (k)
23rd OH—Maj. James M. Comly	Maj. Lyman J. Jackson
30th OH—Lt. Col. Theodore Jones (w & c)	28th OH—Lt. Col. Gottfried Becker
Maj. George H. Hildt	36th OH—Lt. Col. Melvin Clarke (k)
	Maj. Hiram F. Duvol

Gilmore's Co., ([W]V) Cavalry—	Artillery
Lt. James Abraham	1st Battery, OH Light Artillery—
Harrison's Co., ([W]V) Cavalry—	Capt. James R. McMullin
Lt. Dennis Delaney	(6 10 lb. James rifles)
Schambeck's Co., Chicago Dragoons—	Simmonds's Battery, KY Light Artillery—
Capt. Frederick Schambeck	Lt. Arthur Erenburgh (w)[11]
	(2 20 lb. Parrotts,
	3 10 lb. Parrotts,
	1 12 lb. howitzer)

12TH ARMY CORPS—MAJ. GEN. JOSEPH K. F. MANSFIELD (MW)
MAJ. GEN. ALPHEUS S. WILLIAMS

Escort
Company L, 1st MI Cavalry—Capt. Melvin Brewer

1st Division—Brig. Gen. Alpheus S. Williams
Brig. Gen. Samuel W. Crawford (w)
Brig. Gen. George H. Gordon

1st Brigade—Brig. Gen. Samuel W. Crawford (w)	3rd Brigade—Brig. Gen. George H. Gordon
Col. Joseph F. Knipe	Col. Silas Colgrove
5th CT—Capt. Henry W. Daboll[12]	27th IN—Col. Silas Colgrove
10th ME—Col. George L. Beal (w)	2nd MA[13]—Col. George L. Andrews
Lt. Col. James S. Fillebrown[14]	13th NJ—Col. Ezra A. Carman
Maj. Charles Walker	107th NY—Col. Robert B. van Valkenburgh
28th NY—Capt. William H. H. Mapes	3rd WI—Col. Thomas H. Ruger

11. Capt. Seth Simmonds reported sick on Aug. 15 and was not present at Antietam. See "1863," box 9, folder 7, Henry Hunt Papers, LC. Thanks to Jim Rosebruck.

12. Detached at Frederick on Sept. 15.

13. The Pennsylvania Zouaves d'Afrique were attached. They consisted of a small company and were also known as Collis's (PA) Independent Company.

14. Injured when kicked in the stomach by his horse.

46th PA—Col. Joseph F. Knipe
        Lt. Col. James L. Selfridge
124th PA—Col. Joseph W. Hawley (w)
        Maj. Isaac L. Higgins
125th PA—Col. Jacob Higgins
128th PA—Col. Samuel Croasdale (k)
        Lt. Col. William W. Hammersly (w)
        Maj. Joel B. Wanner

2nd Division—Brig. Gen. George S. Greene

1st Brigade—Lt. Col. Hector Tyndale (w)
        Maj. Orrin J. Crane
5th OH—Maj. John Collins
7th OH—Maj. Orrin J. Crane
        Capt. Frederick A. Seymour
29th OH[16]—Lt. Theron S. Winship
66th OH—Lt. Col. Eugene Powell (w)
28th PA—Maj. Ario Pardee Jr.

3rd Brigade—Col. William B. Goodrich (k)
        Lt. Col. Jonathan Austin
3rd DE—Maj. Arthur Maginnis (w)
        Capt. William J. McKaig
Purnell Legion (MD)—
        Lt. Col. Benjamin L. Simpson
60th NY—Lt. Col. Charles R. Brundage
78th NY—Lt. Col. Jonathan Austin
        Capt. Henry R. Stagg

2nd Brigade—Col. Henry J. Stainrook
3rd MD—Lt. Col. Joseph M. Sudsburg
102nd NY—Lt. Col. James C. Lane
109th PA[15]—Capt. George E. Seymour
111th PA—Maj. Thomas M. Walker

Artillery—Capt. Clermont L. Best
4th Battery, ME Light—
        Capt. O'Neil W. Robinson Jr.
        (6 3-inch rifles)
6th Battery, ME Light—
        Capt. Freeman McGilvery
        (3 Napoleons, 1
        3-inch rifle)
Battery M, 1st NY Light—
        Capt. George W. Cothran
        (4 10 lb. Parrotts,
        2 3-inch rifles)
10th Battery, NY Light—Capt. John T. Bruen
        (6 Napoleons)
Battery E, PA Light—Capt. Joseph M. Knap
        (6 10 lb. Parrotts)
Battery F, PA Light—
        Capt. Robert B. Hampton
        (4 10 lb. Parrotts)
Battery F, 4th U.S.—
        Lt. Edward D.Muhlenberg
        (6 Napoleons)

15. Detached on Sept. 13 and not at Antietam.
16. Detached on Sept. 9 and not at Antietam.

Cavalry Division—Brig. Gen. Alfred Pleasonton

1st Brigade—Maj. Charles J. Whiting
5th U.S.—Capt. Joseph H. McArthur
6th U.S.—Capt. William P. Saunders

2nd Brigade—Col. John F. Farnsworth
8th IL—Maj. William H. Medill
3rd IN—Maj. George H. Chapman
1st MA—Col. Robert Williams
8th PA—Capt. Peter Keenan

3rd Brigade—Col. Richard H. Rush
4th PA—Col. James H. Childs (k)
        Lt. Col. James K. Kerr
6th PA—Lt. Col. C. Ross Smith

4th Brigade—Col. Andrew T. McReynolds
1st NY—Maj. Alonzo W. Adams
12th PA—Maj. James A. Congdon

Horse Artillery
Battery A, 2nd U.S.—Capt. John C. Tidball
                (6 3-inch rifles)
Batteries B & L, 2nd U.S.—
                Capt. James M. Robertson
                (4 3-inch rifles)
Battery M, 2nd U.S.—Lt. Peter C. Hains
                (6 3-inch rifles)
Batteries C & G, 3rd U.S.—
                Capt. Horatio G. Gibson
                (6 3-inch rifles)

Unattached Cavalry
1st ME—Col. Samuel H. Allen[17]

Confederate Army of Northern Virginia
Gen. Robert E. Lee, commanding

LONGSTREET'S COMMAND—
MAJ. GEN. JAMES LONGSTREET

Jones's Division—Brig. Gen. David R. Jones

Toombs's Brigade—Brig. Gen. Robert Toombs (w)
                Col. Henry L. Benning
2nd GA—Lt. Col. William R. Holmes (k)
        Maj. Skidmore Harris (w)
        Capt. Abner M. Lewis

Drayton's Brigade—
        Brig. Gen. Thomas F. Drayton
50th GA—Lt. Col. Francis Kearse
51st GA—unknown
15th SC—Col. William D. DeSaussure

---

17. Detached at Frederick on Sept. 13. Also had company detachments to the 5th and 9th Corps' headquarters.

15th GA—Col. William T. Millican (k)
   Capt. T. H. Jackson
17th GA—Capt. J. A. McGregor
20th GA—Col. John B. Cumming

Pickett's Brigade—Brig. Gen. Richard Garnett
8th VA—Col. Eppa Hunton
18th VA—Maj. George Cabell
19th VA—Lt. William N. Wood
28th VA—Capt. William L. Wingfield
56th VA—Capt. John B. McPhail

Jenkins's Brigade—Col. Joseph Walker
1st SC—Lt. Col. Daniel Livingston (w)
2nd SC Rifles—Lt. Col. Robert Thompson
5th SC—Capt. Thomas C. Beckham
6th SC—Capt. Edward B. Cantey (w)
4th SC Battalion—Lt. William T. Field
Palmetto Sharpshooters—
   Capt. Alfred H. Foster (w)
   Capt. Franklin W.
   Kilpatrick

Artillery
Wise (VA) Artillery—
   Capt. James S. Brown (w)
   (4 guns of unknown caliber and type)

Hood's Division—Brig. Gen. John B. Hood

Hood's Brigade—Col. William T. Wofford
18th GA—Lt. Col. Solon Z. Ruff
1st TX—Lt. Col. Philip Work
4th TX—Lt. Col. Benjamin Carter
5th TX—Capt. Ike N. M. Turner
Hampton (SC) Legion—Lt. Col. Martin Gary

3rd SC Battalion—Capt. George M. Gunnels
Phillips (GA) Legion—Lt. Col. Richard T. Cook

Kemper's Brigade—Brig. Gen. James Kemper
1st VA—Capt. George F. Norton
7th VA—Capt. Philip S. Ashby
11th VA—Capt. Robert M. Mitchell Jr.
17th VA—Col. Montgomery D. Corse (w)
   Maj. Arthur Herbert
24th VA—Col. William Terry

G. T. Anderson's Brigade
1st GA Regulars—Col. William J. Magill (w)
   Capt. Richard A. Wayne
7th GA—Lt. Col. George H. Carmical
8th GA—Lt. Col. John R. Towers
9th GA—Lt. Col. John C. L. Mounger
11th GA—Maj. Francis H. Little

Law's Brigade—Col. Evander M. Law
4th AL—Capt. Lawrence Scruggs (w)
   Capt. William M. Robbins
2nd MS—Col. John M. Stone (w)
   Lt. Col. D. W. Humphreys (w)
   Maj. John Blair (w)
   Lt. William C. Moody
11th MS—Lt. Col. Samuel Butler (w)
   Maj. Taliaferro S. Evans (k)
6th NC—Lt. Col. Robert Webb (w)
   Maj. Samuel Tate (w)

Evans's Brigade—Brig. Gen. Nathan G. Evans
             Col. Peter F. Stevens
17th SC—Col. Fitz McMaster
18th SC—Col. William H. Wallace
22nd SC—Maj. Miles L. Hilton
23rd SC—Lt. Edwin R. White
Holcombe Legion—Col. Peter F. Stevens
             Maj. William J. Crawley
Macbeth (SC) Artillery—Capt. Robert Boyce
             (6 guns of unknown
             caliber and type)

Artillery—Maj. Bushrod W. Frobel
German (SC) Artillery—
             Capt. William K. Bachman
             (4 Napoleons, 2
             12 lb. Blakely rifles)
Palmetto (SC) Artillery—Capt. Hugh R. Garden
             (2 12 lb. howitzers,
             2 6 lb. guns)
Rowan (NC) Artillery—Capt. James Reilly
             (2 10 lb. Parrotts, 2
             3-inch rifles, 2 24 lb.
             howitzers)

Anderson's Division—Maj. Gen. Richard H. Anderson (w)
Brig. Gen. Roger Pryor

Wilcox's Brigade—Col. Alfred Cumming (w)
             Maj. Jere Williams (w)
             Maj. Hilary A. Herbert (w)
             Capt. James M. Crow
8th AL—Maj. Hilary A. Herbert (w)
9th AL—Maj. Jere Williams (w)
             Capt. James M. Crow
             Lt. Alexander C. Chisholm
10th AL—Capt. G. C. Whatley (k)
11th AL—Maj. John C. C. Sanders

Armistead's Brigade—
             Brig. Gen. Lewis A. Armistead (w)
             Col. James G. Hodges
9th VA—Capt. William J. Richardson
14th VA—Col. James G. Hodges
38th VA—Col. Edward C. Edmonds
53rd VA—Capt. William G. Pollard (k)
             Capt. Joseph C. Harwood
57th VA—Capt. William H. Ramsey

Mahone's Brigade—
             Lt. Col. William A.Parham
6th VA—Capt. John Ludlow
12th VA—Capt. Richard W. Jones Jr.
16th VA—unknown
41st VA—unknown

Pryor's Brigade—Brig. Gen. Roger A. Pryor
             Col. John C. Hately
14th AL—Maj. James A. Broome
2nd FL—Capt. William D. Ballantine (w)
             Sgt. Henry C. Geiger (c)[18]
5th FL—Col. John C. Hately
             Lt. Col. Thomas B. Lamar (w)
             Maj. Benjamin F. Davis
8th FL—Lt. Col. George Coppens (k)
             Capt. Robert A. Waller (k)
             Capt. William Baya
3rd VA—Col. Joseph Mayo (w)
             Lt. Col. Alexander D. Callcote[19]

18. Capt. Alexander Moseley assumed command of the regiment on Sept. 18.
19. Capt. Charles F. Urquhart is also identified as commanding the regiment on Sept. 17. He was killed in action.

Featherston's Brigade—Col. Carnot Posey
12th MS—Col. William H. Taylor
16th MS—Capt. Abraham M. Feltus Jr.
19th MS—unknown[20]
2nd MS Battalion—Maj. William Wilson (mw)

Wright's Brigade—Brig. Ambrose R. Wright (w)
     Col. Robert Jones (w)
     Col. William Gibson
44th AL—Lt. Col. Charles A. Derby (k)[21]
3rd GA—Lt. Col. Reuben Nisbet (w & c)
    Capt. John F. Jones
22nd GA—Col. Robert Jones (w)
    Maj. Lawrence D. Lallerstedt
48th GA—Col. William Gibson

Artillery—Maj. John S. Saunders
Donaldsonville (LA) Artillery—
     Capt. Victor Maurin
     (2 10 lb. Parrotts, 1
     3-inch rifle, 3 6 lb. guns)
Huger's (VA) Battery—Capt. Frank Huger
     (1 10 lb. Parrott, 1
     3-inch rifle, 2 6 lb. guns)
Moorman's (VA) Battery—Capt. Marcellus
     Newton Moorman
     (2 10 lb. Parrotts,
     1 gun of unknown
     caliber and type)
Grimes's (VA) Battery—Capt. Cary F. Grimes (mw)
     Lt. John H. Thompson
     (1 10 lb. Parrott, 2 12
     lb. naval howitzers)
Dixie (VA) Battery—
     Capt. William H. Chapman
     (1 3-inch rifle, 1
     Napoleon)

Attached Reserve Artillery

Washington (LA) Artillery—
     Col. John B Walton
1st Company—Capt. Charles W. Squires
     (2 3-inch rifles, 2 10 lb.
     Parrotts)

Lee's Battalion—Col. Stephen D. Lee
Ashland (VA) Battery—
     Capt. Pichegru Woolfolk Jr.
     (2 10 lb. Parrotts,
     1 12 lb. howitzer)

20. A list of casualties for the 19th MS in the *Richmond Enquirer*, Oct. 7, 1862, named a Capt. J. Hardie, who was slightly wounded in the groin, as the senior officer, but there was no J. Hardie in this regiment. A James Hardy was a private. It is possible that Adjut. Robert H. Allen, who was wounded in the arm, commanded.

21. C to *Daily Constitutionalist*, Oct. 18, 1862, ANBL, stated that Derby was the only field officer with the regiment at Sharpsburg.

2nd Company—Capt. John B. Richardson
  (2 Napoleons, 2 12 lb.
  howitzers)
3rd Company—Capt. M. B. Miller
  (4 Napoleons)
4th Company—Capt. Benjamin F. Eshleman
  (2 12 lb. howitzers, 2 6 lb.
  guns)

Bedford (VA) Battery—Capt. Tyler C. Jordan
  (1 3-inch rifle, 1 10
  lb. Parrott, 1 12 lb.
  howitzer, 1 6 lb.
  gun)
Brooks's (SC) Battery—Lt. William Elliot
  (2 10 lb. Parrotts, 2
  12 lb. howitzers)
Eubank's (VA) Battery—Capt. John L. Eubank
  (1 3-inch rifle, 1
  rifle of unknown
  type, 1 12 lb.
  howitzer, 1 6 lb. gun)
Madison (LA) Battery—
  Capt. George V. Moody
  (2 3-inch rifles,
  2 24 lb. howitzers)
Parker's (VA) Battery—Capt. William W. Parker
  (2 3-inch rifles, 2
  12 lb. howitzers)

JACKSON'S COMMAND—
MAJ. GEN. THOMAS J. "STONEWALL" JACKSON

Ewell's Division—Brig. Gen. Alexander R. Lawton (w)
Brig. Gen. Jubal A. Early

Lawton's Brigade—Col. Marcellus Douglass (k)
  Maj. John H. Lowe
  Col. John H. Lamar
13th GA—Lt. Divany A. Kidd
26th GA—Col. Edmund N. Atkinson (w)
31st GA—Lt. Col. John T. Crowder (w)
  Maj. John H. Lowe
38th GA—Capt. William H. Battey (k)
  Capt. Peter Brennan
  Lt. John W. McCurdy (w)[23]
60th GA—Capt. Waters B. Jones

Trimble's Brigade—Col. James A. Walker
15th AL—Capt. Isaac B. Feagin (w at
  Shepherdstown)
12th GA—Capt. James G. Rodgers (k)
  Capt. John T. Carson
21st GA—Maj. Thomas C. Glover (w)
  Capt. James C. Nisbet (w)
21st NC[22]—Capt. Francis P. Miller (k)

22. The 1st NC Battalion, consisting of two companies, was attached to the 21st NC.

23. The succession of commanders in the 38th GA is uncertain. Battey definitely commanded at the opening of the fighting. He may have been succeeded by McCurdy, and Brennan possibly arrived to take command after the battle action.

61st GA—Col. John H. Lamar[24]
        Maj. Archibald P. McRae (k)
        Capt. James D. van Valkenburg

Early's Brigade—Brig. Gen. Jubal Early
        Col. William Smith (w)
13th VA—Capt. Frank W. Winston
25th VA—Capt. Robert D. Lilley
31st VA—Col. John S. Hoffman
44th VA—Capt. David Anderson
49th VA—Col. William Smith (w)
        Lt. Col. John C. Gibson
52nd VA—Col. Michael Harman
58th VA—Capt. Henry W. Wingfield

Hays's Brigade—Brig. Gen. Harry T. Hays
5th LA—Col. Henry Forno[25]
6th LA—Col. Henry B. Strong (k)
7th LA—Col. Davidson Penn (w)
8th LA—Maj. Trevanion D. Lewis (w)
14th LA—Lt. Col. David Zable (w)

Artillery—Maj. Alfred R. Courtney
Louisiana Guard Battery—Capt. Louis E. D'Aquin
        (1 10 lb. Parrott, 2 3-inch rifles)
Johnson's (VA) Battery—Capt. John R. Johnson
        (3 guns,
        combination of
        12 1b. howitzers
        and 6 lb. guns)
Staunton (VA) Battery—Lt. Asher W. Garber
        (2 6 lb. guns)
Courtney (VA) Battery—Capt. Joseph W. Latimer
        (2 3-inch rifles)
Chesapeake (MD) Battery[26]—
        Capt. William D Brown
        (2 10 lb. Parrotts, 1
        3-inch rifle)
1st MD Battery—Capt. William F. Dement
        (4 Napoleons)

Hill's Light Division—Maj. Gen. Ambrose P. Hill

Branch's Brigade—
        Brig. Gen. Lawrence O. Branch (k)
        Col. James H. Lane
7th NC—Col. Edward G. Haywood

Archer's Brigade—Brig. Gen. James J. Archer
        Col. Peter Turney
5th AL Battalion—Capt. Charles M. Hooper
19th GA—Maj. James Neal

---

24. Lamar does not appear to have been present at Sharpsburg, but he arrived to command the brigade at Shepherdstown on Sept. 19.

25. Forno was wounded at Second Manassas and may not have been present at Sharpsburg.

26. Left at Harpers Ferry.

18th NC—Lt. Col. Thomas J. Purdie
28th NC—Col. James H. Lane
        Maj. William J. Montgomery
33rd NC—Lt. Col. Robert F. Hoke
37th NC—Capt. William G. Morris

Gregg's Brigade—Brig. Gen. Maxcy Gregg (w)
1st SC Provisional Army—
        Col. Daniel H. Hamilton
1st SC Rifles—Lt. Col. James M. Perrin
12th SC—Col. Dixon Barnes (mw)
        Maj. William H. McCorkle
        Lt. Col. Cadwallader Jones III[28]
13th SC—Col. Oliver E. Edwards
14th SC—Lt. Col. William D. Simpson

Pender's Brigade—
        Brig. Gen. William Dorsey Pender
16th NC—Lt. Col. William A. Stowe
22nd NC—Maj. Christopher C. Cole
34th NC—Lt. Col. John L. McDowell
38th NC—Lt. Col. Robert F. Armfield

Artillery—Maj. Reuben L. Walker
Crenshaw's (VA) Battery—
        Capt. William G.Crenshaw
        (1 Napoleon
        1 12 lb. howitzer,
        2 6 lb. guns)
Fredericksburg (VA) Battery—
        Capt. Carter M.Braxton
        (2 3-inch rifles, 4 6 lb. guns)
Pee Dee (SC) Battery—Capt. David G.McIntosh
        (1 10 lb. Parrott, 1
        3-inch rifle, 1
        Napoleon, 1 12 lb.
        howitzer)
Purcell (VA) Battery—Capt. William J. Pegram (w)
        (2 10 lb. Parrotts,
        2 Napoleons)

Capt. Tilghman W. Flynt (w & c)
Capt. Frank M. Johnson
1st TN—Col. Peter Turney
7th TN—Maj. Samuel G. Shepard[27]
        Lt. George A. Howard
14th TN—Lt. Col. William McComb (w)
        Maj. James W. Lockert

Field's Brigade—Col. John M. Brockenbrough
40th VA—Lt. Col. Fleet W. Cox
47th VA—Lt. Col. John W. Lyell
55th VA—Capt. Charles N. Lawson
22nd VA Battalion—Maj. Edward P. Tayloe

Thomas's Brigade—Col. Edward L. Thomas
14th GA—Col. Robert W. Folsom
35th GA—Lt. Col. Bolling C. Holt
45th GA—Maj. Washington L. Grice
49th GA—Lt. Col. Seaborn M. Manning

27. Shepherd fell out on the march from Harpers Ferry, and Adjut. Howard commanded at Sharpsburg.
28. Arrived at Sharpsburg after the regiment's battle action.

Letcher (VA) Battery—
  Capt. Greenlee Davidson[29]

Jackson's Division—Brig. Gen. John R. Jones (w)
  Brig. Gen. William E. Starke (k)
  Col. Andrew J. Grigsby

Winder's Brigade—Col. Andrew J. Grigsby
  Lt. Col. Robert D. Gardner (w)
  Maj. Hazael J. Williams
4th VA—Lt. Col. Robert D. Gardner (w)
5th VA—Maj. Hazael Williams
  Capt. Edwin L. Custis (w)
27th VA—Capt. Frank C. Wilson
33rd VA—Col. Edwin G. Lee (c)
  Capt. Jacob B. Golladay (w)
  Lt. Daniel H. Walton

Jones's Brigade—Capt. John E. Penn (w)
  Capt. Archer C. Page (w)
  Capt. Robert W. Withers
21st VA—Capt. Archer C. Page (w)
42nd VA—Capt. Robert W. Withers
  Capt. David W. Garrett
48th VA—unknown
1st VA Battalion—Lt. Charles A. Davidson

Taliaferro's Brigade—Col. James W. Jackson (w)
  Col. James L. Sheffield
47th AL—Col. James W. Jackson (w)
  Maj. James A. Campbell
48th AL—Col. James Sheffield[30]
23rd VA—Lt. Col. Simeon T. Walton (w)
37th VA—Lt. Col. John F. Terry (w)

Starke's Brigade—Brig. Gen. William Starke (k)
  Col. Jesse Williams (w & c)
  Col. Leroy Stafford (w)
  Col. Edmund Pendleton
1st LA—Lt. Col. Michael Nolan (w)
  Capt. William E. Moore
2nd LA—Col. Jesse Williams (w)
9th LA—Col. Leroy Stafford (w)
  Lt. Col. William R. Peck
10th LA—Capt. Henry D. Monier
15th LA—Col. Edmund Pendleton
1st LA Battalion—Lt. Col. Marie A. Coppens

Artillery—Maj. Lindsay M. Shumaker
Alleghany (VA) Battery—Capt. Joseph Carpenter
  (1 3-inch rifle,
  1 10 lb. Parrott,
  1 Napoleon)

---

29. Left at Harpers Ferry.
30. Sheffield was reported as present with his regiment, but he was in a Charlottesville hospital until Sept. 6 from a wound received at the Battle of Cedar Mountain. He may have been captured and paroled at Sharpsburg, but there is no evidence of that in his military service records.

Cutshaw's (VA) Battery—Capt. Wilfred E. Cutshaw
    (1 or 2 3-inch
    rifles, 2 12 lb.
    howitzers)

2nd Baltimore Battery—Capt. John B. Brockenbrough
    (1 3-inch rifle, 1
    Blakely rifle, 1 10
    lb. Parrott, 1 12 lb.
    howitzer)

Danville (VA) Battery—Capt. George W. Wooding
    (2 10 lb. Parrotts,
    1 3-inch rifle,
    1 Napoleon)

Lee (VA) Battery—Capt. Charles J. Raine
    (2 3-inch rifles, 2 12 lb.
    howitzers)

Rockbridge (VA) Battery—Capt. William T. Poague
    (2 10 lb. Parrotts, 1
    Napoleon)

Hampden (VA) Battery—Capt. William Henderson Caskie
    (1 10 lb. Parrott)

Rice's (VA) Battery[31]—Capt. William H. Rice
    (1 10 lb. Parrott, 1
    3-inch rifle, 1
    Napoleon)

UNATTACHED DIVISIONS

McLaws's Division—Maj. Gen. Lafayette McLaws

Kershaw's Brigade—
    Brig. Gen. Joseph B. Kershaw
2nd SC—Col. John D. Kennedy (w)
    Maj. Franklin Galliard
3rd SC—Col. James D. Nance
7th SC—Col. D. Wyatt Aiken (w)
    Maj. William C. White (k)
    Capt. John S. Hard
8th SC—Lt. Col. Axalla J. Hoole

Cobb's Brigade—
    Lt. Col. Christopher C. Sanders
    Lt. Col. William MacRae

Semmes's Brigade—Brig. Gen. Paul J. Semmes
10th GA—Capt. Philologus H. Loud (w)
    Capt. William Johnston (w)
53rd GA—Lt. Col. Thomas Sloan (mw)
    Capt. Samuel W. Marshborne
15th VA—Capt. Emmett M. Morrison (w & c)
    Capt. Edward J. Willis
32nd VA—Col. Edgar Montague

Barksdale's Brigade—
    Brig. Gen. William Barksdale
13th MS—Lt. Col. Kennon McElroy

31. Posted to cover a ford between Shepherdstown and Williamsport and not present at Sharpsburg.

16th GA—Lt. Col. Henry Thomas
24th GA—Maj. Robert E. McMillan (w)
15th NC—Lt. Col. William MacRae
Cobb's (GA) Legion—Lt. Col. Luther Glenn

Artillery—Maj. Col. Henry C. Cabell
Manly's (NC) Battery—Capt. Basil C. Manly
                 (1 3-inch rifle, 2 12
                 lb. howitzers, 3 6 lb.
                 guns)
Pulaski (GA) Battery—Capt. John P. W. Read
                 (1 10 lb. Parrott, 1
                 3-inch rifle, 1 6 lb.
                 gun, 1 12 lb.
                 howitzer)
Richmond "Fayette" (VA) Battery—
                 Capt.Miles C. Macon
                 (2 10 lb. Parrotts,
                 4 6 lb. guns)
1st Co., Richmond Howitzers—
                 Capt. Edward S. McCarthy
                 (2 10 lb. Parrotts, 2
                 6 lb. guns)
Troup (GA) Artillery—Capt. Henry H. Carlton
                 (2 10 lb. Parrotts, 1 12
                 lb. howitzer, 2 6 lb. guns)

17th MS—Lt. Col. John C. Fiser
18th MS—Maj. James C. Campbell (w)
        Lt. Col. William H. Luse[32]
21st MS—Capt. John Sims
        Col. Benjamin Humphreys[33]

Hill's Division—Maj. Gen. Daniel Harvey Hill

Ripley's Brigade—Brig. Gen. Roswell S.
                Ripley (w)
                Col. George Doles
4th GA—Col. George Doles
        Maj. Robert Smith (k)
        Capt. William H. Willis
44th GA—Capt. John C. Key
1st NC—Lt. Col. Hamilton Brown
3rd NC—Col. William DeRosset (w)
        Maj. Stephen D. Thruston (w)

Garland's Brigade—Col. Duncan K. McRae (w)
5th NC—Capt. Thomas M. Garrett (w)
12th NC—Capt. Shugan Snow
13th NC—Capt. Joseph H. Hyman
20th NC—Col. Alfred Iverson
23rd NC—Col. Daniel H. Christie[34]
        Lt. Col. Robert D. Johnston

---

32. Arrived after the main battle action.
33. Arrived with Lt. Col. Luse.
34. Christie was detached to temporarily command G. B. Anderson's brigade late on Sept. 17 and on Sept. 18.

Rodes's Brigade—Brig. Gen. Robert E. Rodes
3rd AL—Col. Cullen A. Battle
5th AL—Lt. Col. Edwin L. Hobson
6th AL—Col. John B. Gordon (w)
      Lt. Col. James N. Lightfoot (w)
12th AL—Capt. Exton Tucker (k)
      Capt. William Meroney (w)
      Capt. Adolf Proskauer (w)
26th AL—Col. Edward O'Neal[35]

Anderson's Brigade—
      Brig. Gen. George B.Anderson (mw)
      Col. Charles C. Tew (k)
      Col. Risden T. Bennett (w)
      Maj. William W. Sillers
      Col. Daniel H. Christie
2nd NC—Col. Charles C. Tew (k)
      Capt. John Howard (mw & c)
      Capt. Gideon M. Roberts
4th NC—Capt. Edwin A. Osborne (w & c)
      Capt. William T. Marsh (mw)
      Capt. Daniel P. Latham (mw)
14th NC—Col. Risden T. Bennett (w)
      Lt. Col. William A. Johnson (w)
      Capt. Andrew J. Griffith
30th NC—Col. Francis Parker (w)
      Maj. William W. Sillers

Colquitt's Brigade—Col. Alfred H. Colquitt
13th AL—Col. Birkett D. Fry (w)
      Lt. Col. William H. Betts (w)
      Capt. Algernon S. Reaves (w)
6th GA—Lt. Col. James M. Newton (k)
      Maj. Philemon Tracy (k)
      Lt. Eugene P. Burnett
23rd GA—Col. William Barclay (k)
      Lt. Col. Emory F. Best (w & c)
      Maj. James H. Huggins (w)
27th GA—Col. Levi Smith (k)
      Lt. Col. Charles T. Zachry (w)
      Capt. William H. Rentfro
28th GA—Capt. Nehemiah H. Garrison (w)
      Lt. James W. Banning

Artillery—Maj. Scipio F. Pierson
Hardaway's (AL) Battery—
      Capt. Robert A. Hardaway
      (2 3-inch rifles, 1
      Whitworth rifle)
Jeff Davis (AL) Artillery—
      Capt. James W. Bondurant
      (3 3-inch rifles, 1
      Napoleon)
Jones's (Peninsula) VA Battery—
      Capt.William B. Jones
      (4 guns of unknown
      caliber and type)
King William (VA) Artillery—
      Capt. Thomas H. Carter
      (2 12 lb. howitzers, 2 6 lb.
      guns, 1 10 lb. Parrott)

Walker's Division—Brig. Gen. John G. Walker

Walker's Brigade—Col. Van H. Manning (w)
      Col. Edward D. Hall
3rd AR—Capt. John W. Reedy

Ransom's Brigade—Brig. Gen. Robert Ransom Jr.
24th NC—Lt. Col. John L. Harris
25th NC—Col. Henry M. Rutledge

35. O'Neal was wounded at the Battle of South Mountain and may not have been present at Sharpsburg.

27th NC—Col. John R. Cooke

46th NC—Col. Edward D. Hall

        Lt. Col. William A. Jackson

48th NC—Col. Robert C. Hill

30th VA—Lt. Col. Robert S. Chew (w)

Branch's (VA) Field Artillery—Capt. James Branch

        (3 10 lb.

        Parrotts, 3

        12 lb. howitzers)

French's (VA) Battery—Capt. Thomas B. French

        (3 10 lb. Parrotts, 3

        12 lb. howitzers)

35th NC—Col. Matt W. Ransom

49th NC—Lt. Col. Lee M. McAfee

Reserve Artillery—Brig. Gen. William N. Pendleton

Cutts's Battalion—Lt. Col. Allen S. Cutts

Blackshear's (GA) Battery—

        Capt. James A. Blackshear

        (5 guns of

        unknown

        caliber and type

Patterson's (GA) Battery—

        Capt. George M. Patterson

        (3 12 lb.

        howitzers, 3

        6 lb. guns)

Lane's (GA) Battery—Capt. John Lane

        (3 10 lb. Parrotts,

        1 12 lb. Whitworth

        rifle, 2 guns of

        unknown caliber

        and type)

Lloyd's (NC) Battery—Capt. W. P. Lloyd

        (2 12 lb. howitzers,

        1 6 lb. gun)

Sumter (GA) Battery—Capt. Hugh M. Ross

        (3 10 lb. Parrotts, 1

        12 lb. howitzer, 1

        Napoleon)

Jones's Battalion—Maj. Hilary P. Jones

Brown's Battalion—Col. J. Thompson Brown

Powhatan (VA) Artillery—Capt. Willis J. Dance

        (1 3-inch rifle,

        1 6 lb. gun)

2nd Co., Richmond Howitzers—

        Capt. David Watson

        (2 10 lb. Parrotts,

        1 12 lb. howitzer,

        1 Hotchkiss

        rifle)

3rd Co., Richmond Howitzers—

        Capt. Benjamin H. Smith Jr.

        (2 10 lb. Parrotts,

        2 12 lb. howitzers)

Salem (VA) Artillery—

        Capt. Abraham Hupp

        (2 12 lb. howitzers, 2

        6 lb. guns)

Williamsburg (VA) Artillery—

        Capt. John A. Coke

        (guns of

        unknown

        caliber and

        type)

Nelson's Battalion—Maj. William Nelson

Morris (VA) Artillery—Capt. Richard
 C. M. Page
 (4 12 lb. howitzers)
Orange (VA) Artillery—Capt. Jefferson Peyton
 (1 3-inch rifle, 1 12
 lb. howitzer, 3 6 lb.
 guns)
Turner's (VA) Battery[36]—
 Capt. William H. Turner
 (guns of unknown
 caliber and type)
Wimbish's (VA) Battery—
 Capt. Abram Wimbish
 (guns of unknown
 caliber and type)

Amherst (VA) Artillery—
 Capt. Thomas J. Kirkpatrick
 (2 6 lb. guns, 2 12
 lb. howitzers)
1st Fluvanna (VA) Battery—
 Capt. Charles T. Huckstep
 (4 6 lb. guns)
2nd Fluvanna (VA) Artillery—
 Capt. John Ancell
 (2 6 lb. guns)
Johnson's (VA) Battery—Capt. Marmaduke
 Johnson
 (2 6 lb. guns,
 2 howitzers)
Milledge's (GA) Battery—Capt. John Milledge
 (3 3-inch rifles, 1
 Hotchkiss rifle, 1
 12 lb. howitzer)
Pegram's (VA) Battery (detachment)[37]—
 Capt. John G. Barnwell
 (1 Whitworth rifle)

Unattached Artillery

Yorktown "Magruder" (VA) Artillery—Capt. T. J. Page Jr. (guns of unknown caliber and type)

CAVALRY DIVISION—MAJ. GEN. JAMES E. B. STUART

Hampton's Brigade—
 Brig. Gen. Wade Hampton
1st NC—Col. Lawrence S. Baker
2nd NC—Col. Matthew C. Butler
Cobb's (GA) Legion—Maj. W. G. Delony
Jeff Davis Legion—Lt. Col. William T. Martin
10th VA—Lt. Col. J. Lucius Davis

Lee's Brigade—Brig. Gen. Fitzhugh Lee
1st VA—Lt. Col. L. Tiernan Brien
3rd VA—Lt. Col. John T. Thornton (k)
 Capt. Thomas H. Owen
4th VA—Col. William C. Wickham
5th VA—Col. Thomas L. Rosser
9th VA—Col. William H. F. Lee

Robertson's Brigade—Col. Thomas T. Munford
2nd VA—Lt. Col. Richard H. Burks
6th VA—Col. Thomas S. Flourney

Artillery
Pelham's (VA) Battery—Maj. John Pelham
 (2 3-inch rifles,

---

36. Turner's and Wimbish's batteries had a total of either five or seven guns of unknown caliber and type. Both were disbanded in the army's reorganization on Oct. 4, 1862.

37. This detachment was formed with personnel from Pegram's (VA) battery of A. P. Hill's division. Barnwell was a staff officer to Gen. Pendleton.

7th VA—Capt. Samuel B. Myers
12th VA—Col. Asher W. Harman
17th VA Cavalry Battalion—
        Maj. Thomas B. Massie

1 Napoleon, 5 guns of
unknown caliber
and type)
Hart's (SC) Washington Battery—
        Capt. James F. Hart
        (4 Blakely rifles)
Chew's Ashby (VA) Battery—
        Capt. Roger P. Chew
        (2 3-inch rifles,
        1 Blakely rifle, 1 12 lb.
        howitzer)

APPENDIX C

Strengths and Losses at the Battle of Antietam and the Battle of Shepherdstown

In his final report on the Maryland Campaign, George McClellan gave the strength of the Army of the Potomac at Antietam as 87,164. This figure is its aggregate strength—in other words, every man in uniform in the army. Approximately 17% of this number were detailed to non-combat duties, such as teamsters, cooks, hospital stewards, stretcher bearers, and the like. As the accompanying table shows, its fighting strength was approximately 72,199 men. The losses of the Union army at Antietam and Shepherdstown, as published in volume 19 of *War of the Rebellion: A Compilation of the Official Records of the Union and Confederate Armies*, are generally quite accurate. There was one anomaly: the 16th Connecticut, whose officially reported losses at Antietam were 42 killed, 143 wounded, and 0 missing or captured. Subsequent research revealed that their actual number of casualties was 43 killed, 164 wounded, 20 captured, and 19 missing (who were deserters). There may be other discrepancies that continuing research will reveal, but in general, the Union army maintained reliable records of their battle losses.

The same cannot be said for the Army of Northern Virginia, either for their losses or their strengths. Record keeping was quite poor, partly due to high attrition among company and field officers. Arriving at accurate numbers for Confederate troops or casualties for the Battle of Sharpsburg, as they called this conflict, is a maddening exercise. The following table should be considered simply as a starting point. We will never know with any precision precisely how many men Robert E. Lee had that day. Some units had stragglers trickling in throughout the day, so their strength fluctuated. This was particularly true for A. P. Hill's division. Nevertheless, the numbers for the Confederate army, as shown in the table, are close to Lee's engaged strength.

The official casualty figures the Confederates released, which are published in the *War of the Rebellion* records, volume 19, part 1, pages 810–813, are so inaccurate that they are of limited value. For example, the 6th Georgia was reported to have had 10 killed and 13 wounded, when their actual loss was 81 killed, 115 wounded, and 30 missing or captured. Figures for the 5th Florida, which sustained 159 casualties, were not reported at all. No missing or captured men were included for any unit in the entire army, even though there were hundreds. The records also included losses at the Battles of South Mountain and Shepherdstown in this tabulation. Ezra Carman, the colonel in the 13th New Jersey and, later, the historian for the Antietam National Battlefield, did yeoman work in assembling strength and loss figures for the Army of Northern Virginia, and my efforts build off his. In most instances I have accepted Carman's numbers for total losses for brigades, divisions, and wings, unless I felt that the contrary evidence I had discovered was solid. This can lead to some odd situations, such as my acceptance of Carman's figures for D. H. Hill's wounded and missing men, but not for those killed. This was because the numbers I found for those in the division who were killed, while still slightly low in relation to its actual loss, are higher than what Carman listed, and I have confidence in these amounts. I had less assurance in my figures for the wounded and missing in the division, however, since we have no casualty records for some regiments. Here I used Carman's numbers, since his information always came from veterans. It should also be noted that the "Total" columns for brigades, divisions, and wings will sometimes not agree with the figures that exist for individual regiments. I used the best sources available, but their cumulative totals might differ from Carman's amounts. An example is Drayton's brigade. Carman's figure—142—is 4 higher than the total of the regimental losses in the table. Unfortunately, we do not always know where Carman's information came from, but a rule of thumb for the Army of Northern Virginia is that the highest casualty totals from a reliable source are usually correct, since that army consistently undercounted its losses. The figures in the accompanying table should be considered the *minimum* number of casualties for the Confederates. They may have been as high as 11,000.

A good online source to consult for the strengths and losses in both armies, as well as for personnel known to have been present in the battle, is Brian Downey's Antietam on the Web, at https://antietam.aotw.org, which is continually updated.

Strength and Casualties—Army of the Potomac

	Sept. 17 strength[1]	Killed	Wounded	Missing & captured	Total
1st Corps—Hooker	9,582	417	2,051	122	2,590 (27%)
1st Division—Doubleday	3,403	140	638	34	812 (24%)
1st Brigade—Phelps Jr.	407[2]	30	120	4	154
84th NY (14th Brooklyn)	80[3]	6	21	0	27
22nd NY	67	2	28	0	30
24th NY	57	3	15	1	19
30th NY	53	6	5	1	12
2nd U.S. Sharpshooters	150[4]	13	51	2	66
2nd Brigade—Hoffman	750	0	9	1	10
7th IN		0	4	0	4
76th NY		0	3	1	4
95th NY		0	1	0	1
56th PA		0	1	0	0
3rd Brigade—Patrick	825	30	187	17	234
20th NY State Militia	132[5]	6	40	8	54
23rd NY	238[6]	4	35	3	42
21st NY	225[7]	12	57	2	71
35th NY	230[8]	8	55	4	67
4th Brigade—Gibbon	971	68	275	5	348
2nd WI	150[9]	19	67	0	86
6th WI	314[10]	26	126	0	152
7th WI	190[11]	10	23	5	38
19th IN	317[12]	12	57	0	69
Artillery—Monroe	450	12	46	8	66
1st Battery, NH Light		0	3	0	3
Battery D, 1st RI Light		3	7	8	18
Battery L, 1st NY Light		0	5	0	5
Battery B, 4th U.S.		9	31	0	40
2nd Division—Ricketts	3,331	172	946	86	1,204 (36%)
1st Brigade—Duryée	1,100	59	233	35	327
107th PA	190[13]	19	45	0	64
97th NY	203[14]	24	74	9	107
104th NY		7	60	15	82
105th NY		9	54	11	74
2nd Brigade—Christian	1,000[15]	28	197	29	254
88th PA	350[16]	10	62	5	77
90th PA	264[17]	13	82	3	98
26th NY		5	41	20	66
94th NY		0	12	1	13
3rd Brigade—Hartsuff	1,110[18]	82	497	20	599
12th MA	334[19]	49	165	10	224
13th MA	301[20]	14	119	3	136
83rd NY (9th Militia)	240 est.	6	105	3	114
11th PA	235[21]	13	107	4	124

(continued)

	Sept. 17 strength[1]	Killed	Wounded	Missing & captured	Total
Artillery	121	3	19	2	24
Battery F, 1st PA Light		3	8	0	11
Battery C, PA Light		0	11	2	13
3rd Division—Meade	2,848	105	466	2	573 (20%)
1st Brigade—Seymour	1,000 est.	24	131	0	155
1st PA Reserves		5	22	0	27
2nd PA Reserves		3	21	0	24
5th PA Reserves		3	7	0	10
6th PA Reserves		8	61	0	69
13th PA Reserves		5	20	0	25
2nd Brigade—Magilton	800 est.	41	181	0	222
3rd PA Reserves		12	34	0	46
4th PA Reserves		5	43	0	48
7th PA Reserves	180[22]	12	60	0	72
8th PA Reserves		12	44	0	56
3rd Brigade—Anderson	800 est.	37	136	2	173
9th PA Reserves	260[23]	17	66	0	83
10th PA Reserves		0	9	0	9
11th PA Reserves		7	15	0	22
12th PA Reserves		13	46	2	61
Artillery	248	3	18	0	21
Battery A, 1st PA Light		1	3	0	4
Battery B, 1st PA Light		0	2	0	2
Battery C, 5th U.S.		2	13	0	15
2nd Corps—Sumner	16,475	883	3,856	396	5,135 (31%)
1st Division—Richardson	4,305	210	939	16	1,165 (27%)
Staff		0	2	0	2
1st Brigade—Caldwell	1,343 est.	44	268	2	314
5th NH	321[24]	8	46	1	55
61st NY	228[25]	6	34	1	41
64th NY	214[26]	8	42	0	50
81st PA		7	44	0	51
7th NY		15	46	0	61
2nd Brigade—Meagher	1,340	113	422	5	540
Staff		0	1	0	1
63rd NY	341[27]	35	165	2	202
69th NY	317	44	152	0	196
88th NY	302[28]	27	75	0	102
29th MA	380[29]	7	29	3	39
3rd Brigade—Brooke	1,376	52	244	9	305
52nd NY	119[30]	4	12	2	18
57th NY	309[31]	19	79	3	101
2nd DE	350[32]	12	44	2	58
66th NY	310[33]	11	91	1	103
53rd PA	288[34]	6	18	1	25

(continued)

	Sept. 17 strength[1]	Killed	Wounded	Missing & captured	Total
Artillery	246	1	3	0	4
Battery B, 1st NY Light		1	0	0	1
Batteries A & C, 4th U.S.		0	3	0	3
2nd Division—Sedgwick	6,050	373	1,593	244	2,210 (37%)
1st Brigade—Gorman	1,691	134	539	67	740
15th MA	606[35]	57	238	23	318
1st MN	435[36]	15	60	15	90
34th NY	311	33	111	10	154
82nd NY	339	21	92	15	128
1st Co., MA Sharpshooters[37]		8	17	1	26
2nd Co., MN Sharpshooters[38]		0	21	3	24
2nd Brigade—Howard	2,169	93	379	73	545
69th PA	486[39]	19	58	15	92
71st PA	510	26	95	18	139
72nd PA	681	38	163	36	237
106th PA	492	10	63	4	77
3rd Brigade—Dana	1,946	142	652	104	898
7th MI	402[40]	39	178	4	221
19th MA	418[41]	8	108	30	146
20th MA	400	12	84	28	124
42nd NY	345	35	127	19	181
59th NY	381	48	153	23	224
Artillery	244	4	21	0	25
Battery A, 1st RI Light	109	4	15	0	19
Battery I, 1st U.S.		0	6	0	6
3rd Division—French	6,120	300	1,324	136	1,760 (29%)
1st Brigade—Kimball	1,751	121	510	8	639
132nd PA	750[42]	30	114	8	152
14th IN	320[43]	30	150	0	180
8th OH	341[44]	32	129	0	161
7th [W]V	340[45]	29	116	0	145
2nd Brigade—Morris	2,240	78	356	95	529
130th PA	690[46]	32	146	0	178
108th NY	750[47]	26	122	47	195
14th CT	800[48]	20	88	48	156
3rd Brigade—Weber	1,740	100	449	33	582
1st DE	650[49]	31	182	17	230
5th MD	550[50]	25	123	15	163
4th NY	540[51]	44	142	1	187
Artillery	389	1	9	0	10
Battery G, 1st NY Light	123	1	4	0	5
Battery G, 1st RI Light	135	0	5	0	5
Battery B, 1st RI Light	131	0	0	0	0

(continued)

	Sept. 17 strength[1]	Killed	Wounded	Missing & captured	Total
4th Corps	7,219[52]				
1st Division—Couch		0	9	0	9
1st Brigade—Devens Jr.		0	0	0	0
2nd Brigade—Howe		0	0	0	0
3rd Brigade—Cochrane		0	9	0	9
65th NY		0	1	0	1
67th NY		0	1	0	1
122nd NY		0	0	0	0
61st PA		0	5	0	5
82nd PA		0	2	0	2
Artillery		0	0	0	0
5th Corps—Porter	9,476[53]	17	90	2	109 (0.01%)
1st Division—Morell	5,607[54]	0	0	0	0
1st U.S. Sharpshooters	234[55]				
1st Brigade—J. Barnes	1,711[56]				
118th PA	737				
1st MI	153[57]				
22nd MA	166				
2nd ME	173				
18th MA	282				
13th NY	160				
25th NY	153				
2nd Co., MA Sharpshooters					
2nd Brigade—Griffin	2,017[58]				
4th MI	288				
14th NY	300				
9th MA	379				
62nd PA	435				
32nd MA	315				
2nd DC[59]					
3rd Brigade—Stockton	1,300 est.[60]				
12th NY	159				
17th NY	115				
16th MI	112				
83rd PA	101				
44th NY	95				
20th ME					
MI Sharpshooters					
Artillery	345				
2nd Division—Sykes	3,846	12	85	1	98 (0.03%)
1st Brigade—Buchanan	1,748	4	35	0	39
3rd U.S.	290[61]	0	0	0	0
4th U.S.	318[62]	3	29	0	32
1/12th U.S.	250[63]	1	3	0	4
2/12th U.S.	250	0	0	0	0

(continued)

	Sept. 17 strength[1]	Killed	Wounded	Missing & captured	Total
1/14th U.S.	320[64]	0	2	0	2
2/14th U.S.	320	0	1	0	1
2nd Brigade—Lovell	1,288	8	47	1	56
1st & 6th U.S.					
2nd & 10th U.S.	402	8	46	1	55
11th U.S.		0	1	0	1
17th U.S.					
3rd Brigade—Warren	523				
Artillery	287	0	3	0	3
Battery I, 5th U.S.		0	3	0	3
3rd Division—Humphreys[65]	7,000				
1st Brigade—Tyler	3,500				
2nd Brigade—Allabach	3,500				
Artillery Reserve—Hays	973	5	5	1	11
1st Battery, NY Light		1	0	1	2
Battery K, 1st U.S.		4	5	0	9
6th Corps—Franklin	11,862[66]	70	335	33	438 (0.04%)
1st Division—Slocum	5,915	5	58	2	65
1st Brigade—Torbert	1,300	2	17	0	19
1st NJ		0	6	0	6
2nd NJ		2	7	0	9
3rd NJ		0	1	0	1
4th NJ		0	3	0	3
2nd Brigade—Bartlett	2,500	1	8	0	9
5th ME		0	5	0	5
16th NY	300[67]	0	2	0	2
27th NY		0	0	0	0
121st NY		0	0	0	0
96th PA		1	1	0	2
3rd Brigade—Newton	1,600	1	20	0	21
18th NY		0	4	0	4
31st NY		0	3	0	3
32nd NY		0	4	0	4
95th PA		1	9	0	10
Artillery—Upton[68]	515	1	13	2	16
Battery A, MD Light		1	11	2	14
Battery D, 2nd U.S.		0	2	0	2
2nd Division—Smith	6,670[69]	65	277	31	373
1st Brigade—Hancock	2,500	0	6	0	6
6th ME		0	2	0	2
49th PA		0	4	0	4
2nd Brigade—Brooks	2,100	1	24	0	25
2nd VT		0	5	0	5
3rd VT		1	3	0	4

(continued)

	Sept. 17 strength[1]	Killed	Wounded	Missing & captured	Total
4th VT		0	6	0	6
5th VT		0	2	0	2
6th VT		0	8	0	8
3rd Brigade—Irwin	1,684	64	247	31	342
7th ME	181[70]	12	63	20	95
20th NY	680[71]	38	96	11	145
33rd NY	380	6	41	0	47
49th NY	268	2	21	0	23
77th NY	175[72]	6	26	0	32
Artillery—Ayres	386				
9th Corps—Cox	12,241	439	1,816	154	2,409 (20%)
1st Division—Willcox	3,264	46	285	7	338 (10%)
1st Brigade—Christ	1,395	43	198	3	244
28th MA	200[73]	12	36	0	48
17th MI	525	18	89	0	107
79th NY	300	5	27	0	32
50th PA	370	8	46	3	57
2nd Brigade—Welsh	1,623	3	86	4	93
8th MI	435[74]	0	29	2	31
46th NY	278	2	14	0	16
45th PA	560	1	36	1	38
100th PA	350	0	7	1	8
Artillery	246	0	1	0	1
8th Battery, MA Light		0	1	0	1
Battery E, 2nd U.S.		0	0	0	0
2nd Division—Sturgis	2,909	136	532	11	679 (23%)
1st Brigade—Nagle	1,126	39	160	5	204
2nd MD	162[75]	17	47	3	67
6th NH	104[76]	4	13	1	18
9th NH	710[77]	10	49	0	59
48th PA	150	8	51	1	60
2nd Brigade—Ferrero	1,601	95	368	6	469
21st MA	150[78]	7	41	0	48
35th MA	780	48	160	6	214
51st NY	335	19	68	0	87
51st PA	336	21	99	0	120
Artillery	182[79]	2	4	0	6
Battery D, PA Light	123	0	3	0	3
Battery E, 4th U.S.	59	2	1	0	3
3rd Division—Rodman	2,914	221	807	109	1,137 (39%)
1st Brigade—Fairchild	943	87	321	47	455
9th NY	373[80]	45	176	14	235
89th NY	370	18	77	8	103
103rd NY	200	24	68	25	117

(continued)

	Sept. 17 strength[1]	Killed	Wounded	Missing & captured	Total
2nd Brigade—Harland	1,848	134	483	62	679
8th CT	421[81]	34	139	21	194
11th CT	430[82]	36	103	0	139
16th CT	750	43	164	39	246[83]
4th RI	247	21	77	2	100
Artillery					
Battery A, 5th U.S.	123	0	3	0	3
Kanawha Division—Scammon	3,154	36	192	27	255 (8%)
1st Brigade—Ewing	903	28	134	20	182
12th OH	200[84]	7	26	0	33
23rd OH	360[85]	8	59	2	69
30th OH	343[86]	13	49	18	80
2nd Brigade—Crook	2,005	8	58	7	73
11th OH	430[87]	4	12	5	21
28th OH	775	2	19	0	21
36th OH	800	2	21	2	25
Artillery	246	0	6	0	6
1st Battery, OH Light		0	0	0	0
Simmonds's Battery, KY Light		0	6	0	6
12th Corps—Mansfield	8,020	275	1,386	85	1,746 (22%)
1st Division—Williams	4,735	159	864	54	1,077 (23%)
1st Brigade—Crawford	2,525	88	315	27	430
10th ME	297[88]	21	50	1	72
28th NY	68	2	9	1	12
46th PA	150	6	13	0	19
124th PA	700	5	42	17	64
125th PA	700	28	115	2	145
128th PA	700	26	86	6	118
3rd Brigade—Gordon	2,210	71	548	27	646
27th IN	443[89]	18	191	0	209
3rd WI	345[90]	27	173	0	200
2nd MA	220[91]	12	58	3	73[92]
13th NJ	600[93]	7	75	19	101
107th NY	600	7	51	5	63
2nd Division—Greene	2,577	114	507	30	651 (25%)
1st Brigade—Tyndale	1,213	61	308	7	376
5th OH	171[94]	11	35	2	48
7th OH	156[95]	5	33	0	38
66th OH	120[96]	1	23	0	24
28th PA	766[97]	44	217	5	266
2nd Brigade—Stainrook	587	32	128	16	176
3rd MD	148[98]	1	25	3	29
102nd NY	196[99]	5	27	5	37
111th PA	243[100]	26	76	8	110

(continued)

	Sept. 17 strength[1]	Killed	Wounded	Missing & captured	Total
3rd Brigade—Goodrich	777	21	71	7	99
60th NY	231[101]	4	18	0	22
78th NY	221[102]	8	19	7	34
3rd DE	120[103]	6	11	0	17
Purnell Legion	205[104]	3	23	0	26
Artillery—Best	708[105]	1	15	1	17
Battery M, 1st NY Light	124	0	6	0	6
Battery F, 4th U.S.	98	0	0	0	0
4th Battery, ME Light	104	0	0	0	0
6th Battery, ME Light	85	0	0	0	0
10th Battery, NY Light	117	0	0	0	0
Battery E, PA Light	101	1	6	1	8
Battery F, PA Light	79	0	3	0	3
Cavalry Division—Pleasonton	4,543[106]	6	23	0	29
1st Brigade—Whiting					
5th U.S.		0	1	0	1
2nd Brigade—Farnsworth		0	6	0	6
8th IL		0	1	0	1
3rd IN		0	5	0	5
3rd Brigade—Rush		3	10	0	13
4th PA		3	7	0	10
6th PA		0	3	0	3
Horse Artillery	451	3	6	0	9
Battery A, 2nd U.S.		1	3	0	4
Battery M, 2nd U.S.		2	3	0	5
Independent—15th PA Cavalry		1	0	0	1
Sept. 17 strength and losses	72,199	2,108	9,549	753	12,410 (17%)
Sept. 18 reinforcements	14,219				

Note: Where cells are blank, no data could be found.

1. These figures are for the numbers of men carried into action. To arrive at an estimate of the aggregate amount present, add 17%.

2. *OR* 19, 1:234.

3. All strengths for Phelps's brigade, except the 2nd U.S. Sharpshooters, are from the New York State Military Museum and Veterans Research Center website, https://museum.dmna.ny.gov/unit-history/conflict/us-civil-war-1861-1865/ [accessed Oct. 2017].

4. Edwin H. Chadwick to Dear Friends, Sept. 25, 1862, ANBL.

5. "From the XXth Regiment," in *Kingston (NY) Democratic Journal*, Oct. 1, 1862. In his after-action report, Lt. Col. Theodore Gates estimated his strength at about 150. See *OR* 19, 1:246.

6. Carman's notes on a letter from John Borleau, 23rd NY, AS.

7. Carman, 572.

8. Carman, 572.

9. Letter from Capt. George B. Ely, in Quiner, *Correspondence*, vol. 2, 307.

10. Dawes, *Service*, 92.

11. *OR* 19, 1:258.

12. The strength has been derived by subtracting the known strength of the 2nd, 6th, and 7th WI from Carman's reported strength for the brigade.

13. *OR* 19, 1:262.

14. Lt. Rush P. Cady to Uncle Gustavus, Sept. 25, 1862, Rush Cady letters, Hamilton College Library digital collections, http://elib.hamilton.edu/cady/ [accessed Nov. 2017].

15. The strength is an estimate from Ricketts's report that he carried 3,158 men into action, after deducting the strengths of Hartsuff's and Duryée's brigades.

16. 88th PA, AS.

17. 90th PA, AS.

18. Carman gave their strength as 1,100. See Carman, 64.

19. Carman, 83.

20. Warren H. Freeman to Father, Sept. 21, 1862, in Warren H. Freeman, *Letters from Two Brothers Serving in the War for the Union to Their Family at Home in West Cambridge, Mass.* (Cambridge, MA: H. O. Houghton, 1871), 52.

21. Locke, *Story*, 130.

22. Griffin Baldwin gave the regiment's strength as 167 muskets. Adding an estimate of 13 officers raises the regiment's strength to 180. See Griffin L. Baldwin to Gould, Nov. 5, 1893, GP.

23. Alexander Murdoch to Gould, Dec. 30, 1892, GP.

24. Carman, 573.

(continued)

25. Carman, 574.

26. Carman, 574.

27. For both the 63rd and 69th NY, see Carman, 573.

28. *OR* 19, 1:298.

29. Carman, 574.

30. *OR* 19, 1:301.

31. *OR* 19, 1:303. Capt. Charles B. Curtis, Company A, gave the strength as 325. See Curtis to Friend Cleveland, Sept. 17, 1862, in *Yates County Chronicle* (Penn-Yan, NY), Oct. 2, 1862.

32. *Delaware State Journal and Statesman* (Wilmington), Sept. 26, 1862. Carman gave the strength as 310. See Carman, 574. The *Delaware Republican* (Wilmington), Sept. 25, 1862, listed the strength of the 2nd DE as approximately 400.

33. Carman, 574.

34. Carman, 574.

35. Attached to the 15th MA.

36. Attached to the 1st MN.

37. Carman, 574. Edward Chapin gave the strength as 574, but this probably did not include officers. See Edward Chapin diary, quoted in Olney, "Chapin," 450.

38. Return Ira Holcombe, *History of the First Regiment Minnesota Volunteer Infantry, 1861–1864* (Stillwater, MN: Easton & Masterman, 1916), 221.

39. The strengths for all of Howard's regiments are from ANBL regimental files for the 69th, 71st, 72nd, and 106th PA.

40. Frederick Oesterle, in Jack Dempsey and Brian James Egan, *Michigan at Antietam* (Charleston, SC: History Press, 2015), 98, gave the strength as 636. "7th Michigan at Antietam," *Detroit Free Press*, Sept. 27, 1862, 3, listed the strength as 363.

41. Waitt, *History*, 147, gave the strength as 347.

42. Edward T. Henry [Company K] letter, Oct. 2, 1862, 132nd PA file, ANBL.

43. *Western Sun* (Vincennes, IN), Sept. 26, 1862.

44. *OR* 19, 1:330.

45. Carman, 575. Sgt. Calvin Bell gave the strength of the regiment as "only about two hundred and fifty." See Bell to Father and Mother, Oct. 13, 1862, in Calvin Bell's widow's file, Case Files of Approved Pension Applications of Widows and Other Veterans of the Army and Navy, RG 15, NA.

46. 130th PA file, ANBL.

47. Carman, 576.

48. H. Goddard, *Good Fight*, 58.

49. Seville, *History*, 51.

50. 5th MD file, ANBL.

51. 4th NY file, ANBL.

52. This is the aggregate of those present from the Sept. 20 return. To arrive at a combat strength, deduct 17% for non-combat and detached personnel. See *OR* 19, 2:336.

53. GBM gave Porter's strength as 12,930 on Sept. 17, but this was an aggregate. With Humphreys's 3rd Division, Porter's strength was about 16,000 on Sept. 18.

54. Morell's fighting strength was probably slightly less than this, since some strength figures are from the Sept. 1 return.

55. This is the strength of the 2nd U.S. Sharpshooters on Sept. 1. It was probably slightly smaller on Sept. 17 and during the operations near Shepherdstown on Sept. 19 and 20. See *OR* 12, 3:795.

56. *OR* 12, 3:795. The 2nd Company MA Sharpshooters probably only numbered about 20 to 30 men.

57. All the strengths for Barnes's regiments, except the 118th PA, are from a Sept. 1 strength report. Based on Barnes's report of a strength of 1,711 men on Sept. 20, we know that all the numbers for veteran regiments were slightly less than those given here. See *OR* 12, 3:795.

58. This regiment was added to the brigade after the Sept. 1 strength return was compiled. Its strength is unknown, but the 2nd DC probably was similar in size to the other regiments in the brigade.

59. Griffin's numbers are from his Sept. 1 strength report and were almost certainly slightly less on Sept. 17 and during the operations at Shepherdstown on Sept. 19 and 20. See *OR* 12, 3:795. The 2nd DC was not attached to the brigade when this report was made, and their strength is estimated at 300.

60. An estimate for the 20th ME would be 800, and 20 to 30 for the MI Sharpshooter company.

61. This is an estimate, based on the average for the other five regiments.

62. Carman, 577.

63. On Sept. 21, Sgt. Charles T. Bowen wrote that the two battalions of the 1/12th U.S. Infantry would not number over 500 men. See C. Bowen, *Dear Friends*, 150.

64. The strengths for the 14th and 4th U.S. are from Carman, 577.

65. Arrived Sept. 18. Not engaged at Antietam.

66. *OR* 19, 2:336.

67. [Lt. Col.] Frank Palmer to Carman, Oct. 19, 1899, stated that the 16th NY lost heavily at Crampton's Gap, but their strength had been greatly recovered by a large number of recruits who reached the regiment on Sept. 15.

68. Carman gave the strength of the 6th Corps' artillery at 21 officers and 880 enlisted men. This amounts to an average of 129 men per battery.

69. The strengths for Hancock's and Brooks's brigades are estimates, after deducting for casualties at Crampton's Gap.

70. Thomas Hyde to Gen. Hodson, Sept. 22, 1862, 7th ME Correspondence, Adjutant General Records, MNSA.

71. The strengths for the 20th, 33rd, and 49th NY are all from Carman, 578.

72. Robert F. Morrow Jr., *77th New York Volunteers* (Shippensburg, PA: White Mane Books, 2004), 60.

73. All figures for Christ's brigade are from Carman, 579.

74. All strengths for Welch's brigade are from Carman, 579, except for the 46th NY, which is from *OR* 19, 1:442.

75. Carman, 580.

76. *Peterborough (NH) Transcript*, Sept. 27, 1862. The source is Capt. J. A. Cummings. Carman gave their strength at 150, but this is almost certainly too high.

77. Figures for both the 9th NH and the 21st MA are from Carman, 580.

78. All figures for Ferrero's brigade are from Carman, 580.

79. Carman gave the strength as 241 for the two batteries, but C. Johnson and Anderson, in *Artillery Hell*, 77–78, show that their strength on the Sept. 22 muster was 5 officers and 177 men. They incurred only 3 casualties in battle.

80. Fairchild's regimental strengths are from Carman, 581.

81. The strengths for the 8th and 16th CT and the 4th RI are from Carman, 581.

82. This is Carman's strength for the regiment. The *Morning Bulletin* (Norwich, CT), Sept. 27, 1862, listed the regiment's strength as 440 on the morning of Sept. 14. Lt. George W. Davis, the regiment's quartermaster, gave it as 550 on Sept. 17, however. See "The Statement of an Eyewitness of the Late Battles," *New York Tribune*, Sept. 22, 1862.

83. L. Gordon, "All Who Went," 177. Deserters made up 19 of the missing, and the balance were captured. The officially reported losses of the 16th CT were 42 killed, 143 wounded, and 0 missing.

84. *OR* 19, 1:466.

85. Carman, 582.

86. Carman, 581.

(continued)

87. All figures for Crook's brigade are from Carman, 582.

88. All strengths are from Carman, 583. He estimated those of the 124th, 125th, and 128th PA at 670 each. I have rounded this number up to 700.

89. "3rd WI Infantry," Antietam on the Web, https://antietam .aotw.org/officers.php?unit_id=102/ [accessed Nov. 2017]. This website maintains a database of known participants in the battle.

90. Quiner, *Correspondence*, vol. 3, 61.

91. C. Mills, *Through Blood and Fire*, 32.

92. Estimate for the 13th NJ and the 107th NY have been arrived at by subtracting the strength of three veteran regiments from Gordon's stated strength for the brigade.

93. This includes the Zouaves d'Afrique, a Pennsylvania independent company attached to the 2nd MA. This company had 2 wounded and 1 missing.

94. Carman gave the combined strength for these three regiments as 425. The strength of the 5th OH has been derived by subtracting the known strength of the 7th and 66th OH from this figure. Daniel Mc-Cloud in Company D wrote that the regimental strength was 270. See McCloud [5th OH] to Gould, n.d., GP. Sgt. Martin Barringer, Company I, noted that the regiment only had about 100 men reporting for for duty. See Barringer to Gould, Mar. 10, 1892, GP.

95. *Jefferson (OH) Democrat*, n.d., ANBL.

96. John A. Purinton to Mr. Saxton, Sept. 18, 1862, in *Urbana (OH) Citizen and Gazette*, Oct. 2, 1862. Purinton was a commissary sergeant.

Also see Eugene Powell to Gould, Nov. 18, 1893, who gave the strength as 98.

97. The strength has been arrived at by subtracting the strengths of the Ohio regiments from Carman's stated brigade strength.

98. *OR* 19, 1:511.

99. Capt. Aaron P. Bates to Gould, Mar. 18, 1892. Bates wrote that the regiment mustered 1 field officer, 10 line officers, and 148 enlisted men on Sept. 18, with 5 killed, 27 wounded, and 5 missing, which gives a Sept. 17 strength of 196.

100. John R. Boyle, *Soldiers True*, 61. Private Lemuel H. Hitchcock, in a Sept. 22 letter to his father, gave the regiment's engaged strength as 215. See *Windham (NY) Journal*, Oct. 9, 1862.

101. The strength has been arrived at by subtracting the known strength of the other three regiments in the brigade from Carman's stated brigade strength.

102. "78th NY Infantry," Antietam on the Web, https://antietam .aotw.org/officers.php?unit_id=422/ [accessed Nov. 2017].

103. "78th NY Infantry," Antietam on the Web, https://antietam .aotw.org/officers.php?unit_id=422/ [accessed Nov. 2017].

104. Carman, 158.

105. The strengths for all of the 12th Corps' batteries are from C. Johnson and Anderson, *Artillery Hell*, 81–82.

106. This strength is from the September 20 return. See *OR* 19, 2:336.

Strength and Casualties—Army of Northern Virginia

Command/division/brigade	Strength[1]	Killed	Wounded	Missing & captured	Total
T. J. "Stonewall" Jackson	9,365	427	1,942	109	2,478 (26%)
Lawton	3,723	196	1,096	69	1,361 (37%)
Douglass	1,150[2]	106	438[3]	21	565
13th GA	330[4]	48	166	2	216
26th GA		6	49	6	61
31st GA		6	42	5	53
38th GA		18	52	1	71
60th GA		12	48	0	60
61st GA	350[5]	16	81	7	104
Early	1,100	18	167	9	194
13th VA		0	5	0	5
25th VA		3	20	0	23
31st VA		1	7	0	8
44th VA		2	32	0	34
49th VA		8	69	8	85
52nd VA		4	24	1	29
58th VA		0	10	0	10
Hays	550[6]	44	281	31	356
5th LA	100[7]	9	40	5[8]	54
6th LA		11	41	6[9]	58
7th LA		11	56	9[10]	76
8th LA		7	96	11[11]	114
14th LA		6	47	0	53
J. A. Walker	700	26	192	8	226
15th AL		8	65	6	79
12th GA		13	45	1	59
21st GA		3	64	0	67
21st NC		2	16	1	19
Lawton Artillery (Courtney)	223	2	20	0	22
D'Aquin		1	8	0	9
J. R. Johnson		1	10	0	11
Garber		0	2	0	2
Latimer		0	0	0	0
Dement		0	0	0	0
J. R. Jones	2,435[12]	162	492	33	687 (28%)
Grigsby	400[13]	20	119	0	139
4th VA		3	21	0	24
5th VA	230[14]	11	77	0	88
27th VA		3	5	0	8
33rd VA		3	16	0	19
Penn	300[15]	18[16]	15	2	35
21st VA		9	8	2	19
42nd VA	120[17]	5	4	0	9
48th VA		3	1	0	4
1st VA Battalion		1	2	0	3

(continued)

Command/division/brigade	Strength[1]	Killed	Wounded	Missing & captured	Total
J. W. Jackson	500	41[18]	132	0	173
47th AL	115[19]	10	53	0	63
48th AL		10	32	0	42
23rd VA	120[20]	9	29	0	38
37th VA		12	36	0	48
10th VA[21]					
Starke	925[22]	81	189	30[23]	300
1st LA	250[24]	16	45	10	71
2nd LA	120[25]	21	41	3[26]	65
9th LA		25	57	7[27]	89
10th LA	218[28]	16	34	7	57
15th LA		3	12	3[29]	18
1st LA Battalion[30]	12				
Jones Artillery (Shumaker)	310	2	37	1	40[31]
Carpenter		1	5	0	6
J. B. Brockenbrough		0	8	0	8
Wooding		1	13	1	15
Raine		0	5	0	5
Poague		0	6	0	6
A. P. Hill	3,207[32]	69	354	7	430[33] (13%)
Pender	410	2	28	0	30
16th NC					
22nd NC					
34th NC					
38th NC					
Archer	350[34]	15	90	0	105[35]
19th GA					
1st TN	400[36]				
7th TN	150[37]				
14th TN	300[38]				
5th AL Battalion[39]					
J. M. Brockenbrough	410	0	0	0	0
40th VA					
47th VA					
55th VA					
22nd VA Battalion					
Gregg	800[40]	28[41]	135	2	165
1st SC Provisional Army	140[42]	4	30	0	34
1st SC Rifles	194[43]	3	9	0	12
12th SC	162[44]	20	82	2	104
13th SC		1	14	0	15
14th SC		0	0	0	0
Thomas					
14th GA					
35th GA					

(continued)

Command/division/brigade	Strength[1]	Killed	Wounded	Missing & captured	Total
35th GA					
49th GA					
L. O. Branch	900[45]	20	79	4	103[46]
7th NC					
18th NC	50[47]				
28th NC	300[48]				
33rd NC					
37th NC					
Artillery (R. L. Walker)	337	4	22	1	27[49]
Crenshaw		1	4	0	5
Braxton		1	2	1	4
McIntosh		1	2	0	3
Pegram		1	13	0	14
Longstreet	10,069	512	2,448	313	3,273 (33%)
D. R. Jones	3,457	103	656	48	807 (23%)
Kemper	434	11	88	10	109[50]
1st VA	45[51]	0	8	0	8
7th VA	117[52]	2	10	0	12
11th VA	111	3	38	0	41
17th VA	55[53]	8	23	10[54]	41
24th VA	106	0	2	0	2
Drayton	710[55]	32	106	4	142[56]
15th SC	270	13	43	0	56
3rd SC Battalion	37	0	1	1	2
50th GA	98	2	22	3	27[57]
51st GA	99				18
Phillips (GA) Legion	206				35
Garnett	242[58]	9	69	0	78[59]
8th VA	22[60]				11[61]
18th VA	75[62]	4	27	0	31
19th VA	50[63]				8
28th VA	55[64]	2	18	0	20[65]
56th VA	40[66]	0	8	0	8
Toombs	641	16	117	25	158
2nd GA	120[67]	6	28	8	42[68]
20th GA	250	4	47	17	68[69]
15th GA	115[70]	6	30	0	36
17th GA	156[71]	0	12	0	12
G. T. Anderson	597[72]	8	77	2	87
1st GA Regulars					
7th GA					
8th GA					
9th GA					
11th GA					

(continued)

Command/division/brigade	Strength[1]	Killed	Wounded	Missing & captured	Total
Jenkins (J. Walker)	755[73]	26	195	6	227[74]
Palmetto Sharpshooters	189	9	55	0	64
5th SC	108	5	28	0	33
6th SC	145	8	56	0	64
2nd SC Rifles	106	2	39	0	41
1st SC	106	2	16	0	18
Artillery					
Brown	81	1	4	1	6
Hood	2,304	174	747	87[75]	1,008 (44%)
Law	1,146	50	379	25	454[76] (40%)
4th AL	270[77]				
6th NC		8	105	0	113[78]
11th MS					
2nd MS					
Wofford	854[79]	118	357	32	562[80] (66%)
18th GA	176	27	64	3	94[81]
Hampton (SC) Legion	77				55[82]
1st TX	226	50	132	4	186[83]
4th TX	200	25	86	20	131[84]
5th TX	175	16	75	5	96[85]
Artillery (Frobel)	304	6	11	0	17
Garden		1	10	0	11[86]
Reilly		3	0	0	3[87]
Bachman	115	2	1	0	3
Evans	365[88]	13	60	11	84[89]
17th SC	59[90]	4	12	3	19[91]
18th SC	50[92]	1	13	5	19[93]
22nd SC	50	0	4	2	6[94]
23rd SC	50	6	6	1	13
Holcombe Legion	41[95]	0	6	0	6
Boyce	115	2	17	0	19[96]
R. H. Anderson	3,712	210	896	165	1,271 (34%)
Cumming	500–550 est.	34+	191+	29+	272[97]
8th AL					78[98]
9th AL	120[99]	8	42	9	59[100]
10th AL	130[101]				100[102]
11th AL	200[103]				35[104]
Wright	466	47	200	33	280[105]
3rd GA	138[106]	23	68	5	96[107]
22nd GA	72[108]	2	25	8	35[109]
48th GA	118[110]	9	43	14	66[111]
44th AL	138[112]	13	64	6	83[113]
Parham	82	3	18	3	24
6th VA					

(continued)

Command/division/brigade	Strength[1]	Killed	Wounded	Missing & captured	Total
12th VA					
16th VA					
41st VA					
Posey	700	45	224	28	297
12th MS	170[114]	6	39	6	51[115]
16th MS	228[116]	27	100	20	147[117]
19th MS		7	30	2	39[118]
2nd MS Battalion		5	55	0	60[119]
Pryor	855	71	223	70	365
2nd FL	240[120]	14	29	19	62[121]
5th FL	240	30	93	36	159[122]
8th FL	125	19	53	10	82[123]
3rd VA	50	4	9	0	13[124]
14th AL	200	8	41	0	49[125]
Armistead	735[126]	5	29	1	35
9th VA					
14th VA					
38th VA					
53rd VA					
57th VA					
Artillery (Saunders)	328	5	11	0	16[127]
Maurin		0	0	0	0
Huger		1	2	0	3
Moorman		1	7	0	8
Grimes		3	2	0	5
Reserve Artillery	596	12+	89+	2	103+
Washington (LA) Artillery	278	4	27	2	33
Squires		1	12	0	13
Richardson		1	5	0	6
Miller		2	10	2	14
Eshleman		0	0	0	0
S. D. Lee's Battalion	318	8+	62+	0	70 + [128]
Woolfolk					
Jordan		1	2	0	3
Elliot		0	18	0	18
Eubank					
Moody		4	24	0	28
Parker		3	18	0	21
Army Reserve					
McLaws	3,264	161	934	26	1,121 (34%)
Semmes	787	53	251	6	310[129]
10th GA	148[130]	16	67	0	83
32nd VA	158[131]	15	57	0	72
15th VA	128[132]	11	64	0	75
53rd GA	276[133]	11	63	6	80

(continued)

Command/division/brigade	Strength[1]	Killed	Wounded	Missing & captured	Total
Kershaw	936[134]	53	282	6	341
2nd SC	253	17	77	0	94[135]
3rd SC	266	11	71	2	84
7th SC	268	23	117	0	140
8th SC	71	2	17	4	23
Barksdale	891[136]	32	256	4	292
13th MS	202	6	54	2	62
17th MS	270	9	77	2	88
18th MS	186	11	69	0	80
21st MS	200	6	56	0	61
Cobb (Sanders)	400	16	121	10	147
16th GA		5	21	0	26
24th GA		4	39	2	45
Cobb's (GA) Legion		4	9	0	13
15th NC		3	52	8	63
Artillery (Cabell)	250[137]	7	24	0	31
Read	78	4	10	0	14
Manly		0	4	0	4
Macon		1	1	0	2
Carlton	27	1	8	0	9
McCarthy	33	1	1	0	2
J. G. Walker	3,946	184	839	97[138]	1,120 (28%)
Ransom	1,600	41	141	4	186[139]
24th NC		20	44	0	64
25th NC		2	13	0	15
35th NC		3	23	0	26
49th NC		16	61	0	77
Walker (Manning)	2,164	140	684	93	917[140]
27th NC	325[141]	31	168	3	202[142]
46th NC	320	5	60	0	65[143]
48th NC	907	31	186	0	217[144]
30th VA	262	39	121	0	160
3rd AR	350[145]	27	155	33	215[146]
Artillery	230	3	14	0	17[147]
T. B. French		1	1	0	2
J. Branch		2	13	0	15
D. H. Hill	5,845	368+	1,439[148]	519[149]	2,326 (40%)
Garland (McRae)	756	9	42	32	84[150]
5th NC					
12th NC					
13th NC					
20th NC					
23rd NC					
G. B. Anderson	1,174	102	218	205	525
2nd NC	255[151]	29	32	53	114[152]
4th NC	194	5	23	29	57[153]

(continued)

Strength and Casualties—Army of Northern Virginia (*continued*)

Command/division/brigade	Strength[1]	Killed	Wounded	Missing & captured	Total
14th NC	475	52	123	103	278[154]
30th NC	250	16	40	20	76[155]
Ripley	1,349[156]	114+	277+	22	743
1st NC	315	50	75	21	146[157]
3rd NC	547				330[158]
4th GA	325[159]	38	134	0	172[160]
44th GA	162	26	68	1	95[161]
Rodes	850	45	150	24	219[162]
field and staff		0	3	0	3
3rd AL	100[163]	2	16	2	20
5th AL		4	13	2	19
6th AL	265[164]	25	60	13	98
12th AL		12	48	6	66
26th AL		2	10	1	13
Colquitt	1,370	95+	179+	30+	718
6th GA	300	81	115	30	226[165]
23rd GA	150[166]	14	64	0	78[167]
27th GA	400[168]				154[169]
28th GA	220[170]				110[171]
13th AL	300[172]				150[173]
Artillery (Pierson)	346	3	45	1	49[174]
Bondurant		1	8	0	9
W. B. Jones	52	1	25	0	26
Carter		1	3	1	5
Hardaway		0	9	0	9
Stuart	4,500	10	28	11	49
Hampton					
F. Lee					
Munford					
Artillery					
Reserve Artillery (Pendleton)	621	4	47	0	51
Cutts	319	2	32	0	34[175]
Blackshear		1	7	0	8
Lane		0	2	0	2
Lloyd					
Patterson		1	5	0	6
Ross		0	18	0	18
H. P. Jones	302	2	15	0	17[176]
Page		2	7	0	9
Peyton		0	8	0	8
Turner					
Wimbish					
Army Total	37,610	1,666	7,677	1,075	10,418 (28%)

(continued)

Note: Where cells are blank, no data could be found.

1. Unless otherwise noted, all strength and loss figures are from Carman, 585–611.

2. *OR* 19, 1:968.

3. *Columbus (GA) Enquirer*, Oct. 8, 1862. A writer from the regiment, in a Sept. 22 letter in the *Daily Morning News* (Savannah), Oct. 4, 1862, gave the regiment's strength as 230. He added that just 15 men came out of the battle, and that the brigade numbered only 95 men after the action that morning. He also mentioned that the regiment lost their flag, because "no one was left to bear it away."

4. F. N. Graves to Carman, Feb. 26, 1895, map, AS.

5. Carman gave the number of wounded as 440, which probably included Douglass and a staff officer.

6. *OR* 19, 1:968.

7. *Memphis (TN) Daily Appeal*, Oct. 11, 1862, 2.

8. "15th Louisiana Infantry," Antietam on the Web, https://antietam.aotw.org/officers.php?unit_id=567&from=results/ [accessed Feb. 2021], lists 5 unwounded POWs. The official return gave 0 missing.

9. "6th Louisiana Infantry," Antietam on the Web, https://antietam.aotw.org/officers.php?unit_id=710/ [accessed Feb. 2021], lists 6 unwounded plus 7 wounded POWs. The official return gave 0 missing.

10. "7th Louisiana Infantry," Antietam on the Web, https://antietam.aotw.org/officers.php?unit_id=716/ [accessed Feb. 2021], lists 9 unwounded POWs. The official return gave 2 missing.

11. "8th Louisiana Infantry," Antietam on the Web, https://antietam.aotw.org/officers.php?unit_id=725/ [accessed Feb. 2021]. The official return listed 0 missing.

12. Jones gave his strength as 1,600. See *OR* 19, 1:1008. Carman estimated the division's strength, including the artillery, at 2,094. See Carman, 595.

13. This is an estimate. Carman gave Grigsby's and Penn's brigades a combined strength of 450, but based on the two regimental strengths we have data on, this seems low. In the case of Grigsby, if each of the regiments other than the 5th VA averaged only 50 men—a reasonable number, given how small many of these units were—we would arrive at a strength of approximately 400.

14. H. Williams to Carman, Mar. 2, 1895, AS.

15. The same formula used for Grigsby (see note 13) has been applied to Penn. This would give a strength of 270, and I have rounded this number up to 300. For Carman's estimate of a combined strength of 450 to work, it would mean that the six regiments/battalion in Grigsby's and Penn's brigades that we do not have strength figures for averaged only 16 men each.

16. Fleming Saunders to Mother, Sept. 20, 1862, 42nd VA file, ANBL.

17. Penn's brigade made no casualty report. All known losses are from "Jones' Brigade," Antietam on the Web, https://antietam.aotw.org/officers.php?unit_id=65&from=results/ [accessed Feb. 2021], which maintains a database of known participants in the battle. The only wounded listed for the 42nd and 48th VA and the 1st VA Battalion were those who died of their injuries. The actual losses for the brigade in wounded men and POWs is definitely higher than these numbers.

18. Detached with the 2nd VA at Martinsburg and not present at Sharpsburg. Col. Edward T. H. Warren was detached with his regiment, so Col. Jackson commanded the brigade at Antietam.

19. See 47th AL file, ANBL. The regiment mustered 17 men, commanded by a sergeant, on the morning of Sept. 18.

20. "23rd Virginia Infantry," Antietam on the Web, https://antietam.aotw.org/officers.php?unit_id=617/ [accessed Feb. 2021].

21. *OR* 19, 1:1009. The brigade probably had some missing or captured men who were not included on the casualty returns.

22. The battalion did not report its losses independently. Because of its size, it was probably attached to one of the other regiments.

23. Carman gave Starke's strength as 650, but based on the strengths we know for three of the regiments and the one battalion, this would have meant that the two remaining regiments, combined, only had about 50 men. Given that the 9th LA incurred 89 casualties, the figure of 650 cannot be correct. Based on the percentage of casualties versus engaged strength, the 9th LA probably had 250 to 300 men, and the 15th LA, around 75. W. E. Moore in the 1st LA wrote to Carman that the brigade had 1,400 to 1,500 men, which is too high. If the 9th LA had 300 men, the brigade's strength would be about 975.

24. Starke's brigade folder, AS. The strength comes from a letter to Carman from W. E. Moore in the 1st LA, in "Starke's Brigade," Starke's brigade folder, AS. Moore said that the 2nd, 10th, and 15th LA were all larger than the 1st LA. W. C. Harris to Carman, in "Starke's Brigade," Starke's brigade folder, AS, said the 2nd LA did not muster over 120 men.

25. Starke's brigade folder, AS.

26. N. Bartlett, *Military Record*, 43.

27. *OR* 19, 1:1015, noted that only 17 men were missing or captured, but personnel database records in "Starke's Brigade," Antietam on the Web, https://antietam.aotw.org/officers.php?unit_id=111&from=results/ [accessed Feb. 2021], fill in some of the POWs for the regiments who reported none. The number of missing or captured men is probably higher than 30.

28. "2nd Louisiana Infantry," Antietam on the Web, https://antietam.aotw.org/officers.php?unit_id=634/ [accessed Feb. 2021].

29. "2nd Louisiana Infantry," Antietam on the Web, https://antietam.aotw.org/officers.php?unit_id=634/ [accessed Feb. 2021].

30. "2nd Louisiana Infantry," Antietam on the Web, https://antietam.aotw.org/officers.php?unit_id=634/ [accessed Feb. 2021].

31. All of Jones's divisional artillery losses are from C. Johnson and Anderson, *Artillery Hell*, 95–96.

32. Carman gave A. P. Hill's engaged strength at Antietam as 2,000 enlisted men, 231 officers, and 337 artillery, but there is no evidence in Hill's report that he deducted officers from his estimate of his infantry strength in the three brigades he engaged. He left Thomas's brigade at Harpers Ferry. The five other brigades, with a total strength of 2,050, thus have an average strength of approximately 410 per brigade. Applying this questionable estimate to Pender's and Brockenbrough's brigades, plus the artillerymen, has produced the number for Hill's approximate total strength.

33. *OR* 19, 1:983. Hill's casualty report tallied 389 men who were either killed or wounded, which does not agree with the statistics his brigades reported and omits his artillery losses. No missing are reported, although there undoubtedly had been a small number.

34. Not present at Sharpsburg. Left at Harpers Ferry.

35. *OR* 19, 1:1000. This was Archer's estimate for his engaged strength. The strength numbers that Turney, Howard, and McComb gave Carman are probably regimental strengths, after stragglers from the march rejoined the brigade. Thus, while Archer was engaged with only 350 men, he may have had nearly 1,000 by nightfall.

36. [Col.] Peter Turney to Carman, Aug. 4, 1898, AS.

37. [Lieut.] George A. Howard, adjut. to Carman, Aug. 12, 1898, AS.

38. William McComb to Carman, Aug. 5, 1898, AS.

39. *OR* 19, 1:1001.

40. Alexander C. Haskell to Carman, June 16, 1896, AS. Haskell was the chief of staff for Gen. Gregg.

41. Sgt. Maj. W. L. Delph to Carman, July 26, 1898, AS. Delph also gave the regiment's casualties as 34 killed or wounded.

42. *OR* 19, 1:995.

43. Maj. W. H. McCorkle to Carman, Mar. 2, 1895, AS.

44. All losses for Gregg are from *OR* 19, 1:989.

(continued)

45. This is an estimate, based on A. P. Hill's statement that his three engaged brigades numbered 2,000 effectives. Gregg had 800, and Archer 350, which gives Branch approximately 900.

46. The strength is from Lt. Iowa M. Royster, quoted in Hardy, *General Lee's Immortals*, 89.

47. Maj. William J. Montgomery to Carman, Oct. 8, 1897, AS.

48. *OR* 19, 1:986.

49. All artillery losses are from C. Johnson and Anderson, *Artillery Hell*, 93–94.

50. Carman, 589. Carman added a ratio of 1 officer to 8⅔ enlisted men to the "musket" strength of each regiment in the brigade, in order to arrive at a total strength.

51. David E. Johnston, *The Story of a Confederate Boy in the Civil War* (1914; repr., Ann Arbor: Univ. Microfilms, 1972), 149, a reprinting of D. Johnston, *Four Years*, copy in AS. In David Johnston to Henry Heth, Sept. 18, 1897, AS, Johnston gave the regiment's strength as 113 muskets. The number of officers is unknown. Carman listed the regiment's strength as only 43. See Carman, 589.

52. *OR* 19, 1:905.

53. *Richmond (VA) Enquirer*, Sept. 30, 1862.

54. These figures are probably low. A number of prisoners were known to have been taken by Fairchild's brigade.

55. J. Evans Edings diary, Edward Willis Papers, LC. Edings was the AAG for Drayton. All of his strengths figures are considerably higher than Carman's.

56. Kurt Graham shared the figures for losses in all of Drayton's regiments, except the 50th GA, with the author. Carman gave Drayton's losses as 32 killed, 106 wounded, and 3 missing or captured. See Carman, 603. The single difference is the number of missing or captured from the 3rd SC Battalion, which comes from Graham's research.

57. *Savannah Republican*, Oct, 1, 1862, 2. The article listed the regiment's strength as 200, but this probably was their South Mountain strength.

58. Carman estimated the brigade's strength as 261, because he believed the strength figures given by Garnett's regimental officers were for muskets, not officers and men. Carman may have been correct, but there is no evidence that the figures in the various reports and letters he received giving regimental strengths were for enlisted men only. Carman also estimated the 28th VA's strength at 47.

59. Capt. William N. Berkeley to wife, Sept. 25, 1862, 8th VA file, ANBL.

60. *OR* 19, 1:900.

61. *OR* 19, 1:901.

62. Frank E. Fields Jr., "The 28th Virginia Infantry Regiment, C.S.A.," master's thesis, Virginia Polytechnic Institute and State Univ., 1984, 37. Fields estimates the regiment's strength at the Battle of South Mountain, where it had 41 casualties, as 96, giving it an estimated 55 men present at Sharpsburg.

63. *OR* 19, 1:904.

64. Carman gave Garnett's loss as 75. See Carman, 601.

65. All losses for Garnett are from *OR* 19, 1:898, 901, 902, 904.

66. *Lynchburg Virginian*, Oct. 2, 1862, ANBL, gave the losses for the Battles of South Mountain and Sharpsburg as 7 killed, 52 wounded, and 16 missing or captured.

67. Carman's notes on Toombs's brigade, AS. Capt. Abner M. Lewis, in his report, gave the engaged strength of the 2nd GA as 18 officers and 89 enlisted men, for a total of 107. Benning estimated the strength of the 20th GA as "no more than 250" in his official report (*OR* 51, 1:161) and as "about 220 or 230" in "Notes by General H. L. Benning," 393. He also gave varying strengths for the 2nd GA in his two documents, first as "only 97," and then as "120 or 130."

68. *OR* 51, 1:166.

69. Carman, 590.

70. *OR* 51, 1:165.

71. *OR* 51, 1:168.

72. The 11th GA was detached, and their strength was not included in Carman's estimate.

73. *Charleston (SC) Mercury*, Oct. 3, 1862. All strength and casualty figures for the brigade are from this article.

74. The losses are from the *Charleston (SC) Mercury*, Oct. 3, 1862, although it did not report the number of missing. Col. Walker gave his brigade's losses as 26 killed, 184 wounded, and 6 missing. His casualty figures for all regiments were different from those reported in the *Mercury*. He gave the losses for the 1st SC as 4 killed and 36 wounded. Since the report in the *Mercury* almost certainly came from the brigade, it is difficult to discern which casualty report is more accurate. The figures of 0 missing from the *Mercury*'s report, and 6 missing from Walker's, are both suspiciously low, in light of the nature of the brigade's engagement. Walker reported that the 1st SC entered the battle with 106 officers and enlisted men and had 40 of them killed or wounded, yet it only mustered 1 officer and 15 men at the end of the engagement, which means that 50 were missing. These individuals may have rejoined the brigade before it recrossed the Potomac River, but Walker did not indicate that they did so.

75. Carman gave the numbers of missing or captured as 62 for Wofford and 25 for Law. See Carman, 605.

76. William Robbins to John Gould, Mar. 25, 1891, Law's brigade folder, AS.

77. *OR* 19, 1:925.

78. *Hillsborough (NC) Recorder*, Oct. 8, 1862.

79. Wofford's brigade strength, and the strengths for all regiments except the 5th TX, are from *OR* 19, 1:929–935.

80. Hood gave the total loss for Wofford as 548, which would have included artillery. This broke down into 69 dead, 417 wounded, and 62 missing or captured. See *OR* 19, 1:925. Carman also gave the same figures for these losses. See Carman, 605.

81. "18th Georgia Infantry," Antietam on the Web, https://antietam.aotw.org/officers.php?unit_id=580/ [accessed Feb. 2021]. The website's personnel database for the 18th GA shows 3 captured on Sept. 17.

82. Carman, 109.

83. Work, "1st Texas Regiment," ANBL.

84. "4th Texas Infantry," Antietam on the Web, https://antietam.aotw.org/officers.php?unit_id=685/ [accessed Feb. 2021]. I have counted "missing or wounded in action" as "wounded" for this calculation, in order to be consistent with how other units initially reported their casualties. Carman gave the 4th TX losses as 107. See Carman, 109.

85. "5th Texas Infantry," Antietam on the Web, https://antietam.aotw.org/officers.php?unit_id=703/ [accessed Feb. 2021]. J. M. Smither to Gould, Feb. 26 and Mar. 24, 1891, GP, gave the losses as 86.

86. C. Johnson and Anderson, *Artillery Hell*, 89.

87. The figures for Reilly's and Bachman's casualties are those verified in "Hood's Division Artillery," Antietam on the Web, https://antietam.aotw.org/officers.php?unit_id=187/ [accessed Feb. 2021]. They were probably higher than these numbers, however.

88. Carman gave the brigade's infantry strength as 284, but Col. McMaster in the 17th SC wrote that his regiment was the largest in the brigade, which would mean that, at best, the other regiments each had no more than 50 officers and men. See McMaster to D. H. Hill, July 11, 1888, D. H. Hill Papers, LV.

89. *OR* 19, 1:946.

90. The strengths for the 18th, 22nd, and 23rd SC are all estimates. See note 88.

(continued)

91. Col. F. W. McMaster gave the strength of his regiment as 59 and reported that his regiment and the Holcombe Legion numbered "about 100 men." See *OR* 19, 1:945.

92. Carman, 605. Carman's figures for the wounded, by regiment, were 2 less than what he recorded for the brigade.

93. *OR* 19, 1:946, 950. "17th South Carolina Infantry," Antietam on the Web, https://antietam.aotw.org/officers.php?unit_id=577/ [accessed Feb. 2021], lists 8 killed for Sept. 16 and 17.

94. Carman, 605n19. This is an estimate that Carman arrived at by taking one-third of the losses reported for the regiment in the Maryland Campaign. His calculation seems logical, since Evans's regiments suffered most of their losses at the Battle of South Mountain. "18th South Carolina Infantry," Antietam on the Web, https://antietam.aotw.org/officers.php?unit_id=583/ [accessed Feb. 2021], lists 4 killed on Sept. 17.

95. Carman, 605n19. Maj. Miel Hilton's after-action report, Oct. 15, 1862, ANBL, gave the total losses for three companies—A, B, and C—as 1 wounded. The final page of the report is missing. Based on the losses in these three companies, Carman's estimate appears to be correct. The roster for the "22nd South Carolina Infantry," Antietam on the Web, https://antietam.aotw.org/officers.php?unit_id=612/ [accessed Feb. 2021], lists 4 killed for Sept. 17.

96. Carman, 605n19. This number may be low, particularly in the category for missing men.

97. H. Herbert, "History," 84.

98. *Richmond (VA) Whig*, Sept. 24, 1862.

99. H. L. Stevenson to R. D. Parker, Dec. 9, 1899, R. Parker Papers, CPL.

100. H. Herbert, "History," 84. Herbert gave the losses for the brigade as 215, but this figure is low, based on sources for each regiment. The minimum loss for the brigade should be 272. The figures shown in the table for those who were killed, wounded, and missing are from Carman, 602. They actually total 254.

101. H. Herbert, "History," 84.

102. *Richmond (VA) Whig*, Sept. 24, 1862.

103. "Tenth Alabama Infantry Regiment," ADAH, http://www.archives.alabama.gov/referenc/alamilor/10thinf.html [accessed Dec. 2017; internal web page link discontinued]. The losses were over 50%, but no specific percentage is given. "10th Alabama Infantry," Antietam on the Web, https://antietam.aotw.org/officers.php?unit_id=537/ [accessed Feb. 2021], has an incomplete personnel database for the 10th AL, with 15 killed.

104. "Eleventh Alabama Infantry Regiment," ADAH, http://www.archives.alabama.gov/referenc/alamilor/11thinf.html [accessed Dec. 2017; internal web page link discontinued].

105. *Daily Constitutionalist* (Augusta, GA), Friday morning, [date missing but probably Oct. 17 or 24, 1862], ANBL; C to *Daily Constitutionalist* (Augusta, GA), Oct. 18, 1862, ANBL, listed the strength as 108.

106. *Daily Constitutionalist* (Augusta, GA), Friday morning, [date missing but probably Oct. 17 or 24, 1862], ANBL. *Rome (GA) Tri-Weekly Courier*, Oct. 14, 1862, listed the strength as 60.

107. *Daily Constitutionalist* (Augusta, GA), Friday morning, [date missing but probably Oct. 17 or 24, 1862], ANBL.

108. *Daily Constitutionalist* (Augusta, GA), Friday morning, [date missing but probably Oct. 17 or 24, 1862], ANBL.

109. Carman gave the brigade losses as 32 killed, 192 wounded, and 34 missing, for a total of 258. See Carman, 603. The Confederate official returns recorded these losses as 16 killed, 187 wounded, and 0 missing, for a total of 203 casualties.

110. American Civil War Research Database, http://civilwardata.com [requires a subscription; accessed Sept. 2020]. The *Daily Constitutionalist* (Augusta, GA), Friday morning, [date missing but probably Oct. 17 or 24, 1862], ANBL, gave the losses as 9 killed, 58 wounded, and 5 missing. With Confederate casualty figures, typically the highest reported loss is the most accurate.

111. *Daily Constitutionalist* (Augusta, GA), Friday morning, [date missing but probably Oct. 17 or 24, 1862], ANBL.

112. *Daily Constitutionalist* (Augusta, GA) Friday morning, [date missing but probably Oct. 17 or 24, 1862], ANBL. The American Civil War Research Database, http://civilwardata.com [requires a subscription; accessed Feb. 2021], gives the losses as 18 killed, 34 wounded, and 4 missing.

113. *Daily Constitutionalist* (Augusta, GA), Friday morning, [date missing but probably Oct. 17 or 24, 1862], ANBL. "44th Alabama Infantry Regiment," Civil War in the East, http://civilwarintheeast.com/confederate-regiments/alabama/44th-alabama-infantry/ [accessed Dec. 2017], gives the losses as 11 killed and 65 wounded, but it does not include the number of missing. The colors were captured by the 61st NY.

114. This is an estimate. The strength of the regiment on Sept. 18 was 100 effectives. Calculating the loss of roughly 65 men on Sept. 17 results in an approximate strength of 170. See "So Reduced: The 12th Mississippi Infantry after the Battle of Sharpsburg," Mississippians in the Confederate Army, June 7, 2013, https://mississippiconfederates.wordpress.com/2013/06/07/so-reduced-the-12th-mississippi-infantry-after-the-battle-of-sharpsburg/ [accessed Feb. 2018].

115. *OR* 19, 1:885.

116. The losses for this regiment are also given as 6 killed and 53 wounded. The colonel of the regiment reported 12 killed on Sept. 17, so it is possible that the losses were 12 killed, 53 wounded, and an unknown number missing. See "So Reduced."

117. *Richmond (VA) Enquirer*, Oct. 7, 1862. Carman gave the number of wounded as 117.

118. *Richmond (VA) Enquirer*, Oct. 7, 1862.

119. "Mississippi in the Civil War," Research OnLine, http://www.researchonline.net/mscw/unit38.htm [accessed Dec. 2017; internal web page link discontinued].

120. All strengths for Pryor are from Carman's notes on Pryor's brigade, Wright's brigade folder, ANBL. The estimate for the 5th FL is an average of the strengths for the 2nd and 8th FL.

121. The American Civil War Database, http://civilwardata.com [requires a subscription; accessed Dec. 2017], gives the losses as 15 killed, 44 wounded, and 11 missing. A list of casualties from the Consolidated Service Records, ANBL, however, recorded the losses as 19 killed and 53 wounded, noting that 10 of the wounded died of their injuries.

122. Lt. Col. C. A. Bryan wrote that the regiment lost two-thirds of their men at Sharpsburg, which means that the regiment was approximately 240 strong. See *Florida Sentinel* (Tallahassee), Oct. 7, 1862.

123. "Men in the 8th Florida Regiment killed, wounded, or captured at the Battle of Sharpsburg, Sept. 17, 1862, from Compiled Service Records and Other Sources," 8th FL file, ANBL.

124. American Civil War Research Database, http://civilwardata.com [requires a subscription; accessed Dec. 2017].

125. "14th Alabama Infantry," Antietam on the Web, https://antietam.aotw.org/officers.php?unit_id=559/ [accessed Aug. 2022].

126. See Carman, 588. The average strength, which has been derived from known regimental strengths, is 147. This formula was also used to estimate Armistead's strength.

127. C. Johnson and Anderson, *Artillery Hell*, 87.

128. C. Johnson and Anderson, *Artillery Hell*, 91–92. It is known that Woolfolk had substantial losses, but there is no record of them. There is no record for Eubank, either. The losses for Elliot have been derived from the database for the battery, in "2nd Battalion, Longstreet's Corps Artillery," Antietam on the Web, https://antietam.aotw.org/officers.php?unit_id=75&from=results/ [accessed Feb. 2021].

(continued)

129. *OR* 19, 1:862. Capt. Charles Kibbee wrote that they carried only 120 into action and had 86 killed or wounded. See Charles C. Kibbee letter, Sept. 21, 1862, in *Macon (GA) Weekly*, Oct. 1862, 10th GA file, ANBL.

130. *OR* 19, 1:862.

131. *OR* 19, 1:862.

132. *OR* 19, 1:862.

133. All losses for McLaws's division are from *OR* 19, 1:861–862.

134. *OR* 19, 1:861–862.

135. Wyckoff, *History*, 49. Wyckoff gives the losses for the 2nd SC as 20 killed and 60 wounded. The discrepancy between his figures, which are from the muster rolls, and the official tabulation is probably due to 3 of the injured who died of their wounds and some of the lightly wounded who were counted on the casualty return but whose injuries did not appear in their service records.

136. *OR* 19, 1:861.

137. Part of Carlton's and McCarthy's batteries were left behind at Leesburg, accounting for their small manpower numbers. Two of Macon's guns were on detached duty at Bolivar Heights.

138. Carman, 611.

139. *OR* 19, 1:811. Carman listed 4 as missing. See Carman, 604.

140. *Hillsborough (NC) Recorder*, Oct. 8, 1862.

141. *Richmond (VA) Enquirer*, Oct. 14, 1862.

142. The official returns listed 134 killed, 700 wounded, and 0 missing or captured. See *OR* 19, 1:811.

143. "27th North Carolina Infantry," Antietam on the Web, https://antietam.aotw.org/officers.php?unit_id=626/ [accessed Feb. 2021], shows that 3 of the captured men were unwounded.

144. According to the *Greensboro (NC) Patriot*, Oct. 23, 1862, the regiment had 72 casualties.

145. Capt. W. H. H. Lawton, in "48th North Carolina," 48th NC file, ANBL, stated that the regiment lost "about one-half of our men," which would mean close to 400 casualties. This is probably an exaggeration, but the losses in the regiment most likely are still higher than those officially reported.

146. *Richmond (VA) Enquirer*, Oct. 14, 1862. The official returns listed 0 missing or captured, but the *Enquirer*'s total was 33.

147. Carman, 604nn15–16.

148. Carman, 611.

149. Carman, 611.

150. Carman, 607. Carman's numbers add up to 83, but he gave 84 as the total.

151. Carman, 597–598.

152. Mast, *State Troops and Volunteers*, vol. 1, 330, 359–360. Mast is the source for the 30th NC casualties, as well.

153. American Civil War Research Database, http://civilwardata.com [requires a subscription; accessed Apr. 2018].

154. Mast, *State Troops and Volunteers*, 360n5.4.30.

155. R. K. Krick, "It Appeared," 257n57.

156. Ripley's regimental strengths are all from Carman, 595.

157. The *Savannah Republican*, Oct. 8, 1862, 1, gave the engaged strength as 278.

158. R. Williams, "'I Longed for Night,'" 26.

159. DeRosset, "Third North Carolina," AS. DeRosset did not break down the losses by the numbers of men killed, wounded, and missing.

160. *Savannah Republican*, Oct. 8, 1862, 1.

161. "44th Georgia Infantry," Antietam on the Web, https://antietam.aotw.org/officers.php?unit_id=669/ [accessed May 2019]. The mortally wounded are included in the wounded count.

162. Sgt. Gordon Sharpe, "Letter from the Potomac," in *Mobile Advertiser and Register*, Oct. 4, 1862. Sharpe wrote that they had "less than 100" in the fight. Carman gave the strength of this regiment as around 300. See Carman's notes on Rodes's brigade, Wright's brigade folder, ANBL.

163. R. K. Krick, "It Appeared," 228.

164. All of the losses for Rodes's regiments are from the *Selma (AL) Daily Reporter*, Oct. 8, 1862.

165. Carman stated that their loss was 50%, which would give the regiment about 150 effectives. See Carman, 145.

166. C. T. Zachry to Gould, Dec. 14, 1897, GP.

167. Carman, 145.

168. Carman, 145.

169. Ben Witcher to Gould, May 25 and June 22, 1891, and Thomas Marshall to Gould, Feb. 23, 1892, GP. The number killed might have been as high as 84.

170. "23rd Georgia Infantry," Antietam on the Web, https://antietam.aotw.orr/officers.php?unit_id=614/ [accessed May 2019]. Carman gave the total loss as 75 killed, wounded, and missing. See Carman, 145.

171. Folsom, *Heroes and Martyrs*, 66. "27th Georgia Infantry," Antietam on the Web, https://antietam.aotw.org/officers.php?unit_id=625/ [accessed May 2019], gives the losses as 15 killed and 89 wounded. If this is true, then the regiment had 50 men who were captured.

172. Carman, 145.

173. This is an estimate, based on the losses in the 28th GA, which was adjacent to the 13th AL. Carman merely stated that the regiment lost a large percentage of its 300 men. See Carman, 145.

174. All artillery losses for Hill's batteries are from C. Johnson and Anderson, *Artillery Hell*, 96–97.

175. C. Johnson and Anderson, *Artillery Hell*, 98–99.

176. C. Johnson and Anderson, *Artillery Hell*, 99–100.

Casualties at the Battle of Shepherdstown, September 19–20, 1862

	Killed	Wounded	Missing & captured	Total
Army of the Potomac	71	161	131	363
5th Corps	70	156	130	356
1st Division—Morell	69	147	130	346
1st U.S. Sharpshooters	2	5	0	7
1st Brigade—J. Barnes	66	125	130	321
118th PA	63	101	105	269
1st MI	1	1	2	4
22nd MA	0	2	0	2
2nd ME	0	2	0	2
18th MA	2	10	2	14
13th NY	0	6	12	18
25th NY	0	3	9	12
2nd Company, MA Sharpshooters				
2nd Brigade—Griffin	1	10	0	11
4th MI	1	6	0	7
32nd MA	0	2	0	2
2nd DC	0	2	0	2
3rd Brigade—Stockton	0	7	0	7
12th NY	0	1	0	1
83rd PA	0	1	0	1
44th NY	0	2	0	2
20th ME	0	3	0	3
2nd Division—Sykes	1	9	0	10
2nd Brigade—Lovell	1	8	0	9
1st & 6th U.S.	0	2	0	2
2nd & 10th U.S.	1	2	0	3
11th U.S.	0	3	0	3
17th U.S.	0	1	0	1
3rd Brigade—Warren	0	1	0	1
5th NY	0	1	0	1
Artillery	1	4	1	6
5th U.S.	0	1	0	1
Army of Northern Virginia	36	256	2	306[1]
Lawton	0	7	0	7
13th GA	0	2	0	2
26th GA	0	0	0	0
31st GA	0	1	0	1
38th GA	0	1	0	1
60th GA	0	0	0	0
61st GA	0	3	0	3
LA Guard Battery	2	0	0	2
A. P. Hill	32	245	1	292
Pender	8	55	0	63
Archer	6	49	0	55

(continued)

Casualties at the Battle of Shepherdstown, September 19–20, 1862 (*continued*)

	Killed	Wounded	Missing & captured	Total
Brockenbrough	2	5	0	7
Gregg	10	54	0	64
Thomas	2	9	0	25[2]
L. O. Branch	3	71	0	74
Artillery (Walker)	1	2	1	4
Longstreet				
Artillery	1	3	1	5
Reserve Artillery (Pendleton)				
Nelson	1	1	0	2

Note: Where cells are blank, no data could be found.

1. The total Confederate losses include the uncategorized 14 casualties in Thomas's brigade.

2. The categories for the other 14 casualties in Thomas's brigade are unknown.

ABBREVIATIONS

AAG	assistant adjutant general
ABB	Antietam Battlefield Board
ADAH	Alabama Department of Archives and History, Montgomery, Alabama
ADC	aide-de-camp
AIG	assistant inspector general
ANBL	Antietam National Battlefield Library, Sharpsburg, Maryland
Antietam NB	Antietam National Battlefield, Sharpsburg, Maryland
AS	Antietam Studies Collection, Record Group 94, National Archives, Washington, DC
B&L	Robert U. Johnson and Clarence C. Buel, *Battles and Leaders of the Civil War*, 4 vols.
Bn	Battalion
BPL	Boston Public Library, Boston, Massachusetts
BU	Boston University, Boston, Massachusetts
c	captured
C&O	Chesapeake and Ohio Canal
Carman	Ezra A. Carman, *The Maryland Campaign of 1862*, ed. Thomas Clemens, vols. 2–3
CCW	U.S. Congress, *Report of the Joint Committee on the Conduct of the War*
CHS	Connecticut Historical Society, Hartford, Connecticut
Cos	Companies
CPL	Chicago Public Library, Chicago, Illinois
CSR	consolidated service record
CV	*Confederate Veteran*
CWLM	Civil War Library and Museum, Philadelphia, Pennsylvania
CWTI	*Civil War Times Illustrated*
DHS	Delaware Historical Society, Wilmington, Delaware
DPA	Delaware Public Archives, North Dover, Delaware
DU	Duke University, Durham, North Carolina
EU	Emory University, Atlanta, Georgia
GBM	George B. McClellan
GDAH	Georgia Department of Archives and History, Morrow, Georgia
GNMP	Gettysburg National Military Park Library, Gettysburg, Pennsylvania

GP	John M. Gould Papers, Dartmouth College, Hanover, New Hampshire
HEPL	Harris-Elmore Public Library, Elmore, Ohio
HL	Henry P. Huntington Library, San Marino, California
HSP	Historical Society of Pennsylvania, Philadelphia, Pennsylvania
HU	Harvard University, Cambridge, Massachusetts
IG	inspector general
IHS	Indiana Historical Society, Indianapolis, Indiana
ISL	Indiana State Library, Indianapolis, Indiana
k	killed
LC	Library of Congress, Washington, DC
Leg	Legion
LHS	Litchfield Historical Society, Litchfield, Connecticut
LV	Library of Virginia, Richmond, Virginia
m	missing
MCHM	Monroe County Historical Museum, Monroe, Michigan
MDAH	Mississippi Department of Archives and History, Jackson, Mississippi
MHS	Massachusetts Historical Society, Boston, Massachusetts
ML	Morgan Library, New York, New York
MNHS	Minnesota Historical Society, St. Paul, Minnesota
MNSA	Maine State Archives, Augusta, Maine
MOLLUS	Military Order of the Loyal Legion of the United States
MP	George B. McClellan Papers, Library of Congress
MSA	Maryland State Archives, Annapolis, Maryland
MSR	military service record
mw	mortally wounded
NA	National Archives, College Park, Maryland
NC Regts	Walter Clark, ed., *Histories of Several Regiments and Battalions from North Carolina in the Great War*, 5 vols.
NHHS	New Hampshire Historical Society, Concord, New Hampshire
NJHS	New Jersey Historical Society, Newark, New Jersey
NLCHS	New London County Historical Society, New London, Connecticut
NT	*National Tribune*
NYHS	New-York Historical Society, New York, New York
NYPL	New York Public Library, New York, New York
OR	U.S. War Department, *The War of the Rebellion: A Compilation of the Official Records of the Union and Confederate Armies*, 70 vols.
OR Suppl.	Janet B. Hewett, Noah A. Trudeau, and Bruce A. Suderow, eds., *Supplement to the Official Records of the Union and Confederate Armies*, 100 vols.
OSU	Oregon State University, Corvallis, Oregon
PCHS	Potter County Historical Society, Coudersport, Pennsylvania
PHS	Providence Historical Society, Providence, Rhode Island
PMNC	Pearce Civil War Collection, Pearce Museum, Navarro College, Corsicana, Texas
POHS	Portsmouth Historical Society, Portsmouth, New Hampshire

POW	prisoner of war
PR	Pennsylvania Reserves
PSA	Pennsylvania State Archives, Harrisburg, Pennsylvania
PWP	*Philadelphia Weekly Press*
RG	Record Group
SANC	State Archives of North Carolina (formerly the North Carolina State Archives), Raleigh, North Carolina
SCHS	South Carolina Historical Society, Charleston, South Carolina
SCL	South Carolina Library, University of South Carolina, Columbia, South Carolina
SHC	Southern Historical Collection, University of North Carolina, Chapel Hill, North Carolina
SHSP	*Southern Historical Society Papers*
SHSW	State Historical Society of Wisconsin, Madison, Wisconsin
SUL	Shorter University Library, Rome, Georgia
THC	Eugene C. Barker Texas History Center, University of Texas, Austin, Texas
THM	Texas Heritage Museum (formerly the Confederate Research Center), Hill College, Hillsboro, Texas
UM	University of Michigan, Ann Arbor, Michigan
USAHEC	U.S. Army Heritage and Education Center (formerly the United States Army Military History Institute), Carlisle, Pennsylvania
USS	U.S. Sharpshooters
UVA	University of Virginia, Charlottesville, Virginia
UW	University of Wyoming, Laramie, Wyoming
VHS	Virginia Historical Society, Richmond, Virginia
w	wounded
WCPL	Wilson County Public Library, Wilson, North Carolina
WMR	Western Maryland Room, Washington County Library, Hagerstown, Pennsylvania
WMU	Western Michigan University, Kalamazoo, Michigan
WRHS	Western Reserve Historical Society, Cleveland, Ohio

Prologue

1. Rufus R. Dawes, *Service with the Sixth Wisconsin Volunteers* (1890; repr., Dayton, OH: Morningside Bookshop, 1984), 87; Edward Bragg to Ezra A. Carman, Dec. 26, 1894, AS; Rufus R. Dawes journal, SHSW.

2. Dawes, *Service*; Edward Bragg to Ezra A. Carman, Dec. 26, 1894, AS; Dawes journal, SHSW.

3. John Sedgwick, *Correspondence of John Sedgwick, Major General*, ed. George W. Curtis (New York: De Vinne Press, 1903), 80.

4. Eric Foner, *The Fiery Trial* (New York: W. W. Norton, 2010), 169–171; James McPherson, *Battle Cry of Freedom* (New York: Oxford Univ. Press, 1988), 355–356.

5. Foner, *Fiery Trial*, 179.

6. Foner, *Fiery Trial*, 197–198; McPherson, *Battle Cry*, 498–500.

7. Foner, *Fiery Trial*, 206.

8. Foner, *Fiery Trial*, 206–207; OR 14:341.

9. *Vermont Phoenix* (Brattleboro), May 22, 1862.

10. Elisha Hunt Rhodes, *All for the Union*, ed. Robert Hunt Rhodes (Lincoln, RI: Andrew Mowbray, 1985), 66.

11. George B. McClellan, *The Civil War Papers of George B. McClellan*, ed. Stephen W. Sears (New York: Ticknor & Fields, 1989), 344–345, 346, 348.

12. David Donald, *Lincoln* (New York: Simon & Shuster, 1995), 360; Frederick Douglass, *Frederick Douglass*, ed. Philip S. Foner (Chicago: Lawrence Hill Books, 1999), 490; Lincoln to August Belmont, Aug. 31, 1862, in McPherson, *Battle Cry*, 503; Lincoln to Cuthbert Bullitt, July 28, 1862, Abraham Lincoln Papers online, LC.

13. "An Ordeal That Tests," *New York Daily Tribune*, July 5, 1862.

14. Donald, *Lincoln*, 362–363; Foner, *Fiery Trial*, 215–216; McPherson, *Battle Cry*, 500.

15. Donald, *Lincoln*, 365–366.

16. For a fuller examination of this period, see the author's previous volume on the Maryland Campaign, *To Antietam Creek* (Baltimore: Johns Hopkins Univ. Press, 2012).

17. John R. Hennessy, *Return to Bull Run* (New York: Simon & Shuster, 1993), 14–18.

18. Hennessy, *Return*, 16–17; McClellan, *Civil War Papers*, 383–383, 388; OR 11, 3:362–364.

19. Hennessy, *Return*, 19, 16; Philip Kearney, *Letters from the Peninsula*, ed. William B. Styple (Kearny, NJ: Belle Grove, 1988), 86, 109; Charles Harvey Brewster, *When This Cruel War Is Over*, ed. David W. Blight (Amherst: Univ. of Massachusetts Press, 1992), 132–133.

20. *Richmond (VA) Daily Dispatch*, May 22, 1862, https://dispatch.richmond.edu/view/secondary-section-view.php?doc=D_023_022/ [accessed Sept. 2015]; Joseph T. Glatthaar, *General Lee's Army* (New York: Free Press, 2008), 153; Harry Lewis to Nancy Lewis [mother], Aug. 9, 1862, in Robert G. Evans, ed., *The Sixteenth Mississippi Infantry* (Jackson: Univ. Press of Mississippi, 2002), 98–99; Peter Wellington Alexander, *Writing and Fighting the Civil War*, ed. William B. Styple (Kearny, NJ: Belle Grove, 2000), 90; Lafayette McLaws,

A Soldier's Genera, ed. John C. Oeffinger (Chapel Hill: Univ. of North Carolina Press, 2002), 132; Glatthaar, *General Lee's Army*, 150; *Richmond (VA) Daily Dispatch*, July 29, 1862.

21. Glatthaar, *General Lee's Army*, 165; Hodijah L. Meade to mother, Sept. 5, 1862, Hodijah L. Meade Papers, VHS; Al P. Kindberg, ed., *A Soldier from Valley Furnace* (Clairsville, OH: R & M's Home Office, 1997), 47; P. Alexander, *Writing and Fighting*, 97.

22. Wilder Dwight, *Life and Letters of Wilder Dwight* (Boston: Ticknor & Fields, 1868), 233.

23. McClellan, *Civil War Papers*, 463; Signal Station at Washington Monument to GBM, 12:40 p.m., Sept. 15, 1862, reel 31, MP.

24. *New York Daily Tribune*, Sept. 19, 1862.

25. John C. Ropes, *The Story of the Civil War*, vol. 2 (New York: G. P. Putnam's Sons, 1898), 349; Edward Porter Alexander, *Fighting for the Confederacy*, ed. Gary W. Gallagher (Chapel Hill: Univ. of North Carolina Press, 1989), 145.

26. On Sept. 15, William M. Owen, a member of the Washington Artillery, overheard Lee express "his belief that there would not be much fighting on the morrow." See William Miller Owen, *In Camp and Battle with the Washington Artillery of New Orleans* (1885; repr., Gaithersburg, MD: Butternut & Blue, 1982), 139.

27. *OR* 19, 2:307–308.

Chapter 1. Into the Corn

1. John Gibbon, *Personal Recollections of the Civil War* (New York: G. P. Putnam's Sons, 1928), 81–82; *OR* 19, 1:248.

2. *OR* 11, 1:465; Walter H. Herbert, *Fighting Joe Hooker* (Lincoln: Univ. of Nebraska Press, 1999), 97; Charles S. Wainwright, *A Diary of Battle*, ed. Allan Nevins (Gettysburg, PA: Stan Clark Military Books, 1993), 161; Kearney, *Letters*, 86.

3. W. Herbert, *Fighting Joe Hooker*, 90; Wainwright, *Diary of Battle*, 66; McClellan, *Civil War Papers*, 450.

4. Joseph Hooker, unfinished Antietam report, Nov. 8, 1862, Joseph Hooker Papers, HL.

5. "The Opposing Forces at the Second Bull Run," *B&L*, vol. 2, 497–498; Holmes W. Burlingame, "Personal Reminiscences of the Civil War, 1861–1865," 104th NY file, ANBL; John B. Sherman to his parents, Sept. 28, 1862, 105th NY file, ANBL; George Cramer letter, Sept. 21, 1862, 11th PA file, ANBL.

6. Capt. Joseph Dickinson to Brig. Gen. John Hatch, Sept. 9, 1862, and Maj. Gen. Joseph Hooker to Brig. Gen. Seth Williams, Sept. 9, 1862, Letters Sent: 1862–1865, entry 3801, pt. 2, *Records of U.S. Army Continental Commands*, RG 393, NA, quoted in Daniel J. Vermilya, "Perceptions, not Realities: The Army of the Potomac in the Maryland Campaign," Joseph L. Harsh Scholarship Award 2012, Save Historic Antietam Foundation.

7. Abner Doubleday report, *U.S. Army Generals' Reports of Civil War Service*, vol. 6, roll 4, RG 94, NA.

8. Wainwright, *Diary of Battle*, 91, 93. 121.

9. The woodlots were part of the property of several different farmers: Poffenberger, Miller, Morrison, Mumma, and others. Rather than confuse the text with numerous owners' names for the parts of these woodlots they owned, they will be referred to by their post-battle names: North Woods, East Woods, and West Woods.

10. Penn's brigade had been commanded by Col. Bradley T. Johnson at the beginning of the Maryland Campaign. Johnson was appointed provost marshal of Frederick during the Confederate occupation and then was sent to Richmond, so he was not at Antietam.

11. See Hartwig, *To Antietam Creek*, 624, 767n38; John R. Jones to Ezra A. Carman, Feb. 25, 1896, 47th AL file, ANBL.

12. John R. Jones to Carman, Feb. 25, 1896, ANBL.

13. John B. Hood, *Advance and Retreat* (1880; repr., New York: Da Capo, 1993), 42; *OR* 19, 1:955.

14. Carman, 53.

15. Carman, 53–55; "Map accompanying letter of W. H. Harrison, May 24, 1895," and "Sketch of Col. J. W. Beck [60th GA]," Lawton brigade

folder, AS; J. D. T. [initials of correspondent], in *Southern Confederacy* (Atlanta), Oct. 8, 1862, 13th GA folder, ANBL. For some reason the Carman-Cope maps of 1904 and 1908 do not show any fence where Douglass's brigade deployed. The Oliver C. Gould map of the early 1890s, however, which was a revision of the 1867 Michler map of Antietam, does show a fence here, as does the 1894 ABB base map. Both of these maps are in GP. A Sept. 19 photograph by Alexander Gardner in Capt. Joseph Knaps's Battery E, PA Light Artillery, taken near Smoketown Road looking north toward the Cornfield, clearly shows a fence line where Gould and the ABB map locate one.

16. For a detailed examination of each Confederate battery and the armaments that were present on this part of the field, see Curt Johnson and Richard C. Anderson Jr., *Artillery Hell* (College Station: Texas A&M Univ. Press, 1995), 90–99. S. D. Lee had Woolfolk's (3, possibly 4 guns), Jordan's (4 guns), Elliot's (4 guns), and Parker's (4 guns) batteries on the Dunker Church plateau. Johnson and Anderson note that Woolfolk may have had a single gun from the Middlesex (VA) Battery attached, which would have given Lee 16 guns. These authors estimate that there were 53 guns in all, including 30 rifled pieces on this part of the field, while Carman arrived at 56 guns, with 31 rifled pieces. The problem with determining an accurate count is that the Confederate artillery reorganized after Antietam, and some batteries that were in the battle were disbanded, so arriving at a precise number of guns is nearly impossible.

17. *OR* 19, 1:819; Robert M. Macknall to Ezra A. Carman, Mar. 15, 1900, AS.

18. Robert E. L. Krick, "Defending Lee's Flank," in Gary W. Gallagher, ed., *The Antietam Campaign* (Chapel Hill: Univ. of North Carolina Press, 1999), 200; Jno. W. Bryan recollections of the Battle of Sharpsburg, A. W. Garber to Carman, Apr. 1, 1896, John J. Block to Carman,

May 30, 1899, and Edwin Marks to Carman, May 31, 1899, Lawton brigade folder, AS.

19. There is disagreement on precisely how many guns were present in the four batteries that were initially massed on Nicodemus Heights. R. E. Krick, in "Defending Lee's Flank," 200, estimates that there were "about fifteen guns." C. Johnson and Anderson, in *Artillery Hell*, 93, 94–95, 100, give the number as 11 guns, and Carman counted 14.

20. "Lieutenant Asher Waterman Garber," Antietam on the Web, https://antietam.aotw.org /officers.php?officer_id=892&from=results/ [accessed July 2014]; A. W. Garber to Carman, Apr 1, 1896, and Sept. 16, 1898, and Jno. W. Bryan recollections, Lawton brigade folder, AS.

21. Gibbon, *Personal Recollections*, 80; Dawes, *Service*, 87. Each gun in a battery had a limber, which pulled the gun and carried an ammunition chest, as well as a caisson, which carried a spare wheel and three additional ammunition chests. Capt. J. Albert Monroe, commanding Battery D, 1st RI Light Artillery, however, wrote that because action was expected in the morning, his battery's caissons, battery wagon, and forge were all parked "quite a long distance" to the rear and under cover. This was often done to keep the caissons, with the bulk of a battery's ammunition, protected from enemy artillery. Since Monroe was the acting artillery chief for the 1st Division's artillery, all its batteries may have done likewise. See J. Albert Monroe, *Battery D, 1st Rhode Island Light Artillery at the Battle of Antietam, September 17, 1862*, Personal Narratives of Events in the War of the Rebellion, Ser. 3, No. 16 (Providence, RI, 1886), 12. The batteries parked in the vicinity of Poffenberger Hill were those of Campbell, Monroe, Reynolds, Edgell, Ransom, and Thompson.

22. W. H. Humphreys to John M. Gould, Mar. 23, 1893, GP.

23. Monroe, *Battery D*, 13–14.

24. Monroe, *Battery D*, 13–14. Gibbon was the author of *The Artillerists Manual*, published in 1859, which became the standard text on gunnery for both armies. See *OR* 19, 1:227.

25. G. W. Beale, *A Lieutenant of Cavalry in Lee's Army* (Baltimore: Butternut & Blue, 1994), 48; George W. Beale to Carman, June 6, 1897, Fitz Lee's brigade folder, AS; William R. Carter, *Sabres, Saddles, and Spurs*, ed. Walbrook D. Swank (Shippensburg, PA: Burd Street, 1998), 16. Carter served in Thorton's regiment. Carter also wrote that the brigade's camp "was just behind Stuart's Battery, in range of the enemy's guns." The battery firing on them was probably Reynolds's Battery L, 1st NY.

26. C. Johnson and Anderson, *Artillery Hell*, 95; Garber to Carman, Sept. 16, 1898, Lawton brigade folder, AS. Garber wrote that he came under fire from both his left and right flanks. This was impossible, as no Federal batteries could have gained a flanking fire on him.

27. The batteries were Battery A, 1st Battalion, NY Light, Lt. Bernhard Wever; Battery C, 1st Battalion, NY Light, Capt. Charles Kusserow; and Battery D, 5th U.S., Lt. Charles E. Hazlett. Also see *OR* 19, 1:976; *Columbus (GA) Enquirer*, Oct. 8, 1862; George Ring to Virgie, Sept. 20, 1862, George Ring Collection, TU, copy in ANBL.

28. *OR* 19, 1:956.

29. E. Alexander, *Fighting*, 239; S. D. Lee to Carman, Nov. 1, 1898, and Jan. 16, 1895, Wm. P. Gibbs to Carman, Oct. 28, 1899, and J. Thompson Brown to Carman, Aug. 6, 1898, AS. There was disagreement among veterans of the battalion over the order of the batteries on the ridge. For example, J. Thompson Brown, a lieutenant in Parker's battery, thought it was (from left to right) Parker's, Woolfolk's, Jordan's, and Moody's. William Gibbs gave the alignment (from left to right) as Jordan, Parker, and then the other two batteries. As Gibbs was in the far left section of Jordan's battery, near the Dunker Church, his locating Jordan on the left of the battalion was no doubt correct. Robert K. Krick, in his history of Parker's battery, places Parker to Jordan's right, as Gibbs did, and also notes that Woolfolk was on the far right of the battalion. This would give an alignment of Jordan, Parker, Moody, and Woolfolk when the action opened. See E. T. Woolfolk to Carman, Feb. 10, 1898, and Wm. Gibbs to Carman, Oct. 24, 1899, AS; Robert K. Krick, *Parker's Virginia Battery, C.S.A.* (Berryville: Virginia Book, 1975), 51–52.

30. R. K. Krick, *Parker's Virginia Battery*, 9, 24–25; J. Thompson Brown to Carman, Aug. 6, 1898, AS.

31. Royal W. Figg, *"Where Only Men Dare to Go"* (Richmond, VA: Whittet & Shepperson, 1885), 42–43; R. K. Krick, *Parker's Virginia Battery*, 49, 54–55.

32. O. R. Howard Thompson and William H. Rauch, *History of the Bucktails* (Philadelphia: Electric, 1906), 211, 216.

33. Thompson and Rauch, *History*, 211; *OR* 51, 1:146; Angelo Crapsey to Dear Friend, Sept. 30, 1862, PCHS.

34. Thompson and Rauch, *History*, 211; *OR* 51, 1:146; Angelo Crapsey to Dear Friend, Sept. 30, 1862, PCHS.

35. Carman, 56–57; Gregory C. White, *A History of the 31st Georgia Volunteer Infantry* (Baltimore: Butternut & Blue, 1997), 49.

36. Ujanirtus Allen, *Campaigning with "Old Stonewall,"* ed. Randall Allen and Keith Bohannon (Baton Rouge, LA: LSU Press, 1998), 169; Capt. James G. Rodgers obituary, in *Macon (GA) Telegraph*, Oct. 23, 1862; *OR* 19, 1:976.

37. *OR* 51, 1:147–148.

38. Joseph Hooker, unfinished Antietam report, Nov. 8, 1862, Hooker Papers, HL; Carman, 57.

39. George Lucas Hartsuff biography, George Hartsuff folder, ANBL.

40. Carman, 63–64.

41. "Poor Bill Christian . . . ," 48th Pennsylvania Volunteer Infantry, Nov. 5, 2007, http://48thpennsylvania.blogspot.com/2007/11/poor-bill-christian.html [accessed Dec. 2013]; Geo. W. Watson to Jno. M. Gould, Apr. 22, 1893, GP.

42. John Vautier journal, USAHEC; Samuel Moore diary, ANBL; Wm. Halstead to Gould, Mar. 3,

1893, and Wm. P. Gifford to Gould, Mar. 7, 1893, GP.

43. George W. Watson to Gould, Apr. 22, 1893, GP; S. Moore diary, ANBL.

44. Carman, 57–58; Henry Wineman to Carman, Mar. 13, 1898, and James Thompson to Carman, Sept. 23, 1897, AS.

45. John Delany to Gould, Mar. 27, 1891, GP. Carman wrote that Duryée's brigade advanced in front of the guns to the fence at the northern edge of the Cornfield and lay down, while the batteries fired several rounds of canister into the Cornfield, but contemporary and postwar accounts from Duryée's brigade make it clear that the brigade halted in the rear of the artillery.

46. *OR* 19, 1:218.

47. John Delany to Gould, Mar. 27, 1891, GP; Carman, 58; John C. Whiteside to Mother, Oct. 2, 1862, Michigan Historical Collections, Bentley Library, UM; Frederick Bennewitz to Gould, Mar. 20, 1890, GP. Bennewitz was carried on the rolls of the 105th as "Frederick Bennewait." Rufus Dawes in the 6th Wisconsin described the height of the corn in a letter to Ezra Carman, July 7, 1896, AS.

48. Thomas A. Maddox, "War Reminiscences," 13th GA file, ANBL; Annette McDonald Suarez, *A Source Book on the Early History of Cuthbert and Randolph County, Georgia*, ed. & comp. William Bailey Williford (Atlanta: Cherokee, 1982), 183; "Alumni," Catalogue [of] Trustees, Officers, Alumni and Matriculates, Univ. of Georgia, http://genealogytrails.com /geo/athens-clarke/uog1906alumni5.html [accessed June 2014].

49. Maddox, "War Reminiscences," ANBL; Suarez, *Source Book*, 183; "Alumni." The Oct. 8, 1862, edition of the *Columbus (GA) Enquirer* referenced a member of the 13th Georgia as carrying an Enfield rifle.

50. [Author unknown], in *Black River Herald* (Boonville, NY), Oct. 23, 1862; Henry J. Sheafer to Gould, Feb. 25, 1897, and Sheafer to Gould, n.d., GP; John C. Whiteside to Mother, Oct. 2, 1862, Michigan Historical Collections, Bentley Library, UM; Carman, 59; George Hundredmark to Gould, Nov. 30, 1893, GP. Carman was quite specific on the distance the 104th and 105th NY advanced south of the corn, giving it as 120 and 160 yards, respectively. Isaac Hall, in *History of the Ninety-Seventh Regiment New York Volunteers* (Utica, NY: L. C. Childs & Son, 1890), 92, claimed that neither side paid any attention to cover, but instead stood and blazed away at one another until the lines melted away. While this may be true for the 97th, the bulk of evidence made it clear that most of the combatants lay prone after coming under fire.

51. Carman, 60; *Columbus (GA) Enquirer*, Oct. 8, 1862; White, *History*, 51–53; John T. Crowder CSR, RG 109, NA.

52. Carman, 60–62; *OR* 19, 1:976–977; J. C. Reed to Carman, Oct. 26 and Oct. 28, 1899, and March 17, 1900, AS. The section probably consisted of Jordan's 6 lb. gun and 12 lb. howitzer, which would be effective at short range.

53. "The Civil War Letters of Charles Harvey Hayden—97th New York Infantry Regiment," New York State Military Museum and Veterans Research Center, https://museum.dmna .ny.gov/application/files/2715/5309/0239 /97thInf_Letters_Hayden.pdf [accessed Sept. 2014]; Charles Barber, *The Civil War Letters of Charles Barber*, ed. Raymond G. Barber and Gary E. Swinson (Torrance, CA: Gary E. Swinson, 1991), 94–95.

54. Letter from "H," Sept. 24, 1862, ANBL; Abram Duryée report, *U.S. Army Generals' Reports of Civil War Service*, vol. 6, roll 4, RG 94, NA; Henry J. Sheafer to Gould, n.d., GP.

55. Carman, 62.

56. Henry J. Sheafer to Gould, n.d., GP.

57. John C. Delany to Gould, Mar. 27, 1891, GP. Curiously, McThompson's report made no mention of the colors being shot down, or that they were rescued by Sheafer, Delany, and Kennedy. See *OR* 19, 1:262.

58. Isaac Hall to Gould, Apr. 8, 1891, John R. Strang to Gould, Jan. 19, 1892, and F. N. Bell to Gould, Oct. 24, 1893, GP.

59. F. N. Bell to Gould, Oct. 24, 1893, GP. Cain was promoted to 1st lieutenant effective Sept. 17, 1862.

60. F. N. Bell to Gould, Oct. 24, 1893, GP; *OR* 19, 1:190; John Whiteside to Gould, Dec. 5, 1890, GP; John Sherman to Parents, Sept. 28, 1862, ANBL; John Whiteside to Mother, Oct. 4, 1862, Michigan Historical Collections, Bentley Library, UM. The size Whiteside gave for his company may be an error.

61. Ujanirtus C. Allen to Boykin, Oct. 15, 1862, Troup County Archives, courtesy of Keith Bohannon; *Columbus (GA) Enquirer*, Oct. 8, 1862; J. D. T., in *Southern Confederacy* (Atlanta), Oct. 8, 1862. J. D. T., the correspondent (who is otherwise unidentified) to the *Southern Confederacy* reported that the 13th Georgia had only 25 men when they left the field. The fate of the color bearer was not recorded.

62. Capt. James G. Rodgers obituary, in *Macon (GA) Telegraph*, Oct. 23, 1862; Carman, 60, 555.

Chapter 2. Men of Iron

1. Dawes, *Service*, 88; Kevin Walker and K. C. Kirkman, *Antietam Farmsteads* (Sharpsburg, MD: Western Maryland Interpretive Assoc., 2010), 37; 1860 Federal Census, RG 29, NA.

2. Gibbon, *Personal Recollections*, 79–80; Alan T. Nolan, *The Iron Brigade* (Berrien Springs, MI: Hardscrabble Books, 1983), 130; Lance J. Herdegen, *The Iron Brigade in Civil War and Memory* (El Dorado Hills, CA: Savas Beatie, 2012), 235–238.

3. Stephen J. Wright, "John Gibbon and the Black Hat Brigade," in *Giants in Their Tall Black Hats*, ed. Alan T. Nolan and Sharon Eggleston Vipond (Bloomington: Indiana Univ. Press, 1998), 53–54. The skirmishers around Miller's farm were probably from Douglass's brigade, as the Hagerstown Pike seems to have served as a dividing line for respective skirmish deployments.

4. Wright, "John Gibbon," 55–56; Gibbon, *Personal Recollections*, 38; Nolan, *Iron Brigade*, 51–54; Dawes, *Service*, 45.

5. Nolan, *Iron Brigade*, 80–112; John Pope, quoted in Wright, "John Gibbon," 59; Hugh Perkins to Herbert, Sept. 21, 1862, in author's collection. Copies of Perkins's letters to Herbert Frisbie are in USAHEC.

6. *OR* 19, 1:254; George Fairfield diary, quoted in Alan Gaff and Maureen Gaff, "The Dread Reality of War," in Nolan and Vipond, *Giants*, 82.

7. William J. Hardee, *Rifle and Light Infantry Tactics* (Philadelphia: J. B. Lippincott, 1860), vol. 1, 171–213.

8. Dawes, *Service*, 88; Dawes journal, SHSW; *OR* 19, 1:254–255; Edward Bragg to Carman, Dec. 26, 1894, AS.

9. Dawes, *Service*, 88, Rufus R. Dawes, "On the Right at Antietam," in *Service*, 333; Bragg to Carman, Dec. 26, 1894, AS; Edwin B. Quiner, *E. B. Quiner Papers* (Madison: State Historical Society of Wisconsin, n.d.), vol. 3, 263–264; Herdegen, *Iron Brigade*, 212, 252n66.

10. Dawes, *Service*, 88; Bragg to Carman, exhibit A, Dec. 26, 1894, AS; Dawes, "On the Right," 334.

11. Dawes to Carman, July 7, 1896, AS.

12. Carman, 74; *OR* 19, 1:255; Bragg to Carman, Dec. 26, 1894, AS; Thomas A. Graham [Ross's battery] to Carman, Mar. 14 and Mar. 19, 1900, AS.

13. Dawes, *Service*, 13, 93; "Captain Werner von Bachelle," Antietam on the Web, https://antietam.aotw.org/officers.php?officer_id=1186/ [accessed Dec. 2014]; Herdegen, *Iron Brigade*, 245. Dawes's accounts seem to imply that Kellogg's Company I re-formed in the regimental line after the regiment cleared Miller's farm buildings.

14. Bragg to Carman, Dec. 26, 1894, AS; Dawes, *Service*, 93. Werner von Bachelle's dog was killed in the subsequent fighting and found beside the captain after the battle.

15. Thomas R. Dunn to John Worsham, Mar. 16, 1895, AS; Robert W. Withers to Carman, Mar. 14, 1895, ANBL; John Worsham to Carman, May 6, 1895, AS; John R. Jones to Carman, Jan. 25, 1896, ANBL. Dunn used curious language in describing Jones's injury from the bursting shell, writing that the general "left the field and ordered me to inform General Starke that he had done so." Dunn wrote nothing derogatory about Jones, but "left the field" was not the language typically used to describe someone genuinely wounded. See "Brigadier General John Robert Jones," Antietam on the Web, https://antietam.aotw.org/officers.php?officer_id=75/ [accessed Dec. 2014]. Although Jones's departure from the army was probably performance related, after the war he fathered a daughter with a former enslaved woman and fully embraced and supported the child, which rendered him an outcast in Lynchburg, Virginia, where he was living. The story is told in Carrie Allen McCray, *Freedom's Child* (Chapel Hill, NC: Algonquin Books, 1998). This raises the possibility that Jones's views on race may have influenced his standing in the Confederate army.

16. *OR* 19, 1:255; Bragg to Carman, Dec. 26, 1894, AS; Bragg to Wife, Sept. 21, 1862, Edward Bragg Papers, SHSW.

17. Dawes, *Service*, 89; Dawes journal, SHSW. Dawes's published accounts of the battle made no mention of the friendly fire. Instead, he simply stated that "shells burst around us." This is another example of the value of unpublished journals, letters, diaries, etc., where soldiers tended to be more frank.

18. Gibbon, *Personal Recollections*, 148; Dawes, *Service*, 92. Hooe seems to have been relatively popular in the regiment. In his detailed 1894 letter to Ezra Carman, Bragg did not mention Hooe by name but instead wrote, "The Captain commanding the skirmishers on the right showed the white feather that morning." See *OR* 19, 1:255; Bragg to Carman, Dec. 26, 1894, AS.

19. *OR Suppl.*, pt. 1, 3:540; James Stewart, "Short Stories," in *Milwaukee Sunday Telegraph*, Jan. 26, 1895; Stewart to Carman, Sept. 18, 1896, AS; *OR* 19, 1:248; Carman, 75.

20. *OR* 19, 1:233.

21. Thomas Clemens, "'Black Hats' Off to the Original Iron Brigade," *Columbiad* 1, no. 1 (Spring 1997), 46–58; Thomas Clemens, ed., "A Brigade Commander's First Fight," *Civil War Regiments* 5, no. 3 (1997), 63. Phelps gave his strength as 425 in his after-action report. See *OR* 19, 1:234. Also see appendix C, however.

22. Clemens, "Brigade Commander," 64.

23. Clemens, "Brigade Commander," 67. Phelps prepared charges against Searing, but the case never went to court-martial. For confirmation that O'Brien commanded the regiment at Antietam, see S. E. Chandler to Gould, Apr. 15, 1891, GP. John Bryson, another member of the regiment, lost his right arm at Second Manassas. He visited the regiment about a month after Antietam and recalled that, even then, Searing was "sick in his tent" and not commanding the regiment. This raises the question of whether Searing was suffering from some form of traumatic shock or depression, but it is impossible to know the answer. See Bryson to Gould, Oct. 18, 1893, GP.

24. Edwin H. Chadwick to Dear Friends, Sept. 25, 1862, ANBL; W. H. Humphrey to Gould, Mar. 23, 1893, GP; Joseph Pettiner to Carrie, Sept. 20, 1862, in "A New Yorker at Antietam," *CWTI* 19, no. 8 (Dec. 1980), 29.

25. *OR* 19, 1:224, 243; Carman, 73.

26. George H. Otis, *The Second Wisconsin Infantry*, ed. Alan D. Gaff (Dayton, OH: Morningside Bookshop, 1984), 31–32, 57, 62–63; *OR Suppl.*, pt. 3, 1:540–541; Dawes journal, SHSW; Dawes to Carman, July 7, 1896, AS; Dawes, *Service*, 90.

27. Dawes, *Service*, 90; Dawes journal, SHSW. In his journal, Dawes only mentioned that Huntington failed to give Kellogg the discretionary part of the order. He said nothing about it in his published accounts.

28. Dawes, *Service*, 90.

29. Geo. H [probably George H. Otis] to Father, Sept. 21, 1862, in Quiner, *Correspondence*, vol. 2, 307–308; Suarez, *Sourcebook*, 184; *OR* 19, 1:974; *Daily Morning News* (Savannah), Oct. 4, 1862. Contemporary sources gave two different figures for the strength of the 13th GA. Suarez, in *Sourcebook*, quoting an undated column from a Savannah paper, gives their strength as 330, with 34 uninjured. E. T. C., the correspondent (who is otherwise unidentified) from the brigade to the *Daily Morning News*, gave their initial strength as 230, with only 15 remaining. The 61st GA suffered 104 casualties. If their strength was around the average, then they lost 67%. Maj. John H. Lowe did not learn that he was the only remaining senior officer until the brigade fell back from its engagement with Doubleday's and Ricketts's divisions. See *OR* 19, 1:975.

30. J. M. Day to Carman, Mar. 14, 1895, AS; Fleming Saunders to Mother, Sept. 20, 1862, ANBL; James M. Garnett [spelled "Garrett" on the typescript] to Carman, Feb. 25, 1895, AS; *OR* 19, 1:1012; A. T. to unknown, Sept. 22, 1862, in *Richmond (VA) Daily Dispatch*, Sept. 27, 1862. Also see A. J. Grigsby to Carman, May 7, 1895, AS. Grigsby's recollections do not fully agree with Garnett's, and his sequencing of events seems to be off.

31. John H. Eicher and David J. Eicher, *Civil War High Commands* (Stanford, CA: Stanford Univ. Press, 2001), 506; *OR* 11, 2:839; *OR* 12, 2:667–668.

32. Napier Bartlett, *A Soldier's Story of the War* (New Orleans: Clark & Hofeline, 1874), 31; Robert Stiles, *Four Years Under Marse Robert* (New York: Neale, 1903), 80–81.

33. R. P. Jennings to Carman, Mar. 25, 1895, AS; James W. Jackson to My Dear Wife, Sept. 21, 1862, in "'Providence has been kind,'" *Military Images* 20, no. 4 (Jan.–Feb. 1999), 22–23.

34. Carman, 77; *OR Suppl.*, pt. 3, 1:541; *OR* 19, 1:233; Dawes, *Service*, 90–91. The precise movements of Phelps's brigade are difficult to pin down. Both Dawes and Capt. George Otis (in

the 2nd Wisconsin) mentioned men from the 14th Brooklyn in their ranks, who were conspicuous because of their red trousers. It is also clear that the 14th advanced to the 2nd and 6th WI's support before the counterattack of Starke's and Jackson's brigades. Phelps's report indicated that he kept the main body of his brigade—except for the 2nd U.S. Sharpshooters, who deployed to protect the 6th WI's right flank—in the rear of Gibbon's line, until that line fell back into the corn after their engagement with Starke's counterattacking brigades. See Geo. H to Father, Sept. 21, 1862, in Quiner, *Correspondence*, vol. 2, 307–308; *OR* 19, 1:233–234; Dawes journal, SHSW.

35. Stewart to Carman, Sept. 18, 1896, AS; Stewart, "Short Stories."

36. Jackson to My Dear Wife, in "'Providence has been kind'"; W. E. Moore to Carman, Feb. 16, 1896, AS. It seems clear from Jackson's account that Starke was not mounted. Also, Capt. W. E. Moore, 1st LA, in his letter to Carman, wrote, "Genl. Starke was on foot and was in advance of the wavering line." The belief that he was mounted is from the diary of Maj. Henry C. Monier, 10th LA, which was published in Napier Bartlett, *Military Record of Louisiana* (1875; repr., Baton Rouge, LA: LSU Press, 1964), 32–33. Monier wrote that while "endeavoring to restore the line of battle [Starke] is shot from his horse." Bartlett, who was an artilleryman and not in Starke's brigade, also claimed that Starke seized Virginia's regimental colors to rally Jackson's brigade, but no eyewitnesses mentioned this. It possibly is an invention of Bartlett's.

37. *OR* 19, 1:1017.

38. *OR Suppl.*, pt. 3, 1:540–541; Geo. H to Father, Sept. 21, 1862, in Quiner, *Correspondence*, vol. 2, 307–308.

39. W. E. Moore to Carman, Feb. 7, 1896, and R. P. Jennings to Carman, Dec. 15, 1897, AS.

40. Edwin H. Chadwick to Dear Friends, Sept. 25, 1862, ANBL; Joseph Pettiner to Carrie,

Sept. 20, 1862, in "A New Yorker at Antietam," *CWTI* 19, no. 8 (Dec. 1980), 29.

41. Edwin H. Chadwick to Dear Friends, Sept. 25, 1862, ANBL; W. H. Humphrey to Gould, Mar. 9, 1893, GP. This fence, and the Confederates behind it, was also mentioned by Joseph C. Dickey, Company C, 2nd U.S. Sharpshooters, and Hugh Perkins, 7th WI. See Dicky to One and All, Nov. 23, 1862, Appendix C, in possession of Steve Stottlemeyer; Hugh Perkins to Friend Herbert, Sept. 26, 1862, copy in author's collection. Perkins's letters are available in the T. R. Stone Collection, USAHEC. The fence can be seen in the middleground distance in a Sept. 19 Alexander Gardner photograph of a Union burial detail on Miller's farm. It appears as a rail fence, but of the type that is known as a stake-and-rider fence—a rail fence laid over a low stone wall.

42. *OR Suppl.*, pt. 3, 1:541; Dawes, *Service*, 91, 93, 214–215; Dawes journal, SHSW.

43. Dawes, *Service*, 91.

44. Alan D. Gaff, *On Many a Bloody Field* (Bloomington: Indiana Univ. Press, 1996), 30, 100; Gibbon, *Personal Recollections*, 28; John Gibbon testimony, *CCW*, 38th Congress, vol. 1, 447.

45. Wm. W. Dudley to Carman, July 16, 1895, AS; Nolan, *Iron Brigade*, 115; *OR* 19, 1:251; George S. Hoyt to Carman, Jan. 22, 1895, AS.

46. George S. Hoyt to Carman, Jan. 22, 1895, and Wm. W. Dudley to Carman, July 16, 1895, AS; *OR* 19, 1:251. Hoyt, in the 7th WI, recalled that Page's men drove their skirmish line back on the main body of the two regiments, but no one in 19th IN reported this.

47. *OR* 19, 1:257–258; George S. Hoyt to Carman, Jan. 22, 1895, AS; Robert H. Scales, "Gun Trouble," *Atlantic* (Jan.–Feb. 2015), https://www.theatlantic.com/magazine/archive/2015/01/gun-trouble/383508/; Donald Knox, *The Korean War, Pusan to Chosin* (San Diego: Harcourt Brace Jovanovich, 1985), 349.

48. Hugh Perkins to Friend, Sept. 21, 1862, USAHEC; George S. Hoyt to Carman, Jan. 22, 1895, AS.

49. Hugh Perkins to Friend Herbert, Sept. 26, 1862, USAHEC.

50. Hugh Perkins to Friend, Sept. 21, 1862, and Hugh Perkins to Friend Herbert, Sept. 26, 1862, USAHEC.

51. *OR* 19, 1:229; Stewart, "Short Stories." Stewart stated that Campbell was wounded immediately after ordering the two sections he brought up to unlimber, but Gibbon's and Stewart's own after-action reports made it quite clear that Campbell was wounded later in the action. See Gibbon, *Personal Recollections*, 84; *OR* 19, 1:229.

52. *OR* 19, 1:1017; Oli Claffey reminiscences, ANBL; W. E. Moore to Carman, Feb. 16, 1896, and Nov. 2, 1898, AS.

53. Jackson to My Dear Wife, in "'Providence has been kind.'" In his letter home, Jackson claimed that his brigade held its line for 2 hours, which is a considerable exaggeration, but not uncommon. It was difficult for soldiers under fire to accurately estimate the length of the time they were engaged in combat.

54. W. E. Moore to Carman, Nov. 2, 1898, AS; W. H. Humphrey to Gould, Mar. 9, 1893, GP; Edwin H. Chadwick to Dear Friends, Sept. 25, 1862, ANBL. Chadwick, writing only 8 days after the battle, is the source for Parmelee taking the 2nd U.S. Sharpshooters' colors in their advance. Obviously he handed this off to someone else when he picked up the flag of the 1st LA.

55. Dawes journal, SHSW; Dawes, *Service*, 91.

56. Dawes journal, SHSW; Dawes, *Service*, 91.

Chapter 3. The Pinch of the Fight

1. John H. Eicher and David J. Eicher, *Civil War High Commands* (Stanford, CA: Stanford Univ. Press, 2001), 187; George Kimball, *A Corporal's Story*, ed. Alan D. Gaff and Donald H. Gaff (Norman: Univ. of Oklahoma Press, 2014), 107,

293; Phil K. Faulk, "South Mountain," *NT*, Aug. 12, 1882; Austin C. Stearns, *Three Years with Company K*, ed. Arthur A. Kent (London: Associated Univ. Presses, 1976), 121.

2. G. Kimball, *Corporal's Story*, 107–108.

3. *New York Tribune*, Sept. 19, 1862.

4. Benjamin F. Cook, *History of the Twelfth Massachusetts Volunteers (Webster Regiment)* (Boston: Twelfth [Webster] Regiment Assoc., 1882); William H. Locke, *The Story of the Regiment* (Philadelphia: J. B. Lippincott, 1868); R. B Henderson to Gould, Apr. 24, 1894, and David Chenery to Gould, Mar. 12, 1894, GP.

5. *OR* 19, 1:978.

6. *OR* 19, 1:978; George Lovick Pierce Wren diary, typescript, ANBL; George Ring to Virgie, Sept. 20, 1862, George Ring Collection, TU.

7. William Penn Snakenberg memoir, ANBL.

8. *Memphis (TN) Daily Appeal*, Oct. 11, 1862. Fitzsimmons was killed. David Jenkins's military service record indicates that he was killed, and there is no further data on him after Sharpsburg.

9. Terry L. Jones, *Lee's Tigers* (Baton Rouge, LA: LSU Press, 1987), 17–18, 31–32, 37.

10. T. Jones, *Lee's Tigers*, 111, 240.

11. T. Jones, *Lee's Tigers*, 100, 230, 236–242. Desertion rates of over 20% were not uncommon in some regiments. The 6th LA had the highest desertion rate in the brigade, at 27%, which is extremely high. To provide some perspective, the 2nd and 7th WI, which both saw a great deal of service and combat in the war, had desertion rates of 3.91% and 2.39%, respectively. See the American Civil War Research Database, civilwardata.com [requires a subscription]. Also see George Ring to wife, quoted in James P. Gannon, *Irish Rebels, Confederate Tigers* (Campbell, CA: Savas 1998), 131.

12. *OR* 19, 1:978; G. Wren diary, ANBL.

13. David Chenery to Gould, Mar. 12, 1894, and George Kimball to Comrade Rollins, Dec. 17, 1891, GP; G. Kimball, *Corporal's Story*, 176.

14. G. Kimball, *Corporal's Story*, 109; Kimball to Rollins, Dec. 17, 1891, and Robt. Shearer to Gould, Nov. 15, 1892, GP.

15. *OR* 51, 1:140.

16. Stearns, *Three Years*, 126–127. Also see Hovey to Gould, Mar. 16, 1894, and Fox to Gould, Mar. 8, 1892, GP.

17. G. Kimball, *Corporal's Story*, 172, 177.

18. Kimball to Rollins, Dec. 17, 1891, GP; G. Kimball, *Corporal's Story*, 177.

19. Kimball to Rollins, Dec. 17, 1891, GP; G. Kimball, *Corporal's Story*, 177; Lewis Reed to Gould, Apr. 29, 1894, GP. Reed wrote, "We suffered a heavy loss from a rebel battery a short distance north of Dunker Church." Kimball also mentioned this artillery fire but misidentified it as Stuart's. Also see Joseph E. Blake to Brother Stephen, Oct. 21, 1862, Civil War Miscellaneous Collection, USAHEC; Abram B. Dyer journal, ABB Papers, NA; Robt. Shearer to Gould, Nov. 29, 1892, GP.

20. Lewis Reed to Gould, Apr. 13, 1894, GP; G. Kimball, *Corporal's Story*, 178. The soldier probably was Nathaniel H. Dyer, who was the only individual killed in Kimball's company.

21. G. Kimball, *Corporal's Story*, 178.

22. Joseph E. Blake to Brother Stephen, Oct. 21, 1862, Civil War Miscellaneous Collection, USAHEC.

23. Robt. Shearer to Gould, Apr. 29, 1892, GP.

24. P. A. Dunton to Friend Byron, Sept. 24, 1862, 13th MA file, GNMP; letter from a private soldier, Sept. 23, 1862, in *Boston Evening Transcript*, Oct. 1, 1862. The soldier only identifies himself as "B." Also see Stearns, *Three Years*, 127–128. Stearns did not identify his friend who died. It was either Joshua T. Lawrence, a 21-year-old painter from Roxbury, or David S. Thurber, a 24-year-old clerk from Mendon, the only two men killed in Company D.

25. Stearns, *Three Years*, 128, 130. Tom Gassett, who may have been William's older brother, was also killed that day.

26. Charles Hovey to Gould, Mar. 16, 1894, GP.

27. *OR* 19, 1:978; G. Wren diary, ANBL; Snakenberg memoir, ANBL.

28. Alpheus S. Williams, *From the Cannon's Mouth*, ed. Milo M. Quaife (Lincoln: Univ. of Nebraska Press, 1995), 130; T. Jones, *Lee's Tigers*, 130.

29. T. Jones, *Lee's Tigers*, 130; George Ring to Virgie, Sept. 20, 1862, George Ring Collection, TU; G. Wren diary, ANBL. Richardson survived his wound.

30. *OR* 19, 1:968, 974, 979; Robert E. L. Krick, *Staff Officers in Gray* (Chapel Hill: Univ. of North Carolina Press, 2003), 215, 230.

31. *OR* 19, 1:977.

32. *OR* 19, 1:974.

33. *OR* 19, 1:977.

34. Carman, 81; Enoch Jones to Gould, Feb. 28, 1893, and Charles Ackerman to Gould, Mar. 15, 1893, GP.

35. Oliver P. Clarke to Gould, Oct. 26, 1893, GP.

36. *OR* 19, 1:190; Charles Ackerman to Gould, Mar. 15, 1893, Enoch Jones to Gould, Feb. 28, 1893, and William H. Holstead to Gould, Mar. 9, 1893, GP. William DeRosset, in a letter to Stephen D. Thruston, July 12, 1886, GP, mentioned that the 3rd NC were armed with smoothbores and buck-and-ball ammunition.

37. Wm. P. Gifford to Gould, Mar. 7, 1893, and Charles Sloat to Gould, Mar. 8, 1894, GP.

38. John Vautier to Gould, Nov. 21, 1892, GP; John Vautier diary, USAHEC; *OR* 19, 1:190; *Yonkers (NY) Examiner*, Oct. 10, 1862.

39. George Kimball to Gould, Dec. 17, 1891, GP; Alfred J. Sellers to My Dear General, Sept. 30, 1897, AS.

40. Gannon, *Irish Rebels, Confederate Tigers*, 136; John Heil CSR, RG 109, NA.

41. Kimball, *A Corporal's Story*, 179–180. Dehon was killed at Fredericksburg while serving on George Meade's staff.

42. Carman, 64; *OR* 51, 1:139; James Thompson to Carman, Sept. 27, 1897, "Battery C, PA Light Artillery" [with Carman's notes on the battery], William Turpin to Carman, n.d., and William Turpin to Carman, Sept. 29, 1898, AS. Thompson thought he followed Duryée's brigade into the Cornfield. Carman established that he followed Hartsuff.

43. Col. Richard Coulter after-action report, Sept. 21, 1862, GP; Lewis Reed to Gould, Apr. 13, 1894, GP. Reed was a 20-year-old stitcher (garment maker) from East Abington. He spent months recovering from his wound but survived to be promoted numerous times, eventually to captain in the 54th MA, and survived the war.

44. George Kimball to Rollins, Dec. 17, 1891, GP; *OR* 11, 1:217–219.

45. *OR* 51, 1:141; Cook, *History of the Twelfth*, 69; George Kimball to Rollins, Dec. 17, 1891, GP; Kimball, *A Corporal's Story*, 179–180.

46. *OR* 19, 1:190, Cook, *History of the Twelfth*, 68–69; Kimball to Rollins, Dec. 17, 1891, GP; Joseph Blake to Brother Stephen, Oct. 21, 1862, Civil War Miscellaneous Collection, USAHEC. Kimball believed that most of the missing in the 12th were, in fact, killed.

47. Kimball, *A Corporal's Story*, 181–182; Kimball to Rollins, Dec. 17, 1891, GP.

48. Alfred J. Sellers to My Dear General, Sept. 30, 1897, AS; "Colonel Peter Lyle, Commander of the 90th Pennsylvania," Student of the American Civil War, Sept. 5, 2012, https://studycivilwar.wordpress.com/2012/09/05/colonel-peter-lyle-commander-of-the-90th-pennsylvania/ [accessed Feb. 2015].

49. *OR* 19, 1:956, 968–969, 975, 1017.

50. *OR* 19, 1:975. Although Seymour's brigade was not part of Hooker's initial assault, part of his brigade could be added to the strength of the Federals attacking Jackson's line, since they were engaged with Walker's brigade and part of Douglass's brigade early on in the action.

51. Gibbon and Phelps had 1,378 men combined. Jones had approximately 2,100 in his four brigades. The reference to the 1st Corps being in the "kinks" is from GBM to Mary Ellen, Sept. 12, 1862, in McClellan, *Civil War Papers*, 450.

52. *OR* 19, 1:923. 968–969, 1022.

53. Hood made it clear that the request for support came from Lawton, not Jackson, who frequently gets the credit for ordering Hood into action. See *OR* 19, 1:23; Hood, *Advance and Retreat*, 42; Carman, 88.

Chapter 4. Hood Strikes Back

1. John Cheeves Haskell, *The Haskell Memoirs*, ed. Gilbert E. Govan and James W. Livingood (New York: Putnam, 1960), 16; Richard M. McMurray, *John Bell Hood and the War for Southern Independence* (Lexington: Univ. Press of Kentucky, 1982), 3, 6, 10, 22.

2. Hood, *Advance and Retreat*, 16, 19.

3. McMurray, *John Bell Hood*, 35.

4. McMurray, *John Bell Hood*, 39–40; Stephen W. Sears, *To the Gates of Richmond* (New York: Ticknor & Fields, 1992), 85–86; J. H. L., "Hood 'Feeling the Enemy,'" *B&L*, vol. 2, 276.

5. McMurray, *John Bell Hood*, 46.

6. McMurray, *John Bell Hood*, 48–49; Sears, *To the Gates*, 240–241.

7. McMurray, *John Bell Hood*, 49–50. Once, when a staff officer mentioned Hood's name to Jackson, the latter responded, "Oh! He is a soldier!" See James I. Robertson Jr., *Stonewall Jackson* (New York: Simon & Shuster, 1997), 609.

8. McMurray, *John Bell Hood*, 50; Hood, *Advance and Retreat*, 36–37. A statement on page 37 is telling regarding Hood's tactical philosophy: "While I lost many valuable officers and men, as shown by the official reports, my two brigades *true to their teaching* [author's italics], captured five guns in addition to fourteen stands of colors."

9. Douglas S. Freeman, *Lee's Lieutenants* (New York: Charles Scribner's Sons, 1943), vol. 2, 147; Hartwig, *To Antietam Creek*, 361–362, 732n.

10. *OR* 19, 1:923; James Carr Murray to Father, Oct. 17, 1862, THM. Murray served in the 4th TX. Whether he was a courier at division headquarters or knew someone there is unknown, but he had detailed knowledge of Hood's efforts to get reinforcements.

11. Eicher and Eicher, *High Command*, 578;

12. Eicher and Eicher, *High Commands*, 340; 1860 Federal Census, Darlington County, South Carolina, RG 29, NA; Clement A. Evans, ed., *Confederate Military History* (Dayton, OH: Morningside Bookshop, 1975), 8:422; Hennessy, *Return*, 159.

13. Hood, *Advance and Retreat*, 31.

14. James H. Hendrick to Mother, July 13, 1862, ANBL; H. Waters Berryman to Mother, Sept. 4, 1862, THM; "Civil War Diary of August L. P. Varin, 2nd Mississippi Infantry, C.S.A.," RootsWeb, http://www.rootsweb.ancestry.com/-mscivilw/vairindiary.htm [accessed May 2015]; James O. Moore, "The Men of the Bayou City Guards," master's thesis, Univ. of Houston–Clear Lake, 1988, THM, copy in ANBL; R. T. Coles, *From Huntsville to Appomattox*, ed. Jeffery D. Stocker (Knoxville: Univ. of Tennessee Press, 1996), 67.

15. McMurray, *John Bell Hood*, 42.

16. D. C. Love to Gould, Apr. 29, 1897, and J. M. Smither to Gould, Feb. 26, 1891, GP; James L. Lemon diary, 18th GA file, ANBL.

17. D. C. Love to Gould, Apr. 29, 1897, and O. P. Putnam to Gould, Aug. 30, 1895, GP; L. A. Daffan autobiography, Brake Collection, box 8, USAHEC; William Robbins to Gould, Mar. 25, 1891, GP; William Pritchard, quoted in George E. Otott, "Clash in the Cornfield: The 1st Texas Volunteer Infantry in the Maryland Campaign," *Civil War Regiments* 5, no. 3 (1997), 92.

18. Typically, when a unit in combat marched by the flank, it simply faced right or left and moved in a column of fours, unless commanded otherwise. W. T. Hill in the 5th TX was clear that Wofford's brigade formed a column of fours, and Law's brigade no doubt did likewise. See W. T. Hill to Gould, July 21, 1891, GP.

19. W. T. Hill to Gould, July 21, 1891, GP. Also see Lemon diary, 18th GA file, ANBL; Carman, 88; David Love to Gould, Apr. 29, 1891, William Robbins to Gould, June 19, 1894, and William Robbins map, Mar. 25, 1891, GP. Robbins's map

made it clear that Law's brigade crossed the pike north of the church.

20. William Robbins to Gould, Mar. 25, 1891, and William Robbins map, Mar. 25, 1891, GP; Coles, *From Huntsville*, 67, 259n21. Frame managed to remain with the regiment until he was captured in Tennessee in Oct. 1863 and held as a POW until the end of the war. He took the Oath of Allegiance on June 14, 1865. See Joseph Frame CSR, RG 109, NA.

21. *OR* 19, 1:923, 928–932, 935, 937; Lt. Col. B. F. Carter, 4th TX, reported that his regiment was directly in the rear of the 11th MS, which would mean that the 1st TX initially was in the rear of the 2nd MS, and the 5th TX was in the rear of the 6th NC.

22. Hood, *Advance and Retreat*, 43; Carman, 89.

23. "Battery C, PA Lt. Artillery," 1st Corps Artillery folder, AS; William L. Turpin to Carman, n.d., AS; Carman, 89–90.

24. Jno. W. Stevens, *Reminiscences of the Civil War* (1902; repr., Powhatan, VA: Derwent, 1982), 74; Andrew J. Baker to Gould, Apr. 7, 1897, GP; *OR* 19, 1:931, 935.

25. Dawes, *Service*, 91; Dawes journal, SHSW.

26. Dawes journal, SHSW; Geo. H. to Father, Sept. 21, 1862, in Quiner, *Correspondence*, vol. 2, 307; W. H. Humphrey to Gould, Mar. 27, 1893, GP; Edwin H. Chadwick to Dear Friends, Sept. 25, 1862, ANBL.

27. Dawes, *Service*, 91; Dawes to Carman, Mar. 4, 1898, AS.

28. *OR* 19, 1:928; Carman, 90, 99–101. Carman stated that the two "regiments" that Wofford reported were the 14th Brooklyn (NY), with elements of Phelps's brigade, and the 2nd WI. Carman forgot the 6th WI, which was intermingled with the 14th Brooklyn, but from the accounts of members of these units, they were badly disorganized and comingled. How Carman was able to discern who was in which group is difficult to determine. More likely, the two groups were the 2nd WI and elements of Phelps's brigade in one, and the 6th WI, 14th Brooklyn, 2nd U.S. Sharpshooters, and

members of Phelps's other regiments in the other.

29. Lemon diary, 18th GA file, ANBL; Stephen E. Welch, Herod Wilson, James Estes, Christopher P. Poppenheim, and J. Hervey Dingle Jr., CSR, NA; 1860 Federal Census, NA. Dingle had a wife and five children and owned 31 enslaved people. Also see "Clarendon County, South Carolina: Largest Slaveholders from 1860 Slave Census Schedules and Surname Matches for African Americans on 1870 Census," RootsWeb, https://freepages.rootsweb .com/~ajac/genealogy/scclarendon.htm [accessed June 2015]; *OR* 19, 1:931.

30. Stephen Welch to Parents, Sept. 22, 1862, ANBL.

31. *OR* 19, 1:928, 932, 935, 936; Carman, 94, 101; J. M. Smither to Gould, Feb. 26, 1891, AS. Lt. Col. Carter's report states that he halted in the rear of Law's brigade and then was ordered by Hood to move to the right and drive off some Federal troops that were observed near the edge of the East Woods.

32. J. M. Smither to Gould, Feb. 26, 1891, AS; *OR* 19, 1:936. J. M. Smither's letter to Gould made it clear that the 5th TX moved up directly in the rear of the 1st TX, which meant that it moved with the 4th TX. While the 5th TX was in the rear of the 1st TX, they were ordered by Hood to attack in the direction of the East Woods.

33. Carman, 90; D. C. Love to Gould, Apr. 29, 1891, GP.

34. William Robbins to Gould, Mar. 25, 1891, GP; Robbins to Carman, Oct. 9, 1896, AS. Scruggs claimed that he was wounded later in the morning, when the 4th AL withdrew from the East Woods, but his memory clearly failed him here. See Scruggs to Gould, Jan. 9, 1891, GP. Robbins was positive that he was hit in the first fire and never entered the East Woods. The regimental adjutant, Robert Coles, concurred and wrote to Gould that he remembered "<u>distinctly</u> where & when he [Scruggs] was wounded, and he <u>certainly</u>

never entered the wood with us." See Coles to Gould, Feb. 19, 1891, and J. C. Nisbet to Carman, Jan. 10, 1895, GP.

35. S. Moore diary, ANBL.

36. S. Moore diary, ANBL; A. J. Sellers to Gould, Dec. 31, 1894, AS; *OR* 19, 1:265–266; Walter F. Beyer and Oscar F. Keydel, eds., *Deeds of Valor from Records in the Archives of the United States Government* (Detroit: Perrien Keydel, 1907), 1:90. If Paul exaggerated his actions for *Deeds of Valor*, he would not be the exception. Many others who were awarded medals in the postwar years did so, as well. See "Medal of Honor Citation, Private William H. Paul," Antietam on the Web, https://antietam.aotw.org/moh.php?citation_id=17/ [accessed June 2015]; James Durkin, *The Last Man and the Last Life* (Glenside, PA: J. M. Santarelli, 2000), 14, 90, 92, 94; George W. Watson to Gould, Apr. 22, 1893, AS; Alan Sessarego, *Letters Home, IV* (Gettysburg, PA: Americana Souvenirs & Gifts, 2003), 11. For an example of the undocumented statements that Ricketts was injured when his horse was killed, and that he had two horses killed under him, see "Union Brigadier General James B. Ricketts," Monocacy National Battlefield, MD, https://www.nps.gov/mono/learn/historyculture/james_ricketts.htm [accessed June 2015]. Ricketts left active field service on Nov. 1, 1863, and served on commissions and court-martials until the spring of 1864, when he resumed command of a division in the 6th Corps. Charles Wainwright, the 1st Corps' Chief of Artillery, wrote that Ricketts was "politely relieved," which implies the it was not due to wounds, but instead to poor performance. See Wainwright, *Diary of Battle*, 121.

37. Durkin, *Last Man*, 92.

38. A. J. Sellers to Gould, Dec. 31, 1894, AS; Durkin, *Last Man*, 94; George W. Watson to Gould, Apr. 22, 1893, AS.

39. Carman, 92; William Turpin to Carman, Sept. 29 and Nov. 3, 1898, and n.d., AS; *OR* 51, 1:139; Thomson to Carman, Mar. 8, 1891, AS. Also

see "Battery C, PA Lt. Artillery," 1st Corps Artillery folder, AS, which is the source for information on the timed fuses Thompson's crews used.

40. Carman, 93; Lt. George Breck, "The Late Battles in Maryland," *Rochester (NY) Union and Advertiser*, Sept. 26, 1862.

41. Carman, 93; Breck, "Late Battles."

42. Adoniram J. Warner, "Minutes of the Battle of Antietam," WRHS. Warner's "minutes" were transcribed and published by James B. Casey, ed., "The Ordeal of Adoniram Judson Warner: His Minutes of South Mountain and Antietam," *Civil War History* 28, no. 3 (Sept. 1982), 213–236.

43. Frank Holsinger, "How It Feels to Be Under Fire," in Henry Steele Commager, ed., *The Blue and the Gray* (Indianapolis: Bobbs-Merrill, 1973), vol. 1, 315–316. Mangle's name was misspelled "Maugle" in the published muster roll.

44. John W. Burnett [4th PA Reserves] to Gould, n.d., GP; Holsinger, "How It Feels," 315.

45. John W. Burnett to Gould, n.d., GP; Meade to Margaret, Nov. 16, 1862, George Meade Papers, PHS.

46. *OR* 19, 1:269, 274; Carman, 93; Casey, "Ordeal"; John W. Burnett to Gould, n.d., GP; Lieut. H. S. Gansevoort to parents, Sept. 22, 1862, in *Albany (NY) Atlas and Argus*, Oct. 3, 1862.

47. J. P. George to Gould, Apr. 21, 1892, GP; Casey, "Ordeal"; *OR* 19, 1:269–270; Carman, 93–94. Carman wrote that the 10th PA Reserves were detached from Robert Anderson's brigade when they moved out of the North Woods, but Colonel Warner made it clear that his regiment was not detached until they reached the ravine north of the Cornfield.

48. William Wall [1st TX] to Gould, May 28, 1894, GP. For the involvement of Starke's brigade, see W. E. Moore to Carman, Feb. 16, 1896, and Nov. 2, 1898, AS.

49. Gibbon, *Personal Recollections*, 82; *OR* 19, 1:243–244, 246; Marsena Rudolph Patrick,

Inside Lincoln's Army, ed. David S. Sparks (New York: Thomas Yoseloff, 1964), 144.

50. *OR* 19, 1:246–247; Gibbon, *Personal Recollections*, 82; Enos B. Vail, *Reminiscences of a Boy in the Civil War* (privately printed, 1915), 84; "Letter from the 20th Regiment," *New York Courier*, Oct. 3, 1862. The writer of this latter piece was Lt. John McEntee of Company K. Both McEntee and Gates claimed that the regiment's left wing advanced through the corn beside the Hagerstown Pike, implying that this occurred before Hood's principal attack, but it is clear from Vail's account and evidence from other participants outside the 20th NY State Militia that this advance was made to help cover the retreat of Gibbon's and Phelps's brigades. See Ira M. Slawson to Friend Cleland, Oct. 12, 1862, in *Yates County Chronicle* (Penn-Yan, NY), Oct. 23, 1862. Slawson was detached from the 23rd NY Infantry to Battery B.

51. *OR* 19, 1:931; Stephen E. Welch to Parents, Sept. 22, 1862, ANBL; Lemon diary, 18th GA file, ANBL; Carman, 103.

52. Augustus Buell, *The Cannoneer* (Washington, DC; *National Tribune*, 1890), 38–39; John Gibbon to Wife, Sept. 21, 1862, HSP.

53. Gibbon, *Personal Recollections*, 84; Beyer and Keydel, *Deeds of Valor*, 75–76.

54. James Stewart to Gould, Jan. 16, 1893, GP; James Stewart to Gibbon, Aug. 22, 1893, AS; Buell, *Cannoneer*, 38.

55. Beyer and Keydel, *Deeds of Valor*, 78; *OR* 19, 1:229; Ira M. Slawson to Friend Cleland, Oct. 12, 1862, in *Yates County Chronicle* (Penn-Yan, NY), Oct. 23, 1862; Theodore B. Gates, *The "Ulster Guard" (20th N. Y. State Militia) and the War of the Rebellion* (New York: Benj. H. Tyrrel, 1879), 318–319; Buell, *Cannoneer*, 39. For Hogarty's Medal of Honor citation, which differs in some details from his account in *Deeds of Valor*, see "Medal of Honor Citation, Private William P. Hogarty," Antietam on the Web, https://antietam.aotw.org/moh.php ?citation_id=11/ [accessed June 2015]. Curiously, Stewart's report did not mention either Hogarty or Cook in the list of men he deemed worthy of special notice. See note 56 regarding the flag Slawson saw captured. What regiment it came from is unknown. Cook was badly wounded in the leg, below the knee, but recovered. See Cook to his brother, Sept. 21, 1862, in *Hartford (WI) Home League*, Oct. 4, 1862.

56. Gibbon, *Personal Recollections*, 83; [McEntee],"Letter"; Dawes, *Service*, 91.

57. Carman, 101; J. P. George to Gould, Mar. 4, 1892, GP; *OR* 51, 1:150–151; Dawes, *Service*, 91; Dawes journal, SHSW; Dawes to Carman, Nov. 10, 1898, AS. For the action of the left wing of the 20th NY State Militia, see *OR* 19, 1:246–247; "From the XXth Regiment," *Kingston (NY) Democratic Journal*, Oct. 1, 1862. Gates also claimed that one of his men shot a Confederate color bearer and brought his colors off the field, but Gates did not identify the unit it belonged to. Both this claim and the one that his men recovered the national colors of the 6th WI were disputed afterward by Gibbon, Stewart, and Lt. Col. Bragg. Gibbon wrote that during the fight, someone brought in one of the Confederate colors. He ordered the man to throw it down and help defend the battery. It was this flag that Gibbon believed someone in Gates's regiment had picked up. Gibbon also disputed Gates's report of saving the 6th WI's national colors. "I knew that was not true, for I saw them come off the field myself," he wrote. Both Gates and Lt. John McEntee, however, wrote about recovering the 6th WI's national colors immediately after the battle, with Gates including it in his after-action report. Since all the color guard of the 6th WI were wounded, it seems likely that this was not an invention to burnish the reputation of the 20th NY State Militia, but instead confirmed that Hardenbergh's left wing did recover the colors and returned them to someone in the 6th WI soon after coming out of the Cornfield. Hence the period in which the colors were out of the hands of the 6th WI was probably

quite brief. It seems likely that the Confederate colors "captured" by the 20th NY State Militia was the one Gibbon ordered the soldier who brought it in to throw down. Dawes also disputed Gates's claim of recovering the 6th WI's national colors, but in the intense excitement of the moment, with multiple events occurring simultaneously, it was impossible for anyone to know about or see every incident that occurred, or to even be aware, because of the corn, that the color bearer had been shot. See Gibbon to Stewart, Aug. 4, 1893, and Dawes to Carman, Feb. 14, 1898, AS.

58. *OR* 19, 1:251, 257–258; Carman, 105. My interpretation of these events differs slightly from Carman, as I discovered no evidence that the 7th WI moved again after their change of front to engage Starke's counterattack. See George Hoyt to Carman, Jan. 2, 1895, AS; Hugh Perkins to Friend, Sept. 21 and Sept. 26, 1862, USAHEC.

59. *OR* 19, 1:928, 935; Carman, 101, 104–105; Daffan autobiography, Brake Collection, box 8, USAHEC.

60. Daffan autobiography, USAHEC; J. M. Polk, quoted in Susannah J. Ural, *Hood's Texas Brigade* (Baton Rouge, LA: LSU Press, 2017), 123.

61. W. R. Hamby, "Hood's Brigade at Sharpsburg," *CV* 16, no. 1 (Jan. 1908), 19; James C. Murray to Sister, Sept. 22, 1862, THM.

62. *OR* 19, 1:244; M. Smith, "Reminiscences," 22, ANBL; Patrick, *Inside Lincoln's Army*, 148. Lord was court-martialed in 1863 and resigned. He apparently had political capital in New York State, for in Sept. 1863, he was commissioned colonel of the 20th NY Cavalry and commanded the regiment until the end of the war. For details on his court-martial, see "*Daily Reformer*, Feb. 10, 1863," 35th New York Infantry Regiment's Civil War Newspaper Clippings, https://museum.dmna.ny.gov/unit-history/infantry/35th-infantry-regiment/newspaper-clippings/ [accessed June 2015].

63. "War Correspondence," *Louisville (NY) Journal and Republican*, Oct. 1, 1862.

64. *OR* 19, 1:244; Patrick, *Inside Lincoln's Army*, 148. Patrick claimed credit for maneuvering the 7th WI and the 19th IN to the ledge, along with his regiments, but there is no evidence that either of these units received any orders from him.

65. Murray, *New Yorkers*, 77; Putnam, "Patrick's Brigade."

66. *OR* 19, 1:928, 930, 931, 811; Susan P. Lee, *Memoirs of William Nelson Pendleton, D.D.* (Philadelphia: J. B. Lippincott, 1893), 216; M. Smith, "Reminiscences," 22, ANBL.

67. *OR* 19, 1:811; Carman, 109. A descriptive list of the 4th TX casualties appeared in the *Houston Weekly Telegraph*, Oct. 29, 1862.

68. *OR* 19, 1:244, 251; Patrick, *Inside Lincoln's Army*, 148; Murray, *New Yorkers*, 77. The writer of this account was possibly Sgt. James C. Otis. See Carman, 106. Why Carman determined that the 7th WI advanced with the 19th IN and was repulsed by the 4th TX is a mystery. There is no evidence that the 7th WI advanced beyond the limestone ledge.

69. William E. Barry to Gould, Mar. 12, 1891, GP. Barry was confused about the New York regiment that captured him, stating that it was the 33rd NY. It could only have been the 23rd NY, as the 33rd was in the 6th Corps. To underscore the circumstances Wofford's left flank faced, Lt. James Lemon, 18th GA, wrote in his journal that his regiment was out of ammunition and going through the cartridge boxes of the dead to keep up the fight. In reference to the counterattack of the 19th IN and Patrick's brigade, he wrote, "At length we were forced to flee by the left flank so as to prevent our total destruction." See Lemon diary, 18th GA file, ANBL.

70. *OR* 19, 1:251; William W. Dudley to Carman, July 16 and July 18, 1895, AS; Robert "Bob" Patterson, "Personal Recollections of the Scenes and Incidents of the Battle of Antietam," in *Muncie (IN) Morning Star*, Sept. 18, 1912; Henry Marsh to Father, Sept. 23, 1862, Henry C. Marsh Papers, ISL.

71. *OR* 19, 189, 244, 251; John H. Mills, *Chronicles of the Twenty-First Regiment, New York State Volunteers* (Buffalo, NY: John M. Layton, 1867), 290, 292–293; Louis C. Greenleaf to Carman, Dec. 13, 1894, and William F. Rogers to Carman, Jan. 10, 1895, AS. Also see William F. Rogers, "Antietam," AS; "23rd New York" [with Carman's notes], AS. Louis Greenleaf, in the 5th NY, wrote that the flag captured by his regiment was the left guidon of one of D. H. Hill's regiments, but he was told this by some Texas prisoners, probably from the 4th TX. Since the 35th NY did not fight with Ripley's brigade, the flag was more likely a guidon of the 4th TX, or possibly the 1st TX, the Hampton Legion, or the 18th GA. Private Stanislaus Barreaux of Company E captured the flag, which was described by one 35th NY correspondent as a battle flag, but it definitely was not. See Murray, *New Yorkers*, 77–78.

72. *OR* 19, 1:932; Philip A. Work, "The 1st Texas Regiment of the Texas Brigade . . . at the Battles of Boonsboro Pass or Gap and Sharpsburg or Antietam, MD, in September 1862," ANBL. In his after-action report, Work said he sent Capt. John R. Woodward to Wofford. But Woodward was acting as major in command of the left wing and was unlikely to be sent on such a mission. In his recollection of the action, Work stated that it was Shropshire, which indicates that the report was incorrect. Work also wrote that Shropshire was killed and Hanks lost a leg. The former was not killed, but instead had his arm fractured and later resigned as a result of his injury. Hanks was wounded and captured, and he had his right leg amputated. See Winkfield Shropshire and Amos G. Hanks MSR, NA.

73. Carman, 102; *OR* 19, 1:269–270; *OR* 51, 1:151; Casey, "Ordeal"; J. P. George to Gould, Jan. 21, 1892, GP. All Model 1842 firearms were originally smoothbore, but a number of them were rifled and issued to Union infantry regiments. The rifled version could also fire round balls.

74. Casey, "Ordeal"; J. P. George [11th PA Reserves] to Gould, Jan. 21 and Mar. 4, 1892, GP; Carman, 102–103; "A Letter," Second Wisconsin Volunteer Infantry, http://secondwi.com/wisconsinpeople/john.htm [accessed Feb. 2016]; Otott, "Clash," 77.

75. J. P. George to Gould, Mar. 4, 1892, GP; *OR* 51, 1:150–151,154, 155; O. T. Hanks, "History of Captain B. F. Benton's Company, 1861–1865," THM; Work, "1st Texas Regiment," ANBL.

76. H. Walters Berryman to Mother, Sept. 22, 1862, THM; Hood's Brigade Historical Papers, GP; R. W. Cotton MSR, NA.

77. Work, "1st Texas Regiment," ANBL. Private Hicks was not killed, as Work claimed. In fact, his military service records do not even indicate that he was wounded. See Charles H. Hicks MSR, NA. Dale's first name was spelled "Mat" in the 1860 Federal Census and occasionally in his military service records. He was a printer in Palestine, Texas. See Matt Dale MSR, NA; 1860 Federal Census, NA.

78. Work, "1st Texas Regiment," ANBL; *OR* 19, 1:932–934; Carman, 102–103. The initial casualty report filed by Work gave the regiment's losses as 45 killed and 141 wounded. See *OR* 19, 1:811. The number of dead rose to 57 when the mortally wounded are added. See Otott, "Clash," 111. In an 1891 letter to Robert Burns, a former major in the 1st TX, Work stated that out of the detail of 24 men who were detached to cook rations for the regiment during the night of Sept. 16, less than half of them had returned to the regiment when they went into action, so Work thought he carried only 211 officers and men into the fight. The colonel was drawing on memory, but there is no reason to doubt his statement. Hood's Brigade Historical Papers, GP, however, which listed the casualties of the regiment at Sharpsburg, gave its effective strength as 26 officers and 218 enlisted men, or 244 in total. It is fruitless to play the numbers game—did they have 211, 226, or 244 men on Sept. 17?—because whatever number

is correct, the regiment suffered horrendous losses. The losses of the 1st TX were not exceeded officially, but it is possible that the 6th GA of Colquitt's brigade suffered a higher percentage loss. Because of the poor records, due to heavy casualties, we will probably never know.

79. *OR* 19, 1:186; H. Walters Berryman to Mother, Sept. 22, 1862, THM.

80. *OR* 51, 1:151, 154, 155; Carman, 107. Capt. Samuel Dick, commanding the 9th PA Reserves, reported that Gibbon personally ordered him to advance. Since the rest of the brigade followed, it seems likely that Gibbon ordered or convinced Robert Anderson to do so with the rest of his brigade.

81. Samuel McDowell Tate to Gould, May 7 and May 15, 1891, GP; Carman, 95.

82. David C. Love to Gould, Apr. 29, 1891, GP; Carman, 96.

83. Carman, 95–96; I. Thropp [probably Isaac Thropp Jr., a corporal] to Gould, Apr.10, 1893, GP; Holsinger, "How It Feels," 314; Frank Holsinger to Gould, Feb. 29, 1893, and Edwin H. Minor to Gould, Sept. 8, 1894, GP.

84. Frank Holsinger, "War Stories by the 'Woodbury Kid,'" in possession of Steve Stottlemeyer; Holsinger, "How It Feels," 315; Holsinger to Gould, Feb. 29, 1893, GP.

85. Carman, 96; Bates Alexander, "Seventh Regiment," Save the Flags Collection, USAHEC; Griffin Lewis Baldwin diary, 7th PA Reserves file, ANBL; unidentified 7th PA Reserves' soldier's letter to parents, Sept. 29, 1862, ANBL; *OR* 19, 1:191; Griffin L. Baldwin to Gould, Nov. 5, 1893, GP.

86. D. C. Love to Gould, Apr. 29, 1891, GP; Dunbar R. Ransom to Carman, Feb. 5 and Feb. 18, 1895, and Dunbar R. Ransom to Edwin E. Bryant, Feb. 22, 1895, AS; Lieut. H. S. Gansevoort letter, Sept. 22, 1862, in *Albany (NY) Atlas and Argus*, Oct. 3, 1862.

87. D. C. Love to Gould, Apr. 29, 1891, GP.

88. *OR* 19, 1:938; Carman, 98; David C. Love to Gould, Apr. 29, 1891, GP; James Steptoe Johnston to Mary Green, Sept. 24, 1862, Mercer-Green-Johnston Papers, LC.

89. *OR* 19, 1:938; Carman, 98; David C. Love to Gould, Apr. 29, 1891, and Griffin L. Baldwin to Gould, Nov. 5, 1893, GP.

90. Holsinger, "How It Feels," 316.

91. Carman, 99; David C. Love to Gould, Apr. 29, 1891, GP; David C. Love to Carman, Sept. 22, 1897, AS; William Kidd MSR, NA; *OR* 19, 1:811, 925.

92. "Civil War Diary of August L. P. Varin," RootsWeb, http://www.rootsweb.ancestry.com /-mscivilw/vairindiary.htm; *OR* 19, 1:923, 934, 938; Hood, *Advance and Retreat*, 44; M. Smith, "Reminiscences," 21, ANBL. Also see Hood to Carman, May 27, 1877, AS.

93. *OR* 19, 1:923; Nicholas A. Davis, *The Campaign from Texas to Maryland* (Richmond, VA, 1863), 91–92.

94. N. Davis, *Campaign*, 92.

95. Lafayette McLaws to Hood, May 31, 1863, folder 7, Lafayette McLaws Papers, SHC; McMurray, *John Bell Hood*, 72–73.

Chapter 5. The Death of a General

1. Robert M. Green, *History of the One Hundred Twenty-Fourth Regiment* (Philadelphia: Ware Bros., 1907), 148; Dione Longley and Buck Ziadel, *Heroes for All Time* (Middletown, CT: Wesleyan Univ. Press, 2015), 63.

2. Eicher and Eicher, *High Commands*, 363; Jeremiah Taylor, *Memorial to General J. K. F. Mansfield* (Boston: T. R. Marven, 1862), 66, 67; *OR* 5, 755.

3. Taylor, *Memorial*, 67; A. Williams, *Cannon's Mouth*, 125, 133.

4. *OR* 19, 2:214; Laurence Freiheit, *Major General Joseph King Fenno Mansfield* (Iowa City: Camp Pope, 2019), 565n51; Taylor, *Memorial*, 49–50.

5. *OR* 19, 2:297; Hartwig, *To Antietam Creek*, 137.

6. Henry Stager diary, in Green, *History*, 151, 155; Charles J. Mills, *Through Blood and Fire*, ed. Gregory A. Coco (Gettysburg, PA: Gregory Coco, 1982), 27; Ezra A. Carman diary, NJHS.

7. Earl Hess, *Civil War Infantry Tactics* (Baton Rouge, LA: LSU Press, 2015), 80.

8. *Cleveland Morning Leader*, Oct. 2, 1862. At age 65, Edwin Sumner was the oldest general officer in the Army of the Potomac.

9. Ario Pardee to Pa, Sept. 8, 1862, Pardee-Robison Papers, USAHEC; Alpheus Williams to Ezra Carman, May 16, 1877, Ezra A. Carman Papers, NYPL; A. Williams, *Cannon's Mouth*, 255; Green, *History*, 120.

10. Regimental Committee, *History*, 171, 56; Gould, *Joseph F. K. Mansfield*, 8–9.

11. A. Williams, *Cannon's Mouth*, 123, 125; Jonathan H. Keatley to Gould, Nov. 18, 1892, GP.

12. Gould, *Civil War Journals*, 193; John R. Rankin, "What I Thought at Antietam," Benjamin W. Smith Papers, IHS; W. F. Goodhue, "The Morning of Antietam," in *Proceedings of the 17th Annual Reunion of the 3d Wis. Vet. Association* (n.p., 1907); Miles C. Huyette, *The Maryland Campaign and the Battle of Antietam* (Buffalo, NY: Miles C. Huyette, 1915), 28; Regimental Committee, *History*, 62; Green, *History*, 120.

13. Goodhue, "Morning of Antietam."

14. *Lewiston (ME) Falls Journal*, Oct. 2, 1862; Goodhue, "Morning of Antietam"; A. Williams, *Cannon's Mouth*, 125; Hess, *Infantry Tactics*, 51.

15. John M. Gould memorandum diary, John Mead Gould Papers, Rubenstein Library, DU; Green, *History*, 120–121; Goodhue, "Morning of Antietam."

16. Gould, *Civil War Journals*, 193–194; Gould, *Joseph F. K. Mansfield*, 9; Van R. Willard, *With the 3rd Wisconsin Badgers*, ed. Steven R. Raab (Harrisburg, PA: Stackpole Books, 1999), 89; John M. Gould, *History of the 1st-10th-29th Maine Regiment* (Portland, ME: Stephen Berry, 1871), 233–234.

17. Goodhue, "Morning of Antietam."

18. Rankin, "What I Thought," IHS; Gould, *History*, 234; Huyette, *Maryland Campaign*, 35; E. R. Brown, *The Twenty-Seventh Indiana Volunteer Infantry in the War of the Rebellion, 1861 to 1865* (Monticello, IN, 1899), 239.

19. Rankin, "What I Thought," IHS; Bryant, *History*, 126; Gould, *History*, 235; Gould, *Joseph F. K. Mansfield*, 9.

20. Robbins to Gould, Mar. 25, 1891, GP; Carman, 91–92.

21. Robbins to Gould, Mar. 25, 1891, GP; Carman, 92; J. M. Smither to Gould, Feb. 26, 1891, GP. Robbins remained unaware of the 5th TX's presence until well into his fight in the East Woods and only discovered them when he visited his right flank to see how they were managing. He also never knew the identity of the 21st GA until the 1890s.

22. *OR* 19, 1:922–924, 937–938.

23. *OR* 19, 1:1022, 923.

24. *OR* 19, 1:1032.

25. Samuel D. Thruston, "Historical Sketch of the 3rd NC at Antietam," July 27, 1886, AS.

26. Thomas A. Vitanza, *Samuel Mumma House, Park Building 45, IDLCS No. 08045* (Sharpsburg, MD: Historic Preservation Training Center, National Park Service, U.S. Dept. of the Interior, 1999); Samuel Mumma Jr. to James Clark, Mar. 22, 1906, and James Clark to Sharpsburg postmaster, Mar. 17, 1906, in Francis F. Wilshin, *Historic Structures Report, History Data, Antietam National Battlefield Site, Maryland* (Washington, DC: National Park Service, U.S. Dept. of the Interior, 1969); William DeRosset, "The Third North Carolina at Sharpsburg," AS. DeRosset also claimed that he ordered the burning of the farm in a letter to Samuel Thruston, a captain in the 3rd NC, July 12, 1886, AS. James Clark wrote to Samuel Mumma Jr. that it was Ripley who ordered the destruction. Ripley's report merely stated that some farm buildings in his brigade's front were set on fire to prevent them from being used by the enemy. See *OR* 19, 1:1033.

27. *Valley Register* (Middletown, MD), Sept. 26, 1862; DeRosset, "Third North Carolina," AS; Samuel D. Thruston account of 3rd NC at Sharpsburg, July 27, 1886, AS; *OR* 19, 1:1033.

28. Allen Johnson and Dumas Malone, eds., *Dictionary of American Biography* (New York: Charles

Scribner's Sons, 1946), 25–26, 626; Roswell Ripley to Genl. Gist, Nov. 7, 1860, CSR, RG 109, NA.

29. A. Johnson and Malone, *Dictionary of American Biography*, 25–26, 626; William DeRosset to D. H. Hill, June 18, 1885, D. H. Hill Papers, LV. Also see D. H. Hill to DeRosset, June 22, 1885, and D. H. Hill to Stephen Thruston, June 12, 1886, AS. For Ripley's actions at the Battle of South Mountain, see Hartwig, *To Antietam Creek*, 345–347, 479–480.

30. William DeRosset to D. H. Hill, June 18, 1885, D. H. Hill Papers, LV.

31. *OR*, 19, 1:1033; *OR Suppl.*, pt. 1, 3:586; C. T. Furlow to Gould, Nov. 1, 1893, GP; DeRosset, "Third North Carolina"; William DeRosset to D. H. Hill, June 18, 1885, D. H. Hill Papers, LV.

32. DeRosset, "Third North Carolina," AS; John C. Key [4th GA] to Carman, Sept. 29, 1897, AS; Carman, 119.

33. Carman, 119–120; William DeRosset to D. H. Hill, June 18, 1885, D. H. Hill Papers, LV; William L. DeRosset to Colonel [S. D. Thruston], July 12, 1886, in DeRosset, "Third North Carolina," AS. Robert Smith may have been mortally wounded and not killed outright. There is a document in Smith's CSR stating he was mortally wounded, taken prisoner, and died at David Smith's farm. This was a Confederate field hospital, so it is more likely that he died at Dr. Otho Smith's farm, a Union field hospital. See Robert S. Smith CSR, RG 109, NA.

34. Carman, 107; J. P. George statement, GP. George thought they passed over the colors of the 4th TX. He also wrote that they captured a flag of an Alabama regiment. Since there was no Alabama regiment in this area, it might have been the colors of the 11th MS. See *OR* 51, 1:151; Carman, 108, 120.

35. J. B. R. to *The Countryman*, Sept. 24, 1862, *Countryman* (Eatonton, GA), Oct. 6, 1862, ANBL; *OR* 51, 1:151, 155.

36. J. P. George statement, GP; *OR* 51, 1:154. Lt. Col. Samuel Jackson's report stated that the regiment did not advance beyond the corn and was relieved by a portion of the 12th Corps, but Lt. George made it clear that the regiment did advance south of the corn.

37. *OR* 51, 1:151; Carman, 120; Hamilton A. Brown to Carman, Aug. 27, 1897, AS. Brown stated that the entire 1st NC was moved to the left of the brigade, but Carman stated that it was only part of the regiment. Carman is sustained by 2nd Lt. Thomas D. Boone, who wrote to Carman that his company was beside the 3rd NC throughout the engagement. See Boone to Carman, Sept. 27, 1897, GP; Robert Williams, "'I Longed for Night to Come': The First North Carolina State Troops in the Maryland Campaign," *Company Front* 26, no. 1 (June 2013), 21–23.

38. *OR* 19, 1:191.

39. *OR* 19, 1:475, 484, 487; A. Williams, *Cannon's Mouth*, 125; Gould, *Joseph F. K. Mansfield*, 11; Carman, 115.

40. Carman, 115–116; *OR* 19, 1:484, 486–487; James Forsyth to Gould, Sept. 23, 1892, and C. H. Dyer to Gould, Jan. 28 1891, GP.

41. Williams to General [Carman], May 16, 1877, Carman Papers, NYPL.

42. "Colonel George Lafayette Beal," Antietam on the Web, https://antietam.aotw.org/officers .php?officer_id=211&from=results/ [accessed Dec. 2015]; 1860 Federal Census, NA.

43. Gould, *Joseph F. K. Mansfield*, 11; "The 10th Maine at Antietam," Gould memorandum diary, DU; Gould, *History*, 235–236; Gould, *Civil War Journals*, 194.

44. Gould, *History of the 1st-10th-29th*, 236–237; Gould, *Joseph F. K. Mansfield*, 11; Gould, *Civil War Journals*, 194; 1860 Federal Census, NA.

45. Gould, *History*, 236–237.

46. W. T. Hill to Gould, July 21, 1891, GP; Gould, *History*, 237; Gould, *Joseph F. K. Mansfield*, 13–14; James Fillebrown to wife, Sept. 19, 1862, in *Lewiston (ME) Falls Journal*, Oct. 2, 1862; William Robbins to Gould, Mar. 25, 1891, GP.

47. George L. Beal report, *U.S. Army Generals' Reports of Civil War Service*, vol. 10, 561, RG 94, NA; James Fillebrown to wife, Sept. 19, 1862, *Lewiston (ME) Falls Journal*, Oct. 2, 1862; Gould, *History*, 240; Edwin W. Fowler to Gould, Feb. 22, 1870, Gould Papers, DU.

48. Gould, *History*, 238–239. The combustible paper cartridge was developed in 1855 by Colt Firearms. The cartridge never became common in the army, although Gould indicated that they worked well at Antietam.

49. Carman, 118; *OR* 19 1:487, 489.

50. Frederick Crouse, "An Account of the Battle of Antietam," ANBL.

51. Carolyn J. Mattern, "A Pennsylvania Dutch Yankee: The Civil War Letters of Private David William Mattern," *Pennsylvania Folklife* (Autumn 1986), 7, copy in ANBL. Mattern's name was misspelled as "Maddern" in the published regimental muster roll. Also see Crouse, "An Account," ANBL; *OR* 19, 1:487, 493.

52. To "refuse"—such as in "refuse the line" or "refuse the flank"—is a common military term. It is a maneuver where a unit bends its line back to protect a flank.

53. Gould, *Joseph F. K. Mansfield*, 15–16; Gould memorandum diary on Mansfield's death, Dec. 2, 1862, and "The 10th Maine at Antietam," Gould Papers, DU; Gould, *History*, 240; Gould, *Civil War Journals*, 194–195. Also see Gould to Mansfield's widow, Dec. 1862, part of "Joseph King Fenno Mansfield," in the Battlefront section, Hard & Stirring Times Exhibit, Middlesex County Historical Society, https://mchsctorg.wordpress.com /exhibits-displays/hard-stirring-times-online -exhibit/battlefront/ [accessed Jan. 2017]. Gould's many accounts of Mansfield's death, dating from his wartime journal to his subsequent paper on Mansfield's death, are all highly consistent.

54. Gould, *Civil War Journals*, 195; Gould, *History*, 240–241; Gould, *Joseph F. K. Mansfield*, 15–16; Gould memorandum dairy on Mansfield's death, Dec. 2, 1862, DU.

Chapter 6. The 12th Corps Sweeps the Field

1. Williams to Carman, May 16, 1877, Carman Papers, NYPL; A. Williams, *Cannon's Mouth*, 126; C. D. M. Broomhall to Carman, May 16, 1900, Carman Papers, NYPL; James Forsyth to Gould, Sept. 21, 1897, GP.

2. A. Williams, *Cannon's Mouth*, 126; Williams to Carman, May 16, 1877, Carman Papers, NYPL.

3. Williams to Carman, May 16, 1877, Carman Papers, NYPL; *OR* 19, 1:475; Carman, 124; Alpheus Williams, "The Battle of Antietam," Carman Papers, NYPL.

4. Carman, 120.

5. *OR* 19, 487, 493; Robbins to Gould, Mar. 25, 1891, GP; Crouse, "An Account," ANBL; Henry A. Shenton to Gould, May 2, 1894, GP; Peter Noll, Sept. 17, 1862, letter in *Reading (PA) Daily Times*, Sept. 25, 1862.

6. Gould note, "128 PA," on the regiment's field officers, and Hugh Jameson [1st sgt. in Company K, 28th NY] to Gould, Feb. 5, 1892, GP; John S. Dougherty to Friends, Sept. 21, 1862, ANBL.

7. Surgeon's Certificate, DeRosset CSR, folder 3, p. 41, NA; DeRosset, "Third North Carolina," AS; DeRosset to Thruston, July 12, 1886, AS; DeRosset to D. H. Hill, June 18, 1885, GP. Thruston to DeRosset, July 28, 1886, GP; 1860 Federal Census, NA.

8. Thruston letter to Carman, Sept. 3, 1898, AS; DeRosset, "Third North Carolina," AS. Thruston located the right flank of the 3rd NC after they had changed front to beside (west of) the rock outcropping where the 90th PA monument is located today. Alexander Gardner photographed the site after the battle, showing the area littered with Confederate dead.

9. DeRosset estimated that the 3rd NC suffered three-quarters of their total loss of 354 during the period when they changed front to the rear, which would be approximately 265 men. See DeRosset, "Third North Carolina," AS.

10. *OR* 19, 1:487, 489–490, 493; Robert Andrews to Mother, Sept. 21, 1862, in *Bucks County Intelligencer* (Doylestown, PA), copy in ANBL; Crouse, "An Account," ANBL; Robbins to Gould, Mar. 25, 1891, GP; Mattern, "Pennsylvania Dutch Yankee," 7, copy in ANBL; Frank Holsinger to Gould, Feb. 29, 1893, GP.

11. Carman, 124–125; *OR* 19, 1:494.

12. E. Brown, *Twenty-Seventh Indiana*, 242; Julian W. Hinkley, *A Narrative of Service with the Third Wisconsin Infantry*, Wisconsin History Commission Original Paper No. 7 ([Madison]: Wisconsin History Commission, 1912), 54.

13. *OR* 19, 495; Rankin, "What I Thought," IHS.

14. E. Brown, *Twenty-Seventh Indiana*, 243; Rankin, "What I Thought," IHS.

15. Wilbur D. Jones, *Giants in the Cornfield* (Shippensburg, PA: White Mane Books, 1997), 5.

16. Rankin, "What I Thought," IHS; E. Brown, *Twenty-Seventh Indiana*, 243. Some of Robert Anderson's PA Reserves may have returned to the fight, along with Gordon's regiments, but the bulk of these regiments retired to the North Woods.

17. Rankin, "What I Thought," IHS.

18. Bryant, *History*, 126; Hinkley, *Narrative*, 55.

19. *OR* 19, 498. Lt. Col. Hamilton Brown, commanding the 1st NC, in a letter to Gould, wrote that his regiment was transferred to the left of the brigade during the action, which Carman interpreted as part of the regiment having shifted to the left, since it was known that not all of the 1st NC moved. Brown's letter, however, indicates his faulty memory on other matters, and there is no other evidence that part of the 1st NC was ever shifted to the left of the brigade. Stephen Thruston thought that Brown was "entirely in error as to all his positions on the field." He found Brown and part of the 1st NC behind his right flank when his regiment fell back out of the corn. But it is possible that Brown was correct in stating that his regiment was divided, with one wing supporting Thruston's advance into the corn, and the other

wing maintaining a connection with the rest of the brigade, and that, years later, his memory failed him on specific details. See Carman, 120; Brown to Gould, Aug. 27, 1897, GP; Thruston to Carman, Sept. 3, 1898, AS.

20. Carman, 126; Charlie Mills to Aunt Mary, Oct. 28, 1862, Houghton Library, HU; Rankin, "What I Thought," IHS.

21. Carman, 126; E. Brown, *Twenty-Seventh Indiana*, 246–247; Hinkley, *Narrative*, 55–56.

22. E. Brown, *Twenty-Seventh Indiana*, 247; Thruston to Carman, Sept. 3, 1898, AS.

23. Ben Milikin to Gould, Mar. 1, 1895, GP.

24. Richard H. Clark, *The Memoirs of Judge Richard H. Clark*, ed. Lollie B. Wylie (Atlanta: Franklin, 1898), 339–348; Alfred H. Colquitt CSR, Confederate Generals and Staff Officers, RG 109, NA; "Colonel Alfred Holt Colquitt," Antietam on the Web, https://antietam.aotw.org/officers.php?officer_id=20/ [accessed Mar. 2016].

25. Carman, 128; Ben Milikin to Carman, Sept. 8, 1897, AS; Ben Milikin to Gould, Mar. 1, 1895, GP. The skirmish battalion was composed of one company from each regiment in the brigade. They were armed with rifles and commanded by Capt. William Arnold of the 6th GA. Carman wrote that the battalion joined Robbins's regiments in the East Woods, but a letter from Sidney Lewis to Gould made it clear that the battalion was not in the East Woods, but instead was along a fence line north of Roulette's farm, partially concealed by one of Roulette's cornfields and facing northwest. See Lewis to Gould, June 4, 1892, GP; Carman, 126–127. Carman also wrote that Colquitt's brigade obliqued across the front of Ripley's brigade before they fronted and formed line, but veterans from the brigade, in their correspondence with Gould, made it clear that they formed line almost immediately after crossing Smoketown Road, which had to have been south of, or possibly parallel with, part of Ripley's line. Lt. Col. C. T. Zachry, commanding the

27th GA, wrote that they formed a "junction" with Ripley, then fronted and formed line. See Zachry to Gould, Dec. 14, 1897, GP. Also see George Cain to Gould, Mar. 4, 1893, GP.

26. Stallings to Gould, July 9, 1892, GP. George Cain, 28th GA, wrote that after forming line, they advanced 150–200 yards to a rock ledge, which could only be the rock outcropping, before they were ordered into the Cornfield. See Cain to Gould, Mar. 4, 1893, GP; Thruston to Carman, Sept. 3, 1898, AS; Thruston to Gould, May 11, 1891, GP.

27. Ben Witcher to Gould, May 25 and June 22, 1891, GP.

28. *OR* 19, 1:1054.

29. Wm. Robbins to Gould, June 10, 1891, GP; Madison Robbins and Ireneous A. Marshall CSR, RG 109, NA.

30. S. D. Hale to Gould, Mar. 27, 1891, and Wm. Robbins to Gould, June 14, 1892, GP; *OR* 19, 1:936.

31. George Smith to Gould, Apr. 18, 1894, Hollis Turner to Gould [re. interview with Xavier Martin], Apr. 8, 1891, Edwin Fowler to Gould, Jan. 5, 1891, and Granville Blake to Gould, Mar. 6, 1891, GP. In Gould's interview with Sgt. David Jumper of Company H, Jumper repeated several times, "I saw very few rebs in the woods." See Gould notes with Jumper interview, Apr. 18, 1891, GP.

32. George Nye to Gould, Mar. 15, 1890, GP.

33. George Nye to Gould, Mar. 15, 1890, Jere Dempsey to Gould, Mar. 10, 1893.

34. Charles Harris interview, Nov. 23, 1893, GP; Edwin Fowler to Gould, Feb. 22, 1870, Gould Papers, DU; Henry F. Smith to Gould, Mar. 24, 1870, and Ben Redlon interview, May 14, 1892, GP.

35. For example, see Elias Libby to Gould, Dec. 18, 1890, and Gould to Libby, Dec. 12, 1890, GP.

36. Robert J. Wynstra, *The Rashness of That Hour* (New York: Savas Beatie, 2010), 52–58.

37. Wynstra, *Rashness*; 56; Frederick C. Winkler, *The Letters of Frederick C. Winkler* (Madison:

presented by William Winkler to the State Historical Society of Wisconsin, 1963), 52.

38. Duncan McRae to Gould, Dec. 27, 1870, GP. McRae wrote that, between Ripley, Colquitt, and McRae, the delay in moving toward the front was 15 minutes to a half hour. Also see Carman, 132.

39. *OR* 19, 1:1040, 1043–1044; McRae to Gould, Dec. 27, 1870, and Jan. 21, 1871, Elijah Withers to Gould, Feb. 13 and Aug. 15, 1892, GP.

40. *OR* 19, 1:1040, 1043–1044; McRae to Gould, Dec. 27, 1870, and Jan. 21, 1871, GP; Elijah Withers to Gould, Feb. 13 and Aug. 15, 1892, Veines E. Turner to Gould, Apr. 6, 1892, and J. M. Smither to Gould, Mar. 24, 1891, GP.

41. Carman, 124; Williams to Carman, May 16, 1877, Carman Papers, NYPL.

42. Carman, 134–135; *OR* 19, 1:475–476.

43. E. Brown, *Twenty-Seventh Indiana*, 247; Rankin, "What I Thought," IHS.

44. E. Brown, *Twenty-Seventh Indiana*, 249.

45. Quiner, *Correspondence*, vol. 3, 61; Rankin, "What I Thought," IHS.

46. Rankin, "What I Thought," IHS; Josiah C. Williams to Parents, Sept. 22, 1862, ISL; W. F. Goodhue, "The History of the Colors of the Regiment," The Third Wisconsin Volunteer Infantry, http://3rdwisconsin.com/the-history-of-the-colors/ [accessed Aug. 2015]; Quiner, *Correspondence*, vol. 3, 61–62.

47. E. Brown, *Twenty-Seventh Indiana*, 249; John Bloss to Friends, Sept. 25, 1862, Special Collections & Archives, OSU, copy in ANBL; W. Jones, *Giants*, 12; Quiner, *Correspondence*, vol. 3, 62.

48. W. Jones, *Giants*, 5. This was one of four wounds Bloss received during the war. Also see E. Brown, *Twenty-Seventh Indiana*, 249, 252; *OR* 19, 1:499.

49. Carman, 131; Bryant, *History*, 128; C. D. M. Broomhall to Carman, May 16, 1900, Carman Papers, NYPL; Charlie Mills to Aunt Mary, Oct. 28, 1862, Houghton Library, HU; Andrews to Gould, May 19, 1894, GP.

50. Eugene Powell to Gould, Nov. 18, 1893, GP; Carman, 135.

51. Powell to Gould, Nov. 18, 1892, GP; *OR* 19, 1:509; Carman, 136. Powell wrote of a morning mist, which was surely battle smoke.

52. A. Williams, *Cannon's Mouth*, 127.

53. Powell to Gould, Nov. 18, 1892, GP.

54. Ben Witcher to Gould, June 22, 1891, GP; Ben Witcher to Carman, Sept. 8, 1897, AS; Thomas Marshall to Gould, Feb. 23, 1892, GP.

55. *OR* 19, 1:508.

56. Joseph A. Moore reminiscences, *CWTI* Miscellaneous Collection, USAHEC; "The Battle of Antietam," *Philadelphia Weekly Press*, Apr. 12, 1888.

57. John O. Foering to Gould, June 22, 1891, and William Armor to Gould, May 6, 1891, GP; J. Moore reminiscences, USAHEC; Joseph H. Cornet, "The 28th Penna at Antietam," in *Grand Army Scout and Soldiers' Mail* (Philadelphia), Sept. 22, 1883, copy in USAHEC.

58. William Armor to Gould, May 6, 1891, GP; "Battle of Antietam"; E. B. Withers [13th NC] to Gould, Feb. 13, 1892, Thomas McCormick Walker to Gould, Apr. 18, 1891, Edwin A. Fowler to Gould, Jan. 5, 1891, and George Nye to Gould, Mar. 15, 1890, GP.

59. *OR* 19 1:1043–1044; Duncan McRae to Gould, Dec. 27, 1870, GP. There is a typescript of both this letter and a Jan. 21, 1871, letter from McRae to Gould in AS. Carman probably produced the typescript, but McRae's difficult handwriting caused Carman to make two important word errors. He thought McRae wrote "unutterable," when it is surely "unaccountable," and "a brigade formed," when it is clearly "a brigade famed." E. B. Withers, commanding the 13th NC, and Veines E. Turner in the 23rd NC, both maintained that the break began on the right and that they did not join in the general stampede, but instead were ordered to fall back, since the rest of the brigade was retreating. This may be true, as D. H. Hill specifically mentioned that the 23rd NC maintained its integrity and that he ordered it to take position in the Sunken Lane. Also see Withers to Gould, Feb. 13,

1892, and Veines E. Turner to Gould, Apr. 6, 1892, GP; *OR* 19, 1:1023. The boulders and rocks that McRae mentioned his men took cover behind were evidently removed after the war, for there are very few left in the remnants of the East Woods. The woods where McRae's right and center were located are gone. As of this writing, they are in private hands and under cultivation. Where McRae's left would have been, the National Park Service is currently restoring the woods.

60. J. M. Smither to Gould, Mar. 24, 1891, GP.

61. Gen. Matthew Ridgeway, quoted in Thomas E. Ricks, *The Generals* (New York: Penguin, 2012), 178; Veines E. Turner to Gould, Apr. 6, 1892, GP; *OR* 19, 1:1023.

62. Gould notes on Gilbert P. Robinson interview, Sept. 1891, GP. The 3rd MD had a desertion rate of slightly over 24%, which meant that nearly a quarter of the regiment deserted during the war, an extremely high number. See American Civil War Research Database, http://civilwardata.com/active/index.html [requires a subscription]. Also see Lewis Stegman to Gould, Apr. 4, 1892, and Lyman B. Welton to Stegman, probably Mar. 1892, GP. Lane was wounded at Gettysburg. It was this wound that apparently led to his resignation in 1864.

63. *OR* 19, 1:511–512; G. M. Elliot account of Antietam, GP; Milton Wing [3rd MD] to Gould, June 9, 1892, Aaron P. Bates to Gould, Mar. 18, 1892, Lewis Stegman to Gould, Apr. 1 and Apr. 4, 1892, and Lyman B. Welton to Stegman, 1892, GP. Welton wrote that the 3rd MD were "badly rattled" and sent a "sharp fire" into the 102nd NY. Also see Isaac VanSteenbergh to Gould, Mar. 27, 1892, GP; Lemuel H. Hitchcock to Father, Sept. 21, 1862, in *Windham (NY) Journal*, Oct. 9, 1862.

64. Robbins to Gould, Mar. 25 and June 5, 1891, GP; "5th Texas Infantry," Antietam on the Web, https://antietam.aotw.org/officers.php?unit_id=703/ [accessed Feb 2018]; J. M. Smither to Gould, Feb. 26 and Mar. 24, 1891, GP; *OR* 19, 1:937. In his June 5 letter to Gould,

Robbins wrote that the regiment's losses were much higher than what was reported (7 killed and 37 wounded), because he was sick for nearly a month after the battle and, as a result, the losses were not accurately transmitted.

65. Ben Witcher to Gould, May 25 and June 22, 1891, Thomas Marshall to Gould, Feb. 23, 1892, and Robert G. Johnson Jr. to Gould, May 23, 1891, GP; Carman, 144–145. Carman believed the 6th GA might have suffered as much as 90% casualties, which would be the highest percentage for any regiment in a single battle in the war. There are varying figures for how many men the regiment took into action. Witcher and Marshall both gave the amount as 300, but Carman found veterans who estimated the strength to be as low as 200. He took an average of the figures he received (between 200 and 320) and estimated its strength at 260.

66. Ben Milikin to Gould, Mar. 1, Apr. 27, and May 27, 1895, GP; Ben Milikin to Carman, Dec. 20, 1897, AS; C. T. Zachry to Gould, Dec. 14, 1897, GP; Carman, 145. Carman gave the 27th GA's loss as 30%, which would be 120 men. His figures came from James M. Folsom, *Heroes and Martyrs of Georgia* (Macon, GA: Burke, Boykin, 1864), which reported the casualties as 154 killed or wounded, a 38% loss. Lt. Col. Zachry thought only about 100 of the 400 men carried into action came out of the fight, but Silas Crosby, a sergeant at Antietam, was specific, stating that only 37 men had mustered on Sept. 18. This is a loss of 92%. See Milikin to Gould, May 27, 1895, GP. Many of those missing on the morning of Sept. 18 might have returned later that day or on the 19th. If Zachry's figures are correct, the regiment suffered a 75% loss.

67. James A. Hunt to Gould, July 18, 1892, GP; Carman, 145, 564–565; "Record of Events on Muster Roll Co. D," AS.

68. Ben Witcher to Carman, Sept. 8, 1897, AS; W. W. Holbert to Carman, Sept. 18, 1897, GP;

S. Joseph Lewis Jr., "Letters of William Fisher Plane, C.S.A. to His Wife," *Georgia Historical Quarterly* 48, no. 2 (1964), 225.

69. *OR* 19, 1:845; Carman, 145–146. The two guns were a 12 lb. howitzer and probably a 6 lb. gun from Fleet's battery, which was attached to Woolfolk's battery. See C. Johnson and Anderson, *Artillery Hell*, 91.

70. William H. H. Fithian [28th PA] diary, ANBL; J. Moore reminiscences, USAHEC; *OR* 19, 1:845; Carman, 146; Carman notes and map with W. D. Terrell letter, n.d., and S. D. Lee to Carman, Nov. 1, 1898, AS. Lee believed Woolfolk lost only one howitzer, and Lt. Colonel P. T. Manning's ordnance report also indicated that only one howitzer was lost by Woolfolk, but Manning and Lee probably overlooked the attached 6 lb. gun that had belonged to Fleet's battery. See *OR* 19, 1:844. The abandoned limber belonged to Rhett's battery and can be seen in Alexander Gardner's photograph of Sept. 19.

71. Josiah Lewis, "An Account of Some Incidents of My Life," in possession of Zack Waters; Thomas Walker to Gould, Apr. 18, 1891, and Sidney Lewis to Gould, June 4, 1892, GP.

72. Spencer Viall to Brother, Sept. 24, 1862, in Richard E. Cies, ed., *Too Soon Forgotten* (Ocala, FL: Special Publications, 1994), 75; Rankin, "What I Thought," IHS; E. Brown, *Twenty-Seventh Indiana*, 250; Carman, 162; Bryant, *History*, 128.

73. Charles Morse to Mother, Sept. 21, 1862, Charles Morse Papers, MHS.

74. Robert G. Shaw to Father, Sept. 21, 1862, in Robert Gould Shaw, *Blue-Eyed Child of Fortune*, ed. Russell Duncan (Athens; Univ. of Georgia Press, 1992), 240.

75. George Andrews to Gould, Mar. 5, 1891, GP.

76. Eugene Powell to Gould, Nov. 18, 1893, GP; Eugene Powell to Father, Sept. 18, 1862, in *Urbana (OH) Union*, Oct. 1, 1862.

77. Rankin, "What I Thought," IHS; Carman, 161.

78. James Wheeler [102nd NY] to Gould, Jan. 22, 1892, GP; Monroe, *Battery D*, 19–20; E. K. Parker statement to Gould, Mar. 1894, AS;

S. W. L. [Stephen W. Lockwood] to Messrs. Richardson and Barker, Sept. 30, 1862, in *Lockport (NY) Daily Journal & Courier*, Oct. 6, 1862.

79. Carman, 141; Fithian diary, ANBL; Eugene Powell to Gould, Nov. 18, 1893, GP; Monroe, *Battery D*, 21–22.

80. E. K. Parker statement to Gould, Mar. 1894, and Christopher Carpenter to Carman, Dec. 5, 1899, AS; Monroe, *Battery D*, 23.

81. Carman, 142, 144. Sgt. Crosby's statement about Colquitt's strength on Sept. 17 is in Ben Milikin to Carman, Dec. 20, 1897, AS. Also see DeRosset, "Third North Carolina," AS; R. Williams, "'I Longed for Night,'" 46.

82. *OR* 19, 1:1054.

83. *OR* 19, 1:1037.

84. Williams to GBM, Apr. 18, 1863, Carman papers, NYPL; *OR* 19, 1:30, 56–57.

85. *OR* 19, 1:1022, 1054.

86. *OR* 19, 1:219; Joseph Hooker, "Report of the Battle of Antietam," July 21, 1877, Hooker Papers, HL; E. Brown, *Twenty-Seventh Indiana*, 251; Bryant, *History*, 128; Robert G. Shaw to Father, Sept. 21, 1862, in Shaw, *Blue-Eyed Child*, 241; Charles Morse to Mother, Sept. 21, 1862, Morse Papers, MHS; Williams to GBM, 9 a.m., Sept. 17, 1862, reel 32, MP.

Chapter 7. To the West Woods

1. GBM to Mary Ellen, May 6, 1862, in McClellan, *Civil War Papers*, 257; "Reminiscences of General Sumner," in Frank Moore, *Anecdotes, Poetry and Incidents of the War* (New York, 1866), 189–190.

2. Marion V. Armstrong, *Unfurl Those Colors!* (Tuscaloosa: Univ. of Alabama Press, 2008), 59.

3. Kearney, *Letters*, 86, 146; Wainwright, *Diary of Battle*, 264.

4. *OR* 51, 1:839; Carman, 43–44.

5. Carman, 576.

6. Frederick L. Hitchcock, *War from the Inside* (Philadelphia: J. B. Lippincott, 1904), 56; Blake McKelvey, "The Civil War Letters of Francis Edwin Pierce of the 108th New York Volunteer Infantry," in *Rochester in the Civil War*, ed. Blake McKelvey (Rochester, NY: Rochester Historical Society, 1944), 152.

7. Hitchcock, *War*, 55; Daniel Bond reminiscences, MNHS; Benjamin Hirst, *The Boys from Rockville*, ed. Robert L. Bee (Knoxville: Univ. of Tennessee Press, 1998), 19.

8. Deposition of Peleg F. Murray, Archibald B. Hudson pension file, NA. Hudson proved to be a good soldier. He reenlisted as a veteran volunteer in 1864, was captured at the Battle of Spotsylvania Court House, and endured imprisonment at Andersonville. He survived and lived until 1907. Also see Daniel McAdams, "A Short History of the Service of Daniel McAdams," Houghton Library, HU; S to Friends' Editor, Sept. 27, 1862, in *Nantucket (MA) Weekly Mirror*, Oct. 11, 1862. The writer of this letter probably was Sgt. John W. Summerhayes, who rose to become a captain.

9. Richard F. Miller, *Harvard's Civil War* (Hanover, NH: Univ. Press of New England, 2005), 168; Roland E. Bowen, *From Ball's Bluff to Gettysburg—and Beyond*, ed. Gregory A. Coco (Gettysburg, PA: Thomas, 1994), 133.

10. Samuel S. Sumner, "The Antietam Campaign," in Military Historical Society of Massachusetts, *Civil War and Miscellaneous Papers* (Boston: Military Historical Society of Massachusetts, 1918), 10; Samuel S. Sumner to George B. Davis, Apr. 4, 1897, John C. Ropes Papers, BU; Carman, 171; Rufus R. Dawes to Cox, Apr. 30, 1887, box 8, Jacob Dolson Cox Papers, Oberlin College.

11. S. S. Sumner to George B. Davis, Apr. 4, 1897, J. Ropes Papers, BU; *OR* 19, 1:419, 424, 434.

12. S. S. Sumner to George B. Davis, Apr. 4, 1897, J. Ropes Papers, BU; George F. Noyes, *The Bivouac and the Battlefield* (New York: Harper & Bros., 1864), 196.

13. Noyes, *Bivouac*, 196; Carman, 171.

14. See *OR* 19, 1:122 for the location of the signal station on Hooker's front and at Pry's farm. Also see Edwin Vose Sumner testimony, *CCW*, 37th Congress, pt. 1, 368.

15. Marcy to Sumner, Sept. 17, 1862, Telegrams Received, 1862–1865, *Records of U.S. Army Continental Commands*, entry 45, pt. 2, RG 393, NA.

16. Sumner testimony, *CCW*, 37th Congress, pt. 1, 368; S. S. Sumner to George B. Davis, Apr. 4, 1897, J. Ropes Papers, BU.

17. J. R. Jones and Alexander Lawton, wounded; Douglass and Starke killed; Walker, James Jackson, Penn, Ripley, and McRae wounded.

18. Daniel W. Crofts, "Virginia's Bad Old Man," Opinion Pages, *New York Times*, Apr. 5, 2011, https://opinionator.blogs.nytimes.com/2011/04/05/virginias-bad-old-man/ [accessed April 2011]; D. Freeman, *Lee's Lieutenants*, vol. 2, 86.

19. *OR* 19, 1:968; *OR* 19, 1:244; Carman, 153; R. E. Krick, "Defending Lee's Flank," 203–204. "Alfred Poffenberger's farm" was actually owned by Mary Locher, who rented it to Poffenberger. To avoid a complicated explanation, it will be referred to in the text as "Poffenberger's farm."

20. Casey, "Ordeal," 227. Warner identified this unit as a company from Gibbon's brigade, but only the 23rd NY was detached to watch the flank.

21. Casey, "Ordeal," 228; A. J. Warner to Gould, Oct. 19, 1894, GP; *OR* 19, 1:820, 969. Stuart claimed he displaced to Hauser's Ridge because the enemy had advanced too far into the West Woods toward the Dunker Church, and his guns could not continue to fire "without danger of harming our own men." Perhaps, but there were many targets outside this particular field of fire for Stuart's guns to shoot at. Early's explanation for why they moved is more convincing. Also see R. E. Krick, "Defending Lee's Flank," 204–205.

22. Brockenbrough had 3 rifles and 1 howitzer; Raine, 2 rifles and 2 howitzers; Poague, 2 guns (probably his 10 lb. Parrott rifles); D'Aquin, 1 howitzer; and Pelham, 6 guns, 5 rifles, and 1 Napoleon. Brockenbrough and Raine may not have brought their howitzers into action because of their short range, and it is uncertain at what point D'Aquin's gun arrived.

Hence the variance in the number of guns in action on the ridge. For Pelham's armament, see Stirling Murray to Carman, June 23 and July 25, 1898, AS. In the first letter, Murray wrote that the battery had 2 3-inch rifles, 2 howitzers, a Napoleon, and a Blakely rifle, but in his subsequent letter, he revised this and gave its equipment as 4 3-inch rifles, 1 Napoleon, and 1 Blakely. Carpenter's, Wooding's, and Balthis's batteries, who were with Stuart on Nicodemus Heights, all withdrew to reorganize and resupply with ammunition, and they were not present on Hauser's Ridge.

23. R. E. Krick, "Defending Lee's Flank," 207, 213; W. W. Blackford, *War Years with Jeb Stuart* (New York: Charles Scribner's Sons, 1945), 149–150. Shumaker took medical leave for neuralgia and "intercoastal rheumatism" in 1863 and was probably sick during Sharpsburg. See Lindsay M. Shumaker CSR, NA.

24. *OR* 19, 1:969; Carman, 153; Casey, "Ordeal," 228–229.

25. *OR* 19, 1:969; Carman, 153.

26. Carman, 158; *OR* 19, 1:244.

27. Carman, 155; *OR* 19, 1:244. Carman called this lane the "wood road." It was probably the original roadbed of the old road from Hagerstown to Sharpsburg, which was subsequently supplanted by the Hagerstown Turnpike. For simplicity, I will refer to this as the "Poffenberger farm lane" for Alfred Poffenberger's farm. It served the farm traffic for Hauser, Poffenberger, and Nicodemus. Maryland Route 65 closely follows part of this old roadbed and, unfortunately, cuts right through an important part of the battlefield. See Carman, 195n36.

28. *OR* 19, 1:970. Early reported that Jackson said "he would send for reinforcements." Early wrote his report three months after the battle, and he may not have correctly remembered what Jackson said. Jackson had already sent Sandie Pendleton to Lee to request reinforcements, so it is unlikely that he told Early he would send for reinforcements. Also see R. E. Krick, *Staff Officers*, 306.

29. S. P. Lee, *Memoirs*, 216; James Wylie Ratchford, *Memoirs of a Confederate Staff Officer*, ed. Evelyn Ratchford Sieburg and James E. Hansen II (Shippensburg, PA: White Mane Books, 1998), 27. Ratchford's memoir, written around 1908, suffers from some memory lapses. The major wrote that Hill sent him to Lee when they could see "massive reinforcements" arriving for the enemy, which described the arrival and attack of the 12th Corps. Since it is known that Ratchford accompanied Colonel Walter Taylor to order McLaws's division to the left at 8 a.m., Ratchford must have been sent when Ripley's brigade went into action, or shortly after 7:30 a.m.. See *OR* 19, 1:923. Hood reported that he dispatched numerous messages to Longstreet requesting reinforcements, although he did not indicate when these requests were sent. Joseph Harsh, in *Sounding the Shallows* (Kent, OH: Kent State Univ. Press, 2000), believes that D. H. Hill went to Lee personally around the time of Hood's counterattack to ask that his entire division be sent in. Since Hill's entire division did move or was moving toward the left, this may have happened, but I can find no evidence that Hill ever made this request.

30. *OR* 19, 2:610.

31. Henry L. P. King diary, SHC. Douglas Freeman, in *Lee's Lieutenants*, has been one of the most notorious critics of McLaws and his alleged slowness. For a full examination of McLaws's march to Sharpsburg, see Hartwig, *To Antietam Creek*, 633–636. Also see McLaws to Heth, Dec. 13, 1894, AS. This is a wonderful, detailed letter that highlights the command confusion in the Army of Northern Virginia, with orders coming from both Jackson and Longstreet, even though McLaws was not officially attached to either of their commands.

32. McLaws to Heth, Dec. 13, 1894, AS; *OR* 19, 1:858.

33. Harsh, *Sounding*, 199–200; Armistead L. Long, *Memoirs of Robert E. Lee* (London: Samson, Lowe, Marston, Searle, & Rivington, 1886), 221; *OR* 19, 1:909, 914. In his article for *B&L*, Walker claimed that Lee sent him orders at 4 p.m. on Sept. 16 to move at 3 a.m. on the 17th and take position on the extreme right of the army. Walker's two articles on the Maryland Campaign are so riddled with errors that they are quite unreliable. In his own after-action report, Walker wrote that he moved to the right at daylight, not at 3 a.m. Second, Lee would not have moved Walker from his reserve position until he knew McLaws and R. H. Anderson were up. See John G. Walker, "Sharpsburg," *B&L*, vol. 2, 679–680. For more on Walker's numerous fictions, see Harsh, *Sounding*, 167, 179, 194, 205.

34. *OR* 19, 1:909.

35. McLaws to Heth, Dec. 13, 1894, AS; *OR* 19, 1:858; Ratchford, *Memoirs*, 27.

36. McLaws to Heth, Dec. 13, 1894, AS; Carman, 185. Among those criticizing McLaws was Ratchford, who wrote in his memoir that it was he "who finally" got McLaws's division in motion, and that the division was commanded by a "very slow man." See Ratchford, *Memoirs*, 27. Ratchford had nothing to do with getting McLaws's division moving, however, and despite the extreme fatigue of the division and its commanders, they responded promptly and efficiently to Taylor's orders to march. McLaws marked the route of his division on a map for the ABB, AS.

37. *OR* 19, 1:970.

38. Colonel William B. Goodrich biographical sketch, in John Gilmary Shea, *The American Nation Illustrated in the Lives of Her Fallen Brave and Living Heroes* (New York: Thomas Farrell & Son, 1862), 409–417, copy in ANBL.

39. Carman, 78n159; Patrick, *Inside Lincoln's Army*, 149.

40. John O. C. Redington to Carman, Jan. 4, 1900, Carman Papers, NYPL; Goodrich biographical sketch in Shea, *American Nation*, 415–416, copy in ANBL.

41. Patrick, *Inside Lincoln's Army*, 149.

42. Carman, 157; *Delaware County American* (Media, PA), Sept. 24, 1862, in Green, *History*, 157; C. D. M. Broomhall to Carman, May 16, 1900, Carman Papers, NYPL.

43. David Herring to Carman, July 2, 1900, Carman Papers, NYPL.

44. *Delaware County American* (Media, PA), Sept. 24, 1862, in Green, *History*, 156–157; David S. Wilkinson diary, in Green, *History*, 110–111; William Potts reminiscences, in Green, *History*, 121; C. D. M. Broomhall to Gould, June 29, 1891, GP; Broomhall to Carman, May 16, 1900, Carman Papers, NYPL; Carman, 157.

45. Carman, 157–158.

46. *OR* 19, 1:970; Carman, 157.

47. *OR* 19, 1:970.

48. Carman, 161; Regimental Committee, *History*, 20–21.

49. Thomas McCamont, "From Organization to the Close of the Battle of Antietam," in Regimental Committee, *History*, 68–69; Milton Lytle to Gould, Oct. 27, 1892, GP; *OR* 19, 1:492. During the 125th PA's advance south of the Cornfield, one of their men found a glove belonging to Colonel Strange, 6th LA, which was given to Col. Higgins.

50. Carman, 178; Jacob Higgins, "At Antietam," *NT*, June 3, 1886; *OR* 19, 1:492; Milton S. Lytle, "History of the 125th Regiment Pennsylvania Volunteers," *Monitor* (Huntington, PA), June 19, 1902.

51. Carman, 179; Higgins, "At Antietam"; Lemuel Stetson to Friend, Sept. 27, 1862, in *Albany (NY) Atlas and Argus*, Oct. 2, 1862. Lemuel Stetson was a distinguished member of the New York State Democratic party and the father of Lt. Col. John L. Stetson, 59th NY, who was killed in action.

52. Higgins, "At Antietam."

53. Carman, 179; John Keatly to Gould, Nov. 18, 1892, and Milton Lytle to Gould, Oct. 27, 1892, GP; Lytle, "History"; *OR* 19, 1:492; Higgins, "At Antietam."

54. Numerous accounts gave the depth at Pry's Ford as knee deep. For example, see George Washington Beidelman, *The Civil War Letters of George Washington Beidelman*, ed. Catherine H. Vanderslice (New York: Vantage, 1978), 102; R. Bowen, *From Ball's Bluff*, 124, 133; William McLeon journal, ANBL; *OR* 19, 1:305, 311, 319. Howard gave the distance between brigades as 60–70 paces. Gorman reported that they were 50 yards apart, and Dana wrote that he was directed to keep his line 75 yards behind Gorman. The length of the column is derived from a column of 5,446 men in column of fours, with no intervals, which would extend for about 1,360 yards (3 feet per man), or three-quarters of a mile. There were always intervals between brigades, and sometimes between regiments, so on the road the column would have been nearly a mile long.

55. "A Short History of the Service of Daniel McAdams," Houghton Library, HU; Edward Walker [to unknown], fragment of letter, n.d., Edward Walker Papers, PMNC, copy in 1st MN file, ANBL.

56. Isaac J. Wistar, "The Philadelphia Brigade at Antietam," *Philadelphia Weekly Times*, Feb. 17, 1882; Samuel Chase Hodgman to Father, Nov. 17, 1862, U.S. Civil War Collection, WMU, http://name.umdl.umich.edu/USCW0023 .0001.001/ [accessed Mar. 2018]; *OR* 19, 1:311; "Letter from the Army," unidentified Boston newspaper, n.d., 15th MA file, ANBL. The newspaper correspondent did not identify Studley, but he was the company commander at the time. Also see R. Bowen, *From Ball's Bluff*, 133–134; John Reynolds, "Antietam," *Boston Journal*, n.d.; "A Short History of the Service of Daniel McAdams" Houghton Library, HU.

57. *OR* 19, 1:305; Edward Chapin diary, quoted in Peter B. Olney, "Edward Chapin," in Thomas

Wentworth Higginson, *Harvard Memorial Biographies* (Cambridge, MA: Sever & Francis, 1866), vol. 2, 448–450; *Weekly Pioneer and Democrat* (St. Paul, MN), Oct. 3, 1862; Lt. Robert Park, Company K, 72nd PA, statement in William M. Runkel, "The Philadelphia Brigade, Its Part, Under Sedgwick and Howard, at the Battle of Antietam," *PWP*, Apr. 8, 1882.

58. Sumner testimony, *CCW*, 37th Congress, pt. 1, 368; Joseph Hooker testimony, *CCW*, 37th Congress, pt. 1, 581.

59. Albert V. Colburn to Sumner, Sept. 17, 1862, and Colburn to Hooker, 8:30 a.m., Sept. 17, 1862, Telegrams Received, 1862–1865, *Records of the U.S. Army Continental Commands*, entry 45, pt. 2, RG 393, NA. Sumner's orders have no time signature, but both messages were certainly written at the same time.

60. Sumner testimony, *CCW*, 37th Congress, pt. 1, 368; *OR* 19, 1:476; Carman, 172. In the several wartime and postwar letters Williams wrote about Antietam, he never mentioned meeting with Sumner, so this may have been something he told Carman, since the two men served together and knew one another.

61. For an alternative argument, positing that Sumner conducted a thorough reconnaissance before committing Sedgwick, see Armstrong, *Unfurl*, 172–179. I found no evidence that Sumner conducted anything more than a cursory reconnaissance, or that he made any effort to fully inform himself about the positions of the 1st and 12th Corps. Alpheus Williams thought that this was the case, writing to his daughter after the battle that Sumner sent Sedgwick attacking toward the West Woods "with too much haste, I thought, and too little reconnoitering of the ground and positions held by us." See A. Williams, *Cannon's Mouth*, 128.

62. Sumner testimony, *CCW*, 37th Congress, pt. 1, 368.

63. Hammerstein to Colburn, no time signature, Sept. 17, 1862, reel 32, MP. The mention that "Sumner is moving up" places this message at

around 9 a.m. The 1st Corps' signal station was on Poffenberger Hill. Alpheus Williams's message was probably sent from a station near the East Woods.

64. *OR* 51, 1:842–843.

Chapter 8. Disaster in the West Woods

1. *Weekly Pioneer and Democrat* (St. Paul, MN), Oct. 3, 1862. The writer is not identified, but it was possibly Sgt. A. J. Underwood, Company L, 1st MN Sharpshooters. Also see Edward Chapin diary, quoted in Olney, "Chapin," 448–450; Edward A. Walker to Friend Knight, Oct. 5, 1862, MNHS; Frederick Oesterle, "Incidents Connected with the Civil War Years as Recorded by One of the Veterans" (Pontiac, MI, 1911), typescript, MCHM; R. Bowen, *From Ball's Bluff*, 134.

2. Charles Whittier, "An Egotistical Memoir," typescript, BPL. Sedgwick's direct quote to Sumner, as Whittier remembered it, was "You don't want them up here?"

3. Whittier, "Memoir," BPL.

4. Sedgwick, *Correspondence*, 80–81.

5. Edward Walker [to unknown], fragment of letter, n.d., E. Walker Papers, PMNC, copy in 1st MN file, ANBL; Edmund Robins to Carman, Apr. 5, 1900, Carman Papers, NYPL; Carman, 193.

6. Jasper N. Searles and Matthew F. Taylor, *History of the First Minnesota Volunteer Infantry, 1861–1864* (Stillwater, MN: Easton & Masterman, 1916), 221; Carman, 193.

7. Chapin diary, quoted in Olney, "Chapin"; R. Bowen, *From Ball's Bluff*, 128; Edward Walker [to unknown], fragment of letter, n.d., E. Walker Papers, PMNC, copy in 1st MN file, ANBL.

8. Edward Walker [to unknown], fragment of letter, n.d., E. Walker Papers, PMNC, copy in 1st MN file, ANBL; Carman, 193–194.

9. *OR* 19, 1:313, 317; Carman, 194. Carman gave the range as 25 yards. Also see Chapin diary, quoted in Olney, "Chapin."

10. Chapin diary, quoted in Olney, "Chapin."

11. R. Bowen, *From Ball's Bluff*, 128; "Letter from the Army," n.d., unidentified Boston newspaper, 15th MA file, ANBL.

12. *OR* 19, 1:857, 865, 874; Robert Shand, "Incidents in the Life of a Private Soldier in the War Waged by the United States against the Confederate States, 1861–1865," Robert Shand Papers, SCL; James Nance to Laura, Sept. 24, 1862, SCL; McLaws to Heth, Dec. 13, 1894, ABB Papers, copy in ANBL.

13. *OR* 19, 1:858; McLaws to Henry Heth, Dec. 13, 1894, ABB Papers, copy in ANBL; King diary, SHC.

14. *OR* 19, 1:872; Pierre Beauregard, quoted in Glatthaar, *General Lee's Army*, 352; Mac Wyckoff, *A History of the 2nd South Carolina Infantry* (Fredericksburg, VA: Sergeant Kirkland's Museum & Historical Society, 1994), x.

15. Carman, 185; Lafayette McLaws map, AS. McLaws reported that he formed his division, from right to left, with Cobb's brigade (Sanders), then Kershaw's, Barksdale's, and Semmes's brigades. Based on this order, Kershaw should have followed Cobb's brigade, but his report suggests that he did not. See *OR* 19, 1:858, 868; Wm. J. Stores [32nd VA] to John Daniel, Jan. 29, 1906, John Daniel Papers, UVA; Stores to Carman, Dec. 30, 1899, AS; J. J. McDaniel, *Diary of the Battles, Marches and Incidents of the Seventh S.C. Regiment* (privately printed, 1862), 15.

16. *OR* 19, 1:858, 865, 871, 874; McLaws to Heth, Dec. 13, 1894, ABB Papers, copy in ANBL. In his letter to Heth, McLaws wrote that Jackson ordered him to send a brigade to support Early. Semmes's report, however, written 7 days after the battle, stated that he was ordered to support Stuart. What seems likely is that Jackson advised McLaws about Early's presence but ordered the brigade to support Stuart.

17. *OR* 19, 1:874, 883; Stores to John Daniel, Jan. 29, 1906, Daniel Papers, UVA; Stores to Carman, Dec. 30, 1899, AS; King diary, SHC.

18. McLaws to Heth, Dec. 13, 1894, ABB Papers, copy in ANBL.

19. Carman, 180; *OR* 19, 1:909; W. H. Andrews to Carman, Feb. 6, 1899, AS; W. H. Andrews, "Gen. 'Tige' Anderson's Brigade at Sharpsburg," *Atlanta Journal*, Aug. 24, 1901; Thos. D. Gilham, "Oglethorpe Rifles: A Full History of the Celebrated Company [Company K, 8th GA]," ANBL.

20. *OR* 19, 1:971.

21. Carman, 188; *OR* 19, 1:865; Creswell A. C. Waller to Carman, Dec. 14, 1899, and June 7 and June 13, 1901, AS; Charles Kerrison Jr. to Sister, Sept. 18, 1862, SCL. Kerrison wrote that the Federals were lying down. Also see W. H. Andrews, "Battle of Antietam," AS.

22. Creswell A. C. Waller to Carman, Dec. 14, 1899, and June 7 and June 13, 1901, AS; Shand, "Incidents," SCL.

23. *OR* 19, 1:883; Carman, 200; James Dinkens to Carman, May 26, 1898, AS. Dinkens also authored *1861 to 1865, by an Old Johnnie* (1897; repr., Dayton, OH: Morningside Bookshop, 1975) and "Griffith-Barksdale-Humphrey Mississippi Brigade," *SHSP* 32 (1904), 258–263. His accounts are prone to exaggeration and a poor memory, and Carman ignored his more outlandish statements.

24. C. C. Cummings, "Mississippi Boys at Sharpsburg," in Lamar Rifles, MDAH; Dudley T. Peeble memoir, ANBL; Edward Burress [21st MS] letter, n.d., ANBL; Carman, 200.

25. Carman, 199; *OR* 19, 1:874, 882; William J. Stores to John W. Daniel, Jan. 29, 1906, Daniel Papers, UVA.

26. Carman, 199; *OR* 19, 1:874, 878, 879, 880, 882; William J. Stores to Carman, Oct. 30, 1899, P. H. Loud to Carman, Sept. 2, 1898, and Jno. Parham to Carman, Oct. 5, 1899, AS; John T. Parham, "Thirty-Second Virginia at Sharpsburg," *SHSP* 34 (1906), 252.

27. Carman, 198; *OR* 19, 1:865, 868; W. Andrews, "Battle of Antietam," AS. Also see W. Andrews, "'Tige' Anderson's Brigade at Sharpsburg," *CV* 16 (1908), 579.

28. *OR* 19, 1:320; Whittier, "Memoir," 5, type-script, BPL; Carman, 195.

29. Samuel Hodgman to Father, Nov. 17, 1862, U.S. Civil War Collection, WMU, http://name .umdl.umich.edu/USCW0023.0001.001/ [accessed Mar. 2018]. One of the two men Hodgman identified was Phendlon B. Homan, who was wounded in the thigh. Homan was 41. He was discharged on Apr. 10, 1863, and reenlisted in the 11th MI Cavalry on Sept. 23, 1863.

30. Carman, 197–198; unidentified [7th MI] to Carman, n.d., box 9, folder 2, Oliver Chapman to Carman, Apr. 16, 1905, Carman Papers, NYPL.

31. Huyette, *Maryland Campaign*, 39; *OR* 19, 1:198, 492; Higgins, "At Antietam"; William W. Wallace to J. Simpson Africa, Oct. 5, 1862, in *Globe* (Huntington, PA), Sept. 30, 1862, "Another Hero Gone," *Journal and American* (Huntington, PA), Sept. 24, 1862, and Walter W. Greenland to J. Simpson Africa, Sept. 18, 1862, in *Monitor* (Huntington, PA), Sept. 24, 1862, all in "Letters to Huntington County Newspapers," 125th PA file, ANBL.

32. *OR* 19, 1:316.

33. Unidentified [7th MI] to Carman, n.d., box 9, folder 2, Carman Papers, NYPL. This soldier related that the 7th MI was flanked after the 125th PA retreated. The only regiments who could have flanked them were Barksdale's two right regiments. See Carman, 201; W. Andrews, "'Tige' Anderson's Brigade," 579; David P. Krutz, *Distant Drums* (Utica, NY: North Country Books, 1997), 69; *OR* 19, 1:316; M. O. Young, "History of the First Brigade," Dr. Spencer King Collection, Civil War Miscellaneous Collection, GDAH. Barton survived his wounds and became a policeman in Corey, Pennsylvania, after the war.

34. McLeon journal, ANBL; Krutz, *Distant Drums*, 68; W. Andrews, "'Tige' Anderson's Brigade," 579.

35. McLeon journal, ANBL; *OR* 19 1:192, 862, 888.

36. *OR* 19, 1:193, 320; Carman, 205–206.

37. Oliver W. Holmes to parents, Sept. 17, 1862, in "Battle, Antietam, Notable Personalities," 20th MA file, ANBL; Lt. Henry Ropes to Father, Sept. 20, 1862, BPL; Col. William Tidball to father of Lt. Col. Lemuel Stetson, in *Plattsburgh (NY) Express and Sentinel*, Oct. 11, 1862, ANBL; *OR* 19, 1:313; Carman, 210.

38. Eicher and Eicher, *High Commands*, 305–306.

39. Beidelman, *Civil War Letters*, 102. Col. Joshua T. Owen, commanding the 69th PA, reported that the Confederate battery was located on their extreme left, so it probably was somewhere on Reel Ridge. See *OR* 19, 1:318; Lt. Robert Park statement, in Runkel, "Philadelphia Brigade."

40. *OR* 19, 1:305, 318.

41. Carman, 196; Sylvester Byrne to Carman, Mar. 17, 1905, Carman Papers, NYPL.

42. Carman, 202; Lt. Robert Park statement, in Runkel, "Philadelphia Brigade"; Sylvester Byrne to Carman, May 22, 1905, Carman Papers, NYPL. Byrne was a very reliable eyewitness, as he was part of the burial detail sent to the woods on Sept. 18, visited the field again in 1863, and went back to it several times after the war. Also see Byrne to Carman, Mar. 15 and Mar. 17, 1905, Carman Papers, NYPL.

43. "Narrative of the 7th Mich. on the 17th at Antietam," Carman Papers, NYPL, also in ANBL; Samuel Hodgman to Father, Nov. 17, 1862, and Samuel Hodgman to Brother, Sept. 17, 1861, U.S. Civil War Collection, WMU.

44. Oesterle, "Incidents," MCHM; Frank Spencer to Father, Sept. 19, 1862, in *Livingston (MI) Republican*, Oct. 14, 1862; Eicher and Eicher, *High Commands*, 477; *OR* 19, 1:193, 320.

45. *OR* 19, 1:192, 193, 198, 861, 862, 888. Confederate losses here include the 3rd SC, which received most of its casualties later in the action.

46. Carman, 206; Marion V. Armstrong, *Opposing the Second Corps at Antietam* (Tuscaloosa: Univ. of Alabama Press, 2016), 49–50; *OR* 19, 1:883, 909.

47. *OR* 19, 1:971. Early's report, while highly detailed, is confusing and has some exagger-

ated claims. He stated that before Barksdale, Kershaw, and G. T. Anderson came up, his own brigade drove the enemy—that is, the 125th PA, the 34th NY, and the other regiments—completely out of the woods, which it did not.

48. *OR* 19, 1:313; Carman, 207, 210; Ernest L. Waitt, comp., *History of the Nineteenth Regiment Massachusetts Volunteer Infantry, 1861–1865* (Salem, MA: Salem Press, 1906), 137. Carman has Sumner ordering the 59th NY to cease firing and fall back after Maj. Philbrick pointed out the Rebels flanking the division. Kimball's report made it clear that Sumner did this before they saw Barksdale in their rear.

49. Carman, 208; *OR* 19, 1:306, 318; John E. Reilly [69th PA] to Carman, Mar. 4, 1905, and Joseph R. C. Ward [106th PA] to Carman, Feb. 17, 1905, Carman Papers, NYPL; Oliver O. Howard, "Personal Reminiscences of the War of the Rebellion," *NT*, Apr. 3, 1884.

50. Howard, "Personal Reminiscences"; Howard to Wife, Sept. 26, 1862, Oliver O. Howard Papers, Bowdoin College; Joseph R. C. Ward [106th PA] to Carman, Feb. 17, 1905, Carman Papers, NYPL. Howard also made the incredible statement that had he been in charge of his old brigade—the one he had commanded on the Peninsula—he could have executed the change of front, implying that the Philadelphia Brigade was either not well drilled enough or not sufficiently familiar with Howard to execute the movement. This is nonsense—an example of Howard attempting to deflect criticism to his men, which he also did at Chancellorsville. For Sedgwick's positive opinion of the brigade, see Sedgwick, *Correspondence*, 67, 72.

51. James Peacock to Son, Oct. 27, 1862, 59th NY file, ANBL; David S. Moore, ed., *I Will Try and Send You All the Particulars of the Fight* (Albany: Friends of the New York State Newspaper Project, 1995), 104; "Death of Lt. Colonel Stetson," *Malone (NY) Palladium*, Oct. 16, 1862; *OR* 19, 1:193.

52. R. Bowen, *From Ball's Bluff*, 127, 135; *OR* 19, 1:313; Samuel L. Fletcher, "A Short Account of My Life," 15th MA file, ANBL; Andrew E. Ford, *The Story of the Fifteenth Regiment Massachusetts Volunteer Infantry in the Civil War, 1861–1864* (Clinton, MA: W. J. Coulter, 1898), 200; Lyman H. Ellingwood to Charlie, Sept. 19, 1862, in *Beverly (MA) Citizen*, Sept. 27, 1862; Carman, 213n74.

53. Henry Ropes to Father, Sept. 18 and Sept. 20, 1862, and Ropes to Brother John, Sept. 27, 1862, J. Ropes Papers, BPL; Henry Patten letter, Sept. 27, 1862, quoted in Edward Blake Robins to Carman, Apr. 5, 1900, Carman Papers, NYPL; Miller, *Harvard's Civil War*, 174.

54. Herbert Mason to Father, Sept. 19, 1862, HSP; Henry Patten letter, Sept. 27, 1862, quoted in Edward Blake Robins to Carman, Apr. 5, 1900, Carman Papers, NYPL.

55. Francis W. Palfrey, *The Antietam and Fredericksburg* (1881; repr., Harrisburg, PA: Archive Society, 1992), 87; Ropes to father, Sept. 20, 1862, and Ropes to Brother John, Sept. 27, 1862, J. Ropes Papers, BPL; Henry Patten letter, Sept. 27, 1862, quoted in Edward Blake Robins to Carman, Apr. 5, 1900, Carman Papers, NYPL; Miller, *Harvard's Civil War*, 175; *OR* 19, 1:193.

56. Carman, 211; Austin Carr diary, USAHEC; Patrick I. Kane to Brother, Sept. 21, 1862, in *Brooklyn (NY) Daily Times*, Oct. 1, 1862. Kane was a private in Company F.

57. *OR* 19, 311, 314; Edward Walker [to unknown], fragment of letter, n.d., E. Walker Papers, PMNC, copy in 1st MN file, ANBL; Edward A. Walker to Friend Knight, Oct. 5, 1862, MNHS; *Weekly Pioneer and Democrat* (St. Paul. MN), Oct. 3, 1862; Bond reminiscences, MNHS. Company L was with the 1st MN Sharpshooters, who were attached to the 1st MN Infantry at Antietam.

58. Waitt, *History*, 138; William B. Hoitt to Harry, Sept. 22, 1862, book 36, Lewis Leigh Collection, USAHEC. I found no evidence that the 19th MA fired a few rounds to their front

after the retreat of the 82nd NY, which Carman claimed they did, but they withdrew immediately when it became evident that the division was flanked and stampeding to the north. See Carman, 211.

59. Isaac J. Wistar, *Autobiography of Isaac Jones Wistar, 1827–1905* (Philadelphia: Wistar Institute of Anatomy and Biology, 1937), 407; Wistar, "Philadelphia Brigade."

60. Wistar, *Autobiography*, 407–408; Beidelman, *Civil War Letters*, 102; John M. Steffan to Guss, Sept. 23, 1862, John M. Steffan letters, Civil War Miscellaneous Collection, USAHEC.

61. Joseph R. C. Ward, *History of the One Hundred Sixth Regiment Pennsylvania Volunteers* (Philadelphia: F. McManus Jr., 1906), 105; Joseph R. C. Ward to Carman, Feb. 17, 1905, Carman Papers, NYPL.

62. J. R. Ward, *History*, 105–106; "Extract from the 'History of the 106th' as corrected for republication," Joseph Ward to Carman, n.d., and Ward to Carman, Feb. 15, 1905, Carman Papers, NYPL.

63. *OR* 19, 1:883, 861.

64. *OR* 19, 1:869, 883; Carman, 213; Y. J. Pope to Carman, Mar. 20, 1895, AS; W. G. Peterson to Carman, Jan. 17, 1898, NA. Carman measured the distance where the 3rd SC took cover as 165 yards west of the Hagerstown Pike.

65. Carman, 224–225; *OR* 19, 1:971; C. B. Coiner to Carman, Nov. 27, 1892, and Dec. 5, 1899, AS. Also see C. B. Coiner map, Dec. 1, 1899, and D. W. Anderson map, March 13, 1895, AS.

66. Wm. J. Stores to John Daniel, Jan. 29, 1906, Daniel Papers, UVA; Parham, "Thirty-Second," 252; Stores to Carman, Dec. 30, 1899, AS; "Semmes" [Carman's notes on Semmes's brigade], AS; Carman, 215–216; *OR* 19, 1:874, 878, 882.

67. Carman, 212; R. Bowen, *From Ball's Bluff*, 127; J. R. Ward, *History*, 105; John W. Kimball to Carman, May 26, 1899, and Feb. 17, 1900, AS. Kimball thought they remained there for "thirty or more minutes," which is impossible, as it could only have been a few minutes.

68. Carman, 216; *OR* 19 1:244; Patrick, *Inside Lincoln's Army*, 150; Louis C. Greenleaf to Carman, Dec. 13, 1894, and William F. Rogers, "Movements of the Twenty-First Regiment New York State Volunteers at the Battle of Antietam," AS. Rogers's memory concerning the order of events was clearly confused. See J. Mills, *Chronicles*, 292.

69. Carman, 212, 217; Searles and Taylor, *History*, 213–214.

70. Waitt, *History of the 19th Regiment*, 139–140; Edward A. Walker [to unknown], fragment of letter, n.d., E. Walker Papers, PMNC, copy in 1st MN file, ANBL.

71. Edward A. Moore to Carman, Oct. 12 and Oct. 19, 1899, and Jan. 8, 1900, William Poague to Henry Heth, May 18, 1893, Poague to Carman, Apr. 18, 1895, John T. Block to Carman, May 30, 1899, and Jno. H. O'Conner to Carman, June 14, 1899, AS; Edward A. Moore, *The Story of a Cannoneer Under Stonewall Jackson* (New York: Neale, 1907), 152–154. C. Johnson and Anderson, in *Artillery Hell*, 92, list D'Aquin's ordnance as one 10 lb. Parrott and two 3-inch rifles, but Block's and O'Conner's letters stated that the battery also had one or two howitzers. Also see John Catlett Gibson to Carman, Sept. 16, 1899, AS. Gibson was lieutenant colonel of the 49th VA.

72. Carman, 218–219; Edward A. Walker [to unknown], fragment of letter, n.d., E. Walker Papers, PMNC, copy in 1st MN file, ANBL; *OR* 19, 1:314. Also see William Colvill Jr. to Carman, Dec. 10, 1892, AS.

73. William Colvill Jr. to Carman, Dec. 10, 1892, AS; Carman, 219.

74. Carman, 219; *OR* 19 1:236, 314, 879; Colvill [Jr.] to Carman, Dec. 10, 1892, and James Gardner to Carman, July 31, Oct. 15, and Oct. 18, 1895, AS.

75. Patrick, *Inside Lincoln's Army*, 150; Henry C. Hoffman after-action report, Sept. 20, 1862, AS; Carman, 217, 219–221.

76. *OR* 19, 1:874, 878, 880, 882; Wm. J. Stores to John Daniel, Jan. 29, 1906, Daniel Papers, UVA; Stores to Carman, Dec. 30, 1899, and

Jan. 18, 1900, "Semmes" [Carman's notes on Semmes's brigade], n.d., and Callow Jones to Carman, Oct. 13, 1899, AS; John M. Steffan to Guss, Sept. 23, 1862, Steffan letters, USAHEC.

77. *OR* 19, 1:230; George Breck to the *Union*, Sept. 18, 1862, in *Rochester (NY) Union and Advertiser*, Sept. 27, 1862. Stewart underestimated the distance. From his second position on Reynolds's left, it was 400 yards to the pike.

78. Edward A. Moore to Carman, Oct. 12, 1899, and John T. Block to Carman, May 30, 1899, AS; Breck to the *Union*.

79. *OR* 19, 1:874, 878, 879, 880, 882, 862; Stores to Carman, Dec. 30, 1899, and Jan. 18, 1900, AS; Wm. J. Stores to John Daniel, Jan. 29, 1906, Daniel Papers, UVA.

Chapter 9. Attack and Counterattack

1. Carman, 234; Cresswell A. C. Waller to Carman, Dec. 14, 1899, AS.

2. Carman, 226; *OR* 19, 1:309–310, 869. Carman identified the Purnell Legion, two companies of the 124th PA, and some men of Howard's brigade as the units that engaged Nance. Woodruff, though, made it clear in his report that he had no support at this time. Any friendly infantry was "broken, and was retreating rapidly and in great disorder."

3. Carman, 234–235; Cresswell A. C. Waller to Carman, Dec. 14, 1899, AS.

4. Cresswell A. C. Waller to Carman, Dec. 14, 1899, AS; *OR* 19, 1:862, 865; C. Johnson and Anderson, *Artillery Hell*, 86. The time of Kershaw's advance is found on the Kershaw ABB Tablet, no. 387.

5. R. C. [probably Adjut. John R. Carwile], "In Memoriam: Major William Caspers White, 7th South Carolina Vols.," *Charleston (SC) Mercury*, Dec. 3, 1862; *OR* 19, 1:310, 865. Kershaw's claim that they drove "column after column of enemy" is obviously a reference to what the 2nd SC and other Confederate units had achieved before the 7th SC and 8th SC arrived.

6. Carman, 214, 233; Carman's notes on Battery M, 1st NY Artillery, and Battery E, PA Artillery, Carman Papers, NYPL. Both Cothran's and Knap's batteries mentioned passing the ambulance carrying Hooker, although Knap's men were uncertain whether it was Hooker or Mansfield.

7. *OR* 19, 1: 308, 483, 505, 506, 513; Carman's notes on Battery M, 1st NY Artillery, and Battery E, PA Artillery, Carman Papers, NYPL; Eugene Powell to Gould, Nov. 18, 1893, GP; John Foerning [28th PA] diary, HSP; Fithian diary, ANBL; Gideon Woodring to Gould, Jan. 8, 1892, GP.

8. *OR* 19, 1:506, 862; Shand, "Incidents," SCL; McDaniel, *Diary*, 15; Charles Kerrigan to Sister, Sept. 18, 1862, SCL.

9. Carman's notes and map with J. D. McLucas correspondence, Apr. 27, 1895, and Duncan McIntyre to Carman, Feb. 19, 1895, AS; *OR* 19, 1:862. Carman wrote that the 8th SC not only crossed the Hagerstown Pike, but they advanced beyond the 2nd SC and 7th SC, came to a point overlooking Mumma's cornfield, and fired on Weber's brigade of French's division, causing confusion. This is contrary to what McIntyre wrote to Carman. If the 8th SC had advanced this far, they would have been directly in front of Tompkins's left half battery and the 102nd NY, neither of which mentioned any infantry reaching this point. Carman may have been in error here. See Carman, 247–248, 248n13.

10. *OR* 19, 1:310, 862, 864; Henry W. Addison to Carman, Nov. 3, 1898, AS; R. C., "In Memoriam"; Theodore Reichardt, *Diary of Battery A, First Regiment, Rhode Island Light Artillery* (Providence, RI: N. Bangs Williams, 1865), 65; "Our Army Correspondence," *Charleston (SC) Daily Courier*, Oct. 14, 1862; Gideon Woodring to Gould, Jan. 8, 1892, GP; Fithian diary, ANBL; W. C. Armor to Gould, May 6, 1891, GP. Armor claimed that they captured three flags, one of them, he thought, from the 7th SC. Possibly the other two were guidons, as neither the 2nd SC or 8th SC lost any flags.

John Foerning's diary, HSP, also mentioned Tompkins's cannoneers being driven from their guns. Some of the dead that can be seen in Alexander Gardner's series of Sept. 19 views of the Dunker Church plateau are almost certainly from the 7th SC, which passed directly through this area in their charge.

11. Carman, 233; Y. J. Pope to Carman, Mar. 20, 1895, AS; Shand reminiscences, Shand Papers, SCL; J. to Father, Sept. 22, 1862, in *Charleston (SC) Daily Courier*, Oct. 17, 1862. Based on the content of the letter, "J" is probably Capt. John Stewart Hard, who commanded Company F and was killed at the Battle of Chickamauga.

12. *OR* 19, 1:308, 866–867; Shand reminiscences, Shand Papers, SCL.

13. H. H. Carlton to Carman, May 20, 1893, and Dec. 2, 1899, and McLaws to Heth, Nov. 13, 1894, AS; Carman, 235. I believe both Carman and Carlton were in error as to the timing of Carlton's deployment. It did not occur before Kershaw's brigade came into action but, rather, after that brigade retreated. In his Dec. 2 letter, Carlton thought it was about 10 a.m. when he was in action, which would be about correct. Capt. Tompkins's report also made it clear that he engaged Carlton with two guns after repulsing Kershaw's attack.

14. H. H. Carlton to Carman, May 20, 1893, and Dec. 2, 1899, and McLaws to Heth, Nov. 13, 1894, AS. In recalling his location, Carlton wrote to Carman that at one point during the engagement, he stood on the steps of the Dunker Church to observe his fire.

15. *OR* 19, 1:477, 495.

16. Carman, 230–231; Sebastian Duncan Jr. journal and letterbook, Duncan Papers, NJHS; Rev. E. Livingston Allen, *Both Sides of Army Life* (Poughkeepsie, NY: J. S. Schepmoes, 1885), 2.

17. Duncan journal, NJHS; *OR* 19, 1:501–502; Carman, 231.

18. Charles Morse to Mother, Sept. 21, 1862, Morse Papers, MHS; Shaw, *Blue-Eyed Child*, 245; *OR* 19, 1:500.

19. *OR* 19, 1:914; J. Walker, "Sharpsburg," in *B&L*, vol. 2, 679–680, is not to be relied on.

20. Carman, 228; Robert T. Knox to Carman, Dec. 10, 1899, AS; Samuel H. Walkup journal, SHC; Benjamin Cason Rawlings, *Benjamin Cason Rawlings*, ed. Byrd B. Tribble (Baltimore: Butternut & Blue, 1995), 55. Armstrong, in *Opposing*, 52, believes the division went through Sharpsburg. This was the most direct route to the left, but the evidence we have indicates that the division avoided the village and went around it.

21. *OR* 19, 1:920; Carman, 228–229.

22. *OR* 19, 1:915, 920; Carman, 228–229.

23. Duncan journal, NJHS; Carman, 231.

24. Carman, 231; Duncan journal, NJHS; F to Dear Ones at Home, Sept. 21, 1862, in *Massachusetts Spy* (Boston), Oct. 1, 1862. Based on the content of this letter, John A. Fox is probably the author. Fox identified his company as the one that picked up the flag of the 11th MS. See Fox to Gould, Mar. 11, 1891, GP.

25. *OR* 19, 1:500; Carman, 231–232; F to Dear Ones at Home, Sept. 21, 1862, in *Massachusetts Spy* (Boston), Oct. 1, 1862; Charles F. Morse to Mother, Sept. 21 and Sept. 22, 1862, Morse Papers, MHS; Andrews to Gould, Mar. 5, 1891, GP; Charley Mills to Aunt Mary, Oct. 28, 1862, Houghton Library, HU.; Andrews to Wife, Sept. 23, 1862, Geo. L. Andrews Collection, USAHEC; Shaw, *Blue-Eyed Child*, 241–242, 245.

26. Duncan journal, NJHS, in which he wrote, "The Rebs who were pursuing us were most terribly cut by our batteries and driven again to the woods." Also see Charles F. Morse to Mother, Sept. 22, 1862, Morse Papers, MHS; Shaw, *Blue-Eyed Child*, 241. Dwight died of his wounds on Sept. 19.

27. *OR* 19, 1:915, 918; Knox to Carman, n.d. [probably 1897 or 1898], AS; Rawlings, *Benjamin Cason Rawlings*, 55; Walkup journal, SHC.

28. Knox to Carman, n.d. [probably 1897 or 1898], AS; Walkup journal, SHC; Constantine A. Hege to Father, Aug. 13, 1862, book 11, Lewis

Leigh Collection, USAHEC; Manning's brigade ABB Tablet, no. 388.

29. Knox to Carman, Dec. 10, 1899, Nov. 10, 1897, and undated, AS; Rawlings, *Benjamin Cason Rawlings*, 57; *Free Lance* (Fredericksburg, VA), Sept. 16, 1892; Robert K. Krick, *30th Virginia Infantry* (Berryville, VA: Virginia Book, 1983), 26–27.

30. Knox to Carman, Nov. 10, 1897, and Dec. 10, 1899, AS; R. K. Krick, *30th Virginia*, 26–27; Rawlings, *Benjamin Cason Rawlings*, 59.

31. Walkup journal, SHC.

32. Palfrey, *Antietam*, 89; *OR* 19, 1:192–193. An example of the lack of credit given to McLaws can be found in Robert E. Lee's report, where he credited Walker's division with driving the enemy back "with great slaughter," an event that never happened. Jackson's report did not mention McLaws, other than stating that Semmes's and part of Barksdale's brigades participated in the attack that drove the enemy from the woods. See *OR* 19, 1:149, 956.

33. Francis A. Walker, *History of the Second Army Corps in the Army of the Potomac* (1886, repr., Gaithersburg, MD: Butternut Press, 1985), 117–118.

34. Carman, 308; Thomas M. Walker to Gould, Apr. 18, 1891, GP; *OR* 19, 1:505, 918.

35. *OR* 19, 1:869.

Chapter 10. General French Assaults the Sunken Lane

1. *OR* 19, 1:1037.

2. *OR* 19, 1:1023; Carman, 239; V. E. Turner to Gould, Apr. 6, 1892, GP.

3. *OR* 19, 1:1037.

4. *OR* 19, 1:1037, 1050; Carman, 241–242; E. B. Withers to Gould, Feb. 13 and Aug. 15, 1892, GP. Col. Risden T. Bennett, commanding the 14th NC, wrote that D. H. Hill in person gave the command to Rodes and G. B. Anderson to defend the Sunken Lane. See Bennett to Gould, Dec. 26, 1892, GP.

5. D. H. Hill to George Randolph, June 6, 1862, George B. Anderson CSR, NA; *Mobile Adver-*

tiser and Register, Dec. 14, 1862; G. Ward Hubbs, ed., *Voices from Company D* (Athens: Univ. of Georgia Press, 2003), 27, 34, 90.

6. *Mobile Advertiser and Register*, Dec. 14, 1862; *Selma (AL) Daily Reporter* Oct. 8, 1862.

7. "Gen. George Burgwyn Anderson," *The Land We Love* 3, no. 2 (June 1867), 96–97; E. Alexander, *Fighting*, 154.

8. Carman, 243–244.

9. Bennett to Gould, Dec. 7 and Dec. 26, 1892, GP; *OR* 19, 1:1051.

10. *OR* 19, 1:1030; Carter to Carman, Apr. 30, 1896, AS; Carman, 241. Patterson's battery had six guns, but Carman stated that only three guns were present at this location. See John W. Tullis to Carman, Apr. 3, 1896, and Mar. 19 and Apr. 6, 1900, AS. Capt. Robert Hardaway was sick during the Maryland Campaign, and Tullis commanded the battery. Tullis's map of his battery's position, AS, places his guns south of Mumma's farm and about opposite to the middle of Mumma's cornfield. Carman wrote that Patterson was "a few yards" in the rear of Mumma's corn. See Carman, 147, 275–276; *OR* 19, 1:943–944; C. T. Scaife to Carman, Aug. 6, 1901, Carman Papers, NYPL; William M. English to Gould, Sept. 27, 1897, GP. English is the source for the statement that four guns were dismounted in the exchange with Tompkins's battery, which English referred to as "Benjamin's battery," writing that "the men who served them were made out of steel."

11. *OR* 19, 1:1030; Thomas Henry Carter, *A Gunner in Lee's Army*, ed. Graham T. Dozier (Chapel Hill: Univ. of North Carolina Press, 2014), 142; Carman, 482; *OR* 19, 1:1030; Carter to Carman, Apr. 30, 1896, AS. In this letter, Carter wrote, "Just where I found Genl. Lee before crossing the Hagerstown road I cannot now recall. It was a hill and he on foot; it may have been near the town."

12. Robert K. Krick, "It Appeared as Though Mutual Extermination Would Put a Stop to the Awful Carnage: Confederates in Sharpsburg's Bloody Lane," in Gallagher, *Antietam*

Campaign; "In Memoriam," *Selma (AL) Daily Reporter*, Dec. 18, 1862; John B. Gordon, *Reminiscences of the Civil War* (New York: Charles Scribner's Sons, 1904), 84. Curiously, the "In Memoriam" article about Lt. Perry made no mention of Lee's presence, and no one else besides Gordon mentioned seeing the Confederate army's commander.

13. "Recollections of Sgt. Maj. Newsome Edward Jenkins," SANC, copy in ANBL; John C. Gorman, "Memoirs of a Rebel: Part I, South Mountain and Sharpsburg," ed. George Gorman, *Military Images* 3, no. 3 (Nov.–Dec. 1981), 4–6. It is not known if Rodes deployed skirmishers.

14. *OR* 19, 1:1037; Gorman, "Memoirs."

15. Theodore Lyman, *With Grant and Meade from the Wilderness to Appomattox* (Lincoln: Univ. of Nebraska Press, 1994), 10; Robertson, *Stonewall Jackson*, 100–109.

16. Jack C. Mason, *Until Antietam* (Carbondale: Southern Illinois Univ. Press, 2009), 168. Richardson was hoping to be assigned to a division of Michigan troops, and he wanted French to take command of the 1st Division in the 2nd Corps.

17. Armstrong, *Unfurl*, 64–65; Nathan Kimball file, ANBL; Thomas Loundsdale, "The Story of Antietam as Told to My Son," 14th IN file, ANBL; Charles H. Merrick to Myra, Sept. 24, 1862, WRHS. West Virginia was not yet a state, and the 7th [West] VA was officially the 7th VA at this point of the war. To avoid confusion for the reader, it will be referred to as the "7th [West] Virginia," which it became in 1863.

18. Dwight Loomis and Joseph Gilbert Calhoun, eds., *The Judicial and Civil History of Connecticut* (Boston: Boston History 1895), 320; George H. Washburn, *A Complete Military History and Record of the 108th N.Y. Volunteers from 1862 to 1864* (Rochester, NY: E. R. Andrews, 1894), 203–204; Charles D. Page, *History of the Fourteenth Regiment Connecticut Volunteer Infantry* (Meridan, CT: Horton, 1906), 14–15; Henry Perkins Goddard, *The Good Fight That Didn't End*, ed. Calvin Goddard Zon (Columbia: Univ. of South Carolina Press, 2008), 43; Armstrong, *Unfurl*, 80–81.

19. Washburn, *Complete Military History*, 106. The extract from Capt. Andrew H. Boyd's diary (he was commanding Company H) indicated that they only had two definite days of drilling.

20. Armstrong, *Unfurl*, 150–151; "20th Infantry Regiment," New York State Military Museum and Veterans Research Center, http://dmna.ny.gov/historic/reghist/civil/infantry/20thInf/20thInfMain.htm [accessed Oct. 2017].

21. William P. Seville, *History of the First Regiment Delaware Volunteers* (Wilmington: Historical Society of Delaware, 1884), 29, 45; Michael D. Doubler, *Closing with the Enemy* (Lawrence: Univ. Press of Kansas, 1994), 292–293. Although Doubler wrote about World War II GIs, his comments about training and soldiers in combat are just as applicable to 1862 as they were in 1944.

22. Hitchcock, *War*, 55; Edward W. Spangler, *My Little War Experience* (York, PA: privately printed, 1904), 22.

23. Carman, 245; "The Eighth Ohio at Antietam," *Sandusky (OH) Daily Register*, Nov. 10, 1862; Armstrong, *Unfurl*, 207.

24. Chaplain H. S. Stevens, *Souvenir of the Excursion to Battlefields by the Society of the Fourteenth Connecticut Regiment and Reunion at Antietam, September 1891* (Washington, DC: Gibson Bros., 1893), 49; Hirst, *Boys from Rockville*, 22; Washburn, *Complete Military History*, 24; George R. Graham, "The Fifth Maryland at Antietam," AS. Graham claimed that this incident took place after the 3rd Division reached the East Woods, but it undoubtedly occurred before the division crossed Antietam Creek. Graham also claimed that the adjutant's messenger found their ordnance wagon near Boonsboro. It would be impossible for an individual to ride to someplace around Boonsboro, collect roughly 30,000–40,000 rounds

of cartridges, and return in the time that Graham states. Also, a single horse and rider could not carry this many cartridges. There was no reason for Graham to invent this story, but it is unlikely that it unfolded as he remembered it 30 years later.

25. Hirst, *Boys from Rockville*, 22; Hitchcock, *War*, 56–57.

26. Hitchcock, *War*, 66; John P. Smith scrapbook, 132nd PA file, ANBL; Oakford to Frances [wife], Sept. 6, 1862, Oakford to Frank, Sept. 12, 1862, and Oakford to Mother, Sept. 12, 1862, PSA. Oakford had three children, ages 13, 10, and 3. His mother lived with Oakford's family. See 1860 Federal Census, NA.

27. Thomas Francis Galwey, "At the Battle of Antietam with the Eighth Ohio Infantry," in MOLLUS, *Personal Recollections of the War of the Rebellion* (1891; repr., Wilmington, NC: Broadfoot, 1992), 72–73; Thomas Francis Galwey, *The Valiant Hours*, ed. W. S. Nye (Harrisburg, PA: Stackpole Books, 1961), 40–42. Curiously, although Galwey devotes considerable space to Shepherd's story in his reminiscences, Galwey did not identify him by name in his MOLLUS paper and gave different circumstances for his death later that morning.

28. Carman, 246; Galwey, "At the Battle," 73; H. Stevens, *Souvenir*, 49; Hirst, *Boys from Rockville*, 22–23; Spangler, *My Little War Experience*, 33; William F. Smith to Mother, Oct. 3, 1862, box 35, Lewis Leigh Collection, USAHEC.

29. Carman, 246. The only Confederates that French could have seen were part of Rodes's brigade. See Daniel Woodall, "A Memory of the Battle of Antietam," Sept. 18, 1873, ANBL; *OR* 19, 1:323. I found no evidence that French received any other orders from Sumner until his attack on the Sunken Lane was fully underway. The language in his report, that he formed "adjacent to and contiguous with Sedgwick's" division, while not technically correct—since Greene's division was between French's and Sedgwick's—was accurate in that in lieu of any new orders from Sumner,

Greene was on Sedgwick's line. Therefore, forming beside Greene followed the spirit of his orders.

30. Seville, *History*, 48; Carman, 246–247, 249.

31. G. Graham, "5th Maryland," AS; Carman, 247.

32. *Roulette House Historic Structure Report*, U.S. National Park Service Report No. PMIS No. 49366 (Mar. 2006), 36, 48, copy in ANBL; Carol Reardon and Tom Vossler, *A Field Guide to Antietam* (Chapel Hill: Univ. of North Carolina Press, 2016), 162–163.

33. G. Graham, "5th Maryland," AS; "Major Leopold Blumenberg," Antietam on the Web, http://antietam.aotw.org/officers.php?officer_id=371&from=results/ [accessed Oct. 2017]; Page, *History*, 36.

34. G. Graham, "Fifth Maryland," AS; Carman, 247; Woodall, "Memory," ANBL.

35. "Recollections of Sgt. Maj. Jenkins," SANC, copy in ANBL.

36. Gorman, "Memoirs"; "Tew at Sharpsburg," *Hillsboro (NC) Recorder*, June 14, 1888. Gorman was probably the author of this article. For the Tom Taylor letter, see Dr. Harlan Eugene Cross Jr., *Letters Home* (Fairfax, VA: History4All, 2008), 74.

37. J. Gordon, *Reminiscences*, 84.

38. Carman, 247; James K. P. Racine [his name was spelled "Rosine" on his Military Service Record], *Recollections of a Veteran* (Elkton, MD: Appeal, 1894), 31; G. Graham, "5th Maryland," AS. Carman wrote that during Kershaw's assault on Greene's position, the 8th SC struck the right flank of the 1st DE and created confusion before the South Carolinians were driven back. Not a single Delaware account of the battle mentioned a flank attack, and we must assume that Carman was in error.

39. John Carey, n.d., post-battle letter, General Correspondence No. 623, Civil War Correspondence and Personal Papers, DPA; Woodall "Memory"; Carman, 247–248. Nearly every account of the 1st DE mentioned a second line of Confederates posted above the Sunken

Lane, in the corn. For other examples besides Woodall, see Seville, *History*, 48; William F. Smith to Mother, Oct. 3, 1862, box 35, Lewis Leigh Collection, USAHEC.

40. "Tew at Sharpsburg"; J. Gordon, *Reminiscences*, 87; Soldier, *Montgomery (AL) Weekly Advertiser*, Nov. 19, 1862; Carman, 248; Racine, *Recollections*, 31–32; G. Graham, "5th Maryland," AS.

41. Albert F. Kennelly to Father, Sept. 24 and Sept. 29, 1862, *Sunday Mercury* (New York City), Oct. 5, 1862; Colonel F. M. Parker, "Thirtieth Regiment," in Walter Clark, *NC Regts*, vol. 2, 499–500; Carman, 249.

42. Colonel E. A. Osborne, "Fourth Regiment," in W. Clark, *NC Regts*, vol. 1, 247; G. Graham, "5th Maryland," AS. Graham wrote that the color bearer was wounded in the head during this back-and-forth movement. He recovered but never rejoined the regiment. The point where the colors advanced to is about where the 5th MD monument stands today.

43. *OR* 19, 1:871–872. The brigade's strength was given as 357, but this did not include officers. After the action at Crampton's Gap, 43 officers were left. Sgt. Oliver Hardy, the future father of Oliver Hardy Jr., part of the comic duo of Laurel and Hardy, was a sergeant in Cobb's 16th GA and was wounded.

44. William F. Smith to Mother, Oct. 3, 1862, box 35, Lewis Leigh Collection, USAHEC; Woodall, "Memory," ANBL; Woodall to Mrs. R. W. Jones, Oct. 2, 1862, Woodall folder, DHS; Seville, *History*, 48; "Correct Account of the Part Taken by the First Delaware in the Battle of Antietam," *Smyrna (DE) Times*, Oct. 2, 1862.

45. "Army Correspondence," *Brockport (NY) Republican*, Oct. 2, 1862; Stevens, *Souvenir*, 49.

46. John S. Hays to Carman, Oct. 29, 1894, ANBL; John D. Hemminger diary, Michael Winey Collection, USAHEC; Spangler, *My Little War Experience*, 33.

47. Hemminger diary, USAHEC; Morris R. Darrohn, "Recollections of My Army Life,"

108th NY file, ANBL; Hirst, *Boys from Rockville*, 20; *Waterbury (CT) American*, Oct. 17, 1862.

48. Page, *History*, 36–38; Samuel H. Davis to father, Sept. 20, 1862, in *New London (CT) Chronicle*, Oct. 2, 1862; Hirst, *Boys from Rockville*, 20; Samuel Wheelock Fiske, *Mr. Dunn Browne's Experiences in the Army*, ed. Stephen W. Sears (New York: Fordham Univ. Press, 1998), 8–9. H. Stevens, in his *Souvenir*, 49, also mentioned how difficult it was to see the enemy.

49. *OR* 19, 1:335–336; Carman, 250; Hemminger diary, USAHEC; Spangler, *My Little War Experience*, 30–31.

50. Washburn, *Complete Military History*, 26, 31, 155.

51. McKelvey, "Civil War Letters," 153; Washburn, *Complete Military History*, 25, 193.

52. Washburn, *Complete Military History*, 225, 270, 330.

53. Washburn, *Complete Military History*, 31, 155, 226; George Goff to Brother, Sept. 17, 1862, in *Rochester (NY) Evening Express*, Sept. 25, 1862.

54. Washburn, *Complete Military History*, 226, 330; Jno. Bloss to Mrs. W. W. Bloss, Sept. 21, 1862, in *Rochester (NY) Evening Express*, Sept. 23, 1862.

55. Samuel H. Davis to father, Sept. 20, 1862, in *New London (CT) Chronicle*, Oct. 2, 1862.

56. *Rochester (NY) Union and Advertiser*, Sept. 27, 1862; H. Stevens, *Souvenir*, 54, 61.

57. *OR* 19, 1:1037; Carman's notes on Rodes's brigade, Wright's brigade folder, ANBL. A. Fuller, a private in Company B of the 12th AL, wrote in a letter published in the *Southwestern Baptist* (Marion, AL), on Oct. 26, 1862, that "our right wing did not sustain us, and we fell back." The 12th AL only had about 140 men, so it is unlikely that he meant the right wing of his regiment, but, rather, the right wing of the brigade.

58. *OR* 19, 1:872, 1037; Carman, 250. It seems evident in Rodes's report that he was somewhat incredulous about Longstreet ordering the attack, given the reduced strength of Rodes's brigade.

59. For a brief biography of Simons, see the description of his papers in "James Simons Personal Papers, 1875–1919," South Carolina Historical Society, http://schistory.org/wp-content/uploads/2015/06/Simons-James_-personal-papers-478.18.pdf [accessed Oct. 2017)]; James Simons Jr. diary, AS; Simons [Jr.] to Dear Sirs [probably Carman and the Antietam BB], May 25, 1896, and Simons [Jr.] to Carman, Dec. 23, 1899, AS.

60. Simons diary, AS; Simons [Jr.] to Dear Sirs [probably Carman and the Antietam BB], May 25, 1896, and Simons [Jr.] to Carman, Dec. 23, 1899, AS. The trees Simons mentioned can be seen in the Alexander Gardner photograph that shows the dead of either the 6th AL or the 2nd NC.

61. Carman, 275–276; *OR* 19, 1:943–944; C. T. Scaife to Carman, Aug. 6, 1901, Carman Papers, NYPL; William M. English to Gould, Sept. 27, 1897, GP. Boyce did not mention any stand by the battery south of the Sunken Lane, but Scaife made it clear that they were there. On his 10:30 a.m. map, Carman indicated that they withdrew from this position at 10 a.m., but see note 64.

62. *OR* 19, 1:849; Carman's notes on the 3rd Company, Washington (LA) Artillery, AS; George McNeil to Andrew Hero Jr., May 8, 1896, AS. McNeil was a 1st sergeant and Hero was a 1st lieutenant at Sharpsburg.

63. *OR* 19, 1:849; Carman's notes on the 3rd Company, Washington (LA) Artillery, AS. The guns Miller passed were probably some of the damaged pieces Boyce sent to the rear.

64. Simons diary; Simons [Jr.] to Dear Sirs [probably Carman and the Antietam BB], May 25, 1896, and Simons [Jr.] to Carman, Dec. 23, 1899, AS. It is possible that Boyce withdrew during Kimball's assault. Members of the 14th IN mention a battery firing canister at them, and Boyce's was the most likely unit to have had the range and field of fire to do this. See John C. Hahn and Fritz Kassler CSRs, NA.

65. Gorman, "Memoirs"; Benjamin B. Ross reminiscences, USAHEC.

66. Carman, 251–252; S. Sumner, "Antietam Campaign," 11–12; *OR* 19, 1:324. French's report is a curiosity and is not particularly accurate.

67. Loundsdale, "Story of Antietam," ANBL; Thos. McEbright to Friend Estill, Sept. 24, 1862, in *Holmes County (OH) Farmer*, Oct. 9, 1862; Galwey, "At the Battle," 75; A. H. N., "The Eighth Ohio at Antietam," *Sandusky (OH) Daily Register*, Nov. 10, 1862; Charles H. Merrick to Myra, Sept. 24, 1862, WRHS. Merrick also mentioned the 8th OH fixing bayonets to drive back the retreating men of Weber's and Morris's brigades. Capt. William Houghton, 14th IN, also wrote about the frightened men from Weber's and Morris's brigades, although he specifically identified them as Marylanders: "They ordered the cowards back with threats called them cowards and asked them if they were not ashamed to see the stars & stripes moving from the Rebel flag finding some to cowardly to shame." See Houghton to Mother, Sept. 21, 1862, IHS.

68. Galwey, *Valiant Hours*, 40; A. H. N., "Eighth Ohio"; Loundsdale, "Story of Antietam," ANBL. Truckey's wound required the amputation of his leg, and he was discharged from the army in March 1863.

69. Galwey, "At the Battle," 75; Hitchcock, *War*, 59; *OR* 19, 1:331; G. W. W. to Friend Handy, Sept. 19, 1862, in *Mauch Chunk (PA) Gazette*, Oct. 2, 1862.

70. Francis Galwey diary, LC; A. H. N., "Eighth Ohio"; William Houghton to Mother, Sept. 21, 1862, IHS.

71. B. F. Ogle to Mr. A. V. Ogle, Sept. 18, 1862, in *Tiffin (OH) Tribune*, Oct. 10, 1862; Houghton note, in Nancy N. Baxter, *The Gallant Fourteenth* (Traverse City, MI: Pioneer Study Center, 1980), 99; Augustus VanDyke to Angie, Sept. 21, 1862, box 1, folder 4, IHS. George S. Smith and Creighton Thompson both survived their wounds. Smith was promoted to captain and resigned in Aug. 1863.

Thompson resigned on Feb. 10, 1863. The two men whose horrible deaths Augustus Van-Dyke referred to in his letter were Privates Raleigh Kelso and John J. Landeman.

72. Carman, 253–254.

73. Hitchcock, *War*, 60–61. Hitchcock did not name Palmer, but it is clear that this is who it was. Some parts of Hitchcock's account are incorrect. He mentioned a major, who could only have been with the 108th NY, who was conspicuous for attempting to rally the regiment and was decapitated by an artillery round. Maj. George Force, 108th NY, died early on in the action of that regiment, and no other major of any regiment in this locale was killed. There seems to be no reason for Hitchcock to invent the story, but his memory may have been confused as to when and where it occurred. Although Hitchcock implies that the 108th NY was not doing its duty, the letters of Capt. Francis Pierce in the 108th NY make it clear that part of this regiment remained in the fight until relieved by Caldwell's brigade of Richardson's division.

74. McKelvey, "Civil War Letters," 156.

75. McKelvey, "Civil War Letters," 154.

76. William F. Smith to Mother, Oct. 3, 1862, box 35, Lewis Leigh Collection, USAHEC; Seville, *History*, 48. Capt. Daniel Woodall also mentioned the group that assembled in the Mumma farm lane. See Woodall, "Memory," ANBL; H. Stevens, *Souvenir*, 54. There is disagreement in the 1st DE accounts of where Rickards was killed. Some had it occurring during the effort to retrieve the colors of the regiment earlier in the action. Lt. Smith's account is more contemporary than these, and I have accepted his location of Rickards's death.

77. Galwey, *Valiant Hours*, 41.

Chapter 11. The Sunken Lane Falls

1. C to *Daily Constitutionalist* (Augusta, GA), Oct. 18, 1862, ANBL.

2. C to *Daily Constitutionalist*, Oct. 18, 1862, ANBL; Col. R. F. Floyd to Governor John Milton, Sept. 22, 1862, Governor's Office letterbooks, ser. 32, vol. 6, 462, in possession of Zack Waters; Marshall B. Hurst, *History of the 14th Alabama Regiment* (Richmond, VA, 1863), 11, ADAH; Westwood A. Todd Papers, SHC; Carman, 257.

3. James J. Kirkpatrick diary, THC; J. W. Lindsey and C. H. Andrews "Third Georgia Regiment: History of Its Campaigns from 26 April 1861 to 9 April 1865," Charles H. Andrews Papers, SHC.

4. William B. Hesseltine, "The Potter-Pryor Duel," *Wisconsin Magazine of History* 27, no. 4 (June 1944), 449–452, https://archive.org/details/jstor-4630191/page/n3/mode/2up/ [accessed Jan. 2018].

5. Eicher and Eicher, *High Commands*, 441; Glatthaar, *General Lee's Army*, 192; Hartwig, *To Antietam Creek*, 93; R. E. Krick, "Defending Lee's Flank," 239; Roger Pryor, CSR of Confederate Generals and Staff Officers, NA. Pryor eventually resigned his commission and reenlisted as a private.

6. Officers of the 16th Mississippi to Pres. Jefferson Davis, Nov. 29, 1862, CSR of Confederate Generals and Staff Officers, NA.

7. Carman, 257; C. Johnson and Anderson, *Artillery Hell*, 87–88.

8. Carman, 257; Frank Huger to Carman, Dec. 23, 1893, AS; Galwey, *Valiant Hours*, 43. Galwey thought the Confederate battery was near the Dunker Church. This was probably Maurin's battery, which was on the far left of Grimes's battalion. Thomas Loundsdale, in "Story of Antietam," ANBL, also mentioned receiving fire from a Confederate battery to their right.

9. Carman, 257; John H. Thompson to Carman, Apr. 9, 1896, R. D. Parker Papers, CPL; John S. Saunders to Henry Heth, June 8 and Nov. 21, 1893, AS.

10. C to *Daily Constitutionalist*, Oct. 18, 1862, ANBL; Lindsey and Andrews, "Third Georgia Regiment," Andrews Papers, SHC; Robert H.

Little memoirs, 44th AL file, ANBL; Hurst, *History*, 11; James J. Kirkpatrick diary, THC; Alexander C. Chisholm to Gould, Sept. 24, 1892, GP.

11. Robert K. Krick, "It Appeared," 239; Col. William Gibson after-action report, Wright's brigade folder, ANBL. Gibson wrote that R. H. Anderson was wounded "long before reaching our advanced position." See *OR* 19, 1:1023.

12. Hilary A. Herbert, "History of the Eighth Alabama Volunteer Regiment, C.S.A.," ed. Maurice S. Fortin, *Alabama Historical Quarterly* 39, nos. 1–4 (1977), 78; Colonel F. M. Parker, "Thirtieth Regiment," in W. Clark, *NC Regts*, vol. 2, 499–500. John F. Bagarly, Company G, 4th NC—whose name was also spelled "Bagalry," "Bagely," and "Baggarly"—served as a courier for much of the war. See John F. Bagarly CSR, NA; Rev. A. D. Betts, *Experience of a Confederate Chaplain, 1861–1864* (n.d.), Gregory Coco Collection, GNMP. Although Carman's detailed order of battle listed Bennett as the next in command after Tew, Parker was the next in seniority to Bennett. Also see Fred Philips to Henry Heth, Aug. 25, 1894, GP. Philips confirmed that Tew "rose up" and was wounded when Philips delivered his message to him. In addition, see Parker to R. D. Parker, Nov. 30, 1899, R. Parker Papers, CPL. In this letter, Parker related that he was shot as soon as he rose up to go to the left, which differs from his account in his history of the regiment in *NC Regts*.

13. Ezra A. Carman, summary of Pryor's brigade's operations, Wright's brigade folder, ANBL; Carman, 259, 269. Carman's summary and his manuscript contradict one another. In the summary, he wrote that Hately deployed where they halted, but his manuscript made it clear that they did not deploy until the brigade advanced, minutes later. The Piper barn today is a restoration and resembles its appearance in 1917. The original barn was smaller.

14. Carman, 260; Reuben Nisbit to Gen. A. R. Wright's son, n.d., Wright's brigade folder, ANBL; Gibson after-action report, Wright's brigade folder, ANBL.

15. R. Little memoirs, ANBL; C to *Daily Constitutionalist*, Oct. 18, 1862, ANBL; Reuben Nisbit to Gen. A. R. Wright's son, n.d., Wright's brigade folder, ANBL; Lindsey and Andrews, "Third Georgia Regiment," Andrews Papers, SHC.

16. W. B. Judkins, "Colonel R. H. Jones War History," in possession of Zack Waters; C to *Daily Constitutionalist*, Oct. 18, 1862, ANBL. The latter is the source stating that Jones was wounded very soon after Wright. Also see R. K. Krick, "It Appeared," 243.

17. Carman, 261–262; Gibson after-action report, Wright's brigade folder, ANBL; C to *Daily Constitutionalist*, Oct. 18, 1862, ANBL; James Shinn journal, Edwin A. Osborne Papers, SHC.

18. R. Little memoirs, ANBL; *OR* 19, 1:327; Commodore P. Mears to Friend Amsey, Sept. 25, 1862, HSP; William H. Osborne, *History of the Twenty-Ninth Regiment of Massachusetts Volunteer Infantry, in the Late War of the Rebellion* (Boston: A. J. Wright, 1877), 184; Charles A. Fuller, *Personal Recollections of the War of 1861* (1906; repr., Hamilton, NY: Edmonston, 1990), 58; Lindsey and Andrews, "Third Georgia Regiment," Andrews Papers, SHC. Sgt. Little was concussed by a shell burst but managed to crawl back to Piper's farm.

19. C to *Daily Constitutionalist*, Oct. 18, 1862, ANBL; Gibson after-action report, Wright's brigade folder, ANBL; Lindsey and Andrews, "Third Georgia Regimen," Andrews Papers, SHC.

20. *OR* 19, 1:1037; Carman, 269–270. Rodes was diplomatic in his report, giving credit to Pryor for immediately ordering his brigade forward. Ballentine added details to Carman that Rodes left out, which reflect poorly on Pryor. See John B. Hughes [11th AL] to Parker, Feb. 25, 1900, R. Parker Papers, CPL; Lindsey and Andrews, "Third Georgia Regiment," Andrews Papers, SHC.

21. *OR* 19, 1:1037; Carman, 259, 270; James J. Kirk-patrick diary, THC; John B. Hughes to Parker, Feb. 25, 1900, R. Parker Papers, CPL. Carman wrote that Cumming's and Posey's brigades both initially formed on a ridge running south from Piper's house, but there is no evidence that supports this. Kirkpatrick [16th MS] and Hughes [11th AL] both indicate that they initially halted near the Piper barn before moving up through the orchard to the front.

22. Carman, 270; David Lang to Carman, July 14, 1896, 8th FL folder, Florida Archives, ANBL; *Florida Sentinel* (Tallahassee), Oct. 7, 1862; Hurst, *History*, 11. It appears that the only regimental commander who was unscathed was Maj. James A. Broome [14th AL], but there is a question about whether he was present. His service records do not provide evidence one way or the other. Marshall Hurst did not mention Broome and wrote that Capt. G. W. Taylor in Company K took command of the regiment when Wood assumed command of the brigade.

23. R. Evans, *Sixteenth Mississippi*, 117; J. J. Wilson to father, Sept. 20, 1862, Jefferson J. Wilson Papers, MDAH; Ross reminiscences, USAHEC. Also see Carman, 259, 259n33 [Clemens note].

24. J. J. Wilson to father, Sept. 20, 1862, J. J. Wilson Papers, MDAH; *OR* 19, 1:884; Galwey, *Valiant Hours*, 41; Loundsdale, "Story of Antietam," ANBL. Edward Spangler [130th PA] described how a dozen or so Confederates came out of the lane and attempted to advance along the Roulette farm lane to get on his regiment's flank. "All these brave men were killed," he wrote. This might have been part of the advance beyond the lane by Posey's brigade. See Edward W. Spangler, *My Little War Experience*, 35.

25. Carman, 281; H. Herbert, "History," 78; Zachariah Abney to R. D. Parker, Dec. 8, 1899, R. Parker Papers, CPL. The *Richmond (VA) Whig*, Sept. 24, 1862, contains details of Williams's wound and Wilson's death. Also see Bailey George McClelen, *I Saw the Elephant*, ed. Nor-man E. Rourke (Shippensburg, PA: Burd Street, 1995), 30.

26. H. Herbert, "History," 78.

27. Galwey, *Valiant Hours*, 42.

28. Gus to Angie, Sept. 21, 1862, Augustus Mortimer Van Dyke Papers, IHS; Galwey, *Valiant Hours*, 42.

29. Carman, 255.

30. Galwey, "At the Battle," 77; Loundsdale, "Story of Antietam," ANBL.

31. Loundsdale, "Story of Antietam," ANBL.

32. Galwey, *Valiant Hours*, 41–42. Jack Shepherd's real name was Victor Aarons. He was a Jewish sailor who had lived a colorful life before the war.

33. Loundsdale, "Story of Antietam," ANBL; Commodore P. Mears to Friend Amsey, Sept. 25th, 1862, HSP. A soldier in the 108th NY saw what might have been this same soldier and found 17 bullet wounds in his body afterward. See "Army Correspondence," *Brockport (NY) Republican*, Oct. 2, 1862.

34. Loundsdale, "Story of Antietam," ANBL; Galwey, *Valiant Hours*, 43; Hemminger diary, USAHEC; Oliver H. Palmer to Wife, Sept. 19, 1862, Civil War Miscellaneous Collection, USAHEC; "Army Correspondence," *Brockport (NY) Republican*, Oct. 2, 1862.

35. Sphinx to *Brockport Republican*, Sept. 21, 1862, in *Brockport (NY) Republican*, Oct. 2, 1862; Loundsdale, "Story of Antietam," ANBL; Galwey, *Valiant Hours*, 43; Oliver H. Palmer to Wife, Sept. 19, 1862, Civil Was Miscellaneous Collection, USAHEC. "Sphinx" appears to have been an officer in Company H. No regiment in R. H. Anderson's or D. H. Hill's divisions during the fighting in the Sunken Lane lost their colonel and lieutenant colonel and had their major captured. Palmer's letter, however, confirms much of what Sphinx related in his Sept. 21 letter.

36. "Recollections of Sgt. Maj. Jenkins," SANC, copy in ANBL; "From Our Army," *Raleigh (NC) Standard*, Oct. 1, 1862. The author of this newspaper article is John Gorman. Passages

of it are, word for word, the same as Gorman's postwar reminiscences, published as John C. Gorman, "Memoirs," 4–6. Also see Ross reminiscences, USAHEC.

37. Loundsdale, "Story of Antietam," ANBL; A. H. N., "Eighth Ohio"; Hitchcock, *War*, 62.

38. J. Mason, *Until Antietam*, 5, 8–9, 74–77.

39. J. Mason, *Until Antietam*, 79–80.

40. J. Mason, *Until Antietam*, 85–109.

41. J. Mason, *Until Antietam*, 125–126.

42. J. Mason, *Until Antietam*, 164–166.

43. J. Mason, *Until Antietam*, 167–169.

44. C. Fuller, *Personal Recollections*, 57; William F. Fox, ed., *New York at Gettysburg*, vol. 2 (Albany, NY: J. B. Lyon, 1902), 512; W. Osborne, *History*, 184–185; Edward Ephraim Cross, *Stand Firm and Fire Low*, ed. Walter Holden, William E. Ross, and Elizabeth Slomba (Hanover, NH: Univ. Press of New England, 2003), 45.

45. W. Osborne, *History*, 184; Fox, *New York*, 512; E. Cross, *Stand Firm*, 47.

46. The official reports of GBM, French, and Hancock (who wrote the report for the 1st Division) offer no evidence of any orders to Richardson or request for his support. That Sumner was unaware of where both French and Richardson were is evident from his 10:15 a.m. signal message to GBM: "I am hunting French's and Richardson's divisions, and cannot find them. If you know where they are, send them to me." See entry 13, Signal Corps Messages Sent and Received, Jan. [18]62–May [18]63, RG 111, NA.

47. Carman, 263–264; *OR* 19, 1:277, 293; *Irish American Weekly* (New York City), Oct. 18, 1862; Henry H. Robbins letter, Sept. 21, 1862, in *Old Colony Memorial* (Plymouth, MA), Oct. 4, 1862, ANBL. Robbins wrote that they deployed "within 500 yards of the fighting." Carman stated that they deployed in the cornfield, but Meagher's report made it clear that they deployed on the edge of the corn.

48. *OR* 19, 1:277.

49. Susannah Ural Bruce, *The Harp and the Eagle* (New York: New York Univ. Press, 2006), 102.

50. Frank A. Boyle, *A Party of Mad Fellows* (Dayton, OH: Morningside Bookshop, 1996), 166–167; Timothy Egan, *The Immortal Irishman* (New York: Houghton Mifflin, 2016), 220.

51. F. Boyle, *Party*, 111–112. Meagher had tried unsuccessfully to have an Irish regiment transferred to the brigade.

52. *Irish American Weekly* (New York City), Oct. 18, 1862; Maj. Richard C. Bentley to Father, Sept. 18, 1862, *Albany (NY) Times and Courier*, Sept. 30, 1862; *OR* 19, 1:294; Fox, *New York*, 512. The clump of trees and bushes was probably around one of the limestone outcroppings, approximately 200 yards north of where the observation tower stands today.

53. *OR* 19, 1:294.

54. *Pittston (PA) Gazette*, Oct. 2, 1862; Hitchcock, *War*, 63; Carman, 267.

55. Maj. Charles Chipman to wife Lissie, Sept. 25, 1862, in Joseph G. Bilby and Stephan D. O'Neill, eds., *"My Sons Were Faithful and They Fought"* (Hightstown, NJ: Longstreet House, 1997), 60; Richard C. Bentley to Father, Sept. 18, 1862, in *Albany (NY) Times and Courier*, Sept. 30, 1862; Capt. Michael O'Sullivan letter, in *Albany (NY) Morning Express*, Sept. 26, 1862; Sgt. Maj. William Quirk letter, n.d., in *Irish American Weekly* (New York City), Oct. 25, 1862; "63rd Infantry Regiment," New York State Military Museum and Veterans Research Center, https://dmna.ny.gov /historic/reghist/civil/infantry/63rdInf /63rdInfCWN.htm. Both Bentley and Quirk wrote that the initial volley destroyed the entire right wing of the 63rd NY. Also see *OR* 19, 1:295; John Dougherty to Mother, Sept. 4, 1862, Case Files of Approved Pension Applications of Widows and Other Veterans of the Army and Navy, RG 15, NA. Dougherty's name was also spelled "Doherty."

56. Cpl. John Dillon to Dear Sir, Mar. 27, 1895, Civil War Miscellaneous Collection, USAHEC; "Color Sergeant William Daly, 63rd Regiment, N. Y. S. V." and "Letter from Capt. Michael O'Sullivan, of the 63d

Regiment—An Interesting Account of the Battles in Maryland—On the Battle-Field, Sharp's Farm, Maryland—Sunday, Sept. 21," 63rd New York Infantry Regiment's Civil War Newspaper Clippings, New York State Military Museum and Veterans Research Center, https://museum.dmna.ny.gov/unit-history/infantry-1/63rd-infantry-regiment/newspaper-clippings/ [accessed Mar. 2018].

57. F. Boyle, *Party*, 131; Maj. Charles Chipman to wife Lissie, Sept. 25, 1862, in Bilby and O'Neill, "*My Sons*," 60. The armament of Meagher's regiments can be found in "Army of the Potomac Armament," Antietam Brigades Blog, https://antietambrigades.blogspot.com/p/army-of-potomac-armament.html [accessed July 2022].

58. Fox, *New York*, 512; Robert McLernon, "Casualty List, the 88th New York Volunteer Infantry, Meagher's Irish Brigade, Antietam, Maryland, September 17, 1862," New York State Military Museum and Veterans Research Center, https://museum.dmna.ny.gov/application/files/4415/5240/5169/88thInf_Casualty_Antietam_McLernon.pdf [accessed Mar. 2018].

59. *Plattsburgh (NY) Republican*, Oct. 18, 1862; Carman, 267.

60. Carman, 269.

61. *OR* 19, 1:295–296; Carman, 267–268.

62. *OR* 19, 1:298; Carman, 268; "Antietam—the Dead of the Brigade," 63rd New York Infantry Regiment's Civil War Newspaper Clippings, New York State Military Museum and Veterans Research Center, https://museum.dmna.ny.gov/index.php/?cID=2361/ [accessed Mar. 2018].

63. *OR* 19, 1:298; Carman, 268–269. Kelly made no mention of his wound in his after-action report. See *Irish American Weekly* (New York City), Oct. 18, 1862; Bilby and O'Neill, "*My Sons*," 41.

64. Sgt. Maj. William Quirk letter, n.d., in *Irish American Weekly* (New York City), Oct. 25, 1862; Hitchcock, *War*, 63–64; Cross, *Stand Firm*, 51; C. Fuller, *Personal Recollections*, 58; Thomas

Hamill to My Dear Kane, Sept. 30, 1862, *Brooklyn (NY) Daily Times*, Oct. 4, 1862.

65. *OR* 19, 1:285, 289; Carman, 279.

66. Eicher and Eicher, *High Commands*, 159; George Barr to Vinnie, Dec. 23, 1862, Schoff Civil War Collection, Clements Library, UM.

67. *OR* 19, 1:289; Ephraim E. Brown diary, in possession of Patricia A. Murphy; Maria Lydig Daly, *Diary of a Union Lady, 1861–1865*, ed. Harold E. Hammond (New York: Funk & Wagnalls, 1962), 228.

68. Brown diary, in possession of Patricia A. Murphy.

69. C. Fuller, *Personal Recollections*, 59. There is considerable confusion over precisely where Caldwell's brigade went in, but Barlow's report made it clear. He came up on the left of the 63rd NY, and, therefore, in the rear of the 88th NY. Further evidence of his position is in a letter he wrote to the ABB in 1893, in which he mentioned that he thought the first troops he engaged with were Georgians. This was Wright's brigade. See *OR* 19, 1: 289; Francis Barlow to ABB, May 20, 1893, 61st NY file, ABB Papers, ANBL; Brown diary and Ephraim Brown to Parents, Sept. 18, 1862, in possession of Patricia A. Murphy.

70. *OR* 19, 1:289; Brown diary and Ephraim Brown to Uncle, Oct. 1, 1862, in possession of Patricia A. Murphy. Barlow's report did not include the maneuver related in the chapter text, but Brown was quite specific in describing it. Barlow did mention it, however, in his letter to the ABB (cited in note 69), as did Charles Fuller. See C. Fuller, *Personal Recollections*, 59. This explanation of Barlow's movements differs from Carman's, but we have sources that were not available to him. There is a question of where Barlow's regiments outflanked the Confederates in the Sunken Lane: either near where the 132nd PA monument is now or by the current the observation tower. It is impossible to say with certainty, but these regiments were probably closer to the tower than the monument.

71. Gibson after-action report, Wright's brigade folder, ANBL; C to *Daily Constitutionalist*, Oct. 18, 1862, ANBL; Joshua S. Pittenger to wife, Oct. 23, 1862, J. S. Pittenger letters, American Heritage Center Collection, UW.

72. McClelen, *I Saw*, 30; William L. Fagan to R. D. Parker, Dec. 25, 1899, R. Parker Papers, CPL; J. J. Wilson to John N. Wilson [brother], Oct. 2, 1862, in R. Evans, *Sixteenth Mississippi*, 119.

73. Ross reminiscences, USAHEC; *OR* 19 1:1048; Shinn journal, SHC; *OR* 19, 1:1051.

74. Brown diary, in possession of Patricia A. Murphy; C. Fuller, *Personal Recollections*, 59. For details on Greig, see "Medal of Honor Citation, Lieutenant Theodore W. Greig," Antietam on the Web, https://antietam.aotw.org /officers.php?officer_id=991/ [accessed May 2018]. Greig received a Medal of Honor in 1887 for the capture of this flag, which was mistakenly identified as that of the 4th AL.

75. "The 6th Alabama Regiment," *Montgomery (AL) Weekly Advertiser*, Nov. 19, 1862; "Our Army Correspondence," *Mobile Advertiser and Register*, Oct. 8, 1862; J. Gordon, *Reminiscences*, 90; H. Cross, *Letters Home*, 74.

76. *OR* 19, 1:1038.

77. H. Cross, *Letters Home*, 74.

78. *OR* 19, 1:1048; Risden Bennett to Gould, Dec. 2, 1892, GP; Gorman, "Memoirs."

79. Ephraim Brown to Uncle Emory Morris, Oct. 1, 1862, in possession of Patricia A. Murphy; C. Fuller, *Personal Recollections*, 59; Greg Mast, *State Troops and Volunteers*, vol. 1 (Raleigh: North Carolina Dept. of Cultural Resources, 1995), 359. After the Civil War, Tew's sword eventually made its way into Canada. It was returned to the Citadel in 2015. For more details about Tew's death and the tragic rumors that he had survived the war, which prolonged the suffering of his family, see R. K. Krick, "It Appeared," 238–239.

80. Ephraim Brown to Uncle Emory Morris, Oct. 1, 1862, in possession of Patricia A. Murphy; C. Fuller, *Personal Recollections*, 59; Charles A. Hale, "The Story of My Personal Experience at the Battle of Antietam," *CWTI* Miscellaneous Collection, USAHEC.

81. *OR* 19, 1:288, 285; E. Cross, *Stand Firm*, 48; Thomas L. Livermore, "Thomas Livermore Puts On His War Paint," in Commager, *Blue and the Gray*, vol. 1, 225.

82. T. Livermore, "Thomas Livermore," 219; E. Cross, *Stand Firm*, 47–48, 51; George Barr to Vinnie, Dec. 23, 1862, Schoff Civil War Collection, Clements Library, UM. Cross charged Caldwell with cowardice, and the general requested a court of inquiry. Surgeon George Barr's testimony was particularly damning, but because Barr was a surgeon, not an infantry officer, and did not know or understand tactics, Caldwell avoided being dismissed from the service. Whatever happened to him at the Battle of Antietam did not repeat itself. Caldwell performed extremely well at Gettysburg. In the reorganization of the army in 1864, however, Hancock removed Caldwell from division command, believing he did not have the leadership ability for this post.

83. *OR* 19, 1:290; Carman, 288. Carman wrote that this quote was from F. Walker, *History*, but he must have read a draft of the history, as the quote does not appear in the published edition, possibly because it was so harsh against Caldwell.

Chapter 12. The Confederate Center Imperiled

1. *OR* 19, 1:1024, 943; H. Herbert, *History*, 79; Elias Davis letter, Aug. 3, 1864, Elias Davis Papers, SHC.

2. Carman, 284–287; *OR* 19, 1:872, 910, 915, 920; Longstreet, *Manassas*, 249–250. While Longstreet's memoir is superior to his after-action report, both reflect poorly on his memory of the sequence of events and have limited value in understanding Longstreet's decisions. Carman implied that D. H. Hill ordered Cobb's brigade to advance before Cooke's two regiments charged, but MacRae's report for

Cobb's brigade made it quite clear that the brigade made only one attack at this time, which was in support of the charge by Cooke's regiments.

3. Thomas, *Bold Dragoon*, 95.

4. Sloan, *Reminiscences*, 44; Joseph C. Webb, "An Old Army Letter," 27th North Carolina file, ANBL.

5. Carman, 311; Sloan, *Reminiscences*, 44; J. Webb, "Old Army Letter," ANBL. It was common for soldiers to imagine they did much greater damage than, in fact, had occurred. For example, Capt. Webb wrote that when they fired, half of the Federal artillerymen and all their horses fell.

6. Carman, 284–286, 318–319.

7. *OR* 19, 1:325–326; Carman, 304–318.

8. Carman, 286–287; H. Stevens, *Souvenir*, 55–57.

9. *OR* 19, 1:872; Carman, 285–286.

10. J. Graham, "Twenty-Seventh," 435; *OR* 19, 1:284.

11. Carman, 319; J. Graham, "Twenty-Seventh," vol. 2, 435; Joseph C. Webb letter, Oct. 9, 1862, *Hillsborough (NC) Recorder*, Oct. 29, 1862; J. Moore reminiscences, USAHEC. Capt. Webb wrote that the 27th NC's flag had 27 bullet holes in it and the staff had been struck four times, but Campbell was untouched. Webb added, "Col. Cooke was so well pleased by Campbell's performance, that he called him up after the battle, and told him that he might go when and where he pleased, just so he was always about to carry the flag and lead the 27th into battle." Campbell did so until he was killed at the Battle of Bristoe Station in 1863. See William H. Campbell CSR, RG 109, NA.

12. J. Graham, "Twenty-Seventh," vol. 2, 435.

13. Galwey, "At the Battle," 83; Galwey, *Valiant Hours*, 56–57.

14. *OR* 19, 1:299; 304; Wilson to Parents, Sept. 21, 1862, in possession of Margurite Finney, copy in 53rd PA file, ANBL. The author is probably Commissary Sgt. J. Wilson Barnett, 53rd PA. Also see Carman, 286–287; Hyde, *Following*, 95. Hyde said nothing about advancing to the northern fence of Mumma's cornfield, but he

did mention the movement against Cooke, stating that his regiment lost 12 men in the action.

15. *OR* 19, 1: 290; Joshua S. Pittenger to wife, Oct. 23, 1862, Pittenger letters, UW; C. Fuller, *Personal Recollections*, 60; Frank Higbe to R. D. Parker, Aug. 9, 1899, R. Parker Papers, CPL.

16. J. Graham, "Twenty-Seventh," vol. 2, 435–436; Joseph C. Webb letter, Oct. 9, 1862, in *Hillsborough (NC) Recorder*, Oct. 29, 1862; C. Fuller, *Personal Recollections*, 60. The plowed field was south of Roulette's orchard and east of Mumma's cornfield.

17. Benjamin Hyatt to Parents, Sept. 30, 1862, 3rd AR file, ANBL; Carman, 286–287; Joseph C. Webb letter, Oct 9, 1862, in *Hillsborough (NC) Recorder*, Oct. 29, 1862; "Orange Guards." There is no listed author, but it is clearly Lt. James Graham. Also see Longstreet, *Manassas*, 250.

18. *OR* 19, 862, 872; Carman, 287.

19. Hale, "Story," USAHEC; T. Livermore, "Thomas Livermore," 227; H. Herbert, "History," 79.

20. Hale, "Story," USAHEC; E. Cross, *Stand Firm*, 49; T. Livermore, "Thomas Livermore," 227; H. Herbert, "History," 79.

21. Hale, "Story," USAHEC.

22. E. Cross, *Stand Firm*, 49; Cross to Henry Kent, Sept. 20, 1862, in E. Cross, *Stand Firm*, 121. Cross identified the regiments of Cumming's brigade and the 4th NC as the units mounting the flank attack. Also see Cross to Rev. E. R. Wilkins, Nov. 10, 1862, in E. Cross, *Stand Firm*, 129.

23. T. Livermore, "Thomas Livermore," 221; Hale, "Story," USAHEC.

24. T. Livermore, "Thomas Livermore," 221–222.

25. *OR* 19, 1:292; James H. Mitchell to Father, Sept. 28, 1862, James H. Mitchell Collection, USAHEC.

26. Carman wrote that only the 57th and 66th NY participated in this advance into Piper's cornfield, but post-battle accounts from the 2nd DE make it clear that they also participated. See unidentified soldier to *Delaware Inquirer*, Sept. 20, 1862, in *Delaware*

Inquirer (Georgetown), Oct. 1, 1862; Cross to Henry Kent, Sept. 20, 1862, in E. Cross, *Stand Firm*, 121; James H. Mitchell to Father, Sept. 28, 1862, James H. Mitchell Collection, USA-HEC. Although Maj. Alford B. Chapman's after-action report stated that the 57th NY captured the colors of the 12th AL, Col. Samuel Zook's report to the adjutant general of New York for the year 1862 identified the colors as those of the 11th AL. For Zook's report, see "Report of the Operations—57th New York Infantry Regiment," New York State Military Museum and Veterans Research Center, https://museum.dmna.ny.gov/index.php/?cID=2298/ [accessed May 2018]; Josiah M. Favill, *The Diary of a Young Officer Serving with the Armies of the United States During the War of the Rebellion* (Chicago: R. R. Donnelly & Sons, 1909), 186. Favill's account contains some exaggerations, and his statement about the bayoneting of men who did not surrender quickly enough may be one. Also see John B. Hughes, Company G to Parker, Feb. 25, 1900, R. Parker Papers, CPL.

27. H. Herbert, "History," 79; Alexander C. Chisholm to Gould, Sept. 24, 1892, GP. Robison's name was also spelled "Robinson" and "Robeson" in his service records. Herbert wrote that Pvt. W. G. McCloskie in Company G took the flag after Robison, but no one by that name served in the regiment. The closest possibility is Mathias J. McCosker in Company G, who was captured at Gettysburg, escaped from Fort Delaware Prison, deserted, and was not heard of again. See Robison and McCosker CSR, RG 109, NA. Herbert implied that the Company G private carried the colors throughout the rest of the battle, but the capture of the 8th AL's flag was documented by Cpl. James Mitchell, 81st PA. See note 26.

28. *OR* 19, 1:850, 943–944, 1024. D. H. Hill reported that Boyce's battery "with grape and canister drove the Yankees back," but Longstreet wrote that Boyce's guns withdrew to avoid being cut off by the Union's advance.

Boyce's report made no mention of this part of the action, which indicates that he was not there for long and may not have contributed as materially as Hill claimed. Also see Carman, 294; Napier Bartlett, *A Soldier's Story of the War* (New Orleans: Clark & Hofeline, 1874), 138–139; James Longstreet, "The Invasion of Maryland," *B&L*, vol. 2, 669; Longstreet, *Manassas*, 251.

29. Carman, 291–293; Westwood Todd reminiscences, Todd Papers, SHC; *OR* 19, 1:850, 910; Longstreet, *Manassas*, 250.

30. *OR* 19, 1:302–303; Cross to Rev. E. R. Wilkins, Nov. 10, 1862, in E. Cross, *Stand Firm*, 129; *Delaware State Journal and Statesman* (Wilmington), Sept. 26, 1862; "History of the 57th Regiment," 57th New York Infantry Regiment's Civil War Newspaper Clippings, New York State Military Museum and Veterans Research Center, https://museum.dmna.ny.gov/index.php/?cID=2296/ [accessed Jan. 2018]; Francis Barlow to Antietam Board, May 20, 1893, ABB Papers, 61st NY file, ANBL. Barlow wrote that the projectile that struck him was about the size of an English walnut. He did not know if it was a canister ball or a piece of case shot (shrapnel ball), and "even after all these years he could not tell the difference anyway."

31. *OR* 19, 1:1024, 1038; Carman, 290, 293–294. Since there is no evidence that Miller's guns in Piper's orchard withdrew until the action ended, the elements of the 57th and 66th NY who reached the Piper farm lane must have advanced across the meadow east of the orchard. Also see Walter Battle to Mother, Sept. 28, 1862, "Civil War Letters," WCPL.

32. Carman, 290, 294.

33. Carman, 295; Jim Rosebrock, "The Horse Artillery at Antietam," South from the North Woods, July 13, 2012, http://southfromthenorthwoods.blogspot.com/2012/07/horse-artillery-at-antietam.html.

34. Carman, 295; *OR* 19, 1:343. Carman mentioned that Capt. Victor Maurin's Donaldsonville (LA) Artillery was positioned near some

haystacks, but these were west of the Hagerstown Pike and nearly 1,500 yards away. Therefore the guns Graham engaged with could not have been Maurin's. See Carman, 296.

35. Carman, 296. Carman did not show Manly's battery on Reel Ridge on his noon–12:15 p.m. map, but he placed the battery near Reel's barn in his narrative. Also, although he did not include Macon's guns in his narrative, Carman did put them on his noon map and, earlier in the narrative, mentioned that they were near Reel's barn. Carman included Maurin's battery on his noon–12:15 p.m. map and had them being in action during Richardson's advance beyond the Sunken Lane. All the rifled guns of Saunders's battalion were supposedly dismounted when the battalion first came into action. Carman may be in error here, but he might have received new information regarding Maurin when he revised his map that he did not have when he wrote his manuscript. See Carman, 186, 282; John W. Tullis to Carman, Mar. 19, 1900, AS; *OR* 19, 1:343–344; J. Mason, *Until Antietam*, 189.

36. *OR* 19, 1:344; J. Mason, *Until Antietam*, 189; Carman, 295–296; H. Stevens, *Souvenir*, 9.

37. Hirst, *Boys from Rockville*, 21; Page, *History*, 43–44; H. Stevens, *Souvenir*, 58.

38. Page, *History*, 44; H. Stevens, *Souvenir*, 59.

39. J. Wilson Barnett to Parents, Sept. 21, 1862, in possession of Marguerite Finney, copy in 53rd PA folder, ANBL; E. Cross, *Stand Firm*, 50; Blake McKelvey, "Civil War Letters," 154.

40. *OR* 19, 1:279–280. Chaplain Stevens in the 14th CT helped establish the time when Hancock arrived to take command. Stevens wrote that the regiment was in support of Graham's battery for nearly an hour before Hancock arrived and ordered them to move forward to the top of the ridge. This places Hancock's arrival between 1:30 p.m. and 2 p.m. See H. Stevens, *Souvenir*, 59.

41. R. K. Krick, "It Appeared," 229n57, 257; Gorman, "Memoirs," 6; William W. Sillers to Sister, Oct. 1, 1862, Sillers-Holmes Family

Correspondence, Rare Books and Special Collections, Univ. of Notre Dame, https://rarebooks.nd.edu/digital/civil_war/letters/sillers-holmes/5025-02.shtml [accessed May 2018].

42. *OR* 19, 1:1038; "Letter from a Mobile Rifleman," *Mobile Advertiser and Register*, Oct. 18, 1862 [the writer was probably Joseph B. Belt in Company K].

43. The flags lost were those of the 8th, 11th, and 44th AL; the 16th MS; the state colors of the 4th NC; and one of the flags—unit unknown, but probably in Wright's brigade—taken by Barlow's 61st and 64th NY. The 7th NY claimed to have captured three colors, and Caldwell reported that his brigade captured six colors. If this is true, then nine colors were lost. Whether they were battle flags or state flags (which very few Confederate units carried), or whether some colors were claimed by the same unit, is unknown. See *OR* 19, 1:285–286, 289; Cross to Henry Kent, Sept. 20, 1862, in E. Cross, *Stand Firm*, 121. The Confederate forces that were engaged were D. H. Hill's two brigades, with 2,224 men (G. B. Anderson, 1,174; Rodes, 850; Colquitt/McRae, about 200); R, H. Anderson, 2,603 (Cummings, 500; Wright, 466; Posey, 700; Pryor, 855; Parham [attached to Pryor], 82); Cobb, 400; and Cooke, 675 for a total of 5,902. This does not include artillerymen, which would probably bring the overall strength to over 6,000. G. T. Anderson reinforced this number with about 500 men.

44. *OR* 19, 1:1024, 1026.

45. Galwey, *Valiant Hours*, 42; Spangler, *My Little War Experience*, 37.

46. Robert Grandchamp, *Colonel Edward Cross, New Hampshire Fighting Fifth* (Jefferson, NC: McFarland, 2012), 112.

47. C. Fuller, *Personal Recollections*, 71–72.

48. Loundsdale, "Story of Antietam," ANBL; Galwey, *Valiant Hours*, 44.

49. The two batteries were Battery B, 1st NY, and Battery B, 1st RI.

50. Carman, 304; Sumner to GBM, 10:15 a.m., 10:20 a.m., and no time signature, Sept. 17, 1862, "Signal Corps Messages Sent and Received, Jan. [18]62–May [18]63, RG 111, NA. The untimed message is identical to the 10:15 a.m. message, but it also contains two more sentences: "Reinforcements are badly wanted. Our troops are giving way." It may have been sent immediately after the 10:20 message, to convey additional urgency to the 10:15 message, or it may have been that the first two sentences of the 10:15 a.m. message took more time to decode. See Nelson H. Davis to GBM, Jan. 31, 1876, box A95, reel 38, MP; *OR* 19, 1:61.

51. *OR* 19, 1:61. For McClellan's opinion of Sumner, see GBM to Mary Ellen, May 6, 1862, in McClellan, *Civil War Papers*, 257.

52. *OR* 19, 1:61.

Chapter 13. Stalemate in the North

1. Lt. Joseph B. Molyneaux letter, Sept. 22, 1862, in *Cleveland Morning Leader*, Oct. 2, 1862; Carman, 306.

2. Carman, 307–308.

3. William Armor to Gould, May 6, 1891, GP; John A. McLaughlin, comp., *A Memoir of Hector Tyndale* (Philadelphia, 1882), 56. Tyndale wrote that it was a six-gun battery. Armor said it only had two guns.

4. *OR* 19, 1:918; John M. Hudgin to Carman, n.d., AS.

5. John M. Hudgin to Carman, n.d., AS; A. C. Jones to Carman, Jan. 20, 1903, Carman Papers, NYPL; Carman, 302, 314.

6. Carman, 308; Samuel Toombs, *Reminiscences of the War* (Orange, NJ, 1878), 20; Williams to GBM, Apr.18, 1864, Carman Papers, NYPL; *OR* 19, 1:476.

7. Carman, 308–309; Sebastian Duncan Jr. to Mother, Sept. 21, 1862, Sebastian Duncan Jr. Papers, NJHS; Charles A. Hopkins to Carman, Jan. 15 and Jan. 17, 1900, AS.

8. Carman, 312; *OR* 19, 1:971. Although Carman placed Early on Ransom's left at this time, it is clear from Early's report that he did not move up there until after Armistead's brigade had arrived.

9. Walter M. Clark to Carman, Jan. 3, 1900, AS.

10. Walter Clark to Carman, Apr. 24, 1899, and Jan. 3, 1900, AS; Carman, 312; *OR* 19, 1:971.

11. Carman, 315.

12. Carman, 310; *OR* 19, 1:505; "Battery E, PA Artillery" [with Carman's notes], Carman Papers, NYPL.

13. *OR* 19, 1:505; Carman, 310; "Battery E, PA Artillery" [with Carman's notes], Carman Papers, NYPL.

14. "Battery E, PA Artillery" [with Carman's notes], Carman Papers, NYPL; David Nichol to Father and Home, Sept. 21, 1862, in James P. Brady, ed., *Hurrah for the Artillery* (Gettysburg, PA: Thomas, 1992), 157; Carman, 311.

15. "Battery E, PA Artillery" [with Carman's notes], Carman Papers, NYPL; David Nichol to Father and Home, Sept. 21, 1862, in Brady, *Hurrah*, 157; Carman, 311.

16. James P. Stewart to Mother, Sept. 21, 1862, *CWTI* Miscellaneous Collection, USAHEC. Stewart was a corporal on the No. 2 piece. See Carman, 311.

17. Pennock J. Cole to Carman, Oct. 13, 1900, Carman Papers, NYPL. Although Lt. Col. Benjamin L. Simpson wrote the report for the Purnell Legion, he was not present at the battle. See William T. Fulton to Carman, Dec. 21, 1899, Carman Papers, NYPL.

18. Charles A. Hopkins to Carman, Jan. 15, 1900, AS.

19. Carman, 316. Nearly every account from the 13th NJ mentioned the Confederates marching with trail arms, which the Federals perceived as an intent to surrender. See Toombs, *Reminiscences*, 20–21; Sebastian Duncan Jr. to Mother, Sept. 21, 1862, Duncan Papers, NJHS. Also see *Daily Guardian* (Paterson, NJ), Sept. 25, 1862; E. Allen, *Both Sides*, 2.

20. Pennock J. Cole to Carman, Oct. 13, 1900, Carman Papers, NYPL; Sebastian Duncan Jr. to Mother, Sept. 21, 1862, Duncan Papers,

NJHS; Charles N. Ritchie, "A Newark Soldier in the Civil War," *Newark (NJ) Evening News*, July 15, 1903; Surgeon John H. Love to Frank, Sept. 18, 1862, John H. Love Papers, NJHS; Carman diary, Oct. 31, 1862, NJHS.

21. *OR* 19, 1:509.

22. Carman, 318; Ambrose Henry Hayward, *Last to Leave the Field*, ed. Timothy J. Orr (Knoxville: Univ. of Tennessee Press, 2010), 101; J. Moore reminiscences, USAHEC; Sebastian Duncan Jr. to Mother, Sept. 21, 1862, Duncan papers, NJHS.

23. Brady, *Hurrah*, 157, 162.

24. J. Moore reminiscences, USAHEC; Maj. Ario Pardee to Father, Sept. 8, 1862, Pardee-Robison Papers, USAHEC; McLaughlin, *Memoir*, 57. Tyndale survived his wound but did not return to duty until late July 1863.

25. Carman, 317–318; A. Williams, *Cannon's Mouth*, 129.

26. A. Williams, *Cannon's Mouth*, 129.

27. *OR* 19, 1:376; *OR* 51, 1:839–840. Although Franklin wrote that the 6th Corps was underway by 5:30 a.m., nearly every account of the march that gave a start time said it was 6 a.m. See Mark A. Snell, *From First to Last* (New York: Fordham Univ. Press, 2002), 57, 69.

28. Lyman, *With Grant*, 140; Gordon Rhea, *Cold Harbor* (Baton Rouge, LA: LSU Press, 2002), 109.

29. Hyde, *Following*, 94; Carman, 304; Smith to Maj. Davies, May 9, 1897, Ezra A. Carman Papers, LC; entry 13, Signal Corps Messages, RG 111, NA. General Smith marked the cross-country route of his division to the Boonsboro Pike on a map titled "Route of Smith's Division," AS.

30. Entry 13, Signal Corps Messages, RG 111, NA.

31. Christoph Niederer journal, Civil War Miscellaneous Collection, USAHEC; P. J. C. to the *Journal*, Sept. 22, 1862, in *Jamestown (NY) Journal*, Oct. 3, 1862. The *P* in "P. J. C." is probably a typo. There was no one with those initials in Company K, but there was an "R. J. C.," Robert J. Cowden. See John M. Priest, ed., "'Vivid in My Memory': A Com-

mon Soldier and the Battle of Antietam," *CWTI* 24, no. 8 (Dec. 1985), 22; Thomas W. Hyde to Mother, Sept. 24, 1862, in Thomas W. Hyde, *Civil War Letters* (privately printed, 1933), 49.

32. Hyde, *Following*, 94; John Conline, "Recollections of the Battle of Antietam and the Maryland Campaign," in MOLLUS, *War Papers*, vol. 2 (Wilmington, NC: Broadfoot, 1993), 117; T. Abel Crane to Friend Earle, Sept. 20, 1862, in *Orleans Independent Standard* (Irasburgh, VT), Oct. 3, 1862. The printed name is probably an error. The letter writer most likely was T. Abel Chase, a sergeant in Company B. See Anders Henriksson, trans. and ed., "The Narrative of Friedrich Meyer: A German Volunteer in the Army of the Potomac," *Civil War Regiments* 6, no. 2 (1998), 13.

33. Smith to Maj. Davis, May 9, 1897, Carman Papers, LC; Smith to Maj. Davies, July 31, 1897, AS; Smith to John C. Ropes, Dec. 29, 1896, J. Ropes Papers, BU.

34. Smith to Maj. Davis, May 9, 1897, Carman Papers, LC; Carman, 305; Cowan to Carman, Aug. 8, 1895, AS.

35. *OR* 19, 1:406; Carman, 305.

36. Thomas P. Lowry, *Tarnished Eagles* (Harrisburg, PA: Stackpole Books, 1997), 92–93.

37. Carman, 321–322.

38. *OR* 19, 1:402; Smith to Franklin, Jan. 13, 1898, AS; Charles E. Stevens to Carman, Jan. 1, 1898, AS; A. Williams, *Cannon's Mouth*, 135.

39. Carman, 322. Two members of the 20th NY mentioned passing through a cornfield during their advance or engaging Rebels in the corn. This could only be the Mumma cornfield. See Henriksson, "Narrative," 13; Niederer journal, USAHEC.

40. Gary Kappesser, "A Brief History of the 20th Regiment New York Volunteers United Turner Rifles," 20th NY file, ANBL; Bart Muller, "The Twentieth New York," 20th NY file, ANBL.

41. "Departure of the Twentieth Regiment, German Turners," 20th New York Infantry

Regiment's Civil War Newspaper Clippings, New York State Military Museum and Veterans Research Center, https://museum.dmna.ny.gov/unit-history/infantry/20th-infantry-regiment/newspaper-clippings/ [accessed Oct. 2018].

42. "Departure"; Kappesser, "Brief History," ANBL; Henriksson, "Narrative," 4, 9; Ernst von Vegasack and Michael J. McAfee, "20th New York Volunteer Infantry, the United Turner Rifles: 'Let Them Wave. They Are Our Glory,'" *Military Images* (May–June 1999), 44–45; Hyde, *Following*, 68; William C. Alberger to Carman, Feb. 20, 1905, Carman Papers, NYPL.

43. Von Vegasack and McAfee, "20th New York," 45; Henriksson, "Narrative," 10; Hyde, *Following*, 89. The other field officers Hyde saw, although he may have been unaware of it, were Lt. Col. Alberger and Maj. George Johnson in the 49th NY. Alberger wrote that but for the exertions of Johnson, Col. Vegasack, and himself, he did not think the 20th NY would have gone "as far to the front as they eventually did." See William C. Alberger to Carman, Feb. 20, 1905, Carman Papers, NYPL.

44. Niederer journal, USAHEC; Henriksson, "Narrative," 13; P. J. C. to the *Journal*, Sept. 22, 1862, in *Jamestown (NY) Journal*, Oct. 3, 1862.

45. P. J. C. to the *Journal*, Sept. 22, 1862, in *Jamestown (NY) Journal*, Oct. 3, 1862; Niederer journal, USAHEC; Henriksson, "Narrative," 13.

46. Henriksson, "Narrative," 13; William C. Alberger to Carman, Feb. 20, 1905, Carman Papers, NYPL; Niederer journal, USAHEC; P. J. C. to the *Journal*, Sept. 22, 1862, in *Jamestown (NY) Journal*, Oct. 3, 1862.

47. Hyde, *Civil War Letters*, 49; Hyde, *Following*, 95; *OR* 19, 1:196.

48. Hyde, *Civil War Letters*, 49; Hyde, *Following*, 95. There were three Knoxes in Company K, so which one was the sharpshooter is unknown.

49. Carman, 323; Charles E. Stevens letter, n.d., typescript, AS; *OR* 19, 1:196, 409, 415;

Edward H. Fuller [77th NY] to Carman, Mar. 5, 1905, Carman Papers, NYPL.

50. *OR* 19, 1:326, 402, 409, 414, 416; Carman, 325; C. E. Stevens letter, n.d., typescript, AS.

51. Smith to Maj. Davis, July 31, 1897, AS; Charles C. Morey to [unknown], Jan. 11, 1863, Charles C. Morey letters, Stuart Goldman Collection, USAHEC; T. Abel Crane to Friend Earle, Sept. 20, 1862, in *Orleans Independent Standard* (Irasburgh, VT), Oct. 3, 1862.

52. *OR* 19, 1:402–403; Smith to Maj. Davis, May 9, 1897, Carman Papers, LC; Smith to Maj. Davis, July 31, 1897, AS; Conline, "Recollections," 117; C. to Father, Sept. 20, 1862, in *Brandon (VT) Monitor*, Oct. 3, 1862.

53. *OR* 19, 1:411; Carman, 325; Robert Sawin to George, Sept. 26, 1862, copy in author's collection.

54. Carman gave Slocum's time of arrival as 12 noon, which he probably took from Slocum's report. This is simply impossible, as it would mean they reached the East Woods at the same time as Smith. Slocum probably meant that they reached Keedysville at noon, which was the time William Westervelt in the 27th NY gave for their arrival there. It would have taken nearly an hour for a division to ford Antietam Creek and cover the distance from there to the East Woods. See Carman, 326; *OR* 19, 1:381; William Westervelt memoir, Civil War Miscellaneous Collection, USAHEC; Stephen W. Sears, *Landscape Turned Red* (New York: Ticknor & Fields, 1983), 271; William B. Franklin, "Notes on Crampton's Gap and Antietam," *B&L*, vol. 2, 597; Snell, *From First*, 194.

55. H. P. Cooke [1st NJ] to Carman, Aug. 31, 1899, and E. B. Williston to Carman, Oct. 12, 1891, AS; Carman's summary of Otis S. Neal [Battery A, MA Light Artillery] letter, Aug. 13, 1894, AS; Carman note on "MD Light, Battery A," AS; *OR Suppl.*, pt. 3, 1:550. Carman's correspondents from Porter's and Wolcott's batteries did not agree with Upton's statement that Wolcott was initially placed immediately to

the right of Smoketown Road. They situated him on Porter's right. See Carman, 325–326; Edward Williston to John Stearns, Oct. 7 and Oct. 12, 1891, ABB Papers, NA.

56. *OR* 19, 1:377; William B. Franklin testimony, *CCW*, 37th Congress, pt. 1, 626; Franklin, "Notes," 597; Snell, *From First*, 194.

57. Franklin testimony, *CCW*, 37th Congress, pt. 1, 626; Franklin, "Notes," 597.

58. Sumner testimony, *CCW*, 37th Congress, pt. 1, 368; *OR* 19, 1:270; F. Walker, *History*, 117–118. Also see James H. Wilson, *Under the Old Flag* (New York: D. Appleton, 1912), 112–113.

59. *OR* 19, 1:226. The number of guns Sumner massed on the right represented slightly over 20% of the Army of the Potomac's artillery.

60. J. H. Wilson, *Under*, 113–114. Wilson claimed he informed Sumner that Burnside had carried the Rohrback Bridge. Since this did not occur until about 1 p.m., he could not have told Sumner this on his first visit, but he might have done so on his second. Nonetheless, Wilson allowed many events he learned about afterward to infiltrate his story.

61. McClellan, *Civil War Papers*, 314–315; *OR* 19, 2:312.

62. *OR* 19, 1:62.

63. Franklin testimony, *CCW*, 37th Congress, pt. 1, 627. Stonewall Jackson concurred with Franklin's and Smith's opinion of Nicodemus Heights. In his report, Jackson described the heights as "an important position, which, if the enemy possessed, might have commanded our left." See *OR* 19, 1:957.

64. Franklin testimony, *CCW*, 37th Congress, pt. 1, 627; Snell, *From First*, 195–196; Henry Keiser diary, USAHEC; Smith to Maj. Davis, May 9, 1897, Carman Papers, LC; *OR* 19, 1:62. Sumner had signaled to GBM at an unknown time: "Do you think it proper to countermand the order to send Slocum's division to Richardson's support, as I shall need it on the right if I advance." See entry 13, Signal Corps Messages, RG 111, NA. Given Sumner's strong argument against any advance from the right,

it is highly unlikely that this message was sent before GBM arrived. The reference by Sumner to needing Slocum on the right if Sumner advanced possibly meant a Sept. 18 advance. There is no evidence that Sumner contemplated or suggested any advance on the afternoon of Sept. 17.

65. *OR* 19, 2:610.

66. *OR* 19, 1:151, 956; Joseph L. Harsh, *Taken at the Flood* (Kent, OH: Kent State Univ. Press, 1999), 406–407. Harsh believes that Lee may have met with Jackson, and the two discussed a turning movement. While this is possible, there is no contemporary evidence that placed the two commanders together.

67. Hunter McGuire, "General T. J. (Stonewall) Jackson, Confederate States Army," *SHSP* 25 (1897), 101.

68. Harsh, *Taken*, 408. Lee's orders for Hill to advance to Sharpsburg were received at 6:30 a.m. Hill's division marched at 7:30 a.m. If Hill communicated his starting time to Lee, then Lee would have known that the earliest Hill could arrive was around 1:30 p.m.. This would have been a march moving at 3 miles per hour—possible, but difficult to maintain consistently for a distance of 17 miles. A 2:00 or 2:30 p.m. arrival was more likely. Whether Hill sent a staff officer to communicate his expected arrival time to Lee is unknown, but it seems inconceivable that he did not.

69. J. Walker, "Sharpsburg," *B&L*, vol. 2, 679–680; *OR* 19, 1:916.

70. *OR* 19, 1:859. Carman identified the guns accompanying Stuart as one from Poague's Rockbridge (VA) Battery, two from Raine's Lee (VA) Battery, three from Brockenbrough's 2nd Baltimore Battery, and three from batteries he did not name. He also stated that French's (VA) Battery and Branch's (VA) Field Artillery in Walker's division accompanied the movement, although Walker wrote that they had no long-range ammunition. Robert E. L. Krick, in his careful study of Confederate artillery on the left in this battle, identifies only

two guns from Brockenbrough and three from Turner's (VA) battery in Hilary P. Jones's Battalion, along with Poague's and Raine's batteries, for a total of eight guns. See Carman, 337; R. E. Krick, "Defending Lee's Flank," 212. Only the 4th and 5th VA of Lee's brigade, the 7th VA of Munford's brigade, and the 1st and 2nd SC Cavalry of Hampton's brigade are positively known to have participated in this movement. See Carman, 61n, 337.

71. R. E. Krick, "Defending Lee's Flank," 212; Carman, 337; William T. Poague, *Gunner with Stonewall*, ed. Monroe F. Cockrell (Jackson, TN: McCowat-Mercer, 1957), 47.

72. George C. Sumner, *Battery D, 1st Rhode Island Light Artillery in the Civil War, 1861–1865* (Providence, RI, 1897), 35; *OR* 19, 1:1010; Poague, *Gunner*, 47; Rufus R. Dawes, *Service*, 94.

73. Carman, 338; G. Sumner, *Battery D*, 35.

74. Carman, 332–333. There were four Hoods in the 35th NC. Based on their service records, Benjamin Hood seems to be the most likely one present at Sharpsburg. He deserted to the enemy from the trenches in 1864. See Benjamin F. Hood CSR, NA.

75. *OR* 19, 1:916, 920; J. Walker, "Sharpsburg," 680; Carman, 332. Walker wrote that he found Longstreet in the rear of the Confederates' position when Col. Cooke's two regiments launched their noon counterattack. This would place Longstreet in the vicinity of Reel's farm, which offered him the best view of the field.

Chapter 14. The Middle Bridge

1. *OR* 19, 1:55.

2. David Strother, "Personal Recollections of the War," *Harpers New Monthly Magazine* 36 (February 1868), 281–282, https://babel.hathitrust.org/cgi/pt?id=coo.31924079637561&view=1up&seq=283&skin=2021&q1=strother. Strother also mentioned this was the same position in which GBM conducted his Sept. 15 observation.

3. *OR* 19, 61–62; Sears, *Landscape*, 270.

4. Alexander Webb to Father, Sept. 24, 1862, and undated Webb letter [written before Sept. 24], Alexander Webb Papers, Yale Univ.; Stephen Weld to Father, Sept. 18, 1862, in Stephen Minot Weld, *War Diary and Letters of Stephen Minot Weld 1861–1865* (1912; repr., Boston: Massachusetts Historical Society, 1979), 138.

5. On his maps, Carman gave the time of Pleasonton's advance as noon, but numerous accounts from the cavalry division placed the time when they advanced at around 10 a.m. See Tidball after-action report, in *OR Suppl.*, pt. 1, 3:516; Capt. Samuel B. M. Young [4th PA Cavalry] statement, Apr. 8, 1898, AS; Carman's notes on "3rd IN Cavalry," AS.

6. Carman, 358–359; S. Young statement, Apr. 8, 1898, AS. Young was 22 years old, and after the war he was commissioned into the Regular Army. He rose to the rank of general and commanded a brigade of cavalry in the Spanish American War that included the 1st U.S. Volunteer Cavalry, known as the Rough Riders. He subsequently served as the first president of the Army War College and the first chief of staff of the U.S. Army. He also was the acting superintendent of Yellowstone National Park in 1897. Carman wrote as if only Young's squadron crossed the Middle Bridge with Dennison, but Hugh Crawford in Company B, in an undated statement to Carman in Carman's notes, "4th PA Cavalry," AS, made it clear that Tombler's squadron also crossed it. Also see A. G. Wilkins, "Fourth Pennsylvania Cavalry," *NT*, Jan. 9, 1903.

7. Charles Thomas Bowen, *Dear Friends at Home*, ed. Edward K. Cassedy (Baltimore: Butternut & Blue. 2001), 153; H. D. D. Twiggs to Carman, Dec. 28, 1898, AS. Newcomer Ridge is not a name used during the war or by Carman in his history of the battle. It is used here as a means to identify an otherwise nameless landscape feature.

8. Carman, 373; C. Johnson and Anderson, *Artillery Hell*, 89–90, 99; H. D. D. Twiggs to Carman, Feb. 4, 1899, AS.

9. *OR* 19, 1:897, 942, 945–946.

10. Maj. Miel Hilton after-action report, Oct. 15, 1862, 22nd SC file, ANBL; Capt. S. A. Durham, 23rd SC after-action report, Oct. 16, 1862, Confederate States Armies Casualties, NA.

11. The batteries south of the Boonsboro Pike were Capt. Elijah D. Taft's 5th Battery, NY Light; Lt. Alfred von Kleiser's Battery B, 1st NY Light; Capt. Stephen H. Weed's Battery I, 5th U.S.; Capt. George W. Durell's Battery D, PA Light; and Capt. Joseph C. Clark Jr.'s Battery E, 4th U.S. See *OR* 19, 1:896, 947–948; William N. Wood, *Reminiscences of Big I* (Charlottesville, VA: Michie, 1909), 38.

12. Carman, 359; Carman's notes on "4th PA Cavalry," AS; S. Young statement, Apr. 8, 1898, AS. Young wrote to Carman that a shell from the Rebels killed or mortally wounded four men in his squadron in the place where the road crests the first hill. Since the regiment had only one man killed besides their colonel, it seems likely that the major's memory was incorrect. Hugh Crawford, whose memory seems quite good, remembered that there was only one man killed and one wounded, and two horses killed. It is also evident that this incident occurred after Young's forward element was driven back by Twiggs's riflemen.

13. H. D. D. Twiggs to Carman, Feb. 4, 1899, AS; Eugene C. Tidball, *"No Disgrace to My Country"* (Kent. OH: Kent State Univ. Press, 2002), 25.

14. Carman's notes, "4th PA Cavalry," AS; Samuel P. Bates, *History of the Pennsylvania Volunteers, 1861–5*, vol. 2 (Harrisburg, PA: B. Singerly, 1868), 25; Carman, 360–361.

15. Bates, *History*, vol. 2, 525.

16. *OR Suppl.*, pt. 1, 3:516; Carman's notes on Tidball, with reference to Tidball to Carman, Nov. 15, 1896, AS; E. Tidball, *"No Disgrace,"* 25. The National Park Service has installed a trail to Tidball's position that is well worth the climb, both for the excellent view and to appreciate how difficult it would be to push a one-ton cannon up the slope.

17. Albert Payson Morrow to Carman, Apr. 14, 1898, AS; Carman's notes on "3rd IN Cavalry," AS; Carman's notes on "1st MA Cavalry," AS; *OR* 19, 1:199–200.

18. Carman, 363. The regiments that crossed Antietam Creek were the 4th and 6th PA, the 1st MA, the 8th IL, the 3rd IN, a squadron of the 8th PA, and the 5th U.S. See Benjamin W. Crowninshield, *History of the First Regiment of Massachusetts Cavalry Volunteers* (Boston: Houghton Mifflin, 1891), 79; Flavius Bellamy diary, ISL; Charles Francis Adams Jr. to Mother, Sept. 25, 1862, in Worthington Chauncey Ford, ed., *A Cycle of Adams Letters, 1861–1865* (New York: Houghton Mifflin, 1920), vol. 1, 188; Henry Lee Higginson to Carman, Aug. 28, 1899, AS.

19. Carman's notes on "3rd IN Cavalry," AS; Wilkins, "Fourth Pennsylvania."

20. H. D. D. Twiggs to Carman, Feb. 4, 1899, AS; *OR* 19, 1:945–946.

21. *OR Suppl.*, pt. 1, 3:525. Hains only had two of his four sections at this time. One of his sections was detached. See C. Johnson and Anderson, *Artillery Hell*, 83; Carman, 364. Profiles of battery commanders are from Thomas Clemens, "Biographical Dictionary," unpublished manuscript.

22. Sears, *Landscape*, 270–271; *OR Suppl.*, pt. 1, 3:518.

23. *OR* 19, 1:358; Carman, 366.

24. Timothy J. Reese, *Regulars*, rev. ed. (n.p., Timothy J. Reese, 2006), 40–41, CD-ROM; Eicher and Eicher, *High Commands*, 151, 576. For an example of the lobbying on Winthrop's behalf, see the Sept. 19, 1861, letter from Robt. Winthrop, Fred's older brother, bearing the signatures of prominent Republicans in New York City, endorsing Fred's application for a commission in the Regular Army, in Main Series, 1861–1870, Letters Received by the Office of the Adjutant General, NA.

25. Reese, *Regulars*, 3, 43–45. The original plan that expanded the size of the Regular Army also called for reorganizing the existing regi-

ments on the same pattern as the new regiments, but this proposal failed. Only the new regiments were organized under the French system.

26. Reese, *Regulars*, 46–55; C. Bowen, *Dear Friends*, iv–v, 13, 28.

27. Reese, *Regulars*, 59.

28. C. Bowen, *Dear Friends*, 34, 36, 63, 65, 166.

29. C. Bowen, *Dear Friends*, 150, 154. Bowen stated that the 3rd GA and the 9th LA were in his front. Neither regiment fought the 12th U.S., so Bowen did not learn the exact identity of the unit in combat against him. Based on his description of the action and the fact that he mentioned the 3rd GA, the prisoners most likely were from Twiggs's detachment. In *Dear Friends at Home*, editor Edward Cassedy has a note on page 150 stating that iron marker no. 88 on the Antietam battlefield is incorrect in placing Company G (Bowen's company) south of the Boonsboro Pike, as well as in listing Capt. Winthrop as the commander of the company. Nonetheless, the tablet, written by Carman, is correct. Both the after-action report for the 1/12th U.S. and Bowen's own account made it clear that the company operated south of the pike. Bowen wrote that Company B and Company G were deployed as skirmishers. Company B was commanded by Winthrop, who was also in charge of the skirmish line, which accounts for the narrative on the tablet. Also see *OR* 19, 1:358. The strength of the two companies is derived from Bowen's statement that the two battalions of the 12th U.S. did not number over 500 men, or about 250 per battalion, which averages to 25 per company.

30. *OR* 19, 1:362; Carman, 366.

31. *OR* 19, 1:351, 357, 360; Carman, 368–369. For Sykes's illness and his fear that the enemy had a large force hiding behind Cemetery Hill, see Gromontulh [*sic*], Capt. and ADC to Porter, no time signature, Sept. 17, 1862, reel 31, MP.

32. *OR* 19, 1:353; Carman, 369.

33. Francis Bernard Heitman, *Historical Register and Dictionary of the United States Army*, vol. 1 (Washington, DC: U.S. Gov't. Printing Office, 1903), 983; Tidball to Carman, Sept. 26, 1896, AS.

34. Reese, *Regulars*, 109; "Hiram Dryer," Fort Larned, National Historic Site, Kansas, https:// www.nps.gov/fols/learn/historyculture/hiram -dryer.htm [accessed Feb. 2019]; Thomas M. Anderson, "The Reserve at Antietam," *Century Magazine* 32 (n.s., 10), no. 5 (Sept. 1886), 783. An extended excerpt from Anderson's article is in *B&L*, vol. 2, 656.

35. Pleasonton to GMC, 2:30 p.m., Sept. 17, 1862, reel 31, MP; *OR* 51, 2:845.

36. Tidball to Carman, Sept. 26, 1896, AS; Gromontulh [*sic*], Capt. and ADC to Porter, no time signature, Sept. 17, 1862, reel 31, MP.

37. *OR* 19, 1:357, 362; Carman, 371.

38. *OR* 19, 1:357, 362; Carman, 371.

39. *OR* 19, 1:939, 1044; Carman, 376. For details about Garrett before the war, see "Untitled Story #1," Fold3, https://www.fold3.com /memorial/637307081/thomas-m-garrett /stories#26a0eb00-62aa-11e4-154b -52553f4d6d74/ [requires a subscription] [accessed July 2022]. Garrett was killed on May 12, 1864, at the Battle of Spotsylvania Court House.

40. Carman, 377; Hugh Garden to Carman, May 1, 1896, AS; C. Johnson and Anderson, *Artillery Hell*, 89; *OR* 19, 854–865, 926.

41. *OR* 19, 1:896, 903.

42. *OR* 19, 1:362; C. Bowen, *Dear Friends*, 153; Carman, 378. Carman did not count the companies of the 1/12th U.S. who accompanied this advance. Charles Bowen is the authority for this information. The 1/12th U.S. probably had an average of 25 men in each company, which gives the total skirmish line a strength of 400 in the 2nd and 10th U.S., 120 in the 4th U.S., and 50 in the 1/12th U.S.

43. C. Bowen, *Dear Friends*, 150, 153; Twiggs to Carman, Dec. 28, 1898, AS; *OR* 19, 1:946.

44. *OR* 19, 1:362–363; C. Bowen, *Dear Friends*, 154; Carman, 378–379.

45. *OR* 19, 1:896, 898–899; Carman, 383; George C. Cabell to Carman, May 10, 1895, AS; Wood, *Reminiscences*, 39.

46. Carman, 379; *OR* 19, 1:357, 359, 360.

47. Carman, 380; *OR* 19, 1:939–940, 1044–1045.

48. *OR* 19, 1:940, 1024–1025.

49. *OR* 19, 1:942, 947–948, 1044–1045.

50. Carman, 383.

51. Carman, 383.

52. Carman, 383; S. D. Lee to Carman, Mar, 19, 1900, and Oct. 24, 1901, AS.

53. Carman, 384–385; Wm. H. Powell, "More Light on 'The Reserve at Antietam,'" *Century Magazine* 33 (n.s., 11), no. 5 (Mar. 1887), 804; Anderson, "Reserve," 783; Thomas M. Anderson to George Davis, Jan. 31, 1897, box 3, item 650, ABB Papers, RG 92, NA; *OR* 19, 1:339, 357, 358. The Regular officers did not discuss this internal dispute over Dryer's planned attack in their reports. Only Porter alluded to it by writing that the Regulars were sent across Antietam Creek merely to support the batteries and keep the Confederate skirmishers from harassing the artillerymen: "They were, however, diverted from that service, and employed to drive the enemy's skirmishers to their reserves. Their many losses attest the serious work they had to perform." This was a formal way of saying that the 5th Corps' leadership was proud of their performance, but that Dryer exceeded his orders. Thomas M. Anderson's letter to George Davis claimed that Dryer's message was received around sunset and that Buchanan, after reading it, told him, "Dryer reports center very weak and wants leave to attack." Anderson's memory was probably foggy on both points. The message would have arrived at least an hour or more before sunset, and Dryer was not asking leave to attack. Instead, he wanted Blunt to support the attack he intended to make. See May H. Stacy journal, 12th U.S. Infantry file, ANBL.

54. Anderson, "Reserve," 783; Carman, 392–393; Thomas M. Anderson to George W. Davis, Jan. 31, 1897, box 3, item 650, ABB Papers, RG 92, NA.

55. Editors, "The Reserve at Antietam," *Century Magazine* 33 (n.s., 11), no. 3 (Jan. 1887), 472.

56. Porter to GBM, 4:30 p.m., Sept. 17, 1862, MP.

57. *OR* 19, 2:212, 339; Carman, 387–388.

58. *OR* 19, 2:316.

59. Strother, "Personal Recollections," 284; Thomas M. Anderson to George W. Davis, Jan. 31, 1899, item 650, box 3, ABB Papers, RG 92, NA; *New York Tribune*, Sept. 20, 1862, 5.

60. *New York Tribune*, Sept. 20, 1862, 5.

61. Carman, 393, 349.

62. Powell, "More Light," 804; Carman, 385; *OR* 19, 1:896.

63. William N. Berkeley to Adjut. Wood, n.d., AS; Eugene Granville Taylor to W. N. Wood, Mar. 31, 1900, AS; *OR* 19, 1:897, 900, 902. Capt. Brown's role with the 19th VA on Sept. 17 is something of a mystery. He was present but not recognized as being in command. See Wood, *Reminiscences*, 38–40; Reardon and Vossler, *Field Guide*, 207.

64. *OR* 19, 1:194, 351; Carman, 389.

65. *OR* 19, 1:1031; Carman, 488–489.

66. Carman, 274; *OR* 19, 1: 940, 942.

67. Carman, 388–389; *OR Suppl.*, pt. 1, 3:518; C. Bowen, *Dear Friends*, 167.

Chapter 15. The Bridge

1. *OR* 19, 1:888–893. The surname Rohrback was also spelled "Rohrbach." This is the spelling that Ezra Carman adopted. The 1860 Federal census record and Henry Rohrback's gravestone, however, spell his last name "Rohrback," and this is the spelling I have adopted in the text.

2. Mark Scroggins, *Robert Toombs* (Jefferson, NC: McFarland, 2011), ix, 6.

3. 1860 Federal Census, NA; Thomas R. Martin, *The Great Parliamentary Battle and Farewell Addresses of Southern Senators on the Eve of the*

Civil War (New York: Neale, 1905), 171; "Robert Toombs's Speech to the Georgia Legislature, Nov. 13, 1860," Causes of the Civil War, http://www.civilwarcauses.org/toombs.htm [accessed June 2019].

4. Scroggins, *Robert Toombs*, 134; Ullrich B. Phillips, *The Correspondence of Robert Toombs, Alexander Stevens, and Howell Cobb* (Washington, DC: U.S. Gov't. Printing Office, 1913), 573; Hennessey, *Return*, 47, 423.

5. *OR* 19, 1:888.

6. "Letter from Henry Benning to Howell Cobb," Causes of the Civil War, http://civilwarcauses.org/benning.htm [accessed June 2019]; "Speech of Henry Benning to the Virginia Convention," Causes of the Civil War, http://civilwarcauses.org/benningva.htm [accessed June 2019].

7. Jack F. Cox, *The 1850 Census of Georgia Slave Owners* (Baltimore: Clearfield, 1999), 24; 1860 Federal Census, NA.

8. *OR* 51, 1:161–162; George McRae, "Benning's Brigade in the Wilderness," *Atlanta Journal*, Aug. 17, 1901.

9. *OR* 51, 1:161–162; *Mexico (NY) Independent*, Oct. 9, 1862.

10. *OR* 19, 1:888–889.

11. *OR* 51, 1:161; McRae, "Benning's Brigade."

12. Theodore T. Fogle to Parents, Sept. 16, 1862, Theodore T. Fogle Papers, EU; William Lokey, *My Experiences in the War between the States*, microfilm copy, GDAH, 10; Helen E. Terrill, *History of Stewart County, Georgia*, vol. 1 (Columbus, GA: Columbus Office Supply, 1958), 276–277.

13. *OR* 19, 1:888–893; Carman, 407.

14. *OR* 19, 1:888–893; Carman, 407.

15. *OR* 19, 1:888–893; *OR* 51, 1:161–162, 168; Carman, 407.

16. *OR* 19, 1:30; Jacob D. Cox, *Military Reminiscences of the Civil War* (New York: Charles Scribner's Sons, 1900), 301; Hartwig, *To Antietam Creek*, 609–613.

17. David Thompson, "With Burnside at Antietam," *B&L*, vol. 2, 660. The three batteries were McMullin's 1st Battery, OH Light Artillery; Roemer's Battery L, 2nd NY Artillery; and Muhlenberg's Battery A, 5th U.S.

18. J. D. Cox, *Military Reminiscences*, 305; "Autobiography of George Crook," Crook-Kenan Papers, USAHEC.

19. Carman's 1908 "Map of the Battlefield at Antietam," daybreak, LC; C. Johnson and Anderson, *Artillery Hell*, 77–79.

20. J. D. Cox, *Military Reminiscences*, 303.

21. J. D. Cox, *Military Reminiscences*, 304, 174–181. There were volunteer officers, such as Alpheus Williams, who were every inch the equal of professionally trained officers. But the professionals had an edge in their knowledge of engineering, reconnaissance, and logistics that volunteers only gained by practical experience. More volunteers in higher ranks failed at this than succeeded during the Civil War.

22. Eicher and Eicher, *High Commands*, 460, 518, 570; J. R. Cole, "History of Washington and Kent Counties, Rhode Island," 1889, USGenWeb, http://theusgenweb.org/ri/washington/Bios/sk2.html [accessed June 2019].

23. Charles A. Cuffel, *History of Durell's Battery in the Civil War (Independent Battery D, Pennsylvania Volunteer Artillery)* (Philadelphia: Craig & Finley, 1903), 77; *OR* 19, 1:443.

24. J. D. Cox, *Military Reminiscences*, 333.

25. "The 11th Connecticut at Antietam," *Hartford (CT) Daily Courant*, Sept. 26, 1862; *Mexico (NY) Independent*, Oct. 9, 1862; "Concerning the Battle of Antietam," Lt. Matthew J. Graham to Rush Hawkins, Sept. 27, 1894, Rush Hawkins Papers, BU; Charles F. Johnson, *Long Roll* (East Aurora, NY: Roycrofters, 1911), 190.

26. Wolcott P. Marsh to Ana, Sept. 24, 1862, Wolcott P. Marsh Family Papers, Clements Library, UM, copy in 8th CT file, ANBL; *Mexico (NY) Independent*, Oct. 9, 1862; C. F. Johnson, *Long Roll*, 190; Nathan Mayer to Brother Louie, Sept. 29, 1862, in *Hartford (CT) Daily Courant*, Oct. 7, 1862; *OR* 19, 1:451, 452. McKinley, Shultz, and Dennis all survived their wounds.

27. Cuffel, *History*, 78; B. F. Eshleman to Carman, Jan. 5, 1899, AS; John B. Richardson to B. F. Eshleman, Mar. 22, 1894, AS.

28. Cuffel, *History*, 78; Samuel H. Rhoads to Carman, Mar. 16, 1896, Carman Papers, NYPL; *OR* 19, 1:436.

29. *OR* 19, 1:31, 63, 419; George B. McClellan, *McClellan's Own Story* (New York: Charles L. Webster, 1887), 609–611.

30. J. H. Wilson, *Under the Old Flag*, 110; McClellan, *Own Story*, 609–611; John M. Wilson to Genl. David Stanley, Nov. 30, 1894, J. Ropes Papers, BU. Stanley had a beef with Jacob Cox over Stanley's role in the Nov. 30, 1864, Battle of Franklin and was soliciting any evidence he could find that might damage Cox's reputation. Also see Stanley to John Ropes, Dec. 1, 1894, J. Ropes Papers, BU.

31. *OR* 19, 1:30, 424–426.

32. *OR* 19, 1:424–426.

33. J. D. Cox, *Military Reminiscences*, 333; Cox to Carman, Mar. 13, 1896, Carman Papers, NYPL. J. D. Cox's map, which accompanied this letter, places Burnside's headquarters directly north of Rohrback's farm and to the right of Durell. He was mistaken about the position of Benjamin's battery, which was on a higher ridge southeast of the ridge Burnside's headquarters was on, and Cox probably confused Durell with Benjamin.

34. *OR* 19, 2:308.

35. J. D. Cox, *Military Reminiscences*, 386–388.

36. *OR* 19, 2:314.

37. *OR* 19, 2:51; *OR* 51, 1:842.

38. *OR* 19, 2:19; *OR* 51, 1:31, 419, 424; J. D. Cox, *Military Reminiscences*, 338.

39. *OR* 51, 1:844.

40. Stephen Sears to author, Dec. 28, 2012, in author's collection.

41. J. D. Cox, *Military Reminiscences*, 341.

42. *OR* 19, 1:424.

43. *OR* 19, 1:419; Carman, 404. What I have referred to as "Hill 415," from its elevation, is purely for identification purposes. The hill had no name in 1862.

44. Mary Elizabeth Sergent, *They Lie Forgotten* (Middletown, NY: Prior King, 1986), 152–153.

45. "Reminiscences of the Eleventh: Griffin A. Stedman," *Connecticut War Record* 2, no. 4 (Nov. 1864), 303–304; Sergent, *They Lie Forgotten*, 153–154..

46. Charles W. Rouse diary, 11th CT file, ANBL; Ojos Negros [pseudonym], "Lieutenant Kingsbury's Death," *NT*, July 30, 1885; "The 11th Connecticut at Antietam," Sept. 20, 1862, in *Hartford (CT) Evening Press*, Sept. 26, 1862. The writer may have been Capt. Joseph H. Converse.

47. Griffin A. Stedman after-action report, Sept. 23, 1862, CHS; Mary A. Livermore, *My Story of the War* (1889; repr., New York: Da Capo, 1995), 351. In his report, Stedman's handwriting appears to give Kittler's name as "Sergt. Keatles." It could also be read as "Sergt. Keattler," which may be how his name was pronounced. Mary Livermore somehow learned the full story of this incident and the names of those involved. Kittler appears to have had personal issues. He was reduced to private two times during the Civil War, but also promoted to sergeant twice. Eastman survived the Battle of Antietam and was promoted to captain by the end of the war.

48. Rouse diary, ANBL; Stedman after-action report, CHS; John Banks, *Connecticut Yankees at Antietam* (Charleston, SC: History Press, 2013), 153–155.

49. "The 11th Connecticut at Antietam," *Hartford (CT) Evening Press*, Sept. 26, 1862. The author of this piece, J. H. C., was Adjut. Joseph H. Converse. See Stedman after-action report, CHS; "Philo Pearce's 1925 Antietam Remembrance," John Banks' Civil War Blog, Sept. 15, 2018, https://john-banks.blogspot.com/2018/09/teens-antietam-close-calls-slumber-on.html [accessed July 2019], original in HEPL.

50. "Captain John Griswold: In Memoriam," *Connecticut War Record* 1, no. 11 (June 1864), 212. The author is Asst. Surgeon Nathan Mayer, who used the pseudonym "Horse John"; "Philo Pearce's Remembrance"; George F. Till-

inghast, "Antietam Bridge," *NT*, Dec. 30, 1886; Dr. Nathan Mayer, Asst. Surgeon, to Brother Louie, Sept. 29, 1862, in *Hartford (CT) Daily Courant*, Oct. 7, 1862; "The Statement of an Eye Witness of the Late Battles," *Hartford (CT) Daily Courant*, Sept. 23, 1862; "A Father and Five Sons in the Army," *NT*, May 30, 1889, 3. Homer Barnum's sons were in different regiments, and their fate is unknown. He was killed at Petersburg in 1864. Company losses for the 11th CT were printed in the *Hartford (CT) Daily Courant*, Sept. 26, 1862.

51. Rouse diary and George Bronson to Wife, Sept. 21, 1862, ANBL; S. O. C. to Dear Friends, Sept. 21, 1862, in *New Haven (CT) Daily Palladium*, Sept. 30, 1862. The writer of this letter to the *Palladium* was in Company K. There was no one in Company K with these initials, and this was probably a pseudonym. The *Hartford (CT) Daily Courant*, Sept. 26, 1862, listings for Company D had six killed; for Company E, five; and for Company H, nine. Company D had only one man wounded, a highly unusual ratio of killed to wounded, which may reflect their particular exposure, as well as the accuracy of the Georgians.

52. Stedman after-action report, CHS; Francis T. Brown, Company E, to Friend Henry, Sept. 30, 1862, ANBL; "One of the Most Wounded Soldiers," 11th CT file, ANBL. The story about Maynard did not relate where the fifth bullet struck him, so it may have been a flesh wound.

53. Carman, 411; "The Battles of South Mountain and Antietam: Cox's Division," *Dayton (OH) Daily Empire*, Oct. 17, 1862. The writer is probably John D. Kenney, a 25-year-old private in Company A.

54. "Autobiography of George Crook," USAHEC; *OR* 19, 1:471–472; Reardon and Vossler, *Field Guide*, 217–218.

55. Carman, 412.

56. Carman, 412; Joshua H. Horton and Solomon Teverbaugh, comps., *A History of the Eleventh Regiment (Ohio Volunteer Infantry)* (Dayton,

OH: W. J. Shuey, 1866), 74; Rev. W. W. Lyle, *Lights and Shadows of Army Life* (Cincinnati: R. W. Carroll, 1865), 154; Dr. Nathan Mayer, Asst. Surgeon, to Brother Louie, Sept. 29, 1862, in *Hartford (CT) Daily Courant*, Oct. 7, 1862; "The Statement of an Eye Witness of the Late Battles," *New York Tribune*, Sept. 22, 1862.

57. Carman, 412; *OR* 19, 1:471–472. In the "Autobiography of George Crook," USAHEC, Crook was selective in what he chose to tell and he was also inaccurate.

58. Dr. Nathan Mayer, Asst. Surgeon, to Brother Louie, Sept. 29, 1862, in *Hartford (CT) Daily Courant*, Oct. 7, 1862; Banks, *Connecticut Yankees*, 152–153; "Captain John Griswold," 212; "Philo Pearce's Remembrance." Mayer sought no glory for himself in his account concerning the collecting of Griswold's body, which gives it the ring of truth.

59. "The 11th Connecticut at Antietam," *Hartford (CT) Evening Press*, Sept. 26, 1862; Negros, "Lieutenant Kingsbury's Death"; Francis T. Brown to Friend Henry, Sept. 30, 1862, ANBL; Stedman after-action report, CHS.

Chapter 16. The Bridge Captured

1. David Strother, "Personal Recollection," 283.

2. Carman, 414; Jacob Eugene Duryée, "My Three Regiments," in possession of Brian Pohanka.

3. Carman, 414.

4. *OR* 19, 1:444; James I. Robertson Jr., ed., "A Federal Surgeon at Sharpsburg," *Civil War History* 6, no. 2 (1960), 140; J. Duryée, "My Three Regiments."

5. "'Lt. Col. Duryée Will Oust Every One of Us if Possible!': Marylanders in the Army of the Potomac, Part 2," Tales from the Army of the Potomac, Apr. 19, 2020, https://talesfromaop.blogspot.com/2020/04/lt-col-duryee-will-oust-every-one-of-us.html [accessed April 2020]; C. H. Bowen to Governor Bradford, June 4 and July 1, 1862, Adjutant General's Records, MSA.

6. Robertson, "Federal Surgeon," 137.

7. Robertson, "Federal Surgeon," 137–138.

8. J. Duryée, "My Three Regiments." Why Sturgis gave orders directly to a regimental commander, rather than through Nagle, is unknown.

9. J. Duryée, "My Three Regiments."

10. Carman, 415, 417; *OR* 19, 1:444; Edward O. Lord, *History of the Ninth Regiment, New Hampshire Volunteers, in the War of the Rebellion* (Concord, NH: Republican Press Assoc. 1895), 109; Sam Rhoads to Carman, Mar. 16, 1896, Carman Papers, NYPL. Naming hills by their elevations is a twentieth-century creation and was not used during the Civil War. My identifying these various hills by their heights is only for readers' ease of understanding.

11. Robertson, "Federal Surgeon," 140, 143.

12. J. Duryée, "My Three Regiments"; Lyman Jackman, *History of the 6th New Hampshire Regiment*, ed. Amos Hadley (Salem, MA: Higginson, 1998), 34, 38. The regiment's dog survived all the battles until the one at Poplar Springs Church in 1864, when it was believed to have been killed. Carman wrote that the two regiments were lined up side by side before the charge, and he probably drew this information from Lyman Jackman's history of the 6th NH. See Carman, 415. But Jacob Duryée's account and Theodore Dimon's wartime journal were both positive that the 2nd MD led the advance, followed by the 6th NH.

13. J. Duryée, "My Three Regiments"; Robertson, "Federal Surgeon," 141.

14. Robertson, "Federal Surgeon," 141.

15. J. Duryée, "My Three Regiments"; Robertson, "Federal Surgeon," 141; John A. Cummings to Friends, Sept. 1862, in *Peterborough (NH) Transcript*, Sept. 27, 1862; John A. Cummings to Friends, Sept. 29, 1862, in *Peterborough (NH) Transcript*, Oct. 11, 1862; Otis F. R. Waite, *New Hampshire in the Great Rebellion* (Claremont, NH: Tracy, Chase, 1870), 320–321.

16. Captain Oliver C. Bosbyshell letter, Sept. 21, 1862, in *Miner's Journal* (Pottsville, PA), Oct. 4, 1862; Oliver C. Bosbyshell, *The 48th in the War* (Philadelphia, 1895), 79; James Wren, *Captain James Wren's Diary*, ed. John M. Priest (Shippensburg, PA: White Mane Books, 1990), 71; Robertson, "Federal Surgeon," 142.

17. *OR* 19, 1:197.

18. McRae, "Benning's Brigade"; Charles Frederick Terrill to his brother, Sept. 25, 1862, in Terrill, *History*, 276.

19. Carman, 425. Burnside did receive a signal message of a "strong force" moving to the Confederates' left, but this was McLaws's division, since the message states that the enemy were coming up from Shepherdstown. See Myer to Burnside, no time signature, Sept. 17, p. 96, no. 660, Signal Corps Messages Sent and Received, Jan. [18]62–May [18]63, RG 111, NA.

20. Carman, 425; *OR* 19, 1:419; "Concerning the Battle," BU; Wolcott P. Marsh to Ana, Sept. 24, 1862, W. Marsh Family Papers, Clements Library, UM, copy in 8th CT file, ANBL.

21. Carman, 425–428; *OR* 51, 1:165, 168; William A. Croffut and John M. Morris, *The Civil and Military History of Connecticut During the War of 1861–1865* (New York, 1868), 267; C. F. Johnson, *Long Roll*, 191. Johnson wrote that Rodman "procured a guide to show him the ford" but gave no other information.

22. J. D. Cox, *Military Reminiscences*, 333–343; McClellan, *Own Story*, 603, 609.

23. John William Hudson to Dear Sophy, early Oct. 1862, WMR, copy in 35th MA file, ANBL.

24. Thomas H. Parker, *History of the 51st Regiment P.V. and V.V.* (Philadelphia: King & Baird, 1869), 231–232; William J. Bolton, *The Civil War Journal of Colonel William J. Bolton*, ed. Richard A. Sauers (Conshohocken, PA: Combined, 2000), 86.

25. T. Parker, *History*, 232.

26. H. G. to Editor, Oct. 1, 1862, *National Defender* (Norristown, PA), Oct. 15, 1862. "H. G." is either Henry L. Gerhart or Henry M. Groff. Both were Company F privates. See "Sixth Annual Meeting of the Association of the 51st Regiment P.V.," copy in 51st PA file, ANBL.

27. "The Fifty-First Penna. Reg't. and its Marches and Battles in Virginia and Maryland," *National Defender* (Norristown, PA), Nov. 18, 1862. The writer was Major Edwin Schall, who was killed in action at the Battle of Cold Harbor in 1864.

28. Carman, 417, 422.

29. Albert Pope journal, ML; Charles Hawes to Maria, Sept. 17, 1892, 35th MA file, ANBL; "Fifty-First Penna."; T. Parker, *History*, 232–233; John William Hudson to Dear Sophy, early Oct. 1862, WMR, copy in 35th MA file, ANBL.

30. T. Parker, *History*; "Sixth Annual Meeting," 6, ANBL; Robert Potter, "51st New York at Antietam," Carman Papers, NYPL.

31. Carman, 417; Charles F. Walcott, *History of the 21st Regiment Massachusetts Volunteers in the War for the Preservation of the Union, 1861–1865* (Boston: Houghton, Mifflin, 1882), 200. Walcott's history was incorrect in certain particulars of the engagement, however. See John William Hudson to Dear Sophy, early Oct. 1862, WMR, copy in 35th MA file, ANBL.

32. *OR* 51, 1:161–162; Theodore Fogle to Father and Mother, Sept. 28, 1862, Fogle Papers, EU; Terrill, *History*, 276–277.

33. *Southern Confederacy* (Atlanta), Oct. 9, 1862; *OR* 51, 1:161–162; "Notes by General H. L. Benning on the Battle of Sharpsburg," *SHSP* 16 (1888), 393.

34. Martin G. Reed, "How the 51st Pa. Took the Bridge," *NT*, June 10, 1886; John William Hudson to Dear Sophy, early Oct. 1862, WMR, copy in 35th MA file, ANBL; Potter, "51st New York," NYPL; George Washington Whitman to Mother, Sept. 21, 1862, in George Washington Whitman, *Civil War Letters of George Washington Whitman*, ed. Jerome M. Loving (Durham, NC: Duke Univ. Press, 1975), 65–69.

35. T. Parker, *History*, 234; "Sixth Annual Meeting," 6, ANBL; Bolton, *Civil War Journal*, 86; Potter, "51st New York," NYPL; John William Hudson to Dear Sophy, early Oct. 1862, WMR, copy in 35th MA file, ANBL; Reed, "How the 51st Pa."

36. Carman, 421. In his autobiography, Crook made the absurd claim that this crossing of Antietam Creek by the 28th OH, along with enfilading artillery fire, was responsible for causing the Confederates to evacuate their position. He gave no credit to Ferrero's brigade: "Two Pennsylvania regiments crossed it without loss and got the credit of taking the bridge and I understood that both of their colonels were made brigadier generals for this service." Out of 775 men, the 28th OH had 21 killed or wounded on Sept. 17. The 51st NY and 51st PA lost 207. See J. E. Walton [30th OH] to Carman, Nov. 7, 1902, and Feb. 17, 1905, and David Cunningham [30th OH] to Carman, Feb. 3, 1905, Carman Papers, NYPL. Toombs reported that he was satisfied with the behavior of the 50th GA, but Benning complained that they had abandoned their position soon after the fighting began and went to the rear. See *OR* 19, 1:890; *OR* 51, 1:161–162; "Notes by General H. L. Benning," 393.

37. R. B. Wilson [12th OH] to Carman, Jan. 27, 1905, and David Cunningham [30th OH] to Carman, Feb. 3, 1905, Carman Papers, NYPL; Theodore Fogle to Father and Mother, Sept. 28, 1862, Fogle Papers, EU. "Notes by General H. L. Benning," 393, mentioned the envelopment of his position, as did George McRae [20th GA] in "Benning's Brigade." Spivey apparently died of his wounds. See J. C. Spivey CSR, RG 109, NA.

38. Carman, 428; "Concerning the Battle," BU.

39. Carman, 428; "Concerning the Battle," BU; C. F. Johnson, *Long Roll*, 191; David Wilson to Mother and Sister, Oct. 1, 1862, in *Mexico (NY) Independent*, Oct. 9, 1862; William H. Reylea, "History of the 16th Connecticut Volunteer Infantry," William H. Reylea Papers, CHS.

40. "Concerning the Battle," BU; Matthew J. Graham, *Ninth Regiment, New York Volunteers (Hawkin's Zouaves)* (New York: E. P. Coby, 1900), 289–290, 317. Graham's regimental history included Lt. Col. Kimball's after-action report on pp. 316–322, which is not in the *OR*.

41. *OR* 19, 1:456; Lesley J. Gordon, "All Who Went into That Battle Were Heroes," in Gallagher, *Antietam Campaign*, 173; Reylea, "History," CHS.

42. *OR* 19, 1:456; Henry J. Spooner, "The Maryland Campaign with the Fourth Rhode Island," in MOLLUS, *Personal Narratives of Events in the War of the Rebellion*, vol. 9 (1903; repr., Wilmington, NC: Broadfoot, 1993), 229–230.

43. Carman, 429–430; *OR* 19, 1:453, 456. Carman had Ewing's brigade arriving after Fairchild's New Yorkers, but accounts from the Kanawha Division indicated that the Ohioans made contact with regiments of Sturgis's 2nd Division before Rodman arrived.

44. Carman, 425.

45. E. S. [Edwin Schall] to Editor, *National Defender* (Norristown, PA), Nov. 18, 1862; H. G. to Editor, Oct. 1, 1862, *National Defender* (Norristown, PA), Oct. 14, 1862.

46. *OR* 19, 1:197; "Sixth Annual Meeting," 6, ANBL; E. S. [Edwin Schall] to Editor, *National Defender* (Norristown, PA), Nov. 18, 1862; T. Parker, *History*, 237.

47. T. Parker, *History*, 238.

48. Carman, 420; McClellan, *Own Story*, 603.

49. John William Hudson to Dear Sophy, early Oct. 1862, WMR, copy in 35th MA file, ANBL.

50. John William Hudson to Dear Sophy, early Oct. 1862, WMR, copy in 35th MA file, ANBL.

51. T. Parker, *History*, 238.

52. Pope journal, ML; Regimental Assoc. Committee, *History of the Thirty-Fifth Regiment Massachusetts Volunteers, 1862–1865, with a Roster* (Boston: Mills, Knight, 1884), 42,

53. George W. Silvass to Carman, Apr. 1, 1896, and Samuel H. Rhoads to Carman, Mar. 16, 1896, Carman Papers, NYPL. Special thanks to Tom Clemens for identifying McKibben, who was detached from the 51st NY. He became assistant adjutant general for the division in Oct. and was promoted to captain. He was probably an aide-de-camp at the Battle of Antietam.

54. George W. Silvass to Carman, Apr. 1, 1896, and Samuel H. Rhoads to Carman, Mar. 16, 1896, Carman Papers, NYPL; Cuffel, *History*, 81.

55. Cuffel, *History*, 81.

56. Walcott, *History*, 201; Carman, 420.

57. George W. Silvass to Carman, Apr. 1, 1896, Carman Papers, NYPL; Carman, 422; *Oswego (NY) Commercial Times*, Sept. 26, 1862. The newspaper article stated that two other lieutenants were wounded, but the battery's casualty figures indicated that one officer and one enlisted man were killed, and one officer wounded. With just four guns, Clark should only have had two lieutenants. Silvass made it clear that Clark and both of his lieutenants were the ones hit by this shell. See "Concerning the Battle," BU.

58. Cuffel, *History*, 82–83.

59. *OR* 19, 1:425, J. D. Cox, "The Battle of Antietam," *B&L*, vol. 2, 653.

60. John William Hudson to Dear Sophy, early Oct. 1862, WMR, copy in 35th MA file, ANBL. The 21st MA had 150 officers and men, with an estimated 130 enlisted men firing 40 to 60 rounds each.

61. Henry K. Douglas, *I Rode with Stonewall* (Chapel Hill: Univ. of North Carolina Press, 1940), 172; *OR* 19, 1:31. The area of Burnside's operations was the first part of the battlefield President Lincoln visited with GBM. Surely, had GBM thought Burnside had failed here, he would have used this opportunity to make the president aware of it, but there is no evidence that McClellan uttered a negative word.

62. *OR* 19, 1:63–64; McClellan, *Own Story*, 603, 608.

Chapter 17. A Famous March and a Desperate Assault

1. Capt. Andrew B. Wardlaw [commissary officer] diary, Andrew B. Wardlaw Collection, USAHEC. Other members of A. P. Hill's Light Division also mentioned this Sept. 16 march. See Harsh, *Sounding*, 19.

2. *OR* 19, 1:981; Wardlaw diary, USAHEC; R. T. Mockbee, "Historical Sketch of the 14th Tenn. Regt. of Infantry," Eleanor S. Brockenbrough Collection, VHS. Hill's troops were described by Federal soldiers and a newspaper correspondent captured at Harpers Ferry as a "mongrel, bare-footed crew"; "Ireland in her worst straights [*sic*] could present no parallel"; "they were rugged and shoeless and guns rusty and dirty"; and "they are a dirty, ragged, ignorant set of men." See "New York 'Times' Narrative," in Frank Moore, ed., *The Rebellion Record*, vol. 6 (1863; repr., New York: Arno, 1977), 447–448; Henry B. Curtis Jr. to Lucy, Sept. 18, 1862, GNMP; Mark to Sister, Sept. 24, 1862, *Ontario (NY) Repository and Messenger*, Oct. 8, 1862.

3. Casualties in the division are from *B&L*, vol. 2, 317, 496, 500; *OR*, 19 1:981.

4. James H. Lane to J. G. Harris, June 5, 1896, AS; James F. J. Caldwell, *The History of a Brigade of South Carolinians*, ed. Lee A. Wallace Jr. (Dayton, OH: Morningside Bookshop, 1984), 45; David G. McIntosh reminiscences, David G. McIntosh Papers, SHC.

5. For details about Hill's arrest, see Hartwig, *To Antietam Creek*, 94; "A Letter from the Army," *Raleigh (NC) Semi-Weekly Standard*, Oct. 3, 1862; Caldwell, *History*, 45; Mockbee, "Historical Sketch," VHS.

6. Mockbee, "Historical Sketch," VHS; Ambrose [or Ambrus] Rufus Collins to wife and children, Sept. 8, 1862, ANBL. There was no one by the name of Ambrose or Ambrus Collins in the 18th NC, but he appears in the 1860 Federal census. See *OR* 9, 1:1000.

7. Andrew Wardlaw to Wife, Sept. 24, 1862, 14th SC file, ANBL; William Dorsey Pender, *The General to His Lady*, ed. William H. Hassler (Chapel Hill: Univ. of North Carolina Press, 1962), 179–180; McIntosh reminiscences, SHC.

8. See Hartwig, *To Antietam Creek*, 224, 226; Ivy Duggan letter, in *Central Georgian* (Sandersville), Oct. 1, 1862, Ivy Duggan, "Army Correspondence," Ivy Duggan Papers, Hargrett Rare Book and Manuscript Library, Univ. of Georgia Libraries, Digital Library of Georgia, https://dlg.usg.edu/record/dlg_turningpoint_hargo342-001-001/ [accessed Jan. 2020].

9. Brig. Gen. James L. Kemper to Genl. Samuel Cooper, Aug. 11, 1864, and Joseph Walker CSR, 5th SC Infantry, NA; Dr. James R. Boulware [6th SC] diary, James Boulware Papers, LV; Frank M. Mixson, *Reminiscences of a Private* (Columbia, SC: State, 1910), 29.

10. Boulware diary, LV; James Lide Coker, *History of Company G, Ninth S.C. Regiment, Infantry, S.C. Army and of Company E, Sixth S.C. Regiment, Infantry, S.C. Army* (1899; repr., Greenwood, SC: Attic Press, 1979), 109, ANBL. Coker was an acting field officer at Sharpsburg. He wrote that "apples and green corn were our sole dependence for food," and that no rations were issued to the men.

11. "Loss of the Fiftieth Georgia Regiment at Antietam," in F. Moore, *Rebellion Record*, vol. 6, 18–19; George D. Wise, *History of the Seventeenth Virginia Infantry, C.S.A.* (Baltimore: Kelly, Piet, 1870), 115.

12. Carman, 435–46. Also see Carman's 1908 "Map of the Battlefield of Antietam," 3 p.m., LC.

13. Benjamin F. Powell to Carman, Jan. 17, 1898, AS. Powell was a 1st sergeant in Company H, 24th VA. Also see David E. Johnston to Carman, Jan. 28, 1898, AS, in which Johnston includes a letter he received from Powell about the 24th VA's movements and position. In addition, see Richard L. Maury to Carman, Oct. 29, 1897, AS. Maury was the 24th VA's major, and he included a passage from correspondence also received from Powell, in which Powell wrote that Longstreet in person ordered the regiment to the right. This is entirely possible, but it seems likely that D. R. Jones would have accompanied his wing commander. See David E. Johnston to Carman, Sept. 21 and Sept. 23, 1897, B. F. Eshleman to Carman, Jan. 5, 1899, John B. Richardson to B. F. Eshleman, Mar. 22, 1894, and John B.

Richardson to Carman, Feb. 2, 1899, AS. Eubank's battery may have been somewhere along Jones's front as well, but it seems to have disappeared after it was shelled out of its position west of the Rohrback Bridge in the morning. Carman did not show it on any of his 1908 afternoon maps.

14. *OR Suppl.*, pt. 1, 3:571–572; "Notes by General H. L. Benning," 393; Carman, "Toombs 1 p.m. to bivouac," AS; Enos R. Tate [15th GA] to Carman, Aug. 2, 1898, AS; Ivy Duggan letter, in *Central Georgian* (Sandersville), Oct. 1, 1862, Ivy Duggan Papers, Digital Library of Georgia.

15. Munford to Carman, Mar.[?] 24, 1894, and Dec. 19, 1894, AS.

16. The Confederate batteries and guns facing the 9th Corps were Benjamin Eshleman's four guns; John B. Richardson's four guns; James S. Brown's four guns; James Reilly's two guns; and, on Cemetery Hill, George Moody's four guns, Charles Squires's four guns, and Hugh Garden's four guns. Carman also mentioned that Eubank's (VA) Battery [but Carman did not show it on his afternoon maps], Moody's Madison (LA) Battery, and two of Squires's guns were engaged exclusively with the 5th Corps and the horse artillery. See Carman, 437.

17. Thomas Welsh to Wife, Sept. 23, 1862, ANBL; Todd, *Seventy-Ninth Highlanders*, 242.

18. *OR* 19, 1:430; Carman, 438.

19. Carman, 438–439.

20. Henry W. Woodbury to Carman, June 12, 1905, Carman Papers, NYPL; *OR* 19, 1:434–435; Cox to Carman, Mar. 13, 1896, Carman Papers, NYPL; C. Johnson and Anderson, *Artillery Hell*, 77–81. The figure of 22 guns is arrived at by counting four guns in Cook's battery and 6 each for Roemer, Simmonds, and McMullin.

21. Cox to Carman, Mar. 13, 1896, Carman Papers, NYPL.

22. "Concerning the Battle," BU; Cuffel, *History*, 83.

23. C. F. Johnson, *Long Roll*; "Concerning the Battle," BU.

24. Lt. Col. Edgar Kimball's after-action report, Sept. 20, 1862, in *New York Times*, Oct. 1, 1862; William Reylea, "History," 26, CHS; Jonathan Edward Shipman to Friend Hubbard, Sept. 14, 1862, book 5, Lewis Leigh Collection, USAHEC.

25. John Ryan, *Campaigning with the Irish Brigade*, ed. Sandy Barnard (Terre Haute, IN: AST Press, 2001), 62.

26. William H. Palmer to Jed Hotchkiss, Apr. 22, 1895, and Hugh R. Garden to Carman, May 1, 1896, AS; John Dooley, *John Dooley, Confederate Soldier, His War Journal*, ed. Joseph T. Durkin (Washington, DC: Georgetown Univ. Press, 1945), 45. Dooley's wording implies that Kemper and his staff did not return before the Union attack.

27. Todd, *Seventy-Ninth Highlanders*, 243; Carman, 441; Reardon and Vossler, *Field Guide*, 234.

28. Frederick Pettit to Parents, Sept. 17, 1862, Fred Pettit letters, *CWTI* Miscellaneous Collection, USAHEC; Marinus King McDowell memoirs, 100th PA file, ANBL.

29. Elisha J. Bracken diary, Timothy Brooks Collection, USAHEC; Frederick Pettit to Parents, Sept. 17, 1862, *CWTI* Miscellaneous Collection, USAHEC. Elisha Bracken noted that he used up most of his ammunition in the efforts to dislodge the Confederates from the stone walls, indicating that these were not brief engagements.

30. C. F. Johnson, *Long Roll*, 192; Carman, 441.

31. *OR* 19, 1:891; Carman, 463–464.

32. *OR* 19, 1:891; Carman, 426; J. D. Cox, *Military Reminiscences*, 336, 340–341, 345.

33. *OR* 19, 1:425, 138.

34. *OR* 19, 1:138. There are no time signatures on these messages, other than the final one at 3 p.m. Given the amount of time it would take to signal and decode each message, this series of messages probably was sent between 2:30 and 3 p.m.

35. Carman, 463; *OR* 19, 1:981; Alexander C. Haskell to Carman, Oct. 12, 1896, AS. James Caldwell, the author of the history of Gregg's brigade in the war, believes that they reached the Potomac at 2 p.m. See Caldwell, *History*, 45.

36. Caldwell, *History*, 45; Berry Benson, *Berry Benson's Civil War Book* (Athens: Univ. of Georgia Press, 1992), 27; McIntosh reminiscences, SHC. For Hill's route, see the map from Tilghman W. Flynt [19th GA] to Carman, May 23, 1896, AS.

37. *OR* 19, 1:438; Maj. Edward Overton to ABB, June 21, 1893, ABB Papers, copy in ANBL; S. K. [Samuel Klinger] Schwenk, 1st L[ieu]t., Company A, to the Editor, Sept. 30, 1862, in *Miner's Journal* (Pottsville, PA), Oct. 18, 1862.

38. Thomas Welsh to Wife, Sept. 23, 1862, ANBL; Rick Wiggin, "Profile of a Historic Figure: Answers and Questions About Thomas Welsh," Pride of Columbia: The Life and Legacy of Brig. Gen. Thomas Welsh, https://sites.google.com/site/generalwelsh/profile/ [accessed Feb. 2020].

39. Wiggin, "Profile"; Allen D. Albert, ed. *History of the Forty-Fifth Regiment Pennsylvania Veteran Volunteer Infantry, 1861–1865* (Williamsport, PA: Grit, 1912), 38, 63; Thomas Welsh to Wife, Sept. 14, 1862, ANBL.

40. Thomas Welsh to Wife, Sept. 14, 1862, ANBL.

41. Thomas Welsh to Wife, Sept. 23, 1862, ANBL; *OR* 19, 1:441; Horatio Belcher to [indiscernible], Dec. 15, 1862, in possession of John Fuller, copy in author's collection; Carman, 441–442.

42. Mixson, *Reminiscences*, 29; James R. Hagood, "Memoirs of the First South Carolina Regiment of Volunteer Infantry in the Confederate War for Independence from April 12, 1861, to April 10, 1865," SCL; Daniel Livingston MSR, NA. How Livingston kept his commission as long as he did is a wonder. His regiment was singled out for misbehavior at the Battles of South Mountain and Sharpsburg.

43. Hagood, "Memoirs," SCL; *OR* 19, 1:907; Carman, 442.

44. Carman, 442–443; *OR* 19, 1:907–908; Mixson, *Reminiscences*, 29. Mixson wrote that he never saw Knotts at the stone wall. See Joseph E. Knotts MSR, NA.

45. "Concerning the Battle," BU.

46. David L. Thompson, "With Burnside at Antietam," *B&L*, vol. 2, 661.

47. D. Thompson, "With Burnside," 661; Carman, 449; C. F. Johnson, *Long Roll*, 192.

48. D. Thompson, "With Burnside," 661; C. F. Johnson, *Long Roll*, 192; "Concerning the Battle," BU.

49. D. Thompson, "With Burnside," 661; David E. Johnston to Carman, Sept. 21, 1897, AS.

50. Carman, 457; *OR* 19, 1:453; George Merriman Jr. to Mary, Sept. 24, 1862, ANBL; John Russell Bartlett, *Memoirs of Rhode Island Officers Who Were Engaged in the Service of Their Country During the Great Rebellion of the South* (Providence, RI: Sidney Rider, 1867), 235; Captain Newton Spauling Manross document, typescript, 16th CT file, ANBL; Banks, *Connecticut Yankees*, 85–87.

51. George Merriman Jr. to Mary, Sept. 24, 1862, and George Robbins to Sister, Sept. 23, 1862, ANBL; Wells A. Bigham to Father, Sept. 20, 1862, in Sessarego, *Letters Home*, 14–16.

52. Carman, 457; *OR* 19, 1:453.

53. David E. Johnston to Carman, Sept. 21, 1897, AS; "Notes by General H. L. Benning," 393; Carman, 460.

54. J. L. Napier to Carman, Jan. 13, 1897, and Napier to Col. D. G. McIntosh, Nov. 30, 1896, AS; McIntosh reminiscences, SHC.

55. J. L. Napier to Carman, Jan. 13, 1897, and Napier map to accompany this, AS; McIntosh reminiscences, SHC; McIntosh to Harry Heth, Dec. 3, 1892, AS.

56. Napier to Col. D. G. McIntosh, Nov. 30, 1896, Napier to Carman, Jan. 13, 1897, Napier map to accompany this, and Richardson to Eshleman, Mar. 22, 1894, AS.

57. McIntosh reminiscences, SHC; McIntosh to Harry Heth, Dec. 3, 1892, and Napier to Col. D. G. McIntosh, Nov. 30, 1896, AS.

58. Carman's notes on "1st SC," AS. In these notes, Carman stated that Alexander C. Haskell, Gregg's chief of staff, wrote or told him that Gregg was in the advance for A. P. Hill's division. See Benson, *Civil War Book*, 26; Munford to Carman, Dec. 19, 1894, AS. Munford wrote that Hill's command post was near a large

strawstack in a field immediately north of Blackford's farmhouse.

59. "Gregg, Maxcy," *South Carolina Encyclopedia*, http://www.scencyclopedia.org/sce /entries/gregg-maxcy/ [accessed Feb. 2020]; Edward A. Pollard, *Southern History of the War* (New York: Charles B. Richardson, 1865), vol. 2, 196–197. Also see William W. Freehling, *The Road to Disunion* (New York: Oxford Univ. Press, 1990), 511–535.

60. A. C. Haskell to Carman, June 16, 1896, AS; Carman, 464; *OR* 19, 1:987–991.

61. "Branch, Lawrence O'Bryan," NCpedia, https://www.ncpedia.org/biography/branch -lawrence-obryan/ [accessed Feb. 2020]; Michael C. Hardy, *General Lee's Immortals* (El Dorado Hills, CA: Savas Beatie, 2018), 51.

62. Hardy, *General Lee's Immortals*, 102. Hardy believes Branch carried as few as 250–300 men into action at Sharpsburg, due to straggling from exhaustion. Major William J. Montgomery in the 28th NC, however, wrote to Ezra Carman that he believed his regiment alone carried 300 men into action. The difficulty in determining the strength of any of A. P. Hill's brigades is that stragglers were constantly rejoining their regiments throughout the action. See Montgomery to Carman, Oct. 8, 1897, J. S. Harris to Carman, Feb. 1 and Feb. 13, 1900, and W. G. Morris to Carman, June 1, 1896, AS; Carman, 463, 471. Captain Frederick M. Barber's company was Company H.

63. Lane to Carman, Mar. 22, 1895, and Feb. 10 and 17, 1900, James H. Lane to J. G. Harris, June 5, 1896, and Maj. William J. Montgomery to Carman, Oct. 8, 1897, and July 10, 1900, AS. Montgomery thought the 28th NC led the brigade, but Carman concluded that it was the 7th NC. See Carman, 471. The 5th AL Battalion was left at Harpers Ferry and did not accompany their brigade to Sharpsburg.

64. Eicher and Eicher, *High Commands*, 107; Ural, *Hood's Texas Brigade*, 48–49.

65. Eicher and Eicher, *High Commands*, 107; Jack D. Welsh, *Medical Histories of Confederate* *Generals* (Kent, OH: Kent State Univ. Press, 1995), 10.

66. *OR* 19, 1:1000–1001; Wm. McComb to Carman, Aug. 18, 1898, Carman to Col. Wm. McComb, Feb. 9, 1900, Tilghman Flynt [19th GA] to Carman, Oct. 19, 1898, and George W. Gleaton [19th GA] to Carman, Feb. 10, 1900, AS; Carman, 472.

67. Carman, 443; James H. Rice to Mother, Nov. 12, 1862, SCL; Hugh R. Garden to Carman, May 1, 1896, AS; C. Johnson and Anderson, *Artillery Hell*, 89.

68. *OR* 19, 1:431, 435; Carman, 443; Alfred H. Foster [Palmetto Sharpshooters] to Carman, Jan. 23, 1900, AS. Colonel John Miller owned the mill and rented it to Solomon Lumm.

69. Carman, "45 Penn." map and notes, Carman Papers, NYPL; *OR* 19, 1:441, 946; Thomas Welsh to Wife, Sept. 23, 1862, ANBL.

70. *OR* 19, 1:438–439; John Frederick Holahan, *Civil War Diary of John Frederic Holahan*, ed. Anna M. Holohan Roach Anderson (Lake Park, FL: privately printed, 1970), SUL; Hugh R. Garden to Carman, May 1, 1896, AS; Carman, 444.

71. *OR* 19, 1:439; Carman, 444.

72. Carman, 443; [unidentified] writer, Company K, Oct. 3, 1862, in *Columbia (PA) Spy*, Oct. 11, 1862; *OR* 19, 1:441.

73. Carman, 452. Brown's Wise (VA) Battery incurred only six casualties, but both Maj. William H. Palmer and John Dooley in the 1st VA described the battery as badly wrecked by the Federals' artillery. See Maj. William H. Palmer to Jed Hotchkiss, Apr. 22, 1895, AS; Dooley, *John Dooley*, 46; Barton P. Harper to Sister, Sept. 22, 1862, in *Broome (NY) Republican*, Oct. 8, 1862; Eli Crocker to Friend, Sept. 20, 1862, in *Havana (NY) Journal*, Oct. 4, 1862; E. Kimball after-action report, in *New York Times*, Oct. 1, 1862; Lt. Matthew J. Graham to Rush Hawkins, Sept. 27, 1894, Hawkins Papers, BU. The company that had eight killed from the shell burst was probably Company E, which had a total of nine dead and three mortally wounded.

74. D. Thompson, "With Burnside," 661; David Thompson to Elias, Oct. 1862, ANBL.

75. Carman's notes on "17th VA," AS; Alexander Hunter, "The Battle of Antietam," *SHSP* 31 (1903), 41.

76. Matthew J. Graham to Rush Hawkins, Sept. 27, 1894, Hawkins Papers, BU; Brian Pohanka, *Always Ready* (1996), historical reference for Keith Rocco's painting, "Always Ready," 9th NY folder, ANBL; Carman, 453.

77. Hunter, "Battle" 41; *OR* 19, 1:905; Napier to Col. D. G. McIntosh, Nov. 30, 1896, AS; Dooley, *John Dooley*, 46; Carman, 453–454.

78. Jardine was assigned to command the 89th NY, due to a lack of field officers in that regiment. A characteristic of his leadership was that he gave full credit to Hare for capturing the flag. See *OR* 19, 1:452; C. F. Johnson, *Long Roll*, 193–194; Asa Howard to unknown, Sept. 2, 1862, in *Union (NY) News*, Oct. 9, 1862.

79. Asa Howard to unknown, Sept. 2, 1862, in *Union (NY) News*, Oct. 9, 1862; Carman, 454; C. F. Johnson, *Long Roll*, 193; Matthew J. Graham to Rush Hawkins, Sept. 27, 1894, Hawkins Papers, BU.

80. Carman, 454; *OR* 19, 1:886; C. F. Johnson, *Long Roll*, 193; Matthew J. Graham to Rush Hawkins, Sept. 27, 1894, Hawkins Papers, BU. The actions of the 103rd NY are poorly documented. Carman showed them in a support position behind the 89th and 9th NY when those regiments charged the wall Kemper and Drayton were behind. Their casualties confirm, however, that they were heavily engaged.

81. David Wilson to Mother and Sister, Oct. 1, 1862, in *Mexico (NY) Independent*, Oct. 9, 1862; Wolcott Pascal Marsh, *Letters to a Civil War Bride*, ed. Sandra Marsh Mercer and Jerry Mercer (Westminster, MD: Heritage Books, 2006), 470–471.

82. Carman, 457.

83. McIntosh to Harry Heth, Dec. 3, 1892, AS; McIntosh reminiscences, SHC; Napier to Col. D. G. McIntosh, Nov. 30, 1896, and J. L. Napier to Carman, Jan. 13, 1897, AS; Henry C. Hall to Sister, Oct. 5, 1862, DU.

84. Carman, 458–459; Mattie M. Brunson, "The Flag of the Pee Dee Battery," *CV* 34, no. 3 (1926), 94–95; McIntosh reminiscences, SHC; Napier to Col. D. G. McIntosh, Nov. 30, 1896, AS. Napier wrote of the effectiveness of Durell's fire: "I think most of the carnage sustained by us was from this battery."

85. Carman, 459; L[ieu]t. Roger M. Ford [Company K] diary, ANBL.

86. W. Marsh, *Letters*, 470–471; Carman, 446–447; Charles S. Buell to Parents, in *Waterbury (CT) American*, Oct. 3, 1862; *OR* 19, 1:453. Carman believed Rodman had accompanied the 8th CT in its advance and was riding back to the 16th CT and the 4th RI to bring them up to the 8th CT's support. Based on Harland's report, this seems unlikely. What is more plausible is that Rodman was coming from these two regiments, whom he had just directed to face the Confederates' flank attack, and was riding both to inform Harland of this and to possibly pull the 8th CT back from its exposed position. See Carman, 463.

Chapter 18. The Counterattack

1. Reardon and Vossler, *Field Guide*, 254; John H. Perry to Mother, Sept. 21, 1862, 16th CT file, ANBL; Carman, 462.

2. Carman, 465; Caldwell, *History*, 45; Robert K. Krick, *Lee's Colonels* (Dayton, OH: Morningside Bookshop, 1992), 174. While nearly all of the regiments in the Army of Northern Virginia were raised as part of the Army of the Confederate States, a handful were formed as part of the Provisional Army, authorized in Feb. 1861. This created some confusion and resulted in three 1st SC regiments in the Army of Northern Virginia: the 1st SC Volunteers in Walker's brigade of D. R. Jones's division, and the 1st SC Rifles and 1st SC Provisional Army in Gregg's brigade. There was no difference between these units, except that the Provisional Army was initially intended as a temporary measure. As more

states seceded and joined the Confederacy, it was replaced by the act creating the Army of the Confederate States.

3. *OR* 19, 1:453–454; Bernard F. Blakeslee, *History of the Sixteenth Connecticut Volunteers* (Hartford, CT, 1875), 15–16.

4. William H. Reylea, "History," CHS; George Robbins to Sister, Sept. 23, 1862, 16th CT file, ANBL; John H. Burnham to Mother and Family, Oct. 4, 1862, CHS. Nearly every existing wartime account from the 16th CT mentioned that the Confederates displayed the U.S. colors. Also see Jacob Bauer to Wife, Sept. 18, 1862, 16th CT file, ANBL.

5. John H. Burnham to Mother and Family, Oct. 4, 1862, CHS; Jacob Bauer to Wife, Sept. 18, 1862, 16th CT file, ANBL; Robert Kellogg to Father, Sept. 20, 1862, and Robert Kellogg diary, CHS. Talcott died of his wounds on Dec. 3, 1862.

6. *OR* 19, 1:455–456; Bartlett, *Memoirs*, 235.

7. *OR* 19, 1:992; Benson, *Civil War Book*, 28.

8. *OR* 19, 1:993.

9. Spooner, "Maryland Campaign," 232; Wells A. Bigham to Father, Sept. 20, 1862, in Sessarego, *Letters Home*, 14–16; Reylea, "History," CHS; Sept. 19 entry, Elizor D. Belden diary, and Jacob Bauer to Wife, Sept. 18, 1862, ANBL.

10. *OR* 19, 1:454, 457; Jacob Bauer to Wife, Sept. 18, 1862, ANBL

11. Spooner, "Maryland Campaign," 234; Kellogg to Father, Sept. 20, 1862, CHS; Reylea, "History," 26–28, 43, CHS.

12. William H. McCorkle to Carman, Jan. 23, 1890, AS; *OR* 19, 1:994; Benson, *Civil War Book*, 28; *OR* 19, 1:463.

13. J. Bartlett, *Memoirs*, 236; *OR* 19, 1:457; Carman, 478.

14. *OR* 19, 1:197; L. Gordon, "All Who Went," 177; *OR* 19, 1:991; Maj. Wm. S. Dunlop, "Company B Twelfth S.C.V. in Bivouac and Battle," in *Yorkville (SC) Enquirer*, Nov. 6, 1889; Wardlaw diary, USAHEC.

15. Carman, 468–470; Wayne J. Jacobs, "Memorandum on the Marches of Company A of the

30th Ohio Regiment O.V.I. Commencing July 29, 1861," 30th OH file, ANBL; *OR* 19, 1:470.

16. *OR* 19, 1:466, 470; Carman, 482.

17. David Wilson to Mother and Sister, Oct. 1, 1862, in *Mexico (NY) Independent*, Oct. 9, 1862; Carman, 460.

18. John A. Coffee to Carman, Feb. 10, 1900, AS; "The Fiftieth Georgia Regiment in Virginia and Maryland," *Savannah Republican*, Oct. 16, 1862; *OR* 51, 1:164.

19. *OR* 51, 1:164; W. Marsh, *Letters*, 470–471; "A Fighting Minister from Connecticut," *Medina (NY) Tribune*, Oct. 9, 1862; *OR* 51, 1:164.

20. Carman, 471; "Letter from the Army"; W. Marsh, *Letters*, 470–471; David Wilson to Mother and Sister, Oct. 1, 1862, in *Mexico (NY) Independent*, Oct. 9, 1862; "Lieutenant Marvin Waitt," *Connecticut War Record* 1, no. 5 (Dec. 1863), 96–97, copy in NLCHS; "A Fighting Minister"; Charles S. Buell to Parents, in *Waterbury (CT) American*, Oct. 3, 1862.

21. Carman, 471; *OR* 51, 1:164; Sgt. Frank Spaulding, Sept. 17, 1862, in *Windham County Transcript* (Danielson, CT), Oct. 2, 1862; Banks, *Connecticut Yankees*, 34; *OR* 19, 454–455. Rodman may have communicated with Ward via an aide-de-camp. As Sergeant Wilson wrote in his Oct. 1 letter (see note 20), "Presently an aide rode up with orders for us to retreat in good order." Also see Henry C. Hall to Sister, Oct. 5, 1862, DU; W. Marsh, *Letters*, 470–471; Ford diary, ANBL.

22. Ivy Duggan letter, in *Central Georgian* (Sandersville), Oct. 1, 1862, Duggan, "Army Correspondence," Duggan Papers, Digital Library of Georgia; *Savannah Republican*, Oct. 1, 1862; *OR* 51, 1:167–168. E. McCleod, a Company K private, did not show up on the muster rolls of the regiment.

23. *OR* 19, 1:891–892; *OR* 51, 1:164.

24. *OR* 19, 1:451; Robert E. Bowne, "The 89th Regiment N. Y. S. V.," May 17, 1863, 89th New York Infantry Regiment's Civil War Newspaper Clippings, New York State Military Museum and Veterans Research Center, https://

museum.dmna.ny.gov/index.php/?cID=2491/ [accessed Apr. 2020].

25. *OR* 19, 1:451; Bowne, "89th Regiment N. Y. S. V."; M. Graham, *Ninth Regiment* (New York: E. P. Coby, 1900), 305–306.

26. *OR* 19, 1:451; Bowne, "89th Regiment N. Y. S. V."; M. Graham, *Ninth Regiment*, 305–306; *OR* 19, 1:197.

27. J. D. Cox, "Battle of Antietam," *B&L*, vol. 2, 656; *OR* 19, 1:431; Horatio Belcher to [indiscernible], Dec. 15, 1862, in possession of John Fuller, copy in author's collection. Elisha Bracken, 100th PA, wrote in his diary, "About this time we had used all our ammunition." William Todd, in his history of the 79th NY, stated, "We maintained our position here till we were out of ammunition." See Bracken diary, Timothy Brooks Collection, USAHEC; Todd, *Seventy-Ninth Highlanders*, 243. Belcher was killed in action at Weldon Railroad on Aug. 19, 1864.

28. Carman, 471; William G. Morris to Carman, June 1, 1896, AS; *OR* 19, 1:468, 470.

29. Carman, 472; George W. Gleaton [19th GA] to Carman, Feb. 10, 1900, Tilman Flynt [19th GA] to Carman, Oct. 19, 1898, and Col. Wm. McComb to Carman, Aug. 18, 1898, AS.

30. George W. Gleaton to Carman, Feb. 10, 1900, and Tilghman Flynt to Carman, Oct. 19, 1898, AS.

31. *OR* 19, 1:892.

32. Carman, 475; *OR* 19, 1:468, 470; Jacobs, "Memorandum," ANBL; Carman, 464–465. Several 9th Corps soldiers mentioned the Confederates firing "railroad iron," but they did not describe what they meant by this term.

33. *OR* 19, 1:470; Jacobs, "Memorandum," ANBL; Carman, 475.

34. Carman, 475–476; Tilghman W. Flynt to Carman, Oct. 19, 1898, AS; *OR* 19, 1:468.

35. Carman, 482; *OR* 19, 1:466; D. Cunningham and W. W. Miller, *Report of the Ohio Antietam Battlefield Commission* (Springfield, OH: Springfield, 1904), 62–63.

36. *OR* 19, 1:198; George Crook, *General George Crook*, ed. Martin F. Schmitt (Norman: Univ. of Oklahoma Press, 1946), 100–101.

37. Carman, 447; Cunningham and Miller, *Report*, 90–91.

38. Carman, 484–485; J. D. Cox, "Battle of Antietam," 656. Durell's battery did not take its caissons across Antietam Creek, which limited its ammunition supply. See Sam Rhoads to Carman, Mar. 16, 1896, Carman Papers, NYPL. Possibly Clark did the same. Either Cox or the battery commanders may have felt that there was not enough room for the caissons in the shallow bridgehead.

39. Carman, 480–481; *OR* 19, 1:850–851, 943–944. It is extremely difficult to track the movements of Confederate batteries, sections of batteries, and even individual guns within batteries in the Rebels' counterattack. It is unlikely that we will ever know precisely how many guns were in action.

40. *National Defender* (Norristown, PA), Nov. 18, 1862; Regimental Assoc. Committee, *History*, 46; John William Hudson to Dear Sophy, early Oct. 1862, WMR.

41. Regimental Assoc. Committee, *History*, 46. Carman identified the battery section that drove through the 35th MA as Lieutenant Coffin's. See Carman, 484; *Chelsea (MA) Telegraph and Pioneer*, Sept. 27, 1862; Albert Pope journal, Gregory Coco Collection, USAHEC.

42. T. Parker, *History*, 239; Henry W. Brown to Parents, Oct. 2, 1862, 21st MA file, ANBL.

43. Regimental Assoc. Committee, *History*, 46–47; *Chelsea (MA) Telegraph and Pioneer*, Sept. 27, 1862.

44. Regimental Assoc. Committee, *History*, 48–49; Pope journal, Gregory Coco Collection, USAHEC.

45. Bosbyshell, *48th in the War*, 81.

46. Charles H. Little diary, SHC; Daniel E. Hurd, "My Experiences in the War," William Marvel Collection, USAHEC; Curtis C. Pollock to Ma, Sept. 21, 1862, *CWTI* Miscellaneous Collection, USAHEC.

47. W. G. Morris to Carman, June 1, 1896, J. S. Harris to Carman, Feb. 1 and 13, 1900, and Spier Whitaker Jr. to Carman, Feb. 16, 1900, AS; Carman, 478–479.

48. Wm. McComb to Carman, Aug. 18, 1898, AS; Ivy Duggan letter, in *Central Georgian* (Sandersville), Oct. 1, 1862, Duggan Papers, Digital Library of Georgia; Maj. W. H. McCorkle to Carman, Jan. 23, 1890, and Mar. 2, 1895, William J. Montgomery to Carman, Oct. 8, 1897, and James Lane to Carman, Mar. 22, 1895, AS.

49. John William Hudson to Dear Sophy, early Oct. 1862, WMR; *OR* 19, 1:421; A. E. Burnside testimony, *CCW*, 37th Congress, 1:641. There are no known written communications between Cox and Burnside during the battle, but since Burnside maintained his headquarters near Rohrback's farm, he could only have known about the need for reinforcements if Cox had communicated this to him.

50. Strother, "Personal Recollections," 284; *New York Tribune*, Sept. 20, 1862, 5.

51. Strother, "Personal Recollections," 284; *New York Tribune*, Sept. 20, 1862, 5; Burnside testimony, *CCW*, 37th Congress, 1:641.

52. Strother, "Personal Recollections," 284; *OR* 19, 1:31.

53. J. D. Cox, "Battle of Antietam," 657; *OR* 19, 1:31, 426.

54. *OR* 19, 1:31, 65; McClellan, *Own Story*, 604.

55. Orlando B. Willcox, *Forgotten Valor*, ed. Robert Garth Scott (Kent, OH: Kent State Univ Press, 1999), 361, 366–367.

56. Robert Kellogg to Father, Sept. 20, 1862, CHS; Reylea, "History," CHS; "An Account of the Battle: Diary of Charles S. Buell, 8th CT," Antietam on the Web, https://antietam.aotw .org/exhibit.php?exhibit_id=369/ [accessed Apr. 2020]; W. Marsh, *Letters*, 470–471.

57. *National Defender* (Norristown, PA), Nov. 18, 1862.

58. *Roxbury (MA) City Gazette*, Sept. 25, 1862; Regimental Assoc. Committee, *History*, 49–50.

59. Regimental Assoc. Committee, *History*, 49–50; Pope journal, Gregory Coco Collection, USAHEC; *OR* 19, 1:197. Sgt. S. G. B. [Samuel G. Berry] to Editor, Oct. 5, 1862, *Lynn (MA) Weekly Reporter*, Oct. 18, 1862. Sergeant Berry, who rose to 1st lieutenant and was killed at Petersburg, wrote that the regiment had only 5 officers and 200 enlisted men on the morning of Sept. 18, but by the end of the day, the strength of the regiment had risen to 500.

60. Carman, 480.

61. *OR* 19, 1:897; *Savannah Republican*, Oct. 16, 1862; Boulware diary, LV; Mixson, *Reminiscences*, 34; James R. Hagood, "Memoirs of the First South Carolina Regiment of Volunteer Infantry in the Confederate War for Independence from April 12, 1861 to April 10, 1865," 88, SCL.

62. Henry E. Young to Dear Louis, Sept. 22, 1862, Gordon Collection, EU.

63. Regimental Assoc. Committee, *History*, 51.

Chapter 19. Return to Virginia

1. Capt. John B. Cook letter, Sept. 21, 1862, in *Lewiston (ME) Journal*, Oct. 2, 1862.

2. *OR* 19, 1:408–410; *OR Suppl.*, pt. 3, 1:551.

3. Carman, 344; *OR* 19, 1:410, 910; *OR Suppl.*, pt. 3, 1:520–521, 551.

4. Lowry, *Tarnished Eagles*, 90–93; Robert S. Westbrook, *History of the 49th Pennsylvania Volunteers* (Altoona, PA, 1897), 92–93. For examples of Irwin's troubles with Hancock, see Westbrook, *History*, 102, 104, 111.

5. Hyde, *Following*, 100, 104–105; Hyde, *Civil War Letters*, 50; Carman, 345; *OR* 19, 1:410, 412. Hyde reported that 15 officers and 166 enlisted men participated in the attack. In *Following the Greek Cross*, Hyde gave his regiment's strength on the morning of Sept. 17 as 15 officers and 225 enlisted men, yet he never explained the discrepancy between his Sept. 19 report and his reminiscences.

6. Hyde, *Following*, 100.

7. *OR* 19, 1:412; Hyde, *Following*, 100, 104; Hyde, *Civil War Letters*, 52.

8. *OR* 19, 1:412; Hyde, *Following*, 101.

9. Hyde, *Following*, 101.

10. Carman, 347.

11. Carman, 347; Hilary A. Herbert to General [probably Henry Heth], Jan. 15, 1902, Carman Papers, NYPL; Alexander Chisholm [9th AL] to Gould, Nov. 22, 1892, GP. Initially, Herbert's scratch force had marched down in the direction of the Boonsboro Pike, thinking they could be of some service in the effort to contain the 5th Corps' advance on Cemetery Ridge, but they found no employment there. When they returned to the Piper farm lane, just east of the farmer's house, they saw Confederate skirmishers retreating from the orchard and Hyde's regiment entering it at the southwestern corner.

12. *OR* 19, 1:412–413, 885, 910, 1038; Hyde, *Following*, 102; Carman, 347–348.

13. Alexander Chisholm to Gould, Nov. 22, 1892, GP.

14. Hyde, *Civil War Letters*, 50–51; Hyde, *Following*, 103.

15. Hyde, *Civil War Letters*, 50–51; Hyde, *Following*, 103.

16. *OR* 19, 1:410, 910; *OR Suppl.*, pt. 3, 1:520–521, 551.

17. *OR* 19, 1:412–413; Hyde, *Civil War Letters*, 51; Hyde, *Following*, 104.

18. Hyde, *Civil War Letters*, 51–53; Hyde, *Following*, 107; *OR* 19, 1:402. Irwin was wounded at Fredericksburg and resigned his commission in Oct. 1863.

19. Carman, 584–585; Max Hastings, *Overlord* (New York: Simon & Schuster, 1984), 102.

20. *OR* 19, 1:812–813; Carman, 611; Longstreet, "Invasion," 669; Harsh, *Taken*, 433.

21. S. D. Lee's account, printed in Carman, 504–505; Owen, *In Camp*, 157; Longstreet to Carman, Feb. 11, 1897, and Carman's notes on Charles Marshall interview, Mar. 9, 1897, Carman Papers, NYPL. For a good analysis of the sources documenting this meeting and their reliability, see Harsh, *Sounding*, 207–210.

22. Longstreet to Carman, Feb. 11, 1897, Carman Papers, NYPL; Carman, 504–505; Owen, *In Camp*, 157; Longstreet, "Invasion," 671–672.

23. Carman, 504–505; Longstreet, "Invasion," 671–672; Longstreet to Carman, Feb. 11, 1897, Carman Papers, NYPL.

24. Longstreet, *Manassas*, 291; *OR* 19, 1:151.

25. Strother, "Personal Recollections," 284; entry 13, no date, no time signature, Signal Messages Sent and Received from Elk Mountain, Jan. [18]62–May [18]63, RG 113, NA. The officer on duty at Elk Mountain was Lt. Joseph Gloskoski. The messages in the Signal Corps' ledger book are copies or extracts of original messages sent and received. The message reporting an immense train on the road from Sharpsburg to Shepherdstown has a date of Sept. 16 below it, but this is incorrect and was probably added afterward, as most signal messages contain no date. This message is the only signal note GBM could have been referencing in his communication to Burnside. The other messages before and after this one in the ledger were all sent or received on Sept. 17. See *OR* 19, 1:32.

26. Burnside testimony, *CCW*, 37th Congress, pt. 1, 641–642.

27. *OR* 19, 1:31, 66; McClellan, *Own Story*, 607.

28. Sackett to GBM, Mar. 9, 1876, in McClellan, *Own Story*, 610.

29. *OR* 19, 1:65–66; Cox, quoted in Sears, *Landscape*, 300; Willcox, *Forgotten Valor*, 366–367. In *Forgotten Valor*, 361–363, Willcox made the bizarre claim that A. P. Hill never appeared on the field.

30. Sumner testimony, *CCW*, 37th Congress, pt. 1, 368–369; Franklin testimony, *CCW*, 37th Congress, pt. 1, 627; Franklin, "Notes," 597. Franklin wrote that GBM visited him a second time, later on in the afternoon of Sept. 17, and this was when Franklin suggested an attack on Nicodemus Heights the next morning. But GBM did not return to his right on the 17th, and this was clearly a memory lapse on Franklin's part. See Franklin to his wife, Sept. 20, 1862, quoted in Snell, *From First*, 197; Patrick, *Inside Lincoln's Army*, 151; Webb to Father, Sept. 24, 1862, Webb Papers, Yale Univ.; Weld to Father, Sept. 18, 1862, in Weld, *War Diary*, 138.

31. Carman, 502; Sumner testimony, *CCW*, 37th Congress, pt. 1, 369.

32. *OR* 19, 2:312–313.

33. *OR* 19, 1:372–373; *OR* 51, 1:843–844.

34. *OR* 51, 2, 844; Patrick Lyons, "Partial History of Co. E, 2nd Regt., R.I. Vols., 1861–1864," POHS; Augustus Woodbury, *The Second Rhode Island Regiment* (Providence, RI: Valpey, Angell, 1875), 112–113; Alfred S. Roe, *The Tenth Regiment Massachusetts Volunteer Infantry, 1861–1864* (Springfield, MA: Tenth Regiment Veteran Assoc., 1909), 136; Tockwotton to Editors, Sept. 26, 1862, in *Providence (RI) Evening Press*, Oct. 3,1862.

35. *OR* 19, 2:306; George G. Meade, *Life and Letters of George Gordon Meade*, vol. 1 (New York: Charles Scribner's Sons, 1913), 314.

36. *OR* 19, 1:32, 65–66.

37. Strother, "Personal Recollections," 285; Patrick, *Inside Lincoln's Army*, 151.

38. G. Meade, *Life and Letters*, vol. 1, 311.

39. McLaws to Heth, Dec. 13, 1894, ABB Papers; Shand, "Incidents," SCL; J. J. McDaniel reminiscences, in United Daughters of the Confederacy, South Carolina Division, *Recollections and Reminiscences 1861–1865 through World War I*, vol. 12 ([South Carolina]: South Carolina Division, UDC, 2002), 351; Shinn journal, SHC; William W. Sillers to Sister, Oct. 1, 1862, Sillers-Holmes Family Correspondence, Univ. of Notre Dame; Fleming Saunders to Mother, Sept. 20, 1862, 42nd VA file, ANBL; R. Williams, "'I Longed for Night,'" 26; Charles C. Kibbee letter, Sept. 21, 1862, in *Macon (GA) Weekly*, Oct. 1862, 10th GA file, ANBL; Dawes, *Service*, 98.

40. Melvin Dwinell to the *Courier*, Sept. 16, 1862, in *Weekly Courier* (Rome, GA), Sept. 27, 1862.

41. Felix Viskniskki reminiscences, June 1904, 49th NY file, ANBL; Captain Edwin Drake to Father, Sept. 28, 1862, in *Winsted (NY) Herald*, Oct. 16, 1862.

42. Henry Royer to father, Sept. 18, 1862, in *Norristown (PA) Herald and Free Press*, Sept. 23, 1862; Viskniskki reminiscences, ANBL; R. B. Y. [Roger B. Yard] to Editor, Oct. 11, 1862, in *Monmouth (NJ) Democrat*, Oct. 23, 1862; *Daily Constitutionalist* (Augusta, GA), ANBL. The date of the newspaper is not discernable on the copy, but it is after Oct. 17, 1862.

43. King diary, SHC; Brown diary, in possession of Patricia A. Murphy; R. B. Y. to Editor, Oct. 16, 1862, *Monmouth (NJ) Democrat*, Nov. 6, 1862; An unknown Confederate command on Slocum's front also requested a truce to bury their dead that morning, which Slocum refused and sent back. See Slocum to GBM, no time signature, Sept. 18, 1862, reel 32, MP. For an example of Lee's rigid interpretation of official truces between armies, see Gordon C. Rhea, *On to Petersburg* (Baton Rouge, LA: LSU Press, 2017), 114–121.

44. King diary, SHC.

45. King diary, SHC; "Personne" [Felix G. DeFontaine] to Editors, Sept. 26, 1862, in *Charleston (SC) Mercury*, Oct. 14, 1862; R. B. Y. to Editor, Oct. 16, 1862, in *Monmouth (NJ) Democrat*, Nov. 6, 1862. Chaplain Yard did not identify the officer and only stated that he was looking for a major from a South Carolina regiment. This could only have been Major William C. White. White's body was brought to the Confederates' lines by Federal soldiers, and it is likely that Adjut. Blythe arranged this.

46. R. H. Brett to Sister Kate, Sept. 24, 1862, copy in author's collection.

47. James Steptoe Johnston to Mary Green, Sept. 22, 1862, Mercer-Green-Johnston Papers, LC; Howard J. Huntington diary, 6th WI file, ANBL. Capt. King's statement in his diary reflected the nonlethal nature of the shooting: "Tho' skirmishers were ordered to fire on every one, yet many bodies were recovered by both sides within range without molestation." See King diary, SHC; Samuel H. Walkup journal, Rubenstein Library, DU; James L. Lemon diary, 18th GA file, ANBL.

48. Strother, "Personal Recollections," 285–286.

49. Edward Burruss letter, n.d., typescript, 21st MS file, ANBL. Burruss's father was from Virginia and his mother was from New York.

His father's property included 93 enslaved people, and he claimed a value of $100,000 in real estate and $200,000 in his personal estate in the 1860 Federal census. See Shand, "Incidents," SCL.

50. Gibson after-action report, ANBL; Thomas Hamill to my Dear Kane, Sept. 30, 1862, in *Brooklyn (NY) Daily Times*, Oct. 4, 1862; C. Fuller, *Personal Recollections*; Brown diary, in possession of Patricia A. Murphy; "Masonic Incident," *Penn-Yan (NY) Democrat*, May 15, 1863. For the identity of the Alabama lieutenant, see "Lieutenant John Oden," Antietam on the Web, https://antietam.aotw.org/officers.php?officer_id=12676/ [accessed July 2020]. Oden survived his wounds but, as a result of them, resigned his commission in June 1863. Nisbet was the only Georgia lieutenant colonel wounded in the Sunken Lane area. The 132nd Pennsylvania also claimed credit for removing him, although he believed it was men in the Irish Brigade who rescued him. See Lindsey and Andrews, "Third Georgia Regiment," Andrews Papers, SHC.

51. Brown diary, in possession of Patricia A. Murphy.

52. *OR* 19, 1:994; John Dooley, *John Dooley*, 50; William Powers to Children, Sept. 23, 1862, in *New York Union News*, Oct. 9, 1862; David E. Johnston, *Four Years a Soldier* (Princeton, WV, 1887), AS; William H. Reylea, "History," 40–41, CHS.

53. Henry Pratt to J. N., Sept. 23, 1862, in *Havana (NY) Journal*, Oct. 4, 1862; Lane to Carman, May 15, 1896, AS.

54. S. K. [Samuel Klinger] Schwenk, 1st L[ieu]t., Company A, to the Editor, Sept. 30, 1862, in *Miner's Journal* (Pottsville, PA), Oct. 18, 1862.

55. *OR* 51, 1:846–848.

56. *OR* 19, 1:32, 67, 370–374.

57. *OR* 19, 2:322.

58. McClellan, *Civil War Papers*, 469; Strother, "Personal Recollections," 287.

59. McClellan, *Civil War Papers*, 469; *OR* 19, 1:374; Sumner testimony, *CCW*, 37th Congress, pt. 1,

369; Strother, "Personal Recollections," 286. Strother left the meeting to ride around the battlefield. When he returned, he was told that Sumner "was opposed to a renewal of the battle." GBM's testimony before the joint congressional committee on Mar. 2, 1863, closely agreed with Sumner's statement regarding the perceived condition of the army: "The next morning I found that our loss had been so great, and there was so much disorganization in some of the commands, that I did not consider it proper to renew the attack that day, especially as I was sure of the arrival that day of two fresh divisions, amounting to about 15,000 men." See George B. McClellan testimony, *CCW*, 37th Congress, pt. 1, 441.

60. Strother, "Personal Recollections," 286; Franklin to GBM, 10 a.m., Sept. 18, 1862, reel 32, MP; *OR* 19, 1:32.

61. Strother, "Personal Recollections," 286; Couch's division, Fourth Army Corps, ABB Tablet no. 76.

62. King diary, SHC; William L. Fagan to R. D. Parker, Dec. 25, 1899, R. Parker Papers, CPL; *OR* 19, 2:610; James Nance to Laura, Sept. 24, 1862, SCL; Lafayette McLaws, "The Capture of Harpers Ferry," *Philadelphia Weekly Press*, Sept. 19, 1888; Carman, 507.

63. Longstreet to Carman, Feb. 11, 1897, Carman Papers, NYPL; *OR* 19, 1:841; Carman, 506–507; Carman's notes on Charles Marshall interview, Mar. 9, 1897, Carman Papers, NYPL. S. D. Lee claimed that Robert E. Lee seriously considered offensive action on Sept. 18, but there is no evidence for this.

64. William W. Sherwood journal, VHS.

65. William Reylea, 16th CT, wrote that it "rained terribly" in the late afternoon and evening of Sept. 18. See Reylea, "History," CHS; *OR* 19, 1:123; Francis A. Donaldson, *Inside the Army of the Potomac*, ed. J. Gregory Acken (Harrisburg, PA: Stackpole Books, 1998), 125.

66. Harsh, *Sounding*, 21; Owen, *In Camp*, 159–160.

67. Osmun Latrobe diary, VHS; Melvin Dwinell to the *Weekly Courier*, Sept. 21, 1862, in

Tri-Weekly Courier (Charleston, WV), Oct. 4, 1862; Herman Humphrey Perry [Company D, 2nd GA] to Carman, Jan. 22, 1896, AS. Perry placed the incident between midnight and 1 a.m. on Sept. 17, but Latrobe and Dwinell, whose accounts were contemporary, recorded that it occurred on the night of the 18th. Dwinell's detailed letter differs significantly from Perry's, and although Dwinell was not an eyewitness, he wrote it only 3 days after the event. Also see Ivy Duggan letter, in *Central Georgian* (Sandersville), Oct. 1, 1862, Ivy Duggan Papers, Digital Library of Georgia. Duggan wrote that the incident occurred while the brigade was forming up to march. In addition, see Crowninshield, *History*, 80.

68. Boulware diary, LV; *OR* 19, 1:972; Walkup journal, DU; Latrobe diary, VHS; E. B. Tate [15th GA] to Carman, Aug. 2, 1898, AS; *Macon (GA) Daily Telegraph*, Oct. 4, 1862.

69. Thomas McGrath, *Shepherdstown* (Lynchburg, VA: Schroeder, 2007), 21; *OR* 19, 1:830; Owen, *In Camp*, 160; Andrew B. Wardlaw diary, USA-HEC; Jedediah Hotchkiss, *Make Me a Map of the Valle*, ed. Archie P. McDonald (Dallas: Southern Methodist Univ. Press, 1973), 83; Wm. T. Field to Carman, May 2, 1895, and July 21, 1898, AS. Lieut. Field wrote that his battalion was detailed on Sept. 16 "as a pioneer Corps to repair the roads to and a ford on the Potomac River." Also see George B. Davis, Leslie J. Perry, and Joseph W. Kirkley, *Official Military Atlas of the Civil War*, comp. Calvin D. Cowles (Washington, DC: U.S. Gov't. Printing Office, 1891), plate 29. The army's trains may have followed Shepherdstown Road before turning south to Boteler's Ford, about a half mile past Grove's home. This is the route marked on the plate.

70. Walkup journal, DU; Dooley, *John Dooley*, 51; Douglas, *I Rode*, 177; Hotchkiss, *Make Me a Map*, 83; Hotchkiss to G. F. R. Henderson, Mar. 24, 1896, in Robertson, *Stonewall Jackson*, 620.

71. *OR* 19, 1820; W. H. Cheek to Carman, June 14, 1897, AS; Carman summary of J. M. Monie letter to Carman, June 3, 1897, AS.

72. Dooley, *John Dooley*, 51; King diary, SHC. King mentioned that General Kemper, acting as provost marshal, was with Lee. See Joseph J. Norton diary, SCL; Varina D. Brown, *A Colonel at Gettysburg and Spotsylvania* (Columbia, SC: State, 1931), 43.

Chapter 20. Shepherdstown

1. *OR* 19, 1:32, 67; *OR* 51, 1:848.

2. *OR* 51, 1:850–852; David Strother, "Personal Recollections," 284. Pleasonton's orders were sent at the same time as Sumner's, at 4 a.m.

3. *OR* 19, 1:212; Joseph W. Brown, *The Signal Corps, U.S.A., in the War of the Rebellion* (Boston: U.S. Veteran Signal Corps Assoc., 1896), 334; *New York Times*, Sept. 25, 1862, 1; McClellan, *Civil War Papers*, 469–470.

4. *New York Times*, Sept. 25, 1862.

5. McGrath, *Shepherdstown*, 35–36; Abner Hard, *History of the Eighth Cavalry Regiment, Illinois Volunteers, During the Great Rebellion* (Aurora, IL, 1868), 187; *OR Suppl.*, pt. 1, 3:515, 523, 526, 529; *New York Times*, Sept. 25, 1862; *OR* 19, 1:212.

6. Pleasonton to Marcy, 10:20 a.m., Sept. 19, 1862, and Myer to Marcy, 10:45 a.m., Sept. 19, 1862, reel 32, MP; Louis R. Fortescue, *Service with the Signal Corps*, ed. J. Gregory Acken (Knoxville: Univ. of Tennessee Press, 2015), 133–134.

7. Allen S. Cutts, quoted in Peter S. Carmichael, "We Don't Know What on Earth to Do with Him: William Nelson Pendleton and the Affair at Shepherdstown, September 19, 1862," in Gary Gallagher, ed., *The Antietam Campaign* (Chapel Hill: Univ. of North Carolina Press, 1999), 263–264; John H. Chamberlayne, *Ham Chamberlayne—Virginian* (Richmond, VA: Dietz, 1932). 118.

8. *OR* 19, 1:830–831, 838; S. P. Lee, *Memoirs*, 213; Carmichael, "We Don't Know," 262.

9. *OR*, 19, 1:830–831, 838; Carmichael, "We Don't Know," 270; Clark to Carman, Apr. 24, 1899, and Jan. 3, 1900, AS; *Daily Morning News* (Savannah), Oct. 4, 1862. Of the batteries that reinforced Pendleton, two were from R. H. Anderson's division: Capt. Victor Maurin's Donaldsonville (LA) Artillery, with one 10 lb. Parrott and two 3-inch rifles (probably), and Captain William Henry Chapman's Dixie (VA) Battery, with one rifle and one Napoleon. From Lawton's division, there was Capt. Louis E. D'Aquin's LA Guard Battery, with two 10 lb. Parrotts, and from A. P. Hill's division, Capt. Carter Braxton's Fredericksburg (VA) Battery, with two 10 lb. Parrotts. D. H. Hill's division provided Capt. Robert A. Hardaway's (AL) Battery, with two 10 lb. Parrotts; and Lt. Thomas A. Maddox, who had one 10 lb. Parrott. Capt. Barnwell's report identified him with Cutts's battalion. Maddox served with Hamilton's battery earlier in the war, and, after it was disbanded in July 1862, with Milledge's (GA) Battery, but he may have been detailed to Cutts's battalion. What battery his gun was from is unknown. The battery positioned by Col. Armistead Long consisted of four 6 lb. guns, but its organizational affiliation is also unknown.

10. *OR* 19, 1:831–832, 835, 838.

11. S. P. Lee, *Memoirs of William Nelson Pendleton*, 225.

12. Robert E. Lee to Mrs. Thomas J. Jackson, Jan. 25, 1866, quoted in Carmichael, "We Don't Know," 266; S. P. Lee, *Memoirs*, 213.

13. *OR* 19, 1:339, 421; *OR* 19, 2:330; *OR* 51, 1:851, 853; McClellan, *Civil War Papers*, 470.

14. Fitz John Porter notes, reel 3, frame 56, and Richard T. Auchmuty to Carswell McClellan, Jan. 12, 1892, reel 31 (container 63), frames 88–89, Fitz John Porter Papers, LC [courtesy of John Hennessy].

15. John M. Bancroft diary, Auburn Univ.; S. S. Partridge to Dear Mac, Sept. 26, 1862, in McKelvey, *Rochester*, 89; Daniel G. McNa-

mara, *The History of the Ninth Regiment, Massachusetts Volunteer Infantry* (Boston: E. B. Stillings, 1899), 221; Donaldson, *Inside*, 127.

16. Donaldson, *Inside*, 127; John L. Parker, *Henry Wilson's Regiment* (Boston: Rand Avery, 1887), 197.

17. *OR* 19, 1:343, 353–354; C. Johnson and Anderson, *Artillery Hell*, 74–75.

18. C. Bowen, *Dear Friends*, 154–155, 157; *Yates County Chronicle* (Penn-Yan, NY), Oct. 2, 1862.

19. *OR* 19, 1:339, 345; J. Parker, *Henry Wilson's Regiment*, 197; *Yates County Chronicle* (Penn-Yan, NY), Oct. 2, 1862; C. A. Stevens, *Berdan's United States Sharpshooters in the Army of the Potomac, 1891–1895* (St. Paul, MN, 1892), 207.

20. Joshua L. Chamberlain to Fanny, Sept. 21, 1862, PMNC; *OR* 19, 1:832; S. P. Lee, *Memoirs*, 213; Merit Seay, quoted in Carmichael, "We Don't Know," 267.

21. *OR* 19, 2:612–613; *OR* 19, 1:832.

22. *OR* 19, 2:612–613; *OR* 19, 1:832.

23. *OR* 19, 1:339–340; McGrath, *Shepherdstown*, 72; Carman, 509.

24. *OR* 19, 1:345; *Yates County Chronicle* (Penn-Yan, NY), Oct. 2, 1862.

25. George M. Barnard to Mother, Sept. 21, 1862, MHS.

26. *OR* 19, 1:345; *Yates County Chronicle* (Penn-Yan, NY), Oct. 2, 1862; C. Stevens, *Berdan's Sharpshooters*, 207.

27. D. H. Hill to Robert L. Dabney, July 19, 1864, quoted in Carmichael, "We Don't Know," 270; *OR* 19, 1:833; Douglas, *I Rode*, 184; Weld, *War Diary*, 139. Carmichael notes that Jubal Early, the acting division commander of Lawton's division, held Lamar responsible for the poor performance of the brigade at Shepherdstown. Whatever inquiries into Lamar's competence occurred did not result in any action against him, and he remained in command of the 61st GA until he was killed at the Battle of Monocacy in 1864. See Carmichael, "We Don't Know," 29n, 285; *OR* 19, 1:973. No question seems to have been raised on the performance

of Col. James Hodges, commanding Armistead's brigade. Hodges continued in command of the 14th VA until he was killed on July 3, 1863, at the Battle of Gettysburg.

28. *OR* 19, 1:833; Martin N. Bertera and Kim Crawford, *The 4th Michigan Infantry in the Civil War* (East Lansing: Michigan State Univ. Press, 2010), 107.

29. *OR* 19, 1:833, 848; S. P. Lee, *Memoirs*, 214; Carmichael, "We Don't Know," 271.

30. *OR* 19, 1:833–834, 838, 848; S. P. Lee, *Memoirs*, 214.

31. Bertera and Crawford, *4th Michigan*, 107.

32. Carmichael, "We Don't Know," 272; *OR* 19, 1:833–834; S. P. Lee, *Memoirs*, 214; Emily V. Mason, *Popular Life of Gen. Robert E. Lee* (Baltimore: John Murphy, 1872), 151. That the staff officer was unidentified in Mason's account is cause for suspicion about the accuracy of the alleged quotations from Lee and Pendleton.

33. *OR* 19, 1:833–834; S. P. Lee, *Memoirs*, 214; Carmichael, "We Don't Know," 273.

34. Carmichael, "We Don't Know," 273.

35. *OR* 19, 1:142, 957, 982; Douglas, *I Rode*, 184. James I. Robertson, in *Stonewall Jackson*, 621–622, notes that in 1896, Surgeon Hunter McGuire wrote that Jackson drove the enemy into the Potomac River on Sept. 20, "before General Lee ever came over or before Gen. Jackson ever heard from him." McGuire, of course, could not have been privy to all that transpired between Lee and Jackson. Robertson also relates that Jackson had time to conduct a personal reconnaissance before ordering his troops to march, adding greater evidence to the conclusion that this was not an impulsive or hasty action. When Robert L. Dabney, with whom D. H. Hill shared his recollections in 1864, published his biography of Jackson in 1866 and included Hill's story of Lee's befuddlement that night, he drew a strong rebuttal from Lee, who rarely entered into debates about the war.

36. Porter to Marcy, 9 p.m., Sept. 19, 1862, image 167, Correspondence I: Sept. 16–22, MP. It is

possible that General John Buford suggested to Porter that Pleasonton's cavalry was in need of refitting and reshoeing. This would explain why Porter issued the order in the name of GBM, through Buford.

37. [Norman M. Smith] to General, 6:30 a.m., Sept. 19, 1862, and Voss to Seth Williams, Sept. 19, 1862, images 173 and 175, Correspondence I: Sept. 16–22, MP; *OR* 51, 1:851–852.

38. *OR* 51, 1:850, 853; Pleasonton to Marcy, 12:15 a.m., Sept. 20, 1862, image 202, Correspondence I: Sept. 16–22, MP.

39. Carman, 79; *OR* 19, 1:350; Bancroft diary, Auburn Univ.

40. *OR* 19, 1:340, 346, 351, 361.

41. *OR* 19, 2:334.

42. *OR* 51, 1:854; Porter to Marcy, no time signature, Sept. 20, 1862, and Porter to Marcy, 8 a.m., Sept. 20, 1862, images 215 and 212, Correspondence I: Sept. 16–22, MP. It is clear that the untimed dispatch was sent first, during General Charles Griffin's crossing of the Potomac River to retrieve the Confederates' abandoned artillery and equipment.

43. *OR* 19, 1:361; McGrath, *Shepherdstown*, 97.

44. *OR* 19, 1:361, 363, 365, 366; Amaziah Barber to Father and Mother, Sept. 28, 1862, 11th U.S. file, ANBL.

45. Pleasonton to Marcy, 10:30 a.m. and noon, Sept. 20, 1862, images 209 and 210–211, Correspondence I: Sept. 16–22, MP; *OR* 19, 1:351. McGrath, in *Shepherdstown*, 101, writes that when Barnes's brigade crossed the Potomac River, they passed the 3rd IN and some horse artillery returning from Virginia and watering their horses, but he did not give the source for this information. This would have been the force Pleasonton sent across to Virginia.

46. *OR* 19, 1:361; Pleasonton to Marcy, 10:30 a.m., Sept. 20, 1862, image 210–211, Correspondence I: Sept. 16–22, MP.

47. *OR* 19, 1:346; Donaldson, *Inside*, 129.

48. Donaldson, *Inside*, 129. Thomas Coane recovered himself and was eventually promoted to 1st lieutenant. John Kenner was promoted to

quartermaster sergeant in Oct. 1862 but was reduced to the ranks in Feb. 1863.

49. Donaldson, *Inside*, 127; "Shepherdstown Cement Mill," Jefferson County Historic Landmarks Commission, http://jeffersoncountyhlc.org/index.php/landmarks/botelers-cement-mill/ [accessed Sept. 2020]. Alexander Boteler acquired the mill before the Civil War and owned the property on the Virginia side of the ford that bore his name. He was a colonel in the Confederate service, although a claim of poor health kept him from active duty. Boteler was also a member of the Confederate House of Representatives. The burning of his mill, although allegedly done for military reasons, probably resulted from his well-known Confederate sympathies.

50. Robert G. Carter, *Four Brothers in Blue* (Washington, DC: Gibson Bros., 1913), 20–21, 28; *OR* 19, 1:346; Carman, 125.

51. *OR* 19, 2:334–335.

52. *OR* 12, 3:795; *OR* 19, 1:346, 348; Donaldson, *Inside*, 129–130; John L. Smith, *History of the Corn Exchange Regiment, 118th Pennsylvania Volunteers* (Philadelphia, 1888), 59.

53. *OR* 19, 1:346.

54. *OR* 19, 1:957, 973, 982. Many stragglers had rejoined their units on Sept. 19, so A. P. Hill's strength may have been closer to 4,000.

55. Carman, 142, 160; *OR* 19, 1:982; Marion Hill Fitzpatrick, *Letters to Amanda*, ed. Jeffrey C. Lowe and Sam Hodges (Macon, GA: Mercer Univ. Press, 1998), 21–22.

56. *OR* 19, 1: 982, 995; Wardlaw diary, USAHEC; V. Brown, *A Colonel*, 43; Benson, *Civil War Book*, 29; Caldwell, *History*, 50.

57. *OR* 19, 1:1001, 1004.

58. *OR* 19, 1:340, 351–352, 361, 363–368; Amaziah Barber to Father and Mother, Sept. 28, 1862, 11th U.S. file, ANBL.

59. *OR* 19, 1:347; R. Carter, *Four Brothers*, 29; Edwin C. Bennett, *With Musket and Sword* (Boston: Coburn, 1900), 100–101.

60. *OR* 19, 1:346–347.

61. R. Carter, *Four Brothers*, 29; Bennett, *With Musket*, 101.

62. Donaldson, *Inside*, 127, 132; J. L. Smith, *History of the Corn Exchange*, 59.

63. Donaldson, *Inside*, 106, 132. Passmore officially resigned on Dec. 13, 1862. Donaldson's scathing indictment of his performance can be found in *Inside the Army*, 144–145.

64. Donaldson, *Inside*, 132–133.

65. Donaldson, *Inside*, 133; J. L. Smith, *History of the Corn Exchange*, 60–61.

66. Donaldson, *Inside*, 133; McGrath, *Shepherdstown*, 143.

67. J. L. Smith, *History*, 63; Donaldson, *Inside*, 133.

68. McGrath, *Shepherdstown*, 144; J. L. Smith, *History*, 63–65; Donaldson, *Inside*, 133; *OR* 19, 1:349.

69. Donaldson, *Inside*, 133; J. L. Smith, *History*, 65–66.

70. Donaldson, *Inside*, 133–134; J. L. Smith, *History*, 67.

71. J. L. Smith, *History*, 66–67; *OR* 19, 1:1001–1002, 1004; Andrew J. Proffit to Mother and Father, Sept. 22, 1862, Proffit Papers, SHC; Lemuel Crocker to Parents, Sept. 22, 1862, in *Advocate* (Buffalo, NY), Oct. 2, 1862; Donaldson, *Inside*, 134.

72. J. L. Smith, *History*, 68; Donaldson, *Inside*, 135.

73. Donaldson, *Inside*, 134–135; J. L. Smith, *History*, 68; Fortescue, *Service*, 136.

74. Lemuel Crocker to Parents, Sept. 22, 1862, in *Advocate* (Buffalo, NY), Oct. 2, 1862; Donaldson, *Inside*, 136.

75. J. L. Smith, *History*, 69–72; Lemuel Crocker to Parents, Sept. 22, 1862, in *Advocate* (Buffalo, NY), Oct. 2, 1862; Donaldson, *Inside*, 136.

76. *OR* 19, 1:204. Colonel James Barnes received considerable criticism for his handling of operations on Sept. 20. Lt. Louis Fortescue, a signal officer, was particularly harsh in his assessment, writing about the "unpardonable stupidity of the officer, Barnes." See Fortescue, *Service*, 136–137. For a detailed examination of Barnes and the criticism leveled at him, see McGrath, *Shepherdstown*, 201–202. Barnes's critics did not understand that

Prevost had received orders to retreat but ignored them, since Prevost believed they came from outside official channels.

77. *OR* 19, 1:983. The most detailed accounting of casualties is in McGrath, *Shepherdstown*, 211–217.

78. *OR* 19, 1:821; Carman, 269. For correspondence on Couch's and Franklin's orders and movements, see *OR* 51, 1:851–856. For the 12th Corps' time of arrival in Pleasant Valley and Maryland Heights, see A. Williams, *Cannon's Mouth*, 131, 132. Williams confused the dates of his march. He marched on Sept. 19, not the 18th, and arrived early in the morning of the 20th.

79. *OR* 19, 2:142–143.

80. *OR* 51, 1:856–858.

81. GBM to Mary Ellen, Sept. 20, 1862, in McClellan, *Civil War Papers*, 473; *OR* 19, 1:68.

82. J. L. Smith, *History*, 76; Donaldson, *Inside*, 138–139; Lemuel Crocker to Parents, Sept. 22, 1862, in *Advocate* (Buffalo, NY), Oct. 2, 1862. Crocker was remarkably modest in describing his exploit on Sept. 21 to his parents. Even though it is well documented that he carried out the effort alone, he wrote to his parents that he and "a volunteer force" crossed the Potomac River, so he may have received some assistance.

83. J. L. Smith, *History*, 76–77; Donaldson, *Inside*, 138–139. Crocker thought the Confederate officer was "Lee," and it might well have been, just not Robert E. Lee. Private Mishaw survived his wound.

84. J. L. Smith, *History*, 76–77; Donaldson, *Inside*, 138–139. Ironically, on Sept. 22, Porter sent over a flag of truce with Col. Alexander Webb, his chief of staff. He also dispatched some paroled Confederate prisoners and applied for leave to bury the dead. See Weld, *War Diary*, 139.

Chapter 21. Aftermath

1. A. M. Waddell, "General George Burgwyn Anderson," *SHSP* 14 (1886), 395; Walter R. Battle to Mother, Sept. 29, 1862, in Hugh B. Johnston, "The Civil War Letters of George Boardman Battle and of Walter Raleigh Battle of Wilson, North Carolina," WCPL; R. K. Krick, "It Appeared," in Gallagher, *Antietam Campaign*, 236, 253nn31–32.

2. Walter R. Battle to Mother, Sept. 29, 1862, in H. Johnston, "Civil War Letters," WCPL; R. K. Krick, "It Appeared," 236, 253nn31–32; Seaton Gales, "Gen. Geo. Burgwyn Anderson," *Our Living and Our Dead* 3 (July–Dec. 1875), 334; Alfred J. Bollet, *Civil War Medicine* (Tucson, AZ: Galen, 2002), 152–154; *Raleigh (NC) Register*, Oct. 18, 1862.

3. McDowell memoirs, 100th PA file, ANBL. This is probably the same barn that Dr. Nathan Mayer in the 11th CT used temporarily as an aid station during his regiment's effort to capture the bridge. Mayer later evacuated it as being too dangerous: "The old barn was very unsafe; shell fell about it constantly, and musket balls whistled through the straw." See Dr. Nathan Mayer to Brother Louie, Sept. 29, 1862, *Hartford (CT) Daily Courant*, Oct. 7, 1862.

4. McDowell memoirs, 100th PA file, ANBL.

5. McDowell memoirs, 100th PA file, ANBL. For general information on what was referred to as "antisepsis," see Bollet, *Civil War Medicine*, 211–213.

6. G. Wren diary, Woodruff Library, EU.

7. G. Wren diary, Woodruff Library, EU; George L. P. Wren MSR, RG 109, NA. Wren was wounded again at the Battle of Chancellorsville on May 4, 1863, and he was captured on May 12, 1864, at the Battle of Spotsylvania Court House. He remained a POW at Fort Delaware until he took the Oath of Allegiance on June 16, 1865. He died in 1901.

8. James R. Simpson recollections, 125th PA file, ANBL; John H. Nelson, *"As Grain Falls Before the Reaper"* (Hagerstown, MD: John H. Nelson, 2004), 18–19.

9. Nelson, *"As Grain Falls,"* 12; Charles C. Coffin, "Antietam Scenes," *B&L*, vol. 2, 683; Simpson recollections, ANBL.

10. Simpson recollections, ANBL; J. W. Cursy[?] telegram to John Simpson, Sept. 20, 1862,

125th PA file, ANBL; 1860 Federal Census, NA. Before the war, Simpson lived with his father John, a 64-year-old farmer; his sisters Anna, age 30, and Lydia, age 25; and his brother George, age 22.

11. G. Merrill Dwelle to Sister Carrie, Sept. 18 and Oct. 18, 1862, G. Merrill Dwelle Papers, MNHS; Nelson, *"As Grain Falls,"* 14–15; *OR* 19, 1:112. Kathleen Ernst describes Smoketown as "a tiny settlement consisting of 'three small houses and a pig pen.'" See Kathleen Ernst, *Too Afraid to Cry* (Harrisburg, PA: Stackpole Books, 1999), 171.

12. G. Merrill Dwelle to Sister Carrie, Oct. 18, 1862, Dwelle Papers, MNHS.

13. G. Merrill Dwelle to Sister Carrie, Oct. 18, 1862, and Feb. 17, 1863, Dwelle Papers, MNHS. Dwelle survived the war and lived until 1915.

14. Samuel C. Hodgman to Brother, Sept. 17, 1862, U.S. Civil War Collection, WMU; Hodgman to Father, Nov. 17, 1862, in "'Gone a Sogerine': The Civil War Experiences of Samuel Chase Hodgman," WMU; George Merriman to Mary, Sept. 24, 1862, 16th CT file, ANBL; Edwin R. Coghill diary, 30th VA file, ANBL.

15. Boulware diary, Boulware Papers, LV; George Barr to My Dear Vinnie, Dec. 23, 1862, Schoff Civil War Collection, Clements Library, UM; Isaac Scott to My Dear Colonel, Oct. 8, 1862, *Wheeling (WV) Daily Intelligencer*, Oct. 14, 1862. Given the number of wounds Scott helped dress, his aid station was probably at Roulette's farm. Also see George Bronson to Wife, Sept. 21, 1862, 11th CT file, ANBL; Dr. Nathan Mayer to Brother Louie, Sept. 29, 1862, *Hartford (CT) Daily Courant*, Oct. 7, 1862; J. Franklin Dyer, *The Journal of a Civil War Surgeon*, ed. Michael B. Chesson (Lincoln: Univ. of Nebraska Press, 2003), 39–40. Surgeon William J. H. White, medical director of the 6th Corps, was also killed, but White was not treating the wounded at that time. He was mistaken for a combat officer. See "Surgeon William James Harrison White," Antietam in the Web, http://antietam.aotw.org

/officers.php?officer_id=13824&from=results/ [accessed Dec. 2020].

16. Ludolph Logenhery diary, 7th WI file, ANBL; William Bolton journal, CWLM, copy in 51st PA file, ANBL; *OR* 19, 2:659.

17. Wardlaw diary, USAHEC; William M. Clark to Brother, Sept. 22, 1862, 28th PA file, ANBL; C. to Father, Sept. 20, 1862, in *Brandon (VT) Monitor*, Oct. 3, 1862; Nelson, *"As Grain Falls,"* 12, 30–31; Joseph K. Barnes, *Medical and Surgical History of the Civil War*, vol. 2, pt. 1 (Wilmington, NC: Broadfoot, 1990), 108; H. Stevens, *Souvenir*, 61. The two-wheeled ambulances were phased out as the war progressed and replaced with four-wheeled models with springs. See Bollet, *Civil War Medicine*, 105–106.

18. James Kent Lewis to Mother, Sept. 18, 1862, 16th NC file, ANBL; *Athens (GA) Southern Banner*, Oct. 10, 1862; P. Alexander, *Writing and Fighting*, 112–113.

19. J. M. Greene to Annie Shoemaker, Sept. 21, 1862, 17th MS file, ANBL.

20. *OR* 19, 2:606, 659.

21. *OR* 19, 1: 107, 109; Barnes, *Medical and Surgical*, 104–105; "Appeal to the Public, with Letters Concerning Army Operations and the Relief Work of the Commission in Maryland (Sept. 24, 1862)," 13, U.S. Sanitary Commission, *Documents of the U. S. Sanitary Commission* (New York, 1866), vol. 1, no. 48, 13; James M. Greiner, Janet L. Coryell, and James R. Smither, eds., *A Surgeon's Civil War* (Kent, OH; Kent State Univ. Press, 1994), 24.

22. Robertson, "Federal Surgeon," 141, 145; Nelson, *"As Grain Falls,"* 38–41. Nelson writes that the location of Millard Redhouse Hospital, as Dimon's hospital was later named, is unknown, but a U.S. Sanitary Commission map placed it at the present-day intersection of Dogstreet and Geeting Roads, east of Keedysville.

23. Robertson, "Federal Surgeon," 145–146, 148–149.

24. Robertson, "Federal Surgeon," 148–151. Dr. Jonathan Letterman reported that "the

difficulty of supplying the hospitals with food was a much greater one than that of providing articles belonging to the medical department, and was a matter of very great concern." See *OR* 19, 1:109.

25. Hitchcock, *War*, 1904), 73; Spangler, *My Little War Experience*, 39.

26. Ben Milikin to Gould, Mar. 1, 1895, GP; Tilghman W. Flynt to Carman, Feb. 29, 1898, AS.

27. Nelson, *"As Grain Falls,"* 5, 46, 76. Also see Gordon Dammann and John W. Schildt, *Islands of Mercy* (Brunswick, MD: E. Graphics, 2019); "Appeal," 7; "A Union Soldier—Casualty at Antietam—September 17, 1862," 19th MA file, ANBL.

28. *OR* 19, 1:110. As an example of the numbers of wounded men being moved, Surgeon C. F. H. Campbell, the director of transportation at Frederick, reported that he sent 6,362 from Frederick to Washington, DC, Baltimore, and Philadelphia during his time there. See Barnes, *Medical and Surgical*, 106.

29. *OR* 19, 1:111; Bernard Rostker, *Providing for the Casualties of War* (Santa Monica, CA: Rand, 2013), 82–83, 87–88. A 1:19 ratio for nurses is consistent with Marinus McDowell's experience in Frederick, where his tent had 18 patients to 1 nurse.

30. Jonathan Stowe diary, USAHEC.

31. Barnes, *Medical and Surgical*, 107; *Lancaster (PA) Daily Inquirer*, Sept. 22, 1862; Gregory A. Coco, *A Strange and Blighted Land* (Gettysburg, PA: Thomas, 1995), 241, 245; Rostker, *Providing*, 79; Allan Nevins and Milton H. Thomas, eds., *The Diary of George Templeton Strong*, vol. 3 (New York: Macmillan, 1952), 257; "Appeal," 9–14.

32. "Appeal," 9.

33. Ernst, *Too Afraid*, 168–169; Nelson, *"As Grain Falls,"* 53; John Banks, *Connecticut Yankees*, 74; "Remembering Their Ancestor: Nurse Maria Hall," Oct. 26, 2013, John Banks' Civil War Blog, https://john-banks.blogspot.com/2013 /10/remembering-their-ancestor-civil-war .html [accessed Dec. 2020].

34. Banks, *Connecticut Yankees*, 70–76; "Remembering Their Ancestor."

35. The total number of men killed in action or those who died from their wounds for the 29 Union regiments was drawn from William F. Fox, *Regimental Losses in the American Civil War, 1861–1865* (Albany, NY, 1889). The number who died from wounds was then divided by the officially reported number of wounded, in order to arrive at an average. The regiments included in this average were the 97th NY; the 8th and 11th CT; the 7th ME; the 5th and 9th NH; the 2nd, 12th, 19th, 20th, and 28th MA; the 8th, 9th, 11th, and 13th PA Reserves; the 11th, 28th, 45th, 72nd, 111th, and 118th PA; the 1st DE; the 19th IN; the 7th MI; and the 2nd, 3rd, and 6th WI. The mortality rate for the 13th PA Reserves and the 45th PA was drawn from their losses at South Mountain. Also see Bollet, *Civil War Medicine*, 89, 151–152. The Confederate mortality rate from wounds was probably higher than 13%, and the estimate of 1,000 men who died from their wounds is conservative.

36. Maj. J. Edward Ward after-action report, Sept. 22, 1862, 8th CT file, ANBL.

37. Robertson, "Federal Surgeon," 151.

38. Nelson, *"As Grain Falls,"* 17, 39.

39. H. Waters Berryman to mother, Sept. 22, 1862, 1st TX file, ANBL; *Bradford Reporter* (Towanda, PA), Oct. 2, 1862. GBM reported that his army buried 2,700 Rebels after the battle. Estimates of burials of the Confederates' dead were notoriously unreliable and often exaggerated. The Army of Northern Virginia's mortality rate was probably more than 1,546 but less than 2,000. See *OR* 19, 1:67.

40. Henry Ropes to John, Sept. 20, 1862, Henry Ropes letters, BPL.

41. *Brandon (VT) Monitor*, Oct. 3, 1862. The writer, as well as which regiment of the brigade he belonged to, is unidentified. Also see Charles Goddard [1st MN] to Mother, Sept. 19, 1862, Charles Goddard Papers, MNHS; Nelson Miles to Brother, Sept. 24, 1862, Gary Ecelberger's

Antietam files, ANBL; E. Cross, *Stand Firm*, 121; William E. MacDonald, "The Long Roll Diary of a Yankee Mudsill," ed. Robert E. Elsden, 2nd MA file, ANBL; Dawes, *Service*, 94–95.

42. William A. Frassanito, *Antietam* (New York: Scribner, 1978), 51–54. Frassanito writes that the record is unclear for precisely when the photographers reached the battlefield. Frassanito thought Sept. 18 was the most likely date.

43. *New York Times*, Oct. 6, 20, 1862.

44. "Camp of the 36th Regt. N. Y. S. V. near Sharpsburg, Md., Oct. 1st, 1862," 35th New York Infantry Regiment's Civil War Newspaper Clippings, New York State Military Museum and Veterans Research Center, https://museum.dmna.ny.gov/index.php/?cID=2127/ [accessed Dec. 2020]; James M. Smith to Friends, Sept. 27, 1862, 5th PA Reserves file, ANBL; Favill, *Diary*, 190.

45. Oliver Wendell Holmes Sr., "My Hunt After 'the Captain,'" *Atlantic Monthly* (Dec. 1862), 748–749.

46. "In Memoriam, 130th Regiment," 25, 130th PA file, ANBL; Edwin H. Chadwick to Dear Friends, Sept. 25, 1862, NHHS; Baldwin diary, ANBL; Fletcher, "Short Account," ANBL.

47. R. Bowen, *From Ball's Bluff*, 128.

48. Fletcher, "Short Account," ANBL; "In Memoriam," 25, ANBL; Burnham to A. N. Clark, Sept. 19, 1862, in *Hartford (CT) Courant*, Sept. 30, 1862. Burnham wrote this letter at 11 p.m., immediately after finishing the burials.

49. Favill, *Diary*, 190; John H. Burnham to Mother and Family, Oct. 4, 1862, CHS; Reylea, "History," CHS.

50. David Frantz diary, 130th PA file, ANBL; *Bradford Reporter* (Towanda, PA), Oct. 2, 1862; Leander Davis to Wife, Oct. 2, 1862, Battery M, 1st NY Light Artillery file, ANBL

51. Nelson Stanton to Friend, Oct. 4, 1862, 15th MA file, ANBL; Carr diary, USAHEC; Seth Plumb to Friends, Sept. 20, 1862, Plumb Family Papers, LHS. Also see Sgt. Frank Spaulding, Sept. 17, 1862, in *Windham County Transcript* (Danielson, CT), Oct. 2, 1862.

52. H. Waters Berryman to Mother, Sept. 22, 1862, 1st TX file, ANBL. Cook was killed in action.

53. *Bradford Reporter* (Towanda, PA), Oct. 2, 1862; Hitchcock, *War*, 71–72; Frantz diary, ANBL; Oliver H. Roe to Sister Mary, Sept. 21, 1862, GNMP.

54. *Globe* (Huntington, PA), Oct. 9, 1862. The writer identified himself only as "soldier."

55. David H. Hackworth and Julie Sherman, *About Face* (New York: Simon & Shuster, 1989), 76.

56. Bollet, *Civil War Medicine*, 317–318.

57. Thomas Welsh to Wife, Sept. 23, 1862, 45th PA file, ANBL; Hitchcock, *War*, 74; William H. S. Burgwyn, *A Captain's War*, ed. Herbert M. Schiller (Shippensburg, PA: White Mane Books, 1994), 20, 23; William M. Robbins to John Gould, June 5, 1891, GP; Dawes, *Service*, 99; Nelson E. Dodge to Friend, Sept. 23, 1862, [item] 2163, Gilder Lehrman Collection, NYHS; Eli Pinson Landers, *In Care of Yellow River*, ed. Elizabeth W. Roberson (Gretna, SC: Pelican, 1997), 97–98; Jonathan Peacock to Son, Oct. 27, 1862, 59th NY file, ANBL; Sidney Spaulding to Father, Sept. 20, 1862, 9th NH file, ANBL; James P. Stewart to Mother, *CWTI* Miscellaneous Collection, USAHEC

58. Henry Livermore Abbott, *Fallen Leaves*, ed. Robert G. Scott (Kent, OH: Kent State Univ. Press, 1991), 143; Henry Ropes to brother, Sept. 27, 1862, H. Ropes letters, BPL; Miller, *Harvard's Civil War*, 182.

59. D. Thompson, "With Burnside," 662; Abner Ralph Small, *The Road to Richmond*, ed. Harold A. Small (Berkeley: Univ. of California Press, 1959), 185.

60. William Houghton to Mother, Sept. 21, 1862, IHS; Augustus VanDyke to Angie, Sept. 21, 1862, box 1, folder 4, IHS; David E. Beem to Wife, Sept. 20, 1862, David E. Beem Papers, IHS; *Memphis (TN) Daily Appeal*, Oct. 11, 1862.

61. Combat stress led Dawes to take a discharge in Aug. 1864. On Sept. 1, shortly after his discharge, he wrote that "it seems almost certain to me that I could never have lived through another such carnival of blood." See Dawes, *Service*, 305.

Chapter 22. Civilians

1. *Roulette House*, 36, 48, copy in ANBL; 1860 Federal Census, Washington County, MD, Sharpsburg District, typescript, ANBL; Richard E. Clem, "Face of the Civil War: Remembering Nancy Campbell," John Banks' Civil War Blog, July 25, 2017, https://john-banks.blogspot.com/2017/07/face-of-civil-war-remembering-nancy.html [accessed Dec. 2020]; Jacob Rohrbach, "The Farmsteads at Antietam—William Roulette Farm," Jacob Rohrbach Inn, https://jacob-rohrbach-inn.com/blog/2017/06/farmsteads-antietam-william-roulette-farm/ [accessed Dec. 2020]; K. Walker and Kirkman, *Antietam Farmsteads*, 66, 70.

2. Francis F. Wilshin, *Historic Structures Report, History Data, Antietam National Battlefield Site, Maryland*, U.S. National Park Service Report (Aug. 28, 1969), 127–130, https://irma.nps.gov/DataStore/DownloadFile/590781/ [accessed Dec. 2020]; Jacob Rohrbach, "The Farmsteads at Antietam—Henry Piper Farm," Jacob Rohrbach Inn, https://jacob-rohrbach-inn.com/blog/2017/07/the-farmsteads-of-antietam-henry-piper-farm/ [accessed Dec. 2020]; Harsh, *Sounding*, 112.

3. Barbara Jean Fields, *Slavery and Freedom on the Middle Ground* (New Haven, CT: Yale Univ. Press, 1985), 106, 117.

4. Reardon and Vossler, *Field Guide*, 118; Jacob Rohrbach, "The Farmsteads at Antietam—Samuel Mumma Farm," Jacob Rohrbach Inn, https://jacob-rohrbach-inn.com/blog/category/farmsteads-at-antietam/?s=Mumma/ [accessed Dec. 2020].

5. Reardon and Vossler, *Field Guide*, 189; Rohrbach, "Henry Piper Farm"; Ernst, *Too Afraid*, 120.

6. H. Stevens, *Souvenir*, 49.

7. H. Stevens, *Souvenir*, 65.

8. *Roulette House*, appendix F, 3–12. Roulette filed two claims, on Oct. 3 and Nov. 1, 1862. Also see Rohrbach, "William Roulette Farm." Roulette's damage claim, in 2022 dollars, would be approximately $108,549.

9. Elizabeth Piper to Friend, Oct. 4, 1862, in "Elizabeth Piper and the Battle of Antietam," Dan Masters' Civil War Chronicles, Sept. 29, 2017, https://dan-masters-civil-war.blogspot.com/2017/09/elizabeth-piper-and-battle-of-antietam.html [accessed Dec. 2021].

10. Reardon and Vossler, *Field Guide*, 189; Rohrbach, "Henry Piper Farm."

11. Ted Alexander, "The Civilians of Sharpsburg," *Civil War Regiments* 6, no. 2 (1998), 156; Jacob Rohrbach, "The Farmsteads at Antietam—Phillip Pry Farm," Jacob Rohrbach Inn, http://jacob-rohrbach-inn.com/blog/2020/02/the-farmsteads-of-antietam-phillip-pry-farm/ [accessed Dec. 2020]. Piper's failure to receive payment probably was linked to his not having signed a certificate of loyalty to the government. Others were denied compensation for the same reason.

12. Rohrbach, "Samuel Mumma Farm"; Ernst, *Too Afraid*, 195; Alexander, "Civilians," 155; Steven Cowie, *When Hell Came to Sharpsburg* (El Dorado Hills, CA: Savas-Beatie, 2022), 81; *Athens (OH) Messenger*, Aug. 20, 1863.

13. Ernst, *Too Afraid*, 145; *Lancaster (PA) Daily Inquirer*, Sept. 22, 1862; *Columbus Daily Ohio State Journal*, Sept. 30, 1862; Bancroft diary, Auburn Univ.; S. S. Partridge to Dear Mac, Sept. 26, 1862, in McKelvey, *Rochester*, 89; *Altoona (PA) Tribune*, Oct. 2, 1862. For more specific details of the damage that was caused, see Cowie, *When Hell Came*.

14. Bracken diary, USAHEC.

15. John T. Trowbridge, *The South* (Hartford, CT: L. Stebbins, 1866), 51–52.

16. Alexander, "Civilians," 152; Ernst, *Too Afraid*, 117; *OR* 19, 2:618.

17. *OR* 19, 2:602; Donaldson, *Inside*, 127.

18. *Richmond (VA) Daily Dispatch*, Sept. 24, 1862. The number of African Americans captured with the Union garrison at Harpers Ferry fluctuated, depending on the source. Numbers ranged from 500 to 1,200, but a figure of 1,000 or more was common. What happened to

those individuals who were not transported to Richmond is unknown.

19. Nelson, *"As Grain Falls,"* 15–16, 19, 23, 24.

20. *OR* 19, 2:374; *Altoona (PA) Tribune*, Oct. 2, 1862. Baltimore's population in the 1860 Federal census was 212,418, and Frederick's was 8,142. See Harsh, *Sounding*, 126.

21. *OR* 19, 1:95; Small, *Road to Richmond*, 52; *OR* 19, 2:376.

22. Wainwright, *Diary of Battle*, 116.

23. *Mansfield (OH) Semi-Weekly Herald*, Sept. 27, 1862; *Altoona (PA) Tribune*, Oct. 2, 1862; Henry W. Brown to Parents, Oct. 1, 1862, 21st MA file, ANBL.

24. Austin C. Stearns, *Three Years in Company K*, ed. Arthur A. Kent (London: Associated Univ. Presses, 1976), 134; Ernst, *Too Afraid*, 191–192.

25. Nelson, *"As Grain Falls,"* 22–23; Greiner, Coryell, and Smither, eds., *Surgeon's Civil War*, 24; *OR* 19, 1:657.

26. Ernst, *Too Afraid*, 184–185; Alexander, "Civilians," 157–158; Rohrbach, "William Roulette Farm"; Nelson, *"As Grain Falls,"* 24–25; 1860 Federal Census, NA. Adam Michael's real estate was worth $8,600, and his personal estate, $1,850, both of which were higher than the average in his Sharpsburg district.

27. H. Stevens, *Souvenir*, 65–66; Carman diary, NJHS; *Athens (OH) Messenger*, Aug. 20, 1863; *Portland (ME) Daily Press*, May 11, 1863.

28. *Western Democrat* (Charlotte, NC), Sept. 30, 1862; *Memphis (TN) Daily Appeal*, Oct. 1, 1862; *New York Herald*, Sept. 18, 1862; *Daily Journal* (Evansville, IN), Sept. 19, 1862; Dawes, *Service*, 94.

29. *New York Tribune*, Sept. 19, 1862; J. Cutler Andrews, *The North Reports the Civil War* (Pittsburgh, PA: Univ. of Pittsburgh Press, 1955), 283; "Army Correspondence," *Savannah Republican*, Oct. 1, 1862; *Charleston (SC) Daily Courier*, Sept. 29, 1862; *Athens (GA) Southern Banner*, Oct. 8, 1862; J. Cutler Andrews, *The South Reports the Civil War* (Princeton, NJ: Princeton Univ. Press, 1970), 214.

30. *Daily Reporter* (Selma, AL), Oct. 9, 1862; *Savannah Republican*, Sept. 26, 1862; *Globe* (Huntington, PA), Oct. 1 and 8, 1862; *Philadelphia Public Ledger*, Sept. 24, 1862.

31. Holmes, "My Hunt," 738–764; Chaplain Wm. Earnshaw to Annie, Sept. 17, 1862, James Colwell to Annie, Sept. 13 and 14, 1862, and Annie to James, Sept. 18, 1862, folder 2, Civil War Miscellaneous Collection, USAHEC; Baldwin diary, ANBL; David G. Colwell, "The Bitter Fruits: The Civil War Comes to a Small Town in Pennsylvania," master's thesis, California State Univ., Los Angeles (1995), copy in 7th PA Reserves File, ANBL. Annie Colwell raised her four children, two of whom received appointments to the U.S. Naval Academy. She died at age 74 in Carlisle, PA.

32. David Beem to Emaline Lundy, Sept. 20, 1862, Beem Papers, IHS. Beem spelled her name "Amaline," which is probably how it was pronounced, but her widow's pension file spells her name "Emaline." The couple had two boys, ages 9 and 4. See Case Files of Approved Pension Applications of Widows and Other Dependents of Civil War Veterans, ca. 1861–ca. 1910, RG 15, NA.

33. *Broome (NY) Republican*, Oct. 8, 1862; Drew Gilpin Faust, *This Republic of Suffering* (New York, Alfred A. Knopf, 2008), 146.

34. Faust, *This Republic*, 185–186.

35. Dawes, *Service*, 99; J. L. Conklin telegram, Sept. 21, 1862, and John Gibbon to My Dear Madam, Oct. 1, 1862, Bragg Papers, SHSW.

36. *Elyria (OH) Independent Democrat*, Oct. 8, 1862; James Carr Murray to Sister, Sept. 22, 1862, James Carry Murray Papers, THM; Thomas Hamill to My Dear Kane, Sept. 30, 1862, in *Brooklyn (NY) Daily Times*, Oct. 4, 1862.

37. Bruce, *Harp*, 105–106, 107–113.

38. Nelson M. Stetson, comp., *Stetson Kindred of America*, Booklet No. 4, 2nd ed. (Rockland MA: A. I. Randall, 1914), copy in 59th NY file, ANBL; Wm. L. Tidball to Stetson, Sept. 20, 1862, *Plattsburgh (NY) Express and Sentinel*, Oct. 11, 1862, 59th NY File, ANBL; *Malone (NY)*

Palladium, Oct. 16, 1862; Lemuel Stetson to Friend, Sept. 27, 1862, in *Albany (NY) Atlas and Argus*, Oct. 2, 1862. According to Nelson's *"As Grain Falls,"* 54, the hospital for Sedgwick's division was probably at the Simon Wyand farm, located on the western edge of Keedysville, which was being rented by Joshua Wyand.

39. Ernst, *Too Afraid*, 176–177; Anna M. Holstein, *Three Years in Field Hospitals of the Army of the Potomac* (Philadelphia: J. B. Lippincott, 1867), 17; *OR* 19, 1:112. The army also disliked allowing the wounded to recover at home, because it was difficult to monitor the healing process and, hence, their return to their units.

40. Case Files, roll WC7148-Eaglesfield-George, RG 15, NA.

41. Case Files, roll WC78683–WC78699-Shepherd Brown, RG 15, NA.

42. Joseph R. Herring and Benjamin Frank Vickers CSR, RG 109, NA; J. Gordon, *Reminiscences*, 66. Vickers was listed in the 1860 Federal census as "Frank Vickers." He appears to have been a brick mason. He, Victoria, and their 8-month-old child lived at the residence of Nancy Robinson. Gordon thought Vickers had previously served in Mexico and Nicaragua during one of the filibustering expeditions in the 1850s. He may have been in Nicaragua, but he was too young to have served in Mexico.

43. *Boston Saturday Evening Express*, Sept. 27, 1862; Quiner, *Correspondence*, 309.

44. *Charleston (SC) Mercury*, Dec. 3, 1862; Faust, *This Republic*, 163; Quiner, *Correspondence*, vol. 2, 309. The writer of White's memorial is unknown, but it may have been Capt. Eldridge C. Goggins in Company M.

45. Frassanito, *Antietam*, 234–235.

46. Frassanito, *Antietam*, 234–235.

Chapter 23. Emancipation

1. GBM to Mary Ellen, Sept. 20, 1862, in McClellan, *Civil War Papers*, 473; Gideon Welles, *Diary of Gideon Welles*, vol. 1 (Boston: Houghton Mifflin, 1911), 143–144; Foner, *Fiery Trial*, 231; McPherson, *Battle Cry*, 557.

2. Foner, *Fiery Trial*, 230–247; McPherson, *Battle Cry*, 546–557; Douglass, *Frederick Douglass*, 519.

3. McPherson, *Battle Cry*, 546–557.

4. Fear of a slave insurrection was not an abstract worry, and it resulted in lethal consequences in some instances. The *Monmouth (NJ) Democrat* carried a story of the execution by hanging of 17 Blacks in Culpepper County, Virginia. Most of the individuals were free but were found with copies of Northern newspapers containing the Emancipation Proclamation. The refugee who carried this story to Union authorities declared "that there is the greatest consternation imaginable among the whites in that section, in consequence of an apprehended negro insurrection." See *Monmouth (NJ) Democrat*, Oct. 23, 1862.

5. *OR* 19, 2:644; *OR* 21, 1:1086; "U.S. Brigadier General R. H. Milroy's Order to Citizens of Winchester and Frederick County, Virginia, in Reference to the Emancipation Proclamation of President Abraham Lincoln," Jan. 5, 1863, War Department Collection of Confederate Records, RG 109, NA.

6. Joseph T. Glatthaar, *General Lee's Army*, 153–154; John F. Shaffner to Mr. C. F. Pfohl, Oct. 3, 1862, Pfohl Papers, SHC; Samuel A. Burney, *A Southern Soldier's Letters Home*, ed. Nat Turner (Macon, GA: Mercer Univ. Press, 2002), 214–215; Aaron Sheehan-Dean, *The Calculus of Violence* (Cambridge, MA: Harvard Univ. Press, 2018), 141.

7. GBM to Mary Ellen, Sept. 25, 1862, and GBM to Wm. H. Aspinwall, Sept. 26, 1862, in McClellan, *Civil War Papers*, 481–482; Ethan Sepp Rafuse, *McClellan's War* (Bloomington: Indiana Univ. Press, 2005), 340.

8. Zachery A. Fry, *A Republic in the Ranks* (Chapel Hill: Univ. of North Carolina Press, 2020), 26; McClellan, *Civil War Papers*, 325; Rafuse, *McClellan's War*, 342; Porter to Marble, Sept. 30–Oct. 2, 1862, vol. 3, Manton Marble Papers, LC; William Marvel, *Radical Sacrifice*

(Chapel Hill: Univ. of North Carolina Press, 2021), 251.

9. Sears, *Landscape*, 320; Roy P. Basler, ed., *Collected Works of Abraham Lincoln*, vol. 5 (New Brunswick, NJ: Rutgers Univ. Press, 1953), 442–443, 508–509. Montgomery Blair's Sept. 27, 1862, letter to GBM provided details of the Maj. Key case. It seems unlikely that GBM did not share this with Porter before Sept. 30. See Montgomery Blair to GBM, Sept. 27, 1862, image 129–131, Correspondence I: Sept. 23–30, MP, https://www.loc.gov/search/?fa=partof:ge orge+brinton+mcclellan+papers:+correspond ence+i,+1783–1888/ [accessed Jan. 2021].

10. Snell, *From First*, 199; G. Meade, *Life and Letters*, vol. 1, 317, 319; A. Williams, *Cannon's Mouth*, 142.

11. *Harrisburg (PA) Patriot*, Oct. 2, 1862; Wainwright, *Diary of Battle*, 109; Fry, *A Republic*, 49; Quiner, *Correspondence*, 317; Dawes, *Service*, 126; Alan D. Gaff, *On Many*, 214.

12. R. Bowen, *From Ball's Bluff*, 136; C. Bowen, *Dear Friends*, 158; Lt. Col. Charles Albright to Lincoln, Oct. 20, 1862, Lincoln Papers, LC, copy in 132nd PA file, ANBL; Donaldson, *Inside*, 146.

13. Montgomery Blair to GBM, Sept. 27, 1862, images 129–131, Correspondence I: Sept. 23–30, MP; Francis P. Blair to GBM, Sept. 30, 1862, images 200–201, Correspondence I: Sept. 23–30, MP; Rafuse, *McClellan's War*, 339–341; McClellan, *Civil War Papers*, 326–327.

14. J. D. Cox, *Military Reminiscences*, 356, 359–361.

15. McClellan, *Civil War Papers*, 490; J. D. Cox, *Military Reminiscences*, 355, 361.

16. OR 19, 2:395; Rafuse, *McClellan's War*, 348–349; Welles, *Diary*, 163. Welles met with Governor Edwin D. Morgan of New York on Oct. 8. Morgan told Welles he had met Aspinwall the day before, and that Aspinwall "had seen and got from GBM the general army order just published sustaining the Emancipation Proclamation." Morgan also perceived that although GBM did not necessarily want to become a presidential candidate, the army's commander did not believe he could avoid becoming one.

Chapter 24. Recovery

1. OR 19, 1:974; OR 12, 3:966; Glatthaar, *General Lee's Army*, 198. The estimate of a 30% loss of leadership at Sharpsburg is derived from the number of officers listed as present for duty on the Sept. 22 return. The true percentage of this loss may have been higher, since many officers who had previously been absent returned to the army between Sept. 18 and Sept. 22. Also see Hartwig, *To Antietam Creek*, 79.

2. OR 19, 1:969, 1038; Col. R. F. Floyd [8th FL] to Governor John Milton, Sept. 22, 1862, Governor's Office letterbooks, in possession of Zack Waters; "Letter from a Mobile Rifleman," *Mobile Advertiser and Register*, Oct. 18, 1862 [the writer was probably Joseph B. Belt in Company K]; Robert G. Johnson Jr. to Gould, May 23, 1891, GP; Shinn journal, SHC; William W. Sillers to Sister, Oct. 1, 1862, Sillers-Holmes Family Correspondence, Univ. of Notre Dame.

3. Charles Kibbee letter, Sept. 21, 1862, in *Macon (GA) Weekly*, Oct. 1862, 10th GA file, ANBL. Also see *Western Sentinel* (Charlotte, NC), Oct. 17, 1862, and John F. White to Nat, Oct. 12, 1862, VHS; Lemon diary, 18th GA file, ANBL; *Athens (GA) Southern Banner*, Oct. 8, 1862; P. Alexander, *Writing and Fighting*, 114.

4. Henry E. Young to Dear Louis, Sept. 22, 1862, Gordon Collection, EU; OR 19, 1:143.

5. OR 19, 2:597–598, 617–618.

6. Glatthaar, *General Lee's Army*, 176–177; Cadmus Wilcox, quoted in Glatthaar, *General Lee's Army*, 180; OR 19, 2:627.

7. John F. Shaffner to Mr. C. F. Pfohl, Oct. 3, 1862, Pfohl Papers, SHC; [unknown] to Parents, Sept. 16, 1862, 5th AL File, ANBL; *Lockport (NY) Daily Journal & Courier*, Oct. 6, 1862. The writer of the newspaper letter is probably Sergeant Stephen W. Lockwood, who was discharged, due to a disability, on Oct. 10, 1862. Also see Daly, *Diary*, 190; Donaldson, *Inside*, 143.

8. Rufus Felder to Sister, Oct. 1, 1862, THM; James Steptoe Johnson to Mary Green, Sept. 22, 1862, Mercer-Green-Johnston Papers, LC; E. Alexander, *Fighting*, 155; Donaldson, *Inside*, 143.

9. *OR* 19, 1:143, 2:622. For some opinions within the Confederate army advocating shortening the line of communications, see Gary W. Gallagher, "The Net Result of the Campaign Was In Our Favor: Confederate Reaction to the Maryland Campaign," in Gallagher, *Antietam Campaign*, 28–29; *OR* 19, 2:622.

10. *OR* 19, 2:626–627, 640, 641, 659. For evidence of how successful Lee's strategy was in making GBM believe the Confederates were seeking battle, see GBM to Halleck, Sept. 23, 1862, in McClellan, *Civil War Papers*, 479–480. Lee could also receive supplies and other items via the railhead at Culpepper Court House, but this route was more exposed to enemy raids and had to cross the Blue Ridge Mountains to reach the Valley Turnpike.

11. *OR* 19, 2:51–55

12. *OR* 19, 2:614, 635, 623, 633, 635, 663, 637; Glatthaar, *General Lee's Army*, 214, 215. In a Sept. 29 letter to George Randolph, Lee explained that he had his supply officers make payments for requisitioned supplies with Confederate banknotes—that is, promissory notes, which were not backed by hard assets and would only be redeemable for payment after the war. There were "capitalists in the country, and persons, perhaps, inimical to us" who refused to accept these notes. Lee asked whether Confederate currency could be used as legal tender—in other words, as a form of money recognizable as the satisfactory payment of a debt in a court of law—and thereby prevent "the attempt to depreciate it on the part of men inimical to our cause." Randolph responded that the executive branch had no authority to make Confederate money legal tender between individuals, but that the army should continue to procure supplies and pay for them with Confederate currency. If anyone refused to accept this form of pay-ment, "they may be considered as hostile to the Government, and may be arrested and removed from the vicinity of the army." This policy differed little from what the Confederates condemned John Pope for during the Second Manassas Campaign. See *OR* 19, 2:635–636. Also see William W. Sillers to Sister, Nov. 15, 1862, Sillers-Holmes Family Correspondence, Univ. of Notre Dame.

13. *OR* 19, 2:618–619.

14. *OR* 51, 2:631; Robertson, *Stonewall Jackson*, 625.

15. Robert Rodes, quoted in Glatthaar, *General Lee's Army*, 193.

16. Glatthaar, *General Lee's Army*, 183, 197.

17. *OR* 19, 2:629–630.

18. Charles F. Terrill to brother Samuel, Sept. 25, 1862, in Terrill, *History*, 276.

19. *Savannah Republican*, Oct. 16, 1862; Coker, *History*, 114; T. Harry Williams, ed., "The Civil War Letters of William L. Cage," *Louisiana Historical Quarterly* 39, no. 1 (Jan. 1956), 124; Shinn journal, SHC; *OR* 19, 2:621, 639, 660, 674, 713. An excellent study for understanding how units can recover quickly from severe losses if they retain a core cadre of officers and noncoms is Robert S. Rush, *Hell in Hurtgen Forest* (Lawrence: Univ. Press of Kansas, 2001). On page 291, Rush writes, "Only when units become battle-hardened around a cadre of survivors does combat power increase, and as long as there is a continual influx of new soldiers around this battle-hardened core, units keep going and keep fighting."

20. *OR* 19, 2:633–634, 683–684. For more on the Army of Northern Virginia's reorganization, see D. Freeman, *Lee's Lieutenants*, vol. 2, 250–283. One caveat to Freeman's analysis is his evaluation of McLaws's performance. Freeman has a dislike of McLaws, possibly because Lee never fully understood or appreciated the Georgian's role at Harpers Ferry or Sharpsburg and failed to give him the credit he deserved. McLaws outperformed every other division commander in the Confederate army, with the exception of A. P. Hill and

Hood, but he faced greater challenges than either of them during the Maryland Campaign, and his division inflicted greater damage with fewer losses than did Hood. Freeman is ambivalent about D. H. Hill, although his commentary is generally favorable.

21. *OR* 19, 2:647–654.

Chapter 25. End of an Epoch

1. *OR* 19, 1:68; *OR* 19, 2:339, 342–343; GBM to Halleck, Sept. 20, 1862, in McClellan, *Civil War Papers*, 475. For Halleck's response and an explanation for the tenor of his Sept. 20 message, see *OR* 19, 2:339.
2. *OR* 19, 2:348–349.
3. John Bigelow Jr., *Chancellorsville* (New York: Smithmark, 1995), 47; Marvel, *Radical Sacrifice*, 250; Henry Royer to Father, Sept. 18, 1862, in *Norristown (PA) Herald and Free Press*, Sept. 23, 1862; [unknown] to Mr. Mirror, Sept. 20, 1862, in *Bloomville (NY) Mirror*, Oct. 7, 1862; John H. Burnham to Mother and Family, Oct. 4, 1862, CHS.
4. GBM to Halleck, Sept. 27, 1862, in McClellan, *Civil War Papers*, 482–483; Couch to Marcy, Oct. 7, 1862, image 145, Correspondence I: Sept. [?]–Oct. 9, MP.
5. GBM to Halleck, Sept. 27, 1862, in McClellan, *Civil War Papers*, 482–483.
6. GBM to Halleck, Sept. 27, 1862, in McClellan, *Civil War Papers*, 482–483.
7. GBM to Halleck, Sept. 19, 1:30 pm, in McClellan, *Civil War Papers*, 470; *OR* 19, 2:360, 371, 380, 421.
8. GBM to Mary Ellen, Sept. 22, 25, and 29, 1862, in McClellan, *Civil War Papers*, 477, 481, 485.
9. GBM to Mary Ellen, Sept. 20, 1862, 8 a.m. and 9 p.m., in McClellan, *Civil War Papers*, 473, 476; McClellan, *Civil War Papers*, 324; *New York Herald*, Sept. 26, 1862, 4.
10. Donald, *Lincoln*, 385–386.
11. *OR* 19, 1:10.
12. GBM to Mary Ellen, Oct. 2, 1862, in McClellan, *Civil War Papers*, 488.
13. Wainwright, *Diary of Battle*, 109–110; H. G. [either Henry Gerhart or Henry Groff] to Mr. Editor, Oct. 12, 1862, in "Letters from the 51st," *Bulletin of the Historical Society of Montgomery County*, 51st PA file, ANBL; Snell, *From First*, 199; G. Meade, *Life and Letters*, vol. 1, 317; J. D. Cox, *Military Reminiscences*, 365.
14. A. Williams, *Cannon's Mouth*, 136; J. D. Cox, *Military Reminiscences*, 365–366; Marvel, *Radical Sacrifice*, 252.
15. GBM to Mary Ellen, Oct. 5, 1862, in McClellan, *Civil War Papers*, 489–490; G. Meade, *Life and Letters*, vol. 1, 317.
16. Brooks D. Simpson, "General McClellan's Bodyguard: The Army of the Potomac after Antietam," in Gallagher, *Antietam Campaign*, 58; Donald, *Lincoln*, 387. For examples of feelings about Burnside, see Edwin Schall to Editor, "Letters from the 51st," in *National Defender* (Norristown, PA), Oct. 11, 1862; Henry C. Hall [8th CT] to Wife, Oct. 5, 1862, in "Civil War Letters of Henry Clay Hall, 1840–1864," transcribed by Carol Hall, 8th CT file, ANBL; John H. Burnham [16th CT] to Mother, Oct., 4, 1862, CHS.
17. *OR* 19, 1:10–11.
18. *OR* 19, 1:11–12.
19. Burlingame, "Personal Reminiscences," ANBL; John B. Sherman to parents, Sept. 28, 1862, 105th NY file, ANBL; "For the *Delaware Republican*," *Delaware Republican* (Wilmington), Oct. 9, 1862; G. Meade, *Life and Letters*, 320; Wainwright, *Diary of Battle*, 114–115.
20. Wainwright, *Diary of Battle*, 115; *OR* 19, 1:19. On Oct. 18, Gideon Welles wrote of Stanton, "The Secretary of War is reticent, vexed, disappointed, and communicates nothing. Neither he or McClellan will inspire or aid one another." See Welles, *Diary*, 176.
21. McPherson, *Battle Cry*, 568; A. Williams, *Cannon's Mouth*, 136–137; Wainwright, *Diary of Battle*, 114.
22. G. Meade, *Life and Letters*, 320; Thomas Welsh to Wife, Sept. 23, 1862, 45th PA file, ANBL; Lt. Col. Charles Albright to Lincoln, Oct. 20,

1862, Lincoln Papers, LC, copy in 132nd PA file, ANBL.

23. *Chicago Tribune*, Oct. 11, 1862, 1; Welles, *Diary*, 169; Marvel, *Radical Sacrifice*, 254; Snell, *From First*, 200.

24. G. Meade, *Life and Letters*, 320; Wainwright, *Diary of Battle*, 115; *OR* 19, 2:417; Stephen Z. Starr, *From Fort Sumter to Gettysburg, 1861–1863* (Baton Rouge, LA: LSU Press, 1979), 318, 321; *OR* 19, 2:421.

25. *OR* 19, 1:13–14.

26. *OR* 19, 1:13–14; Donald, *Lincoln*, 389; George C. Rable, *Fredericksburg! Fredericksburg!* (Chapel Hill: Univ. of North Carolina Press, 2002), 42.

27. *OR* 19, 2:464, 484–485.

28. McClellan, *Civil War Papers*, 511, 515; Donald, *Lincoln*, 389.

29. McClellan, *Civil War Papers*, 510; *OR* 19, 2:336, 470. GBM included Whipple's and Stoneman's divisions, who were added to the Army of the Potomac from the capitol's defenses, in his figure of 116,000. The influx of 20,000 men was Halleck's estimate for the 3rd Corps, the 11th Corps, and Bayard's cavalry brigade. Their actual strength was probably closer to 27,000. See Rafuse, *McClellan's War*, 355; A. Williams, *Cannon's Mouth*, 140.

30. Rafuse, *McClellan's War*, 362.

31. McClellan, *Civil War Papers*, 515, 516.

32. *OR* 19, 2:545; G. Meade, *Life and Letters*, vol. 1, 325.

33. *OR* 19, 2:545; G. Meade, *Life and Letters*, vol. 1, 325; Rable, *Fredericksburg!*, 43; Marvel, *Radical Sacrifice*, 159–160; Stephen W. Sears, *George B. McClellan*, 340. General Orders No. 182 did not include Porter's removal or the reassignment of Hunter and Hooker. These came in a separate order.

34. McClellan, *Civil War Papers*, 518–519; Rable, *Fredericksburg!*, 43; Marvel, *Radical Sacrifice*, 159–160.

35. Sears, *George B. McClellan*, 340–341; Marvel, *Radical Sacrifice*, 160; McClellan, *Civil War Papers*, 486.

36. Donald, *Lincoln*, 390; A. Williams, *Cannon's Mouth*, 151.

37. McClellan, *Civil War Papers*, 486.

38. G. Meade, *Life and Letters*, vol. 1, 325.

39. C. Bowen, *Dear Friends*, 186–187; Donaldson, *Inside*, 162–163; Alonzo H. Quint, *The Potomac and the Rapidan* (Boston: Crosby & Nichols, 1864), 223; Dawes, *Service*, 105, 107; J. Wren, *Diary*, 86.

40. Wainwright, *Diary*, 125; Donaldson, *Inside*, 164–165; *Maryland Free Press* (Hagerstown), Nov. 21, 1862. The *Free Press* article about the review mentioned that GBM rode 4 to 5 miles to where the 6th Corps were drawn up to be reviewed.

41. McClellan, *Civil War Papers*, 522.

42. Donaldson, *Inside*, 163; *New York Herald*, Nov. 13, 1862.

43. *OR* 19, 1:14.

44. *OR* 19, 2:490.

45. Welles, *Diary*, 169, 177.

46. Sears, *George B. McClellan*, 339.

47. Horace Porter, quoted in Gordon C. Rhea, *The Battle of the Wilderness, May 5–6, 1864* (Baton Rouge, LA: LSU Press, 1994), 421–422.

48. Henry Ropes, quoted in Fry, *A Republic*, 72, 73–74, 111–117; Donaldson, *Inside*, 298.

49. Fry, *A Republic*, 77–78, 162, 179.

50. Dawes, *Service*, 153.

ESSAY ON SOURCES

The essay below provides a survey of some of the most important, or interesting, sources associated with the Maryland Campaign that were consulted in the preparation of this book. A full bibliography is available online at www.press.jhu.edu/books. Search for the book title to find the webpage, and then look for the bibliography in the additional resources section.

Manuscripts

For the Union Army of the Potomac, one of the most important collections are the extensive George B. McClellan papers at the Library of Congress, which are also available on microfilm and online at the library's website, https://www.loc.gov. While much of McClellan's correspondence appears in *War of the Rebellion: The Official Records of the Union and Confederate Armies*, volume 19, parts 1 and 2, McClellan's papers contain a considerable amount of daily army communications not included in the *Official Records*. Perhaps the most significant Antietam collection in the country is the Antietam Studies collection in Record Group 94 at the National Archives. It consists of hundreds of letters written principally to Ezra Carman, a veteran of the battle, who was the historian of the Antietam Battlefield Board from 1894 to 1898. Carman sought to document the position of every regiment and battery in the Battle of Antietam and carried on an extensive correspondence with Union and Confederate veterans. Although the letters were written nearly 30 years after the battle, they are a treasure trove of detailed, eyewitness accounts for the Battle of Antietam. There is a project underway, as of this writing, to publish this collection, which will be an important addition to Antietam's historiography.

The majority of Ezra Carman's extensive papers are housed in the Manuscript Division of the Library of Congress, but there is an important Carman collection at the New York Public Library, which contains many letters from Union and Confederate veterans about the battle. His wartime diaries and other correspondence are at the New Jersey Historical Society. Carman's papers at the Library of Congress include his massive and neatly handwritten manuscript of the Maryland Campaign, which is indispensable for any serious study of it. Thomas Clemens, an authority on the campaign, published a copiously annotated edition of Carman's manuscript in three volumes, titled *The Maryland Campaign of September 1862*.

Equaling the Antietam Studies collection in importance is the John M. Gould Antietam Collection at Dartmouth College in Hanover, New Hampshire. Gould was an officer in the 10th Maine, and he initially set out to establish where the 12th Corps' commander, Major General James K. Mansfield, was mortally wounded in the fighting on September 17. His extensive correspondence with Union and Confederate veterans, which grew to be voluminous, spilled beyond this narrow focus to cover all the fighting in the vicinity of the East Woods and the Cornfield. Gould was incredibly thorough in trying to track down veterans from nearly every unit engaged on this part of the battlefield, and because he was a fellow veteran, his correspondents were unusually frank and honest with him.

Among institutions with substantial manuscript collections, two that stand out are the United States Army Heritage and Education Center in Carlisle, Pennsylvania, and the Southern Historical Collection at University of North Carolina at Chapel Hill. The USAHEC collections include manuscripts from both Union and Confederate soldiers, and their holdings for men in the Army of the Potomac are massive. The same is true for the Army of Northern Virginia holdings in the Southern Historical Collection, which also includes the papers of several important Confederate officers, such as D. H. Hill, Longstreet, McLaws, and William Pendleton.

Maps

The most important maps for any study of Antietam are in Ezra Carman's *Atlas of the Battlefield of Antietam*, a series of 14 maps at a scale of approximately 1 inch to 250 yards, available on the Library of Congress website. Carman published two editions, in 1904 (https://www.loc.gov/item/map05000006/) and 1908 (https://www.loc.gov/item /2008621532/). The latter reflected corrections Carman made to the 1904 version. Bradley M. Gottfried's *The Maps of Antietam* (2012) includes 124 color maps covering not only the Battle of Antietam, but also the entire campaign.

Newspapers and Periodicals

Wartime newspapers, particularly local papers in small and midsized locales, are rich with primary source material relating to Antietam and the Maryland Campaign. In that era, it was not unusual for soldiers to send letters from the field to their hometown newspaper, or for people to provide a private letter from one of their family members to the paper. Numerous small town and major city newspapers were consulted in the research for this book. For those from small and midsized towns, which are a virtual gold mine, I have my friend Jeff Stocker to thank, who read through hundreds of them and shared items in them with me. Citations from specific papers can be found in the notes. Postwar newspapers are also a valuable source. One of the most important is the *National Tribune*, a Union veterans' paper, started in the late 1870s, that continued into the 1930s. Besides feature articles that were often written by retired officers, during the 1880s and 1890s the newspaper included a section titled "Picket Shots," where veterans wrote about—and frequently argued about—campaigns and battles. The *Philadelphia Weekly Press* ran a series of articles from former Union and Confederate officers and enlisted men in the 1880s that are quite valuable. Because they were written after the war, they must be used with some caution, as these authors often had agendas to advance, as well as sometimes faulty or selective memories.

Among periodicals, the *Confederate Veteran* magazine and the *Southern Historical Society Papers* both contain considerable Confederate material relating to Sharpsburg. *Confederate Veteran* was not founded until the late 1890s, and while many former soldiers who wrote for the magazine still possessed clear memories of the war, the Lost Cause powerfully influenced such recollections during the life of this publication. Some veterans exaggerated or invented their experiences, while others suffered from poor memory. The same is true, to a lesser degree, for the *Southern Historical Society Papers*.

Published Primary and Secondary Sources

The foundation for any serious research on Antietam, its aftermath, and the end of the Maryland Campaign is *The War of the Rebellion: The Official Records of the Union and Confederate Armies*. The Maryland Campaign is covered in series 1, volume 19, parts 1 and 2 (1887). The *OR*s, as they are called, contain after-action reports of Union and Confederate officers, ranging from battery and regimental command on up to army command, as well as army-level correspondence.

The limitation of the *OR*s is that they only included reports and correspondence that the compilers had copies of. As diligent as these individuals were in acquiring Union and Confederate war records, reports are missing (in some cases they were never submitted), and some valuable correspondence was lost or never found its way into the records. Some of what was missed is included in volume 51, parts 1 and 2 (1897), and in Janet B. Hewett, Noah A. Trudeau, and Bruce A. Suderow, eds., *Supplement to the Official Records of the Union and Confederate Armies*, part 1, vol. 3 (1994).

One might imagine that the importance of the Maryland Campaign and the Battle of Antietam would have produced an outpouring of books on a par with those about the Battle of Gettysburg. This is not the case, although in the past 20 years there has been a considerable increase in tomes about this battle. The first published book-length account of the campaign was Francis W. Palfrey's *The Antietam and Fredericksburg* (1882). This remained the only study on the topic until the 1965 publication of James V. Murfin's *Gleam of Bayonets: The Battle of Antietam and the Maryland Campaign of 1862*. Murfin has since been replaced by Stephen Sears's superbly written *Landscape Turned Red: The Battle of Antietam* (1983) and Joseph Harsh's *Taken at the Flood: Robert E. Lee and Confederate Strategy in the Maryland Campaign of 1862* (1999), an outstanding analysis of Confederate strategy in the campaign. Harsh also produced an indispensable companion volume, titled *Sounding the Shallows: A Confederate Companion for the Maryland Campaign of 1862* (2000). Gary W. Gallagher edited a collection of essays on the campaign in *The Antietam Campaign* (1999). Already mentioned above are Tom Clemens's annotated three volumes of Ezra Carman's *The Maryland Campaign of September 1862* (2010–2016). William Frassanito's *Antietam: The Photographic Legacy of America's Bloodiest Day* (1978) examines the photographs taken by Alexander Gardner and Timothy H. O'Sullivan after the battle and is indispensable. *Artillery Hell: The Employment of Artillery at Antietam* (1995), by Curt Johnson and Richard C. Anderson Jr., is essential for any study of the artillery forces in the battle. Civilian experiences regarding the campaign and the battle are told by Kathleen Ernst in *Too Afraid to Cry: Maryland Civilians in the Antietam Campaign* (1999), and Steven Cowie, *When Hell Came to Sharpsburg: The Battle of Antietam and Its Impact on the Civilians Who Called It Home* (2022). Any account of the battle's aftermath should consult John H. Nelson's *"As Grain Falls Before the Reaper": The Federal Hospital Sites and Identified Federal Casualties at Antietam* (2004). This study is difficult to find but well worth the effort to do so. *Antietam Farmsteads: A Guide to the Battlefield Landscape* (2010), by Kevin M. Walker and K. C. Kirkman, is also out of publication, although the Save Historic Antietam Foundation did have copies for sale.

There are two modern biographies of McClellan that represent the most thorough and balanced scholarship on the general. These are by Stephen Sears, *George B. McClellan: The Young Napoleon* (1988), and Ethan Sepp Rafuse, *McClellan's War: The Failure of Moderation in the Struggle for the Union* (2005). Sears also edited the highly useful *Civil War Papers of George B. McClellan* (1989), and his *Lincoln's Lieutenants: The High Command of the Army of the Potomac* (2017) is quite helpful in understanding the command culture of the Union army at Antietam. For the Confederates, Joseph T. Glatthaar's *General Lee's Army: From Victory to Collapse* (2008) is simply the best book for understanding the Army of Northern Virginia.

Biographies of Robert E. Lee abound, but a highly recommended one to grasp the type of person Lee was is Elizabeth B. Pryor's *Reading the Man: A Portrait of Robert E. Lee Through His Letters* (2007). Gary Gallagher's anthology, *Lee the Soldier* (1996), is also valuable in providing an understanding of Lee's generalship.

Memoirs, reminiscences, and regimental histories abound, but they frequently must be used with caution, as veterans writing for a Gilded Age audience often obscured war's realties and portrayed their Civil War experiences in heroic, romantic, and (sometimes) fanciful narratives. Two Union titles that stand out are Rufus R. Dawes, *Service with the Sixth Wisconsin Volunteers* (1984 reprint)—which contains one of the finest descriptions about the Battle of Antietam ever penned by a Civil War veteran—and J. Gregory Acken, who edited *Inside the Army of the Potomac: The Civil War Experience of Captain Francis Adams Donaldson* (1998). The latter contains the unvarnished wartime letters of a captain in the 118th Pennsylvania, which provide an accurate picture of soldiering, stripped of nostalgia. Although this regiment was not engaged at Antietam, Donaldson's description of its baptism by fire at Shepherdstown is unforgettable. Another set of letters that provides an unembellished and grim account of the Battle of Antietam and the war, is Roland E. Bowen, *From Ball's Bluff to Gettysburg—and Beyond: The Civil War Letters of Private Roland E. Bowen, 15th Massachusetts Infantry, 1861–1864*, edited by Gregory A. Coco (1994). The original is out of print, but a new edition will be published in the near future. Alan D. Gaff and Donald H. Gaff edited *A Corporal's Story: Civil War Recollections of the Twelfth Massachusetts* (2014). On the Confederate side, there is Jeffery D. Stocker, who edited *From Huntsville to Appomattox: R. T. Cole's History of the 4th Regiment, Alabama Volunteer Infantry* (1996), and Edward P. Alexander's *Fighting for the Confederacy: The Personal Recollections of General Edward Porter Alexander*, edited by Gary W. Gallagher (1989). Although Alexander, as Lee's ordnance officer, was not present on the battlefield at Sharpsburg, his appraisal of the campaign and his overall honesty make this one of the finest publications by a former Confederate officer. Confederate war correspondent Peter

Alexander's detailed reports, which he wrote throughout the Maryland Campaign, are remarkable for their frankness about the war's reality. They can be found in *Writing and Fighting the Confederate War: The Letters of Peter Wellington Alexander, Confederate War Correspondent*, edited by William B. Styple (2002).

For those wishing to visit the battlefield sites covered in this book, two excellent titles are Carol Reardon and Tom Vossler, *A Field Guide to Antietam: Experiencing the Battlefield Through Its History, Places, & People* (2016), and Ethan Sepp Rafuse, *Antietam, South Mountain, and Harpers Ferry: A Battlefield Guide* (2008).

Brian Downey's Antietam on the Web, https://antietam.aotw.org, is an outstanding internet resource. I also regularly made use of Fold3, Ancestry's subscription website, at https://www.fold3.com/collection/us-civil-war/, which contains digital copies of all surviving Confederate service records, as well as many Union records from the National Archives, which the latter is still working to digitize. Widows' pension files, often a mother lode for researchers, are also available, in addition to the 1860 Federal census and many other useful collections from the National Archives. The extensive American Civil War Research database for Union and Confederate regiments, at civilwardata.com [requires a subscription], is also quite useful and includes images of a number of individuals.

INDEX